THE ★★★★★★★★★★★★★★★★★★★
PRESIDENTS

A Reference History

THE
PRESIDENTS

A Reference History

Third Edition

HENRY F. GRAFF, EDITOR

CHARLES SCRIBNER'S SONS®

THOMSON
™
GALE

New York • Detroit • San Diego • San Francisco • Cleveland • New Haven, Conn. • Waterville, Maine • London • Munich

The Presidents

Henry. F. Graff

REF
973
PRE

Project Editor
Matthew May

Editorial
Cynthia Crippen, Melissa Dobson, Paul Kobel,
Deanna Raso, Eleanor Stanford

Permissions
Lori Hines

Imaging and Multimedia
Robert Duncan, Leitha Etheridge-Sims,
Lezlie Light, Michael Logusz, Kelley Quin

Product Design
Tracey Rowens
Michael Logusz

Manufacturing
Rhonda Williams

LIBRARY OF CONGRESS CATALOGING-IN-PUBLICATION DATA

The presidents : a reference history / Henry F. Graff, editor.— 3rd ed.
    p. cm.
        Includes bibliographical references and index.
        ISBN 0-684-31226-3 (hardcover)
        1. Presidents—United States—History. 2. Presidents—United
        States—Biography. 3. United States—Politics and government. I.
        Graff, Henry F. (Henry Franklin), 1921-
E176.1
973'.09'9—dc21

2002001440

Printed in the United States of America
10 9 8 7 6 5 4 3 2 1

Contents

THE PRESIDENTS

Introduction

to the 3rd Edition

This latest edition of *The Presidents: A Reference History*, coming only six years after the Second, is a tribute to its ever-enlarging role as a standard resource for students and the general public alike. This revision features important additions; they include an early assessment of President George W. Bush's administration, already marked by unprecedented challenges to national security, and, of course a full account of President Bill Clinton's two terms. One new essay views the history of the presidency as a whole, and another provides an authoritative history of the White House. The highly admired essay on First Ladies has been brought up to date as have the instructive Appendices: the General Bibliography on the Presidency, The Table of Presidential Data, and profile of The Executive Office of the President. All of the articles on the individual presidents were reviewed and revised where needed to accommodate fresh interpretations. Evaluations of recently published books update the bibliographies. Two full-color inserts vividly portray the social history of the presidency and election-related memorabilia, making more tangible how the U.S. Chief Executives are chosen and their daily life in office.

As the twenty-first century opened, it was clear that any president might be caught in the toils of changes in the way fellow Americans perceive him—or conceivably—her. The huge amount of information daily offered to the public about the occupants of the White House is now a potent factor in shaping the conduct of the presidential office. Inevitably, the historic role of the Chief Executive as "leader" has been recast—and made more arduous. The news and entertainment media are unquenchable streams of tidbits of every kind about the First Family. Added to the press conferences, releases, and leaks, this boundless public knowledge about the inner workings of the Oval Office, for all its salutary value to a democratic society, has sometimes bred in the popular mind a dismaying cynicism about national government. Because the president of the United States—the POTUS in recent insider jargon—remains the only voice in the country that at any moment commands attention, the ability of the incumbent to maintain the prestige of the White House is vital to his work as executive. Readers of this book will find that presidential esteem and power have had their ups and downs as forty-three holders of the office have handled its inherent difficulties. A comparison with past events may provide sufficient cause to believe that the presidency will remain vigorous and adaptable and continue to serve as the trustworthy pilot of the Great Republic.

HENRY F. GRAFF
Columbia University, April 2002

Introduction

to the Second Edition

In the twelve years since the First Edition of this book was published, the office of the president has continued in its extraordinary fashion to reflect the nation's constantly changing assessment of its needs and priorities. This Second Edition, however, does more than simply fill in with inclusive essays on the presidencies of that period—those of Ronald Reagan, George Bush, and Bill Clinton. It also presents the original essays freshly reviewed and vetted for accuracy and up-to-dateness, in almost every instance by the author. This task produced a good number of corrections and emendations. All of the bibliographies have been similarly reexamined and revised.

Taking into account the expanding public awareness of how White House business is conducted, we have included a comprehensive chapter on the influence that First Ladies have exerted on the presidencies. We have aimed, too, at making all the essays in the book more "personalized" by including portraits of each of the chief executives, and more useful by providing an appendix with a series of details on the presidents' lives and administrations which the user might care to know but which could not be allowed to clutter the main body of the text. Also included is a bibliography of the presidency, a unique guide to further exploration of the endlessly alluring subject of the nation's executive leadership. In a word, this book is now a work of reference that will still more fully serve alike the ordinary reader seeking enlightenment, the high school or college student preparing a paper, and the experienced researcher looking for answers to recondite questions.

In the very eye of almost every national and international issue, the White House is on duty twenty-four hours a day, as the American people sit in judgment on its every move. The role of the presidency in national life described in the introduction to the First Edition seems no less valid today. A tendency noted then has become even more pronounced: the office grows increasingly democratic with each passing year. By means of talk radio and talk television, its occupant has become as familiar to the electorate as a next–door neighbor. Official presidential documents signed with a "Jimmy" or sometimes a "Bill" show one of the ways the chief executives themselves have responded to the development. When the Clinton administration instituted E-mail in 1993 it did not anticipate that it would receive about 125,000 messages on the system in the first seven months alone. Whatever the effect of this latter-day intimacy on the once remote and august office, the ready accessibility of its occupant is opening a new era in the life of the White House. The outcome cannot be foretold. *The Presidents: A Reference History*, Second Edition, is a quasi-encyclopedic source for perceiving what the presidency has been until the present, and a template for gauging what it may become.

HENRY F. GRAFF
Columbia University, February 1996

A

rising (though less splendid),
cance for free people abides.

The degree of detail with
impressed upon every reader
well documented from its be
may be probed exhaustively
no significant presidential sec
try, moreover, including the g
idle curious as well as to the

The articles in this boo
sources. The authors are pro
ist on the president of whom
individual presidency he is
American history, with all its
light they shed on the indivi
ident. They may also be rea
subject of modern history: ;
and most successful republi

Introduction

to the First Edition

The president of the United States at any given moment personifies to the world no less than to the American people the nation's power, purpose, and prestige. Taken together, the acts of the thirty-nine men who have occupied the presidency constitute the story of the national political leadership of the country during the nearly two centuries since the creation of the office. These men each emerged out of the bewildering chaos and conflict of their day by some fortuitous or unexpected turn of the wheel of history; for despite youthful dreams of reaching the White House, no youth can lay out and follow a sure road to it. Yet regardless of the contingent circumstances that bring presidents to power, they manage magically to become the symbols of the people's hopes and expectations. More fully than the nation is aware, presidents reflect the public temper that elevates them to office; and the people, time and again, discover in the man in the White House the qualities that their condition seems to demand.

Possibly only through the working of such reciprocal feeling was Abraham Lincoln metamorphosed from Honest Abe, a well-meaning but unknown politician, into a revered Father Abraham, defender of the Union and the voice of the loftiest American ideals. Possibly only through such an interaction between the leader and the led did Franklin D. Roosevelt, a victim of polio, unable to walk unaided, bring succor and reassurance to a paralyzed nation striving to go to work and be normal again.

The advent of television in the same period as the rapidly expanding scope of presidential duties brought the people into closer contact with the president than the Founding Fathers could have imagined. And despite the lengthening line of the presidents and the frequent turnover in the White House in the last twenty years, each president still gives his name to an era, however brief it may be, because every chief executive exhibits to the country and to his time a distinctive way of conducting affairs and puts his stamp on the urgent problems of the day. The crises, foreign or domestic, that can convulse an administration may leave a president's reputation

THE creation of the presidency wa
grand achievements of the Constitutio
tion that met in Philadelphia in 1787. A
controversy between the large and sma
garding their representation in Congress
order of business, the delegates did not
in taking up the subject of the executiv
hesitation they referred to the executive
establishing as *the president*. The C
names as *president* the presiding officer
ate, but the appellation is understood to
long alone to the chief executive of the Un
The word *presidency* to describe the offi
dent was already current in 1800.

Earliest Presidents

The designation *president* had long been t
Americans; it was used in the colonies an
the states to denote the chief executive,
magistrate, as he was often called. By 1800
in all the states the title of president had g
in popular usage to *governor*. It had not se
markable that from the First Continental Co
1774 to the last session of the Second Cor
1789, the chairman was "President of the Co
and under the Articles of Confederation fro

damaged or even in ru
inauguration is a rite o
gle and risk.

Presidents have alw
attention, scrutinized
rewards and honors of
available and visible. Pr
fest itself in an infinite
the will of the people
comes when what the
The most tumultuous
this truth—and they gi

The terms and co
Indeed, of the eight an
them concern the pres
Americans are still tin
Washington launched
understood that every
might set a precedent
lowed him has recogn
relishes the opportuni
ald of a new foreign po
as a memento a foldin
who had preceded l
Republican chiefs, set
gural address some w
Republicans.

All the men discu
they had in the life of i
tains of the ship of st
eled in marble, may n
presidency, he wrote,
rise, it can only be ex
the burden and respo
States," Harry S. Trur
ly, very lonely at the t
dent, who walked the
audience: "In the Mid
of trouble and sin. Ma
mental wardrobe of e
a more extensive war

Weighed down o
is specifically limited
The occupant must d
were barely speaking
Johnson was meetin
about to take the oat
tions of presidential
the reins of authorit
hended the significa
and he wrote about i

John A. Garraty
Columbia University
Grover Cleveland

Paul W. Glad
University of Oklahoma
William McKinley

Norman A. Graebner
University of Virginia
Zachary Taylor and Millard Fill

Henry F. Graff
Columbia University
Lyndon B. Johnson
A History of the Presidency

Fred I. Greenstein
Princeton University
Dwight D. Eisenhower

David M. Kennedy
Stanford University
Franklin D. Roosevelt

Ralph Ketcham
Syracuse University
James Madison

Richard S. Kirkendall
University of Washington
Jimmy Carter

Louis W. Koenig
New York University
Benjamin Harrison

Nicholas D. Kristof
The New York Times
George W. Bush

Richard B. Latner
Tulane University
Andrew Jackson

Arthur S. Link
Princeton University
Woodrow Wilson

Richard P. McCormick
Rutgers University
William Henry Harrison and John Tyle

Donald R. McCoy
University of Kansas
Calvin Coolidge

Sense, published in 1776, had affixed to George III the label "the Royal Brute of Britain." The fear of a new brute was ineradicable in the public mind. So, how much power should the proposed executive have? A deeply concerned delegate unhesitatingly declared that he regarded "the executive magistracy as nothing more than an institution for carrying the will of the legislature into effect." The legislature, he maintained, "was the depository of the supreme will of the people." This view of a president as dominated by Congress swiftly lost favor among the delegates.

As the work of the Convention proceeded, one of the most influential in shaping the executive was James Wilson of Pennsylvania, a Scotsman who had emigrated to America as a young man and had ardently supported the break with the Mother Country; in 1776 he had signed the Declaration of Independence. Wilson had no fear that a new monarchy was in the making, for he was confident, he said, that republican instincts were too well rooted in the public mind. He was convinced that there must be a single magistrate who would give "most energy, dispatch, and responsibility to the office." Wilson keenly favored also the direct popular election of the president, another idea that the Convention was not willing to accept. George Mason, a Virginian, was adamant: allowing the people to choose the president, he insisted, would be "as unnatural as it would be to refer a trial of colors to a blind person."

A second shaper of the emerging presidency was James Madison of Virginia, who, holding the view that Congress could become as oppressive as George III had been, also argued for a strong executive. Such an officer would serve as a counterweight to the legislature which, experience had shown, did not shrink from exerting its power. Madison supported a single seven-year term for the president—yet another idea that was rejected.

Early in September, a Committee on Unfinished Business, chaired by David Brearley of New Jersey, added precise touches to the specifications for the new executive. The proposals were honed in a vigorous but not prolonged series of discussion. The term of office would be four years. The president would be required to be a "natural-born citizen" and at least thirty-five years of age. An electoral college—with the number of each state's electors equaling the number of its congressional representatives plus its two senators—was devised for the election of the president, both to make election indirect and to bal-

ance the interests of the large and the small states. The electors chosen by the state legislatures in a manner determined by each state, would vote for two persons, not inhabitants of the same state. While this design gave the advantage to the large states it was assumed, as one delegate said, that "nineteen times in twenty" no individual would win a majority of the votes. The decision would then devolve upon the House of Representatives, where each state, regardless of the size of its delegation, would have one vote.

Electoral College

The electoral college has long been a contentious feature of the presidential elections. The opposition to it was especially clamorous after disputed canvasses, as those of 1824 and 1876 were, and that of 1888 when Benjamin Harrison (1889–1893) won in the electoral college despite receiving 100,000 fewer popular votes than Grover Cleveland (1885–1889; 1893–1897), his chief opponent, and that of 2000, when the Republican, George W. Bush (2001–), defeated Albert Gore although the Democrat received 540,000 more popular votes. In his inaugural address, Bush made no mention of how narrow his victory had been, but later conceded sardonically: "I wasn't exactly a landslide winner." Andrew Jackson (1829–1837), when he was finally in the White House after being bested in the electoral college in the election of 1824, proposed the direct election of presidents by the people in each of his Annual Messages to Congress. (He also wished to restrict presidents to one term of four or six years.)

When the Convention came to the end of its deliberations, the final phrasing of the finished document was referred to a Committee of Style that turned the work over to Gouverneur Morris of New York. Morris was the third major figure in the making of the presidency. A few years earlier he had had a large part in the writing of his state's constitution, which provided for a strong executive. Among many delegates in Philadelphia, New York's arrangement seemed an ideal model to follow. With respect to the presidency, Morris left standing the language already agreed upon, which is the heart of Article II of the Constitution: "The executive power shall be vested in a President of the United States of America," with no qualifying statement whatsoever. The explanation was not far to seek. One delegate put it this way: "I do [not] believe the [executive powers] would have been so great had not many of the members cast their eyes toward General Washington as President; and shaped their Ideas of the Powers to be given a President, by their opinions of his Virtues." The expectation that Washington, who inspired unbounded confidence in his integrity and probity, would fill the chair of president, likely spurred the convention to make the president commander-in-chief and to provide for a four-year term renewable without limit.

The Presidency at Work

Combining today the roles of head of government and chief of state, the president is the very symbol of the United States, its premier statesman, and its resounding voice in the family of nations. From the White House flow the major initiatives for domestic and foreign policies. As titular head of the party in power, the president is likewise the chief politician of the country, the designated unifier of the competing constituencies and regions. He is also incomparably the principal newsmaker. But what the world takes for granted about the stability of America's presidential system of government was by no means assured when George Washington (1789–1797) took the oath of office on 30 April 1789. Its words spoken by him—and by presidents-elect every four years since—are a sample of republican simplicity, then an unfamiliar concept in the governance of nations. His hand on the Bible, the chief executive-to-be pledges: "I do solemnly swear (or affirm) that I will faithfully execute the Office of President of the United States, and will to the best of my Ability, preserve, protect and defend the Constitution of the United States."

For many years, people the world over wondered how the United States would fare under a president, often referring to the remarkable provision and powers of its chief leader as the "American experiment." From time immemorial, monarchies—many of them absolute in power—had been almost universally the preferred form of government. Few people, indeed, would have guessed that the success of the American presidency would become an inspiration for peoples throughout the world.

Washington had no wish to be a king and did not act like one, but republics were rare in history and there were no guides to how a president ought to conduct himself. Washington was acutely conscious of the novelty of his position as the first of its kind in the history of the world, and he understood that almost every step he took would set a precedent for

those who filled the office after him. The public also was keenly aware that the country was breaking fresh ground. Even how to refer to President had to be decided. One Senator suggested: "His Highness the President of the United States of America and Protector of their Liberties"; another proposed: "His Elective Highness." In the end the simple "Mr. President" seemed august enough.

The presidency has continued to grow in complexity along paths that the founding fathers could not have imagined. Washington altered the conduct of the office as laid out in the Constitution through the creation of the cabinet, a body of advisers who also head the administrative subdivisions of the government. The cabinet was in its way the equivalent of the council of state that Madison had proposed at the Constitutional Convention for the purpose of keeping a watchful eye on the president. The cabinet that Washington established was not a monitor above him but, on the contrary, being his appointees, the members were subservient to him.

The cabinet arrangement began when Washington directed that the heads of the executive departments—state, treasury, and war—meet in his absence from the capital city. They met in this way only once, but beginning in 1793 these officials along with the attorney-general began to meet with Washington periodically. James Madison, then a member of the House of Representatives, was the one who first referred to the group as the cabinet. Washington had in mind taking votes on public issues at the cabinet sessions in order to establish that he was not an authoritarian. But the conflict between Jefferson, the secretary of state, and Hamilton, the secretary of the treasury, was so intense that the idea died quickly.

Because the cabinet has no constitutional foundation, presidents have used it variously. It has grown in size as new federal departments have been created, and is accordingly unwieldy as a vehicle for making decisions. Dwight D. Eisenhower (1953–1961) found it useful for vetting policy proposals, but John F. Kennedy (1961–1963) regarded it as of little value. Some presidents have used it chiefly for political purposes: James K. Polk (1845–1849) filled its places with possible successors; Abraham Lincoln (1861–1865), on the other hand, filled it with four members of his party who had been his rivals for the nomination in 1860. When it was suggested to him that they would eat him up, he replied that they would eat each other up. By the end of the Civil War he was not consulting the cabinet at all, to the dismay of the members. This has increasingly been the history of presidential cabinets.

Presidents have come to rely on groups of intimates for their advisers. Andrew Jackson's coterie of cronies, mostly journalists, were designated the "Kitchen Cabinet" because they met in the kitchen of the White House. Theodore Roosevelt's (1901–1909) insider group of friends and agency heads was his "Tennis Cabinet" because they discussed public business on the White House tennis court. Franklin D. Roosevelt (1933–1945) had as his closest aides a "brain trust," a designation describing the scholars, economists, and lawyers who played significant roles in shaping New Deal policies. In conducting the Vietnam War, Lyndon B. Johnson (1963–1969) brought together his principal associates for lunch on Tuesdays in the private quarters of the White House. This group has been referred to as the Tuesday Cabinet. George W. Bush relies heavily on a group of "insiders," some of whom had their first national political experience in the administration of his father.

Political Parties

Even before Washington's presidency ended, the rise of political parties had commenced to alter the workings of the office. Although Washington detested the idea of parties, two groups had arisen in response to the national problems his administration was addressing. One group, guided by Thomas Jefferson and James Madison, was called the Democratic-Republicans. They had support in rural parts of the North and South and on the frontier. The other group, which had its strength among business and manufacturing interests, designated themselves the Federalists. They were generally pro-England and the Jeffersonians pro-France; at the time, the French Revolution was convulsing Europe. Washington in 1793 issued a neutrality proclamation stating that the United States would be impartial in foreign relations, that the nation would take no sides. This position set the basic policy for presidents in their conduct of international affairs for the next century.

When Washington's second term was coming to an end in 1796 he announced that he would not seek a third term. In tribute to Washington's decision, the next two-term presidents, Jefferson (1801–1809) and Madison (1809–1817) both forswore a third term. Ulysses S. Grant (1869–1877) sought a third term in 1880, and Theodore Roosevelt ran again in 1912, but the tradition was not actually broken until 1940. That year Franklin D. Roosevelt sought and won a third term—and in 1944 a fourth term. Today the Twenty-second Amendment to the Constitution forbids the president from serving more than two terms. Ratified in 1951, it was a kind of posthumous rebuke to FDR. Both Ronald Reagan (1981–1989) and William Jefferson Clinton (1993–2001) felt frustrated by the provisions of the amendment.

The early presidents had been chosen by congressional leaders of the emerging parties in party "caucuses." At first these decisions were made in secret meetings, then for a while openly. The supporters of Jackson, representing a new spirit in politics, railed against "King Caucus" as undemocratic. After the savage presidential contest of 1824, the day of the caucus system was over, to be succeeded by a unique American institution, the national nominating convention. It was first convened in 1831 by the Anti-Masons, a small, single-issue party that is remembered now only for that contribution. Today, delegates of the major parties gather quadrennially in June or July to select their standard-bearers. The Republican delegates that gathered in Philadelphia in 2000 were 2,066 strong, with an equal number of alternates. A few weeks later when the Democrats met in Los Angeles, they assembled 4,366 men and women and 610 alternates. Both parties had chosen their delegates in state primary elections, state conventions, and state committees of the parties.

The system has grown more complicated in our own time, owing to the fact that the choosing of the next presidential candidates begins almost as soon as Inauguration Day is over. Would-be presidents announce that they are throwing their hats in the ring: they establish what are called exploratory committees, which promptly metamorphose into fundraising organizations.

The testing time is the primary season, which commences in January in Iowa and continues in other states until June. Invariably, however, most of the primary votes are cast before April, and the nominations are clinched long before the final primaries. The number of delegates that each state party sends to its convention depends on the party's performance in the previous election, bonuses being granted for the number of the party members elected to Congress, the state legislatures, and the governorships. The delegates whom the Republicans at present send to their convention are pledged to vote for a particular candidate.

The Democrats' delegates are divided in accordance to the way each state voted in the previous three elections. Seventy-five percent of them represent electoral districts; the rest are at-large. Party leaders and certain elected officeholders constitute an additional 15 percent of the total number. On top of this number, there are several hundred so-called superdelegates, chosen because they are high officials of the party or because of the importance of the elective office they hold. Superdelegates are unpledged. The Republicans assign all the delegates of a particular state or congressional district to the candidate who wins the most votes in that region. The Democrats assign the delegates in proportion to the votes the candidates received in the primaries.

Campaign Dramas

Some of the struggles that have taken place in conventions are legendary. The Democratic convention of 1844 produced Candidate Polk in a wild session, making him the first "dark horse" to run for the White House. Not even mentioned in the first seven ballots, he, rather than the better-known leaders of the party, was nominated on the ninth. Franklin Pierce (1853–1857) was not a candidate when the Democrats met in the summer of 1852, and his wife was firmly opposed to his becoming one. He was chosen on the thirty-fifth ballot. In 1880 James A. Garfield (1881) was not mentioned on the first ballot of the Republican convention. On the second to fifth ballots he had only one vote. His strength rose and fell on successive ballots; even on the thirty-fifth he had only fifty votes. But a sudden flood of support made him the nominee on the thirty-sixth. In 1912 Woodrow Wilson (1913–1921), the governor of New Jersey, was eventually nominated by the Democrats on the forty-sixth ballot.

The Democratic convention of 1924 was the monster of all conventions. The nominee for president, John W. Davis was finally named on the 103rd ballot, as people with radios—then new-fangled—listened intently for the result they thought would never come. Today, the convention has become somewhat of an anachronism. Franklin D. Roosevelt in 1932 was nominated by his party on the fourth ballot. Since then, every president has been nominated by his party on the first ballot. The last major party nominee for the presidency not chosen on the first ballot was Wendell L. Willkie, named by the Republicans on the sixth in 1940.

Campaign Trails

Presidential campaigns since almost the beginning have been a source of wonder and of public entertainment. The first campaign that displayed the vitriol and half-truths that are the stuff of today's was that of 1800. John Adams (1797–1801) was battling for reelection against Thomas Jefferson. In the back-and-forth between their respective newspaper supporters (for only in print did the verbal fireworks take place) Adams was reviled as a fool and a tyrant, and once again as in 1796, as an "avowed friend of monarchy." Jefferson was denounced as an atheist, a Franco-maniac, and sometimes simply as Mad Tom. He was, it was said, an infidel whose passions posed untold, indeed unimaginable danger to the republic.

The Federalists and the Democratic-Republicans acted as if they were foreign adversaries, constantly at each other's throat in the public prints and using denunciatory language that even now is rarely used. No citizen of that day would have predicted that in their old age Adams and Jefferson would correspond with each other on the great questions of republican government in a body of letters that is today a national treasure. Despite the heat of the political struggles, voters have always seemed able to see beyond the rhetoric of the combatants and their followers. Notice, for example, that all incumbent presidents running for office during wartime have been reelected. Although James Madison was fiercely blamed for the War of 1812, which was denounced as "Mr. Madison's War," he was reelected in 1812. Lincoln won a second term in 1864, even though the outcome of the Union cause was still in doubt.

Personal assaults have never been absent from presidential canvasses. But they are usually ineffective. Despite a rumor of Jefferson's amorous connection with his slave Sally Hemings that was circulated in 1804, the issue evaporated quickly and did not defeat its target in the election. (The story never died, however, and in the late 1990s DNA testing has confirmed that the descendants of Sally Hemings had a Jefferson ancestor, possibly Thomas.) As for Andrew Jackson in 1828, he was stung by the scorpion charge which had long shadowed him that Rachel, his dear wife, had lived with him in adultery. She had mistakenly assumed she was divorced from her first husband at the time that she and the hero of the Battle of New Orleans (1815) were married. That she and Jackson were remarried when the facts were revealed mattered not at all to the supporters of John Quincy Adams. Rachel Jackson's death before her husband's inauguration left Jackson bereft, and he never ceased to put the blame for it on his opponents' scurrility. The story plainly did not weaken Jackson's candidacy.

Martin Van Buren (1837–1841), when he ran for president in 1836, was said to be an illegitimate son of Aaron Burr—thus, a bastard sired by a traitor who had killed Alexander Hamilton in 1804. Lincoln in the election of 1860 felt the pain of hearing that he was an illegitimate child, too. Such personal calumniation reached new heights during the election of 1884. The Democratic candidate, Grover Cleveland, was said to be the father of a child born out of wedlock, and his opponents made the most of the story. Cleveland had not been sure he was the father of the little boy—it might have been the responsibility of a friend of his—but being a bachelor he took on the obligation of supporting the child and his mother. In the end, his determination to tell the truth, as he also urged his supporters to do, carried the day and won him the election. Nevertheless, the impertinent jingle "Ma, Ma, where's my pa? Gone to the White House, ha ha ha" lingers in presidential history.

In the new century, possibly because Victorian moralism in America was at its zenith, coupled with big-power responsibilities and the sobering effect of World War I, Americans came to think of their presidents as high-minded, flawless men. For years salacious gossip ceased to be a part of presidential campaigns, although Wilson's possibly adulterous trysts and the infidelity of Warren G. Harding (1921–1923) were well-known to intimates and to many newspaper reporters. Franklin D. Roosevelt's longtime affair with Lucy Mercer Rutherford, which had commenced in 1917 when he was assistant secretary of the Navy, was not general knowledge until after his death in 1945. His relations with Margaret ("Daisy") Suckley, a distant cousin, came to light only in the 1990s. John F. Kennedy's promiscuous womanizing likewise played no part in his campaign of 1960.

The old restraint broke down during the 1980s, and today presidential privacy is no more. Bill Clinton's affair with Monica Lewinsky, an intern in the White House, opened the way to his impeachment in 1998. His earlier entanglement with an Arkansas nightclub singer, Gennifer Flowers, was a featured story during his first campaign in 1992. And the lawsuit that a former Arkansas state employee, Paula Jones, brought against Clinton in 1994 for sexual misconduct (which he eventually settled) contributed

heavily to the tabloidization of newspapers and other media, as well as the denigration of the presidency. Without apparent embarrassment, he and Hillary Rodham Clinton, soon to be the First Lady, readily discussed their marriage on national television during the campaign of 1992. A candidate's life is now a more or less open book, with income tax returns and medical records and every kind of rumor and report quickly turned into a national—or even international—story.

The first presidents did not "campaign" in the way modern Americans think of a run for the White House. It was regarded as unseemly for a potential president to appear to be seeking the office. Indeed, the myth was general that the office seeks the man. Still, the ferocious jostling for political primacy is an essential ingredient of the office. Lincoln, for example, was pleased to be everybody's second choice at the Republican convention of 1860 in Chicago. He rightly expected that none of his opponents was strong enough to carry the day and that the party would come to him. His appetite for the office was hard to hide; he had said with barely feigned zest: "The taste is in my mouth a little." When Adlai Stevenson was approached for the Democratic nomination in 1952, his first response was, "Let this cup pass." He was not posing as a modest man but rather shrinking from a contest against General Eisenhower, a sure winner.

The eye of the television camera combined with modern investigative reporting has made it impossible any longer to hide or cover up a candidate's real or perceived shortcomings. Although Franklin Roosevelt suffered paralysis in his legs after contracting polio in 1921, and often had to be carried by Secret Service agents, the general public was unaware of his incapacity. Every effort was made to hide it from the public—in the belief, apparently, that FDR's ability to govern might be deemed impaired. Yet today the public seems to have given up such taboos as would once have militated against presidential candidates. Adlai Stevenson, the Democratic nominee, who ran against General Eisenhower in 1952 and 1956, was the first candidate of a major party who was a divorced man, and Ronald Reagan was the first divorcé elected to the presidency. In neither case did the marital status of the man become an issue. But the fact that Democratic nominee Alfred E. Smith was a Roman Catholic had played a major part in his defeat in 1928. Only when John F. Kennedy, also a Roman Catholic, sought the office in 1960 did this so-called handicap no longer apply. In 2000, Democrat Al Gore chose Senator Joseph Lieberman, an Orthodox Jew, to be the nominee for vice president; Lieberman's religion did not seem to be a deciding factor in the outcome of the election.

As the public began more and more to participate in the hoopla of naming a president, the campaigns became dramatic and picturesque—full of parades, songs, banners, and slogans. Some of the slogans are indelible markers in the nation's history: "Tippecanoe and Tyler, too" (the Whigs in 1840 with William Henry Harrison for president); "We Polked 'em in '44, we'll Pierce them in '52" (the Democrats in 1852); "McKinley and the Full Dinner Pail" (the Republicans in 1900); "He kept us out or war" (the Democrats in 1916 with Woodrow Wilson for president); "Keep Cool with Coolidge" (the Republicans in 1924); "I Like Ike" (the Republicans in 1952 with Eisenhower for president); "Nixon's the One" (the Republicans in 1972).

Until the end of the nineteenth century the principals did not themselves take part in the noisy ballyhoo. Their surrogates and the party faithful did the dirty work. When there were issues at stake—as became commonplace after the Civil War—the candidates' positions on them would be made known by letters published in the newspaper, or by the candidate announcing his support of the party platform. Between 1865 and 1900 controversy revolved chiefly around the tariff (should it be high or low?) and about the currency (should it be backed by silver or by gold or by both?). These hotly disputed questions were really old ones much debated in antebellum days, but now they masked others that did not enter presidential campaign discourse. Deep-lying concerns, such as the conditions of those who toiled in the fields and the swelling industrial centers, the slums in which millions were forced to live, the lack of supervision of the food and drug supply, and, not least of all, the treatment of people of color, including not only the freedmen but also Native Americans and people of Asian descent—none of these found any echo in presidential campaigns.

In office, chief executives have sometimes uttered words of complaint about the burden they bear. Jefferson came to call the presidency "a splendid misery." "A bed of thorns," was how John Tyler put it. "Dignified slavery," was Andrew Johnson's phrase. Beset by office-seekers, James A. Garfield declared: "My God! What is this place that a man should ever want to get into it." Harry Truman labeled the executive mansion a "big white jail." Grover Cleveland was the most candid when he confessed that being president is "a self-inflicted penance," for nobody has yet been dragged kicking and screaming into the White House. Indeed, few presidents, excepting perhaps James Buchanan (1857–1861), in 1861 and Herbert Hoover (1929–1933), though fully aware that they occupy the White House only temporarily, can resist bemoaning their departure on moving day.

The Vice President

John Adams of Massachusetts, Washington's successor in 1797, had been the Vice President. As such he was the first to suffer under the restrictions a vice president has generally confronted, lacking any stated duty except to preside over the Senate, and vote there only to break a tie. At the Constitutional Convention, Elbridge Gerry, who was destined to serve as vice president (1813–1814) under Madison, insisted there was no need for the office. Adams regarded himself as "a mere mechanical tool to wind up the clock." Notwithstanding, he had seen, he wrote his wife, that he was invested with "two separate powers-the one *in esse* [in actuality] and the other *in posse* [in potential]." In actuality he was nothing; in potential he could be everything.

So it has been in the entire history of the office. Although Adams as president viewed Jefferson, his vice president, as "the first prince of the country, and the heir apparent to the sovereign authority," Jefferson complained that no one was consulting him "as to any measure of government." Charles G. Dawes, the vice president under Calvin Coolidge (1923–1929) told then Senator Alben W. Barkley, who later would be vice president under Harry S. Truman (1945–1953): "I can do only two things: one is to sit up here and listen to you birds talk, without the privilege of being able to answer you back. The other is to look at the newspapers every morning to see how the President's health is!" Still, despite these derisive words, eight vice presidents, by office only men standing in the wings, have succeeded to the presidency.

Although he felt useless, Adams still holds the record for breaking tie votes (twenty-nine). By comparison, in his eight years as vice president under Ronald Reagan, George H. W. Bush (1989–1993) cast only eight such ballots, and Albert Gore, vice president from 1993 to 2001, only four. By a quirk of fate, it became Gore's last official duty to announce from the chair in the Senate in January 2001 the electoral vote making the victor in the canvass just ended his opponent, George W. Bush.

When Jefferson and Aaron Burr were tied in the electoral college in the presidential election of 1800, the House of Representatives was called upon to choose between them. Since the Twelfth Amendment, added to the Constitution in 1804, electors must mark their ballots to show separately their choices for president and vice president. The result has been the choosing of a person not as a potential successor to the presidency but in order to bolster the chances of the head of the ticket. The office was shortly used to "balance" a presidential ticket with a politician from another part of the country. Thus Jefferson and Madison, both from Virginia, served with George Clinton of New York. Sometimes it is personalities that have been "balanced": the sophisticated New Yorker Martin Van Buren, for instance, had as his running mate Richard Mentor Johnson of Kentucky, who boasted that he "was born in a cane brake and cradled in a sap trough." Sometimes the choice has been used to neutralize the stance of the presidential candidate. Thus when William Jennings Bryan, ardent advocate of free silver, was nominated in 1896, the Democratic convention named Arthur Sewall of Maine, a bank president, to run with him. Sometimes the vice presidential nominee settles a political debt, as in 1932 when John Nance Garner of Texas was repaid for helping make Franklin D. Roosevelt the standard-bearer. In 1984 the Democratic nominee, Walter F. Mondale, in a bow to the rising tide of feminism, named Geraldine Ferraro, a congresswoman from New York, to join him at the top of the ticket. She became thereby the first woman designated by a major party for one of the two highest elective offices. General Eisenhower's selection in 1952 of the young Richard Nixon to be his vice president owed something to Ike's eagerness to blunt criticism that he was too old to be president. Bill Clinton's naming of Al Gore as his running mate in 1992 was aimed in part at projecting an image of youth in the Democratic party leadership. Presidents who have served more than one term have sometimes changed their vice president. Of the fifty-four presidential elections since the first, only eight resulted in the reelection of the entire ticket.

In the nineteenth century Martin Van Buren was the only vice president who succeeded to the White House without the death of his president, Van Buren being elected in 1836. Today it is assumed that the vice president is "in the succession," and from the outset of an administration he is an adviser and consultant to the president—the only other nationally elected official. Since 1960 it has been the practice for the presidential nominees to select the other half of their ticket, rather than leave the choice to the convention, and upon election to give the vice president a medley of tasks, mostly ceremonial but increasingly substantial. For example, President Jimmy Carter (1977–1981) insisted that Vice President Walter F. Mondale attend every policy meeting that he himself did. This arrangement took on new form under President George W. Bush (2001–) when his vice president, Dick Cheney, was given four offices in Washington to deal with the wide range of responsibilities laid upon him. These tasks made him seem a kind of prime minister, the most powerful holder of the second highest office in history. After the terrorist attacks of 11 September 2001, Cheney was reported to be performing his duties from a "secure and undisclosed location." He and the president were hoping to ensure the continuity of government in the event that either became a victim of a terrorist attack. Cheney remained "the coach to Mr. Bush's quarterback," and through video conferences and frequent use of the telephone, Cheney kept a close watch on policies.

Presidents by Accident

Remarkably, the Constitution was in force for more than half a century before a president died in office. When William Henry Harrison (1841) succumbed to pneumonia a month after his inauguration, John Tyler (1841–1845), his vice president, immediately took the presidential oath and claimed his full rights as chief executive. No member of the Constitutional Convention was still living to say what the framers might have intended otherwise in such an eventuality. Like many contemporaries, John Quincy Adams, a former president (1825–1829), was appalled. He wrote in his diary: "I paid a visit this morning to Mr. Tyler, who styles himself President and not Vice President acting as President." Efforts in Congress to argue that Tyler was somehow not entitled to exercise the powers of the office failed to carry the day.

Other "accidental" presidents have seemed to mean surprisingly good luck for the country. The second such was Millard Fillmore (1850–1853), vice president under Zachary Taylor (1849–1850), who had not even consulted him in selecting his cabinet. After Taylor's death in office, Fillmore helped bring about the Compromise of 1850 that forestalled for a decade the looming disruption of the Union. When Lyndon Johnson succeeded to the presidency upon the assassination of John F. Kennedy in 1963, civil rights legislation that had languished in Congress was put on the road to enactment in a notable burst of presidential energy, by a man who had been a recognized master of the Senate when he was the majority leader. Two of the outstanding presidencies in the twentieth century, Theodore Roosevelt's and Harry S. Truman's, followed satisfactorily the demise of their principals. Yet the transition has not always been smooth. When James A. Garfield was critically wounded by a gunshot in 1881 and Vice President Chester A. Arthur met the next day with the cabinet, no one rose to greet him and they stared at him dumbly.

Several times the succession to the presidency after the vice president has been dealt with by legislation. A law passed in 1792 put the president pro tempore of the Senate, usually spoken of as president pro tem, next in line; a new law in 1886 removed the president pro tem from the line of succession and substituted the cabinet officers. President Truman in 1947 signed into law the Succession Act that remains in effect today. It places the Speaker of the House and then the president pro tem next after the vice president, to be followed by the secretary of state and the other cabinet officers in the order of their departments' creation.

Finding the Candidates

The recruitment of presidents has changed over time. The first presidents were those who helped to found the nation. Washington's role is memorialized forever as the "Father of His Country" and as "First in peace, first in war, and first in the hearts of his countrymen." John Adams, the second chief executive, was already known to fame as the "Atlas of Independence" for his Herculean labors in the cause of liberty during the 1770s and 1780s. Then followed a group of luminous Virginians: Jefferson, the third president, was the principal author of the Declaration of Independence; Madison, Jefferson's close friend, had earned the sobriquet "Father of the Constitution," and James Monroe (1817–1825), who had been wounded as a soldier in the War for Independence, and was said to look like George Washington,

is remembered as the "last of the cocked hats"—the last president who wore the tricorne of the Revolutionary era. Jefferson, Madison, and Monroe all had served as secretary of state—Jefferson under Washington, Madison under Jefferson, and Monroe under Madison. Consequently, the office of secretary of state came to be regarded as preparation for the presidency and its holder as next in line to the White House.

This pattern became a factor in the election of 1824 when Monroe's second term in office was coming to an end. The three leading candidates were Andrew Jackson of Tennessee who won 99 electoral votes, John Quincy Adams of Massachusetts who won 84, and Henry Clay of Kentucky who won 37. Because none of them had a majority, the House of Representatives had to select the winner. Clay was in the position of president-maker because he could choose to throw his support to either Jackson or Adams. Clay found it congenial to side with Adams, and Adams was thereupon elected. Soon afterward Adams made Clay his secretary of state. The Jackson supporters were outraged, shouting "bargain and corruption." They believed that with that appointment Adams had "paid off" Clay by putting him in succession to the presidency—in accordance with the established practice since the beginning of the office, with the single exception of John Adams's presidency.

In his inaugural address, Adams admitted: "Less possessed of your confidence in advance than any of my predecessors, I am deeply conscious of the prospect that I shall stand more and oftener in need of your indulgence." He got little of it: Jackson's backers during the next four years waged a tireless campaign to avenge their man's defeat. Many observers could see that the nature of politics was changing. The older aristocratic view that leadership is to be found in an elite class only was beginning to be supplanted by the notion that "the people" must rule. Whereas only about 20 percent of the eligible voters went to the polls in 1824, four years later the number had quadrupled.

The Jacksonians, maintaining that they were the true successors of Jefferson, called themselves Democratic-Republicans. Soon they shortened the name to Democrats. They touted Jackson as "the people's choice" and elected him in 1828. He had once said, "I know what I am fit for. I can command a body of men in a rough way, but I am not fit to be President." Nevertheless, on his inauguration day hordes of his partisans overran the White House in their certainty that a glorious new time for the nation was at hand. John Quincy Adams, still smarting that Jackson had not called on him to pay his respects after his election, refused to attend Jackson's oath-taking. A few years later when Adams's alma mater, Harvard College, bestowed an honorary doctor of laws degree on Jackson, Adams was incensed, calling his successor "a barbarian who could not write a sentence of grammar and hardly could spell his own name." Harvard's president might have been speaking for the emerging new outlook when he responded to Adams: "As the people have decided that this man knows laws enough to be their ruler, it is not for Harvard College to maintain that they are mistaken."

The age of Jackson commenced a new time in the history of the presidency, for it was in the 1830s that what we call "public opinion" began to form and to become an element in national politics. "Public opinion" was not always easy to divine, but every vote-seeker knew that somehow it was the pulse of the electorate. More and more, politicians came to respond to the views of the people and to keep a wet finger to the wind.

Getting Out the Vote

In the era before the modern media changed the way the news was circulated, people would usually make their choice of president by following the decision of their local party chieftains. For the book-reading public there were the campaign biographies of the principal candidates.

This genre first appeared in 1824. In one way or another, all of the literary trumpeters made their subjects out to be "heralds of destiny"; some were also provided with exalted ancestries. In 1852 Nathaniel Hawthorne, a Bowdoin College classmate of Franklin Pierce, composed a campaign biography of his fellow-alumnus that was quickly printed in huge quantities. Five thousand copies were distributed free in New York City alone. The same year a million copies of a biography of Pierce's opponent, General Winfield Scott, were said to have been handed out.

During the campaign of 1860 Lincoln was so little known in the eastern part of the country that newspapers sometimes simply referred to him as "the Westerner." When he came to New York to deliver an address at Cooper Union Institute, he traveled uptown to the studio of the photographer Mathew Brady, where he had his picture taken. The

Republican party thereupon distributed hundreds of thousands of copies of it, making it a "first" for millions of people: seeing what their would-be president looked like. Nevertheless, the circumstances of his life were made known through campaign biographies widely circulated. Another literary lion, William Dean Howells, was the author of one of the best of them, dwelling heavily on how Lincoln had educated himself and embedding that fact in the voter's sense of the future Emancipator's character and worth.

Yet another literary light, General Lew Wallace, best known for his novel *Ben Hur* (1880), wrote Benjamin Harrison's campaign biography. And John Dos Passos, later the author of the acclaimed *U.S.A.* trilogy (1937), touted McKinley for reelection in 1900. In 1952, the popular writer John Gunther wrote a worshipful life of Dwight D. Eisenhower. When he was a candidate for the governorship of New York in 1928, Franklin Roosevelt wrote a campaign biography of Alfred E. Smith, the Democrats' choice for president.

Before the Civil War, candidates were invariably revealed to have been paragons of virtue as children; after the 1870s Tom Sawyer provided the model boyhood-pranks and artfulness mingled with unmistakable good-heartedness. In the twentieth century candidates have also been depicted as outdoor types—Hoover, for instance, was portrayed as an avid fisherman. The Horatio Alger theme of "rags to riches" also had its place: thus Wendell Willkie, the Republican candidate in 1940, was reported to have peddled newspapers as a boy, James A. Garfield was presented as the "canal boy" working on the waterways of his native Ohio, and Eisenhower was said to have sold vegetables on the streets of Abilene, Kansas. These desirable attributes seem not to have been verified. One of Grant's biographers affirmed that the general never drank anything "stronger than cold water."

Boasting that the candidate was a farmer has always seemed advantageous. Franklin Roosevelt enjoyed contending that his Hyde Park homesite was really a farm. Voter-readers learned that Harry Truman had hardened his hands on the levers of a gangplow. Garfield was depicted "working in the hay-field with his boys."

But above all, military heroism has been the choice card of admission, for, like most peoples who applaud their war heroes, Americans have given their triumphant army leaders open sesame to the White House, from Washington to Jackson to Zachary Taylor to Theodore Roosevelt to Eisenhower. Sometimes the campaign biographer has had to find a substitute for the real thing. Thus it was recalled that William Jennings Bryan, the Democrats' candidate in 1896, 1900, and 1908, *trained* a regiment in Nebraska during the Spanish-American War. Thomas E. Dewey, the Republican candidate in 1944 and 1948, was hailed as the successful chairman of the first U.S.O. fund drive, providing aid and entertainment to service men and women. And the Republicans called attention to Ronald Reagan's World War II service, which consisted chiefly of making training films for the troops. Lord Bryce writing in 1880 in his classic commentary *The American Commonwealth* offered the judgment that what the party desires in not a good president but a good candidate. Voters must wrestle with the implications of this assessment every four years.

The campaign biography has become less important today because the media present the candidates in such intimate detail that no mystery attaches to them and no myth about them can be sustained. William Jefferson Clinton's history of womanizing and his experiment with marijuana were the stuff of conversation well before he took the oath of office. George W. Bush's need to give up alcohol was public knowledge and turned into a virtue when his campaign for the presidency was only beginning.

Today, biographies of the candidates issued in presidential years are sometimes searching and critical. Two of the kind in 2000 were David Maraniss and Ellen Nakashima's *The Prince of Tennessee: The Rise of Al Gore* and Molly Ivins and Lou Dubose's *Shrub: The Short but Happy Political Life of George W. Bush.* For many years, too, prospective presidents have forsaken the older style of seeming to be reluctant candidates and proclaimed their own merits for voter support in books usually put together hastily by ghost writers. The titles are indicative. Calvin Coolidge's supporters aiming to make him a dark horse candidate in 1920 brought together a collection of his speeches entitled *Have Faith in Massachusetts* (1919). Likewise Richard Nixon (1969–1974) put out in 1960 a compilation of his speeches called *The Challenges We Face.* Barry Goldwater, the Republican candidate in 1964, published *Where I Stand.* Four years earlier he had turned out *The Conscience of a Conservative.* In 1964 Lyndon Johnson proudly distributed a little book entitled *My Hope for America.* Jimmy Carter attracted national attention in 1975 after he released *Why Not the Best?* The year 1988 saw

the Democratic candidate, Michael S. Dukakis bring out *Creating the Future: The Massachusetts Comeback and Its Promise for America.* It was, in its way, a response to his opponent, George H. W. Bush, who had written (with Victor Gold) *Looking Forward* (1987). The title was identical to a book written by Franklin Roosevelt in 1933. The Republican candidate, Robert Dole, tried something fresh in 1996 when he made use of Jack Kemp, his popular vice presidential candidate, in *Trusting the People: The Dole/Kemp Plan to Free The Economy and Create a Better America.* Dole also produced a joint autobiography with his accomplished wife, Elizabeth, that they fetchingly called *The Doles: Unlimited Partners* (1988). In 1999, George W. Bush contributed to the species *A Charge to Keep.* Aside from being of interest to historians, these books and their kind quickly gather only dust on the shelves of libraries.

Rise of the Modern Media

Changing technology also played a part in creating a new political culture. Whereas in 1801 it was considered extraordinary that Jefferson's inaugural address had appeared in a Washington newspaper almost immediately (he had given a copy of it beforehand to the editor), William Henry Harrison's forty years later was distributed by railroad, and people in Philadelphia could read it the evening of the day it had been delivered in the capital. When James K. Polk was nominated in Baltimore in 1844, the news was received in Washington on the first telegraph line in the country. Before Polk's term ended, the wire service the Associated Press had been created, linking major newspapers in their coverage of events. Already the penny press, begun modestly in 1833, was placing newspapers in the hands of "the common man" and opening the way to making the populace politically informed. By the time that the telephone was in widespread use in the 1890's, news could be disseminated everywhere, and practically instantaneously, and presidential politics became one of its alluring staples. The new Linotype machine made it possible to set the stories quickly, supplying constantly updated editions of newspapers, heightening the interest in news, notably accounts of presidential activities.

In the 1890s the general use of the halftone method of reproducing pictures enabled magazine and newspaper editors to illustrate cheaply the articles they ran. This development allowed people at last to know what their president looked like. Up to then, for the most part, only woodcuts had been used, and they only occasionally. As a result, the majority of Americans only knew the faces of Washington and Lincoln. At the beginning of the twentieth century the rotogravure process improved the tonal quality of reproduced photographs, and the facial features of public figures became familiar to millions, especially in the big cities, through the Sunday supplements printed in sepia. For the first time the general public became accustomed to the looks and public doings not only of the president, but also of his family.

The first radio broadcast of election results was heard in 1920 on the Pittsburgh station KDKA. Four years later, moviegoers saw the presidential candidates for the first time in newsreels. In 1925 millions heard on the radio Calvin Coolidge's inaugural address, another first. Franklin D. Roosevelt was the first president to be televised—at the New York World's Fair of 1939. William Jefferson Clinton's inauguration was the first that was broadcast live on the Internet. After World War II, television became the chief vehicle of presidential news, and the amount of money spent on presidential campaigns, mostly to pay for time on television, became a major factor and issue in national politics. Critics of the way this money was being raised argued that the sums contributed damaged the democratic process by constituting veritable bribes from interested donors.

Presidents and the Press

Presidents only gradually responded to the call and needs of the media. Their attentiveness has been in proportion to the growth of democracy which has more and more made it de rigueur for the chief executive to seem to be in tune with the voice of the people. But from early on, the press and the presidents have had a love-hate relationship. George Washington had considered himself a unifying force for the new nation, seeking to provide a standard "to which the wise and honest may repair." The incendiary partisan newspapers of the day irked him, because they reflected the factionalism he despised. He canceled his subscription to thirty of them when he left his Virginia estate at Mount Vernon for his inauguration, although he was reading one on the last day of his life. On a tour of the South in 1791 he was followed about by reporters, experiencing what every president since then has known: an unquenchable limelight. In

1798 John Adams supported the Alien and Sedition Acts designed to silence his critics. And Jefferson, who spoke feelingly of the importance of freedom of the press, nevertheless could declare: "Newspapers present for the most part only a caricature of disaffected minds." Although Madison was the author of the First Amendment, which guarantees freedom of the press, he felt wounded by the press's carping about his conduct of the War of 1812. During the Mexican War, Polk regarded newspaper criticism as nothing less than treason. So it has been as presidents and writers for the media wrestle with each other like scorpions in a bottle.

Lincoln owed his nomination to two editors of Chicago newspapers; yet he punished editors of Confederate sheets. His relations with the press were often stormy, and cartoonists pilloried him relentlessly. Ulysses S. Grant, seared by the revelation of corruption in his administration, felt obliged to say as he closed his second inaugural address that from the time of his first campaign in 1868 he had "been the subject of abuse and slander scarcely ever equaled in political history."

Grover Cleveland, a secretive man, was openly hostile to the press, too. In his day newsmen did not even have working space in the White House. They were forced to stand outside in all kinds of weather and hope to buttonhole visitors as they entered or departed. When a journalist asked the president to appoint a new secretary who might be good to newspapermen, Cleveland responded: "I have a notion to appoint a man who will be good to me." Cleveland remains the only president who refused to attend the annual dinner of the Gridiron Club, the insider association of Washington journalists founded in 1885 where the president and the press attired in white tie and tails "singe but do not burn" each other with more or less good-natured sallies. His successor, William McKinley (1897–1901), had the same wariness toward the press. Talking to journalists a few days after having spoken before a gathering of patent experts, he said wryly: "This is the second time that I have been called upon this week to address a congress of inventors."

Theodore Roosevelt opened yet another new day in the history of the presidency, one in which the president is the head of his party as well as chief executive. TR had a press secretary and one of the president's closest friends was the Kansas newspaperman William Allen White. Roosevelt had learned early that self-promotion was an indispensable tool of the modern White House. He often talked to newspapermen while he was being shaved in the morning. Woodrow Wilson held the first press conference as it is known today—eleven days after his inauguration in 1913. Suggested by his press secretary, Joseph P. Tumulty, it was attended by about 125 newsmen. Previously only favored journalists had had access to the president. The questions were submitted in writing. Wilson himself chose when to hold these sessions and would not yield to a demand for them, even in the unlikely event that journalists should make such a call. Still, like his predecessors, Wilson was convinced that newspaper reports were not trustworthy.

Despite all, the public continued to rely on newspapers for judging their leaders. Horace Greeley, the editor of the *New York Tribune* in Lincoln's day, was nominated by the Democrats and the Liberal Republicans in 1872 and received substantial support in the election. In 1920 the two major-party candidates were active newsmen: Warren G. Harding for the Republicans was the editor and publisher of the *Marion* (Ohio) *Star,* and James M. Cox for the Democrats, also from Ohio, was the editor and publisher of the *Dayton Daily News.*

Presidential suspicion of journalists persisted none the less: Herbert Hoover, for instance, continued to hold press conferences in what was then the usual way, taking questions submitted in writing. Under Franklin D. Roosevelt, press conferences became less formal as journalists gathered around the president who was seated at his desk. At ease with the press (he maintained he was a journalist himself, claiming the status by virtue of having served on the *Harvard Crimson* as an undergraduate), he often teased his interrogators. And those whom he regarded as wrongheaded or otherwise irritating to him he consigned to his "Dunce Club." Even so, it was still forbidden to quote the president directly. Blessed with a mellifluous speaking voice, FDR gave "fireside" chats on the radio, which was becoming an everyday appliance in millions of homes. These talks are remembered today as a hallmark of his administration, allowing him to go over the heads of the print media and giving him unique access to the public mind.

Harry Truman, considerably less effective as a public speaker than his predecessor, was certain that newspaper editorials did not reflect popular opinion. He could feel vindicated when, despite almost universal predictions by the media that his Republican opponent, Thomas E. Dewey, would win the presidency in 1948, he was elected in his own right to a term in the White House. Dwight D. Eisenhower allowed his words at press conferences to be quoted directly and tape recordings of them to be released. On 19 January 1955 his news conference was recorded on television and on movie film—a groundbreaking event. Ike began by saying: "Well, I see we are trying a new experiment this morning. I hope it doesn't prove to be a disturbing influence." On the fortieth anniversary of Eisenhower's graduation from West Point, his address to the class of 1955 was telecast in color—another first for a president.

The presidential debates between competing candidates beginning in 1960, when Vice President Richard M. Nixon and Senator John F. Kennedy went toe to toe, inaugurated a now expected feature of campaigns. The electorate wants to judge not only what the opponents are espousing but also their demeanor and facial expressions. When Kennedy became president, his ready wit made some of his press conferences entertaining as well as informative, and he scheduled them for evening hours. As talk radio and talk television began to fill the airwaves, candidates and presidents took advantage of the opportunities to deliver their message.

New Uses of the Media

One of the first to use talk television was George H. W. Bush when he was vice president. With unusual skill Bill Clinton took advantage of his articulateness to go one-on-one with ordinary citizens at "town meetings." During his first campaign in 1992, Clinton's playing of a saxophone on a late-night television show appeared to make a favorable impression on many voters by thus dramatizing the message that he belonged to a new generation prepared to innovate. Others were aghast and insisted that such a performance was undignified—not recalling that President Truman once played the piano in the White House with Lauren Bacall, a famous actress, sitting on the lid displaying her shapely legs. In recent campaigns, candidates, especially from the major parties, have arranged to meet so-called focus groups to probe and keep in touch with public opinion. And the constant polling of the citizenry on questions large and small has raised "public opinion" to new heights of importance, even as it appears to diminish the function of the president as "leader." Modern press secretaries have become skilled in massaging the president's words to give them the best possible slant for public consumption. The press secretary is now known informally and critically as "the spinmeister"—the master interpreter.

Most Americans may be only dimly aware that before each press conference presidents are exposed to "dry runs" at which they and their staff collectively attempt to anticipate the issues on the minds and tongues of the media questioners. At these sessions the president and his people fashion answers they deem appropriate—including humorous sallies—hoping thereby to furnish the public with a clarifying or, from time to time, an obfuscating proposition. Where presidents seek to manipulate the media to their advantage, the media representatives strive constantly to draw "a story" out of the chief executive's words. The growth of "24/7" news distribution—twenty-four hours a day, seven days a week—has made the thirst for breaking news unquenchable.

Presidential Ghost Writers

By the same system, presidential speeches are rarely the work of the president himself. George Washington's celebrated Farewell Address, which was so influential during the long period of American isolation from world affairs, was the work mostly of Alexander Hamilton, the secretary of the treasury. When James K. Polk asked Congress for a declaration of war against Mexico in 1846, his words were written by Secretary of the Navy George Bancroft, the most distinguished American historian of the time. Years later Bancroft was again the presidential amanuensis, this time of Andrew Johnson. Understandably, being able to write well is not an ordinary requirement in a chief executive. The most accomplished penman among all the presidents was Theodore Roosevelt, who earned substantial royalties for his works of history.

The last president who wrote his own speeches was Woodrow Wilson, using a typewriter that he had used as a productive scholar in earlier years. Franklin Roosevelt leaned heavily on the poet Archibald MacLeish, the playwright Robert Sherwood, Judge Samuel I. Rosenman, and Harry Hopkins, who was often called the president's alter ego. Hopkins wrote FDR's third inaugural address. Still the many drafts of some of Roosevelt's speeches extant in the FDR Library at Hyde Park, New York, show how much the phrasing was in fact the president's. Roosevelt himself was the author of his powerful "day of infamy" speech delivered before Congress the day after the attack on Pearl Harbor on 7 December 1941.

Speechwriters often are the men and women who have the "passion for anonymity" that Franklin Roosevelt hoped to find in his intimates. Their identity becomes known, though, and deserves to be, for they are the makers in a substantial way of the nation's patriotic slogans and political maxims. Eisenhower, who was a superior writer himself, leaned nevertheless on several helpers including Edward Mead Earle, an historian who labored on Ike's first book, *Crusade in Europe* (1948), a memoir of the conquest of Nazi Germany. As chief executive, Eisenhower relied on a team, as all recent presidents have done. His included particularly Emmet John Hughes of *Life* magazine, and C. D. Jackson, a former editor of *Time*. Eisenhower's Farewell Address in January 1961 contained his memorable warning against the corrosive influence of the "military-industrial complex." The text was substantially the work of Malcolm C. Moos, a political scientist and newspaper editor, and a friend of Eisenhower's brother, Milton, then president of Johns Hopkins University. Theodore Sorensen, a Nebraska-born lawyer, was the principal author of some of President Kennedy's best speeches including his distinguished inaugural address. Kennedy's book, *Profiles in Courage* (1955), which earned him a Pulitzer Prize and was so influential in helping enlarge his reputation on the eve of his campaign for the presidency, was the product of skillful ghostwriting by Sorenson and others.

Richard Nixon was admirably served by William Safire, who later became a widely read political columnist for the *New York Times*. Presidents Reagan and George H. W. Bush used the talent of Peggy Noonan as their writer. Noonan was responsible most notably for Bush's promise not to raise taxes—"Read my Lips!"—that may have helped cost the president the election of 1992. George W. Bush has the services of Michael Gerson and Susan Hughes, who like their recent predecessors, have the ability to mesh their own style of writing with the speaking cadences as well as the thoughts of their principal.

None of these facts should suggest that the president is a ventriloquist's dummy. All the recent presidents have worked over the drafts submitted to them for important speeches so that when the finished product becomes public the president can say, in most cases, it is his own. The public was recently surprised to learn that despite the general impression that he delegated the task, Reagan often prepared even first drafts of his own speeches. The president must deliver so many talks today and meet so many foreign guests who often are accorded state dinners that he could not possibly spend his time researching appropriate remarks, greetings, and toasts that have to come from the head table. Assistant speechwriters draft these ceremonial comments.

Post-Presidencies

The country has been notably unable to make use of its former chief executives. The day a president leaves the office his executive power is gone and he becomes a has-been overnight. He reappears at the White House only at the invitation of the incumbent. The most publicized return of an ex-president followed Kennedy's call to Eisenhower to join him at Camp David, the presidential retreat in the Catoctin Mountains of Maryland, after the failure of the ill-conceived Bay of Pigs invasion of Cuba in 1961. New in office, Kennedy was clearly hoping to have not only Eisenhower's counsel but also the prestige of one of the most popular presidents on his side. Herbert Hoover, however, did not set foot in the Oval Office throughout the twelve years that Franklin Roosevelt, his successor, occupied it. In 1945, when Harry Truman, who had succeeded FDR, invited Hoover, who happened to be in town, back to the White House, Hoover wept with amazement and pleasure.

Jefferson in retirement became famous as the Sage of Monticello occupied with the planning and the building of the University of Virginia. James Monroe in his post-presidency spent much of his public energy in lawsuits against the federal government. He claimed real and imagined expense-money as due him for his services abroad as a diplomat. Although Congress twice voted him substantial sums, he continued to feel short-changed. After an unhappy presidency full of frustrated plans and hopes, John Quincy Adams returned to Washington as a member of the House of Representatives and served with distinction for seventeen years. He earned there the reputation of "Old Man Eloquent," the most insistent antislavery voice in Congress. John Tyler at the request of the Virginia legislature accepted the chairmanship of the "peace convention" in Washington in 1861, seeking to find a way out of the secession crisis. When the Senate ignored the convention's proposals, Tyler became himself a secessionist and won election to the Confederate House of Representatives.

Retired presidents, despite the variety of their pursuits, have shown that exercising power leaves an

The presidency's burdens are understood and shared by those who have held the seat of power. Harry Truman (left) and Herbert Hoover, though members of opposing political parties, enjoyed a warm friendship and are shown at the White House during Truman's term. CORBIS

addiction that appears to be irreversible. In a now-famous quip, Harold Ickes, who served in Franklin Roosevelt's cabinet, said: "When a man has been bitten by the presidential bug, he begins to suffer from a terrible disease that is only cured by embalming fluid." President Grant, following an around-the-world tour in 1879, wanted to run again in 1880. Failing in his goal, he spent his last years writing what would prove to be the most widely sold book ever written by a president—his remarkable *Memoirs,* still in print today. They cover not his terms in the White House but his years on the battlefields of the Civil War. Theodore Roosevelt, who was only fifty years old when he left the presidency in 1909, had expressed the hope even as he entered the office eight years earlier that he would not be "a loose cannon on the deck" when his term of service was over. But he spent the next years working to win the presidency again. One of his opponents was William Howard Taft (1909–1913), recently his closest friend, whom he had turned into a resolute foe. Taft had said privately in the run-up to the election: "If you were to remove Roosevelt's skull now, you would find written on his brain '1912.'" The winner that year was the Democrat, Woodrow Wilson. Shortly Roosevelt was harassing him, too, maintaining that Wilson was not sufficiently active in countering Germany's violation of American rights on the high seas. Soon after Wilson's reelection in 1916 and the entry of the United States into World War I, Roosevelt applied to Wilson—in vain it proved—for a commission to lead an American army into Berlin.

Taft in his after-presidency gave a series of instructive lectures on the office at Columbia University, published as *Our Chief Magistrate and His Powers* (1916). Yet his heart and mind were bent on returning to the judicial bench where he had once sat. Indeed, in Taft's days in Roosevelt's cabinet, the president, speaking in the manner of a fortune-teller had one evening teased him and Mrs. Taft: "I see a man standing before me weighing about 350 pounds. There is something hanging over his head. I cannot make out what it is. At one time it looks like the presidency—then again it looks like the chief justiceship." With unfeigned glee Mrs. Taft shouted: "Make it the presidency." "Make it the chief justiceship," responded Taft in a quiet voice. In 1921 President Harding appointed Taft to be chief justice. Taft is still the only man to have served in two of the three highest offices in the land. And drawing on the immense prestige this singular fact appeared to entitle him to, he continually irritated Harding and Harding's successor, Calvin Coolidge, with suggestions respecting vacancies to be filled on the Supreme Court.

Hoover, in his long post-presidency, rendered valuable service on two national commissions he headed to streamline the operation of the federal government. Nixon, the only president forced to resign his office, spent his last years writing not only his memoirs but also a series of works on foreign affairs. They were planned both as instruction to the public and to help rehabilitate their author's reputation by highlighting what he regarded as his expertness on international politics. Carter kept a high profile as an ex-president. Having created the Carter Center in Atlanta, a nonprofit organization to promote peace and human rights, he took on various projects including helping to encourage and supervise elections in other countries. Through the Jimmy Carter Project of Habitat for Humanity International, he and his wife, Rosalynn, helped construct houses in New York City slums.

In the television era, former chief executives do not disappear from the public eye, as Truman did. They may be seen every so often on talk shows and occasionally they are rounded up as a group—as, for instance, on the occasion in November 2000 of the two hundredth anniversary of the White House. With the exception of Ronald Reagan, all of the living former presidents were prominently present at the memorial service in Washington's National Cathedral for the victims of the 11 September 2001 terrorist attacks in New York City, Washington, D.C., and the hijacked airplane that crashed in western Pennsylvania.

Past presidents are in demand as public speakers, not so much for what they have to say, but as glamorous attractions at business and charitable gatherings. Reagan was widely criticized for accepting $2 million for two appearances in Japan, soon after he left the White House in 1989. But the practice of "cashing in" is now accepted. The commander-in-chief in his post-presidency is recognized as a celebrity-in-chief. George H. W. Bush earns around $4 million annually in fees for about fifty such appearances. Even before he left office, Bill Clinton was being booked for talks for as much as $150,000 apiece.

Illness and Disability

Presidential illness since the beginning has been a factor in the life of the nation. Nevertheless, the health of presidents until relatively recently was rarely spoken of; it was regarded as nobody's business but the president's. Moreover, even after the advent of modern medicine, the unspoken proscription against speaking about the body in Victorian America played a role in keeping off limits the details of the chief executives' physical condition. Consequently, facts are known today that contemporaries were unaware of. George Washington, for example, was barely in office in 1789 when he developed a painful carbuncle on his left thigh. He may have been near death from the staphylococcal infection and high fever that accompanied it. His intense suffering, which in the end included the surgery he had to endure without anesthetic, necessitated rebuilding the carriage he traveled in so that he could lie in it at full length. The following year he contracted a cold, which, it was said, then turned into influenza and pneumonia—bringing despair for his recovery. We may only speculate on how the national history might have been different if the Father of His Country had died on either occasion: the first when the government was being launched under his hand as the indispensable man, and the second when the critical struggle over the first Bank of the United States was being played out.

When Andrew Jackson came to office in 1829 heralded as formidable, indestructible Old Hickory, he was in truth a debilitated man. He was still feeling the effects of a pistol shot long before lodged in his left shoulder, and suffering perpetually from intestinal bleeding, possibly caused by the calomel he took for his recurrent dysentery. We can never know how his frailty affected his performance as Chief Executive.

Presidents Polk and Truman, even though they served a century apart, have sometimes been compared as unexpected presidents who showed themselves to be feisty leaders forced to take the country into war. Both had been sickly children. Polk suffered as a boy from a bladder stone, eventually removed by surgery, that robbed him of a normal childhood. He was proud that his career as president and war leader proved he was no longer, as he once called himself, "the meager boy, with pallid cheeks, oppressed and worn with disease."

Truman, too, endured a boyhood blighted by illness. At the age of eight, paralyzed by the effects of diphtheria, he had to be wheeled around in a baby carriage. Amply coddled, he became, simply stated, a sissy. Indeed, he liked to believe that he could arrange his sister's curls better than his mother could. But he was determined to be manly. Growing up he set his heart on winning an appointment at the Military Academy at West Point, but this ambition was frustrated by his "flat eyeballs" (his own designation). In World War I he showed his mettle as an officer in an artillery unit and this service in uniform had an abiding influence on his political life. As president he demonstrated enormous respect for military men, including especially Generals Mark Clark, George C. Marshall, and Dwight D. Eisenhower.

The question of how far the president's health ought to come officially and contemporaneously to the public's knowledge did not trouble the country in earlier days. When, for instance, word leaked out in the 1880s that President Chester A. Arthur was suffering from Bright's disease, a usually fatal kidney ailment, the White House silenced public speculation by denouncing the story as malicious gossip. A notable case occurred in 1893, shortly after Grover Cleveland's second inauguration. He had begun to suffer

from a lesion in his mouth that was soon diagnosed as a cancer, requiring immediate attention. Apart from the president's personal stake, the political stakes were enormous. Cleveland was a committed defender of the gold standard; if he should die, his vice president, Adlai E. Stevenson of Illinois (a grandfather of the Adlai E. Stevenson who twice ran unsuccessfully for president against Dwight D. Eisenhower in the 1950s), who was a fervent advocate of the free silver policy would be president. Because it would be risking exposure to take Cleveland to a clinic or hospital, the work was done aboard a friend's yacht anchored in New York's East River near Bellevue Hospital. The medical staff was ordered to stay out of sight lest they be recognized by Bellevue's resident doctors. To keep the president steady during the procedure, as the boat sailed slowly up the river, his chair was lashed tight to the mast. To avoid doing external surgery, one of the doctors, William W. Keen, a Philadelphia man, who had served in the Civil War and had studied abroad, employed a cheek retractor he had brought home from Paris in 1866. Operated on a second time a few weeks later, the president was fitted with a prosthesis that did not show on his face. The public was none the wiser until 1917—almost a quarter of a century later—when Dr. Keen, in an article in the *Saturday Evening Post,* finally broke the embargo on the story.

Although one in four presidents has been disabled at some time during his term of office, the disability of a president was not dealt with appropriately even after Woodrow Wilson was stricken by a massive stroke in 1919 that severely affected his gait and speech. His wife, Edith Galt Wilson, screened his mail and the list of his visitors, and is sometimes referred to, therefore, as the "first woman president." Wilson's medical history, had it been known in 1912 when he ran for the White House the first time, would have raised a flag of caution. The public was unaware that he had been suffering strokes since 1898. Many Americans will always believe that although the nation as a whole was bent on being quit of Europe after the end of the World War I, the failure of the Senate to ratify the Treaty of Versailles was in some measure related to the personality deficits the president had undergone.

A generation later, Franklin D. Roosevelt, aided as Wilson had been by a White House doctor willing to cover up what he knew, was an ailing man even as he presented to the world his smiling, confident face. At the end of 1943 when the Allied landings in

Normandy were being planned, the president was suffering acutely from hypertensive congestive heart disease, and hypertension that resisted efforts at reduction. The medical people in the president's entourage well knew that by D-Day in 1944, the president was barely able to concentrate on affairs of state. When he traveled to the Pacific to visit the American commanders and ostensibly to lay plans for the final assault on Japan later in the year, he was actually seeking surcease from the daily cares of his office.

Although there was much gossip in 1944 when FDR ran for a fourth term that he was mortally ill, the voters, ignorant of the truth, elected him handily. During the canvass, though, when the invasion of France was in its critical moments, the president at a private lunch with his running mate, Harry Truman, urged him for his own safety and for the good of the country, to avoid campaigning by airplane. "This time, we may need you," the president told him presciently. Still, talking to the press after this portentous meeting, Truman offered traditional words of reassurance, saying that he found the president well and hearty. Not until 1970 was a full account of FDR's medical condition made public—in an article in the *Annals of Internal Medicine,* a medical journal, by Dr. Howard Bruenn, the young naval aide who had been called in to treat the president.

After Eisenhower suffered a heart attack in 1955, he and Vice President Nixon came to an informal agreement that the vice president would take over the responsibilities of the presidency in a comparable emergency in the future. In the next years first when Eisenhower underwent bowel surgery and then after he suffered a "brain spasm" there was, he would say, "a gap when I could not carry out the duties of my office." The openness of the Eisenhower administration in reporting on the various ailments the general came down with while in the White House, was no example for the Kennedy administration. It followed the style of the Cleveland and Wilson administrations. President Kennedy suffered, beginning when he was thirty years old, from adrenal insufficiency, or Addison's disease, a fact confirmed by the autopsy performed after his assassination, but kept secret at the behest of the Kennedy family. When Kennedy underwent back surgery in 1954 because of his disease, he received the last rites of the Roman Catholic Church. Kennedy had kept fit by taking regular supplements of cortisone and similar drugs in replacement of the adrenal hormone. Still,

victims of the disease taking cortisone and its ilk are subject to mood swings and stomach inflammation, including ulcers. Moreover, the face is sometimes made fuller by the medicines.

In his quest for the nomination in 1960, Kennedy had declared himself "the healthiest candidate for President in the country." This was a backhanded reference to his opponent, Senator Lyndon B. Johnson, who had suffered a severe heart attack in 1955. When the truth about JFK's medical condition was finally revealed in the *Journal of the American Medical Association* in 1967, many people declared that if it had been known in 1960, it is doubtful that he would have been nominated, let alone elected.

Johnson's heart condition was constantly on his mind. He liked to say that he had had "the worst heart attack you could have and still live." He confessed that every time he passed Wilson's portrait, he trembled at the thought of himself lying helpless in the White House. He saw to it that there was defibrillation equipment on every floor, and he carried with him a copy of his electrocardiogram for emergency reference. The frenetic way in which he managed the Great Society legislation led some people to conclude that he felt instinctively he had no time to lose. Johnson and House Speaker John McCormack, who was next in line of succession, came to an agreement similar to the Eisenhower-Nixon arrangement. When President Reagan underwent surgery for colon cancer in 1985, he temporarily transferred the powers of his office to Vice President George H. W. Bush.

At last the Twenty-fifth Amendment, ratified in 1967, aimed at dealing officially with the vexing matter of presidential and vice presidential succession and disability. It provided formally for the first time that when death or resignation removes a president, the vice president becomes president. When a vice president is similarly removed, the president will choose a successor who takes office at once upon confirmation by a majority vote of both houses of Congress. And when a president writes to the president pro tem of the Senate and to the Speaker of the House that he is unable to perform the duties of his office—and until he informs them otherwise—the vice president becomes acting president. Similarly, if a majority of the cabinet (or of any other body that Congress designates) declares that the president cannot discharge his duties, the vice president becomes acting president. When the president declares that he is able to resume his office, he must so inform the president pro tem of the Senate and the

Speaker of the House. If there is disagreement as to whether he is so able, Congress under specific time restraints must respond appropriately. In recent elections it has been common for candidates to issue medical reports on their physical condition, but these are not always complete.

Presidential Children

The constant presence of the presidents in the public eye has also generated a continuing interest not only in First Ladies, but also in the children of presidents. The offspring have played the role of stand-ins for the princes and princesses of monarchies and fairy tales. Indeed, Alice Roosevelt, the child of Theodore Roosevelt and Alice Lee Roosevelt, his first, late wife, was often referred to in the press as Princess Alice, her name given to a popular shade, labeled Alice blue. She wrote later: "I was the daughter of an enormously popular President and I looked upon the world as my oyster." Other First Daughters have not fared as well. Molly Garfield, just turned fourteen years old in 1881, was only in the White House eight months when her father succumbed to an assassin's bullet. And Gerald Ford's (1974–1977) daughter Susan lamented that living there was like living in a "cross between reform school and a convent."

Presidential children are treated with deference when they are young and regarded as extensions of their parents when they are older. The son of President Kennedy and Jacqueline Bouvier Kennedy, known affectionately to the public as John-John, became world famous as a mere three-year old in a picture published around the world that showed him saluting the casket of his martyred father. Years later John junior's death in an airplane crash in 1999 evoked national mourning. The one presidential son who as a boy may have altered American history was Robert Todd Lincoln. Having failed the entrance examination to Harvard College in fifteen out of sixteen subjects, he was enrolled in Phillips Exeter Academy in New Hampshire in order to "bone up." Eager to visit and encourage him there, his father came east in 1860, lured by a fortuitous invitation to address the Cooper Union Institute in New York City for a fee of $200 and expenses. That address became a key factor in spreading Lincoln's fame and making possible his nomination for the presidency the following month.

Presidents and the First Ladies have all kept keenly in mind the difficulties that their prominence creates for their sons and daughters. But for her father's presidency, Jenna Bush's brush with the law involving an underage drinking violation in Texas in 2001 would not have been public knowledge. Several first families have made earnest efforts to shelter their children not only from public exposure but also from the effects of the flattery and luxury that flow toward them. Chester A. Arthur notably tried to shield his daughter Nell from the world. The Kennedys hoped that the media would keep the spotlight off their daughter, Caroline. The media were respectful of the similar strong wishes of Bill and Hillary Rodham Clinton for their only child, Chelsea.

Still, the doings of children in the White House especially in times of crisis have added to the president's appeal by making him seem ordinary even though the public expects him also to be extraordinary. During the Great Depression, Sistie and Buzzie Dahl, the children of the Roosevelts' daughter, Anna, and her husband, came to be national personages. Even during the agony of the Civil War, the Northern public was amused to hear that Tad Lincoln, only eight years old in 1861, had led a team of goats through the executive mansion. And a generation later, Theodore Roosevelt did not object when his lively children introduced a pony into the Blue Room and walked on stilts across the elegant broadloom carpeting. Amy Carter, just turned nine years old when her father became president, "slept over" occasionally in the tree house her parents had had constructed for her on a White House lawn.

No one can seriously believe that the children of presidents serve as models for the nation's young people. Still, their doings are constantly on display. And they think of themselves as a group with a special bond. Susan Ford said recently "I know when I run into Luci [Johnson] and Lynda [Johnson] and Julie [Nixon] and we all go, 'And do you remember this?' there's only a few people who realize what it's like." In 1959 the largest gathering of the offspring of presidents took place at a "Life with Father" luncheon hosted by the Women's National Press Club in celebration of its fortieth anniversary. Afterward the Eisenhowers received the invitees at the White House. Nine of the sixteen living presidential children, and grandchildren up to six "greats" dating back to John Adams attended. It was a non-political get-together but Helen Taft insisted that the children of the conservative presidents before World War I had had more fun than the children of the later liberal chief executives. She recalled that they slid down the state stairways on trays and had played hide and seek all over the White House.

A few presidential sons may have added special luster to their parents' reputation by virtue of their military service. Quentin Roosevelt, the youngest son of Theodore and Edith Roosevelt, perished in an air duel over France in 1918 during World War I, the only child of a presidential couple killed in action for his country. Two other Roosevelts were wounded in the war, leading Roosevelt to say proudly, "Haven't I bully boys, one dead and two in the hospital." Theodore Roosevelt, Jr. landed in the first wave at Normandy in 1944 at the age of fifty-seven, and died of a heart attack a month later. He was awarded posthumously the Congressional Medal of Honor.

This highest military decoration had been won also by Webb C. Hayes, son of Rutherford and Lucy Hayes (1877–1881), for gallantry in the Philippines campaign during the Spanish-American War when he infiltrated the enemy lines alone at night. In the Civil War, sons of presidents fought on both sides. Five presidential sons were active in the Confederate cause. Two of John Tyler's sons, David and John, left school as mere striplings to wear the gray uniform. The only son of Zachary and Margaret Taylor, Robert Taylor, saw heavy action as a brigadier general in the Confederate army, having been appointed by Jefferson Davis. He was killed when he was thrown from his horse. He had served as military aide to his father during the Mexican War and as his private secretary during his presidency. Charles Johnson, the son of Andrew and Eliza McCardle Johnson, was an assistant surgeon with the Middle Tennessee Infantry. Shortly before the end of the war he, too, was thrown by his horse and killed. Son Robert was a Union Army colonel who resigned after his father became president in order to serve as his secretary. Frederick Dent Grant was only eleven years old when the Civil War broke out but he often accompanied his father into battle, and was slightly wounded in the Battle of Vicksburg. He was a seasoned soldier at the time he entered the United States Military Academy at West Point in 1866. All four of Franklin and Eleanor Roosevelt's sons were in uniform during World War II, and all of them saw heavy action.

John Eisenhower, the only child of Dwight and Mamie Eisenhower, also a West Pointer, was a major in combat in Korea when his father was nominated by the Republican party in 1952. John's superiors immediately forbade him to lead hazardous patrols lest he be captured and turned into an invaluable hostage. An effect was to damage his chances for promotion. Subsequently, Truman sent for him to be present at his father's inauguration. As Eisenhower rode with Truman to the Capitol, keenly aware of the likely damage done to his son's career, he angrily asked the outgoing president who had ordered his son home. Truman bluntly answered that he had taken that action as commander-in-chief.

Sons of presidents have served in high places in presidential administrations after their fathers', no doubt trading on their name. Robert Lincoln served as secretary of war for Presidents Garfield and Arthur. James R. Garfield was secretary of the interior under Theodore Roosevelt. Herbert Hoover, Jr. was undersecretary of state for three years in the Eisenhower presidency. Franklin D. Roosevelt, Jr. was undersecretary of commerce in the Kennedy administration and was elected to Congress from New York three times in the 1980s. James Roosevelt, another son, served in the House from his district in California for six terms beginning in 1954. Harry A. Garfield, the president's eldest son, was for twenty-five years president of Williams College in the early twentieth century. In the same era, John Tyler's youngest son, Lyon Gardiner Tyler, born after his father's term, was president of William and Mary College. John Eisenhower, who has written some well-regarded books of military history, was named by Nixon as ambassador to Belgium.

In general, presidential children have not cast discredit on their parents reputation, even when they have not reflected glory on them. In a more straitlaced time than the present, the many divorces of Franklin and Eleanor Roosevelt's five children (they accumulated fourteen among them) caused no political repercussions. And Ronald Reagan's widespread popularity was not affected by the pinpricks he endured from his offspring. Maureen, a child of the president's first marriage to Jane Wyman, raised the eyebrows of many Americans when she reported having seen Lincoln's ghost in the White House. The president's adopted son, Michael, wrote an exposé of his troubled childhood that he tellingly called *On the Outside Looking In* (1988). And in 1986 Patricia Ann Reagan (known professionally as Patti Davis) published a devastating roman à clef about the Reagans entitled *Home Front*.

Several presidential children died while their fathers were in the White House. Willy Lincoln, eleven years old, succumbed to a "bilious fever" in 1862. Calvin Coolidge, Jr., sixteen years old in 1924, fell a victim of blood poisoning that resulted from a blister on his foot after playing tennis on a White House court. Patrick Bouvier Kennedy, two days old, in 1963 succumbed to hyaline membrane disease, an ailment of newborns. John Quincy Adams's son, George Washington Adams, while mentally deranged, jumped or fell from a steamer in Long Island Sound at the age of twenty-eight in 1829. Young Adams's uncle Charles, the second son of John Adams, had died a drunkard's death in 1800. With characteristic candor the second president had expressed his unspeakable anguish over the youth: "I renounce him. King David's Absolom had some ambition and some enterprise. Mine is a mere rake, buck, blood, and beast." Franklin and Jane Appleton Pierce's only surviving son, Benny, eleven years old, was killed before his parents' eyes in a railroad accident two months before the father took office. Mrs. Pierce was so grief-stricken that she did not attend the inauguration, and forever blamed her husband's political ambition for their irreparable loss.

The effect on the presidencies of which these sons were a part cannot be measured. The Lincolns were famously inconsolable, and Coolidge wrote in his autobiography that "when [young Calvin] went, the power and glory of the Presidency went with him....I don't know why such a price was exacted for occupying the White House." The Clevelands' first child, Ruth, whose death of diphtheria at the age of twelve, a few years after they left the White House, crushed her parents, had been known as Baby Ruth. Her memory survives in the name of a candy bar still popular.

In pre-feminist days, presidents' daughters were sometimes judged by the kind of marriages they made. Zachary Taylor's daughter Sarah Knox Taylor was wedded to Jefferson Davis in 1835—despite her parents' impassioned objection—this before either her father or her husband had become a national figure. Eleanor Wilson in 1914 married William Gibbs McAdoo, the secretary of the treasury, a marriage that later ended in divorce. She died a recluse in India. In an elaborate White House wedding in 1906, Alice Roosevelt became the bride of Nicholas Longworth, a congressman from Ohio who years later served as Speaker of the House of Representatives.

Margaret Wilson, Woodrow and Ellen Axson Wilson's second daughter, and Margaret Truman, Harry and Bess Wallace Truman's only child, were aspiring concert singers. In a moment of pique, Truman denounced in a well-publicized letter the hostile review on Margaret's talent that appeared in the *Washington Post*. She would afterward write of the difficult position her father's office placed her in: "If some critics condoned or over praised me because of my political position, others accused me of trading on my father's prestige." In later years she was the author of several books of crime fiction. Helen Taft served as hostess in the White House during her mother's incapacity. She made her social debut there in 1910 in a pink chiffon dress, a color that came to be labeled "Helen pink." She earned a Ph.D. from Yale and had a notable career as dean and professor of history at Bryn Mawr College, where her authoritarian style became legendary.

Only two presidential sons have returned to the White House as presidents themselves. John and Abigail Adams's son, John Quincy, was elected in early 1825 in the House of Representatives. On that occasion his father said: "No man who ever held the office of President would congratulate a friend on obtaining it." Still, he could not suppress his boundless pride: "The multitude of my thoughts and the intensity of my feelings are too much for a mind like mine, in its ninetieth year." When George W. Bush, the son of George and Barbara Bush, was elected in 2000, the elder Bush's emotions were no less intense, and he playfully referred to his son for a while as "Quincy" or simply "Q." Father and son also joshed each other as "41" and "43," a reference to their numbered places on the roll of the presidents. When the war against terrorism began in 2001, the elder Bush said he and the embattled commander-in-chief talked to each other regularly. "It's not always about policy. It's not, 'What do you think, Dad, I should be doing?' It is more the relationship of a very close family staying in touch."

In 1848, John Van Buren, the second of the four sons of Martin and Hannah Van Buren, was prominently mentioned as a potential candidate for the Free Soil Party. He withdrew from consideration in favor of his father. An earnest band of Whigs in 1856 had boomed for president, John Scott Harrison, son of William Henry Harrison and Anna Symmes Harrison. In dismissing the notion of his candidacy the younger Harrison said forthrightly that his backers efforts were "calculated too largely on the potency of a name." He served in the House for two terms in the 1850s as a Whig. And he and his wife, Elizabeth Irwin Harrison were the parents of President Benjamin Harrison, making him the only son and father of a president. In a bizarre incident in 1878, John Scott

Harrison's body was stolen by grave robbers who sold it to a medical school in Cincinnati, where his horrified son John by chance discovered it hanging from a rope.

Robert Todd Lincoln, the sole surviving son of the Lincolns, in 1884 received eight votes for president at the Republican National Convention. Four years later a group of Republican planners imagined that he could be an admirable running mate for a ticket headed by Frederick Dent Grant and that a Grant-Lincoln ticket would be a sure winner. In the 1940s and early 1950s Senator Robert A. Taft of Ohio, the son of William Howard and Helen Herron Taft, widely regarded as "Mr. Republican," ardently sought the Republican nomination. He was overwhelmed at successive conventions by Wendell L. Willkie of Indiana in 1940, Thomas Dewey of New York in 1944 and 1948, and Dwight D. Eisenhower in 1952.

Transitions

The peaceful transfer of power from one president to another on inauguration day is a phenomenon that Americans take for granted, but in truth it is a remarkable tribute to the success of republican government in the United States. When John Adams succeeded Washington on 4 March 1797, he wrote his beloved Abigail: "The sight of the sun setting...and another rising (though less splendid), was a novelty." It has remained a novelty in many nations of the world. Nevertheless, the transition from one administration to another has not always been smooth. John Adams, still smarting over the outcome of the election of 1800, did not remain in Washington to witness the inauguration of Jefferson, his successor. And John Quincy Adams in 1829 also fled the town, unwilling to be present to see Andrew Jackson's accession to the White House. In 1869, Andrew Johnson was angrily conducting a cabinet meeting even as his successor, General Grant, was being inaugurated.

Periodically there has also been bad blood between presidents and aspiring successors within the same party. In the presidential canvass of 1928 Calvin Coolidge gave only lukewarm support to the Republican nominee, Herbert Hoover, his secretary of commerce, because he disliked him intensely. He often referred to Hoover derisively as the "Wonder Boy," and sometimes said of him: "That man has given me nothing but advice, and all of it bad." Lyndon John-

son prized his so-called idea folder containing his collection of constantly growing possible proposals for public initiatives. In 1968 he adamantly refused to lend it to Vice President Hubert H. Humphrey, the Democratic party nominee to succeed him, lest it be helpful to him in the campaign. Bill Clinton in his post-presidency remained highly critical of former vice president Al Gore, his successor as Democratic party nominee, believing that Gore would have won in 2000 if he had invited Clinton to go on the campaign trail for him. The two men who began their era at the helm as seemingly boon companions were barely on speaking terms. By the time of the presidential election of 1912, the former intimate friendship between Theodore Roosevelt and William Howard Taft, his successor in office (whose election in 1908 TR was largely responsible for) had broken apart, in Taft's words, "like a rope of sand."

Incoming presidents of the same party as the outgoing one invariably emphasize in their public utterances their aim to continue ongoing policies. At the same time, they try to establish their own identity quickly. When there is a party turnover, the incoming president typically asserts that sweeping changes are in the offing. Still, the comity between the president arriving and the one departing befits their inseparable place together in the line of the chief executives. Although Eisenhower and Truman were at odds at the time of Ike's inauguration, Eisenhower discovered in his first moments in the Oval Office that Truman had left for him a collection of memoranda on vital issues he might have to deal with immediately.

This transfer of power was once conducted informally according to the taste of the incumbent. Millard Fillmore, for example, invited President-elect Franklin Pierce to join him at a lecture by the famed English writer, William Makepeace Thackeray, then a "hot ticket" in Washington. Afterward, Thackeray and Washington Irving, who had come to Washington to hear him, were, in company with Pierce, guests at a dinner the Fillmores hosted at the White House.

In 1944, at the zenith of World War II, Franklin D. Roosevelt began the practice of giving national security briefings to his opponents. After the election of 1960, Dwight D. Eisenhower initiated the custom of creating a presidential liaison group to work with his successor's team. Lyndon B. Johnson gave personal briefings to the men running to succeed him and, under the direction of one of his staff, elaborate briefing books were prepared in every major segment of the executive branch to help orient the incoming Nixon administration. Johnson was eager that the period of transition not provide a moment of weakness in national security, believing that Soviet missiles had been moved at the time of Kennedy's assassination.

George H. W. Bush spoke these words to President-elect Clinton after showing him around the White House following the election of 1992: "Bill, I want to tell you something. When I leave here, you're going to have no trouble with me. The campaign is over, it was tough and I'm out of here. I will do nothing to complicate your work and I just want you to know that." When Taft and Wilson rode to the Capitol for Wilson's inauguration in 1913, they were on such cordial terms that Taft confided to his successor he had been able to save $100,000 out of his salary as president. And nothing showed off better the amity of a transition than the picture of Grover Cleveland in 1889 holding an umbrella over the head of Benjamin Harrison as he delivered his inaugural address in a drenching rain.

Ex-presidents have usually but not always spoken without criticism or rancor about their successors—even those who defeated them at the polls. During the campaign of 2000, ex-President Bush felt constrained to say that he would finally have to speak his mind about President Clinton if Clinton persisted in disparaging Bush's son, George, the Republican nominee for president. When President George W. Bush was in office only six months, Jimmy Carter sharply scorched him for his conservative bent, particularly in foreign affairs: "I am disappointed in almost everything he has done." President Clinton made it clear even before he left office in 2001 that he believed Vice President Gore had won the election of 2000 and that the Supreme Court's decision preventing a recount in Florida and giving the victory to Bush was faulty. Speaking in Washington State he said sarcastically to cheering Democratic party partisans: "They have this unusual system [here]. They actually count all the votes."

Before the Twentieth Amendment, which changed the day of inauguration from 4 March to 20 January, a president had nine months of grace before the new Congress took office. The change brings the new Congress into office on 3 January, so the president-elect now has only about ten weeks in which to prepare to take over the White House. In 1952 to finance his transition task force Eisenhower had used money provided by a special Republican party com-

mittee. In 1960 Kennedy used leftover campaign funds to finance his transition task force. Recognizing the ad hoc nature of this arrangement, Kennedy appointed a Commission on Campaign Costs to examine the problem and to make recommendations. As a result, Congress passed the Presidential Transition Act of 1963, which authorized payment for office space, transportation, travel, and staff. The sum allowed was $900,000 and it has been increased from time to time.

Under the Presidential Transition Act of 2000, signed by President Clinton, the sum rose to $7,100,000: $1,830,000 for the outgoing administration, with the understanding that $305,000 would be returned to the Treasury if Vice President Gore was elected, and $4,270,000 for the incoming administration. The newcomers' portion would be available from the day after the election to thirty days after the inauguration. For the outgoing president and vice president the money would be at their disposal for seven months, beginning one month before the inauguration. The disputed election of 2000 made immediate payment impossible: no "apparent victor," as the law requires, had been identified. Both parties, therefore, were forced to raise private money. The law, incidentally, requires that the names of donors be made public and that no gift exceed $5,000.

Clearly the transfer of the presidency is more complicated than ever. Ideally the money appropriated enables a new administration to "hit the ground running." But the exigencies of modern government make that impossible. Today there are 3,000 presidential positions requiring neither a civil service examination nor confirmation by the Senate. Some of them are in the Senior Executive Service, a roster of high rank civil servants, usually consisting of people with special qualifications. As for the remainder of these jobs, in the last fifteen years, between 1,100 and 1,500 of them have been filled at any one time under Schedule C—posts outside the civil-service merit system and regarded as policy determining or involving a close and confidential relationship with a key official in the administration. These important and valued offices, despite a 25 percent vacancy rate, require security clearance, and the time this process consumes varies from a few weeks to several months.

The Clinton administration was not truly in place until October, 1993—about nine months after Clinton took office. The predecessor administration under George H. W. Bush had required about the

The April 1994 funeral for President Nixon was attended by the former presidents and their wives. From left, Presidents Clinton, Bush, Reagan, Carter, and Ford along with the former first ladies. ARCHIVE PHOTOS

same length of time. When Richard Nixon went to Washington for his inauguration in January 1969, he had in hand about seventy-five appointees despite earnest efforts at recruiting that included circularizing the likely entries in *Who's Who in America*. Five months after becoming secretary of state in the administration of George W. Bush, Colin Powell felt himself handicapped by still having a mere skeleton staff in place. By January 2002, the administration had made only 920 Schedule C appointments. In recent years a steady call has been heard to reduce the size of Schedule C, but no incoming president has yet seen fit to limit this vestige of the spoils system.

The Presidents' Papers

The presidential library system was created in 1939 when Franklin D. Roosevelt, aware of the swelling

quantity of presidential documents, donated his papers and a portion of his private estate at Hyde Park, New York, to the federal government. His plan was to establish a repository open to the public for the study of the presidency. Previously, presidential papers were handled on an ad hoc basis by presidents and their heirs and thus scattered throughout the country, to be found today in the collections of various museums, libraries, and historical societies. Some, like Millard Fillmore's and Chester Arthur's, were deliberately destroyed. Many presidents' papers are to be found in the Library of Congress.

Today there are ten libraries in the presidential library system. The quantity of papers, now supplemented by extensive electronic records, seems to grow with each succeeding presidency. Incredible as it may seem, Lyndon Johnson took back with him to his library in Austin, Texas, twenty-five hundred five-drawer filing cabinets. Under an act of Congress passed in 1955, the libraries are constructed by private and nonfederal means but are maintained by public funds. Under the Presidential Records Act of 1978, a president's papers belong to the nation, and as soon as an administration ends the Archivist of the United States takes possession of them. No longer may presidents consider the papers generated in their time in the White House as their private property. So when an administration leaves office, it leaves no files behind.

Salary and Pension

In 2001, the president's salary was raised to $400,000 a year, and it is expected that no former president will be strapped for money, a condition that has not always obtained. Jefferson was so impoverished that in 1815 he felt forced to sell his library to the government—forming the nucleus of today's Library of Congress—in order to pay his creditors. Monroe was in such dire straits that, after his wife's death, he moved in with his daughter in New York City. He was buried there because there was no money to send his remains back to Virginia. Not until 1858, in celebration of the centennial of his birth, was he re-interred, in Richmond, thanks to admirers. Ulysses S. Grant was forced into poverty in his last years by a colossal stock fraud that swallowed his savings. The $450,000 advance he received for his *Memoirs* proved to be the only way to provide for his family. It came as he was suffering from throat cancer and hoping to finish his book before he died.

Harry Truman was so poor upon his return to Missouri that he had to move into his mother-in-law's house. He hoped for some relief through the passage of a pension bill, but, for inexplicable reasons, Sam Rayburn, the Speaker of the House, sat on the proposal year after year. When it finally became law during the Eisenhower administration, the pension amounted to $25,000—much welcomed by Truman. The only other living ex-president was Herbert Hoover, a millionaire many times over, who had never taken a salary as president. But he accepted the pension anyway, because, he said, he did not wish to embarrass his friend, Harry Truman. Their friendship transcended their differing party affiliation, as has been the case among most former presidents. They considered themselves equal members of the most exclusive club in the land. When Truman

invited Hoover to attend the dedication of the Truman Library in Independence, Missouri, he inquired whether politics would stand in the way of his accepting. According to Truman, Hoover responded: "Of course not, that soldier boy in the White House [General Eisenhower] isn't listening to either of us."

Under the Former Presidents Act that Eisenhower signed, ex-presidents are entitled to a pension tied in amount to the salary of members of the cabinet. In 2001 this was $161,000. In addition they receive the franking privilege—free mailing—for all nonpolitical correspondence, government paid-for office space and office staff, and allowances for travel. The sum is now a $2.5 million annual entitlement. In addition they have lifetime Secret Service protection for themselves and their spouse and for their children until they reach the age of sixteen. Widows are protected until they remarry.

POTUS—Unofficial Designation

The acronym POTUS (the "O" being long, as in "toe") is in common parlance in the White House today, used by in-the-know staffers to refer to the President of the United States. It is never uttered in addressing him face-to-face. POTUS long ago existed in the telegraph code that was a bible of the major news wires. And it is said that when President Franklin D. Roosevelt traveled on the Pennsylvania Railroad in his private car, *Magellan*, POTUS was the cover word employed to identify this important passenger. "POTUS to PRIME" was sometimes the heading of FDR's aides—not the president himself—placed on his correspondence with Prime Minister Churchill in the era of World War II.

POTUS's public emergence began when buttons on White House phones linked directly to the president were labeled thus in President Lyndon B. Johnson's time. The word came into currency during President Jimmy Carter's term, and it was picked up as shorthand by the Secret Service, matching SCOTUS which was becoming the favorite acronym for the Supreme Court of the United States. Nancy Reagan inspired but may not have originated FLOTUS (rhyming with POTUS) to specify the First Lady. VPOTUS (pronounced vee-potus) to indicate the vice president was occasionally heard in the same era to refer to George Bush, then holding office. Its use became ordinary when Al Gore was vice president in Bill Clinton's administration. The word VEEP to describe the vice president became popular in President Harry Truman's day as a nickname for Vice President Alben W. Barkley, being simply a contracted pronunciation of VP, the common abbreviation for vice president.

Kinds of Presidencies

The staffing of a presidency is vital in shaping its character. But each presidency is ultimately stamped by the personality and inclinations of the incumbent, modified by the fortuitous circumstances that force themselves upon his term. Kennedy said that to judge a president one has to know "what he had going for him." George Washington cut the pattern for the early presidencies which were aimed at making a nation by constructing a sense of national unity out of the varying sectional interests. Above all, aware of the mode of British politics in his day, he was opposed to factionalism—although in the end he could not prevent its rise—and the development of "the demon of party spirit." John Adams, too, tried to eschew politics. Nevertheless, the election of Jefferson in 1800 forced a change. He was the leader of the party—although the president as his party's leader was not accepted for another century. However, the role of the president as leader in foreign affairs and in military matters—foreshadowed by Washington's handlings of the Whiskey Rebellion in 1794—was firmly set by Jefferson's purchase of the Louisiana territory in 1803 and by Madison's unambiguous role as commander-in-chief of the army during the War of 1812.

Jackson's election in 1828 after a long and celebrated military career, brought to the White House the first "man of the people." As such Jackson could sway Congress and shape legislation, so that he may be regarded as the maker of the modern presidency. Even so, its character has been constantly refashioned. The emergence of the slavery issue dwarfed the presidents and the candidates for the office for a long generation. None of Jackson's eight successors was reelected. The power of the presidency was reasserted and dramatized by Lincoln in his ultimately successful conduct of the Civil War. He drew to himself greater power than any that had ever been exercised. Although he had come into politics as a Whig who believed that the president is entitled only to limited authority, Lincoln became, in practice, a Jacksonian. His immediate successors, enveloped in domestic questions, including the racial upheaval caused by emancipation, tended to offer few programs for Congress to act upon. Rather, they saw the presidency as coordinate with Congress, not its director.

Social problems at the beginning of the twentieth century offered new opportunities for a creative presidency. The need and the man were combined in the Republican Theodore Roosevelt, a war hero and dynamo of energy, who used the penny press and the muckraking magazines to make himself a leader of popular causes, including the management of overseas "possessions" and the assault on overweening trusts. He regarded the presidency as a "bully pulpit," an unmatched place from which to advocate a program. TR made himself the undisputed leader of the nation and his party, the source of innovation in public policies and the principal maker of political news. This conception of the presidency transcended party lines. The Democrat Woodrow Wilson, who came to the White House in 1913, was a former professor of political science who admired immensely the British parliamentary system. Still, he came to accept the Rooseveltian view of the presidency and to believe that if the president correctly interprets the public temper and sets forth appropriate programs, he is "irresistible."

In the 1920s and early 1930s the successive presidents were relatively supine. Calvin Coolidge said that it was not the role of the president to send bills to Congress but the business of Congress to send the president bills to sign. However, the example of Jackson, Lincoln, Theodore Roosevelt, and Wilson remained in the bloodstream of the office. The terrible force of the Great Depression allowed Franklin D. Roosevelt to exceed even his distant cousin Theodore's broadened presidency. He regarded the White House as essentially a place for moral leadership. Nevertheless, in his inaugural address he promised to seek "broad Executive power to wage war against the emergency." When the threat of the totalitarian powers to the security of the United States came to seem an even greater emergency, his unprecedented use of the prestige of his office made the presidency more powerful than ever. The high point came in 1942 when FDR said that if Congress did not repeal a certain law, he himself would repeal it.

In the aftermath of World War II, the power of the office was potentially greater than ever. President Truman's remarkable initiatives in foreign policy which included the Marshall Plan, the Truman Doctrine, and participation in the Korean War, extended more tangibly than ever the leadership of the presidency beyond the borders of the United States. Subsequently, Eisenhower's immortal name as the Liberator of Europe enabled him to be less aggressive and strident in exercising leadership during the cold war than Truman had been. Kennedy's inheritance from Ike of an all-powerful office made possible his now-famous defy to "every nation, whether it wishes us well or ill, that we shall pay any price, bear any burden, meet any hardship, support any friend, oppose any foe, in order to assure the survival and the success of liberty."

This vastly enlarged conception, labeled by critics the "Imperial Presidency," came to grief in Kennedy's abortive invasion of the Bay of Pigs, and it suffered disgrace in the administration of Richard Nixon, tarnished by the Watergate episode and related crimes. Next, the failed war in Vietnam and the hostage crisis in Iran stained respectively the Johnson and Carter administrations and further weakened the hand and authority of the presidency abroad. Although President Reagan by his ebullient style and rhetoric could insist that it was once more "Morning in America," the presidency had been shorn of some of its power, and substantially lessened in prestige.

A number of events further sullied the office, notably the Iran-contra affair in the 1980s and the personal acts of President Clinton that led to his impeachment and trial in 1998. But by the serendipity of history, the terrorist attacks on the United States on 11 September 2001 showed once again the vitality and power of the presidential office. President George W. Bush, in masterly fashion, drew the country together for the long twilight struggle that lay ahead. Shifting gears from domestic concerns that had almost exclusively dominated his plans, he transformed his presidency overnight, employing the explicit and implied powers of the office to meet the mortal threat to the homeland. The president of the United States had become, like some of his great predecessors, the voice of hope and inspiration for freedom-loving people everywhere in the world.

Editor's Note: For further reading on the institution of the presidency, consult the classified bibliography in Appendix A. In addition, the annotated bibliographies at the end of each presidential essay identify works that may illuminate the impact of individual presidents on the office.

The White House

William Seale

The White House NATIONAL PARK SERVICE

THE White House is perhaps the most remarkable artifact of the American nation. The concept of an official home for the president originated with the constitutional government in 1789, and in 1790 such a home was prescribed in the Residence Act calling for the creation of a permanent federal city. In 1791 this proposed city was named for the nation's first president, George Washington. Thus by law the White House—and the federal city and Capitol as well—was set down by Congress, written into the Constitution.

The act presented the issue of what sort of a house the president of the United States should have. Congress provided a rented town house for President Washington in New York and then, after the temporary capital was relocated in 1790, in Philadelphia. Washington wanted the new capital city to be built on the Potomac River, for reasons of security and commerce. He engaged the services of the French engineer and architect Pierre Charles L'Enfant to design the city. L'Enfant designed what is essentially the Washington, D.C., we know today. His plan included a "presidential palace." Little is known about this structure, except that the plan was for a building about four times the ground dimensions of the White House as built, and some twenty feet higher. The plan was approved by Washington, and like the design for the city itself, the proposed residence suggested Washington's initial vision of the nation's capital as a place of grandeur and pomp.

The President's House

L'Enfant, ultimately dismissed for insubordination in 1792, left the layout of the federal city complete on paper, but it is generally believed that there were no building plans for the proposed structures, only lines of demarcation that indicated the buildings on their sites. Washington, acting on the suggestion of his secretary of state, Thomas Jefferson, announced a national competition for plans for the design of the Capitol and President's House (as it was then typically called). While the competition was being advertised, Washington contacted James Hoban, a builder he had met in Charleston, South Carolina, and consulted with him about the type of design Washington envisioned for the presidential residence. Hoban, an Irish American schooled in monumental building arts in Dublin, had followed his trade in Philadelphia and Charleston. He ultimately won the competition as Washington's man. Other entries were for structures that suggested palaces. Hoban's entry shows how Washington's ideas had changed in only a few years in favor of a building less palatial, yet by American standards still very grand.

Hoban almost certainly held up models before his presidential patron. The chosen design was based on a house that had been familiar to Hoban in Dublin, the palace of the Duke of Leinster. It was about fifty years old at the time, a broad stone mansion rising two stories above a rustic base. More the house of a squire than a lord, the image appealed to Washington. The commissioners charged with overseeing construction of the city attempted to modify the plan by changing the material to brick; Washington disallowed this. When they respectfully protested the scale, Washington omitted the raised rustic base story and increased the volume of the house by twenty percent. He insisted that the stonework be elaborately rendered in the grand Anglo-Palladian manner.

The commissioners, unpaid government appointees, were left with the responsibility of getting so ambitious a house built. A sandstone quarry was purchased downriver on the Potomac at Aquia Creek. Stonemasons were engaged in Scotland, a party from the Highlands and one from Edinburgh. Both were expert; both had worked to plans of the celebrated Scottish architects Robert and James Adam. They put their best efforts into the President's House, which must have seemed very out of style to them, having recently worked on the restrained neo-classical buildings of New Town in Edinburgh.

By 1798 the building stood much as we know it today. Washington never lived there. He set the stakes for it, establishing the north wall, in cellars already dug out for L'Enfant's "palace." In moving the building north, Washington took it out of view in the axis down Pennsylvania Avenue to the Capitol, a vista filled by the Treasury portico today. He violated the eighty-two acre preserve, called from the outset "the President's Park," by mandating that the government offices be built there, flanking the executive mansion. Thus Washington started the pattern of change with respect to the White House that would be followed by presidents for two centuries to come.

History's Stage

As prescribed in the Residence Act, John Adams, who had become president in 1797, moved into the new house on November 1, 1800. His wife, Abigail, remarked innocently that the East Room was larger than a New England meetinghouse. Because the house was as yet unfinished, lacking sufficient stairs, service bells, some plasterwork, and kitchen fittings, and was sparsely furnished, neither Adams can have been very comfortable, but the rhythms of great events came in with them. In the house on 12 December 1800, Adams heard the election results from South Carolina that put his party, the Federalists, out of the presidency forever; Adams lost to Thomas Jefferson in a contest that pitted the Federalist ideology of a strong central government against that of the more democratic "Republicans," who favored more limited government. In a small second floor room just east of his bedroom on his last night in office, Adams made his famous Midnight Appointments, commissioning several federal judges who were sympathetic to his views. It was Adams who, in a letter to his wife, wrote the timeless benediction for the White House: "I pray Heaven to bestow the best of Blessings on this House, and on all that shall hereafter inhabit it. May none but honest and wise men ever rule under this roof!"

Adams's use of the word "rule" might have given his successor pause. Jefferson, president from 1801 to 1809, brought a new tone to government, reducing it where possible and largely stripping it of ceremony. The White House—for it was first called that in Jefferson's time—could be seen as a glaring anachronism in an era dedicated to "republican simplicity." In various improvements Jefferson made the house seem less august. He built low-lying wings to the east and west that made the house seem not so tall and guant; they contained the "offices" that typically served such a residence in scattered outbuildings. He made no effort to complete the unfinished East Room, and put his office squarely in the State Dining Room, which the Federalists had used for their levees or formal receptions. Jefferson's usual entertaining consisted of small dinners.

He opened the house to the public in the spring of 1801, and it has remained open to tours, except in wartime and for reasons of national security, as following the 11 September 2001 terrorist attacks, ever since. The Marine Band, early-on an Italian family orchestra rescued by the Marine Corps from Mediterranean pirates, was brought in for concerts; the Marine Band, titled by Jefferson the "President's Own," remains the source of White House music today. One continuing White House ceremony was established by Jefferson: When a foreign diplomat presents his credentials to the president, the exchange takes place in the center of the Blue Room.

By the time of Jefferson's departure, British military provocation against the United States at sea was creating great public tension. As the second greatest maritime power in the world, the new United States considered itself a plumb Britain might one day return and pluck. James Madison came to the presidency in 1809 as a man of action. Needing political support, he turned the White House into a most formidable rival to every tavern in Washington. In the able hands of Dolley Payne Madison, his wife, the public rooms were redecorated in sumptuously theatrical elegance that was, oddly enough, *British* high style. Politicians and officials scrambled to attend the weekly receptions of Dolley Madison, providing Madison with opportunities to make political hay.

The quiet that followed the United States' declaration of war on Britain in 1812 soon ended in 1814, when the British, free to turn their attention from European conflicts after the defeat of Napoléon Bonaparte that year, sailed for American shores. On 24 August, British sailors under Rear Admiral George Cockburn marched toward Washington, entering the city after dark. Meanwhile, the White House was the scene of pandemonium, with the packing of papers and valuables. Fearing that the British might make a mockery of Gilbert Stuart's portrait of George Washington, Mrs. Madison entrusted it to two visitors, who removed it from the frame and fled with it through Georgetown. Mrs. Madison departed in a carriage with her coachman, some baggage, and her macaw, and began a wandering journey through the Virginia countryside that would last until nearly dawn. Madison returned to the White House at about dark, had a glass of port with secretary of state James Monroe and other officials, then went to join American troops.

Cockburn's detail of 150 sailors entered the White House at about eleven. Finding the table set for dinner for forty, the officers dined and drank and took souvenirs (Cockburn ordered that these be of no value) and generally enjoyed themselves while Lieutenant Richard Pratt, who had been the fire expert under the command of General Arthur Wellesley, the Duke of Wellington, during Britain's Spanish campaign of 1812, prepared the house for its fate. At last the sailors stood in a circle around the house and hurled flaming javelins through the broken-out windows, igniting the house and burning it to its stone walls.

The loss of the White House had an even more profound effect upon the Americans than the burning that same night of the Capitol, which was unfinished and had yet to achieve its visual identity. After a brief effort to remove the capital to Cincinnati, Congress approved the repair of the public buildings in Washington, and Madison insisted that the White House be rebuilt to match the original structure. What was ultimately salvaged was the central pedimented section of the north front, the basement level, and the entire south front. The rest of the structure was rebuilt, and finished in time for the New Year's Reception in 1818 of a new president, James Monroe.

Monroe was a popular president. The period was called the Era of Good Feelings, due to explosive national prosperity. Monroe ordered furniture for the White House state rooms from France. Pieces of the suite of gilded furniture designed by the French cabinetmaker P. A. Bellangé remain in the oval Blue Room. Many other purchases were made at this time: silver, statuary, chandeliers, carpets, clocks, urns, and a pair of elegant decorative ostrich eggs set up upon golden stands are items included in Monroe's invoices from Paris and later inventories of the house. Some of the silver purchased during Monroe's tenure continues to be used at White House tables, and the French clocks, although not allowed to chime, still tick away White House hours. While the Era of Good Feelings collapsed in the Panic of 1819, Monroe's popularity did not. His most memorable marks on the White House are the South Portico—so-called, when in fact the unpedimented colonnade is a porch—and the large stone gate piers on Pennsylvania Avenue. A pair of iron gates installed under Monroe's direction in 1818 stood in place until 1976. The present-day fence and gates were designed after Monroe's originals.

The People's House

The tempo of politics surrounding the White House rose to a fever pitch in the 1820s with factions in a newly expanded nation battling for control. John Quincy Adams ultimately paid dearly for what was termed a fixed election in 1824, that paved the way for Andrew Jackson's election in 1828. Jackson's inaugural on 4 March 1829, amounted to mass hysteria, as thousands accompanied him from the Capitol to the White House. Jackson, professing to take his mandate from the people rather than from politicians, rode to the White House on horseback in what became the first inaugural parade. The teeming crowd did not disperse when the doors of the executive mansion opened. Where once a few supporters had come to toss back a glass with the new president, now crowds flowed in. Jackson eventually had to flee the White House; he was held up and carried down the steps of the new South Portico to a carriage and then on to a hotel for the night. The unruly crowd, unaware that the president was gone, celebrated on; the steward of the house eventually had washtubs full of whiskey-laced orange juice put out on the south grounds, to draw the visitors outside so that the doors of the residence could be locked.

It was during Jackson's administration that the White House was at last finished. Construction of the North Portico commenced at once, having been planned along with the South Portico in the rebuilding of the White House after the 1814 fire. It was completed in 1831. The vast East Room, which up until then had been furnished somewhat arbitrarily, was now given a proper presidential decor. Major William B. Lewis, a Jackson crony who lived at the White House, went to Philadelphia and selected wallpaper, curtains, chandeliers, colossal mirrors, carpets, tables, lamps, and "twenty-two spittoons" to complete the room. Not least, he ordered 150 gilt stars to be pasted over the room's arched door; the

stars formed a galaxy over Old Hickory as he entered the room to attend receptions.

Jackson built a new stable for his numerous horses, including the racehorses that he regularly ran in competition. Probably to rescue a sago palm extracted from the burning greenhouses at Mount Vernon in 1835, President Jackson ordered an orangery built in the garden just southeast of the house. This became a delightful private retreat inaccessible to the public, where on snowy days the president and his company could enjoy not only the warmth of the tropics, but camellias, lilies, oranges, and lemons. Formal gardens soon extended beyond the tall, southward glass windows of the orangery. Garden and orangery stood where the south wing of the Treasury building now stands.

It was also in the decade of the 1820s and the early 1830s that the setting of the White House developed into a more or less permanent configuration. Originally Pennsylvania Avenue did not pass in front of the White House. In L'Enfant's conception, the avenue and New York Avenue, both diagonals in the city plan, were to terminate in each direction at the grounds of the presidential residence, which, with Sixteenth Street going due north, was to have radial avenues to a forecourt at its north or principal facade. When L'Enfant's "palace" was scrapped and Hoban's design built, these plans were altered, and what was to have been a forecourt was simply open land, used for a time as a common and market place. James Monroe ordered it marked off into a park in 1820; this space became Lafayette Park in 1824, named for the nation's first guest of state. Pennsylvania Avenue was at about that time brought in front of the White House.

The British had burned George Washington's two executive office buildings the morning after the White House. These were replaced with four new buildings, each with columned porches. East of the White House stood the State Department, to the north, and Treasury, to the south; west of the White House were the Navy Department, which faced south, and the War Department facing north. During the time these buildings stood, a large sand-bottom pool existed between the two buildings on the east, a feature of the running water system Andrew Jackson installed in the White House in 1833.

When the Treasury building burned in 1836, the architect Robert Mills designed a grand new structure that is the Treasury building we know today, occupying the entire space on the east. The buildings on the west, together with the State Department, were combined into the gigantic granite building on the west, completed about 1873 in the French Second Empire or "General Grant" style by Supervising Architect of the U.S. Treasury, Alfred Mullet. Known for many years as the State, War, and Navy building, it is today the Old Executive Office Building (OEOB in White House jargon), housing the vice president and part of the president's staff. Very little of a radical character was done to the White House for many years after Jackson. The residence had two distinct parts, the office in the east end of the second floor and the family quarters, seven or eight rooms in the west end, both parts connected by the long, tall transverse corridor, itself divided into three sections by fan-transomed glass doors. The state rooms on the main floor were generally for entertaining and receiving, although the Red Room and the small dining room on the north were often used by the presidential families in their everyday lives.

The rooms were all wallpapered, with carpets wall to wall and heavy window hangings crowned by gilded cornices. Furniture was mostly mahogany, upholstered in satin or silk, damask or brocade, with fringe and tassels. Interior decorating is continual in such a place, where wear and tear is accelerated far beyond that in the average house. Monroe had painted one of the parlors green in 1818 and made it forever the Green Room; Martin Van Buren followed in 1838 with the oval Blue Room; and James Knox Polk in 1846 with the Red Room.

Jefferson installed the first waterclosets in 1801, one at each end of the second floor, and while many subsequent fixtures replaced his, there were not more than three waterclosets in the house until after the Civil War. The first kitchen range was also Jefferson's, although many followed. As late as Lincoln's time the old brick bread ovens remained, although since Polk the White House had received its bread supplies from local bakeries. Under Madison, central heating (a furnace in the basement) was installed in the parlors and dining room, but neither Madison nor Monroe apparently cared to replace this system after the fire. Van Buren had the major rooms centrally heated with a gravity system, which relied on rising heat to distribute warm air. Sarah Polk ordered gas lighting, and the lights of the White House went out at nine at night when the gas company closed. At receptions, Sarah Polk, the First Lady, strategically positioned herself beneath the candle chandelier in the Blue Room, and her guests, plunged into darkness at nine, were drawn through the dark rooms to the light.

Polk had a marble statue of Jefferson erected on the north lawn, so that Polk, who had seen the nation expand to the Pacific, might be identified with so great a founding father. Sarah Polk checkmated this effort by hanging a captured portrait of the Spanish conquistador Hernán Cortés in the Blue Room. And so the White House changed in small ways through the 1830s, 1840s, and 1850s, but the familiar image of the house remained unaltered.

Management of the house initially fell to a steward, who hired and managed the servants. Southern presidents brought slaves to the White House and they lived in the private quarters with the family; slaves were continually in conflict with the stewards, from whom they refused to take orders. The early stewards were European; most had seen duty in domestic service before. President Tyler brought armed Metropolitan Police officers into the house in plainclothes as the first guard force. In idle time these officers would supervise cleaning, preparation for receptions, and purchasing from merchants and suppliers. So much were they a part of the running of the White House by the late 1850s that President Buchanan changed their titles from "doorkeepers" to "ushers." Today the head official is the chief usher, who is in charge of the residence and grounds. All household staff is under this person's jurisdiction.

Like any place where legendary people have lived, the White House gained a mystique, especially during and after the tenure of Abraham Lincoln. Lincoln's brief time in the residence, a little over four years, presented a domestic melodrama that paralleled the greater movements of the age and put in human terms for Americans the incomprehensible devastation of the Civil War. The Lincolns—rather than just Lincoln—sanctified the White House by epitomizing the American family in a time of personal and national crisis. After the triumph of Lincoln's attaining of the presidency, the family was torn apart by death and sacrifice. Major Elmer Ellsworth, a close friend of Lincoln's who had lived with the family at the White House, in 1861 became the first Union casualty of note in the war. In 1862 the Lincolns' twelve-year-old son William ("Willie") died of typhoid fever. Throughout her time in the White House Mary Todd Lincoln was vilified by the opposition press, which among other things accused her of spying for the Confederacy. In 1865 President Lincoln was assassinated, martyred to a world far wider than his own domestic circle, and his wife, left the White House, grief-stricken and mentally unstable. So compelling a story touched chords north and south. The White House had been Lincoln's home and and would be cherished for that ever after.

Restoration

The U.S. Army Corps of Engineers, charged with maintenance and public building in the District of Columbia, took a great interest in public improvements after the Civil War. Various officers traveled to Europe and studied public works; a nationalistic industrial age was flourishing, notably in France and Germany. Among the many projects of the Corps of Engineers that never got far from the drawing table was a new White House. Plans had been drawn up for a "suburban palace" located in the picturesque area now known as Rock Creek Park. President Andrew Johnson approved the idea in 1867. But when President Ulysses S. Grant came to office in 1869 as the peacemaker, he recognized the symbolic power of the White House and would entertain no notions of a new one.

The existing White House instead became the focus of improvements. The aftermath of the Lincoln assassination had left the house (which had been overused during the war) fairly well torn up, with the public moving idly in and out while Mrs. Lincoln lay upstairs consumed by grief. President Johnson, knowing he would never live in a new mansion if one was begun, accomplished a complete refurbishing of the interior. The office was refurnished except for Andrew Jackson's portrait and desk, and a telegraph was installed in the southeast corner room of the office suite. A greenhouse built on the roof of the west terrace in 1857 to house plants from the former orangery caught fire in 1867 and was replaced with a greenhouse of iron, opening directly into the house. This was enlarged by Grant, who had a billiard room constructed between the house and the greenhouse; other glass extensions rambled over the west wing. Subsequent presidents had additional greenhouses built. Palms, cactus, orchids, camellias, spring bulbs, water plants, all flourished under the care of expert gardeners. A rose house stood on the site of today's open-air Rose Garden.

The presidents welcomed the privacy that the greenhouses afforded. For some they were a promenade and for others a place for rest beneath the glass ceilings. First Ladies liked their floral bounty. Bouquet makers were employed making gift bouquets to send by coachman to hotels and boarding houses, substituting for the personal calls First Ladies traditionally made to congressmen and senators' wives and important women visiting town. If any one feature characterized the Victorian White House it was the "glass houses" or "conservatories" that stood as large and exotic companions to the historic building.

Efforts by President Chester A. Arthur in 1881 to demolish and replace the White House came to nothing and even raised some hackles. He proposed a modern wing, with a "bridge of sighs" connecting it to the original structure, and various plans survive. The Corps of Engineers continued to await its moment to improve the presidential complex; if one thing had been learned, it was that the old White House would remain. With this in mind, the Corps began preparing plans for adding to the house in the architectural manner established by the original building. When her husband, Benjamin Harrison, came to office in 1889, First Lady Caroline Harrison oversaw various improvements to the White House, including the installation of electricity in 1891. She met with the engineers to discuss a major expansion of the house, to mark the one hundredth anniversary of George Washington's inauguration as president. With her participation, the Corps produced detailed plans for such an expansion.

The idea was to create a quadrangle to the south, faced on one side by the south façade of the White House and on the east and west, with new space for art galleries, presidential offices, and guest rooms, and at the far south end with new greenhouses, which, because the grade slopes downward, would not obstruct the historic view of the river. Congress was not entirely opposed and a bill was born. However, Harrison appointed a certain postal official in Maine without consulting Speaker Thomas Brackett Reed from Maine (known in his day as "Czar Reed"), and Reed retaliated for what he considered a slight by obstructing passage of the bill. The celebration of Washington's inauguration went on with considerable glitter but without a new White House.

Encouraged by construction of the massive Jefferson Building of the Library of Congress in the 1890s and the building projects of the 1893 World's Columbian Exposition in Chicago, the Corps of Engineers in collaboration with the architectural designer Frederick Owen, continued to refine their plans for an enlarged White House. Grover and Frances Cleveland gave an idle nod to the idea. Cleveland's successor William McKinley, president from 1897 to 1901, was generally agreeable, and the Corps, under the public buildings commissioner Colonel Theodore Bingham, planned to present its new project as part of the one hundredth anniversary of the first occupation of the White House by John Adams. In 1900 the Corps unveiled an elaborate model, tailored to please McKinley with its inclusion of a press wing. Mrs. McKinley's remark, "There won't be any hammering while I live here," was hardly heard amid the enthusiasm of Bingham and his supporters.

Objections were soon voiced by various political figures, not the least of whom was Senator James McMillan of Michigan, chairman of the District Committee and Centennial Committee of Washington City. Urged on by the American Institute of Architects and his aide Charles Moore, McMillan rallied support for a comprehensive parks system for Washington, which took the form of an Act of Congress on 8 March 1901. The issue of White House expansion, although pushed by the Corps, receded, and McKinley's assassination in September put the plan in limbo.

The Modern White House

Leading figures in the design and architectural community sought access to the new president, Theodore Roosevelt. Roosevelt and his wife, Edith Carow Roosevelt, sought a house that would provide a more suitable background for the newly "international" presidency than the old Victorian mansion that the White House had become. Moreover, the Roosevelts had a big family, and as Mrs. Roosevelt's notes and sketches showed at the time, the area of the second floor that was allocated for their living quarters was not adequate to accommodate them. The offices on the second floor had to go.

By the summer of 1902 a renovation of the White House was in the hands of Charles F. McKim of the prominent Manhattan architectural firm McKim, Mead and White. McKim's advisor was the Washington architect Glenn Brown, who had sparked much of the public controversy against the Corps of Engineer's expansion plan. While McKim always insisted that the Roosevelt renovation was the work of his firm, all written sources make it clear that he and Glenn Brown did the designing. What they did was to rethink the White House and the manner in which it functioned.

They faced an old stone house with an interior largely of wood and plaster. Two stories and an attic rose above a basement that was beneath ground on the north and entirely out of ground on the south. The basement was for services, and housed dingy kitchens, pantries, a "meat room" where meat was stored, servants' bedchambers, a housekeeper's apartment, and storage rooms piled with discarded furnishings. On the main floor were the state rooms, East Room, and two dining rooms, with the three parlors in between; on the west side of it the greenhouses rambled, occupying more ground space than the house itself. The second floor held offices and living quarters, and the attic was a forgotten space, entirely isolated from the rest of the house when an elevator was installed in place of the back stairs in 1881, cutting off access.

The architects first declared the White House to be historic and thus sacrosanct. They did not want to expand it, but to bring it back in line with its original conception. By that standard, some spaces would be eliminated and new space would be found in the existing envelope. Plans to remove the greenhouses initially met with resistance from the Roosevelts, but McKim's gentle persuading as well as, perhaps, the intervention of a cousin, the novelist Edith Wharton, finally caused the president to assert, "Smash the glass houses!" Jefferson's west terrace would be retained. His east terrace, demolished in the Grant administration, would be reconstructed. The house and its wings would be repaired to look as they had originally, without Victorian additions.

An office building would be added to the end of the west wing to accommodate the thirty employees who had previously had their offices on the second floor of the White House. The entire second floor would thus be renovated as family living quarters, while the first or state floor would remain the official and ceremonial heart of the White House, with support facilities in a completely revised basement, now to be the "ground floor." A program of interior decoration was also planned.

Entrance to the White House was now to be through the East Wing, as it is today. Visitors would pass along the colonnade of Jefferson's reconstructed wing into the basement, now a "ground floor," its magnificent structural vaulting plastered smooth and painted white, giving it a monumental and dramatic character. Coatrooms, rest rooms, a modern kitchen, and offices were on the ground floor, which now featured a special entrance into the oval room named the Diplomatic Reception Room, which was located directly beneath the first floor's Blue Room.

President Roosevelt insisted that the White House renovation take no more than ninety days from inception to completion, and he planned to remain in the house while the work was being done. This last edict was quickly rescinded, and in a haze of plaster dust Roosevelt moved across the street to a rented row house. The work was completed in time for the first state dinner of the season, in December 1902.

It was a house transformed. Even in black-and-white photographs its attributes are clear. The interior of the state rooms was given a European flair, with the grand East Room made over in Louis XVI style, featuring parquet floors and white-painted paneling, and the State Dining Room refitted with dark-polished Georgian-style oak paneling. The parlor walls were covered in silk and arrangements of cream-colored English- and French historical-style furniture graced the rooms. Modern plumbing, heating, and wiring were installed; the upstairs now housed an abundance of bedrooms, and the gleaming bathrooms showcased nickel-plated faucets and white tile.

The new West Wing—the so-called Temporary Executive Office Building—made the greatest change in affording the family privacy and the office staff more room. Although the president was allocated work space there, the West Wing was intended for use primarily by the president's secretary and staff. Bill signings and important meetings in which the president was in attendance continued to be held in the White House proper, in the president's study on the second floor. Some congressmen refused to use the West Wing, thinking it inferior. In 1909 Taft doubled the size of the West Wing, building the first Oval Office, the shape chosen to reflect the most familiar—and distinctive—room in the main house.

Roosevelt's renovation prepared the White House for the twentieth-century presidency. Ever greater crowds, more numerous events, larger staff, and greater public attention to the residence were to characterize White House life from then on. Very little was done to change the house during the next half century. In 1927 President Calvin Coolidge presided over replacement of the attic; the roof was raised to accommodate a full third floor, while the outside facade of the house remained unchanged. The solarium or "sky parlor" was built over the South Portico at this time, and guest and service rooms were added to serve the second-floor family quarters, as the ground floor served the first, or state, floor.

Herbert Hoover's plans to double the size of the West Wing were laid aside when the wing was dam-

aged by fire on Christmas Eve 1929. The nation was in the initial stage of the Great Depression, and Hoover decided that a reconstruction of the West Wing was more appropriate than an expanded building. Where Coolidge had delivered an occasional radio address from the West Wing, Hoover gave many such addresses, noting that they were being broadcast from his office. This was the first time that the general public became aware of the West Wing as a significant feature of the White House. Franklin D. Roosevelt (president from 1933 to 1945) carried the idea a step further by issuing cozy "fireside chats" (although these addresses were typically broadcast from the Diplomatic Reception Room, which had no fireplace.)

FDR's interest in the White House was great and change was undertaken soon after he became president. Roosevelt, who had been stricken with polio in 1921, had an indoor swimming pool installed at the White House for his exercise therapy; its construction was paid for largely by schoolchildren in New York State who donated dimes and pennies in the first wave of the fundraising effort for polio aid and research that became known as the March of Dimes. The pool was boarded over during the Nixon administration in order to accommodate the present press room. Roosevelt loved old houses, and had remodeled the family estate at Hyde Park and helped design Eleanor Roosevelt's Val-Kill cottage, both in the Hudson River Valley of New York. At the White House a National Park Service architect, Lorenzo Winslow, met with him frequently on projects. Together they designed the ground-floor library and would have overseen renovation of the West Wing had Mrs. Roosevelt not intervened to ensure that her friend and sometimes colleague Eric Gugler have the job. In enlarging the West Wing in 1934, Roosevelt doubled its size, but because the addition was mostly underground, the facade of the building was unchanged. Gugler designed the Oval Office that we know today.

Roosevelt had long wanted an extension of the East Wing to house a White House museum, but he was unable to raise sufficient funds. He continued to collect artifacts, and after the United States entered World War II in 1941, ordered the wing begun as an emergency action. Winslow designed it; Congress funded it, and the construction was conducted behine high wooden fences in utmost secrecy. Unknown to the public, the new addition included a bomb shelter, a grim series of concrete rooms several stories beneath the ground, with a presidential chamber in the center furnished with a cot and desk. Roosevelt is said to have refused to return to the room after seeing it once.

Preserving the Symbol

After Roosevelt's long tenure, a new president faced a White House showing fifty years of quick alterations and structural neglect. A U.S. Army Corps of Engineers report made the week after the Japanese bombed Pearl Harbor on 7 December 1941, had pronounced the White House a firetrap. Roosevelt had dismissed the report, saying that he had lived in old houses all his life and they all had aches and pains. When President Harry S. Truman moved to the residence in 1945 from a small apartment in Washington, the barren family quarters never looked more in need of help. There were deep cracks in the walls, and now and then the heavy chandeliers on the state floor swayed slightly, accompanied by a falling snow of plaster dust. In 1948, after a leg of the grand piano belonging to the president's daughter, Margaret, sank between two boards in the floor of her room, the president called in the Corps of Engineers.

Truman and his family moved to Blair House across the street—which had been rescued from demolition by FDR for use as a guest house—and the Corps went to work inspecting the White House. Not long after, the Corps ordered the house emptied. One engineer recalled crawling between the upstairs floor and the East Room ceiling and finding the plaster ceiling unlocked from its lath as much as eighteen inches—in other words, the eighty-five-foot ceiling was like a hammock, largely suspended between its two ends.

Major work was required to fix the structural problems. The original interior framing of the house was constructed of wood covered with wood lath, all dry wood that indeed made it a firetrap. It could be restored, its parts carefully pieced and repaired, but it would be of use then only as a museum. Truman wanted the White House to remain the home of the presidents. For this it had to be fireproof and bombproof. Many project designs were put forth. The plan that the president favored had been carried out on a historic building at Yale University, which had been gutted, its outer walls preserved. Truman was determined to undertake just this type of renovation, to save George Washington's original walls and otherwise empty the vessel, building a new, structurally sound White House without altering the historic facade.

Restoration was carried out between 1948 and 1952. The third floor, built during Coolidge's tenure in 1927, was retained; permanent steel legs were built through the old house and down to the level of cellars yet to come to support it. Underpinning for the outside walls of the house extended twenty-four feet into a new foundation, and a steel framework was constructed to support the reconstructed walls of the interior. At first an effort was made to preserve old doors and paneling, but as the job progressed, most of the material was discarded or made into souvenirs. Some old wainscoting was retained, along with some window surrounds and various other woodwork. Truman was intent that the project not be seen as a violation of the historic site. Once while making his daily inspection of the work, he came upon laborers preparing to enlarge a doorway to admit a bulldozer and dump truck needed to dig the new basement. He stopped them at once, ordering that the bulldozer and truck be dismantled outside and reassembled within to accomplish the task.

Toward the end of the work, Truman cracked the whip. He wanted to occupy the house before his administration was over. The work proceeded in haste and was completed by the spring of 1952. Inside the changes were subtle, but the house did have a more monumental feel due to generous use, relative to the original White House, of such materials as marble where plaster had been before. The rooms were stylishly furnished, mostly with reproductions of American antiques. The former First Lady, Eleanor Roosevelt, in her syndicated newspaper column "My Day," wrote that it reminded her of a Sheraton Hotel.

The reconstruction carried out under Truman could be dismissed as a desecration, but any judgment must be tempered by the fact that Truman was dealing with the White House, home and office of the world's most powerful leader. He saved the image and enough of the substance to lend the restored White House historical credibility. It was not an easy decision; not nearly as easy as his decision, in 1948, to install a balcony over the South Portico, with access from the family quarters; he did this to fire a volley at the Congress, which had refused to fund a new executive office wing. But Truman's view of history was sweeping, and he was conscious of the symbolic power of the White House, and committed to preserving that symbol. His decision in the renovations of 1948 to 1952 stands the test of time.

Enduring Image, New Challenges

Truman was the first president to understand the burgeoning power of television and the impact that this technology would have on the presidency. He insisted that the historic White House be his backdrop during televised addresses to the nation. He added a broadcast room to the residence for this purpose. Television did have a dramatic impact on the presidency, and in rescuing the physical White House, Truman preserved an American icon that, with the help of the broadcast media, became known throughout the world.

Dwight D. Eisenhower, president from 1953 to 1961, was heir to the Truman renovations. The only change that he and First Lady Mamie Eisenhower made was in the Diplomatic Reception Room, which was furnished with American antiques under the direction of the American Society of Interior Designers. Alterations to the White House were, however, a main issue in the administration of Eisenhower's successor, John F. Kennedy.

During the brief Kennedy administration, the White House was rethought in a major way for the first time since Theodore Roosevelt's renovation. With the advice of Letitia Baldridge, Jacqueline Kennedy's social secretary, White House ceremony was reconsidered. For example, visiting heads of state had previously been met at the airport and driven down Constitution Avenue through crowds of government workers waving small flags distributed for the purpose. Now visiting dignitaries were transported from the airport via helicopter; at the White House, some 600 spectators were admitted to mark the occasion. The Marine Band played, and the President and guest each made brief addresses and retired to the house, the entire ceremony taking about twenty minutes.

Kennedy sought a background for his presidency that would reflect the United States' postwar international prestige. Mrs. Kennedy envisioned a solution in refurbishing the rooms of the White House; she began making plans for redecoration even before they moved to the residence in 1961. But the idea gained new meaning when, on an official trip to France, President and Mrs. Kennedy were struck by President Charles de Gaulle's "historically accurate" interior restorations at the palace of Versailles and its outdoor pavilion, the Grand Trainon, as well as the restoration of Empress Josephine's chateau, Malmaison. The decorator responsible for

these, Stephane Boudin, was brought to the United States to oversee interior design of the White House. Boudin's role was a well-kept secret for fear that the public and press would criticize the president's going to Europe to find talent sufficient for the American White House. Henry Francis du Pont, founder of the Winterthur Museum in Delaware, was the name publicly associated with the renovations at the Kennedy White House, but the decisions were Boudin's, subject to Mrs. Kennedy's approval.

The refurbished state rooms were dramatic in their period attire, and gained the approbation of the American public. A particular sort of personal attention was drawn to the White House and its occupants as it had not been in many years. The First Lady showcased the reenvisioned interior of the White House in a nationally televised tour, as Truman had done in 1952; President Kennedy made a cameo appearance, praising the work. Not only was the house redecorated along historical lines, but longtime government plans to bulldoze the houses around Lafayette Park so that high-rise offices could be built were scrapped in favor of restoring and reconstructing the old houses and building executive and judicial office buildings behind them. Designed and carried out by the architect John Carl Warnecke, an intimate of the Kennedys, this work was completed after Kennedy's death in 1963.

President Kennedy, who took an interest in gardening, named the White House Reservation One of the National Park Service, and put the Park Service in charge of the grounds. Kennedy had the Rose Garden redesigned by Rachel Lambert Mellon and the horticulturist Perry Wheeler; he wanted the garden to be tranquil and private and yet able to accommodate five hundred spectators at a bill signing. Every Kennedy endeavor to update the White House was governed by the concept of historical accuracy. To further interest the public in the White House and its history, Mrs. Kennedy founded the White House Historical Association, a nonprofit organization that today funds acquisitions of antiques and many publications about the White House, including guide books and the journal *White House History*.

Mrs. Kennedy's renovations were completed under the administration of President Lyndon B. Johnson (1963–1969). The Committee for the Preservation of the White House was established by Executive Order in 1964 and given jurisdiction over the state rooms. Lady Bird Johnson's program of beautification extended to the White House grounds in the planting of many trees and creation of the Children's Garden, a space tucked away in the south grounds and featuring a fish pool.

During the administration of Richard M. Nixon (1969–1974), the West Wing, notably the basement, was remodeled, and a columned porch was added to the north side. The President and Mrs. Nixon were also interested in history and antiques and greatly expanded the Kennedy program. Most of the antique furnishings in the White House today were acquired by gift or purchase during the Nixon administration. All of the state rooms were redecorated, their contents enhanced with valuable furnishings of antique or historical value.

Interest in the White House under Presidents Gerald Ford (1974–1977) and Jimmy Carter (1977–1981) centered in art, and fine American pictures were acquired, including notable portraits, busts, and genre scenes. President Ronald Reagan (1981–1989) had the family quarters, some thirty-two rooms on the second and third floors entirely remodeled under the direction of interior designer Ted Graber of Los Angeles. His successor, President George Bush (1988–1993), showed little particular interest in redecorating an already many times redecorated White House, although he did refurbish the Oval Office, keeping with a relatively recent trend of updating this room by administration, to reflect a president's personal tastes.

The presidency of Bill Clinton (1993–2001) saw many stylish changes in the decoration of the family quarters, but little with respect to the state areas of the house, except for the Blue Room, which was refreshed and redecorated along the lines Nixon had introduced. Hillary Rodham Clinton sought historical authenticity in following the preferences of James Monroe even with respect to the paint specifications. She removed everything that was not reflective of Monroe's original purchases and personally refitted some reproduced period wallpaper to better suit the room. Her "restoration" perhaps begins a trend. In the administration of President George W. Bush, which began in 2001, the family quarters have been more rearranged than redecorated, although some colors have been changed.

Access to the People's House was restricted in the late twentieth and early twenty-first centuries due to security threats at home and abroad. The block of Pennsylvania Avenue in front of the White House was closed to vehicular traffic in May 1995, during the Clinton administration, after several security breaches on White House grounds and the car bombing of the Oklahoma City federal building in April 1995. Secret Service officials had been urging closure of the avenue since the mid-1980s.

The National Park Service has planned a large-scale underground expansion to the south under the Ellipse, a large open field behind the White House, and on the north, under Pennsylvania Avenue, for parking, offices, meeting rooms, and storage. Plans were being made for an ever greater pedestrian area north of the White House, and perhaps eventually on the surrounding streets. Plans had also been put forward regarding construction of a traffic tunnel beneath Pennsylvania Avenue; an alternate plan is for such a tunnel to be built beneath K Street, to the south. All of this, of course, is pending the security adjustments that will be necessary in the aftermath of 11 September 2001.

In retrospect, it seems unfortunate that the original eighty-two acre President's Park was not preserved in Washington's day, for if it was still intact, the problems of the White House with respect to security would be fewer. History has brought change to the White House over two centuries, as have the aims, conceptions, and preferences of the individuals residing under its roof. But the image itself is one of continuity. One thing seems certain: The White House and even its grounds within the iron fence will always look about as they do, whatever may be done to alter the broader surroundings. In a nation with little ceremony beyond the courtroom, symbols are especially important. The White House is the foremost symbol of the American presidency, and one of the most familiar symbols in the world of American democracy.

Editor's Note: For further reading on the institution of the presidency, consult the classified bibliography in Appendix A. In addition, the annotated bibliographies at the end of each presidential essay identify works that may illuminate the impact of individual presidents on the office.

George Washington

Jacob E. Cooke

George Washington THE LIBRARY OF CONGRESS

O N 4 February 1789 the electoral college, entrusted by the newly adopted United States Constitution with the election of a president and vice president, voted unanimously for George Washington as the new nation's first chief executive. Since Washington was almost universally regarded as the indispensable man, neither his election nor his acceptance of the post was ever in doubt. It was for this reason that the framers adopted Article II of the Constitution, the section providing for, and broadly stipulating, the duties of the president. There was no problem in granting general and undefined powers to an office that most delegates believed would be filled

by a man as universally admired and respected as Washington.

When official word of his election reached him on 14 April 1789 (a delay due to the slowness with which Congress assembled), Washington reluctantly and unhappily acquiesced in his countrymen's wishes. "I bade adieu to Mount Vernon, to private life, and to domestic felicity," he confided to his usually matter-of-fact diary, "and with a mind oppressed with more anxious and painful sensations than I have words to express, set out for New York."

On the long eight-day trip to New York, then the nation's capital, the president-elect had ample time to reflect on his reservations about satisfactorily filling the office, particularly in view of its predictable problems. Fifty-seven years old, weary of official cares, and in poor health, Washington believed that he had already given too much of his life to public service. Resigned, nevertheless, to rendering the best possible "service to my country in obedience to its call," he realized that a principal contribution would be to diminish promptly the opposition to the new central government that had been revealed in the stormy debates over its ratification, a task that he, more than any other American, was best qualified to accomplish. He was also aware that "the first transactions of a nation, like those of an individual upon his first entrance into life, make the deepest impression, and . . . form the leading traits in its characters." Time has borne him out. The imprint of Washington's two terms in office has been of lasting importance not only in the history of the American presidency but also in the development of a viable national government. Perhaps only he could so successfully have accomplished these goals. Because of temperament, training, and, above all, his prominent status as the architect of American independence, he was the right man, at the right time, in the right job.

Early Years

Washington was born on 22 February 1732, the first son of Augustine Washington and his second wife, Mary Ball, in Westmoreland County, Virginia. A moderately well-to-do planter, Augustine had a large family—four children by his first marriage and six by his second. Soon after George was born, his family moved to a plantation in Stafford County, on the east side of the Rappahannock River, where he acquired a sparse education in what would now be called a private school. He later mastered surveying. His favorite sibling and his idol was his eldest half brother, Lawrence, who became George's father surrogate when Augustine Washington died in 1743, the same year in which Lawrence married a daughter of Colonel William Fairfax, head of one of the most socially prominent and influential families in Virginia. At the age of seventeen, George became a member of Lawrence's household at Mount Vernon, a part of which estate George inherited when his elder brother died in 1752.

The only military experience that Washington had preceding the American Revolution was acquired in the 1750s. Appointed adjutant general of a military district in Virginia with the rank of major in 1751, Washington was sent two years later by Governor Robert Dinwiddie to the Ohio Valley to alert the French to the dangers of trespassing on lands claimed by the English. The French were not deterred, and in the ensuing French and Indian War, Washington, now a lieutenant colonel, served as aide-de-camp to General Edward Braddock, in which post he took part in the disastrous expedition against Fort Duquesne. Following this defeat, Washington served from 1755 to 1758 as commander of the Virginia militia raised to defend the colony's western frontier. In this capacity, he gratifyingly commanded a successful expedition against Fort Duquesne.

On 6 January 1759, Washington married Martha, wealthy widow of John Parke Custis, and daughter of John Dandridge. With Martha and her children he settled down at Mount Vernon, becoming a typically prosperous country squire. His status was mirrored by his service in the House of Burgesses from 1759 to 1774.

A cautious and prudent Virginia aristocrat, Washington was nevertheless among the first Virginians to protest British colonial policy. He publicly emphasized his opposition by accepting appointment as a delegate to the Continental Congress during 1774–1775. On 15 June 1775 he was chosen by that body as commander in chief of the Continental army.

The saga of Washington's Revolutionary War exploits has been recounted many times and need not be repeated here. Among the highlights of his extraordinary military career were the successful siege of Boston in 1775–1776; the crossing of the Delaware on Christmas night 1776 and defeat of the redcoats at Trenton; the depressing defeats in the autumn of 1777 at Brandywine and Germantown, Pennsylvania; the bitterly cold winter that the dispirited Continental army endured at Valley Forge in 1777–1778; the skillfully commanded victory at Monmouth, New Jersey, in June 1778; and the famous Yorktown campaign in 1781, which brought the war to an end. By this time, Washington was the foremost hero of the Revolution, virtually canonized by his countrymen and widely respected abroad.

After eight and a half years as commander in chief of the revolutionary army, Washington resigned his commission and resumed his former life as a planter at Mount Vernon. He was enormously satisfied to be relieved of the heavy duties of official life and happy to be once again a private citizen. But the feebleness of government under the Articles of Con-

General George Washington visits with wounded soldiers of his Continental Army at Valley Forge during the bitter winter of 1777–1778. THE LIBRARY OF CONGRESS/CORBIS

federation and the imperativeness of strengthening the Union quickly convinced him that his dream of serene retirement at Mount Vernon was likely to be shattered. It soon was. Convinced that "we are fast verging to anarchy and confusion," Washington accepted his selection as a delegate to the Constitutional Convention, which assembled in Philadelphia in May 1787, and was chosen its president. Once the new Constitution was written and ratified, there was, as has been said, no doubt as to the identity of the new nation's first president.

Washington's journey to the new capital in April 1789 was physically arduous, but it was a triumphal procession then unparalleled in the country's history. At major coach stops along his route, he was hailed in a manner befitting a Roman conqueror or a European sovereign—bells were rung, guns fired, countless congratulatory speeches made, odes recited, and parades and public banquets held. As he sailed across New York Bay on the last leg of his journey, he was accompanied by a sloop crowded with choristers who sang odes—one of them set to the

tune of "God Save the King"—in his honor. When he reached the Battery, the cheers of a dense crowd and the peals of church bells competed with the thunder of thirteen-gun salutes from ship and shore batteries.

Such adulation suggests a major difficulty in objectively assessing the accomplishments and shortcomings of the first president. Since his retirement in 1783 as commander in chief of the Continental army, he had been hailed as "Father of His Country," heralded as an American Atlas or Fabius, and honored as the Cincinnatus of his nation's successful revolution. The most famous American of his day, at home and internationally, he was already a legendary figure and, as such, virtually immune from the critical or partisan barbs and shafts hurled at many of his presidential successors. He is still remembered primarily as the hero of the Revolution, the military leader most responsible for establishing on the field of battle a new and ultimately powerful nation. Even now, as for almost two centuries, his presidential stewardship is considered a postscript to his renowned generalship. It is also true, as one close student of his career, J. A. Carroll, commented, that "the biographers of George Washington either have found him a paradox and made him a paragon, or found him a paragon and left him a paradox."

The enduring image of Washington remains the one popularized by famous sculptors and portraitists, especially Gilbert Stuart, who painted him at least one hundred twenty-four times. Washington was variously depicted as a Roman imperator with sword and toga; Cincinnatus at the plow; or, less frequently, as in Stuart's "Lansdowne" portrait, a republican statesman attired in black velvet. In sum, as Marcus Cunliffe perceptively commented, Washington "has become entombed in his own myth—a metaphorical Washington Monument that hides from us the lineaments of the real man."

On 30 April 1789, Robert R. Livingston, chancellor of the state of New York, administered the oath of office to the nation's first president. The ceremony took place on a small portico of the remodeled Federal Hall, just off the Senate chamber where the two houses of Congress had assembled. Arriving in a canary-colored coach drawn by six horses, Washington, tall, erect, his hair powdered, was dressed in a suit of domestically spun brown broadcloth, his attire adorned by shoe buckles of silver and a dress sword in a steel scabbard. As he swore to preserve, protect, and defend the Constitution of the United States, he looked down from the balcony of Federal Hall upon throngs of people who lined Wall and Broad Streets. The crowd cheered, from the Battery came a thirteen-gun salute, and the president, bowing in acknowledgment, withdrew.

Having taken his place on the dais of the Senate chamber, Washington, his voice low, his gestures awkward, his hands trembling, delivered his brief inaugural address. Although the occasion was inspiring and his audience dazzled by the president's courtly and imposing appearance, the address itself, like so many of its successors, was, when read in cold print, not particularly impressive. He repeated his oft-made assertions regarding the conflict between duty and inclination, his consciousness of his "inferior endowments," and his lack of practice "in the duties of civil administration," and (perhaps to compensate for these deficiencies) invoked the care of "that Almighty Being who rules over the Universe" and whose "providential agency" had solicitously guided the people of the United States. Turning to affairs of state, the president merely declared his intention to

defer to congressional judgment. His one specific request was that he receive no salary and that his compensation "be limited to such actual expenditures as the public good may be thought to require."

First Term

One of the most important developments of Washington's first months in office was congressional creation of executive departments and the president's appointments to head them. An act establishing the State Department became law on 27 July; a measure creating the Department of War was approved early in August; and the Treasury Department was created on 2 September.

Congress also provided for two executive officers who lacked a department: an attorney general and a postmaster general. To fill the former, the president chose Edmund Randolph, a Richmond lawyer, former governor of Virginia, and Antifederalist apostate of whom Washington was particularly fond personally. As postmaster general, Washington designated Samuel Osgood, whose assignment in those comparatively simple days was carried out in a single room with the aid of two clerks.

The president's predictable candidate for the War Department was Henry Knox, who had administered the corresponding office under the Confederation. Although genial and cooperative, Knox proved to be the cabinet's least capable administrator and least independent and forceful member. Washington's choice for secretary of state came as something of a surprise: Thomas Jefferson, a fellow Virginian, who was on the eve of returning from France, where his service as United States minister since 1784 had earned him diplomatic distinction and Washington's esteem. To head the Treasury Department, the president called on a former aide-de-camp and one of the nation's foremost nationalists, Alexander Hamilton.

The practice of presidential consultation with the cabinet collectively was to develop only slowly. At the outset, Washington solicited advice from his principal ministers individually, sometimes asking for reports on designated issues or occasionally inviting one or another to discuss matters over the breakfast table. By the end of 1791, the president had begun to convene meetings of heads of the executive departments (the attorney general included, largely because most high-level problems often involved legal issues). The group met with increasing frequency during the remainder of Washington's first term and frequently during his second.

Washington went to cabinet meetings with an agenda in mind, thus restricting discussion to issues of his choosing and discouraging the introduction of unrelated subjects. He did not actively participate in cabinet meetings, leaving debate to his ministers, whose opinions he occasionally requested in writing. Once he reached a decision, he expected his heads of departments to carry it out without dissent.

Although he no doubt would have liked unanimity, the president more often than not was obliged to choose from among sharply divided views of his principal ministers, notably those of Hamilton and Jefferson (who, the secretary of state later recalled, were "daily pitted . . . like two cocks"). Knox almost always slavishly sided with the treasury secretary, Jefferson usually disagreed with both, and Randolph steered an erratically independent course, which, although closer to that of his fellow Virginian than to Hamilton's and Knox's, prompted Jefferson to describe him as "indecisive" and a "chameleon."

Of greater historical consequence than cabinet dissension was its secure establishment as an advisory body to the president. This was not an inevitable development, for no such function was prescribed by the Constitution. But it was a predictable one for reasons that the first president had set forth at the end of the Philadelphia convention: "The impossibility that one man should . . . perform all the great business of state I take to have been the reason for instituting the great departments, and appointing officers therein to assist the supreme magistrate in discharging the duties of his trust." And such a view has remained the rationale for an extraconstitutional body that has been a major government institution from that day to this.

Many other developments of Washington's presidency established precedents that permanently shaped the structure of the federal government. As Washington himself put it, "Few who are not philosophical spectators can realize the difficult and delicate part which a man in my situation has to act. . . . I walk on untrodden ground. There is scarcely any part of my conduct which may not hereafter be drawn into precedent." This was because the Constitution provided only the skeleton of a government and because the new government had few established guidelines on which to rely.

Instead of viable precedents, the Confederation bequeathed merely a small number of unpaid clerks, a large debt, worthless paper money, and, in effect, a bankrupt and weak Union. Major problems, old and new, urgently required solutions. North Carolina and Rhode Island, for example, stubbornly remained outside the new Union; citizens of Vermont still schemed with Canada; Great Britain continued to refuse to relinquish its posts in the American West; and there was only a minuscule army and no navy at all. Virtually every effort of the administration to settle these difficulties constituted a precedent, as did its decisions and actions on most other issues, particularly those involving interpretation of the Constitution.

In the process of establishing precedents, Washington proved to be an uncommonly able executive. "In his daily administrative tasks," Leonard D. White, a distinguished authority on American public administration, commented, "he was systematic, orderly, energetic, solicitous of the opinion of others but decisive, intent upon general goals and the consistency of particular actions with them." Washington, in sum, demonstrated his mastery of administrative detail and reserved for himself the final say in major affairs of state.

This did not ordinarily include legislative affairs. Although Congress—despite the virtually unanimous belief in the separation of powers—was initially receptive to presidential direction, Washington was not inclined to offer forceful leadership personally. He did, of course, obey the constitutional injunction that the chief executive advise Congress on the state of the Union and "recommend to their consideration such Measures as he shall judge necessary and expedient." In performing this duty, Washington chose to appear in person at the opening of each session of Congress in order to review the record of the preceding year and to recommend subjects for congressional consideration. During the course of sessions he occasionally submitted special messages, chiefly informational, on important issues as they arose. At the outset elaborate protocol was observed, with Congress drawing up formal replies to the president's annual messages, although it did not always respond favorably to his recommendations.

During his first administration, Washington's department heads also played an active role in advising Congress on legislative policy. This was particularly true of the secretary of the treasury. Although the House was unwilling to allow Hamilton to appear before it in person, he nevertheless exercised instrumental legislative leadership. This included the submission of written reports and the use of influence over members of congressional committees.

But the trend toward executive leadership of Congress—especially as exercised by Hamilton—drastically changed during Washington's second administration. The alteration was not due to revised views of Washington or his ministers on presidential leadership but rather to Congress' less friendly response, which was, in turn, tied in with the gradual development of political parties, the Federalists and the Democratic-Republicans.

Despite Hamilton's attempt to exercise decisive influence, the First Congress initiated most of the legislation that it enacted. So it was with the stipulation of salaries for public officials; the adoption of titles, forms, and ceremonies consonant with what Senator William Maclay of Pennsylvania called "republican plainness"; the provision of a bill of rights; and the enactment of tariff legislation.

In one conspicuous instance, Congress also enhanced the powers of the presidency. In question was the right of the chief executive to remove unilaterally from office those public officials for whose appointment the Constitution mandated approval of the Senate. James Madison of Virginia, one of the ablest and most influential members of the House of Representatives, sought to deprive the Senate of any claim to veto executive dismissals, by moving that department heads could be removed by the president solely on his own authority. The House approved Madison's motion, but the Senate was less easily persuaded. The vote on the resolution was a tie that was broken by its presiding officer, Vice President John Adams, in favor of exclusive executive authority. An important source of presidential power was thus established, although the silence of the Constitution on the subject led to a century and a half of sporadic controversy concerning it.

Rather less precedent-setting was Washington's position on the chief executive's veto power. As he saw the issue, that power had been conferred to enable the president to preserve the Constitution by blocking legislation that in his view violated it, a function that subsequently would be assumed primarily by the Supreme Court. So far as executive power itself was concerned, Washington had no need to use the veto to safeguard it from inroads by Congress (as Hamilton, in *The Federalist*, had predicted he would), largely because Congress' confidence in Washington forestalled any such attempts. Further, it never would have occurred to Washington to veto legislation because he disagreed with it on political grounds, if only because he did not consider himself

a party leader. In short, during his eight years in office, Washington, adhering to his resolve that the separation of powers required him to pursue a hands-off policy toward Congress, vetoed only two comparatively minor pieces of legislation.

Although the relationship between the executive and legislative branches of government would in the future turn out to be more consequential, issues of presidential protocol seemed to Washington to be of similar, if not greater, importance. He established a social schedule comprising three types of affairs: his "levees" for men only, staged on Tuesday afternoons; his wife's tea parties (which he also attended), held on Friday evenings; and official dinners, held on Thursdays at four in the afternoon. The dinners and the levees were stiff and formal affairs, leading some disgruntled Republicans to complain that Washington's style of entertaining was more regal than George III's—the harbinger, more radical critics complained, of an American monarchy.

Washington's entertainment schedule was designed to harbor his time by sparing him the otherwise constant intrusion of callers; the stilted quality of presidential entertainment was due to his own reserve and formality. (That silence prevailed at official dinners, for example, was because the president, who was expected to initiate table talk, was no dazzling conversationalist.) The president's critics, as Marcus Cunliffe has remarked, were "unfair in not realizing that the presidency was more than the man who occupied it. It was a symbolic office, which the majority of Americans then and later expected to see maintained with a degree of decorum."

The ceremonial aspects of Washington's presidency were also demonstrated by tours of the country. Although they were simple and brief by comparison to similar trips by much later presidents, they were, like so many seemingly inconsequential acts of the first president, precedent-setting. Washington took two such tours, one through New England in the fall of 1789 and another of the southern states in April 1791. The trips not only set a precedent but taught Washington what many later presidents would discover: the deep satisfaction derived from personal contact with the generality of Americans, who in his case manifestly admired, respected, and even revered him. It should be emphasized that Washington, unlike many of his successors, did not seek partisan advantage or personal popularity from such tours.

Nevertheless, it was largely because of Washington's enormous popularity that he was instrumental in establishing an effective administration and reconciling most Americans to the new government and, concomitantly, national authority. It was Hamilton who gave what he himself described as "executive impulse" to Washington's presidency. In appointing Hamilton, Washington, on whose staff the young New Yorker had served during the Revolution, realized that he was tapping the best financial talent the country could offer.

The president's satisfaction was the greater because he properly perceived that the Treasury Department would be the nerve center of the new government. Fiscal ineptitude had been chiefly responsible for the series of events that had toppled the Confederation and led to the adoption of the Constitution. Among the most important provisions of that document was the pledge that "all debts contracted and engagements entered into before the adoption of the Constitution shall be as valid against the United States under this Constitution as under the Confederation." The most pressing problem of the new government was the fulfillment of this pledge, and it fell to Hamilton to propose the ways and means.

His recommendations created the most bitter controversy of Washington's presidency. Hamilton's proposals were submitted to Congress on 14 January 1790, in his *Report Relative to a Provision for the Support of Public Credit*, which was also his blueprint for a prosperous, strong, even preeminent, central government. The report began an acrimonious controversy that preoccupied Congress for the rest of its session. In this famous state paper Hamilton divided the public debt—comprising accrued interest in addition to principal—into three categories: first, the foreign debt, totaling around $11.7 million; second, the domestic debt, amounting to $40.4 million; third, the debts of the states, approximately $25 million. He called for a discharge of the foreign debt (plus interest) in full; payment of the face value of the principal of the domestic debt but with a reduction of stipulated interest rates; and assumption of state debts on the same terms as public securities but with interest payments to be postponed until 1 January 1792. To maintain the price of public securities and to manage any government surplus the treasury secretary proposed the establishment of a sinking fund.

Initially, the debate on Hamilton's report centered on the national domestic debt and was sparked by James Madison, who in mid-February 1790 offered

an amendment to Hamilton's recommendations. At issue was the question, To whom should payment be made, those to whom certificates had originally been issued or, as the treasury secretary proposed, the present owners, many of whom were speculators? Madison's plan was intended to do justice to the original holders of the debt and also satisfy the cupidity of assignees. Let those who bought up government securities be paid the highest value they had reached, he proposed. Let the difference between this amount and par value of the stock be paid to the original holders. In rebuttal, Hamilton's supporters argued that discrimination, as Madison's plan was termed, would mean an unacceptable increase in the already swollen national debt and that the task of distinguishing between original holders and assignees would involve the government in an administrative quagmire. Primarily for these reasons, discrimination was decisively defeated on 22 February.

Congress now centered its attention on a bill for the assumption of state debts by the federal government, an issue on which it was deadlocked until the eve of its adjournment, some six months later. Those states whose revolutionary debts remained for the most part unpaid championed the measure, those whose financial obligations had been largely discharged opposed it, and those with moderate and funded debts were uncommitted or unpredictable. Congress had also reached an impasse over the site of the nation's capital city, then New York City, an issue that at the time appeared to many legislators as important as Hamilton's fiscal measures. Boosters of the country's major cities (Baltimore and Philadelphia chief among them) eagerly sought the coveted prize, as did southerners, who insisted that it be located in a wilderness near the Potomac River. The situation was ripe for a compromise or compromises that would break the congressional logjam on this issue and on assumption. The votes of congressmen from Pennsylvania, widely believed to be the swing state, assured the success of a residence bill providing that Philadelphia should serve as the capital for a decade, at the end of which time the government would move to a permanent location near Georgetown, on the Potomac. Hamilton's timely concessions to make assumption more palatable to its opponents provided the votes necessary for passage of that measure.

As was his wont, Washington did not intercede on behalf of either bill or even publicly comment on them. Their passage was left to the administration's congressional allies and to Hamilton's behind-the-scenes legislative leadership. But the president favored both measures and, on 4 August 1790, unhesitatingly signed them into law, no doubt pleased that such divisive issues had been satisfactorily settled.

Had he known about it at the time, Washington would have been anything but happy over the gradually widening rift between his principal cabinet members, Hamilton and Jefferson. During the months immediately following Jefferson's arrival in New York in March 1790, the official association and personal relationship between the two men was on the surface harmonious. But viewed in retrospect, an eventual clash between two such egocentric, strong-willed, and ambitious men who were divided by political philosophy, divergent family backgrounds, social status, personality, and manner was inevitable.

Soon after the convening of the Second Congress in 1790, the two men's initial but superficial stance of personal forbearance and official cooperativeness was replaced by undisguised mutual suspicion. It surfaced during the controversy that was provoked by Hamilton's *Report on a National Bank*, the single most important issue debated by the Congress that assembled in Philadelphia on 6 December 1790, the first session to be held in the temporary capital. Hamilton called on Congress to charter a national bank capitalized at $10 million, one-fifth of the total to be provided by the government on its own account and the rest by individual investors. Although principally "under a *private* and not a *public* direction," the bank was based on the resources and credit of the United States, and a major purpose was to assist in the nation's financial operations. It was designed not only to aid but also to strengthen the new government, objects that were not lost on the treasury secretary's opponents, notably Madison and Jefferson. A majority of Congress, however, accepted Hamilton's argument: a bill chartering the Bank of the United States sailed smoothly through the Senate, and in mid-February the House gave its assent after only two weeks of debate. The measure was presented to the president on 14 February 1791.

Although brief, the debate in the House was heated enough and the opposition's arguments were plausible enough to make Washington uneasy about the measure's constitutionality. To dispel such misgivings, he solicited the advice of Attorney General Edmund Randolph, who pronounced the bank unconstitutional. Still undecided, Washington turned to his secretary of state. A constitutional fundamentalist and fiscal conservative, Jefferson set forth in his opinion on the bank a rigidly literal and strict construction of the Constitution that would have virtually strangled the national government in its infancy. Still undecided, the president sent copies of Randolph's and Jefferson's opinions to the secretary of the treasury, implicitly requesting him to refute them. Although he was confident of Hamilton's ability to do so, Washington could not have forecast the masterfulness of the essay in constitutional law that he received in reply.

While demolishing Jefferson's position point by point, the major thrust of Hamilton's argument was that his antagonist's constitutional literalness would destroy "the just and indispensable authority of the United States." Rejecting almost scornfully Jefferson's negative approach, the treasury secretary set forth a boldly affirmative view, one that emphasized the scope, rather than the limits, of government power. The president may or may not have fully perceived the drift of Hamilton's thought, but he was persuaded by the treasury secretary's argument that the proposed bank was a constitutional exercise of the government's enumerated powers to regulate trade, collect taxes, and provide for the common defense. On 25 February, Washington signed the bill chartering the Bank of the United States.

By siding with the secretary of the treasury on the establishment of a national bank, Washington unintentionally brought out into the open and intensified the rivalry between the prima donnas of his official family, Hamilton and Jefferson. But as many historians have long insisted, this contest was largely the personal expression of a deep-seated and intense sectional conflict between slaveholders and other agrarians of the South versus mercantile and related commercially oriented interests of the North.

Since Washington sided with Hamilton on the bank as well as on other economic issues, he has often been depicted as the unwitting supporter of northern business. The first president actually represented neither one section nor the other, nor any particular class. Rather, as James Thomas Flexner perceptively commented, he "visualized a mixed economy in which agrarianism and business activity would move together." He supported Hamilton's program because he believed that it would benefit all sections by promoting national prosperity and a more closely knit union. The restoration and firm establishment of public credit, moreover, was a means to the same goal. Far from being disturbed by the speculation engendered by the sale of government bonds and bank stock (which horrified Jefferson), Washington congratulated himself and his countrymen that "our public credit stands on that ground" which at the time of the launching of the new government "would have been considered as a species of madness to have foretold."

Although the president thus approved of most of Hamilton's policies, he by no means automatically endorsed them all. Believing that the United States would remain for generations to come an agricultural nation, he did not, for example, share his treasury secretary's vision of a powerful, industrialized nation, as attested by his refusal to back Hamilton's most ambitious (and in the event prescient) report—his plea for the encouragement of manufactures. In sum, the stereotyped view of Washington as merely a figurehead whose administration was actually run by Hamilton (a view first and most forcefully set forth by Jefferson) is inaccurate. Washington not only made the major decisions of his administration (usually, as has been said, after soliciting and pondering the opinions of his advisers), but he also skillfully and patiently tried to establish some semblance of harmony between his prickly principal secretaries.

No diplomat, however adroit, could have accomplished that assignment. By the summer of 1792 the conflict between the two secretaries had ripened into open warfare. Late in July 1792 the treasury secretary began an anonymous (although his authorship was no secret) newspaper crusade designed to discredit his rival and to drive him from office. As article after article appeared, Hamilton's attack on the secretary of state became increasingly shrill. Jefferson was an "intriguing inceniary" whose tenets tended to promote "*national disunion, national insignificance, public disorder and discredit,*" the perpetrator of "the most wanton and flagitious acts that ever stained the annals of a civilized nation." Jefferson publicly ignored such vicious assaults, confining himself to the excoriation of his rival in his personal and official correspondence. To Washington, for example, he charged that Hamilton's program "flowed from principles adverse to liberty, and was calculated to undermine and demolish the republic." For his part, Jefferson was determined that his own retirement, on which he soon planned, not "be clouded by the slanders of a man whose history, from the moment history can stoop to notice him, is a tissue of machinations against the liberty of the country which has not only received and given him bread, but heaped honors on his head."

Washington was greatly disturbed by the deadly warfare conducted by advisers he personally liked and officially trusted. Persuading himself that the differences between the two were not irreconcilable, he decided to write essentially the same letter to both, pleading with them to subordinate personal antagonism to the national interest. Since neither secretary shared the president's equitable temperament and willingness to subordinate private pique to disinterested public service, the attempt was predictably futile. Both Hamilton and Jefferson politely acknowledged the soundness of Washington's advice and then proceeded to ignore it. Jefferson was especially testy, insisting that rather than continue to battle with an antagonist he scorned, he would soon resign as secretary of state, which he in fact did a year and a half later.

Washington was upset by the recalcitrance of his chief ministers not only because of personal concerns but because of practical and political considerations: The feud between Hamilton and Jefferson could prove irreconcilable and consequently increase party strife. Furthermore, the rift in his official family might oblige him to reconsider his firm decision to retire at the end of his first term. Additionally, disunity within his official family might adversely affect the conduct of foreign affairs, always to Washington an object of overarching concern.

During his first term in office, Washington's principal diplomatic difficulties concerned the Indian tribes, Great Britain, and Spain. The most immediate menace to national security came from Native Americans, who roamed and largely controlled the western frontier. Had they been able to effectively deploy their manpower and exploit their skill in guerrilla warfare, they would have presented an even graver danger, one that the sparsely manned American military forces could not have readily parried. But individual Indian tribes often appeared more intent on fighting each other than the white man, on whom they also were hazardously dependent for guns and gunpowder. For their protection and security they acquired them by playing the three contending North American empires against each other. Of these, Native Americans most trusted Spanish Louisiana and British Canada and most distrusted the United States. The former two not only supplied them with munitions but were also less interested in seizing territory than in pursuing the mutually profitable fur trade; fellow Americans in the United States were less interested in trading with the natives than in acquiring their lands, often by treaties fraudulently obtained.

Although the Spanish attempted to block U.S. expansion in the Southwest by negotiating profitable trade alliances with Indian tribes that served as a buffer against attempts of the United States to seize Louisiana and to open the Mississippi River to its commerce, the British posed the greater threat to the new nation's sovereignty. The northwestern frontier was the scene of seemingly endless warfare between Native Americans (aided and abetted by their British allies) and American frontiersmen (intent on retaliation against murderous assaults on U.S. settlements in the West). The crux of the problem, as the United States saw the matter, was that redcoats of His Majesty's Canadian regiments still occupied seven forts in the Old Northwest, posts that England had by the terms of the 1783 peace treaty ceded to the United States. England justified its refusal to abide by this provision of the treaty by pointing to stipulations that the United States had failed to honor: the repayment of revolutionary debts due to British merchants and the return of Tory property. Britain's true reason for holding on to the forts was to safeguard the route along which Indian furs were shipped to Canada.

Washington did not immediately perceive the nature and extent of British machinations in the West. When he belatedly did so, he swiftly asked Congress to enlarge the small regular army by one regiment. That done, he decided in 1791 to restore peace to the area by sending a punitive expedition against the warring tribes. Commanded by General Arthur St. Clair, the army advanced from Fort Washington into present-day Indiana. On 4 November, St. Clair's forces were, despite Washington's warnings about such an eventuality, ambushed and humiliatingly defeated by a confederated Indian army. Although he was charitably exonerated by Washington as well as by a committee of the House of Representatives, St. Clair resigned his commission. The United States Army, reorganized and enlarged, was now placed under the command of General Anthony Wayne, a leading Revolutionary War commander. During 1792 and 1793, Wayne postponed an active campaign while he patiently instructed his troops in the tactics of forest warfare.

In the meantime, Washington took the initiative in another type of training program by seeking to convince Congress and the state governments that the solution to the problem of Indian-American relations was not war but a change in attitude and the resultant adoption of policies that would assure justice to Native Americans. The murder of a Native American, for example, should be judged as the murder of a white person, measures should be taken to protect natives' property, and "such radical experiments . . . as may from time to time suit their condition" should be launched in order that Indians might gradually be integrated into U.S. culture. The period was not auspicious for the acceptance of such ideas, particularly in view of the persistence of Native Americans in conducting savage raids against U.S. settlers on the frontier.

For Washington, a more immediate and personal problem was the approaching presidential election of 1792. Early in his first administration he had made the decision to retire at the end of a single term, and wishing above all else "to return to the walks of private life," he balked at reversing it, the more so since for the moment the foreign scene appeared serene and domestic developments, particularly the success of Hamilton's economic program, gratifying. But would the rift in his official family oblige him to reconsider his earlier decision to retire? Pressure to do so crowded in from every quarter, from north and south, from private citizens and official colleagues. Among the latter, none were more importunate than the principal rivals of his cabinet, who suspended their acrimonious disagreement on everything else political to urge the president to stand for reelection.

Neither Hamilton's nor Jefferson's pleas, nor those of many other prominent Americans, had any effect on the president's unwillingness to announce his candidacy for reelection. Nevertheless, over the months following his return to Philadelphia from Mount Vernon in October 1792, Washington continued to remain mute. Predictably no rival candidate presented himself, and there was not even a whisper that one would. Aware that he was in a field of one, Washington certainly knew that the electorate would take his silence for assent, and it did. On 13 February 1793 the electoral college unanimously elected him to a second term. His running mate, John Adams, was also returned to office, although by a vote of only seventy-seven to fifty. To Washington, now past sixty and in poor health, what others saw as an electoral triumph was rather another four-year sentence to what he described to Jefferson as "the extreme wretchedness of his existence."

Second Term

Washington's second inauguration, 4 March 1793, was a simple affair, particularly in contrast with his first. Acting on the advice of his cabinet, whose opinion on the ceremony attending his swearing-in he had asked for, Washington rode alone in his coach to the Senate chamber, where he took the oath of office and delivered his second inaugural address. Its brevity (it consisted of only two short paragraphs) and its stern and self-righteous tone perhaps reflected his chagrin at being obliged to remain in office for another four years. Washington then took the presidential oath and without fanfare promptly returned to the executive mansion. His misgivings and forebodings about his second term were not misplaced. Within a few weeks of his inauguration it seemed that the United States was inexorably being drawn into the conflict sparked in Europe by the French Revolution.

Some three months earlier, disturbing news of developments in France during the summer of 1792 had reached the State Department—the defeat of French armies that had led to mass Jacobin demonstrations in Paris, including the storming of the Tuileries; the imprisonment of the king; and the suspension of the constitution and establishment of a revolutionary government, all followed by the revival of French military successes. Then during the weeks following the onset of Washington's second term came yet more ominous news—Louis XVI had been guillotined, the Girondin party had gained power, France had declared war on Great Britain and Spain, a great European coalition was being formed to resist the Revolution, and a new minister plenipotentiary of the French republic was being sent to the United States.

A great many, perhaps most, Americans enthusiastically acclaimed the transformation of their monarchical revolutionary war ally into a sister republic. The French Revolution, in other words, seemed a replay of the American revolutionary scenario: a battle against royal absolutism and aristocratic privilege was another chapter in the story of man's struggle for justice, freedom, and equality. Such ardent pro-French sentiment was not dampened by the violence that raged in Paris nor even by the monotonous regularity with which aristocratic heads fell into the executioner's basket. Jefferson spoke for the more extreme defenders of the French Revolution when he commented that it was only to be expected that the tree of liberty must sometimes be watered by

President Washington is depicted with his cabinet in this Currier and Ives lithograph. THE LIBRARY OF CONGRESS/CORBIS

human blood and expressed his willingness to see "half the earth desolated" if that were necessary for the triumph of human freedom.

Washington emphatically disagreed. Studiedly impartial, he deplored the pro-French sentiment that prevailed among so many of his countrymen. His ardent wish, as he had written in 1790, was for America to be "unentangled in the crooked politics of Europe." Neither was he enthusiastic about the Reign of Terror and the concomitant bloodbath. He rather believed that "cool reason" alone could "establish a permanent and equal government" and deplored the fact that such dispassion "is as little to be expected in the tumults of popular commotion as an attention to the liberties of the people is to be expected in the dark divan of a despotic tyrant." The grave threat that the war in Europe posed to American sovereignty must, he believed, be safeguarded by a policy of neutrality.

But in view of the Franco-American Revolutionary War treaties, how could such a policy be pursued? By the terms of those treaties the United States had promised to come to the aid of France if that nation became involved in a war; its prizes (but not those of its enemies) might be brought into United States ports, and its West Indian possessions were guaranteed. Was not the sacrifice of national honor the price of reneging on commitments made to America's ally? Was not England's enmity, or even war with that nation, the inevitable consequence of meeting treaty obligations to France? Washington sought to avoid the risk of armed confrontation with England and the danger of diplomatic retaliation by France by eschewing a formal suspension of the French alliance while informally disregarding its stipulations. This was the implicit intent of his famous Proclamation of Neutrality, issued in April 1793, in which he announced his determination to pursue "a conduct friendly and impartial toward the belligerent Powers" and enjoined his countrymen against aiding either combatant.

The turmoil and attendant changes in France posed for the president another and, from the standpoint of precedent, more important problem: Should the United States recognize the republic that had replaced the monarchy, with which, in theory anyway, the Franco-American treaties of alliance and commerce concluded in 1778 had been negotiated or did the overthrow of the monarchy annul those treaties? Whichever way Washington decided, important groups or interests would be alienated. If recognition were accorded the new regime, the Federalists at home and the aristocratic powers in Europe would be resentful; if recognition were denied, the Jeffersonians at home and the revolutionaries in France would be outraged. After careful deliberation, Washington directed his secretary of state to recognize the revolutionary government, arguing that "we surely cannot deny to any nation the right whereon our own government is founded, that every nation may govern itself according to whatever form it pleases." Thus was established a vitally important precedent for the chief executive's right to extend—or, by implication, to refuse—recognition to a foreign government.

Washington's insistence on American aloofness from the wars of the French Revolution was perhaps his greatest accomplishment as president. Pushed in one direction by the partisans of France, shoved in another by the supporters of Great Britain, Washington believed that during the critical years of its youth as a nation the United States must remain free to grow in its own way, to continue to prosper, to consolidate, and thus to perpetuate national union. He thus steadfastly held to the belief that the diplomatic desideratum of his day was for Americans to forswear partiality for one power or the other and to pursue an unswervingly neutral policy. To do otherwise would be to court the single gravest danger confronting the new nation: foreign entanglements that might lead to United States participation in foreign wars and ultimately to the loss of its independence.

The point needs to be underscored. J. A. Carroll has said that in no other "instance during his tenure as chief executive did Washington demonstrate his role in government so abundantly, or his greatness in statecraft so dramatically. In the year 1793 he forged the neutral rule in its fundamental form, and through the next four years his every policy was built on it."

A severe test not only of American neutrality but also of presidential patience was provided by the reception of the new French minister, Citizen Edmond Genet. Aware that Genet would insist that America honor its treaty obligations and do whatever else it could to aid an embattled sister republic, the Washington administration was squarely confronted with the difficulty of maintaining the nation's neutrality in the face of its diplomatic vulnerability. Genet, "brash, egotistic, extravagant in his ambition," was certain that he could make the United States into "an outpost of French revolutionary sentiment and also of recrudescent French imperialism." A great number of Americans, blithely unaware of the Frenchman's unneutral expectations, warmly welcomed Genet as the symbol of a steadfast ally and beleaguered sister republic. Enthusiastically greeted on his leisurely tour from Charleston, South Carolina, to the nation's capital, Genet arrived in Philadelphia on 16 May 1793, hailed by a salvo of cannon and the ringing of bells.

The president's treatment of the French emissary was in sharp contrast: Washington's icy manner would have frozen the enthusiasm of all but the most insensitive of diplomats. Genet was singularly obtuse. Disregarding the president's cautionary signal, the advice of sympathetic Republicans, and the laws of the United States, Genet stuck to the belief that the Americans need only hear his clarion call to rally around the standard of the French Revolution. Thus self-deceived, he pursued policies suggesting that the United States was France's satrapy rather than the nation's sovereign ally. He organized expeditions against Florida and Louisiana, outfitted and armed privateers, directed that their prizes be returned to American ports, and sought to popularize the notion that the survival of American republicanism hinged on the success of French arms.

Washington was indignant and angry at Genet's flagrant abuse of his ministerial post, behavior of which the secretary of state was astonishingly indulgent. Having convinced himself that the emissary of America's close republican ally could do no wrong, Jefferson insisted on giving Genet the benefit of every doubt. But the doubts soon became irrepressible, and by early August the secretary of state was ready to join his cabinet colleagues in approving the president's decision to request Genet's recall. Until the French had time to respond, Washington was obliged to put up with Genet, whose brashness was as unbridled as before.

To make sure that the president was kept informed of exactly how reckless the Frenchman was, two prominent Federalists, Senator Rufus King of New York and Chief Justice John Jay, published in a New York newspaper the following succinct accusation: "Mr. Genet, the French Minister, had said he would appeal to the people from certain decisions of the President." Far from denying the charge, Genet addressed a public letter to Washington saying that he had done just that and was prepared to do so again. Although pleased by the overwhelmingly favorable public support accorded him, Washington remained ostensibly impartial: he extended no thanks to King and Jay, much to their chagrin, and, at the request of Genet, ordered an inquiry to determine whether the French minister had been libeled. For six more months Washington continued to endure patiently Genet's uncurbed efforts to undermine the American government. Finally, early in 1794, a new French minister, Jean Antoine Joseph Baron Fauchet, arrived with orders to arrest his predecessor and send him back to France. Washington charitably granted asylum to Genet, who thus kept his head while giving his heart to one of Governor George Clinton's daughters, with whom he settled in rural New York.

In the meantime, Genet's onetime patron had retired to rural Virginia. Jefferson, fed up with political abuse and squabbles, had submitted his resignation on 31 July 1793 (to become effective at the end of December) and left for Monticello a month later. Since he did not return to the capital until November, this September departure marked all but the end of his tenure as secretary of state. He was replaced by Attorney General Edmund Randolph.

For Washington, Jefferson's departure would prove a major liability. Not only was the latter now free to head the political opposition to Washington's administration, but the president was also deprived of a counselor whose opinions had often been the necessary counterweight to those of the secretary of the treasury. As Flexner concluded, "The very essence of Washington's decisionmaking process was set awry. Since he endeavored, before he reached a conclusion, to balance all points of view, he found it immensely valuable to have laid before him the arguments of the ablest members of both principal factions. Now, when Hamilton spoke, there was no equally strong voice to answer."

This was tellingly demonstrated by the course of Anglo-American relations during the final years of Washington's presidency. The administration scarcely had time to breathe a collective sigh of relief over the soothing of relations with France that followed the forced retirement of Genet when it was confronted with distressing evidence of a revival of England's hostility. For one thing, the British government was manifestly determined to cut off the flourishing American trade with the French Caribbean ports that followed France's decision in February 1793 to throw open its previously guarded West Indian trade to the United States. Britain's determination took the form of a number of orders-in-council that cavalierly ignored neutral—and this meant particularly American—rights. By January 1794 the British were making wholesale captures of vessels flying the flag of the United States while systematically ignoring the government's protests.

Such high-handed assaults on American commerce channeled congressional energy during the winter and early spring of 1794 into a "flood of legislation aimed at war," despite the repeal in January of the most objectionable of the orders-in-council and the diminution of the indiscriminate condemnation of American vessels by British admiralty courts in the West Indies. Such minor concessions were counterbalanced by other grievances of longer standing— exclusion of American ships from British West Indian ports, retention of American fur-trading posts in the Northwest, refusal to settle the Maine boundary, unwillingness to grant compensation for slaves carried off by the British army in 1783, and the search of American ships for British deserters and their impressment on flimsy evidence. To most congressmen, Federalists and Republicans alike, the time had come for yet another successful chastisement of imperial presumption. Accordingly, on 28 March 1794 a one-month embargo (later extended) on all foreign shipping was imposed, followed by an unsuccessful effort to sequester debts due from American to British subjects. These punitive measures were accompanied by a Federalist-sponsored program of national preparedness calling for harbor fortifications, an increase in the army, and the building of warships.

Although Washington shared the view that the injuries inflicted on the United States by Great Britain must be redressed, he believed that the proper policy was neither military strutting nor retaliatory measures but diplomacy. Successful negotiations, he was convinced, were the only sensible alternative to a ruinous war. To whom should they be entrusted? Could Washington have had his wish, the American negotiator would have been his most trusted adviser. But Hamilton's presumed Anglophilia (allegedly extending even to monarchism), his controversial position in American politics, and the resultant storm that his designation would raise precluded the New Yorker's nomination. After canvassing the other qualified envoys—John Adams, Chief Justice John Jay, and Jefferson among them—Washington bowed to Hamilton's insistence that "Mr. Jay is the only man in whose qualifications for success there would be thorough confidence."

Although Jay's instructions were drawn up by Secretary of State Edmund Randolph, they incorporated some of Hamilton's suggestions (especially his insistence that those instructions be largely discretionary rather than narrowly prescriptive) but faithfully reflected the president's ideas. The American envoy was directed to persuade England to perform the unexecuted parts of the Anglo-American peace treaty of 1783, to secure indemnification for the capture and condemnation of American vessels, and to win acceptance of an Anglo-American commercial treaty. Jay was firmly instructed to sign no treaty that conflicted with American engagements to France or failed to give American ships entry to ports of the British West Indies. The outcome of the diplomatic mission by which Washington had successfully countered congressional bellicosity was now up to Jay and, more instrumentally, to Lord Grenville, the British foreign secretary. On 12 May 1794, Jay left for London, where month after month he sought concessions that Grenville only stingily allowed.

While Jay was seeking to wrest from England respect for America's sovereign status and recognition of its rights as a neutral, the Washington administration was attempting to assure the supremacy of federal law against delinquent taxpayers. At issue was the excise on whiskey, authorized by a law of March 1791, which encountered strong opposition among distillers, especially in the westernmost counties of Pennsylvania. There in 1792 violence erupted, to which Washington reacted by issuing on 15 September a proclamation admonishing all citizens "to refrain and desist" from obstructing the enforcement of federal laws. For over a year and a half the Wash-

ington administration pursued a policy of pacification that seemed to allay active resistance to the excise, but beginning in the spring of 1794, news reached Philadelphia of discontent and occasional violence. By midsummer, these had been replaced by a systematic and popularly supported campaign to shut down operation of the federal revenue system in the disaffected area—or so it appeared to the president and his Treasury Department advisers. At a cabinet meeting on 2 August also attended by Pennsylvania's Governor Thomas Mifflin, Washington elicited advice on how to handle a seemingly imminent insurrection.

The cabinet discussion was inconclusive, and Washington requested the conferees to submit written opinions. Hamilton called for the use of troops to quell what he unhesitatingly termed treason, a position endorsed by the attorney general and the secretary of war. Secretary of State Edmund Randolph and Mifflin dissented. The decision was up to the president. Aware that even as the cabinet deliberated, some five thousand dissidents, many of them armed, were assembling at Braddock's Field near Pittsburgh, Washington promptly made up his mind: the citizens of the western counties were not only flagrantly defying federal law that must be upheld but also contemplating an insurrection that must be countered by force. Before ordering the army to march west, Washington issued a proclamation commanding the insurgents to disperse and exhorting all inhabitants of the area to "prevent and suppress dangerous proceedings." He then awaited the report of commissioners that had been appointed to negotiate with the insurgents.

By 9 September the president, despairing of an amicable settlement and worried that the season during which military operations were feasible was rapidly passing, approved orders for a general rendezvous of troops at Carlisle. Conscious of the prestige his presence would lend the punitive expedition, he decided personally to assume command of the expected fifteen thousand militiamen from Pennsylvania and the neighboring states of Maryland, New Jersey, and Virginia. Hamilton insisted on going along, rationalizing that since measures of his own department were the ostensible cause of the insurrection, it could not "but have good effect" for him to share in the "danger to his fellow citizens." On 30 September 1794 the president, with characteristic terseness, recorded in his diary, "I left the City of Philadelphia about half past ten o'clock this forenoon accompanied by Colo. Hamilton."

Some hours after they left the capital city, they were overtaken by a messenger bearing an official packet for the president. It contained highly gratifying news from General Anthony Wayne, describing a series of stunning victories over the Indians in the Northwest. These had culminated on 20 August in Wayne's resounding triumph in the Battle of Fallen Timbers, a victory that opened up the Ohio country and diminished, although it did not destroy, Anglo-Canadian influence over Native Americans in that region. Encouraged that the far western frontier was for the time being strife-free, Washington could more resolutely turn his attention to armed resistance by westerners on the nearer frontier.

On 4 October the presidential coach arrived in Carlisle, where the troops were beginning to assemble, and from there Washington journeyed westward to Fort Cumberland and then to Bedford, where all the militia would soon rendezvous. Having bestowed on the expedition the prestige of his personal presence, Washington returned to Philadelphia to deal with other pressing business. As his replacement as commander of the federal troops, he designated Governor Henry Lee of Virginia, whose instructions were prepared by Hamilton, who remained with the army to assist in the successful completion of the mission. Hamilton was no doubt delighted, but the advantages of his remaining were lost on virtually everyone except himself and the president. The treasury secretary's presence provided ammunition for Republican critics, who charged that the entire military mission had been arranged by him for personal political advantage. To Washington, whose confidence in Hamilton was by this time unalloyed, such a charge was nonsense; the president, rather, believed that the opposition to the western Pennsylvania expedition was fomented by his partisan opponents.

Whether the latter belief was true or not, Washington's conviction that the expedition would serve actually and symbolically as a reminder of national supremacy was well placed; the militia encountered no armed opposition and even the extremists of the antitax movement were dissuaded from further active resistance to the excise. The dispatch of troops to enforce obedience to federal law was, moreover, a precedent of indeterminable, but certainly consequential, historical importance, as the history of southern school integration in the mid-twentieth century, among other later developments, would attest.

Washington returned to Philadelphia in late October in expectation of delivering his sixth annual message to Congress, which was scheduled to assemble on 3 November. A quorum could not be counted until 18 November, and the president addressed Congress on the following day. Most of his twenty-five-minute address was given over to the background, immediate causes, and suppression of the so-called Whiskey Rebellion (more accurately, "Insurrection"). His comments on the then-mushrooming "democratic societies" or "Jacobin clubs," promoted for partisan ends by some prominent Republicans of the day, were far and away the most controversial part of his message. Washington spoke derogatorily of "certain self-created societies" and asked the people to determine whether the Whiskey Rebellion "had not been fomented by combinations of men who, careless of consequences and disregarding the unerring truth that those who rouse cannot always appease civil convulsions, have disseminated, from ignorance or perversion of facts, suspicions, jealousies, and accusations of the whole government?"

Although in the context of succeeding presidential speeches Washington's remarks were innocuous enough, they created at that time strong reverberations throughout the country. It was the first time the nation's revered hero had spoken disparagingly in public of the political opposition. The effect was immediate: the democratic societies virtually disappeared, and those Republicans who had encouraged the societies were reduced to grumbling in private because they dared not confront the president openly. For his part, Washington presumably regretted having even implicitly chided his opponents—much less, as was privately thought by some critics at the time, having attempted to abridge freedom of speech and assembly. He never again publicly criticized his political opponents or even thus referred to them.

Ignoring the opposition was probably easier than having to do without two of his most trusted advisers. On the last day of 1794, Henry Knox stepped down as secretary of war to try to salvage what he could from his imprudent land speculations. At the end of January 1795, Hamilton resigned as secretary of the treasury largely because he was no longer willing to oblige his family to live on his meager official income but also because he was weary of the calumnies heaped upon him and his policies. It was not easy to find officials of similar ability. But Oliver Wolcott, Jr., Hamilton's successor, had extensive experience as the second-ranking Treasury Department official and proved to be a competent finance minister. Timothy Pickering, Knox's replacement, was a professional civil servant with useful experience and proven resourcefulness in negotiations with Indian tribes, then the principal task of the War Department.

Washington's principal problem in 1795 was the treaty that John Jay negotiated with Great Britain. Unhappily aware that he had been forced to bargain from a position of weakness, Jay believed that he had secured all that was then possible. Britain had promised to give up the northwestern posts by June 1796, to pay for the spoliations on American commerce, and to sign a commercial treaty granting the United States certain limited trading privileges with India and with the British West Indies. In return, Jay had renounced maritime principles that the United States had hitherto considered inviolable—the familiar insistence of neutral nations on freedom of the seas—and had instead accepted Great Britain's interpretation of international law. Although many of their respective countrymen did not see the matter that way, Jay and Lord Grenville, the British foreign secretary, had in fact worked out a quid pro quo based on a realistic assessment of the prevailing power situation. They were convinced, moreover, that the treaty was as important for the machinery it established for settling further disputes as for what it formally stipulated.

To a good many Americans the true measure of Jay's Treaty was not its provisions but its omissions and shortcomings. The oversights that aroused the greatest furor were the absence of any offer of compensation for slaves freed by the British in 1783 and silence on the issue of impressment of bona fide American sailors by the English navy. The shortcomings most often lamented were Britain's refusal to grant the United States an unrestricted, rather than a partial, privilege of trading with the British West Indies and the stipulation that American ships would not carry molasses, sugar, coffee, cocoa, and cotton to any other part of the world.

Soon after the treaty was delivered to the secretary of state in early March 1795, President Washington called for an emergency meeting of the Senate on 8 June, stipulating also that the provisions of the treaty should until then be kept secret. Over the next few months, Washington closely studied the document negotiated by Jay, particularly its commercial sections, of which he conceded that he needed a more "intimate" knowledge. Whether he acquired it,

he kept to himself: when the Senate convened, he submitted the treaty without any opinion of his own.

On 24 June, after two weeks of debate conducted in secret session, the Senate, by a vote of twenty to ten (precisely the constitutionally necessary two-thirds majority), advised him to ratify Jay's handiwork, on the condition that the clause restricting American trade with the British West Indies (article 12) be suspended, pending "further friendly negotiations." For Washington, such a condition posed a perplexing problem: Should he ratify promptly in confident expectation of excision or revision of that article, or should ratification await such changes? His decision was rendered more difficult by receipt of news that the British were again seizing American vessels bound for France. Despite his angry reaction to that report and his dissatisfaction at the high price exacted by England for agreeing to a limited rapprochement, Washington signed the treaty on 18 August 1795, in the face of fierce partisan opposition to it and his awareness that his still-glowing popularity might be greatly dimmed.

The decision was in fact one of disinterested statecraft and was based on his clear perception of the new nation's diplomatic situation. The proper goal of its foreign policy, Washington believed, was avoidance of a war that America was unprepared to fight. Its primary need was not so much a particularly favorable treaty or even an advantageous foreign alliance but time—a long period of peace to develop America's resources, to diversify and expand its growing economy, to create a great common market, to cement a still shaky union, and in these ways to establish a powerful nation capable of challenging the war machines and naval strength of Europe's foremost powers.

Washington's political opponents did not agree, and the protracted fight over Jay's Treaty was an important milestone in American political history. The conclusion reached in the 1950s by Joseph Charles is still generally accepted: "In its political effects [the treaty was] the most important measure . . . between the institution of Hamilton's financial program and the election of 1800." Not only did the controversy over Jay's Treaty signify the maturity of the country's first political parties, but it also occasioned fundamental shifts in partisan loyalties. An influential number of prominent public figures who had steadfastly supported the Washington administration now openly embraced the Republican opposition. This was tellingly displayed in the spring of

1796, when Republican leaders in the House of Representatives decided to abort implementation of the treaty.

Their initial maneuver was adoption of a motion introduced by Edward Livingston of New York on 2 March 1796, requesting the president to submit to the House copies of Jay's instructions and related correspondence. Washington, convinced that such a request was unconstitutional, sought confirmation of his belief by consulting the highest-ranking government officials and the nation's foremost Federalist leader, Hamilton, who advised his former boss "to resist in totality" the congressional request. And so the president, courteously but emphatically, did. Washington's terse message to the House concluded, "A just regard to the Constitution and to the duty of my Office . . . forbids a compliance with your request."

Aware of Washington's heroic standing among his countrymen, Republican leaders in Congress did not openly challenge the president's contention, but they obliquely retaliated by attempting to persuade their colleagues to withhold the necessary appropriation for carrying out key provisions of the treaty. During several weeks of intense debate it appeared that they might succeed. Federalist leaders, in and out of Congress, energetically sought some means of salvaging the treaty. Popular clamor and a deluge of protreaty petitions provided the way. A number of defections destroyed the hitherto united Republicans, and on 29 April the Speaker of the House broke a tie vote to approve an appropriation for carrying the treaty into effect. The episode was manifestly important for the enduring precedents that it established, particularly the exercise of executive privilege. As Washington saw the matter, the decision was a triumph for viable nationhood.

The president could also congratulate himself that the concessions made to Great Britain in Jay's Treaty were compensated for by the conciliatory spirit displayed by Spain in the Treaty of San Lorenzo, negotiated by American envoy Thomas Pinckney in 1795. An impressive American diplomatic victory, that treaty gained for the United States acceptance at long last of its demand for free navigation of the Mississippi and the right of deposit at New Orleans free of duty for oceangoing American goods. Spain also recognized the Mississippi as the new nation's western boundary and the thirty-first parallel as the northern boundary of Florida. As Washington hoped it would, the treaty helped to cement the loyalty of westerners to the Union and opened the way to steady American expansion in the South and West.

Support of Pinckney's successful negotiations was bipartisan, but Jay's Treaty remained a controversial partisan issue (although the furor it initially aroused abated), subtly affecting Washington's last two years in office. Following his endorsement of the latter treaty in August 1795, Washington was for the first time during his presidency subjected to personal abuse, not only on that but also on other issues. Typical were anonymous contributors to the Philadelphia Aurora, then the most fiercely partisan and scurrilous of Republican newspapers. One such writer dubbed the president "Saint Washington," a political leader distinguished merely by "the seclusion of a monk and the supercillious [sic] distance of a tyrant," and another chided him with the offer of a crown.

Washington was most disturbed by the anonymous accusation that he was overdrawing his annual presidential allowance of $25,000. It would have been altogether out of character for Washington to have publicly replied to such attacks, but he did express his reaction in private correspondence, complaining that he was being compared to a Nero or even to a common pickpocket. After forty-five years of public service, he commented, he was weary of being "buffeted in the public prints by a set of infamous scribblers," and he now yearned for retirement.

Partisan abuse did not prompt Washington to endorse the acceptability of political parties in the American constitutional system, much less to profess his allegiance to any party. On the contrary, he continued to caution his countrymen against "the baneful effects of the spirit of party," which, to use the words of his farewell address, "serves always to distract the public councils and enfeeble the public administration."

Although Washington never thought of his administration as representing a party or of himself as a party leader, the facts were somewhat at variance. During his final years as president he appointed to office only those whose political ideas were in accord with his own. As he wrote a member of his cabinet, "I shall not, whilst I have the honour to administer the government, bring a man into any office of consequence knowingly, whose political tenets are adverse to the measures, which the general government is pursuing; for this, in my opinion, would be a sort of political suicide." So it was that

Washington not only initiated a practice that would be permanent but also indirectly set an unintended precedent for which there was no constitutional warrant: the president's role as party leader.

Although Washington denied that he was a party leader, he repeatedly affirmed presidential leadership in foreign affairs. During the final years of his administration, as throughout his presidency, diplomatic problems plagued him. The nation had weathered the tempest of Anglo-American relations of the years 1794–1796 only to find itself locked in conflict with France. Claiming that by Jay's Treaty the United States had allied itself with Great Britain and reneged on its treaty obligations to its Revolutionary War ally, the French began in 1796 a systematic policy of maritime harassment and diplomatic coercion designed to bring the allegedly ungrateful and unruly new nation into line. In July 1796, Washington, to appease domestic critics while also leaving the door open to friendly negotiations, designated Charles Cotesworth Pinckney of South Carolina as American minister to France, replacing James Monroe, whose ardent Francophilia had brought no moderation of French policy but had antagonized Federalist leaders. The futility of Pinckney's ministership would be demonstrated under the nation's second president.

Happily aware that his successor would soon be chosen, Washington turned his attention to the form and timing of the announcement of his retirement. His first inclination was to use a modified version of a valedictory message that James Madison, at the president's request, had drawn up in September 1792. Tailoring his work to fit the heroic mold of the foremost American of his day, Madison had avoided controversial issues and focused instead on commonly cherished national sentiments, such as the perfection of the Constitution and the necessity of preserving the Union. Upon rereading Madison's draft some four years later, Washington concluded that it only needed to be updated in order to take into account the "considerable changes" that had subsequently taken place, particularly in foreign affairs.

The president himself undertook the assignment, penning a terse supplement (actually a list of what he called "wishes"), which he merely tacked onto Madison's draft. The most perceptive student of the farewell address, Felix Gilbert, has described Washington's appendix as a "collection of diverse thoughts and ideas" that were "neither closely integrated nor systematically organized." Nevertheless, the views that he expressed faithfully reflected his current preoccupations and long-standing fundamental principles. Washington pointed to the personal indignities he had endured as chief magistrate, the lamentable party divisions and other domestic difficulties he had encountered, and the centrality of foreign policy problems that he had wrestled with during his second administration.

Apropos of the last subject, Washington indicated the dangers to be confronted, the pitfalls to be avoided, and the proper policies to be followed. Among the dangers Washington warned against was foreign influence in American domestic affairs. The pitfalls he pointed to included avoidance of both political connections with other nations and the falseness of the notion that in international relations nations are guided by altruistic motives. The most important policies to be followed were fidelity to treaty commitments, pride in America's distinctive nationality, adherence to a policy of genuine neutrality, and preservation of the Union.

At this point, Washington, as he had so often done, called on Hamilton for advice. The New Yorker was requested either to revise the rough draft of the valedictory address (essentially, Madison's original version plus Washington's addendum) or, if he considered it necessary, "to throw the whole into a different form." Hamilton did both, counting on the president to accept the New Yorker's declared preference for what he termed his own "Original Major Draft." Although about one-half of the latter was Hamilton's work (the rest was a paraphrase of the Madison-Washington essay), he included nothing that was at variance with Washington's ideas, on which Hamilton, because of long firsthand experience, was an authority. Thus, the most famous presidential valedictory message in American history, despite Hamilton's important contribution to it, has always been properly described as Washington's Farewell Address. It is still read in both the Senate and House of Representatives every 22 February, a tribute to its and the first president's enduring importance.

The Constitution did not, of course, preclude a presidential third term (or virtual lifetime tenure for that matter) and many of Washington's supporters doubtless fantasized that he might run again. But constantly aware, as he complainingly put it, that he had spent "all the prime of his life in serving his country" and ever eager to return to the tranquillity of Mount Vernon, Washington never even fleetingly entertained the possibility of another term. He thus established the precedent that a president should relinquish office after two terms, a tradition that was not breached until Franklin D. Roosevelt's presidency and one that subsequently was institutionalized in the Twenty-second Amendment to the Constitution. Another outstanding feature of Washington's conduct during the election of 1796 was emphatically not copied by most of his successors: He resolved to play no role at all in the choice of his possible successor or in the ensuing campaign. He not only stuck to his resolve but also made no recorded statement on the election of the Federalist candidate John Adams as president and the Republican candidate Thomas Jefferson as vice president.

On 4 March 1797, John Adams was sworn in as the second president of the United States. Among those seated alongside Adams on the elevated dais in Congress Hall was his presidential predecessor, who, attired in an old-fashioned black coat, was, much to the president-elect's chagrin, the center of attention. Characteristically composed, seemingly impassive, Washington was inwardly delighted to be relinquishing an office that he had neither sought nor ever really wanted. Adams understood. His inauguration, the new president wrote, was "a solemn scene . . . made affecting to me by the presence of the General, whose countenance was as serene and unclouded as the day. He seemed to enjoy a triumph over me. Methought I heard him say, 'Ay, I am fairly out and you fairly in! See, which of us will be happiest.' " Whatever Adams himself may have thought, Washington was certain that he would be.

Following the inaugural ceremonies, the former president went to the Francis Hotel, where Adams was temporarily lodging. After congratulating his successor, Washington emerged to be greeted by the enthusiastic cheers of the throng that had assembled outside. The applause that rang out was symbolic of that which would be bestowed on him through proceeding decades.

Last Years

Eager to return home as soon as possible, Washington quickly got rid of disposable possessions and rented a sloop to ship the sizable remainder to his plantation wharf. On 15 March 1797 his coach drew up in front of Mount Vernon. As he alighted, Washington happily assured himself that he now would experience "more real enjoyment than in all the business with which I have been occupied for upwards of forty years." Such business, he reflected, had been "little more than vanity and vexation."

He presumably overlooked the fact that private life also entailed vexations. Chief among them was the dilapidated situation into which Mount Vernon had fallen and the deteriorating condition of his farms, due to manifest mismanagement. After many months of repair work, his mansion was restored to its former solid and handsome state, but the reconversion of his farms to a profitable status was a problem that he wrestled with, largely unsuccessfully, until his death. A situation that otherwise would have created "debts and difficulties" was alleviated by the sale of lands that Washington had bought for speculative purposes. In July 1799 he estimated that his still unsold lands were worth $488,137 (several millions in present-day currency).

Certainly Washington needed a large outside income. Not only did he support a large household staff and live in the style befitting a Virginia gentleman but Mount Vernon was continually thronged with guests—local friends, former official acquaintances, and strangers who wished to meet America's foremost hero. Washington did not object. Although his days—whatever the weather—were spent riding around and supervising his lands, he welcomed diversionary company at dinner and on into the early evening.

Neither management of his farms nor entertainment of his friends crowded out his interest in affairs of state, which he closely followed, especially the worsening relations with France, which by the late spring of 1799 had turned into a quasi war. His confident expectation that involvement in public affairs would be merely vicarious was shattered when, on 2 July 1799, President Adams appointed him lieutenant general and commander of the newly augmented American army. Consulted about the appointment before it was made, Washington had agreed to accept only on the condition that he would not assume active command unless "it became indispensable by the urgency of circumstances." Otherwise, actual command would be exercised by his former much trusted finance minister, Hamilton, who at Washington's insistence and to Adams' chagrin was appointed a major general and the inspector general of the army. Although Washington dutifully performed his necessary military duties, these were minimal and soon nominal. Adams, jealous of Hamilton and an exponent of naval rather than military preparedness, not only saw to it that the army was only marginally augmented but also began negotiations—in time successful—to end the Franco-American undeclared war.

In the meantime, Lieutenant General Washington continued his characteristically calm schedule at Mount Vernon. He also tidied up his affairs by drawing up a will that left the bulk of his estate to his wife, Martha, "for the term of her natural life." The provision was long since determined on and unexceptionable. What was exceptionable was the stipulation that upon Martha's death all his slaves be freed. Washington was the sole Virginian founding father to make this humanitarian decision. As the days glided by, Washington's unruffled routine was reflected in his diary, which uniformly noted the weather. On 13 December 1799 his diary recorded that the thermometer had dropped and that there was slight frost. On the same day, the general developed a sore throat. In the middle of the following night he suddenly became acutely ill, his speech almost inaudible and his breathing labored. On 14 December, his condition quickly worsened. The three physicians called to his bedside repeatedly bled and purged him (standard practice of the time). Near midnight, America's first and still foremost hero died.

BIBLIOGRAPHY

Of the many biographies written in the nineteenth century, three retain historical interest: John Marshall, *The Life of George Washington*, 5 vols. (London, 1804–1807), a strongly pro-Federalist account much of whose background material was lifted from the British *Annual Register*; Washington Irving, *George Washington*, 5 vols. (New York, 1855–1859), in which the well-known novelist dramatically and effectively portrayed his nation's foremost hero; and Henry Cabot Lodge, *George Washington*, 2 vols. (Boston and New York, 1889), which is factually sound but reflects the exalted status Washington continued to enjoy in the late nineteenth century.

The twentieth century has produced a long list of Washington biographies. Still interesting, because of its novelty, is W. E. Woodward, *George Washington: The Image and the Man* (New York, 1926), a muckraking attempt to cut Washington down to human size. The monumental biography of the century and indispensable to scholars is Douglas Southall Freeman, *George Washington: A Biography*, 7 vols. (New York, 1948–1957), the most ambitious attempt ever made to demonstrate that Washington deserves his exalted position in American history. Richard Harwell edited a one-volume edition of Freeman's work: *Washington* (New York, 1968). A more recent multivolume study is James Thomas Flexner, *George Washington*, 4 vols. (Boston, 1965–1972). Flexner provided a one-volume abridgement in *Washington: The Indispensable Man* (Boston, 1974). The best one-volume biography is Marcus Cunliffe, *George Washington: Man and Monument* (Boston, 1958). This slender book is a brilliant and fascinating account of the myth and the man, which, Cunliffe explains, "can never be entirely separated."

Primary material on the first president abounds. Of principal importance are John C. Fitzpatrick, ed., *The Writings of George Washington from the Original Manuscript Sources, 1745–1799*, 39 vols. (Washington, D.C., 1931–1944), and Donald Jackson and Dorothy Twohig, eds., *The Diaries of George Washington*, 6 vols. (Charlottesville, Va., 1976–1979).

Far and away the finest study of Washington's presidency is Stanley M. Elkins and Eric L. McKitrick's encyclopedic and masterful account *The Age of Federalism* (New York, 1993). Also valuable is John C. Miller's stimulatingly interpretive and uncommonly well written *The Federalist Era, 1789–1801* (New York, 1960). A full-scale treatment of Washington's exercise of the executive office is Forrest McDonald, *The Presidency of George Washington* (Lawrence, Kans., 1974), a study marred by some novel theses that are undocumented or implausible. Particularly commendable are the germane sections of Ralph Ketcham, *Presidents Above Party: The First American Presidency*, 1789–1829 (Chapel Hill, N.C., 1984). For the administrative history of Washington's presidency, see Leonard D. White, *The Federalists: A Study in Administrative History* (New York, 1948).

An impressive list of books deals with selected aspects of Washington's presidency, in particular the development of the new nation's first political parties. For an example of the traditional account, consult Wilfred E. Binkley's popular work, *American Political Parties: Their Natural History* (New York, 1943). More plausible and interpretatively original is William N. Chambers, *Political Parties in a New Nation: The American Experience, 1776–1809* (New York, 1963). The pertinent sections of Richard Hofstadter, *The Idea of a Party System: The Rise of Legitimate Opposition in the United States, 1780–1840* (Berkeley, Calif., 1970), is characteristically excellent.

For party ideology, see Joyce Appleby, *Capitalism and a New Social Order: The Republican Vision of the 1790s* (New York, 1984); Lance Banning, *The Jeffersonian Persuasion: Evolution of a Party Ideology* (Ithaca, N.Y., 1978); and Drew R. McCoy, *The Elusive Republic: Political Economy in Jeffersonian America* (Chapel Hill, N.C., 1980).

The diplomatic record of the Washington years has been thoroughly explored. Outstanding contributions include Samuel Flagg Bemis's studies *Jay's Treaty: A Study in Commerce and Diplomacy* (New York, 1923) and *Pinckney's Treaty: A Study of America's Advantage from Europe's Distress, 1783–1800* (Baltimore, 1926). The former is significantly revised by Jerald A. Combs, *The Jay Treaty: Political Battleground of the Founding Fathers* (Berkeley, Calif., 1970). An excellent account of Anglo-American relations is Bradford Perkins, *The First Rapprochement: England and the United States, 1795–1805* (Philadelphia, 1955), which argues that underlying the diplomatic squabbles between the United States and Great Britain was a successful and statesmanlike effort on both sides to maintain cordial relations and to settle differences amicably.

Franco-American diplomacy has not been as exhaustively explored as Anglo-American relations. Alexander DeConde's *Entangling Alliance: Politics and Diplomacy Under George Washington* (Durham, N.C., 1958), is comprehensive but marred by the author's sympathy for the Franco-American alliance, which leads to an unnecessarily critical view of President Washington. More objective is Albert H. Bowman, *The Struggle for Neutrality: Franco-American Diplomacy During the Federalist Era* (Knoxville, Tenn., 1974).

The economic history of the 1790s has been comparatively neglected. The most thorough survey may be found in the relevant sections of Curtis P. Nettels, *The Emergence of a National Economy, 1775–1815* (New York, 1962). Volumes 1 and 2 of Joseph Dorfman's five-volume study *The Economic Mind in American Civilization* (New York, 1946–1959) afford an excellent analysis of economic thought. The most invaluable and interpretatively original studies of economic growth, works that integrate traditional economic history and economic theory, are Stuart Bruchey, *The Roots of American Economic Growth, 1607–1861* (New York, 1965), and Douglass C. North, *The Economic Growth of the United States, 1790–1860* (Englewood Cliffs, N.J., 1961).

For books that offer a cultural perspective on the period, see the pertinent parts of Robert H. Wiebe, *The Opening of American Society: From the Adoption of the Constitution to the Eve of Disunion* (New York, 1984), and Stephen Watts, *The Republic Reborn: War and the Making of Liberal America, 1790–1820* (Baltimore, 1987).

An annotated bibliographical essay (definitive at the time of its publication) is Jacob E. Cooke, ''The Federalist Age: A Reappraisal,'' in George A. Billias and Gerald N. Grob, eds., *American History: Retrospect and Prospect* (New York, 1971).

Recent works include Richard Brookhiser, *Founding Father: Rediscovering George Washington* (New York, 1996), William M. S. Rasmussen and Robert S. Tilton, *George Washington: The Man Behind the Myths* (Charlottesville, Va., 1999), and John Ferling, *Setting the World Ablaze: Washington, Adams, Jefferson, and the American Revolution* (New York, 2000).

John Adams

Charles W. Akers

John Adams THE LIBRARY OF CONGRESS

J OHN ADAMS became the second president of the United States when he took the oath of office in the packed House of Representatives on 4 March 1797. As he described this moving scene to his wife, there was "scarcely a dry eye but Washington's" at "the sight of the sun setting full orbed, and another rising, though less splendid." The new president understood well that no one could fill the role of the godlike father of the nation whose eight years in the presidency had ensured respect for the newly created federal government. The true test of the Constitution was at hand: Could the office be transferred by the first contested presidential election to another from whom there emanated no aura of superhuman

greatness? Adams hoped that at least some of the tears had come from the "pleasure of exchanging Presidents without tumult." But he also knew that Washington's successor faced unresolved problems that could quickly tear the young republic apart.

Early Life

Born on 19 October 1735, Adams was sixty-one when he took office. He had behind him thirty years of distinguished public service. His father, a respected farmer and artisan of Braintree, Massachusetts, had pointed him toward Harvard College and a career in the Congregational ministry. He took his degree in 1755, but by then theological uncertainty had turned him toward a secular vocation. He taught school briefly, then read law, and was admitted to the bar in 1758. Within a dozen years he became the colony's preeminent and busiest lawyer.

In defending such clients as John Hancock and other merchants accused of smuggling and sailors charged with rioting against press gangs of the Royal Navy, he was drawn into the local resistance movement. The Stamp Act of 1765 provoked him to argue in speech and in print against this parliamentary statute, which he termed an unconstitutional violation of colonial liberty. In 1770 he masterfully defended the British soldiers accused of murder in the Boston Massacre. He secured their acquittal while protecting the town's reputation against the charge that the soldiers had been unmercifully harassed. He held several local offices and served a term in the Massachusetts House of Representatives. In retaliation for Adams' opposition to royal government, the governor twice vetoed his election to the Massachusetts Council. His law practice ended in 1774 when the colony and the developing nation began to demand all of his talents and energy.

In 1764, Adams had married Abigail Smith of neighboring Weymouth, Massachusetts, who was to make a major contribution to his public career. Without attending school, she had mastered the literature of the day and developed a remarkably perceptive intellect and an unquenchable spirit. As John Adams became absorbed in politics and diplomacy, he increasingly left to her the responsibility of raising their four surviving children and managing the family's finances. At first impatient with the limitations of the private sphere to which women were confined, she in time accepted her husband's successes as her own and gladly took her place as his confidante and defender. Theirs was a marriage of equals as far as the roles society assigned men and women would permit. But his services for their country kept them apart during most of the ten years after 1774.

Revolution and Confederation

His participation in the First Continental Congress at Philadelphia in the fall of 1774 marked the beginning of John Adams' career as an American statesman. He spent much of the next three years as a member of the Second Continental Congress, where his influence was apparent in such important developments as the election of George Washington to be commander in chief, the recommendation that the colonies establish state governments, the decision for independence, and the establishment of the diplomatic service. His hurried visits home from Philadelphia brought urgent demands on his time from the revolutionary government of Massachusetts. When Congress appointed him one of the commissioners to France, he abandoned thoughts of reopening his law practice and set sail in February 1778. Returning home after eighteen months abroad, he became the principal draftsman of the Massachusetts Constitution of 1780, which was to be an important model for the United States Constitution. But before the Massachusetts convention had completed its work, Congress sent him back to Europe to negotiate peace with Great Britain.

Congress appointed additional peace commissioners in 1781, but only Benjamin Franklin and John Jay arrived in time to join Adams in negotiating the Treaty of Paris (1783), by which Great Britain acknowledged American independence and awarded generous boundaries to the new nation. Adams' wife then joined him, and he remained in Europe until 1788, serving as the first American minister to the British court and saving the credit of the United States by negotiating loans from the Netherlands. He returned home the year after the Constitutional Convention of 1787 uncertain of how, if at all, the country would use his unequaled experience in diplomacy and republican government.

Vice Presidency

Knowing that Washington was certain to be president, Adams believed himself entitled to the second office as a reward for his services. But he considered his election with only thirty-four out of sixty-nine electoral votes to be a humiliation, for Washington had been chosen unanimously. With some anguish of mind he swallowed his pride and took his place in the government being formed. His eight years as vice president provided few opportunities for executive leadership. He conscientiously carried out the tedious duty of presiding over the Senate, in which role he broke several tie votes in favor of the administration. Despite being consulted only rarely on major decisions, he maintained cordial relations with the president. But Alexander Hamilton, Washington's secretary of the treasury, had been wary from the beginning of Adams' well-deserved reputation for independence. After his resignation in January 1795, Hamilton sought to continue and extend his political influence from his New York law office. Unable to deny Adams the vice presidency, Hamilton had succeeded in reducing his vote in the first election and then unsuccessfully sought to replace him in Washington's second term. By 1796, only John Adams stood in the way of Hamilton's domination of the Federalist party, as the supporters of the administration were now known.

Election of 1796

The European war resulting from the French Revolution led many Federalists and other citizens to plead for Washington to accept a third term. He finally refused and announced his retirement on 17 September 1796 in the farewell address. As vice president for eight years and the man who had twice received the second-highest electoral vote, Adams was obviously the heir apparent. But unlike the elections of Washington, this time there was a contest. James Madison, leader of the opposition party in Congress—the Republicans—pushed the candidacy of Thomas Jefferson, to save, so he believed, the country from the aristocratic principles of the Federalists. Although increasingly fearful of Hamilton, Jefferson proved to be such a reluctant candidate that he advised Madison to favor Adams in case of a tie, for the vice president had always been, in Jefferson's words, "my senior." As much as he craved elevation to the first position, Adams' principles would not let him campaign for the office; electioneering was left to others.

As usual, Hamilton sought to play kingmaker. He understood that Adams was too popular in New England to be openly pushed aside, and he regarded Jefferson as the greater evil of the two candidates. But he saw in the electoral college the possibility of electing a Federalist president, who would be more likely to follow his leadership than Adams. Each elector was required to cast two ballots without designating which was for president and which for vice president. Hamilton advanced the vice presidential candidacy of Thomas Pinckney of South Carolina, who had concluded the popular Pinckney Treaty of 1795 with Spain. If New England divided its votes between the two and the South cast a solid vote for Pinckney while scattering its second ballots, the southerner might come in ahead of Adams.

Hamilton's strategy backfired. It produced confusion among Federalist leaders and resentment in New England, whose electors withheld some votes from Pinckney. When the ballots were opened in the Senate on 8 February 1797, John Adams performed his vice presidential duty of announcing his own election. He had received seventy-one votes, Jefferson sixty-eight, and Pinckney fifty-nine. The nation had chosen a president and vice president of opposite parties. More ominous was the sectional nature of the results. Adams had won only thirteen votes south of New Jersey, and seven of these had come from the single state of Maryland. Jefferson had received none north of Pennsylvania.

Political Theory

By the time he took office, no American had read or written more about government than John Adams. It is difficult to discover an important volume on law, political theory, moral philosophy, or economy from classical Greece and Rome to Enlightenment Europe that had escaped his critical eye. He was not an abstract political thinker; rather, he read and wrote to understand and solve the problems of society in his own day. At the outset of the Revolution he believed that the superior virtue of the American people would prove sufficient to maintain a balance between liberty and order in the new republics being formed by the states. In his *Thoughts on Government*, written early in 1776, and in his draft of the Massachusetts Constitution three years later, he advocated popular governments with checks on the abuse of power adequate to maintain their republican purity.

As he viewed the American experiments in government from Europe during the 1780s, Adams lost faith in the political virtue of his countrymen. He saw them repeating the mistakes of Europe, especially in the feverish pursuit of luxury, with its inevitable social and political corruption and its nurturing of class antagonisms. More controls and authority were now needed to govern a society dividing into the aristocratic few and the democratic many. In his last two years abroad he hastily wrote the three volumes of *A Defence of the Constitutions of Government of the United States of America*. This cumbersome work declared that a strong, independent executive was essential to mediate between opposing interests. The continued growth of corruption would in the distant future make free elections impossible and a hereditary executive preferable. This concept in the *Defence* would plague the remainder of Adams' career with the charge of being a monarchist, even though he never advocated hereditary succession for his own day. The French Revolution further strengthened his belief that political freedom could be preserved only by a balanced government effectively controlling the natural rivalry of men for wealth and distinction. The quest for equality, he predicted, would inevitably bring chaos and the loss of the freedom that the French revolutionaries sought.

By the time he returned home in 1788, Adams had transferred his hope for the future of American republicanism from the states to the national government. He readily approved the new federal Constitution, which so much resembled his handiwork in the Massachusetts Constitution of 1780, but he wanted an even stronger executive than provided for by the Philadelphia convention. The president, he thought, should be freed from the shackles of the Senate in making appointments and approving treaties. He wrote to Jefferson of his fear that Congress was certain to encroach on the powers of the president in these and other areas where executive independence was essential; the president needed an absolute veto over acts of the legislature if he was to mediate effectively between opposing interests. Vice President Adams argued in the Senate that the president should be addressed by some such title as "His Highness" or "His Majesty, the President," in keeping with the near-monarchical office to which he had been elected.

Conception of the Presidency

His two terms under Washington appear to have eased somewhat Adams' concern over the weakness of the presidential office, and he took pains in his inaugural address to deny that he advocated radical changes in the Constitution. Yet his view of the president as an independent mediator between contending factions left him largely incapable of bridging the constitutional separation of powers by working closely with Congress to enact his program. His constitutional duty as he construed it was to alert Congress to the nation's problems and to judge its solutions but not to intervene otherwise in the legislative process.

Even had Adams' concept of the presidency permitted him to use the powers of his office to influence Congress, the lack of a Federalist party structure would have thwarted him. Like Washington, Adams had deplored the rise of parties in the first two administrations. In his inaugural address he pronounced the "spirit of party" to be one of the "natural enemies" of the Constitution. Refusing to recognize that he was the leader of a party, he could not command a loyal following. Under Adams the Federalist majorities in Congress were a loose combination of three groups: moderates with whom Adams was popular; independents, or "half-Federalists," who ran under the party banner but voted according to local interests; and the Hamiltonians, who took their lead from the former secretary of the treasury. Insofar as the Federalist party had a vigorous center, it was in the New York City law office of Alexander Hamilton.

At the outset of the new government in 1789, Adams had given full support to Hamilton's plan to establish the credit of the United States, but he soon developed serious doubts concerning the secretary's sponsorship of the Bank of the United States and other measures favoring commercial and manufacturing interests. He preferred a federal government that through frugality kept its credit high and its taxes low. In economic philosophy he stood between the commercialism of Hamilton and the agrarianism of Jefferson. Here, as on other issues, President Adams attempted to balance clashing interests. He retained a faint hope that he might be able to draw the moderate men of both parties toward a nonpartisan center and thus return the Republic to the course on which it had been launched by the framers of the Constitution.

By retaining Washington's cabinet, Adams made what some historians have considered to be the major mistake of his administration, but to him, the reasons for doing so were compelling. He believed that government officials should not be removed except for cause. To dismiss the cabinet he inherited might appear to be an affront to Washington and further split the Federalists. The salaries and prestige of these offices were so low that even Washington had experienced great difficulty in filling them during his second term. Though he lamented the decline in the quality of the secretaries since the resignations of Hamilton and Jefferson, Adams appears not to have considered forming his own cabinet.

Three of the four cabinet members proved disloyal to the president they served. Of these, Secretary of State Timothy Pickering caused Adams the most trouble. An unsuccessful lawyer turned zealous but honest bureaucrat, Pickering held this president in low esteem and did not hesitate to oppose him openly when they differed on domestic and foreign issues. The secretary of the treasury, Oliver Wolcott, Jr., of Connecticut, ably administered his office and refused to oppose his chief openly but remained an intimate of Hamilton. As secretary of war, James McHenry was acknowledged to be incompetent even by Hamilton, whom he subserviently followed. Of the original cabinet, only the attorney general, Charles Lee, demonstrated any loyalty to the president. But this office was still only a part-time position, held by a lawyer who also engaged in private practice. With the creation of the Navy Department in 1798, Adams at last appointed a secretary of his own choosing. The lack of cabinet solidarity weakened the Adams administration, especially since the president was absent from the capital for long periods. It was typical of John Adams that he saw his duty in working with cabinet officers whose loyalty he suspected from the outset of his presidency.

The Crisis with France

In an era of peace, a president with Adams' view of the office might have enjoyed a tranquil four years. He did not regard his election by a margin of three votes as a mandate from the American people but only as a duty to be performed. He had no program for the nation other than the "continuance in all its energy" of the government under the Constitution. "What other form of government, indeed, can so well deserve our esteem and love?" he queried in his short inaugural address, which stressed his dedication to the principles upon which the American governments were founded. But the presidency of John Adams was dominated not by tranquillity but by a single issue that threatened to destroy the Union before the end of its first decade. It was fortunate for the nation—and for Adams' claim to presidential greatness—that this single issue concerned foreign policy, the area in which the president had the most independent authority and the one for which Adams was best prepared by experience.

The course of the French Revolution since 1789 had plunged Europe into war. Despite President Washington's policy of official neutrality, Americans increasingly divided over whether to remain loyal to their ally in the War of Independence or to support the British effort to prevent French domination of all Europe. The leaders of republican France saw in the treaty that John Jay had negotiated with Great Britain in 1794 not only shameful ingratitude for their coun-

try's aid to the struggling colonies during the American Revolution but also a de facto alliance with Great Britain that repudiated the Franco-American alliance of 1778. The treaty became the main issue in the election of 1796 as the Republicans generally denounced it. On the eve of the election, the French minister to the United States, Pierre Auguste Adet, openly acknowledged his government's support for Jefferson. At his inauguration Adams declared his "personal esteem for the French nation" and his determination to maintain "neutrality and impartiality among the belligerent powers of Europe." But already the Directory, the five-man executive of the French republic, had interpreted Adams' succession to the presidency as another act of hostility toward France.

Since 1795, French armed ships preying on American shipping, particularly in the West Indies, had captured hundreds of vessels flying the flag of the United States. On 2 March 1797, two days before the inauguration, the Directory stepped up the maritime war by a decree that legitimized nearly any seizure of an American ship and fell just short of a declaration of war. Furthermore, the Directory had in effect broken off diplomatic relations with the United States by refusing to accept Charles Cotesworth Pinckney as the replacement for James Monroe, the American minister to France recalled by Washington for his opposition to Jay's Treaty.

As Adams took office, he had to pick up the pieces of Washington's shattered neutrality policy. The first president was fortunate, thought Jefferson, to have retired "just as the bubble is bursting." Following three weeks of deliberation, Adams called a special session of Congress for the middle of May. In a message to Congress on 16 May, he denounced the Directory's slighting of Pinckney and honoring of the departing Monroe as an attempt to "separate the people of the United States" from their freely elected government. It was time to convince France and the world that Americans could not be "humiliated under a colonial spirit of fear and inferiority." He pledged a "fresh attempt at negotiations" and a willingness to correct any real wrong done France. But in the meantime the nation must look to "effectual measures of defense." He recommended the building of a navy as the first line of defense and the expansion of the armed forces to protect the long coastline against French raiding parties.

This address ended the brief period of political peace enjoyed by the president. His inaugural address had been praised by even some Republican leaders and editors, but now Jefferson concluded that Adams had been captured by a circle of Federalists pushing for a war against France and close ties with Great Britain. The Republican press generally denounced the "gasconading speech" for exaggerating the danger of war in order to achieve such sinister goals as deceiving the nation into accepting a standing army that could be used to institute an American monarchy. Yet even Hamilton favored another attempt at reconciliation and so instructed his followers in the cabinet. Pickering, Wolcott, and McHenry, more inclined to war than negotiation, gave way to Hamilton on the sending of a peace commission but rejected his advice that it should include a friend of France.

Adams, too, wanted to send a bipartisan commission to France. Ideally, he thought, it should include either Jefferson or Madison. But both refused, and there was growing opposition in the cabinet and among other Federalists to sending any Republican. Finally, on 31 May 1797, the president nominated a geographically balanced commission of Pinckney, Francis Dana, and John Marshall. When Dana declined because of health, Adams defied his cabinet by replacing Dana with Elbridge Gerry, a close Massachusetts friend and a political independent. Following weeks of heated debate, the special session adjourned on 8 July, after approving the commission and passing some feeble defense measures.

Marshall and Gerry soon sailed to join Pinckney and attempted to open negotiations, but no word could be expected from them for many months. The president and Mrs. Adams left the capital in July for their home in Quincy, Massachusetts, and did not return until November. Meanwhile the debate raged in the press. Republican publications described in detail a conspiracy of warmongers, while Federalist editors attacked the cowardly American Jacobins for quivering in fear before insults to the nation's honor by French atheists. The president's annual message to Congress on 23 November added fuel to the flames. He held out little hope of an immediate peace. Defense measures, he insisted, were now more essential than before and should be supported as much as possible by taxation rather than by loans.

With instructions that asked for much and gave little, the commissioners had feeble bargaining power in France. They faced the new French foreign minister, the wily Talleyrand, who, although more inclined to peace than the Directory, saw the negotia-

tions as an opportunity for personal gain. Working through confidential agents, Talleyrand demanded, as preconditions for negotiating, a bribe of £50,000 for himself and the assumption by the United States of all American claims against France. Pinckney answered the demand for a bribe with an emphatic "No, no, not a sixpence." Meanwhile, Adams' speech of 16 May 1797 had increased the Directory's anger over Jay's Treaty, and an apology was demanded.

The commissioners continued in unofficial negotiations for another five months. Their first report reached Adams on 4 March 1798. A shocked president sent the one uncoded letter to Congress the next day, and his anger rose as the others were deciphered. He asked his cabinet if he should lay all the dispatches before Congress and then request a declaration of war. Deciding not to go that far, on the nineteenth he informed the legislature that the mission was hopeless and called for strong defense measures.

Skeptical of the president's "warmongering," Republicans demanded to see the dispatches and in so doing fell into a trap of their own making. After a formal request from the House, the president released the papers on 3 April, substituting the letters *W, X, Y, Z* for the names of the agents who had delivered the request for a bribe. News of the XYZ affair, as it became known, quickly spread throughout the nation and aroused patriots to turn Pinckney's "No, no, not a sixpence" into the toast "Millions for defense, but not one cent for tribute!" Suddenly John Adams became, as his wife proudly noticed, "wonderfully popular." She wrote her son John Quincy Adams, the American minister to the court of Berlin, that the supporters of France had received a "death wound."

President Adams judged that a declaration of war was inevitable, but he was in no hurry to ask Congress for it. While some extreme, or High, Federalists pressed for an immediate declaration, the majority in Congress preferred to wait until further provocation from France united an overwhelming majority of Americans behind a declared war. For several months addresses and resolutions of support from communities and societies all over the nation poured into the president's house. He gave much of his time to answering each address in fervid language, calling for patriotic sacrifice and reproaching the American friends of France. Published in the newspapers and in part as *A Selection of the Patriotic Addresses, to the President of the United States*, these addresses and replies inflamed the passion for war. Federalists now flaunted the black cockade of the American Revolution to shame those Republicans who sometimes wore the tricolor cockade of the French revolutionaries. From pulpit and press, rabid Federalists spread the fear of a worldwide conspiracy, hatched in France, against Christianity and political freedom. Rumors of impending French raids and even a full-scale invasion alarmed the unprotected coastal towns.

Preparations for War

Even without a declaration of war, the XYZ crisis moved Congress in the spring and early summer of 1798 to pass a long series of defense measures. Since 1789, protracted debate over the need for a navy had pitted legislators from the commercial and agrarian sections against each other. In 1794, Congress had authorized the building of six frigates, only three of which had been started, and they were still unfinished when Washington retired. At the request of President Adams, Congress in 1797 had voted to complete the three frigates. Then, in his 19 March 1798 message, Adams announced that he had authorized the arming of private merchantmen. The Republicans unsuccessfully attempted to curb the president's power to take such offensive measures against France by introducing three resolutions, known as the Sprigg Resolutions. After Republican opposition was crushed by the XYZ revelations, Congress promptly voted to procure additional vessels, to arm private merchant ships, to establish the Marine Corps, and to permit the seizure of French armed vessels in any ocean. To take naval affairs out of the overburdened and inefficient hands of the secretary of war, the Department of the Navy was created on 30 April. Adams appointed a capable secretary of the navy, Benjamin Stoddert of Maryland, who quickly became the president's chief ally in the cabinet.

By the end of 1798, the United States Navy had undertaken the protection of American shipping on its side of the Atlantic. In his messages to Congress and his replies to the patriotic addresses, Adams had consistently urged that the "wooden walls" of the navy be the nation's first line of defense. Mrs. Adams fondly thought of her husband as the father of the American navy. He perhaps deserved the honor as much as any single individual, although other major voices had also been raised in the long naval debate

and the actual policy had been worked out by the Federalist majority in Congress. More important than any attribution of credit, the United States for the first time had a navy.

This momentous second session of the Fifth Congress also created a large paper army. Late in May a bill was passed giving the president temporary authority to raise a provisional army in case France declared war or threatened invasion. In June he was directed to appoint officers for the eighty thousand militiamen requested of the states the previous year. Before Congress adjourned in July, it passed legislation to bring the regular army up to full strength and to add ten thousand men to it. These forces appeared to fulfill Adams' request for land defenses made in his 16 May 1797 message. It took him only a few weeks, however, to realize that Congress had presented him with a political rather than a military force.

The crisis intensified Adams' conviction that the president should hold himself above party politics. He had in mind a nonpartisan army headed by Washington and staffed by high-ranking officers drawn from both parties. The former president reluctantly agreed to assume nominal command, provided that he did not have to take the field until the fighting started. In accepting this condition, Adams did not seem at first to understand that Washington would have the choice of his second in command, the general given the responsibility for organizing and training the army. With the full support of Hamilton's followers in the cabinet, Washington not only refused to have any "Jacobin" generals from the ranks of the Republicans but made as a condition of his service Hamilton's appointment as second in command.

In asking Washington to emerge from retirement, Adams had placed himself in the hands of the one public figure in the United States of whom he stood in awe. Never fully able to suppress his jealousy of Washington's primacy in war and peace, Adams had nevertheless understood perfectly the symbolic importance to the Republic of its revered revolutionary hero and first president. He was so troubled by being commander in chief without any military experience that he seems briefly to have regretted that there was no constitutional way to let Washington resume the presidency. Thus, once Washington had stated his terms, Adams could do nothing but surrender on the question of military appointments. As a result, when the issue was finally resolved in October

1798, the president had to place the enlarging army under the de facto command of his Federalist rival, a man whose ambition he had come to fear. Mrs. Adams likely expressed her husband's thoughts when she wrote that Hamilton would "make an able and active officer" but was capable of turning into the American Bonaparte. At the head of the army, he, like Napoleon, could use military force to overpower the government and launch an invasion of neighboring lands to establish an empire. The president's already slight enthusiasm for land defenses began to weaken rapidly.

The Alien and Sedition Acts

The Federalist majority in Congress also erected defenses against domestic enemies and thereby hoped to cripple the Republican party. It became Federalist doctrine that the spread of French radicalism in the United States was largely the work of revolutionaries from Great Britain and the Continent. To many, the most conspicuous symbol of this pernicious influence was Albert Gallatin, a Swiss immigrant who now headed the opposition in the House. But in the "democratic societies" or "Jacobin clubs," which had mysteriously sprung up around 1794, and in the unrestrained opposition press, it was believed, were concentrated less respectable foreigners. These undesirables had fled their inhospitable native lands only to corrupt the foundations of the free republic that had given them asylum. During five weeks in June and July 1798, Congress extended the naturalization period to fourteen years, provided for the control of enemy aliens in a declared war, and gave the president for two years the power to deport any foreigner he suspected of being engaged in subversive activity.

Without being enforced, the Alien Acts intimidated a few foreigners but otherwise had slight consequences. Infinitely more serious was the Sedition Act, passed on 14 July. Since the beginning of party warfare under Washington, the Federalist and Republican newspapers had increased their levels of vituperation. Even after the XYZ revelations, Republican editors had continued the abusive attack on Adams, Hamilton, and their party as tools of England seeking to drag the United States into an unnecessary and destructive war against a loyal ally to whom gratitude for past aid was due. They asserted that the president had repeatedly deceived the people into supporting a war for commerce that would

harm the farmers, who formed the heart of the country. How, they asked, could a party that in 1794 had sold the nation's soul to Britain in the shameful Jay's Treaty now appeal to national honor as an excuse for a war against France?

Such language, interspersed with personal vilification, was treason to many Federalists. When it proved impossible to define *treason* as words alone, they turned to the English common-law doctrine of seditious libel. After the bitterest debate of this heated session, a sedition act was passed by a narrow majority formed almost entirely of northern legislators. The act, to remain in force until the end of the current presidential term, included a provision for a fine of as much as $2,000 and imprisonment not exceeding two years for "writing, printing, uttering or publishing any false, scandalous and malicious writing" with unlawful intent against the president or Congress.

President Adams signed the Alien and Sedition Acts. His attitude toward them at the moment of signing went unrecorded. He had not recommended such measures to Congress, although some of his replies to the addresses had condemned foreign influences and the "thousand tongues of calumny" that threatened the country. Thus, he could be charged with having helped to create the climate in which the bills were written. In July 1798 he had not yet seen clearly his duty in this national crisis. He had set as his life's goal the achievement of fame, which in the eighteenth-century concept meant acting through disinterested public service to shape history in such a way as to win the approbation of future generations. He lost a great opportunity to increase that fame by not vetoing the most severe restrictions on freedom of expression ever passed by Congress.

The Retreat from War

Before Congress adjourned in July, President Adams also signed an act abrogating the 1778 treaties of alliance with France. To pay for the defense measures, Congress levied a direct property tax on houses and slaves and authorized the president to borrow in anticipation of these tax revenues. In this session Adams suffered an embarrassing personal defeat when the Senate refused to confirm his nomination of his son-in-law, Colonel William S. Smith, as adjutant general of the army. Smith's commendable record in the War of Independence had been clouded by his current reputation as a speculator and political opportunist. Even so, he might have been confirmed had not the Hamiltonians in the cabinet warned the senators of Smith's recent troubles.

Late in July 1798, President and Mrs. Adams left the oppressive heat of Philadelphia and headed for Quincy. Along the way he learned the full extent of his newfound popularity. Demonstrations of support repeatedly delayed their journey as town after town turned out to display for the president and First Lady the patriotism of its citizens. A popular new patriotic song, "Adams and Liberty," celebrated the president as the living symbol of the nation's determination to resist foreign intrigues against its liberty.

By the time they reached Quincy on 8 August, Abigail Adams had taken so seriously ill that for weeks she appeared near death. The president remained close to her bedside and conducted the business of his office by mail. His protracted absence from the capital gave the disloyal members of the cabinet a free hand but also afforded Adams time to reflect on the crisis with France. In September the British ambassador, Robert Liston, came to Quincy to offer an alliance against their common enemy. Adams expressed interest without making a commitment. He then learned from his son and from Elbridge Gerry, who had remained in France after the other commissioners had returned home, that the Directory did not desire war with the United States and was making conciliatory gestures. On 22 October he wrote to the secretary of war that "at present there is no more prospect of seeing a French army here, than there is in heaven."

Adams welcomed the softening of France's position. He knew that Hamilton no longer waited for French action to bring on a full-scale war; instead, the general now proposed that Great Britain and the United States join in stripping France's ally, Spain, of its American possessions. As additional reports of Talleyrand's peace overtures reached Quincy, it became apparent that the need for the enlarged army headed by Hamilton was rapidly vanishing. But in Trenton, New Jersey, where the federal capital was temporarily located to escape the yellow fever epidemic in Philadelphia, Hamilton and Pickering attempted to rally Federalists to support an enlargement of the conflict by maintaining that the news from France had been merely Talleyrand's scheme to deceive the United States into letting down its guard. Adams' friends urged him to return to the capital without delay.

Mrs. Adams had sufficiently recovered that the president could return to Philadelphia in late No-

President John Adams is depicted in this 1799 Amos Doolittle engraving, surrounded by the coats of arms of each state, the eagle holding a banner reading "Millions for Our Defence, Not a Cent for Tribute." THE LIBRARY OF CONGRESS

vember. In preparing his annual message to Congress, he solicited the opinion of the cabinet but rejected its judgment, on which Hamilton had exerted a strong influence, that the nation should continue to prepare for war without making any gesture of peace toward France. Instead, in the message of 8 December, Adams called for "vigorous preparations for war," especially the strengthening of the navy, as the way to avoid war: "An efficient preparation for war can alone insure peace. It is peace that we have uniformly and perseveringly cultivated, and harmony between us and France may be restored at her option." But it must be peace with honor. He would not send another minister to France without firm assurances that he would be well received.

In the next two months reports of France's peaceful intentions continued to reach the president. He received Washington's private endorsement of an honorable peace. In the middle of February he was handed solid evidence that France had repealed its decrees authorizing the seizure of

American ships. This information came just as Congress empowered the president to raise an additional army of thirty thousand men. Meanwhile, the British navy so thoroughly enforced its government's policy of capturing American vessels trading with the French West Indies that doubts were raised as to which country was the more dangerous enemy.

Always in the background of the Franco-American crisis remained the unsettled points of contention with Great Britain. The former colonies had enjoyed friendlier relations with the mother country since Jay's Treaty, but irritations remained on questions of the impressment of American seamen, citizenship, and neutral rights in time of war. Republicans charged Federalists with sacrificing American interests out of favoritism for England with the same vigor that Federalists asserted the Republicans to be the advocates of French revolutionary radicalism.

When, in 1799, Adams turned over to the Royal Navy a mutineer who falsely claimed American citizenship, a Republican effort to censure the president failed in Congress. Preoccupied with the threat from France, Adams followed a middle-of-the-road policy that took advantage of Anglo-American friendship without subservience to British might. American privateers fitted out in English ports, the Royal Navy sometimes convoyed American merchantmen out of danger zones, and the ministry headed by William Pitt permitted the United States to purchase large quantities of naval and military equipment and supplies. At the same time, the ministry refused to recognize the right of neutral nations to trade with Britain's enemy. With a quarter century of diplomatic experience, Adams understood the limits of Great Britain's professed friendship in this struggle. He knew that a declared war with France would of necessity increase his country's dependence on English aid, with a resulting loss of American freedom of action.

On 18 February 1799, Adams notified the Senate that Talleyrand appeared willing to receive an envoy from the United States. Consequently, he nominated William Vans Murray, American minister at The Hague, to be minister plenipotentiary to France, with the provision that he not undertake the mission until the French government gave additional assurances of its readiness to enter serious negotiations. The High Federalists responded to this provisional nomination with shock and anger. Pickering was furious that he, the secretary of state, had not been consulted. Adams held out against strong pressure from several leading members of his party to withdraw the nomination, but he quickly accepted a compromise proposal by which two negotiators were joined with Murray. Refusing to add Hamiltonians, he named Chief Justice Oliver Ellsworth and Patrick Henry, and they, along with Murray, were confirmed by the Senate before Congress adjourned on 3 March. The president soon left for Quincy to rejoin his wife and to await the reaction of both France and his own countrymen to his "master stroke of policy," as Abigail Adams described her husband's nomination of a peace commission.

Adams had correctly interpreted the mood of the country. A declaration of war soon after the XYZ revelations might have rallied a majority of citizens to the flag. Now only the High Federalists wanted military action against France. The direct tax, the Alien and Sedition Acts, and the recruitment of soldiers proved more and more irritating in all sections. Before leaving the capital, Adams had issued a proclamation against a tax rebellion among the German communities of eastern Pennsylvania and ordered federal troops to assist the militia in restoring order and seizing the ringleaders. The rebellion was easily suppressed, with twenty-nine persons arrested and brought to trial. Of these, the major leader, John Fries, and his two principal subordinates were convicted of treason and sentenced to be hanged. Adams would eventually pardon this trio and recommend clemency for the others. Nonetheless, the Fries Rebellion publicized the burden of the "window tax," as the direct tax was popularly known because it was in part based on the number and size of the windows in a house. The suppression of this minor uprising by federal troops struck fear into the hearts of many at the prospect of an army led by Hamilton wiping out all opposition to the policies of the High Federalists.

Despite his tacit approval of the Alien and Sedition Acts, Adams only halfheartedly carried out his duty to enforce these measures. He signed a few alien warrants that were never executed, but he refused to give Pickering signed blank warrants to be used in the president's absence or to apply the acts against French consuls still on American soil. And he overruled Pickering's desire to deport Joseph Priestley, the English scientist and political radical, of whom the Adamses had been fond during their stay in England.

The Sedition Act was of more consequence to the Adams administration. By accepting it as a temporary war measure, the president appeared to side with those Federalist newspaper editors whose vitriolic language denounced in every issue the Republican papers as instruments of foreign subversion. Adams approved of at least two prosecutions of opposition editors, and he made no effort to halt the trials or to grant the petitions for pardon of the convicted. Particularly conspicuous was his rejection of the petition of several thousand Vermonters asking a pardon for Congressman Matthew Lyon, who had been convicted of sedition but reelected to Congress while in jail.

In keeping with his independence, Adams expressed a desire to charge some of the most outrageous Federalist editors with sedition. His main culpability lay in turning over enforcement of the Sedition Act to Pickering and permitting him to interpret the law as broadly as possible. Pickering's zeal resulted in at least fourteen indictments under the act in addition to three under common law. The secretary's attempt to wipe out criticism of the Federalist regime ensured that the Sedition Act would be a major issue in the next presidential election and actually increased the number of opposition newspapers. Criticism of the government could not be suppressed among a people who had fought for freedom of speech and press for a century before the First Amendment was written into the Constitution.

The Republican response to the Alien and Sedition Acts included the Kentucky Resolutions (drafted by Jefferson) and the Virginia Resolutions (drafted by Madison). Challenging the constitutionality of the Sedition Act, these resolutions implied the natural right of a state to nullify the enforcement of such an act within its boundaries. In reply the High Federalists raised the specter of disunion, and Hamilton expressed his willingness to march his army south to test Virginia's resistance. In the middle stood John Adams, increasingly more trusted by some Republicans than by the anti-French element in his own party.

Recovered from his defeat on the question of Hamilton's military rank, Adams by 1799 was using his power as commander in chief in the interests of peace. The provisional army, intended only as a temporary emergency measure, had not been brought into existence by the time its authorization expired in December 1798. The president was left with authority to increase the regular army, raise militia forces, and accept the services of voluntary military companies. While deliberately slowing the recruit-

ment of enlisted men, Adams saw political advantage in appointing moderate men from both parties to be officers in an army that he never expected to take the field. High Federalists charged him with obstructing preparedness for war, while Republicans pointed to the slowly growing army as a threat to civil liberties. Once again Adams stood in the middle and attempted to draw others to him.

In Adams' mind the navy remained the first line of defense, but the army was now necessary only to exert diplomatic pressure on France. Following the president's orders, the navy since early in 1799 had been assisting Toussaint L'Ouverture in extending his control over St. Domingue (Hispaniola) after the slaves on that West Indian island had driven out most of their French masters and repelled a British invasion. The continued success of the *Constellation,* one of the recently completed frigates, against French naval vessels in the West Indies confirmed the president's faith in the "wooden walls" of the navy.

In October 1799, John Adams rode out of Quincy and headed back to Trenton, which was again the temporary capital. During the seven months the president had been away, the three cabinet members loyal to Hamilton would have welcomed the creation of a ministerial government to wrest power from the absent and, in their opinion, incompetent chief executive. But there was no constitutional way to turn the president into a figurehead. Adams knew it and rejected several pleas that he return to the seat of government. In August he had received the additional assurances he sought from France that the American envoys would be well received. Consequently, he ordered Pickering to prepare the instructions for the peace commission. The secretary reluctantly obeyed without ceasing his efforts to block the mission. A change in the French government appeared to strengthen Pickering's hand. Stoddert and Lee finally convinced the president that he must hasten to the capital to take personal charge of dispatching the commissioners.

When Adams reached Trenton, he found Hamilton there to join Pickering, McHenry, and Wolcott in demanding that he not send the peace mission. They argued that a treaty with France would bring retaliation from Great Britain and would stain America's national honor. But Adams stood his ground. On 16 October 1799, without advance notice to the cabinet, he ordered Ellsworth and William Richardson Davie to join Murray in Europe. The following March the three met in Paris and opened negotiations with the French government, now headed by First Consul Napoleon Bonaparte.

Adams' peaceful gestures had temporarily revived the popularity of the Federalist party and enabled it to make significant gains in the House and Senate elections of 1799. Then the dispatch of the commissioners irreparably split the party between the aggressive minority headed by Hamilton and the more politically obscure majority supporting Adams. The president's third annual message to Congress on 3 December struck hard at the program of the High Federalists. He called for a "just execution of the laws" to ensure that "individuals should be guarded from oppression," for peace with honor, and for economy in government without inordinate expenditures for defense. The death of Washington on 14 December further weakened the Hamiltonians, who had hoped to secure his endorsement of their military objectives. This great man's death, Hamilton wrote, had removed a "control" on the "perverseness and capriciousness" of the president.

Election of 1800

The presidential election of 1800 brought the Federalist split into the open. Adams wanted the second term for which he had been nominated by congressional caucus; thus, he appeared willing to endure the enemies in his party as long as he had a hope of reelection. That hope was considerably lessened on 1 May when the Republicans captured the New York legislature, which would cast the state's electoral vote. Adams then moved quickly. He confronted McHenry with the charge of disloyalty and accepted his resignation on 6 May. The following week Adams demanded Pickering's resignation and dismissed him when he refused to resign. John Marshall, a Virginia Federalist loyal to Adams, was immediately confirmed as secretary of state. Apparently fond of Wolcott despite his disloyalty, Adams permitted the secretary of the treasury to remain in office until the end of 1800. The president had refused to raise Hamilton to the top command of the army after Washington's death, and in May he gladly signed the congressional acts that provided for a drastic reduction in the army.

By now Hamilton was determined to end Adams' political career, regardless of the consequences to the Federalist party. He wrote, "If we must have an *enemy* at the head of Government, let it be one whom we can oppose, and for whom we are not responsible, who will not involve our party in the disgrace of his foolish and bad measures." He urged Pickering to gather as he left office any material in the archives that could be used against Adams. From Wolcott he also sought "the facts which denote unfitness in Mr. Adams."

In July, Hamilton abandoned his plans for military conquest and returned to his law practice. He advised his followers to manipulate the electoral votes in their states so that the Federalist vice presidential candidate, Charles Cotesworth Pinckney, would receive more votes than Adams and thus be elected president. His final stroke in this campaign marked the conclusion of his decline from brilliant statesman to bungling, vindictive politician. Against the advice of his closest supporters, he wrote and printed the *Letter . . . Concerning the Public Conduct and Character of John Adams.* Ostensibly prepared only for private circulation, the *Letter* somehow reached the press, and Hamilton then published it as a pamphlet. For nearly fifty pages, he reviewed the "great and intrinsic defects" in Adams that rendered him "unfit" for the presidency. The *Letter* had little apparent effect on the outcome of the election, and numerous replies from men of both parties applauded Adams' refusal to bend to the will of the former secretary.

The division among Federalists left Adams annoyed and discouraged but undaunted. In May 1800, after Congress had adjourned and Mrs. Adams had set out for Quincy, he traveled by a circuitous route to inspect the capital being built at Washington. The enthusiastic receptions he received along the way buoyed his spirits and led him to regard more highly his chance of reelection. As he journeyed from Philadelphia to Washington and then to Quincy, he defended his administration and himself with such vigor that one historian of his presidency has concluded that Adams was "the first presidential candidate in history to carry his appeal directly to the people." Then he spent the summer at home, conducting the nation's business by mail and addressing only those delegations that called on him at Quincy.

By 1 November he was in Washington, where he took up residence in the President's House, later known as the White House. In this unfinished but habitable building, he felt at once a sense of destiny as he prayed, "May none but honest and wise Men ever rule under this roof." Mrs. Adams joined him after two weeks and endeavored to preserve the dignity of the presidential household while living in a house with still damp plaster walls and lacking stairways, firewood, and bells to summon the inadequate number of servants. This remarkable woman, on whose strength her husband had constantly depended, would perhaps be pleased to know that posterity did not forget that the First Lady had hung her laundry to dry in the "great unfinished audience room"—later the East Room—of the White House.

The president's fourth annual message to Congress on 22 November radiated pride in the results of his administration. The nation had a permanent seat of government, the provisional army had been disbanded, the victories of the navy had increased the self-esteem of Americans, a treaty of amity and commerce had been concluded with Prussia, negotiations were under way to settle the remaining issues with Great Britain, and a peaceful accommodation with France was expected. But this message proved to be his valedictory. By the second week in December, Adams knew that he would not have another term. News had arrived that South Carolina had deserted its favorite son, Pinckney, to choose electors favoring the Republicans. Although the electoral ballots would not be formally counted until February, the unofficial tally revealed the Republican victory.

The bitterness of defeat mingled with elation in the Adams household, for at about the same time as the news from South Carolina, Commissioner Davie arrived in Washington bearing the treaty concluded with France at the end of September. In the exalted language of diplomacy, this Convention of Môrtefontaine called for "a firm, inviolable, and universal peace, and a true and sincere Friendship between" the two nations. It provided for the restoration of commercial relations on the most-favored-nation principle and the ending of the Quasi-War. The president promptly submitted the treaty to the Senate, where the High Federalists delayed its ratification until 3 February. But the country as a whole, especially the merchants, welcomed peace. The necessary two-thirds vote for ratification was finally obtained when the Senate accepted reservations on the most objectionable points. Unhappy with the reservations, Adams nevertheless approved the ratification and ordered the navy to cease hostilities against French ships.

When the electoral votes were counted in the Senate on 11 February 1801, Adams had sixty-five, Pinckney sixty-four, and Burr and Jefferson seventy-three each. Despite the split of the Federalists, the Alien and Sedition Acts, the Fries Rebellion, the gall of the opposition press, and above all the heavy taxes for defense, the president had run remarkably strongly. A shift of a few hundred votes in the New York legislative election would have given a second term to the president from Massachusetts, who had received all of New England's electoral vote and had improved his vote of 1796 in Pennsylvania and North Carolina.

President Adams took no public part in the political crisis created by the inadvertent tie in the Republican electoral vote for Jefferson and Burr. When Burr, the vice presidential candidate, refused to step aside, the decision fell to the lame-duck House of Representatives, with its Federalist majority. In keeping with his view of his office, Adams let the House fulfill its constitutional responsibility without the influence of the chief executive.

Both the Adamses much preferred Jefferson to Burr. Mrs. Adams likely spoke her husband's mind when she wrote that "neither party can tolerate Burr." The Republican leadership counted on a presidential veto of any congressional bill that attempted to take advantage of the tie to thwart the Republican victory. Adams could hardly have failed to learn that Virginia and Pennsylvania threatened civil war if the Federalists used the deadlock to remain in power. Yet he refused to commit himself in his one recorded meeting with Jefferson. He feared not so much Jefferson, whose integrity he had come to respect while they had been together in France during the Revolution, as he feared the horde of radicals who, he believed, would come into office on Jefferson's coattails. Nonetheless, when the House finally ended the crisis on 17 February by selecting Jefferson, Adams was relieved that he could leave office with the nation intact.

Reform of the Judiciary

John Adams' last three months in office were largely taken up with the reform of the federal judiciary. The country had soon outgrown the judicial structure created in 1789. That system provided for a Supreme Court of six justices, regional circuit courts, and district courts, with a Supreme Court justice required to preside over each session of a circuit court. The result was a nearly impossible schedule of travel for the justices, and one might be called upon to hear an appeal of a case he had helped to decide at a lower level. Frequent petitions from the justices had brought only minor relief, and it had become difficult to get able lawyers to accept appointment to the highest court.

In his annual messages of 1799 and 1800, the president had recommended judicial reform, but Congress proved unable to agree on a bill until after the results of the presidential election were known. Then the Judiciary Act of 1801 moved rapidly through Congress and was signed by Adams on 13 February. It reduced the Supreme Court from six to five at the next vacancy and created six new circuit courts presided over by sixteen new circuit judges, thus relieving the Supreme Court justices of circuit duty. A related act in the last week of February provided for an additional district court with three judges for the District of Columbia.

While Congress debated the Judiciary Act, Adams hurried to appoint a new chief justice of the Supreme Court. After serving on the peace mission, Chief Justice Ellsworth had remained in Europe to recover his health, and his resignation had reached the president in December. Unless a replacement could be confirmed before the Judiciary Act became law, there would be no vacancy and one of the associate justices would have to become chief justice. By appointing a Federalist and thus keeping the Court at six, Adams could make it unlikely that the incoming Republican president would be able to place a member of his own party on the bench for many years.

The favorite of many Federalists, Associate Justice William Paterson, was too close to Hamilton to please Adams. Instead, he nominated, and the Senate confirmed, John Jay, the first chief justice, who had left the Court to be governor of New York. Not in the best of health and regarding the judicial system as seriously "defective," Jay declined. It then dawned on Adams that his secretary of state, John Marshall, possessed the ideal qualities of age, diligence, and legal talent. He appointed Marshall on 20 January. The Senate delayed his confirmation a week while supporters of Paterson sought to change the president's mind. In February 1801 the chief justice whom history would acknowledge as the nation's greatest presided over his first session of the Supreme Court.

Altogether in the last ten weeks of his term, Adams appointed more than two hundred new judges, clerks, marshals, attorneys, and justices of the peace. He filled nearly all of these positions with Federalists of various shades, but most were moderate men of considerable ability. Thus he made one last great effort to put into practice his view of the presidency. On Tuesday evening, 3 March 1801, he signed the final three commissions. At four the next morning he left for Quincy, not waiting to witness the inauguration of Jefferson. Grieving over the recent death of his wayward son Charles and believing his duty finished, he headed into a retirement that would last until 4 July 1826, when both he and Jefferson died on the fiftieth anniversary of the independence of the nation in whose creation they had played such a major part.

Evaluation

Coming between the administrations of two presidents of immortal fame, the presidency of John Adams has been difficult for historians to evaluate and for posterity to appreciate. He had neither Washington's ability to inspire reverence nor Jefferson's understanding of democratic ideas. In his own view, his greatest achievement had been to make peace with France, but modern research has emphasized that Talleyrand and Napoleon neither wanted nor expected a military encounter with the United States and, therefore, that a stronger settlement with France might have been possible. He also took great pride in his elevation of John Marshall to the Supreme Court; yet in 1801 he could not have foreseen the strength that Marshall would infuse into the federal judiciary for the next three decades.

The contribution of the Adams presidency lay not so much in its specific accomplishments as in its strengthening the office at a critical time when it might easily have veered off the course set by Washington. Adams' conception of a strong, independent president who mediated between contending interests enabled him to withstand the violent political passions of the time, which threatened to tear apart the young republic.

Adams' view of the office and his detestation of parties and factions rendered him incapable of bridging the constitutional separation of powers through party leadership. But had he tried, he could not have succeeded, for the Federalists were not a party in the modern sense. As Adams expressed it, his party was "composed of the most heterogeneous ingredients that ever were put together." Only such an independent president as Adams could have prevented the various Federalist factions from further splintering the party and possibly the nation itself during the four years after the retirement of Washington. No one can be entirely certain of Hamilton's intentions in this period, but the available evidence strongly suggests that any president following his lead would have provoked civil war. Or had Jefferson been elected in 1796, when he fell short by only three electoral votes, he could scarcely have convinced the northern states that he was not a tool of France. In this respect, Jefferson owed far more to Adams than he seems to have realized. As Joseph Charles has pointed out, the four years under Adams provided the correct balance of motivation and time for Jeffersonian democracy to develop as a political movement and for the Republicans to gain experience, clarify their principles, and perfect the organization with which they were to govern the nation for the next twenty-eight years.

When, seven years after leaving Washington, John Adams expressed approval of his son John Quincy Adams' switching parties from Federalist to Republican, he provided testimony to the success of his own administration.

BIBLIOGRAPHY

The voluminous manuscripts of Adams and his family are being published in a modern edition that has not yet reached his presidential years. Those volumes already published are essential for the period before 1797. These include Robert J. Taylor, ed., *Papers of John Adams*, vols. 1–10 (Cambridge, Mass., 1977–1995); L. H. Butterfield, ed., *Diary and Autobiography of John Adams*, vols. 1–4 (Cambridge, Mass., 1961); and Butterfield, ed., *Adams Family Correspondence*, vols. 1–6 (Cambridge, Mass., 1963–1993). Still useful is Charles Francis Adams, ed., *The Works of John Adams*, 10 vols. (Boston, 1850–1856). James D. Richardson, ed., *A Compilation of the Messages and Papers of the Presidents*, vol. 1 (New York, 1897), is a convenient source of the communications between the president and Congress.

Page Smith, *John Adams*, 2 vols. (Garden City, N.Y., 1962), is the fullest biography. John Ferling, *John Adams: A Life* (Knoxville, Tenn., 1992), is a comprehensive one-volume biography. John R. Howe, Jr., *The Changing Political Thought of John Adams* (Princeton, N.J., 1966), gives a full account of Adams's political theories. Stephen G. Kurtz, *The Presidency of John Adams: The Collapse of Federalism, 1795–1800* (Philadelphia, 1957), is a major study

of the politics of the Adams presidency. Ralph Adams Brown, *The Presidency of John Adams* (Lawrence, Kans., 1975), is a favorable account of the Adams presidency. James Roger Sharp, *American Politics in the Early Republic: The New Nation in Crisis* (New Haven, Conn., 1993), argues that the Adams presidency suffered from flaws in the Constitution. Stanley M. Elkins and Eric L. McKitrick, *The Age of Federalism* (New York, 1993), discusses the conflicting views of Adams and his presidency. Joseph J. Ellis, *Passionate Sage: The Character and Legacy of John Adams* (New York, 1993), views Adams's thought from the perspective of the period after he left office.

Joseph Charles, *The Origins of the American Party System: Three Essays* (Williamsburg, Va., 1956), offers important insights into the origin of parties. Leonard D. White, *The Federalists: A Study in Administrative History* (New York, 1948), is a topical study of the administrative functions of the federal government under Washington and Adams. Manning J. Dauer, *The Adams Federalists* (Baltimore, 1953), contains useful statistical information on the Federalists. James Morton Smith, *Freedom's Fetters: The Alien and Sedition Laws and American Civil Liberties* (Ithaca, N.Y., 1956), is the major study of the Alien and Sedition Acts. Donald H. Stewart, *The Opposition Press of the Federalist Period* (Albany, N.Y., 1969), is a source book of newspaper attacks on the Federalists. Dan Sisson, *The American Revolution of 1800* (New York, 1974), develops the relationship between the Adams presidency and Jeffersonian democracy.

George Athan Billias, *Elbridge Gerry: Founding Father and Republican Statesman* (New York, 1976), is a biography of Adams's major Republican friend. Gerard H. Clarfield, *Timothy Pickering and American Diplomacy, 1795–1800* (Columbia, Mo., 1969), is a full study of Adams's secretary of state. Harold C. Syrett et al., eds., *The Papers of Alexander Hamilton*, vols. 20–25 (New York, 1974–1977), provides a major documentary source for the Adams administration with important annotation. Jacob E. Cooke, *Alexander Hamilton* (New York, 1982), is an outstanding interpretive work. Broadus Mitchell, *Alexander Hamilton*, vol. 2 (New York, 1962), covers Hamilton's years in the federal government. Gilbert L. Lycan, *Alexander Hamilton and American Foreign Policy: A Design for Greatness* (Norman, Okla., 1970), provides an extensive treatment of Hamilton's influence on American foreign policy.

Marshall Smelser, *The Congress Founds the Navy, 1787–1798* (South Bend, Ind., 1959), is a full study of the creation of the American navy. Bradford Perkins, *The First Rapprochement: England and the United States, 1795–1805* (Philadelphia, 1955), describes the relations of the Adams administration with Great Britain. William Stinchcombe, *The XYZ Affair* (Westport, Conn., 1980), presents new research on this episode. Alexander DeConde, *The Quasi-War: The Politics and Diplomacy of the Undeclared War with France, 1797–1801* (New York, 1966), is the major study of the undeclared war. Michael A. Palmer, *Stoddert's War: Naval Operations During the Quasi-War with France, 1798–1801* (Columbia, S.C., 1987), describes the importance of the navy in Adams's view.

Leonard Baker, *John Marshall: A Life in Law* (New York, 1974), contains an extensive account of Marshall's part in the Adams administration. George Lee Haskins and Herbert A. Johnson, *History of the Supreme Court of the United States*, vol. 2, *Founda-tions of Power: John Marshall, 1801–1815* (New York, 1981), offers an extensive treatment with bibliographical references of the restructuring of the federal judiciary under Adams.

Charles W. Akers, *Abigail Adams: An American Woman* (Boston, 1980), examines her role in the Adams presidency. Stewart Mitchell, ed., *New Letters of Abigail Adams, 1788–1801* (Boston, 1947), contains letters of Abigail Adams to her sister that often detail political developments. Edith B. Gelles, *Portia: The World of Abigail Adams* (Bloomington, Ind., 1992), examines other recent biographies of Abigail Adams and attempts to place her in a female rather than a political culture.

Recent works include David McCullough, *John Adams* (New York, 2001), and Bernard A. Weisberger, *America Afire: Jefferson, Adams, and the Revolutionary Election of 1800* (New York, 2000).

Thomas Jefferson

Merrill D. Peterson

Thomas Jefferson THE NATIONAL PORTRAIT GALLERY/
SMITHSONIAN INSTITUTION

THOMAS JEFFERSON was inaugurated third president of the United States on 4 March 1801 in the infant capital on the Potomac. Raw, brash, and eager, a sprawling village of three thousand people—"a place with a few bad houses, extensive swamps, hanging on the skirts of a too thinly peopled, weak and barren country"—Washington was a fitting symbol of the new nation itself. Two "shining objects" relieved the dismal scene: the President's House, gleaming under its coat of whitewash, and the Capitol, looking like some truncated Roman monument, its north wing alone awkwardly perched on the summit of a hill.

Surrounded by friends, Jefferson walked to the Capitol from a nearby boardinghouse; at noon, without pomp or ceremony, he entered the crowded Senate chamber and took his place on the platform between Aaron Burr, his successor as vice president, and John Marshall, the chief justice of the United States. The election that brought Jefferson to the presidency had been bitterly contested by the two political parties, Federalists and Republicans, and only finally terminated on 17 February in the choice by the House of Representatives between himself and his Republican running mate, Burr. Now, after Marshall administered the oath of office, the fifty-seven-year-old Virginian, tall and lanky, with a ruddy face, bright hazel eyes, and graying hair, rose to deliver his inaugural address.

The address—a political touchstone for a century to come—combined a lofty appeal for the restoration of "harmony and affection" with a brilliant summation of the Republican creed: "We have called by different names brethren of the same principle. We are all republicans: we are all federalists." Believing that the mass of Americans, regardless of party, were fundamentally united in their political sentiments, Jefferson hoped to extinguish the strife, hatred, and fanaticism—the spirit of European politics—that had rocked the Republic during its first decade.

The new president looked to the disappearance of parties and "a perfect consolidation of political sentiments" as the government was restored to its true principles. These principles he traced back to the American Revolution. Equal justice to all men; freedom of speech, press, and religion; majority rule and minority rights; supremacy of the civil over the military authority; economy in the public expense; the encouragement of agriculture and commerce; peace and commerce with all nations, but entangling alliances with none—these should be "the creed of our political faith," said Jefferson. He spoke of preserving "the whole constitutional vigor" of the general government yet called for "a wise and frugal government, which shall restrain men from injuring one another, which shall leave them otherwise free to regulate their own pursuits of industry and improvement, and shall not take from the mouth of labor the bread it has earned." His point was not to place liberty and government in irreconcilable opposition but, rather, to declare his conviction that a free and democratic government, for all its weakness by Old World standards, was, in fact

the strongest government on earth. I believe it is the only one where every man, at the call of the law, would fly to the standard of the law, and would meet invasions of the public order as his own personal concern. Sometimes it is said that man cannot be trusted with the government of himself. Can he, then, be trusted with the government of others? Or have we found angels in the form of kings to govern him? Let history answer this question.

In retrospect, Jefferson called the Republican ascendancy "the revolution of 1800." It was, he said, "as real a revolution in the principles of our government as that of 1776 was in its form; not effected indeed by the sword, as that, but by the rational and

peaceable instrument of reform, the suffrage of the people."

Early Career

Born on 13 April 1743 in Goochland (now Albemarle) County, Virginia, and educated at the College of William and Mary, Jefferson rose to fame as the draftsman of revolutionary state papers, first in Virginia and then in the Continental Congress, where, of course, he became the author of the Declaration of Independence. In the Declaration's celebrated preamble, Jefferson reduced the "natural rights" philosophy of the age to a set of first principles that had a profound influence on the course of the American Revolution. Proceeding from these principles, Jefferson himself sought far-reaching reforms in his native state. He was only partially successful. The Virginia assembly in 1786 enacted his Statute for Religious Freedom; it rejected much more, including his comprehensive plan of public education, although in Jefferson's opinion it was essential to the citizen-republicanism of the new nation. He was governor of Virginia (1779–1781)—his first executive office—during the trying circumstance of war and invasion, and left office under a cloud of criticism that was never completely dispelled.

In 1784, after a brief turn in Congress, Jefferson was sent to Europe on a diplomatic mission. The following year he succeeded Benjamin Franklin as American minister to France. From that vantage point, he observed the coming of the French Revolution. Closely associated with liberal, enlightened circles in Paris, he sympathized with the revolutionary impulse but sought to direct it into moderate and pacific channels of reform. Although he never confused France with America, Jefferson became an ardent friend of the French Revolution and in time assimilated some of its radical doctrine into his political philosophy.

In 1790, Jefferson was named secretary of state in the new national government. He had approved of the Constitution, especially with the promised addition of a bill of rights, and accepted high office under President George Washington out of a sense of loyalty to him and responsibility to the new experiment. In the conduct of the nation's foreign affairs, Jefferson sought to lessen American dependence on British commerce and to open freer channels of trade in a commercial system centered on France. He sought to redeem the trans-Appalachian West from the colonialism of the Spanish to the south and the British to the north, which would contribute as well to the pacification of the Indian tribes. He also sought to take advantage of any war that might occur between European powers by the manipulation of American trade and neutrality.

Pursuing these goals, Jefferson was frustrated by events and also by the secretary of the treasury, Alexander Hamilton, whose fiscal system turned on British trade, credit, and power and who was as hostile to the French Revolution as Jefferson was friendly. The conflict with Hamilton extended to domestic policy and came to involve fundamentally different conceptions of republican government under the Constitution. Along this division, opposing political parties formed. Washington tried to keep peace in his official family, but the task proved to be impossible. At the end of 1793, Jefferson, who had little taste for political combat, resigned and retired to his Virginia home, Monticello.

Elected vice president in 1796, Jefferson at first hoped for a restoration of political concord in the administration of his old friend John Adams. Instead, partisanship reigned as the nation was again plunged into a foreign crisis growing out of the protracted war between the French republic and the monarchical coalition headed by Great Britain. The administration was Federalist; and Jefferson, who had expected that the vice presidency would be "honorable and easy," while the presidency was but "splendid misery," found himself thrust into the leadership of the opposition party. Passage of the Alien and Sedition Acts in the war hysteria of 1798 brought the conflict between these infant parties to a head.

Considering the laws oppressive, unconstitutional, and designed to cripple the Republican party, Jefferson went outside the general government, fully controlled by the Federalists, to start "a revolution of opinion" against them. The Virginia and Kentucky resolutions (1798–1799), authored respectively by Madison and Jefferson, invoked the authority of these two state legislatures to declare the Alien and Sedition Acts unconstitutional. The resolutions were assertions of states' rights doctrine, and as such they posed the issue on which the Civil War would later be fought. More important, however, they originated in a desperate struggle for political survival and addressed the fundamental issue of freedom and self-government descending from the American Revolution. By going outside the government, opening peaceful channels of change through the agitation of public opinion, and building a party in the broad electorate, the Jeffersonian Republicans rose to power in 1800.

Jefferson's Presidential Leadership

Jefferson's inaugural address was a commitment to ongoing change through the democratic process. He named "absolute acquiescence in the decisions of the majority the vital principle of republics, from which there is no appeal but to force." The principle demanded freedom of opinion and debate, including the right of any minority to turn itself into a new majority. "If there be any among us," Jefferson said, "who would wish to dissolve this Union or to change its republican form, let them stand undisturbed as monuments of the safety with which error may be tolerated where reason is left free to combat it." This was the authentic revolution of 1800. Because of it, the Constitution became an instrument of democracy, change became possible without destruction, and government could go forward with the continuing consent of the governed.

The new president named to his cabinet men known to be moderate Republicans. The Federalists' fears were assuaged; Republicans of a more radical persuasion were disappointed. James Madison, the secretary of state, had been Jefferson's political friend and partner for many years. Secretary of War Henry Dearborn and Attorney General Levi Lincoln were Massachusetts Republicans appointed, in part, to nudge that important state into the Republican column. Robert Smith, the secretary of the navy, owed his appointment to his brother, Samuel Smith, the influential representative of Baltimore's mercantile Republican interests. Albert Gallatin of Pennsylvania was the only controversial appointment. His Swiss birth, forensic prowess, and wizardry with treasury figures had combined to make the forty-year-old congressman a Federalist whipping boy. But Jefferson prized Gallatin's abilities, and the new secretary, who had been a sharp critic of Hamilton's fiscal policies, proved to be a force for moderation in the administration. The stability and harmony of this cabinet would never be equaled. In the eight years of Jefferson's presidency, only the part-time office of attorney general changed hands.

The model of executive unity, concentrating all powers of decision in the president, had been established by Washington, then had broken down under

Adams. Jefferson restored it, but he dominated his administration more surely and completely than Washington had done. To the formal authority of the office, Jefferson added the authority of party leader. He had enormous public prestige as the spokesman of republican principles and national ideals. By some personal magnetism he drew men to him, persuaded them to follow, and inspired their loyalty. His style of leadership was averse to dissension and controversy. He sought to engender amiability and, wherever possible, to grasp "the smooth handle." Business was conducted through day-to-day consultation with the secretaries. The cabinet met infrequently, but when it did, usually on critical foreign problems, Jefferson invariably managed to produce a consensus. He led without having to command; he dominated without ruling.

Jefferson also dominated Congress. In 1801, for the first time, the Republicans controlled both houses of Congress. The Federalists were a shrinking minority, yet they were by no means powerless. Their obstructionist tactics would have proved very damaging if the Republicans had not stuck together. In Republican theory, borrowed from the Whig theory of the Revolution, Congress was superior to the executive and the executive should not interfere in legislative business. Jefferson honored the theory, at least in official discourse, but he recognized that practically the government demanded presidential leadership if any majority, whether Federalist or Republican, was to carry out its program. Congress could not lead. During the Federalist decade it had performed best under Hamilton's ministerial guidance. The problem had been easier for the Federalists, for they had no "least government" dogmas to overcome, no deep-seated fears of "monarchical" power; and compared to the Republicans, they formed a fairly cohesive body. The Republican majority was a loose coalition of jarring interests, experienced only in opposition and jealous of executive power.

How, then, could the Republican president overcome the "separation of powers" and make Congress an effective instrument for realizing the administration's objectives? The solution was found partly in the personal influence Jefferson commanded and partly in the network of party leadership outside constitutional channels. As the unchallenged head of the Republican party, Jefferson acted with an authority he did not possess—indeed, utterly disclaimed—in his official capacity. His long arm reached out, usually through cabinet officers, to Capitol Hill, where the leaders of both houses were his political lieutenants. Presidential leadership was thus locked into congressional leadership. And despite the weak structural organization of the Republican party in Congress, it was a pervasive functional reality. The president chose a newspaper, the *National Intelligencer,* in the capital as the administration organ; he kept up a steady stream of communication with Congress and party leaders; he turned his house into a kind of social club and spent countless weary hours and a substantial part of his $25,000 salary entertaining congressmen. (A widower, he had no "first lady", Dolley Madison sometimes performed that role, as did Jefferson's elder daughter, Martha, on her visits to the capital.)

The president was not only chief magistrate but chief legislator as well. Nearly all the legislation during eight years originated with the president and his secretaries. Lacking staff support of any kind, Congress depended on executive initiatives and usually followed them. Federalist congressmen complained of the "behind the curtain" or "backstairs" influence of the president. Eventually some Republicans rebelled. But the system of presidential leadership worked with unerring precision during Jefferson's first term. It worked less well once the Republicans, with virtually no opposition to contend against, began to quarrel among themselves, as they did during Jefferson's second term; and it would not work at all under his successor, Madison, who lacked both his public authority and personal magnetism.

During the early months, Jefferson found the task of making appointments to office exceedingly irksome. Not counting military officers, postmasters, and other minor civil functionaries, there were 316 major offices in the gift of the federal executive. They were monopolized by Federalists. Jefferson's preference was to remove as few as possible, with a view to converting the mass of Federalists to the Republican cause. He was repelled by the principle, already reduced to practice in New York and Pennsylvania, of making party affiliation the sole or primary test of public appointment. The politics of spoils and proscription degraded republican government. Nothing more should be asked of civil servants, he said, than that they be honest, able, and loyal to the Constitution. As important as the principle was in the abstract, it was more important in practice because of its obvious fitness to the attainment of the political harmony and consolidation envisioned in the inaugural address.

Many Republicans, whether from partisan principle or interest, disagreed with this strategy. The Federalist leaders, some said, were incorrigible; any temporizing with them would only disgust the mass of Republicans and jeopardize the administration. Others hungered for the spoils of victory. If the expulsion of Federalists and the appointment of Republicans "should not be the case, for what, in the name of God, have we been contending?" they asked. At the outset, Jefferson held his ground. He limited removals to two classes of officeholders. The first was Adams' "midnight appointments"—indeed, all appointments except judgeships in good behavior made after 12 December 1800, when the president knew he had been defeated. This office-packing by a lame-duck administration was intolerable, and Jefferson considered all these appointments "nullities." The second class included officials found guilty of misconduct. Jefferson especially had in mind federal marshals and attorneys who had forfeited the public trust by their enforcement of the Sedition Act. By January 1802 he counted twenty-one removals of midnight appointments and fifteen removals for misconduct of any kind.

Within a few months partisan pressures from both sides caused the president to modify his patronage policy. The issue came to a head in Connecticut, where the Federalists controlled everything; the Republicans were weak, systematically excluded from the state government, and treated as outcasts of society. Only by federal appointment could they get a political foot in the door. When Jefferson removed a midnight appointment and named a Republican in his place as collector of the port of New Haven, the local merchants and Federalists angrily remonstrated. In reply, Jefferson defended his actions and the right of the Republicans to a fair share of the federal offices. Continued Federalist monopoly defeated the will of the people. "If a due participation of office is a matter of right, how are vacancies to be obtained?" he asked. "Those by death are few; by resignation, none. Can any other mode than that of removal be proposed?" Heretofore the answer had been yes, the mode of conciliation and conversion; and the idea that party allegiance alone was just ground for removal or that the subordinate offices should rotate with the popular will had been rejected. Proposing now, in the summer of 1801, before this demonstration of Federalist intransigence to give the Republicans "a proportionate share" of the offices, Jefferson introduced the partisan standard of removal and appointment in the federal government. In practice, he showed a good deal of flexibility, adapting the policy to varying local situations. By the end of 1803, he had appointed Republicans to one-half the major offices. Federalist patronage, like the party, had been elitist. Jefferson broadened the base of the civil establishment, taking in more westerners and more men of talent without wealth, privilege, or status, thereby making it more representative of American society.

The Republican ascendancy embittered the shrinking Federalist minority. Thomas Paine's return to the United States at the president's invitation in 1802 started up the old slanders of Jacobinism and infidelity. At the same time Jefferson faced a new libel by the grubstreet journalist and disappointed office-seeker James T. Callender, adopted by some of the Federalists, that he had for many years kept an "African concubine," Sally Hemings, at Monticello and was the father by her of several slave children. Thus began the prolific career of a story that would on occasion figure prominently in accounts of Jefferson's personal life, which were necessarily speculative because of his care in guarding his privacy. As with other libels about him, he never replied publicly to this one, doubtless on the theory that any reply would only stimulate rather than arrest it. Moreover, he was committed to what he called his "experiment" in unfettered freedom of the press; and although he twice acquiesced in state prosecutions for libel, he did no injury to that experiment. Almost two centuries later, in the fall of 1998, the results of DNA testing of Jefferson and Hemings descendents provided support for the idea that Jefferson was the father of at least one of Sally Hemings' children, Eston. But in the absence of direct documentary evidence either proving or refuting the allegation, nothing conclusive can be said about Jefferson's relations with Sally Hemings.

Fiscal and Judiciary Reform

Republican reform was grounded on fiscal policy. In the Jeffersonian scripture, public debt and taxes were evils of the first magnitude. The debt drained money from the mass of citizens, diverted it from the productive enterprise of individuals, and led to a system of privilege, coercion, and corruption that was the bane of every government and fatal to a free one. The alternatives were clear: "Economy and liberty, profusion and servitude." The debt, which had actually increased under the Federalists, stood at $83 million and consumed in annual interest almost half the federal revenue. Gallatin developed a plan to extinguish the debt in sixteen years by large annual appropriations but, amazingly, to reduce taxes at the same time. All the internal taxes—Hamilton's whiskey excise, the land tax of the Adams administration—would be repealed. The government would depend entirely on the revenue of the customhouses. The plan required deep retrenchment: reductions in the army and navy, in foreign embassies, and in civil offices, beginning with the tax collectors.

The plan, which Jefferson outlined in his first annual message to Congress, was liable to two main objections. It assumed peace, and although the principles of the Peace of Amiens had been agreed upon, this was a risky assumption in the world of William Pitt and Napoleon Bonaparte and seemed to jeopardize the nation's defense in favor of niggardly economy. Moreover, the plan rested on a doubtful theory of political economy for a developing nation. The theory looked to economic growth through release of the energies, talents, and resources of free individuals without the direct aid or favor of the government. The opposite theory, of which Hamilton was an early practitioner, assigned to the government a positive role in economic development. It supposed that a nation might grow out of debt by going deeper into debt to promote development. The logic of this escaped Jefferson, but he knew that Hamilton's system of debt and taxes involved powers and privileges that were incompatible with republican government under the Constitution.

Jefferson's fiscal program placed the administration on unassailable ground with Republicans in Congress. Men rubbed their eyes in disbelief at the spectacle of the chief magistrate renouncing taxes, patronage, and power. It promised, said an English observer, "a sort of Millennium in government." The program was rapidly put in place. During the next seven years the nation was liberated of $33 million of debt. In the end, of course, the program was derailed by foreign crisis and war. Thirty-four years would pass before retirement of the national debt.

Pitched on the horns of his dilemma, reformation or reconciliation, the president agonized a good deal about the Hamiltonian fiscal system. He reflected in 1802,

> When the government was first established, it was possible to have kept it going on true principles, but the contracted, English, half-lettered ideas of Hamilton destroyed that hope in the bud. We can pay off his debt in 15 years, but we can never get rid of his financial system. It mortifies me to be strengthening principles which I deem radically vicious, but the vice is entailed on us by the first error.. . . What is practicable must often control pure theory.

A clear case in point was Hamilton's Bank of the United States. Jefferson thought it an institution of "the most deadly hostility" to republican government, yet the bank's national charter ran to 1811. Gallatin, meanwhile, found the bank a highly serviceable institution and actually expanded its operations. The demand for credit in a thriving economy was insatiable. State-chartered banks multiplied, and a banking interest grew up in the Republican party. Although it played havoc with his ideal of a plain and dignified republican order, Jefferson could neither injure nor ignore it. "What is practicable must often control pure theory."

The federal judiciary furnished the principal political battleground of Jefferson's first term. There were three battles and many skirmishes in the so-called war on the judiciary. The first was fought over the Federalist Judiciary Act of 1801. This eleventh-hour act of a dying administration created a whole new tier of courts and judgeships; extended the power of the federal judiciary vis-à-vis the state courts; and reduced the number of Supreme Court justices beginning with the next vacancy, thereby depriving Jefferson of an early opportunity to reshape the court.

Republicans were enraged by the act because of its manifest partisanship and its wanton increase of judicial power. Jefferson promptly targeted the act for repeal. The Federalists had retired to the judiciary as a stronghold, he said. "There the remains of Federalism are to be preserved and fed from the treasury and from that battery all the works of Republicanism are to be beaten down and erased." The experience of the Sedition Act had demonstrated, in his opinion, the prostration of the judiciary before partisan purposes.

Soon after assuming office, Jefferson took executive action to pardon victims of the Sedition Act, which he condemned as null and void, and to drop pending prosecutions. He wished to make judges more responsible to the people, perhaps by periodic review of their "good behavior" tenure; and while conceding the power of judicial review, he did not think it binding on the executive or the legislature. It was his theory—a corollary of the separation of powers—that each of the coordinate branches of

THOMAS JEFFERSON

government is supreme in its sphere and may decide for itself on the constitutionality of actions by the others. Congress, after heated debate, repealed the offensive act and, with minor exceptions, returned the judiciary to the footing it had occupied in 1800.

The second battle centered on the case of *Marbury* v. *Madison*. William Marbury and three others alleged that they had been appointed justices of the peace for the District of Columbia on 3 March 1801 but that their commissions, complete in every respect, had been withheld by the incoming administration. They sued Madison, in whose department the matter belonged, and the Supreme Court granted a "show cause" order on delivery of the commissions. Finally, in 1803, Chief Justice Marshall ruled that the plaintiffs had a legal right to the commissions and, moreover, that the requested writ of mandamus to the secretary of state was the appropriate remedy. He went on to read the executive a lecture on the duty of performing valid contracts but chose to avoid a showdown with Jefferson by declaring that the power of the court to issue writs of mandamus, contained in the Judiciary Act of 1789, was unconstitutional.

In later years the decision would be seen as the cornerstone of the whole edifice of judicial review, but in 1803 it was understood essentially as a duel between the executive and the judiciary. The Republicans criticized Marshall not because of theoretical claims of judicial power but because he traveled outside the case, pretending to a jurisdiction he then disclaimed, in order to take a gratuitous stab at the president. Politics alone could explain such behavior. Obviously, although they were constantly at swords' points, neither Jefferson nor Marshall wanted to press the issue to conclusion.

The Jeffersonian campaign, halting though it was, also contemplated the impeachment of federal judges who violated the public trust. In 1803–1804, Congress impeached, tried, and convicted Judge John Pickering of the federal district court in New Hampshire. The case was a hard one because Pickering's bizarre conduct on the bench proceeded less from his politics than from intoxication and possibly insanity, but in the absence of any other provision for removal, the Republicans took the constitutional route of impeachment and convicted him of "high crimes and misdemeanors." In 1804–1805 the House impeached, and the Senate tried, Supreme Court Justice Samuel Chase. A high-toned Federalist, he had earned Republican enmity as the presiding judge

in several sedition trials and in harangues to grand juries assailing democracy and all its works. Inevitably, Chase's impeachment was a political act.

The fact that Chase was indicted the same day the Senate convicted Pickering seemed to substantiate Federalist fears of wholesale prosecution. Actually, this was never the president's intention. He sought only to make an example of a particularly obnoxious Federalist justice. And when the Senate finally voted to acquit Chase, Jefferson turned away from impeachment in disgust. He remained anxious about the unchecked power of the judiciary. He faced still other encounters with John Marshall. But the Jeffersonian war on the judiciary, if such it was, ended without serious disturbance to the foundations of judicial power. Jefferson could rule the cabinet; he could charm, persuade, and cajole Congress; he could provide inspirational leadership for the American people; but in dealing with the judiciary he found little scope for these talents and, of course, felt awkward in a confrontational role.

Louisiana Purchase

When Jefferson became president, peace was pending in Europe and he could look forward to disentangling the nation from the vices and alliances of foreign politics. "Peace is my passion," he repeatedly affirmed. Yet he was no pacifist. One of his first executive acts was to send a naval squadron to the Mediterranean to enforce peace without tribute on the piratical Barbary states. The Tripolitan War, as it was called, met with partial success: a treaty with Tripoli in 1805.

Far more important, of course, was the burgeoning crisis on the Mississippi, which would end in the triumph of the Louisiana Purchase. By the secret Treaty of San Ildefonso in October 1800, as Jefferson learned six months later, Spain ceded the great province of Louisiana (Jefferson suspected the Floridas as well) to France, conditional on an Italian throne for the duke of Parma, Charles IV's brother-in-law. The retrocession of Louisiana, which France had lost in 1763, announced the revival under Napoleonic auspices of old French dreams of empire in the New World. Over the years the United States had worked out an accommodation with Spain on the Mississippi. The Pinckney Treaty (or Treaty of San Lorenzo) of 1795 granted the Americans free navigation of the river through Spanish territory to the mouth, together with the privilege of deposit and reshipment of goods at New Orleans. This was an enormous, indeed essential, boon to western development. American trade at New Orleans dwarfed that of the Spanish.

Spain was a weak and declining power, and given the pace of American expansion across the continent, Jefferson confidently expected that the river, the Floridas, and Louisiana would all fall to the Americans in due time. But Louisiana in the hands of France was another matter. In Napoleon's grand design, Louisiana and the Floridas would provide the necessary economic and strategic support for an overseas empire centered on St. Domingue (Hispaniola), the richest of the French colonies, then in the control of rebel blacks led by Toussaint L'Ouverture. The reconquest of the island was therefore the first step toward realizing the design. This would not be short work, as Jefferson recognized.

Considering all the difficulties and imponderables of Napoleon's plan, the president made as little noise as possible, kept his patience, and put Louisiana in the track of diplomacy. His strategy was one of delay and maneuver improvised to meet events as they unfolded. His first and minimal concern was to ensure that if France did actually come into power at New Orleans, Americans in the West would be accorded the same commercial rights and privileges as under the Spanish. In Washington the secretary of state constantly drummed into the French envoy the grave danger to his country of making enemies of the American people on the Mississippi issue; and the envoy, Louis Pichon, transmitted these perturbations to Paris. In Paris the American minister, Robert R. Livingston, composed a memoir setting forth in detail the great American interest in Louisiana and the Floridas. He was unheeded and unheard, however. "There never was a government in which less could be done by negotiation than here," he wrote home. "There is no people, no Legislature, no councillors—One man is everything."

In April 1802, Jefferson decided it was time to strike out on a bold new course. Through the good offices of a mutual friend, Pierre-Samuel du Pont de Nemours, who was returning to France, Jefferson gave stern warning to Napoleon:

There is on the globe one single spot, the possessor of which is our natural and habitual enemy. It is New Orleans, through which the produce of three-eighths of our territory must pass to market, and from its fertility it will ere long yield more than half of our whole produce, and contain more than half our inhabi-

tants.. . . The day that France takes possession of New Orleans fixes the sentence which is to restrain her forever within her low water mark. It seals the union of two nations who in conjunction can maintain exclusive possession of the ocean. From that moment we must marry ourselves to the British fleet and nation.

The fact that Jefferson, whose foreign politics had always been friendly to France and hostile to Britain, could contemplate a diplomatic turnabout of this kind—even an alliance with Britain—disclosed the gravity of the situation.

While Jefferson flourished this thunderbolt, Madison quietly worked up the project to purchase New Orleans and the Floridas, assuming the latter were France's to sell. This was a startling idea, which could only have originated with an administration bent on settling international disputes without resort to military force. Jefferson was still playing for time, which in this affair, as in all things, he believed was on the American side. Napoleon had yet to make good his policy. Yellow fever and rebel arms annihilated one French army after another in St. Domingue. The expedition mounted for New Orleans never sailed. Spain remained in control there and, it was reported, sickened at the bargain it had made with France. War clouds again gathered in Europe.

In October 1802 the clock was turned ahead dramatically for the United States. The intendant at New Orleans abruptly closed the port to the Americans. Had he acted on Napoleon's dictate or was Charles IV trying to create havoc for the French? The Spanish minister in Washington, the Marqués de Casa Yrujo, assured Jefferson that the intendant had acted on his own authority, in response to abuses of entrepôt privileges; and before much damage could be done Yrujo and Madison negotiated an end to the crisis.

Meanwhile, westerners threatened to take their fate into their own hands, and Federalist congressmen, always eager to embarrass the administration, clamored for war against France and Spain. Something tangible was needed to calm the West and deflate the Federalists. Jefferson moved to appoint his friend James Monroe, who was popular in the West, minister extraordinary to join Livingston in treating for the purchase of New Orleans and the Floridas for up to $10 million. Monroe was instructed to take the country's problem to London if he failed in Paris.

But the problem would be resolved just as Monroe arrived in Paris in April 1803. Neither he nor Livingston had much to do with the result. The

Louisiana Purchase was made in France, not in America, and it owed more to the vagaries of Napoleon's ambition than to Jefferson's cautious diplomacy. With his dream of New World empire fading, Napoleon revived his older dream of empire in the East—Egypt, the Levant, India—and he renounced Louisiana. He could not defend, or even possess, Louisiana while marching to the East; he needed assurances of American neutrality in that venture; and he needed money to fuel his war machine.

The purchase treaty was quickly arranged. It was neither the bargain Jefferson had sought nor within the price he had authorized. It included the whole of Louisiana, which had never been contemplated, together with New Orleans, but omitted the Floridas, which remained Spanish. "They ask for only one town of Louisiana," Napoleon remarked, "but I already consider the colony completely lost." The United States thus acquired an immense uncharted domain, stretching from the Mississippi to the Rocky Mountains or beyond. No one knew its exact boundaries or size, but at one stroke the Louisiana Purchase practically doubled the land area of the United States. The total price, which included the government's assumption of about $3 million worth of debts owed to France by American citizens, was $15 million.

Jefferson never boasted that he bought Louisiana, but he resented the grumblers and doubters who, from one side of the mouth, denounced him for acquiring a "howling wilderness" and, from the other side, denied him any credit for the good it might contain. The whole proceeding was, in truth, an impressive demonstration of the ways of peace in American affairs. In the end Jefferson was saved by the return of European war. But the probability of renewed warfare, like the probability of French defeat in St. Domingue, had entered into Jefferson's calculations from the beginning. He weighed the imponderables in the European power balance, shrewdly threatened to throw the country into the British scale, worked up an attractive proposition for Napoleon, and was therefore prepared to take advantage of the démarche when it came. It came sooner than he had expected, and it brought the United States much more than he sought. The trans-Mississippi West had not been an object. The United States was not threatened there; it lay almost a thousand miles from the frontier in Ohio. This is not to say that Jefferson had no eyes for Louisiana. In his inaugural address he spoke of the United States as "a chosen country, with room enough for our descendants to the thousandth and thousandth generation." Surely he did not mean the country bounded by the Mississippi but rather the country of his continental vision, which would materialize as Americans multiplied and pressed westward. Louisiana, coming all at once in 1803, altered the timetable of American expansion but not its destination.

For several months Jefferson had been planning a voyage of discovery across the continent. Now, by happy coincidence, Captain Meriwether Lewis, whom he had chosen to lead this expedition, set forth from Washington on 5 July 1803 amid public rejoicing over the Louisiana Purchase. The plan of the expedition was thoroughly characteristic of the president. Presenting it to Congress and hoping to head off constitutional objections, he emphasized its commercial purpose: to chart a continuous line of navigation along the Missouri River route to the Pacific. But Jefferson had larger scientific ends in view. Much of the country was terra incognita, so he instructed Lewis to observe everything:

> . . . the soil and face of the country . . . the animals . . . the remains . . . the mineral productions of every kind . . . volcanic appearances . . . climate . . . the dates at which particular plants put forth or lose their flower, or leaf, times of appearances of particular birds, reptiles or insects.

The expedition proved to be a spectacular success. Lewis, Lieutenant William Clark, and their crew went up the Missouri, crossed the Stony Mountains, and in 1805 descended the Columbia River to its mouth. After wintering there, the expedition returned overland to St. Louis in 1806. Many years would be required to absorb the knowledge gathered by the expedition. Of course, it failed in its commercial aim. The gap between the Missouri and the Columbia turned out to be 350 miles of formidable terrain. Jefferson and the many Americans who shared his continental vision of an "empire of liberty" were not discouraged. In its appeal to the imagination, the Lewis and Clark expedition foreshadowed the American future.

Senate ratification of the Louisiana treaty was a foregone conclusion. Yet it did not escape opposition. "Adopt this Western World into the Union," warned a Federalist senator, "and you destroy at once the weight and importance of the Eastern States and compel them to establish a separate and independent empire." Feelings of this kind contributed to an abortive New England disunionist conspiracy in 1804.

Jefferson himself worried about the constitutionality of the treaty. As he explained to a Republican senator, John Breckinridge of Kentucky,

> The Constitution has made no provision for our holding foreign territory, still less of incorporating foreign nations into our Union. The executive in seizing a fugitive occurrence which so much advances the good of this country, have done an act beyond the Constitution. The Legislature in casting behind them metaphysical subtleties, and risking themselves like faithful servants, must . . . throw themselves on their country for doing for them unauthorized what we know they would have done for themselves had they been in a situation to do it.

Jefferson therefore drafted a constitutional amendment to sanction the acquisition retroactively. The amendment also sought to control the future of the trans-Mississippi West by, among other things, prohibiting settlement above the thirty-third parallel, which would become a vast Indian reserve.

The proposed amendment found little support either in the cabinet or in Congress. Spain, still in possession of Louisiana, expressed unhappiness with the treaty, raising fears it might be lost by delay. Weighing the risks, Jefferson backed away from the amendment. He was still troubled, however. "Our peculiar security is in the possession of a written Constitution," he observed. "Let us not make it a blank paper by construction." As his friends felt differently in this instance, he yielded the point while reserving the principle. A revolution in the Union perforce became a revolution in the Constitution as well.

Jefferson spent much time and effort gathering information on the new territory and its people—the Indian tribes scattered throughout but especially the Creoles of the more thickly inhabited portion below the thirty-third parallel, the northern boundary of the later state of Louisiana. To the territory as a whole, the treaty gave no precise limits. Not surprisingly, Jefferson tried to make the most of the situation. After a detailed inquiry into the boundaries, he concluded that there were respectable grounds for claiming Texas to the Rio Grande, West Florida to the Perdido, and the westernmost limits of the Stony Mountains. From this position he would offer Spain $2 million and half of Texas for East Florida. Spain disdained the overture, of course, insisting that the lower boundaries were the Iberville (now Bayou Manchac) and the Sabine. Jefferson's relentless scheming for the Floridas vitiated his diplomacy abroad and exposed him to attack at home for the next five years.

The treaty provided for the incorporation of Louisiana, with its "foreign" and slave populace, into the Union; but Jefferson concluded from his study of the Creoles—their laws, institutions, and manners—that they were unprepared for republican citizenship. A period of apprenticeship was necessary during which Americans would be encouraged to settle in Louisiana, and society there would be gradually reformed.

The Creole sugar planters reacted angrily to this plan, demanding immediate self-government and admission to the Union, together with retention of most of their customary laws and institutions. They threw back at Jefferson his own eloquent words in the nation's birthright on human rights and liberties and self-government. In this potentially dangerous conflict, the president again showed flexibility and moderation. In 1805 he yielded to the demand for a representative assembly in the territory. With the loyal assistance of his handpicked governor, William C. C. Claiborne, Jefferson found the path of political conciliation in Louisiana, and the Territory of Orleans—the first of many from the purchase lands—would be admitted to the Union as the state of Louisiana in 1812. This was a vindication of his own principles, even in the face of doubt, including the idea of an expanding union of equal self-governing states.

An event of the magnitude of the Louisiana Purchase affected everything to come after. The prospects of the Union were at once grander and more terrifying than before, and the government would have to assume new responsibilities addressed to this condition. The nation's destiny was firmly oriented westward; hundreds of millions of acres of land—the heartland of the continent—guaranteed that the economy would remain primarily agricultural for decades to come and that dispersal rather than concentration would characterize American society and government. All this undergirded Jeffersonian ideals. The United States acquired much greater security on its own borders as well as greater power and self-assurance in international affairs. Finally, the Louisiana Purchase enabled the Republicans to tighten their political grip on the nation, causing them to grow bold in power and making bigots and bunglers of the opposition.

Jefferson's reelection to a second term was never in doubt. The Republican caucus in Congress renominated him in February 1804. Burr was replaced as the vice presidential candidate by George Clinton, his rival in New York politics. Burr's undoing began with the suspicions that he had solicited Federalist votes in the House election of 1801. The Twelfth Amendment, then in the course of ratification, would prevent a repetition of that election, with more Federalist maneuvering to defeat Jefferson, by requiring separate votes for president and vice president. The factional struggle between Burrites and Clintonians culminated in the New York gubernatorial election of 1804, featuring Burr as a candidate. Jefferson pleaded neutrality in this contest, although he secretly favored the Clintonians and stood by silently as they drove Burr out of the Republican party.

The Federalist caucus nominated Charles Cotesworth Pinckney of South Carolina and Rufus King of New York. They were little noticed, as the Republicans again ran against the record of John Adams. The contrast between four years of Adams and four years of Jefferson was striking: new taxes versus no taxes; profusion versus economy; mounting debt versus debt retirement; oppressive army and wasteful navy versus defensive arms only; multiplication of offices versus elimination of judges, tax collectors, and useless functionaries; alien and sedition laws versus freedom and equality; judicial arrogance versus judicial chastisement; monarchical forms and ceremonies versus republican simplicity; war and subservience to foreign power versus peace, independence, and national expansion.

The election resulted in 162 electoral votes for Jefferson and Clinton against 14 for Pinckney and King. Only Delaware and Connecticut, with two stray Maryland electors, voted Federalist. Even Massachusetts entered the Republican column. This was particularly gratifying to Jefferson, who saw in it proof that the "perfect consolidation" he had prophesied four years before was indeed coming to fruition.

A self-congratulatory tone pervaded Jefferson's second inaugural address. Contrasting it with the first, he said, "The former was *promise*; this is *performance*." Because of the rapid liberation of the revenue from debt it was not too soon to plan for national internal improvements—"rivers, canals, roads, arts, manufacturing, education, and other great objects"—and he subsequently proposed a constitutional amendment to this end. The Louisiana Purchase gave an urgency to this undertaking that overrode the restraints of Republican dogma. Jefferson rebuked the fainthearted who feared that the

Union would become too big to survive. "But who can limit the extent to which the federative principle may operate effectively?" he asked.

Jefferson spoke glowingly of his policy of peaceful acquisition of Indian lands and of drawing Indians into the paths of civilization. The policy would result, during eight years, in fifteen treaties with Indian tribes and the cession of 95 million acres of land to the United States—an astounding achievement. Jefferson boasted, too, of the "experiment" he had made in freedom of the press to determine whether, despite the reign of falsehood and defamation, the people were able to detect the truth and act upon it. The experiment had been tried, and the election had given the verdict—"honorable to those who had served them, and consolatory to the friend of man, who believes he may be intrusted with his own affairs."

But if Jefferson's first term was a triumph, his second proved to be an ordeal. His method of working with Congress through unofficial channels of personal and party leadership lost its charm. The Republicans began to quarrel among themselves, especially after Jefferson's decision against seeking a third term became known, and the Federalists grew more desperate as their numbers shrank.

In 1805 president and cabinet worked up a secret diplomatic project to obtain the Floridas through Napoleon's influence with Spain. The policy was one of peace and bargain; its effectiveness required, however, a warlike posture in public. It required, too, the silent appropriation of $2 million by Congress in behalf of the secret project. John Randolph of Roanoke, the Republican leader in the House, balked at this. He objected to "this double set of opinions and principles—the one ostensible, the other real," and believing the money would flow into Napoleon's coffers, he denounced the project as "a base prostration of the national character, to excite one nation by money to bully another nation out of its property."

The Two Million Bill was enacted over Randolph's opposition. But the ensuing diplomacy failed, mainly, the president thought, because Randolph had "assassinated" the project in its infancy. Only a handful of doctrinaire Republicans followed Randolph into opposition. Jefferson continued to control Congress. His loss was less one of followers than of prestige—the aura of invincibility that had surrounded him—and as prestige waned, so did the zeal, the trust, and the unity of the Republicans.

Conflict with Britain and the Burr Trial

The Burr conspiracy presented Jefferson with problems of another kind. With his political career ruined in New York and under indictment for the murder of Alexander Hamilton in a duel, Burr turned his adventuresome gaze to the broiling southwestern frontier. He enlisted a bizarre following: General James Wilkinson, commander of the United States Army in the West; John Smith, senator from Ohio; and Harmon Blennerhassett, a romantic Irishman whose island in the Ohio River was the staging area of the conspiracy. Whether Burr plotted western separation and the creation of a new confederacy on the Mississippi or the filibustering conquest of Mexico, or both together, it is difficult to say. But when Burr, with his flotilla carrying sixty or more plotters, descended the Ohio in the fall of 1806, it became the president's duty to hunt him down and bring him to justice. The Burr conspiracy ran through Jefferson's second term like a disquieting minor theme.

The major theme, of course, and Jefferson's heaviest burden, was in foreign affairs. With the formation of the Third Coalition against Napoleon in 1805, all Europe was engulfed in war. The United States became the last neutral of consequence, in effect the commercial entrepôt and the carrier for the European belligerents. The neutral trade was exceedingly profitable. It was, superficially, a perfect case of America profiting from Europe's distresses. In 1790, American exports were valued at $2 million; they rose steadily during the wars of the French Revolution and then in 1805 began to soar, until they reached $108 million two years later—a peak not again scaled for twenty years. Unfortunately, each side, the British and the French, demanded this trade on its own terms, and submission to one entailed conflict with the other.

While Jefferson might try, as in the past, to play off one power against the other, little leverage was left for this game. After Admiral Horatio Nelson's victory at Trafalgar in the fall of 1805, Britain was supreme at sea, and after Napoleon's victory at Austerlitz in November, France was all-powerful on land. "What an awful spectacle does the world exhibit at this instance," Jefferson observed. "One nation bestriding the continent of Europe like a Colossus, and another roaming unbridled on the ocean." One could play fast and loose with the United States in the Atlantic, while the other lay beyond the reach of retaliation. Neither nation feared war with the United

States, whose president prided himself on peace and had neither army nor navy to speak of. Both nations willfully violated American neutrality, although Britain, the sea monster, was the chief aggressor in Jefferson's eyes, with much more power than France to injure the United States.

In his annual message to Congress in December 1805 the president called attention to British aggressions at sea and moved to counteract the mistakenly pacifistic reputation of the administration. Without abandoning his conviction that nations would be led by their own reason and interest to treat the United States justly, he went on to say, "But should any nation deceive itself by false calculations, and disappoint that expectation, we must join in the unprofitable contest of trying which party can do the other the most harm." And he called upon Congress for defensive preparations: harbor fortifications, a fleet of gunboats, and a revitalized militia.

The conflict with Britain turned on two main issues: the neutral trade and impressment of seamen. The decision of a British vice admiralty court in the case of the ship *Essex* in 1805 marked a return to strict interpretation of the so-called Rule of 1756, under which a colonial trade closed in time of peace could not be opened in time of war. Thus ended British acquiescence in the burgeoning reexport trade of West Indian cargoes—Spanish and French as well as British—from American ports. In 1805 over half of American exports—the basis of prosperity—were, in fact, reexports. The United States government claimed that these belligerent cargoes were "neutralized" after passing through American customs and, upon reexport, were protected under the rule of "free ships make free goods." But Britain now declared this American trade fraudulent, representing "war in disguise" in tacit alliance with the French enemy, since its effect was to negate British maritime and naval superiority. British survival, it was said, demanded this more rigorous policy.

Jefferson viewed the *Essex* decision as only the latest chapter in the prolonged British campaign to subvert American wealth and power. The real aim was to put down a dangerous commercial rival and force the Atlantic trade back into channels profitable to Britain. Reason revolts, Jefferson observed, at the idea "that a belligerent takes to itself a commerce with its own enemy [France and the Continent] which it denies to a neutral, on the ground of its aiding that enemy in the war." After the *Essex* decision British cruisers hovered off American harbors and plundered American trade. Every ship, not only those carrying cargoes of colonial origin, was at risk; and the losses were heavy.

No less irritating and, in principle, more important was the British practice of impressment. Especially in wartime, British subjects were forcibly impressed into His Majesty's Navy. Many American seamen were caught in the net. In 1806, three years after the resumption of hostilities, Madison reported that 2,273 known American citizens had been impressed. Britain argued that many of them were in fact British subjects who had deserted, enlisted in the American merchant marine, and perhaps been furnished with fraudulent naturalization papers, all with the connivance of the government. There was some truth in this. The United States did not claim that the American flag protected absconding British subjects; neither did Britain claim the right to impress American citizens. But who was British and who was American? They spoke the same language, physical identification was impossible, and efforts to persuade seamen to carry nationality papers were unavailing.

The root of the problem lay in a conflict of laws. No natural-born British subject could throw off his allegiance. American naturalization laws were therefore ineffectual. In Jefferson's view, impressment assaulted the very existence of American nationality. "Certain it is," he wrote indignantly, "there can never be friendship, nor even the continuance of peace with England so long as no American citizen can leave his own shore without being seized by the first British officer he meets." Every seizure was a stinging reminder of past colonial servitude.

American diplomatic initiatives to settle these issues in 1806 produced a treaty negotiated by James Monroe and William Pinkney, the team of envoys in London. Pitt's sudden death and the formation of a new government that brought Charles James Fox, a longtime friend of the United States, into the foreign ministry, had brightened the prospects for reconciliation. They were quickly dashed, however, by Fox's untimely death. Negotiations were resumed under his successor, Lord Howick, but Jefferson abandoned hope of a favorable outcome.

When the Monroe-Pinkney treaty finally reached Washington in March 1807, Jefferson took one look at it, saw that it omitted the American ultimatum to end impressment and failed to secure crucial neutral rights claims as well, and angrily refused even to send it to the Senate. What Congress or the people might have thought of it would never be known; but in the present-day judgment of some diplomatic historians, the treaty went a long way toward meeting American claims and, had it been ratified, might have restored amicable relations between the two countries.

Instead, relations rapidly deteriorated. In June the *Chesapeake-Leopard* affair inflamed the entire country against Britain. The frigate *Leopard*, one of a British squadron patrolling off Hampton Roads, ordered the American frigate *Chesapeake* to submit to search for deserters, and when refused, the *Leopard* poured repeated broadsides into the defenseless frigate, killing three and wounding eighteen before its flag could be struck. Four alleged deserters were removed from the *Chesapeake* before it limped back to port.

The country rose up in wrath, regardless of party or section. There had been nothing like it since the Battle of Lexington, said Jefferson. War only awaited the snap of his fingers. He wanted no war, however, and chose to cool the crisis. Quietly, without fanfare, Jefferson ordered certain military preparations, but he declined to convene Congress immediately and, unlike his predecessor Adams, manufactured no war hysteria. Jefferson's hope, rather, was to use the affair as a potent new lever in negotiations with Britain—alas, to no avail.

"I suppose our fate will depend on the successes or reverses of Bonaparte," the president mused that summer. This was a hard fate indeed. "It is really mortifying that we should be forced to wish success to Bonaparte and to look to his victims as our salvation." Several months earlier the French emperor had issued the Berlin Decree, inaugurating his own system of economic warfare, the Continental System. The decree purported to place the British Isles in a state of blockade, making lawful prize of all ships trading with Britain. American carriers were exempted, so the decree did not overtly attack American neutrality. The fact that Napoleon could not possibly enforce such a blockade scarcely lessened its nuisance value.

Britain retaliated by an order-in-council throwing a blockade over that portion of the continental coast under French control. Then, in November 1807, after the surrender of Czar Alexander I to the Continental System, Britain closed all Europe to American trade except on monopolistic British terms. Only vessels that passed through British customs would be given clearance to open ports on the Continent. Napoleon replied by extending the Berlin

Decree to the Americans and by issuing, in December, the Milan Decree, declaring that all vessels adhering to the British orders would be "denationalized" and made subject to seizure and condemnation as British property. Between the emperor's tightening Continental System and the British orders, American commerce was caught in the jaws of a vise, a maniacal war of blockades from which there seemed to be no appeal to reason or justice.

Meanwhile, Aaron Burr was pursued and captured with his fellow conspirators; he was then brought to trial at Richmond, Virginia, in April 1807. Jefferson had been slow to move against Burr, partly because of the mystery surrounding his plans and partly because of the risk of arresting the evidence of crime before it was ripe for execution; but once he became satisfied of Burr's complicity in treason, he moved with vigor and dispatch.

Never doubting that the conspiracy would fail, Jefferson made its suppression a clear test of the loyalty of the West and of the strength of republican government over a vast territory. The outcome vindicated his faith in both. Announcing suppression of the conspiracy to Congress, Jefferson unfortunately declared that Burr's guilt had been "placed beyond question." This was certainly the popular verdict. "But," as John Adams remarked at Quincy, "if his guilt is as clear as the noonday sun, the first magistrate of the nation ought not to have pronounced it so before a jury had tried him."

Jefferson busied himself in the difficult task of securing evidence to convict Burr. He was, in a sense, his own attorney general, and when Burr and his confederates came to trial at Richmond, Jefferson directed the prosecution from the White House. John Marshall was the presiding judge. Toward him Jefferson could not be detached, for he distrusted, even feared, Marshall more than he did Burr, and from the first moment, when Marshall decided to hold the culprit on no higher charge than misdemeanor and to release him on bail, Jefferson believed the trial would be made a party question. The little sect of Richmond Federalists, of whom Marshall had long been the chief, lionized Burr and made his cause their own.

During the grand jury proceedings, Marshall subpoenaed the president to appear in court with certain letters bearing on the actions of General Wilkinson, the conspiracy's chief betrayer. Jefferson refused to appear, citing his responsibilities as chief executive: "The Constitution enjoins his constant agency in the concerns of six millions of people. Is the law paramount to this, which calls on him on behalf of a single one?" The court backed off. Nothing required Jefferson's presence. He cooperated fully in the request for papers and offered to give testimony by deposition, but this was never requested.

The grand jury, heavily freighted with Republicans, returned an indictment for treason on 24 June. Under the Constitution conviction for treason required the testimony of two witnesses to the same overt act. As the trial went forward that summer, it gradually became apparent that the prosecution could not furnish the requisite testimony to such an act as constituted "levying war" against the United States. Marshall, in effect, instructed the jury to bring in a verdict of acquittal, which it did on 1 September.

Jefferson was angry but hardly surprised. In his opinion, the whole conduct of the trial had been political, and the verdict had been in view from the beginning. It was, he said, "equivalent to a proclamation of impunity to every traitorous combination which may be formed to destroy the Union." Counting on the public backlash against the decision, he proposed to mount a new campaign to restrain the power of the federal judiciary. That fall he laid the trial proceedings before Congress and urged it to furnish some remedy. Several state legislatures instructed their respective delegations to work for a constitutional amendment rendering judges removable by the president on the address of both houses of Congress. Since both president and Congress were preoccupied with foreign affairs, nothing came of this effort. This was fortunate, for in the long run the nation was better served by Marshall's political bias in the Burr case than by Jefferson's. Better that the scoundrel go free than be convicted on evidence that would introduce into American law the ancient English principle of "constructive treason." Jefferson could not indulge the luxury of this philosophy, of course. He had invested too much—politically, emotionally, ideologically—in another outcome.

Embargo of 1807–1809

Jefferson and his cabinet met for several days near the end of November 1807 to survey the deteriorating foreign situation. Diplomacy had failed, leaving three possible courses of action open to the United States: acquiescence in the commercial decrees, war against one or both belligerents, or a total embargo of American trade. Three weeks later Jefferson sent to Congress a confidential message recommending the embargo. Congress moved swiftly and, virtually without debate, passed the Embargo Act on 22 December 1807. A self-blockade of the nation's commerce, it prohibited American vessels from sailing to foreign ports and foreign vessels from loading cargo in the United States. At the same time, the selective Nonimportation Act, adopted in 1806 but heretofore suspended, went into effect. The government thus launched an experiment of incredible magnitude, one that dwarfed all previous undertakings and held momentous consequences for the peace of the United States and perhaps the world.

At the outset no one, certainly not Jefferson, fully understood the implications, or foresaw the problems, of the embargo. The aims and purposes of the policy were unclear. In part, it was simply an honorable alternative to war. In part, however, it was a measure preparatory to war, for almost six months would be required to bring home American ships, cargoes, and seamen on the high seas—a vital resource in the event of war—during which time the resources already at home would be secure. Finally, it was in some part an experiment to test the effectiveness of "peaceable coercion" in international affairs.

The idea that the United States might enforce reason and justice on European nations by restraining or withholding its commerce was a first principle of Jeffersonian statecraft and a leading article of Jeffersonian Republicanism. The dependence of European colonies in the West Indies on American provisions, especially in wartime; the importance of American neutral carriers and their cargoes for European belligerents; and the enormous value of access to the American market, above all to Great Britain, placed in American hands an ultimate weapon of peace, "another umpire than arms," Jefferson believed, that might not only secure his own country from the ravages of war but also, when put to the test, demonstrate the efficacy of peaceable coercion to peoples everywhere. With the passage of time, as the administration persisted in the embargo long after its short-range purposes were achieved, this larger moral and philosophical aim became the primary one.

Jefferson never explained his experiment to the American people. So often ridiculed as a "visionary," he had no desire to run that gauntlet again. As a result, the people were asked to bear hardships and sacrifices for the sake of a policy they never really understood. This was a critical failure of leadership, which was surprising in a president who had a keen appreciation of the educational function of the office.

Jefferson and Secretary of the Treasury Gallatin, with the corps of customs officers, labored diligently to enforce the embargo. As loopholes were disclosed, as problems of control arose, Congress enacted supplementary legislation. Coastal infractions were serious from New York eastward. Along the Canadian frontier, smugglers carried on a brisk trade by boat, wagon, and sled. In April, Jefferson issued a proclamation placing the Lake Champlain region in a state of insurrection. Escalating penalties for violation of the embargo, combined with arbitrary actions to enforce it, ill comported with Jefferson's political principles. Normal federal law enforcement machinery finally proved inadequate in the eastern states, although the embargo was remarkably well obeyed elsewhere.

Measured in economic terms, the embargo's effectiveness was all too obvious. Treasury receipts dwindled, wiping out the large surplus Jefferson had committed to a program of national improvements. Agricultural prices plummeted, with particularly devastating effects in the southern states. As many as thirty thousand seamen were thrown out of work. Although stories of ships rotting at the wharves and grass growing in the streets were doubtless exaggerated, the most dramatic effects of the embargo could be seen in the seaports. Merchants who had made their fortunes in foreign trade began to divert their capital to new manufacturing enterprises. Jefferson rejoiced in this development, appeared at his Fourth of July reception in 1808 in a suit of homespun, and amid all the loss and suffering caused by the embargo found its redeeming economic virtue in the rise of domestic manufactures.

Politically, the embargo had no redeeming virtue. New England Federalists mounted the dragons of discontent in a bold bid to return to power. Their reckless leaders bitterly assailed the embargo as a national disaster. Why had Jefferson called for it? First, they said, because Napoleon had demanded it and Jefferson was his puppet. Second, because of Virginia Republicanism's hostility to northern commerce. Jefferson expressed little concern about political damages at home from the Federalists' attack, but he was deeply worried about its effects abroad. "They are endeavoring to convince England that we suffer more by the embargo than they do, and if they will hold out awhile, we must abandon it." This was a dangerous game, for if they succeeded, Jefferson said, war with Britain must follow—the unintended outcome of their propaganda.

Although enacted as an impartial measure, operating equally on the belligerents, the embargo actually had very unequal effects. Britain necessarily felt it more than France. Jefferson hoped that Napoleon would understand this and, as if in gratitude, revoke his decrees against American commerce and force Spain to cede the Floridas. Instead, the emperor toyed with Jefferson. When American vessels—fugitives from the embargo—entered French ports, he confiscated them and then declared he was only helping Jefferson enforce the embargo.

In the president's diplomatic strategy, success with one power would likely produce success with the other, since neither could risk war with the United States; and if neither power recognized American rights, and the time came to lift the embargo, the United States would choose the enemy. British colonials, merchants, and manufacturers began to feel the effects of the embargo in the spring. A group of liberal Whigs—bankers, merchants, members of Parliament—launched a campaign against the orders-in-council, but they were no match for George Canning and the Tory ministry. Jefferson attributed British obstinacy to two causes. First was the false belief aroused by New England Federalists that the embargo must produce a political revolution in the United States. Second was the astonishing Spanish revolt against Napoleonic domination, which not only revived Great Britain's fortunes in the war but opened vast new markets, in Spain and the colonies, to British commerce.

In this "contest of privations," as Jefferson called it, time was not on the American side. The pressures on Jefferson to yield were both greater and more urgent than the pressures on Canning or Napoleon. How long could the end of peaceable coercion abroad be supported in the face of economic deprivation, loss of liberty, disobedience to law, division of the Union, and Republican collapse at home? Despite rising opposition, Jefferson stood firmly by the policy. Perhaps he recalled his experience in another crisis, when he, as Virginia's governor, was accused of jeopardizing the safety of the commonwealth by feeble and temporizing measures. To Gallatin, who complained that the embargo could be saved only by new and arbitrary enforcement powers, Jefferson replied, "Congress should legalize all *means* which may be necessary to obtain its *end*," not excluding military force.

A storm of protest rolled over New England in the fall, and Federalists trooped back to Congress demanding embargo repeal. Soon several New England Republicans joined them. Unhappily, the president reported the failure of embargo diplomacy in his last State of the Union message, on 8 November 1808. Without indicating any new direction, he asked Congress "to weigh and compare the painful alternatives out of which choice is to be made."

Abandoning the policy to Congress was an act of folly. His own choice was to continue the embargo for six months, with war to follow if necessary; but for the first time in his presidency, he abdicated leadership. Why? "On this occasion," he explained, "I think it is fair to leave to those who are to act on them, the decisions they prefer, being . . . myself but a spectator." Jefferson's retreat from responsibility was hardly a favor to James Madison, his chosen successor. As president-elect, Madison had no authority, and lacking Jefferson's prestige and a sure sense of the right course, he could not give direction to Congress. As a result, policy formation fell to a leaderless herd of the fainthearted, the demoralized, and the disgusted. Finally, Congress enacted repeal of the embargo; it would expire with the expiration of Jefferson's presidency. Its replacement, the Nonintercourse Act, reopened trade with all countries except Britain and France. Neither Jefferson nor Madison approved of this feeble measure. A trade open to the rest of the world was in fact a trade open to Britain and France. Yet Jefferson signed the measure into law. It exposed the United States to all the risks of war without the coercive benefits of the embargo. Its only merit was profit.

Jefferson went into retirement convinced that the embargo, if borne for a while longer, would have forced justice from Britain and therefore put a stop to the long train of degradation that led to the War of 1812. Such an outcome was not absolutely foreclosed, although it found little support in the actual circumstances. Jefferson became a victim of his own idealism. Henry Adams observed, "Few men have dared to legislate as though eternal peace were at hand, in a world torn by wars and convulsions and drowned in blood; but this was what Jefferson aspired to do." And as it failed abroad, the "peace policy" produced at home most of the evils Jefferson feared from war: debt, distress, disobedience, dis-

THOMAS JEFFERSON

unionism—in short, the debauchery of Republican principles and hopes. Continued adherence to the embargo in these circumstances would have required more power than the government could command and more obedience than a free people could give.

Retirement

Jefferson's popularity, though shaken, remained high to the end, and he retired to his beloved Monticello with the gratitude and the affection of the overwhelming majority of his countrymen. Not the least of his political accomplishments was the control of the presidential succession, first to Madison and then to Monroe, so that the next sixteen years continued the Republican dominance he began. More than most former presidents he exercised an influence on his successors, although the extent of this was often exaggerated by political enemies. He rejoiced at "shaking off the shackles of power," wanting nothing so much as to return to his farm, his family, and his books, which had always been his supreme delights.

For three years the nation drifted toward war. When it finally came, Jefferson expressed mingled feelings of satisfaction and disappointment. On the one hand, the war would be "the second weaning from British principles, British attachments, British manners and manufactures," and in that light would introduce "an epoch in the spirit of nationalism." On the other hand, what was war itself but the curse of the Old World blighting the hopes of the New? The country was meant to be "a garden for the delight and multiplication of mankind," Jefferson mournfully observed. "But the lions and tigers of Europe must be gorged in blood, and some of ours must go, it seems, to their maws, their ravenous and insatiable maws."

Monticello was more than a home, it was a republican mecca. Men came from far and near to see the renowned Sage of Monticello, who was not only a statesman but a scientist, architect, agriculturist, educator, and man of letters. In retirement, as throughout his life, mind and hand were never idle. Jefferson kept up a lively correspondence; that with John Adams, the revolutionary friend and then political foe, with whom he was reconciled in 1812, stands as a literary monument of the age.

Beginning in 1814, Jefferson concentrated his energies on the "holy cause" of education in his native state. In his philosophy, freedom and enlightenment depended on each other; education, therefore, was a paramount responsibility of free government. He revived the general plan of education he had proposed for Virginia during the Revolution. Again the legislature rejected Jefferson's farsighted plan. It approved, however, a major part, the state university, which was close to his heart.

Jefferson was the master planner and builder of the University of Virginia in all its parts, from the grounds and the buildings to the curriculum, faculty, and rules of governance. When it came time for him to write his epitaph, "Father of the University of Virginia" was one of the three achievements, together with authorship of the Declaration of Independence and the Virginia Statute for Religious Freedom, for which he wished to be remembered. Many have often remarked upon his omission of the presidency and much else besides. Perhaps in that he silently testified to his own sense of values.

Jefferson's declining years were etched with sadness. His health began to fail in 1818. At the same time, his personal fortune was doomed. He owned a large estate—ten thousand acres of land and the slaves to work them—but years of embargo, nonintercourse, and war had crippled Virginia agriculture, and recovery had only begun when the Panic of 1819 struck. New debts were piled upon old, some descending from before the Revolution, some descending from his years in the White House, and drove Jefferson into bankruptcy. In the end, even Monticello would be lost.

Jefferson was also deeply troubled by the course of national affairs. The Missouri Compromise "fanaticized" politics on a sectional line dividing free and slave states; the Supreme Court, realizing his worst fears, became "a subtle corps of sappers and miners" of the Constitution; and the drift toward consolidation in the national government threatened both individual liberty and the federal balance on which the Union depended. Under these blows, Jefferson retreated to the safety of old Republican dogma and gave aid and comfort to the revival of states' rights politics in Virginia. Through all this, nevertheless, he preserved his deep faith in freedom, self-government, enlightenment, and the happiness and the progress of mankind.

The Sage of Monticello died there on the fiftieth anniversary of American independence, 4 July 1826. Ten days earlier, barely able to hold pen in hand, he had declined an invitation to attend ceremonies in

[55]

Washington marking this golden anniversary. Seizing as if by foreknowledge this last opportunity to embellish a legend, Jefferson made his letter an inspiring last testament to the American people:

> All eyes are opened, or opening, to the rights of man. The general spread of the light of science has already laid open to every view the palpable truth, that the mass of mankind has not been born with saddles on their back, nor a favored few booted and spurred, ready to ride them legitimately, by the grace of God. These are grounds of hope for others. For ourselves, let the annual return of this day, forever refresh our recollections of these rights, and an undiminished devotion to them.

Death would not end Jefferson's influence. Generations of Americans turned to him for inspiration and guidance in the successive crises of the nation's affairs. And thus it was that John Adams, who also died on that fateful day of jubilee, uttered a prophetic truth in his last words, "Thomas Jefferson still survives."

BIBLIOGRAPHY

Julian P. Boyd et al., eds., *The Papers of Thomas Jefferson*, 30 vols. to date (Princeton, N.J., 1950–1995), promises to be the definitive edition of Jefferson's writings. As of this writing the project has not yet reached the period of Jefferson's presidency, for which two earlier works remain serviceable: Paul L. Ford, ed., *The Writings of Thomas Jefferson*, 10 vols. (New York, 1892–1899), and A. A. Lipscomb and A. E. Bergh, eds., *The Writings of Thomas Jefferson*, 20 vols. (Washington, 1904–1905). See also Thomas Jefferson, *Writings* (New York, 1984), ed. by Merrill D. Peterson.

Among biographies, the fullest and most authoritative is Dumas Malone, *Jefferson and His Time*, 6 vols. (Boston, 1948–1981). Merrill D. Peterson, *Thomas Jefferson and the New Nation: A Biography* (New York, 1970), runs to 1,000 pages, while Noble E. Cunningham, Jr., *In Pursuit of Reason: The Life of Thomas Jefferson* (Baton Rouge, La., 1987), runs to 350 pages. Peterson is the editor of the multiauthored *Thomas Jefferson: A Reference Biography* (New York, 1986). Peter S. Onuf, ed., *Jeffersonian Legacies* (Charlottesville, Va., 1993), is a contemporary assessment by sixteen scholars. Other studies of Jefferson's thought include Garrett Sheldon, *The Political Philosophy of Thomas Jefferson* (Baltimore, 1991), and David N. Mayer, *The Constitutional Thought of Thomas Jefferson* (Charlottesville, Va., 1994). A seminal study is I. Bernard Cohen, *Science and the Founding Fathers: Science in the Political Thought of Jefferson, Franklin, Adams and Madison* (New York, 1995).

For the presidency, Henry Adams, *History of the United States of America During the Administration of Thomas Jefferson*, 2 vols. (New York, 1930), is still an important and immensely readable source. Other more specialized or broadly interpretive books on the subject are Forrest McDonald, *The Presidency of Thomas Jefferson* (Lawrence, Kans., 1976); Robert M. Johnstone, Jr., *Jefferson and the Presidency: Leadership in the Young Republic* (Ithaca, N.Y., 1978); and Noble E. Cunningham, Jr., *The Process of Government Under Jefferson* (Princeton, N.J., 1978). See also Leonard D. White, *The Jeffersonians: A Study in Administrative History, 1801–1829* (New York, 1951), and James Sterling Young, *The Washington Community, 1800–1828* (New York, 1966). Foreign affairs are the focus of Bradford Perkins, *The First Rapprochement: England and the United States, 1795–1805* (Philadelphia, 1955), and *Prologue to War: England and the United States, 1805–1812* (Berkeley, Calif., 1961); Burton Spivak, *Jefferson's English Crisis: Commerce, Embargo, and the Republican Revolution* (Charlottesville, Va., 1979); and Robert W. Tucker and David C. Hendrickson, *Empire of Liberty: The Statecraft of Thomas Jefferson* (New York, 1990).

Merrill D. Peterson, *The Jefferson Image in the American Mind* (New York, 1960), pursues the Jefferson theme and symbol in American thought and imagination. The best guide to the historical literature is Frank Shuffelton, *Thomas Jefferson: A Comprehensive, Annotated Bibliography of Writings About Him, 1826–1980* (New York, 1983), with a supplement (1992).

Recent works include Joseph J. Ellis, *American Sphinx: The Character of Thomas Jefferson* (New York, 1997).

James Madison

Ralph Ketcham

James Madison THE LIBRARY OF CONGRESS

J AMES MADISON, was born on 16 March 1751 of a family that had been in Virginia since the mid-seventeenth century. Tradesmen and farmers at first, his forebears quickly acquired more lands and soon were among the "respectable though not the most opulent class," as Madison himself described them. The family moved to Orange County in the Virginia Piedmont about 1730 and settled on a plantation that over the next century grew to five thousand acres, produced tobacco and grains, and was worked by perhaps a hundred slaves. Although Madison abhorred slavery, he nonetheless bore the burden of depending all his life on a slave system that he could never square with his republican beliefs.

Madison learned the fundamentals at home and then went to preparatory school before entering the College of New Jersey at Princeton. There he got a fine classical and Christian education, receiving his bachelor of arts degree in 1771. He studied for six months more under President John Witherspoon, whose intellectual independence, practicality, and moral earnestness profoundly influenced him. Madison read John Locke, Isaac Newton, Jonathan Swift, Joseph Addison, David Hume, Voltaire, and others whose Enlightenment world-view became his own. He considered becoming a clergyman or a lawyer but never entered either profession.

While Madison was small and unimpressive physically, he had bright blue eyes, a quiet strength of character, and a lively, humorous way in small groups that made him a welcome and influential colleague in many endeavors. He had some serious illnesses during his life, many bouts of a probably nervous disorder that left him exhausted and prostrate after periods of severe strain, and a hypochondriacal tendency to "fear the worst" from sickness, but he actually lived a long, healthy life free from the common scourges of his day and was capable of sustained, rigorous labors that would have overwhelmed many seemingly more robust men.

As the Revolution approached, Madison served on the Orange County Committee of Safety from 1774, and two years later he was elected to the Virginia convention that resolved for independence and drafted a new state constitution. There he sought successfully to change the clause guaranteeing religious "toleration" only to one proclaiming "liberty of conscience for all." From 1777 to 1779 he served on the Virginia Council of State under two governors, Patrick Henry and Thomas Jefferson.

Elected to the Continental Congress in 1780, Madison became one of the leaders of the so-called nationalist group, which saw fulfillment of the Revolution possible only under a strong central government. He thus supported the French alliance and worked persistently to strengthen the powers of Congress. When he retired from Congress in 1783, he was regarded as its best informed and most effective debater and legislator. Madison then served for three years in the Virginia legislature, where he worked to enact Jefferson's Statute for Religious Freedom and other reform measures. Six years of legislative experience, as well as his studies, increasingly convinced him that weak confederacies were prey to foreign intrigue and domestic instability.

Legislative and Executive Leader

Madison came to see that a vigorous, responsible executive officer, even within republican principles that generally emphasized legislative powers, might be essential to effective government by consent. Revolutionary hostility to the last royal governors, who had been the agents of British tyranny, further heightened American suspicions of executive authority. Yet, by 1787, Madison had also been given many lessons in the liabilities of executive impotence. As a member of the Virginia Council of State, he had observed a government in which the executive not only had very little power overall but was forbidden to act except with the approval of the eight-member council. The delays and inability to act in the exigencies of war eventually convinced Madison that this construction of the executive department was "the worst part of a bad Constitution."

The same executive weakness existed in the Continental Congress. Standing committees conducted much of the executive business, plagued by uncertain authority, dispersed responsibility, rotating personnel, and spotty attendance. Madison supported the creation of "executive departments" of foreign affairs, finance, war, and marine in January and February 1781, and he sought to fill the new offices with able men.

Madison was never among those who suspected that any person given the power to do anything would invariably act badly. Such a proposition, when applied indiscriminately to officials deriving their election or appointment from the people, Madison later charged, "impeached the fundamental principle" of republican government by holding that officers chosen by the people "will immediately and infallibly betray the trust committed to them." Despite this basic faith, in the years immediately preceding the Convention of 1787, Madison observed that in the Virginia and other state legislatures many unjust and unwise laws were passed by popularly elected assemblies.

The dilemma of finding the basic principle of republican government—majority rule—working against the even more fundamental need for just laws was for Madison especially difficult because the source of this malfunction was to be found not only in the tendency toward imprudence and corruption in the representatives but "more fatally [in] . . . the people themselves." That is, a host of private interests, real and imagined, divided the people of the states into groups whose rivalry generally vitiated whatever virtuous motives might be expected to arise from "a prudent regard to their [the people's] own good as involved in the general and permanent good of the community," from a "respect for character," or from religious conviction. Madison concluded that the states, when left to themselves, seemed invariably to trample on both private rights and the public good, despite the fact that the states more fully embodied the principle of legislative supremacy than any other governments in the world. To cope with this discouraging development, Madison argued that in "an extended republic," on the continental scale of the United States, "a greater variety of interests, of pursuits, of passions [would] check each other." Thus, the general government would be less likely to act unjustly and should therefore have "a negative" on the laws of the states, a power he advocated throughout the federal convention. "The great desideratum," he concluded, was "such a modification of the Sovereignty as will render it sufficiently neutral between the different interests and factions." But *neutrality* meant for Madison a point of view that was impartial, disinterested, above party, such as "the prince . . . in absolute Monarchies" had in judging among his subjects.

At the convention, Madison met powerful advocates of restraint on executive power. Roger Sherman of Connecticut "considered the Executive Magistracy as nothing more than an institution for carrying the will of the Legislature into effect." The legislature, Sherman insisted, "was the depository of the supreme will of the Society" and was therefore "the best judge of the business which ought to be done by the Executive department." Sherman sought definition of executive powers by the legislature, proposed various schemes for a plural executive and for its election by the legislature, and objected to an executive veto. Madison, James Wilson, Gouverneur Morris, and others protested immediately and vigorously that such proposals strengthened, rather than diminished, the power of faction and of provincial interests in government. They admitted that any form of monarchy was out of the question in the United States, but they nonetheless sought somehow to retain the benefit of its ability to check legislative corruption and of its supposed nonpartisanship.

Madison revealed his train of thought to the convention when, defending executive veto, he noted the danger that a republic faced from diversity of interests, demagoguery, and the power of a selfish majority. "In this view," Madison concluded, "a negative in the Executive is not only necessary for its own [protection], but for the safety of a minority.. . . The independent condition of the Executive who has the eyes of all Nations on him will render him a just Judge."

Madison even sought some way to combine the judiciary with the executive in the veto power to increase the sense of wisdom and respectability in this vital restraint on a legislature presumed to be fac-

tious. Two days later he noted the difficulty of finding in a republic a source of power that, like "an hereditary magistrate," would have a "personal interest against betraying the national interest." He urged further that the executive have the power to appoint federal judges because he would be "a national officer, acting for and equally sympathizing with every part of the United States." Throughout the debates, Madison sought consistently to protect the executive department from the factious legislature, and insofar as that independence was secure, he was willing to grant wide powers to the executive.

In fact, responding to Wilsons' reasoning, Madison came to see increasingly that in a republic where even executive power rested, directly or indirectly, on the people, there might be less to fear in its exercise than under a monarchy. The more clearly the executive was held responsible to the people, Wilson argued, the more power he could safely be given. This view suited Madison's sober optimism that a self-governing system could be devised that would exercise power wisely and his sense of the need for vigor and responsibility in government. Thus, he supported a single executive, his power to appoint officials in his department, his powers as commander in chief and in foreign affairs, his long term in office, and his eligibility for reelection.

Election of the executive posed a seemingly insoluble problem. Madison shared some of George Mason's fear that to allow election directly by the people was like referring "a trial of colours to a blind man," and Gouverneur Morris' fear that if a legislative body chose the executive "it will be like the election of a pope by a conclave of cardinals." Madison eventually supported the idea of an electoral college as a hedge against both dangers. Altogether, then, the definition of executive power as it emerged from the convention suited Madison as a reasonable compromise between the needs of authority and the need to limit the power of government. He defended the new constitution in his contributions to *The Federalist Papers* in 1787–1788 and as a delegate to the Virginia Ratification Convention in June 1788.

Everything depended, of course, upon the early precedents established and the conduct of the first presidents. Washington's vast prestige gave crucial support to the dignity and authority of the office, most of which Madison supported. In fact, as Washington's chief adviser in the critical years 1788–1789, Madison had a large role in the organization of the executive branch, its etiquette, and its relations with the other branches.

Especially critical was Madison's defense (in the House of Representatives, where he served from 1789 to 1797) of the president's inherent power to remove his appointees from office. Madison scorned arguments that the president should be denied such power because he would infallibly abuse it by removing faithful public servants; such fears, and the consequent denials of power, would hopelessly hamstring governments. Rather, he insisted upon the more basic, self-regulating "principle of unity and responsibility in the Executive department, which was intended for the security of liberty and the public good. If the President alone should possess the power of removal from office, those employed in the execution of the law will be in their proper situation, and the chain of dependence therefore terminates in the supreme body, namely, in the people." That is, the president needed to have the power of removal for profoundly republican reasons: the people would then be able to hold him responsible for the malfeasance of his appointees and could then be justified in refusing him reelection (or in extreme cases, even impeaching him) for inefficiency or corruption in his department. By 1789, Madison had achieved a maturing idea of what it meant to exercise executive power in a republican government.

Yet, despite his admiration for President Washington, Madison was first amazed and then appalled at what the executive branch became under Secretary of the Treasury Alexander Hamilton's guidance during the 1790s. Madison's desire for a vigorous executive, an efficient civil service, and a sound public credit led him to support many of Hamilton's proposals taken by themselves, but it was the totality of his program that the Virginian opposed.

The growth of the executive branch, especially the Treasury Department, allowed its secretary to take the initiative. To this power Hamilton quite candidly added the force and support he could derive from granting privilege to bankers and merchants. Sharing the largesse and financial prospects with congressmen and their friends, furthermore, gave him great influence in the legislature. These consolidating moves, mobilized under the doctrine of loose construction, devised to legitimize the Bank of the United States, instituted, in Madison's view, a veritable "phalanx." Far from shaping an executive who took his lead in policy from the legislature and was the executor of its will, as republican theory required, Hamilton had created a machine to lead and dominate the nation. The parallel with the means

that George III and his ministers had used to control Parliament in the 1770s and Hamilton's conception of himself as a proconsul or prime minister on the order of Richelieu, Colbert, or the elder Pitt were all too apparent. The ease and speed with which Hamilton achieved this model of the executive, under the Constitution, was a sobering lesson for Madison. Phrases about separation of power, and even what he thought were explicit limitations, seemed to mean little when confronted by someone of Hamilton's energy, wile, and brilliance.

Federalist response to the renewal of war between France and Great Britain in 1793—arguments that the president, not Congress, could "proclaim" neutrality (the counterpart, after all, to declaring war) and calls for a buildup of the armed forces, special diplomatic missions, higher taxes, and so on—frightened Madison because the "needs" of war so perfectly promoted the executive tendencies Hamilton had already set in motion. It seemed to him that American "monocrats" (as Jeffersonian Republicans increasingly, although unfairly, termed the Federalists) used shrill accounts of the excesses of the French revolutionary government in 1793–1794 to slander republicanism generally and to strengthen ties with England that would draw American government and society closer to its aristocratic, imperial model.

When Hamilton urged Washington to gather an army in the fall of 1794 to suppress the Whiskey Rebellion, Madison saw in the making "a formidable attempt . . . to establish the principle that a standing army was necessary for *enforcing the laws.*" After Hamilton had persuaded Washington to criticize publicly the "democratic societies" or "Jacobin clubs," which had mushroomed in opposition to Federalist policies in 1794, Madison retorted that "in the nature of republican government the censorial power is in the people over the government, and not in the government over the people."

During John Adams' administration, Madison continued to fret and fume over executive excess. He saw in the president's florid addresses in the war crisis of 1798 only "violent passions and heretical politics," and he labeled the Alien Enemies Act "a monster that must forever disgrace its parents." He wrote Jefferson, "Perhaps it is a universal truth that the loss of liberty at home is to be charged to provisions against danger real or pretended from abroad." In the "Report on the [Virginia] Resolutions of 1798" (1800), Madison scored an enlargement of the executive by "excessive augmentation of . . . offices, honors, and emoluments" that seemed bent on "the transformation of the republican system of the United States into a monarchy." Thus, by 1801, Madison had witnessed the Constitution he had helped draft and had enthusiastically recommended to his countrymen used—indeed, abused—in ways he was sure would destroy the whole notion of free self-government. The chief engine for this ruin, moreover, built by Hamilton from a domestic coalition of mercantile, anti-republican forces and a consolidation of the powers of government spurred by foreign danger, was the executive branch.

Service as secretary of state in Jefferson's cabinet (1801–1809), though, had the not surprising effect of reviving Madison's sense of the legitimate use of executive power—so much so, in fact, that more doctrinaire Republicans such as John Randolph of Roanoke saw him as a dangerous "crypto-Federalist" betraying Jeffersonian principles. Madison, however, was discriminating. He agreed thoroughly with Jefferson and Secretary of the Treasury Albert Gallatin that a prime Republican responsibility was to reduce the apparatus of federal government and especially of the executive branch. But, as Jefferson stated in his first inaugural address, among the "essential principles of our government [is] . . . the preservation of the General Government in its whole constitutional vigor."

Madison undertook his own campaign for "mild" government by firing one of the eight clerks in the State Department (its entire personnel in 1801) and by abandoning virtually all ceremony in conducting his office. He approved Republican measures to reduce the diplomatic establishment, lower the number of federal employees, put the national debt "on the road to extinction," diminish the military, reduce taxes, and repeal the Federalist Judiciary Act of 1801. He agreed, though, that Federalist institutions that had proved useful, such as the Bank of the United States, should remain undisturbed, and he participated willingly in the informal leadership Jefferson exercised through his influence over key members of Congress.

In two major events of Jefferson's presidency, the Louisiana Purchase and the embargo of 1807–1809, Madison showed his willingness to use executive power to achieve important republican ends. He agreed with Gallatin that the Louisiana Purchase was constitutional because "the existence of the United States as a nation presupposes the power

enjoyed by every nation of extending their territory by treaties" and that the Constitution clearly gave the executive the authority to conduct such treaties. The critically important republicanizing results of the purchase—the doubling of agricultural lands, the removal of great power rivalry from the Mississippi Valley, and the reduction thus permitted in defense expenditures—more than compensated for a departure from the letter of Jefferson's self-imposed strict constructionism.

The embargo was a similarly bold effort to achieve a momentous republican breakthrough—nothing less than the substitution of economic pressure for war in international relations—by the orderly processes of a law passed by Congress and its faithful administration by the executive. Jefferson and Madison underestimated the sectional inequity of the measure and the consequent unwillingness of the nation to accept the required sacrifices, and overestimated the dependence of international trade (especially Britain's) on American exports. Thus, enforcement of the embargo, and the apparent need for its long-range continuance, soon entailed a considerable extension of executive power.

At this point, the Republican leaders—Madison most reluctantly—made a revealing decision: they gave up a policy proven ineffective in its intended objective and, even worse, sure to erode seriously their republican values if maintained in the face of widespread public opposition. They resisted the temptations to prove determination and "creditability" by enlarging executive authority and to overpower rather than conciliate deeply felt opposition. There was a critical need, in Madison's mind, to balance the positive uses of executive power against the constant danger of that power becoming oppressive.

Madison as President: The Road to War

Having long pondered the complex question of how to provide leadership in a system of government deriving its "just powers from the consent of the governed" and having gained wide experience in public office, Madison became president on 4 March 1809. Although painful intraparty opposition by his long-time friend James Monroe and by Vice President George Clinton, as well as by a Federalist party revived by anger at the embargo, denied him the political domination enjoyed by Jefferson, Madison nonetheless won comfortably with 122 votes in the electoral college to 47 for Federalist Charles C. Pinckney, 6 for Clinton, and none for Monroe.

Trying to adjust to his diminished political position and perhaps too little inclined to exert his will on Congress, Madison accepted one of the weakest cabinets in American history. Thwarted by the Senate from moving Gallatin to the State Department, Madison instead appointed affable but incompetent Robert Smith, who, through alliance with a group of hostile senators led by his brother, Samuel Smith of Maryland, became a center of disaffection within the cabinet. Madison endured this disloyalty and covered up for Robert Smith's incompetence by in effect continuing to do the work of the secretary of state himself for two years, but he finally had to replace Smith in a storm of factional invective in April 1811.

The new secretaries of war and the navy, William Eustis of Massachusetts and Paul Hamilton of South Carolina, were second or third choices for their posts and were appointed largely to achieve regional balance. Eustis proved utterly unsuited to the administrative needs of the War Department, while Hamilton became an alcoholic, ordinarily unable to perform any duties after noontime. Even Gallatin, although a most able secretary of the treasury and entirely loyal, was restive, resentful, and politically damaged at being barred by the Senate from the State Department.

Two men carried over from Jefferson's administration in offices not yet accorded cabinet status were scarcely better: Attorney General Caesar Rodney was seldom in the capital, while Postmaster General Gideon Granger, because of disputes over appointments, was increasingly estranged from, and hostile to, the president. Madison began his presidency, then, laboring under severe political difficulties and surrounded by less-than-ideal colleagues.

The ill effects of these appointments might have been avoided in normal times, but Madison faced the climactic years of the Napoleonic Wars. Britain and France were locked in a life-and-death combat that made neutrality difficult and infringed the rights of nonbelligerents. Both great powers plundered American vessels on the high seas, issued arbitrary decrees to damage American commerce, and otherwise took what advantage they could of the scorned and unarmed upstart nation. But it was Britain—with warships that ruled the seas; arrogant naval officers who ruthlessly impressed American sailors; sharp-dealing merchants who were eager to keep the former colonies in a state of economic dependence; and a fleet that could harass, blockade, and bombard the American coast with impunity—that could, and did, most injure and offend the United States. Thus, Madison saw Britain as the principal threat to the nation and came increasingly to feel that standing up to her might require a "second War of Independence."

The tangled diplomacy and stop-and-start legislation to impose economic sanctions on one or both of the belligerents that preoccupied Madison during his first three years as president—the signing and repudiation of the Erskine Agreement, the two Macon bills, protests of British orders-in-council and Napoleonic decrees, and so on—all failed because both France and Britain, fighting for survival, were prepared to use any means to win any advantage they could.

In the summer of 1811, Madison, by then ably supported by James Monroe, who had replaced Robert Smith as secretary of state, and buttressed in Congress by energetic young members soon dubbed War Hawks (Henry Clay and John C. Calhoun foremost among them), decided that if final efforts at favorable diplomatic settlement with each belligerent failed, war with the worst offender (almost sure to be Britain) would be necessary. In the spring of 1812, as Madison, Monroe, and their congressional allies pushed war preparations, intransigent dispatches arrived from Europe, so on 1 June, Madison asked Congress to declare war on the former mother country. With Federalists (dominant only in New England) solidly in opposition, the House of Representatives voted for hostilities (seventy-nine to forty-nine) and the Senate followed suit (nineteen to thirteen); on 18 June, Madison signed the declaration of war.

Madison viewed the declaration with sadness and regret, although he had for nearly a year been working with his cabinet and with Clay and others in Congress to prepare the country for battle. In reviewing the course toward war, Madison observed that Britain's notice of July 1811 that it would require humiliating concessions before withdrawing orders-in-council had made hostilities virtually inevitable. Writing to antiwar John Taylor "of Caroline" even before the final declaration, Monroe had explained that upon joining the cabinet in April 1811, he had found erroneous his conviction that Britain would make concessions if properly approached. Nothing, he added, "would satisfy the present Ministry of England short of unconditional submission which it was impossible to make." Thus, after July 1811, "the only remaining alternative was to get ready for fighting, and to begin as soon as we were ready. This was the plan of the administration when Congress met [in November 1811]; the President's message announced it; and every step taken by the administration since had led to it."

Asked to assess Madison's state of mind as the war approached, his private secretary, Edward Coles, noted that "it was congenial alike to the life and character of Mr. Madison that he should be reluctant to go to war, . . . this savage and brutal manner of settling disputes between nations," while diplomacy afforded any peaceful hopes at all. Coles agreed with Monroe that Britain's notice of July 1811 "closed the door to peace in Mr. Madison's opinion" and observed further that during the long session of Congress from November 1811 to July 1812, "a class of irritable men, . . . hotspurs of the day," declaimed for war, heedless of the need for preparation and scornful of "sound, prudent and patriotic men" who wanted delay and further diplomatic initiatives. Madison stood in the middle, Coles said, trying "to moderate the zeal and impatience of the ultra belligerent men, and to stimulate the more moderate and forbearing. To check those who were anxious to rush on hastily to extreme measures without due preparation and to urge those who lagged too far behind." The president restrained his own determination to go to war to bring to his side "tardy and over cautious members of Congress" and thus be able to declare war "by a large and influential majority."

Viewed in this perspective, Madison's course during the year preceding the war declaration and even during the whole seven-year period following full-scale resumption of the Napoleonic Wars in 1805, appears straight and consistent, if not always wise and well executed. He thought throughout that his goal, a genuine republican independence for the United States, found its worst menace in the commercial and maritime arrogance and power of Great Britain. To have submitted to her unilateral decrees, her discriminatory trade regulations, or her naval outrages would have restored the colonial dependence Madison had fought for half a century. It would, moreover, have ratified unjust principles of international law and emboldened antirepublican forces in Britain and the United States, thereby threatening, in Madison's opinion, the survival of free government anywhere in the world.

War was deemed so corrosive to republican principles that only the direst emergency could condone it. Thus, Madison tried every conceivable and even

some inconceivable ways of peaceful resistance until many men less patient, less subtle, and less earnestly republican than he thought him hopelessly irresolute or a tool of Napoleon. Madison pronounced this latter charge "as foolish as it is false." If the war coincided with the views of the enemy of Great Britain and was favored by Napoleon's operations against the British, he observed coolly,

that assuredly could be no sound objection to the time chosen for extorting justice from her. On the contrary, the coincidence, though it happened not to be the moving consideration, would have been a rational one; especially as it is not pretended that the United States acted in concert with [Napoleon], or precluded themselves from making peace without any understanding with him; or even from making war on France, in the event of peace with her enemy, and her continued violation of our neutral rights.

Although in retrospect it may seem Madison underestimated Napoleon's global ambitions, he had no illusions about the French tyrant. Britain's greater capacity to injure the United States was the steady, realistic base of Madison's policy.

Less defensible is Madison's relentless, sometimes innocently implausible reliance on peaceful coercion—such as embargo, selective trading with the belligerents, or alliances with other neutral nations—which instead of persuading the belligerents to deal honorably with the United States, only convinced them they had nothing to fear from it. Thus, insult followed depredation, year after year. Shifting from one kind of nonviolent coercion to another and offering the carrot and then the stick first to one belligerent and then to the other, instead of persuading either of them to accept American support in exchange for commercial justice, led each country to think it could, by intrigue and maneuver, get all it wanted while granting nothing. As a result, by 1812 the United States was neither trusted nor respected by the warring powers. At home, Madison's patient, subtle efforts to unite the country behind him often had the doubly debilitating effect of disgusting those impatient for war and encouraging those opposed to it to think he would ultimately flinch from hostilities. Although, even in retrospect, better alternatives are not readily apparent, Madison's course seldom had the effect he intended.

Least defensible of all is the unfitness of the nation for war in June 1812. In response to those who charged that Britain, not the United States, had to fight at long distance and therefore would benefit from delay and warning, Madison insisted that "it was, in fact, not the suddenness of war as an Executive policy, but the tardiness of legislative provision" that left the nation unprepared. He had, he pointed out, recommended a military buildup in early November 1811, and it was more than two months before Congress took even ill-conceived steps. Although Congress did indeed hang back in this and many other ways during the twelve years of Republican rule, Madison seldom did more than call vaguely for "attention to the nation's defenses," and Secretary Gallatin insisted repeatedly that military expenditures be limited by his plans to discharge the national debt. From 1805 on, while Madison talked loudly and unyieldingly of neutral rights, the chasm widened between the obvious military peril of the European war and the pitiful state of the country's armed forces. He often spoke loudly and carried no stick at all.

Madison correctly pointed out the host of difficulties he faced in placing the nation on a war footing. Officers for the army had to be chosen from among "survivors of the Revolutionary band," many of whom "were disqualified by age or infirmities," or from among those untried on the battlefield. Furthermore, to appoint any executive officer, "an eye must be had to his political principles and connections, his personal temper and habits, his relations . . . towards those with whom he is to be associated, and the quarter of the Union to which he belongs." Add to this, Madison concluded, "the necessary sanction of the Senate" (often denied) and the large "number of refusals" of office by the most qualified prospects, and the reasons for a poorly staffed register were painfully obvious. Madison did not lack will, or understanding of what needed to be done, or courage to face war, but rather, as his own apologies verify, the capacity to disentangle himself from republican pieties, political crosscurrents, and organizational weaknesses.

Calhoun wrote a friend in April 1812 that "our President tho a man of amiable manners and great talents, has not I fear those commanding talents, which are necessary to controul those about him. He permits division in his cabinet. He reluctantly gives up the system of peace." The South Carolinian observed further that "this is the first war that the country has ever been engaged in; there is a great want of military knowledge; and the whole of our system has to be commenced and organized." Eight months later, after disasters caused by "errors and misman-

agement . . . of most incompetent men," Calhoun noted that the difficulties "lie deep; and are coeval with the existence of Mr. Jefferson's administration."

Jeffersonian republicanism, with its hostility to economic regulation, deficit financing, and militarism, simply was not a vehicle designed for effective travel down the road to war. What Clay, Calhoun, and other War Hawks did in 1811 and 1812 was not browbeat the president into war or give the impulse to it from their expansionist predilections but rather to provide the legislative leadership in Congress, the effective attention to preparedness, and the sharp propaganda sense needed to arouse the country. Madison saw too clearly all the variables of a complex situation, knew too well the traps awaiting him in every direction, and understood too profoundly the anti-republican tendencies of arming for war to accept readily the reckless and unsubtle needs of girding for battle. What undermined Madison's policy of upholding American rights by peaceful means was, first and foremost, the absence of effective armed force, which again and again prevented him from being able to confront his opponents with a plausible threat and made skeptics on both sides of the Atlantic doubt he could have any ultimate intention of going to war. Second, an impression of irresolution grew from the shifting terms of his policies of commercial retaliation and peaceful coercion—embargo, nonintercourse, nonimportation, and so on—which often, at the very moment of effective pressure, freed trade long enough for Britain to fill its warehouses. Madison underestimated, too, the flexibility of international trade, the endurance of the belligerents, and the amount of damage some of his policies inflicted on the United States. Thus, the nation, especially New England, saw no credible and effective policy around which to rally. Although Madison, striving for domestic unity, both tempered his policy and manipulated his channels of communication, his stance was inevitably regarded as unwarlike.

Reflecting on the causes of the war, Republican Congressman Jonathan Roberts wrote that "there had all along been an idea cherished by the opposition, that the majority would not have nerve enough to meet war. This I believe, mainly induced Britain to persist in her aggressions. If she could have been made to believe . . . that we were a united people, and would act as such, war might have been avoided." As the *London Independent Chronicle* pointed out, "in every measure of government, the [Federalist] faction have rallied in opposition, and urged the

British Ministry to persist in their Orders. They forced the United States to the alternative, either to surrender their independence, or maintain it by War."

Thus, although these misjudgments, too subtle policies, and republican predilections may paradoxically have made more likely the war that Madison tried to avoid and certainly left the nation dangerously unprepared, he was perfectly clear, as he stated in his first wartime message to Congress, on the basic cause and ultimate need for hostilities:

> The war in which we are actually engaged is a war neither of ambition nor of vainglory.. . . It is waged not in violation of the rights of others, but in maintenance of our own.. . . To have shrunk [from it] . . . would have struck us from the high rank where the virtuous struggles of our fathers had placed us, and have betrayed the magnificent legacy which we hold in trust for future generations. It would have acknowledged that on [water] . . . where all independent nations have equal and common rights, the American people were not an independent people but colonists and vassals.

Madison as Wartime President

Madison and his advisers hoped that American zeal for the war (especially in the West), and the vulnerability of Canada as Britain strained its resources in the climax of the desperate struggle with Napoleon, would lead swiftly to American victory. He therefore ordered an American invasion of Canada at Detroit and an assault on the lightly defended borders at Niagara and in the direction of Montreal, with the intent of gaining advantages that could then be traded for British concessions on the high seas and along the Atlantic coast, where its naval power was overwhelming. Disaster ensued, for on 16 August one poorly led and ill-trained American army surrendered to a much smaller British and Indian force at Detroit and on 13 October another was badly beaten at Queenston Heights opposite Buffalo. A third army, commanded by an old, tired, timid, fumbling Revolutionary War general, William Dearborn, hampered by near-treasonable avoidance of duty by New England militia, retreated to winter quarters near Albany without even attempting to cut the vital, undefended British supply lines strung out westward from Montreal. Spectacular but isolated victories by the *Constitution* and other frigates boosted American morale but did not challenge overall British command of the seas.

These reversals made it necessary (and possible) for Madison to appoint new leaders for the Navy and War departments and to begin finding younger, more able, and more vigorous commanders for the army. His choice for the Navy Department, William Jones, turned out to be able and loyal, serving with distinction until the end of the war, but the War Department "solution" was more problematic. Madison finally settled on General John Armstrong, a New York politician who had wide military and administrative experience but was quarrelsome, imperious, and almost sure to be disloyal politically, especially to a Virginia-led administration. The president was well aware of the liabilities but hoped Armstrong's "known talents" and military experience, together with "a proper mixture of conciliating confidence and interposing control would render objectionable peculiarities less in practice than in prospect." Political considerations seemed still to compel appointment of some incompetent commanders in the army, but a move toward improvement was made by putting William Henry Harrison in command in the Northwest Territory and by promoting Winfield Scott, Jacob Brown, and Andrew Jackson to posts of enlarged responsibility.

In the election of 1812, Madison survived a political challenge from De Witt Clinton, who gathered support from a motley collection of Federalists and discontented Republicans, some of whom wanted a more vigorous and some a less vigorous prosecution of the war. After a scurrilous, even disgraceful campaign, Clinton carried all of New England except Vermont, as well as New York, New Jersey, and Delaware, but Madison's strength elsewhere gave him a 128–89 victory in the electoral college.

Two years of anxiety, frustration, and defeat still faced Madison. Financial and diplomatic headaches increased throughout 1813 as Britain felt emboldened by the effects of Napoleon's disastrous retreat from Moscow, and American armies continued to flounder in the swamps west of Lake Erie. Only toward the end of the year did prospects for successful campaigns against Canada arise, following Commodore Oliver Hazard Perry's naval victory on Lake Erie on 10 September and Harrison's defeat of a British and Indian army on the Thames River, north of the lake, on 5 October.

Meanwhile, another inept campaign in New York State and bold excursions by British naval forces in the Chesapeake Bay and elsewhere along the Atlantic coast left the nation frustrated and apparently defenseless. Disheartened, Madison suffered a near-fatal illness in the summer of 1813, provoking tactless political enemies to wonder how he could "appear at the bar of Immortal Justice" with the "bloody crime" of an unnecessary war on his hands and to hope publicly that the vice president, "scant-patterned old skeleton" Elbridge Gerry, as one Federalist labeled him, would soon follow the "lingering incumbent" to the grave so that a Federalist president of the Senate might rescue the country from its woes. (Gerry did indeed die in November 1814.)

News of Napoleon's defeat at Leipzig and of Wellington's victories in Spain, reaching Washington late in 1813, made it certain, moreover, that Britain would soon have thousands of battle-hardened troops free to assault and punish its former colonies, which, British leaders felt, had attacked treacherously when England was in desperate struggle against the French tyrant. British transports soon brought a fresh army to Canada, and another one appeared in the Chesapeake Bay in the summer of 1814 accompanied by an awesome naval force. An issue of the *Times* of London that arrived in Washington in June 1814 threatened, "Oh, may no false liberality, no mistaken lenity, no weak and cowardly policy, interpose to save the United States from the blow! Strike! Chastize the savages, for such they are! With Madison and his perjured set no treaty can be made.. . . Our demands may be couched in a single word—Submission!" The French minister to Washington wrote, "The Cabinet is frightened.. . . It has a consciousness of its weakness and of the full strength of its enemy."

Madison tried to organize the defense of the capital, but Secretary Armstrong refused either to heed the president's suggestions or to formulate alternate plans. To make matters worse, the army commander in the region, General William Winder, although earnest and loyal, was inexperienced and incompetent. When British forces landed near Washington on 19 August 1814, Madison, Monroe, and Winder sought to muster and position the untested, largely militia forces. The Americans were outmaneuvered, fought a losing battle at Bladensburg on 24 August, and gave up the capital that afternoon.

The Madisons packed what state papers, valuables, and belongings they could and fled on horseback to Virginia as the British force burned the Capitol, the White House, and other public buildings. For seventy-two hours the exhausted president roamed the Virginia and Maryland countryside, searching for his family, sleeping wherever he could, and trying desperately to keep his army and govern-ment in being. He was personally courageous during the crisis and exerted a steadying influence on those around him. For a man of sixty-three, in uncertain health, his physical exertions were remarkable if not foolhardy or heroic.

The British, having humiliated the American government and not intent on permanent occupation, soon withdrew, and Madison returned to the charred and dispirited city on 27 August. He at once, quite properly, dismissed Armstrong and Winder for their serious unfitness in the crisis, and although his own shortcomings were not always those his detractors have charged against him, he does bear ultimate responsibility for the disaster. Sooner than any of his advisers, he warned of the likely motivation for, and place of, the British attack. As Monroe later observed, Washington "might have been saved, had the measures proposed by the President to the heads of departments on the first of July, and advised by them, and ordered by him, been carried into effect."

Madison's faults of conception lay mainly in supposing the militia could be mustered effectively after the British forces appeared and in trusting military command to Winder. A Jackson or a Winfield Scott would almost certainly have foiled the hesitant, poorly executed British campaign against the capital. Madison must bear the blame for Winder's unfortunate appointment as well as for the retention of Armstrong during a period of crisis. Whatever uproar might have followed dismissal of the politically powerful secretary of war, it would have been preferable to his vitiating presence.

Furthermore, if, as is generally warranted by the record, Madison knew that the preparations he deemed essential to the defense of Washington were not being made, he failed as commander in chief in not correcting the situation by whatever means necessary. The dangers and liabilities of almost any course of action likely to lead to correction were as grave as Madison supposed, but it was nevertheless incumbent on him to do something. The events of the summer of 1814 illustrate all too well the inadequacy in wartime of Madison's habitual caution and tendency to let complexities remain unresolved when no clear course of action was available. Although such inclinations are ordinarily virtues, in crises they are calamitous.

Madison's fault was more profound than personal predisposition or the accident of being in the wrong position at the wrong time. Shortly after the president's return to Washington, Navy Secretary

Jones, who had worked with him closely for a year and a half and had been with him almost constantly during the preparations, attack, and flight, observed, "The President is virtuous, able and patriotic, but . . . he finds difficulty in accommodating to the crisis some of those political axioms which he has so long indulged, because they have their foundation in virtue, but which from the vicious nature of the times and the absolute necessity of the case require some relaxation." That is, it was, ironically, Madison's very republican virtue that in part unsuited him to be a wartime president.

Madison's understanding of executive conduct did not require or even allow him single-handedly to make up for the reluctance of the people to be ready to defend themselves, for the hesitations of the states to adopt forthright measures, for the ineffectiveness of other executive officers, or for the failure of Congress to authorize and pay for a sufficient war machine. To have done so would, according to Madison's "political axioms," have corroded every virtue necessary to republican government: a responsible citizenry, vital state governments, self-reliant public servants, and respect for legislative leadership. It was, of course, impossible for him to be a Caesar or a Cromwell, but it was also against his nature and deeply held principles to become even a William Pitt or a Hamilton.

Earnest congressmen such as Nathaniel Macon, former President Jefferson, and even, in a lesser way, Gallatin himself managed, with good luck and without becoming gravely irresponsible, to evade the confrontation of republican pieties with the hounds of war thrust painfully and unavoidably on Madison by British arms in the summer of 1814. Madison believed, with much justification, that he could not conduct a war to validate a republican independence in the manner of an imperial proconsul without destroying that cause in the process. Had he done that, his failure would have been a moral one, permanently disastrous to the country. As it was, he only failed, pathetically in many ways, to find the proper blend, discerned by Washington and Lincoln, of stern, vigorous leadership and of republican deference necessary in wartime. The result was a merely temporary anxiety and destruction, perhaps a small price to pay to save the vital political character of the nation.

Although the repossession of the capital, the repulse of British forces before Baltimore (where Madison's prisoner—exchange envoy, Francis Scott Key, saw "by the dawn's early light" on 14 September that

"the star-spangled banner yet waved" over Fort McHenry), hard-fought battles on the Niagara frontier, and, most important, the defeat of a British land-and-water invasion of the Champlain Valley on 11 September cheered and heartened Americans, and in fact would eventually cause Britain to seek an end to the war, months were to pass before Madison knew the crisis was over. American commissioners were in Europe with instructions for seeking peace, but in the summer and fall of 1814, British diplomats were still insisting on harsh terms. In the meantime, as another powerful British force gathered in the Gulf of Mexico menacing New Orleans, an enlarged war seemed likely amid heightened domestic difficulties.

Although some Federalists in Congress gave loyal if grudging support of the war effort, extremists, still vociferous and strong, reacted differently. To one plea for support of the administration, a leading Federalist retorted:

> How often, in the name of God, will you agree to be cheated? What are you to gain by giving Mr. Madison Men and Money? . . . An union of the commercial states to take care of themselves, leaving the War, its expense and its debts to those choice spirits so ready to declare and so eager to carry it on, seems to be now the only rational course.

Not surprisingly, one visitor in Washington found Madison's thoughts and conversation "full of the New England sedition." To an old friend he wrote:

> You are not mistaken in viewing the conduct of the Eastern States as the source of our greatest difficulties in carrying on the war; as it is certainly the greatest, if not the sole, inducement with the enemy to persevere in it. The greater part of the people in that quarter have been brought by their leaders, aided by their priests, under a delusion scarcely exceeded by that recorded in the period of witchcraft; and the leaders are daily becoming more desperate in the use they make of it. Their object is power. If they could obtain it by menaces, their efforts would stop there. These failing, they are ready to go to every length.

In this atmosphere Madison faced more New England resistance to war measures. Massachusetts refused to send militia to meet a British invasion of Maine; Vermont smugglers drove herds of cattle into Canada to feed British troops; Connecticut Federalists talked of a New England army free from federal control; and the Massachusetts legislature called for a convention to plan regional "self-defense" and to decide whether "to lay the foundation for a radical reform in the national compact," a resolution that led to the Hartford Convention of December 1814.

Acting Secretary of War James Monroe found these moves so threatening that he sent the hero of the Battle of Lundy's Lane, Colonel Thomas Jesup, to Hartford, ostensibly as a recruiting officer but actually as a federal agent to watch for possible treason and rebellion. Jesup's unreassuring reports caused Monroe to authorize New York's Governor Daniel D. Tompkins and General Robert Swartwout to send in loyal troops in case of a New England uprising. Only the triumph of relative moderates at the Hartford Convention persuaded Monroe and Madison to relax from a posture of armed preparedness against potential domestic insurrection.

All this watchful concern by the administration occurred without whipping up the public against the dissenters, without attempting to interfere with the Hartford Convention, and without any special declarations of emergency or other measures that might have led to detentions, strictures on the press, threats to public meetings, or other curtailments of civil liberties. It might be argued, of course, that to praise such restraint is to make a virtue of necessity, since the degree of disaffection in New England was such that Madison could not have coerced the home territory of Daniel Shays even if he had tried. At the very least some stiff fighting might have ensued, but the temptation and perhaps the force for a repressive policy existed.

For the time being at least, British forces in Canada were discouraged and quiescent as attention focused on New Orleans, so the veterans of Plattsburg and the Niagara frontier, now battle-tested and under vigorous, young leadership, were available for service. A few regiments marched to Hartford, Springfield, or even Boston might have cowed the dissidents and emboldened national sentiment in the region. Furthermore, politically the Republicans might have relished an opportunity to brand their foes as traitors and perhaps discredit them for a generation. Again one need only imagine what Hamilton, who had mobilized an army against the whiskey rebels, might have done in New England in 1814 to see the point.

On 4 February 1815 long-delayed news of climactic events that had happened thousands of miles away finally reached the gloomy, anxious capital. First came word of an astonishing American victory on 8 January at New Orleans: Andrew Jackson's frontier army, drawn up behind breastworks and ably prepared and commanded, had destroyed a battle-hardened British army that advanced courageously but fruitlessly against the American lines. The British lost seven hundred killed, fourteen hundred wounded, and five hundred captured, to American casualties of seven killed and six wounded. Then, on 14 February, came news that a peace treaty with Britain had in fact been signed at Ghent, Belgium, on Christmas Eve, 1814.

For Madison, these events were immensely gratifying. Jackson's victory not only rescued the nation from a sense of military inferiority but also achieved a goal Madison had sought for thirty-five years: secure American possession of New Orleans and the great valley it controlled. Now, with Spain prostrate, France conquered, and Britain utterly defeated at the very gates of New Orleans itself, a century and a half of strife and changing control had ended; the red sea of British dead created by the fire of Jackson's men dramatically and finally underscored American possession of the western empire. Madison knew the cheering throngs that filled the streets of Washington were celebrating the most important triumph of American arms since Yorktown.

The Treaty of Ghent contained not one of the humiliating conditions insisted upon by the British the previous August and thus restored all American territory occupied by British forces; recognized American rights on the Mississippi, the Great Lakes, and the Newfoundland fishing banks; placed the two countries on equal grounds commercially; and, by neither confirming nor denying impressment and other maritime rights, left these matters to the almost surely benign consequences of peace. Thus, although the treaty in one way seemed to settle nothing, merely restoring the status quo antebellum, ignoring the maritime grievances so often proclaimed as the cause of the war, and leaving many disputed matters to be settled later by commissions, in fact the United States, by standing up to Britain, had won a second war of independence.

The Senate ratified the treaty unanimously, and on 17 February, Madison declared the conflict ended. Celebrations again resounded throughout the nation, as not only were its independence and honor rescued but, with dazzling trade prospects opened, an era of growth and prosperity seemed assured. Furthermore, these glorious events, coming as they did when internal dissension and financial chaos threatened but before the Madison administration had to take repressive steps, seemed to vindicate the whole republican concept of government. This, of course, was Madison's only real war aim and the crowning achievement of his public life.

Madison as National Leader and Elder Statesman

With the return of peace, Madison sought out policies that would allow the nation to fulfill its potential. He gave top civilian and military appointments to able and proven colleagues—Monroe, Gallatin, John Quincy Adams, Commodores John Rodgers and David Porter, and Generals Jackson and Winfield Scott, for example—in whom the whole nation took pride. He also provided leadership to Congress in his annual message of December 1815, recommending a rechartered Bank of the United States, an equitable commercial treaty with Great Britain, a mildly protective tariff, a small but high-quality defense establishment, a national university, and a program of internal improvements authorized by a constitutional amendment.

This broad, national program was for Madison a propitious return to the high hopes he had shared with Jefferson and Gallatin in 1801–1804, before the ten-year hiatus forced on the nation by the traumatic, nearly overwhelming effects of the Napoleonic Wars. With the Hamiltonian engine in part restrained or dismantled and the nation's republican institutions validated and strengthened by their wartime testing, it was possible to use them for the public interest, and it was the responsibility of the president to articulate that interest. Although it was the task of Congress to legislate, the need for both practical and symbolic leadership was still crucial. Madison thus furnished steady, principled guidance during two years of national euphoria.

Viewed in this light, Henry Adams' often repeated criticism that Madison found himself forced to become a federalist in order to govern properly becomes a half-truth. He was, as Jefferson had claimed for himself, a federalist in that he saw virtue in active national leadership and other federalist principles, but Madison neither abandoned republican precepts nor sought to embrace federalism in its partisan guise. Rather, he intended to eliminate party itself from public life. It was not only safe but essential in 1815 to provide presidential leadership, within widely acknowledged republican guidelines, for the nation as a whole; and in order to do this, the president would have, as much as possible, to rise above partisanship.

Madison (and the other pre-Jackson presidents), rather than supposing it was necessary for the chief executive, even in the White House, to be a vigorous, unabashed party leader, accepted the view that good leadership had to be nonpartisan. Madison knew, of course, that no human being can entirely transcend a partial view, but he would also have insisted that, especially in executive office, it is important to de-emphasize party and faction and neutralize them as much as possible, as he had argued in *The Federalist* (paper no. 10). He further recognized there that special-interest, pluralist politics were "sown in the nature of man" and were "nourished" by the very air of free government. But Madison also believed that the serious intention and the obvious stance of the president to subordinate party (partial) interests and needs, if consistently kept in mind and in public view, would make a difference both in how he acted and in how the nation responded to him. Such an intention and such a stance, moreover, were especially important in a republic because they might influence public perceptions of the presidency and thus affect the range and character of leadership possible in the nation.

Madison's realism about the irrepressible causes of faction led him, in framing the Constitution, to guard against their influence and against any concentration of power that would allow greed and ambition to be dangerous to liberty. But he also regarded virtuous (that is, nonpartisan) leadership as vital to the public good, and he was willing, indeed determined, to encourage such leadership even if it meant putting some restraint on direct, popular government. In so acting, moreover, Madison believed not that he showed hostility to self-government but rather that he was being a wise and creative democrat. As his collaborator Jefferson said so clearly and so often, the true test of a republic was whether or not it cultivated talent and virtue. Neither he nor Madison, furthermore, ever doubted that wise leadership, above party, could provide critical assistance in meeting that test. Such, at any rate, was the aspiration, the republican commitment, and the conception of the presidency that guided Madison as he first devised and later filled the office that for two centuries has focused the hopes as well as the forebodings of the American people.

In retirement at Montpelier, his plantation in Orange County, Virginia, Madison and his vivacious, supremely sociable wife, Dolley, enjoyed twenty years of happy visiting with family, old friends, and semiofficial guests (most notably, the Marquis de Lafayette in 1824) who wanted to see and talk with the sage soon to be known as the Father of the Constitution. Madison remained active politically both as an adviser to public officials and as a participant in some especially favored activities. As long as Monroe was president, Madison wrote and conferred with him regularly, especially on the intricate and momentous settlements in foreign policy with Europe and Latin America that culminated in the Monroe Doctrine of 1823.

Letters exchanged and visits enjoyed with Gallatin, Richard Rush, John Quincy Adams, Henry Clay, and Martin Van Buren kept Madison in close touch with the nation's affairs well into the Jacksonian era. Most important, he took a leading role in combating the nullification movement, especially in denying, directly and authoritatively, that the Virginia Resolutions of 1798 had advocated that doctrine.

He continued a lifelong interest in scientific farming as president of the Agricultural Society of Albemarle, served for a time as president of the antislavery American Colonization Society, and attended the Virginia Constitutional Convention of 1829, where he sought both to diminish the power of Tidewater slaveholders and to extend the franchise. His most sustained public service, however, was to assist Jefferson in founding the University of Virginia and then to serve as its rector for eight years following Jefferson's death in 1826.

Although for ten years or so after his retirement Madison's health remained good enough to allow him to supervise his own farm daily and to make journeys to see many Virginia friends (including semiannual visits with Jefferson and Monroe near Charlottesville, twenty-five miles away), rheumatism and stomach disorders gradually confined him to Montpelier. There he spent most of his time arranging his voluminous papers and especially preparing his full and uniquely valuable notes on the debates of the Convention of 1787 for posthumous publication (published in three volumes in 1839, they became the leading source for understanding that signal event). In wide correspondence and frequent visits with dozens of historians and scholars, the learned, well-informed former president exerted a profound and judicious influence on the recording of the early history of the United States. In 1833 and 1834 his health failed seriously and he was confined to the fireside of his sitting room, where he died quietly on 28 June 1836, the last survivor of those who had played a leading role in the founding of the Republic.

BIBLIOGRAPHY

William T. Hutchinson and William M. E. Rachal, eds., *The Papers of James Madison*, 23 vols. (Chicago and Charlottesville, Va., 1962–), is the full, definitive publication of Madison's papers, including letters written to him, now complete in 17 volumes to 1801, and with beginning volumes in the Secretary of State Series ed. by Robert J. Brugger, et al. (5 vols.) and the Presidential Series, ed. by Robert A. Rutland et al. (4 vols.). Gaillard Hunt, ed., *The Writings of James Madison*, 9 vols. (New York, 1900–1910), is the best source for Madison's writings not yet reprinted in *The Papers of James Madison*. Marvin Meyers, ed., *The Mind of the Founder: Sources of the Political Thought of James Madison* (Indianapolis, Ind., 1973), provides a useful selection of Madison's writings.

Irving Brant, *James Madison*, 6 vols. (Indianapolis, Ind., 1941–1961), gives a detailed, fully sympathetic account of Madison's life. Ralph Ketcham, *James Madison: A Biography* (New York, 1971; Charlottesville, Va., 1990), is a full-length biography. Robert A. Rutland, *The Presidency of James Madison* (Lawrence, Kans., 1990), is a sympathetic account of that subject. William Lee Miller, *The Business of May Next: James Madison and the Founding* (Charlottesville, Va., 1992), and Jack N. Rakove, *Original Meanings: Politics and Ideas in the Making of the Constitution* (New York, 1996), are excellent studies of Madison's uniquely important role during the founding era, 1786–1791.

J. C. A. Stagg, *Mr. Madison's War: Politics, Diplomacy, and Warfare in the Early American Republic, 1783–1830* (Princeton, N.J., 1983), is the authoritative study of both the coming and the conduct of the War of 1812. Drew R. McCoy, *The Last of the Fathers: James Madison and the Republican Legacy* (New York, 1989), provides a valuable interpretation of the last parts of Madison's career. Robert A. Rutland, ed., *James Madison and the American Nation, 1751–1836: An Encyclopedia* (New York, 1994), contains four hundred entries on Madison and his times.

Recent works include Garry Wills, *James Madison* (New York, 2002), and Gary Rosen, *American Compact: James Madison and the Problem of Founding* (Lawrence, Kans., 1999).

James Monroe

Harry Ammon

James Monroe THE LIBRARY OF CONGRESS

INAUGURATION day, 4 March 1817, was one of those rare late winter days in Washington with more than a hint of spring—sunny and balmy. Throughout the morning a steady stream of citizens hastened along the dusty, rutted streets toward the temporary congressional quarters in a frame structure across from the burned-out Capitol. The crowd, largely composed of residents of the city, included visitors from as far away as New York who had taken advantage of the cheaper rapid transportation offered by the newly introduced steamboats. By noon a crowd estimated at eight thousand, the largest ever assembled in Washington, had gathered.

The circumstances that occasioned an outdoor ceremony were entirely fortuitous. Usually inaugurations were held in the House chamber, but the refusal of the representatives to let the senators bring with them their new red upholstered armchairs had culminated in a deadlock broken only by deciding to move the ceremony outdoors. The managers were so distracted by this dispute that they forgot to invite the diplomatic corps, which was conspicuously absent. President-elect James Monroe and his vice president, Daniel D. Tompkins, arrived shortly before noon, escorted by a troop of volunteer cavalry. After being greeted by retiring President James Madison, the party entered the House chamber, where the vice president was sworn in, before returning to the outdoor platform. Monroe was then administered the oath of office by Chief Justice John Marshall, a friend of his youth but since alienated by political differences.

The new president, who stepped forth to deliver his inaugural address, was a familiar figure to Washingtonians, who were accustomed to seeing him go about the city clad in the smallclothes of an earlier age—a black coat, black knee breeches, and black silk stockings. On ceremonial occasions he often wore a blue coat and buff knee breeches, an outfit reminiscent of Revolutionary War uniforms. Now in his fifty-ninth year, Monroe was erect in bearing, robust and vigorous in manner. His hair (worn long and tied behind with a black ribbon) had grayed, and his face had become deeply lined during the recent war. Nearly six feet tall, with dignified and formal manners, he was an impressive figure but by no means handsome—his face was plain, the nose large though regular. His wide-set gray eyes were his most striking feature, exhibiting a generosity of spirit confirmed by the warmth of his smile. Never arousing the same passionate devotion as Jefferson, Monroe was admired for his heroism during the Revolution and for his long service to the nation.

In his inaugural address—described by one auditor as of a "plain homespun character"—Monroe spoke of the renewed sense of national unity apparent after the difficulties of the war years. Espousing a course of moderate nationalism, he recommended the continued protection of domestic manufactures. He also stressed the need for the construction of roads and canals to facilitate the movement of commerce, but failed to clarify his position on the constitutionality of federally funded internal improvements. He devoted the lengthiest portion of his message to a project in which he took a personal interest—the need to improve the defenses of the nation by maintaining a larger peacetime army and by the construction of a chain of coastal fortifications to avert the danger of future invasion.

Early Political and Diplomatic Career

James Monroe, the fifth president and the last of the great trio of Virginia Republicans who had held the presidency since 1801, was born in Westmoreland County, Virginia, on 28 April 1758. His father's family, of Scottish origin, had been settled in the county for a century, but with modest holdings of only six hundred acres the Monroes had never cut a large figure in colonial affairs. When his father, Spence, died in 1774, Monroe, his sister, and two younger brothers were placed under the guardianship of his uncle, Joseph Jones of King George County, one of the most influential leaders during the revolutionary era. Jones, who was then childless, took an active interest in his nephew, and it was with Jones's encouragement that Monroe entered William and Mary College in 1774—the first of his family to attend college, as he later proudly recalled—but his residence there was brief.

Caught up in the enthusiasm for the revolutionary cause, he enlisted in the Third Virginia Regiment in the spring of 1775. Within months the young lieutenant was fighting with Washington at New York. He won fame and promotion to major for his heroism when he and a handful of men put out of action the British cannons blocking Washington's advance at Trenton. As aide-de-camp to General William Alexander, Monroe wintered at Valley Forge and fought at Monmouth. Preferring a field command to the routine of a staff officer, Monroe returned to Virginia in the summer of 1779, in the hope of raising a regiment.

Unable to obtain recruits, Monroe's spirits were at a low ebb when he met Thomas Jefferson, the governor of Virginia. This meeting constituted a turning point in Monroe's life, establishing a close and enduring friendship, cemented by common intellectual interests and political objectives. Jefferson sensed in Monroe not only a warm and generous character but also a powerful determination to be of service to his country no matter what the cost might be. Monroe's close association with one of the most original and best informed minds of the day was a decisive influence in his intellectual development.

In 1782, Monroe entered the House of Burgesses from King George County, where he had begun to practice law. His abilities were immediately recognized by the established leaders in the state and the next year won him membership in the Virginia delegation to the Continental Congress, along with Jefferson. When Jefferson left in July 1784 to take up his post as minister to France, he left for Monroe a collection of books and his French cook, but his most valuable gift was a letter of introduction to James Madison. Jefferson's praise of Monroe to his old friend was unstinted: "The scrupulousness of his honor will make you safe in the most confidential communications. A better man cannot be." Thus was forged the final link in the great collaboration that shaped the future of the early Republic.

In Congress, Monroe moved rapidly to the fore-front of the leaders committed to strengthening the Articles of Confederation. His most constructive work as a delegate was the drafting of the plan of ter-ritorial government incorporated in the Northwest Ordinance of 1787 and the blocking of the move to close the Mississippi to American navigation in re-turn for commercial concessions from Spain.

When his term ended in 1786, Monroe was not alone on his homeward trip to Virginia. Beside him in his carriage was his bride of eight months, the for-mer Elizabeth Kortright, daughter of a once wealthy New York merchant. Much admired for her beauty, the elegance of her dress, and the refinement of her polished, if rather formal, manners, she brought to Monroe the happiness of family life so much prized by his generation. In the terms of the age, she con-ducted herself as an ideal wife should, devoted to her children and never obtruding in political concerns. The Monroes lived for two years in Fredericksburg, where he opened a law office. Then, in 1789, they moved to a plantation he purchased in Albemarle County, thus realizing Monroe's cherished dream of living within a few miles of Jefferson's estate, Monti-cello. Since the Madisons lived but twenty miles away in Orange County, social visits and political confer-ences were easily arranged. It was in Virginia that Monroe's two daughters were born—Eliza in 1786 and Maria Hester in 1802.

At home in Virginia, Monroe combined an active county law practice with the management of his plantation and membership in the state legislature. As a member of the Virginia ratifying convention, he opposed the Constitution, objecting to the excessive power granted to the Senate and the president. The law had little appeal for Monroe, and he readily aban-doned his practice after his election to the United States Senate in 1790. He continued, nonetheless, to supervise his plantation, which remained the princi-pal source of his income. He always considered farm-ing his profession and politics but an avocation.

As a senator, Monroe worked closely with Madi-son, then in the House, in combating the Hamilto-nian fiscal program. He aided Jefferson and Madison in laying the groundwork of opposition to Washing-ton's policies, which culminated in the formation of the Republican party. In 1794, President Washington appointed Monroe to succeed Federalist Gou-verneur Morris as minister to France in the hope that the selection of a Republican would improve rela-tions strained by France's conviction that the Wash-ington administration was pro-British. The ratification of Jay's Treaty in 1795 confirmed the French government in its belief that Washington was hostile to the revolutionary movement and rendered ineffective Monroe's efforts at reconciliation. Irritat-ed by Monroe's open enthusiasm for the revolution-ary regime, Washington abruptly recalled him in 1796. Monroe responded with a lengthy pamphlet at-tacking the administration. His *View of the Conduct of the Executive in Foreign Affairs* . . . (Philadel-phia, 1798) was approved by fellow Republicans and won him the governorship of Virginia in 1799.

Just before leaving for France in 1794, Monroe had purchased a more extensive estate adjacent to Monticello. Selling his earlier holdings, he now made his home on his new plantation of twenty-five hun-dred acres, which he named Highlands (now known as Ashlawn). Until his election as president, he and his family lived in a simple frame house at Highlands.

As Virginia's governor from 1799 to 1802, Mon-roe improved the administrative organization of the state government, providing stronger leadership than his predecessors. He was the first governor to use the annual message to outline matters needing legislative action. His effective handling of the abor-tive slave uprising known as Gabriel's Rebellion was highly praised.

Monroe's third term as governor had no sooner ended than Jefferson, in January 1803, appointed him as special envoy to France to negotiate the pur-chase of a site on the lower Mississippi as a port of deposit. The abrupt suspension of the right of de-posit by the Spanish authorities made the mission an urgent one. Accompanied by his wife and daughters, Monroe reached Paris on 12 April 1803, to be coolly greeted by the resident minister, Robert R. Living-ston, who had just learned after months of importun-ing that Napoleon was willing to sell all Louisiana. Faced by the fact that it was all or nothing, Livingston and Monroe ignored the limitations of their instruc-tions and signed an agreement. Monroe rightly as-sumed that his friendship with President Jefferson and Secretary of State Madison would ensure the ac-ceptance of the treaty.

After completing his mission to France, Monroe was named minister to Great Britain, where he re-mained until 1807 except for a foray to Madrid in a vain effort to purchase Florida. His main objectives in England were to secure recognition of American principles of neutral rights and a cessation of impressment. Not until 1806, when Charles James Fox became foreign secretary after twenty years in opposition, did Monroe see any hope of a modification of long-standing British policy. He at once began negotiations but had to postpone them, pending the arrival of special envoy William Pinkney.

Fox's illness and death a few months after Pinkney's arrival so weakened the cabinet that major policy changes could not be undertaken. Nonetheless, Monroe and Pinkney concluded an agreement that modified British commercial restrictions but contained no provision on impressment. The best they could obtain from the British commissioners was a note appended to the treaty promising that the "strictest care" would be taken "to preserve the citizens of the United States from any molestation or injury." In accepting this informal statement, Monroe assured Madison that it meant the end of impressment. Although the British, he said, would never abandon a basic principle, they would alter policy through admiralty orders.

Monroe was truly shocked when Jefferson rejected the treaty without submitting it to the Senate. Having been absent so long, Monroe did not realize that the administration regarded impressment as the central issue. Madison, expecting Monroe to return much earlier, had failed to make the point clear in his instructions. The treaty had the misfortune to arrive in Washington at the same time as the news of the British orders-in-council of January 1807, which banned neutral trade with the Continent.

When Monroe returned home in 1807, he was warmly received by Jefferson and Madison but disappointed at their failure to seek his advice on foreign affairs. During the next few years his relations with Madison, whom he blamed for the rejection of the treaty, were strained. No longer did the Madisons stop at Highlands on their regular visits to Monticello. It was through Jefferson's good offices that the friendship was restored, for, as Jefferson told Monroe, if he were to lose the friendship of either he would regard it as the "greatest of calamities which could assail my future peace of mind."

Secretary of State, 1811–1817

With Madison's foreign policy subject to rising criticism from Republicans and Federalists alike, in March 1811 he replaced Secretary of State Robert

Smith with Monroe. Both critics and friends of the administration welcomed the appointment of Monroe, an experienced diplomat, for Smith was widely regarded as incompetent. In bringing Monroe into the cabinet, Madison had decided to take a firmer stand with the European belligerents by refusing to settle minor issues unless major concerns were first resolved. As Monroe explained to John Taylor of Caroline, the time had come for the nation to "cease dealing in the small way of embargoes, non-intercourse, and non-importation" and prepare to defend its rights by force. Since neither the French minister nor his British counterpart had authority to make concessions, Monroe's efforts to press them for alterations in policy proved fruitless.

During August 1811 the president and Monroe met while in Virginia and agreed that unless the 1807 orders-in-council were repealed, the only recourse would be to declare war. When Congress met, Monroe worked closely with Speaker Henry Clay and John C. Calhoun, chairman of the House Committee on Foreign Affairs. Their cooperation, as well as the support of younger War Hawks, enabled Madison to secure the approval of defense measures. Monroe, in fact, helped Calhoun's committee draft a response to Madison's war message of 1 June 1812. The House responded promptly, but not until 18 June did the Senate concur.

Monroe preferred a field command during the war rather than the relative inactivity of the State Department, but this proved impossible, since it would have meant placing him over officers who had held higher ranks during the Revolution. When Secretary of War William Eustis, overwhelmed by the increased administrative burden, resigned late in 1812, Madison had to abandon his plan of appointing Monroe after it was learned that confirmation would encounter opposition from northern Republicans and Federalists critical of continued Virginia domination of the national government. To mollify his critics, Madison turned to John Armstrong, Robert Livingston's brother-in-law.

From the outset friction was evident between the two secretaries, for Armstrong felt that Monroe had deprived Livingston of the proper credit due for the Louisiana Purchase. Armstrong vigorously opposed the recommendation made by Monroe and others that the defenses of the capital and Chesapeake Bay area needed strengthening against the possibility of an invasion. Preferring to direct the affairs of his department from the field with the northern army, Armstrong continued to minimize the threat even after it was learned in the spring of 1814 that the British were amassing a large force in the West Indies.

On 2 July, disregarding Armstrong's objections, Madison created a new military district for the bay area under the command of General William Winder, whose preparations were persistently obstructed by the secretary of war. Thus, when a large British force appeared in the bay, no arrangements had been made for reconnaissance. It was Monroe, riding out with a troop of volunteer cavalry, who brought the first reports of the British movement.

Armstrong was blamed for the resultant fiasco at Bladensburg—where the president, Monroe, and Armstrong were all on the field—and the subsequent British occupation of Washington and burning of the public buildings in August 1814. Armstrong's resignation and his replacement by Monroe, who continued as acting secretary of state, were greeted enthusiastically by the citizens of Washington and the military.

Working long hours—frequently sleeping in his office—Monroe brought order into the confused state of affairs in the War Department. His service came too late to affect the outcome of the war, for the Treaty of Ghent arrived in February 1815. As secretary of state, Monroe had drafted the original instructions for the peace commissioners as well as the later modification authorizing them to abandon the American demands on impressment and neutral rights. After relinquishing the War Department in March 1815, Monroe left for a much needed rest in Virginia. Not until six months later was he well enough to return to the capital and begin the negotiations that culminated in the Rush-Bagot agreement to demilitarize the Great Lakes.

With the war over, public interest promptly focused on the coming presidential election. It was generally assumed that Monroe, because of his close association with Jefferson and Madison and long service to the nation, would be the Republican nominee. However, the nomination was by no means assured, for many northern politicians were weary of Virginia domination. New Yorkers were the most outspoken, feeling that they had too long been relegated to the second place on the ticket. Without a northern candidate of national stature, they turned to the secretary of the treasury, William H. Crawford. A former senator from Georgia, Crawford owed his prominence to the fact that his easygoing, jovial manner had made him immensely well liked by con-gressmen; since the nomination was in the hands of a congressional caucus, his personal popularity was a major asset. He also had the backing of Jefferson's secretary of the treasury, Albert Gallatin, to whose influence Crawford owed his elevation to the Treasury.

Monroe and his congressional supporters were sufficiently worried by Crawford's candidacy that they considered boycotting the congressional caucus in favor of a state nomination. Madison, following Jefferson's example, was outwardly neutral, but his preference for Monroe was well known. The columns of the *National Intelligencer*, the semi-official administration paper, were full of pro-Monroe items. Crawford, only forty-four, was reluctant to challenge his senior colleague but did not publicly withdraw his name. Consequently, when the caucus met in March 1816, Monroe was nominated by the disappointingly small margin of sixty-five to fifty-four. In effect the caucus was the real election, since the Federalists were so weakened by their opposition to the war that they mustered only minimal support for Rufus King, who received 34 electoral votes to the 183 cast for Monroe.

The disparity in the electoral count marked the end of the first two-party system, a development welcomed by leaders of Monroe's generation in both parties. They had long regarded party conflict as a divisive element tending to destroy republican institutions. They cherished the ideal expressed by Washington in his farewell address of a nation without parties, governed by men chosen on their merits. Shortly after his election Monroe expressed his commitment to this goal when he observed that the "Chief Magistrate of the Country ought not to be the head of a party, but of the nation itself." However, he did not fall in with Andrew Jackson's suggestion that the process of party amalgamation be facilitated by appointing Federalists to high office. Free government, Monroe told Jackson, must still depend on its "decided friends, who stood firm in the day of trial."

Monroe as President: The "Era of Good Feelings" Begins

In choosing his cabinet Monroe honored established precedent, reappointing his predecessor's secretaries and preserving a geographical balance. Crawford was continued in the Treasury, although he had hoped for a transfer to the State Department as the probable successor to Monroe. Benjamin Crowninshield, a New Englander with a mercantile background, remained in the Navy Department, and Richard Rush of Pennsylvania continued as attorney general until late in 1817, when he was named minister to Great Britain, a post more to his liking. Rush's replacement was William Wirt, a successful Baltimore lawyer celebrated for his popular biography of Patrick Henry. Having no political ambitions, Wirt continued to busy himself with his private practice, since the attorney generalship was a part-time office.

In an effort to broaden the geographical basis of his administration, Monroe wanted to place a westerner in the War Department. After a series of refusals, including one from Henry Clay, who, as a presidential aspirant, was unwilling to enter the cabinet in a lesser post than that held by Crawford, Monroe selected John C. Calhoun. The South Carolinian had demonstrated a command of military affairs while a member of the House during the war. Intellectually gifted, tall, and handsome, the thirty-five-year-old Calhoun presented an image vastly different from the gloomy one of his later years. He gave the War Department an efficient administration that effected substantial economies.

The major post, that of secretary of state, went to John Quincy Adams, who had been absent from the United States since 1809 on a series of diplomatic appointments that had taken him from St. Petersburg, to Ghent, and then to London. The son of a Federalist president and himself a former Federalist, he had been one of the moderate Federalists who had entered Republican ranks during Jefferson's administration. Monroe chose Adams because of his extensive diplomatic experience, a consideration Monroe felt had been ignored by previous administrations. Monroe also intended to disabuse people of the notion that the incumbent in the Department of State was necessarily the president's hand-picked successor. In this Monroe failed. Within a year Adams had developed a solid core of supporters in Congress and was considered a major candidate for the presidency.

Adams—a cold, pedantic man, ill at ease in large gatherings and unprepossessing in appearance (he was short, plump, and balding)—proved the ablest of the secretaries and intensely loyal to his chief. Adams' passion for work, concern for detail, and ability to draft forceful and logical state papers made him invaluable. He genuinely admired Monroe for his sound judgment, although he was frequently irked by the deliberate processes of the president's mind. Sharing, as they did, a common view of American for-

eign policy goals, their working relationship was extremely harmonious. While Monroe kept full control over policy decisions, he entrusted Adams with all discussions with foreign diplomats. Because Monroe felt that Jefferson's and Madison's habit of casual discussion with diplomats had been a source of confusion, the president restricted his contact with diplomats to formal and ceremonial occasions. Adams' lengthy political diary provides an intimate view of the workings of the Monroe administration.

The only significant change in the cabinet during Monroe's two terms was in the Navy Department. Crowninshield resigned in 1818 and was replaced by Smith Thompson of New York, who remained until 1823, when he was shunted to the Supreme Court at the request of Senator Martin Van Buren of New York. Van Buren, a rising power in the Republican party, was committed to Crawford and felt it essential to squelch Thompson's ambitions. Thompson was succeeded (probably at Calhoun's suggestion) by former Senator Samuel L. Southard of New Jersey. Personally agreeable, Southard was a close friend of Samuel L. Gouverneur, the New Yorker who married Monroe's younger daughter, Maria Hester.

To signalize the coming era of party harmony and the renewal of national unity, Monroe followed George Washington's example by embarking on a tour of the nation. This he completed in two segments, visiting New England and the Middle Atlantic states in 1817 and making a less extensive tour in the West and South two years later. His purpose was clearly understood. Fittingly, it was in a Federalist newspaper, as the editor welcomed the approaching end of party warfare, that the phrase "Era of Good Feelings" made its appearance. Monroe's northward journey was the occasion of unprecedented demonstrations—troops of militia, parades, banquets, and delegations of citizens who greeted him fulsomely not only as president but as a celebrated hero of the Revolution.

The high point was reached in Boston, where the streets were lined with a crowd estimated at forty thousand. After a public banquet attended by leading Federalists, Monroe made a round of private visits to old opponents of his party. So great was the rush of Federalists to do him homage that, as Abigail Adams shrewdly remarked, it was like an "expiation" for sins. She attributed Monroe's success in winning approval to "his agreeable affability . . . unassuming manners . . . [and] his polite attentions to all orders and ranks."

Monroe had every reason to feel that his tour had succeeded in its objectives. By 1819 every New

England state but one was in the hands of the Republicans. The presidential election of 1820, in which he received all but one of the electoral votes, seemed another proof that party conflict had ceased to be a factor in national political life.

The president and his family did not move into the executive mansion until September 1817, for not until then were the renovations after the fire completed. It was at this time that the mansion, covered with white paint to conceal the scars of fire, became widely known as the White House. At first the Monroes used their own furniture, awaiting the arrival from France of draperies, china, furniture, wall coverings, marble mantelpieces, and ormolu clocks (ordered without nudes). During their residences in France, Monroe and his wife had acquired a preference for French styles not only in furnishings but in social usages.

The presidential family consisted of Mrs. Monroe; Eliza and her husband, George Hay; and the president's youngest brother, Joseph, who acted as a private secretary. Until he returned to New York in 1820 after marrying Maria Hester, Monroe's youngest daughter, Samuel L. Gouverneur was a frequent resident and occasional secretary to the president. Since funds were not provided for staffing the White House, Monroe employed his own servants. With the Monroes a note of formality reminiscent of the Washington years reappeared. At official dinner parties, strict precedence, much to the pleasure of the diplomats, replaced Jefferson's pell-mell. Dinners were served in the formal French manner, with the dishes handed around by the servants. It took official and social Washington some time to recover from Mrs. Monroe's announcement that she, unlike Dolley Madison, would neither return nor make calls. She would, however, be at home in the mornings to receive callers. During Monroe's second term his wife was frequently ill, and so her duties as hostess were filled by her daughter Eliza.

Monroe continued the custom of biweekly evening receptions (known as drawing rooms), which had been abandoned by Jefferson but resumed by the Madisons. The doors were open to all citizens properly dressed. The president received guests standing in the Oval Room. His wife and Eliza, whose stylish dresses were the envy of every Washington lady, were seated beside him. As the guests walked about the rooms, servants passed trays of refreshments and music was usually provided by the marine band. Apart from these occasions, the president and his family led a very private life. When his daughter Maria Hester was married in the White House, only members of the family were present. The president, again following Washington's usage, did not accept invitations from the diplomatic corps, members of the cabinet, or members of Congress.

During the sessions there might be as many as twenty at dinner, for every caller was usually invited to dine. On these all-male occasions Mrs. Monroe was not present. Since the president's salary of $25,000 without any supplements was inadequate to cover the cost of entertaining, Monroe's indebtedness, already large, increased rapidly.

During the war years Monroe had been able to make infrequent visits to Albemarle. He preferred to stay at Oak Hill, a property he had acquired many years earlier, only thirty miles from the capital. Although the plantation was not as large as Highlands, he regarded the Oak Hill estate as more fertile and potentially more productive; consequently, after his election to the presidency, he decided to make it his principal residence and constructed a handsome porticoed mansion.

In response to the disappearance of political parties, Monroe developed new methods of executive leadership. Every president since Washington had relied upon party loyalty to ensure congressional approval of administration measures. Bereft of party support, Monroe turned to the members of his cabinet as a source of power. Three of the secretaries—Adams, Crawford, and Calhoun—as aspirants to the presidency had substantial followings in Congress. Of the leading hopefuls only Henry Clay had elected to remain outside the administration. It was not until Monroe's second term that Andrew Jackson's strength as a candidate was evident. As John Quincy Adams' diary makes abundantly clear, Monroe's frequent cabinet meetings were not held to secure advice but to hammer out a consensus. It is noteworthy that Monroe was able to win congressional approval for every measure that had the support of the cabinet. He never consulted the secretaries when he knew agreement was impossible.

To a greater extent than his predecessors, Monroe used his annual messages to outline concerns needing legislative attention rather than merely as a general report on the main events of the past years. Personal contact with congressmen played an important role, and here Monroe's openness and personal warmth were effective. Every day during the sessions of Congress there was a constant stream of visitors to the White House; no appointments were needed, the president received all, and, as was expected, he usually invited his callers to dinner.

Economic Policy

Although foreign affairs, which the Constitution placed directly under the control of the executive, occupied much of his attention, a variety of domestic issues required executive involvement. In his first annual message, Monroe startled the members of Congress by recommending that the Constitution be amended to authorize federal construction of roads and canals. In making this proposal Monroe was attempting to resolve the dilemma created when Madison, just before leaving office, vetoed as unconstitutional a bill appropriating dividends from the federally owned stock in the Bank of the United States for internal improvements. Madison's action had seemed inconsistent to many, for Madison, like Jefferson, had signed bills for the construction of the Cumberland Road. When Monroe queried Madison, he received the unsatisfactory response that the earlier bills had been signed hastily, without full consideration of the issue.

Monroe's recommendation produced some acrimonious debates, but action on an amendment was blocked by those who insisted that Congress had adequate power. Monroe, to his surprise and pain, was vigorously criticized for meddling in a purely legislative matter. In the next few years Monroe contributed to the confusion by signing bills for the extension of the Cumberland Road. Not until 1822, when he vetoed a bill for the collection of tolls on the Cumberland Road, did he have an opportunity to clarify his position. In a lengthy essay he argued that the collection of tolls was an invasion of the police power of the states. It was true that the road had been built with federal funds, but jurisdiction had remained in the hands of the states that had cleared the right of way. This finespun argument did not strike contemporaries as very convincing, no matter where they stood on the issue.

Monroe took a particular interest in the strengthening of the defenses of the nation. Just before leaving the War Department in 1815, he had submitted a report to Congress recommending that the army be retained at twenty thousand men rather than returned to the prewar figure of ten thousand. He also outlined an extensive plan for constructing coastal fortifications. Although Congress reduced the army to its prewar level, the substantial sum of $400,000 was appropriated in 1818 for coastal fortifications. The next year the sum was increased to $800,000. However, the decline in federal revenues following the Panic of 1819 led to a cutback in 1821 to $220,000. Only after revenues improved in 1822 did Congress raise the annual appropriation to $400,000, in response to Monroe's plea for the need to defend Florida.

Midway in his first term Monroe was confronted by two unexpected domestic crises. During his western tour in 1819, Monroe had become aware of the distress precipitated by the first peacetime depression—the so-called Panic of 1819. There was large-scale unemployment in urban areas, farm prices were depressed, and business failures were numerous in the new industries established during the war. The depression was the result of complex factors ill understood at that time. Monroe shared the prevailing opinion that the major causes were the influx of cheap European manufactures, which forced the closing of factories, and the financial instability resulting from excessive note issues and careless loan practices by state-chartered banks. Neither Monroe nor his contemporaries appreciated the role of the extensive speculation in western lands nor the impact of the catastrophic drop in cotton prices in 1818.

Contemporaries unjustly blamed the financial distress on the policies of the second Bank of the United States (rechartered in 1817), admittedly badly managed by William Jones, its first president. Monroe, who considered the bank essential to ensure a sound currency and to control the careless habits of state banks in making loans, succeeded in 1819 in persuading the directors to replace Jones with Langdon Cheves, a far abler financier. Monroe approved Chief Justice Marshall's decision in *McCulloch v. Maryland* (1819), which upheld the constitutionality of the bank.

Within the limitations of current thinking about the role of government in the economy, there was little that Congress could do to ameliorate the suffering caused by the depression. In his annual message of 1819, the president urged citizens to respond to the current difficulties, which he considered temporary, by practicing industry and economy—a policy also considered proper for the federal government. In response to his suggestion that Congress "give encouragement to domestic industries," a bill was introduced providing for increased duties on textiles, the industry most hurt by imports. This mild protectionist measure encountered immediate opposition from southern congressmen, many of whom had eagerly supported the tariff of 1816. The bill passed the House but failed in the Senate by one vote.

The only form of governmental intervention familiar to Americans during economic crises was in the form of debtor relief provided by the states. Although debtor problems lay mostly within the jurisdiction of the states, the federal government was faced with extensive defaults in payments for purchases of public land. In his annual message of 1820, Monroe recommended that purchasers who acquired the land when prices were high be granted a "reasonable indulgence." Following a specific plan submitted by Crawford, a bill was passed permitting debtors unable to pay the balance to secure title for that portion for which they had already paid. A discount was granted those making their payments on time.

Since government revenues from customs and land sales had declined so sharply, the Treasury in 1820 was faced with a deficit of $7 million, a sizable sum in a budget of only $25 million. Calhoun had made substantial economies in the operation of the War Department, which absorbed nearly a third of the budget in 1818, but they were insufficient to reduce the deficit substantially. Regarding the depression as only temporary, Monroe accepted Crawford's recommendation that the deficit be met by loans. However, as Monroe noted in his second inaugural, if the depression continued, he would request additional taxes.

Not until after the Missouri question (see below) had been laid to rest near the end of the session of 1820–1821 did Congress move to enact measures to reduce governmental expenditures. The main thrust of the economizers was against the War Department, not only because it absorbed such a large share of the budget but because supporters of rival candidates used it as a means of attacking Calhoun. Republicans of the old school, who had always been hostile to military expansion, were only too happy to join the attack. In addition to cutting appropriations for fortifications, in March 1821 Congress approved a bill reducing the army from a complement of ten thousand men to six thousand, to effect a saving estimated at $2 million. Even after the revenues improved, the reduction in the army was made permanent.

The Missouri Question

In the winter of 1819–1820 the president and Congress engaged in the more serious, protracted conflict over the effort to prevent the admission of Missouri as a slave state. Nearly the whole session was consumed in this bitter controversy while the two houses remained deadlocked. The lower house insisted that slavery be banned as a condition for the admission of Missouri, but the Senate stubbornly rejected all measures imposing restrictions. Although deeply concerned over this issue, which threatened to divide the nation into two hostile sections, Monroe never raised the question with his cabinet prior to the passage of the final compromise, knowing that an agreement on the issue would be impossible. Monroe genuinely believed, and this was a widely held opinion, that the restrictionists, among whose leaders were many former Federalists, were trying to revive the old two-party system on a sectional basis.

Within the framework of the then current interpretation of the relationship between the executive and legislative branches, it was impossible for Monroe to intervene directly in the controversy. From the outset he let it be known that he would veto any measure restricting slavery in Missouri, since this would be contrary to the provision of the Constitution requiring that new states be admitted on an equal footing with the older states. Slavery was a legal institution and imposing limitations on Missouri would deprive that state of the right to determine a basic institution. In opposing restriction, Monroe was not only concerned with the constitutional issue: he shared the common view of many southerners that confining slavery to a few states would ensure its perpetuation. Slavery, he believed, would be more easily eliminated if it were diffused throughout the nation.

Monroe was himself a slaveholder. Like most southerners of the revolutionary generation, he condemned it as evil and anticipated its eventual destruction. He agreed with Jefferson, with whom he corresponded on the subject, that the only solution was the removal of blacks to Africa. He was a member of the American Colonization Society, which had this objective as its ultimate goal, and in 1821 he assisted the society in acquiring title to Liberia as a refuge for freed slaves. It was in gratitude for his efforts that the directors named the capital Monrovia.

While the Missouri debates were raging in Congress, Monroe was kept informed of developments by Senator James Barbour of Virginia. Through Barbour, Monroe let it be known that he would approve Henry Clay's compromise admitting Missouri as a slave state and Maine as a free state and banning slavery in territory north of 36°30'. When Monroe finally consulted his secretaries after the passage of the compromise, he received only a qualified approval.

When the compromise was pending Monroe enlisted the aid of George Hay, his son-in-law (then in Richmond), to calm the Virginia hotheads who loudly talked of secession if southern interests were sacrificed. As Monroe told Jefferson, the plot to destroy the Union had been prevented only by the "patriotic devotion of several members of the non-slave-owning states, who preferred to sacrifice themselves at home, to a violation of the obvious principles of the Constitution." Monroe—and this was typical of most southerners—failed to grasp the intensity of northern antislavery sentiment.

In spite of the furor over the Missouri question and the problems created by the depression, the presidential election of 1820 aroused scant popular interest. Fewer voters turned out than for local elections in which there was a real contest. As the only candidate (there was no caucus, the nomination being left to state legislatures), Monroe received all the electoral votes but one. The only conflict over the election took place in Congress when northern restrictionists objected to the inclusion of Missouri's electoral vote in the final count, since the state had not as yet been formally admitted. The issue was solved by reporting two sets of electoral votes, one with, and the other without, Missouri's three votes. This was by no means the end of the dispute over Missouri. During the session of 1820–1821 there was a prolonged conflict over provisions in the Missouri constitution making it illegal for free blacks to enter Missouri and forbidding manumission without specific authorization of the state legislature. Clay worked out a compromise providing that no provision of the Missouri constitution should be construed as denying any citizen the privileges and immunities of citizens of the United States. While Clay labored in Congress, Monroe quietly helped round up the votes needed to ensure the passage of what has been termed "the second Missouri Compromise."

In view of the responsibility the Constitution assigned to the executive for the conduct of foreign relations, Monroe understandably gave close attention to this aspect of his office. When Monroe and Adams were in the capital, daily conferences were the rule,

for the State Department was but a few minutes—walk from the White House. When the president was at Oak Hill during the summer, messengers regularly brought him dispatches. Monroe read all the diplomatic correspondence, scrutinizing and frequently revising Adams' notes.

Foundations of the Monroe Doctrine

Now that the wars precipitated by the French Revolution were over, Monroe had an opportunity to develop foreign policy in new directions. No longer need the executive be preoccupied with the protection of neutral rights and the need to preserve American neutrality. Among Monroe's major objectives, fully supported by Adams, was the recognition of the United States as the only republic of consequence in the world and the strongest power in the Americas. The nation no longer would seek its aims through the patronage of European powers, as Jefferson had relied on France, but would pursue an independent course. Monroe shared the expansionist aims of his generation and with Adams' help fully exploited every opportunity for expanding American territories.

The most immediate problems demanding attention after his inauguration were those arising from the revolutionary movements in Spain's Latin American colonies. Some had been resolved while he was secretary of state, when he had helped formulate a policy of neutrality highly beneficial to the insurgents. Monroe, deeply sympathetic to the revolutionary movements, was determined that the United States should never repeat the policies of the Washington administration during the French Revolution, when the nation had failed to demonstrate its sympathy for the aspirations of peoples seeking to establish republican governments. He did not envisage military involvement but only the provision of moral support. To go beyond this would do the colonies more harm than good, since it would invite European intervention to restore them to Spain. Monroe's caution was justified, for the European powers had intervened in Europe to suppress revolutions in Spain itself and in the Kingdom of the Two Sicilies.

Monroe's policy was also shaped by his desire to obtain from Spain the long-sought cession of Florida and a definition of the boundaries of the Louisiana Purchase. Premature action in extending recogni-

President James Monroe is depicted with his cabinet as he outlines the Monroe Doctrine, a new direction in U. S. foreign policy that demonstrated American resolve and power in the hemisphere. THE LIBRARY OF CONGRESS

tion to the former colonies would jeopardize the possibility of a settlement with Spain. Still, recognition had to be considered. In order to obtain more accurate information than that appearing in the press, Monroe, shortly after he entered office, sent a special commission to South America to report on the stability of the newly independent states.

As soon as Adams arrived in October 1817 to take his place in the cabinet, Monroe discussed a more immediate issue than recognition. The various insurgents had freely issued letters of marque to privateers, many of whom were Americans. Behaving more like pirates than privateers, they had made their headquarters on Amelia Island, within the jurisdiction of Spanish Florida. With the approval of his cabinet, Monroe authorized an expedition to occupy the island and end this annoyance.

In December, Monroe took more drastic action, authorizing Andrew Jackson to lead an expedition into Florida to pursue Indians raiding the southern frontier. This invasion was justified by the provision of Pinckney's Treaty of 1795, in which Spain had promised to restrain the Indians living under its jurisdiction. Because Jackson had been specifically instructed not to occupy Spanish posts, his seizure of St. Marks and Pensacola was truly embarrassing for the administration. Moreover, his execution of two British traders after a summary trial on the grounds that they were inciting the Indians threatened to create a major international crisis.

Jackson's conduct created a furor, for it was widely alleged that by his actions he had infringed on the congressional power to declare war. The cabinet was sharply divided on this issue. Calhoun and Crawford were among the many who urged that the general be repudiated, while Adams, sensing that at last Jackson had given the administration the lever needed to pry Florida from Spain, recommended that his conduct be approved.

Sensitive to the constitutional issues and yet unwilling to give Spain an advantage by an outright condemnation of the general, Monroe found a middle course acceptable to the secretaries. In reporting on events in Florida in his annual message, he informed Congress that Jackson had indeed overstepped his orders but had done so on information received during the campaign that made the action necessary. Monroe added that the posts had promptly been restored once Jackson had achieved his objectives. Monroe's position was effective in checking the massive anti-Jackson campaign launched in Congress by states' rightists and those anxious to weaken Jackson's standing as a presidential candidate. Jackson was not pleased with Monroe's formula, which fell short of the positive approval he believed he merited. His sensitivity on this point was a major factor in his breach with Calhoun in 1830.

The congressional debate on the resolutions condemning Jackson were under way at the very time that Adams and the Spanish minister were concluding a treaty for the cession of Florida and the extension of Louisiana's western boundary line northward and westward to the Pacific. The administration's concern that Jackson's execution of British subjects might lead to war proved unfounded. The British, having more important concerns on the Continent, made no protest. When Spain failed to ratify the treaty within the six-month time limit, the president contemplated asking Congress in his annual message of 1819 for immediate authority to occupy Florida. However, after he learned that France and Britain were exerting pressure on Spain to ratify, he requested instead contingent authority, suspending action until the arrival of a special emissary from Spain. Although Clay and other advocates of immediate recognition of the new Latin American states were critical of Monroe's delay, they were too much absorbed in the Missouri debates to raise serious objections in Congress.

Spain ratified the treaty late in 1820, but Monroe still held back from immediate recognition of the new Latin American regimes because of doubts about their stability. Not until March 1822 did he inform Congress that permanent governments had been established in the United Provinces of La Plata (present-day Argentina), Chile, Peru, Colombia, and Mexico. He requested an appropriation for diplomatic missions to these nations.

Adams' instructions for the new ministers, drafted under Monroe's careful supervision, declared that the policy of the United States was to uphold republican institutions and to seek treaties of commerce on a most-favored-nation basis. The new diplomats were also instructed to let it be known that the United States would support inter-American congresses dedicated to the development of economic and political institutions fundamentally differing from those prevailing in Europe. The articulation of an "American system" distinct from that of Europe was a basic tenet of Monroe's policy toward Latin America. Monroe took pride in the fact that the United States was the first nation to extend recognition and to set an example to the rest of the world for its support of the "cause of liberty and humanity."

Monroe was aware that recognition did not provide an effective shield against foreign intervention to restore Spain's colonies. This threat became an immediate concern in October 1823 when dispatches arrived from Richard Rush, the minister in London, informing the president that Foreign Secretary George Canning was proposing that the United States and Great Britain jointly declare their opposition to European intervention. This astounding proposal from so recent an enemy was given the closest consideration.

Monroe at once wrote Madison and Jefferson, who both urged him to accept. In spite of their endorsement, Monroe had serious doubts. To accept the British proposal would make the nation once again seem subordinate to a European power and would not enhance American prestige among Spain's former colonies. Acceptance would also involve a declaration repudiating further territorial expansion at Spain's expense and thus rule out the prospect of acquiring Cuba, an event Adams and many others thought most likely. Monroe also sensed that the people were not yet ready for such close cooperation with Great Britain.

Monroe explored the proposal in detail with his secretaries at lengthy cabinet meetings in November 1823. (Crawford, then seriously ill, was absent.) All agreed that joint action was neither possible nor essential, since the British cabinet had obviously already decided on its policy. At first Monroe felt that a circular diplomatic note would be sufficient to state American opposition to intervention. This had the disadvantage that as a private communication it would not be publicized.

It was the president who hit on the means of announcing the American position to the world: he would include a general statement in his annual message of 2 December 1823. Putting forward the principle that "the political system of the allied powers is essentially different . . . from that of America," he announced that the United States would view any interference in the internal affairs of the American states as an "unfriendly" act. He coupled this with the statement that the United States itself adhered to a policy of noninterference in the internal affairs of other nations. A third principle, the work of Secretary Adams, concerned Russian expansion on the West Coast and declared that the United States considered the Americas closed to European colonization.

A few days after Monroe delivered his message, the American press reported that a large expedition destined for South America was being collected at Cádiz. This report, which later proved erroneous, led Monroe to review the position of the administration and to inform Rush that the United States would undertake further discussions with the British on the possibility of cooperation, should intervention take place. This did not mean, as he explained in a private letter to Rush, that he was committing the nation to "engage in war." What Monroe did not know in December 1823 was that the threat of intervention had vanished in the face of the express opposition of the British government. (In the early twentieth century President Theodore Roosevelt and his successors employed the Monroe Doctrine to justify American intervention in the internal affairs of Latin American states—an interpretation never intended by its author.)

The rejection of the British proposal in regard to Spain's colonies did not mean that Monroe was averse to joint action that did not make the nation seem to be playing a subordinate role. Since the end of the War of 1812 there had been tentative moves by Great Britain toward a rapprochement. The Great Lakes had been demilitarized by the Rush-Bagot Agreement in 1817, and the following year American negotiators had obtained a concession on the fisheries as well as an agreement compensating Americans for slaves removed by British forces at the end of the war. Efforts to obtain concessions for American trade in the British West Indies had been repeatedly rejected.

A more hopeful step was undertaken in the summer of 1823 when Monroe and Adams negotiated an agreement to establish an international patrol to suppress the slave trade. Monroe had rejected the initial proposal in 1819 because it would have required the

United States to abandon its position on neutral rights by permitting British ships to stop and search American ships on the high seas. This objection was apparently lessened in 1822 when the House, yielding to the pressure of the American Anti-Slavery Society, adopted a resolution condemning the slave trade as piracy. Since pirates could not claim the protection of any national flag, suspect ships could be stopped and searched by the international patrol established by the British. Congressman Charles Fenton Mercer, a friend and neighbor of the president's, had been the principal agent in securing the adoption of the resolution. Acting on this basis, Monroe, who had long sought to open the way to a rapprochement with Great Britain, was prepared to make a major change in American policy on neutral rights and participate in the international patrol, a measure long urged by the British. In 1823 an agreement to this effect was negotiated with the approval of all the cabinet except Adams, who suspected (correctly) that he would be blamed for what many would regard as a sacrifice of a basic American right.

The Senate ratified the treaty early in 1824 with such crippling amendments that the British government withdrew its ratification. The opposition was directed by supporters of Crawford seeking to damage Adams' presidential ambitions. Monroe was deeply offended, since Crawford had been one of the most ardent advocates of the proposal. Crawford was too ill to have actively directed the maneuvering against the treaty, but it was not the first instance that Monroe felt that the secretary of the treasury had been disloyal. The year before, Monroe had seriously considered dismissing Crawford from the cabinet but held back, realizing that it would simply exacerbate political rivalries.

Final Years

During Monroe's last two years as president the struggle over the succession degenerated into what could be called the Era of Bad Feelings. Although Monroe was not a candidate, he was subjected to criticism—often of a petty nature. Crawford, Clay, and Jackson all saw it to their advantage to oppose administration policies. Adams and Calhoun (who withdrew from the campaign early in 1824) remained loyal to Monroe and restrained their supporters. The Crawfordites were especially bitter, since they felt that Monroe owed a particular debt to Crawford for not opposing him in 1816. Monroe remained neutral but the impression prevailed that he preferred Adams.

It was a combination of congressional supporters of Jackson and Crawford who raised questions impugning the president's integrity in the management of the so-called Furniture Fund, money appropriated in 1817 and 1818 for the refurnishing of the White House. The investigation was handled in such a way as to leave a cloud of suspicion, although it was apparent that the only error had been inadequate bookkeeping by the agent Monroe engaged to manage the fund.

The Crawfordites managed to generate considerable embarrassment for the president over the discovery that Ninian Edwards, a Calhoun supporter, had been the author of the "A.B. Letter," which questioned Crawford's management of the Treasury. The subsequent investigation, controlled by Crawford's friends, left the basic issues unanswered but placed the administration in the position of prodding Edwards, just appointed the first minister to Mexico, to resign. A further unpleasantness, stirred up by the Georgia delegation, was aimed at Calhoun but involved an attack on Monroe for refusing to force the Cherokee to agree to land cessions stipulated in earlier treaties.

After the harassments of his last two years in office, it was with a sense of relief that Monroe relinquished the office to Adams in March 1825, happy to retire to Oak Hill and the life of a country gentleman, which he so much loved. He stayed aloof from the political squabbles of the day in spite of all efforts to involve him. He busied himself with the affairs of the University of Virginia, Jefferson's cherished educational project, attending the meetings of the Board of Visitors and serving as rector. Visits to Charlottesville were occasions of joyous reunions with Madison, the two being drawn together in an even closer bond after Jefferson's death in 1826. Monroe's last public service was as a member of the Virginia constitutional convention of 1829, also attended by Madison. Monroe was chosen president but was too feeble to preside, although he did speak on several occasions.

After Monroe's retirement his most pressing concern was to lift the heavy debt, now amounting to $75,000, which had been accumulating since his first mission to France. The depressed state of Virginia land values made it impossible for him to sell Highlands. His efforts to obtain recompense for expenses of his past diplomatic missions (his accounts had never been settled with the State Department) were frustrated by the opposition of Jacksonians and Crawfordites. Finally, in February 1831, as news of the former president's financial plight became generally known, Congress appropriated $30,000 in settlement of his claims. The Bank of the United States took over Highlands in lieu of a $25,000 debt.

The death of Monroe's wife early in 1830 prostrated him with grief; rarely had they ever been separated since their marriage. Monroe's health began to fail so rapidly that he moved to New York to live with his younger daughter, Mrs. Samuel L. Gouverneur. Oak Hill was put up for sale to pay the balance of his debts. Sadly he notified Madison in April 1831 that he would not be able to attend the meeting of the Board of Visitors. When Adams saw his predecessor at that time, he found Monroe extremely weak but nonetheless anxious to discuss the recent revolutions in Europe. On 4 July 1831—the fifth anniversary of the deaths of John Adams and Thomas Jefferson—Monroe died. The funeral, which took place in New York City, was attended by state and civic officials. Vast crowds lined the streets as the cortege made its way to the cemetery. Throughout the country his passing was observed by days of mourning, memorial services, and eulogies, the most moving of which was delivered in Boston by John Quincy Adams. In 1858, Governor Wise of Virginia planned to have Jefferson, Madison, and Monroe reburied in Hollywood Cemetery in Richmond, but only Monroe's remains were reinterred.

BIBLIOGRAPHY

Stanislaus Murray Hamilton, ed., *Writings of James Monroe*, 7 vols. (New York, 1898–1903), the only printed edition, is of limited value and has now been fully supplanted by microfilm editions of all major collections of Monroe's papers. Harry Ammon, *James Monroe: The Quest for National Identity* (New York, 1971; rev. ed., Charlottesville, Va., 1990), is a full-scale biography based on primary materials. George Dangerfield, *Era of Good Feelings* (New York, 1952), is a limited study depicting Monroe as a dullard and time-serving politician. Noble E. Cunningham, Jr., *The Presidency of James Monroe* (Lawrence, Kans., 1996), contains the latest scholarship on the last of the Virginia presidents.

Leonard D. White, *The Jeffersonians: A Study in Administrative History, 1801–1829* (New York,

1951), superbly details the operation and organization of federal administration under Monroe. Norman K. Risjord, *The Old Republicans: Southern Conservatism in the Age of Jefferson* (New York, 1965), is a scholarly account of the opposition to Monroe's policies from within his own party. Charles M. Wiltse, *John C. Calhoun*, 3 vols. (New York, 1944–1951), includes an extensive account of Monroe's Indian policy based on original sources.

Alexander DeConde, *Entangling Alliance: Politics and Diplomacy Under George Washington* (Westport, Conn., 1974), is essential for understanding Monroe's mission to France. Bradford Perkins, *Castlereagh and Adams: England and the United States, 1812–1823* (Berkeley, Calif., 1964), depicts the close working relationship between Monroe and his secretary of state. Samuel Flagg Bemis, *John Quincy Adams and the Foundations of American Foreign Policy* (New York, 1949), is a definitive study of Monroe's foreign policy. Hugh G. Soulsby, *The Right of Search and the Slave Trade in Anglo-American Relations, 1814–1862* (Baltimore, 1933), is a basic study of a major issue confronting Monroe's presidency.

Dexter Perkins, *The Monroe Doctrine, 1823–1826* (Cambridge, Mass., 1927), is still the definitive monograph about the origins of the doctrine. Ernest R. May, *The Making of the Monroe Doctrine* (Cambridge, Mass., 1975), is a revisionist study arguing that it was issued solely to influence the outcome of the presidential election of 1824. Arthur P. Whitaker, *The United States and the Independence of Latin America, 1800–1830* (Baltimore, 1941), is indispensible for understanding Monroe's Latin American policy.

Dumas Malone, *Jefferson and His Time*, 6 vols. (New York, 1948–1981), is a splendid biography with a full account of the impact on American politics of Jefferson and Monroe's lifelong friendship. Irving Brant, *James Madison*, 6 vols. (Indianapolis, Ind., 1941–1961), touches extensively on his relationship with Monroe. Robert V. Remini, *Andrew Jackson and the Course of American Empire, 1767–1821* (New York, 1977), *Andrew Jackson and the Course of American Freedom, 1822–1832* (New York, 1981), and *Andrew Jackson and the Course of American Democracy, 1833–1845* (New York, 1984) are scholarly pro-Jackson works highly critical of Monroe's treatment of Jackson; Remini's *Martin Van Buren and the Making of the Democratic Party* (New York, 1959) is a fascinating account of Van Buren's reorganization of the Democratic party in its depiction of Monroe as an apostate. Lucius Wilmerding, Jr., *James Monroe, Public Claimant* (New Brunswick, N.J., 1960), contends that Monroe's postretirement claims for expenses as a diplomat were unjustified.

Harry Ammon, ed., *James Monroe: A Bibliography* (Westport, Conn., 1991), is a comprehensive annotated bibliography.

John Quincy Adams

Edward Pessen

John Quincy Adams THE LIBRARY OF CONGRESS

J OHN QUINCY ADAMS, the sixth president of the United States, was one of the most brilliant, learned, and able men who has ever held high office in the nation. Blessed with a strong character, high principles, unswerving integrity, an iron constitution, and a flair for hard work, Adams enjoyed not one but several luminous careers. Commencing as a precocious but strikingly able young diplomat whose work was invaluable to his father, John Adams, and earned the praise of President George Washington, Adams went on to great political and academic successes. An excellent student while at Harvard and a devoted reader of the classics, Adams later was for a time simultaneously Boylston Professor of Rhetoric and

Oratory at Harvard and United States senator. A forceful nationalist and indomitable patriot, he established himself during the years of the Monroe administration as one of the truly great secretaries of state. After leaving the White House for what he mistakenly thought would be the quiet years of retirement and contemplation, he carved out still another illustrious career: as "Old Man Eloquent," he championed the antislavery cause in the House of Representatives, where he served for seventeen years as congressman from Massachusetts. And yet Adams was neither a great nor a successful president.

In this respect, Adams was very much like his father, for John Adams too was a man of the highest

[87]

intellectual and characterological endowment who, although he served his country well and even brilliantly during a time of troubles, served it only with indifferent success when he was named to its highest office. Son, like father, lacked the common touch, appeared to suffer fools badly, and had neither zest for nor skill in playing the political games that evidently had to be played if a chief executive hoped to achieve success, whether in securing the enactment of a program or in assuring his continuation in the nation's highest political office. Both Adamses were one-term presidents.

Since the criteria for "presidential greatness" are indeterminate, historians' and political scientists' evaluations inevitably differ. Yet, interestingly, even one of John Quincy Adams' most knowledgeable as well as warmest scholarly admirers, Samuel Flagg Bemis, concedes the failure of his presidency, devoting no more than twenty-two words to it in his thirty-five-hundred-word essay on Adams in a recent edition of the *Encyclopaedia Britannica*. In the conventional historians' wisdom, John Quincy Adams' presidency is worth remembering less for anything Adams may have done in administering the office than for the unprecedented manner by which he came to occupy it and the fascinating, if dismaying, political campaign by which, after one dismal term, he came to lose it.

Early Career

As the first president in American history whose father had also held the office, Adams, who was born on 11 July 1767 in that part of Braintree, Massachusetts, which later became Quincy, had every advantage as a youngster. At the time of his birth, his father was an increasingly admired and prospering lawyer, and his mother, Abigail Smith Adams, was the daughter of an esteemed minister, whose wife's family combined two prestigious and influential lines, the Nortons and the Quincys. Accompanying his father on diplomatic missions in Europe, young John Quincy Adams received a splendid education at private schools in Paris, Leiden, and Amsterdam, early developing his penchant for omnivorous reading. From youth on, he began each day with a reading of several chapters of the Bible, first in one language and then another, and meticulously kept a diary that has endeared him to historians. For this careful and often fulsome record provides both an accurate description of important historical events and Adams' some-

times sour but always discerning and interesting responses to these events.

He seemed to serve an ideal apprenticeship for the office of chief executive, for in common with most of the presidents, he trained for the law after graduating from college and he made a "good marriage." The young woman Adams wed was Louisa Catherine Johnson, whose father had been a substantial merchant and whose uncle was the governor of Maryland. In addition to the positions already mentioned, Adams served as minister to the Netherlands and then to Prussia between 1797 and 1801. After serving in the Senate from 1803 to 1808, he was appointed the first United States minister to Russia in 1809, turning down an offer of membership on the Supreme Court during his half decade in St. Petersburg. Adding to his reputation was his brilliant and tough-minded performance as chief American peace commissioner in the negotiations at Ghent that ended the War of 1812 and his effectiveness as minister to Great Britain during the last two years of the Madison administration.

If Adams was in 1824 widely regarded as the most able and deserving of presidential candidates, it was not merely because he had held high diplomatic and political positions but because he had displayed such outstanding ability and such independence of mind and character in executing his assignments. The son of a leading Federalist and himself an early champion of the Federalist party, Adams proved to be anything but a slavish devotee to that political cause. When he thought the party was in the wrong, he stood ready to oppose it. In fact, as he told his father, if he thought the country was in the wrong, he could not bring himself to solicit God's approval for its course. President James Madison, a good Jeffersonian, awarded Adams the diplomatic plum of a ministry to Russia as a form of political reward for his break with his party in supporting the Jeffersonian Embargo Act of 1807, an act that was bitterly opposed throughout Adams' New England. The infuriated Massachusetts Federalists prematurely ended Adams' senatorial career. By 1808, Adams was attending the Republican party caucus that nominated Madison for the presidency.

Adams had also demonstrated his stubborn sense of independence while he was secretary of state. An uncompromising nationalist and patriot, he alone in President Monroe's cabinet opposed the censure of General Andrew Jackson for the latter's behavior in 1817. Jackson had violated the borders of Spanish Florida and came near embroiling the nation in another crisis with Great Britain over his execution of two British subjects during the course of his foray. Adams stuck to his guns, the censure motion was deflected, and within a year Florida fell into American hands for a song. And it was Adams who spurned the subsequent British offer that the two nations engage in a joint declaration against European intervention in South America; it was thus because of Adams that the Monroe Doctrine was put forward as a purely American conception.

A typical Adams in his evident conviction that he was not exceptional and that his performance of his various public tasks was inadequate, John Quincy Adams at age forty-five confided to his diary that with his life two-thirds completed, he had "done nothing to distinguish it by usefulness to [his] country or to mankind." In fact, he had demonstrated great capacity, high character, and much promise of yet greater achievement in whatever responsibilities might lie ahead. The portrait he drew of himself as a "man of reserved, cold, austere, and forbidding manners" whose adversaries ostensibly regarded him as a "gloomy misanthropist" and an "unsocial savage" may have had some point. He certainly seemed to believe that these were actual defects in his character and that he lacked the "pliability" to reform them. In truth, John Quincy Adams was not a pliable man. But in view of the austerity and near rigidity of Washington and the lack of what is nowadays called charisma in other of Adams' predecessors, Adams' defects of personality, if they were indeed that, were neither unique nor a certain obstacle to his rise.

Election of 1824

In the judgment of many historians, Adams' presidency was doomed to failure because of the manner in which he gained the high office. Adams never lived down the charge by his leading opponent that he had secured the necessary majority in the House only by agreeing to a "corrupt bargain," by which Adams allegedly rewarded Henry Clay with the post of secretary of state—then the stepping stone to the presidency—in return for Clay's intriguing and manipulating in the House to switch votes to Adams.

The fascinating presidential election of 1824 was a turning point in many ways. It followed a succession of three two-term presidents, Thomas Jefferson, James Madison, and James Monroe—the famous "Virginia Dynasty"—each of whom was identified with Jefferson's Republican party. Monroe had run unopposed in 1820, for the Federalist party of Washington, Hamilton, and John Adams had finally given up the ghost, unable to shake off the popular belief that, in opposing as it had the War of 1812, it had skirted perilously close to treason.

Even before the disintegration of Federalism, the Republicans had the presidential field pretty much to themselves, as party members in Congress would meet in closed caucus to name the candidate for the forthcoming presidential election. As Monroe's second term approached its end, the Republican congressional caucus by an almost unanimous vote recommended William H. Crawford of Georgia, secretary of the treasury in Monroe's cabinet, as its candidate for president. According to Martin Van Buren, the political genius who controlled Republican politics in New York State, acceptance of the caucus' choice for office was an "article of faith" or fundamental tenet of the Republican party. Not in 1824. Van Buren and not too many others dutifully threw their energies into the election of Crawford. But a number of other men, Republicans all, sensing that the caucus selection could this time be successfully opposed, threw their own hats into the ring. John Quincy Adams was one of this ambitious quartet.

By 1824, Crawford's rivals no doubt agreed with the newly skeptical attitude toward caucus selection that was expressed by Adams in his diary entry for 25 January 1824. He had come to believe that "a majority of the whole people of the United States, and a majority of the States [were] utterly averse to a nomination by Congressional caucus, thinking it adverse to the spirit of the Constitution and tending to corruption." Adams was no doubt sincere in his insistence that since he agreed with this sentiment, he could not accept a caucus nomination for the presidency, but he would have sounded more convincing had he had a realistic chance of securing such nomination. But he must have known that there was no such chance. Motivated as he was by soaring ambition, this pillar of rectitude sought to convince himself that he was breaking with tradition only for the loftiest and most principled of reasons. The other contestants simply saw their chance and took it.

Adams' several rivals constituted one of the most impressive constellations of political luminaries that ever vied for the presidency in any single election. In addition to the estimable Crawford, the group included John C. Calhoun of South Carolina, the brilliant Yale-educated nationalist who served as secretary of war under Monroe; Henry Clay of Kentucky, the master politician who had been the chief architect of the Missouri Compromise; and General Andrew Jackson of Tennessee, a man of slight political achievement, little education, and notorious temper, but widely admired for his exploits as an Indian fighter and above all for his stunning victory in 1815 over the British at New Orleans. Withdrawing from the race when it became clear that he had no real chance to win, Calhoun and his backers settled for second place under the presidency of either of the two leading candidates—Adams, the only northerner in the competition, and Jackson, the darling of the South and West.

The election returns make clear how decisively the latter two candidates outdistanced Crawford and Clay. The tallies were as follows:

Candidate	Popular vote	% of total	Electoral vote	% of electoral vote
Jackson	153,544	44	99	38
Adams	108,740	31	84	32
Crawford	46,618	13	41	16
Clay	47,136	13	37	14

Since no candidate had won the required majority of electoral votes, the choice was turned over to the House of Representatives, in accord with Article II of the Constitution. Since, by Article XII, only the top three vote-getters qualify in such a circumstance, Clay's name was dropped from the list presented to the lower house. Since Crawford was known to have become physically incapacitated and unable therefore to perform the duties of the high office, there was very little chance that many in Congress would join the diehards who appeared ready to stand by Crawford, near-dead or fully alive. In his diary entry for 9 February 1825, Adams wrote, "May the blessing of God rest upon the event of this day," for earlier that day, Adams had been selected by the approving vote of thirteen states, with Jackson supported by seven states and Crawford by four.

Three weeks and two days later, Adams reported that he had suffered through two sleepless nights prior to inauguration day. His excitement and unease were induced not only by the fact that he was about to assume the great burden of the presidency but by the vilification that the Jacksonians had heaped on him for what they claimed were the sordid means by which he had won the election to the office in Congress.

The Corrupt Bargain

The charge of "corrupt bargain" began to be heard throughout the land as soon as Clay let it be known early in 1825 that he was supporting Adams for the presidency. What was earlier a murmur became a roar when Adams proffered, and Clay accepted, the position of secretary of state in Adams' cabinet. In a rage at the outcome of the House's "election," Jackson said of Clay that "the Judas of the West has closed the contract and will receive the thirty pieces of silver," and in Clay's home state he charged that "the people [had] been cheated," their will defeated by "corruptions and intrigues at Washington." The following year Clay engaged in a duel with Senator John Randolph of Virginia, putting a bullet through that erratic man's cloak after the Virginian had publicly denounced the "stinking" corruption and bargain between the "puritan and the black leg."

Nothing Adams or Clay might do or say thereafter ever removed completely the taint resulting from the incessant braying of "corruption" by their enemies. Jackson was understandably upset at faring so poorly in the House after getting the substantial popular vote he did. But if a substantial plurality were sufficient to election, the Constitution would have so indicated. The lower house of Congress had every right to consider the runoff as a brand new election and to choose, as it did, the man widely regarded as the best and most responsible candidate. Neither Jackson nor his allies were able, then or afterward, to offer a scintilla of evidence backing up their charge of a bargain.

Adams had every right to appoint the gifted and experienced Kentuckian to the State Department, just as Clay had every right to support Adams and to try to influence others to follow suit. Thomas Hart Benton and Francis P. Blair, ardent Jacksonians both, testified that Clay, to their personal knowledge, had indicated his preference for Adams over Jackson well before the matter was placed before the House. Clay had differed with Jackson over matters of policy and principle and had understandable reason to oppose a natural rival, popular with the same sectional constituency as the Kentuckian.

It is not at all certain either that the Jacksonians fully believed the charge or that they were as horrified as they pretended to be over a pragmatic arrangement of the sort many of them had themselves entered into. What is more clear is that they derived great political capital out of the charge. There is much evidence indicating that Adams' opponents would have opposed his administration and the measures it proposed no matter how it was installed or whom it named secretary of state. But with the appointment of Clay, supporters of Jackson, Calhoun, and Crawford had a marvelous pretext for mounting what was to be four years of incessant opposition to the Adams administration and all its works. John Quincy Adams had glaring faults as a political leader in an increasingly democratic and materialistic republic, but in view of the unyielding nature of his enemies, their cleverness in entering into their own dubious bargains in order to unify and solidify their opposition to him, and the broad geographical and financial support they were able to muster, it is doubtful that his administration would have been a success or he him. self reelected no matter how admirable his political program or how consummate his political skills.

Adams' Qualities as President

One outmoded interpretation held that "the victory of John Quincy Adams gave the business community its last chance," suggesting that the sixth president favored the propertied over the popular interest. In fact, Adams was an independent, as well as intelligent, thinker, a patriot who thought in national rather than class terms. His views were uncommonly humane for the major party politician that in a sense he was. This was a man who rejected the comforting notion that the United States was a classless society; who believed, as did few of his male contemporaries, that women in America were denied the equal opportunities that were their due; who, unlike the slaveholding Jackson, believed that slavery was "the great and foul stain upon the North American Union" and that "the Constitution's protection of slavery was intolerable" and that it should be amended. Like his predecessors in the chief executive's office, he believed that the presidential veto was a potentially despotic power that was to be rarely exercised (in accord with Hamilton's promise to this effect in *The Federalist*).

In addition to his learning, intelligence, and independence of mind, Adams had a capacity for hard work that one would have thought boded well for the prospects of his presidency. His description of a day's work, written a month after he took office, tells something of his approach to the job:

> Since my removal to the Presidential mansion, I rise about five; read two chapters of Scott's Bible and

Commentary, and the corresponding Commentary of Hewlett; then the morning newspapers, and public papers from the several departments; write seldom and not enough; breakfast an hour, from nine to ten; then have a succession of visitors, upon business, in search of place, solicitors for donations, or from mere curiosity, from eleven till between four and five o'clock. The heads of department of course occupy much of this time. Between four and six I take a walk of three or four miles. Dine from about half past five to seven, and from dark till about eleven I generally pass the evening in my chamber, signing land grants or blank patents, in the interval of which, for the last ten days I have brought up three months of arrears in my diary index. About eleven I retire to bed. My evenings are not so free from interruption as I hoped and expected they would be.

By his fourth year in office he was, if anything, putting in an even longer day. His diary entry for 31 May 1828 notes that he would "rise generally before five—frequently before four" and "retire usually between eleven and midnight." When weather permitted, Adams would swim in the Potomac, tend his garden, and ride horseback. By the end of his tenure, perhaps because he was worn down—more by the unremitting sniping at his heels by political foes than by the tasks of office—he was nodding off, briefly but often, on his sofa.

Sadly, neither high intelligence nor hard work availed to ensure a successful presidential tenure. It has become a historian's commonplace to observe that once in the high office, Adams' stiffness of personality, his inability to make the necessary small compromises, and the fancifulness of his proposals combined to defeat his hopes, whether for a great presidency or for reelection. Yet the evidence can be otherwise interpreted. It is not necessary to distort the historical record to conclude that Adams' political rivals and enemies were simply intent on bringing him down, ready to exploit or distort every issue; magnify any error, no matter how trivial; and distort every statement and every action, all with an eye toward undermining his administration and ruining his chances for succession. That they succeeded with a vengeance doubtless indicates that Adams lacked at least some of the things that it takes to achieve a successful presidency. The success of Adams' enemies also suggests, disturbingly, that a successful presidency may be beholden more to an incumbent's opportunism and amorality than to intelligence and integrity.

The Adams Administration

Apart from the controversial Clay, Adams' cabinet appointments were unexceptional. Adams was practical politician enough to try to mend his fences with Crawford by offering him continued tenure in the Treasury Department; the Georgian was too ill to continue. Cabinet offers went to men who, as a group, represented a geographical cross section of the nation: Henry Clay (State), James Barbour (War), Richard Rush (Treasury), Samuel L. Southard (Navy), and William Wirt (Attorney General).

Adams' promise, in his inaugural message, ceaselessly to devote all of his faculties to the "faithful performance of the arduous duties" he was about to undertake was similarly unexceptional. But that Adams also said that he was "deeply conscious" that he was "less possessed of [the people's] confidence" than had been any of his predecessors betrayed his continuing anxiety about his unimpressive popular vote. Perhaps, too, it betokened his unease concerning the unprecedented route he had followed to reach the highest office and the dark mutterings that followed in its wake.

In his first annual message, delivered on 6 December 1825, Adams presented his administration's program to the Nineteenth Congress. A clue to the unrelenting hostility evoked by his almost every suggestion is afforded by the suspicion with which his opponents greeted what would appear to have been an unexceptionable and glittering generalization, to the effect that "the great object of the institution of civil government is the improvement of those who are parties to the social compact." To hear how some devotees of laissez-faire and states' rights republicanism told it, "improvement" came close to being subversive, if not un-American. Adams, of course, had some champions in Congress—the Clay-Adams "coalitionists," above all. But the great majority consisted of Jackson, Calhoun, and Crawford supporters—the last group led by the wily Martin Van Buren—all of them listening with jaundiced ears to Adams' proposals.

The conflict between John Quincy Adams and his congressional opposition was not entirely a matter of office and power, of simple hostility by the "outs" to the "ins." An element of political principle or ideology, broadly construed, was also present. Although their earlier and subsequent careers demonstrated the opportunism of Adams' chief opponents and their readiness to switch from one political position to another when they thought it expedient to do so—as Calhoun reversed himself on the tariff or as Jackson did on the propriety of appointing former Federalists to office—they did tend to be unsympathetic to the idea of activism by the federal government, whether in economic or other matters. The issue of slavery did not arise directly during the years of Adams' presidency, yet it rose indirectly, in the sense that many champions of the South's "peculiar institution" appear to have been hostile to federal intervention in any area of American life, largely because they feared that recognition of such a right might in the future lead to federal interference with slavery.

Anti-Adams men, in Congress and out, who both before and after his message displayed readiness to utilize federal funds to promote internal improvements, now professed to be shocked at his suggestion that the national government facilitate "communications and intercourse between distant regions and multitudes of men" by building and improving roads and canals. The president's enemies had a field day ridiculing his advocacy of scientific investigation and of "public institutions and seminaries of learning" as the essential instruments for achieving the "moral, political, [and] intellectual improvement" of the American people. Singled out for special scorn was his call for the "erection of an astronomical observatory [for] observation upon the phenomena of the heavens." They lampooned the suggestion that the United States build its first such observatory, although no one deigned to challenge the president's report that Europe had more than 130 of these "light-houses of the skies." Even a modern critic of Adams and his administration, while finding the message politically inept, concedes that it was "one of the great presidential papers sent to any Congress." But, inspired as they were by opportunism, unshaking determination to destroy the Adams administration, and what a modern historian calls their anti-intellectualism, Adams' congressional opponents were oblivious to any of the message's charms.

Adams did slip badly in one passage of his message. In urging that the Congress not be "palsied by the will of [their] constituents" in enacting the "public improvement" he called for, he left himself open to the charge that he had thereby revealed his contempt for democracy and the obligation of government to guide itself by the will of the people. The Jacksonians never let up in their subsequent campaign to portray Adams as an aristocrat at heart. His enemies took these words out of a context in which they were part of a ringing nationalistic appeal for the United States not to doom itself to "perpetual inferiority" to foreign nations "less blessed with . . . freedom." Actually, Adams was demonstrating his accord with the well-known proposition, earlier offered by Edmund Burke, that the responsible political leader owes his constituents not his industry but his talents. Andrew Jackson and other of Adams' enemies more than once acted in accord with this elitist principle. But Adams, characteristically, was frank and impolitic enough to state his beliefs openly and put them in the public record. Not surprisingly, in view of the circumstances, Adams' "bold proposals" got absolutely nowhere in Congress.

As the year ended, Adams confided to his diary that it had been a year "without disaster to the country; with an unusual degree of prosperity, public and private." He was right, yet he derived little political capital from the fact, for, as he discerningly noted, public opinion toward him continued to be negative. Aware of his own flaws as a public man, Adams put much of the blame for his lack of popularity on his personal deficiencies. Certainly he was woefully inept, whether at building an organized movement to agitate for his measures or at punishing foes, even when he had the power to do so because they had been appointed by and should have been beholden to him. But the lack of success of his administration appears to have been due above all to the amoral behavior of his political enemies. Its fate was sealed when under the masterful leadership of Martin Van Buren, Adams' opponents all across the country organized what has been called the first truly mass party in American history. Dedicated to the twin propositions of destroying the reputation of John Quincy Adams and his administration and electing Andrew Jackson president of the United States in 1828, the new Democratic party was to have its way, fortified by lavish expenditures of money, brilliant grassroots organization, a national press network that undeviatingly preached the new party's line, the constant reminder that Adams owed his presidency to a "corrupt bargain," unremitting congressional warfare against every administration measure, and Adams' own blunders.

Adams' Nonpartisan Appointments

It throws an interesting, if not strange, light on the politics of the time that one of Adams' chief blunders was simply his fair and high-minded treatment of his political enemies. The era of the "spoils system" did not reward political integrity of the sort that refused to kick men out of office merely because they were performing their jobs ably. The Jacksonians and their Whig successors judged political appointees not so much by the quality of their public performance as by their loyalty to the man or the party in power. Adams had the quaint notion that appointments should go not to the politically friendly but to the worthy.

At the outset of his administration, Adams said that he was "determined to renominate every person against whom there was no complaint"—no complaint, that is, about his professional performance. And he lived up to his promise, despite being importuned to serve his friends and reproved for overlooking them. He indeed would not—and did not—replace "able and faithful political opponents to provide for [his] own partisans." By Adams' old-fashioned standards, partisan appointments would have been a misuse of his presidential powers. He removed only twelve officeholders during his presidency and did so in each case on the grounds of the incumbent's "gross negligence." Clay and other of Adams' astute supporters bemoaned the president's unwillingness to remove John McLean, the postmaster general, and a host of lesser-known officials, all of them working behind the scenes to undermine the Adams administration. Adams brushed aside all evidence of the political disloyalty of these men as irrelevant: the only thing that mattered was whether they were performing their jobs ably. Of course, as Clay rightly argued, it mattered a great deal to Adams' chances for success in the 1828 presidential election that his administration was in effect filled with traitors to his cause, men working to bring about his downfall.

Adams was not unaware of the force of this argument, but he was too principled to let it affect his appointments policy. He appears to have contemplated his forthcoming political disaster reflectively, fortified by his conviction that the path he had taken was the moral one. Indeed it was and therein lay one of the chief causes of his subsequent undoing. That one of the Jacksonian leaders regaled the Senate with a thundering denunciation of Adams' allegedly partisan appointments policy only provides an example of the indifference of the president's enemies to the facts of the case.

The Panama Congress

Some of what historians have called Adams' blunders were blunders only in a manner of speaking; that is, they were proposals or policies that failed and even hurt him politically not because of their lack of merit but because his congressional opponents artfully and effectively made them objects of ridicule. Adams' support of American participation in the Panama Congress of 1826 is a nice case in point.

In a special message on 26 December 1825, Adams told Congress that he had accepted the invitation from Simón Bolívar, the "Liberator" of South America, that the United States send a delegation to the congress of American nations called for the early summer of 1826 in Panama. As Adams carefully explained, although he "deemed [his acceptance of the invitation] to be within the constitutional competency of the Executive," he thought it advisable to ascertain Congress' opinion of the expediency of participating in the proposed congress before naming delegates to it. In an attempt to help the United States Congress better understand the value of attendance, Adams presented a number of reasoned arguments: it would, among other things, be in the national interest; it would strengthen commercial ties with, and opportunities in, South America; it would fortify the Monroe Doctrine's warnings against European intervention in the hemisphere; and it would enhance the popularity of the United States among the nations south of the border. The response of the anti-Adams majority in Congress was predictable.

House and Senate alike denounced the alleged subversion of the powers of Congress and the betrayal of George Washington's warning against foreign entanglements. They claimed to discern, too, a plot to enter, unconstitutionally, into a secret alliance. Southern congressmen warned that the Panama Congress would doubtless express criticism of the slave trade, and they voiced dark forebodings about the presence of black Haitians in Panama and the dangers that would flow from recognition of Haitian independence from France. Adams responded by avowing his veneration of Washington's Farewell Addressington's farewell address, his continuing opposition to foreign entanglements, and his doubts that Haiti "ought to be recognized as an independent sovereign power," in view of its continued economic subservience to France. But what was wrong, he asked, with the United States cementing ties with its southern neighbors, strengthening the Monroe Doc-

trine, further dissuading European intervention, and enhancing American financial prospects?

Of course, nothing Adams said could mollify his critics. But on 22 April 1826 he won what Samuel E Bemis calls his "first and only victory in Congress," when the House of Representatives approved the appropriation of $40,000 to cover the expenses of sending an American delegation to Panama. The victory was a hollow one, since nothing came of it. One of the delegates Adams selected, Richard Anderson, died en route; the other delegate, John Sergeant, did not arrive until the congress was essentially over. At Henry Clay's request, Adams, on his very last day in office, communicated to the United States Congress the administration's instructions to Anderson and Sergeant in order to include in the enduring record proof of the baselessness of the smears and innuendos leveled against the Adams administration's role in the matter.

Toward the end of his life, Adams, in a reflective mood, dismissed the event and the controversy it engendered as a slight thing at best and a fiasco at worst. Bemis is more appreciative, viewing Adams' support of the Panama Congress and the administration's Latin American policy, of which attendance in Panama was a part, as a "noble experiment that led to nothing in its [own] day." But the underlying idea of United States involvement in Latin America was to bear fruit at a later day.

The Last Two Years

It is not clear whether the last two years of John Quincy Adams' presidency are better described as tragedy or farce. A sympathetic biographer, Marie B. Hecht, faults him for what she calls the "sin of pride," not only in failing to exercise the powers available to him in order to marshal support for his programs but for failing to build an effective party machinery that might have organized support for the Adams programs. Although Henry Clay and other Adams supporters did belatedly create a fairly efficient organization to wage Adams' election campaign in 1828, the criticism of Adams no doubt has merit. And yet, in view of the unrelenting efforts of his opponents in Congress, out to ridicule his administration and to frustrate its every initiative, one wonders whether his employment of even the most artful tactics could have sufficed to turn the tide. In a letter to his son, Charles Francis Adams, Adams described the majority in both houses of the Twentieth Congress as a coalition of factions "united by a common disappointment into one mass envenomed by one spirit of bitter and unrelenting persecuting malice" against him. These were, of course, the words of a beaten man. Interestingly, Robert V. Remini, a historian highly sympathetic to Adams' enemies, agrees that the sole object of the pro-Jackson Twentieth Congress either in passing or opposing legislation was to bring about the victory of Jackson over Adams in 1828.

In his third annual message, presented at the end of 1827, Adams proposed a modest program, urging that sympathetic attention be given to the remaining debt the nation owed veterans of the Revolutionary War and to the need for enlarging the judiciary in order to meet the expanding nation's needs. This man, ostensibly unsympathetic to the plight of the needy, also advocated amelioration of the nation's harsh bankruptcy laws. But it mattered not whether his proposals were slight or weighty, reflective of this ideological viewpoint or that. They were all given equally short shrift by a Congress seemingly indifferent to the merits of legislative proposals, in its preoccupation with undermining the administration that presented them.

Adams appears to have been worn down by the unrelenting harassment of his political enemies. In a diary entry for 1827, Adams complained about the unending chores and the unceasing stream of visitors that made his life so irksome. Yet one feels that his malaise was caused more by his growing conviction that his presidency was doomed to failure than by the mundane burdens of the high office— burdens that he, as a highly experienced national leader, had every reason to know were unavoidable in the performance of the job. It seems unlikely that a successful president would have been quite so distraught at the multitude of chores, no matter how mundane or monotonous, to have felt that nothing could be "worse than this perpetual motion and crazing cares" or that the "weight grows heavier from day to day." Ever the gentleman, Adams continued to receive gracefully the constant stream of congressmen who paid social visits to the White House or sought favors from its chief occupant, many of whom were not only hostile but, in his own phrase, "bitter as wormwood" in their opposition to him. Only what Adams called the "besotted" and violent John Randolph, the calumniator of Adams and Clay, was not welcome.

Randolph may not have been personally acceptable to Adams, but no one described as well the true purpose of the complicated tariff measure constructed and steered through the Twentieth Congress in 1828 by Van Buren and the Jacksonians than did the erratic Virginian. An inconsistent and seemingly contradictory set of protective schedules that was transparently designed to widen further the breach between the president and the nation's diverse sectional and economic interests, the tariff was characterized by Randolph as a measure truly concerned with no manufactures except the manufacture of the next president of the United States.

Remini, the modern authority on this "Tariff of Abominations," has described the bill as a "ghastly, lopsided, unequal bill, every section of which showed marks of political preference and favoritism," and as the "supreme example of political horsetrading in the 20th Congress." He has refuted the long-accepted notion that the authors of the measure actually sought its defeat. Its managers frankly conceded that their chief purpose was to overthrow Adams in 1828 by bringing Ohio, Kentucky, and Missouri into the Jackson camp while keeping New York and Pennsylvania within the military hero's fold.

An unanticipated political effect of the bill was the sharp reaction its passage evoked from South Carolina and its leading statesman. In 1828, John C. Calhoun's *South Carolina Exposition and Protest* argued that a tariff for protection rather than for raising revenue was unconstitutional; the passage of the tariff left his state no alternative but to assert its right of "interposition" against the "despotism of the many." Four years later, the nullification crisis erupted. Adams, who for all his nationalism and the loose constructionism of some of his principles was no champion of protectionism, was simply bypassed throughout the controversy over the tariff. There can be no doubt that he was badly hurt by the Tariff of Abominations.

The cynicism of Adams' congressional opponents manifested itself, too, in other measures. The same men who expressed their horror at the alleged unconstitutionality of Adams' nationalistic economic proposals thumbed their noses at the strict-constructionist proposals they professed to revere, passing a great array of "pork barrel" bills, which tapped the federal treasury in order to finance construction, bonuses, land giveaways, and harbor installations that were dear to their hearts because they were likely to be politically useful. Committed as they were to harassing the president, Van Buren's legions deluged Adams as no earlier president ever had been, with requests for official statements from his office to justify his position on issues. It has been estimated by Hecht that committees of the Twentieth Congress "sent to the executive office about five times more requests for facts and opinions" than had been sent by earlier Congresses to Adams' predecessors.

Although Adams had shown himself a great secretary of state, ready to resort to vigorous measures to enlarge both the nation's territorial expanse and its influence in the world, he fared as poorly in foreign policy as in domestic. His presidency must have been a disappointment to nationalists, who expected even greater successes of him when he was able to make, rather than merely execute, foreign policy. His attempts to secure Texas peacefully were thwarted, in part because of the excessively aggressive, meddlesome behavior of Joel Poinsett, the first United States minister to Mexico. In this instance, it is possible that Adams refused to punish an errant appointee not out of a high-minded insistence on disregarding the politics of officials but out of private agreement with Poinsett's blatant interference in Mexico's internal politics.

Although Adams did succeed in inducing Great Britain to pay an indemnity of more than $1 million for the slaves it carried away during the War of 1812, he failed to achieve the more significant objective of bringing Great Britain to the bargaining table to negotiate the restoration of trade by American ships with the British West Indies. Bemis, the outstanding authority on the subject, attributes the defeat of Adams' attempt to retaliate against British shipping to Van Buren's "sniping." Adams' refusal to back off from the forty-ninth parallel as the dividing line between Britain and the United States in the Oregon Territory killed chances for an agreement on the issue in Adams' own time, but of course, it meant that the United States two decades later would secure most of what became the new state of Washington.

A nice example of the conflict between principle, represented by President Adams, and amorality, represented by his Jacksonian opponents, is afforded by the controversy that arose between the Creek Indians and the state of Georgia. Like his presidential predecessors, Adams was no inveterate or humanitarian champion of Indian rights. He, too, sought the removal of the southern tribes to west of the Mississippi, and he countenanced threats and unlovely inducements to accomplish it. But, unlike his

successor in the White House, Adams recognized limits to the American disregard of Indian rights guaranteed by federal treaties. When in 1827 Georgia improperly conducted surveys in treaty-guaranteed Indian lands, Adams issued an ultimatum warning that "the Executive of the United States [would] enforce the laws . . . by all the force committed for that purpose." The House of Representatives supported Adams, insisting that purchase, not crude annexation, was the only proper means by which Georgia might acquire Indian lands. But the Senate, led by arch-Jacksonian Thomas Hart Benton, thwarted the president.

Election of 1828

Confronted by a brilliantly organized opposition that had created the first truly modern political party network in American history, Adams harbored no illusions about his chances for reelection in 1828. He would not stoop to making personal appearances before citizens whose votes he needed. In turning down a proposal that he speak to German farmers on the occasion of the opening of a canal in Pennsylvania, Adams said he thought such behavior "unsuitable to [his] personal character and to the station in which [he was] placed." To the modern critics who attribute Adams' decisive defeat in the presidential election largely to his own failure to match the organization and the tactics of his opponents, Adams would have answered that his principles meant more to him than did reelection. It was Henry Clay who later said he would rather be right than president, but it was John Quincy Adams who best lived up to the ideal. Certainly Adams would have rudely dismissed any suggestion that he should have modified or watered down the proposals his administration presented to Congress, with an eye toward broadening the base of his electoral support in 1828. He labored under the antique notion that there were things more important to a president than his reelection.

The 1828 campaign was a vicious one. A political ally of Adams' wrote him that he had never seen an opposition so "malignant and unprincipled as that which is organized against you." Over seventy years ago the historian Edward Channing, in attributing Adams' defeat to Jackson's overwhelming support in the South "combined with the employment of most unjustifiable methods by his partisans in Pennsylvania and New York," concluded that "possibly it was more honorable to have been defeated in 1828 than to have been elected." Writing a half century later, Remini concurs with this estimate, concluding that "this election splattered more filth . . . upon more innocent people than any other in American history." Jackson's opponents did not wear kid gloves, charging the Hero of New Orleans with murder and adultery, among other things. (Both charges were true, if only in a technical sense.) But these attacks paled in comparison to the smears leveled at Adams, who was charged, falsely, with adultery, using public funds to buy personal luxuries, and pimping for the czar during his ministry in Russia. Neither was the infamous "corrupt bargain" neglected.

Inevitably, the election returns can be variously interpreted. Jackson won a decisive victory in the electoral college, 178 to 83. When the popular vote is examined, Jackson's small majority in the West and the Middle Atlantic states and his decisive defeat in the New England states suggest that his smashing three-to-one majority in the South was the vital element in his election. Jackson's friends congratulated him on the outcome, one claiming that it was a victory for virtue. It was more surely a victory for the South. The popular totals also suggest that voters were not altogether indifferent to what they discerned as the principles of the two candidates—one a large slaveholder, the other a critic of slavery—for all the campaign's emphasis on parades, rallies, the dispensation of liquor, and other forms of ballyhoo.

Arthur Schlesinger, Jr., the author of perhaps the most popular and influential book on the age of Jackson, attributes Adams' "overthrow in 1828" to his failure "to meet the problem" of an alleged widespread discontent among the American people. Historians' interpretations of such matters are bound both to differ and to change over time. The weight of the evidence seems to be that the chief "problem" Adams failed to confront was one posed not by the discontent of the people but rather by the ambition of political rivals determined under no circumstances to permit the sixth president to succeed himself in office.

Adams as Congressman

Adams himself appears not to have regarded his defeat in 1828 as a tragedy. When his Quincy neighbors elected him to the House of Representatives in 1830, he proceeded to throw himself heart and soul into

Following his presidency, John Quincy Adams served as a member of the U.S. House of Representatives. On 21 February 1848, he collapsed in the Capitol due to a stroke and died a few days later. BETTMANN/CORBIS

the performance of his new duties for the last seventeen years of his life. When friends wondered whether acceptance of membership in Congress might be degrading for a former president, Adams responded that no one could be degraded for serving the people, no matter in what capacity. It would be understatement to say that Old Man Eloquent served with distinction in Congress.

As congressman, John Quincy Adams was the stuff of legend. He spoke truth when he said of his congressional years, "I shall be as I have been—a solitary." But the stubbornness, devotion to principle, willingness to go it alone, and the seeming indifference to hostile critics that had availed him so little when he occupied the White House, served to make him the center of attention and controversy when he sat in the House of Representatives. Where his presidential performance earned him contempt or disdain, his congressional labors won him either bitter opposition or enthusiastic acclaim, but never indifference.

The lofty principle he now championed was antislavery. In fairness to his total congressional record, it must be said that Adams was a heroically conscientious representative, actively participating in debate on issues ranging from tariffs and banking to crucial foreign policy controversies. He was awarded the sobriquet Old Man Eloquent for a nationalistic speech urging military appropriations during the war crisis with France of the mid-1830s. But his claim to a place in the pantheon of Congress rests almost entirely on his twin campaigns to win congressional acceptance of the antislavery petitions he presented in behalf of his constituents (and other Americans) and to end the "gag rule" under which the House regularly voted to table petitions bearing on slavery or its abolition.

Commencing on 9 January 1837, when he presented an antislavery petition in behalf of 150 women from his district, Adams persisted in his one-man campaign in behalf of thousands of subsequent petitioners, year after year defying votes to table, insults, censure resolutions, and even death threats until finally, on 3 December 1844, the House passed a resolution rescinding the gag rule. Although he had for a while been decried by abolitionists because of his opposition to what he felt was the impractical goal of an immediate, uncompensated end to slavery, Adams ultimately won the respect of almost all persons who believed as did he that slavery was "a sin before the sight of God." He died dramatically after he suffered a stroke almost immediately after voting on 21 January 1848 to oppose a resolution thanking military officers for their services during what he regarded as the proslavery Mexican War. He lapsed into a coma and died on 23 February 1848.

Adams' onetime political opponent, Martin Van Buren, called him honest and incorruptible, the least venal of men. The praise may be justified, but it has, of course, done nothing for the reputation of the Adams administration. Undervalued in his own time, Adams' service to the nation as president continues to be undervalued in the present age. It is a disquieting testimony to our scale of values that honoring, as we do, political "success" achieved at whatever price and for whatever small or unlovely purposes, we continue to be indifferent to great integrity and devotion to lofty principles displayed by our highest officeholders—even when their failures seem largely to have been due precisely to their manifestation of these admirable qualities.

BIBLIOGRAPHY

Charles Francis Adams, ed., *Memoirs of John Quincy Adams, Comprising Portions of His Diary from 1795 to 1848*, 12 vols. (Philadelphia, 1874–1877), is an indispensable record of Adams's reactions to events. Allan Nevins, ed., *The Diary of John Quincy Adams, 1794–1845: American Diplomacy, and Political, Social, and Intellectual Life, from Washington to Polk* (New York, 1969), is a selection from the diary by an informed historian. Walter La Feber, ed., *John Quincy Adams and American Continental Empire: Letters, Papers, and Speeches* (Chicago, 1965), contains other important documents. Marie B. Hecht, *John Quincy Adams: A Personal History of an Independent Man* (New York, 1972), is competent, fact-filled, and sensible. Mary W. M. Hargreaves, *The Presidency of John Quincy Adams* (Lawrence, Kans., 1985), is a useful single-volume summary of his term. Lynn H. Parsons, *John Quincy Adams: A Bibliography* (Westport, Conn., 1993), is a thorough book-length list of sources for further research.

Marcus Cunliffe, *The Nation Takes Shape, 1789–1837* (Chicago, 1959), is a well-written account of the political background. George Dangerfield, *The Era of Good Feelings* (New York, 1952), and *The Awakening of American Nationalism, 1815–1828* (New York, 1965), are gracefully written, highly informed, and intellectually sophisticated. Daniel Walker Howe, *The Political Culture of the American Whigs* (Chicago, 1979), is an unconvincing but interesting analysis of Adams's beliefs. Samuel Flagg Bemis, *John Quincy Adams and the Foundations of American Foreign Policy* (New York, 1949), and *John Quincy Adams and the Union* (New York, 1956), present perceptive evaluations of Adams's contributions by a pioneer American diplomatic historian. A more recent consideration is William E. Weeks, *John Quincy Adams and American Global Empire* (Lexington, Ky., 1992).

Robert V. Remini, *The Election of Andrew Jackson* (Philadelphia, 1963), and *Andrew Jackson and the Course of American Freedom, 1822–1832* (New York, 1981), provide respectively an invaluable study of how the new Jacksonian party organized to defeat Adams and an informed and controversial interpretation of the politics of the period. Edward Pessen, *Jacksonian America: Society, Personality, and Politics*, rev. ed. (Homewood, Ill., 1978), gives the social, cultural, and economic as well as political background of the antebellum decades. Glyndon G. Van Deusen, *The Jacksonian Era, 1828–1848* (New York,

1959), is a balanced account of national politics during that period.

Recent works include Paul C. Nagel, *John Quincy Adams: A Public Life, A Private Life* (New York, 1997), which draws extensively upon the lifelong journals kept by Adams. Richard Brookhiser, *America's First Dynasty: The Adamses, 1735–1918* (New York, 2002), profiles four generations of the Adams family, focusing on the two presidents, John Quincy's son Charles, and Charles's son Henry. See also Robert V. Remini, *John Quincy Adams* (New York, 2002).

Andrew Jackson

Richard B. Latner

Andrew Jackson THE LIBRARY OF CONGRESS

THE familiar labels "The Age of Jackson" and "Jacksonian Democracy" identify Andrew Jackson with the era in which he lived and with the advancement of political democracy. This honor may exaggerate his importance, but it also acknowledges the important truth that Jackson significantly contributed to shaping the American nation and its politics. Just as contemporaneous artists so often depicted him astride his horse overseeing the battlefield, Jackson bestrode some of the key currents of nineteenth-century American political life.

Jackson's presidency began on a sunny, spring-like day, 4 March 1829. Dressed in a simple black suit and without a hat, partly out of respect for his re-

cently deceased wife, Rachel, and partly in keeping with traditions of republican simplicity, Jackson made his way on foot along a thronged Pennsylvania Avenue. From the east portico of the Capitol, he delivered his inaugural address—inaudible except to those close by—in which he promised to be "animated by a proper respect" for the rights of the separate states. He then took the oath of office, placed his Bible to his lips, and made a parting bow to the audience. With great difficulty, he made his way through the crowd, mounted his horse, and headed for the White House and what had been intended as a reception for "ladies and gentlemen."

What next took place has become a part of American political folklore. According to one observer, the White House was inundated "by the rabble mob," which, in its enthusiasm for the new president and the refreshments, almost crushed Jackson to death while making a shambles of the house. Finally, Jackson was extricated from the mob and taken to his temporary quarters at a nearby hotel. "The reign of King 'Mob' seemed triumphant," one cynic scoffed. There was little doubt that Jackson's presidency was going to be different from that of any of his predecessors. Daniel Webster put it best when he predicted that Jackson would bring a "breeze with him. Which way it will blow I cannot tell."

Webster's uncertainty is readily understandable because Jackson was a relative newcomer to national politics. Jackson was born on 15 March 1767, in the Waxhaw settlement, a frontier border area between North and South Carolina, where his early life was marked by misfortune and misadventure. His Scotch-Irish father had joined the tide of immigrants seeking improved economic and political conditions in the New World, only to die after two years, leaving his pregnant wife and two sons. The third son, whom she named Andrew after her late husband, was born just days later. As a young man during the Revolutionary War, Jackson also lost both his brothers and his mother.

Despite these inauspicious beginnings, Jackson received some formal education at local academies and schools, and following the Revolution, he left the Waxhaw community to study law with two prominent members of the North Carolina bar. In the 1780s, after finding little legal work in North Carolina, he migrated to Tennessee, where he showed the good sense to identify himself with the Blount-Overton faction, a group of prominent men bound together by politics, land speculation, and, increasingly, financial and banking interests.

The eager, hardworking, and talented young Jackson soon received a host of political rewards. He became a public prosecutor, attorney general for the Mero District, delegate to the Tennessee constitutional convention, a member of Congress, a United States senator, and a judge of the Superior Court of Tennessee. By the year 1800, he was the leader of the Western branch of the Blount-Overton faction.

Military positions also came Jackson's way, and he gradually advanced from his appointment as judge advocate for the Davidson County militia in 1792 to be elected major general of the Tennessee militia a decade later. At the same time, he accumulated significant amounts of property, establishing himself as a member of the Tennessee elite by purchasing a plantation, first at Hunter's Hill and then, in 1804, at the Hermitage, near Nashville.

Jackson's enormous military success during the War of 1812, culminating in the Battle of New Orleans, made him a national hero, and during the winter of 1821–1822, political friends placed his name before the country as a presidential candidate in the election of 1824. His first presidential bid fell short, for in a four-way contest, Jackson won a plurality of the popular vote but failed to receive an electoral majority. The decision rested with the House of Representatives, and John Quincy Adams emerged victorious after receiving the support of Henry Clay. When Adams appointed Clay as his secretary of state and heir apparent, Jacksonians alleged a "corrupt bargain." Jackson himself always believed that the will of the people had been corruptly overturned, and he denounced Clay as "the *Judas* of the West." Although it is unlikely that Adams and Clay actually made a secret deal, Jackson had a telling point in that Clay's action deprived the most popular candidate of the presidency. The incident strengthened Jackson's conviction that a republic should be based on the democratic principle of majority, not elite, rule.

Four years later, Old Hickory was vindicated. In the election of 1828, he received about 56 percent of the popular vote and carried virtually every electoral vote south of the Potomac River and west of New Jersey. Yet Jackson's victory was the product of a diverse coalition of groups rather than of a coherent political party. In addition to the original Jackson men from the campaign of 1824, there were the followers of New York's Martin Van Buren and Jackson's vice president, South Carolina's John C. Calhoun; former Federalists; and groups of "relief men," who during the Panic of 1819 had bucked the established political interests by advocating reforms to help indebted farmers and artisans.

Further, there were few clear-cut issues dividing the candidates. Instead, popular attention was captured by a host of scurrilous charges that dragged the contest down to the level of mud-slinging. Rachel, for example, was accused of bigamy in marrying Jackson while she was legally attached to another man. Jackson men, in addition to harping on the corrupt-bargain charge, accused Adams of pimping for the czar while he was minister to Russia.

Nevertheless, there were signs even in that campaign of Jackson's future course. The Jackson men

General Andrew Jackson's victory over the British at the Battle of New Orleans in 1815 catapulted him to national fame and a future in politics. BETTMANN/CORBIS

of 1828 already displayed elements of the political organization that would emerge during his presidency. Significantly, his followers showed themselves more adept than the opposition at appealing to the people and organizing grassroots sentiment. The center of the Jackson campaign was the Nashville Central Committee, whose key members were Jackson's earliest and closest associates in Tennessee politics, such as John Eaton, John Overton, and William B. Lewis. This committee linked together the numerous state and local Jackson organizations and worked closely with political leaders in Washington.

The Jackson committees encouraged a more popular and democratic style of politics by organizing rallies, parades, and militia musters; helping to sustain Jackson newspapers; and encouraging voters to cast their ballots for Jackson on election day. This was the first election in which gimmicks such as campaign songs, jokes, and cartoons were extensively used to arouse popular enthusiasm. Years before,

Jackson's soldiers had given him the nickname Old Hickory to signify both his toughness and their affection for him. During the 1828 campaign, his followers ceremoniously planted hickory trees in village and town squares, and sported hickory canes and hats with hickory leaves. Hickory poles, symbolically connecting Jackson to the liberty poles of the revolutionary era, were erected "in every village, as well as upon the corners of many city streets." Jackson himself, while avoiding overt electioneering displays, carefully supervised this political activity.

The election of 1828 also hinted at Jackson's future program. Until recently, Jackson was rarely considered a man with any coherent political views. Most accounts treated him as a confused, opportunistic, and inconsistent politician. Jackson, to be sure, had no formal political philosophy, but he adhered to certain underlying values and ideas with a degree of consistency throughout his long political career.

Jackson's philosophy owed much to the teachings of Thomas Jefferson and to the tradition of republican liberty of the revolutionary generation. One of the unique products of the American Revolution was the new and distinctive definition it gave to classical and Renaissance traditions of republicanism. Revolutionary thinkers taught that liberty was always jeopardized by excessive power and that a proper balance and limitation of governmental powers was essential to assure freedom. In addition, this ideology of republicanism also emphasized that the character and spirit of the people—what was called public virtue—were fundamental to maintaining a free society. A virtuous citizenry was necessary to liberty, and whatever corrupted the people thereby corrupted their institutions. Rooted in an agrarian, premodern society, traditional republican thought warned of the competing dangers inherent in an expansive market economy, such as stockjobbing, paper credit, funded debts, powerful moneyed interests, a swollen bureaucracy, and extreme inequality of condition.

During the nineteenth century, Americans accommodated republicanism's precapitalistic bias to the dramatic changes in transportation, communication, and economic activity that have been called the Market Revolution. Especially after the War of 1812, Americans acknowledged that it was no longer possible or even desirable to maintain a rigid agrarian social order. They increasingly accepted as beneficial certain material and moral aspects of a developing economy. Economic ambition, for example, need not breed only luxury and corruption; it could also promote industriousness, frugality, and other republican virtues. Nevertheless, many Americans continued to harbor anxieties that the emerging world of commerce, banking, and manufacturing endangered the conditions essential to maintain liberty. In short, the language of republicanism remained potent throughout the Jacksonian era, but its diagnosis of the condition of the American republic was subject to different interpretations.

These ideas left their mark on Jackson. It was evident in his highly moralistic tone; his agrarian sympathies; his devotion to the principles of states' rights and limited government; and his fear that speculation, moneyed interests, and human greed would corrupt his country's republican character and institutions. At the same time, he was not a rigid traditionalist. He accepted economic progress, a permanent and expanding Union with sovereign authority, and democratic politics. His philosophy,

therefore, brought together the not entirely compatible ideals of economic progress, political democracy, and traditional republicanism.

In the campaign of 1828, Jackson's sentiments distinguished him from Adams. While Adams viewed an active and positive government as promoting liberty, Jackson preferred to limit governmental power and return to the path of Jeffersonian purity. The comparison was by no means perfect. Jackson intended no states' rights crusade, and he dissatisfied some idealists, particularly in the South, by endorsing some tariff protection and the distribution of any surplus revenue back to the states. Yet it was evident that, compared to his opponent, Jackson would qualify federal activity. He considered his victory a moral mandate to restore "the real principles of the constitution as understood when it was first adopted, and practiced upon in 1798 and 1800." His specific program was to become clear only as his presidency unfolded.

Administration and Appointments

Among Jackson's first responsibilities as president was the administration of government, including his selection of cabinet and other personnel. Some Jackson men, like the Virginia editor Thomas Ritchie, wanted Jackson to share power with an "old fashioned . . . consultative" cabinet, reflective of the cabinet's increased status in the period following the War of 1812. But Jackson refused; he intended, instead, to control his cabinet. More than that, he was prepared to alter fundamentally the whole basis of presidential power by resting his authority directly upon the people. The president, Jackson claimed, was "the direct representative of the American people."

The idea that the chief executive was the people's special representative became an established part of the presidential office, though not all occupants were as skilled as Jackson in making political capital of it. At the time, it was controversial. One prominent editor complained that whereas formerly the president's essential duty was to execute the law made by other government branches, it had come to be claimed as "the true democracy, that the *president* is THE 'GOVERNMENT.' " But Jackson's supporters parried such protests. "That the practice is not usual is no objection to it," responded Jackson's official newspaper, the *Washington Globe*.

As befit a president who intended to lead, Jackson wanted a cabinet composed of "plain, business men" who would sustain a moderate states' rights program, rather than prominent politicians who might undercut his authority and use their office as a stepping-stone to higher position. He also had to navigate carefully between the rival camps of Van Buren and Calhoun, both of whom were considered competitors for the succession. In the end, Jackson selected Van Buren as secretary of state, his friend Eaton as secretary of war, Samuel Ingham of Pennsylvania as secretary of the treasury, John Branch of North Carolina as head of the Navy Department, John McPherson Berrien of Georgia as attorney general, and Kentucky's William T. Barry as postmaster general.

The selections generally fit Jackson's criteria. There were no radical antitariff or protariff zealots who might stir trouble, and none, with the exception of Van Buren, was a major political figure. Both the Calhoun and Van Buren men felt disappointed, a sign of Jackson's ability to maintain his independence of both groups. Almost unnoticed in the din of protest by dissatisfied office seekers was that Jackson had drawn the line against the followers of Adams and Clay. His would be, applauded one Jackson man, "a party administration."

Jackson's first cabinet proved a keen disappointment. Its members soon divided into hostile factions, and Jackson called it into session only rarely before it dissolved in the spring of 1831. But, contrary to most historical accounts, this was the exception, not the rule. Later cabinet appointments were generally more felicitous, and Jackson ordinarily met his cabinet on a regular basis, usually once a week, except when crises called for more frequent, even daily, sessions. Yet Jackson never granted his cabinet great formal power. Individual members like Van Buren might accumulate considerable influence, but Jackson looked to his cabinet primarily to inform and discuss, not to decide. The more important the issue to him, the more he used his cabinet only to gain political support for a predetermined policy.

From the outset, Jackson looked for advice from friends and associates not necessarily in the cabinet. He asked William B. Lewis, who held a job in the Treasury Department, to live in the White House, and he retained his nephew Andrew Jackson Donelson as his private secretary, while Donelson's wife, Emily, served as White House hostess. More significantly, he gave special attention to a Kentucky editor and former relief leader named Amos Kendall, who landed an appointment as an auditor in the Treasury

Department. In December 1830, Kendall was joined among Jackson's close advisers by another Kentucky relief man, Francis Preston Blair, who arrived to edit the *Globe*. Along with Van Buren, the two Kentuckians constituted Jackson's inner circle of advisers, though others would from time to time join them.

The opposition soon dubbed Jackson's advisers the "kitchen cabinet," by which they meant a close-knit group of "favorites who controlled and directed" him. The charge was unfounded. In reality, Jackson established a flexible advisory system composed of many people with overlapping responsibilities. The system was well suited to an active president who disliked official councils and preferred to consult informally with whomever he thought able to give useful advice.

The arrangement also left Jackson entirely free to make the final judgment and assume full responsibility for a decision. Jackson vigorously denied that others made policy for him, and his own closest aides agreed. Kendall summed it up best when he explained that influence depended on agreement with Jackson's objectives and style: "There are a few of us who have always agreed with the President in relation to the Bank and other essential points of policy, and therefore they charge us with having an influence over him! Fools!! They can not beat the President out of his long-cherished opinions, and his firmness they charge to our influence."

Jackson's handling of administrative matters also refutes opposition charges that he was incompetent and irresponsible. In Jackson's day, presidents were expected to oversee the day-to-day conduct of public business, such as appointments and removals, department reports, budgetary appropriations, and other administrative chores. Jackson showed the attention to detail, consistency, and tact required of good administrators. One observer reported that the president "looks personally into every thing.. . . He frequently visits the executive offices, supervises the proceedings of the subordinate functionaries, and directs and stimulates them by his presence." Little wonder that Jackson could report that his labors employed him "day and night" and that his situation was one of "dignified slavery."

Meanwhile, economic growth, an increased and more widely dispersed population, and new government initiatives such as Indian removal strained old administrative arrangements. In the preceding forty years of constitutional government, there had been only two formal administrative reorganizations worthy of notice; but during Jackson's presidency, almost every federal department was overhauled at least once, and the Post Office and General Land Office, which accounted for more than three-quarters of the civilian manpower employed by the executive branch, underwent major reorganizations. The civil service was enlarged, and new formal and elaborate bureaucracies appeared. Administrative rules better defined jurisdictions and responsibilities, and official duties were carefully checked and separated from private activities. According to Matthew A. Crenson's prominent study, Jackson's administrative legacy was the beginning of real government bureaucracy.

No aspect of Jackson's administrative performance has been subjected to as much criticism as his policy of rotation in office. It has been viewed as a euphemism for the spoils system and as a major culprit in the decline of administrative standards during the Jacksonian period. During the campaign of 1828, there was an expectation among many Jackson supporters that his victory would be followed by the wholesale removal of Adams officeholders. To some extent, this reflected the wider participation by citizens in government and the practice of party politics in some states like Pennsylvania and New York, which had well-developed party organizations. No politician of Jackson's skill could ignore the need to inspire and reward efforts made in his behalf. As his presidency progressed, Jackson found further justification in having loyal friends in office. Faithful officeholders brought the government closer to the people and assured that the people's will, as expressed in his policies, was dutifully carried out. In short, partisanship was democratic.

But removals also resulted from Jackson's concern for republican virtue. Jackson sincerely believed that his election was a victory over "the corrupting influence of executive patronage" and that the "corrupt bargain" between Adams and Clay was symptomatic of the extensive decay imbedded in the government. Jackson affirmed the reforming impulse behind removals in his first annual message. "Corruption in some and in others a perversion of correct feelings and principles divert government from its legitimate ends and make it an engine for the support of the few at the expense of the many," he asserted. "Rotation" would prevent officeholders from assuming a permanent right to their positions, and public duties should be made simple enough so that all "men of intelligence" could perform them. Implicit in this message was Jackson's idea that "rotation in office . . . will perpetuate our liberty."

There was much outcry among officeholders and opposition spokesmen who feared a mass beheading of all who would not swear fealty to Old Hickory. Even some of Jackson's own supporters, particularly in the South, expressed disapproval of large-scale dismissals and the appointment of inappropriate personnel, especially low-status newspaper editors. Jackson's critics had a point. Partisanship explicitly entered more fully into the appointments process than ever before. In his first year in office, Jackson removed more officials than all his predecessors combined, and the purges and partisan appointments doubtless contributed to a decline in ethical standards. Certainly, no previous officer managed to bilk the government of as much money as Jackson's collector of the Port of New York, Samuel Swartwout, who absconded with over $1 million and fled to Europe. While Jackson did not intend to introduce a spoils system, his policy opened the way for his successors to institute a more systematic policy of party patronage.

Yet, there was no wholesale proscription during Jackson's presidency, and there were many positive aspects to his policy. Jackson made clear from the outset that reform would proceed "*judiciously . . . and upon principle.*" Only about one-tenth of federal officeholders were removed during his presidency, and not all of these were for political reasons. Especially in the upper echelons of the civil service, key figures remained in their positions, retaining their subordinates and giving stability to the system.

Although a few of Jackson's appointments proved to be disasters—Postmaster General Barry's tenure was marked by inefficient service and escalating debts—many of Jackson's appointments were excellent. From his position in the Treasury Department, for example, Amos Kendall zealously lopped off excess expenditures, unmasked corruption, and improved efficiency. He boasted of saving thousands of dollars and shocked many opposition leaders by exposing his predecessor, Tobias Watkins, a furious Adams partisan, for defalcation. Even Adams conceded that "some of the dismissions are deserved," and though he considered most of the new appointees "less respectable, he acknowledged that some were "good."

The wrongdoing that did occur should also be seen within the context of a general deterioration of ethical standards in American society. The legal profession, the business community, and organized religion all showed a similar decline in internal discipline, and it is likely that Jackson's administrative reforms were designed in part to counteract this slide. In the outcry over removals, it is often forgotten that Jackson's presidency marked an era of creative administration.

The Eaton Affair

Jackson had barely taken office when he confronted his first political crisis. The trouble revolved around Secretary of War Eaton and his wife, Peggy. For various reasons, Eaton's appointment was unpopular with many Jackson supporters. Compounding this difficulty was Eaton's marriage on New Year's Day 1829 to Margaret O'Neale Timberlake. Peggy, the daughter of a Washington tavern keeper, had gained an unsavory reputation for being too forward with her father's boarders when her first husband, a naval officer, was away. Eaton was a frequent guest at the O'Neale tavern. When her husband died at sea, probably a suicide brought on by drinking, Eaton married Peggy after receiving Jackson's opinion that marriage would disprove the charges of impropriety.

Washington society, already fearful that Jackson would have as little regard for its conventions as he had for Indians or British troops, saw Eaton's appointment as a challenge and responded by snubbing Mrs. Eaton. Although some prominent Washington leaders, particularly Van Buren, associated with the Eatons, many did not. Among the families that excluded her were those of Calhoun, Ingham, Branch, Berrien, and Donelson. Doubtless recalling the slanderous attacks against his own wife during the recent campaign, Jackson decried the baseness of those who, in the name of morality, dragged the intimate and private relations of marriage into the public arena. "*Our society wants purging here,*" he concluded.

Jackson devoted an inordinate amount of time during his first year in office gathering evidence to prove Mrs. Eaton's virtue and laboring to have his family and cabinet harmonize. His efforts had little effect, and the social war against Peggy Eaton continued unabated. Jackson was furious and miserable, but he continued to support the Eatons and insisted that loyalty to them was essential to his own success.

The Eaton affair inevitably spilled over into politics. Initially, Jackson assumed that Clay and the opposition were responsible. However, by the late fall of 1829, he had identified Calhoun as the archconspirator. Because Eaton, who was a Van Buren partisan, had refused to back Calhoun's presidential aspirations, Jackson alleged, Calhoun thought it necessary to destroy him, whatever the consequences to the administration.

In retrospect, it is clear that Jackson exaggerated Calhoun's responsibility. The Eaton controversy involved matters of decorum that would have made it difficult under the best of circumstances to harmonize the cabinet. Much opposition to the Eatons also emanated more from political hostility to Eaton and Van Buren than from devotion to Calhoun.

Yet if Jackson simplified, he also struck a core truth. While there is no direct evidence that Calhoun initiated the quarrel to strengthen his claims to the succession, he was doing nothing to put a stop to a scandal that was damaging Jackson's credibility. One close Jackson associate put the issue squarely when he judged Calhoun a "madman" if he promoted the maneuvers against Eaton, and not a wise man if he does not put an end to it."

Soon other difficulties mixed with the Eaton incident to separate Calhoun from Jackson. In the fall of 1829, Jackson learned that, as a member of Monroe's cabinet, Calhoun had recommended that Jackson be punished for defying the president's orders and pursuing the Seminole Indians into Spanish Florida. In May 1830, when Jackson received confirming evidence in written form, he forwarded the material to Calhoun and expressed his "great surprise" at these allegations. Calhoun began a correspondence in which he attempted to blame Van Buren's friends for reviving the issue, but he was still forced to concede his opposition to Jackson's Florida invasion. Jackson denounced Calhoun as a "hypocrite" who had "attempted to stab me in the dark."

Jackson also grew increasingly irritated by Calhoun's political independence, particularly his prominent position among the radical antitariff nullifiers. Their deteriorating relationship came to a head at the Jefferson Day Dinner in April 1830, which some Calhounites intended to use as an occasion to identify nullification with Jeffersonian principles. Jackson suspected that the proceedings would prove irregular, and he made the impending dinner the subject of "frequent conversations" with Van Buren. Having seen the list of regular toasts beforehand, he prepared his own and carefully rehearsed it with aides.

After the regular toasts were given, Jackson rose to provide the first volunteer statement. Tradition has it that he stared sternly at Calhoun and announced, "Our Union—*it must be preserved.*" The words struck home with great force, and one nullifier rushed to ask Jackson to insert the word *federal* before *Union*. Jackson readily agreed, saying that he had written the phrase that way but had inadvertently omitted the word. Even so, Jackson's declaration contrasted starkly with the sentiment offered by Calhoun: "The Union: Next to our liberty, the most dear; may we all remember that it can only be preserved by respecting the rights of the States and distributing equally, the benefit and burden of the Union." This overly long toast did nothing to dispel the idea that he was not in accord with Jackson's convictions.

Jackson's alienation from Calhoun was largely complete by this time. Thereafter, occasional efforts were made to reconcile the two men, but never successfully. In February 1831, Calhoun placed himself totally outside the pale by publishing his correspondence with Jackson concerning the Seminole controversy. The effect was to challenge Jackson in public and to give the impression that Jackson was weak and had been manipulated by Calhoun's enemies. "Mr. Calhoun does not attack the President, he says; yet he makes him out a dupe!" Kendall observed. The administration drew the line against "false friends," and Calhoun was effectively read out of the party.

The final scene of the Eaton drama was played out a few months later, in April 1831, when Van Buren paved the way for a general cabinet reorganization by resigning from his position. While Calhoun had been losing Jackson's confidence, Van Buren had been gaining it. The New Yorker, by showing the Eatons the same social consideration he gave to others and by lending his support to Jackson's political goals, earned Jackson's trust and affection. By January 1830, Jackson had concluded that Van Buren should be his successor. Van Buren's enemies charged him with manipulating the Eaton affair to undermine Calhoun, but the truth is that Van Buren needed only to let events take their course and take advantage of "the indiscretions of Calhoun's friends." Jackson noted approvingly that Van Buren "identified him [self] with the success of the administration." He could not say the same for Calhoun.

Yet Van Buren's prominence placed him in a distressing situation. So long as he remained in the cabinet, he was certain to bring continued attention to himself as a possible intriguer. The public might blame him for the Jackson-Calhoun split and for the disturbances over the Eatons. Van Buren, consequently, hit upon the idea of resigning from the cabinet as a way to restore harmony to the party and cabinet and to remove himself from a precarious position.

Jackson reluctantly accepted Van Buren's resignation, along with that of Eaton, and then discharged Branch, Berrien, and Ingham. Only Barry remained, leaving Jackson with virtually a free hand to select new members who would work better together. Jackson also appointed Van Buren minister to Great Britain, but on 25 January 1832, the Senate rejected his nomination. A tie was arranged so that Calhoun could cast the deciding vote against his rival. It may have been Calhoun's hope that this act of revenge would weaken Van Buren and the administration. One senator overheard Calhoun reassuring his followers that the vote would hurt Van Buren: "It will kill him, sir, kill dead. He will never kick, sir, never kick." But in the end, the rejection made Van Buren a political martyr and the inevitable choice for Jackson's vice president at the upcoming Democratic National Convention.

Despite the extraordinary discord and division of Jackson's first two years, he emerged from the fray with a more coherent and loyal following. The loss of Calhoun was more than compensated by the firmer attachment of the Van Buren interest. Similarly, the establishment of Blair's *Globe* in December 1830, replacing Duff Green's pro-Calhoun *United States Telegraph*, provided new energy for the administration. To be sure, Blair's arrival from Kentucky was not auspicious: his already thin, cadaverous-looking frame was disheveled and bandaged from a mishap to his coach, leading a disappointed Lewis to comment, "Mr. Blair, we want stout hearts and sound heads here." But Blair and his paper were all that Jackson could wish. Unlike Green, Blair was fully devoted to Jackson and his objectives, particularly on banking and currency matters. Blair also made the *Globe* a clearinghouse for party information and propaganda, by exchanging copies with over four hundred other papers and by extending its circulation. The paper gave Jackson greater control over his administration, greater authority with Congress, and closer ties to the voters.

Indian Removal

Not all of Jackson's energy was diverted by political rivalry and intrigue. Even as he was preoccupied with Eaton and Calhoun, he began to move forward with his program. Among the first issues to be addressed was the situation of the Indian tribes.

When Jackson took office, relations between the southern tribes, the state governments, and the United States had reached a critical juncture. Georgia had clashed with the federal government when President John Quincy Adams refused to implement a controversial treaty removing the Creek Indians. Although Adams backed down and negotiated another treaty ceding the disputed land to the state, the incident highlighted the plight of the remaining southern tribes, particularly the Cherokee. Perhaps no issue more clearly distinguished the two presidential candidates in 1828, for Jackson's imposing record of conquest over the Indians, both by arms and treaty, contrasted dramatically with Adams' protective posture.

In his first annual message of December 1829, Jackson proposed that an area west of the Mississippi River be set apart and guaranteed to the Indian tribes. There they could be taught "the arts of civilization" and perpetuate their race. Emigration to this new territory would be "voluntary," but those who remained in the East would be subject to the laws of the states in which they lived and would "ere long become merged in the mass of our population."

The idea of removing Indians westward had a long history and the federal government had made numerous treaties for the removal of Indians. But Jackson's statement represented a shift in emphasis of sufficient magnitude to mark a new era in Indian-white relations. He proposed that efforts at civilizing the tribes now take place only in Indian territory, where the tribes would be free from corrupting contact with the advancing tide of frontiersmen. Determined to pursue removal with unprecedented vigor and directness, Jackson threatened that those Indians who remained behind would lose their tribal status and be considered individuals subject to state authority.

The administration's Indian removal bill encountered stiff resistance in Congress, where humanitarian and political objections nearly defeated it. Only by skillfully mobilizing their forces did Jackson's followers narrowly succeed in passing the measure on 26 May 1830. The final vote showed a considerable degree of party loyalty, making it the first important measure of Jackson's presidency that distinguished the emerging Democratic party from the opposition.

Despite the public outcry against removal, the program had many defenders, among them Jackson himself. Disputing the idea that the Indian tribes could establish separate nations within the borders of existing states, he promised liberal and equitable exchanges for their present lands. He contended that only in the West could Indians avoid demoralization and even complete annihilation at the hands of an expanding "mercenary" white population. With the Indians secure in their new territory, the federal government could exercise "parental control" over their interests and make them "civilized."

However sincerely intended, Jackson's humanitarian concerns were laced with an ethnocentrism and paternalism that devalued Indian culture and advances. No matter that some Indians had adopted many of the trappings of white society, Jackson considered the tribes as obstacles to the progressive spread of a superior civilization over the continent. "What good man would prefer a country covered with forests and ranged by a few thousand savages to our extensive Republic, studded with cities, towns, and prosperous farms . . . and filled with all the blessings of liberty, civilization, and religion?" he asked. When Indians also protested against leaving their traditional and sacred lands, Jackson facilely compared their fate to the experience of the highly mobile white society. "Doubtless it will be painful to leave the graves of their fathers," he acknowledged, "but what do they more than our ancestors did or than our children are now doing." Thus, if Indians assumed white ways, as had many Cherokee, Jackson disregarded it; if Indians desired to retain their traditional values, Jackson treated them as potential men on the make. Jackson was no Indian-hater, but his proposed philanthropy was virtually as damaging as outright hostility.

Efforts to make removal treaties with the Indians began as soon as Jackson took office and continued throughout his presidency. Jackson himself occasionally participated in the negotiations. The administration focused on the southern tribes, beginning in September 1830 with the Treaty of Dancing Rabbit Creek with the Choctaw, and proceeding with the Creek, Chickasaw, and, in 1835, the Cherokee. Less well known are the treaties made with the generally weaker tribes of the Old Northwest, such as the Chippewa, Ottawa, and Potawatomi. Over the period of Jackson's presidency, the United States ratified some seventy treaties, affecting approximately forty-six thousand Indians.

Jackson hoped removal would be humane, but the process was often harsh and violent. Treaties were concluded with leaders who represented only a portion of the tribe and who often benefited personally from the agreement; food and transportation for the westward journey were contracted with the lowest bidder; and those staying behind generally found themselves deprived of their landholdings and treated as second-class citizens. When Indians refused to remove or when, disappointed in their new lands, they tried to return, violence broke out. The Black Hawk War of 1832 and the Creek War and the beginning of the long and bloody Seminole War in 1835 are examples of the coercion inherent in removal. Finally, Jackson's promise of Indian self-government in the West never materialized, and federal authority remained intrusive in Indian affairs. Under pressure of a rapidly expanding agricultural and commercial frontier, Jackson's respect for states' rights and reduced federal expenditures produced an arrangement that was neither just nor humane.

Internal Improvements

Indian removal showed that Jackson's goal of assuring a virtuous yet progressive society was circumscribed by race. At the same time, he clarified other aspects of his program by reversing the trend toward expanded federal assistance for internal improvements. In his first annual message in December 1829, Jackson brought the issue to Congress' attention by announcing that many people considered previous policy unconstitutional or inexpedient. "The people expected reform, retrenchment and economy in the administration of Government," he explained privately. "This was the cry from Maine to Louisiana, and instead of these the objects of Congress, *it would seem*, is to make mine one of the most extravagant administrations since the commencement of the Government."

Bogged down in the Eaton affair, Indian removal, and other matters, Jackson left it to Van Buren to choose an appropriate measure to initiate his new policy. Van Buren waited until April 1830, when a Kentucky congressman introduced a bill calling upon the federal government to purchase stock in a corporation to construct a road in Kentucky from Maysville to Lexington. The Maysville Road was considered by its advocates as part of a more extensive interstate road system and, therefore, deserving of federal support. The bill readily passed the House of Representatives at the end of April, with the backing of many Jackson men. Van Buren then brought it to

Jackson's attention during one of their daily horseback rides, and Jackson promptly agreed that since the road was located entirely within one state, it would serve admirably.

Rumors circulated that Jackson might veto the Maysville bill, and a group of western Democrats appealed to Representative Richard M. Johnson of Kentucky to present their case for the road. Johnson explained that the improvement was needed and that a veto would severely damage the Jackson party in Kentucky. Warming to his subject, Johnson dramatically declaimed, "General! If this hand were an anvil on which the sledge hammer of the smith was descending and a fly were to light upon it in time to receive the blow he would not crush it more effectually than you will crush your friends in Kentucky if you veto that Bill!"

Jackson rose to his feet and responded in equally fervent language, bluntly remarking that there was "no money" for the expenditures desired by the friends of internal improvements. "Are you willing— are my friends willing to lay taxes to pay for internal improvements?—for be assured I will not borrow a cent except in case of absolute necessity!" he heatedly proclaimed. Jackson soon ended the interview on a more amicable note, promising to examine the bill from all angles before making up his mind, but Johnson left the White House convinced that the bill was as good as dead. "Nothing less than a voice from Heaven would prevent the old man from vetoing the Bill," Johnson explained to his colleagues, and he "doubted whether that would!"

Johnson was right, for Jackson handed down his veto, rejecting the bill on grounds that were both constitutional and pragmatic. Affirming that internal improvements could be constitutionally appropriated only for purposes of national defense and national benefit, Jackson condemned the measure as "of purely local character." He also skillfully argued against the expediency of such proposals even if they fell within his constitutional rule. Recalling the American responsibility to perpetuate "the republican principle," Jackson urged lightening public burdens, ending wasteful expenditures, and eliminating the corruption and special privilege associated with government investment in private corporations.

Over the eight years of his presidency, Jackson elaborated and refined his objections to internal-improvements projects. He warned that federal involvement risked jurisdictional clashes with the states and that government investment in private transportation companies delegated public responsibilities to private agencies and led to charges of "favoritism and oppression." He also protested against the "flagicious logrolling" that encouraged inequities of burdens and benefits and was destructive of legislative harmony. Jackson was not against economic progress, but he maintained that demands for an extensive, federally sponsored system of improvements endangered republican government and distorted natural economic growth.

Internal-improvements spending did not cease during Jackson's administration. Indeed, he spent more money—about $10 million—than all previous administrations combined. But given the pressure for improved communication and transportation facilities placed on all levels of government by economic expansion, evidence of Jackson's commitment to restraint can be found in the lack of new proposals emanating from his administration and the discouragement of new pet projects caused by actual or threatened vetoes. Most of the money approved by Jackson was for projects already begun under earlier administrations or involved activities and locales that were clearly under federal jurisdiction. Jackson therefore halted the drive for a national system of improvements and located the major responsibility for projects on state and local governments and on private funding.

More than the Indian removal bill, Jackson's internal-improvements policy began the process of identifying Jackson's followers with a party platform. Jackson himself broadcast the idea that his position on internal improvements was a testing ground for the emerging party divisions. "The line . . . has been fairly drew," he announced after issuing the Maysville message.

The veto also signaled a significant change in presidential power. Prior to Jackson's presidency, the veto had been resorted to only nine times, generally on grounds of unconstitutionality or to protect the executive against legislative encroachment. Jackson exercised the veto on more occasions, a total of twelve times; frequently employed the pocket veto, by which a president withholds a bill, unsigned, until Congress adjourns; and expanded the grounds for vetoing a measure. Indeed, it was the portions of Jackson's veto messages dealing with nonconstitutional matters that generally contained the most authentic examples of Jacksonian rhetoric and had the greatest popular appeal. In directing his vetoes to the people, moreover, Jackson enhanced presidential power and made the chief executive substantially the equivalent of both houses of Congress.

The Bank of the United States

Jackson's style of reaching out for political issues was never better illustrated than his attack on the Second Bank of the United States. The bank had been chartered in 1816 to restore the country to a sound fiscal condition after near financial catastrophe during the War of 1812. It was a large corporation, managed and operated under both private and public auspices. Its capital was $35 million, partly subscribed by the United States government, and it was permitted to establish branches and issue bank notes. It was a profit-making institution that also provided public services such as transferring government funds around the country and functioning as a depository for the Treasury. Although it possessed no monopoly over the money supply, it exerted great influence over the nation's financial affairs.

After a shaky start, the bank earned a reputation for fiscal responsibility under the presidency of Nicholas Biddle. It even gained considerable popularity among state bankers, who might have looked upon their giant relative as an enemy. Still, the bank's support did not run deep; Jeffersonian constitutional scruples, traditional republican anxieties, and practical objections lingered among numerous Americans who considered its monetary policies either too lenient or too restrictive and its powers a potential threat to republican government.

Foremost among the doubters was Jackson. Having once been brought to the brink of insolvency by speculative adventures, Jackson became suspicious of all banks and their paper-money issues. His opposition to the national bank, therefore, was part of a broader antibanking and hard-money perspective. "I have been opposed always to the Bank of the U.S. as well as all state Banks of paper issues, upon constitutional ground," he insisted. He also suspected that the bank had intervened in local and national elections and thereby constituted a danger to free government. Thus, when preparing his first annual message, Jackson rejected pleas that he exclude reference to the bank, responding to one worried counselor, "Oh! My friend, I am pledged against the bank."

It is unlikely that Jackson thought in terms of the immediate destruction of the Bank of the United States. Rather, he intended to curb its abuses and explore possible alternatives. In his first message, he briefly observed that the bank's charter was scheduled to expire in 1836 and that its stockholders would probably apply for a renewal. Claiming that both the constitutionality and expediency of the bank were "well questioned by a large portion of our fellow-citizens" and that the bank had failed to establish a uniform and sound currency, he tentatively suggested that Congress consider substituting an institution more closely attached to the government. A year later, he reiterated his apprehensions about the "dangers" of the bank and elaborated on his proposal for a modified national bank that would be an adjunct of the Treasury.

Yet the pace of events remained like a minuet with both sides eyeing each other warily. Jackson's new cabinet, organized in the spring of 1831, contained two highly regarded figures, Louis McLane at the Treasury Department and Edward Livingston at the State Department, who sympathized with the bank. An all-out assault would doubtless have precipitated another cabinet crisis, something Jackson could ill afford. Perhaps, too, he preferred to delay further action until after the 1832 presidential election. Whatever his reasons, Jackson's third annual message, delivered in December 1831, was more modest than his earlier ones. While affirming his continued misgivings about the bank, he ambiguously left the whole subject "to the investigation of an enlightened people and their representatives."

Jackson's moderation troubled antibank Democrats. They need not have worried, for events favored their cause. In January 1832, Biddle, acting on the unfortunate advice of political friends, submitted to Congress a memorial for renewing the bank's charter. The timing was obviously calculated to make the bank a political issue. The National Republican party had nominated Clay as its presidential candidate in December 1831, and he was eager to test Jackson's strength on this very question. The bank's transparent political design further convinced Jackson that it was indeed a "monster" that threatened to corrupt the nation. As Roger Taney, Jackson's new attorney general, explained, the bank's application meant that "the Bank says to the President, your next election is at hand—if you charter us, well—if not, beware of your power."

The recharter bill passed the Senate on 11 June and the House on 3 July 1832. Jackson met it with a veto that pulsed with the language of Jacksonian democracy. It pronounced the institution a private and privileged corporation whose concentration of political and economic power promoted corruption and threatened liberty. Jackson scored the bank for its "exclusive privileges," claiming that most of its stock was held by foreigners and Americans "chiefly of the richest class." He accused it of operating inequitably, particularly against the West, and of "gross abuse" of its charter. Most especially he warned that the principles embodied in the bill contravened the basic principles of republican equality. Government, Jackson proclaimed, should confine itself "to equal protection, and, as Heaven does its rains, shower its favors alike on the high and the low, the rich and the poor." It should not add "artificial distinctions" to the inevitable natural and just differences among men and "make the rich richer and the potent more powerful."

Jackson's opponents assailed the veto as "the very slang of the leveller and demagogue." They had a point. Superficially, the message implied conflict between the rich and the poor. Yet its ideas were more complex. The veto did not call for the redistribution of wealth or for class war. Instead, it blended a progressive regard for equal opportunity and "competition," with the apprehension that special privilege and monopoly promoted corruption, concentration of power, and a dangerous degree of inequality. The bank veto appealed to concerns that were both contemporary and nostalgic, as Jackson tried to reconcile an expanding and increasingly market-oriented society, of which the bank was a key agent, with the Revolution's ideal of a virtuous republic.

Inevitably, the bank became the paramount issue in the 1832 presidential election. Illustrating the rapid development of party organization during this period, the Democratic party's first national convention met in Baltimore in May 1832 and nominated Jackson and Van Buren. Although it was more fully attended than its rivals', the Democratic meeting was not the first national political convention. The previous December, the National Republicans had assembled in Baltimore to select Clay and John Sergeant of Pennsylvania as their standard-bearers. Even earlier, in September 1831, the nation's first major third party, the Anti-Masons, convened in Baltimore. This party originated in upstate New York in 1826 when an itinerant stonemason named William Morgan disappeared after threatening to publish the secrets of Freemasonry. When local Masons obstructed the investigation into Morgan's kidnapping, a storm of grassroots protest erupted in western New York and spread throughout New England, Pennsylvania, Ohio, Michigan, and other northern states. Anti-Masons soon organized politically and, inspired by moral and egalitarian ideals, advocated the eradication of the Masonic order as well as a variety of other reforms. Finding that the likely presidential contenders in 1832, Jackson and Clay, were both high-ranking Masons, Anti-Masonic leaders decided to nominate their own candidate. In September 1831, delegates from thirteen states nominated William Wirt of Maryland for president and Amos Ellmaker of Pennsylvania for vice president.

The two opposition parties proved no match against Jackson's popularity and his party's organizational efforts. During the campaign, special-edition newspapers, parades, barbecues, and rallies supplemented an extensive network of Hickory Clubs and state and local organizations. Jackson, while carefully avoiding overt efforts at soliciting votes, managed to make numerous public appearances when returning to Washington in the early fall from a summer stay in Tennessee. The campaign, therefore, advanced the movement toward a popular, voter-oriented style of politics.

Jackson won a smashing reelection victory. His estimated 55 percent of the popular vote and 219 electoral votes demonstrated his continued special appeal to the voters. In contrast, Clay received 37 percent of the popular vote and 49 electoral votes, while Wirt gained only 8 percent of the popular vote and 7 electoral votes. The Anti-Masonic party soon dissolved, its members being absorbed by both the Democratic party and the new Whig party. But there was no time to savor the triumph, for even as the results were recorded, Jackson's attention was primarily focused on South Carolina and the issue of nullification.

Nullification

The nullification crisis was precipitated by South Carolina's bitterness at Jackson's failure to urge a major downward revision of tariff rates. Protective tariffs were considered unconstitutional, inexpedient, and inequitable throughout the South, but resentment was most extreme in South Carolina. There, the tariff was a great symbol of southern oppression, and nullification became the appropriate remedy. As devised by Calhoun, nullification's chief theoretician, in his *Exposition* (1828) and Fort Hill Address (1831), each

state retained the final authority to declare federal laws unconstitutional. Acting through a convention, a state could pronounce a federal law null and void within its limits while remaining in the Union.

Jackson was a moderate on the tariff issue. He considered modest protection necessary to ensure the production of goods necessary for national defense and security, to establish a parity with European manufacturers, and to raise sufficient revenue to pay the national debt. He did not doubt the constitutionality of tariff protection. He vowed, therefore, to pursue "a middle and just course" on the tariff, a policy that was also politically expedient because of the lack of consensus among Democrats on the subject.

As for nullification, Jackson's contempt was unreserved. He declared it an "abominable doctrine" that struck at the very roots of the Union, which he considered "perpetual," and it violated the principle of majority rule. He distinguished nullification from traditional states' rights principles. States' rights "will preserve the union of the states," Jackson explained, but nullification "will dissolve the Union."

In the spring of 1831, nullifier leaders went on the offensive. They organized themselves to take control of South Carolina and issued increasingly hostile attacks against the tariff and the administration. When Congress assembled in December, Jackson tried to defuse the controversy by recommending that tariff rates be lowered. Certainly pressure from South Carolina forced his hand on this matter, but tariff reform also comported with his evolving program. The approaching end of the national debt made excessive rates appear to be a special privilege of manufacturers, at the expense of ordinary citizens. High tariffs also provoked sectional strife and undermined "liberty and the general good."

Congress responded with a reform tariff in 1832, returning schedules to approximately what they had been in 1824. The measure was unacceptable to nullifiers, however, who won more than two-thirds of the seats in the South Carolina legislature the following October and called a state convention. Meeting in Charleston on 19 November 1832, the delegates approved the Ordinance of Nullification, which declared that the tariffs of 1828 and 1832 were null and void and that after 1 February 1833 it would be illegal to enforce the payment of import duties within the limits of South Carolina. The convention further warned that any use of force against the state would provide grounds for secession.

Jackson viewed the situation as grave. He regarded the nullifiers as reckless and disappointed demagogues who sought to ride to power on the ruin of the nation. Republican government was always susceptible to subversion from within, and the nullifiers seemed hell-bent on a separation of the Union. Jackson therefore developed a strategy designed to avoid provoking war while isolating and intimidating South Carolina. He sent arms and equipment to the loyal Unionists in the state, readied the army and navy, orchestrated expressions of patriotism throughout the nation, and promised prompt federal military intervention if nullifiers resisted federal laws and overawed South Carolina loyalists.

When Congress convened in December 1832, Jackson made a new conciliatory gesture by announcing his commitment to further tariff reform. Yet it seems unlikely that he had much confidence that this would placate South Carolina. Instead, he probably hoped to isolate the state from southern moderates, who would now have little reason to sympathize with extremism.

Indeed, to show his determination to hold fast against nullification, Jackson issued the Nullification Proclamation on 10 December. Composed with the assistance of Kendall, Blair, and especially Secretary of State Edward Livingston, whom Jackson charged to use his "best flight of eloquence," the proclamation pronounced nullification *"incompatible with the existence of the Union, contradicted expressly by the letter of the Constitution, unauthorized by its spirit, inconsistent with every principle on which it was founded, and destructive of the great object for which it was formed."* He urged South Carolinians to retrace their steps and called upon all Americans to give their undivided support to the Union and "to inspire new confidence in republican institutions."

Led by Van Buren's followers, moderates in Congress sought to end the conflict by supporting a lower tariff bill introduced by Gulian C. Verplanck of New York. But to Jackson the situation remained critical, and on 16 January he sent Congress a message, informing it of South Carolina's actions and requesting explicit confirmation of his right to employ state militias and federal forces against the dissidents.

The resulting Force Bill, as it became known, received bipartisan support—its floor manager in the Senate was Daniel Webster—and though many southerners disliked the measure, its passage was all but assured from the time it was introduced. Jackson considered the act necessary to "show to the world" that the United States was prepared "to crush in an instant" rebellion and treason. At the same time, he made no effort on behalf of the Verplanck bill, preferring to postpone tariff revision until nullification was put down.

Prospects for compromise brightened considerably toward the end of January 1833, when a public meeting in Charleston resolved to delay nullification until Congress completed deliberations on tariff reform. A few weeks later, Clay and Calhoun made public their agreement to underwrite a compromise tariff that would provide a face-saving retreat for the nullifiers. The Clay tariff proposal sacrificed the principle of tariff protection for time, by slowly bringing rates down to a revenue standard. Jackson conspicuously refused to shift his priorities by making Clay's bill an administration measure. But most legislators considered the Compromise Tariff of 1833 as essential as the Force Bill, and by the beginning of March, both proposals had passed Congress. Significantly, Jackson signed the Force Bill first, declaring that it gave "the death blow" to nullification.

The threat to the Union was over, and most Americans breathed a sigh of relief. Yet there were those who, like Jackson, had doubts that the new tariff would bring enduring sectional peace. In the spring of 1833, when some nullifiers denounced the new tariff and called for continued and unceasing efforts to protect the South and slavery from prejudicial legislation, Jackson predicted that the nullifiers, having failed to break up the Union on the tariff issue, would now grasp "the negro, or slavery question" as their "next pretext." Additional signs of restiveness in the South were evident among many Democrats, who considered Jackson an unreliable guardian of states' rights.

Even so, the nation had weathered the storm. Jackson had vindicated the Union, demonstrated that states' rights principles were compatible with nationalism, and displayed remarkable skill in wielding presidential power. One leading Democrat remarked at this time, "He is a much abler man than I thought him. One of those naturally great minds which seem ordinary except when the fitting emergency arises."

Shortly afterward, in June 1833, Jackson departed from Washington on a tour of the East Coast, providing himself with a refreshing break from the recent arduous responsibilities of office and permitting the country to renew its commitment to the Union through patriotic celebration. The response in Baltimore, Philadelphia, New York, Boston, and elsewhere was magnificent. The enthusiasm was genuine and almost universal. In Cambridge, Jackson was awarded an honorary degree of doctor of laws from Harvard. When Adams complained about this debasement of Harvard's reputation, he was met with a telling response from the president of Harvard: "As the people have twice decided that this man knows law enough to be their ruler, it is not for Harvard College to maintain that they are mistaken." But Jackson was compelled to cut short his itinerary when he collapsed from fatigue and bleeding from the lungs. He was taken by steamer back to Washington, where his life remained in danger for two days, before he rallied.

Removal of Deposits

Even as the tour proceeded, Jackson was deeply immersed in politics, for the issue of the Bank of the United States again pressed upon his attention. The bank's charter continued in effect until 1836 and then permitted the institution two years more to wind up its affairs, during which time it could try to reverse its fate. Indeed, Jackson thought there was sufficient evidence that Biddle would neither acknowledge defeat nor work harmoniously with the government. He alleged that since the veto, Biddle had circulated propaganda for the bank, aided Clay's presidential campaign, and mismanaged bank funds.

Equally ominous, the recent alliance of Clay and Calhoun gave new life to the opposition, which, Jackson predicted, would seek recharter as the centerpiece of a system of expanded governmental powers. He considered the situation a "crisis," and he determined to remove the government's deposits from the bank, relying instead on a system of selected state banks, called pet banks. In preparation, he shuffled his cabinet personnel, shifting the conservative McLane from the Treasury Department to the State Department and appointing the Pennsylvanian William Duane to replace McLane.

Throughout the summer of 1833, Jackson confronted evidence of serious resistance to removal from probank Democrats, cabinet members, and even good friends like Van Buren and Ritchie. At the end of July, he fled the sultry capital for his Virginia vacation resort at the Rip Raps to ponder the situation. As the steamboat conveyed the party down the Chesapeake, an incident occurred that showed Jackson's unflagging self-assurance. The Chesapeake waves were unusually high, seemingly endangering the old vessel and its occupants. An aged passenger

exhibited a good deal of alarm, but Jackson retained his composure. "You are uneasy," Jackson said to the gentleman. "You never sailed with *me* before, I see."

Deciding to put to rest further discussion of his intentions, Jackson returned to Washington, called his cabinet together, and explained that there could now be "no excuse for further delay." Though most cabinet members swung reluctantly to his side, Duane stubbornly resisted issuing the order changing the government's depository. Jackson, who regarded Duane as "either the weakest mortal, or the most strange composition I have ever met with," fired him and replaced him with Roger Taney. On 25 September, Taney ordered that as of 1 October, future government revenue be placed in state banks.

The removal order set off a last, mighty struggle with the Bank of the United States. Biddle retaliated by turning the screws on the economy, reducing loans, calling in debts, and curtailing other activities. "This worthy President thinks that because he has scalped Indians and imprisoned Judges he is to have his way with the Bank. He is mistaken," Biddle fumed.

At the same time, opposition leaders, who were beginning to adopt the name *Whig*, denounced Jackson. "Executive usurpation," they cried, trying to undermine Jackson's popular appeal. During the so-called Panic Session of Congress, Senate Whigs managed to pass two resolutions in February and March 1834, rejecting Taney's reasons for removing the deposits and censuring Jackson's actions as "not conferred by the Constitution and laws."

As economic distress spread throughout the country, many Jacksonians hesitated. But Jackson refused to bend or to lose control of the situation. "Go to Nicholas Biddle," he told complaining delegations seeking redress. The president also turned the tables on the Senate by issuing a "Protest" detailing its own transgressions and disregard of constitutional procedures.

The tide of events soon turned in Jackson's favor. In February 1834, Pennsylvania's governor, George Wolf, turned against the bank, and in Congress the president's backers counterattacked. Finally, on 4 April 1834, after prolonged debate, House Democrats passed four resolutions that sustained both the bank veto and the removal of the deposits. Having failed to alter Jackson's policy, the bank's directors voted in July to end the contraction.

Jackson had once again prevailed. "Biddled, Diddled, and Undone" was the epitaph for the bank penned by one Democratic editor. To be sure, Jackson lost some supporters over the removal issue, mostly among southern states' rights radicals, who used the question of "executive usurpation" as a pretext for joining the Whig party. But like other Jackson policies, removal clarified party lines and firmed the commitment of those who remained loyal.

Destroying the national bank was one thing, but assuring the nation a stable and secure monetary system was another. Following removal, therefore, Jackson began his campaign to reform banking abuses. His administration's fondness for hard money—gold and silver—is probably the most difficult of all Jackson measures for twentieth-century Americans to understand. In an era when banking was virtually unregulated and an expanding economy fueled demands for more and more credit, paper money was an obvious target for reformers, who held it responsible for a cruel economic cycle of booms and busts. They also complained that it sapped public virtue by encouraging speculation, robbing "honest labor" of its earnings, and making "knaves rich, powerful and dangerous." Attacks against excessive paper issues reflected concern for actual banking abuses as well as anxiety and, for some, resistance to the onrushing Market Revolution.

Administration efforts to encourage what the *Globe* called "Jackson money" only partially succeeded. Congress revalued gold in 1834, but the precious metal never became a circulating medium for ordinary commercial transactions. Moreover, Congress dragged its feet for two years before imposing restraints on small bills, so that Treasury Secretary Levi Woodbury, who succeeded Taney, was compelled to take action on his own authority. In April 1835, he ordered that after 30 November the pet banks refuse bank notes under $5 for payment of government dues. In early 1836 the ban was extended to cover notes under $10.

During his second administration, Jackson also turned his attention to the issue of a successor who would perpetuate his program and party. Van Buren had long been his choice, and in the summer of 1834, Jackson informed Van Buren that he was insisting that party leaders take a stand against the Bank of the United States, national banks in general, "and in favor of you." Van Buren, however, had drawbacks. As a northerner, he was suspect to many southerners, and his reputation for political scheming left a trail of political resentment. Rebellion against a Van Buren succession flared throughout the South and consolidated behind the candidacy of a slaveholding Tennessean, Senator Hugh Lawson White.

In order to unite the party behind Van Buren, Jackson urged that a national convention meet early. In response to the administration's call, delegates convened in Baltimore on 20 May 1835 and nominated Van Buren, along with the popular Kentucky military hero and senator Richard M. Johnson. Johnson's earlier open relationship with a mulatto woman and his two daughters by her stirred resistance among many southern Jacksonians who preferred Virginia's William C. Rives for the vice presidency. But Jackson's fiat went forth, and Johnson won the necessary two-thirds vote.

Slavery

Southern apprehensiveness about the Van Buren-Johnson ticket becomes more understandable in light of renewed northern antislavery activity at this time. Jackson's presidency coincided with the formation of state and national antislavery societies, the publication of William Lloyd Garrison's *Liberator*, and the expansion of abolitionist efforts to awaken the nation's conscience. Although abolitionists focused primarily on nonpolitical tactics, their activities inevitably intruded into politics. During the last two years of the Jackson administration, therefore, the slavery issue was reintroduced to American politics for the first time since the fiery Missouri debates of 1819–1821.

In the summer of 1835, shortly after the Democratic convention adjourned, antislavery forces organized a campaign to distribute propaganda tracts through the mails to the South. The southern response was predictable. Southern state legislatures passed laws to keep out such "incendiary literature," and many southern postmasters refused to deliver abolitionist mail. At Charleston, South Carolina, on 29 July, a mob of some three hundred incensed citizens stormed the post office to seize abolitionist material. Although persuaded to disperse, a few Carolinians returned that night and took possession of the literature, which they burned the following evening on the Charleston parade grounds.

The Jackson administration's handling of this controversy has generally been interpreted as evidence of its southern orientation. According to one account, the Democratic party's pro-South and proslavery bias was the "darker side to Jacksonian Democracy." The Jackson administration certainly was hostile to abolitionism and any efforts to disturb the South's "peculiar institution." It showed a continuing solicitude for southern opinion and interests, and it embraced the racial tenets of "herrenvolk democracy," which affirmed the equality of whites and their superiority over non-whites. Jackson himself was a substantial planter, owning many slaves, and while he insisted that they be treated "humanely," he showed no disposition to disturb the legal and constitutional arrangements that maintained the slave system. Yet Jackson's position on the slavery issue was more complex than this.

The Democratic party was a national organization, and northern attitudes about slavery and civil liberties had to be given weight. Moreover, Jackson's denunciation of abolitionism did not signify that he considered slavery a positive or permanent good. Rather, he thought that by maintaining sectional calm, Providence would, in time, somehow eradicate the evil. Indeed, he generally perceived the growing slavery controversy as artificial and political, with both abolitionists and southern extremists seeking to divide the Union to serve their separate ends. The permanency of the Union and the American experiment in liberty went hand in hand; both were directly threatened by agitation over slavery. And so, too, was the Democratic party. The administration therefore sought to put a damper on the slavery issue by placating southern worries while resisting extreme proslavery demands.

With Jackson vacationing in Virginia, the administration's initial response to the mails controversy fell to the recently appointed postmaster general, Amos Kendall. Seeking to intercept the mails with as little noise and difficulty as possible, Kendall adopted an evasive strategy of refusing officially to sanction the action of local postmasters who detained the mail, but also declining to order it delivered. He thus left postmasters to their own discretion.

Upon learning of the situation in Charleston, Jackson angrily denounced the abolitionists as "monsters" and suggested that those who subscribed to the papers have their names recorded by the postmaster and exposed in the public newspapers. Yet Jackson did not justify mob action or the complete interdiction of abolitionist mailings. He denounced the "spirit of mob-law" as evidenced in Charleston and thought that the instigators should be "checked and punished." Reminding Kendall that federal officials had "no power to prohibit anything

from being transported in the mails that is authorized by the law," he suggested that the papers be delivered only to those who were "really subscribers."

The mails controversy became a leading question when Congress convened in December 1835. In his annual message, Jackson noted the "painful excitement" caused by the abolitionist tracts and recommended that Congress prohibit their circulation in the South. His proposal prompted a heated debate in the Senate when Calhoun objected to giving Congress power to exclude material. Such authority, Calhoun alleged, would equally permit the federal government to "open the gates to the flood of incendiary publications."

Calhoun urged that state law, not Congress, be the arbiter of what was incendiary, and in February 1836, he reported a bill declaring it unlawful for postmasters in states and territories to receive and put into the mail any material "touching" the subject of slavery that was addressed to any area where such material was prohibited. Not everyone found Calhoun's distinction clear. At least one key Jacksonian asserted that Calhoun's bill was actually an administration measure because it ultimately relied upon federal authority to enforce the ban.

Northern Whigs led the opposition to Calhoun's bill, protesting that it violated freedom of the press. Significantly, a number of loyal Jacksonians, including Thomas Hart Benton of Missouri and John Niles of Connecticut, also considered the proposal "preposterous and mischievous." After considerable discussion and revision, the bill barely survived a test vote in the Senate on 2 June when a tie was broken by Vice President Van Buren. It then failed on a final vote when enough northern Democrats combined with northern and borderstate Whigs to defeat it. The tally was more sectional than partisan, indicating how slavery jeopardized party unity. Eventually, toward the end of the session, the Senate approved a Post Office Department reorganization plan that explicitly forbade postmasters from detaining the mail. But southern state laws remained on the books, and federal law became, in the words of one historian, "largely a dead letter in the South."

Although Congress had failed to adopt his recommendation, it is hard to think that Jackson was disappointed by this course of events. The mails controversy subsided as southern states quietly nullified federal law without resorting to federal legislation that many northerners found objectionable. The

Democratic party's position was to muffle rather than inflame the slavery issue, and the *Globe*, after blaming defeat for the mails bill on the Whigs, let the subject rest.

A second slavery question proved more nettlesome to the Jackson administration. This was the antislavery campaign to petition Congress for the abolition of the slave trade and slavery in the District of Columbia and in federal territories. The trouble erupted early in the session when, on 18 December 1835, South Carolina congressman James Henry Hammond announced that he "could not sit there and see the rights of the southern people assaulted day after day, by the ignorant fanatics from whom these memorials proceed." He demanded that the petitions not be received by the House.

Hammond's action precipitated a bitter debate that, in one form or another, lasted a decade. Southern radicals like Hammond intended from the outset to use the petitions as a way of ascertaining northern attitudes toward slavery and to establish the principle that slavery lay entirely outside of congressional authority. Aside from the Vermont abolitionist congressman William Slade, no northerners spoke in favor of the prayers of the petitions. Instead, northern spokesmen defended the right to have antislavery memorials respectfully received and handled. Northern Whigs again led the defense of the right of reception, but they were joined by a number of prominent Jacksonians like Samuel Beardsley of New York, who warned that northern freemen would not tolerate having their petitions forbidden or treated with scorn.

As in the mails controversy, Jacksonians tried to "sink the irritating topic into instant insignificance." After weeks of speeches and political maneuvering, Democrats eventually rallied behind a resolution offered by Henry L. Pinckney of South Carolina, calling for a select committee to deal with the materials. Southern radicals were furious that Pinckney had seemingly conceded the power of the House to act upon the subject of slavery at all. But the resolution passed the House handily, with the overwhelming majority of Democrats, particularly from the North, in support.

In May 1836, Pinckney presented his committee's report to the House. Denouncing the "sickly sentimentality" of antislavery reformers, it proposed resolutions denying constitutional authority to interfere with slavery in the states; declaring that Congress "ought not" to interfere with slavery in the

nation's capital; and, finally, tabling with no further action, and without printing or referral, all petitions and other material relating to the subject of slavery or its abolition. The last resolution was the famous "gag rule."

As expected, Pinckney's motions were condemned by some as an invasion of southern rights and by others as a violation of the right of petition. In order to prevent the discord from getting out of control, Jacksonian leaders quickly cut off debate by moving the previous question and rushing a vote on the resolutions. All passed easily, and the slavery issue in Congress was temporarily held in abeyance under the combined restraints of party loyalty and the gag rule.

But the controversy over petitions continued to agitate national politics, in part because the gag rule provided a concrete and attractive target for antislavery advocates who linked their cause to the broader one of civil liberties. Annual debates over the gag rule strained the Democratic party, whose members were torn between sectional allegiance and party loyalty. In 1844 enough northern Democrats refused to go along with their southern colleagues, and the gag rule died. Jackson deplored the increased sectional bitterness that marked national politics during his presidency. He urged Americans to remember that the foundations of the Constitution and the Union were laid in the "affections of the people" and in their "fraternal attachment" as members of one political family. His sentiments were heartfelt, but time would demonstrate that his appeals for moderation, for unionism, and for patience in awaiting Providence's will were ineffectual nostrums for the great moral and legal issues posed by slavery.

While the slavery controversy agitated political waters, Jackson also found rough sailing in his campaign to reform banking excesses and the nation's money supply. Although the deposit system was generally performing well, serious problems were becoming evident. The country was in the midst of an inflationary surge propelled by an influx of silver and by overbanking and speculation, and the pet banks were doing their share in dangerously expanding credit. These conditions produced a surplus of tariff and land revenues, which accumulated in the pets. Other institutions resented the pets' access to federal funds and demanded a portion.

As a result, when the administration proposed a measure to regulate the pet banks, Congress severely modified it. The resulting Deposit Act of 1836 was a multipurposed affair. It provided some needed restrictions on small paper bills but also limited the amount of federal money that could be held in each pet bank. The effect was to increase radically the number of pets and sacrifice control over the deposit system.

Even more objectionable to Jackson was a provision that distributed the surplus federal revenue to the states. Jackson had once supported distribution, though only under certain conditions, but he now considered the measure unconstitutional and inexpedient. It made the states dependent on the federal government for revenue, encouraged speculation and excessive paper issues, and created pressures on Congress to raise the tariff to replace the lost money. Indeed, he considered this measure so harmful that he actually prepared a veto. Only after Congress made federal funds a deposit subject to recall, rather than an outright grant, did he reluctantly sign the bill.

Jackson's approval was clearly motivated by practical concerns. In an election year, Democrats rivaled Whigs in promising states the benefits of the surplus, and a presidential veto would have damaged Van Buren's prospects. Besides, distribution was simply the price that Jackson had to pay for getting some degree of bank regulation.

In the aftermath of the bill's passage, Jackson made it evident that his signature spelled no retreat from his hard-money policy. In July 1836, he issued the Specie Circular, which directed government agents to receive only gold and silver in payment for public lands after December 1836, a measure designed to diminish land speculation and to "preserve the deposit banks" by increasing the specie backing of bank notes. The Specie Circular generated a storm of protest; Congress passed a bill at the close of Jackson's presidency repealing it, but Jackson pocket vetoed the bill. "I have the great republican principles to sustain, the constitution to preserve, protect and defend, and the most vital principle of it is the currency, and I have to maintain a consistency of character in all my acts to make my administration beneficial to republicanism," he explained.

Jackson's banking and currency program must receive mixed grades. The pet-bank system aggravated the inflationary pressures of the mid-1830s and contributed to the inevitable Panic of 1837, shortly after Jackson left office. His efforts to regulate and reform bank paper had only a modest effect in controlling speculation and bringing about economic stability.

Criticism of Jackson's program should be balanced by the realization that economic fluctuations are international in scope and that the federal government had only a limited ability to shape the course of economic affairs. It is doubtful the boom-and-bust cycle of the 1830s would have been avoided if Jackson had rechartered the national bank. Moreover, Jackson should be credited for the social and moral considerations that inspired his actions. He perceived, if only dimly, that the rapid changes associated with the Market Revolution undermined traditional values and relationships, and jeopardized the rough equality of condition that underpinned a republican society. His warnings about concentrations of political and economic power and about the debilitating effects of corruption have become part of the American reform tradition.

Foreign Affairs

The spring of 1836 brought one clear-cut triumph for the president: the successful conclusion of a settlement with France over spoliation claims dating from the Napoleonic era. When Jackson took office, negotiations with France had reached a "hopeless" condition, according to Secretary of State Van Buren. Jackson informed Congress in his first annual message that he intended to break the logjam.

Jackson's minister to France, William C. Rives, prodded and flattered the reluctant French government into signing a treaty in July 1831. By its terms, France agreed to pay the United States 25 million francs, and in return, the United States paid a small sum to extinguish French claims against the American government and reduced the duties on French wines. Jackson happily announced the settlement the following December and submitted the treaty for ratification; it was approved unanimously.

Celebration proved premature when France, embroiled in financial and political difficulties, refused to appropriate money to implement the treaty. At first, Jackson accepted the word of the king and his ministers that the fault lay in the French Chamber of Deputies. But by the summer of 1834, his confidence in the king diminished too, and in October he began talking about taking "strong measures."

Jackson labored with more than usual attention over the foreign affairs section of his December 1834 message to Congress. One evening, he was brought the page proofs as revised by Secretary of State John Forsyth. Donelson began to read them while Jackson paced the floor, pipe in hand. When Donelson seemed to slur over a key passage dealing with France, Jackson paused. "Read that again, sir," he said. Donelson repeated the words more distinctly. "That, sir, is not my language," Jackson exclaimed, striking out the unauthorized revisions and writing his own original phrasing.

The message was direct and to the point. It recapitulated the history of the negotiations and, while disclaiming any desire to intimidate or threaten France, recommended that Congress authorize reprisals against French property. The statement temporarily worsened relations with France, and there was talk of war when the French government recalled its minister. Yet neither side acted precipitately. In France, Minister Edward Livingston explained that Jackson's message was intended to heal the diplomatic breach, not insult the French. Somewhat mollified, the Chamber of Deputies soon appropriated money to pay the claims but attached a proviso that no money should be paid until France received a satisfactory explanation of the language in Jackson's message.

Jackson refused to concede any point of honor. In his message of December 1835 and in a special message the following January, he decried the right of any foreign power to dictate the language used by a president. He would issue, he said, no "servile" apology. Jackson also called for commercial retaliation if France continued to refuse payment. But Jackson, too, carefully avoided provocation by reaffirming his peaceful purposes and reiterating his good opinion of the French people.

Though matters remained in a precarious condition for some weeks, the issue was soon resolved. In February 1836, Great Britain offered to mediate the dispute, and France quickly accepted the accommodating portions of Jackson's December message as a satisfactory explanation. In May, Jackson announced to Congress the termination of the controversy, along with the information that the first four installments of the debt had been paid.

The resolution of the French crisis was only one of Jackson's diplomatic accomplishments. Contrary to popular notions, Jackson actually devoted considerable energy to foreign affairs. About one-third of his annual messages related to foreign policy. Skillfully combining energy, bluster, tact, and patience, Jackson set a course to expand American commerce, resolve long-standing claims, restore American prestige, and enlarge America's territorial boundaries.

As a result of Jackson's leadership, the United States achieved a number of diplomatic triumphs, in addition to the agreement with France. These included the settlement of spoliation claims against Denmark, Portugal, and Spain and trade agreements with Russia, Spain, Turkey, Great Britain, and Siam. The treaty with Great Britain reopened American trade with the British West Indies, while the agreement with Siam was the first between the United States and an Asiatic nation. Partly owing to these diplomatic initiatives, American exports increased more than 75 percent and imports grew 250 percent during Jackson's presidency.

Jackson was not entirely successful in foreign affairs. Missions to China and Japan accomplished nothing, and efforts to dislodge Great Britain's position in South America failed. Most conspicuous, Jackson's attempt to acquire Texas fell short. For years, he had considered Texas essential to the security of the Southwest, and as president, he was willing to spend $5 million to purchase it. He even countenanced the scheming and shady operations of his representative in Mexico, Colonel Anthony Butler, who at one point, for example, proposed that he head a military occupation of Texas. Jackson endorsed the letter "A. Butler: What a scamp," yet he delayed replacing Butler with a more respectable agent until near the end of his presidency.

By that time, events in Texas made further diplomatic efforts impossible. In 1835 fighting broke out between the American settlers and the Mexican government, and by the spring of 1836, the Texans had routed the Mexican army and were appealing to Jackson for recognition and annexation. Despite his desire for Texas, Jackson proceeded cautiously. In part, he was unconvinced that Texas could maintain independence against Mexican military strength. Even more worrisome were possible domestic repercussions, since antislavery forces were already making Texas a slavery and sectional issue. Annexation would further strain national loyalties, divide the Democratic party, and jeopardize Van Buren's election chances.

Jackson therefore rejected annexation and left the initiative for recognition to Congress. Not until 3 March 1837, after Van Buren's election had been safely decided and after Congress had led the way with appropriate resolutions, did Jackson nominate a chargé d'affaires to the Republic of Texas. It was one of his last acts as president. He had not achieved complete success in the Southwest, but he had managed to bring closer to fulfillment his objective of expanding and securing American boundaries in that region.

By the time Jackson retired from the White House, he had significantly altered the office of the president and the course of American history. In expanding the veto power, basing his authority on the will of the people, and intervening in legislative matters, he dramatically enhanced the chief executive's political and legislative powers. The president was now the focal point of national politics.

Jackson also advanced the formation of the Democratic party and, with it, the second American party system. Not only did he encourage the development of such organizational devices as the national convention, but his program and principles became the dividing line that separated Americans into opposing political camps. By the end of his second term, the country had two national political parties, each extending its structure deep into the electorate. This new political system had a distinctly more voter-oriented and democratic style than the previous one. Jackson was by no means exclusively responsible for these changes, but by bringing the presidency and national politics closer to the electorate, he contributed significantly.

Finally, Jackson stamped on the Democratic party a commitment to the principles of limited government, equality, and public virtue as the basis of a healthy republic. Sensing that progress toward a market-oriented society posed dangers to free institutions, Jackson attacked privileged monopolies, paper-money banking, speculation, excessive government expenditures, burdensome taxation, and consolidated power as diseases that sapped republican government and public virtue. He sought to revitalize Jeffersonian principles as a way of reconciling desirable economic advances with the republican ideals of the past.

To be sure, key elements of Jackson's program, such as Indian removal and the gag rule, revealed that his egalitarian rhetoric applied only to whites. Yet in an important way, Jackson succeeded in delineating the conflict between democratic equality and economic development, and he made the kind of defiant effort to reconcile these forces that one would expect of Andrew Jackson.

Retirement

Jackson was almost seventy years old when he retired to the Hermitage. He found comfort in the presence of his family and relations, particularly the children of his adopted son, Andrew Jackson, Jr. The Hermitage again became a seat of hospitality for friends, as well as a shrine to the Democratic faithful who made pilgrimages to visit the General. Jackson gave careful attention to his plantation, which had been poorly managed by Andrew, Jr., in his absence. He also put his religious house in order when, in 1838, he joined the Presbyterian Church. His religious affirmation was not followed by a noticeable decrease in the number or intensity of epithets he hurled at opponents.

But problems also plagued Jackson's retirement. His health, always precarious, deteriorated, leaving him increasingly weak and feeble. He suffered from tuberculosis and dropsy, complaining of headaches, coughing, and swelling. Yet Jackson carried on, giving credit for his continued life to the restorative powers of Matchless Sanative, a cough medicine that he claimed made "a new man" of him. Most likely it was Jackson's will and spirit, not Matchless Sanative or the ministrations of physicians, that held death at bay.

Equally worrisome were the debts that cast a shadow over the Hermitage. They were almost entirely the result of his adopted son's bad business judgment and immaturity. Jackson assumed these obligations, selling land and borrowing money, using the valuable Hermitage as collateral. His indebtedness eventually ran to over $25,000, and the Hermitage began to look neglected.

Ever a politician, Jackson continued his involvement in public affairs. The Panic of 1837 brought hard times until the early 1840s. Whigs and conservative Democrats blamed Jackson's banking and hard-money policy, and urged Van Buren to repudiate the Specie Circular. Jackson responded by denouncing the "perfidy and treachery" of the banks, and he pressed Van Buren to hold firm on the circular. When Van Buren refused to rescind the order and recommended to Congress an independent treasury system by which the government would divorce itself from banks and place its funds in separate repositories, Jackson fully approved. His endorsement strengthened Democratic resolve to pass the so-called divorce bill in 1840.

Jackson also took a keen interest in Van Buren's reelection campaign of 1840. He roundly condemned the Whig party's log-cabin and hard-cider tactics as "an attempt to degrade our republican system," and he even stumped for Van Buren in western Tennessee. When the Whig ticket of William Henry Harrison and John Tyler won, Jackson's spirits temporarily sagged, but they quickly revived as he urged Democrats to unite around Van Buren.

Jackson's greatest influence on public affairs during his post-White House years came after Tyler assumed the presidency following Harrison's sudden death. When Tyler made the annexation of Texas a leading administration measure, Jackson bent his energies toward its accomplishment. Although the Texas issue had volatile political and sectional overtones, Jackson focused only on what he deemed "national" considerations, particularly the benefits of checking English influence over Texas and securing American borders.

Jackson's enthusiasm for expansion strained his political relationship with Van Buren, Thomas Hart Benton, and other Democrats who balked at immediate annexation. But Jackson would not relent; he was "for the annexation regardless of all consequences." In April 1844, Van Buren published a letter opposing immediate annexation, and Jackson reluctantly and painfully withdrew his support and advocated the nomination of "an annexation man." He worked behind the scenes to push the candidacy of his fellow Tennessean James K. Polk, who eventually emerged with the Democratic presidential nomination in 1844.

Increasingly weak and debilitated, Jackson summoned up his reserves of strength to promote Polk's election, scrawling letters of advice and encouragement to party leaders and helping to secure Tyler's withdrawal as an independent candidate. He called Polk's victory "glorious," and when news of the Democratic triumph was followed at the end of February 1845 by word that Congress had passed a joint resolution annexing Texas, Jackson rejoiced. In May he advised the newly inaugurated "Young Hickory" also to uphold American claims to Oregon. "No temporising with Britain on this subject now, *temporising will not do*," he counseled.

The strong words belied the physical deterioration that had set in. "I am I may say a perfect Jelly from the toes to the upper part of my abdome [*sic*]," he informed Blair toward the end of May. Surgery on 2 June brought only temporary relief from the dropsy, and on Sunday, 8 June, Jackson died. He was seventy-eight years old. In accordance with his "republican feelings and principles," he was buried two days later alongside his wife in the Hermitage garden after a service that was as simple as possible. There were nationwide ceremonies in honor of Jackson, and while a few embittered partisans refused to at-

tend, most Americans genuinely sorrowed at the passing of a man who, for half a century, had shaped the nation's destiny.

BIBLIOGRAPHY

A short, highly interpretive biography of Andrew Jackson emphasizing his psychological impulses is James C. Curtis, *Andrew Jackson and the Search for Vindication* (Boston, 1976). The best modern biography of Jackson is a three-volume work by Robert V. Remini: *Andrew Jackson and the Course of American Empire, 1767–1821* (New York, 1977), *Andrew Jackson and the Course of American Freedom, 1822–1832* (New York, 1981), and *Andrew Jackson and the Course of American Democracy, 1833–1845* (New York, 1984). On the influence of republican ideology on Jackson's presidency, consult Richard B. Latner, *The Presidency of Andrew Jackson: White House Politics, 1829–1837* (Athens, Ga., 1979), and Harry L. Watson, *Liberty and Power: The Politics of Jacksonian America* (New York, 1990). For a different view of Jackson's presidency, see Donald B. Cole, *The Presidency of Andrew Jackson* (Lawrence, Kans., 1993). Drew R. McCoy, *The Elusive Republic: Political Economy in Jeffersonian America* (Chapel Hill, N.C., 1980), explains the complexity of republican thinking in an earlier era.

Historians have long debated the meaning of Jacksonian politics. Marvin Meyers, *The Jacksonian Persuasion: Politics and Belief* (Stanford, Calif., 1957), is in many respects the most successful interpretation of Jacksonianism. Arthur M. Schlesinger, Jr., *The Age of Jackson* (Boston, 1945), still offers a vivid portrait of the democratic qualities of Jacksonian politics. Charles Sellers, *The Market Revolution: Jacksonian America, 1815–1846* (New York, 1991), is a learned and comprehensive account of Jacksonian America's confrontation with the market revolution.

On the political issues of Jackson's presidency, Matthew A. Crenson, *The Federal Machine: Beginnings of Bureaucracy in Jacksonian America* (Baltimore, 1975), places Jackson's administrative actions in a broad social framework. Daniel Feller, *The Public Lands in Jacksonian Politics* (Madison, Wis., 1984), thoroughly examines the political and sectional dimensions of this issue. On Indian policy, Michael Paul Rogin, *Fathers and Children: Andrew Jackson and the Subjugation of the American Indian* (New

York, 1975), is both insightful and controversial in its psychological orientation. Ronald N. Satz, *American Indian Policy in the Jacksonian Era* (Lincoln, Nebr., 1974), is an excellent analysis of the many aspects of Indian removal. Anthony F. C. Wallace, *The Long, Bitter Trail: Andrew Jackson and the Indians* (New York, 1993), provides a brief and useful introduction to the process of Indian removal.

Jackson's banking and financial policy is critically examined in Bray Hammond, *Banks and Politics in America: From the Revolution to the Civil War* (Princeton, N.J., 1957). John M. McFaul, *The Politics of Jacksonian Finance* (Ithaca, N.Y., 1972), is more favorable to Jackson, while Peter Temin, *The Jacksonian Economy* (New York, 1969), places economic events in an international and theoretical context. William W. Freehling, *Prelude to Civil War: The Nullification Controversy in South Carolina, 1816–1836* (New York, 1966), is a model historical study of this crisis. Richard E. Ellis's excellent study, *The Union at Risk: Jacksonian Democracy, States' Rights, and the Nullification Crisis* (New York, 1987), argues the strength of nullification. Daniel Walker Howe, *The Political Culture of the American Whigs* (Chicago, 1979), perceptively explores the values and thinking of the Whig opposition, while Merrill D. Peterson, *The Great Triumvirate: Webster, Clay, and Calhoun* (New York, 1987), contains a wealth of information about Jackson's leading opponents.

Two essays that argue that Jackson and the Democratic party tilted toward the South and slavery are Richard H. Brown, "The Missouri Crisis, Slavery, and the Politics of Jacksonianism," in *South Atlantic Quarterly* 65 (1966), and Leonard L. Richards, "The Jacksonians and Slavery," in Lewis Perry and Michael Fellman, eds., *Antislavery Reconsidered: New Perspectives on the Abolitionists* (Baton Rouge, La., 1979). Robert V. Remini, *The Legacy of Andrew Jackson: Essays on Democracy, Indian Removal, and Slavery* (Baton Rouge, La., 1988), provides a useful correction to this view. Russel B. Nye, *Fettered Freedom: Civil Liberties and the Slavery Controversy, 1830–1860,* rev. ed. (East Lansing, Mich., 1964), remains an excellent study of the mail and petition controversies as well as other slavery-related issues. William W. Freehling, *The Road to Disunion: Secessionists at Bay, 1776–1854* (New York, 1990), contains numerous insights about slavery and politics. Two other studies of southern locales show how Jacksonian politics operated on a smaller scale: J. Mills Thornton III, *Politics and Power in a Slave Society: Alabama, 1800–1860* (Baton Rouge, La., 1978), and Harry L. Watson, *Jacksonian Politics and Community Conflict: The Emergence of the Second American Party System in Cumberland County, North Carolina* (Baton Rouge, La., 1981).

Jackson's foreign policy receives careful attention in John M. Belohlavek, *"Let the Eagle Soar!": The Foreign Policy of Andrew Jackson* (Lincoln, Nebr., 1985). Also useful are William H. Goetzmann, *When the Eagle Screamed: The Romantic Horizon in American Diplomacy, 1800–1860* (New York, 1966), and Paul A. Varg, *United States Foreign Relations: 1820–1860* (East Lansing, Mich., 1979).

Recent works include Robert V. Remini, *Andrew Jackson and His Indian Wars* (New York, 2001).

Further reference sources can be found in Robert V. Remini and Robert O. Rupp, *Andrew Jackson: A Bibliography* (Westport, Conn., 1991).

Martin Van Buren

James C. Curtis

Martin Van Buren THE LIBRARY OF CONGRESS

T HE inauguration of Martin Van Buren on 4 March 1837 would long live in the memory of his contemporaries. The thousands who jammed Washington's avenues had come not so much to greet their new leader as to catch a final glimpse of the departing president, Andrew Jackson. They stood respectfully while the new president read his inaugural address and took the oath of office. As the inaugural party began its descent from the platform, the crowd unleashed a thunderous ovation "such as power never commanded, nor man in power received." "For once," recalled Senator Thomas Hart Benton, "the rising was eclipsed by the setting sun."

No one was more keenly aware of the significance of this transition than Martin Van Buren himself. He regarded Jackson as the last of the great revolutionary heroes. "I feel that I belong to a later age," Van Buren told the inaugural crowd, "and that I may not expect my countrymen to weigh my actions with the same kind and partial hand." Within weeks an unprecedented economic depression would cause Van Buren's countrymen to judge him harshly. Historians have been equally severe in their assessment. Depression victim though he would become, Martin Van Buren was superbly qualified for the White House.

More than any other statesman of the age, Van Buren devoted himself to the perfection of party politics grounded on principle and maintained by discipline. His career in both state and national government exemplified a professionalism that would shape the modern two-party system. If Andrew Jackson was the symbol of a political renaissance in the United States, Martin Van Buren was its chief architect and prime beneficiary. Lacking prestigious family connections, martial fame, or substantial wealth, he worked within the party to gain advancement. He was the first professional politician to become president.

Early Career

Born on 5 December 1782 in the small Hudson River community of Kinderhook, New York, Martin Van Buren grew up in an era of political confusion and intense party rivalry. He rose through the ranks of New York Republican (Democratic-Republican) politics in direct opposition to the policies and paternalistic tactics of the state's popular Republican governor, De Witt Clinton. Van Buren and his fellow "Bucktails" (anti-Clintonian Republicans) rebelled against Clinton's favoritism and arbitrary use of appointment powers. They created an efficient organization, known as the Albany Regency. This prototype of the modern political machine based its power on a widespread correspondence network that included local committees, state officeholders, and an aggressive newspaper, the *Albany Argus.*

By the early 1820s, the Albany Regency was a powerful state organization with national ambitions. Van Buren went to Washington in 1821 as New York's junior senator, hoping to create an effective alliance between the states based on a shared commitment to the principles of limited government. To Van Buren, traditional Jeffersonian concepts of states' rights promised an ideal framework for a modern party that would encourage state activism by restraining the power of the federal government. Thus, he favored expansion of the economy through internal improvements like the Erie Canal but insisted that the states should build and finance such projects. Similarly, Van Buren wanted regulation of the nation's currency and improved conditions for the workingman under state, not federal, regulation.

This Jeffersonian outlook endeared him to such prominent southern politicians as Virginia editor Thomas Ritchie, leader of the Richmond Junto, an organization as powerful as the Regency. Ritchie looked to states' rights to protect against federal interference with slavery. These two astute and ambitious politicians failed in 1824 to forge an alliance grounded on states' rights; three years later they endorsed Andrew Jackson, a southerner by birth and a candidate of proven popularity.

Van Buren committed the Regency to the Jacksonian cause with enthusiasm and misgivings. He applauded Jackson's willingness to rely on professional politicians to conduct his campaign. Still, Van Buren worried that "Old Hickory" would win election in 1828 not as champion of states' rights but as a retired military hero. Jackson's triumphant election in 1828 magnified Van Buren's fears. "I hope the General will not find it necessary," Van Buren said, referring to the inaugural message, "to avow any opinion upon Constitutional questions at war with the doctrines of the Jefferson School." Throughout Jackson's two terms as president, Van Buren struggled to balance his own ambitions with his commitment to political orthodoxy.

The standard interpretation of Van Buren as loyal lieutenant and architect of Jacksonian reform has little basis in fact. Awed by Old Hickory's commanding presence, Van Buren never became a close personal friend. Jackson rewarded Van Buren's loyalty by appointing him secretary of state but turned to trusted western colleagues for advice on such matters as the Indian Removal Act, passed by Congress in 1830. This was the only piece of important legislation to emerge from Jackson's first term of office. His strongest acts were those of defiance. At Van Buren's urging, he used the veto power to restrain congressional appropriations for internal improvements.

By defending limited government, Van Buren retained his southern support during the opening years of Jackson's first term when the Eaton affair destroyed party harmony. Angered at the ostracism of Peggy Eaton, the wife of his secretary of war, Jackson embarked on a lengthy campaign to uphold her virtue, in the process reorganizing his cabinet to oust supporters of John C. Calhoun, whose wife was one of Peggy's detractors. Van Buren stepped down as secretary of state to go abroad as minister to England; he departed in the certain knowledge that Calhoun was no longer a threat to his further advancement in the party.

Van Buren did not play such a commanding role during the bank war. Andrew Jackson attacked the Second Bank of the United States and its president,

Nicholas Biddle, for personal and political reasons. Habitually suspicious of paper money, Jackson became convinced that the bank was speculating with government deposits, abusing its congressional charter, and working to defeat his bid for reelection. Key western advisers, such as Amos Kendall, supported Jackson's beliefs and in July 1832 convinced him to veto a bill to renew the bank's charter. Replacing Calhoun as Jackson's running mate, Van Buren dutifully supported the veto message without endorsing its antibank animus or hard-money leanings. Van Buren favored state controls to encourage sound banking practices, establish a reliable paper-money system, and curtail excessive note issues.

Van Buren maintained a similar detachment during the three months of the nullification crisis. Despite his long-standing rivalry with Calhoun, the main theorist of nullification, Van Buren urged a moderate presidential response to avoid offending key southern Democrats. Jackson ignored this advice and abandoned states' rights principles in his proclamation denouncing nullification. The president's failure to work for a legislative compromise weakened Democratic control in Congress and strengthened opponents like Henry Clay, whose compromise tariff bill ended the constitutional crisis. Jackson further undermined Democratic unity by contemplating a new political alliance that would bypass Van Buren to include former opponents like Daniel Webster. This realignment never materialized; Van Buren rescued his credentials as heir apparent by agreeing to a removal of deposits from Biddle's bank, an action that drove a permanent wedge between the president and such bank supporters as Webster.

By selecting Van Buren as his running mate in 1832, Jackson in effect anointed his successor. A man given to anger and strong emotions, Jackson could never have tolerated a successor with a similar temperament or independent spirit. Herein lay the source of his difficulties with prospective allies John C. Calhoun and Daniel Webster. Van Buren was much their opposite, so much so that even friends expressed the fear that the portly New Yorker "lacked the moral courage to meet those exigencies which might require bold and decisive action."

In accepting the Democratic nomination in 1835, Van Buren did not delude himself. He realized full well that he lacked the kind of popular appeal Jackson had brought to American politics. Indeed, his running mate, Richard M. Johnson of Kentucky, was chosen to give the ticket another military hero from the War of 1812. While Van Buren appreciated the need to leaven politics with popularity, he had seen Democratic leadership stray too far from principle during the nullification crisis. As the campaign began, he tried to bring the alliance back to its philosophical base.

Van Buren first sought to reassure his southern supporters. In accepting the nomination, he restated his commitment to states' rights and stood by these principles when abolitionists flooded southern mails with literature denouncing slavery. Van Buren arranged for the Regency to denounce abolitionist extremism first in the columns of the *Albany Argus* and then in the governor's annual message. In the spring of 1836, the Democratic nominee declared that while he recognized the right of Congress to abolish slavery in the District of Columbia, he would "go into the White House the inflexible and uncompromising opponent" of such legislation. Van Buren would not carry his prosouthern sentiments to extremes. He refused to support the Texas Revolution despite appeals from key southern leaders like Thomas Ritchie. Van Buren feared that the Texas question would create sectional discord, and he convinced Jackson to delay any official action until after the election.

Financial fluctuations added to sectional unrest. By removing government deposits and placing them in state banks, Jackson weakened Biddle's political power but destroyed the control the Bank of the United States once exercised over the nation's monetary exchanges. By 1836, the economy was in an inflationary spiral, fueled by an increase in specie and excessive note issues by state banks. Jackson's Treasury Department could not regulate this expansion without assuming powers and functions just stripped from Biddle. In the face of mounting fiscal instability, Jackson issued the Specie Circular in July 1836, requiring that all public lands be paid for in gold and silver. This was a first step in the direction of the hard-money policy that radical Democrats had long been urging. Although uncertain how to supervise state banks without violating precepts of limited government, Van Buren did not believe that his party could survive as antibank champions of a metallic currency. States were too dependent on their financial institutions and the Democrats too committed to states' rights. Van Buren was fortunate that his political opponents lacked the solidarity to capitalize on the unstable economy and the disagreement in Democratic ranks.

Emerging during the early stages of the bank war, the Whig party was still in an embryonic state during the election of 1836. Jackson's bank veto and his defense of executive privilege provided the only substantive issues for Whig candidates. Whig power lay more in Congress than in the countryside. Unable to unite on principle or to find a leader who could appeal to all sections of the country, Whig strategists decided to run several sectional candidates. This strategy allowed Hugh Lawson White, William Henry Harrison, and Daniel Webster to appeal to local constituencies and helped establish strong Whig organizations in Tennessee, New York, Virginia, and Georgia. These state machines were to exert a strong influence on political developments over the next four years.

Van Buren built winning margins in such crucial Democratic strongholds as Pennsylvania, North Carolina, Virginia, and New York. In the final balloting, Van Buren received 170 electoral votes to his opponents' 124. While comfortable, the margin was not cause for self-congratulation. Whig triumphs in Georgia and Tennessee and the close contest in Pennsylvania loomed as large clouds on the political horizon.

Administration and Cabinet

Van Buren hoped that his cabinet appointments would stop Whig momentum in the South and restore confidence in the Democrats as a party of sectional unity, but a legacy of administrative turbulence limited Van Buren's freedom of choice. Indeed, Andrew Jackson had never managed to create a workable relationship with his formal cabinet. During Jackson's first year in office, cabinet factionalism had proved so disruptive that the president ceased formal meetings. He turned instead to a coterie of western advisers, prompting opponents to brand this group a "kitchen cabinet" and charge the president with violating constitutional customs. The president continued to rely on informal advice but resumed regular cabinet meetings in 1831, if only to silence his critics. While Van Buren intended to restore the cabinet to its rightful place in the executive branch, he could not appoint men of his own choosing without removing Jackson's appointees, thereby deepening suspicions of Democratic instability.

As a former secretary of state, Van Buren realized the importance of this premier cabinet post. Georgia's John Forsyth was the last of Jackson's four secretaries of state. A staunch presidential supporter during the nullification crisis, Forsyth had served in both the House and the Senate. Although he decided to retain Forsyth, Van Buren was suspicious of the Georgian's political orthodoxy. The president-elect received numerous letters urging appointment of another southerner to the cabinet to redress Jackson's long neglect. Van Buren tried to satisfy this demand by asking Virginia's senator William C. Rives, disappointed aspirant for the Democratic vice presidential nomination in 1835, to head the vacant War Department. Maintaining that only the State Department interested him, Rives declined and thus made an open break with Van Buren that would have a significant impact on relations with Congress.

Rather than offend Rives further by turning to another Virginian, Van Buren convinced South Carolina's Joel Poinsett to become secretary of war. Whatever gain Van Buren made by adding a second southerner was offset by Poinsett's political views. Like Forsyth, the native of Charleston had been a strong supporter of Jackson's nullification policies.

The retention of Jackson's secretary of the treasury, Levi Woodbury, and postmaster general, Amos Kendall, preserved a sense of continuity and sectional balance, which Van Buren considered essential for party cohesion. New Hampshire's Woodbury had been a cabinet member since 1831, initially as secretary of the navy. Although friendly to Van Buren, he leaned toward the hard-money policies that had become dominant in the last year of Jackson's' presidency. Kentucky's Kendall represented the West and had been the most powerful of Jackson's cabinet members. A skilled political journalist, he had been a key member of the Kitchen Cabinet and instrumental in directing the attack on the bank. Appointed postmaster general in 1834, Kendall had remained fiercely loyal to Jackson and openly suspicious of Van Buren. Like Woodbury, Kendall expected to maintain his status as a member of the inner circle and architect of both fiscal and political strategy.

Van Buren exerted more personal control over the two remaining cabinet posts. He convinced his friend and former law partner, Benjamin F. Butler, to continue as attorney general, a post Butler had accepted at Van Buren's urging in 1833. Van Buren was well aware that Butler felt uncomfortable in Washington and longed to return to Albany. The resignation of a former member of the Albany Regency at the outset of his administration would have embarrassed Van Buren and fed rumors of serious Democratic dissension. While succeeding in his entreaties with Butler, Van Buren failed in his efforts to convince Secretary of the Navy Mahlon Dickerson to retire to

An 1837 political cartoon depicts a modern version of Macbeth, *with President Van Buren recoiling in horror at the sight of the "ghost of commerce" in the midst of the economic crisis of the Panic of 1837.* THE LIBRARY OF CONGRESS

a diplomatic post in Belgium. Van Buren would have preferred to replace the sixty-six-year-old New Jerseyite with a younger man.

Despite the political pressures created by the Panic of 1837, Van Buren managed to restore the cabinet's traditional role. He continued weekly meetings and discontinued the informal gatherings of advisers that had attracted so much attention during Jackson's presidency. Van Buren solicited advice from department heads, especially during times of domestic and foreign turmoil. In such emergencies, the cabinet met daily. Van Buren tolerated open and even frank exchanges between cabinet members, perceiving himself as "a mediator, and to some extent an umpire between the conflicting opinions" of his counselors. Such detachment allowed the president to reserve judgment and protect his own prerogative for making final decisions. These open discussions gave cabinet members a sense of participation and made them feel part of a functioning entity, rather than isolated executive agents. Always an astute politician, Van Buren realized that the cabinet

could communicate official decisions to the states and work to ensure party cohesion.

In his efforts to restore party harmony, Van Buren worked closely with key Democrats in Congress, where divisiveness had reached alarming proportions during the nullification crisis. New York's Churchill Cambreleng, chairman of the powerful House Ways and Means Committee and long an intimate friend, took an active role in fashioning legislation to respond to the Panic of 1837. Van Buren's protégé Silas Wright performed similar duties in the Senate, where he chaired the Finance Committee and was floor manager for Democratic legislation. Cambreleng and Wright were extremely effective leaders. A study of congressional voting behavior in the first two sessions of Congress during Van Buren's administration shows a partisan coherence in both houses of better than 85 percent. Van Buren rarely quarreled with the Senate over appointments, unlike his predecessor. Having assembled a compatible cabinet and a group of advisers with control in Congress, Van Buren looked forward to a cessation of the open political warfare of the past decade.

Panic of 1837

The worst depression the nation had suffered shattered these hopes within weeks of the inauguration. Neither the president nor the American people were prepared for the financial panic that swept across the country in May 1837. Warnings of a major crisis had been in the air since the beginning of the campaign. Storm signals came from the nation's banking institutions and took the form of extreme pressure on the money market. Discount rates approached 25 percent. Inflation soared, fed by a marked increase in cotton prices. On the eve of the inauguration, workers in New York City rioted to protest the price of food. Newspapers contained ominous reports of potential bank closings. Van Buren was inundated with urgent requests that he act to halt the inflationary spiral. Most correspondents urged the new president to reconsider the Specie Circular of 1836.

Van Buren responded with a thorough reconsideration of Jackson's hard-money order. As he had done so often in the past, he asked his closest confidants to solicit advice from state leaders. This style of decision making was thorough but time-consuming. More than a month elapsed before replies reached Washington. All the while, the financial crisis worsened, so much so that Silas Wright contended it was "nonsense to talk any longer" of the Specie Circular "or any action of the sectional or state governments as either having occasioned the mischief, or as being able to furnish the remedy." Similar sentiments came from Cambreleng, who blamed speculators and friends of a new national bank for manufacturing the crisis. Convinced by these letters that repeal would not alleviate the emergency but would only break with previous policy, Van Buren decided to retain the circular.

On 10 May 1837 the storm struck: New York banks, unable to meet continuing demands for specie, suspended payments, and financial houses across the country quickly did the same. Debtors struggled to meet obligations with depreciated currency. Urban workers, already hurt by rising food prices, now faced the prospect of unemployment. "It would be difficult to describe, or render intelligible in Europe," wrote the British minister, Henry Fox, "the stunning effect which this sudden overthrow of the commercial credit and honor of the nation has caused. The conquest of the land by a foreign power could hardly have produced a more general sense of humiliation and grief."

Van Buren was more disoriented than grief-stricken. On 15 May, with state banks in disarray and government deposits in jeopardy, the president finally issued the call for a special session of Congress to meet in September. Throughout the steamy summer months, Van Buren made preparations for this extraordinary meeting. Never before had his party been called upon to develop a legislative program; the chief executive was accustomed to cautious, deliberate action, not to crisis management. Furthermore, he had always been able to depend upon the support of the press to clarify and explain federal policy.

In the spring and summer of 1837, Democratic newspapers were themselves in a panic. Francis P. Blair, editor of the *Washington Globe*, the Democrats' national newspaper, lashed out at New York merchants; Thomas Ritchie's *Richmond Enquirer* rushed to the defense of state banks and refused to consider the president's problems. Even the editor of the *Albany Argus* refrained from printing editorials supporting Van Buren, fearing that such statements would constitute an attack on New York's beleaguered banks. By his failure to restrain Blair and his inability to rally state editors, Van Buren approached this special session deprived of the normal channels of political communication and persuasion.

The Independent Treasury

The president's primary concern was for the safety of government funds entrusted to state banks. When Congress convened, his opponents would demand new safeguards and, if none were forthcoming, would undoubtedly move to dismantle the entire deposit system, leaving the door open for recharter of a national bank. To foreclose this possibility, Van Buren advocated a separation of government funds from state banks and control of these monies by designated federal agents.

The advantages of a separation of bank and state were several. By removing its funds from state banks, the federal government would avoid association with institutions instrumental in bringing on the panic. The government would collect, store, and disburse public revenue through Treasury agents and postal employees and not be open to the charge that these funds were the basis for unchecked speculation. While economically feasible, this plan contained numerous political pitfalls. Even though requiring a minimum of enabling legislation, an independent treasury, or subtreasury, as it would soon be known, carried an implicit criticism of state banks. According to one proponent, these institutions would henceforth be "left to their fate." Furthermore, as Silas Wright warned, the divorce of bank and state would make the president vulnerable to charges that he wanted to "extend executive patronage and power." Although disappointed by the waverings of state leaders, Van Buren realized that he needed their support to succeed in the special session of Congress that convened on 4 September 1837.

In recommending the creation of an independent treasury, the president invoked Jeffersonian rhetoric in an attempt to disguise the radical aspects of his program. He cautiously explained the origins of the panic, being careful not to blame state banks for the collapse. "All communities are apt to look to government for too much," the president told the special session. "If, therefore, I refrain from suggesting to Congress any specific plan for regulating the exchanges of the country, relieving mercantile embarrassments, or interfering with the ordinary operations of foreign or domestic commerce, it is from a conviction that such measures are not within the constitutional province of the General Government." But the government was obliged to safeguard its own funds. It was in this context that Van Buren recommended an independent treasury. In so doing, he was careful to point out that such a program required no increase in government patronage.

Although cautious and couched in familiar terms, the president's proposals constituted a radical departure from the premise upon which the Democratic party was built. As a loose and often factious coalition of state interests, the Jacksonian alliance functioned smoothly so long as state leaders could interpret federal policy to suit their own interests. Van Buren's proposal for an independent treasury contained no encouragement for state initiative. Quite the contrary, the president placed the needs of the federal government ahead of those of the states. He reversed the delicate balance of political priorities that he had struggled so long to maintain. No matter how careful his wording, how respectful his tone, the president had created a dilemma from which there would be no easy escape.

The Congress that listened respectfully to Van Buren's message was fully under Democratic control. The president's supporters had majorities on all twenty-two standing committees in the Senate and on eighteen of thirty committees in the House, where they had only a sixteen-vote advantage. Democrats enjoyed a two-to-one majority on the crucial committees in both houses that would consider the

president's financial proposals. In a normal congressional session, such organization would have given the Democrats firm control of the legislative process. But these were extraordinary circumstances. Conservative Democrats, deeply committed to state banks, threatened to rebel on the subtreasury issue.

This revolt fed on disagreements between the president and his state supporters. Governor William Marcy of New York, once a loyal member of the Regency, refused to endorse Van Buren's special session proposals, despite the pleadings of the attorney general, who made a special visit to Albany. In an angry exchange with Butler, Marcy came right to the heart of the party's dilemma. He asked "if the men at Washington expected that I was to proclaim a divorce between the government of the state and the banks." Butler said no. In that case, Marcy continued, "what sort of supporters of Mr. V. B. shall we be if we repudiate his doctrines as applicable to the states?" To this pointed question, there was no reply. In Virginia, Thomas Ritchie remained outspoken in his criticism of an independent treasury and his defense of the state-bank deposit system.

Despite the growing influence of the conservative cause, the president's legislative spokesmen pushed ahead with their relief proposals. Wright and Cambreleng were able to secure passage of bills postponing the final distribution of surplus revenue, establishing a schedule for recovery of government deposits, granting leniency in the collection of customhouse bonds, and authorizing an issue of Treasury notes to cover government expenses. In both houses, Democrats united to enact these measures after a minimum of debate.

Democratic unity evaporated during the debates on an independent treasury. Pennsylvania's James Buchanan claimed that the president's proposal was perfectly consonant with Jeffersonian principles of limited government. Silas Wright echoed these sentiments. The new voices were those of conservative Democrats who urged reform, not abandonment, of the state banks. Borrowing rhetoric from the Whigs, they charged the president with seeking to enlarge executive patronage and wield new power by the act of collecting and storing revenue. Despite these strong criticisms, Wright's leadership prevailed and the Democrats, on 3 October 1837, secured Senate approval for creation of an independent treasury by the narrow margin of twenty-five to twenty-three.

In the House, Cambreleng lost control of the debate, allowing South Carolina's Francis Pickens to speak on behalf of an independent treasury only to launch into a diatribe against northern capitalism and its war on slavery. Such emotionalism proved infectious. When Cambreleng made his long-awaited defense of the president's proposal, he lashed out against all banks, arguing that an independent treasury "would be a steady and salutary check, in preventing the excess and unwarrantable issues" of these institutions. Cambreleng concluded with a bold declaration: "We fear not the results of this experiment."

By opposing an independent treasury as a radical experiment, conservatives claimed to be the true champions of states' rights and limited government. Their obstructionist strategy proved successful. On 14 October 1837, by a vote of 120 to 107, the House postponed consideration of an independent treasury. The circumstances surrounding this critical vote added to the president's disappointment. John Clark, a congressman from Van Buren's home state, introduced the motion to postpone, reminding his colleagues that even the *Albany Argus* had failed to endorse an independent treasury.

As soon as the special session adjourned, Van Buren tried to allay fears created by the angry congressional debates. Secretary of the Treasury Woodbury wrote to friends in the New York financial community, asking how the administration could make clear that it did not intend to suppress banks or introduce a metallic currency. All the replies sounded the same disturbing theme. "The divorce of Bank and State is a Manifesto from the highest authority in the country," wrote one New York banker, "proclaiming that the State Banks are unsafe as depositories." Whatever gains Van Buren made by such private inquiries were immediately undercut by a series of devastating editorials in the *Washington Globe* denouncing the conservatives and striking at banks in general. This harangue occurred shortly before the fall elections in New York, where Whigs gained sixty-seven seats in the state assembly, thereby establishing a clear majority and destroying a pillar of Regency power.

Although alarmed by the defeat in New York, Van Buren continued to concentrate on what he perceived as a crisis for the federal government alone. In December 1837 he again proposed the subtreasury system, this time adding a special deposit feature to please the conservatives. The president's calm and deliberate message drew praise from all segments of the party but could not overcome the emotionalism generated by the panic.

No sooner had Democrats organized themselves in Congress than a heated sectional debate ensued, caused by John C. Calhoun's introduction of six proslavery resolutions. Van Buren appreciated Calhoun's support for the subtreasury bill at the special session but was not about to let the South Carolina senator disrupt Democratic unity. The president remained firm in his commitment to Jeffersonian principles as they applied to all state issues, including slavery. In accord with this philosophy, Van Buren's Senate supporters modified the resolutions so that the final wording enjoined the government against interfering with states' rights, whereas Calhoun wanted a pledge of federal protection for slavery. Not until early February 1838 did the Senate begin debate on the subtreasury system, only to be interrupted a second time by an oratorical fight between John C. Calhoun and his archrival, Henry Clay. Finally, on 26 March 1838, the Senate approved the independent-treasury bill by twenty-seven to twenty-five.

The narrow margin of victory did not augur well for deliberations in the House. Conservatives picked up support with each delay and took further encouragement from spring elections in Virginia. For the first time in more than a decade, the Richmond junto faced the prospect of an opposing party in control of the state legislature. In May 1838, Congress repealed the Specie Circular of 1836 and New York banks resumed specie payments, thereby increasing conservative momentum. Van Buren realized that the resumption damaged chances for House approval of an independent treasury, but he continued to press the measure as the only alternative to a national bank. Indeed, Nicholas Biddle wrote to a member of Van Buren's cabinet claiming that his bank was ready to resume its role as exclusive depository for government funds. "Its whole machinery can be remounted in twenty-four hours," Biddle claimed.

Cambreleng pushed for passage of the subtreasury bill in mid-June, and this time maintained tight control of debate. He prevented key Democrats from abstaining as they had at the special session and added strength from South Carolina without allowing any of Calhoun's followers to raise the question of slavery. Although highly disciplined, House Democrats could not overcome the results of electoral losses in New York and Virginia. Where once these two state machines had worked closely with members of their congressional delegations, the Whig triumphs made state Democrats reluctant to speak out against their banks and eager to avoid a definite stand on an independent treasury. Once again their wavering had a telling impact: on 25 June 1838, by a vote of 125 to 111, the House defeated the bill.

The resumption of specie payments and the failure of the president's program placed Democrats on the defensive in the fall elections. In New York, under the skillful leadership of Thurlow Weed, the Whigs developed a political organization as sophisticated and extensive as the Regency. Whig editors promised that their gubernatorial candidate, William H. Seward, would restore financial order. These well-orchestrated appeals prompted a huge voter turnout and a Whig victory that captured the legislature and placed Seward in the governor's mansion. Disconsolate, the Democrats blamed their loss on the panic and the federal government. In leaving office, Marcy concluded that "the election was conducted chiefly with reference to the policy of the federal government. If we had had nothing but our own policy to vindicate, I cannot bring myself to doubt that we should have had a different result."

The Whig triumph came as a bitter blow to Van Buren. The Albany-Richmond axis, once the backbone of the Jacksonian alliance, had been broken by the Whigs, who would remember the lesson well. In celebrating their stunning sweep of the Empire State, they were already looking ahead to the next presidential campaign. "Mr. Van Buren's chances for reelection may now be considered desperate," wrote one political observer.

Bowed but not broken, the president continued his efforts to refine his economic proposals. In his second annual message, on 3 December 1838, he argued that an independent treasury would eliminate the possibility of fraud such as the one that had recently occurred when Samuel Swartwout had absconded with over a million dollars in government revenue from the New York Customhouse. Van Buren's congressional opponents seized on this scandal to investigate the handling of Treasury funds. In a lengthy report in late February 1839, a special House committee concluded that Swartwout's defalcation had been aided by a Democratic fiscal policy that had discontinued "the use of banks as depositories."

Having consumed much of their energy on this investigation, Whigs moved for adjournment. Realizing that it would take months to clear the air, House Democrats agreed and abandoned efforts to pass the independent-treasury bill. This truncated session of Congress came to a close on 4 March 1839, the second anniversary of Van Buren's inauguration. The administration was hardly in a mood to celebrate. "We have at last got rid of Congress," wrote the secretary of the treasury, "and a most disreputable one in many respects it has been."

Before the fall elections could bring the president a more cooperative Congress, another financial crisis struck the country. The resumption of specie payments in 1838 triggered an expansion of credit and borrowing that in turn fed an inflationary economy. State governments again promoted internal improvements, often by borrowing from abroad to raise funds. Biddle's bank in Philadelphia, now under Pennsylvania charter, led this expansionist surge, only to be hard hit by sudden credit restrictions in England in 1839. In October 1839, the bank suspended specie payments; nearly half of the nation's 850 banks followed suit. The political consequences were immediate. The fall elections destroyed the conservative Democrats, especially in New York and Virginia, leaving Van Buren in control of a weakened but united party.

The president seized the advantage. In recommending an independent treasury to the new Congress, he abandoned the conciliatory language of the past. He blamed renewed financial failures on foreign investors and state banks, urging Congress to adopt measures to safeguard the country from further speculative crazes. For the first time, he urged that all government revenue be collected and disbursed in gold and silver. This provision, coupled with the proposed subtreasury system, would have "a salutary influence on the system of paper credit with which all banks are connected." Although careful to recognize that some banks were already "sound and well managed," Van Buren advocated the subtreasury system as a mechanism for reform and regulation of the nation's economy. He told supporters that he had taken "strong ground" that he hoped would break the congressional deadlock.

While the president was in a bold mood, his congressional managers were disorganized. Democrats retained control of the Senate, where they passed the subtreasury bill on 23 January by a vote of twenty-four to eighteen. Their margin in the House was so small that they had to await the outcome of six disputed elections before pressing Van Buren's program. In the meantime, the Whigs captured the powerful position of Speaker of the House and, with it, control of a majority of standing committees. Nearly three months elapsed before the House resolved the disputed elections, adding five seats to the Democratic total. Still, floor managers hesitated to close off debate, fearing that defeat of the subtreasury bill would destroy Van Buren's remaining chances for reelection.

The Whigs took advantage of delays to assail Democratic fiscal policy in speeches that were quickly converted into campaign circulars. Finally, on 30 June 1840, the Democrats closed debate and pushed for a vote. Van Buren won his long-awaited victory 124 to 107. At 3:00 P.M. on 3 July 1840, the president received the subtreasury bill. He decided to wait twenty-four hours before signing what the party would thereafter call a "second Declaration of Independence." The president was at last free from a measure that had become an obsession.

Foreign Affairs

The president demonstrated much more certain control over foreign relations than over financial affairs. Although preoccupied with the panic, Van Buren proved to be a shrewd diplomat, preventing the Texas Revolution from inflaming sectional tensions in the United States. Van Buren inherited a Texas policy not totally to his liking. Having avoided a stand on the Texas question during the election, he was disappointed when Jackson, a day before leaving office, recognized the new regime. In the summer of 1837, the Texans went a step further by pressing for annexation. Their formal request appealed to American nationalism, characterized Mexico as a society of "barbarians," and argued that the president should move quickly or Texas would sign treaties with foreign powers that might injure the United States.

At that time, Van Buren was trying to prepare his proposals for the special session and was in no mood to be rushed or pressured. After consulting the cabinet, he decided to reject the proposal. In his reasoned reply, Van Buren argued that there was no constitutional precedent for annexation of a sovereign state; annexation might be construed as an act of war against Mexico. The president concluded that the United States had no objection to commercial treaties between Texas and European powers. The Texans bristled at the reply, threatening to take their cause directly to Congress and venturing the opinion that had Jackson been president, the United States would have welcomed annexation. Van Buren ignored this tactless reply and kept the Texas question out of the special session. By the time Congress con-

vened in regular session, in December 1837, annexation had become intertwined with a dispute between the United States and Mexico over injury claims by American citizens against the Mexican government.

A by-product of the Texas Revolution, the Mexican claims dispute could have propelled the two nations into war. Throughout the first year of his presidency, Van Buren tried to reach agreement on the claims dispute, to no avail. In his first annual message, the president reported the negative results of a special mission to Mexico City and then referred the entire controversy to Congress for it "to decide upon the time, the mode, and the measure of redress." This action alone was a sharp contrast to Jackson's earlier request for force, but Van Buren went further, expressing his confidence that congressional action would be marked by a "moderation and justice which will, I trust, under all circumstances govern the councils of our country."

The president's opponents took advantage of even this pacific passage to charge the Democrats with a secret conspiracy. "The annexation of Texas and the proposed war with Mexico are one and the same thing," claimed former president John Quincy Adams, now a congressman from Massachusetts. Adams privately speculated that annexation was designed to increase the extent of slavery and commit the North to a permanent defense of southern institutions. According to the *National Intelligencer*, the Whig newspaper in Washington, the president sought war with Mexico to divert national attention from the panic.

Although a war might have provided a diversion, the president had no intention of abandoning his quest for a peaceful solution to the claims dispute, one that would avoid sectional discord. By the spring of 1838, Texas realized that it could not outflank the president by going directly to Congress. The waning of annexationist ardor convinced the Mexican government that Van Buren was sincere in his expressed desire for peace. Mexico admitted the legitimacy of the claims and proposed third-party arbitration to reach a final solution. On 11 September 1838, the president signed a convention to this effect.

Van Buren refused to indulge expansionist Democrats, because he wanted to avoid further damage to the North-South axis of the party, which he considered the bulwark of the Union. Ironically, the Texans saw this most clearly. "Many of our friends as well as enemies in Congress dread the coming of the question at this time," wrote the Texan emissary, Memucan Hunt, in 1838, "on account of the desperate death-struggle, which they foresee, will inevitably ensue between the North and the South, a struggle involving the probability of a dissolution of this Union."

A rebellion on the nation's northern border coincided with the Mexican crisis and compounded the president's political problems. The revolt centered in southern Canada, where dissatisfaction with British rule reached a peak in the fall of 1837. William Lyon Mackenzie led an uprising that enlisted American citizens who joined the Canadian rebels in their stronghold on Navy Island, in the Niagara River. Since New York officials seemed unable to restrain their own people, British authorities decided to disarm the outpost. They sent a raiding party to attack the steamship *Caroline*, a forty-six-ton vessel used to supply Navy Island. The British found the *Caroline* at a pier in Schlosser, New York. Ignoring the international boundary, the party boarded the ship, set it aflame, and cast it adrift. The *Caroline* sank before reaching Niagara Falls. In the ensuing confusion, one American died and several were wounded.

Rumors of the raid spread quickly and exaggerated the outcome. "It is infamous," wrote one observer; "forty unarmed Americans butchered in cold blood, while sleeping, by a party of British assassins, and the living and dead sent together over Niagara." The president dispatched General Winfield Scott to Buffalo with strict instructions to call out the militia but employ it only as a last resort and then to avoid placing arms in the hands of border residents who might join the rebellion. The president then issued a neutrality proclamation calling for strict adherence to the law. Senate Democrats overcame Whig attempts to capitalize on the crisis and, in early March 1838, passed a new neutrality law. This measure was to run for two years and empowered civil authorities to prevent border excursions in the future. The president's proclamation, the Senate bill, and the Scott mission combined to defuse the border crisis.

Early in 1839, another conflict arose in a remote area of northern Maine known as the Aroostook Valley. The Peace Treaty of 1783 had left in doubt the exact location of the international boundary dividing Maine from New Brunswick. By the 1830s, American and British citizens alike wanted to develop the more than seven million acres of virgin timber that lay in this disputed territory. Clashes between Maine and New Brunswick developers were inevitable. In January 1839, Canadian authorities arrested a Maine land agent and took him to a New Brunswick jail. New Brunswick's lieutenant governor, Sir John Harvey, justified the arrest and issued a proclamation calling for withdrawal of all American forces from the disputed region. Maine's governor, John Fairfield, assembled nearly a thousand men and asked the state legislature for money and authority to call out another ten thousand. When the president heard of these measures, he appealed directly to the British minister, Henry Fox, and together they drew up a memorandum calling for all parties to withdraw from the Aroostook Valley.

The calm that prevailed in Washington had little impact in Maine. Fairfield denounced peace proposals. "Should you go *against* us on this occasion," he warned the president, "or not espouse our cause with *warmth* and *earnestness* and with true *American feeling*, God only knows what the result would be politically." Van Buren had dealt with too many professional politicians to be upset by the threats of an amateur. Again he turned to Winfield Scott, sending him to Augusta with instructions to calm the angry governor and prevent any warlike actions by the assembled Maine militia. While Scott journeyed north, Congress contributed to the war fever by granting the president more authority and funds than he requested. The legislature that refused to pass a subtreasury bill to safeguard government money gave Van Buren authority to spend $10 million and the power to mobilize fifty thousand militia for defense of the frontier. Once in Augusta, Scott worked swiftly and surely to disarm the crisis.

As president, Martin Van Buren established a solid record as a statesman, acting swiftly and surely in times of international tension. His handling of crises on the northern and southern borders of the country demonstrated a sincere and consistent commitment to neutrality and peaceful settlement of disputes. He displayed none of the aggressive behavior that marred the record of his predecessor. Van Buren passed up several opportunities to embrace expansionist ideology for political advantage. The nation's prolonged and severe financial crisis obscured this record of accomplishment. By the time Van Buren finally earned the respect of foreign governments, his term was nearly over and he was fighting for his political life.

Campaign of 1840

The campaign of 1840 had its origins in the Panic of 1837. Throughout four turbulent sessions of Congress, the Whigs sought every opportunity to strengthen their cause. Whig victories in the Democratic strongholds of New York and Virginia were more than reflexive reactions to the financial chaos. They stemmed from substantial political networks and a sophisticated style of electioneering. Whig managers like New York's Thurlow Weed and Pennsylvania's Thaddeus Stevens were ready to wage an extensive grassroots campaign to capitalize on public excitement aroused by the panic.

The president misread these political signs. He developed a stereotypical view of the Whigs as disorganized and amateurish. Van Buren had tolerated his own party's mass rallies in 1828 as manifestations of the public's fascination with Andrew Jackson. Van Buren intended to take higher ground in his own campaign.

Early in 1840, the president developed a detailed plan for the coming campaign, concentrating on restoring the Regency to power in New York as an example for Democrats nationwide. He drew up a seventy-five-page document, directing his New York supporters to renew their efforts at the grassroots level. He urged them to reestablish local committees of correspondence that could once again serve the vital function of circulating campaign documents. This part of the electoral blueprint showed the Van Buren of old, a man sensitive to the need for discipline, organization, and attention to fine detail. The remainder of this campaign manual revealed an anxious politician struggling to rally the faithful behind traditional principles, all the while fearful that his opponents would succeed by stealth and subversion. Van Buren exhorted his fellow Democrats to attend to the history of political parties, to recognize the Whigs as the Federalists of old. Armed with history, the voters could make informed choices, provided that the polls remained pure. At no point in his outline of campaign plans did the president refer to current economic conditions. Neither did he repeat arguments from his annual message on the use of the subtreasury to reform the banking structure. By charting a strategy that avoided all contemporary issues, especially those that had stimulated voter interest, the president severely limited his own campaign.

Divided between sectional candidates in 1836, the Whigs were united in 1840. To oppose Van Buren, they chose William Henry Harrison, whose southern birth and record of military heroism (especially his 1811 victory over Tecumseh at Tippecanoe) proved malleable elements in a campaign designed

to first mobilize and then unleash popular frustrations pent up during the panic. The choice of Virginia's John Tyler as Harrison's running mate enabled the Whigs to continue their siege of the Old Dominion, thereby demonstrating that the Democratic alliance was crumbling at its strongest point.

Despite the lavish attention he paid to the coming campaign, Van Buren could not bring unity to a party badly divided by economic disagreement. The Democratic convention at Baltimore on 5 May 1840 selected Van Buren but failed to nominate a vice presidential candidate, deciding to leave this selection to the states. This decision was the product of a lengthy disagreement between Van Buren and Jackson. Never the closest of friends, the two men drifted even further apart during the panic. The "Old Hero" confined his criticisms to private correspondence, often lecturing Francis P. Blair on the decline of Democratic solidarity.

As a remedy Jackson proposed that Tennessee's James K. Polk be the vice presidential candidate. Jackson argued that Polk had more appeal in the West than incumbent Richard M. Johnson. While recognizing Polk's admirable record as Speaker of the House, Van Buren was reluctant to drop Johnson from the ticket because the Kentuckian had a martial reputation to rival that of Harrison and strong support in Pennsylvania and New York. With the subtreasury bill still in the House, the president did not want to anger congressional delegations from these key states. Polk eventually withdrew his name, as did several other hopefuls.

The economic wars of the present, not the military campaigns of the past, provided the real issues in the election. Early in 1840, the Whigs added a new dimension to their fiscal attacks by personally ridiculing the president as a dandy and a spendthrift. Congressman Charles Ogle of Pennsylvania spent three days during debate on routine appropriation bills describing the "Regal Splendor of the President's Palace." Ogle maintained that the portly Van Buren had gained weight at public expense by routinely eating off gold plate in the executive mansion.

The charge of executive excess was hardly new. Van Buren had fallen heir to the Whig attacks on "King Andrew," and repeatedly during debates on the subtreasury bill, critics had charged the president with seeking to enlarge his power by manipulation of the nation's currency. Ogle's assault was neatly designed to simplify and personalize the complex economic and constitutional issues generated by the panic.

By contrast, the Whigs portrayed their own candidate as a man of modest means, who was born in a log cabin and imbibed nothing more aristocratic than native cider. At rallies more extensive than those introduced by the Democrats in 1828, Whig managers fed their eager converts a steady diet of such partisan fare.

The president was not so much a victim of such rhetorical assaults as he was a prisoner of his own principles. Having spent a political life denying the power of the federal government to manage domestic affairs, he could hardly have made an abrupt about-face and claim to be a savior of the nation's finances. Such a strategy would have fed the popular fear of executive usurpation. While bound by tradition to eschew offensive tactics, the president might have been more sensitive to the strength of Whig organization and the new party's ability to take advantage of the slightest miscalculation. In 1840, Van Buren erred badly by allowing his secretary of war to propose a thorough reform of the nation's militia system. While designed to place the militia more firmly under state control, Poinsett's proposal generated a storm in the press, where Whig propagandists charged that Van Buren wanted to raise a standing army.

Even after passage of the subtreasury bill, the president failed to change his electioneering strategy. He remained committed to a reasoned defense of Democratic principles, circulated in newspaper editorials and through campaign documents. His followers did their best to match Whig efforts on the campaign trail. For each log cabin the Whigs erected at mass rallies to symbolize Harrison's humble origins, Democrats erected hickory poles at their own gatherings to recall the martial exploits of "Old Hickory." Van Buren viewed these electioneering efforts with a measure of detachment, believing that Whig rhetoric was unprincipled and the precursor of a massive conspiracy to steal the election. He wrote to Jackson of the potential of vote fraud, warning "the mischief will be done before you are apprised of the danger." Van Buren initiated an election-eve investigation of previous state contests, trying to document Whig chicanery.

While the president remained in Washington dutifully answering innumerable requests for policy statements, his opponent took to the stump. Old Tip was by no means a stunning orator, but his appearances created a new bond with the expanding electorate. Here was a man willing to go to the people, to converse with them in simple, understandable language, to recount his military exploits, and to speak out against executive excess in Washington. Harrison's campaigning combined with other Whig innovations paid handsome dividends in the fall election. The party received 234 electoral votes to Van Buren's 60. The popular outpouring, stimulated by the panic, broke all election records. Van Buren actually received 400,000 more popular votes than he had in 1836. But the Whigs proved more adept at recruiting new voters, winning nineteen of twenty-six states. The Democrats' strongest showing came in the South, where they recaptured Virginia and won contests in Alabama, Arkansas, and Missouri. "Never in my experience of twenty-seven years," the Regency's Azariah Flagg wrote Van Buren, "have I seen the rank and file show so much spirit and zeal."

Blinded to these realities, the president accepted defeat calmly but with obvious bitterness. He called the election a "catastrophe," resulting from Whig fraud rather than Democratic collapse. "Time will unravel the means by which these results have been produced," he wrote to Andrew Jackson, "and then the people will do justice to all."

Martin Van Buren looked forward to a vindication that never came. Perhaps the cruelest irony of his presidency was not that he fell victim to a partisan process he helped perfect but that in response to the Panic of 1837, he proposed legislation that violated the cherished concept of states' rights, which he had long insisted was the foundation of the Democratic alliance. Where Jackson had been the target of political charges that he was usurping power, Van Buren acted the part of a strong president. Neither his party nor his contemporaries were prepared for such executive initiative. "Van, Van's a used up man," the Whigs cried during the election of 1840. Stinging though the cry was, it contained elements of truth. Martin Van Buren used all his political prowess while president and still he could not hold together the party he had so carefully constructed. The inauguration in 1841 would usher in the new Whig alliance and herald the arrival of the modern two-party system. That day dawned bright and clear, but not for Martin Van Buren, who left Washington for retirement in his native New York.

Despite the bitter defeat, Van Buren remained active in politics, guarding the principles that had guided his career. In 1844, he once again opposed the annexation of Texas, costing him the Democratic nomination. In 1848, Van Buren deviated from his party by accepting nomination on a free-soil ticket, but only to assist long-time New York allies. The former president devoted his final years to his *Autobiography*, which remains one of the most valuable sources on the development of American political parties. Van Buren died quietly on 24 July 1862, having seen the sectional crisis he had worked so long to prevent become a bloody reality.

BIBLIOGRAPHY

Elisabeth H. West, ed., *The Calendar of the Papers of Martin Van Buren* (Washington, D.C., 1910), provides an introduction to the rich collection of Van Buren's papers at the Library of Congress; the papers are the most important source on Van Buren's presidency. James D. Richardson, ed., *A Compilation of the Messages and Papers of the Presidents 1789–1897*, 10 vols. (Washington, D.C., 1896–1899), includes Van Buren's addresses to Congress and many important state papers. Donald B. Cole, *Martin Van Buren and the American Political System* (Princeton, N.J., 1984), is an excellent biography.

Edward Pessen, *Jacksonian America: Society, Personality, and Politics,* rev. ed. (Homewood, Ill., 1978), provides a sophisticated overview of antebellum America. Richard P. McCormick, *The Second American Party System: Party Formation in the Jacksonian Era* (Chapel Hill, N.C., 1966), is a masterful account of party formation. Lee Benson, *The Concept of Jacksonian Democracy: New York as a Test Case* (Princeton, N.J., 1961), is a quantitative analysis of New York politics that suggests the crucial relationship between local and national party activity.

James C. Curtis, *Andrew Jackson and the Search for Vindication* (Boston, 1976), provides critical insights into Jackson's presidency and the troubled political legacy that Van Buren inherited.

James C. Curtis, *The Fox at Bay: Martin Van Buren and the Presidency, 1837–1841* (Lexington, Ky., 1970), and Major L. Wilson, *The Presidency of Martin Van Buren* (Lawrence, Kans., 1984), study Van Buren's single term in office. Reginald C. McGrane, *The Panic of 1837: Some Financial Problems of the Jacksonian Era* (Chicago, 1924), although dated, is still the best brief introduction to the financial collapse that dominated Van Buren's presidency. Peter Temin, *The Jacksonian Economy* (New York, 1969), challenges long-standing assumptions about Jacksonian finance and provides a thoroughly modern quantitative explanation for the Panic of 1837. John A. Garraty, *Silas Wright* (New York, 1949), neatly summarizes Wright's career but deemphasizes the senator's disillusionment with official economic policy during the Panic of 1837. Charles G. Sellers, *James K. Polk, Jacksonian, 1795–1843* (Princeton, N.J., 1957), is an invaluable guide to congressional maneuvers during Van Buren's presidency.

Robert G. Gunderson, *The Log-Cabin Campaign* (Lexington, Ky., 1957), captures the flavor of the political rough-and-tumble but lacks analytical rigor. John C. Fitzpatrick, ed., "The Autobiography of Martin Van Buren," in *Annual Report of the American Historical Association for the Year 1918*, vol. 2 (Washington, D.C., 1920), was written during Van Buren's retirement; the former president makes perceptive comments on political development but does not carry the narrative beyond 1835.

Also see John Niven, *Martin Van Buren: The Romantic Age of American Politics* (New York, 1983).

William Henry Harrison and John Tyler

Richard P. McCormick

William Henry Harrison THE NATIONAL PORTRAIT GALLERY

John Tyler CORBIS

ILLIAM HENRY HARRISON, the first Whig elected to the presidency, was inaugurated on 4 March 1841. A month later he was dead. John Tyler thus became the first vice president to succeed to the office of president of the United States upon the death of the incumbent. Tyler is most commonly remembered in connection with the 1840 campaign slogan "Tippecanoe and Tyler Too." He also acquired dubious fame as the president who was disowned by his political party because he vetoed important measures enacted with the support of that party in Congress. Because of this circumstance, his administration has often been termed a disaster and Tyler has been placed at, or near, the bottom in rank-

ings of American presidents. Whatever may have been his shortcomings as a political leader, his administration was neither uneventful nor inconsequential. It was, on the contrary, unusually important in the evolution of political parties, in shaping the course of domestic policies, and especially in launching new initiatives in foreign affairs.

Harrison's Presidency

Harrison was born in Virginia on 9 February 1773, the son of a signer of the Declaration of Independence. He served as an officer in the army until he was appointed secretary of the Northwest Territory in 1798. As the territorial governor of Indiana from 1800 to 1813, he won fame for his questionable triumph over the Indians at the Battle of Tippecanoe in November 1811. During the War of 1812, he achieved the rank of major general and added to his military laurels with an important victory at the Battle of the Thames. After resigning from the army early in 1814, he established his residence on a farm at North Bend, Ohio.

A constant seeker of public office, he was successively a member of the House of Representatives, the Ohio Senate, and the United States Senate before his appointment as minister to Colombia in 1828. Recalled from that post in 1829, he returned to his farm burdened with heavy debts, and in 1834 accepted appointment as clerk of the county court of common pleas to relieve his financial distress. From that humble base, he launched his candidacy for president in opposition to Martin Van Buren and ran surprisingly well in 1836, carrying seven states. Because of this strong showing, he was nominated by the Whigs in 1839 in preference to Henry Clay, and in a contest made memorable by an unprecedented turnout of voters, he achieved a huge electoral majority over Van Buren in 1840. As Harrison assumed office, the nation was descending into the worst economic depression it was to experience until 1929. Severe deflationary conditions dried up sources of credit, forced banks to suspend redemption of their bills in specie, and drove prices downward. Nine states that had overinvested in public works were unable to meet scheduled payments on their indebtedness. Because of sharp declines in imports and in land sales, the revenues of the federal government plummeted from $50 million in 1836 to a bare $17 million in 1841, leading to large annual deficits. Not until 1843 did economic conditions improve.

The Whig party had not come to power with a clearly defined program for dealing with the economic crisis. Newly formed of disparate factions, it had promulgated no platform at its national convention, and its candidates had been vague in their campaign pronouncements. The party represented opposition to Van Buren, to the exercise of excessive power by the executive branch, and to the financial policies that had culminated in the establishment of the independent treasury system. Its most conspicuous spokesman had been Henry Clay, longtime senator from Kentucky, who championed the reestablishment of a national bank, a protective tariff,

and the distribution to the states of the revenue from the sale of public lands. Despite his eminence, he was bypassed as a candidate in favor of Harrison, a military hero with ambiguous views on these controversial matters.

Clay expected to dominate the administration through his leadership of the Whigs in Congress, but his relationship with Harrison grew distant when the two men disagreed over patronage questions and the desirability of convening a special session of the new Congress. Clay also had reason to be concerned about the influence of his old rival, Daniel Webster of Massachusetts, who was appointed secretary of state and who favored a more moderate course of action than the impetuous Clay. Behind these personal rivalries lay the question of whether the union achieved by the Whigs in the 1840 campaign could be sustained in support of a legislative program.

Harrison's lengthy inaugural address provided only deceptive clues for divining the future course of the administration. Emphasizing his concern that power had become too greatly concentrated in the executive branch, he declared that he would serve but a single term, would be restrained on the use of the veto, and would not employ patronage to enhance his authority. The president, in his view, should not interfere in the legislative process; in particular, the "delicate duty of devising schemes of revenue" should be left entirely to Congress. He deplored agitation of the slavery question, appealed for national unity, and condemned the evil of excessive partisanship. At no point did he offer his opinions on the tariff, on distribution, or on a national bank, except for the oblique comment that he was opposed to a wholly metallic currency. Clearly, his was a limited concept of presidential leadership, and it was fully in accord with Whig rhetoric attacking "executive usurpation" in the 1840 campaign.

Under intense pressure from Clay, backed by Whig congressmen, Harrison was induced to call the Twenty-seventh Congress into special session, ostensibly to deal with "the condition of the revenue and finance of the country." This session was to convene on 31 May. But on 4 April, worn down by the insatiable demands of hosts of office seekers and a demanding social schedule, Harrison succumbed to pneumonia. His death brought John Tyler—"His Accidency"—to the presidency.

The Accession of Tyler

Tyler shared with Harrison his birthplace in Charles City County, Virginia. Both of their fathers had served as governors of that state. Born on 29 March 1790, Tyler, at fifty-one, was the youngest man up to that point to become president, and Harrison, the oldest. A graduate of William and Mary College and a lawyer, he had served in the Virginia legislature, the governorship, the House of Representatives, and the United States Senate. Never a strong party man, he had reluctantly supported Andrew Jackson for the presidency in 1828 and 1832 but had broken with him in 1833, opposing the removal of the deposits from the Bank of the United States and casting the lone vote in the Senate against the Force Act. In 1836 he resigned his seat in the Senate rather than obey the instruction of the Virginia legislature to vote for expunging the resolution of censure that the Senate had imposed earlier on Jackson.

A strict constructionist, an ardent champion of states' rights, and a defender of the South's "domestic institutions," Tyler had a rigid, even anachronistic, political conscience. He had long opposed the Bank of the United States and a protective tariff, yet he admired Henry Clay. He was sufficiently prominent as a states' rights opponent of Van Buren to be a vice presidential candidate in 1836 on the ticket headed by Hugh Lawson White of Tennessee. After others reportedly had declined the honor, he was the unanimous choice of the Whig national convention for the vice presidential nomination in 1839. A southern man was needed to balance the ticket; and Tyler, with his special appeal to the states' rights element in southern Whiggery, was an appropriate choice. But his unyielding constitutional scruples and his deficiencies as a political leader were to create embarrassments for his party and severe damage to his reputation as president.

Tyler's first official act had lasting constitutional significance. It was unclear whether, upon the death of a president, the vice president would actually become president or be merely vice president acting as president. Tyler promptly decided that he was the president. He subscribed to the presidential oath of office, issued a brief inaugural address, and moved into the White House. Some critics, then and afterward, challenged his view, but it was soon endorsed by Congress and has since prevailed. Decisive though he was on this crucial issue, Tyler generally held to a limited concept of presidential leadership. More specifically, he believed that responsibility for initiating legislation should rest upon Congress and that the president should confine himself to providing Congress with information and, in extreme in-

Americans in mourning over the sudden death of President Harrison in 1841 expressed their grief by wearing armbands such as the above. THE LIBRARY OF CONGRESS

stances, interposing his veto when he felt that the Constitution was being violated or the national welfare was being affected adversely.

Tyler's Conflicts with Clay's Whigs

Tyler's concept of the presidency was to be severely tested and challenged during the course of the special session. The Whigs controlled both houses of Congress, having a thin majority in the Senate and a margin of nearly fifty votes in the House. As enunciated by Clay, Whig political principles required that the executive branch be shorn of the excessive authority it had acquired under Andrew Jackson. Congress should determine the course of public policy; the veto power, wielded so devastatingly by Jackson, should be tightly curbed; and the president should be guided in all his actions by his "constitutional advisers," the members of the cabinet. What Clay envisioned was a crude approximation of the parliamentary model, with himself in the role of party leader.

Soon after the session opened, Clay set forth his legislative agenda. The central feature was the reestablishment of a national bank. But he called as well for the repeal of the Independent Treasury Act, the distribution to the states of the proceeds of public-land sales, an increased tariff, and a loan issue to meet immediate financial exigencies. Later he added a national bankruptcy bill, intended to afford relief to those victims of the economic depression who were unable to discharge their debts. These measures constituted an astutely contrived legislative package designed when taken together to win support from all segments of the congressional Whig party. Tyler had already indicated that he had serious constitutional reservations about a national bank and that he could accept distribution only if the tariff were not raised, but Clay remained fully committed to his program.

A fateful confrontation was not long in developing over the bank issue. A plan for a modified version of the old Bank of the United States, drafted by Secretary of the Treasury Thomas Ewing, was introduced in Congress in the summer of 1841. It was presumed that it had Tyler's approval. Clay, with the support of the well-disciplined Whig caucus, had the bill revised to reflect his own view of what was required. When it appeared that sufficient votes could not be mobilized for the amended measure, a "com-

promise" in the form of restrictions on the power of the bank to establish branches in the states was adopted. In this mangled form, the bill passed both houses by votes that closely followed party lines.

Ten days later, Tyler vetoed the measure, citing specific objections to the compromise amendment and to the discounting power conferred on the bank, while expressing more generally his familiar doubts about the constitutional authority of Congress to charter any national bank. Although the veto was not unanticipated, it produced a sensational reaction. An unruly crowd gathered at the White House that evening to assail Tyler, and Whig spokesmen condemned his un-Whiggish use of the veto. Some charged him with treachery and alleged that he was plotting to create a new party to support him for the presidency in 1844.

Almost immediately, further efforts were made to enact an acceptable bank bill. The product of too many hands and of resultant misunderstandings and suspicions, the new measure was to create a "fiscal corporation" of limited scope. Clay regarded it as too feeble to gain the confidence of potential investors, but Webster worked valiantly for its passage in the hope of preventing a total rupture between the administration and the congressional Whigs. The bill was hurried through Congress, despite last-minute efforts by Tyler to have it postponed. He had by now become wary of any Whig-sponsored bank scheme, and he was drawing closer to his small circle of strict-constructionist Virginia advisers. On 9 September, a week after receiving the bill and only a few days before the special session was to adjourn, Tyler again wielded his veto. His stated objections were minor and unconvincing, and he coupled them with the plea that he be given time for "deep and deliberate reflection" on how best to meet the need for regulating the currency and safeguarding the public funds.

Next to the reestablishment of a national bank, Clay's most cherished objective was distribution. Balked a decade earlier in his efforts to secure federal appropriations for internal improvements—such as roads, canals, and river clearance—Clay had fostered the proposal that monies from the sale of public lands should be distributed among the states, which in turn could carry out essential public works. Moreover, as an exponent of a protective tariff, he saw that with the elimination of land sales as a source of federal revenue, the government would be obliged to keep important duties at a high level.

The bill that took shape in the special session, the Preemption Act of 1841, called for the distribution of 90 percent of the land-sale revenues to the states, with the remaining 10 percent being granted as a bonus to nine of the newer states in which most of the public domain was located. As an inducement to the western Whigs, many of whom were cool to distribution, the measure included provision for preemption. Squatters on surveyed lands could acquire, or preempt, 160 acres at the minimum price of $1.25 an acre. But the most critical feature of the bill, inserted to appease southern Whigs, who feared that distribution would lead inevitably to a higher tariff, decreed that distribution would end if the tariff rose above the maximum level of 20 percent fixed by the Compromise Tariff of 1833. In this form the measure was enacted over the opposition of the Democrats, who argued that it was imprudent to deplete the treasury when there was a large deficit. Tyler signed the act.

Although major attention centered on the bank and on distribution, other matters also engaged Congress. With minimal difficulty, the independent treasury was abolished, leaving no depository for federal funds except the state-chartered banks. A national bankruptcy act that enabled thirty-four thousand persons to discharge $441 million of indebtedness by turning over to their creditors assets worth only one-tenth that amount was enacted, only to be repealed two years later in response to widespread protests. Congress also authorized a three-year loan of $12 million, but the government could sell only $5.5 million of these notes because the terms were unattractive to investors. As another emergency financial measure, articles that had not been subject to import duties or to minimal charges were now to be taxed at the maximum rate of 20 percent of their appraised value. To all of these Whig-sponsored enactments, Tyler gave his approval.

Despite his acquiescence to most of the items on the Whig agenda, Tyler had, with his two bank vetoes, damaged irreparably his relations with the Whig party. On 11 September, two days after the second veto, all the members of the cabinet except Webster resigned, citing the president's lack of candor in connection with the second bank bill. Webster justified his decision to remain in the cabinet on the grounds that the Whig party, including the president, should remain united and expressed the belief that it was still possible to create a satisfactory "fiscal agent." Tyler, who had already contemplated replacing the cabinet he had inherited from Harrison, quickly filled the vacant posts with Whigs who were hostile to Clay and who were disposed to give Tyler loyal support.

Even more dramatic than the cabinet resignations were the actions taken on 13 September by a caucus of Whig congressmen. In a fervent "Address," they expressed their frustration with the bank vetoes, charged that Tyler was seeking to "overthrow the present division of parties in the country," and declared that the Whig party could "be no longer . . . responsible or blamed for the administration of the executive branch of the government." Having thus ostracized Tyler, they pledged their party to seek constitutional amendments that would limit the president to a single term, curb the veto power, and restrict the chief executive's power to remove incumbents from office. Interestingly enough, they also announced their stand for "no government bank, but an institution capable of guarding the people's treasure and administering to the people's wants." According to his repeated declarations, this was what Tyler desired also.

The spectacular clash between the president and his party should not obscure the fact that the Whigs had at last united behind a program and a leader. The disparate factions that had coalesced to nominate "Tippecanoe and Tyler Too" could not have adopted a platform, as their Democratic counterparts did; they were too diverse in their issue orientations. But marshaled by Clay's skillfully contrived package of legislation, which made for intraparty bargaining, and further goaded into unity by their conviction that the president was engaged in "treachery," the party came to stand on a common ground behind Clay. The degree of party unity manifested during the special session was not to be exceeded in the antebellum decades; on most key votes on economic legislation, four-fifths of the Whigs were aligned against an even more solid phalanx of Democrats. Although the Whigs suffered reverses in the 1841 state elections, all blame was attributed to Tyler's perverse behavior; the party showed no loss of confidence in its program or its acknowledged leader.

The struggle between the Whigs and Tyler continued during the first regular session of the Twenty-seventh Congress. Lasting from early December 1841 until the end of August 1842—a total of 269 days—it was the longest congressional session until that time. The matter of greatest interest was the tariff, coupled with distribution. The Compromise Tariff of 1833, which had provided for the gradual reduction of duties from the high levels that had been set by the Tariff of 1832 until they should reach a maximum of 20 percent in 1842, would expire on 1 July 1842. With the government facing a predicted deficit in that year of $14 million—out of a total budget of $32 million—tariff revenues would have to be increased. Tyler recommended such action, but he also made clear his conviction that if the rates rose above 20 percent, distribution must be ended.

Clay, while he recognized the problem of the deficit, was insistent both that the tariff should be raised and that distribution should continue. His position was based in part on his recognition of the political reality that some southern Whigs would not support a higher tariff unless it was tied to distribution. The first test came over the enactment of a "temporary" tariff (25 June 1842), which postponed until 1 August 1842 the final reductions scheduled under the 1833 act and specified that distribution was to continue. Tyler vetoed the measure, arguing that a temporary tariff was unnecessary and condemning the distribution feature.

Despite this indication of the president's views, the Whig majority in August passed a "permanent" tariff and again combined it with distribution. Not surprisingly, the result was another presidential veto. Tyler insisted there should be no distribution so long as the condition of the treasury made it necessary to impose tariff duties in excess of 20 percent. Clay had exulted on the first tariff veto. "The more vetoes now of right measures the better," he had declared. He reveled in Tyler's embarrassment, believing that it would redound to the benefit of the Whigs and of his own presidential ambitions.

But Tyler had his way. Because it was essential that government revenues be increased, Congress finally yielded and enacted the Tariff of 1842 with. out distribution; a separate distribution bill was pocket vetoed by Tyler. Average rates were restored to approximately the level of 1832, and the much abused credit system for the payment of duties was abolished. The measure was passed only with substantial support from northern Democrats and over the opposition of a large majority of southern Whigs, demonstrating that the latter remained cool to a high tariff in spite of their willingness to acknowledge Clay as their leader.

The second tariff veto, like the second bank veto, produced a furious reaction among the congressional Whigs. In an unprecedented move, Tyler's message was referred in the House to a select committee of thirteen headed by the redoubtable John Quincy Adams. The committee promptly brought in a report that rehearsed and deplored Tyler's two bank vetoes, scored his latest betrayal of the Whig concept of the presidency, and concluded that although his "weak and wavering obstinacy" surely merited impeachment, existing political conditions made such an action impractical. In his helpless rage, Adams could only propose the introduction of a constitutional amendment to enable Congress to override a presidential veto by a simple majority. When Tyler sent the House a "solemn protest" against this arraignment, that body indignantly refused to enter it in its official journal.

The issue of restricting the veto had already been raised in the Senate, where Clay had introduced a proposed amendment on lines similar to that of Adams. The move, he insisted, was not motivated by Tyler's actions; it was made to redeem a party pledge and to prevent encroachment by the executive on the legislative branch. After three months of intermittent and often brilliant debate, with the Democrats opposing the change, the proposed amendment was dropped without being brought to a vote. In the House, Adams' measure received a majority vote (99 to 90), but less than the required two-thirds. With much less seriousness of purpose, but in keeping with their campaign pronouncements, Whigs also sponsored amendments to limit the president to a single four-year term and to restrict the president's power of appointment and removal. Given the complexion of Congress, there was no likelihood that these proposals would receive favorable consideration.

Congress did take one momentous action that was to affect its future composition. Down to that time, many states had followed the practice of electing their members of the House of Representatives from the state at large, which meant that the majority party in a state would elect all of that state's congressmen. This was changed by the Apportionment Act of 1842, which reduced the size of the House from 242 to 223 members and required that thereafter each representative be chosen in his own, single-member district. Several states adopted protests against what they termed an assault on their prerogatives, and four refused at first to create the requisite districts. But, in time, the law was accepted, and election by districts became uniform among the states. (In a similar vein, Congress, in the closing days of the Tyler administration, established a uniform date for holding the presidential election. The election had previously been conducted in the states on various days between 30 October and 10 November; henceforth it was to occur in all states on "the Tuesday next after the first Monday in November.")

Except for essential appropriation acts, little more was accomplished in this interminable session. Tyler had brought forth a plan for a "board of exchequer" that would, he maintained, provide for a sound currency and safeguard the public funds, but the Whigs were in no mood to give serious consideration to the plan, which was not without merit.

Harassed by the unrelenting opposition of the Democrats and frustrated by Tyler's vetoes, the congressional Whigs had little to show for their efforts. The reestablishment of a national bank had been balked, and the issue soon receded from the political agenda. Distribution had been achieved for a brief period, during which the states received $600,000; then it, too, passed into oblivion. The bankruptcy bill had proved to be unpopular and was repealed. A tariff had been enacted, but it owed its passage to Democratic votes and had sorely divided the Whigs.

The congressional elections in the fall of 1842 added to the discomfiture of the Whigs. The Democrats captured the House of Representatives with a majority of nearly two to one. The Whigs remained narrowly in control of the Senate. With the two houses thus at odds and with the president allied to neither party, the Twenty-eighth Congress was predictably unproductive. Despite the setback to his party, Clay's fortunes seemed bright. In March 1842 he had resigned from the Senate with a moving valedictory speech in which he reiterated his principles and left no doubt of his availability as a presidential candidate. In April he was nominated by the North Carolina Whig convention, and similar endorsements followed rapidly.

Tyler meanwhile indulged himself in the futile hope that he could head a new party made up of anti-Clay Whigs in the North, conservative Democrats, and southern extremists. The prospect was remote, but if a suitable issue should arise, it was not beyond the realm of possibility, for both major parties were of recent origin and might well disintegrate under the impact of new issues.

Foreign Affairs

Tyler's unfortunate relationship to Congress permitted him little scope for leadership in domestic matters, but he exploited his powers as president effectively in the realm of foreign affairs. Remarkably sensitive to America's strategic and economic opportunities, he was, unlike Clay or Van Buren, a vigorous expansionist. So energetic was he in promoting his policies that he was largely instrumental in shifting popular attention away from the public questions that had dominated the Jacksonian era, to new and ominous issues that were to come to a head in his successor's administration.

Of immediate concern as he assumed office were relations with England. Several explosive issues had combined to produce such tensions between the two nations that there was talk of war on both sides. In the wake of the ill-fated rebellions in Canada in 1837, there had been a series of nasty incidents along the border that resulted from raids by expatriate rebels and their American sympathizers. Other troubles erupted in 1839 with the Aroostook War, in which men from Maine clashed with those from New Brunswick in the disputed area between the two jurisdictions. Southern sentiment was aroused when, in November 1841, an American ship, the *Creole*, carrying slaves from Virginia to New Orleans, was taken into the Bahamas following a mutiny and the British refused to return the slaves to their owners.

Webster, as secretary of state, was eager to compose differences with England and had Tyler's full support and cooperation. With the arrival in the spring of 1842 of a special British emissary, Lord Ashburton (Alexander Baring), amicable negotiations got under way, culminating in the Webster-Ashburton Treaty (August 1842). The most vexatious issue was the northern boundary of Maine, which had remained undetermined since the Treaty of Paris in 1783. Some twelve thousand square miles were in dispute. By clever but not entirely ethical means, Webster induced Maine and Massachusetts, of which Maine had formerly been a part, to yield to a compromise that gave five thousand square miles of the contested region to New Brunswick. Minor adjustments were made in the northern boundaries of New Hampshire, Vermont, and New York. Farther west, the British gave up sixty-five hundred square miles on the border between Lake Superior and the Lake of the Woods, where in 1887 the great Mesabi iron ore deposits were discovered. To reduce tensions between the two nations over efforts to suppress the slave trade, it was agreed that each would accord the other the "right of visit" when the ships of either nation were suspected of carrying slaves and that the United States would maintain a squadron in African waters to cooperate with the British fleet in preventing the traffic in slaves. In supplemental notes, the problem of the border incidents was resolved by an agreement on the mutual extradition of criminals. Although some disappointment was expressed that the negotiations had not resolved the status of Oregon, the treaty was speedily approved by the Senate, and what might have become a serious crisis was averted.

In a more remote sphere, the Tyler administration was successful in establishing treaty relations with China. Although Americans had long conducted a prosperous trade with that ancient nation, Britain's victory over China in the Opium War (1839–1842) seemed to promise even greater commercial possibilities there. Accordingly, Tyler dispatched Caleb Cushing of Massachusetts as a special commissioner to negotiate with imperial officials. His efforts—backed by four warships—resulted in the Treaty of Wanghia (1844), which secured for Americans the same trading privileges that had been extorted by the British. Tyler also manifested interest in Hawaii, then an independent kingdom that saw itself threatened by the intervention of foreign nations. Noting that most of the ships putting into port there were American and that numerous American missionaries had settled there, Tyler, in his annual message to Congress in December 1842, extended the principles of the Monroe Doctrine to Hawaii: the United States, he asserted, would view with "dissatisfaction" any attempt by another nation to take possession of Hawaii or subvert its government.

Closer to home, Tyler declared an end to the costly and inhumane war against the Seminole Indians. The last remaining Indian nation in the South after the others had been forcibly removed to reservations west of the Mississippi by Jackson, the Seminoles had been induced to sign a fraudulent treaty in 1833, giving up their remaining lands. Led by Chief Osceola, they had resisted and for nearly a decade had been harried by American troops until only a small remnant remained. At that point, Tyler announced the termination of hostilities in a message to Congress in May 1842.

Of far larger consequence was Tyler's interest in the vast territory that was known as Oregon. Located west of the Rocky Mountains and extending from the forty-second parallel (the present northern boundary of California) to 54°40' north latitude (the southern boundary of Alaska, then a Russian possession), Oregon was claimed jointly by the United States and Great Britain on the basis of early voyages of discovery. By the Convention of 1818, the two nations, un-

able to decide on a boundary between their claims, had agreed to joint occupation of the region. This agreement was extended indefinitely in 1827, with the provision that it could be terminated by either party upon giving one year's notice to the other. Prior to 1840 there had been negligible American settlement in the area. The British presence was represented by the Hudson's Bay Company, which maintained fur-trading posts in the Columbia River valley and elsewhere north of that river.

By the time of the Webster-Ashburton negotiations, the British were prepared to agree on a division of the territory with the Columbia River as the boundary, but this was unacceptable to the United States, for it was known that the entrance to that river was unsuitable as a harbor. Webster countered with a proposal that Britain persuade Mexico to cede to the United States part of California, including the excellent port of San Francisco, in return for which he would accept the Columbia as the Oregon boundary. When this gambit failed, the Oregon issue was left unresolved.

In the same year, popular interest in Oregon rose markedly as the result of the publication of glowing reports from the exploratory voyage of Lieutenant Charles Wilkes and accounts sent back by the first organized party of settlers to venture over the Oregon Trail. By 1843 hundreds of pioneers were heading for the Willamette Valley. In July 1843 delegates from six western states met in convention in Cincinnati and adopted resolutions asserting that the United States had valid title to all of Oregon and calling for the extension of American jurisdiction over the whole region. Similar pronouncements were soon being made by western spokesmen in Congress.

Tyler shared the rising expansionist sentiment. In December 1841 he had urged Congress to appropriate funds for a chain of forts from Council Bluffs, Iowa, to some point on the Pacific "within our limits" to protect the route of travel to Oregon. A year later he called attention to the Oregon question, indicating that he would press the British for a settlement. In his annual message in December 1843, he was explicit, if not entirely candid, in declaring that "the United States have always contended that their rights appertain to the entire region of country lying on the Pacific and embraced within 40° and 54°40' of north latitude." In actuality, he would have settled for a division along the forty-ninth parallel, including the magnificent harbor of the Juan de Fuca Strait.

This was the boundary that was to be agreed on in 1846. But Tyler was not energetic in pressing for Oregon, because by 1843 his attention was focused on what he regarded as the grandest objective of his administration—the annexation of Texas.

The Effort to Annex Texas

The issue of Texas annexation had been assiduously avoided by the leading politicians of all parties ever since the Texans had succeeded in establishing their independence from Mexico in 1836. They feared that talk of annexation would immediately raise the question of adding greatly to the slaveholding area of the United States, arouse northern foes of slavery extension, and threaten to disrupt existing party alignments. Recognizing the danger posed by the slavery issue to the maintenance of the Union, President Jackson had waited until his last day in office before extending recognition to the new republic. His successor, Martin Van Buren, had abruptly declined Texas' offer to accept annexation. In the campaign of 1840, there was no mention of Texas.

Tyler, a president without a party, was free from the constraints that inhibited such leaders as Clay or Van Buren. He was not concerned about the divisive effect of Texas annexation on the Whig or Democratic party. On the contrary, he saw the possibility that by successfully exploiting the annexation issue he might form a new party supportive of his ambitions for a second term. Moreover, he was in principle an expansionist and saw in annexation an achievement that would add luster to his presidency. He contemplated acquiring Texas after the completion of the Webster-Ashburton negotiation, but Webster, who remained as secretary of state, was hostile to the idea. When Webster finally resigned in May 1843, Tyler replaced him with Abel P. Upshur of Virginia, who shared the president's ardor for annexation.

There were formidable obstacles to be overcome. Mexico had never recognized the independence of Texas and gave notice that annexation would be regarded as an act of war. Great Britain, with support from France, wanted an independent Texas, preferably with slavery abolished there, and was offering alluring inducements to the Texas authorities. Not the least of the obstacles was the likelihood that the Senate would not welcome annexation, because of the threat that it would pose to the unity of both parties. As early as March 1843, when there were rumors of Tyler's intentions, John

Quincy Adams headed a group of northern congressmen who published an "Address to the People of the Free States," warning against a "slaveholders' plot" to extend the bounds of slavery. On the other side, a small number of southern Democratic politicians were scheming to use the Texas issue to deprive Van Buren of the party's nomination in 1844.

Despite the dubious, even threatening, omens, Tyler determined to proceed. He would downplay the slavery issue and emphasize instead the economic advantages that would accrue from annexation. Even more, he would depict the British in the role of the villains, working to frustrate American expansion, posing a threat to the "domestic institutions" of the South, and securing the material advantages of an independent Texas subservient to John Bull. By late 1843, Upshur was in secret negotiation with Texas emissaries, even assuring them that the Senate would be agreeable and that the United States would extend its protection to Texas, pending ratification of a treaty.

On 28 February 1844, matters took an unexpected turn. President Tyler, members of his cabinet, other Washington dignitaries, and their guests accepted an invitation from Captain Robert F. Stockton to take a cruise on the Potomac on the *Princeton*, the most modern ship in the navy. On the homeward trip, the vessel's huge naval gun, the "Peacemaker," was fired for the entertainment of the company. It exploded, with catastrophic effect. Total casualties were eight dead, including Upshur and Secretary of the Navy Thomas W. Gilmer, and eleven injured. With inadequate forethought, Tyler chose John C. Calhoun as Upshur's replacement. A southern extremist, whose most recent candidacy for the presidency had been abandoned in failure a few months earlier, Calhoun was, like Tyler, a man without a party. He, too, was prepared to exploit the Texas issue, in his case by relating it explicitly to the defense of slavery.

Under Calhoun's direction, a treaty of annexation was signed on 12 April, and ten days later it was sent to the Senate. In his message urging approval, Tyler began with the dubious assertion that Texas had been acquired as part of the Louisiana Purchase in 1803, ignoring the fact that if such a claim had any basis, it had been renounced by the Adams-Onís Treaty in 1819. More cogently, he argued the economic benefits to be gained by "reannexation." But his strongest plea was that if the United States did not take Texas, it would "force Texas to seek refuge in the arms of some other power," a thinly veiled reference to Britain.

A few days later he forwarded to the Senate correspondence between Calhoun and Richard Pakenham, the British minister in Washington. In his letter to Pakenham, Calhoun went to extraordinary lengths to tie annexation to a justification of slavery, holding forth on the dire consequences to the South if Britain should be successful in securing the abolition of slavery in Texas. To oppose annexation, as Calhoun defined the issue, was to place slavery in the United States in jeopardy. In mid-May, Tyler continued his campaign for ratification by sending the Senate a letter from Andrew Jackson that argued that if annexation were not accomplished promptly, "Texas might from necessity be thrown into the arms of England and be forever lost to the United States." In South Carolina, an effort was launched to hold a southern convention to rally that region behind annexation.

The treaty met with a negative reception in the Senate. Northern senators denounced it as an overt invitation to war with Mexico and as a slaveholders' plot led by a desperate and repudiated president. Some professed to see it as having been contrived solely for political ends—to deny Van Buren the presidential nomination and to advance the candidacy of Tyler. Almost without exception, the Whigs, regardless of section, opposed the treaty and castigated Tyler for raising the issue. Finally, on 8 June 1844, the treaty was brought to a vote. Only sixteen senators—fifteen Democrats and one Whig—voted affirmatively; thirty-five were opposed. Undaunted, Tyler sent the rejected treaty and relevant documents to the House of Representatives two days later, repeating his warning that Texas would throw itself into the arms of England and intimating that the House should initiate the process of annexation by joint resolution.

Election of 1844

It was against this exciting background that preparations for the 1844 presidential election were reaching their climax. Early in the spring of 1844, there appeared to be little doubt that Van Buren would be the Democratic nominee and that Clay would get the nomination denied him by the Whigs in 1840. Tyler, recklessly utilizing the presidential patronage to weld together a small coterie of supporters, was keeping his options open. He might somehow induce the Democrats to adopt him, run as a third-party candidate, or use the threat of his candidacy to force acceptance of Texas annexation.

When the rumored treaty became a reality, it had a profound impact on the political scene. On 27 April both Clay and Van Buren released letters to the press stating their views on Texas. Both were opposed to "immediate annexation." Both emphasized the dangers to the Union that would result from sharp sectional division over the issue and both predicted that annexation would lead to an unjustifiable war with Mexico. Van Buren, in his usual cautious and intricate language, conceded that if the people and Congress favored annexation, he would yield his own reservations, but this device did not satisfy his opponents among the southern Democrats.

Clay had no rivals for the Whig nomination, and so he was chosen by acclamation at the party's convention early in May. In their enthusiasm for Clay, the Whigs adopted no formal platform. By the time the Democratic National Convention met on 27 May, several southern delegations had withdrawn their support from Van Buren, citing his stand against annexation. It soon became apparent that although he could command a majority of the convention votes, he could not secure the necessary two-thirds. With a deadlock threatening, the convention managers turned to a "dark horse" who was acceptable to the Van Buren forces but who had previously declared himself in favor of immediate annexation—James K. Polk of Tennessee. Polk was nominated on the ninth ballot. News of this unlikely event was transmitted by telegraph over the line between Baltimore and Washington, which had been financed by a federal appropriation. In its closing hours, the convention adopted a platform that included a plank calling for the "re-occupation of Oregon and the re-annexation of Texas at the earliest practicable period." The expansionist issues brought forth by Tyler were now taken up by the Democratic party and would figure prominently in the ensuing campaign.

Tyler's political course reflected his anomalous position. In 1842, having been disowned by the Whigs, he had sought to create a base of support among moderate Whigs and conservative Democrats. When this strategy failed, he turned toward the Democrats, appointing several from that party to his cabinet, but these overtures were rebuffed. Finally he created his own party, built on a core of office-holders. Tyler's obedient partisans held a convention at the same time as the Democrats. A loosely organized affair, it dutifully nominated Tyler for president, neglecting even to select a vice presidential running mate or to frame a platform. With no prospect of success and with the Democrats committed to annexation, Tyler was soon in negotiation with Polk's emissaries, who were seeking his withdrawal from the contest. With assurances that his followers would be welcomed into the Democratic ranks, Tyler announced the end of his candidacy on 20 August and threw his meager support to Polk. He remained convinced thereafter that his action was responsible for Polk's narrow victory, which he saw as a vindication of his own policies.

How much actual influence the Texas issue had on the outcome of the election remains debatable. For the most part, voters held firm to their established party loyalties. Concerned about possible Whig defections in the South, Clay wrote two letters for publication to correspondents in Alabama in which he seemed to modify his opposition to annexation, but in another public letter in September, he insisted that his views on this controversial issue had not changed. His apparent equivocation may have injured him in the North. Polk remained silent throughout the campaign, except for one vague statement on the tariff. Clay lost New York by 5,106 votes, and the vote of that state gave Polk his electoral majority. In the nation as a whole, Clay ran only about 38,000 votes behind Polk and carried eleven of twenty-six states.

Despite the narrowness of the Democratic victory and the uncertainty of the effect of the annexation issue on the outcome, Tyler told Congress when it met in December 1844 that "a controlling majority of the people and a large majority of the states have declared in favor of immediate annexation." Accordingly, he recommended annexation by joint resolution, which would require only a majority vote in each house. Two weeks later he reported that Mexico had engaged in so many unjust and unfriendly acts against the United States as to justify a declaration of war, but he urged instead prompt action on the joint resolution. After intense controversy, a resolution was prepared that left to the president the choice between two courses of action: he could offer Texas prompt admission as a state with certain stated conditions attached, or he could negotiate with the Texas authorities the terms and conditions under which it might be admitted to the Union. In this equivocal form the joint resolution passed the Senate (twenty-seven to twenty-five) on 27 February 1845, with only two Whigs siding with the majority,

and gained approval by a substantial margin in the House in a vote that followed closely party lines. The resolution went to Tyler on 1 March 1845.

It had generally been anticipated that Tyler would leave action on the resolution to Polk, who was expected to exercise the second option. But Tyler was not to be deprived of his triumph. On 3 March he sent an agent to Texas offering statehood under the first option. When Polk came to office on 4 March, he did not recall Tyler's emissary. In due course, Congress formally admitted Texas as a state in January 1846.

Evaluation of Tyler

Contrary to accepted opinion, John Tyler was a strong president. He established the precedent that the vice president, on succeeding to the presidential office, should be president. He had firm ideas about public policy, and he was disposed to use the full authority of his office to gain his ends. Only Jackson exceeded him in the use of the veto. His boldness in seeking the annexation of Texas, whatever the motives or merits of his actions, was extraordinary. He was insistent on maintaining the independence of the executive branch against Whig efforts to make it subservient to Congress. Operating under the peculiar disadvantages of having gained the office by accident and of becoming a president without a party, he conducted his administration with considerable dignity and effectiveness.

His break with the Whigs was unfortunate both for him and for the party. On the two key issues involved—the bank and distribution—his course was not irrational. As a politician, Tyler believed in moderate policies. In his view, which was probably correct, the reestablishment of a national bank was too controversial a measure to be undertaken: its enactment would not end the controversy, for the Democrats remained solidly opposed, and when they returned to office, they might well destroy the bank. As for distribution, there was surely merit in his contention that the government should not be deprived of a source of revenue when it had large deficits. Significantly, neither the bank nor distribution was to be revived as a prominent issue in the future.

Tyler's deficiencies were as a political leader. He lacked Jackson's ability to engender popular support. His bank vetoes, unlike Jackson's, were devoid of demagogic appeal; he did not have Old Hickory's charisma. He failed utterly in his feeble efforts to supplant Clay as leader of the Whig party, and his attempt to form a new party was futile and even pathetic. Paradoxically, it was during his eccentric presidency that the second American party system achieved its greatest vigor. Instead of disintegrating under Tyler's potentially disruptive influence, the two major parties closed their respective ranks, sharpened their differences, and mobilized under their banners in 1844 as had never been done before and was not to be duplicated in the antebellum period.

Tyler departed from Washington as Polk was being inaugurated, with the conviction that he had served the best interests of the nation. He was a genial man, very much at ease in his social relationships, given to writing romantic poetry and performing on the violin. His first wife had died in September 1842, having borne him eight children. In June 1844, after a year of ardent courtship, Tyler married the vivacious Julia Gardiner, who was thirty years his junior. The devoted couple retired to Tyler's Virginia plantation, Sherwood Forest, and in time there were seven more Tyler children. Although he was treated like a pariah, the former president retained his keen interest in political affairs and was pleased to be received back into the ranks of the Virginia Democratic party in 1852. With the approach of the Civil War, he became an advocate of secession, and in June 1861 he was proud to be chosen a member of the provisional Congress of the Confederacy. In November he was the victor in a four-way contest for a seat in the Confederate House of Representatives. He died in Richmond on 18 January 1862. He was, in the end, more faithful to his lifelong principles and to his native state than to the Union over which he had presided.

BIBLIOGRAPHY

The best study, which also supplies a useful bibliography, is Norma Lois Peterson, *The Presidencies of William Henry Harrison and John Tyler* (Lawrence, Kans., 1989).

Freeman Cleaves, *Old Tippecanoe: William Henry Harrison and His Time* (New York, 1939; repr. 1990), is the standard biography. Harrison's election is ably treated in Robert G. Gunderson, *The Log-Cabin Campaign* (Lexington, Ky., 1957).

An admiring biography is Oliver Perry Chitwood, *John Tyler: Champion of the Old South* (New York,

1939). Robert Seager II, *And Tyler Too: A Biography of John and Julia Gardiner Tyler* (New York, 1963), is especially valuable for its depiction of Tyler's personal life. Henry A. Wise, *Seven Decades of the Union . . .: A Memoir of John Tyler* (Philadelphia, 1881), is a worshipful account by a contemporary. The best compendium of Tyler documents is Lyon Gardiner Tyler, *The Letters and Times of the Tylers*, 3 vols. (Richmond, Va., 1884–1896). Indispensable for Tyler's views on the issues of his administration is James D. Richardson, ed., *A Compilation of the Messages and Papers of the Presidents, 1789–1897*, vol. 4 (Washington, D.C., 1897).

William R. Brock, *Parties and Political Conscience: American Dilemmas, 1840–1850* (Millwood, N.Y., 1979), offers a provocative explanation for the failure of the Whigs under Tyler. Outdated but still useful is Oscar D. Lambert, *Presidential Politics in the United States, 1841–1844* (Durham, N.C., 1936). The Democratic opposition is best described in Charles G. Sellers, *James K. Polk, Jacksonian, 1795–1843* and *James K. Polk, Continentalist, 1843–1846* (Princeton, N.J., 1957, 1966). John Ashworth, *"Agrarians" and "Aristocrats": Party Political Ideology in the United States, 1837–1846* (London, 1983), attempts to define opposing party beliefs. A perceptive study by a political scientist is Robert J. Morgan, *A Whig Embattled: The Presidency Under John Tyler* (Lincoln, Nebr., 1954).

Merrill D. Peterson, *The Great Triumvirate: Webster, Clay, and Calhoun* (New York, 1987), is indispensable because of the large roles these giants played during Tyler's administration. Thomas B. Alexander, *Sectional Stress and Party Strength: A Study of Roll-Call Voting Patterns in the United States House of Representatives, 1836–1860* (Nashville, Tenn., 1967), provides analyses of alignments in Congress on key issues. New understandings of Webster's role in the Tyler administration are developed in Sydney Nathans, *Daniel Webster and Jacksonian Democracy* (Baltimore, 1973). George R. Poage, *Henry Clay and the Whig Party* (Chapel Hill, N.C., 1936), is not uncritical of Clay as an opponent of Tyler. Howard Jones, *To the Webster-Ashburton Treaty: A Study in Anglo-American Relations, 1783–1843* (Chapel Hill, N.C., 1977), gives due credit to Tyler for this diplomatic achievement. The best study of a complex problem is David M. Pletcher, *The Diplomacy of Annexation: Texas, Oregon, and the Mexican War* (Columbia, Mo., 1973). Tyler's expansionist policy is also the subject of Frederick Merk,

Fruits of Propaganda in the Tyler Administration (Cambridge, Mass., 1971). The economic problems of the period are examined by George Rogers Taylor, *The Transportation Revolution, 1815–1860* (New York, 1951). Tyler's support for exploratory expeditions is described in William H. Goetzmann, *New Lands, New Men: America and the Second Great Age of Discovery* (New York, 1986). The serious student will want to consult the relevant volumes of the papers of John C. Calhoun, Henry Clay, Andrew Jackson, James K. Polk, and Daniel Webster.

James K. Polk

David M. Pletcher

James K. Polk THE LIBRARY OF CONGRESS

B EYOND a doubt the one-term president who left behind him the greatest record of accomplishment was James Knox Polk. In the area of domestic legislation his administration lowered the prevailing high tariff and established a moderate policy that lasted fifteen years, until the Civil War. It reestablished the independent treasury (sometimes called subtreasury), a system of handling revenues that made the government custodian over its own funds instead of scattering them among private banks, and thereby restored some order to a fiscal system still disorganized from Andrew Jackson's Bank War of the 1830s. It also founded the United States Naval Academy at Annapolis.

But Polk's record of accomplishment depends mostly on his achievements in foreign affairs. His administration completed the annexation of Texas, begun by John Tyler. Under his personal, day-by-day direction, his administration brought the United States into, and out of, a major diplomatic crisis with Britain and a war with Mexico in which the United States did not lose a single major battle. Following his instructions, American diplomats negotiated treaties that added to the national domain the western third of its continental territory—California, Oregon, and the Southwest, a vast area nearly as large as all the nations of Free Europe after World War II. In the process, he restated and partly redefined the Monroe Doctrine. Further, one of Polk's diplomats negotiated a treaty with Colombia (then called New Granada) that was to serve Theodore Roosevelt nearly sixty years later as the legal basis for assisting in the independence of Panama, which led directly to the construction of the Panama Canal. Overall, it would not be too much to say that Polk's administration raised the United States to the level of a second-class power and laid part of the foundation for its later establishment as a great power.

Historians have been slow to recognize Polk's importance. Since he was a narrowly partisan Democrat, it is not surprising that early studies of his administration were mostly party tracts. By the end of the nineteenth century, Henry Clay, John C. Calhoun, and Daniel Webster loomed so far over him that J. T. Morse, Jr., and Ellis P. Oberholtzer failed to include him in two biographical series about American statesmen. The executive leadership of Theodore Roosevelt and Woodrow Wilson made Polk's tribulations and achievements seem more relevant than at any time since 1848, and the appearance in 1922 of a major biography by Eugene Irving McCormac established Polk's reputation. A few twentieth-century historians dismissed him as "Polk the Mediocre," but none could ignore him, and in mid-century the succession of strong presidents forced a historical reevaluation in which Polk was recognized as the major link in the chain of executive dominance between Andrew Jackson and Abraham Lincoln. In the early 1960s a poll of historians ranked Polk eighth in importance among presidents—just below Theodore Roosevelt and above Harry S. Truman. Reaction against the "imperial presidency" may have eroded some of his popularity.

Polk's long obscurity was due partly to the nature of his background and rise to power and partly to his personality and conduct of the presidency. Born in Mecklenburg County, North Carolina, on 2 November 1795, he grew up in central Tennessee. As a boy he was sickly (although he had strength enough to survive, at seventeen, a gallstone operation without modern anesthesia or antisepsis), and as a man he was often ill with fever or diarrhea. With characteristic single-mindedness, he prepared himself for the law, first at the University of North Carolina and then in the law office of the veteran Tennessee politician Felix Grundy. Deciding on a career of public office, Polk made his way upward through the rough, semifrontier politics of Tennessee. In 1825 he progressed from the state legislature

to the United States House of Representatives. By then he had attracted Andrew Jackson's attention and patronage, as well as Old Hickory's many enemies.

For most of the next two decades, Polk perfected his skills in the thick of partisan national politics, being at first a Jeffersonian republican but soon becoming a Jacksonian democrat. He fought with bitter enmity against John Quincy Adams' administration and then against the whole Whig party, in which he could see no redeeming features. (Although Polk later received Henry Clay at the White House with warm cordiality, Adams never forgave or forgot his hostility.) By 1833, Jackson so appreciated Polk's loyalty and ability that he put him in charge of the Bank War in the House and saw to it that he was raised to the chairmanship of the Ways and Means Committee. Two years later Polk won the speakership after an unusually bitter fight with fellow Tennessean John Bell. The residual animosity from the Bank War and this fight, together with the long running battle over the "gag rule" and the frustrations of Martin Van Buren's election and early presidency, made Polk's four-year tenure as Speaker perhaps the noisiest and most vituperative so far in American experience. Polk received the attacks with calm dignity, parried them with an acute command of parliamentary procedure, and remembered them for later reference.

Retiring from the House to become governor of Tennessee (1839), Polk hoped for the nomination for the vice presidency in the Democratic convention of 1840. He failed in this, and after his defeat for reelection as governor the following year, his career in national politics seemed at an end. Undaunted and with Jackson's continued support, he organized a canny group of supporters to make another effort for the vice presidential nomination at the party convention of 1844, at which Van Buren's candidacy for reelection seemed a foregone conclusion. Unfortunately for Van Buren, he chose the wrong side of the Texas question, newly emerged as a burning issue, and after Polk had come out resoundingly for annexation of both Texas and Oregon, his clique was able to obtain his nomination for the presidency by exploiting the convention's two-thirds rule, the resulting deadlock, and Jackson's influence.

The Whigs' jeer "Who is James K. Polk?" has left a wide impression that Polk was the first dark-horse presidential candidate in American history. This is misleading, for Polk's stormy years as Speaker of the House had made him well known within the party.

He was, to be sure, a compromise candidate, and in order to preserve unity, he promised that, if elected, he would serve only one term. The campaign especially featured the expansionist and tariff issues; but since Clay, the Whig candidate, waffled on Texas (whose annexation he really wished to postpone) and Polk waffled on the tariff (which he really intended to reform downward), it is impossible to attribute the result to any issue. Early in the summer Clay seemed to be running ahead, but Polk finally won, with the electoral vote 170 to 105. Votes in all sections of the country were divided; Polk even carried Maine and New Hampshire but lost Tennessee and North Carolina. It has been generally assumed that Clay's hedging on Texas allowed the minority, antislavery Liberty party to absorb enough of his strength to throw New York's 35 electoral votes to Polk, but some have argued that a more forthright stand on Texas would have lost Clay four of the states he won (with 35 electoral votes) by narrow margins.

Administration

No man could have lived through such a nomination and election without being either steeled or broken, and Polk's whole political life produced in him a determination to curb his rebellious party and be absolute master of his administration. At his inauguration he was only forty-nine (making him the youngest president until that time), a short, thin, angular man whose long, graying hair was brushed back from a habitually sad, unsmiling face with high cheekbones and fixed jaw. Everyone remembered his deep-set piercing eyes. The personality beneath this drab exterior was introverted, intense, narrow, and almost humorless, although alert and not without compassion. His mind was quick and shrewd, and his memory for names, faces, and records penetrating and well organized. But he lacked charisma; he might impress doubters with his determination, but he warmed few hearts and stirred few souls.

As a good Jacksonian, Polk brought to the White House a conviction that the president, the only true representative of national interests, must dominate the government and be the very symbol of the common man. More than any other Jacksonian, Polk understood and accepted the hard, grinding work that this responsibility entailed and almost literally drove himself to an early grave. American politicians commonly took long vacations from the summer heat and the year-round strains of the capital, but for one period of thirteen months Polk never traveled more than three or four miles from Washington. He mastered the routine and details of every executive department, delegated power with great reluctance, and called for frequent and full accountings.

While Polk's contemporaries and biographers have given him full credit for determination and scrupulous honesty in personal affairs, they have also recognized a certain indirection or deviousness in his political methods. Allan Nevins has called him "cute" in the Yankee sense, but "by his lights . . . eminently truthful and upright." Literally truthful he may have been, but he kept his own counsel, let others guess (often wrongly) at his intentions, and ignored or privately resented the later recriminations. From his earliest days in the House, Polk was a "good hater." He thought opposition among Whigs natural, if misguided, and came to respect a few whom he recognized as honorable men; but opposition from fellow Democrats, especially John C. Calhoun's faction, was to him simple treason, motivated by selfish ambition, and this he rarely forgave. Beginning in August 1845, he kept a diary of his discussions and reactions. One cannot be sure that he was completely frank, even with himself, but Polk's record brings the historian closer to the arcanum of presidential policy-making than is his usual lot.

Polk's handling of his cabinet reflected the combination of decision and caution that lay at the heart of his character. He chose a moderately able group of men, half of them from Congress and well balanced geographically. Like Polk, Secretary of State James Buchanan came from a Presbyterian farmer's family and rough-and-tumble politics in a state (Pennsylvania) that had contributed heavily to Polk's election. Ambitious, persistent, and calculating like his master, Buchanan was also timid and irresolute (Polk once said that he "sometimes acts like an old maid"). Secretary of the Treasury Robert J. Walker, an excitable, frail little man who was often ill, supported Polk's expansionist and low-tariff policies enthusiastically, reorganized the Treasury Department and the customs service, and implemented the new subtreasury system. Secretary of War William L. Marcy, though hampered by Congress, administered a wartime army with reasonable efficiency. Secretary of the Navy George Bancroft (later minister to Britain) carried through the foundation of the United States Naval Academy on the executive's initiative after Congress had delayed action for years. Other cabinet members—John Y. Mason (attorney general, then navy), Cave Johnson (postmaster general), and Nathan Clifford (attorney general)—supplied Polk with personal friendship (especially Mason and Johnson), party connections, and steady, competent service.

Polk managed to get full advantage from the advice of this experienced cabinet while keeping it under complete control. Holding cabinet meetings twice a week, he opened all subjects to discussion, often keeping his own opinions secret until he was ready to act. Members were encouraged to call frequently at the White House to present departmental problems, and Buchanan, who had the most complex duties of all, made almost daily visits. (Characteristically, being a strong party man, he caused more trouble for Polk over patronage than over foreign policy and at one point agonized for weeks over whether to resign and join the Supreme Court.) When Polk asked Buchanan, like other cabinet members, to forswear presidential ambitions while in the cabinet, he carefully hedged his reply. Polk often doubted his loyalty but never quite reached the point of asking him to resign. While Polk was a demanding master, he was as considerate to his cabinet members as his chilly, unbending nature allowed, and they constituted a more genuine "official family" (as he sometimes called them) than in most other administrations.

In his handling of Congress, Polk was the first president consistently to mount campaigns for administrative measures, and he exercised a degree of control unique in the period between Jackson and Lincoln, when Congress usually dominated the executive. Paradoxically, in some important matters, such as the Oregon question, Polk ostentatiously sought coordinate congressional action so as to share the blame in case of an unpopular decision. (In such cases, he was careful to avoid creating the precedent that the executive must necessarily consult Congress before acting.) Such flexible control, even though it sometimes faltered, was a high achievement, for the Democrats had only a six-vote margin in the Senate from 1845 to 1847, and in the congressional elections of 1846 they lost control of the House of Representatives; furthermore, in both houses the party was seriously divided by regional and other factions.

Polk used a variety of expedients and methods to enforce his will on Congress. He maintained constant touch with both the leadership and the rank and file by opening the White House to them daily and frequently summoning them for conferences, producing a steady stream of legislators up and down Pennsylvania Avenue. He used his cabinet members as go-betweens, especially Cave Johnson, Buchanan, and Walker, and before an important vote several of them might be seen in the Capitol, buttonholing their friends. (At the same time, Polk gravely deplored the developing practice of congressional lobbying by private interests.) Polk put pressure on doubtful Democrats with urgent editorials in the party newspaper, the *Union*, setting forth his arguments. He gave close and unremitting attention to patronage, although no record has been found of specific deals for desired votes.

As with many other presidents, Polk's influence over Congress was most effective early in his term of office. In his first major confrontation, over the Oregon question, Polk could not obtain what he sought, a simple resolution advising him to notify Britain of the abrogation of the 1827 convention on the joint occupancy of Oregon, and he had to be satisfied with a mildly qualified recommendation after a three-month debate that left permanent scars on the party. During the spring and summer of 1846 he enjoyed a string of victories: quick approval of a new Oregon treaty; a declaration of war against Mexico; a new, lowered tariff; and the subtreasury act. The declaration of war was a tour de force for which administration leaders unmercifully pressed a coalition of Whigs and pacifist Democrats with imputations of unpatriotic slackness, which rankled throughout the war. In the case of the tariff, Polk won the narrowest possible victory, thanks to the political and financial blandishments of Secretary Walker; the political expertise of the chairman of the House Ways and Means Committee, James J. McKay; and a complicated series of compromises and votes in which presidential pressure induced more than one high-tariff politician to abandon his principles and support the bill.

During the last half of Polk's term the increasing unpopularity of the Mexican War, the Democratic loss of the House, and the incubus of the slavery question often frustrated his measures. He had trouble obtaining new regiments for the army, and Congress would not authorize the rank of lieutenant general, to which he wished to appoint Senator Thomas H. Benton, a tyro soldier but a loyal Democrat, and thereby put him in command over the skilled but Whiggish Winfield Scott. Worse still, when Polk requested a special fund to hold in reserve for peace negotiations, the House attached to the bill the Wilmot Proviso, which prohibited slavery in any territory to be acquired from Mexico. The Senate rejected this inflammatory proposal, which Polk called "mischievous & foolish," but the proviso haunted him for the rest of his administration, poisoning the atmosphere and obstructing much useful legislation. At the end of his term he managed to obtain a law establishing government in the newly acquired Oregon Territory without reference to slavery (in effect prohibiting it, since Oregon lay well to the north of the Missouri Compromise line); but because his skills were inadequate to put together a compromise for California and New Mexico, he had to leave this problem to his successor.

In his dealings with Congress, the Democratic party, and the American people at large, Polk exploited assiduously both press and patronage with moderate, if not unvarying, success. When he became president, he had long appreciated the power of the press, and not trusting the loyalty of Jackson's old newspaper, the *Globe*, he transferred government business to a new Washington organ, the *Union*. As editor he chose the venerable Thomas ("Father") Ritchie of Virginia, an experienced but old-fashioned journalist who did not have Polk's ruthlessness and sense of timing but leaked confidences in his editorials and let himself be diverted into side issues. The president sometimes intervened to write his own editorials.

Polk also fully realized the value of patronage and surrounded himself with spoils politicians (indeed, Secretary Marcy practically invented the term *spoils system*), but in a factionalized party Polk often made as many enemies as friends with his appointments. Also he soon came to loathe the pressure of office seekers, and although he wrote self-righteously in his diary that he felt obliged to give up hours each day interviewing them (they were citizens, after all), he complained about them on an average of at least once a week. Far more pleasurable to him was the extensive social life he fostered in the White House with the aid of his charming and popular wife, the former Sarah Childress, but even here Polk's stiffness and lack of charisma partly defeated his purpose.

Since Polk made his most notable accomplishments in foreign relations and war, careful examination of his skills and methods in these areas is necessary. He brought no special knowledge or talent to the conduct of foreign relations; indeed, he felt little but contempt for diplomatic protocol. As a nationalist from mid-America, he possessed a strong xenophobia unmitigated by any sophisticated, cosmopolitan appreciation of European culture or institutions. If he had any model for foreign relations, it was that of the brusque, high-handed Jackson. During the Oregon controversy, he formulated what would be called today a recommendation for "eyeball" diplomacy: "I remarked . . . that the only way to treat John Bull was to look him straight in the eye; . . . that if Congress faultered [sic] or hesitated in their course, John Bull would immediately become arrogant and more grasping in his demands." Polk did not bother to make a corresponding recommendation for Mexico, his other adversary, but his writings show that he held both government and people in contempt as hardly worthy of nationality. His feelings toward Britain and Mexico could produce only a policy of bluntness and bluff. Take a bold stand, negotiate from apparent strength, assume what you cannot prove, make no concessions that can be interpreted as weakness, and keep your opponent off balance. Ideas of mutual interest and compromise formed little part of his thinking.

In several ways Polk's handling of the armed forces established precedents for some of his successors. By stationing troops in disputed territory on the Mexican border, he was able—whether intentionally or not—to provoke Mexico into war without prior recourse to Congress or the democratic process. In fighting the war Polk went beyond Madison (in the War of 1812) in the number of detailed orders he issued to his generals and the frequency of reports he expected from them, thereby reasserting the traditional American assumption of civilian control over the military. His lack of experience in military affairs hampered him in personal direction of the war somewhat more than his unfamiliarity with the technicalities of diplomacy. A greater obstacle was his remoteness from the fighting fronts, a remoteness that grew as his armies advanced into Mexico. He might make major strategic decisions in Washington, such as that to send a separate army into central Mexico, but to his great chagrin, he had to entrust most other planning to two Whig generals, Zachary Taylor and Winfield Scott.

Polk was sure that his two generals were trying to undermine his administration and succeed him as president. After unwillingly dispatching Scott to Veracruz, he disloyally tried to get Benton promoted over his head. Congress rescued Polk from this blunder and allowed Scott to complete his career as the most distinguished American soldier between the Revolution and the Civil War. Polk functioned more effectively in other areas than strategic planning, working with Marcy to overhaul an underdeveloped, second-rate army and solve staggering problems of long-distance supply and administration.

Foreign Policy

The best way to understand Polk's accomplishments in diplomacy and war is to study their development, step by step. On taking office, he inherited two major problems of foreign policy, both concerning American territorial expansion. At Tyler's urging, Congress had just passed a joint resolution authorizing annexation of the independent Republic of Texas. Most Texans wanted this, but their government hesitated. Meanwhile, agents of Britain and France urged Texas to remain independent, in order to offset the United States and create a balance of power in North America. Mexico, which still claimed sovereignty over Texas, threatened the United States with war if it went through with annexation and broke relations as soon as Congress passed the joint resolution.

An older controversy with Britain had been smoldering for years on the northwestern frontier. Both Britain and the United States claimed Oregon, a region west of the Rockies stretching from the northern boundary of California to the Alaska panhandle (54°40') and including modern Oregon, Washington, and British Columbia. The conventions of 1818 and 1827 had established joint occupancy of this area, with provision for termination by either party after a year's notice. The Hudson's Bay Company dominated most of Oregon, but along the Columbia River, where fur trapping had greatly declined, American immigrants were establishing a chain of farming settlements, the vanguard of a great frontier movement. Tyler's secretary of state, John C. Calhoun, had opened exploratory negotiations over Oregon, but seeing the progress of American migration, he favored what he called "masterly inactivity" and soon let the negotiations lapse. Meanwhile, the British foreign secretary, the earl of Aberdeen, had come to the conclusion that the best solution to the question would be a compromise boundary along the forty-ninth parallel, reserving all of Vancouver Island to Britain, but he had not convinced the rest of the British cabinet, nor did he know how to suggest the compromise to the United States without weakening Britain's negotiating position.

The American desire for Upper California was also certain to affect Polk's foreign relations. California was undeniably Mexican territory, but distance and Mexico's political instability had allowed the province to drift away from Mexican control. The Californians were a mixture of Mexicans, Indians, Europeans, and Americans. New England traders had established firm economic connections between California's Pacific ports and the east coast of the United States. American explorers had traversed the interior, and early in the 1840s a few of the American emigrants to Oregon began to stray off into central California to take up farming or ranching. By 1845 the Mexican hold on California had virtually disappeared, and many Americans were wondering whether the British would intervene there as they were trying to do in Texas.

When Polk wrote his inaugural address, draft by draft, consulting many advisers as was his custom, he determined to deal explicitly with Texas and Oregon, leaving California for later disposition. He devoted considerable space to Texas, taking annexation for granted and warning foreign powers not to interfere in this purely American problem. He might have passed over Oregon with the remark that delicate negotiations were still pending, but the Democratic platform of 1844 had mentioned the "clear and unquestionable" American title to the whole territory, and this claim had aroused much enthusiasm in the Middle West during the campaign. Polk quoted this categorical phrase in his address without explaining his reference and went on to indicate that the United States government would protect the American emigrants to Oregon with laws and "the benefits of our republican institutions," looking toward annexation in the near future. Undoubtedly he hoped to satisfy the westerners without unduly arousing the British, but in the long run he was disappointed on both counts.

After his inauguration, the new president set out to complete the annexation of Texas. Thinking to secure Mexican acquiescence, he sent an unofficial diplomatic agent to reopen formal relations, hinting at a possible indemnity for Texas. He also sent agents to Texas to join the American chargé d'affaires, Andrew Jackson Donelson (Jackson's nephew and Polk's personal friend), in urging the Texas government to accept the terms of the joint resolution. British and French diplomatic agents were also working for reconciliation between Texas and Mexico. The British agent even persuaded the Mexican government to recognize Texan independence as an inducement to refuse annexation, but he was too late.

By May, Texas public opinion was overwhelmingly annexationist, and in the following months the Texas Congress accepted the joint resolution, and a special constitutional convention drew up a new state constitution for membership in the Union.

Polk's success in Texas drew the United States closer to war with Mexico. On rather dubious grounds Texas claimed the Rio Grande as its boundary with Mexico, and without examining this claim carefully, Polk committed himself to its support. Mexican leaders denounced both the annexation and the boundary claim and threatened to attack the Texas frontier. Having promised to protect the Texans as soon as they accepted annexation, Polk dispatched a naval squadron along the Gulf coast and moved several thousand troops under Zachary Taylor from the Louisiana border to Corpus Christi on the Nueces River, at the northern edge of the disputed boundary zone, with permission to move south if Taylor thought best—a typical Polkian move to share responsibility but a reasonable one, considering the slowness of communications. At the same time, Polk sent private orders to Commodore John D. Sloat, commander of the Pacific squadron, that in case of war, Sloat should seize the principal ports of California.

Some historians believe that at this point Polk was consciously plotting war with Mexico. They rely on the private papers of Commodore Robert F. Stockton, the commander of the squadron protecting the Texas coast and an ultraexpansionist with powerful friends in the government. From certain inconclusive letters of his, it appears that he considered a preventive seizure of Mexican territory south of the Rio Grande. Also, according to President Anson Jones of Texas, Stockton proposed to him that the two of them provoke a war. Without written orders from Polk or some other equally clear evidence, the "plot thesis" rests on surmise. Instructions from Bancroft to Stockton and from Buchanan to Donelson were explicitly defensive, and Polk's correspondence and other factors suggest that at this time he neither desired nor expected war with Mexico.

Perhaps the best reason why Polk should have wanted to keep peace on the border was that Anglo-American relations had taken a turn for the worse during April and May because of the blunt passage on Oregon in his inaugural address. British observers failed to notice that the president had carefully respected the sanctity of treaties and that he was only following the example of the British government and the Hudson's Bay Company in proposing to extend legal protection to American settlers. Instead, the British press focused on Polk's assertion of the "clear and unquestionable" American title and hurled insults and threats at the overbearing Americans. When questions arose in Parliament, the prime minister, Sir Robert Peel, declared that Britain also had clear and unquestionable rights in Oregon. Naturally the American press seized all these statements and returned them with interest.

Behind the scenes the British government began unobtrusively to check Canadian fortifications—as well as Channel defenses, in case France supported the Americans. At the same time, Aberdeen encouraged a few moderates to disparage the value of Oregon in the press and sent instructions to the British minister at Washington, Richard Pakenham, to seek American terms or suggest arbitration of the Oregon question. Privately he encouraged Pakenham to draw from the Americans, if possible, an offer of the forty-ninth parallel and Vancouver Island, with the right to navigate the Columbia River, so that he might propose a compromise to the cabinet in London. Buchanan discouraged Pakenham's talk of arbitration but delayed further reply for several weeks.

At this point both parties blundered. When Buchanan gave Pakenham a formal reply on 12 July he indeed proposed the forty-ninth parallel, conceding to Britain all of Vancouver Island. Even though he made no reference to navigation of the Columbia River, these terms provided an adequate basis for negotiations. Unfortunately (and certainly on Polk's instructions) Buchanan set forth the ramshackle American claim to the whole area up to 54°40' in a manner that made the compromise offer seem an American condescension. Outraged, Pakenham replied with an equally strong statement of the British claim and, carried away by his own rhetoric, rejected Buchanan's offer out of hand instead of referring it to London, as he should have done. Apparently Polk then jumped to the conclusion that the wily British had tricked him into showing his cards without ever intending to compromise. After brooding for several weeks, at the end of August he had Buchanan withdraw the offer altogether and intimated that if the British wished to negotiate, they must assume the initiative with an offer of their own.

Thus, in the first six months of his administration, Polk had widened the breach with Mexico and Britain and limited his freedom of action in both cases. With a little more understanding of diplomacy, he might have managed to put Britain on the defensive without interrupting communications, by giving Aberdeen a chance to explain and excuse his minister's mistake. The situation called for Talleyrand's probing pen; instead, Polk had used an eraser. Since neither party would reopen negotiations for fear of losing face and bargaining leverage, the impasse over Oregon continued through the rest of 1845. When western expansionists learned of Polk's stand, they assumed that he would now carry out the Democratic party plank of pushing the boundary up to 54°40'. As he soon learned, such aroused expectations made any sort of compromise all the more difficult.

Still, the Mexican issue, at least, did not seem beyond peaceful settlement, for Polk's special agent to Mexico City and the American consul there reported throughout the summer that despite public fury at the American annexation of Texas, the government hesitated to start hostilities because of lack of funds and uncertainty about the loyalty of the army. Both thought that the government would receive a special American commissioner to discuss the Texas question (and presumably offer Mexico a disguised indemnity for its loss). It is not clear whether Polk understood the limited nature of the Mexican concession, but, true to his aggressive instincts, he determined to appoint a full minister plenipotentiary; ignore the Texas question, which he regarded as settled; and try to persuade Mexico to sell California. For this mission he chose John Slidell of Louisiana, a rising young politician with some polish and knowledge of Spanish but no previous association with Mexican affairs.

Before Slidell departed from New Orleans in late November 1845, news from the Pacific coast suggested that the California question might require more direct action. In mid-October, Buchanan received an alarming dispatch from Thomas O. Larkin, an American merchant-consul at Monterey. Larkin warned that Britain was apparently preparing to dominate California, for a new British vice-consulate had just been established at Monterey, probably to operate in conjunction with the Hudson's Bay Company; furthermore, there were rumors that Mexico was sending out troops, paid for by British money, to reassert authority. Larkin's report, three months old, was exaggerated or downright wrong, for the Hudson's Bay Company had lost interest in California trapping, the Mexican reinforcement expedition had been given up, and the British government, though deploring American influence there, was not disposed to take

action. Polk and Buchanan, of course, had no way of knowing this.

The alarmed president determined to reinforce the Slidell mission with preventive measures in California. He drew up instructions for Sloat, repeating with emphasis that he should seize the principal Mexican ports in case of war. Polk also instructed Larkin to propagandize among the Californians for union with the United States and resistance to a British protectorate. These instructions Polk sent out with Commodore Stockton in the frigate *Congress*, but since that ship would need several months for the long voyage around Cape Horn, Polk selected a young marine lieutenant, Archibald H. Gillespie—apparently for no other reason than that he spoke Spanish. Polk gave Gillespie duplicates of the orders to Sloat and Larkin and told him to memorize the latter. Gillespie was to follow an overland route to California through central Mexico disguised as a merchant. At this point, Senator Thomas Hart Benton suggested that Gillespie should also carry coded orders and private letters to Benton's son-in-law, the army explorer Lieutenant John Charles Frémont, then conducting a reconnaissance in eastern California. Historians have long argued as to just what was in these orders, but unless their text is found (which now seems unlikely), no one can say definitively whether Frémont's later actions were authorized.

While Polk stood his ground on Oregon and California, he was also composing his first annual message to Congress, one of the most important documents of his whole career. In that message he said nothing of his hopes and plans for California but described the measures he had taken to protect Texas against Mexican aggression, outlined other grievances against Mexico, and characterized the Slidell mission as an effort to collect justifiable claims. Concerning Oregon, he summarized Tyler's negotiations and blamed Britain for their rupture. He called on Congress to provide an armed guard and land grants for emigrants to Oregon. First, however, in order to comply with treaty requirements, he recommended that Congress take steps to give the prescribed year's notice to terminate joint occupation.

After his discussion of Oregon, Polk reaffirmed "the principle avowed by Mr. Monroe"—the first significant presidential reference to the Monroe Doctrine since its original declaration in 1823. This passage has an interesting history. The president included something like it in an early draft of his inaugural address but soon deleted it. During the summer he was much irritated to read a statement by the French prime minister, François Guizot, that France must play an active role in North American affairs in order to maintain "l'équilibre des forces," which the American press translated as "the balance of power," a term embodying to Americans all the decadent, deceitful ways of monarchical Europe. After consulting Senator Benton and getting trial drafts from Buchanan and Bancroft, Polk drew up a statement.

In applying the Monroe Doctrine to Guizot's remarks, Polk was broadening it to include European political intrigue, as well as military action, in the New World, but at the same time, he implied a limitation by suggesting that the nature of the United States action under the doctrine might depend on the circumstances—a hint that Washington would be most concerned about violations near at hand. Guizot had been referring to Texas, for France had little interest in California and none in Oregon, but Polk intended his declaration to reinforce his analysis of the Oregon question and probably also to warn Britain off California.

Polk's annual message was an integral part of his aggressive strategy against Mexico and Britain. By justifying his policies, he sought to demonstrate that he was trying to preserve the peace, whatever the adversaries might do in the future. In the case of Oregon, he called on Congress for prompt, decisive action that would show government and country to be united behind him. Britain, he hoped, would then have to break the impasse at a disadvantage and offer new terms, which he could treat as he chose. What he really accomplished was to limit his actions further by revealing too much of his ambitions to the Mexicans and by making Congress his partner in determining policy toward Britain.

Under the political circumstances of the day it was unrealistic to expect prompt, decisive action from Congress. After the bitterly fought election of 1844, a Whig minority sought revenge and recovery of power. During the last phases of the Texas question, expansionism had become entangled with the antislavery cause; and the resulting confusion of personal ambitions, partisan loyalties, and ideological convictions made it impossible to predict anyone's actions. Rebellious factions threatened to split the Democratic party, especially a group of western expansionists—who now spread a newly coined slogan, "Fifty-four Forty or Fight!"—and a southern bloc led by Calhoun, who had put his whole heart into the campaign for Texas but now favored delay and compromise in Oregon.

The debate dragged on from December 1845 until late April 1846. As everyone realized, abrogation of the joint-occupation agreement would remove the only legal safeguard against war over some trivial local incident in Oregon. Polk wanted a simple, noncommittal statement advising the president to give notice of abrogation; western Democrats, especially in the Senate, wanted to add a shout of rude defiance that would effectively prevent any diplomatic response from Britain; and moderates at first opposed any notice at all. By February, Whigs and antiwar Democrats in the House of Representatives managed to pass a mildly worded resolution of notice that virtually invited Britain to resume negotiations but shifted full responsibility for them to the president. In April, after weeks of thunderous debate that stirred the country to its depths, the Senate finally accepted the House resolution, as Calhoun and his bloc recognized that some sort of notice was necessary. The innocuous wording infuriated western extremists, who foresaw a compromise settlement and suspected (probably with reason) that Polk had encouraged the moderates in the last weeks of the debate rather than have the Senate adjourn without acting.

As long as Congress wrangled, Polk could make no progress in negotiations with Britain during the winter of 1845–1846. Aberdeen was well aware of conciliatory sentiment in the United States through editorials and correspondence of eastern moderates, but he probably underestimated the force of western expansionism pressing on Polk. At first he hoped that Polk might change his mind and offer terms or agree to arbitration, but eventually he reconciled himself to waiting until Congress passed a resolution that would enable Britain to reopen negotiations without loss of face. Meanwhile, he dropped hints that Britain might send naval reinforcements to Canada if pressed too hard. (These hints undoubtedly helped induce Polk to favor compromise in the Senate.) Anglo-American diplomatic communications during the impasse were admirably maintained by the two ministers, Louis McLane in London and Richard Pakenham in Washington, who made as much sense as anyone could out of the complex situation.

At the same time, American relations with Mexico were also worsening. In early December, Slidell arrived in Mexico City, where he found nationalists livid at the idea of selling more territory and a moderate government clinging feebly to power. The foreign minister, unhappy at Slidell's inopportune arrival, refused to receive him, on the grounds that his credentials were those of a full minister plenipotentiary rather than a temporary commissioner. (This distinction was not mere desperate hairsplitting, as Polk thought, for if Mexico agreed to renew formal relations before negotiating, it would have little prospect of obtaining an indemnity or other concession in return for the loss of Texas.) At the end of the month, the nationalists staged a successful revolution and placed a conservative army leader, General Mariano Paredes y Arrillaga, in the presidential chair.

Since Paredes hoped for an Anglo-American war over Oregon, he too refused to receive Slidell. Undismayed at this setback, Polk advanced his position and took another strong stand. He ordered Taylor at Corpus Christi to move his forces across the disputed zone and occupy the north bank of the Rio Grande, avoiding any offensive action against the Mexicans. At the end of January he wrote to Slidell that if Paredes would not see him, "nothing can remain but to take the redress of the injuries to our citizens and the insults to our Government into our own hands."

Some historians have interpreted the strong language to mean that Polk never expected Slidell to succeed but intended the mission merely as an excuse for military attack. At the same time, Polk wrote to his brother that Paredes had probably exaggerated his anti-Americanism in order to gain power and that the order to Taylor was merely "a precautionary measure." Given the uncertain state of the Oregon debate at this time, it is reasonable to suppose that Polk hoped Slidell would sign a treaty but was prepared to increase the pressure if he did not. Nevertheless, his action in risking a Mexican attack might be criticized as compromising the powers of Congress.

During March and April 1846, Polk's relations with both Britain and Mexico reached a turning point. In Texas, Taylor led his army to the bank of the Rio Grande, where the soldiers built a fort within cannon shot of the Mexican border city Matamoros. In Mexico City, Slidell, following instructions, sent a final request for reception, received another refusal, and prepared to leave for home. In London the British government awaited action in Congress on the Oregon question, and in Washington the congressional debate was splitting the Democratic party and threatening Polk's whole legislative program. At the beginning of May, Polk was driven to the expedient of telling the Speaker of the House that if Congress tried to adjourn prematurely, he would forbid the action and force a showdown.

Hitherto, Polk had regarded war with Mexico as possible but unlikely. At some time during April 1846 he seems to have concluded that a short, limited conflict on the Rio Grande might be the best way to reunite his party, impress Britain, and bring Mexico to terms. Learning of Slidell's final rejection, he went over the whole matter with the cabinet, which agreed that he should send a message to Congress recommending that the United States take matters into its own hands. Polk kept delaying action, first waiting for the end of the Oregon debate, then for Slidell's return to Washington, and finally for some sort of Mexican attack that would arouse congressional patriotism.

The crisis came during the weekend beginning 8 May. On Friday morning Slidell arrived in Washington. After talking with him, Polk decided to make his appeal to Congress, but on Saturday morning he and the cabinet decided to wait a few days longer, hoping for further news from the Rio Grande. Four hours later, the adjutant general called at the White House with a dispatch in which Taylor reported that Mexican troops had ambushed one of his scouting parties north of the river, killing or capturing most of its members. Taylor remarked laconically, "Hostilities may now be considered as commenced." Polk agreed and spent most of Sunday composing a war message, which he sent to Congress next day. In this he discoursed on the "fair and equitable" principles the United States had displayed toward Mexico, recited American grievances, and justified Taylor's presence on the Rio Grande. Declaring that Mexico had "shed American blood upon the American soil," he called on Congress to ratify the fact that "war exists . . . by the act of Mexico herself."

Congress received this call to arms with mixed feelings. Nearly everyone recognized the danger to Taylor's men and favored voting reinforcements and supplies, but the Whigs and Calhoun's bloc of Democrats opposed a formal declaration of war or any statement blaming hostilities on Mexico until they could investigate the circumstances leading to bloodshed. Polk's supporters outmaneuvered them at every point, while the president himself pressured Benton, a key figure, to swallow his doubts. The war bill was passed by an impressive margin, but Whigs voted for it unwillingly, lest their party suffer the stigma of disloyalty and go to pieces as the Federalist party had done during the War of 1812.

Polk's War Leadership

For several months Polk's plans succeeded in all theaters of action. On the Rio Grande, Taylor put his troops out of danger by defeating a larger Mexican army in two battles, Palo Alto (8 May) and Resaca de la Palma (9 May). Then he occupied Matamoros and, after receiving reinforcements, moved slowly into northeastern Mexico. At the same time, the Americans were carrying through the occupation of California. When Gillespie arrived with instructions, Larkin began quietly to propagandize among the inhabitants for annexation, but Frémont in the interior determined on more drastic action and assumed the leadership of an independence movement among American settlers in the Sacramento area, to found the so-called Bear Flag Republic. At this point Commodore Sloat of the Pacific squadron received news that war had broken out. Moving his ships to Monterey, he occupied the whole bay area. A little later Stockton and the *Congress* arrived; Polk sent troops overland; and the combined American forces, regular and irregular, completed the occupation. British naval forces off the coast observed the American actions with impotent chagrin, for they could not take counteraction without orders from London, which were never sent.

Meanwhile, the United States and Britain had solved the Oregon problem. By early May the conciliatory wording of the congressional resolution on Oregon made it possible for Aberdeen to renew negotiations. First, the foreign secretary argued the British cabinet into approving an offer of compromise terms; then, he proposed to McLane a treaty dividing the disputed territory at the forty-ninth parallel, with Vancouver Island reserved to Britain and navigation rights on the Columbia River to the Hudson's Bay Company. Polk balked at the navigation rights but agreed to submit the whole matter to the Senate. Buchanan and Pakenham quickly drew up a treaty, and on 18 June the Senate approved it by 41 to 14. (Navigation rights were included but made subject to American law.) While the coming of the war undoubtedly made Polk and Congress more eager for a settlement, it does not seem to have played an important role in forming British policy. During June and July, Britain and the United States further improved their relations by lowering tariffs and thereby increasing their trade.

Success on the Rio Grande, in California, and in Oregon undoubtedly led Polk to expect a short war with Mexico and a quick treaty confirming the annexation of California and some connecting territory. He had reckoned without the Mexican sense of honor. Showing unexpected powers of resistance, the Mexicans were favored by their formidable geography: a belt of semidesert in the north, mountain ranges in the center, and the fever-ridden Gulf coast. Polk put out peace feelers to Antonio López de Santa Anna, an opportunistic spoilsman who had been president of Mexico twice in the past but was then exiled in Havana. Santa Anna hinted that if he were enabled to regain power, he would negotiate with the United States. Polk granted him free passage through the American blockade and meanwhile had Buchanan write to Mexico City suggesting negotiations. Nothing came of either venture. The government bluntly refused to discuss terms; and after Santa Anna had seized power, he ignored his assurances to Polk, issued a call for troops, and organized Mexico's defense against the Americans. Meanwhile, Taylor had advanced beyond the Rio Grande and captured Monterrey (not to be confused with the port in California), only to see its defenders retreat into the dry lands to the south.

Polk resented these frustrations all the more because several forces were pressing him for an early peace. One was the British government, which hoped to mediate before the Americans advanced any farther; Polk politely but firmly refused its advances. More important, the Whig opposition was gaining support for its antiwar campaign in all parts of the country and especially among the northern antislavery bloc—both outright abolitionists and free-soil men, who opposed taking slavery into the territories. They were convinced that Polk, a southerner, had started the war to obtain more slaveholding territory. (The fact that Calhoun also opposed the war impressed few of these men. By then they thoroughly distrusted the South Carolina senator.) When Polk sought a special appropriation of $2 million in order to make a cash offer to Santa Anna if he seemed receptive, the antislavery bloc attached to the bill the notorious Wilmot Proviso, which would have forbidden slavery in any part of the territory to be gained from Mexico. Polk finally obtained his money at the following session of Congress, but his opponents had gained a useful issue for harassment.

By the end of 1846, Polk had to choose between alternate strategies for fighting the war and obtaining a peace. One was to occupy all of northern Mexico as far south as Tampico and San Luis Potosí, establish a line of forts, and wait until the Mexicans gave up. The other was to seize Tampico and Veracruz, the principal Gulf ports; send an army west from Veracruz along the old Spanish road through the mountains; and, if necessary, occupy Mexico City. The first tactic was obviously within American capabilities, for small detached forces had already marched almost at will through New Mexico and Chihuahua. It was the safer and less expensive of the two strategies, but it called for patience from the dynamic American people, already restive at the duration of the war. The second plan was much riskier, for it required a landing and unprecedented supply lines through the fever zone and across a punishing terrain. One victory for the Mexicans might encourage them to hold out indefinitely, and continued American successes would surely arouse the expansionists' appetite for territory. Buchanan and most moderates favored the defense line. Slidell, Benton (who now ardently supported the war), and other activists called for a central invasion.

For several months Polk postponed a final decision, although in November 1846 he authorized the army to make plans for the capture of Veracruz. (Tampico was occupied without Mexican resistance at the same time.) Meanwhile, he sent special agents into Mexico to seek out signs of peace sentiments. In January 1847 a Mexican emissary arrived in Washington to inquire about American terms, armed with letters from Santa Anna and other Mexican officials. Polk replied with a formal proposal for negotiations. When the government in Mexico City returned a demand that the Americans withdraw from all Mexican territory before negotiations would be considered, Polk became furious at what he considered Mexican trickery and committed himself to an invasion of central Mexico.

Polk reluctantly entrusted the invasion to General Winfield Scott, the ranking officer in the army and an excellent choice. After the central campaign had begun, Taylor advanced south of Monterrey without orders and defeated Santa Anna in a hard-fought, close, but strategically insignificant battle at Buena Vista, which established him as a hero in the public eye. Scott landed successfully, captured Veracruz, and, in order to avoid the fever, quickly proceeded into the interior. Meanwhile, Santa Anna, a forceful leader if no great tactician, suppressed a civil war in Mexico City, pulled his army together, and marched

out to meet Scott, taking up a strong defensive position in a mountain pass. In the most spectacular victory of the war, at Cerro Gordo (17–18 April 1847), Scott managed to outflank the Mexicans and drive them back in disorder; then, he occupied the large upland city of Puebla. Beaten for the second time in less than two months, Santa Anna limped back to Mexico City.

Since neither army had enough immediate strength for further fighting, Polk decided on another peace feeler. This time he chose an orthodox, if minor, diplomat, Nicholas P. Trist, chief clerk and de facto undersecretary of the State Department. Trist was a protégé of Buchanan, a certified Democrat (his wife was Jefferson's granddaughter), spoke fluent Spanish, and knew Latin American ways. Polk instructed him that he should obtain at least a boundary line up the Rio Grande and across southern New Mexico at about 32° to San Diego on the Pacific coast. For this he was to offer $15 million; but if Mexico would also cede Lower California or other territory, he might raise the price. These terms represented a compromise between expansionists such as Benton and moderates such as Buchanan.

After an initial period of jealous and puerile bickering, Trist and Scott formed an effective team and tried every expedient they could conceive, straightforward or devious, to bring the Mexicans to terms. First, they established a reliable line of communications to the Mexican government through the British minister at Mexico City, who was eager to end the fighting. Then, at a hint from Santa Anna, they sent him a "sweetener" of $10,000 and promised immediate payment to Mexico of $1 million upon signature of a treaty. (When Polk learned of the thinly disguised bribes, he was scandalized and seriously considered recalling both Scott and Trist.)

After Santa Anna, perhaps losing his nerve, repudiated his overture, Scott led his forces into the Valley of Mexico, defeated the Mexicans in two more battles (Contreras and Churubusco), and encamped just outside Mexico City. Trist then met a commission of Mexicans to discuss terms, but Santa Anna, torn between factions, rejected them. Scott fought and won two more battles (Molino del Rey and Chapultepec) and finally, seeing no alternative, attacked Mexico City itself on 13 September 1847, drove out the government, and prepared for indefinite occupation. Santa Anna, thoroughly discredited, resigned and headed for exile again, while the Mexican Congress and the ranking civilian leaders straggled off to a provincial capital to reorganize. The war had reached another impasse.

Back in the United States the impatient American public was feeling more and more frustrated at the recurring news of Scott's victories and persistent Mexican resistance. Opponents of the war continued to cite mounting casualty lists and appropriations, but a newly active group of ultraexpansionists, northern and southern, used the same casualties and appropriations to justify the United States in demanding more territory—even the annexation of all Mexico. Opponents deplored such ruthless conquest as degrading to the American character and predicted that if absorbed, the "mongrel" Mexican people would corrupt American democracy. Expansionists replied with "Manifest Destiny"—God had provided an opportunity for the United States to regenerate Mexico.

Having learned a few lessons from the Oregon debates, Polk reacted to the all-Mexico movement with caution. He was not unalterably opposed to acquiring territory south of the Rio Grande and 32°; but with every Democratic politician jockeying for position in the presidential race of the following year, he did not want to give up control over his party by taking sides prematurely. For a time he left negotiations to Trist, despite his mounting dissatisfaction. When he learned of the futile dickering at Mexico City, his impatience boiled over, and he decided to take another strong stand. Ordering Trist to come home, the president declared that if the Mexicans decided to discuss terms, they could send a representative to Washington.

By the time this order reached Trist, in mid-November, the situation in Mexico had changed to the American advantage. The civilian government that succeeded Santa Anna was moderate and favored negotiation. Although extremists invoked patriotism to continue the war, the government gradually brought them under control. When the order for Trist's recall arrived, he feared that the chance for negotiations, if not exploited, might disappear. Scott's troops might then have to remain in Mexico indefinitely, surrounded by an increasingly hostile population and fighting off guerrilla bands. Others in Mexico City were also aware of the dangers of indefinite occupation: American army officers, friendly Mexicans, and European residents. Urged by them and after several days of hesitation, Trist decided to disobey his orders and stay. Even after that decision, he had to wait two more months for a settlement, arguing every point at issue with the Mexican commissioners. Finally, on 2 February 1848, they signed the Treaty of Guadalupe Hidalgo, carrying out the most important of Trist's instructions. Through it, the United States obtained Upper California and New Mexico in return for $15 million plus $3.75 million of American claims against Mexico.

Trist's courageous insubordination rescued the president from the impossible task of reconciling American and Mexican ultranationalists. The text of the treaty arrived in Washington just as the all-Mexico movement crested, and Polk lost little time in submitting it to the Senate. Whatever he may have felt about additional annexations, he could not deny that Trist had achieved the original goals of the war, and he had some idea of the dangers to be incurred in continuing it. Except for ultranationalists, the country received the treaty with a collective sigh of relief, and on 10 March 1848, after the Senate had taken time to consider the alternatives, it approved nearly all the terms, by a vote of thirty-eight to fourteen. The Mexicans accepted a few revisions without difficulty, and the American troops were soon on their way home. The triumph was slightly marred by a needless quarrel between Scott and his principal officers. Because of the incident, Polk recalled Scott, to the astonishment of the Mexicans, and set up a military court of inquiry, but no important action was taken. Polk vented his spleen on Trist for disobedience and tactless dispatches by stopping his salary at the point of his recall. The unfortunate envoy, who deserved much better, had to wait over twenty years for full payment or any other recognition of his accomplishment.

During the last year of Polk's administration, he briefly considered other ways of acquiring territory that he mistakenly suspected of being the object of British designs. Soon after the war ended, the rebellious Mexican province of Yucatán sought an American protectorate and intervention in a destructive local Indian war. Polk submitted the proposal to Congress, but before Congress could act, a truce between Indians and whites in Yucatán removed the issue. During the summer of 1848, Polk instructed his minister to Spain, Romulus M. Saunders, to explore the possibility of purchasing Cuba, recently racked by rebellion. The inexperienced Saunders could not prevail against Spanish national pride, and a trial vote in the Senate indicated that the upper house would probably have rejected a purchase treaty anyway. These failures were undoubtedly fortunate for both Polk and the country, as the southwestern annexations and the sectional arguments they aroused strained the national institutions to their limit.

Farther south, in Central America, the influence of Britain was more overt, but the Polk administration had little success in countering it. Polk sent Elijah Hise as chargé d'affaires to Guatemala with instructions to encourage the weak, feuding Central American states to revive their recently dissolved confederacy. Hise was also to negotiate commercial treaties and report on British encroachments. Hise signed two commercial treaties and went beyond his instructions in contracting for perpetual canal rights across Nicaragua, but this treaty was not ratified. A more important action was a treaty of 12 December 1846 with Colombia, which owed little to Polk's direction. Secretary Buchanan had instructed the American chargé at Bogotá, Benjamin A. Bidlack, to negotiate a commercial treaty and guard against European efforts to obtain sole transit rights across the Isthmus of Panama, which was then part of Colombia. Bidlack included in the treaty (article 35) a long statement in which Colombia guaranteed to the United States that the isthmus would always be open and free to Americans. In return, the United States guaranteed the neutrality of the isthmus and Colombia's sovereignty over it.

When the cabinet saw these provisions, its members remarked doubtfully that the American guarantees seemed to violate the country's tradition against entangling alliances, but Polk submitted Bidlack's treaty to the Senate. Busy with the Mexican War, that body delayed action for over a year, while Colombia kept a special envoy in Washington to lobby for the treaty. In June 1848, the treaty was approved with almost no discussion. This casually adopted treaty led to a considerable expansion of American influence: the construction of a successful railroad in the 1850s, repeated American naval interventions on the isthmus during the succeeding decades, and finally, in 1903, Theodore Roosevelt's veiled support for an independence movement in Panama and the digging of the Panama Canal. It is not likely that Polk had any of these developments in mind when he received and submitted the Bidlack Treaty, but he might have applauded Roosevelt's deeds, had he been alive to witness them.

Appraisal of Polk

How should one judge the policies and actions of the Polk administration? In order to arrive at a fair appraisal, one must first weigh the merits and demerits of its greatest accomplishment, the territorial annexations, around which nearly all its other actions revolved. The Polk administration added to the United States about 1.2 million square miles of territory—far more than any other administration before or since—and the enormous value of this territory was at once established by the discovery of gold in California. The victories of the Mexican War won the grudging but genuine respect of Europe. Britain withdrew most of its political influence from Mexico and a few years later, in the Clayton-Bulwer Treaty, agreed to share influence in Central America. The broad frontage on the western coast eventually made the United States a force in Pacific affairs. In effect, the United States was promoted to a second-rank power whose views must be consulted in all international questions relating to the northern half of the New World.

Within the United States the effects of the war and the annexations were more mixed. Like all wars this one cost money, which the prosperous United States could well spare, and lives, which families and friends could not. On the one hand, the war's heroics, superimposed on a rising Romantic movement in popular literature, refurbished American history back to the Revolution and renewed Americans' devotion to their old ideals, which had become a little tarnished. On the other hand, the victories created a spirit of "lick all creation," an overblown chauvinism with strong hints of militarism and racism that coarsened democratic sensibilities and laid American ideologies open to charges of hypocrisy. Europeans, especially conservatives, had long thought American institutions tainted with braggadocio; during the 1850s the whiff thickened to a stench. To Latin Americans, the events of 1843–1848 revealed perhaps for the first time the aggressive potential of their expanding neighbor, and a stereotype began to take shape in Latin American writing about the United States—the Colossus of the North.

But the most alarming effects of western annexations and the Mexican War were felt in American sectionalism, already a threat. By the early 1840s many Whigs had come to believe that further expansion in any direction would place intolerable strains on national unity. To abolitionists, Texas became a moral issue, what Charles Sumner called "our own original sin." Although abolitionists were partly reassured by the apparent evenhandedness of the Democratic party program of 1844 and Polk's inaugural address, the Oregon compromise at 49° struck them as a betrayal by the South and a southern president. When a seemingly unending war for limitless southern annexations followed, this northern sense of betrayal crystallized in the Wilmot Proviso (first introduced by one of Polk's own Democrats), which completed the association of slavery and expansion. The intense opposition to the war, partly Whig and partly antislavery, made it seem not only disruptive, setting one section against another, but sinful. "When the foreign war ends, *the domestic war will begin*," warned the *New York Gazette and Times* in 1847. Ralph Waldo Emerson wrote in his journal that the war was a dose of arsenic, and he might well have applied the term to the acquisition of Texas and Oregon, too.

Given the mixed effects of the Polk administration's accomplishments, we may proceed to a few conclusions about Polk's own nature and methods. In the first place, it seems clear that he placed too great reliance on bold talk and too little confidence in the possibility of compromise. Suspicious by nature, he was inclined to view each offer by his opponents as a trap or an attempt to exploit American amiability and weakness. Although anxious to negotiate from an appearance of strength, he did not seem to think it necessary to build up the army and navy. As a result, he slipped into the dangerous practice of bluffing, not realizing or perhaps not caring how little respect American military forces inspired abroad. He probably counted on distance, trade, and the vulnerability of Canada to deter Britain from action and probably despised the Mexicans as too weak and disorganized to carry out their braggart threats.

Second, beyond these basic attitudes, much of Polk's foreign policy was improvised from month to month in response to events. The statement on Oregon in his inaugural address was a pacifier for the West; Buchanan's offer to Britain, an attempt to draw the fangs of British critics; and the withdrawal of that offer, a startled and indignant reflex. Meanwhile, Polk sought to renew diplomatic relations with Mexico in the hope of keeping peace during the annexation of Texas; but as soon as he understood Mexican weakness and confusion, he advanced his goal to the purchase of California. During his first year in office, he regarded war with either adversary as unlikely, but in March and April 1846, changed circumstances, especially political divisions at home, led him to favor a short tactical war with Mexico. As that war lengthened, he made other political and military decisions in reaction to events.

Third, Polk's largely improvised policies suffered from the phenomenon that twentieth-century analysts have called "escalation." This is a process by which an initial set of decisions starts a chain of causes and effects each more difficult to control than its predecessor, each widening the area of action and requiring increased forces and money. On inauguration day Polk had a fairly wide range of acceptable policies from which to choose. Some of his early actions and the pressure of circumstances gradually reduced this range. Eventually, after Scott had captured Mexico City, Polk found himself boxed in, unable to move, for ultraexpansionists at home would not let him withdraw from central Mexico to a tenable defensive line and he lacked the resources or the desire to extend the conquest over the whole country. Inaction, too, posed grave problems, for a few small guerrilla victories might have revived the Mexicans' morale and enabled them to cut Scott's long supply lines and isolate him in Mexico City. Fortunately, the disobedient Trist seized the fleeting moment of Mexican willingness to negotiate and so rescued the president from his dilemma.

Fourth, Polk failed to understand the deadly combination of the slavery and expansion issues until the explosive results were beyond his control. To this unfortunate outcome both his habit of improvisation and the element of escalation contributed. Before he became president, he shared the convictions of many southerners about slavery—that it was a practical necessity, though in many respects deplorable, and that it was a local matter and so should have no connection with national politics or international diplomacy. The ominous interjection of slavery into the Texas question during 1843 and 1844 seems to have made little impression on him.

Consequently, when the antislavery bloc opposed the war as a slaveholders' plot and seized upon the Wilmot Proviso as a weapon, Polk reacted with irritation at its using a potentially divisive issue for partisan purposes. As soon as it was clear that the proviso could not be shunted aside, he called in its sponsor, Representative David Wilmot, to assure him that in seeking territory from Mexico, he had no intention of extending slavery, for the land was unsuited to it, and that since no slave-state senator could vote for the proviso, its inclusion would defeat necessary war legislation and prolong hostilities indefinitely. As he told Representative Preston King, slavery had "no legitimate connection" with either the war or the peace treaty. Despite the accusations of abolitionists and some early historians, these assurances seem to have accurately represented his views.

Polk managed to end the war without reference to slavery, but the argument continued to simmer, and through 1848 the proviso was attached to every bill for the organization of government in the annexed territories. By now Polk was thoroughly alarmed that the issue might split not only the Democratic party but the country. After accepting the proviso in the Oregon territorial bill, he made it clear that he would agree to any compromise terms that the North proposed for the other territories: settlement of the slavery issue by the inhabitants, extension of the Missouri Compromise line to the Pacific, or submission of the whole matter to a judicial tribunal. Eventually he even favored immediate admission of California as a state without conditions attached (which would virtually guarantee the outlawry of slavery). In his last annual message to Congress he delivered an eloquent plea for tolerance and compromise in the name of "the glorious Union." He spent his final weeks in office making desperate but vain efforts to work out an acceptable formula.

All in all, one is forced to conclude that Polk's policies were much more hazardous than he realized, thanks to his overbold improvising, the phenomenon of escalation, the small forces that the United States deployed in the field, and the likelihood of deep divisions within the American parties, government, and people. Even assuming that Britain had no desire to fight its best customer, Polk could not be certain that a sense of honor over some uncontrollable local conflict in Oregon would not precipitate a general Anglo-American war. Britain had significant economic interests in Mexico, so a Mexican victory over Taylor on the Rio Grande would have facilitated a private loan from British bankers, and a military stalemate in northern or central Mexico would probably have led to British mediation, which rising American opposition to the war might have forced Polk to accept. An indefinite occupation of Mexico City and smoldering guerrilla warfare lasting through the American election of 1848 might well have caused an open break between ultraexpansionists largely supported by the South and pacifists backed by abolitionists.

Without placing too much weight on "contingent history," it is possible to imagine what might have happened had Polk made a different set of choices. An arguable alternative to bold tactics against either Britain or Mexico was the policy that Calhoun had recommended for Oregon—"masterly inactivity." This policy rested on two assumptions:

the continuous, irresistible force of American western migration and Europe's customary involvement in Old World affairs. At Polk's inauguration, he might have refused direct comment on Oregon while examining the possibilities of a negotiated settlement with Britain and completing the annexation of Texas. If he had resisted the impulse to break off discussion with Pakenham, he might have had an agreement to announce in his first annual message, forestalling western resentment with a fait accompli. Failing that, he could have used western resentment to put pressure on Britain but without relinquishing the Oregon question to Congress.

In any case, Polk should have avoided an open break with Mexico before the Oregon controversy was completely settled. There was no need for haste; stationing Taylor at Corpus Christi would have protected Texas settlements adequately with a minimum of provocation to Mexico. As for California, careful analysis of British policy in Europe and in Texas should have reassured Polk that Britain had few designs on the Pacific coast outside of Oregon, where honor was involved. Why not allow American settlers to occupy California, keep American warships cruising off the coast, and see whether the Californians might not repeat the history of Texas? During some later European crisis (such as the revolutions of 1848 or the Crimean War of the mid-1850s), the United States would have been free to open negotiations with an independent California government, which by then might have observed the prosperity of Oregon under American rule.

Perhaps war with Mexico might have been avoided altogether. At worst, it would have been postponed until a more favorable moment, and with the United States already occupying Texas and California, any fighting would have been defensive and limited to border areas. Mexicans, of course, would have resented the loss of California under any circumstances, but they had no means of retaining it, and this course would have spared them the humiliation of a foreign army in their capital. Most important to the United States, a policy of more gradual, peaceful expansion would undoubtedly have avoided many of the bitter debates in Congress and the press that widened the alarming gap between North and South.

Such an alternative set of policies and actions might have won the United States less territory than was gained through war, for modern New Mexico and Arizona might have stayed with Mexico. Also these policies and actions would have required a president who combined Polk's determination, persistence, and knowledge of political machinery with greater sophistication in international affairs, a deeper conviction of the dangers of sectional strife, and greater charismatic appeal to the public, which he would have to carry with him at several crucial points. It would have required him to serve a second term or at least to influence the succession enough to ensure some continuity of policy. Perhaps this was impossible in the party politics of the 1840s. Perhaps also the divisiveness of the Texas issue had pushed the slavery question past the point of no return, as some historians have argued, placing it beyond the influence of rational argument and delaying tactics. In any case, the outline of an unexplored gradualist policy is useful in appraising the actual achievements of the Polk administration.

As in the case of many other presidents, the end of the Polk administration has an element of pathos. While trying in vain to settle the question of government in California and New Mexico, Polk prepared with quiet dignity to wind up his affairs and transfer power to his Whig successor. When General Taylor arrived in Washington to take over from his old commander, there was a day of embarrassed hesitation in the White House, lest Taylor fail to make the prescribed first social call on the sitting president. The inaugural ceremonies over, Polk and his wife left at once for their home in Tennessee, traveling by train and boat through much of the South. The warm welcome he received everywhere was tempered by an onset of his old illness, intensified by fear of cholera as he hurried through disease-ridden New Orleans and up the Mississippi. Arriving in Tennessee, haggard, coughing, and racked with diarrhea, he nevertheless made a round of visits with friends and relatives before settling down in a newly acquired home. In his last diary entry, on 2 June, he told of taking a carriage ride and unpacking books for arrangement in new shelves. Two weeks later, on 15 June 1849, he died.

BIBLIOGRAPHY

A good study, focusing especially on domestic problems, is Paul H. Bergeron, *The Presidency of James K. Polk* (Lawrence, Kans., 1987). Charles A. McCoy, *Polk and the Presidency* (Austin, Tex., 1960), covers much of the same ground.

The first scholarly biography of Polk, Eugene Irving McCormac, *James K. Polk: A Political Biography* (Berkeley, Calif., 1922), is still useful. More personal are two volumes by Charles G. Sellers: *James K. Polk, Jacksonian, 1795–1843* and *James K. Polk, Continentalist, 1843–1846* (Princeton, N.J., 1957, 1966). The first volume is unmatched on Polk's rise to power; the second should be used with McCormac and Pletcher. Polk's own account, *The Diary of James K. Polk During His Presidency, 1845–1849*, edited by Milo Milton Quaife, 4 vols. (Chicago, 1910), gives fascinating insights into Polk's mind as well as an account of his daily activities.

Biographies of Polk's cabinet members show how they worked with their master. John M. Belohlavek, *George Mifflin Dallas: Jacksonian Patrician* (University Park, Pa., 1977), is an able study of Polk's almost ignored vice president. Philip S. Klein, *President James Buchanan: A Biography* (University Park, Pa., 1962), is probably still best on Polk's secretary of state. James P. Shenton, *Robert John Walker: A Politician from Jackson to Lincoln* (New York, 1961), and Ivor D. Spencer, *The Victor and the Spoils: A Life of William L. Marcy* (Providence, R.I., 1959), cover important accomplishments of the Polk administration.

On domestic issues see works by Bergeron, McCoy, McCormac, and Sellers already cited. Sections of several books treat the Polk administration: Joel H. Silbey, *The Shrine of Party: Congressional Voting Behavior, 1841–1852* (Pittsburgh, Pa., 1967); John Tebbell and Sarah Miles Watts, *The Press and the Presidency: From George Washington to Ronald Reagan* (New York, 1985); and Leonard D. White, *The Jacksonians: A Study in Administrative History, 1829–1861* (New York, 1954).

American expansionism, the background to most of Polk's foreign relations, has received much attention. Albert K. Weinberg, *Manifest Destiny: A Study of Nationalist Expansionism in American History* (Baltimore, 1935), the classic analysis, has several chapters on the 1840s. Frederick Merk offers somewhat different interpretations in two books, written with Lois Bannister Merk, *Manifest Destiny and Mission in American History: A Reinterpretation* (New York, 1963), and *The Monroe Doctrine and American Expansionism, 1843–1849* (New York, 1966). About half of the latter is devoted to the Polk adminstration. Norman A. Graebner, *Empire on the Pacific: A Study in American Continental Expansion* (New York, 1955), focuses on Oregon and California. Thomas R. Hietala, *Manifest Design: Anxious Aggrandizement in Late Jacksonian America*

(Ithaca, N.Y., 1985), treats expansionism essentially as a defensive maneuver intended to divert attention from problems at home. Gene M. Brack, *Mexico Views Manifest Destiny, 1821–1846: An Essay on the Origins of the Mexican War* (Albuquerque, N.Mex., 1975), is especially useful on the Texas question and the coming of the Mexican War.

On foreign policy, David M. Pletcher, *The Diplomacy of Annexation: Texas, Oregon, and the Mexican War* (Columbia, Mo., 1973), provides a presentation of the interpretation used in the present article. Glen W. Price, *Origins of the War with Mexico: The Polk-Stockton Intrigue* (Austin, Tex., 1967), is the most detailed exposition of the "plot thesis" concerning the coming of the Mexican War. Justin H. Smith, *The Annexation of Texas*, rev. ed. (New York, 1941), although originally published in 1911 and thus not based on modern scholarship, contains by far the most comprehensive account of the annexation campaign. More recent is Frederick Merk, *Slavery and the Annexation of Texas* (New York, 1972). Merk's *The Oregon Question: Essays in Anglo-American Diplomacy and Politics* (Cambridge, Mass., 1967), contains several chapters on Polk's policies. The second volume of Sellers's biography has chapters on foreign relations.

The classic study of the Mexican War is Justin H. Smith, *The War with Mexico*, 2 vols. (New York, 1919; repr. Gloucester, Mass., 1963), very detailed and still useful, although both anti-Polk and anti-Mexican. Pletcher, cited above, has superseded it in diplomacy. See K. Jack Bauer, *The Mexican War, 1846–1848* (New York, 1974), and John S. D. Eisenhower, *So Far from God: The U.S. War with Mexico, 1846–1848* (New York, 1989), for military history.

Otis A. Singletary, *The Mexican War* (Chicago, 1960), is a short account of the military action, especially useful on the American occupation of Mexico. David Lavender, *Climax at Buena Vista: The American Campaigns in Northeastern Mexico, 1846–1847* (Philadelphia, 1966), provides a good account of the first half of the war. More up-to-date and popularized overviews are Seymour V. Connor and Odie B. Faulk, *North America Divided: The Mexican War, 1846–1848* (New York, 1971), and John Edward Weems, *To Conquer a Peace: The War Between the United States and Mexico* (Garden City, N.Y., 1974). Good biographies of the principal military leaders are Holman Hamilton, *Zachary Taylor*, vol. 1 (Indianapolis, Ind., 1941); K. Jack Bauer, *Zachary Taylor: Soldier, Planter, Statesman of the Old Southwest* (Baton Rouge, La., 1985); Charles Winslow Elliott, *Winfield Scott: The Soldier and the Man* (New York, 1937); and Oakah L. Jones, Jr., *Santa Anna* (New York, 1968). On the last phase of the war and the negotiation of the peace treaty see John Douglas Pitts Fuller, *The Movement for the Acquisition of All Mexico, 1846–1848* (Baltimore, 1936); Robert W. Drexler, *Guilty of Making Peace: A Biography of Nicholas P. Trist* (Lanham, Md., 1991); and Richard Griswold del Castillo, *The Treaty of Guadalupe Hidalgo: A Legacy of Conflict* (Norman, Okla., 1990), which, however, concentrates on post-1848 history. A remarkable study of American public opinion on the war, with emphasis on support and the effects of the war at home is Robert W. Johannsen, *To the Halls of the Montezumas: The Mexican War in the American Imagination* (New York, 1985). It should be balanced, however, by John H. Schroeder, *Mr. Polk's War: American Opposition and Dissent, 1846–1848* (Madison, Wis., 1973).

Zachary Taylor and Millard Fillmore

Norman A. Graebner

Zachary Taylor THE LIBRARY OF CONGRESS

Millard Fillmore THE LIBRARY OF CONGRESS

Zachary Taylor entered the world of politics fresh from his personal triumphs in the Mexican War. Leaders of the Whig party had condemned the war as an inexcusable aggression against Mexico, but they recognized in Taylor's unassuming manner and immense popularity qualities that would make him an ideal presidential candidate to recapture the White House after four years of James K. Polk. The Whigs, no less than the Democrats, had principles, but many wondered whether Taylor, whose entire career had been in the army, either understood or accepted them.

In April 1848, while Taylor was still saying that he was a no-party candidate, several southern friends prepared a letter that he copied and sent to his brother-in-law, Captain John S. Allison. In it Taylor acknowledged that he was not sufficiently familiar with public issues to pass judgment on them. He wrote, "I reiterate . . . I am a Whig but not ultra Whig.. . . If elected I would not be the mere president of a party—I would endeavor to act independent of party domination, & should feel bound to administer the Government untrammelled by party schemes."

Taylor believed that Congress, not the president, should have complete control of the major issues before the country. The Allison letter was sufficiently Whig in doctrine to assure Taylor's fourth-ballot nomination at Philadelphia in June 1848. Not all Whigs were pleased. Horace Greeley, editor of the *New York Tribune*, termed the convention "a slaughterhouse of Whig principles." To balance the ticket, the convention named Millard Fillmore, an old-line Whig from New York, for the vice presidency. The convention adopted no platform.

Whig leaders sought to capitalize on Taylor's stature as a national hero and his broad appeal to Americans everywhere. Still Taylor was a man of the South, born in Virginia (24 November 1784) and raised in Kentucky in an aristocratic slaveholding family. A slaveholder himself at the age of thirty, he soon extended his planting operations into Louisiana and Mississippi. Despite a series of misfortunes caused by invalid land titles, falling cotton prices, bollworms, cutworms, and flooding, he managed by 1847 to enter the select company of planters who owned more than a hundred slaves. But Taylor was not ostentatious. He was of average height, muscular, and heavy-boned. His clothing was ordinary, often ill fitting. He had a temper and sometimes displayed it, but generally he conducted himself with unstudied ease, displaying simple good manners. His personal and family life was untouched by scandal. Despite his apparent wealth, Taylor lived modestly at his cottage in Baton Rouge or at his Mississippi plantation, Cypress Grove.

Political success in 1848 lay in the ability to neutralize a divisive sectional issue already tormenting the nation's politics. Polk had decreed that the Mexican War would bring California and New Mexico into the Union, and the annexation of Texas in December 1845 as a slave state had conditioned the antislavery forces of the North against the further extension of slavery into newly acquired territories. In August 1846, David Wilmot of Pennsylvania moved to amend an administration request for $2 million to aid in negotiating a peace with Mexico by adding the proviso that "neither slavery nor involuntary servitude" should ever exist in any territory acquired from Mexico "except for crime, whereof the party shall first be duly convicted." Northern majorities carried the Wilmot Proviso through the House; Democratic managers kept the antislavery measure off the Senate floor. South Carolina's John C. Calhoun met the sectional challenge in February 1847 with the argument that all states had equal rights in the territories, including the right of importing slaves into them. Congress, as the agent of the states, had no right to legislate slavery into or out of the territories. To prevent a serious

disruption of their party, Democratic leaders bent on expansion searched for a compromise. Polk and Secretary of State James Buchanan favored the extension of the Missouri Compromise line of 36°30' to the Pacific, but Lewis Cass of Michigan, leader of the administration forces in the Senate, produced the celebrated alternative of "popular sovereignty." Cass's plan would permit people of all sections to move freely into any new territory. When that region had sufficient population to warrant a territorial legislature, that legislature would decide the question of slavery in the territory.

Popular sovereignty became the official position of moderate Democrats everywhere, especially in the North and West. Proslavery spokesmen of the South saw immediately that popular sovereignty assured southerners no greater access to the territories than would the Wilmot Proviso. Cass's doctrine, charged the *Charleston Mercury* in January 1848, would merely transfer political control of the territories from northern congressional majorities to "mongrel" territorial populations consisting largely of northerners. In mid-January, D. L. Yulee of Florida introduced a resolution in the Senate declaring that neither Congress nor a territorial legislature had the constitutional right to exclude slavery from any territory of the United States. William L. Yancey of Alabama carried these southern demands into the Democratic convention that gathered in Baltimore in May. When the Democrats nominated Cass for the presidency, northern proviso Democrats bolted the party and, joined by rebellious Whigs who distrusted Taylor, held a convention at Buffalo in August, formed the Free-Soil party, and nominated Martin Van Buren for the presidency.

Throughout the campaign Taylor's doubtful allegiance to Whig principles troubled party leaders, especially when he accepted a local Democratic nomination. Thurlow Weed, the powerful Whig boss of New York, threatened to call a mass meeting to denounce the party's candidate. Fillmore suggested rather that he and Weed address a letter to Taylor. Taylor replied on 4 September in the form of another Allison letter in which he again defined his principles as Whig. This held the party in line.

Taylor's final victory was modest, with 1,360,000 popular votes to 1,220,000 for Cass and 291,000 for Van Buren. Taylor's margin in the electoral college was more decisive (163–127). Van Buren did not carry one state, but his 120,000 votes in New York provided Taylor his victory margin in that key state.

Taylor's triumph at the polls did not assure a successful Whig administration. In the South, Whig orators had campaigned for Taylor as a southerner and Louisiana slaveholder, a man whom the South could trust, while in the North, Whig politicians portrayed him as a proponent of the Wilmot Proviso. Democratic editors advertised the discrepancy but without apparent effect. By avoiding the slavery-extension issue as a united party, the Whigs, unlike the Democrats, had no solid core of party stalwarts committed to a compromise solution of the territorial question. Any national decision on slavery in the territories could break up the Whig party completely.

Taylor could choose from a host of distinguished Whig leaders in filling his cabinet posts. Henry Clay and Daniel Webster scarcely concealed their resentment toward Taylor's election. Both would attempt to manage the affairs of the nation from their seats in the Senate. Taylor asked his close supporter, John J. Crittenden, to join the cabinet, but Crittenden preferred the governorship of Kentucky. For the State Department, Taylor selected John M. Clayton of Delaware, a noted orator but undistinguished administrator. William M. Meredith, a leading member of the Philadelphia bar, became secretary of the treasury and one of the cabinet's most popular members. Taylor placed the noted Ohio Whig, Thomas Ewing, over the Interior Department. He assigned the little-known George W. Crawford to the War Department. William Ballard Preston of Virginia, secretary of the navy, knew little about ships but much about politics. Jacob Collamer, the postmaster general, was a successful Vermont politician who would become Taylor's chief dispenser of the federal patronage. Reverdy Johnson, a wealthy leader of the Baltimore bar, entered the cabinet as attorney general. Whig editors thought the cabinet moderate and able; at least all of its members appeared to be steadfast Whigs. From the outset Fillmore's role in the new administration was almost nonexistent. He faced opposition not only in the cabinet but also in New York, where the two commanding Whigs, Weed and William H. Seward, fought him successfully for control of the New York patronage.

The California Statehood Question

Moderates in both houses of Congress hoped to dispose of the slavery issue in California and New Mexico even before Taylor entered the White House. In

A Taylor–Fillmore campaign poster distributed by the Whig Party in 1848. THE LIBRARY OF CONGRESS

January 1848, James Marshall's discovery of gold in the Sacramento Valley set off a rush for the goldfields. Within weeks thousands of gold seekers moved toward California, some overland by covered wagon, some by ship around South America, and others across the Isthmus of Panama. Convinced that California would soon have more than the sixty thousand inhabitants required for statehood, such House leaders as Clayton and Preston, joined by Stephen A. Douglas of Illinois in the Senate, introduced measures advocating a state government for California. Because any state had the unquestioned right to determine the status of slavery within its borders, statehood for California seemed a sure remedy for the slavery question there. Southern extremists blocked Douglas in the Senate; Preston's measure remained alive until 27 February 1849, when, overloaded with amendments, the House killed it.

Taylor's inaugural several days later contained no forthright approach to the territorial issue. Democratic editors complained that it shaped no policy at all, keeping the public as much in the dark as it had been at the time of Taylor's election. Southerners suspected that the president's failure to define an antiproviso position meant that he secretly favored a northern solution of the territorial question. Political observers noted, moreover, that most cabinet members leaned toward Free-Soilism.

Privately, Taylor, no less than Clayton and Preston as cabinet members, hoped to avoid a sectional conflict by disposing of the California statehood question as quickly as possible. By December 1849, California's population would approach one hundred thousand. California's loosely organized government, a legacy of Mexican rule, was inadequate to cope with the region's crime and insecurity; indeed, California's citizens were eliminating known criminals by administering justice themselves. Taylor planned to resolve all of California's problems permanently by encouraging immediate statehood. As early as April 1849, Clayton predicted that California "will be admitted—free and Whig!" Taylor dispatched Thomas Butler King, a slaveholding member of Congress from Georgia, to California as his personal agent. King reached the west coast in June and proceeded to argue California's need for statehood. Delegates met in Monterey in September to form a constitution. A third of them were southerners, but their addiction to states' rights prevented them from raising the question of slavery. The constitution, adopted unanimously in October, prohibited slavery for all time. Without waiting for congressional approval, Californians elected state officials and a congressional delegation. Meanwhile, New Mexican leaders also demanded a new government. By the autumn of 1849 the president advocated immediate statehood for both California and New Mexico, revealing at last the antislavery outlook of his administration. During a trip through Pennsylvania in July, Taylor had declared at Mercer, "The people of the North need have no apprehension of the further extension of slavery." Conscious of the growing sectional strife in the nation, Taylor would eliminate the territorial issue by bringing the entire Mexican Cession into the Union as states.

Involvements Abroad

As the president planned the nation's escape from the troublesome issue of slavery expansion, the spread of revolution across Europe following the overthrow of the French monarchy in February 1848 captured the American imagination. The outpouring of sympathy centered on Hungary, where the Magyar patriots, under Lajos Kossuth, were struggling against Austria. In June 1849, after the Hungarians had won a succession of victories, Secretary of State Clayton dispatched Ambrose Dudley Mann, then in Germany, to Hungary to report on the progress of the revolution and offer America's encouragement. Crittenden was delighted. He wrote to Clayton,

> Your readiness to recognize Hungary is a forward and bold step. I like it for the sentiment and resolution it implies. Go ahead!—it is glorious and will please our people to see the Majesty of our Republic exhibiting itself on all proper occasions, with its dignity and fearless front, in the eyes and to the teeth of misruling kings, or despots of whatever make or title they may be.

Such sentiments reflected the deep American animosity toward European repression, but the genuine interests of the United States in European politics lay in the balance of power, not in the self-determination of European peoples. Predictably the Taylor administration remained officially silent when Russian troops, coming to the aid of Austria, crushed the Hungarian uprising. Early in 1850, Cass proposed a resolution demanding that the administration sever diplomatic relations with Austria. Clayton, supported by Clay and other traditionalists, ignored Cass's overture to American sentimentalism.

For the Taylor administration the region of immediate concern was Central America. During 1849, thousands of Americans poured across Panama and Nicaragua, traveling largely along two possible canal routes en route to California. Clearly the American interest, then or later, demanded the right to build a canal and control it. As early as June 1848, the Senate approved a treaty with New Granada (now Colombia) that granted the United States transit rights across the Isthmus of Panama. In return, the United States pledged to guarantee the neutrality of the route. The British possessed British Honduras and asserted a protectorate over the Indians of the Mosquito Coast. To offset the American treaty with New Granada, the British seized control of the port of San Juan del Norte, which commanded the entrance to the best canal route across Nicaragua; they renamed the port Greytown. Then, in October 1849, the British seized Tigre Island, near the possible western terminus of the Nicaraguan route. Despite Britain's prompt release of Tigre Island, the British and the Americans were clearly on a collision course in Central America.

Clayton moved to resolve the burgeoning contest by opening negotiations with the able Sir Henry

Lytton Bulwer, who reached Washington in late 1849. Neither the United States nor Britain would permit the other to have sole control of an isthmian canal. Both nations, moreover, feared that the other would attempt to strengthen its position in Central America by seizing territory. The Clayton-Bulwer Treaty, signed on 19 April 1850, resolved the canal issue by asserting that neither country, should it build a canal, had the right to fortify it or exercise exclusive control over it. The territorial arrangements were more ambiguous. Both governments agreed never to occupy, fortify, or exercise any dominion over any part of Central America; neither would they assume any protectorate over a Central American government. Clayton agreed that these limitations did not apply to areas already under British control.

For Whigs and conservatives the self-denying aspects of the treaty served the immediate interests of the United States admirably. Britain, the world's leading maritime power, had agreed not to monopolize a Nicaraguan canal or to extend its holdings along the Caribbean. Expansionist Democrats such as Cass and Douglas condemned the acceptance of the self-denying clauses as an act of national cowardice. Buchanan charged that Clayton, like Bulwer, merited a British peerage. To its partisan critics the Taylor administration had not answered the challenges either of revolutionary Europe or of British ambitions in the Caribbean.

The Territorial Issue

Long before Congress convened in December 1849, Taylor faced a rebellious South prepared to contest California's admission as a free state. In 1849 there were fifteen slave and fifteen free states, giving the South equality in the Senate. The admission of California as a free state would shatter the balance irretrievably. Calhoun's "Southern Address" of the previous January, a strong, uncompromising defense of slavery expansion, became the standard of southern loyalty for Democrats and Whigs alike. Southerners accused the president of manipulating the entire constitution-making process in California. Northern antislavery congressmen lauded Taylor's initiative and returned to Washington determined to bring California into the Union as a free state. Sectional disagreements so splintered the parties that not until Christmas could the House elect a Speaker.

Robert C. Winthrop of Massachusetts was the leading Whig candidate for the speakership. North-ern and southern Whigs had elected him in 1847; thereafter he had commanded the position with fairness and distinction. Assuming that Winthrop might face opposition in the South, northern Whigs sought a southern candidate who might appeal to the North. The likeliest candidate was Charles S. Morehead of Kentucky. On the Democratic side, Howell Cobb of Georgia towered over the rest. He inspired confidence not only as a skilled debater but also as a man of integrity. A Unionist, Cobb was one of the few southerners in Congress who had refused to sign Calhoun's Southern Address.

When the voting began, Cobb secured a strong plurality, but could never gain the needed majority. As the voting continued week after week, no fewer than fifty-three Democrats received votes in the balloting. When Cobb and Winthrop failed to win the speakership, the Democrats turned to northerners while the Whigs turned to southerners. Nine Free-Soilers complicated the balloting. They held the balance of power and stood as a bloc against both Winthrop and Cobb. As the balloting continued, various moderate Democrats from the Old Northwest moved ahead only to reach a stalemate.

Finally, on 21 December, a Whig-Democratic conference agreed on a proposal that the House proceed to elect a Speaker and if no one received a majority in three ballots, then the one with the largest number of votes be declared the victor. Winthrop and Cobb now resumed their places at the head of the balloting. On the third ballot Cobb became Speaker with 102 votes to 99 for Winthrop. At the end, Cobb received one vote fewer than he had at the beginning. The voting demonstrated that no party or section could control the House. Taylor's actions had driven some key southern Whigs into the opposition. Georgia's two leading Whigs, Robert Toombs and Alexander Stephens, turned against the northern Whigs when the president refused to give them any pledge that he would oppose the Wilmot Proviso.

Taylor viewed the congressional turmoil at a distance, determined to do his duty when the time came. Visitors at the White House reported that he remained calm and relaxed. In his first annual message, dispatched to both the House and the Senate on Christmas Eve, Taylor advocated the immediate recognition of California's statehood under its new constitution. He noted that New Mexico would be asking for admission to the Union shortly. To maintain the nation's tranquillity, the president admonished that we should abstain frown the introduction of those exciting topics of a sectional character which have hitherto produced painful apprehensions in the public mind; and I repeat the solemn warning of the first and most illustrious of my predecessors against furnishing "any ground for characterizing parties by geographical discriminations."

Again Taylor asserted his belief that the executive had no authority to dictate to Congress or to counter its will with a veto. For northerners this meant that Taylor would not veto the Wilmot Proviso. The president still hoped that the admission of California and New Mexico as states would eliminate the proviso from congressional consideration. Taylor reminded members of Congress that their first obligation was to the nation and not to slavery. Much of the conservative press praised the president's appeal to nationalism.

Editors predicted another congressional crisis when Senator Henry S. Foote of Mississippi, on 27 December, moved that Congress establish territorial governments for California, New Mexico, and Utah—a clear rejection of Taylor's proposals. In a special message to Congress on 21 January 1850, Taylor explained to southerners his limited role in California's decision to form a constitution. He had sent King to California, he admitted, but he had not instructed King to exercise any influence over the selection of delegates or the drawing of the constitution. Taylor again advocated the admission of New Mexico as a state, not a territory, to permit the residents of the region to settle the question of slavery permanently.

Southern orators spent January churning the emotions of Congress. Even the moderate Whig Thomas L. Clingman of North Carolina termed Taylor's proposals "impudent." They would bring California, New Mexico, Oregon, Utah, and Minnesota into the Union as free states, giving the North a majority of ten votes in the Senate and two-thirds of the House. With the South shorn of its power, the North would abolish slavery in the states. The South wanted a "fair settlement." Clingman would give California to the North in exchange for the extension of slavery into New Mexico. Southerners accused the president of adopting Cass's popular sovereignty, permitting northern majorities to resolve the slavery issue. Elected by southern votes, the president had turned on the South. Thomas Hart Benton of Missouri further antagonized the South when he declared that Texas' claims to New Mexican lands extending to the Rio Grande were unwarranted. Only

the federal government, Benton argued, could resolve this controversy. He recommended a boundary 4° east of Santa Fe. Southerners noted that Benton's proposal would reduce the area of slavery in the Southwest. Even the future Texas boundary had become a subject of serious sectional dispute.

Clay's Compromise Measure and the Great Debate

Such a maze of conflicting sectional interests called for a political compromise. In the waning days of January, Clay, the elder statesman of the Whig party who had recently returned to the Senate, pondered the issues in search of some formula that would resolve the numerous controversies between the free and slave states. One evening he walked to Daniel Webster's quarters to obtain the advice and support of his noted Whig rival, like Clay nearing the end of a long career in public life.

On 29 January, Clay presented eight resolutions to the Senate. One endorsed the president's plan to admit California under its free constitution. The second would establish territorial governments for New Mexico and Utah without regard to slavery. The third and fourth would redraw the Texas boundary to exclude all lands claimed by New Mexico but would compensate Texas with the federal assumption of the Texas debt. The fifth and sixth would abolish the slave trade in the District of Columbia but would guarantee slavery there unless the people of Maryland and the District consented to its abolition with just compensation to the owners. The seventh favored an effective fugitive slave act. The last guaranteed the slave trade between slaveholding states against congressional action. Clay combined these measures into an omnibus bill, hopeful that it would restore health to the Union and strength to the Whig party.

After submitting his resolutions, Clay explained and defended them. He appealed to members of Congress to show "mutual forebearance" and accept a peaceful resolution of the sectional conflict. Clay admitted that his major appeal was to the North. He had asked for more concessions there because the North was numerically more powerful and therefore could afford to be magnanimous. The southern concern over slavery, moreover, was far more pervasive than that of the North. "In one scale, then," said Clay, "we behold sentiment, sentiment, sentiment alone. In the other property, the social fabric, life, and all that makes life desirable." He asked senators to avoid behavior destructive of the Union. Clay returned to the Senate floor on 5 February to open the formal debate on the omnibus bill. Sensing the importance of the occasion, people of power and eminence packed the galleries and floor of the Senate chamber. The House adjourned so that its members could join the throng. Clay spent more than two hours in presenting every argument to uphold his measures. At the end he appealed to the Union now threatened with destruction. Dissolution and war, he cried, were "identical and inseparable."

Clay had challenged Taylor for the leadership of the Whig party and the nation. The attempt was futile. In the North, Clay had the support of Webster and James Cooper of Pennsylvania, but not one other northern Whig followed him. In the South, Clay had four or five staunch Whig supporters, no more. Successful in avoiding the compromise principles of the Democratic party, the Whigs, in the burgeoning crisis, would avoid the territorial question by following the president. The core of compromise strength lay in the Democratic party. Indeed, the majority of Democrats backed Clay completely; it was there that he received four-fifths of his support. Sam Houston of Texas, a Jacksonian Democrat, followed Clay in the Senate with a ringing defense of popular sovereignty and an appeal to the Union. Clay had done nothing to win the adherence of such Democrats, but his measure reflected so substantially the dominant Democratic approach to the sectional controversy that some believed Douglas the real author of the Clay proposals. Taylor Whigs and southern extremists, however, constituted a bloc of opposition that Clay and the Democrats could not overcome.

Northerners expected little of Clay because he was not one of them. It was the South that Clay's moderation offended. Georgia's John M. Berrien, a well-known conservative Whig, opened the southern offensive. Accepting Calhoun's argument, he asserted that he, as a slaveholder, had the right to enter the West with his slave property. Nothing in the Constitution, he argued, denied that slavery could exist in any territory that was the common property of the United States. He would employ his best efforts to avert disunion, but he owed his allegiance, he avowed, to Georgia. One day later, on 13 February, Jefferson Davis of Mississippi drew a packed gallery when he launched the southern Democratic attack. In perhaps the major forensic effort of his career, Davis pledged to uphold the Southland, now losing

its traditional role in American life. He accused the North of sowing the seeds of disunion by attacking southern institutions and society.

Calhoun's famous reply to Clay came on 4 March. Near death and so weak that he could not speak, Calhoun asked James M. Mason of Virginia to read his final plea for the Union—a Union that recognized the rights and institutions of the South. As Mason read, Calhoun sat in his chair directly in front of him, his hands clinging to the armrests like claws. Calhoun, like Davis, saw danger to the South in the gradual destruction of the old balance between the sections. Once, in the days of Washington and Jefferson, the South had felt secure in the Union. Now the North, with its augmented numbers, was on the verge of creating a consolidated government to pursue its advantage. Having gained the admission of Iowa and Wisconsin, northerners now demanded that all the new territories be carved eventually into free states. Against such aggression the South asked for simple justice—equality in the territories, the faithful return of fugitive slaves, the end of agitation on the slavery question, and an amendment that would restore the guarantees of the Constitution. In the absence of such assurances, Calhoun concluded, the future of the Union was fraught with peril. Together Berrien, Davis, and Calhoun reminded the nation that the South had a heavy financial and social investment in slavery, which it would defend at all costs against the onrush of northern numbers, power, and sentiment.

Meanwhile, Taylor's Whigs had not remained silent. Jacob W. Miller of New Jersey took up the defense of Taylor's simple program on 21 February. He supported the president's behavior toward California, arguing that Congress had the right to bar slavery from the territories; but, he added, the question was academic because California would enter the Union as a state. If the South denied Congress the right to act on the question of slavery in the territories, it should permit the people of the West to settle the matter under the president's program. The South would gain nothing and defy its own principles by resisting. That day Taylor visited Richmond to dedicate the cornerstone for the Richmond monument to Washington. His cordial reception in Virginia demonstrated that the debate in Congress had not marred his popular image, although Democrats attributed Taylor's good reception to the country's appreciation of his office, not his leadership.

Through his control of the Whig party, Taylor possessed the power to prevent a compromise on the territorial question, but he could in no way defuse the mounting sectional and legislative crisis. When the Whigs Toombs and Clingman urged Taylor to settle the California question by accepting Clay's compromise, the president retorted that the country would accept his formula for avoiding the territorial issue or end in disunion. He reminded the dissenting South that the federal government would use force to snuff out any rebellion. As in his election campaign, Taylor rejected any necessity to bridge his Unionist, antislavery appeals to the North and his rejection of southern demands.

Daniel Webster entered the debate on 7 March with the year's most memorable oration. The crowd jammed the corridors demanding admittance to the galleries. At sixty-eight, Webster suffered from poor health, but his presence remained commanding. He would not speak, he began, "as a Massachusetts man, nor as a Northern man, but as an American.. . . I speak to-day for the preservation of the Union. 'Hear me for my cause.' " Using historic argument, Webster cautioned extremists of North and South alike to be wary of their claims to righteousness. Webster could be magnanimous to the South in favoring constitutional guarantees of slavery in the states, because he knew that nature had declared both California and New Mexico free. Slavery could survive nowhere in the Mexican Cession. On the matter of fugitive slaves, he agreed with the South. His peroration was a magnificent appeal to the Union. He ridiculed the idea of peaceful secession. I would rather," he said, "hear of . . . war, pestilence, and famine, than . . . hear gentlemen talk of secession.. . . To break up this great Government! to dismember this great country!" Disruption would not be peaceful; it would produce a war, a war that he would not describe. Webster gave ringing affirmation to Clay's arguments, something that the Democrats could not do. Webster's remonstrance to both sections to forgive and forbear in the interest of national harmony antagonized those northerners who expected more of him. Ralph Waldo Emerson rebuked the senator: "Every drop of blood in this man's veins has eyes that look downward." Still, the favorable response to Webster's appeal suggested that much of the country favored compromise.

Several other speakers followed Webster during March and April, but they offered little new to the arguments. Douglas' address was important, not because it changed the trend, but because it revealed the Democratic ties to Clay. Douglas challenged Webster on a minor point and then turned on Taylor, accusing him of cleverly avoiding the territorial issue in 1848 in order to make people of each section believe that his opinions harmonized with their own. Now the president favored nonintervention, permitting him to defend the Wilmot Proviso without asking Congress to act on the issue. Douglas insisted that the situation called for action, that the administration, in dwelling only on California, was exposing the West to anarchy. Like Webster, Douglas acknowledged that geography had settled the question of slavery in New Mexico and Utah. Finally, Douglas praised Clay for proposing a solution of the issues before the country.

Douglas had long been active behind the scenes. Since February he had been negotiating an understanding between House Whigs and Democrats on the territorial issue. He arranged for his Illinois lieutenant, John A. McClernand, to report out of the House Committee on Territories bills providing for the territorial organization of New Mexico and Utah under the principle of popular sovereignty, California's admission as a free state, and slavery's retention in the District of Columbia. Douglas prepared similar bills for the Senate's territorial committee. He avoided the issues of fugitive slaves and the slave trade. In Douglas' preparations lay the foundations of the Compromise of 1850. On 31 March, Calhoun died, and the southern extremists were thus deprived of their most powerful and revered leader.

During April the Senate debate became ill-tempered and personal. Foote, as associate of Calhoun, pressed the Senate to refer the plans of Clay, Douglas, and others to a select committee of thirteen for the purpose of creating a new master plan. Clay and Cass supported the proposal. Benton favored a compromise but opposed Clay's omnibus arrangement. On 17 April the Missourian, whose previous exchanges with Foote had become heated, accused Foote of attempting to blackmail the Senate into action by magnifying the crisis with abstractions. The Mississippian rose to defend the southern leaders as patriots whose names would be venerated when their "calumniators" would be recalled only with contempt. At that statement Benton left his desk and strode toward Foote, who retreated toward the clerk's table, pointing a cocked revolver at Benton. Seeing the weapon, Benton tore open his coat and dared Foote to assassinate him. Senators surrounded the two men and restored order. To recover its dignity, the Senate appointed a committee to study the incident. The committee recommended no action.

On 18 April the Senate provided for the Select Committee of Thirteen to prepare a compromise measure and appointed Clay as chairman. Douglas refused to join the committee, convinced that a compromise would be possible only if the individual bills were voted separately. On 8 May, Clay presented the committee's report to the Senate. The three bills in the committee proposal modified and rearranged the original Clay compromise, but the differences were slight. After presenting the majority report, Clay turned to the minority members to present their objections. The result was confusion.

For three weeks the debate raged while the Taylor forces remained silent. Clay insisted that his committee desired to cooperate with the executive and that his program and the president's were reconcilable. But Taylor stood firm, advocating statehood for California and New Mexico as an independent measure. Against the northern Whigs and the possibility of a presidential veto, Clay had no chance. By July he was no closer to gaining a compromise than he had been in January. Clay faced strong opposition in the South, but the real barrier to his success was in the executive mansion. As the debates in Congress continued with no end in sight, rumors from the White House indicated that the president was ill. Indeed, Taylor had become afflicted with cholera and died on the evening of 9 July 1850.

Fillmore and the Compromise

Vice President Fillmore was spending a sleepless night when the cabinet informed him of the president's death. He took the oath of office the following day at noon in the House of Representatives. The chamber was crowded, but Fillmore made no speech. Newspapers across the country paid tribute to Taylor. The funeral ceremony at the White House on 13 July lasted until early afternoon. Taylor's body was placed in a vault at the Congressional Burying Ground. That evening Mrs. Taylor moved out of the White House. Later the Taylor family moved the body for final burial outside Louisville, near the president's first home.

Fillmore was a man of dignity, good manners, and conciliatory disposition. He was moderately tall, somewhat portly, with attractive features and sparkling eyes. Born in Locke, New York (7 January 1800), into a family of poor farmers, Fillmore was largely self-educated and self-made. He became an apprentice to two carders and cloth dressers; both

men added to his early misery. His exposure to books was so limited that at the age of seventeen he could scarcely read. He purchased a dictionary and stole occasional minutes to read it while tending his machines. After attending an academy at New Hope and studying law briefly under a local judge, Fillmore moved to Buffalo, where he entered a law firm to complete his legal preparation. In 1824 he entered the New York bar, enjoying immediate success as a lawyer. In 1826 he married Abigail Powers, the daughter of a clergyman.

In 1833, Fillmore entered the House of Representatives as a member of the Anti-Masonic-National Republican coalition, soon to merge into the new Whig party. As a three-term member of the House, he developed a reputation for reliability and devotion to Whig causes. As chairman of the Ways and Means Committee, he steered the Whig Tariff of 1842 through the House. Fillmore was a candidate for the vice presidential nomination in 1844. That year he received the Whig nomination for the governorship of New York but lost by a narrow margin. In 1847 he returned to politics as comptroller of New York. His nomination for vice president in 1848 on the second ballot met the needs of the party by adding a northerner and an old associate of Clay to the Whig ticket.

For sixteen months Taylor locked Fillmore out of his councils. The vice president had questioned the administration's effort to dispose of the territorial question by dividing the entire Mexican Cession into states and admitting them to the Union without slavery. The cabinet had proscribed Fillmore's friends and had scarcely been civil to him. With Fillmore's inauguration all members of Taylor's cabinet offered their resignations; Fillmore accepted them without hesitation. The old cabinet agreed to remain in office for one week while Fillmore organized his own administration.

The new president wanted only Whigs of national outlook in his cabinet. Webster now became secretary of state. Crittenden, having accepted the need for compromise, entered the cabinet as attorney general. William Alexander Graham of North Carolina, a staunch Whig on national issues, became secretary of the navy. Thomas Corwin, a popular Ohio Whig, became secretary of the treasury. Fillmore named his former law partner, Nathan K. Hall, as postmaster general. For secretary of war he chose Charles Magill Conrad, a sound Louisiana Whig. Ultimately the Interior Department went to Alexander H. H. Stuart, a Virginia Unionist.

With Fillmore's presidency the drift toward political chaos ended abruptly. Compromisers now controlled the government. Fillmore's cabinet appointments, all reflecting his preference for a compromise settlement, altered wholly the political climate in Washington. Northern Whig delegations that once supported Taylor now shifted to Fillmore. Southern Whigs such as Toombs and Stephens moved back into the Whig mainstream.

Clay, studying the trend, concluded that he could now push his omnibus bill through the Senate. On 29 July, Clay's committee, to strengthen the bill's appeal in the South, offered to modify the proposed Texas boundary and even encouraged southern extremists to believe that Texas would extend westward to the Rio Grande. Fillmore objected to this change and insisted on the restoration of Clay's original measure. The vote to reassert the original proposal failed. Now enemies of the bill struck out the California section, leaving ultimately only the territorial organization of Utah. Douglas' prediction that the omnibus bill would fail proved to be accurate. Clay, disappointed and exhausted, departed for Newport, Rhode Island, to recuperate by the sea.

Douglas was in control. On 3 August he predicted that the Senate would now pass the territorial measures he had reported out of committee four months earlier. By introducing the bills piecemeal, Douglas counted on varying combinations of Democratic and Whig moderates to carry them. The voting began on 9 August with the Texas boundary measure. Texas received more than Clay's committee had planned originally: it got $10 million from the federal government but conceded the Rio Grande above El Paso to New Mexico. That measure carried easily, 30 to 20. Several days later the California statehood bill passed, 34 to 18. The New Mexico territorial bill, which organized the region under the principle of popular sovereignty, won overwhelmingly, 27 to 10. Another bill organized Utah as a separate territory. The fugitive slave bill passed after a week of vigorous debate. Finally the Senate adopted the District of Columbia bill, which abolished only the slave trade, not slavery, in the District, by an ample majority of 33 to 19.

The House, under Douglas' guidance, passed the compromise measures against futile opposition. During September, Congress completed its work on the Compromise of 1850 and adjourned after the then longest session on record. Avoiding the question of the rightness or wrongness of slavery, the Compromise settled the status of the institution on every square foot of United States soil. Douglas and

his colleagues had gained a remarkable legislative triumph, one meriting, they believed, the nation's approbation.

Most Americans, sharing no interest in a sectional conflict, rejoiced over the Compromise of 1850. The individual decisions were direct and uncompromising, but they distributed the costs of accommodation. That some favored the North and others the South, however, enabled the extremist minorities of both sections to condemn what in the arrangement they did not like and attribute it to the determination of their sectional opponents to command the country's future. To some southern editors Fillmore had degraded the South and destroyed its equality in the Union. Taylor's moderate proposal on California and New Mexico might have served southern interests far more effectively than did the extreme proslavery demands of Calhoun and his southern adherents. Had the South accepted Taylor's assumption that slavery could not expand and that the territorial issue merely served to strengthen the antislavery movement in the North, it might have avoided much of the subsequent assault on its institutions.

For the North's antislavery forces, the Compromise was scarcely a triumph at all. The Fugitive Slave Act of 1850 proved to be the major source of sectional bitterness. The act placed federal enforcement agencies at the disposal of the slave-holder. Any black accused of being a runaway slave lost the right of trial by jury and even the right to testify in his own behalf. A federal judge or commissioner could remand him to slavery on the presentation of merely an affidavit of anyone claiming to be the owner. The law required federal marshals to uphold the act and levied heavy penalties against anyone who assisted a slave to escape. For southerners the Fugitive Slave Act was no more than legal recognition of their property rights and their only compensation for the admission of California as a free state. Actually Fillmore's effort to enforce the act produced what one critic termed "an era of slave-hunting and kidnapping."

Throughout the North mass meetings protested against the hated law. Many northern abolitionists refused to obey it. Blacks, aided by vigilance committees and a more effective underground railroad, made their way into Canada. The legislatures of all New England states, as well as those of Pennsylvania, Ohio, Indiana, Michigan, and Wisconsin, passed "personal liberty laws", which, in one form or another, forbade judges to assist southern claimants and extended to blacks claimed as slaves the rights of habeas corpus and trial by jury. These laws placed the burden of proof on the pursuer.

Foreign Relations

Taylor's administration had responded to the challenges of revolutionary Europe and British-American rivalry in the Caribbean without resolving either of them permanently. Austria sought to instruct the United States on its proper relationship to Europe's revolutions when its chargé d'affaires in Washington, Chevalier J. G. Hülsemann, lodged a protest with the United States government. He accused Washington of displaying far too much interest in Hungary's liberation. Fillmore agreed that the United States could not make every European broil an affair of its own. In his annual message of December 1850, he restated the traditional American doctrine that each nation possessed the right "of establishing that form of government which it may deem most conducive to the happiness and prosperity of its citizens.. . . The people of the United States claim this right for themselves, and they readily concede it to others."

In his famous reply to Hülsemann of 21 December 1850, Secretary Webster asserted that the American people had the right to cheer the forces of freedom in Europe, but assured Hülsemann that the United States would engage in no action that might give weight to its words. Neither was Europe to interpret the sympathy of the American people for struggling humanity as a sign of hostility toward any of the parties in the great national uprisings in Europe. Indeed, declared Webster, the United States desired amicable relations with all countries. Webster's references to the growing power of the United States and its right to voice its opinions toward events abroad were designed less to antagonize Austria than to foster Unionism in the United States with an appeal to national pride.

In 1851, Congress invited the exiled Kossuth to visit the United States. His triumphal reception on 5 December set off a Kossuth craze from the Atlantic to the Middle West; articles on Hungary filled the press. American orators used the occasion of his presence to express sympathy for the oppressed of Europe, but critics noted that Kossuth's open appeal for American support exceeded the limits of acceptable international behavior.

Then Kossuth set out for Washington, Webster revealed his deep reluctance to meet the Hungarian or to attend the congressional dinner planned in his honor. When, at the White House, Kossuth failed to resist the temptation to make a statement in behalf of his Hungarian cause, Fillmore responded with a mild rebuke. He reminded Kossuth that the United States had no intention of interfering in Europe's internal affairs. At a subsequent White House dinner, Kossuth's scarcely concealed anger embarrassed all who attended. To protect the administration from congressional charges that it had no concern for humanity, Webster attended Congress' festive dinner for Kossuth. There he exclaimed, "We shall rejoice to see our American model upon the Lower Danube and on the mountains of Hungary." But the obligation to establish that model, Webster added, belonged solely to the Hungarian patriots.

Jacksonian Democrats organized the Young America movement to exploit the cause of Europe's oppression. Douglas made a dramatic appeal for a more effective foreign policy before a Jackson Day audience in January 1852: "I think it is time that America had a foreign policy . . . a foreign policy in accordance with the spirit of the age—but not such a foreign policy as we have seen attempted to be enforced in this country for the last three years." On 20 January, Cass introduced a resolution in the Senate declaring that the United States could not again witness, without deep concern, the efforts of European powers to crush an independence movement. Cass's resolution aroused the fury of congressional conservatives, who reminded him that words and resolutions such as his demeaned the dignity of the country because the moral influence they sought to wield would prove impotent in affairs among nations.

Even before Kossuth left Washington for a tour of the Middle West, the enthusiasm aroused by his presence in the country had begun to evaporate. Clay reminded him pointedly that even if the United States declared war on Russia it could not transport men and arms effectively into the heart of Europe. Kossuth's receptions became more perfunctory the longer he remained in the country. In the South he faced indifference, if not open hostility. At the end he became the victim of the very enthusiasm he had created. Democratic politicians had used him in their appeals to American nationalism, but they would not offer him any effective support any more than Clay would. When, later in 1852, Kossuth sailed for England, he had collected about $90,000; otherwise, his mission had been a failure.

Democrats who had condemned the Clayton-Bulwer Treaty assumed that Britain intended to extend its influence in Central America. When the British in 1852 converted the tiny Islas de la Bahía of Honduras, long under their control, into a crown colony, Democrats charged the British with aggression in the Caribbean. Cass and Douglas declared the British action a defiance of the Monroe Doctrine and demanded that the United States defend the sacred doctrine. Cooler heads in the administration could see no danger to American interests in the British decision and refused to act.

As the debate over the Bay Islands raged on, the Jacksonians found another issue with which to belabor the conservative Fillmore administration. During 1849 and 1850 a Venezuelan adventurer, Narciso López, engaged in filibustering activities against the island of Cuba with the intention of overthrowing the Spanish regime. Polk had tried unsuccessfully to buy Cuba in 1848. When the Senate later that year voted on a purchase resolution, the South revealed a surprising unanimity in favor of acquisition. Thereafter southern expansionists supported López in his efforts to extend American control over the island of sugar and slaves. Among them were Mexican War veterans in search of adventure, planters in search of new lands, and proslavery elements who feared a Spanish policy of emancipation.

During 1849, federal officials prevented López from leaving the United States, but in the spring of 1850, with several hundred followers, he slipped out of New Orleans and landed at Cárdenas. The invaders burned the governor's mansion but failed to ignite a revolt. Soon they retreated to Key West, Florida. Facing only limited reprisals in American courts, the conspirators soon planned another invasion of Cuba. The movement picked up additional support from Cuban juntas in New York and New Orleans. Democratic editor John L. O'Sullivan, who in 1845 coined the phrase "manifest destiny," lent his pen to the crusade. Articles proclaimed the desire of Cubans to free themselves from Spanish rule, awaiting only a propitious occasion to mount their revolt. Much of the northern press denounced the enterprise and predicted its failure. Fillmore issued a proclamation condemning the plan to plunder Cuba. New York authorities prepared to prevent any expedition from leaving that port.

López again transferred his activities to New Orleans. Upon receiving reports of a Cuban uprising, he set off for Cuba with five hundred recruits in August 1851. Again the expedition found itself isolated. Spanish forces overwhelmed the invaders; executed many of them, including López; and sent others into slavery or penal servitude. Southern editors rebuked the Fillmore administration for preventing a successful invasion. Extremists staged anti-Spanish demonstrations, highly destructive of Spanish property, in both New Orleans and Key West. Even northern Jacksonians took up the issue. Douglas denounced Fillmore's policy of neutrality toward Cuba:

> They employ the American Navy and Army to arrest the volunteers and seize the provisions, ammunition, and supplies of every kind which may be sent in aid of the patriot cause, and at the same time give free passage and protection to all men, ammunition, and supplies which may be sent in aid of the royalist, and THEY CALL THAT NEUTRALITY!

Britain and France entered the controversy by sending naval vessels to Cuban waters with the warning that they would stop any further adventuring from the United States for the purpose of conducting hostile operations against the government in Cuba. The State Department objected. At the suggestion of Madrid, Britain and France, in January 1852, offered a tripartite guarantee of Spanish rights in Cuba. Despite Webster's total disapproval of southern filibustering, his replies to London and Paris were not encouraging. Finally, following Webster's death in the autumn of 1852, the administration, working through the new secretary of state, Edward Everett, sent a firm rejection. Everett assured British and French officials that the United States had no intention of seizing Cuba, but he reminded the two European powers that Cuba barred the entrance to the Gulf of Mexico and the Mississippi, that it stood astride the chief American route to California. Under certain contingencies, wrote Everett, the island "might be almost essential to our safety." Everett's letter was sufficiently nationalistic in sentiment to win the approval even of the Jacksonians.

The Election of 1852 and Retirement

Long before Everett disposed of the tripartite offer, Fillmore faced the question of his reelection. Unfortunately his own Whig party was rapidly disintegrating as a national organization. As early as the election of 1850, it had become evident that the Whig party would pay a heavy price for any compromise settlement. In several key Massachusetts, New York, and Ohio elections, antislavery politicians replaced well-known Unionists, while much of the South moved toward moderation on the sectional issues. Only in Mississippi and South Carolina did key leaders persist in the belief that the Compromise of 1850 was a betrayal of southern interests. Southern Whigs accepted the compromise but warned the North that any infringement of this settlement would terminate in disunion. Thus, the Compromise of 1850 was the only platform on which the Whig party could remain united. Yet so unpopular was the compromise among northern Whigs that no one even remotely associated with the Fugitive Slave Act could win northern support. What was to southern Whigs the final measure of forbearance was for the North totally unacceptable. The mass of southern Whigs nevertheless maintained their party allegiance in the caucus of 1852 and secured a campaign platform affirming the compromise.

Fillmore had long regarded his accession to the presidency sufficient reward for his political endeavors; he had little desire for another term. He remained silent on the matter of his candidacy and engaged in no political maneuvering to assure his nomination in 1852. When Webster announced his candidacy, Fillmore decided to withdraw formally from the race. Yet his friends prevailed on him to sustain his candidacy, at least passively, until by campaign time his public support rendered a withdrawal of his name almost impossible. Shortly before his death in 1852, Clay endorsed Fillmore. The Whig convention opened in Baltimore on 16 June. From the outset it was at an impasse as Fillmore, Mexican War hero General Winfield Scott, and Webster, supported only by New England, divided the vote. Finally, on the fifty-third ballot, Pennsylvania bolted to Scott, permitting him to win the Whig nomination. Fillmore accepted the decision with magnanimity; the party did not. The widespread distrust of Scott among the party faithful left the Whig standard in shreds. No longer was the national Whig party capable of fulfilling the political ambitions of its adherents. Weed admitted gravely, "There may be no political future for us." In the subsequent election Scott carried four states—Massachusetts, Vermont, Tennessee, and Kentucky. The Whig party had entered its last presidential campaign.

Fillmore's conservatism on sectional issues had alienated the northern Whigs, but his reputation for earnestness and integrity remained high among the party moderates. Franklin Pierce, who succeeded Fillmore as president, could not prevent the further sectionalization of American politics. The Kansas-Nebraska Act of 1854, which opened Kansas to slavery expansion, sent northern antislavery forces into open rebellion; most joined the new Republican party. By 1856 the Whig party was dead. Its moderates entered the Know-Nothing party, known in 1856 as the American party. Meeting in Philadelphia in February 1856, the American party endorsed the Kansas-Nebraska Act and nominated Fillmore, then traveling abroad, for the presidency. The northern delegates withdrew, limiting the party largely to conservative southern Unionists. The Republicans now dominated the North. The Democrats, in control of the South, gained enough northern votes to elect James Buchanan. Fillmore carried only one state, Maryland.

Fillmore never ran for public office again. He returned to Buffalo to become that city's leading citizen, devoting himself to educational and charitable affairs. He became the first chancellor of the University of Buffalo and the first president of the Buffalo Historical Society. In 1858 he married Caroline McIntosh, the widow of Ezekiel McIntosh of Albany. (His first wife, Abigail, had died in March 1853 as he was preparing to leave the White House.) Fillmore died on 8 March 1874 and was buried in Forest Lawn Cemetery, Buffalo.

BIBLIOGRAPHY

Elbert B. Smith, *The Presidencies of Zachary Taylor and Millard Fillmore* (Lawrence, Kans., 1988), is a judicious account devoted specifically to these two presidencies; it is generally complimentary to both. Avery Craven, *The Coming of the Civil War* (New York, 1942), contains good chapters on the politics and personalities of the Taylor-Fillmore years. Allan Nevins, *Ordeal of the Union*, vol. 1 (New York, 1947), covering the years 1847–1852, includes excellent chapters on Taylor, Fillmore, and the Compromise of 1850, as well as on the external challenges in Europe and the Caribbean. Holman Hamilton, *Zachary Taylor,* vol. 2 (Indianapolis, Ind., 1951), a long and generally sympathetic account of Taylor's presidency, is the standard work on the subject. Brainerd Dyer, *Zachary Taylor* (Baton Rouge, La., 1946), less detailed than Hamilton's study, notes that Taylor was almost lost in the events of his administration. William Elliot Griffin, *Millard Fillmore: Constructive Statesman, Defender of the Constitution, President of the United States* (Ithaca, N.Y., 1915), offers perceptive commentary on most aspects of Fillmore's life. The major study of Fillmore's life remains Robert J. Rayback, *Millard Fillmore: Biography of a President* (Buffalo, N.Y., 1959).

There are excellent biographies of the key congressional actors in the events of the Taylor-Fillmore presidencies. Richard N. Current, *Daniel Webster and the Rise of National Conservatism* (Boston, 1955), includes an excellent treatment of the debate on the Compromise of 1850. Claude M. Fuess, *Daniel Webster*, 2 vols. (Boston, 1930), long the standard biography, contains excellent accounts of Webster's role in the Compromise of 1850 and as secretary of state. Carl Schurz, *Henry Clay*, 2 vols. (Boston, 1899), although old, is still useful for its detailed account of Clay's role in the Compromise; it assigns no role to Douglas. More recent is Glyndon G. Van Deusen, *The Life of Henry Clay* (Boston, 1937). Charles M. Wiltse treats Calhoun's role in the Compromise generously in *John C. Calhoun*, vol. 3 (Indianapolis, Ind., 1951). Robert W. Johannsen, *Stephen A. Douglas* (New York, 1973), is the standard work on Douglas. George Fort Milton, *The Eve of Conflict: Stephen A. Douglas and the Needless War* (Boston, 1934), an excellent treatment of the events of 1850, focuses on Douglas's contribution.

Holman Hamilton, *Prologue to Conflict: The Crisis and Compromise of 1850* (Lexington, Ky., 1964), remains the standard account of the Great Debate of 1850. Edwin C. Rozwenc, ed., *The Compromise of 1850* (Boston, 1957), includes excerpts from the major speeches in the Great Debate, three interpretive studies of the Compromise, and several accounts of the year's events. Richard H. Shryock, *Georgia and the Union in 1850* (Philadelphia, 1926), focuses on the state's reaction to the Compromise, which was instrumental in determining the general acceptance of the settlement in the South. W. Darrell Overdyke, *The Know-Nothing Party in the South* (Gloucester, Mass., 1968), contains a chapter on Fillmore's 1856 campaign as the Know-Nothing candidate.

Recent works include Robert J. Scarry, *Millard Fillmore* (Jefferson, N.C., 2001).

Franklin Pierce

William W. Freehling

Franklin Pierce THE LIBRARY OF CONGRESS

A N intriguing paradox characterizes Franklin Pierce's administration: on the one hand, few administrations exerted such a powerful impact on the social and political life of the American nation, but on the other hand, few presidents exercised such little influence on their administration's policies. Pierce was an inconsequential charmer who staked his claim for presidential greatness on other people's not very charming initiatives. His failure was not just his own but also that of a political culture so fragmented that its factions could agree only on a pleasant nonentity as president yet so convulsed that it demanded a president who would act forcefully. A split culture thus bred a non-actor clinging to more forceful statesmen's actions as if they were his own but who was sure to be destroyed when his adopted initiatives enraged half his civilization.

Early Career

The convivial New Hampshire politician who was caught in this cosmopolitan historical trap had been born and bred to be a delightful provincial. He came into the world in a backwoods log cabin in Hillsborough County on 23 November 1804. His father, Benjamin Pierce, was a rough-hewn local quasi squire who had been something of a Revolutionary War hero. For himself, the elder Pierce aspired to be a leader of the Granite Hills, but for his son, he wished an education a little better than New Hampshire could provide.

Franklin Pierce was accordingly sent to Bowdoin College in Maine. There he studied enough to graduate fifth in his class. More important, he was so attractive a personality as to gain the lifelong friendship of the novelist Nathaniel Hawthorne. Hawthorne's least impressive literary effort would someday be the campaign biography of his college chum turned presidential candidate. Franklin Pierce's affability was even in college pointing the way ahead.

After graduation, Pierce wandered through several law offices in search of training. At this time, his swashbuckling father was reaching the top of New Hampshire politics. Frank Pierce plunged into his father's partisan political campaigns with great zest. The two Pierces rose together, both carried upward in the Jacksonian ascendancy. In 1827, the father was elected governor, and two years later the son was elected to the state legislature. In March 1833, the younger Pierce, not yet thirty, was elected to Congress.

Through it all, Pierce's family, fraternity, faith, and fortune rested in his partisan god, the Democratic party. "A Republic without parties," ran the future president's very first political pronouncement, "is a complete anomaly." For an undereducated young frontiersman without much taste for book learning but with great relish for political combat and camaraderie, the received wisdom of a rough-and-ready father, as embodied in the Democratic party, provided the best preparation for the political life. Or so it seemed to those in the Granite Hills who were charmed by the governor's heir apparent.

In Washington, affability was not enough, even to those who spent months drinking and chatting as residents of Washington's boardinghouses. Frank Pierce spent ten years in Congress, the first four in the House and the last six as a very young senator. In all that time, he made not one noteworthy speech, sponsored not one important bill, emerged not once from the shadows of the congressional hanger-on. He was known chiefly for being the congressman least able to hold his liquor. The reputation came naturally to this man of friendly manner, relaxed joshing, and relish for gossiping and partying. The New Englander, so often so tight-lipped and full of righteous learning, was here as genially openhearted as the stereotypical southerner.

The similarity of manner may explain part of Pierce's one congressional political passion, a whole-hearted adoption of the southerners' hatred for New England abolitionists. Because the Democratic party was so strong in the South and the abolitionists so drawn to northern Whiggery, the northerner with southern principles was most often a Democrat. Nowhere in New England were southern sympathizers so common as in New Hampshire. Frank Pierce was the perfect example of the New Hampshire Democrat as friend of the slaveholder.

Pierce made his feelings clear in the "gag rule" controversy of the 1830s, the beginning of the great contest over slavery for his generation of politicians. He was a passionate advocate of the Democratic party's policy of gagging antislavery proposals without debate. He ridiculed abolitionists as consisting of "children who knew not what they did," ladies who were outside "their proper sphere," and feminized men who outrageously interfered in other people's homes. Congressman Pierce found nothing such fun as having a couple of toddies with southern friends, quickly becoming boisterously tipsy, and then pouring drunken hatred on the fanatics who would break up the Union to abolish bondage.

In the early 1840s, Pierce came to realize such adventures were getting him nowhere. Strident support of the South and automatic acceptance of everything Jacksonian were making for a career of mere competence. Meanwhile, the Washington boardinghouse scene was altogether too tempting for one of his propensity for hard drinking. Residence in Washington was even worse for Mrs. Pierce, who was exactly the kind of righteous, unbending New Englander her husband so little resembled. In 1842, the failed senator and his scoffing wife returned to New Hampshire in search of better fortune.

Back home, Pierce found that his talent for social intercourse could indeed lead to a fortune. He became one of New Hampshire's richest and most successful trial lawyers. His genius was not in legal learning, for he rarely bothered searching the books for precedents. He was, rather, inordinately adept at sizing up a jury and appealing to their most intimate feelings. No opposing lawyer was as likable as Pierce. Few juries could resist his easy manner.

When the Mexican War came in the mid-1840s, Pierce was once again called away from his successes in the Granite Hills, summoned to a duty beyond his talents. A brigadier general, he was to lead his men in the assault on Mexico City but arrived too late for the final battle. He was wounded grievously and ingloriously: when his horse badly stumbled, he faint-ed and fell. His aching frame had to be hoisted into the saddle to ride out too late for the climactic Battle of Chapultepec.

When the war ended, he was once again glad to return to his smiling New Hampshire homeland. He once again became the most ingratiating of trial lawyers and the most pleasant of backwoods talkers. This was the man who one last time was called out of New Hampshire, this time to be president of the United States at a time of grave national peril.

Ascent to the Presidency

The incredible happened because, in the year 1852, only a man of Pierce's soothing mediocrity could satisfy a terribly divided Democratic party. In 1848, Free-Soil Democrats had seceded from the party to support Martin Van Buren's anti-southern third-party effort. After the Compromise of 1850 somewhat settled angry political turmoil, these so-called Barnburners returned to their scorched party. Southerners were not happy about having the fugitives back. Northerners who had stayed were even less happy with the returned "traitors." Everyone was prepared to hate everyone else's candidate, and any candidate with any firm position was bound to excite ire. The result was that none of the Democrats' leading men—especially Lewis Cass of Michigan, James Buchanan of Pennsylvania, and young Stephen A. Douglas of Illinois—could garner the necessary two-thirds majority of the Democratic convention.

The formula for breaking the deadlock was to find a southern man whom the North could trust; a northern man whom the South could trust; or, best of all, a northern man with southern principles whom not even anti-southern northerners could much dislike. It first occurred to a Virginian, on the convention's thirty-fifth ballot, that no one disliked Franklin Pierce. He was that rarity, a New Englander liked even by slaveholders. If the Barn-burners distrusted so southernized a northerner, they knew how pleasant he was and how he, with his easygoing nature, might respect differences. On the forty-ninth ballot, the convention nominated "Young Hickory from the Granite Hills."

In the election, the latest Young Hickory scored an electoral college triumph, 254–42, rivaling Old Hickory's. But his popular vote margin was dangerously thin. Pierce won the presidency despite receiving 14,000 fewer votes than his five opponents in the North. His national popular-vote majority of 44,000 came heavily from the Democratic party's southern power base. (Pierce's popular vote was 1.6 million, and that of his chief rival, the Whig Winfield Scott, was 1.4 million.) His was a mandate to lean a little precariously South, without quite losing a balance wavering in the North. It was the perfect posture for a northern southerner who loved everyone except abolitionists. The man and the hour had met.

Conciliation and Expansion

Providence quickly delivered another message to the Pierces. On the way to Concord from Boston on 6 January 1853, the president-elect's train car derailed and rolled down an embankment. Pierce and his wife escaped injury, but their beloved eleven-year-old son, Benjamin, the only one of their three children to survive infancy, was fatally mangled before their eyes. Mrs. Pierce, always a dour hater of the political life, pronounced the death God's way of leaving an inadequately prepared man free of domestic distraction. Pierce, who knew his credentials, thought she might be right. "No heart but my own," he told the nation in his inaugural, "can know the personal regret and bitter sorrow over which I have been borne to a position so suitable for others." Meanwhile, Mrs. Pierce was in her bedroom, penciling little notes to Bennie apologizing for not loving him enough.

The self-doubting president in the big gloomy house was mercifully presented with initial tasks he had been trained to handle. Pierce, an effective party boss in New Hampshire, knew how to use patronage to build a coalition. Democrats had selected him in part because a man so blandly conciliatory would invite all party factions to share the victory. His assigned task was to fuse both northerners who had bolted the party in 1848 and southerners who had considered breaking up the Union in 1850 with the middling sorts who had championed the Compromise of 1850 as a party-restoring, Union-saving measure. The task required critical patronage plums for Democratic extremists of North and South.

The conciliatory party boss from New Hampshire, predictably, conciliated. He awarded one of the leading southern radicals, Jefferson Davis, the post of secretary of war. He gave one of the leading New York Barnburners, John A. Dix, the assignment of assistant secretary of the treasury. True both to the southern-dominated coalition that had elected him and to his own southern leanings, appointments went more often to slaveholders. The southern tilt was the more pronounced because some of Pierce's important northern appointments, such as that of Caleb Cushing of Massachusetts to be attorney general, predictably went to northerners like himself, who considered abolitionists to be irresponsible Yankees. Cushing and Davis were ultimately the most important cabinet members precisely because Pierce was what he had been selected to be—a northern man with sympathy for slaveholders. But with appointments such as the sensitive Dix selection, the new boss had also been true to the party's need for healing. The politician had fulfilled his mandate.

The great middle of the Democratic party proceeded to wail that this appeaser of extremes had ignored the centrists. The whine echoes in the historical literature. Pierce, the patronage distributor, is often condemned for failing to steer in the middle of the road. The truth is that in the manner of the forgiving diplomat, he was trying to broaden the middle to include both extremes. If the party was to save the Union, he could do no less; if the coalition had needed an unforgiving centrist, he would never have been the politico selected. His patronage gestures to all left few in revolt. The question was whether his policies could equally well keep merely half-loyal extremists in uneasy alliance with the scoffing middle.

Pierce's announced policies combined the party's old unenergetic domestic program with its new energetic foreign policy. This youngest Hickory yet was a champion of the "Young America" program, which sought to extend American energies throughout the hemisphere. "My administration will not be controlled by any timid forebodings of evil from expansion," bragged the new president. Any domestic troubles from hemispheric expansionism would be settled by the soothing principles of the Compromise of 1850. For the rest, his administration would prevent government intervention in the private sector and thus cause no irritations. As with the patronage, he would be a peacemaker, unless perchance expansionism required some new Mexican war.

His first—alas, also his last—triumph was a peaceful extension of American territories. In the Gadsden Treaty of early 1854, so called after its negotiator, James Gadsden of South Carolina, the Pierce administration bought some forty-five thousand square miles of territory from Mexico at a cost of $10 million. The United States received less acreage than

Pierce desired and a great deal less than most ardent southern expansionists would like to have possessed on the slaveholders' flank. But limits on the territorial gain of the South had the unintended effect of limiting the political damage in the North. The more extreme northern antiexpansionists could not stir up a Mexican War-style revulsion against so slight a concession to Young America's appetites. The conciliating character in the White House had brought forth a conciliatory result, largely because the Mexicans had to some degree fulfilled yet blunted his administration's thrust.

Other people were not so kind to Pierce in his pursuance of the larger and more devoutly desired of his Young America policies. Cuba was truly the apple of this president's eye. His southern cronies wished it as an extension of their slaveholding empire. His democratic sympathies went out to Cuban victims of Spanish tyranny. He wanted to extend freedom for whites by buying up a territory enslaving blacks. If the Whig antislavery crowd found that formula grotesquely inhumane, the handsome president here again exuded that style of American humaneness, with a southern accent, that he was elected to serve. He only needed to secure this southern extension as genially as he had secured the Gadsden Purchase.

The president adopted a seductive strategy for bringing a Cuban purchase attractively to the American Congress. August Belmont, the American banker, believed that because the Spanish king was badly in debt, Spain's creditors could discreetly induce the monarch to ease the pressures on him by selling the far-off island. The American public could then be informed that the tyrant had willingly sold a neighboring people into American freedom.

Pierce put some subtle men into the right spots to bring off this delicate public relations coup. Belmont was given a diplomatic post at The Hague, where he would be in close proximity to the financial and political powers whose aid he would need to enlist. This move was suggested by future president James Buchanan, the ambassador to Great Britain and a prime advocate of Belmont's scheme. Pierce waited for the apple to fall deliciously into his lap.

Unfortunately, his Cuban initiative came to national attention with all the delicacy of a herd of buffalo. The chief buffalo was one Pierre Soulé, a swashbuckling Louisiana extremist whom Pierce had appointed ambassador to Spain. He pursued high-handed ways of intimidating the Spanish authorities into selling Cuba. With Spain stiffening against Soulé's public posturing, the Pierce administration decided on a private conference of its foreign ministers at Ostend, Belgium, in October 1854. From that meeting of Buchanan, Soulé, and Minister to France John Y. Mason of Virginia came the notorious Ostend Manifesto.

The manifesto, chiefly composed by Buchanan, largely urged the Belmont-Buchanan plan of quiet negotiations toward purchase. But Soulé insisted on some louder additional phrases concerning the forcible coercion of a monarch who would not voluntarily sell. Should Spanish possession endanger American power and security, declared the ministers, "by every law human and divine, we shall be justified in wresting it from Spain, if we possess the power." This jarring language, so different from Pierce's usually conciliatory approach, doomed Pierce's policy. The Ostend Manifesto, when made public, inspired an outcry in the North. Since the ministers were Pierce's, his administration was undermined.

The responsibility was in fact the president's. He had allowed the notoriously boorish Soulé to attend the European conference, against Buchanan's discreet advice. Pierce had permitted Soulé's presence because his southern friends wanted what they had achieved with the patronage—at least an extremist's input. But this time, indiscreet slave-holders had pushed too hard, and the likable balancer in the White House had been shoved way too far to the South to protect his precarious hold on the North.

The Territorial Question

The same phenomenon transpired in the central drama of the Pierce years. Franklin Pierce started without a policy on the Kansas issue. The vast area to the west of Iowa, soon to be called Nebraska, and the sprawling plains to the west of Missouri, soon to be called Kansas, were without territorial government. The land was ripe for settlement, and squatters were eager to get at the virgin land. Railroad speculators, desiring a central route to the Pacific, also wanted the area organized and populated. Few, least of all Pierce, wanted the resident Indians to remain a hindrance to white settlement. The problem was that the land had been part of the Louisiana Purchase. All of it, being north of the 36°30' line, was declared free territory by the Missouri Compromise. Southerners wanted the ban on slavery removed.

The hardest fighters for removal were Missouri slaveholders. They feared that if their state, already bordered by the free states of Iowa and Illinois, were surrounded on a third side by free territory, slavery in Missouri was doomed. Senator David R. Atchison, the Missouri slaveholders' champion, especially insisted on repeal of the Missouri Compromise before organizing the territory for settlement. Northerners deplored Atchison's insistence.

It had been easy for many years to deal with the problem simply by not legalizing settlement, but the option of doing nothing was no longer available in 1854, because pressures for organizing territorial government were too intense. With the Pierce administration still pursuing the time-honored expedient, the burden of resolving the problem was placed on the shoulders of the Senate Committee on the Territories, chaired by Stephen A. Douglas of Illinois.

Douglas, another Young America northern Democrat, was all for organizing a government to oversee territorial expansion, especially as he had some personal interest in a railroad route to the Pacific through these lands. More important, his Americanism assumed the necessity of establishing local governments in these areas so that white men could decide on their own institutions for themselves. He had no use for big government imposing policy on remote areas. He deplored congressional decisions, such as the Missouri Compromise, negating slavery in far-off places whose inhabitants might desire it. He wished to institutionalize local popular control, which he called popular sovereignty, by providing a territorial government for Kansas and Nebraska and allowing territorial residents to decide on slavery and everything else.

At first, Douglas sought to duck the politically dangerous step of actually repealing the Missouri Compromise and thereby repelling the North. He would say nothing about the old ban. He would merely report out a bill giving settlers in Kansas and Nebraska the right to vote for or against slavery at the time of statehood.

Atchison and other southerners would not permit that evasion. If the Missouri Compromise outlawed slavery in these areas during the territorial phase, no slaveholder would be around to vote for slavery in the statehood phase. According to Douglas' own popular-sovereignty principles, citizens on the spot had the right to decide on their own institutions as soon as they elected any government. If Douglas would not honor his personal creed, the South would block his bill. Douglas finally relented. He added language permitting local inhabitants to vote on slavery during the territorial years.

Southern Whigs, always eager to show that southern Democrats only pretended to be friends of slavery, pointed out Douglas' remaining loophole. Until inhabitants voted, the Missouri Compromise would abolish slavery. Thus, no slaveholding territorial residents would be present to legalize slavery in the territorial phase. Whigs, led by Archibald Dixon of Kentucky, accordingly demanded that the slavery restriction of the Missouri Compromise be repealed.

With pressure on Douglas mounting, Pierce and his cabinet belatedly realized that critical policy was being made outside the administration. The panicky cabinet hurriedly conducted its own discussion of the explosive problem. The debate yielded a solution the president thought just right. Territorial government should be organized with no mention of the Missouri Compromise and the question of slavery in the territories should be left to the Supreme Court. Pierce and the majority of his cabinet thought the Missouri ban was unconstitutional on just the grounds the Supreme Court would use in the Dred Scott decision three years later. Congress, reasoned Pierce, could not outlaw slave property without violating the constitutional ban on seizing property without due process of law. The Court would therefore have to decide to throw out the Missouri Compromise. The Court, not the administration, would take the blame for removing a sacred law, and the sacred Court could withstand criticism more than could an administration already vulnerable in the North.

The cabinet's program, so like the Buchanan-Belmont plan for annexing Cuba, was perfect stuff for a northern man with southern principles. Pierce was sure the Court would give the South everything a southerner could desire in a conciliatory way no northerner would find offensive. But Douglas had gone too far and knew too well that southerners would reject dodges such as Pierce's. On the very day the cabinet decided on an evasive way past the Missouri Compromise, the senator from Illinois caved into Archibald Dixon's demand to stop evading. Having decided that repeal of the Missouri Compromise was necessary to keep southerners behind the bill to provide government for Kansas and Nebraska, Douglas asked Jefferson Davis to arrange a conference at the White House the very next day, a Sunday. Pierce said he could not work on the Sabbath. Douglas insisted. Davis pleaded. The obliging Pierce reluctantly agreed to chat.

What transpired at that historic White House meeting will always remain a mystery. The atmo-sphere appears to have been tense. Pierce probably gently urged his plan. Douglas certainly insisted that political reality demanded his. At any rate, the world quickly knew that Pierce was making Douglas' Kansas-Nebraska bill the centerpiece of administration policy.

Why did Pierce accept the burdens of a pro-southern policy on Kansas, as on Cuba, far more offensive than his own? Because he again had no choice. Just as the Ostend Manifesto was proclaimed before Pierce could disavow it, so the Douglas policy had assumed a momentum of its own before the president could move to stop it. Moreover, in the light of the political realities that Douglas confronted in the Senate, Pierce must have been brought to see that evasion would not work. Pierce's proposal to let the Supreme Court decide on slavery was even more likely to be unacceptable to Atchison than was Douglas' proposal to let state-makers decide, and for the same reasons. Until the Court decided to let slavery into the territories, the Missouri Compromise ban on slavery would prevail; and even if the Court agreed with Pierce, the North would gain a toehold in Kansas before judges removed the restriction. Atchison wanted slavery in Kansas immediately and with no weighty provisos about entrance being legal. Given Atchison's power among southern Democrats, the Missouri Compromise had to be repealed or no Democratic administration could make policy. Douglas meant to make law. The president could choose whether to make war.

Pierce could only choose to make peace. Douglas' popular-sovereignty policy, after all, was Pierce's policy too. Local control was indeed the essence of what the Democratic party stood for. Pierce had not been elected to fight an intraparty battle to retain a big-government ban on slavery in the territories. He was elected to administer Democratic party policy in an amiable southern way. Now Missourians would not permit amiability to interfere with what they saw as a proslavery death struggle. The harsh conflict a southern-leaning coalition had elected Pierce to soothe was producing southern demands too harsh for the soother to handle.

With the two most important northern Democrats joining hands with the South on a proslavery bill, the national majority party proceeded to enact the minority's wishes. A coalition of almost all southerners and over half the northern Democrats controlled the Senate easily and barely secured the House. The Senate passed the Kansas-Nebraska bill by a lopsided 37–14; the House concurred, 113–100. Northern House Democrats were horridly split, 44–42 for the bill. With Northern Whig congressmen, 45 strong, unanimously against Douglas' creation, the North voted against the South's wishes by an overwhelming two-thirds majority.

Thus was enacted perhaps the most important legislation any administration ever sponsored. Perhaps not even the Federal Reserve Act or the Social Security Act had such an enormous immediate impact on the American people. The Kansas-Nebraska Act, which the Pierce administration had finally made its own, led directly to the rise of the Republican party, Bleeding Kansas, the collapse of the National Democratic party, and Abraham Lincoln's election. The inconsequential Mr. Pierce, by joining Stephen A. Douglas in bowing to the South's pressure, had finally become monumentally consequential.

The first price of enacting the South's wishes over the North's protests was the destruction of any possible benefit from Pierce's conciliation of the northern Barnburners. The irrelevance of the earlier uproar about patronage was now apparent. On the one hand, John Dix's appointment was scarcely sufficient to stop another, and this time irretrievable, bolt from the Democratic party by northern Free-Soilers, who were appalled that areas where slavery had been banned were now open to it. On the other hand, the lack of patronage for moderate Democrats in both North and South was scarcely sufficient to provoke men in the middle toward extremist parties. Southern Democrats were delighted with the Kansas-Nebraska Act; northern moderates were frightened by the storm of Yankee Free-Soil fanaticism.

In the midterm elections of 1854, Free-Soil, anti-Nebraska agitation yielded the utter destruction of that fragile northern plurality Pierce had received in 1852. In the congressional election, Democrats lost every Free-Soil state except California and Pierce's own New Hampshire. The president was mystified by all those northern voters beyond his state. Why worry about repealing the Missouri Compromise? The Court would have soon declared it unconstitutional anyway. Why worry about slavery in Kansas? The place was too far north for bondage. Why not appease the South? The law would give the North every opportunity to push its superior numbers into the West. Young Hickory from the Granite Hills, for all his attempts to do things indirectly, simply could not understand why the direct policies stuffed down his reluctant throat seemed so morally atrocious to

other Yankees. The provincial was out of contact with his section.

Bleeding Kansas

The Pierce administration's last two years were anticlimactic and predictable. With the North on fire over the Kansas-Nebraska Act and the president at a loss to understand why, the administration was in no position to keep ahead of an ever-worsening crisis. Moreover, even with all the advantage of hindsight, one cannot see how anyone could have prevented the disaster that came to be known as Bleeding Kansas. The same passion for protecting slavery in Missouri that had led Atchison to insist on repealing the Missouri Compromise inevitably led Missouri ruffians to pour into Kansas, seeking to legalize slavery. The same revulsion for repealing emancipation that had led northerners to turn against the Democratic party led New England settlers to race west, seeking to reinstall freedom. Against all this, the bland president again had but the same blunt weapon—he could appoint conciliatory administrators.

Conciliation again could not be enough. Pierce's compromise choice for territorial governor of Kansas was Andrew Reeder of Pennsylvania, still another northern man with southern principles. Reeder, like Douglas' first Kansas-Nebraska draft, adopted too conciliatory a stance to suit proslavery Missourians. Atchison and other Missouri roughnecks believed that northern "fanatics," organized in the New England Emigrant Aid Company, were invading Kansas to prevent the adoption of slavery. The Missourians accordingly developed what they considered a counterinsurgency policy of pushing more proslavery settlers into Kansas and, failing that, of propelling Missourians over the border at the last moment to vote proslavery on election day, 30 March 1855. They demanded that the governor recognize their elected government, wherever they wished to establish it. With the aid of Missourians in Kansas for the day, proslavery settlers selected a proslavery legislature to meet near Missouri's border.

Northerners, on the other hand, called these transient voters illegitimate. Free-Soilers believed aggressive Missourians were first to cause all Kansas' troubles. Northern settlers accordingly urged Reeder to nullify the election of the first, proslavery Kansas legislature.

Reeder tried to satisfy both sides. On the critical matter of certifying the election of proslavery legislators, the governor accepted most of the southern selections and called the legislature into session. But his call edged toward "fairness" by declaring that the legislature should meet one hundred miles distant from the Missouri border. Atchison protested that the location was too northern to be fair. The Missouri senator also undercut Reeder's pose of fairness by noting that the governor owned the land where he had called the legislature to meet. Atchison brusquely demanded Reeder's ouster. The Missouri titan urged the appointment of a governor more sympathetic with southern attempts to repress northerners' "invasion" of a "southern" homeland.

Pierce, with his lifelong hatred of abolitionists, accepted Atchison's premises. The president thought the Kansas governor remiss for not blaming the origins of the trouble on the "invading" New England Emigrant Aid Company. Pierce also deplored Reeder's inability to demonstrate that local control by the settlers themselves worked fairly and peacefully. In July 1855, after some wavering, the president dismissed Reeder. Pierce then appointed as Kansas governor yet another conciliatory northern man with southern principles, Wilson Shannon, former governor of Ohio.

The territory Shannon was sent out to administer was now simply not administrable. Northern settlers had organized their own government under the so-called Topeka Constitution. With two governments claiming legitimacy and responsibility for law and order, violence could not be avoided. Shannon spent the better part of a year asking Pierce for troops to deter bloodshed.

Not even soldiers could prevent war. In May 1856 the nation's newspapers blazed with the news of a total breakdown of civil peace in Kansas. First came tidings of the southern sack of the Free-Soil town of Lawrence. Then came news of the so-called Pottawatomie Massacre, in which John Brown and seven others murdered five proslavery settlers near Pottawatomie Creek on 24–25 May 1856.

Pierce's bad fortune was to have the Democratic National Convention of 1856 meet in Cincinnati at the very moment the most bloody news was coming east. Whoever was to blame for the breakdown of government in Kansas (and Pierce always blamed the New England Emigrant Aid Company), the president's administration was not providing law and order. The Kansas-Nebraska Act, itself a political horror in the North, was doubling the horror by ushering in a stream of events indicating that the Democratic party's master formula, local control of slavery-related matters, produced not fairness but disaster in the territories.

Pierce dearly wished for another term, for another chance to prove that his administration could yet rescue the principle of popular sovereignty. But his moment had long since passed. In 1852 the party had needed a Yankee who leaned South with a smile. In 1856, Pierce's coalition needed a northern man with southern principles disassociated from policies Pierce had frowned upon but swallowed. James Buchanan, Pierce's man in England, had luckily been out of the country throughout the events that had made the last of the Young Hickories very old very quickly. In June 1856, Buchanan easily wrested the party nomination from the sitting president. That had never happened before in American politics.

Pierce never recovered from this unprecedented repudiation. His presidential term having ended as dismally as his congressional years, he was reduced to wandering over the globe until 1860, wondering what had gone wrong. Thereafter he sank even more deeply into an alcoholic haze, his lifelong battle with the demon drink dismally lost. He died in 1869, almost unnoticed, once again almost unknown. His reputation in the history books is about as bleak. So it had to be for an easygoing New Hampshire backwoodsman who was called forth to keep a party happy but savaged in a conflict fast yielding blood and bullets and old men trying to find laughter at the bottom of a bottle.

BIBLIOGRAPHY

Nathaniel Hawthorne, *Life of Franklin Pierce* (Boston, 1852), the first biography of Pierce, was written by his college friend. Allan Nevins, *Ordeal of the Union*, 2 vols. (New York, 1947), is a massive, wonderfully readable narrative of national history during the Pierce years. Roy Nichols, *Franklin Pierce: Young Hickory of the Granite Hills* (Philadelphia, 1931), the best biography of Pierce and one of the best of any president, is still very reliable. Larry Gara, *The Presidency of Franklin Pierce* (Lawrence, Kans., 1991), is especially informative on foreign policy matters. See also Wilfred J. Bisson, comp., *Franklin Pierce: A Bibliography* (Westport, Conn., 1993).

James Buchanan

Elbert B. Smith

James Buchanan THE LIBRARY OF CONGRESS

JAMES BUCHANAN was neither exciting nor charismatic, but the power of his office and his character, principles, beliefs, and affinities blended with the extraordinary situations and events of his administration to make him a highly significant president. Historians may argue forever over whether or not the Civil War had become inevitable by the time Buchanan took office, but he clearly exercised a powerful influence on the crises leading to war.

When Buchanan was inaugurated in 1857, prosperity and economic expansion marked all sections, but the North and South were bitterly divided over the question of slavery in new territories, most of which were unsuited for slavery because of climate and geography. Most northerners, usually living in states that practiced severe forms of racial discrimination, were willing to tolerate slavery where it already existed but would not risk its expansion into new areas or give it moral approval by granting the legal right of expansion even into areas where it could not exist. Most southern leaders would not settle for tolerance and indeed craved moral approval in the form of equal rights for slavery whether or not any practical advantage was involved. Conversely, the denial of equal rights was a moral condemnation and a threat to the self-esteem of a proud and sensitive people.

[193]

Many northerners believed that the South was trying to spread slavery not only westward but even to the northern states. Many southerners feared that the restriction against slavery in such remote places as Oregon and New Mexico was the first step toward total abolition. Both perceptions were false, and an eloquent president able to understand the situation and the feelings of each area might have contributed much to sectional peace. Harmony was Buchanan's primary goal, but his predilections helped make his dream impossible.

Character and Convictions

Born on 23 April 1791 to hardworking Scotch-Irish parents near Mercersburg, Pennsylvania, Buchanan graduated from Dickinson College in 1809. After a successful legal career in Lancaster, Pennsylvania, and a term in the state legislature, he spent forty years, with brief interruptions, as congressman, senator, secretary of state under James K. Polk, and minister to Great Britain under Franklin Pierce.

Probably eyeing the presidency from the beginning, Buchanan carefully and shrewdly maneuvered his way through numerous controversies and crises, and usually either emerged on the popular side or avoided any public commitment at all. Some historians have considered him indecisive and weak, but his decisions and actions usually served a clear-cut purpose. In 1824 he strongly supported Henry Clay for president, but even after contradicting Andrew Jackson publicly, he was on Old Hickory's winning side by 1828. As a representative and senator, he was regularly elected first as a Federalist and then as a Democrat in a state where each party was usually divided bitterly on both issues and personalities. As secretary of state, he opposed President Polk's demand for 54°40' as the boundary of Oregon; prepared a brilliant argument for 54°40' refused to support his own argument and advocated a compromise; and, finally, on the grounds that 54°40' was correct, refused to help prepare the message submitting 49° to the Senate. During the Mexican War he advocated only limited annexations, opposed Polk's effort to send a prestigious peace commission for fear it would not demand enough territory, and finally opposed the actual peace treaty because it did not annex more territory to the United States. Perhaps he was indecisive, but he emerged from the bitterly controversial Polk administration with no serious political scars.

Buchanan, however, was not without strong feelings and convictions. As a young man he had vowed to remain a bachelor when his fiancée died shortly after an unexplained estrangement. He was an extrovert who craved affection and companionship, and as a congressman and senator he formed close personal friendships with southern colleagues who often left their wives at home and tended to dominate Washington's boardinghouse society. His dearest friend and longtime roommate was Senator and later Vice President William R. King of Alabama, and Howell Cobb of Georgia and Jefferson Davis also occupied strong places in his affections. Buchanan was also the patriarch and chief financial supporter of an enormous brood of orphaned cousins, nieces, and nephews and could appreciate the southern defense of slavery as a paternalistic institution. He ultimately accumulated a fortune of some $300,000 as a lawyer and investor, but his most cherished possession was Wheatland, a manorial estate near Lancaster. He could understand the psychic rewards of a marginally profitable plantation because he shared them. For these and perhaps other reasons, James Buchanan by 1857 had thoroughly identified himself emotionally with the South and its fears and ambitions. He occasionally expressed a dislike for slavery, but at no time did he publicly oppose its expansion or express any repugnance against such a possibility. In 1826 he denounced slavery as a political and moral evil that could not be remedied without the "introduction of evils infinitely greater." Emancipation, he opined, would turn the slaves into masters, and "who could for a moment indulge in the horrible idea of abolishing slavery by the massacre of the high-minded, and the chivalrous race of men in the South? . . . For my own part I would, without hesitation, buckle on my knapsack, and march . . . in defense of their cause."

In 1850 Buchanan supported the Compromise and condemned the Wilmot Proviso, which would have forbidden slavery in the territories taken from Mexico. Serving as minister to England from 1853 to 1857, he avoided the bitter debates over the Kansas-Nebraska Act, which repealed the Missouri Compromise ban on slavery north of 36°30'. With the U.S. ministers to France and Spain (both southerners), however, he co-authored the Ostend Manifesto, which urged the annexation of Cuba by force if necessary to protect American slavery against the threat of abolition in Cuba.

The President and His Administration

In 1856 Buchanan won the Democratic nomination in a grueling convention that rejected its more popular and more controversial candidates. He was elected president with only 45 percent of the popular vote and carried only four of the fourteen northern states. In their campaign platform, the Republicans had condemned the pro-southern President Pierce and his administration as criminals to be severely punished. In return, numerous southern leaders warned that the election of an entirely northern Republican president would justify and require secession. The Republican Frémont had won a northern majority, but Buchanan and the Democrats had won a slim national victory, greatly helped by the Know-Nothing candidacy of Millard Fillmore. Any further defection to the Republicans by northern Democrats in 1860 could easily elect a Republican president and make secession likely. Thus, Buchanan's goal of sectional peace would require first the reunification of the Democratic party.

Party unity would demand of Buchanan a harmonious relationship with Senator Stephen A. Douglas, the party's most popular northwestern leader. Douglas had authored the Kansas-Nebraska Act, which repealed the Missouri Compromise barrier against western slavery and decreed that territorial citizens themselves could decide for or against slavery. Douglas was still popular in the South and had contributed much time and, by his own account, $40,000 to Buchanan's election. Buchanan, however, envied, resented, and disliked Douglas, and southern radicals considered the senator a threat to their ambitions. After thanking the famous senator in a letter addressed to "Samuel A. Douglas," the president awarded the northwestern political patronage, including cabinet posts, to Douglas' most bitter enemies.

Advised primarily by southern friends, Buchanan chose for his cabinet four slaveholding southerners: Howell Cobb, Jacob Thompson, John B. Floyd, and Aaron Brown for the departments of Treasury, Interior, War, and the Post Office, respectively. The State and Navy departments and the attorney general's office went to northerners Lewis Cass, Isaac Toucey, and Jeremiah Black. Cass was senile and useless; Toucey was pro-southern, like the president; and Black would be pro-southern on legal grounds until after the actual secession. The big-city politicians, representatives of commerce and industry, Free-Soil Democrats, and popular-sovereignty followers of Douglas were ignored. The cabinet was a homogeneous group of rural politicians and lawyers still wedded to the America of Andrew Jackson, while the

President Buchanan (center) surrounded by his cabinet. Seated left to right are Jacob Thompson, John B. Floyd, Isaac Toucey, and Jeremiah Black. Standing left to right are Lewis Cass, Howell Cobb, and Joseph Holt. BETTMANN/CORBIS

president himself had been either out of office or serving as minister in England for the past eight years. The group was united by strong southern viewpoints and antiquated and often inaccurate assumptions. Many historians have considered Buchanan a weak president dominated by his cabinet, often called "the Directory," but this is incorrect. Buchanan was an energetic, shrewd, stubborn man who deliberately selected advisers and subordinates whose views he already shared. The unanimity with which they faced their opponents and the disagreement of historians with the wisdom of their policies do not mean that the president was a weakling.

It is true that Buchanan did have a unique relationship with his cabinet. His niece Harriet Lane was his official hostess, but his cabinet members and their wives were his real family. They visited and came to dinner frequently and provided the companionship he needed. Cobb in particular occasionally lived at the White House for weeks at a time. Along with a few like-minded congressmen and senators, they were a clan bound together by intense loyalty and a total inability or unwillingness to recognize the wisdom, integrity, or justice of any opponent or opposing position. To the end of his life, Buchanan blamed the Civil War primarily on the work of a few misguided northern fanatics. The massive northern vote for Frémont in 1856 and for Lincoln in 1860 apparently escaped his attention.

Dred Scott

Preparing his inaugural address, Buchanan faced a serious dilemma. His platform had endorsed popular sovereignty but had conveniently left unspecified the point at which the decision on slavery would be made. Southerners insisted that the matter could be decided only at the point of statehood, after slavery had had at least a chance and when a rejection could be attributed to climate, geography, or other impersonal forces. Northerners, including Douglas, would have the decision made by the territorial constitution before any significant number of slaves could arrive and before the accompanying racial prejudice could work to preserve even a minimal development of the institution. A rejection at this point would deny slavery any chance at all and could be based only on moral grounds insulting to proud southern sensibilities.

Buchanan shared the southern view, but saw an opportunity to shift the decision to a case pending before the Supreme Court. A slave, Dred Scott, had sued for freedom in Missouri on the grounds that he had lived with his late owner, an army officer, for several years in Illinois and Wisconsin, areas free under the Missouri Compromise. By the time the case worked its way through the lower courts, the officer's widow had married an abolitionist. Scott's freedom was assured, but all concerned insisted upon a judicial ruling against Scott for the sake of principle and politics. In response to Buchanan's inquiry, Justice John Catron had informed the president-elect that the five southern justices would probably allow the Missouri court's ruling to stand and would avoid a broad pro-southern statement of principle limited only to themselves. Catron also suggested, however, that if Justice Robert Grier of Pennsylvania would support their position, the southerners might change their minds and deal with the general questions related to territorial slavery. Quite improperly, Buchanan wrote Grier a strong request that he join the southerners. In his inaugural address, Buchanan announced that the Court would soon settle the issue of territorial slavery and predicted that sectional peace would result.

On 6 March 1857 the Court announced two basic principles: First, no Negro could be a citizen, and Scott's suit was therefore invalid. Second, slaves were property protected by the Constitution in all territories; therefore, neither the federal government nor any territorial government could bar slavery from any territory, and the Missouri Compromise therefore had always been unconstitutional. This direct application of the Constitution to territories contradicted all past and future rulings (which granted Congress arbitrary authority over territories) and caused an uproar in the North. In northern eyes, the Supreme Court, in collusion with the president, had destroyed all legal barriers to western slavery and had prepared the way for a complete southern conquest of the region. Nothing could have helped the Free-Soil Republican party more.

The Lecompton Constitution

Buchanan correctly believed that the Dred Scott decision would not expand slavery anywhere, but he promptly rejected an ideal opportunity to prove this to his northern critics. Kansas already had a large antislavery majority and was ready to become a free state whenever a free and fair election could be achieved. Instead, a convention at Lecompton, Kansas, elected by a small fraction of the eligible voters, wrote a proslavery state constitution and ruled that Kansas could vote for it with or without slavery but could not vote against the constitution itself. Only a handful voted in the December 1857 referendum, and the result was an overwhelming victory for slavery. With incontrovertible evidence that the Lecompton Constitution was acceptable only to a small minority of Kansans, Buchanan ignored the pleas of his own appointed Kansas governor and asked Congress to admit Kansas as a slave state. Kansas, he announced, was "as much a slave state as Georgia or South Carolina."

To southerners, Kansas was a slave state won in a fair contest. To northerners, the administration and its Kansas allies had violated the sacred democratic precept that the people of any state should be allowed to accept or reject any constitution in a fair election. In the Senate, Douglas increased Buchanan's hatred and damaged permanently his own presidential chances in the South by opposing the Lecompton Constitution as a fraud. Nonetheless, the administration and the southern leadership mustered enough votes in the Senate to approve the admission of Kansas under the Lecompton Constitution by a vote of thirty-three to twenty-five. In the House, a long and bitter debate punctuated by a free-for-all fistfight on the floor ended in a compromise that ultimately returned the constitution to Kansas for another vote. On 2 August 1858 the people of Kansas rejected the Lecompton Constitution by a six-to-one margin. Southerners were furious over the loss, while northerners were no less angry over what had been attempted. The northern vision of a slavocracy dominating the White House, Senate, and Supreme Court aroused defiance everywhere.

Buchanan responded to Douglas' apostasy on Kansas by using every power at his command against the senator's reelection in 1858. In Illinois, civil servants and newspapers dependent on federal contracts were ordered to oppose Douglas, and an administration Democrat became a third candidate. The contest featured the Lincoln-Douglas debates, which overnight made Abraham Lincoln a national figure but weakened Douglas still further in the South. Lincoln announced a formula on slavery that inspired moral comfort without imposing any disturbing sense of obligation. Slavery, he said, should be left alone in the South, but its containment should be firmly established to put it on the road to "ultimate extinction." This, he argued, would put the northern mind at ease and stop the antislavery agitation, which in turn would stop the southern demands and threats of secession. Douglas in his so-called Freeport Doctrine sought to reconcile popular sovereignty with the Dred Scott decision. Even though the Court had forbidden government action against territorial slavery, he said, a territorial legislature could effectively bar slavery by refusing to pass laws for its protection. Douglas was reelected, but President Buchanan had played a major role in promoting Lincoln's future and weakening the hopes of Douglas for the presidency.

Recession and "Cold War"

Meanwhile, the country had slipped into a brief economic recession in 1857–1858, and in the North new demands for tariffs, homesteads, a more effective banking system, and internal improvements at federal expense had been renewed. Most of these efforts were defeated in Congress, and Buchanan vetoed those that escaped. His solution to the recession was to deliver lectures on the virtues of thrift and the sinfulness of speculation. Thus, the midterm elections of 1858, which produced Republican landslide victories throughout the North, were probably a referendum on the economy and on James Buchanan as much as a vote against slavery, but many southerners thought otherwise. Also, Senator William H. Seward of New York, in response to northern Democratic efforts to minimize the party differences on slavery,

cited an "irrepressible conflict" between freedom and slavery in which only the Republicans supported freedom. Seward, a moderate prone to indulge in reckless language just for effect, promptly denied the implications of his words, but the South was not mollified.

In the background throughout the Buchanan administration a "cold war" of symbolic situations and events also developed. The actual number of runaway slaves was slight, and most were returned without incident; but many northern states still maintained laws in opposition to federal fugitive-slave laws. Several runaways were helped to escape under dramatic and well-publicized circumstances, and the Wisconsin legislature actually passed an ordinance of nullification against the federal law of 1850. The border states, from which most runaways escaped, were relatively quiet, but the Deep South, which rarely lost a slave, was in constant turmoil.

The corollary northern grievance was the refusal of southern federal juries to convict slave traders caught importing slaves in violation of federal law. *Uncle Tom's Cabin* (1852) continued to circulate widely, and Hinton Rowan Helper of North Carolina published *The Impending Crisis* (1857), a devastating attack on slavery for its crushing effects on nonslaveholding southern whites and a call for violent revolution. Frederick Law Olmsted proposed no action, but his essentially friendly volumes describing his southern travels were an equally severe indictment of the overall effects of slavery. On the southern side, George Fitzhugh offered two books on the humane and paternalistic characteristics of slavery as opposed to the vicious cruelties of northern capitalistic free labor. Fitzhugh was certain the North would ultimately see the light and adopt a modified version of southern slavery for its own white labor. In other books and newspapers, southerners were told that the North was siphoning off a major portion of the wealth produced by their work and talent. Northerners wrote of southern backwardness. Southerners denounced northern industrialism and its accompanying reform movements as fountains of socialism and atheism. Most of the Protestant churches painfully split into northern and southern divisions.

John Brown's Raid

Still, the common bonds of language, tradition, patriotism, economic interdependence, and religion appeared to be holding firm until October 1859, when the fiery abolitionist John Brown invaded Harpers Ferry, Virginia, with 22 men and some 950 iron-tipped spears. The effort was promptly crushed, but Brown had clearly intended to rouse the slaves to revolt, arm them with guns and spears, and begin an all-out war against the whites. Governor Henry A. Wise of Virginia refused to have Brown examined for insanity, and Brown insisted on the martyrdom Wise was eager to confer. Still suffering from wounds, Brown was carried into the courtroom on a cot, and he flatly denied any purpose beyond helping slaves to escape. He lied with magnificent eloquence and dignity, and the circumstances of his trial, along with his courage on the scaffold, helped mitigate the initial northern feeling that he was a monster and a madman. The abolitionists promptly canonized him. Thoreau compared his execution to the crucifixion of Christ, and others took up the comparison. More important, because Brown had been financed by a handful of rich northerners, southern radicals emphasized the intent, rather than the result, to convince perhaps hundreds of thousands of previously moderate southerners that the North really did intend to invade the South and start a horrible race war similar to that in Haiti from 1791 to 1804.

The Election of 1860

No one was more shaken by Brown's raid than James Buchanan. In his memoirs he listed Seward, Helper, John Brown, and the Republican party generally as the chief authors of the Civil War, and 1860 found him and his White House family still convinced that they were an island of sanity and justice in a cruel and unfair world. Thus, when southern Democrats demanded a southern presidential nominee and a presidential platform guaranteeing federal protection for slavery in all territories regardless of majority public sentiment within such territories, Buchanan lost touch with reality and agreed. Some of his closest friends warned that the election of a Republican president in 1860 would bring secession, and Buchanan should have believed them. While a moderate southern Democratic candidate might gain a significant northern vote, he could not possibly do so on a platform including a federal slave code for the territories, and under any circumstances he would need the support of Stephen A. Douglas. Indeed, the election of Douglas seemed to many the best possible hope for peace. He was pledged to allow the people of any territory to have slavery if they wanted it, and he had studiously refrained from any moral condemnation of the institution. He had also, however, refused to help Buchanan and the South saddle antislavery Kansas with a proslavery constitution, and Buchanan's personal hatred for him had become a mania. Buchanan had vowed publicly in 1856 that he would serve only one term, but he probably resented the total absence of any requests that he break his pledge. He knew that like his predecessor, Franklin Pierce, he could not be renominated, but he was determined to play a vital role in the immediate future of the Democratic party.

As a reward for southern good behavior at the Democratic convention of 1856, Charleston, South Carolina, had been selected for the convention of 1860. Radical southerners, led by William Lowndes Yancey of Alabama, were determined to split the Democratic party by demanding federal protection for territorial slavery, and they were shrewd enough to know that the northern Democratic delegates could not accept such a platform and still hope to win the federal and state offices for which many of them were candidates. But the "Fire-Eaters," as extreme advocates of southern interests were known, needed at least some northern support to prevent a reasonable platform and the nomination of Douglas, and this was provided by James Buchanan. Much of the Northeast had already fallen to the Republicans, and most of the delegates from this region, therefore, were federal officeholders beholden to the Buchanan administration. Also, it should be remembered, a considerable residue of southern support existed in numerous northern cities, where working people feared the possible competition of both foreign immigrants and newly freed slaves. Thus, the convention was essentially managed by friends of the president, for whom the defeat of Douglas was the primary object and a territorial slave code was entirely acceptable.

In the spring of 1860 the Democratic delegates arriving by sea, coach, and train found Charleston a beautiful city graced by blooming flowers and lovely young women in from the plantations to enjoy the social season, attend the convention, and supply adrenaline to the more eloquent radical orators. Southerners and northerners of the Buchanan camp met gracious hospitality everywhere, while the Douglas supporters were housed in a hot, uncomfortable dormitory. Tempers were shredded, and reason gave way to emotion almost immediately. The so-called Buchaneers and the southerners delayed the selection of a candidate until the adoption of the platform, and the platform committee recommended the southern program. In the ensuing debate, the great southern orator William L. Yancey roused the convention and galleries to a fever pitch by a long recitation of northern aggressions and by accusing northern Democrats of supporting slavery for constitutional rather than moral reasons. If northern Democrats would not make a moral commitment to slavery by supporting his platform, said Yancey, they would deserve even greater condemnation than the hated Republicans. Senator George E. Pugh of Ohio spoke for most northern Democrats when he replied bitterly that after years of losing elections at home by defending the South, northern Democrats were now being asked to avow publicly the righteousness of slavery to save the party. The Democratic party, shouted Pugh, would not be "dragged at the chariot wheel of 300,000 slave masters," and its leaders would not "put their hands on their mouths and their mouths in the dust."

On 30 April 1860 the national Democratic party ran aground, having been steered onto the reef in large part by the party helmsman, James Buchanan. The Charleston convention rejected Yancey's platform and voted for popular sovereignty. The delegates from eight southern states bolted the convention. Several weeks later, meeting in Baltimore, the northern Democrats nominated Douglas, while the southerners nominated Vice President John C. Breckinridge of Kentucky to run on their extremist platform. Buchanan and former president Pierce promptly endorsed Breckinridge, and the White House in effect became his campaign headquarters.

Meanwhile, a collection of former Whigs and Unionist Democrats nominated John Bell of Tennessee on a brief platform that spoke only for sectional peace. During the election campaign, this Constitutional Union party circulated a pamphlet outlining the horrendous results that would follow a Lincoln victory and thereby contributed much to southern hysteria.

The Republicans, almost certain of victory against their divided opponents, met in Chicago and rejected Seward, the conservative front-runner who had too often sounded like a dangerous radical, and turned instead to the moderate Abraham Lincoln, who had spoken only for containment of slavery and a hope for its ultimate extinction. With a candidate who fit almost every American stereotype of what a

president should be and a platform that promised tariffs, homesteads, internal improvements, liberal immigration laws, and western railroads—something for almost everyone—the Republicans had an appeal far beyond the question of slavery, and their candidate could be reasonably presented as the one most likely to bring sectional peace. The platform did not even require Lincoln to oppose the expansion of slavery unless a specific situation should arise, and no such event was even on the horizon.

Only Douglas campaigned actively, and placing sectional peace above his ambitions, he assured southern listeners that the election of Lincoln would pose no threat to slavery and begged them to remain calm regardless of the result. When hecklers asked how Douglas would react to secession, the "Little Giant" shouted back that he would suppress it with military force.

Throughout the South the 1860 election campaign was one long rehearsal for secession. Politicians and editors filled the air with warnings of northern conspiracies, new John Brown invasions, slave rebellions, the burning of homes, and the murder of women and children. Congressman Lawrence Keitt of South Carolina would never "permit a party stained with treason, hideous with insurrection, and dripping with blood, to occupy the government." In Dalton, Georgia, thirty-six blacks were arrested and charged with a plot to burn the town and kill all the people. In Talladega, Alabama, two whites and eight blacks were arrested, and one white man was hanged. Rumors that the wells were being poisoned swept through Texas, and a moderate opponent of slavery was hanged. A vendor of Breckinridge campaign badges was almost hanged because a Lincoln button fell from his bag. The threat of mob violence shadowed local conservatives and Unionists who might be tempted to speak out for common sense.

James Buchanan might have supported the contention of Douglas that a Lincoln victory would not justify secession, and he could have combined his support for Breckinridge with warnings that secession would be resisted. He considered the Breckinridge platform a reasonable solution and probably hoped the threats of disunion would do no more than force a northern surrender to southern demands. The administration newspaper, the *Constitution*, subject to Buchanan's orders under pain of immediate dismissal as the recipient of executive patronage, cooperated zealously with the disunionists. Lincoln's election, wrote editor William M. Browne, would put abolitionist officeholders in every community to spread antislavery ideas among whites and foment rebellion among slaves.

Douglas feared a rumored southern plot to seize Washington if Breckinridge should carry the border states, and campaigned vigorously in those areas. In the end, Bell carried Virginia, Kentucky, and Tennessee, while Douglas himself took Missouri. Breckinridge carried Maryland by only 700 votes. The total vote apparently indicated that most southerners still hoped to remain in the Union. Lincoln received 1,866,452 votes; Douglas, 1,376,957; Breckinridge, 849,781; and Bell, 588,879. While Breckinridge carried eleven of the fifteen slave states, he won a majority in only seven of them. The majority in eight of the fifteen voted for Bell and Douglas. The combined slave-state vote was 570,000 for Breckinridge and 705,000 for Bell and Douglas. Even in the states that seceded almost immediately, Bell and Douglas won 48 percent of the vote.

Equally important, the Republicans did not win either house of Congress. As Douglas pointed out, if the southerners would stay in their seats, Lincoln, tied hand and foot by his opposition, would be "an object of pity and commiseration rather than of fear and apprehension by a brave and chivalrous people," and in four short years another election would quickly remedy any real grievances. Also, the Supreme Court remained under firm southern control. Whatever the long-range prospects for slavery, the southern states were clearly in no danger from either Lincoln or the Republican party in 1861 unless they should try to divide a nation that Lincoln and most northerners would be determined to preserve.

Secession

In 1860, Lincoln won only 39.9 percent of the popular vote, the price of slaves remained high, and no one was threatening even to tax slavery, much less abolish it. Also, southern statesmen were fully aware of the northern Jim Crow system of discrimination against free blacks. Free-Soilism depended as much upon racist opposition to blacks in western territories as it did upon moral objections to slavery, and southern leaders knew it. The lower South had announced its ultimata before and during the campaign, however, and there could be no turning back. On 20 December 1860 a South Carolina convention unanimously passed an ordinance of secession with specific indictments of the northern states, and dur-

ing the next several weeks, six more states followed. Of the remaining eight slave states, Delaware ignored the matter, while seven rejected secession for the moment.

Ironically, the reasons cited by those that seceded were far more applicable to those that did not secede. Much was made of northern refusals to return escapees; and with John Brown the only example, the North was accused of inciting slaves "by emissaries, books, and pictures, to servile insurrection." Perhaps most important, the northern states had "assumed the right of deciding upon the propriety of our domestic institutions," had "denounced as sinful the institution of slavery," and had "permitted the open establishment among them of societies whose avowed object is to disturb the peace . . . of other states." And finally, the North had expressed the ultimate condemnation by electing to the presidency a man who not only denounced slavery as wrong but had openly said that the nation could not endure half slave and half free. Economic arguments were conspicuously absent. Southerners were determined to create a new nation that would prove to the world, to the hated Republicans, and perhaps to themselves that their critics were wrong and that slavery really was a humane institution compatible with America's most cherished values. It is important to remember that secession and the ensuing war would have been impossible without the support of the vast southern white population who owned no slaves but would fight for a system designed to keep blacks in an inferior position.

Just as Buchanan had contributed significantly to the election of Lincoln, he now aided the secession effort in states where the issue might have been in doubt. His southern cabinet members stayed in office until events within their respective states or special circumstances forced their withdrawal. All brought every pressure of friendship to bear, and while Cobb resigned on 8 December, after Buchanan publicly denied the right of secession, the others continued for weeks to wield a pro-southern influence and keep the southern leaders informed of his feelings and decisions. Also, southern congressmen and senators remained in Congress up to, and in some cases beyond, the secession of their states. They participated in debates, served on peace-seeking committees, did all they could to block any compromises, and bombarded their friend the president with requests, persuasion, and demands.

At first, both president and cabinet were unanimous in their sympathy for the South. A Pennsylvania judge wrote Attorney General Black a letter justifying secession, and when read to the president and cabinet, "it excited universal admiration and approbation for its eloquence and its truth." As always, Buchanan avoided all contact with Republicans, Free-Soil moderate Democrats, or anyone else willing to discuss the irritations, grievances, and fears of the North. Not until the end of January 1861 did he break with Browne, editor of the party's mouthpiece, who openly advocated and defended secession. His annual message to Congress on 3 December 1860 came before any state had actually seceded, although most of the federal officials in South Carolina had already resigned; and, as always, he ignored completely the northern side of the argument.

Since the Mexican War, an undetermined but clearly significant number of northerners had come to consider the southern territorial demands part of a gigantic slave-power conspiracy to spread the blighting institution and gain absolute control of the government. Northeasterners resented the southern success in blocking tariffs, while north-westerners blamed the slavocracy for their failure to get homesteads and internal improvements. Northerners everywhere had long chafed under the domination of southern and pro-southern presidents, southern cabinets, a southern-dominated Senate, and a southern-minded Supreme Court. Eight of the first fourteen presidents had been staveholders, and among the six northern presidents only John Adams, John Quincy Adams, and Millard Fillmore had expressed any serious criticisms of slavery. Pierce and Buchanan had supported every southern wish. Southern leaders had never grasped the fact that much of the northern enmity they resented so bitterly was a normal response to their own words and actions. They had long needed a president who would at least try to make them understand this, but the task was beyond the comprehension of James Buchanan.

The South needed reassurances, but not a presidential endorsement for secessionist arguments. Buchanan, however, blamed the crisis entirely on the "intemperate interference of the Northern people with the question of slavery." Congressional and territorial efforts to exclude slavery from the territories and state violations of the fugitive-slave laws could have been endured, he said, but "the incessant and violent agitation of the slavery question" had produced its "malign influence on the slaves.. . . Many a matron throughout the South retires at night in dread of what may befall herself and her children be-fore the morning.. . . no political union, however fraught with blessings and benefits" could endure "if the necessary consequence be to render the homes and firesides of nearly half the parties to it habitually and hopelessly insecure. Sooner or later the bonds of such a Union must be severed." Reviewing twenty-five years of "inflammatory appeals," Buchanan announced that peace and harmony could easily be restored if the slave states were "let alone and permitted to manage their domestic institutions in their own way." The Supreme Court, he continued, had ruled that a territorial legislature could not bar slavery, but northern radicals would give such a legislature the (power to annul the sacred rights of property." Furthermore, if the northern states did not immediately repeal their "unconstitutional and obnoxious enactments" against the fugitive-slave laws, "the injured States, after having first used all peaceful and constitutional means to effect redress, would be justified in revolutionary resistance to the government of the Union."

After admitting that certain grievances would justify secession, Buchanan argued rather brilliantly that secession was unconstitutional, saying that the Founding Fathers had never intended any such right and "the solemn sanction of religion" had been added in the oaths of office taken by federal and state officers. He suggested, however, that secession might be justified if it was called revolution instead of an inherent constitutional right. The right of resistance against oppression existed "independently of all constitutions" and was "embodied in strong and express language in our own Declaration of Independence." The federal government, therefore, had no power either to recognize secession or to coerce any state to remain in the Union. And finally, said Buchanan, either Congress or the states should call a constitutional convention that could emphasize the duty of the federal government to protect slavery in all the territories throughout their territorial existence, reconfirm the right of masters to have escaped slaves returned, and declare all northern state laws hindering this process to be null and void.

Buchanan had clearly learned nothing from the election of 1860. John Breckinridge, with a platform that embodied Buchanan's suggestions, had received almost no northern votes and had not even won a popular majority in the slaveholding states. Federal protection for slavery where a popular majority opposed it violated a basic precept of democracy and had already been rejected overwhelmingly by northern voters.

Thus, the president defended the southerners' own excuses for secession, denied them any such right, announced that he would not coerce them, and declared that secession could be prevented only by concessions that every southerner knew would never be made. The impact of his message on the secession conventions cannot be measured, but it must have weakened the Unionists, who were strong in several southern states. To northerners, the message was further evidence that southerners were ruling the country, and it probably made most of them even less receptive to compromise proposals. Southerners, on the other hand, found their radical arguments vindicated but were angered by Buchanan's refusal to admit the right of secession.

To his credit, Buchanan was keenly aware of the bloodshed and mass suffering a civil war would bring. He understood the depth of southern anger, pride, fears, determination, and courage, and he also knew the blood, treasure, and power the north could, and would, expend for the Union if a military confrontation should occur. He hoped the border states could be kept from seceding and prayed that peace could be maintained until the erring sisters recognized their mistake and rejoined the nation voluntarily. He eagerly supported every attempt by Congress to find a compromise, but all such efforts failed.

Just two days before the secession of South Carolina, a Senate committee headed by John J. Crittenden offered a plan to extend the Missouri Compromise line to the Pacific, but southerners and northerners alike rejected it. A House committee headed by Thomas Corwin proposed a repeal of the state personal-liberty laws, a southern jury trial for suspected fugitives, and a thirteenth amendment permanently denying Congress any right to deal with slavery. The amendment ultimately passed both houses and had been ratified by one state before the Battle of Fort Sumter. An ad hoc committee of national leaders chaired by former president John Tyler was equally unsuccessful.

Buchanan sent an emissary to Illinois with a plea for Lincoln to join him in a call for a national referendum on the Crittenden proposals, but the president-elect refused. Lincoln quite correctly believed that the South would accept no concessions less than those already rejected by northerners in the 1860 election. During the Corwin committee deliberations, Lincoln did agree that he would not oppose the admission of New Mexico if it should choose slavery, as long as everyone understood that this would

be the final concession. The seceding states rejected the offer as a plot to add another free state, even though New Mexico was the only territory left where slavery could have survived even temporarily.

Buchanan, meanwhile, continued to act as though the 1860 election had never occurred. Secession, he argued, had been caused by a misapprehension in the South of the true feelings of the northern people and a transfer of the question "from political assemblies to the ballot box . . . would speedily redress the serious grievances which the South had suffered." Unfortunately for Buchanan's aspirations, nothing the North would offer could keep the lower South from seceding, and nothing would induce Abraham Lincoln to accept a division of the Union. Neither James Buchanan nor a national convention could change these facts.

Fort Sumter

Buchanan could either make his successor's task far more difficult or to leave him with a situation uniquely designed to place the burden for beginning a war squarely on the South. Several federal forts located in the South, including those at Charleston, remained in northern hands, and Buchanan was under constant pressure to surrender them peacefully to the South. His southern friends desperately wished to confront the incoming president with a fait accompli, but for once Buchanan's head triumphed over his heart.

In late October 1860, a week before the elections, General Winfield Scott, commander in chief of the army and the Whig candidate for president in 1852, had written Secretary of War John B. Floyd that a broken Union could be reunited only by a civil war and that a lesser evil would be the division of the nation into as many as four new nations. After this startling suggestion, Scott recommended that nine federal forts in the South be immediately garrisoned but added that with most of the army stationed in the West, only four hundred men were available. Scott's "Views" were immediately relayed to Floyd's southern friends, and in January 1861, Scott published them. Throughout the following crises, Scott's advice to both Buchanan and Lincoln continued to be equally inconsistent. If either president had wished to surrender the forts, he could have done so with Scott's publicly expressed support, although the general would later insist that his alternative suggestions expressed his true sentiments.

Scott had correctly recognized the potential of the forts for triggering a war. The secessionists quickly seized all but those at Dry Tortugas and Key West, which could easily be defended, and those at Pensacola and Charleston, which posed serious problems. Fort Pickens, at Pensacola, was vulnerable, but it was located outside the harbor and could be reinforced from the sea without danger from shore batteries. At Charleston, Forts Moultrie and Johnson were shore installations and Castle Pinckney stood on a small island near the shore, while the unfinished Fort Sumter was a brick pentagon only fifty feet high on a rock in the middle of the harbor. Ships trying to reinforce Sumter could be attacked by shore batteries, as could the fort itself, but the shore batteries would be equally clear targets for heavily armed warships if the federal government should decide to use them. If the Carolinians would permit a token Union force to remain in the forts indefinitely, perhaps no explosion would occur, the border slave states would remain in the Union, and peaceful efforts to win back the others could continue. A southern attack could bring northern public opinion immediately up to the point of war.

Shortly after Lincoln's election, Buchanan and War Secretary Floyd gave the Charleston command to Major Robert Anderson, a southerner who was friendly to slavery and presumably would handle the situation with tact and understanding, but the fifty-six-year-old Anderson was first of all a Unionist and a professional soldier. He immediately began calling for reinforcements and argued that making the forts invulnerable would be the best way to avoid bloodshed. Supported by Cass and Black, Buchanan ordered reinforcements over the violent objections of his southern cabinet members. Floyd persuaded his chief to wait for a conference with General Scott. Before Scott reached Washington, Cobb and Thompson promised for South Carolina that the forts would not be molested, and Buchanan, in turn, revoked his order for reinforcements.

At no time was Buchanan ever ready to abandon the forts. They were federal property, not to be taken legally under either the right of secession, which he opposed, or the right of revolution, which he supported. The same constitutional scruples that denied him the right to coerce the seceding states also denied him the right to surrender the forts. Further, the northern press, like almost all other ascertainable public opinion, was angrily opposed to any suggestion that the forts would not be held, and Buchanan had always had a strong instinct for political survival as well as for his place in history. If the forts should

be lost through their neglect, he warned Floyd, "it were better for you and me both to be thrown into the Potomac with millstones tied about our necks."

Until his resignation on 20 December, Assistant Secretary of State William H. Trescot represented South Carolina at the White House, and afterward he remained an official envoy. As Buchanan continued to insist that he could neither make concessions nor recognize Carolina negotiators as accredited diplomats, the forts remained unreinforced and unattacked by mutual consent. On 11 December, Cass resigned when Buchanan refused to send additional men to the forts, even though only two weeks earlier Cass had strongly opposed the right of the government to coerce a seceded state. Scott also urged the dispatch of three hundred men to Fort Moultrie, but Buchanan refused for the same reasons he had given Cass: no state had yet seceded and Congress was still debating possible compromises. Buchanan moved Black to State and promoted Edwin M. Stanton to attorney general. The last three had supported the Dred Scott decision and the candidacy of Breckinridge for president, but recognizing the public temper, they now became the antisecession war hawks in the cabinet.

On 22 December a scandal broke involving corruption in the War Department resulting from the incompetence if not the actual venality of John Floyd, who had also ordered a shipment of heavy guns from Pittsburgh to Texas. Black furiously denounced Floyd on both counts. Five days later, Anderson spiked the guns at Fort Moultrie and moved his command by night into the less vulnerable Fort Sumter. Buchanan's southern friends came singly and collectively to threaten war unless the move should be countermanded. When Buchanan ultimately refused, Floyd resigned in protest from a position already untenable because of his malfeasance in office.

On 31 December, Buchanan, on Scott's advice, ordered the warship *Brooklyn* to sail immediately to Fort Sumter with troops, stores, and provisions. Scott then changed his mind and suggested that the *Brooklyn* might have difficulty maneuvering in Charleston harbor and that a fast, shallow-draft steamer might accomplish the mission with greater secrecy and success. On 5 January 1861 the *Star of the West*, loaded with men and supplies, sailed from New York. On the same day, Anderson reported that he needed no immediate assistance, and Scott himself sent the ship a countermanding order, which arrived after it had sailed. Scott then ordered the

Brooklyn to pursue the *Star of the West* and give aid if it should be damaged. If the Star could not land, it should return to Norfolk. At Charleston on 9 January it was greeted by heavy gunfire and immediately retreated. The shore batteries were within range of Anderson's guns at Fort Sumter, but he had received no warning that the ship was coming and was reluctant to start a battle without orders.

Buchanan was briefly a hero for rejecting the southern demands, but the ill-fated relief expedition brought attacks from every side. Northern editors called him a weakling, secessionists were furious because he had sent the ship at all, and southern Unionists agreed with the northerners. On 18 January, Scott allowed the press to publish his ''Views'' of October 1860, and his suggestion that secession was permissible and preferable to civil war must have encouraged the secessionists in the states still debating the issue. As other southern states seceded one by one, their delegates continued to hound Buchanan for a promise either to withdraw Anderson or refrain from sending reinforcements. For the rest of his term Buchanan kept answering that he would send help only if Anderson requested it. Determined to be prepared, the administration organized a relief expedition of four small steamers in New York with orders to be ready to sail immediately. Scott, Black, and Stanton wished to send this fleet before the harbor defenses could be made stronger, but until the day of Lincoln's inauguration Anderson continued to advise that he was safe and that such an expedition would suffer heavy casualties and do more harm than good.

Congress, meanwhile, refused Buchanan's every request for authority to do the things he probably did not wish to do anyhow. Bills for calling the militia and increasing his military power were quickly defeated, and no bill to raise money for defense was ever proposed. Heavily criticized for inaction, he replied that with Congress in session he could not use military force without congressional authority. Lincoln would later start with the advantage of an adjourned Congress. A congressional committee dismissed as groundless the charge that Floyd had conspired to send huge quantities of arms to the South, but various northern papers continued to stir up suspicions that the president was trying to arm the South. General Scott's first report to Lincoln and his later charges were in the same vein but were quite unfair. Buchanan did strengthen the other forts, and they remained in Union hands. Substitu-

tion of the *Star of the West* for the *Brooklyn* was Scott's own idea, and unlike Scott, Buchanan had never suggested publicly that secession should be accepted.

As his oldest and dearest southern friends vied with northern editors in denouncing him as a traitor, the weary president considered inauguration day on 4 March to be truly a day of deliverance. As he sat in the Capitol signing last-minute bills, a surprising and ominous message arrived. After weeks of reassurances, Anderson had just reported that a successful reinforcement of his command would take twenty thousand men. Buchanan and his cabinet were now vulnerable to unfair charges of gross negligence or worse. As a final act, they prepared a letter for Lincoln summarizing all previous dealings with Fort Sumter and explaining the naval force in readiness in New York. The crisis now belonged to Abraham Lincoln.

Foreign Policy: The Imperialist

Ironically, if the sectional quarrel had not overshadowed all other events, Buchanan might be remembered as a bold and vigorous imperialist, in part for his role in co-authoring the Ostend Manifesto. Futher, in a special message to Congress in 1858 he concluded, ''It is, beyond question, the destiny of our race to spread themselves over the continent of North America, and this at no distant day.''

In 1857 he ordered twenty-five hundred troops under Colonel Albert Sydney Johnston to suppress the Utah Mormons, and only the heroic work and tact of Thomas L. Kane brought the Saints into sufficient submission to avoid a bloody war. Buchanan publicly condemned the filibustering efforts of William Walker in Central America, but the Department of State released Walker, and Buchanan reprimanded Commodore Hiram Paulding for using armed force in the territory of a friendly nation, Nicaragua, while making the arrest. Walker later insisted that Buchanan had offered him secret encouragement, and Nicaragua angrily denounced the president for Walker's activities.

Buchanan boldly defied the British in several controversies. Fortunately, Disraeli and other British leaders had concluded that American control of Central America might increase the productivity of the region and thereby expand the market for British goods. Under Buchanan's pressure, the British made sweeping concessions to local government in the area. Relations with Britain were further complicated by British efforts to stop the African slave trade. Though committed by treaty to assist in this effort, the American government admitted no right of search in peacetime, and most slavers, regardless of nationality, would raise the American flag when British ships appeared. In 1858, when the British sent a small fleet to Cuba and the Gulf of Mexico, Buchanan, with full Senate support, ordered every available vessel to the Gulf "to protect all vessels of the United States . . . from search or detention." Rather than risk war, the British stopped their efforts against ships flying the American flag. In the Northwest, in 1859, a quarrel with Britain over the ownership of San Juan Island ended in a complete American victory after Buchanan sent a naval force and a small army under General Scott to the area.

Annually, Buchanan asked Congress for troops to quell lawlessness and protect travelers in Central America. Congress refused, but the president persuaded both New Granada (now Colombia) and Costa Rica to acknowledge claims against themselves. He bullied Nicaragua into granting transit rights and induced Mexico to grant the right of military occupation in case of disorder. Mexican civil wars continued to take American lives and property, and in 1858, Buchanan asked Congress for authority to assume a temporary military protectorate over northern Mexico. The Senate Foreign Relations Committee approved, but the full Senate refused. In December 1859 the president asked for authority to invade Mexico and obtain "indemnity for the past and security for the future." Fortunately for Mexico, Congress was entirely occupied with John Brown's raid. In 1860 the administration signed a treaty in which Mexico sold the United States transit rights and the right to police the route, but again the Senate balked.

In February 1855 an American helmsman had been killed on the Paraná River by gunfire from the shore. Three years later, Buchanan sent a commissioner with a commodore, nineteen warships, and twenty-five hundred marines and sailors to Paraguay. The expedition collected $10,000 in damages for the sailor's family, an apology, and a useless treaty of trade and commerce. Meanwhile, every effort to get money to buy Cuba or take it by force also fell victim to the slavery quarrel.

If James Buchanan really meant everything he said and really wanted everything he requested from Congress, he was prepared to annex everything from the Rio Grande to Colombia at the risk of war with nations involved or with Great Britain, if necessary. Threatening weaker Latin neighbors may not have required great courage, but if the British had stood their ground in Central America and had defended their right to search suspected slave ships, Buchanan might have had to choose between war and a humiliating retreat. Conceivably, he may have considered such tactics a possible tool for achieving unity between the quarreling sections—Seward would later recommend this to Lincoln—but if so, he was strangely blind to the harshly divisive impact of both the War of 1812 and the Mexican War.

The Final Struggle

Alone among American former presidents, Buchanan was denied a pleasant and honorable retirement. His well-known southern sympathies gave credence to ridiculous Republican charges that he had somehow been responsible for the fall of Fort Sumter and for the war itself. Stores exhibited banknotes picturing a red-eyed Buchanan with a rope around his neck and the word *Judas* written on his forehead. Lincoln's war message of 4 July drew heavily from an inaccurate report by General Scott and unfairly damaged Buchanan's reputation still further. A Senate resolution to condemn Buchanan failed but received wide publicity. Newspapers charged that he had failed to prevent secession and war by not strengthening the fort earlier, had negotiated truces with the enemy, had overruled General Scott by sending the *Star of the West* instead of the *Brooklyn*, had vetoed Scott's proposals to reinforce Sumter, had scattered the fleet around the world, and had tried to arm the South. Buchanan's most recent former cabinet officers could have come to his rescue with true accounts, but five of them had accepted positions with Lincoln, the others were frightened by adverse public opinion, and none would say a word in his defense. On successive days, newspapers announced that he was in England selling Confederate bonds and that he was in Pennsylvania plotting with spies. His portrait was removed from the Capitol rotunda to keep it from being defaced, and he was even accused of stealing pictures from the White House and keeping the gifts brought by a Japanese delegation.

At first, the attacks made him violently ill, but he soon recovered and defended himself vigorously. He demolished the charges of Scott in an exchange of public letters and finished his memoirs in 1866. The book refuted the charges of malfeasance, demonstrated the hypocrisy of his accusers, and restored his peace of mind. It also blamed the Civil War primarily on northern radicalism and clearly revealed the greatest weakness of his presidency—his thorough emotional identification with the South and his inability to understand and deal with northern public opinion on the issues that had separated the sections. He died on 1 June 1868 with no regrets and still certain that history would vindicate his memory.

BIBLIOGRAPHY

John B. Moore, ed., *The Works of James Buchanan*, 12 vols. (repr. New York, 1960), is a splendid original source, containing virtually all of the Buchanan papers extant. Philip S. Klein, *President James Buchanan* (University Park, Pa., 1962), best of the Buchanan biographies, argues that devotion to the Constitution explains Buchanan's policies. George T. Curtis, *Life of James Buchanan, Fifteenth President of the United States* (New York, 1883), a massive biography with much original material, is pro-Buchanan but valuable. Elbert B. Smith, *The Presidency of James Buchanan* (Lawrence, Kans., 1975), attributes Buchanan's policies to southern affinities rather than to personal weakness. Kenneth Bourne, *Britain and the Balance of Power in North America, 1815–1908* (Berkeley, Calif., 1967), is a source for studying Buchanan's relations with the British.

Eugene D. Genovese, *The Political Economy of Slavery: Studies in the Economy and Society of the Slave South* (New York, 1965), presents a tenuous argument that slaveholders had to expand slavery or lose their control of southern society. Alice Nichols, *Bleeding Kansas* (New York, 1954), clarifies a complex story. Don E. Fehrenbacher, *The Dred Scott Case: Its Significance in American Law and Politics* (New York, 1978), is by far the best work on the subject. James P. Shenton, *Robert John Walker: A Politician from Jackson to Lincoln* (New York, 1961), a biography of the governor of Kansas who fought the Lecompton Constitution, portrays an important figure. Louis Ruchames, ed., *A John Brown Reader* (London, 1959), presents differing viewpoints on Brown.

Charles Sellers, ed., *The Southerner as American* (Chapel Hill, N.C., 1960), particularly the essay by Sellers, reveals a sensitive understanding of southern psychology. Ollinger Crenshaw, *The Slave States in the Presidential Election of 1860* (Baltimore, 1945), also is essential to an understanding of the southern state of mind. Thomas P. Kettell, *Southern Wealth and Northern Profits* (New York, 1860), argues the economic disadvantages to the South of being in the Union, while Leon Litwack, *North of Slavery: The Negro in the Free States, 1790–1860* (Chicago, 1961), gives a strong argument against any significant threat to slavery in 1860. Dwight L. Dumond, *The Secession Movement, 1860–1861* (New York, 1931), is still unsurpassed; and *Southern Editorials on Secession* (New York, 1931), some five hundred editorials selected from fifteen hundred gathered by Dumond, is vital to anyone trying to understand the motives behind secession. Edwin C. Rozwenc, ed., *The Causes of the American Civil War* (Boston, 1961; 2d ed. 1972), is an excellent group of essays embodying different historical schools of thought toward the Civil War, including an essay on Buchanan. Avery Craven, *The Coming of the Civil War* (New York, 1942), is a pioneer revisionist work stressing distortions and false perceptions in each section. Harvey Wish, ed., *Ante-bellum Writings of George Fitzhugh and Hinton Rowan Helper on Slavery* (New York, 1960), is easier to read than the originals and omits nothing significant. Robert W. Johannsen, *Stephen A. Douglas* (New York, 1973), is the definitive Douglas biography.

Philip Auchampaugh, *James Buchanan and His Cabinet on the Eve of Secession* (Lancaster, Pa., 1926), brief and strongly pro-Buchanan, contains valuable information. James Buchanan, *Mr. Buchanan's Administration on the Eve of the Rebellion* (New York, 1866; repr. 1999), is his own highly revealing version of his travail. Charles W. Elliott, *Winfield Scott, the Soldier and the Man* (New York, 1937), is pro-Scott, but his facts still give the edge to Buchanan in their wartime controversy. Winfield Scott, *Memoirs of Lieut.-General Scott, LLD*, vol. 2 (New York, 1864), loses the argument to Buchanan even here.

W. A. Swanberg, *First Blood: The Story of Fort Sumter* (New York, 1957), is an excellent study of the problem during Buchanan's administration as well as Lincoln's. Allan Nevins, *The Emergence of Lincoln*, 2 vols. (New York, 1950), brings the period to life and adds significant interpretations. Roy P. Basler, *The Collected Works of Abraham Lincoln*, vols. 2 and 3 (New Brunswick, N.J., 1965), reveals much about the period and northern public opinion. Charles Crowe, ed., *The Age of Civil War and Reconstruction, 1830–1900: A Book of Interpretive Essays* (Homewood, Ill., 1966; rev. ed. 1975), is a superb collection of articles embodying the differing views of numerous talented historians. Thomas Pressley, *Americans Interpret Their Civil War,* rev. ed. (New York, 1962), is a review of almost everything ever written about the Civil War before 1962.

Abraham Lincoln

Gabor S. Boritt with Matthew Pinsker

Abraham Lincoln THE LIBRARY OF CONGRESS

THE date was 11 February 1861. One day short of his fifty-second birthday, Abraham Lincoln, president-elect of the United States, was saying his farewell to his hometown of Springfield, Illinois:

> My friends—No one, not in my situation, can appreciate my feeling of sadness at this parting. To this place, and the kindness of these people, I owe every thing. Here I have lived a quarter of a century, and have passed from a young to an old man. Here my children have been born, and one is buried. I now leave, not knowing when, or whether ever, I may return, with a task before me greater than that which rested upon Washington. Without the assistance of the Divine Being, who ever attended him, I cannot succeed. With

that assistance I cannot fail. Trusting in Him, who can go with me, and remain with you and be every where for good, let us confidently hope that all will yet be well. To His care commending you, as I hope in your prayers you will commend me, I bid you an affectionate farewell.

Lincoln's heart was heavy. His old life was behind him. History tells us that he had very good reason to wonder "when, or whether ever" he would see his home again. The burdens upon him crushed him to the ground.

Humbly he gave credit to his hometown and to his neighbors for all that he was, for all that he had attained. He said, and he knew, that he, by himself, was nothing. But bowed down to the ground though he was, he still could not but fix his eyes on heights heretofore unscaled by any American. He had always looked up thus. Before him he now saw a task greater than Washington's—greater than the founding of the nation. The arrogance of such a view (however obscured by sincere humility), as well as the historical accuracy of it, is striking. Leaving the safe haven of his little western town, Lincoln sensed that if he should succeed at his task, his achievement and, one would suppose, his fame would surpass that of Washington.

The man from Illinois was fit for the task before him. Utter humility and strength rarely matched were his to the full. It is not surprising that he, a product of the Bible more than any American president before him or since, is so well summed up by an old Hasidic saying: "Everyone must have two pockets so that he can reach into one or the other, according to his needs. In his right pocket are to be the words 'For my sake was the world created,' and in his left, 'I am dust and ashes.' "

Lincoln was born on the Kentucky frontier in 1809, at the dawn of the Republic, to the nearly illiterate Thomas Lincoln and the probably illegitimate Nancy Hanks Lincoln. He was thus southern born, as were his parents, though his ancestry reached back to Pennsylvania and New England. In 1816 his family moved to the new state of Indiana and, as he reached adulthood, to Illinois. Raised to farm work in "a wild region," he found around him absolutely nothing to excite ambition for education. "Of course when I came of age," he recounted in his brief autobiography, "I did not know much."

The Bible he did know and in a way and to an extent that are almost unknown to our times. It left deep marks on both his language and his morality. So too, but to a lesser degree, did Shakespeare, some history, poetry, and, as the years went on, Blackstone, Euclid, and liberal texts on economics. Because his reading was so limited and his mind so excellent, he dug very deeply into what he did study. Moreover, what he did study deserved to be studied. Thus it is not romantic to suggest that, his protestations notwithstanding, in fundamental ways Lincoln's education was fortunate.

Lincoln's mother died when her son was nine years old. No small part of the tenderness of both Lincoln's public and private self can be tied to the young boy's loss. Indeed, the "riddle of mortality,"

to quote the historian Robert Bruce, became his intimate companion throughout life.

His first exposure to the wider world came when, in 1828 and 1831, Lincoln traveled in a flatboat down the Mississippi to New Orleans. Thereafter, for many years, he found central Illinois to be good enough to stay in, first in the pioneer village of New Salem and then in Springfield. He volunteered to fight Indians as a citizen soldier, but saw no action. He started studying law. Later, he made fun of his military experience, removing it as far as possible from a real war experience, speaking of it as consisting of "bloody struggles with musquitos" and "charges upon wild onions." Being elected captain of volunteers did give him his first important indication of his gift for leading men—"a success," he wrote in 1859, "which gave me more pleasure than any I have had since."

Early Political Career

After an initial defeat, in 1832, Lincoln was elected two years later to the Illinois House of Representatives. He succeeded to leadership rapidly, earning a local reputation as a follower of Henry Clay and as a capable politician in his own right. For a young man who would rise in life, the Whig party provided a hospitable political home. Indeed, into the 1850s, Lincoln's main political task remained advocating his own brand of an economic vision that called for the development of the United States through the nurturing of banking, commerce, industry, and transportation, and through the movement from a poor sort of farming toward intensive, scientific agriculture. Westward expansion held little appeal for him, westerner though he was, a product of his people's westerning experience.

Like other Whigs, he countered the Jacksonian manifest destiny for America with a call for the internal improvement of the nation. At the heart of his persuasion was an intense and continually developing commitment to the ideal that all men should receive a full, good, and ever-increasing reward for their labors so that they might have the opportunity to rise in life. Lincoln's political emphases would not change until the mid-1850s when, at last, he permitted himself to fully face the fact that slavery subverted the "American dream."

In 1842, after a tumultuous courtship, he married Mary Todd, the lovely, cultured daughter of a Kentucky banker. By then he had transformed himself from the barefoot penniless boy into a lawyer-politician in a frockcoat and, in the eyes of some, into "the candidate of pride, wealth, and aristocratic family distinction." The couple had four children, all boys, only one of whom lived to manhood. The family had a satisfying domestic life until the presidency, the war, and the death of a child destroyed a crucial part of their tranquillity. But love never deserted the Lincolns.

In 1847 the couple moved to Washington, D.C. Lincoln served a single term in the United States House of Representatives supporting governmental aid for the economic development of the country and opposing the Mexican War. He represented his constituency well, but he failed to distinguish himself, became frustrated by tensions within the Whig party, and so began to lose interest in politics. Law became ever more attractive to him; it provided a good middle-class living for his family and, quite important to Lincoln, also "a superior opportunity" for "being a good man."

Then the 1850s brought a revolution to American politics, making slavery the issue of the times. Lawyering again faded into the background as Lincoln seized the opportunity to reenter the political arena and reinvigorate the Democratic opposition in Illinois. He left the old Whig party to help form the new Republican movement. He won election once again to the Illinois House of Representatives but resigned before serving to pursue a seat in the U.S. Senate in 1855. Although Lincoln lost a close contest, he improved his standing as a leader for the new political alignment and emerged in 1856 as a prominent contender for the Republican party's first vice presidential nomination. Two years later, Lincoln ran for the Senate as the endorsed nominee of the Illinois Republicans against the incumbent, Stephen A. Douglas. It was the Lincoln-Douglas debates during their senatorial campaign that made Lincoln a nationally known figure and popularized his views.

The language he spoke and the moral convictions he championed were memorable:

> The ant, who has toiled and dragged a crumb to his nest will furiously defend the fruit of his labor, against whatever robber assails him. So plain, that the most dumb and stupid slave that ever toiled for a master, does *constantly* know that he is wronged.
>
> If slavery is not wrong, nothing is wrong. I can not remember when I did not so think, and feel.
>
> As I would not be a *slave*, so I would not be a master. This expresses my idea of democracy. Whatever dif-

fers from this, to the extent of the difference, is no democracy.

Free labor has the inspiration of hope, pure slavery has not hope.

At rare moments Lincoln proclaimed the full implication of his views:

> I want every man to have a chance—and I believe a black man is entitled to it—in which he can better his condition—when he may look forward and hope to be a hired laborer this year and the next, work for himself afterward, and finally to hire men to work for him!

Free men had to oppose slavery because it subverted the American dream in myriad ways but, perhaps most important, because by denying blacks the right to rise, slavery endangered that right for all. Though Lincoln did not call for the political or social equality of black people, the issue he and the Republicans presented to the America of the 1850s was huge enough: " 'Can we, as a nation, continue together *permanently—forever*—half slave, and half free?' The problem is too mighty for me. May God, in his mercy, superintend the solution."

Lincoln himself gave one answer when he accepted the nomination for senator: "A house divided against itself cannot stand." But Lincoln and the nation were quite unprepared for the violence that came with the answer. Indeed, to fight the political war against slavery, he turned a blind eye toward the probability of a bloody war that would be the price of freedom. He was a pacific man, and as a mature adult he denounced war and military glory as an "attractive rainbow, that rises in showers of blood—that serpent's eye, that charms to destroy." Looking at the future he confused prognosis and preference. Then at age fifty-two he found himself the leader of a nation at war with itself.

Election of 1860

Lincoln's election to the presidency gave him anything but a solid mandate to lead. In 1860 the Democratic party split into northern and southern branches. Douglas of Illinois ran on the northern ticket, and, though the only candidate to win substantial numbers of votes in all the states, he carried only Missouri. John C. Breckinridge, later a Confederate general, carried the southern Democratic banner and won all the slave states except a few on the border. Some former Whigs and Know-Nothings formed the Constitutional Union party, nominated John Bell, and carried Virginia, Kentucky, and Tennessee. The Republicans' Lincoln took every free state except New Jersey, where he received four of seven electoral votes. His honest rail-splitter image, with its connotation of the right to rise blending into his stand opposing slave labor, was enough to give him the electoral college. There being almost no Republican votes in the southern states, his popular vote (1.9 million) was not quite 40 percent of the total. (He received 180, or 59.41 percent, of the electoral vote.) A shift of 25,000 votes, out of a total of 675,000 in New York, an area with a high concentration of swing voters, would have thrown the election into Congress, where his chances would have been very slim. Thirty-nine thousand voters merely staying away from the polls in four smaller strategic states would have done the same.

The votes were barely counted when, in December 1860, South Carolina declared its secession from the Union. It was followed early in 1861 by all the states of the Deep South: Mississippi, Florida, Alabama, Georgia, Louisiana, and Texas. In February these seven states formed the Confederate States of America and adopted a constitution much like that of the United States. They elected Jefferson Davis president, and Alexander H. Stephens, Lincoln's friend from his first stay in Washington, vice president.

The First Term

In his inaugural address, early in March, the president of the United States tried to be conciliatory without giving ground on the Republican principle of opposition to the further growth of slavery. He deprecated war, but war came when Lincoln refused to give up Fort Sumter in Charleston Harbor and the rebels fired upon it on 12 April. Four more states, Virginia, Tennessee, Arkansas, and North Carolina, seceded quickly to join the Confederacy. Its capital was moved from Montgomery, Alabama, to Richmond, Virginia.

Lincoln called for seventy-five thousand volunteers for three months—he still did not understand the magnitude of the struggle he was to lead. Nonetheless, following and enlarging the path of strong presidents like George Washington and Andrew Jackson, Lincoln acted with great vigor. He commenced his "reign," as opponents would quickly label it, by refusing to call Congress into session in

the face of an unprecedented emergency. He proceeded then to double the size of the army and navy; institute an economic blockade of the South on land, as well as at sea; spend treasury funds without appropriations; and suspend both the writ of habeas corpus (where he saw fit) and the freedom from arbitrary arrest and imprisonment. Lincoln was going to save the Union and, more important, as he understood it, the principles it stood for.

His vigorous and seemingly arbitrary actions immediately called into question among many of his contemporaries the character of his presidency. Criticism grew as the years went by, for he added to his list of unprecedented policies presidential conscription, presidential reconstruction, and presidential emancipation until "this most abused of presidents," to quote historian Don E. Fehrenbacher, "suffered his worst abuse as the alleged assassin of his country's freedom."

In a famous episode in the spring of 1861, John Merryman of Maryland, a leading secessionist, was arrested while the allegiance of the state to the Union hung in the balance. Chief Justice Roger B. Taney issued a writ of habeas corpus and, when it was ignored by military authorities, called upon Lincoln to do his duty. For good measure, in a written opinion Taney declared the presidential suspension of habeas corpus, under article I, section 2 of the Constitution, as well as military arrests to be unconstitutional.

Lincoln ignored *Ex parte Merryman*. In doing so, he did less than defy the Court, because the Merryman opinion was solely Taney's. Indeed, the full Court wisely refused to hear a similar case on technical grounds. Over the years Lincoln defended often, in his homely fashion, his stance on civil liberties and their relationship to the Constitution: "Often limb must be amputated to save a life; but life is never given to save a limb." By examining literally thousands of less-publicized cases, historian Mark Neely has shown how Lincoln tried repeatedly to achieve that precarious balance between order and liberty during wartime. Eventually both the Congress and the Court approved the emergency measures. When the war was over, however, Lincoln's good friend David Davis spoke for the Supreme Court in *Ex parte Milligan* (1866), ruling that military trials of civilians while regular courts were functioning were unconstitutional.

In the Merryman case, symbolic of the issue of civil liberties in general, historians tend to defend both Lincoln and Taney because, on the one hand, the Civil War demanded strong practical action to save the Union and, on the other, the affirmation of the fundamental rights of freemen was equally indispensable. Justice Robert H. Jackson summed up matters felicitously in 1955: "Had Mr. Lincoln scrupulously observed the Taney policy I do not know whether we would have had any liberty, and had the Chief Justice adopted Mr. Lincoln's philosophy as the philosophy of the law, I again do not know whether we would have had any liberty."

Though Lincoln is generally seen as a model of the strong president who stood up to Confederates, Peace Democrats ("Copperheads"), Radical Republicans, and a southern-minded chief justice, it is important to clarify that paradoxically he was also a "Whig in the White House," as historian David Herbert Donald has noted. The Whigs, building on the colonial tradition of enmity toward executive usurpations, took their name from the English foes of large royal powers. In the 1830s the American Whigs united against "King Andrew I" (Jackson), and in time Lincoln accepted this central tenet of his party's ideology.

Accordingly, though a Republican by then, President Lincoln made a sharp distinction between executive and legislative powers. In ordinary matters of government, he rarely interfered with the work of Congress; for example, he used the veto sparingly. In matters of patronage, he deferred to the legislators or cabinet officers. On policy matters, too, he gave much leeway to the members of his cabinet, whom he appointed from among the ablest leaders of his party, men like William H. Seward at the State Department, Salmon P. Chase at the Treasury Department, and Edwin M. Stanton in the War Department. Of course, more than theory had guided Lincoln, and he also saw practical short-term benefits to his stance. But over the long run, Lincoln's adherence to the Whig view substantially weakened the powers of the presidency and paved the way for postwar congressional dominance.

Strong president or weak president, despot or Whig—which one was the real Lincoln? It might be said that only the Civil War called forth and justified the despot. The war was the supreme emergency of American history, and, presumably, more ordinary times would have produced a much tamer president. The professions, as well as the record, of the Whig in the White House buttress such a conclusion. The professions and record, however, may mislead. It is tempting and almost inevitable to go beyond them

Abraham Lincoln (right) meets with George McClellan, his first commanding general, in the field during the Civil War. Lincoln was later forced to replace him, and McClellan was the Democratic nominee for president against Lincoln in 1864. CORBIS

and postulate that Lincoln thrived on the wise but broad use of power that the war had "compelled."

The Civil War

The war started badly for the Union. In the first major battle, at Bull Run on 21 July 1861, the inexperienced army of Irvin McDowell was routed by the equally inexperienced Confederates of P. G. T. Beauregard and Joseph Johnston. The slogan "On to Richmond" was shelved, and Lincoln put George B. McClellan in command. But while the general in chief settled down to training the Army of the Potomac, on the diplomatic front danger threatened.

In foreign policy the chief task before the Lincoln administration was to minimize aid from abroad to the Confederacy, especially from Britain and France. Lincoln left much of the task to Secretary of State Seward, though early in his administration it was necessary for him to take charge directly in some crucial cases. At the height of the Sumter crisis, Seward presented Lincoln with a memorandum that not only indicated the desirability of Seward's assumption of the presidential duty but also proposed to avert civil war by resorting to foreign war. Seward wanted to "seek" explanations from Great Britain and Russia, "demand" explanations from Spain and France, "categorically, at once"—because of those nations' supposed violations of the Monroe Doctrine. Presumably war with one or more foreign powers would follow and southerners would join northerners to defend their common country. Though Lincoln had little understanding of diplomacy, his common sense told him to play down the document and give Seward time to calm down. Seward's position was thus saved and he would yet become a great secretary of state.

Indeed, later in 1861, Seward played the pivotal role in defusing the Trent affair. By then Britain had granted "belligerent rights" to the South, but not recognition as an independent nation. The American effort to keep Europe out of the war was succeeding at the diplomatic table, but not on the high seas. In early November, a hotheaded captain of the United States Navy, Charles Wilkes, removed from the British steamer Trent the Confederate emissaries to Britain and France, James M. Mason and John Slidell. As the North, much in need of victories, celebrated, London spoke of war. Then, after a decent interval had passed, Lincoln ordered the release of the southerners. There was to be only one war at a time.

In 1862 and again in 1863 the British and the French pushed mediation attempts that in effect would have meant the recognition of Confederate independence. In the end, the South not only failed to obtain European recognition but was unable to get any truly substantial help. Six raiders were built in British and French shipyards, the most famous of which, the Alabama, caused millions of dollars worth of damage to northern shipping before it was sunk in 1864. Yet northern diplomats, most notably Charles Francis Adams, were competent. Northern grain was important to a Europe that suffered crop failures. Southern cotton in turn was increasingly replaced by the cotton of India and Egypt. The Old World was also beset with uprisings, wars, and threats to the balance of power. By 1863, with the Emancipation Proclamation appealing to Europeans with antislavery sentiments, it was Adams, the American minister to the Court of St. James's, who spoke of Anglo-American war unless the British put an end

to the aid trickling to the Confederacy. Ultimately, success on the diplomatic front depended on the outcome on the battlefield.

In 1862 a string of Confederate victories in the East dazzled the world. The navy remained the one bright spot for Lincoln. Indeed, on 9 March, after the iron-sheathed wooden Virginia (the rechristened Union Merrimack, salvaged by the Confederates) threatened Washington, putting fear into president, cabinet, and the city, it was stopped by the ironclad Monitor. Naval warfare was being revolutionized, and the Union continued its domination of the seas.

On land the picture was different. The Army of Northern Virginia was led by the finest southern generals, Robert E. Lee (who took command in mid-1862), Thomas ("Stonewall") Jackson, and James E. Longstreet. They faced the generally larger Army of the Potomac, led by a succession of second-rate generals. Under McClellan, this army tried to come back from the Bull Run defeat in an elaborate campaign on the Virginia Peninsula but failed. In the Shenandoah Valley, Jackson seemed to play with his opponents, albeit bloodily. At Bull Run again, in late August, the Union troops, under John Pope, repeated their fiasco of the previous year. When Lee invaded Maryland, McClellan, fully in command once more, stopped him at Antietam (17 September 1862) in the single bloodiest day of the war. This, however, was a far cry from victory, though Lincoln chose to treat it as such and issue the Preliminary Emancipation Proclamation in its wake (22 September). The year ended with the Army of the Potomac, now under Ambrose Burnside, suffering a disastrous defeat at Fredericksburg (13–15 December).

The year 1863 promised more of the same as "Fighting Joe" Hooker, his army outnumbering Lee's more than two to one, was beaten back at Chancellorsville, Virginia, on 1–4 May. Not until Lee ventured north again to Gettysburg did the tide appear to turn. There, during the first three days of July, in a bitter encounter, the Army of the Potomac under its newest commander, George G. Meade, decisively defeated the Confederates of invincible repute. Thereafter to the end of 1863 and beyond, the Union side in the East seemed to be satisfied to rest on its Gettysburg laurels, Lincoln's passionate efforts to the contrary notwithstanding.

In the West, by contrast, the finest northern generals, the likes of Ulysses S. Grant, William Tecumseh Sherman, and George H. Thomas, faced weak Confederate generals. Though here, too, the war had its shifting tides, on the whole federal arms proved victorious. In February 1862, Grant captured Fort Henry and Fort Donelson with substantial naval support, only to be stopped at Shiloh, Tennessee, in a very bloody draw (6–7 April). On 1 May the Union navy took New Orleans, and five days later the Mississippi River fleet took Memphis. Indeed, throughout the war the Union navy was largely successful. A high point of the western campaigns, as well as of army-navy cooperation, came with the siege of Vicksburg, Mississippi, and its surrender to Grant on 4 July 1863, the day after the battle of Gettysburg. "The signs look better," Lincoln wrote in a public letter in August. "Peace does not appear so distant as it did."

In its broadest terms, the goal of the war had always been clear to the president (though in its many significant details, change was continuous). In his war message in 1861 he had already explained:

> This is essentially a People's contest. On the side of the Union, it is a struggle for maintaining in the world, that form, and substance of government, whose leading object is, to elevate the condition of men—to lift artificial weights from all shoulders—to clear the paths of laudable pursuit for all—to afford all, an unfettered start, and a fair chance, in the race of life.

In the fall of 1863, Lincoln went to the small Pennsylvania town of Gettysburg to help dedicate the Soldiers' National Cemetery. He gave a two-minute address there to America, the world, and to history:

> Four score and seven years ago our fathers brought forth on this continent, a new nation, conceived in Liberty, and dedicated to the proposition that all men are created equal.
>
> Now we are engaged in a great civil war, testing whether that nation, or any nation so conceived and so dedicated, can long endure. We are met on a great battle-field of that war. We have come to dedicate a portion of that field, as a final resting place for those who here gave their lives that that nation might live. It is altogether fitting and proper that we should do this.
>
> But, in a larger sense, we can not dedicate—we can not consecrate—we can not hallow—this ground. The brave men, living and dead, who struggled here, have consecrated it, far above our poor power to add or detract. The world will little note, nor long remember what we say here, but it can never forget what they did here. It is for us the living, rather, to be dedicated here to the unfinished work which they who fought here have thus far so nobly advanced. It is rather for us to be here dedicated to the great task remaining before us—that from these honored dead we

take increased devotion to that cause for which they gave the last full measure of devotion—that we here highly resolve that these dead shall not have died in vain—that this nation, under God, shall have a new birth of freedom—and that government of the people, by the people, for the people, shall not perish from the earth.

Lincoln understood that one of his chief tasks as president was to keep alive the northern will to fight. The challenge of the task was all the greater because the North had the wherewithal to win the war. Lincoln believed not only that right was on the side of the Union but knew that might was too. Might certainly could be more readily measured.

In his war message in 1861, Lincoln had pointed to the material superiority of the North. More than three years later, in his last annual message, he would emphasize that the North was actually "*gaining* strength, and may, if need be, maintain the contest indefinitely.. . . The national resources, then, are unexhausted.. and, as we believe, inexhaustible." The North had to bring this superiority to bear on the battlefield. Though Lincoln's conduct of the war had many facets—he even considered taking command in the field—his principal military duty was to rally the people.

At the start of the war the North had perhaps 22 million people against the South's 5 million to 6 million whites and 3.5 million blacks. The North's railroad mileage was twice that of the South's; the cash value of its farms two and a half times greater; and the cash value of its manufactured products about ten times greater. More than 25 percent of the population of the free states was urbanized, as against 10 percent of the slave states. Forty percent of the Union population was engaged in agriculture, compared to 84 percent of the Confederate population. The value of northern farmland was two and a half times the value of land in the slave states, and its agriculture was much more mechanized. Twice as many of the free states' school-age children attended school—not counting the slave population of the South, which was not only unschooled but almost wholly illiterate.

Not surprisingly for one who spent the bulk of his public career in Illinois dealing with matters economic, Lincoln's military direction from the White House always carried a large economic ingredient. One of his earliest moves of the war had been the establishment of the blockade of the southern ports, which, by the close of the war, grew to be deadly effective. He insisted that his military make good use of the railroads. He advocated, from late 1862, the use of black troops, in part because the step not only added to northern military strength but also because it weakened southern economic strength. He emphasized the significance of the Mississippi Valley, new weapons, and even the use of reconnaissance balloons.

More subtle links also existed between Lincoln's progressive economic persuasion and his innovative strategic notions, which some historians speak of as his "military genius." Thus, the man who in the 1840s demanded from Congress a centralized and coordinated plan of national improvements in the 1860s made like demands upon his generals for centralization of authority and coordination of plans. And so the Union's unified command system and its central, overall plan of strategy were born. Similarly, Lincoln's decisive championship of cordon offense (advancing on the enemy on every front, thus pitting all the northern resources against all the southern ones) stemmed primarily from his conviction that economic might, more than anything else except morale, would determine the outcome of the war. This oft-attested conviction was fundamental to his recognition that the objective of the Union forces should be not the conquest of territories but the destruction of opposing armies, the destruction of "the most important branch of . . . resources"—men.

Perhaps the most unsettling aspect of Lincoln's military policy was the drastic rate at which federal commanders were replaced. In the East, for example, in a period of two years he removed the general in charge seven times. He was criticized harshly then, and since, for failing to support his commanders in defeat. Yet Lincoln's actions reflected a core aspect of his outlook, which under the pressure of war became extreme: he conducted a ruthless campaign of pushing the successful to the fore. His view that in the Civil War one side stood for the "open field" for all, while the other side was against it, thus received more than symbolic corroboration. In the Confederacy the men who held the chief commands early in the war would, with the exception of those who had been killed, be there at war's end. In contrast, there would not be a single general commanding a main army in the Union service of 1865 who had held high command at the beginning of the struggle. In this respect, Lincoln's American dream had triumphed on the battlefield too.

If the president's outlook ever wavered, the booming prosperity of the wartime North helped strengthen it. Government purchases for military needs stimulated various sectors of industry and much of farming. Expanding industries included transportation, iron and steel, woolen clothing, shoes, munitions, and coal. Farmers increased production greatly. Even though one-third of farmworkers went into the army, exports of wheat, corn, pork, and beef to Europe doubled. Farms and factories made the first widespread use of laborsaving machines such as the reaper and the sewing machine. The war forced the economy into an early form of mass production, and the nation expanded as settlers moved westward.

Though war brought prosperity to the North, financing the war was a most difficult undertaking. Taxes and money borrowed from the people in the form of war bonds became the major sources of northern finance, though paper money and consequent inflation played their part too.

The laboring people's wages did not keep up with inflation through much of the war, and there were strikes. Predictably, Lincoln took the side of the laborers. Almost invariably strikers had "just cause" for their action, he explained, and even as employers were denouncing the supposed illegal nature of unions, Lincoln received union members in the White House. Repeatedly he warned against "the effort to place *capital* on an equal footing with, if not above *labor*." When he sent his ideas to Congress, warning that if working people surrendered their political power "it would be used to close the door of advancement" against them, it grew painfully clear that in these matters the president was not in step with much of the leadership of his country. The House of Representatives, laying the groundwork not only for the modern American economy but also for the abuses of the Gilded Age, snubbed the president's message. Radical Republican Congressman Thaddeus Stevens explained the tabling of Lincoln's message by saying that there was "no appropriate committee on metaphysics in the House." Copperhead Clement Vallandigham agreed: "I presume it will go to the Committee of Unfinished Business." And as one historian added, "Unfinished business it remained for the rest of the century."

Some of the victorious troops fresh from Gettysburg were sent to New York City to put down antidraft riots. Conscription had been employed first in 1862, and more freely in 1863, to stimulate volunteering for the Union army (the same was the case in the Confederacy), and in New York resistance degenerated into the worst riot of American history up to that time. For Lincoln the "most notable feature" of the riots was "the hanging of some working people by other working people." "It should never be so," he stated. "The strongest bond of human sympathy, outside of the family relation, should be one uniting all working people, of all nations, and tongues, and kindreds." The words might have come from one of his European admirers, Karl Marx, indicating the idea's international currency, though Lincoln had something quite American in mind. The workingmen hanged were blacks. The riots of 1863 may have been less a protest against the draft, or class distinctions, than against Lincoln's policy toward black people.

Lincoln had always been egalitarian to the bone and opposed to slavery. As a young politician, he had found the courage to denounce slavery in the Illinois House of Representatives. By the 1850s his sentiments had become the centerpiece of his politics, but as president, his job was to reforge a nation the southern part of which was slave owning. He had to do this by rallying the northern, mostly free part of the nation, which included not only the crucial border states that saw slavery as sacred but also huge numbers of negrophobes in such places as the northwestern heartland of Indiana, Ohio, and Illinois and the city of New York.

Accordingly, the president moved with great caution toward emancipation, starting in late 1861. When, about the same time, his impetuous commander of the western department, John Charles Frémont, declared the slaves of the Missouri rebels summarily freed, Lincoln said no. He requested the repeal of the order, and when he failed to obtain compliance, he fired the general. In April and May of 1862 when General David Hunter issued similar proclamations of emancipation in the southern department the president once again countermanded the orders. Over the years he would often state his determination "not to go forward fast enough to wreck the country's cause."

Exquisite timing and knowing the limits of the possible were key elements in Lincoln's success as a leader. At first, he hoped to bring the great change to America as gently "as the dews of heaven." His desire for gradualism was supplemented with promises of compensation, for the slave owners stood to lose billions of dollars worth of "property." He hoped thus to induce voluntary action on the part of individual states. And he knew, too, that the slaves would need substantial help to enjoy their newfound freedom. Into his hopes Lincoln put his whole "soul," to borrow the word used independently by two of his confidants, Senator Charles Sumner of Massachusetts and Supreme Court Justice David Davis. Toward the end of 1862, too late, he still gave beautiful and oft-quoted expression to these hopes:

> The dogmas of the quiet past are inadequate to the stormy present.. . . As our case is new, so we must think anew, and act anew.. . . Fellow-citizens, *we* cannot escape history.. . . In giving freedom to the *slave*, we *assure* freedom to the *free*—honorable alike in what we give, and what we preserve. We shall nobly save, or meanly lose, the last best, hope of earth.

He had worked with representatives of border slave states, with congressmen, with the general public, but the fact was that the gentle road to drastic change, ever difficult, in a time of civil war and revolution was quite unrealistic. It was bound to fail.

Congress moved ahead, too, with the two separate Confiscation Acts that authorized seizing the private property of Confederate military personnel and civilians. But it was the White House that led the way to African-American freedom. In the summer of 1862, Lincoln decided in favor of immediate abolition of slavery. From then on, he concentrated formidable political powers on bringing as much of the country behind this revolutionary policy as possible.

In August an attack on him by the influential editor of the *New York Tribune* helped his cause. In "The Prayer of Twenty Million," Horace Greeley accused the president of moving too slowly, deferring too much "to Rebel Slavery." Lincoln replied with a thunderous no and an oath of allegiance to the Union:

> If there be those who would not *save* the Union, unless they could at the same time save slavery, I do not agree with them. If there be those who would not save the Union unless they could at the same time *destroy* slavery, I do not agree with them. My paramount object in this struggle *is* to save the Union, and is *not* either to save or destroy slavery. If I could save the Union without freeing *any* slave I would do it, and if I could save it by freeing *all* the slaves I would do it; and if I could save it by freeing some and leaving others alone I would also do that.

Lincoln had thus seemingly rebuffed the abolitionist left, though in fact he was about to take their side. His intended audience was that large conservative segment of the electorate that opposed the freeing of the slaves—some at any cost, except the cost of the Union. The Union was the common cause on which nearly all northerners could agree, and there Lincoln took his stand. When he would make his decision for emancipation public, he would thus do so on conservative grounds.

A second way to make emancipation acceptable to a reluctant northern public was through the advocacy of black colonization outside the United States, most probably in Central America or Africa. Many northerners feared that the end of slavery in the South would inundate the North with blacks. They would accept emancipation only if it were accompanied by the removal of blacks from America. It was therefore good politics for the president to advocate colonization. He managed to follow this political road in part because he himself still had fears about how successfully the two races could break out of their old relationship. Though at some level of consciousness Lincoln understood the impossibility of the colonization idea, for a time in late 1862, he made much of the policy.

Thus, on the surface it was an uncomplicated Unionist and colonizationist who issued the Preliminary Emancipation Proclamation on 22 September 1862—after Lee's armies were repelled in the battle of Antietam. But in a deeper sense Lincoln was more of an emancipator than a Unionist. And even as he issued the Final Emancipation Proclamation on 1 January 1863, freeing the slaves in the areas still in rebellion, he forgot, almost with indecent haste, about colonization. He had spent none of the paltry sum Congress had appropriated for the purpose. Instead, he focused increasing attention on reconstructing a nation of blacks and whites.

Emancipation itself was a central step in reconstructing the United States. The war had begun with the announced goal of restoring the Union as it was in 1860. In 1861, surely by 1862, the goal had shifted toward Reconstruction, the reshaping of the Union without slavery. As the war continued and then veered toward a close, a further shift occurred, expanding the goal of the struggle to include union, emancipation, and movement toward civil rights for the freedman. The interplays between the North and the South, between factions in both, and between Congress and the executive in Washington were complex, but the central issue remained the role of African Americans in American society. Lincoln moved behind a radical vanguard but ahead of northern opinion, not to mention white American opinion in general and at times ahead of the consensus of his Republican party as well. The question to him was not " 'Can any of us imagine better?' but 'Can we all do better?' " With this clear, pragmatic motto before him, he led Americans toward acceptance of ever greater black freedom.

The president consistently refused to recognize the validity of secession ordinances and, in legal terms, looked upon the Union as an unbroken and unbreakable unit. The war constituted a set of problems that he, as commander in chief, had to deal with, and Reconstruction measures fell into this category of problems. At the same time, he was ready to allow Congress a substantial and constitutionally legitimate role in the Reconstruction process.

In the middle of 1863, as parts of Arkansas, Louisiana, Texas, Florida, Virginia, and all of Tennessee came under the control of federal arms, Lincoln brought into being local military governments. Their chief task was to rally southern Unionists, subdue and keep away rebels and their sympathizers, and bring about a new day for blacks.

At the end of 1863 the president proposed his Proclamation of Amnesty and Reconstruction. It included the "10 Percent Plan"—well received in Congress—which called for the formation of civilian governments when one-tenth of the voting population of 1860 took the oath of allegiance to the United States. Emancipation was not to be open for discussion in these states. Many citizens were proscribed from participation in the political process either as voters or officeholders: individuals who had held diplomatic or civil posts in the Confederacy, Confederate officers above the rank of colonel, those who had resigned from the armed forces of the United States or from any branches of the government, and those who had mistreated federal prisoners of war. His proposal notwithstanding, Lincoln insisted that flexibility should be the key to Reconstruction and that different plans might be needed in different times and places.

Louisiana became Lincoln's test case. Initially he had overestimated southern unionism there, as elsewhere in the South. When satisfactory Reconstruction failed to materialize, he increasingly involved himself in personally directing the Louisiana experiment. His style combined daring, strength, and coercion with caution, conciliation, and ambiguity. It demanded movement, but only step by step, and entailed the use of patronage, the military, and other tools of presidential power. It included a precise, lawyerly command of the language, a unique eloquence, and a genius for ambiguity. This last quality, though needed, helped confuse many Radicals in Congress (and later historians as well).

The president created a government, under General Nathaniel P. Banks, that struck down slavery, provided for public schools for blacks and whites, and empowered the state legislature to enfranchise blacks. As white Louisiana Unionists faced the hostile pro-Confederate majority, Lincoln labored with finesse to keep the former united—hence, much of his ambiguity. Yet, as early as August 1863, Lincoln was ready to have the color line on the franchise breached. In March 1864 he wrote his famous letter to Governor Michael Hahn calling for voting rights for "very intelligent" blacks and black veterans because "they could probably help, in some trying time to come, to keep the jewel of liberty within the family of freedom." Rather than being a mere suggestion for "private consideration," this was a "directive," as historian LaWanda Cox has shown, and was understood as such by Louisiana leaders. In short, Lincoln led the Unionists toward black suffrage while pretending to stay in the background.

Ironically, the Radicals in Washington tried to strike down the Louisiana free-state movement in the name of black suffrage and Lincoln's abuse of military power. The conflict that then developed between the executive and the legislature sometimes overshadowed the cooperation between the two, not merely in various areas of governmental work but specifically on Reconstruction. Lincoln had, after all, worked well with Congress to abolish slavery in the territories and the District of Columbia; to admit West Virginia, split off from Virginia, as a new free state; and to smooth out disagreements over the 1862 Confiscation Act. And they would later work together in establishing the Freedmen's Bureau to help care for the freed slaves and, most momentously, in pushing through Congress the Thirteenth Amendment, thereby abolishing slavery under the Constitution.

Nonetheless, early in 1864, Lincoln provoked a split with the Radicals. Congressman Henry Winter Davis of Maryland and Senator Benjamin F. Wade of Ohio produced a somewhat muddled bill in favor of congressional Reconstruction. Though the bill did not call for black suffrage, it had the aura of Radicalism about it. Lincoln pocket vetoed the bill—the only important veto of his presidency—much less because of the larger issues of Reconstruction than because of the upcoming presidential election. While the Wade-Davis bill had wound its way through Congress, the president had remained silent. Then, to the surprise of many, including his friends in Congress, he declined to sign the measure. Probably many of his friends would have refused to support the Wade-Davis bill if they had known his position. As correspondent Noah Brooks summed it up in *Washington in Lincoln's Time* (1895), it was only when the executive acted that "for the first time men who had not seriously opposed the passage of the . . . bill began to wish that it had never gone to the President."

It seems that Lincoln wanted the opportunity to veto the bill and draw a sharp line between himself and the Radicals. A few days earlier, equally surprisingly but to the same effect, he accepted the resignation of Chase, the resident Radical of the cabinet. But then, elections are usually won at the center, and Lincoln did win. Soon after he was quite ready to accept more than the Wade-Davis policy for Reconstruction and appoint Chase chief justice of the United States.

Although the Wade-Davis veto soured Lincoln's relations with an important element of his party, its wider political benefits were much needed. After the military successes of 1863, above all at Gettysburg and Vicksburg, the year 1864 brought reversals, with the end of the war appearing no closer than before. In the western theater Nathaniel Banks led an expedition into the Red River region of Texas and into dismal failure. Sherman, who had succeeded Grant in the western command that spring, commenced to move from Chattanooga against Atlanta, but the able General Joseph Johnston managed to slow his progress significantly. In the East, progress seemed even slower and was extremely costly. Grant, recently appointed general in chief by Lincoln, promptly took up headquarters with the Army of the Potomac to lead it in person. In the Wilderness region of Virginia (5–7 May), around Spotsylvania Courthouse (8–21 May), and at Cold Harbor (3 June), the new general in chief suffered such heavy casualties that some in the North called him "Butcher Grant."

The North could celebrate the death of J. E. B. Stuart, if the death of a gallant foe is a suitable occasion for celebration. But that the Confederates remained very much alive was quickly demonstrated when Jubal Early moved up the Shenandoah Valley toward Washington. At the very time the North had expected the fall of Richmond, Washington was being threatened instead (11 July). Lincoln, as well as assorted cooks and clerks quickly pressed into defensive service, came under fire. To top it all, the Union soldiers, bogged down to a siege at Petersburg, tunneled under the Confederate lines and exploded a section thereof with a mine only to fail in exploiting the advantage. The fiasco was made spectacular by its very novelty.

The president at times despaired of reelection. His own party put up challengers from its Radical wing, first Chase and then Frémont, but Lincoln parried them with relative ease. His aim was to attract the center of the electorate, which would decide the election. The Democrats—themselves divided into various factions, notably for and against war—moved in the same direction and nominated a war Democrat, General George McClellan, as Lincoln's opponent. However, to the Republicans' advantage, the Democrats did so on a peace platform.

The president and his party used their power and considerable political skills to great advantage. They changed the party name from Republican to Union to enlarge its appeal. The vice presidential nomination was taken from the colorless incumbent, Hannibal Hamlin, and given to a loud southern Unionist, Senator Andrew Johnson of Tennessee, a "self-made man" like Lincoln. Nevada was rushed into the Union to gain additional Republican votes. Also, large efforts were made to garner the military vote.

All the same, the president knew that ultimately it was upon the fortunes of war that all else depended and the northern forces began to prevail late in 1864. In August, Tennessee-born Admiral David Farragut, famous for his victory at New Orleans and his pithy "Damn the torpedoes—full speed ahead," won the battle of Mobile Bay; in September, Sherman took Atlanta, and Sheridan purged the Shenandoah Valley of Virginia.

In November, Lincoln won reelection with 2.2 million votes, giving him a convincing majority of 400,000. (The electoral vote was 212–21.) McClellan carried only Kentucky, Delaware, and New Jersey. The war was going to be finished. There were minor irregularities in the election but they were overshadowed, as Lincoln understood, by the stupendous fact that in the midst of a great civil war, elections were held at all. "It shows," he told a group of serenaders, "how *sound*, and how *strong* we still are." Lincoln's understanding of history was as fine as was his leadership.

Yet the war was taking its toll on him. The vigorous middle-aged man who had taken office in 1861 had become the almost old man who appears in his last photograph. Mary Todd, his lovely bride, had grown old too, and after the loss of their twelve-year-old son, Willie, in 1862, she began to lose her grip on reality. Lincoln's heart grew heavy. He said there was a tired spot inside him that nothing could touch. Around him there were death and devastation. The casualties of the war—both North and South—continued to mount, by the end reaching 1.5 million men, including about 620,000 dead—this in a nation of 31.5 million.

Reelected to the presidency, Lincoln said, "I do not impugn the motives of any one opposed to me. It is no pleasure to me to triumph over any one." He added soon after, "So long as I have been here I have not willingly planted a thorn in any man's bosom."

On 15 November, Sherman left Atlanta, beginning the march to the sea. From Atlanta east, the troops lived off the country and destroyed what they could not take. Sherman believed that the Confederacy should not be allowed to live from the southern harvest or have a happy, secure backcountry. Savannah fell before Christmas. Lincoln frankly admitted that he had doubts about Sherman's march and gave all the credit for success to the general. In the new year, Sherman started his march northward through the Carolinas. The war fought there was a newer and uglier kind of war. Columbia, South Carolina, went up in flames—at whose hands, historians still debate.

Sheridan had followed like tactics in the Shenandoah Valley. He seemed ready to use any means to prevent the valley from provisioning Lee's armies or any other army that might try to attack Washington via that route. Bushwhacking southern guerrillas ensured the campaign's deterioration into scorched-earth tactics. The rich, beautiful Shenandoah Valley fell victim to total war. It was a blessing when, at last, Grant broke the grip of Lee, who on 2 April abandoned Richmond. Seven days later Lee surrendered at Appomattox.

Plans for Reconstruction

Lincoln was intent on seeing his Louisiana experiment through but also hoped to work with the Radicals. He had played a crucial role in the adoption of the Thirteenth Amendment by a somewhat reluctant House of Representatives. In his last public address, on 11 April, before the White House, he pleaded for saving the Louisiana government that congressional Radicals opposed: "Concede that the new government of Louisiana is only to what it should be as the egg is to the fowl, we shall sooner have the fowl by hatching the egg than by smashing it.''

What the fowl was to look like he indicated by expressing his personal preference for giving the franchise to blacks who were educated, or propertied, or were Union veterans. How far he was to go beyond that, or with what speed, we do not know, but his course would have depended in no small part on what he judged to be attainable. The direction he took was clear, and though he knew each state to be unique, in his last address he also explained that ''what has been said of Louisiana will apply to other states.''

Lincoln knew and prized the achievement of black soldiers against heavy odds, which he could not always readily lighten. As early as 1863, he had spoken glowingly of the black man who ''with silent tongue, and clenched teeth, and steady eye, and well-poised bayonet, . . . helped mankind'' to the great consummation of freedom. Blacks had fought in more than 190 battles, and about 68,000 black soldiers and sailors had been killed or wounded. Twenty-one blacks won the Congressional Medal of Honor. A black regiment was the first to march into Richmond when the Confederate capital fell, and Lincoln toured the city escorted by black cavalry. No one could misunderstand the significance of his escort. For the postwar era Lincoln was determined to bring both political and economic advancement to blacks. His commitment to black freedom fit into a larger commitment to a democratic, capitalist America. And so his postwar response to black needs would have also depended in no small part on his response to the coming Gilded Age.

Reconstruction for Lincoln meant more than providing a place for blacks in ''a new birth of freedom,'' central though that issue was. He was also concerned with southern whites, even the former slaveholder, and as late as 1865, he gave serious attention to compensating slaveholders. During the war years his numerous peace feelers and reconstruction schemes included strong appeals to the economic interests of the Confederates. He assumed, somewhat naively for a time of bitter war, that materialist enticements could seduce the South into peace. This assumption largely explains the absurdly vast amount of time he devoted to the problems of trading with the Confederacy (the corruption it bred notwithstanding), especially in cotton. The same was true of his secret feelers about the federal takeover of the Confederate war debt (obliquely attacked in the Wade-Davis Manifesto), his persistent offers for large-scale compensation for slaves, his lack of enthusiasm for congressional laws of confiscation, and perhaps even the unrealistic presidential request that the Pacific Railroad be built on the five-foot gauge used primarily in the South.

After the war ended, such economic incentives were likely to have more substantial effects. The blueprint that Congress created during the war for a modern nation was also a blueprint for the new, reconstructed America. Lincoln not only tried to help set the tone for it—though unsuccessfully in the field of labor relations—but in crucial instances he made vital contributions to the revolution that changed the government's role in the American economy. He Whiggishly stayed in the background as a rule, letting Congress shape legislation, but when he was needed, as in the case of the establishment of the national banking system and of the Department of Agriculture, he brought the full weight of the presidency to bear. He also encouraged movement toward graduated income taxes (though such taxes were later declared unconstitutional); uniform paper currency (the greenbacks); higher tariff protection for American industry; internal improvements, notably the Pacific Railroad; immigration; the Land Grant College (or Morrill) Act (1862); and the Homestead Act (1862), which provided free homesteads of 160 acres for those who would work the land in the West for five years. The net result, as the president reported while calling for the support of immigration, was that the nation ''was beginning a new life.''

Nowhere would this new life be more beneficial than in the war-ravaged South. There, Lincoln knew, more than in the rest of the country, the interests of blacks and whites were intertwined, and he had come to nurture a faith that the two races would learn to cooperate. Emancipation, Lincoln believed, did not merely liberate the blacks but also the whites. It made the American dream also a southern dream, with a resultant prosperity for all. In the midst of the hatreds of war, he took pleasure, in private, in creating a ''word painting of what the South would be when the war was over, slavery destroyed, and she had an opportunity to develop her resources.'' Long after one of Lincoln's treasury officials had heard him dream thus, the official found himself listening to a new breed of southerner advocating economic development and a ''New South.'' The official experienced a flash of memory that came with ''the vividness of an electric light," as he "recognized the word-picture of Mr. Lincoln.. . ."

The war had been won, the Union saved. But the Union to Lincoln had not been an end but a means. It had to be upheld, as he had explained in 1861, as it held "that thing for which the Union itself was made." The Union was a ship, and its cargo "the prosperity and the liberties of the people. . . . So long as the ship can be saved, with the cargo, it should never be abandoned."

The idea of a Union is essentially national; that of democracy, the American Dream, the right to rise in the world, is universal. One historical view prizes the Civil War as a "war for nationality" and makes Lincoln into the "Great Nationalist" of the modern historians, a man who had a religious faith in the Union. Another view cherishes him as an American Moses or Christ, one who spoke to mankind.

The first view denies the uniqueness of the United States and sees Lincoln as a New World counterpart of those Europeans whose highest goal was the building of a nation—almost as an end in itself. In contrast, Lincoln's dream helped lead America to the nationalism of Theodore Roosevelt, Woodrow Wilson, and Franklin Delano Roosevelt.

In March 1865, at his second inaugural, Lincoln delivered another speech that might be described as one of the finest in the English language. He again looked ahead:

> Fondly do we hope, fervently do we pray, that this mighty scourge of war may speedily pass away.. . .
>
> With malice toward none, with charity for all, . . . let us strive on to finish the work we are in, to bind up the nation's wounds, . . . to do all which may achieve and cherish a just and lasting peace among ourselves and with all nations.

Six weeks later, on the night of 14 April 1865, Good Friday, the president was shot while attending a performance at Ford's Theater in Washington. He died nine hours later. He thus did not live to see how difficult it would be to create a "new life," a "new birth of freedom," in a new America.

BIBLIOGRAPHY

David Herbert Donald, *Lincoln* (New York, 1995), is by far the finest biography. However, with the book's focus on the pragmatic politician that Lincoln was, his ideas and moral convictions fade. Some of the glory that was Lincoln is missing. Carl Sandburg, *Abraham Lincoln: The Prairie Years and the War Years*, 6 vols. (New York, 1926–1939), is the long-beloved popular biography by a poet of note. William H. Herndon, *Herndon's Life of Lincoln*, ed. by Paul M. Angle (Greenwich, Conn., 1961), is the indispensable life, based on the research of Lincoln's law partner, Herndon, and ghostwritten by Jesse W. Weik. Earl Schenck Miers et al., eds., *Lincoln Day by Day: A Chronology, 1809–1865* (Washington, D.C., 1960; rev. ed., Dayton, Ohio, 1991), an important reference work and the product of a generation of research by a group of scholars, traces Lincoln's daily activities through his entire life. Mark E. Neely, Jr., *The Last Best Hope of Earth: Abraham Lincoln and the Promise of America* (Cambridge, Mass., 1993), is the best brief portrait. Roy P. Basler, Marion Dolores Pratt, and Lloyd A. Dunlap, eds., *The Collected Works of Abraham Lincoln*, 9 vols. (New Brunswick, N.J., 1953–1955); Roy P. Basler, ed., *Supplement, 1832–1865* (Westport, Conn., 1974); and Roy P. Basler and Christian O. Basler, eds., *Second Supplement, 1848–1865* (New Brunswick, N.J., 1990), are standard editions of Lincoln's written and spoken words. See also Don E. Fehrenbacher and Virginia Fehrenbacher, eds. and comps., *Recollected Words of Abraham Lincoln* (Stanford, Calif., 1996).

Richard N. Current, *The Lincoln Nobody Knows* (New York, 1958), consists of judicious essays on some of the controversial subjects of Lincoln's life and career. Charles B. Strozier, *Lincoln's Quest for Union: Public and Private Meanings* (New York, 1982), is a useful psychobiography. Michael Burlingame, *The Inner World of Abraham Lincoln* (Urbana, Ill., 1994), focuses on valuable and rarely used sources. Mark E. Neely, Jr., *The Abraham Lincoln Encyclopedia* (New York, 1982), is the best all-around reference work on Lincoln and associated subjects.

Don E. Fehrenbacher, *Prelude to Greatness: Lincoln in the 1850s* (Stanford, Calif., 1962), is a perceptive analysis of Lincoln's public career in the 1850s. Philip Shaw Paludan, *The Presidency of Abraham Lincoln* (Lawrence, Kans., 1994), is an impressive synthesis. Gabor S. Boritt, *Lincoln and the Economics of the American Dream* (Urbana, Ill., 1994), is an interpretation of Lincoln through the examination of his economic persuasion. Mark E. Neely, Jr., *The Fate of Liberty: Abraham Lincoln and Civil Liberties* (New York, 1991), provides a fine summary of the president's approach to constitutional issues. La-

Wanda Cox, *Lincoln and Black Freedom: A Study in Presidential Leadership* (Columbia, S.C., 1981), is the best analysis of the subject.

Gabor S. Boritt, ed., *Lincoln, the War President: The Gettysburg Lectures* (New York, 1992), is a collection of essays by leading historians on Lincoln's approach to the war. Garry Wills, *Lincoln at Gettysburg: The Words that Remade America* (New York, 1992), is a provocative discussion of Lincoln's most famous speech. William B. Hanchett, *The Lincoln Murder Conspiracies* (Urbana, Ill., 1983), is the best historiographical study of the Lincoln assassination.

Harold Holzer, Gabor S. Boritt, and Mark E. Neely, Jr., *The Lincoln Image: Abraham Lincoln and the Popular Print* (New York, 1984), is the only account of the shaping of Lincoln's image through etchings and lithographs, 1860–1865. Philip B. Kunhardt, Jr., Philip B. Kunhardt III, and Peter W. Kunhardt, *Lincoln: An Illustrated Biography* (New York, 1992), is the best pictorial history. James Mellon, ed., *The Face of Lincoln* (New York, 1979), is the finest work on Lincoln photographs. Merrill D. Peterson, *Lincoln in American Memory* (New York, 1994),

goes beyond historiography to provide a readable appraisal of Lincoln's role in American culture over the past century and more.

The two finest collections of Lincoln manuscripts are available on microfilm from the Library of Congress: Abraham Lincoln Papers, 97 reels; Herndon-Weik Papers, 15 reels. In addition, a major documentary project promises much new insight into Lincoln's career. The Lincoln Legal Papers, directed by Cullom B. Davis in Springfield, Illinois, will be published in upcoming years on CD-ROM.

Recent works include Lerone Bennett, Jr., *Forced Into Glory: Abraham Lincoln's White Dream* (Chicago, 2000); Gabor Boritt, ed., *The Lincoln Enigma: The Changing Faces of an American Icon* (New York, 2001); George P. Fletcher, *Our Secret Constitution: How Lincoln Redefined American Democracy* (New York, 2001); William Lee Miller, *Lincoln's Virtues: An Ethical Biography* (New York, 2002); Ronald C. White, *Lincoln's Greatest Speech: The Second Inaugural* (New York, 2002); and Jay Winik, *April 1865: The Month That Saved America* (New York, 2001).

Andrew Johnson

Albert Castel

Andrew Johnson THE LIBRARY OF CONGRESS

NO president ever became president under more dramatic and tragic circumstances than did Andrew Johnson. On the night of 14 April 1865, Johnson, recently inaugurated as vice president, went to bed in his hotel room in Washington, D.C. Scarcely had he gone to sleep when he was awakened by a friend who informed him that President Lincoln had just been shot by an assassin at Ford's Theater. Johnson promptly dressed and hastened to the boardinghouse where Lincoln lay dying. He remained awhile and then left when it became apparent that the distraught Mrs. Lincoln resented his presence. At 7:30 on the morning of 15 April church bells tolled, signaling Lincoln's death. Shortly after 10 A.M. Johnson took the oath of office as the seventeenth president of the United States.

Personal and Political Background

No president, not even Lincoln, rose from lower depths of poverty and deprivation to reach the height of that office than did Johnson. He was born on 29 December 1808 in a two-room shack in Raleigh, North Carolina; his parents were illiterate tavern servants; and he never attended school. In 1822 he became a tailor's apprentice, learned that trade, and managed to acquire a rudimentary knowledge of reading. At the age of seventeen he moved to east Tennessee, where in 1827 he opened a tailor shop in Greeneville and married Eliza McCardle, a shoemaker's daughter who taught him to write and cipher.

His business prospered, but as soon as he was old enough to vote, he became active in politics, first as an alderman and mayor in Greeneville, then as a state legislator, and next as a Democratic member of the United States House of Representatives from 1843 to 1853. In 1853 and again in 1855 he won election as governor of Tennessee, and in 1857 he went to the United States Senate. By then he was a well-to-do man, owned a few household slaves, and entertained presidential aspirations.

A tireless campaigner, an unsurpassed stump speaker, and a man both shrewd and courageous, Johnson was a staunch advocate of Jacksonian democracy and the champion of the "plebeians" (the small farmers and tradesmen of Tennessee) against the "stuck-up aristocrats" (the wealthy, slaveholding planter class). He also possessed, in the words of a fellow Tennessean who knew him well, a "deep-seated, burning hatred of all men who stood in his way." For him political combat was personal combat, and he engaged in it with uncompromising ferocity.

During the winter of 1860–1861, Johnson strongly opposed secession, both by the South as a whole and by Tennessee. Although he believed in states' rights and defended the right of slavery, he placed preservation of the Union above all else, argued that slavery could be best protected within the Union, and denounced the Confederacy as a conspiracy by the planter aristocracy. For a while he succeeded in keeping Tennessee in the Union, but following the outbreak of war in April 1861, the state seceded and Johnson had to flee for his life to the North. His valiant struggle against secession made him the leading Unionist of the South, won him the acclaim of the North, and caused the South to condemn him as a renegade.

In March 1862, after federal forces captured Nashville, Lincoln appointed Johnson military governor of Tennessee. During the next three years he strove against great obstacles to establish a pro-Union civil government, a goal that was finally achieved early in 1865, when a new state constitution abolishing slavery went into effect. Realizing that the war doomed slavery, Johnson supported Lincoln's emancipation policy and told the blacks of Tennes-

see that he would be the Moses who led them into the promised land of freedom.

Meanwhile, Lincoln, hoping to attract support from northern prowar Democrats and border-state Unionists, arranged for Johnson to be his running mate in the 1864 presidential election. Hence, Johnson returned to Washington, where on 4 March 1865 he was inaugurated as vice president. Unhappily, prior to the ceremony Johnson, who recently had been ill and was feeling faint, drank some whiskey and then delivered a rambling, maudlin, almost incoherent inaugural address. Later on, enemies would seize upon this incident to denounce Johnson as "the drunken tailor," but there is no evidence that he habitually overindulged. As it was, he realized that he had disgraced himself and that there was little chance he would ever again play an important role in national affairs. Then came Lincoln's assassination, and suddenly he was the most important man in the nation.

Johnson's Task

With Lee's surrender to Grant at Appomattox on 9 April 1865, the Civil War to all intents and purposes ended, leaving in its wake over six hundred thousand dead Union and Confederate soldiers, a devastated and demoralized South, and an exultant and dominant North. The great issue now was Reconstruction. The Union was preserved and slavery was destroyed. But by what process and under what terms would the seceded states come back into the Union? And what would be the future legal, political, and social status of blacks? Johnson faced the task of dealing with these questions; on his success or failure in doing so depended the success or failure of his presidency.

During the war both Lincoln and Congress had wrestled with Reconstruction. In 1863, Lincoln instituted in Louisiana and Arkansas a program whereby 10 percent of the voters, on taking an oath of allegiance, could form state governments and elect congressmen; once the latter were seated, these states again would be in the Union. The Republican majority in Congress, feeling that the Ten Percent Plan was inadequate and overly lenient, refused to seat the congressmen elected under it and declared that Reconstruction should be carried out by the legislative, rather than the executive, branch.

In July 1864, Congress passed the Wade-Davis bill, which disfranchised all high-ranking Confederates, required 50 percent of the voters in a rebel state to take a loyalty oath before elections could be held, and made abolition of slavery a condition for readmission to the Union. Lincoln in turn pocket vetoed this measure on the grounds that Reconstruction policy should be flexible—that is, carried out by the president. Finally, to confuse matters even more, just before his death Lincoln hinted that with the coming of peace he might take a different approach to Reconstruction, one in which voting rights would be given to blacks who had served in the Union army or who were "very intelligent."

Thus, April 1865 found the government without an established Reconstruction policy and with the Republicans divided over what the policy should be. One faction, the Radical Republicans, of whom Senator Charles Sumner of Massachusetts and Representative Thaddeus Stevens of Pennsylvania were the outstanding spokesmen, contended that the Confederate leaders should be punished severely, that the rebel states should not be restored to the Union until their future loyalty was assured, and that blacks should receive full civil and political rights both as an act of justice and as a means of securing Unionist (that is, Republican) domination of the South.

Another faction, the Moderate Republicans, was primarily concerned about preventing secessionist leaders from returning to power in the South and about keeping the Democrats from regaining their pre-1861 control of the government. They favored securing for blacks their basic personal and civil rights but were hesitant about granting them political rights. They were more numerous and powerful than the Radicals, particularly in Congress.

Finally, there were the Conservative Republicans, who saw no need to go beyond what the war had already achieved—salvation of the Union and emancipation of the slaves—and who therefore believed that the southern states should be readmitted quickly and that the fate of the blacks should be left to the indefinite future. Although weak in Congress, the Conservatives were strong in the cabinet that Johnson inherited from Lincoln—notably in the secretary of state, the highly experienced and astute William H. Seward. In contrast, only one influential member of the cabinet, Secretary of War Edwin M. Stanton, was sympathetic to the Radicals.

The differences between the Radicals and Moderates were essentially ones of timing and degree, but the Conservatives had more in common with the Democrats. Bitter over their loss of national power in 1860, the Democrats wanted to bring the southern states back into the Union as soon as possible, confident that this would bring their party back to power. Moreover, having opposed emancipation, they likewise opposed "Negro equality"; as far as they were concerned, the status of the former slave should be determined by the former master.

Reconstruction Program

Paradoxically, both the Radicals and the Democrats welcomed Johnson's unexpected accession to the presidency. The latter hoped that Johnson, as a lifelong Democrat, would sympathize or even ally himself with their party. For their part the Radicals, who had considered Lincoln too conservative, believed that Johnson inclined to their viewpoint because of his frequent and vehement denunciations of secessionists as traitors who should be treated as such. Their confidence that the new president was "thoroughly radical" increased as he continued to advocate punishing the rebel leaders and when he repudiated an agreement made by Major General William T. Sherman with Confederate General Joseph E. Johnston that had the effect of leaving Confederates in control of southern state governments.

On 29 May 1865, Johnson announced his Reconstruction program in the form of two proclamations. The Amnesty Proclamation pardoned all participants in the rebellion, restored their property except slaves, and required them to take a loyalty oath. It excluded from amnesty the upper-echelon leaders of the Confederacy and all persons possessing over $20,000 in taxable property. Such people would have to apply to the president for a restoration of their right to vote and hold office.

The other proclamation dealt with North Carolina, but its provisions set the pattern for all of the seceded states except Virginia, Tennessee, Arkansas, and Louisiana, where pro-Union governments already existed. It stated that the president would appoint a provisional governor who would summon a convention to draw up a new constitution, whereupon the state would resume its normal relationship to the Union. Only those men who had been eligible to vote in 1861 and who had taken the loyalty oath could vote for delegates to the constitutional convention; in other words, unpardoned rebels and all blacks were barred from the polls, although the convention or a subsequent state legislature could enfranchise the latter if it so desired.

Johnson's cabinet unanimously approved the proclamations, although the North Carolina one, as drafted by Secretary of War Stanton, originally left the way open for black suffrage. Taken together, they were in accordance with Lincoln's approach to Reconstruction in that they gave top priority to reconciling the North and South and looked to the speedy return of the seceded states to the Union. On the other hand, the disfranchisement clauses of the Amnesty Proclamation had more in common with the Wade-Davis bill than with the Ten Percent Plan, and the North Carolina Proclamation showed no trace of Lincoln's proposal to give the vote to at least some blacks.

Three interlocking motives prompted Johnson's Reconstruction program. First, like Lincoln, Johnson wanted to restore the southern states as functioning members of the Union as soon as possible. To him this was the supreme purpose of the Civil War, whereas the future status of blacks was a secondary matter that, for both constitutional and practical reasons, should be left to the states. Second, he wished to transfer political power in the South from the planter aristocracy to the "plebeian" democracy through the disfranchisement clauses of the Amnesty Proclamation. Black suffrage, as he saw it, would thwart the achievement of this objective, because the majority of blacks, even though free, would remain economically bound to the big planters and so would be controlled politically by that class. Third, he hoped to be elected president in 1868 in his own right by promoting what he was confident most Americans desired—sectional reconciliation—and opposing what he was sure few of them favored—black equality. This approach, he believed, would lead to the formation of a new political party that would combine the moderate majority in both sections; unify and dominate the nation; and, of course, look to him as its leader.

Johnson's proclamations delighted the northern Democrats, pleased Conservative Republicans, and relieved southerners, who had expected the worst from the Tennessee turncoat. The Radicals were disappointed by Johnson's failure to give at least some blacks the vote and began to suspect that they were mistaken about his sentiments. As for the Moderate Republicans, they considered the proclamations satisfactory as far as they went, but worried about unrepentant rebels taking control of the new southern state governments and electing congressmen who would join with the northern Democrats to challenge Republican power nationally. Many of them also had misgivings about leaving the fate of the blacks entirely in the hands of their former masters. For the time being, both Radicals and Moderates withheld overt criticism of Johnson's program and waited to see how it worked in practice.

Implementation of Johnson's Program

Johnson followed the North Carolina Proclamation with identical declarations for Mississippi, South Carolina, Florida, Georgia, Alabama, and Texas. During the summer and fall of 1865, all of these states held constitutional conventions. Through the provisional governors he appointed, Johnson directed each state to nullify its secession ordinance, ratify the Thirteenth Amendment by formally abolishing slavery, and repudiate its Confederate debt. South Carolina refused to carry out nullification, Mississippi balked at ratification, and neither of those states repudiated its debt.

Aware of Republican concern about blacks, Johnson also advised—but did not require—these states to "extend the electoral franchise to all persons of color" who could read, who could write their names, or who owned real estate worth at least $250, and to enact laws "for the protection of freedmen in person and property." By doing this, Johnson pointed out, they would "completely disarm the adversary"—by which he meant the Radicals—and greatly enhance their chances of quick readmission to the Union. It was excellent advice, but the southerners failed to heed it. The very idea of former slaves voting was repugnant to them, and they were resolved to restore by other means the "white supremacy" formerly guaranteed by slavery. Hence, none of the southern states so much as considered limited black suffrage; instead, they began enacting "black codes"—laws that provided some basic rights for blacks but had the effect, as well as the intent, of placing them in a position of legal, economic, and social subordination approaching peonage.

Nor was this all. During the fall of 1865 the South held state and congressional elections in which most of the successful candidates were men who had supported the Confederacy. Furthermore, many of the winners were ineligible to hold office under the terms of the Amnesty Proclamation, but by then, that made little practical difference. At first sparing in conferring pardons, Johnson was granting them almost automatically by the latter part of 1865. By doing so, he undermined his plan of transferring political power in the South to the "plebeian" class, but he advanced his presidential ambitions by gaining the goodwill of the former Confederate leaders, who obviously remained dominant in the South. In keeping with this alteration in his strategy, Johnson directed that lands confiscated from rebels during the war be returned to them, thereby dispossessing several thousand blacks who had been settled on them by the Union army.

Aside from Democrats and Conservative Republicans, northerners became increasingly disturbed by Johnson's program and its consequences. They resented the election of Confederate leaders to office, they considered the black codes an attempt to restore slavery, and they were angered by newspaper reports, sometimes exaggerated but sometimes quite accurate, of violent acts committed against blacks, Unionists, and northerners in the South. To them it seemed that the southerners were not displaying proper repentance for the sins of secession and slavery, that they remained disloyal at heart, and that they were attempting to undo the results of the war.

Most Republican politicians felt the same way. Furthermore, they feared that the newly elected southern senators and representatives would, by uniting with the northern Democratic members, threaten their control of Congress. Hence, when Congress, which had not been in session since March, reassembled early in December 1865, the Republican majority barred the southern congressmen from their seats and set up the Joint Committee of Fifteen on Reconstruction, headed by Senator William Pitt Fessenden of Maine, to investigate conditions in the South and recommend appropriate legislation. In taking these actions, the Republicans signaled that they believed further Reconstruction measures were needed and that they intended to formulate them.

Congress' rejection of the southern delegates did not surprise Johnson, as newspapers had been predicting it for sometime, but he was angered by the establishment of the Joint Committee on Reconstruction, deeming it a direct challenge not only to his Reconstruction policy but also to his authority as president. In his annual message to Congress, delivered on 5 December and ghostwritten by the historian George Bancroft, Johnson sought to rally public opinion behind his program by arguing that to continue military occupation of the South or to try to impose black suffrage on it was contrary to the Constitution and to the very concept of democracy, that the sole legitimate purpose of Reconstruction was the restoration and reconciliation of the southern people to the Union, that this now had been substantially accomplished, and that all that remained to be done to complete Reconstruction was to seat the congressmen from the former rebel states.

Public reaction to the message was, on the whole, favorable, and Johnson felt confident that eventually the Republicans would be compelled to admit the southern delegates or else place themselves in the ruinous position of keeping America divided. The only significant group that openly denounced Johnson for his handling of Reconstruction was the Radicals. Johnson endeavored to counteract them by releasing a report written by General Grant on conditions in the South in which Grant asserted that "the mass of thinking men in the South accept the present situation of affairs in good faith" and by stating in published interviews that giving blacks the vote against the will of the whites would produce a race war in the South.

For a while it seemed that Johnson's strategy would succeed. Then, early in February 1866, Congress, by unanimous vote of the Republicans, passed the Freedmen's Bureau bill. This measure extended indefinitely the life of the Freedmen's Bureau, an agency created near the end of the war to provide aid, education, and legal protection for former slaves. Republican leaders not only hoped but expected Johnson to sign it. Anxious to avoid a split with the president that would play into the hands of the Democrats, they had gone to him prior to its passage and offered to change anything to which he had strong objections; he voiced none and they assumed he had none.

Hence, they and Republicans throughout the nation were stunned when, on 19 February, Johnson vetoed the bill. It was, he declared, unnecessary and unconstitutional; furthermore, it had been passed by a Congress that unjustly excluded the duly elected representatives of eleven states. In totally rejecting the bill, Johnson ignored the advice of some of his advisers, notably Secretary of State Seward, that he propose a compromise. Doing this, he feared, would cost him his recently acquired popularity in the South, where the Freedmen's Bureau was hated as the main obstacle to the restoration of white supremacy, and cause the Democrats to turn against him, thereby ruining his plan to form a new party. He realized that the Republicans would resent the veto, but he calculated that popular sentiment would oblige most of them to accept both it and his leadership.

On 20 February the Senate, by a vote of 30 to 18, failed to achieve the two-thirds majority needed to override the veto; three Moderate Republicans, hoping to forestall an open break with the president, joined eight Democrats and seven Conservatives to sustain it. Johnson exulted in the victory. Ignoring the thin margin by which it had been obtained, he believed that he had successfully defied the "Radicals," as he indiscriminately labeled all Republicans who were not Conservatives. On the evening of Washington's Birthday, he delivered from a White House balcony to a crowd of supporters a speech in which he excoriated his opponents in general, and Sumner and Stevens in particular, as traitors bent on subverting the Constitution and consolidating all power in the central government. So intemperate were his remarks that even friends were embarrassed, and most Northerners felt that he disgraced the presidency.

Less than three weeks later, Congress passed the Civil Rights Act of 1866. Designed to protect blacks against the black codes and southern white terrorism, the bill declared them citizens of the United States entitled to equal protection of the laws and conferred broad enforcement powers on the federal government. As with the Freedmen's Bureau bill, Republican congressional leaders solicited Johnson's views on this measure and again got the impression that he found it acceptable. In spite of the Freedmen's Bureau bill veto and the Washington's Birthday tirade, Moderates still hoped to achieve harmony with the president and within the Republican party.

As before, their hope proved unfounded. On 27 March, Johnson delivered another stern veto. The civil rights bill, he declared, was an unconstitutional intrusion on states' rights and discriminated against whites in favor of blacks. No doubt he was sincere in making these assertions, but as in the case of the Freedmen's Bureau veto, he also was motivated by his desire to retain Democratic and southern support.

The veto outraged most northerners and turned all of the Moderate Republicans against Johnson. They concluded that he had gone over to the Democrats and that in alliance with them and the southerners he was endeavoring to destroy the Republican party. Hence, on 6 April the Senate overrode the veto by 33 to 15, and three days later the House did the

same by 122 to 41. For the first time, a Congress had defeated a presidential veto.

Johnson's rejection of the civil rights bill was the greatest blunder of a presidency filled with blunders. Had he signed the bill or, as most of his advisers urged him to do, returned it to Congress with a request that its enforcement provisions be modified, he could have kept the Moderates and Radicals divided. Instead, he united them in opposition to him, thereby ruining any realistic chance of securing the early readmission of the southern states while setting in motion forces that would render him nearly impotent as president.

Meanwhile, the Joint Committee on Reconstruction had been conducting hearings and considering legislation. On 30 April—the same day a white mob began a three-day rampage against blacks in Memphis, Tennessee—the committee reported a constitutional amendment designed to make permanent the protections given by the Civil Rights Act. Two months of debate ensued, at the end of which Congress adopted the Fourteenth Amendment, which provided that all persons born or naturalized in the United States are to be citizens and that no state may "deprive any person of life, liberty, or property, without due process of law; nor deny to any person . . . the equal protection of the laws." In addition, the amendment provided for reducing the House representation of any state denying adult male citizens the vote, disfranchised former federal and state officials who engaged in rebellion, guaranteed the Union war debt, declared the Confederate debt void, and stated that "Congress shall have the power to enforce, by appropriate legislation, the provisions of this article."

Like the Freedmen's Bureau bill (which, incidentally, Congress repassed in July, overriding another veto) and the Civil Rights Act, the Fourteenth Amendment was a product of the Moderates, who beat back an effort by Sumner and Stevens to incorporate black suffrage per se. By adopting it, the Republicans in effect set forth the peace terms of the North and of Congress. Should the southern states ratify it, thereby indicating acceptance of equal civil rights for blacks, they would be readmitted forthwith to the Union. Should they reject it, then (the Republicans clearly implied) they could expect much more drastic treatment.

Johnson promptly denounced the amendment and called for its defeat. All of the former Confederate states, with one exception, either rejected it or took no action. The exception was Johnson's own Tennessee, which, under the almost dictatorial sway of Governor William ("Parson") Brownlow, ratified it against the will of its largely disfranchised citizens. The vast majority of southerners found the prospect of black legal and civil equality intolerable. Moreover, they believed, as did Johnson himself, that northerners would not impose on their fellow whites of the South something they themselves denied blacks in most of their states.

The Referendum of 1866

On 28 July, Congress adjourned and its members headed home to engage in the upcoming congressional elections. These elections, as everyone knew, would be a de facto referendum on Reconstruction. If the Republicans could maintain or increase their majority in Congress, it would mean the North supported their policy of protecting black rights in the South; if they lost their majority or had it substantially reduced, then they would stand repudiated and Johnson would be vindicated.

Johnson sought to secure Republican defeat and victory for himself in two main ways. The first was to try to form a working coalition of Conservative Republicans and northern Democrats that would back candidates favorable to his Reconstruction policy and serve as a step toward the establishment of a new political party. To this end he arranged for the organization of "Johnson Clubs" throughout the North and the border states, and for the meeting of delegates from all of the northern and southern states in the National Union Convention in Philadelphia on 14–16 August. The Johnson Clubs tended to be dominated by Democrats, and many of the participants in the National Union Convention were prominent Copperheads and Confederates. Consequently, most Republicans regarded both moves as merely devices to trick them into voting for Democrats, and instead of gaining support, Johnson lost it.

Johnson's other major effort to overthrow the Republicans took the form of doing something no previous president had done—making a personal campaign tour. Using as the occasion an invitation to dedicate a monument to Stephen A. Douglas in Chicago, Johnson left Washington on 28 August in a special train that carried him north to upstate New York, west to Chicago, south to St. Louis, and then back east to Washington via the Ohio Valley. Proud of his prowess as a stump orator, Johnson believed that if he could speak directly to the people, he would rally them behind his Reconstruction policy. Instead, this "swing around the circle" proved to be a political and personal fiasco. Everywhere he went, Johnson delivered virtually the same speech; before long, his audiences knew what he was going to say before he said it, and pro-Republican humorists had a field day parodying his repetitious remarks. On several occasions, notably in Cleveland and St. Louis, hecklers caused him to lose his temper, to engage in unseemly debates, and to make indiscreet statements. At Indianapolis, Pittsburgh, and several other cities hostile crowds shouted him down, and Republican newspapers denounced him as a vulgar, drunken demagogue who was disgracing the presidency, accusations with which many northerners agreed. Far from persuading the northern people, he ended up disgusting them.

During September, October, and November the voters of the North went to the polls. When all ballots were counted, the Republicans had retained control of every state in the North and increased their already huge majority in Congress. Quite obviously the course of Reconstruction henceforth would be determined by Congress with little or no reference to the wishes of the president. Any chance that Johnson would be able to form a new party and succeed himself in the White House had been destroyed, although in spite of everything he would continue to harbor the latter ambition.

Congressional Reconstruction

On 3 December 1866, Congress reassembled, with the Republicans resolved to scrap Johnson's Reconstruction program and replace it with a new one. Reinforcing their resolve was the refusal of the ten southern states still outside the Union to ratify the Fourteenth Amendment and the New Orleans riot of 30 July, in which a mob of whites massacred thirty-eight Republicans, thirty-four of whom were blacks.

All through the winter Congress debated and labored. As before, the Radicals pushed for black suffrage, whereas the Moderates held back, fearing that imposing this on the South would indeed outrage the North, where only a handful of states, all with minuscule black populations, permitted blacks to vote. Ultimately, faced with political humiliation if they did not come up with something, the Republicans united to pass the Military Reconstruction Act late in February 1867.

The act divided the ten unreconstructed states into five military districts, each under a general em-

Johnson toured the nation by railway during the 1866 congressional elections in an unprecedented attempt to bolster the campaigns of Democratic candidates and his Reconstruction policies. THE LIBRARY OF CONGRESS

powered to employ military courts and troops to maintain order and enforce federal laws; directed that conventions elected by black voters and eligible whites be held in each of the ten states for the purpose of framing new constitutions that would provide for black suffrage; stipulated that after a state had adopted its new constitution and ratified the Fourteenth Amendment it would be entitled to congressional representation; and, finally, barred from voting for, and serving in, the state constitutional conventions any person guilty of violating an oath to uphold the United States Constitution by voluntarily engaging in rebellion. In sum this was, and remains, the most drastic law ever enacted by Congress, for it placed millions of citizens under military rule in peacetime, deprived hundreds of thousands of them of political rights, and enfranchised a group that the majority of Americans at that time considered unqualified to participate in government. Nevertheless, like the Civil Rights Act and the Fourteenth Amendment, it was largely a Moderate measure; Sumner, Stevens, and other Radicals criticized it because it allowed the readmission of southern states upon ratifi-

cation of the Fourteenth Amendment and did not confiscate "rebel" lands for distribution to blacks.

Congress also passed two bills aimed at Johnson himself. One, which took the form of an amendment to the annual Army Appropriation Act, required the president to transmit all orders to military commanders through General of the Army Grant, whom the Republicans counted on to block or at least report any attempt by Johnson to sabotage the administration of the Military Reconstruction Act. The other measure was the Tenure of Office Act. This prohibited the president from dismissing any official appointed with the Senate's consent without that body's approval. Its purpose was to prevent Johnson from removing Republican officeholders and replacing them with his own supporters.

Needless to say, Johnson vetoed the Military Reconstruction Act, which he accurately described as revolutionary, and the Tenure of Office Act, which he rightly labeled an unconstitutional encroachment by the legislative on the executive branch; as for the Army Appropriation Act, he signed it only because he

Campaigns
and
Elections

TOP

Automobiles became more and more prevalent in American society in the 1920s and thus gave presidential aspirants a new way to attract voters. Here is a license plate accessory advertising Calvin Coolidge's candidacy from 1924. COLLECTION OF DAVID J. AND JANICE L. FRENT

LEFT

Theodore Roosevelt was the first president to host an African-American in the White House. This depiction of his dinner with Booker T. Washington was issued in 1903 to appeal to progressive voters. Note the portrait of Abraham Lincoln in the background. A/P WORLDWIDE

BOTTOM

Labor unions have often thrown their support behind Democratic candidates, as this poster distributed by the New York State American Labor Party indicates; the group was promoting the reelection campaign of Franklin D. Roosevelt in 1936.
COLLECTION OF DAVID J. AND JANICE L. FRENT

BOTTOM
Herbert Hoover hoped to capitalize on the booming economy of the 1920s. However, the 1929 stock market crash and the resulting fallout quickly made this dreamy 1928 campaign poster a sad irony. COLLECTION OF DAVID J. AND JANICE L. FRENT

TOP

The presidential candidates of 1964 are portrayed as comic book characters: Barry Goldwater as the gunslinger from the west, and Lyndon B. Johnson as the superhuman champion of social progress. COLLECTION OF DAVID J. AND JANICE L. FRENT

RIGHT

This poster for 1972 Democratic nominees George McGovern and Sargent Shriver urges a party-line vote. The 1972 election was the first in which eighteen-year-olds were allowed to vote. COLLECTION OF DAVID J. AND JANICE L. FRENT

He's making
us proud again.

TOP

In the wake of Watergate and shattered trust in the presidency, Gerald Ford tried to emphasize his efforts to restore faith in the office during the 1976 campaign. He ultimately lost to Jimmy Carter, who also campaigned on themes of honor and integrity.

COLLECTION OF DAVID J. AND JANICE L. FRENT

BOTTOM

Campaign buttons like this "Kansans for Reagan" button from 1980 are often seen during a party's national convention.

COLLECTION OF DAVID J. AND JANICE L. FRENT

TOP

In 1984 Walter Mondale achieved a historical milestone when he named Rep. Geraldine Ferraro as his vice-presidential running mate, the first woman ever on a major party's national ticket. Mondale and Ferraro lost to Ronald Reagan and George Bush.
COLLECTION OF DAVID J. AND JANICE L. FRENT

BOTTOM

As a former public official herself, Elizabeth Dole often took center stage in reaching out to audiences on behalf of her husband's 1996 presidential campaign. Former senator Bob Dole lost to incumbent President Bill Clinton. BETTMANN/CORBIS

feared that to do otherwise would demoralize the army, but he protested against the provision requiring him to issue orders via the general of the army. And needless to say, Congress overrode his vetoes and ignored his protest. In addition, before recessing at the end of March, the House instructed the Judiciary Committee to prepare a report on the advisability of impeaching the president—a warning to Johnson to behave while Congress was away from Washington. Thus, by the spring of 1867, Johnson's Reconstruction program had been demolished and he, so it seemed, was reduced to virtual impotence.

Johnson Counterattacks

In spite of his defeats and humiliations, Johnson remained determined to fight on until he achieved victory and vindication, just as he had done in his struggle against secession. He believed that although most northerners, duped by Republican propaganda, might agree to civil rights for blacks, they would not support the imposition of black suffrage on their fellow whites of the South or the indefinite prolongation of bayonet rule in the southern states. Sooner or later, he calculated, the Republicans would "hang themselves" with their extreme measures as public opinion in the North turned against them. Meanwhile, until that happened, and in order to help make it happen, he would do everything he could to oppose, cripple, and discredit Military Reconstruction. He also hoped, indeed expected, that the Supreme Court would declare the congressional program unconstitutional. Already, on 17 December 1866, the Court had held in the case of *Ex parte Milligan* that military tribunals had no right to try civilians in areas where the civil courts were functioning—a decision that obviously had negative implications for the Military Reconstruction Act.

On 1 April 1867 an election in Connecticut resulted in the Democrats capturing the governorship and three of that state's four congressional seats— the first Democratic victory in the North since 1864. Johnson saw this as a "turn of the current" of northern public opinion. It also encouraged him to launch an indirect but potentially devastating assault on Military Reconstruction. At Johnson's behest, Attorney General Henry B. Stanbery prepared an interpretation of the legal powers of the district commanders in the South that, in the words of Michael Les Benedict, "virtually emasculated the Reconstruction law." The Republicans, who had anticipated such a move,

quickly reconvened Congress, which on 13 July passed a supplementary Reconstruction bill that overruled Stanbery's interpretation on every important point. Automatically Johnson vetoed the bill, and just as automatically, Congress repassed it over his veto and then again went home, hoping that Johnson finally realized the futility of resisting its will—a vain hope.

Playing a key role in carrying out Military Reconstruction was Secretary of War Stanton. For a long time Johnson had been aware of the fact that Stanton constantly obstructed his policies, that he habitually lied to him, and that he was actively aiding the congressional Republicans. Yet he had held back from dismissing him from the cabinet out of fear of the political and personal repercussions, for Stanton enjoyed great prestige in the North because of his wartime services and possessed strong backing among the Republicans. By the summer of 1867, Johnson had decided that he no longer would tolerate Stanton's disloyalty to his administration. Therefore, on 11 August, after failing to obtain Stanton's resignation, he suspended Stanton from office under the terms of the Tenure of Office Act and named Grant acting secretary of war, a post Grant accepted with great reluctance, as he, too, opposed the president's Reconstruction program and had been secretly collaborating with Congress. In addition, on 17 August, Johnson relieved Major General Philip H. Sheridan as commander of the Military District of Louisiana and Texas, where he had been pursuing a course that Johnson deemed both tyrannical and insubordinate.

As was to be expected, the Republicans reacted to Stanton's suspension and Sheridan's removal with anger and demands for impeachment. Johnson was unmoved, and the outcome of the autumn state elections reinforced his feeling that northern public opinion was shifting in his favor. The Democrats won in New York, New Jersey, and California; gained control of the Ohio legislature; and sharply reduced Republican majorities in several other states. In addition, the voters of Ohio, Minnesota, New Jersey, and Kansas overwhelmingly rejected black suffrage in their states. Unlike in 1866, when most Republican candidates carefully avoided the issue, in 1867 they came out in favor of granting blacks the vote in the North as well as the South. The result was that, in the blunt words of Radical Senator Benjamin Wade, "The nigger whipped us."

When Congress convened in December 1867, Johnson announced to his cabinet, "The time for mere defense is now past and I can stand on the of-

A copy of a ticket to the Senate impeachment trial of President Andrew Johnson, issued on 13 March 1868, the day the Senate ordered Johnson to stand trial. AP/WIDE WORLD

fensive in behalf of the Constitution and the country." Accordingly, in his annual message of 3 December he declared that the effect of Military Reconstruction was to make blacks the rulers of whites, that this could only cause the South to sink into barbarism, and that he intended to resist the unconstitutional usurpations of Congress, "regardless of all consequences," confident that he would be sustained by the people, as demonstrated in the recent elections.

Infuriated, the Radicals called for the House to impeach Johnson. But the Moderates, although likewise angry, stated that unfortunately there was no legal basis for such action, and after an acrimonious debate the House on 7 December defeated an impeachment resolution by 108 to 57, with 66 Republicans joining 42 Democrats in opposition. Radical leaders thereupon began deploring the "surrender of Congress" to the president, whereas one of Johnson's confidants asserted that "the President has Congress on the hip." Further encouraging Johnson while at the same time alarming all Republicans, the case of *Ex parte McCardle*, involving the constitutionality of the Military Reconstruction Act, was now before the Supreme Court; on the basis of the *Milligan* precedent, the Court would almost surely strike down the act.

But if Radicals and Moderates differed as to the feasibility of impeaching Johnson, they did agree that he must not be allowed to displace Stanton permanently as secretary of war. If that happened, the Tenure of Office Act would become a dead letter and Johnson would be free to name a secretary of war

who would cooperate with him in sabotaging Military Reconstruction, thereby threatening Republican domination in the South. Hence, on 13 January 1868 the Senate, applying the Tenure Act, rejected a request from Johnson that it concur in Stanton's dismissal and declared that Stanton was still secretary of war.

Johnson had anticipated this action. Accordingly he had asked Grant not to surrender the secretary of war's office without giving prior notice; in this way Johnson would have an opportunity to appoint someone else to the post so as to bring about a Supreme Court test of the Tenure Act. Grant promised, or at least permitted Johnson to understand that he promised, to do what the president requested. But on 14 January, after the Senate refused to sanction Stanton's removal, Grant went directly to the War Department building, locked the secretary of war's office, and turned over the key to a military aide; an hour later Stanton arrived, obtained the key, and entered his old office.

Johnson accused Grant of "duplicity" both before the cabinet and in the press. Grant heatedly denied the charge and thus the two became open, bitter enemies. Probably Grant did betray Johnson, for although he had warned Johnson that he would quit as acting secretary of war if the Senate rejected Stanton's dismissal, he knew that the president did not expect him to do it so abruptly and in a manner that would make it so easy for Stanton to regain physical possession of the office. On the other hand, Johnson was seeking to exploit for his own purposes Grant's prestige and popularity; and had Grant allowed him to do this, Grant would have been caught in the middle of the struggle between the president and Congress. Realizing this, Grant decided to extricate himself, even though it meant acting in a fashion that at best can be described as slippery.

Foiled in his plan to prevent Stanton from taking possession of the war office, Johnson next tried to force him out of it, his intention still being to bring about a legal test of the Tenure Act. To this end, on 21 February he appointed the adjutant general of the army, Lorenzo P. Thomas, secretary of war and instructed him to go to the War Department and demand that Stanton vacate the office. Thomas, an elderly, ineffectual type, did so twice; each time Stanton adamantly refused and Thomas went away.

The Republicans exploded with anger and joy— anger because Johnson was so brazenly defying the will of Congress and joy because he had at last given them a plausible reason to impeach and remove him from office. On 24 February the House of Representatives, by a vote of 126 to 47, passed a resolution declaring "that Andrew Johnson, President of the United States, be impeached of high crimes and misdemeanors." For the first time in American history a president had been impeached.

Johnson's Impeachment Trial

A special House committee drafted articles of impeachment against Johnson—that is, specific accusations of "high crimes and misdemeanors." Adopted by the House on 2 and 3 March, the articles totaled eleven. The first eight were variations on the charge that Johnson had violated the Tenure Act by attempting to supplant Stanton with Thomas; the ninth and tenth contained petty and patently absurd allegations; and the eleventh, primarily the handiwork of Stevens, combined all of the previous charges. On 4 March seven Republicans, acting as the "impeachment managers," formally presented the articles to the Senate, which sat as a "High Court of Impeachment" presided over by Chief Justice Salmon P. Chase. Two days later, the Senate summoned Johnson to stand trial beginning 13 March.

Johnson reacted to impeachment calmly. "If I cannot be President in fact," he told his personal secretary, "I will not be President in name alone." To defend him, he retained the services of several of the nation's leading lawyers. Pleading the need for more time to prepare their case, they succeeded in getting postponement of the trial. In the meantime, the Republicans passed a bill that deprived the Supreme Court of jurisdiction over cases such as *Ex parte Milligan*. Thus, Johnson was frustrated not only in his effort to challenge the Tenure Act in the courts but also in his hope of having Military Reconstruction declared unconstitutional.

On 30 March the impeachment trial, which the president was not required to attend in person, got under way. Johnson's attorneys argued that the Tenure of Office Act was unconstitutional; that even if it were constitutional, it did not protect Stanton because he had been appointed by Lincoln, not Johnson; that the president had not actually violated it, since Stanton obviously still remained in office; that Johnson's attempt to replace Stanton was motivated by a legitimate desire to test the act's constitutionality and not by criminal intent; and, finally, that since impeachment was a judicial and not a political process and since Johnson had not committed any indictable offense, the president was innocent of "high crimes and misdemeanors." The House managers, with Benjamin Butler of Massachusetts being the main spokesman, rebutted the defense's allegations about the Tenure Act and maintained that impeachment was political in nature; otherwise, Butler sarcastically asked, how could an unfit president be removed unless he was caught "robbing a chicken house" or committing some other statutory crime?

The managers believed that the catchall eleventh impeachment article offered the best prospect for convicting Johnson. Therefore, on 16 May the Senate voted on it first. Thirty-five senators declared Johnson guilty, and nineteen declared him innocent. Since under the Constitution at least two-thirds of the senators present and voting are needed to convict a president, Johnson escaped by the narrowest possible margin. Ten days later, votes on two other articles provided the same outcome, whereupon the impeachment trial ended.

Johnson owed his escape to the fact that seven Republicans joined with the Senate's ten Democrats and two Conservatives to vote for acquittal. A combination of factors explains why these seven "recusants" deserted their party's ranks: they doubted the legal justification of impeachment, feared that deposing the president would ultimately injure the party, and disliked the prospect of the ultra-Radical Senator Benjamin Wade of Ohio replacing Johnson, which under the presidential succession law of that time he would have done by virtue of being president pro tem of the Senate. Johnson also helped his own cause by letting it be known that if he remained in office, he would cease obstructing the implementation of Military Reconstruction and that he would appoint the politically neutral Major General John M. Schofield to be the new secretary of war—promises he kept. (Stanton resigned as soon as the impeachment trial ended.)

Today practically all historians and legal experts agree that Johnson was innocent of the charges brought against him, and in 1926 the Supreme Court did what Johnson had hoped for in 1868—it declared the Tenure of Office Act unconstitutional. On the other hand, the oft-expressed view that Johnson's removal from office would have permanently weakened the presidency probably is erroneous. The circumstances that led to Johnson's impeachment were both extreme and unique, whereas the forces that brought about the emergence of the "imperial presidency" in the twentieth century would have operated regardless of the outcome of Johnson's trial. Finally, although the impeachment as such failed, it did cause Johnson to abandon his struggle against Congress' Reconstruction program. Despite having declared that he did not want to be president in name alone, in effect he settled for exactly that.

Other Events of Johnson's Presidency

Reconstruction was the dominant issue of Johnson's presidency to which, both out of choice and necessity, he devoted most, sometimes all, of his attention and energy. Yet he also had to concern himself with a number of other matters that were highly important in their own right—indeed, would have held center stage under normal circumstances.

When Johnson became president, a war with France over Mexico was a distinct possibility. During the Civil War the French, then ruled by Napoleon III, flagrantly violated the Monroe Doctrine by establishing in Mexico a puppet regime headed by the Emperor Maximilian, an Austrian archduke. Initially Johnson seemed disposed to adopt the approach advocated by General Grant—namely, to tell Napoleon that unless he pulled his troops out of Mexico immediately, the United States Army would drive them out. Fortunately, Secretary of State Seward successfully asserted his control over foreign policy, something in which Johnson had no experience and scant interest. By means of skillful diplomatic prodding, Seward induced Napoleon, who was finding the Mexican intervention costly in money and men, to withdraw his forces beginning late in 1866. Once they all left, the Mexicans, led by Benito Juárez, had little difficulty overthrowing Maximilian. Thus, the greatest challenge to United States interest in the Caribbean prior to the Castro Communist takeover of Cuba was repelled. Ironically, an aggressive policy leading to war with France would have been enormously popular in the United States and would probably have assured the success of Johnson's Reconstruction program.

Seward, who long had been an advocate of Manifest Destiny, tried to pursue an expansionist policy, hoping thereby to gain public support for the Johnson administration and to advance his own presidential aspirations. In large part because of the bitter conflict over Reconstruction, his only solid achievement along this line was the acquisition of Alaska in

1867. Early that year the Russian government, having decided that Alaska was a financial and strategic liability, instructed its minister in Washington, Baron Edouard de Stoeckl, to sell it to the United States. Seward proved more than willing to buy it, and he and Stoeckl quickly negotiated a treaty whereby the United States agreed to pay $7.2 million in gold for the territory. The treaty easily passed the Senate, 37 to 2, on 9 April 1867, but the necessary appropriation bill encountered strong opposition in the House, where many Republicans opposed it simply because they hated Johnson. Finally, on 14 July 1868, after Stoeckl discreetly bribed several key representatives, the House approved it, 114 to 43. Thus, the expansion of the United States across the North American continent, which began in 1803 with the Louisiana Purchase, came to an end.

During the Civil War, Confederate warships, of which the *Alabama* was the most prominent, inflicted tremendous damage on northern merchant shipping. Since these raiders had been built in Britain, the United States government held the British government responsible for their depredations and demanded monetary reparation. In 1868, in an effort to settle these so-called *Alabama* Claims before he left office, Johnson sent a former senator named Reverdy Johnson to London, where he negotiated a treaty whereby the claims of both British and American citizens arising from the Civil War would be settled on an equal basis. It was a poor treaty, but thinking it the best that could be had, Johnson submitted it to the Senate early in 1869, only to see it rejected, 54 to 1. Two years later the United States obtained a much better settlement of the *Alabama* Claims.

On the domestic front the two main problems other than Reconstruction had to do with fiscal policy and the Indians of the western plains. Concerning the first, the Civil War had resulted in a federal debt of nearly $3 billion (an enormous sum by the standards of the day), the issuance of over $600 million in "greenbacks" (paper money unsupported by gold or silver), and unprecedentedly high taxes, especially the tariff. Johnson for the most part left financial policy to Secretary of the Treasury Hugh McCulloch, a holdover from Lincoln's cabinet. McCulloch generally cooperated with the Republican Congress in gradually reducing the number of greenbacks in circulation with a view to restoring a bullion-based currency.

Meanwhile, during the latter part of his presidency, when he was desperately casting about for political allies, Johnson toyed with the thought of embracing the "Ohio Idea," a scheme popular in the Midwest that called for increasing, rather than decreasing, the supply of greenbacks in order to pay off the national debt and stimulate the economy. But Johnson held fast to his fiscal conservatism; furthermore, the Ohio Idea had more opponents than proponents, and so he would have hurt, rather than helped, himself politically by advocating it. For similar reasons he made no serious effort to counter the Republican high-tariff policy, although verbally criticizing it.

As regards the Indians, Johnson's administration adopted a two-pronged approach: the army waged campaigns designed to pacify the hostile tribes and safeguard western settlers, and the Bureau of Indian Affairs responded to the demands of eastern reformers by endeavoring to place the Indians on reservations, where supposedly they would be protected from evil white influences and given an opportunity to acquire white civilization. Although the reservation policy fell far short of the expectations of its idealistic proponents, it was probably the most practical one the government could have adopted at that time, for the Indians' way of life was doomed by the westward push of the American people as incarnated in the construction of the transcontinental railroad, a project nearly completed by the time Johnson left office.

Conclusion of Johnson's Presidency

In May 1868 the Republicans, as everyone expected, nominated Grant for president on a platform that called for black suffrage in the South but discreetly avoided proposing it nationwide. Johnson hoped for and sought the Democratic nomination, believing that his fight against congressional Reconstruction entitled him to it. Most Democrats now considered him, rightly enough, a political liability, and at their convention in July nominated Horatio Seymour, a former New York governor. Although disappointed, Johnson—out of hatred for Grant, if nothing else—did what he could during the campaign to help Seymour. Grant won by 214 electoral votes to Seymour's 80, but his popular majority was only 300,000, and even that was the result of the enfranchisement of blacks and the disfranchisement of whites in the South. Hence, early in 1869, the Republicans placed black suffrage on a permanent foundation by ram-

ming through the Fifteenth Amendment, which stated that no citizen could be deprived of the vote for reasons of "race, color, or previous condition of servitude." This turned out to be the final major measure of congressional Reconstruction, and like the first, it became law over Johnson's futile protests.

Johnson finished his few remaining months as president in relative peace. At noon on 4 March 1869 he left the White House without, as is customary, attending the inauguration of his successor. He returned to Tennessee and soon plunged into politics, making several unsuccessful attempts to secure a seat in Congress. Finally, in January 1875, the Tennessee legislature, now controlled by Democrats, elected him to the United States Senate. On 5 March he took his seat in the Senate, thereby becoming the only former president to serve in that body. He did not serve long. On 28 July, while visiting one of his daughters in Tennessee, he suffered a stroke and three days later died. He was buried near his Greeneville home, his body wrapped in the United States flag and his well-thumbed copy of the Constitution beneath his head.

Johnson Evaluated

Johnson's presidency corresponded with the first and most crucial phase of Reconstruction. Since Reconstruction was intimately linked to the highly controversial issue of the status of blacks in American life, both it and Johnson have been highly controversial also. Accordingly, historians who believe that congressional Reconstruction in general was bad and that in particular it was a mistake to grant blacks equal civil and political rights so soon after being freed from slavery portray Johnson as a heroic champion of the Constitution and true reconciliation between North and South. Historians who feel that the Fourteenth and Fifteenth Amendments were necessary acts of justice and that the only thing wrong with Reconstruction was that it did not go far enough condemn Johnson as a racist villain who deserved to be removed from office. Between these extremes stand yet more historians and their judgments of Johnson; historians never have agreed about him, nor will they ever.

Even so, it seems that this can be said with certainty about the tenacious tailor from Tennessee: Few presidents faced a greater challenge than he did, and none failed more completely than he to meet that challenge successfully. There are several reasons why this was so.

First, Johnson was a southerner and a Democrat heading the government of a nation controlled by northerners and Republicans. Consequently, he miscalculated the attitudes of the North and had no sympathy for, or understanding of, the Republicans. Lincoln, had he lived, would not have suffered from such handicaps and the course of Reconstruction would have been substantially different.

Johnson lacked the moral and political authority of an elected president, yet he acted as if he possessed it. As a result, his refusal to compromise with Congress quickly dissipated the strength he initially enjoyed.

Johnson's dedication to the Union, the Constitution, and democracy as he understood them was as sincere as it was strong; but he did not realize that the Civil War was a revolution that would not end with the defeat of the rebels and the freeing of the slaves, and he failed to see that the pre-1861 power relationship between the federal and state governments had been permanently altered in favor of the former.

Johnson, like the vast majority of American whites of his time, considered blacks inferior. Had his racial attitudes been those of Charles Sumner or of a twentieth-century liberal, possibly the story of his presidency and the outcome of Reconstruction would have been happier. But there is no evidence that racism was the sole or even the main determinant of his policies. Like Lincoln, he perceived the enormous obstacles that lay in the way of equality for blacks; he also believed, given the realities of the situation, that the status of blacks in the South would sooner or later be dictated by the whites. This belief, obviously, was not altogether wrong. By 1875, the year Johnson died, the Fourteenth and Fifteenth Amendments were virtually dead. Eighty years would pass before they came to life again.

Finally, Johnson suffered from serious defects of mind and character. Although he possessed "great natural capacity," he held "few ideas," was "narrow-minded," and lacked flexibility and adroitness. He also was extremely distrustful of others, tended to regard advice as tantamount to dictation, and was overly pugnacious and insufficiently discreet. At the same time, he was often indecisive and hesitant, yet when he did act, he did so hastily and without foresight. Quite likely these traits, more than anything else, caused him to commit the blunders that turned his policies and presidency into a shambles.

To sum up, Johnson quested for power all of his adult life; but when, through tragic circumstance, he gained the highest power, he proved incapable of using it in an effective and beneficial manner.

BIBLIOGRAPHY

George Fort Milton, *The Age of Hate: Andrew Johnson and the Radicals* (New York, 1930), is, from a human-interest and literary standpoint, the best biography of Johnson, although excessively favorable to Johnson and overly critical of the Republicans. Hans L. Trefousse, *Andrew Johnson: A Biography* (New York, 1989), is the latest biography of Johnson and although it provides some useful information and insights not to be found in Milton's biography, it tends to go to the opposite extreme of that work, portraying Johnson not as a champion of democracy and the Constitution but rather as a person who "failed to grow" with his time and so "left a legacy of racism." James E. Sefton, *Andrew Johnson and the Uses of Constitutional Power* (Boston, 1980), is a good, up-to-date short biography. Albert Castel, *The Presidency of Andrew Johnson* (Lawrence, Kans., 1979), endeavors to synthesize modern scholarship on Johnson and Reconstruction. Martin E. Mantell, *Johnson, Grant, and the Politics of Reconstruction* (New York, 1973), sheds fresh light on relations between Johnson and Grant. David Miller Dewitt, *The Impeachment and Trial of Andrew Johnson, Seventeenth President of the United States* (New York, 1903; repr. 1967), is, despite its age, the best account of Johnson's impeachment as such.

Eric L. McKitrick, *Andrew Johnson and Reconstruction* (Chicago, 1960), achieved a revolution in Reconstruction historiography and is still the best work on its subject. Michael Les Benedict, *A Compromise of Principle: Congressional Republicans and Reconstruction, 1863–1869* (New York, 1974), is highly detailed and based on impressive research but is extremely anti-Johnson and pro-Radical. Eric Foner, *Reconstruction: America's Unfinished Revolution, 1863–1877* (New York, 1988), the most recent full-length history of Reconstruction, takes what might be termed a neo-Radical view of its subject and hence is very critical of Johnson, whom it blames in large part for the "failure of Reconstruction." Claude G. Bowers, *The Tragic Era: The Revolution After Lincoln* (Cambridge, Mass., 1929), portrays the Radicals as fiends and Johnson as a great hero. LaWanda Cox and John H. Cox, *Politics, Principle, and Prejudice, 1865–1866* (New York, 1963), is of particular value on

Johnson's relations with the Democrats and his attempt to form a new party. William R. Brock, *An American Crisis: Congress and Reconstruction, 1865–1867* (New York, 1963), is balanced and perceptive in its treatment of both Johnson and Congress.

See also Richard B. McCaslin, comp., *Andrew Johnson: A Bibliography* (Westport, Conn., 1992).

Ulysses S. Grant

John Y. Simon

Ulysses S. Grant THE LIBRARY OF CONGRESS

ULYSSES S. GRANT did not need or want the presidency and entered the White House with considerable reluctance. His dazzling rise to fame during the Civil War had elevated him within three years from a former captain working for a younger brother in their father's leather-goods store in Galena, Illinois, to commander of all the armies of the United States. In one more year, he ended the war and prepared to reap the rewards of victory. Citizens of Galena gave Grant a handsomely furnished house, which he retained as a voting residence and visited occasionally, and for a time the Grants lived in Philadelphia, in another house presented to the victorious general; but command of the army required Grant's presence in Washington, where Grant, happily married and a devoted father to four children, united his family. Promoted to general of the army as of 25 July 1866, Grant held military rank higher than any other American except George Washington, drew a comfortable salary with many perquisites, and fulfilled grave responsibilities. Indeed, grateful citizens of the North intended to honor and reward the man who deserved more credit for the continued existence of the United States than anyone except President Abraham Lincoln.

The advantages of Grant's position as general in chief included lifelong tenure, no small benefit to a man who had encountered grinding poverty in the years between resignation from the army in 1854 and reentry into military service in the Civil War in 1861. As a young officer, he had received promotions during the Mexican War, but the peacetime army offered little hope of advancement. Assigned to Pacific Coast duty in 1852 and prudently leaving behind his pregnant wife, Grant encountered inflated prices and felt the financial pinch of army pay. Unable to make a success of investment or farming, lonely and unhappy, Captain Grant resigned his commission. He left the Pacific Coast to rejoin his family, intending to farm the land in Saint Louis County, Missouri, that his father-in-law had given to his wife, Julia, but despite dogged efforts he succumbed to the Panic of 1857 and eventually lost the farm and the unfinished log house, ruefully named Hardscrabble, which he had built with the aid of neighbors. In the years following, Grant never prospered in anything he tried. At one low point, he pawned his watch two days before Christmas, perhaps so that he could buy gifts for his wife and children. The move to Galena in 1860 to take the job his father provided may have been an even greater humiliation.

Such poverty left scars. For the rest of his life he gratefully remembered friends who had stuck by him in his years of adversity and those who helped him gain command in the Civil War and refuted critics of his generalship. He wanted personal loyalty and returned it overgenerously. Grant valued security and stability above glory and wealth. During the Civil War he began to use his military pay to purchase the land he had once farmed, attempting to re-create his father-in-law's estate, White Haven. An avid horse fancier, Grant looked forward to eventual retirement and the satisfactions of a gentleman farmer, but promotion to lieutenant general in 1864 gave him the prospect of an equally pleasant life in the peacetime army as a desk general with a settled family life.

Politics had no appeal for Grant, perhaps in part because it had fascinated his father. Jesse Root Grant, a self-made man who never allowed others to forget it, had risen from poverty to affluence in the leather business, educating himself along the way. He wrote letters to newspapers on a variety of subjects, plunged into political controversy, and was elected mayor of Georgetown and later of Bethel, Ohio. (Ulysses was raised in Georgetown but had been born in Point Pleasant on 27 April 1822.) Perhaps in reaction his son developed such a taste for privacy and modesty that through a long public career he never corrected the common misapprehension that

his middle name was Simpson, his mother's maiden name (he had been named Hiram Ulysses but his first name was never used); he could not even bring himself to deliver a political speech until several years after leaving the White House. Jesse had insisted that his unwilling eldest son go to West Point and did little to help him start farming in Missouri. As Ulysses rose to fame during the Civil War, the proud father tried to promote his son's career through letters to newspapers; as a result, Grant noted, Cincinnati newspapers, those most accessible to Jesse, gave Ulysses the most unfavorable coverage of any in the North. Writing to a potential biographer of Ulysses, Jesse acknowledged where his son got his character:

> Like his mother, he rarely ever laughs, never sheds a tear or becomes excited—though always in a pleasant humor—never says a profane word, or indulges in jokes—always says what he means and means what he says—always expressing himself in the fewest possible words, and never had a personal controversy with man or boy in his life.

In 1856, Grant voted for Democrat James Buchanan for president, later explaining that he did so to avert secession and because "I knew Frémont." In 1860, although ineligible to vote as a newcomer to Galena, Grant favored Democrat Stephen A. Douglas. Yet Grant received his first commission in the Civil War from a Republican, Governor Richard Yates; and his appointment as brigadier general, which preceded his first encounter with the enemy, came through the efforts of another Republican, Congressman Elihu B. Washburne of Galena. Grant's conversion to the Republican party proceeded imperceptibly as he sought to avoid all involvement in political issues, but by 1864 he understood the importance to battlefield victory of the reelection of Lincoln and allowed Washburne to use his letters as campaign literature. Grant supported the reelection of Lincoln through the Union party, something more than a false front for the Republicans, as evidenced by its nomination of Andrew Johnson, an avowed and unrepentant Democrat, for vice president.

In 1864, political speculation already centered on the military hero, and Grant received exploratory correspondence from Democrats as well as Republicans. Before nominating Grant as lieutenant general, Lincoln had sought an assurance that Grant had no presidential ambitions. At the Union convention, Missouri delegates sought to enter a Radical protest by voting for Grant for the presidential nomination, though all other votes went to Lincoln. Grant's sound reasons for rejecting political overtures in 1864 no longer applied after Appomattox.

Grant met Lincoln for the first time in March 1864, when Grant went to Washington to receive his commission as lieutenant general. They had apparent similarities as products of the new West, but their differences were more important. Lincoln retained the aura of frontiersman while Grant cultivated gentility, with Lincoln winning fame for telling dirty stories, and Grant, a reputation for refusing to listen to them. Lincoln's style was indirect, and it is doubtful whether, in their infrequent meetings, Grant fully understood the man or his policy. While Grant received the impression that the president had put the war into his hands, Lincoln retained his supervisory role as commander in chief. When Grant sought to have the president remove a troublesome and incompetent subordinate, Major General Benjamin F. Butler, Lincoln insisted that Grant take responsibility for this decision. Grant's appointment of Lincoln's son Robert to his headquarters staff relieved Lincoln of the onus of withholding his own son from a war to which he had sent so many other sons. Robert's relatively safe position also solved one of Lincoln's problems with Mary Lincoln, whose increasingly bizarre behavior sometimes took the form of irrational fears about the safety of Robert. Mary's tantrums kept the Lincolns and Grants apart, most notably leading to a declined invitation to Ford's Theater. All in all, Grant learned little from Lincoln.

Grant and Johnson

Unfortunately, the president with whom Grant spent far more time, Andrew Johnson, taught negative lessons. Lincoln did not conceal a vein of coarseness, but Johnson displayed it proudly. By emphasizing his humble origins and rise to prominence through his own efforts, Johnson may have seemed reminiscent of Grant's father, whom, not incidentally, Johnson appointed postmaster of Covington, Kentucky, in an embarrassingly blatant attempt to obligate his son.

Johnson and Grant headed toward a collision over policy. Both men had owned slaves before the Civil War, but Johnson had gloried in his ownership, had once declared his dream that every American family might own one, and based policy upon his firm conviction in the superiority of whites. Grant had worked Hardscrabble with slaves supplied by his father-in-law, and Julia continued to own slaves during the Civil War; but Grant freed one slave he owned himself in 1859, at a time when he desperately needed the money that sale of a slave could bring. At the onset of the Civil War, he dreaded a slave insurrection, which he assumed would have to be suppressed by the armed force of both North and South.

Just as he changed from Democrat to Republican during the Civil War, his attitude toward blacks shifted. From the earliest days of the Civil War, blacks contributed to a Union victory as they flocked through northern lines bringing information of southern strength and plans. Once within the lines, they gratefully accepted employment in support of the army, working at tasks that released white men for combat. Grant saw the first black troops in his army prove their capacity as soldiers by their defense of Millikens' Bend in June 1863. By the close of the Civil War, 10–12 percent of the Union army consisted of black troops; an important component of the armies, they had proved themselves on many battlefields.

Thus, Grant, the last former slaveholder elected president, was forced by his military role to consider blacks both as human beings and as soldiers. If he did not transcend the racism of his day, as commanding general he assumed responsibility for all men who served in the army, white and black. Like Lincoln, he believed that governmental responsibility extended to veterans; denying civil rights and citizenship to men who had fought offended his sense of duty. Yet Grant shared some of Johnson's sympathy with the whites of the South: after all, he had firm friendships with many southern officers of the old army, had married a southerner (a cousin of the Confederate general James Longstreet), and had never participated in the bitter sectional debate before the Civil War.

Johnson, appointed brigadier general at the time he was named military governor of Tennessee, had really served in a civil capacity. Ever the politician, Johnson tried to manipulate the army to serve his goals both in Tennessee and in the White House. Sent on a tour of inspection of the South by Johnson, Grant returned with a report that emphasized the willingness of southerners to reaffirm their allegiance, a view that suited Johnson, but did not recommend withdrawal of troops or elimination of the Freedmen's Bureau, an agency established to care for, and protect, former slaves.

Johnson's policy of rapid restoration of political rights in former Confederate states exposed Union soldiers to suits filed in state courts by their former enemies. Grant issued orders in January 1866, authorizing removal of such cases to federal courts or to those of the Freedmen's Bureau. Johnson soon embarked on open warfare with Congress, which passed the Freedmen's Bureau bill and the civil rights bill over his vetoes. Johnson and Grant soon found themselves in quiet conflict over the enforcement of congressional legislation by the army.

The conflict remained quiet because Grant, as a soldier, was determined to obey the commander in chief and because Johnson needed Grant's popularity to shore up his political power. Johnson dragged Grant along on a "swing around the circle," a trip ostensibly to dedicate the Douglas tomb in Chicago but really a political tour to allow Johnson to argue before the voters his case against congressional Radicals, who demanded sweeping political and social change in the South. Johnson's undignified harangues disgusted Grant, who temporarily left the party at Cleveland, leading staunch supporters of Johnson to charge that Grant had withdrawn to recover from excessive drinking. Recognizing the dangers of their eroding relationship, Johnson tried to send Grant on a mission to Mexico and to bring William T. Sherman to Washington in his place; Grant flatly refused to go, insisting that the president had no authority to order an officer on a civilian mission.

Congressional Republicans took advantage of the estrangement through the first Reconstruction Act, whereby they established five military districts in the former Confederacy in which army officers would supervise compliance with Reconstruction policy. On 2 March 1867, Congress overrode Johnson's veto of the first Reconstruction Act and passed an appropriation bill for the army containing a rider that became known as the Command of the Army Act, requiring that all presidential orders pass through the general in chief and prohibiting his removal or relocation. Soon after the Reconstruction Act went into effect, its rigorous enforcement by Major General Philip H. Sheridan in the Fifth Military District (Louisiana and Texas) irritated Johnson, whose hands were tied by the fact that Sheridan was a great favorite of Grant.

In August, Johnson struck at Secretary of War Edwin M. Stanton, who had long been a Radical agent in the presidential camp and was protected by congressional allies through the Tenure of Office Act, which prohibited removal of cabinet officers without the consent of the Senate. Johnson suspended Stanton and appointed Grant acting secretary of war. Johnson knew that he could not succeed in his high-handed removal of Stanton without replacing him with the most popular man in the country; Grant accepted rather than allow the army to fall into unfriendly hands.

Johnson and Grant managed this uneasy partnership until Congress reassembled at the end of 1867, quickly evincing a determination to reinstate Stanton and placing Grant in the untenable position of obeying either his commander in chief or Congress. Grant told Johnson that he intended to resign the office of secretary of war because to hold firm would make him liable to fine and imprisonment under the Tenure of Office Act. Johnson asked Grant to delay his resignation and believed that he had agreed to do so. Through misunderstanding (as Grant's friends believed) or bad faith (as Johnson believed), Grant surrendered the office to Stanton before Johnson had an opportunity to nominate an alternative candidate who might have garnered enough Republican support to achieve confirmation. The restoration of Stanton led to a stormy cabinet confrontation during which Johnson accused Grant of lying. Publication of the exchange of acrimonious correspondence that followed the cabinet meeting completed the process of rupture between president and general.

Johnson's renewed efforts to remove Stanton led to an impeachment trial, with Grant now considered a firm supporter of the removal of Johnson. The break with Johnson provided adequate evidence to Republicans that Grant could be counted in their party. Grant's dislike of Johnson and his policies had increased to the point that he believed that duty demanded his acceptance of a presidential nomination, despite his personal preference for remaining in the army.

Election of 1868

Grant's nomination by the Republican party was inevitable; nobody else received serious consideration, and the convention vote was unanimous. For its vice presidential candidate, the convention chose Schuyler Colfax, a glib and unimportant Indiana congressman. Grant's nomination served to protect the Republicans from answering such hard questions as the length they intended to push Reconstruction policy and the extent of their commitment to the freedmen. The platform advocated enfranchising blacks in the former Confederacy, leaving the matter elsewhere to the states. War's end endangered the fragile alliance of men with widely differing economic policies; midwestern farmers and eastern manufacturers disagreed on crucial currency issues, the tariff, and much more. The concluding words in Grant's letter accepting the nomination, "Let us have peace," became a Republican rallying cry, valued all the more for its banality.

Democrats possessed all the strengths and weaknesses of a national party. Vociferous support from persons who had so recently fought to overthrow the government proved a mixed blessing. Even in the North, the record of the party during the Civil War proved embarrassing; the party had split into war and peace factions, with the latter denying that the war could be won and sometimes acting to fulfill the prophecy. Accusations of lack of patriotism suggested to some leaders the wisdom of abandoning all war-related issues and focusing instead on economic policy, but Democrats North and South refused to abandon issues that they believed so important; furthermore, questions of Reconstruction demanded attention.

The Democrats had a plethora of candidates for nomination, none of them outstanding. Johnson deserved consideration because of his stubborn defense of Democratic principles, and Chief Justice Salmon P. Chase, who had defected from the Democrats over the slavery issue in 1854, announced his return to the party just in time to seek the nomination. George Pendleton of Ohio advocated redeeming bonds issued to finance the Civil War with greenbacks, the fiat currency introduced as a war measure, and this inflationary scheme had enthusiastic support from hard-pressed debtors, especially midwestern farmers. The nomination of Winfield Scott Hancock presented the option of confronting the victor of Appomattox with the hero of Gettysburg and a general whose Reconstruction administration of Louisiana had even pleased Johnson.

As prominent candidates canceled out each other, the convention dragged on for ballot after ballot. Finally the weary delegates settled for Horatio Seymour, the wartime governor of New York, who was presiding over the convention and had disavowed any interest in the nomination. Seymour's reluctance to furnish troops during the war and his inept conduct during the draft riots in New York City constituted liabilities that the Democrats hoped to counter by nominating Francis P. Blair, Jr., for vice president. Blair negated his asset of having been a commander under Sherman, which should have given him the needed aura of patriotism to balance Seymour, by inflammatory criticism of Reconstruction governments as barbarous and despotic.

Grant ostentatiously ignored the ensuing campaign. At its peak, Grant, accompanied by Sherman and Sheridan, left for a combination inspection and vacation tour of the West, going as far as Denver. When election returns were telegraphed to Grant's home in Galena, he took remarkably little interest in them.

When the votes were all counted, Grant had defeated Seymour with 214 electoral votes from 26 states to 80 electoral votes from 8 states: New York, New Jersey, Oregon, Delaware, Georgia, Kentucky, Louisiana, and Maryland. Yet the Republican popular majority (3 million to 2.7 million) was only slightly more than 300,000. Assuming that 90 percent of the 500,000 votes cast by blacks went to Grant, Seymour received a majority of the votes cast by whites. Nonetheless, Grant profited by the same electoral arithmetic that gave victory to Lincoln in 1860 with under 40 percent of the popular vote.

Election returns in 1868 demonstrated the strength and resilience of the Democratic party, saddled with a deplorable record during the Civil War and unappealing candidates in 1868. Given the facts that no presidential vote was recorded in Mississippi, Virginia, and Texas; that Republican victories in southern and border states depended on black votes (by no means assured as a permanent feature on the political scene); and that the Democrats could carry some northern states and make the race tight in others, the Democratic party could still be considered the majority party in the United States. If black votes had not elected Grant, they had not hurt him either. Black votes put six states of the former Confederacy in the Republican column, and Republican hopes for the future depended heavily on continued black political participation. Republican leaders knew that Grant's personal popularity had served as a major campaign asset; they might have lost with any other nominee.

Grant believed that he owed his election to the American people—not to the Republican party. As he prepared for inauguration, he kept his own counsel about his inaugural address and cabinet appointments, rebuffing politicians eager to assist. Republican leaders thought they had done him a favor by giving him the presidency; Grant thought they had given him a burdensome office with unstable tenure. Republican leaders thought they had created a politician; Grant thought they had created an administrator.

Grant's success as a general owed much to his unmilitary attitude. Sent to West Point against his will, he had never enjoyed the traditions of military life. He believed that laws of war as generally conceived were meant to be broken under new conditions. In the war's final year, he accompanied the Army of the Potomac without displacing its commander, Major General George G. Meade, and took on the responsibilities of overall command without leading troops into battle. He employed Major General Henry W. Halleck, his predecessor as general in chief, as chief of staff, setting the United States Army on the road to modern military bureaucracy. This unmilitary general now chose to become an unpolitical president.

There was a key difference in the situation presented him by the presidency. Grant had spent fifteen years in the army from his entrance into West Point until his resignation in 1854, and during the Civil War he was fully cognizant of those laws of war he disobeyed. He understood the procedural details of conventional military organization and was clearheaded about those he hoped to change. His ability to innovate was based upon a knowledge of the fundamentals of his job, something he lacked when he entered the White House.

Grant's obvious distaste for politics disconcerted the politicians but delighted the public. The long battle between Johnson and Congress had grown wearisome; in this sense, the slogan "Let Us Have Peace" had struck home to the voters. They expected little from the president, and Grant prepared to satisfy them.

The powers of the office had been enormously increased by Lincoln under war conditions. At the start of the conflict, he had not called Congress into session but had immediately issued a call for troops, suspended the writ of habeas corpus, and taken other emergency measures that he expected Congress to ratify. When Congress proved an obstacle to Lincoln's concept of the proper conduct of the war, he set policy through the Emancipation Proclamation and his plan for Reconstruction.

Events proved that Johnson could not wield power as Lincoln had. Grant had cooperated with Congress to curb what both regarded as executive usurpation, and he had no intention of fighting the battle over again, this time unnecessarily. If Grant

had followed this policy consistently, his White House years would have been an uneventful period of careful administration of existing legislation with few presidential initiatives, but he believed that he was the only person elected by all the people of the nation, putting him in a position different from that of congressmen elected from individual states. He had a responsibility to carry out the popular will, which he believed he could discern. As a quintessential American, he could think nothing else. He would have no quarrel with Congress over policy, but he would fulfill what he interpreted as moral imperatives.

In his inaugural address, Grant clearly expressed his views: "The office has come to me unsought; I commence its duties untrammeled." He pledged that "all laws will be faithfully executed, whether they meet my approval or not," a statement that might have seemed a platitude had it not followed Johnson's exit from the White House. He argued that bonds issued during the war should be paid in gold as a matter of national honor, adding that this upright policy would enable the government to borrow at lower interest rates in the future. Perhaps the only major surprise was a statement calling for reform of Indian policy, a matter otherwise on the periphery of popular concern.

The cabinet appointments, announced after much popular speculation, surprised the country. Grant named Elihu B. Washburne as secretary of state, an appointment intended as a courtesy to an old friend, who was expected to leave the post after a few days to become minister to France. In Paris, Washburne could answer proudly when asked about his previous employment. To succeed him, Grant named Hamilton Fish, former governor of New York, a man whose political career seemed to be behind him. For secretary of the treasury, Grant named Alexander T. Stewart, an enormously wealthy New York City merchant, who was quickly found to be ineligible because of a law passed in the early days of the Republic prohibiting anyone engaged in trade or commerce from holding that office. An embarrassed president asked Congress to change the law, and to add to his embarrassment, Congress declined to do so. George S. Boutwell of Massachusetts, a congressional Radical, was appointed instead.

For secretary of war, Grant named John A. Rawlins, a Galena attorney who had joined his staff early in the war and become a close friend. Grant originally intended to send the tubercular Rawlins to

Arizona to recover his health but changed his mind because Rawlins insisted on a major appointment. The nominations of E. Rockwood Hoar of Massachusetts as attorney general and Jacob D. Cox of Ohio as secretary of the interior added men respected for ability and integrity. The choice of John A. J. Creswell of Maryland as postmaster general was also suitable. For secretary of the navy, Grant picked Adolph E. Borie, an elderly and wealthy Philadelphian who had no interest in serving and did so only long enough to save the president embarrassment.

In contrast, Lincoln had appointed to his original cabinet leaders of the Republican party, his chief rivals for the nomination, and had also balanced party factions and geographical regions. Grant risked his political popularity by assuming that choosing able men would suffice.

Republican leaders, mystified by these appointments, too often credited them to ineptitude—certainly a factor—while overlooking their logic. Grant's strong feelings about personal loyalty led to the appointments of Washburne and Rawlins. His choice of Fish, his most successful, reflected his conservatism. Politicians forgot that Johnson made Grant a Republican, not a Radical. During the war, Grant's attitude had been one of sympathy for southerners but not for their rebellion. Only when the South continued to defy the supremacy of the federal government after the war did Grant reluctantly come to support Radical Reconstruction and black suffrage. Grant sought to appoint those most likely to achieve sectional harmony and obedience to law, and so he avoided Radicals. Overlooking prominent Republicans was no accident; the appointment of men whose primary loyalty might shift from the executive to Congress held serious risks, since appointees still had the protection of the Tenure of Office Act, another law Grant unsuccessfully asked Congress to change.

Reconstruction

As Grant took office, Reconstruction issues took precedence. Only a week before Grant's inauguration, Congress proposed the Fifteenth Amendment, which declared that the right to vote could not be denied "on account of race, color, or previous condition of servitude." In his inaugural address, Grant stated that the issue of suffrage was "likely to agitate the public" until settled; "I entertain the hope and express the desire," he declared, that its settlement "may be by ratification of the fifteenth . . . amendment." Grant played a quiet but persistent role in ratification, at one point asking the governor of Nebraska to call a special session of the legislature to speed the process. In almost precisely one year, he could declare that the Fifteenth Amendment was the law of the land, the very law he had sworn to uphold.

On inauguration day, four states—Georgia, Mississippi, Virginia, and Texas—remained unrepresented in Congress and subject to the Reconstruction Acts. One year after Grant's inauguration, all states of the former Confederacy except one were represented in Congress, and on 24 February 1871, Georgia seated its senators, having complied with congressional Reconstruction legislation and with the Fifteenth Amendment, which guaranteed the right of blacks to vote. Reconstruction was, in these respects, complete.

By historical consensus, Reconstruction formally ended in 1877 with the withdrawal of the last United States troops from the South by President Rutherford B. Hayes. Outward compliance of white southerners with Reconstruction, grudgingly given and with many reservations, tied the hands of the conservative administration of President Grant. Any effort to maintain the spirit as well as the letter of Reconstruction legislation collided with older and valued concepts of states' rights.

The years of the Grant administration constituted a gradual retreat from Reconstruction, initiated in the South but increasingly tolerated by the North. Grant certainly wanted as rapid as possible an end to the special status of the former Confederacy as a domain of federal intervention. The basic question for him and his countrymen was what price to pay for this peace. From the start, southerners made clear that the road to reunion lay over the rights of their former slaves.

Although the relationship between black votes and Republican majorities in these states was generally understood, Grant spurned any intervention for political advantage; as president, he could intervene only to uphold the law and could officially recognize only clear-cut violations. Aware of this policy, opponents of Reconstruction governments often tried to subvert it through clandestine means, such as the terrorism of the Ku Klux Klan, which would accomplish the purpose without provoking federal intervention. Using hindsight, critics have argued either that the Grant administration did too much or that it did too little to maintain Reconstruction.

Reconstruction state governments controlled by carpetbaggers (northern whites who went to the

South with a mixture of crass and idealistic motives), scalawags (white southerners who supported Reconstruction, again from a mixture of motives), and former slaves possessed varying degrees of integrity. Critics portrayed these state governments as carnivals of corruption, rarely drawing parallels to cases of malfeasance in the North, such as the notorious Tweed Ring in New York City. Promises that Reconstruction governments would be supplanted by honest, competent, and conservative regimes tempted many northerners to ignore the issue of black civil rights.

While the Grant administration erred in intervening too little to uphold Reconstruction legislation, Grant did not ignore violence, intimidation, and disorder in the South. He used enforcement legislation for the Fourteenth and Fifteenth Amendments, and he asked Congress for the legislation ultimately known as the Ku Klux Act (20 April 1871), which enabled him to suspend the writ of habeas corpus and impose martial law in areas in which local officials did not protect the rights of all citizens. Armed with the law, Grant enforced it in parts of South Carolina, sending in troops and initiating prosecutions. Here and elsewhere he recognized opponents of Reconstruction as the same men he had faced in battle, men determined to use force to reverse the results of the war. In upholding Reconstruction, Grant increasingly acted on his own; in fact, the administration proceeded past the point at which it had adequate popular or congressional support. Enforcement declined as the years progressed, as northerners recognized that frustrating any attempt by southern whites to control state governments and to subjugate the black population accomplished no more than buying time and led to efforts to accomplish the same purpose by other means. Any condemnation of the Grant administration for abandoning Reconstruction requires a general condemnation of the nation. As the war years receded, the whites regained control of the South.

Enforcement of Reconstruction was accompanied by extension of amnesty. In May 1872, an administration-favored bill gave amnesty to all but about five hundred former Confederates who had left the United States government to take arms against it. While Johnson's generosity in granting amnesty had infuriated Radicals, the passage of time enabled Grant to enlarge the policy.

Financial Affairs

The basic conservatism of the Grant administration found fullest expression in the handling of financial issues. On 18 March 1869, Congress passed the Public Credit Act, which pledged the repayment of the bonded debt in gold and thus ended years of uncertainty over whether the nation might follow an inflationary course by redeeming bonds with the greenbacks issued during the Civil War, a policy advocated by some Republicans as well as Democrats. Basically, the government followed a policy of hard currency, economy, and gradual reduction of the national debt.

Grant's own ideas about finance were relatively simple, and he seemed to have absorbed some of them from the wealthy businessmen who so assiduously courted him. Aware of Grant's attraction to the financially successful, James Fisk and Jay Gould devised a plan to snare him into a scheme for their own profit. Greenback currency fluctuated in relation to gold; government could affect the price by selling or withholding gold. Gould and Fisk planned to drive up gold prices by convincing Grant that such an increase would benefit farmers, and they enlisted Abel Rathbone Corbin, who was married to Grant's sister and claimed greater influence with the president than he actually possessed. Corbin assisted Fisk and Gould in gaining social access to Grant, something that enhanced the reputations of the unscrupulous pair in New York financial circles.

Gould and Fisk bought up gold, intending to persuade the president to take steps to drive the price upward. While Grant visited relatives in out-of-the-way Washington, Pennsylvania, Corbin wrote him a letter, delivered by special messenger, that argued the case for the public benefits of higher gold prices. Suspicious at last, Grant asked his wife to write Mrs. Corbin a letter telling her to have her husband stop his speculations. Gould double-crossed his partner by secretly unloading his holdings, while Fisk continued to buy until he had driven the price to unprecedented heights on "Black Friday" (24 September 1869). On that same day, Grant and Secretary of the Treasury Boutwell decided to sell gold, and the price immediately plummeted. In the gyrations, fortunes were made and lost, and the whole affair became the subject of a congressional investigation embarrassing to Grant and his wife. The president, although guilty of indiscretion and naïveté, could not be charged with personal profiteering.

Financial concerns again claimed Grant's interest when the Supreme Court decided *Hepburn* v.

Griswold (7 February 1870) by declaring the Legal Tender Acts unconstitutional as applied to contracts made prior to their enactment. Conservative Republicans who dreaded the inflationary impact of increased issuance of greenbacks equally feared the deflationary shock of their sudden disappearance as lawful currency. Grant soon filled two vacancies on the Court with justices believed to favor the Legal Tender Acts. As a result, the Court reversed its stand in ruling on two additional greenback cases, *Knox* v. *Lee* and *Parker* v. *Davis* (1 May 1871). Inevitably, Grant was accused of packing the Court, a charge justified to the extent that he had some idea in advance of how his appointees would vote. Nonetheless, he had appointed two qualified men and had no obligation to select justices who might create financial upheaval.

Foreign Affairs

The handling of foreign affairs illustrates the uneven record of the Grant administration. The most important problem confronting the incoming president was the settlement of the *Alabama* Claims against Great Britain, a complex of grievances centering on the depredations committed against American shipping during the Civil War by the *Alabama*, a Confederate cruiser improperly purchased in England. During the war, Senator Charles Sumner, chairman of the Foreign Relations Committee, had grown so angry over the lack of true British neutrality that he now demanded immense reparations, perhaps to the extent of annexing Canada to settle the matter. Sumner had taken the lead in rejecting a settlement treaty negotiated by the Johnson administration and later provoked the government to increased militancy.

Fish recognized that American claims against Great Britain for granting belligerent status to Confederates were jeopardized by American pressure to grant the same rights to Cuban rebels, who had less claim under international law to such status but much American support for their revolt against Spain. Grant, inclined to sympathize with the Cubans, a course urged by Secretary of War Rawlins, prodded Fish to recognize Cuban belligerency. Concerned about the effect on negotiations with Great Britain, Fish delayed the process by continuing negotiations in Madrid for a peaceful settlement. Rawlins' death on 6 September 1869 removed the leader of the militants, and the failure of the Cuban insurgents to make solid gains lessened United States enthusiasm for active support. For a time, the divergence between Grant and Fish on Cuban policy threatened to throw the issue to Congress, where recognition of Cuban belligerency commanded strong support. Ultimately threatening to resign, Fish forced Grant to send a message to Congress that averted recognition.

Resolution of the Cuban issue permitted Fish to conclude negotiations with Great Britain. He arranged a meeting of commissioners that resulted in the Treaty of Washington, signed 8 May 1871, which acknowledged violations by Great Britain during the Civil War and provided for monetary settlement of American claims by an international commission in Geneva. Sumner argued that Great Britain had prolonged the war for two years at a cost of $2 billion but did not block Senate ratification. Although the commission eventually awarded the United States only $15.5 million, Americans had reason for pride in the settlement of the controversy in favor of the United States without belligerent actions and in the establishment of a precedent for settling international claims through arbitration.

Yet the diplomatic achievements of the Grant administration were shadowed by the Santo Domingo fiasco, the origins of which lay in United States interest in a Caribbean naval base to protect a future isthmian canal and in the inability of the Dominican government to manage its finances. American promoters working with President Bonaventura Báez approached Fish with an offer to sell the country to the United States. Suspicious of where the money would go and dubious about expansion, Fish tried to shelve the proposition, but Grant expressed interest in pursuing the matter. Grant sent his secretary, Orville E. Babcock, to Santo Domingo to investigate, though Fish ensured that he carried no diplomatic authority. Babcock, the Iago of the Grant administration, returned with a draft treaty of annexation.

The pluck and ambition of his bright young secretary captured Grant's admiration. Properly accredited for a second visit, Babcock returned with a treaty of annexation and, in case this was rejected, an agreement for the lease of Samaná Bay as a naval station. To further the treaty, Grant paid a surprise visit to Sumner's house, where he talked about the advantages of annexation and Sumner argued for a territorial appointment for an old antislavery ally. As Grant left, he understood Sumner to assure him of support; Sumner recalled that he had only promised to consider the matter carefully. In fact, Sumner was adamantly opposed to elimination of black self-government in Santo Domingo and led the Foreign Relations Committee to a 5–2 rejection of the treaty. Despite administration pressure, the full Senate rejected annexation by a 28–28 vote, with 19 Republicans joining the opposition.

Just as Grant had slogged south after Lee had stopped him at the battles of the Wilderness and Spotsylvania, his rebuff on the Santo Domingo issue made him even more determined on eventual victory. Heroism in war became pettiness in peace. He dismissed John Lothrop Motley, minister to Great Britain, an appointment made initially to please Sumner, and played a role in Sumner's deposition as chairman of the Foreign Relations Committee. Attorney General Hoar and Secretary of the Interior Cox, both lukewarm in supporting annexation, eventually left the cabinet, the latter replaced by Columbus Delano, who returned the Interior Department to spoilsmen. While Grant could do nothing to secure annexation, he refused to abandon the cause and even brought it up again in his last message to Congress.

Domestic Affairs

Unfortunately, he lacked such persistence in the cause of reform of Indian policy. In his inaugural address, he had pledged to encourage Indians toward "civilization and ultimate citizenship," and soon astonished the nation by the unprecedented appointment of an Indian, Ely S. Parker, a former staff officer, as commissioner of Indian affairs. He followed this by appointing the Board of Indian Commissioners, an unpaid group of advisers to the secretary of the interior who were charged with implementing the "peace policy," based on the appointment of churchmen as Indian agents. In his zeal to serve the Indians, Parker antagonized both board and bureaucrats; he resigned in 1871. The remainder of the peace policy disintegrated amid denominational squabbling, the counterattack of entrenched economic interests, and the unwillingness of the Indians to surrender their way of life to the concepts of white reformers. By the end of Grant's second term, reservation Indians were again at the mercy of a corrupt Interior Department; others were the charges of a United States Army still smarting from the death of George A. Custer at the Little Big Horn in 1876.

A similar fate awaited civil service reform. Filling government positions with nonpartisan appointees through competitive examination had the enthusiastic support of Congressman Thomas A. Jenckes of Rhode Island, Senator Carl Schurz of Missouri, and George William Curtis, editor of *Harper's Weekly*, and of Cox, Hoar, and Boutwell, who tried to implement reform within their departments. Asked by Grant to legislate reform, Congress returned the problem to the White House by asking the president to appoint a civil service commission to draw up rules. Grant appointed Curtis to head the commission and accepted its recommendations, to take effect on 1 January 1872. Civil service had Republican party support when applied to ill-paid clerkships but encountered resistance when it encroached upon such lush pasturage as the New York Customhouse, the preserve of Senator Roscoe Conkling, a loyal supporter of the president. Repeatedly Congress failed to enact civil service legislation; in 1875, it refused to appropriate funds to maintain the commission. Congressional resistance eventually persuaded Grant himself to abandon civil service procedures.

Reformers cooled toward Grant even before Grant cooled toward reform. Disappointment with failures to implement civil service reform, disgust with Reconstruction governments, and dismay with high-tariff policy (when free trade and laissez-faire represented the best economic thought) brought together a group eventually christened Liberal Republicans, who, embellishing their cause with cries of "Grantism," denounced corruption, inefficiency, and nepotism. Led by Schurz, Cox, Sumner, Lyman Trumbull, Charles Francis Adams, and Horace Greeley, editor of the *New York Tribune*, they moved toward independent political status. In 1872, they passed over such logical presidential nominees as Adams and Judge David Davis to nominate Greeley for president, a choice soon ratified by opportunistic Democrats. Greeley's eccentricities, high-tariff views, and record of unqualified abuse of the Democratic party played into the hands of the Republicans.

Grant won reelection easily. Economic prosperity, combined with debt reduction, temporarily lowered tariffs, and repeal of the income tax, hurt the opposition, as did the initial implementation of civil service. Ku Klux Klan outrages in the South reminded voters of Civil War issues, as did Republican orators. When doubts arose, Grantism seemed a small price for peace and prosperity. Grant received 3.6 million votes to 2.8 million for Greeley, who carried only six states: Missouri, Tennessee, Texas, Georgia, Maryland, and Kentucky. Of 366 electoral votes, the

Greeley states had 66. The electoral college refused to count 14 disputed votes for Grant from Arkansas and Louisiana or 3 cast for Greeley, who had died shortly after the election, so the official tally gave 286 for Grant to 63 divided among four Democrats. Grant received the largest percentage (55.6 percent) of the popular vote of any candidate since Andrew Jackson's 56 percent in 1828. Grant rather smugly proclaimed the victory a personal vindication. Loyal Republicans crowed that their party had been purified by the departure of Liberal Republicans; history later proclaimed the opposite. Charges against Grant in the second election campaign were even nastier than those aired in the first, and some came from former allies, now Liberal Republicans. President Grant ignored the charges in public but inwardly seethed. His tendency to overvalue loyalty increased when he felt betrayed, and after 1872 he established a network of party stalwarts around him, men who seldom questioned his policy but instead furthered it. Ironically, Grantism increased in the second term.

The Grant family had settled comfortably in the White House. Julia's original apprehensions about her social role eased when she received assistance and advice from the wife of Secretary Fish. Fred Grant, the oldest son, graduated from West Point; Ulysses, Jr., scraped through Harvard and served his father as presidential secretary. Daughter Nellie enjoyed a White House wedding in 1874, much publicized throughout the country, even though people would have preferred she not marry an Englishman, and Walt Whitman, unacknowledged poet laureate of the Grant administration, wrote a poem in her honor. Jesse, the youngest son, ran happily through the White House in a manner reminiscent of Tad Lincoln, to the delight of his doting parents.

Grant himself usually worked in his office from ten in the morning until around three in the afternoon and then drove his carriage through Washington. Long summer vacations at Long Branch, New Jersey, drew criticism, as did other trips away from Washington, though none could claim that Grant neglected his duties. In fact, the business of the presidency proved so undemanding that Grant gained some thirty to forty pounds in the White House, apparently the happiest years of his life.

As the nation moved rapidly from an agricultural to an industrial economy, the effects of the business cycle increased. The Panic of 1873 represented the American phase of a depression that spread from Europe and settled over the United States for the remainder of the Grant administration. Railroad overbuilding hastened the onset, and efforts by railroad corporations to maintain profit squeezed farmers already hurt by low prices abroad. Economic distress enabled the Democrats, aided by militant farmers organized as Grangers, to gain control of the House in 1874 for the first time since the firing on Fort Sumter.

The Panic of 1873 raised the greenback issue once again. During the Johnson administration, the Treasury had retired some 10 percent of the $400 million issued; the Grant administration left the remainder in circulation. When the panic struck, Secretary of the Treasury William A. Richardson reissued some of the greenbacks, with mild inflationary effects, but hard-pressed westerners clamored for more. Congress passed legislation (14 April 1874) for the reissue of the remaining $18 million, hardly a large amount of money even then or likely to create inflation, but its reissue was an important symbolic act, demonstrating governmental willingness to acknowledge financial distress.

Grant sympathized with the unemployed and even hoped to create public works programs to provide jobs until he was persuaded to accept the conventional wisdom that government must retrench when revenues fall. His first reaction to the inflation bill was positive, and he drafted a message giving the reasons for his support, but he continued to agonize, found himself unconvinced by his own arguments, and eventually vetoed the bill. Even opponents admired his conscientious approach to the issue and regarded the veto as an act of courage.

The Scandals

During the second term, scandal rocked the Grant administration. Before the second inauguration came the exposure of Crédit Mobilier, a scheme to siphon off the profits made in building the transcontinental railroad, which soiled both Vice President Colfax and his successor, Henry Wilson. Regardless of the fact that the bribery of congressmen took place under Johnson and involved Democrats also, airing the details in 1872 stung the Grant administration. Congressman Benjamin F. Butler's scandalous salary grab paired a reasonable pay increase for government officials (the president's salary was doubled to $50,000) with an outrageous provision making the increase retroactive for two years for congressmen, including those defeated in the last election.

Grant's persistent problems in making suitable appointments were exacerbated by his increased self-confidence after reelection. In this spirit, he reappointed his brother-in-law as collector of the port of New Orleans although the appointee's initial term had drawn criticism. Charges of corruption against "Boss" Alexander R. Shepherd, director of public works for the District of Columbia, did not prevent Grant from appointing him territorial governor. When Chase died, Grant first asked Conkling to serve as chief justice, influenced both by gratitude for his political support and Julia Grant's belief that black robes would set off Conkling's blond curls. When Conkling declined, Grant went to the opposite extreme by approaching Fish, who also declined. Grant finally nominated Attorney General George H. Williams, whose name was withdrawn after discovery that he had used government funds to supply his wife's carriage. Grant next nominated Caleb Cushing of Massachusetts, whose name was then withdrawn because Cushing had written a letter to Jefferson Davis in March 1861, recommending someone for a position in the Confederate government. Grant eventually came up with Morrison R. Waite of Ohio, who served ably.

Unfortunately, Grant had to make a great many appointments. In all, twenty-five men served in seven cabinet posts, and the frequency of changes increased as the administration reached its conclusion: there were five new department heads in 1876. Even good appointments backfired, as Grant learned when he chose Benjamin F. Bristow as secretary of the treasury in 1874. Scrupulously honest, Bristow pursued the trail of fraud wherever it led, even into the White House. His investigators uncovered the "Whiskey Ring," which schemed to avoid taxes on liquor by bribing the agents who should have collected them; some of the payments ended up in Republican party coffers. An especially odious degree of corruption existed in St. Louis, involving men who had known Grant before the Civil War and who traded on his friendship. Informed of this, Grant wrote, "Let no guilty man escape if it can be avoided."

Further probing revealed that Grant's secretary Babcock had dealings with some of the chief culprits in St. Louis. Grant's belief in Babcock's innocence was so strong that he initially refused to believe that one of the ringleaders in St. Louis was guilty, simply because the man was a close friend of Babcock. Even convictions in St. Louis did not shake this faith. As evidence emerged of Babcock's role, Grant believed that political manipulators had devised a plot to strike at him through his trusted secretary, and he blamed Bristow. Grant acquiesced when Babcock, who had retained military status, demanded a court of inquiry to forestall indictment in St. Louis, but the grand jury acted too quickly and refused to surrender its papers to a military tribunal. When Babcock went to the city to stand trial, Grant intended to accompany him to testify in his behalf. Dissuaded by his cabinet, Grant instead prepared a deposition in Babcock's defense before Chief Justice Waite. Although Babcock eventually won acquittal, enough evidence emerged to require his dismissal from the White House, a move Grant made tardily and only after prodding by Fish. Grant eventually forced Bristow to resign, blaming him unfairly for the ruin of Babcock.

A worse scandal followed. William W. Belknap, who had succeeded Rawlins as secretary of war, was charged with receiving bribes from a man who had been appointed to a lucrative tradership at a western army post and who, in turn, let another man actually conduct the business in return for regular cash payments. The case was complicated by the fact that the money paid to Belknap was given to his wife, who died in 1874, and when Belknap married his deceased wife's sister, the payments went to her. As Congress investigated, Belknap realized that he must resign and hurried to the White House one morning, babbling something to the president about protecting a woman's honor, words inducing Grant to accept the resignation immediately. Two Republican senators hurried in, too late, to advise Grant not to accept the resignation. That afternoon the House voted to impeach Belknap. In the ensuing trial, the fact that Grant had accepted the resignation before impeachment played a role in acquittal; even then the Senate voted 37–25 for conviction, which required a two-thirds vote. During the trial, Mrs. Grant continued to receive Mrs. Belknap at the White House; afterward both Belknaps called on the Grants, who received them cordially and continued to express belief in the former secretary's innocence.

Grant believed that the prosecution of Belknap was politically motivated, and surely the fact that 1876 was a presidential election year had not escaped the notice of the Democratic majority in the House, which also investigated the minister to Great Britain, Robert C. Schenck, who had used his position to peddle stock in a dubious silver mine to English investors, and Secretary of the Navy George M. Robeson, who was accused of profiting by awarding contracts to a specially favored firm. Grant had already nipped a budding third-term movement in 1875 by writing a public letter, carrying it to the mailbox himself, and then informing his wife, who would have tried to dissuade him. Republicans nominated Hayes, whose two terms as governor of Ohio gave him a reputation for integrity and kept him away from Washington. Grant somewhat resented Hayes for running as a reformer but consoled himself with the thought that Bristow had not been nominated. The scandals of the Grant administration, however salient in retrospect, appear to have had little influence on the presidential election.

Election of 1876

The abandonment of Reconstruction played a greater role in the outcome of the election. During the 1870s, popular opinion in the North swung away from maintaining Reconstruction governments, some of which fell because Republican infighting gave Democrats their opportunity to "redeem" those states; Grant's intention to uphold the laws was circumvented by more sophisticated opponents who combined outward compliance with outrageous subversion. In Mississippi, redeemers overthrew the carpetbag governor, Adelbert Ames, through quiet intimidation of black voters, avoiding the overt violence of earlier campaigns and working so skillfully that Grant refused to answer Ames's anguished pleas. "The whole public are tired out with these annual autumnal outbreaks in the South," Grant wrote—a statement callous but true.

When the votes were counted in 1876, Democrat Samuel J. Tilden had won a clear majority of the votes cast by whites, and Grant privately stated his belief that Tilden had won the election. But Republican strategists realized that the electoral votes of the remaining Reconstruction governments in South Carolina, Florida, and Louisiana would enable them to claim the election for Hayes, and illegal disfranchisement of blacks and fraud by whites in all three provided grounds for the case. Urged by party leaders to use the army to assist Republicans in the three states, Grant instead argued that "no man worthy of the office of President should be willing to hold it if counted in or placed there by fraud." As the outcome of the election hung in the balance, Grant withstood pressure to intervene and supported the electoral-commission plan devised by Congress that finally ended the stalemate. His position alleviated a potentially explosive situation.

An Appraisal

In 1872, Greeley and Sumner had advocated an amendment to limit the president to one term. Although designed to injure Grant, enactment would have proved a blessing. If Grant had left the White House after his first term, he might rank among the ablest presidents, remembered for his staunch enforcement of the rights of freedmen combined with conciliation of former Confederates, for reform in Indian policy and civil service, for successful negotiation of the *Alabama* Claims, and for delivery of peace and prosperity. Black Friday and Santo Domingo might have appeared as minor blemishes on an otherwise outstanding administration. Babcock and Belknap would have left with him, their sins undiscovered.

The second term was another story, in part because the Liberal Republican movement had deprived the president of the aid and counsel of so many reformers and intellectuals, in part because the Panic of 1873 created a situation Grant could not alleviate but for which he could be blamed. As the issues of war receded, so did much of the idealism they had evoked. Aspects of his first term looked backward to continue the work of the Lincoln administration; much in his second term foreshadowed the administrations of Benjamin Harrison and William McKinley. As Grant settled comfortably into the routine of the presidency, he lost some of his independence of thought, falling prey to the influence of party chieftains.

When President Hayes took office, the age of the Civil War and Reconstruction ended. Much won at Appomattox was lost at the Wormley Hotel in Washington, where southerners confirmed prior negotiations with supporters of Hayes to put a Republican president in office in return for the withdrawal of United States troops from the South. In the presidential election of 1872, southern blacks had voted more freely and safely than they would in any succeeding election for nearly a century. In his second term, Grant had relied more heavily on stalwart Republican politicians, successful businessmen, and Fish, none willing to crusade for black civil rights. The wisdom and steady hand of Fish at the State Department had led to successful diplomacy in 1873 when Spanish authorities seized the *Virginius*, a ship carrying arms to Cuban rebels, even though it flew the American flag (improperly), and summarily executed the crew, which included American citizens. Fish had circumvented the clamor for revenge, in-

Ulysses S. Grant raced against time and painful throat cancer to complete his memoirs, among the most acclaimed of any written remembrance by a historical figure. He finished just a few days before his death. THE LIBRARY OF CONGRESS

stead receiving an apology and indemnity from the Spanish government. Fish's thorough conservatism and aristocratic disdain for Reconstruction governments had played a less helpful role in domestic policy. Although Republican leaders called for executive action in the South to save the 1876 election, Grant recognized that the time for action had been allowed to slip away.

During the Grant administration, the nation moved into an age of industrialization. Like most of his countrymen, Grant understood the old far better than the new. He sympathized with few of the concerns of militant farmers or workers and regarded Grangers and socialists as dangerous troublemakers. Elected with no clear mandate, Grant proceeded to give the nation a minimal presidency, a pattern broken only by the pressure of events and his own personal idiosyncrasies. Grant dreaded a resurgence of the turmoil that had thrown the nation into war, and the tumultuous aftermath of the presidential election of 1876 indicated that such fears were not altogether unrealistic.

Similarities exist between the presidencies of Grant and Eisenhower. Two West Point graduates with long military service elected as wartime heroes after major wars and two Republican presidents who served two full terms in office, both presided over periods of relative political calm, peace, and prosperity. Eisenhower, as a product of the modern bureaucratic army, had a far better grasp of administration and a low-key personal style that enabled him to quell controversy. Grant's two outstanding faults, a tendency to carry personal loyalty too far and unyielding stubbornness, suggest a comparison with President Harry Truman, whom he also resembled in blunt, outspoken honesty.

Historical judgment on the Grant administration has commonly been harsh, with Grant ranked among the great failures in the White House. This may be due in part to the contrast between his military and civilian roles and in part to his saliency in American history. Certainly in 1868 and 1872, Democrats exhibited no greater aptitude for government and produced presidential candidates less suitable than Grant. President Grant was charged with the faults of his countrymen: the willingness of the North to abandon the principles of Reconstruction, the unwillingness of the government to assume responsibility for the economic welfare of its citizens, and the acquiescence of Americans in racism and corruption.

The judgment can stand some modification. Grant proved responsive to the people when they wanted peace and prosperity rather than reform. The pendulum of public opinion had swung from high resolve to complacency. Frequent scandals rocked the administration, none of which blemished the president's integrity, however much they impugned his judgment. In his final message to Congress, Grant acknowledged his errors:

> It was my fortune, or misfortune, to be called to the office of Chief Executive without any previous political training.. . . Under such circumstances it is but reasonable to suppose that errors of judgment must have occurred.. . . Mistakes have been made, as all can see and I admit, but it seems to me oftener in the selections made of the assistants appointed to aid in carrying out the various duties of administering the Government.. . . History shows that no Administration from the time of Washington to the present has been free from these mistakes.. . . Failures have been errors of judgment, not of intent.

Many presidents who could have written something similar did not, and Grant's candid statement of fact has sometimes been misread as an apology for his presidency.

Soon after leaving the White House, the Grants began a two-and-a-half-year tour around the world that combined elements of a private vacation and state visit. After his return, Grant again encountered third-term sentiment, not discouraged this time, that came close to success at the 1880 Republican convention. Somewhat at loose ends, Grant entered the Wall Street firm of Grant and Ward, a partnership of his second son, Ulysses, Jr., and Ferdinand Ward. He settled into a comfortable life in New York City with only minor demands on his attention from the firm, in which he was a silent partner, but the one whose reputation attracted investors. In 1884 the firm collapsed, Ward was exposed as a swindler, and Grant's reputation was sullied. Faced with poverty, Grant began to write accounts of his battles for the Century to provide money for his family and unexpectedly found that he enjoyed writing enough to undertake book-length memoirs. Stricken by cancer, Grant battled excruciating pain to finish his book while the entire nation watched with admiration the final struggle between death and Grant's indomitable will. Grant amazed his physicians by living long enough to complete his memoirs. On 23 July 1885, a few days after the last pages went to the publisher, he died quietly. Grant's friend and publisher, Mark Twain, jotted in his notebook when he learned of Grant's death: "He was a very great man—& superlatively good."

BIBLIOGRAPHY

For a brief, incisive, and highly readable biography of Grant, nothing surpasses Bruce Catton, *U. S. Grant and the American Military Tradition* (Boston, 1954). Lloyd Lewis began a multivolume biography but died after completing *Captain Sam Grant* (Boston, 1950), which covers Grant's life to the outbreak of the Civil War. Catton carried this superb biography through the Civil War in *Grant Moves South* (Boston, 1960) and *Grant Takes Command* (Boston, 1969).

The only major study of Grant focusing on the presidency is William B. Hesseltine, *Ulysses S. Grant: Politician* (New York, 1935), now outdated. Two popular biographies of Grant that cover the presidency are W. E. Woodward, *Meet General Grant* (New York, 1928), and William S. McFeely, *Grant: A Biography* (New York, 1981). Both Woodward and McFeely portray Grant as a symbol of his America. Woodward writes as a neo-Confederate, and McFeely as a modern liberal; both dislike Grant. A biography that goes to the opposite extreme in defending Grant is Louis A. Coolidge, *Ulysses S. Grant* (Boston and New York, 1917). Brooks D. Simpson, *Let Us Have Peace: Ulysses S. Grant and the Politics of War and Reconstruction, 1861–1868* (Chapel Hill, N.C., 1991), also takes a uniformly favorable view of Grant. A better-balanced account is available in John A. Carpenter, *Ulysses S. Grant* (New York, 1970). Hamlin Garland, *Ulysses S. Grant: His Life and Character* (New York, 1898), incorporates information from interviews with people who knew Grant.

Grant told his own story in *Personal Memoirs of U. S. Grant* (New York, 1885–1886), which stops at the end of the Civil War. This important and readable literary classic served as the point of departure for chapter 4 of Edmund Wilson, *Patriotic Gore: Studies in the Literature of the American Civil War* (New York, 1962). A comprehensive edition of Grant's own writings is John Y. Simon, ed., *The Papers of Ulysses S. Grant* (Carbondale and Edwardsville, Ill., 1967–), of which twenty-four volumes have been published to date, with chronological coverage through October 1870. Mrs. Grant's charming autobiography is available in Simon, ed., *The Personal Memoirs of Julia Dent Grant* (New York, 1975).

Allan Nevins, *Hamilton Fish: The Inner History of the Grant Administration* (New York, 1936), a detailed account enriched with numerous extracts from Fish's diary, remains indispensable for both foreign and domestic policy. An anecdotal account by Grant's secretary Adam Badeau, *Grant in Peace* (Hartford, Conn., 1887), not wholly reliable, contains information unavailable elsewhere. Southern policy receives detailed analysis in William Gillette, *Retreat from Reconstruction, 1869–1877* (Baton Rouge, La., 1979). Indian policy has evoked a copious literature, notably Robert H. Keller, Jr., *American Protestantism and United States Indian Policy, 1869–1882* (Lincoln, Nebr., 1983). Standard books for approaching crucial issues include Ari Hoogenboom, *Outlawing the Spoils: A History of the Civil Service Reform Movement, 1865–1883* (Urbana, Ill., 1961), and Irwin Unger, *The Greenback Era: A Social and Political History of American Finance, 1865–1879* (Princeton, N.J., 1964).

Recent works include Geoffrey Perret, *Ulysses S. Grant: Soldier and President* (New York, 1997), and Jean Edward Smith, *Grant* (New York, 2001).

Rutherford B. Hayes

Keith Ian Polakoff

Rutherford B. Hayes THE LIBRARY OF CONGRESS

RUTHERFORD BIRCHARD HAYES entered the White House when the powers and prestige of the presidency were at a particularly low ebb. During the term of Andrew Johnson, Congress had reclaimed the initiative, previously exercised by Abraham Lincoln, in shaping Reconstruction policy. It had restricted the president's authority over appointments and removals of officeholders. It had even seized upon Johnsons' attempt to replace one of his own cabinet advisers as a pretext for impeaching him and almost removing him from office. Then the eight years of the Grant administration that followed were so frequently marked by scandal that in December 1875 an overwhelming majority of both Republicans and Democrats in the House of Representatives voted against the principle of a third term.

Hayes himself was, in an unusual respect, beholden to his fellow Republicans in Congress. The outcome of the 1876 presidential election was the subject of a prolonged and potentially dangerous dispute. Democrats were sure they had elected Samuel J. Tilden. Republicans were equally certain that their opponents had carried several southern states by fraud and intimidation. In three of these states—Louisiana, Florida, and South Carolina—local Republicans used their control of the canvassing boards to throw out questioned Democratic votes and declare both the Hayes electors and the Republican state tickets elected, while the Democrats in turn cried foul.

Normally, the presidential electors met in their respective state capitals long after the actual result was known. Their votes were then transported to Washington and routinely tallied by the president of the Senate before a joint session of Congress. It was strictly a ceremonial occasion. This time the existence of rival sets of electoral votes from the three southern states and the ambiguity of the constitutional language describing the official counting procedure led a bipartisan majority in Congress to create a special electoral commission to determine which votes should be counted. The commission was supposed to be politically balanced, consisting of five senators (three Republicans and two Democrats), five representatives (two Republicans and three Democrats), and five associate justices of the Supreme Court (two Republicans, two Democrats, and independent David Davis; but the one independent refused to serve and was replaced by a third Republican). Only after the commission had ruled—in a series of 8–7 party-line votes—in favor of the Hayes electors and the Republican minority had weathered the threat of a filibuster in the Democrat-controlled House was Hayes officially declared president—on 2 March 1877, two days before he assumed office.

To compound the situation further, Hayes had a limited base of support within his own party. He only emerged as the nominee of the Republican National Convention because a deadlock developed between the supporters of the front-runner, James G. Blaine of Maine, and various lesser contenders. Since Blaine's opponents included men as disparate as machine politicians Roscoe Conkling of New York and Oliver P. Morton of Indiana, and reformer Benjamin H. Bristow of Kentucky, they could only put their full strength behind someone else. That created an opportunity for Hayes, then in an unprecedented third term as governor of Ohio.

Hayes had been a lawyer, a Union officer wounded several times while leading his troops in battle, a dependable supporter of the Radical Republican plan during the early Reconstruction Congresses, and a staunch regular in the election of 1872—all of which reassured the likes of Conkling and Morton. At the same time, the reform elements drew encouragement from his advocacy of the gold standard, freedom from involvement in machine politics, and unquestioned personal integrity. And, of course, Hayes was a proven vote-getter in the pivotal Buck-eye State, which all Republicans believed they had to carry to retain the presidency. He was, in short, supremely "available."

Hayes was the very model of a Victorian gentleman. A native Ohioan (born 4 October 1822), he was a graduate of Kenyon College in his home state. After attending Harvard Law School, he built a solid reputation as an attorney in Lower Sandusky (later Fremont) and, after 1850, in Cincinnati. Already prosperous, in 1875 he inherited the substantial estate of the merchant uncle who had provided for him since infancy. Hayes was by no means a scholar, but he enjoyed reading, mostly American history and biography, and welcomed the company of scholars. Above all, he hungered for respectability. His diary plainly reveals the ambivalence he felt when his political ambition clashed with his strict sense of morality, which told him that a man might gladly accept high office but should not actively seek it. In the White House, Rutherford and Lucy Webb Hayes would decline to serve alcoholic beverages, even at state functions.

That same hunger for respectability helps explain the alacrity with which he accepted the advice of former Senator Carl Schurz of Missouri, whom he had never met, regarding his formal letter of acceptance of the Republican presidential nomination. Schurz was the acknowledged mastermind of the Liberal Republican revolt of 1872 and the foremost spokesman of the "best men," as the highly educated, upper-middle-class reformers modestly thought of themselves. Schurz urged Hayes to express himself boldly on the need for a sound currency, southern reconciliation, and civil service reform. On each issue Hayes did so, even employing some of Schurz's suggested language. He was especially blunt in his denunciation of the spoils system, which, he said, "destroys the independence of the separate departments of government, . . . tends directly to extravagance and official incapacity, . . . [and] degrades the civil service and the character of the government.. . . It ought to be abolished. The reform should be thorough, radical, and complete." The reformers were impressed, but party regulars were not. Senator Conkling sat out the rest of the campaign at his home in upstate New York.

A Contentious Beginning

Throughout his presidency Hayes adhered to the policies enunciated in his letter of acceptance. He also demonstrated a political independence that regained for the presidency some of its lost authority and prestige. Furthermore, he set the tone for his administration right at the outset, when he named the men he wanted in his cabinet. For postmaster general (the richest patronage-dispensing position), he chose David M. Key of Tennessee; for secretary of the interior, Carl Schurz; and for secretary of state, William M. Evarts—respectively, a southern Democrat, a Liberal Republican, and the attorney for the defense in the impeachment trial of Andrew Johnson. Blaine, Conkling, and the other Republicans were outraged. Only the certainty that the Democrats would supply the necessary votes to confirm these choices if the Republicans did not gained their grudging acquiescence.

Almost immediately Hayes prepared to kick over another hornet's nest by implementing his pledge of civil service reform. He ordered an inquiry into the management of the New York Customhouse, the central component of Senator Conkling's machine. The resulting report described a pattern of overstaffing, incompetence, and petty bribery and sharply criticized the collector, Chester A. Arthur, and other officials. This faultfinding was not entirely fair: Conkling's allies in the customhouse were honest and capable, and Arthur had actually improved overall efficiency. When President Grant's short-lived Civil Service Commission proposed regulations to govern the appointment of civil servants, Arthur put them into effect, even though he still required customhouse employees to perform political services in addition to their regular jobs and continued to assess them 2–6 percent of their salaries for partisan purposes. On the whole, New York's merchants were satisfied with Arthur's performance. It was the patrician reformers who complained, because the existing system enabled the Conkling organization, and not them, to control the Republican party in New York.

After reading the report on the customhouse, Hayes wrote his secretary of the treasury, fellow Ohioan John Sherman, in May 1877:

> The collection of the revenues should be free from partisan control, and organized on a strictly business basis.. . . Party leaders should have no more influence in appointments than other equally respectable citizens. No assessments for political purposes, on officers or subordinates, should be allowed. No useless officer or employee should be retained. No officer should be required or permitted to take part in the

management of political organizations, caucuses, conventions, or election campaigns.

Hayes did not specify that employees should not be required to be Republicans, but only that they should not be allowed to use their official positions as a base from which to manage state and local politics. He aimed his blow at the Conkling type of organization, not against the Republican party itself. Moreover, he later made it clear that he did not object to the collection of "voluntary contributions" from officeholders, only forced assessments. In practice, this proved to be a distinction without a difference. Accordingly, Hayes's reforms, even when extended throughout the executive branch, represented no more than a modest beginning.

The Southern Question

Simultaneously with his civil service initiative, Hayes set about charting a new course in regard to the South. The "southern question," as Republicans were apt to refer to it, actually had two distinct components: Could the black people be protected in the enjoyment of the economic, legal, and political rights they had won as a consequence of the Civil War, and could the Republican party prevent the South from being made over into a Democratic monolith?

Few, if any, Republicans believed the two components could be separated. The Democrats had fought the granting of civil rights to blacks with every means at their disposal. In Mississippi and elsewhere they had regained power by instituting a virtual reign of terror. Neither were Republican charges of fraud and intimidation in 1876 without foundation; in a completely free election Hayes would have carried several southern states and his party would have elected at least a score of additional congressmen. Moreover, if the Democratic party succeeded in the future in establishing a "solid South," it would need to carry only New York and either Indiana or Ohio to recapture the presidency. By concentrating their campaign resources in those three northern states, the Democrats could conceivably relegate the Grand Old Party to minority status.

The trouble was that by early 1877 the two surviving southern Republican governments, in Louisiana and South Carolina, were mere shadows of their former selves, able to preserve an illusion of authority only because of the presence of federal troops outside their respective statehouses. And, as President Grant publicly acknowledged near the end of the electoral dispute, "the entire people are tired of the military being used to sustain a State Government." Was there, then, an alternative approach to the South, one that abjured direct federal intervention, that would ultimately bring an accretion of strength to the Republican party by somehow splitting the white vote?

Hayes had given this matter some thought prior to the election and appeared resigned to a negative answer. Schurz had wanted him to include in his letter of acceptance the dual declaration "that the equality of rights without distinction of color according to the constitutional amendments must be sacredly maintained by all the lawful power of the government; but that also the constitutional rights of local self-government must be respected." Hayes immediately recognized the flaw in Schurz's reasoning, objecting to the use of the phrase " 'local self-government,' in *that* connection. It seems to me to smack of the bowie knife and revolver. 'Local self-government' has nullified the 15th amendment in several States, and is in a fair way to nullify the 14th and 13th." But he could find no alternative solution.

In the end, his letter restated Schurz's thoughts in his own words:

> The moral and material prosperity of the Southern states can be most effectually advanced by a hearty and generous recognition of the rights of all by all—a recognition without reserve or exception. With such a recognition fully accorded, it will be practicable to promote, by the influence of all legitimate agencies of the general government, the efforts of the people of those states to obtain for themselves the blessings of honest and capable local government. If elected, I shall consider it not only my duty, but it will be my ardent wish, to labor for the attainment of this end.

During the electoral dispute several friends of Hayes, mostly journalists rather than politicians, explored the possibility of an accommodation with various southern Democrats. They persuaded themselves that many antebellum Whigs, Douglas Democrats, and others with business interests felt straitjacketed by the rigid economic policies of the laissez-faire-minded Democracy. These supposedly disgruntled Democrats could be influenced not only to acquiesce in Hayes's inauguration, but in time perhaps even to change their partisan allegiance. What was needed to bring about this shift was the restoration of home rule, a generous share of the federal patronage, and liberal support for internal-improvement projects, especially an enlarged

subsidy for the Texas and Pacific Railroad. In fact, Hayes's friends were pursuing a chimera. The southerners' overriding concern was the withdrawal of the soldiery from the statehouses in Columbia and New Orleans so that the Democrats could install their own governments. It was Hayes's belated confirmation that he would take such a step that brought the filibuster in the House of Representatives to an end on 2 March 1877.

Nevertheless, the notion of a realignment of southern politics along other than racial lines died hard. It was the dream that inspired Hayes's appointment of Key, a Confederate colonel who had voted for Tilden, as postmaster general. Key became a loyal member of the administration, defending Hayes's policies and advising the president on the appointment of other southern Democrats to lesser positions. But none of the men appointed publicly adhered to the Republican party, so no lasting strength was gained by this new departure. Besides, the majority of southern offices necessarily continued to go to Republicans. For example, nearly all of the state officials who had helped secure southern electoral votes for Hayes were taken care of. The Republican party could not simply turn its back on the past.

Even the promised withdrawal of the troops required careful handling. Republicans Daniel H. Chamberlain of South Carolina and Stephen B. Packard of Louisiana claimed to have been elected governors of their respective states on the basis of essentially the same returns that had placed Hayes in the White House. As one presidential adviser remarked, "You cannot dismiss those gentlemen with a wave of the hand." In particular, Hayes could not afford to alienate the half-dozen southern Republican senators whose terms had not yet expired by appearing too readily to consign them to certain political oblivion; his working majority in the upper chamber was very tenuous.

Proceeding cautiously, Hayes invited Chamberlain and Wade Hampton, the Democratic claimant in South Carolina, to Washington for separate visits in late March. Chamberlain was told frankly what was coming. Hampton was pressed for assurances that black rights would be protected and responded in the desired manner. After both men returned to Columbia, Hayes ordered the soldiers to their barracks. On 10 April, Chamberlain quietly turned over his official papers and effects to Hampton, and the Reconstruction era in South Carolina was over.

Louisiana took a little longer, given its violent history, including a bloody Democratic coup d'état attempt in 1874. Hayes sent a commission to New Orleans to report on the state of affairs there. The commission members understood that the president was seeking more than information. He needed a means to break the impasse created by the existence of two complete rival governments. Hayes's emissaries arranged for local businessmen to provide the inducements that lured enough Republican lawmakers to join the Democratic legislature to give it a clear majority of members whose election was conceded by both sides. Thus, when Hayes finally withdrew the federal troops on 24 April, Packard had no choice but to capitulate.

Amos T. Akerman, a Georgia Republican who had served for eighteen months as President Grant's attorney general during the struggle to suppress the Ku Klux Klan, took a dim view of the new conciliatory approach to southern affairs. "I really wish success to the effort of Mr. Hayes to win the good will of the Southern Democrats to his administration," he wrote, "but I see no signs of success." And he went on to predict, "They will give him some surface compliments and accept office from him and then laugh at him for his folly (as they will deem it) in letting them take him in."

Akerman was right. In May, James M. Comly, one of the journalists who had helped conjure up the vision of a conservative-led, business-oriented southern Republican party, visited Louisiana and reported back to his friend in the White House, "The 'old Whig' sentiment I spoke of petered out before we reached New Orleans. There is nothing to hang an old Whig party on. The truth is there does not seem to be anything except the Custom House to hang *anything* on." Hayes at first refused to believe it. In September, accompanied by a sizable entourage, he traveled to Kentucky, Tennessee, Georgia, and Virginia. Everywhere he went he was warmly received by local political and business leaders. He seemed oblivious to the fact that he was granting official recognition to the southern Democrats, not they to him. Back in Washington, he boasted to his diary, "The country is again one and united! I am very happy to be able to feel that the course taken has turned out so well."

But reality could not forever be denied. In March, Hayes had been confident that enough southern Democrats would break with their party's leadership in the House to choose a Republican as Speaker. In fact, with this prospect in mind he fairly insisted that the House Republican leader, James A.

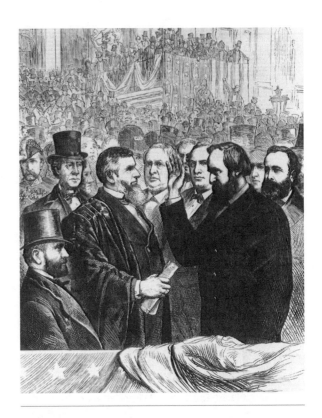

Rutherford B. Hayes takes the oath of office from Chief Justice Morrison Waite on the steps of the U.S. Capitol on 4 March 1877. The election of Hayes remains one of the most controversial in American history. THE LIBRARY OF CONGRESS

Garfield, withdraw as a candidate for the Senate from Ohio. The Democratic party was hardly free of sectional tensions, but no one should have been surprised that the southerners joined in reelecting Samuel J. Randall to the speakership when Congress reconvened in the fall. Garfield was left empty-handed.

During the Hayes administration, as in the years preceding it, no substantial effort was made to establish the kind of infrastructure that would be needed to sustain a southern Republican party, regardless of the nature of its leadership. No newspapers were founded to disseminate Republican ideas. No Republican speakers of national stature ventured southward. Offices were bestowed now on Republicans, now on Democrats, but the two were not required to work together in the interest of revitalizing the party machinery. Most damning of all, only Democrats shared the platform with Hayes on his southern tour. No one remembered how President Jefferson had extended his party's organization into the New

England bastion of Federalism at the beginning of the century.

In the fall elections of 1878 the Republicans paid the price for their lack of foresight. In the entire South only six Republican congressmen survived the Democratic onslaught. The Democrats retained their majority in the House and took control of the Senate. Hayes finally had to admit, "By State legislation, by frauds, by intimidation and by violence of the most atrocious character colored citizens have been deprived of the right of suffrage—a right guaranteed by the Constitution, and to the protection of which the people of those States have been solemnly pledged."

The Depression and Its Effects

Hayes took office in the midst of one of this nation's longest and most severe depressions. Farm prices were low, unemployment was high, manufacturing was stagnant. As always in such conditions, the railroad industry, with its high fixed cost of operation, was particularly hard hit. Long-distance lines engaged in rate wars as they competed for the reduced volume of passenger and freight traffic. In time, weaker companies were forced into receivership when they could not maintain interest payments to bondholders. Inevitably, the railroads sought to retrench their costs by further reducing wages that were already meager. Brakemen in early 1877 received $1.75 a day for twelve hours of exceedingly hazardous work; at the end of a run, moreover, they often either had to lay over at their own expense or pay full passenger fare to return home. Firemen, conductors, and engineers were paid little better. No wonder, then, that when the Baltimore and Ohio declared another 10 percent wage reduction for 16 July of that year, spontaneous strikes began in Baltimore and in Martinsburg, West Virginia, and quickly spread throughout the states of the Middle Atlantic, the Midwest, and the West, bringing much of the nation's freight transportation system to a halt. Worse, the pent-up anger of the strikers and unemployed workers erupted in widespread destruction of railroad property. In Pittsburgh alone a roundhouse, depot, 125 locomotives, 2,000 freight cars, and other equipment were burned. Except in the Civil War, violence on such a scale had never been witnessed in the United States.

State militiamen were too poorly trained and organized to control the situation. In Pittsburgh they fired on people indiscriminately, killing and wounding scores. Immediately, panicky governors appealed to the president for help in restoring order. To his credit, Hayes refused to be stampeded. Without direct precedents to guide him, he checked the language of the Constitution and insisted that the governors specify both that their legislatures were not in session and could not be speedily summoned, and that they were confronted with domestic violence they were powerless to suppress. In every instance the mere appearance of federal troops was enough to halt any continuing disorder.

Yet, the administration inexorably assumed the role of strikebreaker. Postal authorities tried to negotiate an agreement under which the mails in strike-bound areas would be carried on special trains that the workers would allow to move unimpaired. The companies refused. In the end, the government declared any passenger train carrying mail to be a mail train and threatened to prosecute anyone who interfered with it, and the railroad workers acquiesced. Even more one-sided was the action of the judiciary. Federal judges ruled that railroad workers could not strike against lines in receivership without damaging property interests under the custody of the courts. They authorized federal marshals to use military force if necessary to execute their orders. And so the great railroad strike was broken.

In retrospect, the railroad workers did not suffer a total defeat. Once the burning and looting stopped, public opinion was generally favorable to them. The losses sustained by the struck companies were so tremendous that they henceforth treated their employees more respectfully. Within a few years the wage cuts of the depression years were rescinded. Long after he left the White House, Hayes reflected, "Free government cannot long endure if property is largely in a few hands and large masses of people are unable to earn homes, education, and a support in old age." At the time he was not so sympathetic. Still, his handling of the strike had probably kept the government in as neutral a position as the circumstances would permit.

The depressed state of the economy also greatly complicated the task of managing the interrelated issues of the currency and the national debt. During the Civil War the debt had increased forty times over, soaring from less than $2.50 per capita to $75 per capita, or a staggering total of $2.8 billion. Most of this debt was in the form of bonds, but a portion was composed of legal-tender notes (the so-called greenbacks, in practice very much like today's paper currency in that they were non-interest bearing and not explicitly backed by specie). After the war, the government undertook to refund the immensely burdensome bonded debt at a lower rate of interest and over a longer repayment schedule. To make the new terms attractive, treasury officials had to be able to offer firmer assurance than they had in connection with the original bond issues that both principal and interest would be repaid in gold. Making such a promise credible in turn required that the country move toward the resumption of specie payments, whereby citizens holding paper currency could exchange it for gold at full face value.

The question that haunted the postwar years was whether specie payments could be resumed without reducing the volume of legal-tender notes in circulation. Contraction of the currency would make credit tighter and exacerbate the problem of falling prices brought on by the depression. Debtors (who might be farmers, workingmen, shopkeepers, manufacturers, or railroad magnates) quite naturally objected to repaying loans in dollars that were worth more than those they had borrowed. Many of them, in fact, wanted some degree of currency expansion to stimulate higher prices, like the ones they remembered from the prosperous war years.

Hayes was fortunate in this situation to have a secretary of the treasury who well understood both the politics and the economics of these matters, fellow Ohioan John Sherman (who, incidentally, had also been the first politician of national importance to endorse Hayes for the presidency). Sherman was a moderate who cared more for practical results—not least among them, the preservation of the Republican party's political majority—than for abstract principles. As a senator in 1875, he had authored the Specie Resumption Act. This complex measure had been designed, above all, to maintain Republican unity until after the approaching presidential election. Among other things, it authorized the treasury to stockpile a substantial gold reserve by direct purchase or by the sale of additional bonds, in order to cushion a resumption of specie payments on 1 January 1879, a date that was regarded as safely distant.

Meanwhile, the stagnant economy and the continuing downward spiral of commodity prices and wages created growing public pressure for moderate currency inflation. Advocates of an enlarged greenback currency presented the most sophisticated proposals, reasoning that such a flexible circulating medium could be more readily adapted to changing economic conditions and yet would have sufficient strength because it was backed by the collective confidence of the nation in its government and economic system. Neither was the idea lacking in popularity. Independent Greenback and Greenback-Labor candidates for Congress in 1878 captured better than 10 percent of the national vote and ran especially well in the midwestern and southern states. But the simple remonetization of silver was easier to comprehend and quickly outstripped the appeal of greenbackism as an inflationary device.

Sponsored by Democrat Richard P. Bland of Missouri, a bill that provided for the free and unlimited coinage of silver dollars at their traditional ratio of 16 to 1 with gold sailed through the House of Representatives in November 1877. This measure deeply alarmed creditors because a standard silver dollar contained only about 90 cents worth of silver at the metal's current market price. Treasury officials foresaw a flood of silver pouring in upon the mint, resulting not in increasing the currency but rather in driving gold into hiding. Private obligations would then be repaid in cheapened dollars, and specie resumption and refunding of the national debt would be indefinitely postponed. Accordingly, in the Senate, Republican William B. Allison of Iowa amended the Bland bill to restrict the issuance of new silver dollars to between 2 million and 4 million per month. Secretary Sherman recognized that in this form the measure was responsible in its content and beneficial to the Republican party in its principal effects. In view of the overwhelming congressional support, he wondered whether Hayes should not sign it, but Hayes sided with the gold monometallists, such as Schurz, and vetoed the bill on 28 February 1878, calling it "a grave breach of the public faith." Both houses easily overrode the veto the same day.

Hayes reassured investors that the government would continue to meet its obligations in gold, while Sherman concentrated on amassing a gold reserve that reached $130 million. Signs of economic recovery, combined with the growing likelihood that the treasury would in fact be able to redeem any legal-tender notes presented, increased public confidence in the use of paper currency. Two weeks before 1 January 1879, greenbacks at last achieved par with gold in private transactions. On the day set by law, more gold was presented to treasury offices in exchange for paper than paper for gold. Resumption of specie payments was thus achieved without disrupting the economy. Four months later, the refunding of the last Civil War bonds was also completed. Although hardly spectacular, the Hayes administrations' handling of these abstruse problems had certainly been effective.

The Reassertion of Presidential Prerogatives

The long congressional session that began in October 1877 was also marked by the first of two struggles between Hayes and members, now of his own party and then of the opposition, over the prerogatives of the presidential office. Because Hayes prevailed in each instance, the executive branch regained ground that had been lost during the two previous administrations in the perennial power struggle with the legislative branch. The immediate issues of contention were of limited consequence in their own right, but as with so much of what happened during Hayes's term, the implications for the future were considerable.

Hayes initiated the first of these tests of will when he decided that changes had to be made in the management of the New York Customhouse. Grant's appointees continued to take an active part in Senator Conkling's political machine. Alonzo Cornell, in particular, clung to his post as chairman of the New York Republican party even as he served as a naval officer, a direct violation of Hayes's instructions concerning reform of the civil service. So, in October 1877, Hayes nominated Theodore Roosevelt, Sr., Edwin A. Merritt, and L. Bradford Prince to replace collector Arthur, surveyor George H. Sharpe, and Cornell, respectively. Conkling allowed Merritt to be confirmed by the Senate, but he invoked "senatorial courtesy" to block the appointments of Roosevelt and Prince. ("Senatorial courtesy" was the notion, found nowhere in the Constitution, that a nomination to office in one of the states should not be made until after it had been cleared with that state's ranking senator of the president's party.) By a vote of 31 to 25, a majority of the Senate sided with Conkling on this point.

The imperious New York senator and his supporters did not reckon with Hayes's stubbornness in support of a principle—in this case, "the divorce of the Legislature from the nominating power," which he considered "the first step in any adequate and permanent reform" of the civil service because it would keep the offices involved out of politics. After Congress finally adjourned in June 1878, he suspended Arthur and Cornell in accordance with the terms of the almost forgotten Tenure of Office Act and replaced them on an interim basis with Merritt and Silas W. Burt. Finally, in the lame-duck session of the Forty-fifth Congress, Democratic senators, availing themselves of the opportunity to fish in troubled Republican waters, joined a minority of Hayes's own party to end Conkling's obstructionism. Their motivation was frankly partisan, but their action nevertheless had the effect of upholding the principle Hayes repeatedly enunciated.

The Democrats provoked the second battle by attempting to repeal or restrict the president's power to enforce the Federal Elections Law of 1871. This statute provided for the appointment of federal supervisors in congressional districts where there were allegations of irregularity in the conduct of elections. To guarantee that the supervisors would not be impeded in the performance of their duties, they could call on the local United States marshal to deploy as many deputies as the situation required. The law had been invoked not only in the South but in various large northern cities, notably New York, where Tammany Hall had engaged in massive vote fraud in 1868.

The Democrats' strategy was to attach riders to needed appropriation bills in the House of Representatives in the belief that they could then compel the Republican Senate to accept their terms. They first tried this ploy during the hectic last days of the electoral dispute. The House added to the army appropriation bill a rider that prohibited the use of any funds to support the claims of the Republican state governments in Louisiana and South Carolina. The Senate removed the rider, necessitating a conference committee to reconcile the differences between the two houses. The Democratic members of the committee refused to modify their version, and Congress adjourned without the appropriation being approved. This forced Hayes to call a special session in October 1877. By then, of course, the matter of the state governments had been resolved, and an appropriation was more easily adopted.

In the short lame-duck session that began in December, after the elections of 1878 had assured the Democrats control of both houses in the next Congress, they renewed their attempt to destroy the last vestiges of Reconstruction. The House appended to several fiscal 1879 appropriation bills riders repealing the elections law, a measure that permitted the president to employ the army to maintain order at the polls, and the jurors' test oath that barred former Confederates from service on federal juries. The Senate refused to concur, and again Congress adjourned without breaking the deadlock.

Hayes immediately called a special session of the new Forty-sixth Congress for March 1879. With the Senate no longer Republican, the president himself became the key to resisting the Democratic effort to turn back the clock. The Democratic majorities were slender, so it was certain that a veto could not be overridden. But would the Democrats then force parts of the government to shut down in order to get their way?

Hayes readily admitted that the jurors' test oath had outlived its usefulness and that the other statutes in question might legitimately be revised. However, he opposed outright repeal of the elections law and insisted that the federal government had the same obligation to safeguard the polls in congressional elections that the states had in other contests. The Democrats countered that the Constitution made the conduct of all elections primarily a problem for state regulation. Above all, Hayes was determined never to yield to the Democratic scheme to coerce him into accepting provisions of which he disapproved by holding hostage the appropriations needed to operate the government.

In late April, Congress passed an army bill with a rider barring any civil or military official from protecting federal elections from fraud or violence. Hayes returned the bill with a strongly worded veto. Two weeks later, Congress made the same objectionable provisions the subject of a separate bill, which Hayes also vetoed. At the end of May the Democrats in Congress tried again, using an omnibus bill appropriating funds for the executive, judicial, and legislative branches. This time they attached riders that permitted federal supervisors and deputy marshals to observe the conduct of congressional elections but denied them the authority either to prevent fraud and violence or to punish violations of the law after they had occurred. Again, Hayes responded with a veto.

During the last week of June, with the new fiscal year only a few days off, the logjam finally began to break. Congress sent Hayes a bill for the judicial branch alone that repealed the jurors' test oath and forbade any payments to deputy marshals for enforcing the elections law. Refusing to back down, Hayes fired off another veto message. In the meantime, the Democrats passed separate bills for the executive

and legislative branches and for the army. They contained no riders, and Hayes signed them into law. Next he signed a revised bill for the judiciary that repealed the jurors' oath and simply omitted any appropriation for the marshals. He had already indicated his willingness to see the oath dispensed with, so the element of coercion was no longer involved.

In a last defiant gesture before adjourning on 30 June, Congress adopted a separate appropriation bill for the federal marshals that again restricted their use in connection with elections. Once more Hayes vetoed it. As late as May 1880, Congress passed the same bill for the marshals, and Hayes predictably sent it back. Only then did he get an unrestricted appropriation. In the end, the president obtained everything that he wanted, demonstrating that it was possible, by being steadfast, to uphold the independence of the executive branch.

Rethinking Indian Policy

When Hayes was in the White House, the northeastern quarter of the United States was entering the period of its most rapid urban and industrial development. By contrast, the western half of the country was still being staked out. Settlement by ranchers and farmers inevitably meant clashes with nomadic Indians. The annihilation of Custer's regiment at the Little Big Horn dominated the news soon after Hayes's nomination for the presidency. His first year in office witnessed the defeat of the Sioux, mostly by starvation, and the long pursuit of Chief Joseph and his Nez Percé across a thousand miles of the northern Rockies in desperate flight toward refuge in Canada. The next fall the northern Cheyenne slipped away from the army in the Indian Territory in a futile effort to return to their ancestral hunting grounds.

Hayes and Secretary of the Interior Schurz inherited the policy of concentrating the western tribes on compact reservations, but soon came to believe that more humane methods of dealing with the Indians had to be found. Their sympathies were aroused in part by the disaster Schurz unwittingly inflicted upon the eight-hundred-member Ponca tribe. The Grant administration had, by mistake, given the agricultural Ponca's land in Dakota Territory to the Sioux. Schurz ordered the forcible removal of the Poncas to a small tract in the Indian Territory. Numerous members of the tribe died en route. Upon arrival at their strange destination, the survivors found both the climate and the land unsuitable. They, too, tried unsuccessfully to return home.

Genuinely committed to better treatment of Indians, Schurz appointed a commission to investigate the conduct of the Indian Bureau (now Bureau of Indian Affairs). The commission predictably found a pattern of cheating the Indians by unscrupulous agents, compounded by sloppy accounting and inadequate supervision. Schurz moved quickly to remedy the situation. He instituted a code of regulations for bureau employees, revised reporting and accounting systems, ordered unannounced inspections, and for the first time required traders to be licensed and bonded. Because Schurz was the most vigorous of the cabinet secretaries in implementing Hayes's civil service reforms, the caliber of bureau personnel improved. Schurz also supported the experiments in Indian education conducted at Hampton Institute by Richard Henry Pratt, which led to the establishment of the Carlisle Indian School in 1879. When opponents of the new peaceful emphasis sought to transfer the bureau back to the War Department, Schurz helped organize the coalition in the Senate that staved off the move. Thereafter the Interior Department was unquestionably preeminent in determining policies toward the Indians.

In 1881, Helen Hunt Jackson published her stirring protest against American mistreatment of the Indians, *A Century of Dishonor*. Her interest in the subject had first been awakened by the plight of the Poncas, and Schutz fared badly in her interpretation. Her criticism was largely undeserved. Schurz had long been in correspondence with many of the eastern humanitarians who preceded Jackson in their concern. In 1879 and 1880 he undertook two lengthy inspection tours of western reservations to ascertain firsthand what he was dealing with. But it was easier to see the shortcomings in federal policies than to know how to change them. Schurz deserves credit for initiating the process of reform. President Hayes supported him throughout and used his annual messages to Congress to lobby for Indian citizenship, individual farm ownership, and the education of Indian children in American methods of agriculture. Hayes and Schurz thus pointed the way toward the positive, nonexpropriatory aspects of the Dawes Severalty Act of 1887. At the same time, they did not foresee, and probably would not have understood, the negative effects of acculturation.

A Limited Diplomacy

Hayes's presidency was a quiescent period in American foreign relations. The State Department employed only fifty-one people in Washington, from assistant secretaries to clerks. The armed forces were maintained on a similar scale. Congress in 1877 imposed a limit of twenty-five thousand officers and men on the army and seventy-five hundred on the navy. The largely wooden fleet would have been ill matched against some Latin American nations. The country felt so secure behind its ocean frontiers that Hayes used the secretaryship of the navy for his only fully political cabinet appointment: Richard W. Thompson of Indiana, derided as "the ancient mariner of the Wabash," although a decent executive, knew nothing of ships or strategy. Secretary of State Evarts devoted his energies principally to upgrading the quality of the foreign service and improving its efficiency in handling routine matters. He required consuls to study the language and history of their host countries. He also instructed them to gather detailed economic statistics, which were then made available monthly to American merchants and manufacturers in hopes of stimulating increased exports of American products to Europe, Latin America, and Asia.

Only three diplomatic issues of consequence arose in the late 1870s. The most serious dispute was with Mexico. Shortly before Hayes became president, Porfirio Díaz seized power in Mexico City but was unable immediately to extend his control throughout the country. Marauding Indians took advantage of the situation to conduct raids into western Texas and southeastern New Mexico. As a consequence, Evarts and Hayes refused to recognize the Díaz government, while Secretary of War George McCrary authorized army units in Texas to pursue bandits across the border. Unfortunately, no action was better calculated to awaken Mexican fears of further territorial aggrandizement by the United States. Not until April 1878 did Evarts reverse himself and recognize Díaz. Even then, it took another year for Díaz to suppress the border raids and two years for McCrary to withdraw his offensive order. Thereafter, a mutual interest in the economic development of Mexico gradually drew the two countries closer together.

A similar truculence characterized the American response to Ferdinand de Lesseps' French Panama Canal Company. This time Hayes himself set the tone, telling Congress in a special message of March 1880 that "the policy of this country is a canal under

American control." He explained that the canal would be "virtually a part of the coastline of the United States," which was emerging as a two-ocean power. Yet Hayes simultaneously opposed any attempt by the American government to build an isthmian waterway, preferring that it be strictly a private undertaking. Because the French government also declined to involve itself directly, that is what de Lesseps' project became. In need of vast sums of capital, the French promoter then began to sell stock to American investors. To this end he hired Navy Secretary Thompson as the chairman of the American Committee of his Panama Canal Company. A chagrined Hayes was forced to dismiss his wayward cabinet adviser. The staunch nationalism Hayes displayed in this episode was at once a logical extension of past American continental expansion and a forerunner of the more active involvement in world affairs that future Republican presidents would pursue.

Hayes devoted many of his official addresses to the need to overcome sectional and racial prejudices. The problem did not extend just to the South. In 1876, in response to growing agitation in California and Oregon, both major party platforms demanded strict limitations on Chinese immigration. Chinese laborers had built most of the railroads on the west coast and were currently employed in diking and draining the Sacramento delta to create some of California's richest farmland, but that did not endear them to workers of European descent. In 1879, Congress passed a law setting a limit of fifteen Chinese immigrants on any single ship, thus directly contravening the terms of the Burlingame Treaty of 1868, which permitted unrestricted immigration. As he did on other occasions when Congress overstepped its bounds and intruded upon presidential authority; Hayes vetoed the bill. Evarts then sent a commission to China to negotiate both a commercial treaty and an agreement under which the Chinese regulated the immigration of laborers to the United States according to American wishes. Both compacts were ratified shortly before Hayes left office. The effect, of course, was to uphold the sanctity of treaties rather than to protect the equality of peoples.

Evaluation

Considered altogether, the achievements of the Hayes administration were not dramatic. Hayes had not previously been involved in national politics in an important way. He accepted the Republican presidential nomination more as a rare personal honor than as an opportunity to carry into effect a particular agenda. Once elected, he assumed the leadership of a government that, following the failure of Reconstruction, had already retreated to playing a more limited role in the lives of the American people, and he saw no reason to reverse that trend. As he noted in his diary, "We are in a period when old questions are settled, and the new are not yet brought forward." Rather, he contented himself with enhancing the efficiency with which the government carried out the limited functions of the past. Thus, he appointed a strong cabinet loyal to his own views and devoted his attention to such matters as reforming the civil service, resolving the conflict over the southern state governments, and battling for his own understanding of a sound currency. Limited government did not imply a passive presidency, as the many clashes with Congress over the respective prerogatives of the executive and legislative branches showed.

Hayes characteristically pledged in his letter of acceptance to serve only one term. At the end of four years he was satisfied that his performance as chief executive had strengthened his party and enhanced public esteem for the office he held. After James A. Garfield had been nominated by the Republican party to succeed him (Hayes approved of this choice, although he had personally preferred Secretary of the Treasury Sherman), he embarked upon a two-and-a-half-month cross-country excursion to California, Puget Sound, and Santa Fe via railroad, steamship, stagecoach, army ambulance, ferryboat, and yacht. This was the grandest by far of a series of tours, designed to promote national unity, that had taken the president into the Deep South, up to northern New England, and across the Midwest as far as the Dakota Territory to see the wheat harvest.

He returned from the west coast just in time to cast his vote for Garfield. His fellow Ohioan was elected in another close contest, and the Republicans regained control of both houses of Congress—a result for which Hayes rightly believed he deserved some credit. Hayes retired to the life of a private citizen in Fremont, Ohio, as comfortable with his term in office as perhaps any president since. His health was still excellent, and he became the most active former chief executive prior to Jimmy Carter, devoting himself to civic affairs—higher education, prison reform, and veterans reunions—until three days before his death, of a heart attack, on 17 January 1893.

BIBLIOGRAPHY

Ari Hoogenboom, *Rutherford B. Hayes: Warrior and President* (Lawrence, Kans., 1995), is the best biography of the nineteenth president, as Hoogenboom's *The Presidency of Rutherford B. Hayes* (Lawrence, Kans., 1988), is the best overall account of his administration. Arthur Bishop, ed., *Rutherford B. Hayes, 1822–1893* (Dobbs Ferry, N.Y., 1969), contains a useful chronology of Hayes's life and lengthy excerpts from his most important state papers. T. Harry Williams, ed., *Hayes: The Diary of a President, 1875–1881* (New York, 1964), affords the best insight into his character and personality.

Keith Ian Polakoff, *The Politics of Inertia: The Election of 1876 and the End of Reconstruction* (Baton Rouge, La., 1973), details the disputed election of 1876 and its settlement. William Gillette, *Retreat from Reconstruction, 1869–1879* (Baton Rouge, La., 1979), is critical of Hayes's southern policy. Terry L. Seip, *The South Returns to Congress: Men, Economic Measures, and Intersectional Relationships, 1868–1879* (Baton Rouge, La., 1983), compares the voting records of southern Democrats and Republicans of the Reconstruction era. James M. McPherson, "Coercion or Conciliation? Abolitionists Debate President Hayes's Southern Policy," in *New England Quarterly* 39 (1966), illustrates how frustrating this intractable problem could be for those who cared deeply about it. Vincent P. De Santis, *Republicans Face the Southern Question: The New Departure Years, 1877–1897* (Baltimore, 1959), is an excellent account of the Republican attempts to find a substitute for their failed Reconstruction program.

Ari Hoogenboom, *Outlawing the Spoils: A History of the Civil Service Reform Movement, 1865–1883* (Urbana, Ill., 1961), is the best general account of the civil service reform movement from 1865 through the passage of the Pendleton Act in 1883. John G. Sproat, *The Best Men: Liberal Reformers in the Gilded Age* (New York, 1968), incisively analyzes the liberal reformers who had so much influence on Hayes. Hans L. Trefousse, *Carl Schurz: A Biography* (Knoxville, Tenn., 1982), is an excellent biography of the cabinet member closest to Hayes. David M. Jordan, *Roscoe Conkling of New York: Voice in the Senate* (Ithaca, N.Y., 1971), ably portrays one of Hayes's principal opponents.

Robert V. Bruce, *1877: Year of Violence* (Indianapolis, Ind., 1959), is a lively account of the great railroad strike. Walter T. K. Nugent, *Money and American Society, 1865–1880* (New York, 1968), presents the most lucid account of the currency debates after the Civil War. Milton Plesur, *America's Outward Thrust: Approaches to Foreign Affairs, 1865–1890* (DeKalb, Ill., 1971), treats Hayes as one of the forerunners of the more aggressive McKinley and Roosevelt.

Recent works include Ari Hoogenboom, *Rutherford B. Hayes: One of the Good Colonels* (Abilene, Tex., 2000), and Hans L. Trefousse, *Rutherford B. Hayes* (New York, 2002).

James A. Garfield and
Chester A. Arthur

Bernard A. Weisberger

James A. Garfield THE LIBRARY OF CONGRESS

Chester A. Arthur THE LIBRARY OF CONGRESS

IN the history of the presidency, the period from 1865 to 1901 is usually perceived as something of a wasteland. Andrew Johnson is remembered as the only chief executive to be impeached, and Grant, as the one with the most scandal-scarred record; and then come those presidents of whom it has been written that "their gravely vacant and bewhiskered faces mixed, melted, swam together . . . which was which?" Hayes, Garfield, Arthur, and Harrison perfectly fit that image of forgettableness. Cleveland escapes oblivion, for he, at least, held office twice. And McKinley, though popular in his day, is probably best remembered now as the president whose assassination elevated

Theodore Roosevelt, his vice president, to the White House.

This view is a touch—though only a touch—unfair and is typical of the cult of personality, which holds as an article of faith that the character of the president transcends or creates the momentary health of the office itself. That may be so when a political genius like Lincoln is in the White House, but it does not follow that presidents who are not geniuses are necessarily mediocrities. Garfield and Arthur, in particular, may have had only mediocre talents, but in the period from 1881 to 1885, even men of greater gifts would have had a hard time with the presidency.

It was not a time to articulate issues, because they had not yet come into clear focus. The great questions of the Civil War had been settled, but the problems of postwar expansion were not yet in sharp outline. There was no rhetoric to deal with the social problems posed by the city, immigration, labor, the trusts, and the railroads. Nor was there much of a will to do so when times were good. When times were bad, politicians approached the remedies by familiar paths. Arguments over the tariff, monopolies, paper money, and the spoils system went back to the age of Jackson and could be warmed over without much regard to how they fit the facts of the Gilded Age, which were still incomplete and uncatalogued.

The machinery of government under the Constitution, too, was old and in disrepair. The balance of power between president and Congress was still—only twelve years after Andrew Johnson's trial—tipped in the direction of Capitol Hill. The executive office itself lacked anything resembling an information-gathering, planning, or policymaking staff, and presidents still, willingly or not, received the public several times weekly. Congress was not much better: it had gotten too big to be an effective debating society; its rules and committee structure in no way expedited the flow of business; and while it had strong personalities, especially in the Senate, they tended to their own fiefdoms rather than attempting to define a national or even party consensus.

The parties themselves were loose, faction-ridden confederations of state machines, and what was more, neither one had an iron grip on the country. Elections were close, control of Congress swung back and forth almost every two years, and nothing resembling a mandate was visible.

Add to these institutional failings the fact that the truly exciting developments of the age were in business and invention, and it is small wonder that Viscount Bryce could devote an entire chapter of *The American Commonwealth* to explaining why the nation's best men did not go into politics. The most that could realistically be expected from presidents, other than personal integrity, would be a holding action until the country caught up with the implications of the age of steel and steam. If they kept the peace at home and abroad, and took even tentative steps toward getting the country to confront the new order of things, they deserved—as Garfield and Arthur deserve—at least a minimum passing grade from historians.

Portrait of a Winning Dark Horse

Both men were, in a sense, "accidental" chief executives: Garfield was a dark horse who had presidential ambitions but no real expectations of achieving them in the spring of 1880, and Arthur was elevated to the office by the assassin's bullet. The battle of that year's Republican nominating convention was supposed to take place between James G. Blaine and former President Ulysses S. Grant, a sign of a badly factionalized Grand Old Party. Behind Grant's third-term bid was the force of New York's imperious and arrogant Senator Roscoe Conkling, leader of the so-called Stalwart Republicans, undeviatingly loyal to the Radical Republican shibboleths of Grant's presidential heyday—the "bloody shirt," so-called carpetbag and black rule in the South, hard money, and high tariffs. Opposed to Conkling was Senator James G. Blaine, former Speaker of the House, a man of vast charm and, it was persistently suspected, little principle. Blaine's followers were allegedly (but not always actually) less Radical and therefore clubbed Half-Breeds.

The actual contest between the groups was over power and personality rather than ideology. Both Conkling and Blaine wanted control of the patronage, and they were like-minded in their disdain for the good-government and civil-service reformers, who had bolted in 1872 (as Liberal Republicans) and returned in 1876 to exert a strong influence in the administration of Hayes. Because Hayes had publicly condemned the spoils system, pursued corrupt officeholders, and pulled federal troops out of the South (abandoning southern Republicans to their dismal fate), he was anathema to both Stalwarts and Half-Breeds and, although an incumbent, stood no chance of renomination.

None of the three groups—Half-Breeds, Stalwarts, and Reformers, sometimes called Independents—was strong enough to win alone, a fact that became apparent after a few ballots. Convention brokers would have to build a majority (379-vote) coalition behind someone other than Grant or Blaine. One of the contenders was Ohio's John Sherman, brother of the general and secretary of the treasury; but the aging and colorless Sherman had too many liabilities. The politicos began to make overtures instead to his campaign manager, Senator James A. Garfield of Ohio. Garfield was, of course, supposed to be steadfast to his man's cause and to reject such bids, but he did not.

As a candidate, he had far greater assets than Sherman. He was born poor (in 1831) in rural Ohio, helped support a widowed mother, and worked briefly as a barge driver, creating the perfect title for Horatio Alger's campaign biography: *From Canal Boy to President*. He had traveled far from the towpath, too. For a time after graduation from Williams College, he had been a professor of classics and then president of what later became Hiram College. He went into politics as an antislavery Republican in 1859 but left a seat in the Ohio legislature to see action in the Civil War, where he rose to be an unusually competent political general. That gave him first-class credentials to win election to the House (1863) and then to the Senate (1880).

Garfield was, to some extent, a perfect moderate. He read widely (and unobtrusively) without its visibly affecting his Christianity, his Republicanism, or his general laissez-faire orthodoxy. He was not so much a scholar in politics as a politic scholar. He was flexible enough about the tariff and civil service reform to be a Half-Breed but sound enough on the money question and the bloody shirt for the Stalwarts to live with him. He worked hard and was respected by his colleagues. He had enough ambition to move ahead in party ranks and enough self-doubt (well concealed) to avoid the kind of strutting that came naturally to a Conkling and that multiplied enemies.

On the thirty-sixth ballot, Garfield was nominated. Following custom, he immediately made a bid for unity by seeking for the vice presidency a member of the "defeated" Stalwarts. The choice of Chester A. Arthur was somewhat breathtaking, for he was no ordinary Stalwart but Roscoe Conkling's widely known lieutenant—or as many of Conkling's opponents more unkindly put it, his creature. In fact, he had been head of the New York Customhouse, the great fount of Stalwart patronage, and had been fired (to Conkling's undying rage) by President Hayes in a cleanup move. (Interestingly enough, Garfield himself did not make the offer; it came through a lieutenant. Conkling ungraciously and unsuccessfully advised Arthur to "drop it as you would a red hot shoe from the forge," since Garfield was bound to lose.) The reformers in the party had to swallow hard, but as one of their chief journals, the *Nation*, consolingly put it, there was no place in which Arthur's "powers of mischief will be so small as in the Vice-Presidency."

The Democrats nominated a candidate with no previous political experience—General Winfield Scott Hancock, sardonically described by the *New York Sun* as "a good man, weighing two hundred and eighty pounds." Both of the major-party platforms waffled on the issues of the tariff and civil service, and both repeated standard party pieties. A third force was in the field, the Greenback party, demanding not only inflation but such far-reaching measures as the eight-hour day, a graduated income tax, and federal railroad regulation, but its appeal was negligible.

If there was any incident of significance during the election summer, it was a meeting (5 August) of Garfield and Blaine with Stalwart leaders in New York City, at which, apparently, all the Republican factions agreed to cooperate in return for an appropriate sharing of offices. Conkling did not attend but did give his sanction and later visited (and campaigned for) Garfield in Ohio. The terms of the "Treaty of Fifth Avenue" were unrecorded and later disputed, with fateful results for Garfield's short administration. Garfield was also helped by a war chest that came from businessmen and Republican officeholders, who were "assessed" a percentage of their salaries, a practice shared in by the Democrats.

The campaign and election were scarcely noteworthy, except possibly for the closeness of the popular vote. Out of 9.2 million ballots cast, Garfield's final lead was a mere 7,368—not exactly a mandate. When the results were counted, he had won comfortably by 214 to 155 in the Electoral College, without carrying a single southern state, evidence of the final burial of Reconstruction. (The key electoral votes were the 35 of New York; had they gone to Hancock, the decision would have been reversed—a fact that Conkling did not forget.) Moreover, although the Republicans regained control of the House, the Senate was split exactly evenly between the two parties. Garfield therefore began more or less shackled. Even before his inauguration, the problems posed by his initial appointments fully justified one of his diary entries for November: "There is a tone of sadness running through this triumph."

Patronage and Power

The process of cabinet making, not completed until after the inauguration, foreshadowed trouble. For secretary of state, Garfield chose Blaine, first extracting from him a promise not to make the office "the camping ground for fighting the next presidential battle." Blaine gave his word, but temperamentally incapable of keeping it, he was soon busily meddling in Garfield's other appointments. Conkling expected as his reward the right to name the head of the Treasury Department, which carried with it control of the patronage of the customhouses. But Garfield rejected Conkling's candidate, the banker Levi P. Morton, and instead gave New York the position of postmaster general in the person of Thomas L. James, much to Conkling's annoyance.

Other choices reflected a sensible desire to build needed harmony within the contentious party. The War Department went to Robert Todd Lincoln, who was not only the son of the Great Emancipator but the protégé of Senator John A. Logan, an Illinois Stalwart. The choice of Wayne MacVeagh as attorney general pleased the Pennsylvania boss Senator J. Donald Cameron, who had gone to the 1880 convention as a Grant man. William Hunt, who got the navy portfolio, was from the dwindling ranks of southern Republicans. The Treasury and Interior departments went to a pair of moderate midwesterners, William Windom of Minnesota and Samuel J. Kirkwood of Iowa.

Cabinet selection was an exhaustive process, not completed until Garfield had actually delivered his inaugural address, a compendium of platitudes. The only possible hint of future policy was in the reference to the blacks of the South. They were praised for earning "the blessings that gather around the homes of the industrious poor" and were promised that their future would be assured by "the saving influence of universal education."

But with the cabinet completed, Garfield could not yet escape the importunings of hundreds of other office seekers, whose demands caused him to exclaim wearily, "My God! What is there in this place that a man should ever want to get into it!" While his wife, daughter, and four sons seemed to settle happily into the White House, he was finding it a harder battleground than any he had known in uniform.

Shortly after his inauguration, Garfield met with Conkling. The New York senator, never easy to deal with, was especially eager to be placated. He resented Blaine's eminence in the cabinet and influence on Garfield. What was worse for him was a deepening split in the ranks of his own state machine. He wanted Garfield's assignment of federal jobs in New York to reward the friends, and punish the enemies, of Roscoe Conkling. Garfield promised the rewards, but not the punishments, and named five Conkling associates to federal jobs, including the lucrative spot

of United States attorney for the Southern District of New York, on 22 March. The news brought an agitated Secretary Blaine rushing to the White House for a mid-dinner conference. He persuaded Garfield to redress the pro-Stalwart balance by some additional appointments, and the centerpiece of his plan was to replace the collector of the Port of New York, a reformer who had succeeded Chester A. Arthur in the job, with William H. Robertson, the chief New York backer of Blaine in 1880.

When Robertson's name was sent to the Senate for confirmation the next morning, it not only stung reform-minded Republicans but was denounced by Conkling as "perfidy without parallel." To lose control of the customhouse would wreck his machine, and he promised, "There will be hell before Judge Robertson is confirmed." Garfield, who had previously shown no disposition for conflict, suddenly dug in his heels. For a long time he had disliked the practice of "senatorial courtesy," the informal veto allowed each senator over appointments within his state. In 1872 he described it as a "corrupt and vicious" practice that gave the Senate the irresponsible power to thwart the president. The issue, as he saw it, was "whether the President is registering clerk of the Senate or the Executive of the United States." He announced that Robertson might be "carried out of the Senate head first or feet first," but he would not withdraw the nomination.

In pressing what simply appeared to be a shabby intraparty battle on Blaine's behalf, Garfield adorned his short administration with its only achievement. He wooed and threatened, and in the end, a majority of Republican senators realized that the prudent course was to follow him. Confronting defeat, Conkling and the other New York senator, Thomas Platt, resigned in mid-May, just before Robertson's confirmation. They hoped to be vindicated through reelection by the New York state legislature. They failed in that, too.

In winning the battle over Robertson, Garfield had helped to replenish the reservoir of executive power, thoroughly depleted by Congress in Andrew Johnson's day. He had taken a step toward the modern presidency. As Garfield's latest biographer, Allan Peskin, puts it, Blaine and Conkling had more or less forced him into the fight, but "the path upon which he had been pushed led straight to the twentieth century."

The political situation in the Senate was also responsible for a sketchy Garfield initiative on a new southern policy. The Republicans and Democrats were exactly balanced in voting strength there, but the Republicans would be able to organize and control the committees if they could win the vote of a newly elected independent member, Virginia's scrappy little William Mahone. He was a former Confederate general and a former Democrat who had run on the ticket of the Readjusters, a group of dissenters, black and white, from both major parties who wanted to lighten the huge burden of bonded indebtedness that the Reconstruction governments had incurred for the benefit of railroads and other corporations. Mahone could be induced to vote Republican if rewarded with patronage in the Senate and cooperation back in Virginia. Garfield approved the deal, though with misgivings. It meant a partial abandonment of the traditional and heavily black Republican machines in the South in order to woo discontented white Democrats, which accelerated the incoming tide of black disfranchisement. The president consoled himself for this desertion with the thought that the key to the freedmen's future, as he had said on taking office, might be in the schoolhouse rather than the ballot box.

Garfield had time for only one completed domestic achievement. He directed Secretary Windom to refund the national debt, by calling in outstanding United States bonds issued at 6 percent and giving holders the option of cashing them in or holding on to them at 3.5 percent, which was more in line with existing interest rates. The move, it was estimated, saved the taxpayers $10 million—a number better appreciated when set against the fact that total federal expenditures in 1881 were under $261 million.

While the battles over appointments were raging, Secretary Blaine plunged enthusiastically into a new, aggressive hemispheric diplomacy. He threatened to intervene in disputes between Chile and Peru and between Mexico and Guatemala, he brandished the Monroe Doctrine in Great Britain's face, and he proposed a Pan-American conference that would have been dominated by the United States. He also made overtures toward prying open markets for American goods in Europe, Asia, and Africa. None of these adventurous and uncoordinated initiatives was supported by adequate power, and none reached a level where it became the concern of the president before 2 July 1881.

Tragedy, Succession, and Surprise

On that date, Charles J. Guiteau shot his way into American history. Guiteau was one of those self-important, self-anointed cranks who haunt the shadowy fringes of power and are merely nuisances until their potential for violence explodes. A failed Oneida colonist, lawyer, religious journalist, and husband, he hung around Republican headquarters in 1880, distributing privately printed copies of a bizarre pro-Republican speech that he believed entitled him to a diplomatic post after Garfield's victory. Brushed off repeatedly at the White House and State Department, he suddenly received what he believed to be a vision from God, wherein he was told that things were not going well with the Republic and that the problem was the new president, who must be removed. Armed with this commandment and a .44-caliber ivory-handled revolver, Guiteau followed Garfield and his traveling party into the Baltimore and Potomac Railroad station and shot him in the back at point-blank range. Then the assassin calmly accepted his arrest, saying, "I am a Stalwart. Arthur is now president of the United States."

Garfield lingered through a torrid, agonizing summer, wasting away from the effects of blood poisoning caused by the bullet in his spine. It says much about the nature of the federal government in 1881 that there was no problem of carrying on official business during the president's incapacity, which was not to be the case when Woodrow Wilson was fighting for his life in 1919–1920. Congress was in recess, the minimal bureaucracy was virtually shut down in the hot months, and the department heads had no decisions to refer to the president. The basic concern of thoughtful men was what would happen if and when Garfield finally died. The casual way in which the vice presidency was used as a political bargaining chip once again haunted those who believed, with the *New York Times*, that Arthur's previous career had been a "mess of filth." Even among his familiars, it was later testified, the common reaction was, "Chet Arthur, president of the United States? Good God!"

On 19 September the inevitable calamity came. Garfield died that evening, and at 2:15 A.M. the next day Arthur was sworn in as president in his Manhattan home by a New York State judge. What followed would prove surprising to many people, possibly including Arthur himself.

President James A. Garfield was shot by Charles Guiteau on 2 July 1881. Garfield suffered through a painful summer before succumbing. THE LIBRARY OF CONGRESS

Arthur's pre-presidential career was not precisely a "mess of filth"—newspaper editors were then prone to hyperbole—but it did not promise much. Arthur was born in 1829 and raised in a Baptist parsonage in Vermont. He escaped from the icy clutch of New England piety by brainpower. He attended Union College and became successively a schoolteacher, a lawyer, and a Whig (later Republican) politician, having learned the trade from the master, Thurlow Weed. In 1861 he was made quartermaster general of New York State, thereby earning and keeping the useful title "General," and making important friends among contractors and suppliers. The next year he left the service, gradually became Conkling's chief lieutenant, and in 1871 was rewarded by Grant with the New York collector's job. That empire of fees and jobs allowed him to indulge his Victorian gentlemanly taste for fine food, wines, and cigars; elegant clothes; and leisure. As president, he would keep a ten-to-four workday and a five-day workweek and rarely "did today what he could put off until tomorrow." Some of his indolence may have come from bad health; no one knew at the time that he had Bright's disease. (He was to die of it in 1886,

two days after prudently burning all his personal papers.)

As a cultivated and rather aloof man who might have been more at home in London than in Washington, Arthur did not fit the crude image of the party hack. He was, as biographer Thomas Reeves styled him, a "gentleman boss." What the reformers feared was that he would, in effect, turn over the administration of the United States to Roscoe Conkling and the Stalwart machine.

Instead, he scrupulously avoided any taint of jobbery. Conkling got no cabinet seat. (He was offered, but declined, a Supreme Court seat.) Blaine was replaced at the State Department by an experienced and able lawyer and Senate veteran, Frederick T Frelinghuysen of New Jersey. Like several other replacements made by Arthur, he was a Stalwart but one with a clean personal record. The main Half-Breed appointment was that of William E. Chandler, a close ally of Blaine, to the Navy Department. More significant was something Arthur did not do: he made no attempt to replace Robertson in the New York Customhouse or to open up other patronage jobs for his friends by purging earlier appointees. "He has done

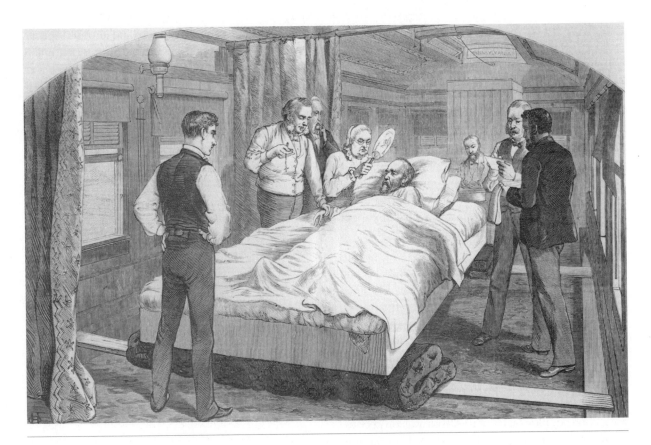

President Garfield returned to Washington by railway car following the attempt on his life. He was attended by his wife and several doctors. THE LIBRARY OF CONGRESS

less for us than Garfield, or even Hayes," one Stalwart lamented.

Arthur also inherited one major controversial issue from Garfield in the form of the star-route cases. Along certain star routes, the Post Office Department had the power to award contracts for mail delivery to private express companies rather than setting up its own systems. It was alleged that under Grant some postal officials and contractors had colluded to bilk the government of several millions in padded charges. Garfield's attorney general was supposed to proceed to trial, which was embarrassing, since two of the defendants, Stephen Dorsey and Thomas Brady, had played prominent parts as Republican fund-raisers in the 1880 campaign. Arthur replaced MacVeagh with Benjamin Brewster and told him, "I desire that these people shall be prosecuted with the utmost vigor of the law." The order was carried out, though one trial was invalidated and a second one resulted in acquittal.

As a onetime Conkling follower, Arthur was expected to resist civil service reform stubbornly. Nothing had exceeded the contempt of Conkling himself for the "carpet-knights and man-milliners" of the clean-government camp. But the shock of the assassination made the merit system a proposal whose time had come, as Arthur recognized. In his maiden speech as president, he damned civil service professionalization with the faintest of praise but said he would sign any measure designed to achieve it. Such a bill, the Pendleton Act, did finally cross his desk in January 1883. It was limited in its application, covering only about 11 percent of all federal employees and leaving wide openings for political assessments and payoffs, but it set up the Civil Service Commission, which could later plug those gaps. Arthur not only signed the act but appointed good men to the commission and was praised in their 1885 official report for his "friendly support."

Arthur also seemed willing to modify Stalwart orthodoxy, which decreed support for a high tariff. His second annual message called for reductions in duties on such important items as cotton, iron, steel, sugar, molasses, silk, wool, and woolen goods. Arthur's conversion was in part a product of his discomfort with a treasury surplus, which tariff collections had helped to generate; he believed it was better to have the money out in circulation, helping the economy. It was also a dutiful follow-up to the report of a special tariff commission created by law in 1882 that, although heavily weighted with protectionists, believed many duties could and should be lowered. Congress, while recognizing a growing pressure for modification, proved customarily susceptible to strong lobbying from special-interest groups, and the result was a weak compromise known as the Mongrel Tariff.

In many of his early actions, as president, Arthur gave the impression of someone who, once he got into the office, felt a sudden responsibility to protect and defend its prerogatives. That transformation—which Arthur was not the last to undergo—was most in evidence when he stamped his veto on legislation. Most nineteenth-century presidents shrank from the political barrage that they knew they would have to endure if they said no to a congressional majority. Some still had constitutional qualms about when it was proper to block a bill, but Arthur was on record in favor of an "item veto," which would have let him cancel unpalatable parts of measures that he otherwise approved—something no president has yet gotten—and he did not hesitate to return a porkbarrel internal-improvements bill of 1882 to the Hill, claiming that it was an "extravagant expenditure of public money."

There was a better-known veto in that same year, one firmly anchored to the executive privilege of defending a treaty. In 1868 the United States and China had signed the Burlingame Treaty, giving the nationals of each power the right of free travel and residence in the other. But as wave after wave of Chinese poured into west coast ports to work in the mines and on the railroads, a backlash of already strong anti-Oriental sentiment built up to politically irresistible levels. Racism and economic anxiety reinforced each other as labor unions and politicians—especially on the west coast—demanded that "coolie laborers" be barred from American shores and that Anglo-Saxon civilization be preserved from opium smoking, gambling, and other heathen vices. The Burlingame Treaty was modified by a new one in 1880, giving Congress some powers over Chinese immigration. Thus armed, the lawmakers, in March 1882, enacted a twenty-year ban on the "importation" of Chinese laborers. The same law denied American citizenship to Chinese and imposed special restrictions and requirements on Chinese nationals visiting the United States.

Arthur struck the bill down. He was not entirely heroic; his message indicated that he would accept a ten-year restriction as an "experiment," and part of his motive was fear that the bill would "repel Oriental nations from us and . . . drive their trade and commerce into more friendly hands." He did note that the law, by overriding a treaty, was "a breach of our national faith" and that parts of it were "undemocratic and hostile to the spirit of our institutions." Congress yielded to the president to the extent of passing a fresh exclusion law, this time reducing the term to ten years, and Arthur went along. (The law was consistently renewed, and the hapless Chinese government could only agree to an accomplished fact.) In one other case in 1882, Arthur vetoed a measure setting safety and health standards for incoming immigrant steamers. His grounds were partly technical, but Congress, as in the case of Chinese exclusion, reworked the law to meet his objections before getting his approval.

These were hardly executive triumphs, but they seem somewhat greater when viewed in context. The presidential office had been emasculated under Johnson and disgraced under Grant, and in the disputed election of 1876 it had been further tainted by cheating, haggling, and a secret deal between Republican and Democratic bosses. That Arthur was able to assert any prerogative at all—even negatively, by veto—was a small foretaste of a better future for the presidency.

For the most part, he lacked the initiative for leadership, but in one single area, naval policy, Arthur made at least some difference, through a strong commitment to the modernization and rebuilding of the American fleet. His aim was to correct a weakness in foreign policy—namely, the lack of adequate power to make a drive for expanded commerce.

A Strong Hand at Sea and Overseas

When Secretary Frelinghuysen replaced Blaine in November 1880, he inherited a set of tangles caused by the Maine politico's robust sense of America's place in the world. Blaine shared William H. Seward's ambitious Whig vision of the national future: the United States should be a great trading power, supreme in the markets of Latin America, linked to the great undeveloped markets of Asia through commercial treaties, and boasting a chain of protective bases in every ocean. Elements of this star-spangled scheme included an American-dominated canal between the Atlantic and the Pacific, a Pan-American union and reciprocity treaties, and a consensus among the "civilized" powers to share equally in trade with the "backward" nations.

The trouble was that in 1881 these imperial fancies were spun on behalf of a United States with a navy of thirty-seven fighting ships (exclusive of thirteen monitors for coastal defense), thirty-three of which were wooden sailing vessels in an age of armor-plated steamers—a United States, moreover, that had never replaced the merchant marine destroyed during the Civil War and that had no professional diplomatic or consular service. The result was thwarted initiatives at every turn. Blaine had tried to intervene in the War of the Pacific between Chile and Peru—won by Chile—with a strong pro-Peruvian stand. But Chile's navy (built, for the most part, in British yards) was stronger than anything the Americans could put to sea. When Frelinghuysen took over, he had to extricate the United States from the situation, and in 1883 the Peruvians were forced by Chile to accept the harsh Treaty of Ancón. In the same fashion, he had to repudiate Blaine's overtures to help Guatemala in a dispute with Mexico in return for bases and concessions. Frelinghuysen also canceled Blaine's planned Pan-American conference as premature and unlikely to win support.

Frelinghuysen was as taken as Blaine had been with the idea of American capital, machinery, and farm products being used to clothe, feed, and uplift the world's millions, but he was more readily made aware by events that the hour had not yet struck. He was not only battling the nation's military weakness but profound congressional apathy. In 1884 he did secure a treaty with Nicaragua that gave the United States canal rights and a virtual protectorate, but it failed in the Senate even before it could create diplomatic problems with the British. (Both nations had promised by the Clayton-Bulwer Treaty of 1850 that neither would exclude the other from Central America.) He negotiated reciprocity treaties with Mexico, Spain, and Santo Domingo, but Congress would not implement them. He attempted, in 1884, to join an international consortium that would ostensibly open trade with the Congo to the United States on equal terms with other nations, but in the last month of the Arthur administration, Congress rejected the plan. In

the words of the Nation, "the people of the United States want[ed] as little of foreign policy as possible."

Frelinghuysen also encouraged the mission of Commodore Robert Shufeldt to negotiate trade concessions in the "hermit" kingdom of Korea, actually a protectorate of China. Shufeldt and the Chinese foreign minister worked out an agreement in 1882, the Treaty of Chemulpo, but within another two years the Japanese moved in on a footing of "equality" with the Chinese. In time, they would shut both the Chinese and the Americans out. Frelinghuysen hoped for some influence in the Indo-Chinese nations of Annam, Tonkin, and Cambodia, but the French, in 1884, completed the process of making the entire area a de facto colony ruled from Paris, with no outsiders admitted to benefits.

It was clear that the United States had the beginnings of a will to join in the process reaching its climax in the early 1880s, whereby Africa and Asia were carved up for the white man's benefit. It was equally clear that the United States lacked the means to join the feast.

Arthur was at least willing to propose that the country begin to acquire the means. In his 1881 annual message he urged a stronger navy, and the next spring he gave full support to William E. Chandler's vigorous administration of the Navy Department. Chandler pruned the officer corps of superannuated wood-and-canvas devotees and created the Naval War College. He set up a naval advisory board that broke with the idea of coastal defense as the navy's major mission, and submitted a plan for a fleet that could project America's power thousands of miles from its shores. The board followed earlier plans for a fleet of sixty-eight ships, most of them steel-hulled, and recommended commencing with the construction of three armor-plated cruisers with good speed, range, and power, plus a dispatch boat. Congress agreed, and Arthur signed the bill authorizing the construction of the *Atlanta*, the *Boston*, the *Chicago*, and the *Dolphin*. The public nicknamed them the ABCD ships. Chandler was especially pleased that the law allowed him to scrap old vessels whose repair bills exceeded 20 percent of their original cost. "I did my best work," he exulted, "in destroying the old navy."

Chandler himself was notoriously entangled with machine politics (the Republican challenge to the vote for Tilden in 1876 had been his idea), and the favoritism of his contract awards created enough Democratic outrage in Congress to block his request

President Chester A. Arthur takes a break from his duties at the White House to enjoy a rustic picnic with a companion. BETTMANN/CORBIS

for seven more cruisers in 1883, even though no graft was proved. In addition, he failed to get the legislators' support for a string of coaling stations around the world. And only one of the ABCD ships, the *Dolphin*, had been put in commission by the last day of Arthur's term in office.

All the same, the accidental president had set the wheels in motion for the naval revolution of the 1890s, the era of Roosevelt and Mahan. He planted at least some of the seeds they watered. And in his final hours as president he had the pleasure of signing a measure authorizing two more cruisers and two more gunboats.

In all other areas, the Arthur record remained relatively barren. He continued to authorize futile ad-

vances toward building a newer, whiter southern Republican party, though he made some routine patronage appointments of black leaders such as P.B. S. Pinchback and Blanche K. Bruce—veterans of Reconstruction's heyday—to federal posts. But his heart was not in maintaining the old commitments, and when the Supreme Court, in the so-called Civil Rights Cases of 1883, gutted 1875 legislation guaranteeing blacks equal protection of the law, Arthur gave no support to proposed new antisegregation legislation. Although he had some liberal (for that day) notions on the subject of protecting and educating the Indians, they were not translated into any policy that he pressed on Congress.

As convention time in 1884 approached, Arthur had neither a strong record nor many friends to support a reelection bid. His appointments had alienated many Stalwarts without appeasing a significant number of Half-Breeds or winning the hearts of the independent reformers. Neither had he built a public image or constituency; on the contrary, he was conspicuous in his efforts to avoid furnishing good copy to the press. Widowed in January 1880, he lived quietly in the White House, with his little daughter and college-age son, giving elegant state dinners and paying considerable attention to menus and furnishings but yielding nothing to democratic curiosity. "Madam," he once snapped to a visitor, "I may be President of the United States, but my private life is nobody's damned business."

Nominations are not won that way, and though Arthur's name was offered as a candidate when the Republicans convened at Chicago, he was quickly buried in an avalanche of votes for Blaine. It was just as well. He would not have survived his second term. He died only twenty months after leaving the White House, and the mists of oblivion at once began to settle around his tall, portly but handsome Gilded Age figure. His contemporaries seem to have been grateful to him for doing better than they expected. Historians, when they thought of him at all, belatedly came to see his administration—joined to Garfield's tragically short one—as a very modest milestone on the road leading to the heights of the imperial presidencies of the succeeding century.

BIBLIOGRAPHY

Allan Peskin, *Garfield: A Biography* (Kent, Ohio, 1978), is the basic contemporary Garfield biography, in which the author portrays his subject as more emotionally complex, intellectually sophisticated, and politically honest than previous twentieth-century historians had allowed. Thomas C. Reeves, *Gentleman Boss: The Life of Chester Alan Arthur* (New York, 1975), like Peskin's study of Garfield, attempts to bring about an awareness of Arthur's strengths, as well as his celebrated limits.

Justus D. Doenecke, *The Presidencies of James A. Garfield and Chester A. Arthur* (Lawrence, Kans., 1981), is the most basic study of the two presidents involved, upwardly revising their previous reputations and furnished with a complete bibliography. John A. Garraty, *The New Commonwealth, 1877–1890* (New York, 1968), a brief, thorough survey of the period described, furnishes a good broad background for understanding the issues of the two administrations. Leonard D. White, *The Republican Era, 1869–1901: A Study in Administrative History* (New York, 1958), part of a general history of the organization and powers of the executive department, is a valuable background for understanding, in administrative terms, what was expected of presidents and the resources available to them in the period during which Garfield and Arthur served. David M. Pletcher, *The Awkward Years: American Foreign Policy Under Garfield and Arthur* (Columbia, Mo., 1962), is the major source for the diplomatic history of the two administrations, contending that the period marked the necessary, if sometimes clumsy, prelude to the more coherent expansionist policies of the century's end.

Morton Keller, *Affairs of State: Public Life in Late-Nineteenth-Century America* (Cambridge, Mass., 1977), sets political behavior in the overall context of American cultural attitudes and expectations, in order to derive fresh understanding of familiar material whose interpretation was long taken for granted. H. Wayne Morgan, *The Gilded Age: A Reappraisal*, rev. ed. (Syracuse, N.Y., 1970), is a collection of essays in which different aspects of the 1877–1896 era are newly examined by different scholars, and long-held stereotypes are challenged; Morgan's *From Hayes to McKinley: National Party Politics, 1877–1896* (Syracuse, N.Y., 1969), focuses on a specific reexamination of party politics in the same revisionist spirit that marks the essays in *The Gilded Age*. These may be usefully supplemented by Ari Hoogenboom, *Rutherford B. Hayes: Warrior and President* (Lawrence, Kans., 1995).

David J. Rothman, *Politics and Power: The United States Senate, 1869–1901* (Cambridge, Mass., 1966), is a penetrating examination of how the powerful bosses in the Senate established, maintained, and defended their prerogatives against presidents, reformers, and other challengers. David M. Jordan, *Roscoe Conkling of New York: Voice in the Senate* (Ithaca, N.Y., 1971), is a biography of Arthur's patron and Garfield's powerful opponent, incorporating recent scholarship to improve on a livelier but older biography by Donald Barr Chidsey. David S. Muzzey, *James G. Blaine: A Political Idol of Other Days* (New York, 1934), a careful, old-fashioned "life and times" of the charismatic and controversial Blaine, who sought to be Garfield's éminence grise, has surprisingly not been supplanted by a modern study and well deserves attention.

Ari Hoogenboom, *Outlawing the Spoils: A History of the Civil Service Reform Movement, 1865–1883*

(Urbana, Ill., 1961), focuses on the political ramifications of the patronage system and of the alliances among its ultimately successful critics. Stanley P. Hirshson, *Farewell to the Bloody Shirt: Northern Republicans and the Southern Negro, 1877–1893* (Gloucester, Mass., 1968), a study of the Republican "change of base" from reliance on black votes after Reconstruction ended, usefully illustrates what dilemmas the move posed for four Republican presidents, including Garfield and Arthur. Two recent works contain the story of how early steps in the modernization of the United States Navy were taken during Arthur's tenure in office: Stephen Howarth, *To Shining Sea: A History of the United States Navy, 1775–1991* (New York, 1991), and Kenneth J. Hagan, *This People's Navy: The Making of American Sea Power* (New York and Toronto, 1991).

Charles E. Rosenberg, *The Trial of the Assassin Guiteau: Psychiatry and Law in the Gilded Age* (Chicago, 1968), though it is somewhat tangential to the story of the Garfield and Arthur administrations, is a fascinating portrait of a disturbed killer and of the still unsolved dilemma of what is "just" in dealing with such a personality.

Grover Cleveland

John A. Garraty

Grover Cleveland THE LIBRARY OF CONGRESS

O F all the presidents, Grover Cleveland is unique in several ways. Only he, having been defeated in a bid for reelection, again won the highest office in the land; thus, he was both the twenty-second president and the twenty-fourth. Actually, he "won" all three of the presidential elections in which he was a candidate, for while Benjamin Harrison carried the Electoral College in 1888, Cleveland had a popular plurality of about 100,000 votes. Cleveland also has the distinction of having won a presidential contest by the smallest popular margin in history—about 30,000 votes in 1884.

Cleveland was unusual, if not unique, in the rapidity of his rise from obscurity to the White House.

In 1881 he was a Buffalo lawyer. He was a diligent worker and modestly successful, but he did not appear to be particularly ambitious. When offered a substantial retainer by a railroad official, he refused on the ground that he already had a comfortable income. "No amount of money would tempt me to add to or increase my present work," he explained. As for politics, he had been an assistant district attorney for a brief period during the Civil War and had served a three-year term as sheriff in the early 1870s. But it was eight years since he had last held office. Outside Buffalo he was unknown.

Cleveland was a bachelor and at forty-four showed no sign of marrying. He spent most of his free time with what was known at the time as a "coarse crowd"—men who frequented saloons and racetracks. He spent weekends and holidays hunting and fishing. Physically he was a squat, bull-like man with a thick neck and a great chest and belly. Although of only medium height, he weighed more than 250 pounds. He was without important intellectual interests.

There were also two skeletons in Grover Cleveland's closet that might have been expected to prevent his achieving important public office. During the Civil War he had hired a substitute when drafted into the army. This was perfectly legal but certainly a disadvantage at a time when most successful northern politicians made much of their military achievements in defense of the Union. More serious still, Cleveland was the father of an illegitimate child. He had provided for the support of the child, but in those Victorian times knowledge of his transgression, should it become widely known, seemed sure to cost him heavily at the polls. Yet three years later he was elected president of the United States.

One of Cleveland's biographers, Horace Samuel Merrill, has explained his political rise simply: "He was lucky—almost unbelievably lucky!" This is true enough, but scarcely an explanation; no one gets to be president without being more than ordinarily favored by Dame Fortune. And his good luck was not merely the kind that comes to the person with a winning lottery ticket. He had the right qualities (and they were not common) for the situations and opportunities that came to him by chance.

A Swift Rise to the Presidency

For years the city government of Buffalo had been corrupt and badly managed, and it seemed to make no difference whether it was run by Democrats or Republicans. In 1881 a group of substantial Buffalonians, seeking a candidate for mayor who was both honest and efficient, hit upon Cleveland, whose record as sheriff was unbesmirched. The current administration was Republican. Cleveland was a Democrat, though unconnected with the then-current Democratic organization. He was not eager for the office but responded to the call to perform his civic duty. He was easily elected.

The reformers sought no more than honesty and efficiency; Cleveland shared their desire, promised to satisfy it, and made good on his promise. In office he devoted himself almost entirely to keeping the fingers of local spoilsmen out of the public till. He did this principally by vetoing measures that misappropriated and wasted city funds, such as a bill giving a street-cleaning contract to a company whose bid was more than $100,000 higher than those of two others. This was enough to bring him statewide fame. Soon Buffalo's "Veto Mayor" was a candidate for governor of New York. Being an upstater, he was independent of the notorious Tammany Hall Democratic machine in New York City. When the Republicans nominated for governor a candidate handpicked by President Chester A. Arthur, the Democrats turned to what one Democratic leader called the "buxom Buffalonian." In November 1882, Cleveland won by nearly 200,000 votes, which in those days of closely contested elections amounted to a landslide.

As with his service as mayor, Cleveland proved to be an enormous, if anything but brilliant, success as governor. His success was the result mainly of his indifference to narrow political advantage. He vetoed a bill lowering fares on the New York City elevated railway because it was a violation of contract. Another measure limiting the hours of streetcar conductors received his veto on similar grounds. Both these bills had wide public support. Yet Cleveland's uncompromising rejection of them, so clearly in disregard of possible political consequences, actually added to his stature in the public eye. His equally uncompromising refusal to grant any patronage to Tammany Hall, despite Tammany's demonstrated ability to swing the balance in state elections, had a similar effect.

Cleveland's achievements as governor were almost entirely negative, but within a matter of months he was being considered a serious candidate for the 1884 Democratic presidential nomination. Of course, more was involved than his reputation for honesty and political courage. Since the Civil War, most of the northern states had voted Republican in presidential elections, and the southern states Democratic. The balance was delicate; victory had depended on carrying a handful of closely contested states—in particular, New York and Indiana. It usually made political sense for the parties to choose candidates from these states because voters tended to favor local men over less-well-known ones. Except in 1880, the Democrats nominated a New Yorker for president in every election from 1868 through 1892.

Although Cleveland fought corrupt machine politicians without regard for party, he was shrewd enough to make solid political alliances with respectable New York Democratic leaders, such as Daniel Manning, a close associate of the aging Samuel J. Tilden, the party's standard-bearer in 1876, and William C. Whitney, another anti-Tammany Democrat. At the national convention in Chicago, Cleveland was nominated on the second ballot. The convention then chose Thomas A. Hendricks, who was a former governor of another key state, Indiana, as the Democratic vice presidential candidate. (Hendricks had run for vice president on the ticket with Tilden in 1876 and was credited with having had much to do with the Democrats carrying Indiana in that contest.)

The 1884 presidential contest was exciting at the time and has fascinated historians ever since. The Republican candidate, James G. Blaine of Maine, was Cleveland's mirror image. Where Cleveland had little previous political experience, Blaine had been Speaker of the House of Representatives, United States senator, and secretary of state. Where Cleveland was blunt, somewhat stiff, unimaginative, and scrupulously honest, Blaine was colorful, hail-fellow-well-met, a font of interesting ideas, and not averse to using his political influence to line his pockets.

Because of this last quality, many Republicans, known as Mugwumps, supported Cleveland. On the other hand, Blaine was popular with Irish-Americans, who usually voted Democratic, because he was thought to be anti-British. Their votes in New York City, where, in addition, the Tammany machine was suspected of giving Cleveland only lukewarm support, might swing the state to the Republicans despite Cleveland's appeal as a native son.

The Democratic strategy was to describe Blaine, who in the face of much hard evidence blandly denied that he had sold political favors, as "the continental liar from the State of Maine" and to stress Cleveland's honesty and efficiency. In this way they hoped to appeal to the Mugwumps and other voters dismayed by Blaine's unsavory reputation and to paper over divisions within their own ranks on issues such as the tariff and currency reform. The Republicans countered by calling Cleveland "the hangman of Buffalo" because, while sheriff, he had personally hanged two criminals rather than turn the task over to an assistant. More important, they exposed his fathering of an illegitimate child: "Ma! ma! Where's my pa? Gone to the White House, Ha! Ha! Ha!" The candidate made the best of this bad situation in typical fashion. "Whatever you do, tell the truth," he advised a friend who asked him how the charge should be dealt with.

Exactly how this and other incidents in an incident-filled campaign affected the result is beyond knowing. Suffice it to say that the election turned on New York's electoral vote, that Blaine did well in Irish-American districts in the state, that there was much Mugwump support for Cleveland, and that Cleveland carried the state by fewer than 1,200 votes. In other words, a shift of 600 votes would have made Blaine president.

First Presidential Term

Cleveland gave the country exactly the sort of administration that might have been expected—honest, conservative, and unimaginative. His cabinet was made up of hardworking and public-spirited men who ran their departments efficiently. Thomas F. Bayard of Delaware was secretary of state, and Daniel Manning of New York, secretary of the treasury. The other members were William C. Whitney, secretary of the navy; William C. Endicott, secretary of war; Augustus H. Garland, attorney general; William F. Vilas, postmaster general; and L. C. Q. Lamar, secretary of the interior. Lamar, who came from Mississippi, and Garland, a resident of Arkansas, were the first southerners appointed to cabinet posts since the Civil War. As the first Democrat in the White House since the Civil War, Cleveland also appointed many other southerners to lesser federal posts.

The change from Republican to Democratic control of the government meant that Cleveland was subjected to enormous pressures from members of his party seeking government posts. Yet, his campaign promises had encouraged Mugwumps to expect him to expand the scope of the new Pendleton Civil Service Act and refrain from discharging Republicans merely to make places for his own supporters. The president found it impossible to satisfy both points of view, in part because he had no clear idea of how the civil service should be staffed. He announced that no one would be fired without cause and that only properly qualified people would replace those who were discharged. In his usual, conscientious way, he devoted much time to going over the records of applicants and weighing the merits of candidates for both major and minor posts. The task both bored and distressed him. He was soon complaining of "the damned, everlasting clatter for office."

His concept of what it meant to be properly qualified was partisan and (still worse) out of date. "Reasonable intelligence" and a decent grade-school education were the only "credentials to office" that most federal jobs required, he told the head of the Civil Service Commission. He also believed in the old Jacksonian system of rotation in office. Since public service was a privilege and a duty in a democracy, any officeholder might be "rotated" after four years to make room for someone else. Starting with what he called "offensive partisans," which in practice came even to include Republicans whose offense had consisted only of campaigning for Blaine, the administration gradually removed most of the government workers who had not been given job security under the Pendleton Act. Mugwumps and others who had hoped that Cleveland would greatly expand the coverage of the act were bitterly disappointed.

Like the other presidents of the era, Cleveland had a rather narrow view of the scope of presidential authority. "The office of the President is essentially executive in its nature," he said. He did not believe it proper "to meddle" with proposed legislation. "It don't look as though Congress was very well prepared to do anything," Cleveland wrote in December 1885. "If a botch is made at the other end of the Avenue, I don't mean to be a party to it." This attitude was a convenient way to avoid getting involved in politically controversial matters, especially for a Democrat, since the party was made up of many disparate and often antagonistic groups. But in his case the attitude was heartfelt.

He was, nonetheless, perfectly willing to resist congressional actions he disapproved of. Just as he had in Buffalo and Albany, he vetoed bills he disliked with evident relish. He repeatedly rejected private bills and pork-barrel legislation. His most significant action of this sort was probably his veto of the Dependent Pension Bill of 1887, a measure that would have granted pensions even to the needy parents of men who had died while in service.

Although a number of important laws were passed during his term, Cleveland had little to do with most of them other than to add his signature after Congress had acted. These included the Interstate Commerce Act of 1887; the Dawes Severalty Act of 1887, which invested Indians with American citizenship and assigned plots of reservation lands to individual, rather than tribal, Indian ownership; and a law of 1889 raising the Department of Agriculture to cabinet status. Cleveland favored these measures but did little to shape them.

Aside from his attitude toward presidential power, which was common in his day, Cleveland lacked some other qualities that make a good leader. He really did not much enjoy being president, and he found the give-and-take necessary for success in politics positively objectionable He got on badly with reporters, resenting their inquisitiveness and tendency to sensationalize the most trivial events. He was poor at delegating authority. Despite—or perhaps because of—his earlier convivial habits, he was something of a loner in the White House. He had no taste for speechmaking and handshaking, or for crowds, official social gatherings, and the punctilio of receptions. Some of this changed after his marriage in 1886 to Frances Folsom, the daughter of his former law partner. He was forty-nine and the bride only twenty-three, but the marriage proved to be happy and fruitful.

The most difficult issue that Cleveland faced during his first term involved the government's finances and their effect on the condition of the nation's economy. The country was expanding in wealth and population at a rapid rate, but the supply of money in circulation was not keeping up with this growth. The result was a steady and apparently relentless deflation that injured anyone who was in debt, a classification that included large numbers of farmers who worked mortgaged land, often with machinery purchased with borrowed money. To deal with this problem, Congress passed the Bland-Allison Act of 1878, which increased the amount of money in circulation by purchasing and coining large amounts of silver. Many conservatives, Cleveland among them, feared that "inflating" the currency in this manner would so frighten investors and businessmen that it would cause a depression.

Cleveland proposed to deal with the problem by ending government purchases of silver and reducing tariffs on foreign goods. Lower duties would mean lower prices for consumers and would reduce the embarrassing surplus that had accumulated in the treasury, which was a further drain on the amount of currency in circulation. When Congress failed to act on the tariff, Cleveland decided to force the issue. He summoned what became known as the Oak View Conference, a series of meetings with Democratic congressional leaders at Oak View, his summer residence outside Washington. At these meetings he persuaded the congressmen to draft an effective tariff-reduction bill. Then he took an unprecedented step: he devoted his entire annual message to Congress on 6 December 1887 to a call for tariff reduction. The current rates were a "vicious, inequitable,

President Cleveland wed Frances Folsom in the White House on 12 June 1886. THE LIBRARY OF CONGRESS

and illogical source of unnecessary taxation." Protected by these high duties, manufacturers were making "immense" profits. If the duties were lowered, "the necessaries of life used and consumed by all the people . . . should be greatly cheapened."

Normally the annual messages to Congress required of presidents by the Constitution were routine summaries of the activities of the various departments and grab bags from which the legislators might draw suggestions for future actions. By centering on one important issue, Cleveland focused national attention on that issue.

Unfortunately he failed to follow up on this dramatic step. In July 1888, Roger Q. Mills of Texas, the chairman of the House Ways and Means Committee, introduced a bill removing the duties on raw wool, lumber, salt, copper ore, tinplate, and several other products, and reducing the duties on such important items as iron and steel, sugar, and woolen cloth. But Cleveland did nothing to press the issue after the bill was introduced. He did not use his influence with congressmen. He refused even to make speeches on

the subject or to issue further statements explaining what he thought should be done. The Mills bill passed the House of Representatives but was defeated in the Senate. The tariff question therefore became the main issue in the presidential election of 1888.

Loss to Benjamin Harrison and Subsequent Reelection

The Republicans responded to Cleveland's challenge. Nominating Senator Benjamin Harrison of Indiana for president and Levi P. Morton of New York as his running mate, they waged an aggressive campaign in which they boldly defended the principle of protective tariffs. Whereas Cleveland considered it beneath his dignity to campaign actively, Harrison made nearly a hundred speeches covering every subject from the tariff and veterans' pensions to the sterling character of Abraham Lincoln and his own fondness for small children. Much money was spent on the campaign, and there was perhaps more than

[285]

the usual amount of corruption and trickery. A clever Republican wrote a letter to the British minister in Washington, Sir Lionel Sackville-West, in which he pretended to be a naturalized citizen of British birth named Murchison. In it he asked the minister if he thought Cleveland would pursue a pro-British policy if reelected. Sir Lionel incautiously responded, his letter (released to the press by the gleeful Republicans) indicating a preference for Cleveland. This "Murchison letter" was thought to cost the Democrats heavily among Irish-American voters. But the tariff was clearly the main issue on which the election was contested.

The outcome was monumentally frustrating for Cleveland and for his party. By carrying both New York and Indiana by narrow margins, Harrison obtained a majority in the Electoral College (233–168) and thus the presidency. But Cleveland won the states of the Deep South by exceptionally large margins. This gave him about 100,000 more popular votes than his opponent.

Some Democratic observers thought that Cleveland would have won if he had waited until after the election to bring forth the tariff issue. He responded to this argument in typical fashion. "I did not wish to be reelected without having the people understand just where I stood," he said. "Perhaps I made a mistake from the party standpoint; but damn it, it was right." After leaving office he settled his growing family in New York City, where he joined a prominent law firm. He made occasional innocuous speeches and maintained his contacts with prominent politicians, mostly through correspondence.

Under Harrison, the Republicans proceeded to raise the tariff and to deal with the surplus by appropriating large sums for pensions and for public works of various sorts and other pork-barrel projects. They also put through the Sherman Silver Purchase Act of 1890, which committed the government to buying 4.5 million ounces of silver a month. Altogether, Congress spent over $1 billion in 1890, by far the largest one-year outlay in the nation's history up to that time.

Public reaction to the work of the "Billion-Dollar Congress"—especially to the new McKinley Tariff, which appeared to raise the cost of many goods—was profound. In the 1890 congressional elections the Democrats swept the House of Representatives and made large gains in the Senate. It seemed likely that they would win back the presidency in 1892.

The McKinley Tariff and the free-spending legislation of the "Billion-Dollar Congress" made Cleveland eager for another term. His identification with tariff reduction and economy in government gave him made-to-order issues. But when large numbers of Democrats voted for a bill providing for the unlimited coinage of silver in 1891, he spoke out strongly against the measure, despite warnings that he would alienate southern and western members of the party. Once again, his frankness in tackling a controversial issue head-on probably helped more than it damaged his chances. In any case, the 1892 Democratic convention nominated him on the first ballot. Adlai E. Stevenson of Illinois was its vice presidential choice.

The campaign of 1892 was a three-cornered contest, for the new Peoples, or Populist, party had entered the race. The Populists nominated James B. Weaver of Iowa and came out for a long list of reforms ranging from the direct election of United States senators and a federal income tax to government ownership of the railroads. The Populist plank that attracted the most attention called for the unlimited coinage of silver.

As was his fashion, Cleveland did not campaign actively. He mended his fences with most of the important Democratic politicians and on election day won a sweeping victory. The electoral vote was 277 to 145, and he polled nearly 400,000 more popular votes than Harrison, the largest plurality in a presidential election since Grant defeated Greeley in 1872—this despite the fact that Weaver received over a million popular votes on the Populist ticket. The Democrats also won control of both houses of Congress.

Cleveland named Walter Q. Gresham of Indiana as his secretary of state. The rest of his second-term cabinet consisted of John G. Carlisle as secretary of the treasury, Daniel S. Lamont as secretary of war, Hilary A. Herbert as secretary of the navy, Wilson S. Bissel as postmaster general, Hoke Smith as secretary of the interior, and J. Sterling Morton as secretary of the new Department of Agriculture.

Domestic Policy in the Second Term

This great victory was partly the result of a serious economic depression, but that depression did not go away merely because the Democrats now controlled the government. The first weeks of the new administration were marked by bank failures, the collapse of important corporations, and a rapid shrinking of the supply of gold in the treasury as worried citizens exchanged paper currency for the precious metal. Unemployment mounted.

Cleveland believed that all would be well if "confidence" could be restored and that the way to restore it was to repeal the Silver Purchase Act of 1890. The steady addition of silver-based money was, he believed, threatening the country with inflation and inhibiting investment. "You cannot prevent a frightened man from hoarding his money," he said. "I want . . . our currency so safe and reassuring that those who have money will spend and invest it in business and new enterprises, instead of holding it."

In Congress resistance to repeal was strong. The Democratic party was badly split on the question, since many southern and western Democrats were being squeezed by the continued price deflation and saw in silver the one hope of ending it. Particularly in the Senate, where the sparsely populated western silver-mining states had more influence than in the House, pressure on the president to accept some compromise grew rapidly.

Cleveland would not yield an inch. Repeat became for him a matter of principle, and opposition to it "shameful." He, who had so vigorously denounced influence peddling and the use of patronage to compel political obedience, used his power to grant or withhold offices and other favors ruthlessly. When Democratic Congressman Willam Jennings Bryan of Nebraska warned him that repeal of the Silver Purchase Act would "injure the party" in his state, Cleveland responded by refusing to appoint Bryan supporters to local offices. "One thing may as well be distinctly understood by Democrats in Congress who are heedless of the burdens and responsibilities of the incoming administration," he explained to a friend. "They must not expect us to 'turn the other cheek' by rewarding their conduct with patronage." In the end he had his way, but only after splitting his own party and reducing drastically his ability to influence later legislation.

The repeal of the Silver Purchase Act on 30 October 1893 marked as fateful a turning point in Cleveland's career as his election as mayor of Buffalo. What he saw as a stand for principle and a do-or-die defense of sound economic policy, others considered stubbornness and arrogance. One Arkansas Democrat called him a "360—pound tool of plutocracy." The governor of South Carolina compared his "betrayal" of the Democratic party to Judas' betrayal of Jesus. A senator predicted that if Cleveland were running for president at that time, he "could not have carried a single electoral vote south of the Potomac." All these charges were as exaggerated as the Arkansan's estimate of the president's weight, which had never much exceeded 250 pounds. (Cleveland's weight was somewhat below that figure in 1893 because he had recently undergone an operation for cancer of the mouth and had lost a considerable amount during his convalescence.)

Cleveland was conservative and he fought hard for what he believed right, but he was not a tool of the rich or an opinionated tyrant. He was certainly not arrogant. His fault was more narrowness of vision than simple stubbornness. He was unable to grasp the fact that others felt as deeply as he about what should be done—that, for example, the farmers in Willam Jennings Bryan's Nebraska district were far more concerned with how their congressman voted on silver than with whether or not he had a few federal jobs to hand out. He could not see beyond the immediate issue of repeal of a bad law or appreciate the possibility that repeal might, on the one hand, have unforeseen bad effects or, on the other, have no effect at all on the nation's economic problems. The historian Stanley L. Jones goes so far as to say that Cleveland failed "to understand the . . . social and economic changes that were taking place in the nation."

Stopping the purchase of silver did not end the drain of gold from the treasury. Since the silver certificates already in circulation could be exchanged for gold, frightened citizens continued to take advantage of that fact. Several times Cleveland had to authorize the sale of gold bonds by the treasury to replenish the reserve. But the drain continued until early 1895, when Cleveland negotiated the sale of $62 million in gold bonds with a syndicate dominated by J. P. Morgan, one of the terms being Morgan's personal promise to find at least half of the gold abroad. This Morgan bond deal brought down a new wave of criticism on the president, the charge being that it was demeaning to make the credit of the United States dependent on the cooperation of a private banker.

More seriously, repeal of the Silver Purchase Act did not restore the confidence of investors or anyone else. The economic situation got worse instead of better. Cleveland might plausibly have argued that the depression had begun before he took office and was caused by the policies of his predecessor. Instead, he continued to insist that no government could do much about the depression beyond making sure that the nation's currency was "sound." His attitude was not unusual. It was probably shared by a large majority of the citizenry. Certainly most of Cleveland's opponents had no better understanding of what could or should be done about the depression than he, but Cleveland seemed to go out of his way to stress his administration's impotence. In his second inaugural address he said, "While the people should patriotically support their Government its functions do not include the support of the people." This was both trite and bad psychology. Experience in office had taught Cleveland that presidents have a great deal of power. He had learned to wield that power but not how to use it constructively.

In forcing through the repeal bill, Cleveland exhausted a good deal of his influence with members of Congress who disagreed with his policies. His heart was set on lowering the tariff and the unpopularity of the high McKinley Tariff of 1890 seemed to make reduction easy. A new bill that embodied the kind of changes he desired was passed by the House early in 1894. But in the Senate, protectionists attached hundreds of amendments that undermined what the House had accomplished. Though Cleveland strove mightily against these changes, he could not command the support of many Democratic senators. He accused these deserters of "party perfidy and party dishonor," but that only caused them to dig in their heels more firmly. In the end the new Wilson-Gorman Tariff became law without his signature.

Cleveland's political ineptness was also demonstrated by his handling of the great Pullman strike that occurred during the spring and summer of 1894. The Pullman company manufactured and operated sleeping and dining cars used on all the nation's railroads. Its workers went on strike in May, in protest against a wage cut. That strike would not have been of concern to the federal government but for the fact that the American Railway Union, responding to the strikers' appeal, refused to move trains carrying Pullman cars. Soon rail traffic west of Chicago was paralyzed.

Cleveland was deeply involved at the time with efforts to reduce the tariff, so he delegated dealing with the strike to Attorney General Richard Olney. Olney, a former railroad lawyer, considered all labor unions undesirable and was determined to break the strike. After consulting with representatives of the railroads, he sought and obtained from a federal judge an injunction forbidding the strikers from in-

terfering with the movement of mail. But the strike continued. The situation in and around Chicago became increasingly tense. Olney had arranged for army units to be sent to the Chicago area, and on 3 July, the day after the issuance of the injunction, Cleveland ordered these troops into the city to preserve order.

The governor of Illinois, John Peter Altgeld, who was personally sympathetic to the strikers, bitterly resented Cleveland's action. He believed that local and state authorities were capable of preserving order. He dashed off a telegram to the president denying his right to use troops without gubernatorial consent.

Cleveland's response was categorical. "I have neither transcended my authority nor duty.. . . In this hour of danger and public distress, discussion may well give way to active efforts on the part of all in authority to restore obedience to the law and to protect life and property."

Cleveland's action was understandable, and he was not a dupe of Olney, as some historians have claimed. Furthermore, his stern defense of the use of troops won wide public support. But the decision to use force was a mistake on two grounds: it did not preserve order, and it further disrupted the already divided Democratic party. For two days mobs rampaged in Chicago, burning railroad cars and buildings. Governor Altgeld, furious at Cleveland both because the president had failed to consult him before sending in troops and because of the federal government's favoritism toward the rail-road owners, threw his formidable influence against the administration. The strike was effectively broken, as perhaps was necessary after the injunction was ignored by the leader of the union, Eugene V. Debs. But the "solution" was entirely too extreme for anyone's good: Debs was thrown in jail, the American Railway Union collapsed, and middle-class opinion turned sharply against organized labor to the ultimate disadvantage of both labor and the middle class.

Foreign Policy in the Second Term

By 1895, Cleveland was almost without a friend in the southern and western wings of the Democratic party. More and more he was identified with the ultraconservative, or Bourbon, faction that dominated the party in the Northeast. Only in matters of foreign policy did his tendency to take an uncompromising stand for what he considered morally right bring him any real popular support.

Shortly before Cleveland's second term began, a group of Americans in the Hawaiian Islands had staged a successful coup, ousting the Hawaiian ruler, Queen Liliuokalani, with the aid of marines from the USS *Boston*. The new government sought annexation by the United States. American public opinion seemed enthusiastic, and a treaty was negotiated and sent to the Senate shortly before Cleveland's inauguration.

Cleveland asked the Senate to delay action until he had time to study the question. He sent a special commissioner, James H. Blount, to the islands to look into the circumstances surrounding the revolution. When Blount reported that the American minister in Hawaii had cooperated with the rebels and that the native population appeared to oppose the new government, Cleveland withdrew the treaty.

Once again Cleveland had taken an "unpopular" stand as a matter of principle, and once again his political courage paid off. Most Americans may have favored the idea of expansion into the Pacific, but they accepted the president's reasoning that it was wrong to overthrow the Hawaiian government in order to do so. One editor described the so-called revolution as an example of "the cheat-your-washerwoman style of diplomacy."

Cleveland's second important diplomatic foray was of a far different character. For many years the boundary between Venezuela and the South American colony of British Guiana had been in dispute. The British government, insisting that there was no substance to the Venezuelan claim, refused to submit the case to arbitration, despite somewhat sporadic pressure to do so by the United States. The territory in question was an almost uninhabited jungle, but when gold was discovered there, it suddenly became important—in part because pressure for coining silver in the United States might ease if the world supply of gold were significantly increased.

In any case, in 1894 and 1895 the Cleveland administration was taking an increasingly stern tone in its communications on the subject with Great Britain. By early 1895 these messages included such phrases as "palpably unjust" and "call a halt." Finally, in July 1895, Cleveland authorized the dispatch of a note drafted by Richard Olney, who was then secretary of state. This note warned that if Britain took or held any territory that was rightfully part of Venezuela, the United States would consider that act a violation of the Monroe Doctrine. If Britain refused to arbitrate the dispute, Cleveland hinted, the United States might well declare war.

The tone of this message was particularly offensive, but the British government was neither offended nor moved by it. The idea of a war between the United States and Great Britain over a relatively minor piece of South American real estate seemed preposterous. The British delayed answering the note until November and then flatly refused arbitration. They denied that the Monroe Doctrine gave the United States any special interest in the matter.

No president could accept such a slap in the face, least of all one like Cleveland. He therefore took the even more extraordinary step of asking Congress for an appropriation to finance an American investigation to determine the proper boundary between Venezuela and British Guiana. After that had been done, the United States would "resist by every means in its power as a willful aggression . . . the appropriation by Great Britain of any land . . . we have determined of right belongs to Venezuela."

Despite its boldness, this strategy was really quite shrewd. No American superpatriot could have asked for a stronger response. Yet by calling for an investigation, Cleveland was postponing indefinitely the possibility of having to enforce his threat. The affair "cannot become serious for some time," one British official noted.

Nevertheless, the threat was there, and faced with it, the British backed down. Obviously, they had not taken Cleveland's original blustering to heart, in part because they had interpreted it as designed primarily for domestic purposes—an attempt to curry favor among Irish-American voters. When they realized that the president was not bluffing, they agreed to arbitration of the boundary dispute.

In the end the affair had a happy resolution for both the United States and Great Britain, though not for Venezuela, because the arbitration tribunal awarded nearly all the disputed territory to Britain. Cleveland, as his biographer Allan Nevins wrote, had been "determined to get a prompt settlement of the question in harmony with his principles of justice and his interpretation of the Monroe Doctrine, and by his smashing blow on the table he got it." The British learned that they must take the United States seriously as a world power; and the Americans, sobered by the thought of an Anglo-American war, ceased to practice so blithely the political sport known as twisting the British lion's tail. Secretary Olney, with Cleveland's approval, was soon mentioning "our inborn and instinctive English sympathies" in communications with British officials.

Whether or not Cleveland took the position he did on the Venezuela boundary in hopes of restoring his political fortunes and papering over the split that had developed in his party over the silver issue is a question still in dispute among historians. If he did so, the tactic failed. By early 1896 his adamant stand against any plan for inflating the currency was rapidly causing him to lose control over his own party. The prolonged depression, the worst the nation had suffered up to that point, made things difficult for the party in power to begin with. But southern and western Democrats, in debt and suffering heavy losses as the prices of farm products sank lower and lower, were turning to leaders who were calling for the free coinage of silver.

The more strident this call, the more determined Cleveland was to resist it. "The line of battle is drawn between the forces of safe currency and those of silver monometallism," he said. He could draw such a line, but he could not hold it. In July the Democrats nominated Willam Jennings Bryan for president and adopted a campaign platform calling for the free coinage of silver.

The Republicans nominated William McKinley and came out squarely for the gold standard. So profound was Cleveland's opposition to free silver that he preferred to see McKinley elected. He heartily approved of the Bourbon Democrats' decision to form what they called the National Democratic party and nominate their own presidential candidate, Senator John M. Palmer of Illinois. Palmer was seventy-nine years old, and no one, least of all Palmer, expected him to do anything except draw off votes of diehard Democrats who opposed Bryan but who were unwilling to vote for a Republican.

Cleveland expressed relief "that the glorious principles of the party have found defenders who will not permit them to be polluted by impious hands." He made no public statement only because he feared that, if he did, he would "further alienate" the pro-silver Democrats in Congress and limit his effectiveness in dealing with other issues.

After McKinley's election—which, Cleveland said, gave supporters of "the cause of sound money . . . abundant reason for rejoicing"—Cleveland eagerly awaited the end of his term. His last significant act was to veto a bill excluding immigrants who could not read and write some language.

Retirement

After he left the White House, Cleveland settled in Princeton, New Jersey. He continued to follow political events closely. During the controversy about annexing the Philippine Islands, he spoke out strongly against the "craze" and "mad rush" for colonial expansion. In 1898 he was one of the original honorary, vice presidents of the Anti-Imperialist League. Over the years he wrote many magazine articles on aspects of his own presidency and on current issues. Some of these were published in his book *Presidential Problems*, but none is memorable. On most questions, as Allan Nevins put it, Cleveland's position was a combination of common sense and conservatism. By far the most interesting of his retirement writings are his articles on hunting and fishing, collected in his *Fishing and Shooting Sketches*.

Cleveland enjoyed a long and happy retirement. The Princeton academic community gave him a warm welcome, and soon he was taking as deep an interest in the affairs of the school as the most enthusiastic alumnus. He accepted an honorary degree (while president he had refused all such honors) and in 1901 was elected to the Princeton board of trustees.

In 1904, Cleveland became chairman of the trustee committee of the graduate school. This made him a central figure in the conflict over the location of the graduate school that developed between Woodrow Wilson, then president of Princeton, and the dean of the graduate school, Andrew Fleming West. In this controversy Cleveland supported West. The dean had been instrumental in bringing Cleveland to Princeton, and the two were fast friends. (Cleveland even named his Princeton home Westland.) But he would probably have opposed Wilson's policies in any case; on university matters, as in nearly all others, he was a staunch conservative.

Cleveland died in Princeton on 24 June 1908. By that date he was admired and almost revered by the public; the bitter feelings generated by his sound-money policies in the 1890s had evaporated. Since his death his reputation has fluctuated with changing national tastes and interests. In the 1920s and 1930s it was at a high point; in the eyes of most historians, he stood among the near-great American presidents. After the Great Depression and World War II, his reputation fell because his deep commitment to limited government and his obsession with maintaining the gold standard seemed hopelessly reactionary. In recent years his place in the presidential hierarchy has risen somewhat, as the national mood has swung again in a conservative direction.

Popularity, of course, was never as important to Cleveland as doing what he considered right. And this commitment and the courage to maintain it remain his most admirable qualities. Cleveland was in many ways remarkably limited; he certainly lacked imagination, and he found it difficult to expose his inner self to all but a handful of close friends. He was anything but creative. But in industriousness and in devotion to principle and to the public good as he saw it, he has had few equals among American presidents.

BIBLIOGRAPHY

The Cleveland papers are in the Library of Congress. The standard biography of Cleveland is Allan Nevins, *Grover Cleveland: A Study in Courage* (New York, 1932); it is accurate, detailed, and well written, but it takes Cleveland too much on his own terms and is consequently rather old-fashioned and lacking in insight on some questions. Nevins also edited a useful volume of Cleveland's correspondence, *Letters of Grover Cleveland, 1850–1908* (New York, 1933). A more critical, if rather brief, life is Horace Samuel Merrill, *Bourbon Leader: Grover Cleveland and the Democratic Party* (Boston, 1957). Robert M. McElroy, *Grover Cleveland: The Man and the Statesman*, 2 vols. (New York, 1923), the first full-length biography, is uncritical. See also George F. Parker, *Recollections of Grover Cleveland* (New York, 1909).

There are many excellent studies of the political events of the Cleveland years. Harold U. Faulkner, *Politics, Reform, and Expansion: 1890–1900* (New York, 1959), is a general survey of the period that also contains a full bibliography listing the principal biographies of Cleveland's contemporaries. These works throw much light on Cleveland as well as their subjects. J. Rogers Hollingsworth, *The Whirligig of Politics: The Democracy of Cleveland and Bryan* (Chicago, 1963), is useful, as is Samuel T. McSeveney, *The Politics of Depression: Political Behavior in the Northeast, 1893–1896* (New York, 1972).

Broader in scope are Matthew Josephson, *The Politicos: 1865–1896* (New York, 1938), which, while overly critical of just about all the political leaders of the time and of the era itself, is lively and insightful, and H. Wayne Morgan, *From Hayes to McKinley: National Party Politics, 1877–1896* (Syracuse, N.Y., 1969), which is up-to-date and more favorably inclined to all concerned. Morton Keller, *Affairs of State: Public Life in Late-Nineteenth-Century America* (Cambridge, Mass., 1977), contains a wealth of fascinating background material on the era.

For Cleveland's foreign policy, see Ernest R. May, *Imperial Democracy: The Emergence of America as a Great Power* (New York, 1961), and Walter LaFeber, *The New Empire: An Interpretation of American Expansion, 1860–1898* (Ithaca, N.Y., 1963), the latter generally critical of American policy, which LaFeber considers to have been dominated by the desire for commercial expansion. John A. S. Grenville and George B. Young, *Politics, Strategy, and American Diplomacy: Studies in Foreign Policy, 1873–1917* (New Haven, Conn., 1966), contains interesting essays on a variety of relevant issues.

Books dealing with specific foreign policy issues of the Cleveland era include Merze Tate, *The United States and the Hawaiian Kingdom: A Political History* (New Haven, Conn., 1965), and A. E. Campbell, *Great Britain and the United States, 1895–1903* (Westport, Conn., 1974).

Recent works include Alyn Brodsky, *Grover Cleveland: A Study in Character* (New York, 2000) Henry F. Graff, *Grover Cleveland* (New York, 2002), and H. Paul Jeffers, *An Honest President: The Life and Presidencies of Grover Cleveland* (New York, 2000).

Further sources are listed in John F. Marszalek, comp., *Grover Cleveland: A Bibliography* (Westport, Conn., 1988).

Benjamin Harrison

Louis W. Koenig

Benjamin Harrison THE LIBRARY OF CONGRESS

THE presidency of Benjamin Harrison attests that the office requires a breadth of personal qualities and political skills and that to fall short in some of these while being strong in others can be fatal to future electoral success. Possessor of an intellect of the first order, high moral principles, statesmanlike perceptions, and commanding skill as a public speaker, Harrison nonetheless failed to stir the public with magnetic responses to its problems and to relate well to fellow party leaders, which impaired his performance of essential party tasks. Elected president in 1888 by the constitutionally required majority of the electoral vote but with a minority of the popular vote, Harrison failed to win reelection in 1892. In-

stead of improving his tenuous political strength, he suffered persistent decline.

Despite his failure to be reelected, Harrison's presidency was well regarded by political connoisseurs of his time. Historian Henry Adams wrote that "Mr. Harrison was an excellent President, a man of ability and force; perhaps the best President the Republican party had put forward since Lincoln's death." In 1927 a longtime Washington journalist, Henry L. Stoddard, after ranking Cleveland, Theodore Roosevelt, and Wilson as the three outstanding presidents between Lincoln and Coolidge, added that "I feel as though I were doing an injustice to Benjamin Harrison not to crowd him into the three, for, intellectually, he outranked them. He was the ablest of them all." If anything, Harrison has come to be less well regarded since these judgments were rendered.

The object of history's mercurial assessments, Benjamin Harrison, is the only grandson of a president (William Henry Harrison) to himself become president. Son of a congressman and great-grandson of a signer of the Declaration of Independence, Harrison was born on 20 August 1833 on his grandfather's farm in North Bend, Ohio, the second of nine children. His father, a farmer, served two terms in Congress. Harrison attended Farmers' College near Cincinnati and completed his education at Miami University in Oxford, Ohio, from which he graduated in 1852. Harrison married Caroline Lavinia Scott, daughter of the president of a woman's college in Oxford; read law in Cincinnati; was admitted to the bar in 1854; and moved to Indianapolis that year to commence his law practice.

Although his father warned him that "none but knaves should ever enter the political arena," Harrison soon occupied a succession of elective offices: city attorney of Indianapolis, secretary of the Republican state central committee, and reporter of the state supreme court. Commander of the Seventieth Regiment of Indiana Volunteers in the Civil War, Harrison rose to the rank of brigadier general. Gaining national distinction as a lawyer after the war, Harrison ran unsuccessfully for the Indiana governorship in 1876. He was nominated shortly before the election, when the prior nominee withdrew because of recently exposed activities that could not bear the scrutiny of the campaign. Harrison turned down an appointment to the cabinet of James A. Garfield, preferring to serve in the United States Senate, to which he was elected in 1881.

As a senator, Harrison supported civil service reform to supplant the traditional spoils system, high protective tariffs to foster industrial development, a strong navy, and regulation of the railroads. He persistently attacked President Cleveland's vetoes of veterans' pension bills. Harrison's popularity with veterans was to be a major factor in winning the presidential nomination in 1888. His bid for a second Senate term was rebuffed when Indiana's Democratic-controlled legislature defeated his continuation by one vote. (United States senators were then chosen by state legislatures.)

A deeply religious man, Harrison taught Sunday school and was a deacon, and later elder, of the Pres-byterian church. The day before he left Indianapolis for his inauguration as president, Harrison passed the collection plate in the First Presbyterian Church, his long practice. As a praying churchman, an ethical lawyer, and an officeholder of sturdy moral courage, Harrison was regarded as an exemplar of political decency, a reputation that accompanied him to the presidency.

Election of 1888

Harrison was an unsuccessful dark-horse aspirant for the Republican nomination in 1884. In 1888 he became a more formidable candidate when Indiana delegates endorsed his nomination and the most preeminent of Republican politicians, James G. Blaine, did not again become a candidate. With a field that at one juncture consisted of nineteen candidates, the organizers of Harrison's race, led by Louis T. Michener, attorney general of Indiana, concentrated on gaining the second-choice votes of the delegates until the final ballot.

Matt Quay, overlord of Pennsylvania Republicans, offered support in return for a blanket promise of a cabinet post. Harrison rebuffed his managers, who urged him to accept the deal, by recalling his instruction at their departure from Indianapolis that "purchasing capacity" must not supersede moral competency in deciding the nomination. A critical juncture in Harrison's progress was reached when Chauncey M. Depew, head of the New York delegation and president of the New York Central Railroad, with the approval of the state's real political boss, Thomas C. Platt, brought the New York delegation into the Harrison fold.

Harrison was nominated on the eighth ballot. The many ballots were telltales of his political weakness. He subsequently acknowledged to Blaine his indebtedness: "Only the help of your friends made success possible." Other factors favoring Harrison were his name, his war record, and his popularity with veterans. Levi P. Morton, a New York banker, was nominated for vice president. The Democrats renominated incumbent President Grover Cleveland, with Allen G. Thurman, a former Ohio senator, as his running mate.

Harrison conducted a "front-porch campaign" from his home. Imaginative pretexts were spawned to bring great crowds of visitors there. On "German Day," large delegations from Chicago and Milwaukee journeyed to Indianapolis, where they heard from

Harrison a eulogy on German virtues. For one of the more imposing receptions, some forty thousand drummers converged from eleven states.

The principal issue in the campaign was the tariff, with Harrison calling for high tariffs and Cleveland, who did not campaign actively because he felt it beneath the dignity of the presidency, advocating lower tariffs. The contrasting positions on the tariff reflected basic differences between the Republican and Democratic parties in the decade 1884–1894, with Republicans espousing doctrines of nationalism and active governmental intervention to promote the expansion of the economy. The Democrats, under Cleveland, advocated states' rights and opposed the employment of national governmental power to speed economic growth. Harrison was severely pressured to make a strong commitment to service pensions for Civil War veterans. Sensing that the public might not welcome costly outlays, he limited himself to general pledges and platitudinous statements about veterans. A skilled formulator of positions on issues that served his political necessities, Harrison promised "liberal treatment" of veterans' pensions.

The Harrison campaign was lavishly financed, and its prime money-raiser was John Wanamaker, the Philadelphia department store magnate and chairman of the campaign's finance committee. Wanamaker was given "unrestricted power in raising and deciding upon the expenditure of funds." As a governing principle, he believed it "right" to solicit businessmen's contributions, and an imposing fund was raised "so quickly," Wanamaker noted, "that the Democrats never knew anything about it." In his expenditures, Wanamaker emphasized a "campaign of education" by salaried speakers and tons of protective tariff literature. His ebullient enterprise prompted charges that he was softening up the public to tolerate expensive favors from the future Harrison administration to business contributors.

As election day neared, Harrison was confident, predicting that "if we can secure an approximately fair election, I think we are safe." His attainment of a majority of the electoral votes—233 to Cleveland's 168—with only a minority of popular votes was aided by his successes in large states. His plurality in New York of 14,000 gained him 36 electoral voles, and he repeated that pattern of narrow popular-vote victories in such major electoral vote states as Indiana, Illinois, Michigan, Ohio, and Pennsylvania. So evenly was the vote distributed nationwide that the election became described as one of "no decision." Cleveland had a slight popular majority of about 100,000, largely because of increased Democratic majorities in southern one-party states.

Another major factor was the Republican campaign fund of over $400,000, the expenditure of which was concentrated in crucial states. Also of prime importance was Tammany Hall's betrayal of Cleveland, which helped Harrison carry New York. Despite Harrison's caution on veterans' pensions, the premier veterans' organization, the Grand Army of the Republic (GAR), was converted by his nomination and campaign into an instrument of the Republican party.

Inauguration

Harrison was inaugurated in a relentless rainstorm, with Grover Cleveland holding an umbrella over his successor's head. His address, after crediting the nation's growth to the benign influences of education and religion, urged that the cotton states and mining territories attain the thriving industrial levels of the states of the Atlantic seaboard, and toward that end, he reaffirmed his promise of a protective tariff. Stressing that "laws are general, and their administration should be uniform and equal," without special regard for sections, Harrison in effect foreclosed special treatment for the South. He urged that blacks be granted the right to vote in both North and South. He lamented the proliferating monopolies and trusts, and he committed his administration to the advancement of social justice.

Harrison also urged early statehood for the territories and in general terms advocated pensions for veterans, a statement that evoked the most enthusiastic applause. He declared that the civil service law would be applied fully and that party service would not become "a shield for official negligence, incompetence or delinquency."

In foreign affairs, Harrison pledged vigilance of national honor and due protection of the personal and commercial rights of American citizens everywhere. He reaffirmed the Monroe Doctrine as a cornerstone of foreign policy and urged the building of a modern navy and a first-rate merchant marine, since the flag would follow every citizen "in all countries and many islands." Although he declared his commitment to international peace through noninterference in the affairs of other governments and the application of arbitration to international dis-

Benjamin Harrison speaks to a crowd. Harrison was a noted orator and relied on his well-crafted skills during his legal and political career. CORBIS

putes, Harrison clearly accorded the development of national strength the foremost priority.

Presidential Style and Appointments

The twenty-third president of the United States, barely five foot six in height and just a bit corpulent, was fifty-five years old when inaugurated. He had piercing blue eyes and a full, meticulously trimmed gray beard. His bearing was energetic, dignified, and graceful. His rival, Grover Cleveland, was one of many who were impressed by Harrison's intellectual abilities and honesty of purpose. Writing in retrospect, editor William Allen White admired his "instinct to do the polite, honest, dignified thing in every contingency."

In making decisions, Harrison was methodical and legalistic, his actions unhurried and maturely deliberated, and he largely kept his own counsel. But many were also disenchanted by aspects of his manner, a list that grew as his administration proceeded.

His legalistic style of thought, strong intellectuality, and summoning of lofty principle provided a ready wherewithal for rebuffing those who sought consideration or favor. Some found him impatient, brusque, and even irascible. Governor Joseph B. Foraker of Ohio called him "grouchy." Others thought him cold. When Speaker of the House Thomas B. Reed was asked if he would board "the Harrison bandwagon," he replied, "I never ride an ice-cart." A governor, calling at the White House with business to transact, was affronted by Harrison's greeting: "I've got all these papers to look after, and I'm going fishing at two o'clock." The president opened his watchcase and awaited the governor's response.

In selecting his cabinet, Harrison emphasized competence and "irreproachable character"; party activity and previous office holding were not prerequisites. For the senior cabinet post, secretary of state, Harrison followed tradition in appointing his party's chief claimant for the presidency, James G. Blaine. He also followed tradition in awarding the postmaster generalship to a principal manager of the campaign, John Wanamaker. Determined to appoint one friend from Indiana of unquestionable loyalty and competence, Harrison chose his law partner, William Henry Harrison Miller, as attorney general. Cabinet making was also an occasion for making enemies. Harrison bypassed two powerful New Yorkers eager for cabinet posts, Platt and Senator Warner Miller. When Harrison appointed Benjamin Franklin Tracy as secretary of the navy and as the new administration's recognition of New York, Platt and Miller became forever hostile.

Harrison's other appointees tolerably approximated his standards, which in effect meant that he chose men much like himself. The final list consisted of six lawyers and two businessmen—all of them regular churchgoers, But Harrison's cabinet making also raised a danger signal for his future. None of the eight cabinet secretaries had worked actively for his nomination, and their selection did not serve the traditional function of placating important party factions to help build consensus for future policy. Harrison, in sum, had a sturdy nonpolitical streak.

Like other presidencies of his era, Harrison's was inundated by office seekers. The problem was compounded by the shakeout of Republicans in the preceding Cleveland administration, the first Democratic incumbency since the Civil War. Republicans now meant to reclaim offices in full number. Despite a plank in the Republican platform promising further civil service reform, a clean sweep of the nonclassified civil service quickly materialized. The chief patronage dispenser, J. S. ("Headsman") Clarkson, removed half of the postmasters. Unlike Cleveland, Harrison removed many officers before they completed their four-year terms.

But Harrison was unable to convert the dispensations of patronage into political advantage. If anything, they became a sizable liability. In awarding offices, the president offended the leading bosses, Quay of Pennsylvania and Platt of New York. Quay, chairman of the Republican National Committee and United States senator from Pennsylvania, presented Harrison with a lengthy list of names to fill various federal offices. When Harrison requested information concerning the fitness and character of each candidate, Quay demurred, noting that the entire matter could be handled by senatorial courtesy with the president simply ratifying what was put before him. But Harrison stood his ground and thus began an enduring enmity. His frequent purpose to represent geographic areas rather than senators' preferences often prompted the legislators to feel humiliated. Unlike other presidents who delegated patronage to subordinates, Harrison handled the task himself. His cool, expeditious management stoked further ill will, especially his requirement that office seekers make their case standing.

While pursuing a vigorous commerce in spoils, Harrison sought to maintain his credibility with a valued constituency, the civil service reformers. He sought to appease them by appointing as civil service commissioner the New York civil service reformer Theodore Roosevelt, who later noted that Harrison "gave me my first opportunity to do big things." Despite Roosevelt's aggressive administration, the Civil Service Reform League denounced Harrison for violating his campaign pledges for civil service reform and the *Nation* characterized him as a "subservient disciple of the spoils doctrine."

Like other presidents of his time, Harrison was caught between the reformers, who pushed him hard and watched for backsliding while advocating extension of the merit system to new offices and agencies, and party leaders and workers, who reminded the president that he owed his election to their work and that their interest could be sustained only by adequate reward. Harrison was unable to devise a formula acceptable to both constituencies, and the compromises he structured badly damaged his standing with party workers.

Cool Relations with Congress

In his dealings with Congress, always a complex, high-risk area for presidents, Harrison was handicapped by the frequent poverty of his relations with Capitol Hill's key power holders. Trouble sometimes sprang from dissatisfaction with Harrison's award of appointments, particularly when party factions other than those of the individual legislators were rewarded with patronage. Harrison's penchant for appointing newspaper editors and publishers to diplomatic and other posts angered senators aggrieved by some past journalistic attack or exposé. The Senate, for example, rejected Harrison's nominee for ambassador to Germany, the distinguished Cincinnati editor Murat Halstead, who had once flayed the chamber for its easy tolerance of corruption in its ranks. Halstead's rejection was Harrison's first defeat from his party.

The president's personality did not wear well with legislators. Senators and congressmen were put off by his ready recourse to high principle and legal niceties. Others were offended by his seeming coldness. "There are bitter complaints," a critic reported. "Senators call and say their say to him, and he stands silent.. . . As one Senator says: 'It's like talking to a hitching post.'" Some legislators were put off by Harrison's displays of a lack of political sense. He once grasped Quay's hand and said solemnly, "Providence has given us the victory." The veteran boss and senator, taken aback, observed afterward that Harrison was "a political tenderfoot. He ought to know that Providence hadn't a damn thing to do with it!" Harrison's most vitriolic detractor was House Speaker Thomas B. Reed. Their severest clashes were over a patronage appointment and the president's exercise of his pardoning power, and the individuals who benefited were the only "two personal enemies" in Reed's life. Imbued with a Whig perspective, especially its precept of legislative supremacy, Harrison did not initiate legislation. His most daring venture was to reecho the Republican platform.

Harrison's approach to legislative leadership was largely one of emphasizing his role as public leader, of presenting policy proposals in his arresting rhetorical and an analytical style, to rally the public behind them. Unfortunately for Harrison, these efforts were of little avail, since public support steadily diminished as his administration proceeded. Nonetheless, Harrison was aggressive in asserting personal influence. He held informal dinners and receptions for legislative leaders, informing them of items he wanted incorporated in bills. He made few vetoes, although he often used the threat of veto profitably. In both legislative houses he was hampered by divisions within his party over the allocation of spoils. In the Senate, where Republicans enjoyed only a bare majority, a "silver bloc" of sixteen western senators held the balance of power. To implement his party's platform on the tariff and the civil rights of blacks, Harrison needed support from Silver Republicans, as they were called, much as they needed his backing for a stronger silver law.

Domestic Affairs

Unlike Cleveland, who was an adamant foe of silver, Harrison was supportive without committing himself to the extreme of free coinage, which Silver Republicans and other advocates of silver desired. With Treasury Secretary William Windom, he developed a bill authorizing the issuance of treasury notes on deposits of silver bullion. A tortuous legislative struggle, with Harrison devising compromises and rallying votes, led to passage of the Sherman Silver Purchase Act (July 1890), which increased the amount of silver to be coined but stopped short of free coinage. The act required the purchase of 4.5 million ounces of silver each month at the prevailing market price, through the issuance of treasury notes redeemable in gold or silver. The greater outpouring of paper money would badly strain the treasury's reserves of gold.

The momentum for silver came from the worsening plight of western and southern farmers who carried a heavy burden of debt. Already the emerging Populist party, which championed their needs and featured among its planks the free coinage of silver, had acquired a strength that would afflict Harrison in future elections. As well, free-silver Republicans from the West frequently were allied with eastern Republicans disaffected by Harrison's patronage policies. The president trod cautiously on the silver issue, aiming to maintain maximum political support. Simultaneously, he wished to avoid what he termed "unsound money." He styled himself a "bimetallist" rather than a gold standard advocate, since he favored expanding the paper currency backed by silver. But his opposition to free coinage cost him the support of western free-silver Republicans.

In campaign speeches, Harrison had proclaimed his belief in a protective tariff, which promised relief from the competition of cheap foreign-made goods. A tariff, he had contended, was beneficial to all—to workers whose jobs in effect were protected "at good wages," to farmers who supplied their needs, to the railroads transporting their goods. The tariff became a reality when Congressman William McKinley of Ohio and Senator Nelson W. Aldrich of Rhode Island became the chief authors of the McKinley Tariff Law of 1890, whose principal schedules were imposed by the National Association of Wool Manufacturers, the Tin Plate and Iron and Steel Associations, Louisiana sugar growers, and other groups. The McKinley bill reached out to farmers by placing protective rates on agricultural products, and it put raw sugar on the free list while compensating Louisiana and Kansas beet growers with a bounty of 2 cents a pound. Harrison helped devise the sugar provision when it threatened to deadlock the bill. He also oversaw the development of a reciprocity provision that empowered the president to impose duties on sugar, molasses, tea, coffee, and hides if he determined that nations exporting them were imposing unequal and unreasonable duties on American goods. No apparent heed was given to the prospect of severely rising prices, which the new law did indeed inflict on consumers. Fortunately, Harrison and Secretary of State Blaine negotiated more than a dozen reciprocal agreements that modified tariff duties with leading trading partners.

A major measure that was responsive to the rising threat of the Farmers' Alliance and the Populist party, and their likely combination with the Knights of Labor, was the Sherman Antitrust Act of 1890. For Harrison, the act redeemed a campaign pledge. He venerated economic competition and disdained monopoly, a sentiment he expressed on inauguration day when he was presented with the gift of a watchdog, an enormous Siberian bloodhound. The dog, he said, "looks very much like an overfed monopolist." The new antitrust law, he thought, might offset to some degree the McKinley Tariff Act by prompting lower prices under freer competition. But Harrison did little to enforce the new law. His inaction was encouraged by Congress' failure to appropriate funds to investigate the trusts. The administration initiated only seven antitrust cases.

In his early policymaking, Harrison was also preoccupied with the rights of blacks in the context of general policy toward the South. His campaign statements were positive but general. Harrison was alert to the necessity of strengthening Republican voting performance in the South, where his own campaign had fared badly. From a series of measures introduced in Congress emerged a consolidating bill known as the Lodge bill or force bill, which sought to protect the rights of blacks at the polls by putting southern elections under federal supervision. The bill left Republican legislators divided, again demonstrating that Harrison could not count on his party's support for prime legislative objectives. Senators Quay and Cameron of Pennsylvania typified a basic cause of Republican recalcitrance by bowing to corporate interests of their state with holdings in the South that the new legislation might impair. Black leaders pressed Harrison to lead a public crusade for "free speech, a free ballot and a fair return of votes at the South." The Lodge bill passed in the House, but the nervous business interests prevailed in the Senate, where an administration advocate of the black cause noted, "We have had too much . . . of what may be called 'strictly business' politics."

Harrison, who considered voting rights for blacks a moral isuse, chose not to go to the people in behalf of the Lodge bill but heeded a traditional demand of black leaders for a share of the patronage. He promptly continued his party's policy of rewarding a few black leaders as a bestowal of recognition on the entire race. Generally, his favors fell on younger leaders rather than old. The president's major coup was the installation of N. Wright Cuney to the important post of collector of the Port of Galveston. The distinguished black leader Frederick Douglass was named United States resident minister and consul general to Haiti. Harrison also sought to name blacks to the postmasterships of larger southern cities, but that policy was deterred when the Senate forced the withdrawal of Dr. W. O. Crum's nomination for postmaster of Charleston. In net effect, Harrison's efforts enhanced his regard in the eyes of the black press and black leaders.

In Congress, Harrison had been known as the "Soldier's Senator" because of his sponsorship of liberal pension legislation for Civil War veterans, and in his presidential campaign he had declared that the nation should not use "an apothecary's scale to weigh the rewards of the men who saved the country." The presence of four generals in the cabinet enhanced the confidence of pension advocates even further, and in addresses on patriotic occasions and to GAR encampments, Harrison reemphasized his commitment to improved pensions for veterans.

One of the president's more promising contributions to the well-being of the veterans was his appointment of Corporal James R. Tanner, GAR commander from New York, who had lost both legs in the Second Battle of Bull Run, as commissioner of pensions. Tanner deemed it his duty "to assist a worthy old claimant to prove his case rather than to hunt for technical reasons under the law to knock him out." Even this was a modest understatement, for Tanner's many critics were soon charging that his handouts to veterans were lavish and illegal. He shot back defiantly that he would "drive a six-mule team through the Treasury." When his administrative superior, Interior Secretary John W. Noble, with the president's encouragement, commenced an investigation of Tanner's prodigal stewardship, Tanner challenged the secretary's authority in a letter released to the press. The intervention of friends of both Tanner and the president induced Tanner to resign, an act that relieved the president of a burgeoning political liability.

Harrison was more successful in moving a new liberal pension law through Congress. Under existing law, wounds or disease traceable to the war entitled the veteran to a pension. At Harrison's urging, Congress adopted in 1890 the Dependent and Disability Pension Act, which provided pensions for all veterans who had served ninety days and who were unable to perform manual labor, regardless of the cause or origin of their disability. The new law also initiated the government's commitment to the principle that its pension system provide for minors, dependent parents, and widows.

An explosion of expenditure promptly followed the enactment of Harrison's measure. Between 1891 and 1895, the number of pensioners rose from 676,000 to 970,000, and by the completion of Harrison's term, the yearly appropriation for pensions increased from $81 million to $135 million. In little more than a decade, the new law cost the government over $1 billion. Ironically, the extravagance of Harrison and Congress far exceeded Tanner's openhandedness. The new pension law confirmed the growing suspicion of citizens that governmental extravagance was moving far beyond bounds. Nonetheless, when critics referred to Congress as the "Billion-Dollar Congress," Speaker Thomas B. Reed retorted, "Yes, but this is a billion-dollar country."

Life in the White House was also on a large scale. Not only President and Mrs. Harrison lived there, but many members of their family. Harrison was described as "the only living ruler who can gather at his table four generations," which he did daily. Those at his board included Mrs. Harrison's father and the Harrisons' daughter, Mary, who helped with her mother's social schedule. With Mary were her two young children. Harrison's son, Russell, divided his time between New York and Montana, but his wife and daughter lived in the White House. Also present was an older sister of Mrs. Harrison. Since the executive mansion had only five bedrooms, the Harrisons found it unduly small.

The household was run methodically, with meals served at their appointed time. Breakfast was followed by prayers led by the president. An hour in the afternoon was reserved for a brisk walk or drive. On Washington's streets, Harrison was often seen conversing with citizens who accosted him. The Harrisons remained regular churchgoers; the president engaged in no business on Sunday and even left his mail unopened. Mrs. Harrison, a lively presence, designed the family china set; decorated hundreds of porcelain dishes, the proceeds of whose sales were donated to charities; engaged a professor of French to instruct the wives and daughters of cabinet families and others; and presided with charm and grace at White House functions. The Harrisons conveyed an easy informality, a relief to many after the stiffness of the Cleveland years. The younger Harrisons restored dancing at the White House, which was said to have been in abeyance since the time of Mrs. Polk.

Harrison's chief aide was Colonel Elijah Walker Halford, his executive secretary and confidant, a former editor of the *Indianapolis Journal*. Like others who served as secretaries to presidents, both before and after Harrison's time, Halford was a factotum who dealt with Congress, the press, and party figures, and the steady march of other White House callers. Halford was overseer of Harrison's daily political well-being. Presidential business was aided by the presence of telephones in the White House, although there was no telephone operator.

Harrison was readily accessible to his cabinet secretaries and followed a regimen of two weekly cabinet meetings and seeing each secretary on a scheduled day each week when, as the president explained, the secretary would come with his papers and a full consultation would proceed concerning appointments and other important business. Harrison devoted cabinet meetings to discussions of items that were of general interest or that at least affected more than one department. Before signing legislation involving a department, Harrison consulted the department head.

Of all his cabinet secretaries, Harrison's most complex relations were with Secretary of State James G. Blaine. For decades the most popular man in American politics, a controlling power of the Republican party, a perennial presidential candidate, and a leader in legislation, Blaine was versatile in both foreign and domestic policymaking. Harrison was slow in offering Blaine the post of secretary. By delaying until mid-January 1889, he sought to avoid any appearance that a deal had been made at the Chicago convention or that Blaine, and not Harrison, was choosing the cabinet.

As secretary of state, Blaine was constrained by the watchful, possibly jealous, Harrison to limited diplomatic initiatives, to concentration on inherited problems and isolated incidents as they arose. Occasionally relations between the two foremost Republicans of the day were brittle. As Mrs. Blaine complained, after a sequence of her husband's disappointments, "All propositions are rejected." Blaine was not invited to accompany the president on his extensive political trips, although other cabinet secretaries and the vice president were. Harrison vetoed a request that Blaine desired above all else, the appointment of his son Walker as assistant secretary of state, for which he was well qualified by ability and diplomatic experience. A lawyer, Walker could have been of estimable assistance to his father, who was not a lawyer, in an administration where legal questions were at the forefront of policymaking.

Despite the rough edges of their relationship, Blaine and Harrison were mutually supportive in the quest for a new and better policy. Blaine, who foresaw great trouble under the McKinley Tariff's high rates, urged, in testimony to congressional committees, sweeping empowerment of the executive to negotiate reciprocity agreements with other countries for individual commodities, instead of general reciprocity treaties.

After initial hesitation, Harrison became more hospitable to reciprocity, influenced by Blaine's tutelage and by his understanding that western farmers welcomed reciprocity as an avenue to enlarged markets for their produce. With agrarian unrest and Populist strength growing, the Republicans patently needed to be more responsive to western sentiment if they were to hold the allegiance of that area.

It was fortunate that Harrison immersed himself in the business of his departments from the outset. An exceptional number of his department secretaries became ill or resigned. Blaine sustained a severe nervous disorder in 1891, a period of intense activity in foreign affairs, and Harrison immediately became his own secretary of state. In the same year, Interior Secretary John W. Noble took extended leave because of health, Secretary of War Redfield Proctor resigned to become senator from Vermont, and Treasury Secretary William Windom died. The heavy burden of additional work prompted Harrison to observe, "The President is a good deal like the old camp horse that Dickens described; he is strapped up so he can't fall down."

A chief preoccupation of Harrison and his colleagues in 1890 was the midterm congressional elections. The fast-developing image of the Harrison administration's extravagance, the hammer blows of the McKinley Tariff on the cost of living, and the distress of agriculture all foreordained that the oncoming congressional elections would constitute a setback to the administration of more severe proportions than the losses a president's party usually sustains in such testings. For Republican congressmen, the elections were a massacre. Before the elections, the Republicans controlled the House; after the elections, only 88 Republicans were returned, with 235 Democrats and 9 Populists. In the Senate, the Republican majority was reduced to 8 undependable votes from the Far West. Staunch Republican states such as Michigan and Massachusetts went Democratic, and McKinley himself was defeated.

The elections, with their crushing impact on Republican fortunes, indicated that the country desired major policy changes. But the result of the elections—the decimation of House Republicans—virtually foreclosed any sizable adjustments of domestic policy. The elections revealed fast-rising Populist strength in the Midwest and South, which alarmed the president's chief political advisers, who anticipated that the Senate's Silver Republicans would become all the more unreliable. The altered congressional party picture stalled most of Harrison's domestic program in his administration's final two years. His strength in the Senate was sufficient to forestall repeal of legislation passed in the first half of his administration.

Foreign Affairs

In the depressed state of the president's political fortunes, the one area in which there might be some hope for a brighter future was foreign policy. Conceivably, the president could set forth appealing prospects and manage crises in ways that would attract the attention and approval of the public, and si-

multaneously diminish its absorption in domestic affairs.

In the initial two years of his term, Harrison had by no means been inattentive to foreign affairs. He entered office intent on abandoning isolation as a cornerstone of foreign policy, and his selection of Blaine as secretary of state augured an era of initiative and creativity. He and Blaine seized the opportunity provided by a law enacted late in the Cleveland administration that requested the president to convene a meeting of Latin American countries. Arrangements begun by Cleveland were completed by Harrison and Blaine. They agreed that the nation's growing industrial production made expansion of foreign markets a principal goal. Discussions preparatory to the conference, scheduled to begin on 2 October 1889, looked toward a customs union, inter-American rail and steamship lines, trademark and copyright laws, and arbitration treaties.

A major feature of this first Pan-American Conference, to which seventeen Latin American nations sent delegates to Washington, was a six-thousand-mile tour to impress the visitors with the size, wealth, and manufacturing capabilities of the United States. When the conference reassembled, with Blaine presiding with brilliance and tact and Harrison watchful of progress and problems, the United States offered its plan for a customs union, through which tariff barriers would be reduced and trade with Europe curtailed.

Despite Blaine's skilled advocacy, the resolution was voted down as unworkable. In a second thrust, Blaine urged that machinery be created for the arbitration of disputes. Again the proposal lost, by a wide margin. National rivalries and fears of United States dominance shaped these decisions. The conference's most signal achievement was the creation of what became known as the Pan American Union, a clearinghouse for disseminating information and fostering cooperation among the member nations. At other junctures, Harrison advocated construction of a Central American canal and increased U.S. presence in Latin America. In both Latin America and the Pacific, Harrison pursued expansionist policies sometimes expressed in a bellicose manner. Although his efforts produced few tangible successes, he heralded the nation's subsequent imperial policies of 1898.

The heritage of foreign policy issues from the Cleveland administration also included the Bering Sea controversy, which centered on the wanton slaughter of fur seals off the Alaskan coast. The sealers, mostly Canadians who stationed their vessels outside the three-mile limit, soon threatened the seals with extinction. Shortly before Harrison's inauguration, the president was authorized by Congress to seize vessels encroaching upon American rights in the "waters of the Bering Sea." Harrison promptly warned all persons "against entering the Bering Sea for the unlawful hunting of fur-bearing animals, "and revenue cutters began intercepting Canadian vessels. An intricate diplomatic controversy ensued, and continued after the termination of the Harrison administration.

More suited to Harrison's need to distract the public from the inadequacies of domestic policy was the Mafia affair in New Orleans. The murder of the local police superintendent on 16 October 1890 was attributed to the Mafia, inspired by the heavy migration of Italians, many from Sicily, where the Mafia Black Hand Society flourished. Numerous Italians in New Orleans were arrested, and fearful of violence, Harrison requested a full report from the governor of Louisiana. In March 1891 a jury found six defendants not guilty and a judge declared a mistrial for the remaining three. An aroused local citizenry stormed the prison and shot down some prisoners and hanged others.

Because Blaine was ill, Harrison composed a telegram to the governor of Louisiana deploring the massacre and requesting protection for Italians in New Orleans. Italian Americans elsewhere in the country called for full and prompt justice. The outraged Italian government demanded indemnity. Harrison directed the American minister in Rome to explain "the embarrassing gap in federalism—that in such cases the state alone has jurisdiction." Although talk of war raged in both countries, in time tempers cooled and the incident was officially closed when Harrison, nudged by Blaine, paid a modest indemnity to the Italian government.

Even more distracting was a stormy interlude in relations with Chile when its government was overthrown in 1891. Harrison disdained the rebels who, he said, "do not know how to use victory and moderation," and he delayed his conferral of recognition. Meanwhile, sailors of the USS *Baltimore* on shore leave in Valparaiso, Chile, engaged in a saloon brawl in which two sailors were killed, seventeen others were injured, and still others were chased by rioters, aided by police, around the city.

The crisis in Chilean relations coincided with Blaine's absence as secretary of state and Halford's illness, a time of many burdens for the president. When Chile made no apology or expression of regret, Harrison directed that a sharp note be dispatched complaining of the delay. With Chilean legal processes moving slowly in dealing with alleged wrongdoers, Harrison declared in his annual message to Congress (9 December 1891) that if the Chilean investigation did not provide satisfaction to the United States, he would again bring the matter before Congress "for such action as may be necessary." When the Chilean foreign minister responded by maligning the president, Harrison, who regarded this new affront as "an atrocious insult to the American government," ordered the navy to prepare for action. Blaine urged caution and understanding for the Chileans amid angry cabinet discussions, and on one occasion, the president leaned forward and with an emphatic gesture declared, "Mr. Secretary, that insult was to the uniform of the United States sailors."

For a time the public was deeply stirred by hostility toward Chile. A new Chilean foreign minister fortunately proved more accommodating and made an unexceptionable apology. Even as the apology was being decoded, Harrison milked the episode for all of its political worth by dispatching another special message to Congress (25 January 1892), detailing the crisis at great length, and submitted the irritating diplomatic papers "for the grave and patriotic consideration" of Congress "and for such action as may be deemed appropriate."

Harrison, in effect, was inviting Congress to declare war at a moment when Chile was about to back down. The Democratic press, agitated by the president's warlike moves, accused him of maneuvering to commence a war to assure his election with the slogan "Don't Swap Horses in Midstream." Soon Blaine, mindful of the lofty sentiments of the Pan-American Conference, induced Harrison to mute his bellicosity, and the controversy petered out when the Chilean apology was released, followed by an indemnity from its government.

Harrison inherited the perplexities of policymaking concerning the distant Samoa Islands, where Britain, Germany, and the United States had long been jockeying for ascendance. Relations with Germany were particularly edgy when Harrison began his administration, but Otto von Bismarck, the Iron Chancellor, who wished to avoid further trouble, convened the Berlin Conference (29 April 1889). Thanks to Blaine's firm and efficient management of negotiations, Samoa's native ruling dynasty was preserved and a tripartite protectorate was established. Germany and Britain were not enthusiastic about the arrangement, but Blaine's skill and tenacity induced their acceptance.

Harrison's top priority in the Pacific was the Hawaiian Islands, which he meant to annex to the United States. Opportunity knocked late in his administration when a revolution toppled Queen Liliuokalani. The upheaval prompted the United States minister, John L. Stevens, to call for troops—which were dispatched—to protect American lives and property. Stevens and Provisional President Sanford Dole prepared a treaty of annexation. In a report to Harrison, Stevens noted that "the Hawaiian pear is now fully ripe, and this is the golden hour for the United States to pluck it."

Harrison was eager to complete the annexation as the crowning achievement of his foreign policy. Although it was late in his term, he placed a treaty before the Senate (16 February 1893) and urged "annexation full and complete." It was essential, the president said, that no other foreign power acquire Hawaii, since "such a possession would not consist with our safety and with the peace of the world." Although Harrison enjoyed the support of most House Republicans and advocates of a big navy and territorial expansion, his project foundered in the Senate, where the Democrats, who controlled the chamber, refused to act before the expiration of Harrison's term. When restored to the presidency, Grover Cleveland, a resolute anti-annexationist, withdrew the treaty.

Although Harrison seemingly used foreign policy to satisfy his own political necessities, and especially the gaining of reelection, much of what he did mirrored basic forces and longings of American society. When he became president, Reconstruction was virtually complete, industrial production was fast expanding, and American manufacturers were eager for foreign markets as outlets for their burgeoning surpluses. National consciousness was growing, patriotic societies were proliferating, and Harrison's plan to build a new and modern navy was widely applauded. In the dawning era of big warships, those built by Harrison's administration were the biggest in the world. A big navy required coaling stations, and Harrison's assertiveness in the Pacific meant to fulfill that necessity.

Although Harrison's handling of foreign policy problems was thoroughly imperial, his use of presidential power in forwarding his designs was, with few exceptions, scrupulously constitutional. He was fastidious in requesting empowerments from Congress, in subjecting his policy initiatives to its approval, and in respecting its constitutionally conferred power to declare war. For major projects, he depended on the treaty power rather than the executive agreement, which can bypass the legislative power. He was solicitous of public approval and alert to the need for informing the public of foreign affairs problems through messages to Congress and his extensive speechmaking across the country.

Foreign policy failed to arouse any tidal wave of demand for Harrison's renomination. Many Republican professionals regarded that eventuality with apprehension and distaste. Minnesota Senator W. D. Washburn represented that opinion when he said, "There are two serious objections to Harrison's renomination; first, no one cares anything for him personally, secondly, no one, as far as I know, thinks he could be elected if nominated." Harrison's most dedicated opponents were the bosses, led by Quay and Platt, who resented the president's handling of patronage.

Election of 1892 and Retirement

The bosses searched for a candidate to oppose the president. They looked eagerly to Blaine, who had resigned as secretary of state for reasons never made clear, but he was plagued by illness and soon made a public statement that his name would not go before the Republicans' Minneapolis convention. The statement also mentioned nothing about Harrison, his record, or his renomination. The omission kept the opposition to Harrison alive, as the bosses turned next to McKinley and John Sherman of Ohio, the two candidates that Harrison's managers feared most.

Harrison did little to help his cause. He was distracted by the serious illness of his wife, a condition first diagnosed as nervous prostration. But as the Minneapolis convention neared, Harrison changed course and sent for his top political adviser, Louis T. Michener. After reviewing the attacks by the bosses and other critics, he declared, "No Harrison ever retreated in the presence of a foe without giving battle, and I have determined to stand and fight." With demonic toil, Harrison's managers struggled to round up delegates and to ward off Mark Hanna's efforts to forestall a first-ballot nomination for Harrison, which might then clear the way for his protégé, McKinley. But Hanna's strategy failed, and Harrison captured the nomination on the first ballot. A potent factor in his success was the belief of rank-and-file Republicans that they could again win with Harrison. The rejected bosses extracted a measure of satisfaction by vetoing the renomination of Levi Morton for vice president and substituting Whitelaw Reid, also of New York and publisher of the *New York Tribune*. The maneuver was laid to the New York delegation and Boss Platt.

With Grover Cleveland as the Democratic nominee, the election of 1892 became the only one in which the nominees of both major parties had served as president. Harrison did little campaigning, with Mrs. Harrison's health in continuing decline, her condition now diagnosed as pulmonary tuberculosis. In deference to Mrs. Harrison, who died midway in the election, Cleveland too did not campaign. The Democratic platform's strongest words were reserved for the McKinley Tariff, which it denounced as the "culminating atrocity of class legislation."

Harrison's cause was gravely injured by a strike at the Homestead Works of the Carnegie Steel Company when twenty men were killed in a battle between locked-out workers and armed Pinkerton detectives. A military force was posted to guard the nonunion labor that was brought in. Harrison's image with labor worsened when he dispatched federal troops to the Coeur d'Alene mines in Idaho in July 1892 at the governor's request. The strike was crushed, and union miners retreated into the mountains.

In the 1892 election, Cleveland avenged the defeat he sustained in 1888. He secured a popular majority of slightly under 375,000 votes and won 277 electoral votes to 145 for Harrison and 22 for Populist party candidate James B. Weaver. Although the Republican party spent $6 million on the campaign, nearly double its outlay for 1888, Harrison, the results implied, failed to respond efficiently to the problems and concerns of labor and farmers in the severe recession of 1893. Their dissatisfactions were reflected in the rapid growth of the Populist party. The McKinley Tariff and the steep increases it wrought in the living costs of the general public helped assure Harrison's downfall.

After completing his presidential term, Harrison returned to Indianapolis and resumed his law practice, which he limited to important and often remunerative cases. He delivered a series of law lectures at Stanford University, which were published in 1901 as *Views of an Ex-President*. The former president, at sixty-two, remarried. His bride, Mary Lord Dimmick, was the daughter of the first Mrs. Harrison's sister and had attended her aunt during her final months of illness. They had one child, Elizabeth. In 1899, Harrison represented Venezuela in the arbitration of its dispute with Great Britain over the British Guiana boundary. He died of pneumonia at his home in Indianapolis on 13 March 1901. The last Civil War general to serve as president, Harrison lived to see his policies vindicated in the Spanish-American War, the termination of the 1893 economic crisis, and Republican recapture of the presidency after Cleveland's term.

BIBLIOGRAPHY

Harry J. Sievers, *Benjamin Harrison: Hoosier Warrior (1833–1865)*, *Benjamin Harrison: Hoosier Statesman (1865–1888)*, and *Benjamin Harrison: Hoosier President (The White House and After)* (Indianapolis, Ind., 1952–1968; Newtown, Conn., 1997), constitute the most detailed biography of Harrison, with an extensive Harrison bibliography. Homer E. Socolofsky and Allan B. Spetter, *The Presidency of Benjamin Harrison* (Lawrence, Kans., 1987), is the leading interpretive study of the Harrison presidency. Leonard D. White, *The Republican Era, 1869–1901: A Study in Administrative History* (New York, 1958), a distinguished administrative history, discusses Harrison and his cabinet and civil service reform. Alice Felt Tyler, *The Foreign Policy of James G. Blaine* (Minneapolis, Minn., 1927), contains an illuminating account of Blaine as secretary of state. David Saville Muzzey, *James G. Blaine: A Political Idol of Other Days* (New York, 1934), the standard biography of Blaine, is still very serviceable. William Alexander Robinson, *Thomas B. Reed: Parliamentarian* (New York, 1930), provides a perspective on the Harrison administration by the Speaker of the House.

D. M. Dozer, "Benjamin Harrison and the Presidential Campaign of 1892," in *American Historical Review* 54, no. 1 (1948), is an excellent analysis of Harrison's strategies and the context in which they evolved. Herbert A. Gibbons, *John Wanamaker*, 2 vols. (New York, 1926), is especially good on Wanamaker's role in the 1888 campaign.

Donald L. McMurry, "The Bureau of Pensions During the Administration of President Harrison," in

Mississippi Valley Historical Review 13, no. 3 (1926), ably presents the pension issue and the administration of the Pension Bureau. Mary R. Dearing, *Veterans in Politics: The Story of the G.A.R.* (Baton Rouge, La., 1952), is extremely useful in its treatment of veterans' pension policy in the Harrison administration. Vincent P. De Santis, *Republicans Face the Southern Question* (Baltimore, 1959), is a valuable treatment of the Harrison administration's relations with black leaders and of pertinent policy questions.

William McKinley

Paul W. Glad

William McKinley THE LIBRARY OF CONGRESS

O NE of the most beloved of American presidents, William McKinley served as the nation's chief executive during a time when the American people surveyed their world with confidence. Recovering from a severe economic depression after his election in 1896, they dreamed of unprecedented economic expansion. Then the stunning military victories over Spain in 1898 reinforced a sense of national purpose as the United States took its place among the great powers. McKinley received much of the credit for achievements at home and abroad as the nineteenth century drew to a close, and under his leadership Americans welcomed the new century optimistically.

McKinley was the first truly modern president, but his enormous popularity derived from something more than his capacity to move with the times. A man of integrity, he firmly believed that the nation must adhere to the fundamental principles on which it was founded. With copybook truisms, uttered no less sincerely because they were truisms, he managed to convey a sense of fidelity to those principles. Thus, despite the momentous events over which he presided, he was able to reassure the American people that they had not broken with the best of their past.

Soldier and Lawyer

William McKinley, Jr., was born in the village of Niles, Ohio, on 29 January 1843, the seventh of nine children. His father, the manager of a charcoal furnace, worked diligently to house, feed, clothe, and educate his growing family. Placing a higher value on education than on creature comforts, the McKinleys moved to Poland on the other side of Youngstown, where young William was enrolled in the Poland Academy. A good student, though not a brilliant one, he succeeded by dint of hard work and exceptional retention. Reserved and reticent in private conversation, he excelled in public speaking and took an active part in the debating societies that were an important extracurricular activity of the time. In 1860 he matriculated at Allegheny College in Meadville, Pennsylvania, but he did not remain there long. He ran short of money, and illness at the end of his first term prevented completion of his classes. Home again, he went to work clerking in the post office and teaching school, hoping that he could earn enough to return to college.

Five years were to pass before McKinley resumed his studies, for the Civil War lengthened the interruption of his formal education. After the fall of Fort Sumter, he enlisted in the Twenty-third Ohio Volunteer Regiment, under the command of Major Rutherford B. Hayes. He remained in the army four years, serving with distinction and winning periodic promotions until finally he was mustered out as a brevet major in July 1865. The war broadened McKinley's experience and strengthened his sense of responsibility, but it drastically modified neither his personal character nor his commitment to the fundamental principles he had learned at home and in school. Like Abraham Lincoln, who became his model, he fought to preserve the Union and to end involuntary servitude. In later years he remained sensitive to human need, and as president he did much to overcome lingering sectional antipathies.

The youthful war hero returned to civilian activities calmly, almost stoically, asking no searching questions about the meaning of life but bearing himself with a grace and dignity that belied his years. He was not without ambition. Indeed, his military accomplishments reinforced his assumption that he could exercise a positive influence in whatever career he chose. The important question for McKinley, then, was what profession he should enter, not whether he would become successful in practicing it. Disdaining the humdrum daily activities of the marketplace, he chose to study law. After reading in the office of Charles Glidden, a well-known Ohio lawyer, he spent a term at Albany (New York) Law School. He was admitted to the bar in March 1867, and he opened an office in Canton, Ohio, later that year.

Entry into Ohio Politics

The young attorney plunged into politics almost immediately, working for Hayes in the gubernatorial campaign of 1867 and for Grant in the presidential campaign of 1868. McKinley's service to the Republican party brought its initial reward with his election as prosecuting attorney of Stark County in 1869, and for the rest of his life he was either campaigning for public office or carrying out the duties of public office. In 1877, having served his political apprenticeship, he entered Congress from the seventeenth Ohio district. His long tenure in the House of Representatives, interrupted only by his being temporarily unseated after a close election in 1882, was to last until 1890, when he was defeated as a result of the gerrymandering of his district. McKinley returned home to enter the Ohio gubernatorial race in 1891. Elected by a comfortable margin, he won reelection in 1893 with an overwhelming majority.

Despite occasional setbacks, McKinley fared well in the politics of Ohio, a key state for anyone seeking national prominence. With its strategic location, industrial growth, and population expansion, Ohio provided a setting in which the forces shaping modern America could be observed in microcosm. The characteristics that made it a bellwether state imposed unusual demands on political leaders. Having to satisfy northerners and southerners, immigrants and American-born, Catholics and Protestants, laborers, industrialists, and farmers—in short a diversity of economic and cultural interests—a politician in Ohio could seldom afford the luxury of campaigning on a single issue. To become successful in politics required transcending limited causes and defining attainable objectives for a complex, protean society. No one ever performed that service for the state better than did McKinley, and by espousing a form of benign economic nationalism, he appealed to a broad range of interests in the nation as a whole.

The stand McKinley took on issues important to his constituency was never determined by economic considerations alone. Neither was he motivated solely by a desire to win votes. McKinley was a decent, honorable man who genuinely respected people and took pleasure in working with them. To the delight of cartoonists, he resembled Napoleon. His facial features and his sturdy frame were, in fact, strikingly like those of the emperor, but even his harshest critics could find in his manner little that was autocratic or imperial. He carried himself with a decorum that did not interfere with his sensitivity to human need.

The traits of character that attracted nearly all who had personal dealings with McKinley were severely tested early in his career. In 1871 he married vivacious Ida Saxton, whose father was one of Canton's leading bankers, and within a year the couple announced the birth of a daughter, Katherine. Awaiting the arrival of their second child in 1873, the McKinleys suffered a reversal of fortune. Ida's mother died, the young wife underwent labor in a state of extreme grief, and there were complications. The infant lived less than a year. Then, to compound McKinley's anguish, little Katie died of typhoid fever a few months later, and Ida was never again to enjoy good health.

Politics proved therapeutic for McKinley, and he devoted himself wholeheartedly to them. Yet he remained attentive to his wife's needs, and his humanitarian concern repeatedly led him to identify with persons in difficulty. At the time of his daughter's death, the nation was undergoing an economic depression resulting from the Panic of 1873. The hard times brought a profound social unrest that often gave way to violence.

Disturbances developed close to home when, in March 1876, coal miners in the Tuscarawas Valley struck for higher pay and better working conditions. Mineowners responded by bringing in strikebreakers from Cleveland, a move that incited the miners to riot. Local authorities were unable to keep the peace, Governor Hayes called out the militia, and a group of miners was arrested for disorderly conduct. Upon hearing of the miners' troubles, McKinley took up their cause. In a well-prepared legal defense, he argued that, had the operators been reasonable, no strike would have occurred. His persuasiveness secured the acquittal of all but one of the strikers and, characteristically, he accepted no fee for his services. The workers never forgot, and in his political campaigns McKinley could always count on significant support from labor.

McKinley in Congress

After his election to the United States House of Representatives, McKinley quickly found himself faced with the necessity of taking a position on two issues that had emerged as important ones during the economic troubles of the middle 1870s: the silver and tariff questions. The first pitted the advocates of bimetallism against proponents of the gold standard. Although never a defender of unrestricted inflation, McKinley favored the remonetization of silver. Aware of silver sentiment among his constituents, he sought some means of securing bimetallism without inflation. He therefore rejected the advice of fellow Republicans and voted for the Bland-Allison Act of 1878, which authorized limited silver purchases and instructed the treasury secretary either to coin the silver or to issue silver certificates. Bimetallists hailed the act as only the first step toward remonetization of silver. Yet, with the return of prosperity and with limited silver purchases assured, agitation for soft money declined. When bimetallism again became the center of political controversy, McKinley was a candidate for the presidency of the United States.

While his vote for bimetallism was to cause him some embarrassment, McKinley concentrated his energies on the tariff, a matter he considered of far greater importance than silver. Upon entering Congress, he had wasted no time in making his position clear. He insisted that until the United States was able to meet foreign competition, high tariffs were necessary to the welfare of all classes. The tariff produced high wages, he asserted, and the laboring man had as great an interest in protection as did the manufacturer. McKinley's first action in the House was to submit a petition from workers who opposed tariff reductions, and in later years his name became synonymous with protection. An admirer of Henry Clay, he urged the extensive collaboration of all sections and classes in a harmonious new American system. The tariff was, in his view, a key measure for achieving national order and tranquillity.

McKinley helped write a protectionist plank for the Republican platform of 1888, and after Republican successes in the election that year, he presided over the House Ways and Means Committee. Because tariff duties were producing a treasury surplus and because disposing of the surplus invited corruption, reformers were demanding that rates be reduced. His mind again moving toward synthesis, McKinley saw the problem as one of reducing revenues without lowering the rates. He therefore proposed to resolve the issue not by accepting tariff reductions but by increasing duties on key items to the point where they became prohibitive.

Passed by Congress in 1890, the McKinley Tariff contained three innovative provisions. To prevent the importation of wheat and other foodstuffs from Canada and Europe, it established a schedule of duties on agricultural products. To satisfy consumer demand for lower sugar prices and to reduce the treasury surplus, it placed raw sugar on the free list while compensating domestic growers with a bounty of 2 cents a pound. Finally, at the insistence of Secretary of State James G. Blaine, it included a reciprocity section permitting the imposition of duties on products from Latin American countries that refused free entry to American products. Although the new tariff met criticism from reformers, who saw it as a measure to favor special interests, it at least helped to reduce the surplus while continuing protection. More important, McKinley became a convert to the idea of reciprocity, and to the end of his life, he urged such commercial agreements with other nations.

The Politics of Depression

The McKinley Tariff, together with lavish expenditures on pensions and pork-barrel schemes, aroused resentment against the "Billion-Dollar Congress," and as a consequence the elections of 1890 brought a Democratic landslide. Yet the Republican losses, including his own, proved a blessing for McKinley. He quickly rebounded to become governor of Ohio for two terms, thereby gaining administrative experience while avoiding the stigma of further association with unpopular national policies. His growing prominence in the party led to his serving as chairman of the Republican National Convention in 1892 and to his winning enough support to be mentioned as a nominee for the presidency. Aware of unrest throughout the land and within Republican ranks, he rejected the suggestion that he throw his hat into the ring. He thus remained in relative safety in Columbus as Grover Cleveland returned to the White House and as the depression that began in 1893 deepened into one of the worst economic disasters in American history.

The depression brought business failures, industrial unemployment, and low farm prices. As economic conditions worsened, social tensions increased. Heated debates over causes of the nation's problems pitted the urban East against the rural West and South, the conservative against the radical, and labor against capital. As in any depression, explanations for hard times multiplied. Ultimately, the debates concentrated on money and currency. The Sherman Silver Purchase Act, passed

the same year as McKinley's tariff legislation, had been inadequate to meet the demand for better prices or for an increase in the stock of money. Once again the segments of society that stood to gain from higher prices, especially the farmers of the West and South, reiterated their cries for free and unlimited coinage of silver.

To Grover Cleveland, the arguments of the silverites were anathema. Securing repeal of the Sherman Act, he learned to his sorrow that while repeal did not halt the depression, his stand on the currency question divided the Democratic party. Silver Democrats listened to orators such as William Jennings Bryan elaborate on the iniquities of gold and on ways in which the gold standard benefited the financiers of Wall Street.

Silver was not the only issue that divided the Democrats during the depression of the 1890s. For years officials in the Treasury Department had considered a gold reserve of at least $100 million essential to sound fiscal policy, but that reserve dwindled to $62 million in 1894 and to less than $42 million early the next year. Cleveland's response was to negotiate an agreement with J. P. Morgan and a syndicate of New York bankers to obtain gold for the treasury by selling bonds. Such maneuvering simply confirmed suspicions that Watt Street was in league with conservative Democrats who remained loyal to the president. To compound the problems of the Cleveland administration, labor unrest summoned up the specter of revolution. Jacob Coxey led an army of jobless workers in a march on Washington to demonstrate for unemployment relief, and violence broke out in Chicago when Attorney General Richard Olney issued an injunction to halt a strike at the Pullman Palace Car Company.

Blaming Grover Cleveland for the depression and facing a divided Democratic party, the Republicans anticipated a return to their winning ways in the elections of 1894. They were not disappointed. After electing a lopsided majority in both houses of Congress as well as in state and local offices, they were confident that with the right candidate they would recapture the presidency in 1896. As plans for the campaign began to take shape, William McKinley clearly emerged as the favorite of most Republicans. Although he had voted for the Bland-Allison Act and the Sherman Silver Purchase Act, his work on the tariff demonstrated an understanding of economic problems that put monetary manipulation in its proper place and satisfied the party faithful.

Content with McKinley's record in politics, Republicans might have shown greater concern for the depression's effect on his personal affairs. He had unwisely endorsed the notes of a friend whose tin-plate business failed and left him liable for debts amounting to more than $100,000. Fortunately, with the help of Mark Hanna, William R. Day, Myron Herrick, and Herman H. Kohlsaat, who took it upon themselves to manage his affairs, McKinley weathered the financial crisis. He made no secret of his difficulties, and sympathetic Democrats as well as Republicans contributed to a fund for his relief. If anything, adversity again worked to his advantage, for it brought him into a closer relationship with Mark Hanna. McKinley first met the Cleveland industrialist in the early 1870s, and Hanna had proved himself to be a reliable associate. Now, having helped to rescue McKinley from financial misfortune, Hanna was prepared to devote his incomparable organizational skills to his friend's campaign for the presidency.

The Election of 1896

The party conventions of 1896 set the tone for one of the most exciting political campaigns in American history. Meeting in St. Louis in June, the Republicans drafted a platform calling for high tariffs, a large navy, the annexation of Hawaii, and independence for Cuba, but the delegates were most interested in the currency plank. Declaring the party to be "unreservedly for sound money," the plank opposed bimetallism "except by international agreement with the leading commercial nations of the earth." McKinley could endorse the phrasing without reservation, but the prosilver faction of the party sought less equivocal wording. When they did not get it, they departed the hall, leaving the convention united behind the gold standard and free to proceed with the nomination of candidates.

The people, thundered Ohio Senator Joseph B. Foraker in steamy St. Louis, wanted something more than a good businessman or fearless leader; they wanted "the exact opposite of the present free-trade, deficit-making, bond-issuing, laborsaving Democratic administration." In short, they wanted McKinley, and the convention nominated him on the first ballot. Soon after the Republicans had chosen their candidate, the Democrats selected Willam Jennings Bryan at a stormy convention in Chicago. Nominated on a platform that contained a demand for the free and unlimited coinage of silver as its most important plank, Bryan became the standard-bearer of the Populist party as well.

The ensuing campaign developed into one that provided abundant material for a study in contrasts. Determined to take his cause to the people, Bryan traveled eighteen thousand miles, delivering six hundred speeches to an estimated 5 million persons. McKinley remained at home in Canton to greet and talk informally with a series of delegations brought in by the Republican campaign committee. As McKinley's campaign manager, Hanna was as untiring as the itinerant Bryan. With the help of a well-staffed speakers' bureau, he made sure that voters heard all the arguments for gold. Identifying McKinley as "the advance agent of prosperity," Republican orators addressed sympathetic audiences of voters dissatisfied with business stagnation and unemployment. Bryan, the Democrats, and the Populists found themselves constantly on the defensive as they sought to clarify the intricacies and the importance of monetary policy.

In general, the campaign for silver attracted farmers seeking higher crop prices, but urban workers and ethnic groups that had traditionally supported the Democratic party could not be persuaded that they had much to gain from bimetallism. Nothing in McKinley's campaign alienated ethnic blocs; nothing he said to workers seemed so divorced from realities of the depression as did Bryan's plea for silver. Neither did McKinley neglect the farmers. His kindly nature, his imperturbable nationalism, and his long experience in Ohio politics had produced a broker politician of consummate skill.

McKinley did not offer a new heaven and a new earth, but as his campaign pronouncements indicate, he at least offered hope for every interest group in a troubled society. "The farmer is suffering today because the number of his competitors has increased and his best customers are out of work," he told a delegation of farmers. Raising tariff rates would reduce competition and set factories to operating again. Everyone would benefit. "You don't get customers through the mint; you get them through the factory" was his refrain. For a delegation of Pennsylvania coal miners, he summed up his argument against silver: "We do not want cheap money, any more than we want cheap labor in the United States."

At the close of the campaign, Republicans had good reason to be optimistic. When the returns were in, McKinley had polled 7,104,779 popular votes to 6,502,925 for Bryan. The geographic distribution of the vote indicates that McKinley's strength lay in the Northeast, the area of greatest urban and industrial

A campaign poster trumpets the candidacy of William McKinley, emphasizing a prosperous economy and strength abroad. CORBIS

development. Three-fourths of American industry centered in the manufacturing belt east of the Mississippi River and north of the Ohio River and Mason-Dixon Line, where three-fourths of the manufacturing wage earners lived. It was in this region that McKinley won the election. He captured all of its electoral votes as well as those of the upper South (Delaware, Maryland, West Virginia, and all but one in Kentucky), those of rural states in the upper Middle West (Iowa, Minnesota, and North Dakota), and those of Oregon and California.

Forming a New Administration

During the interval between his election and his inauguration, McKinley busied himself with selecting a cabinet and setting his administration in place. Cabinet appointments are never easy to make, for they involve considerations that may have little to do with qualifications of candidates. The president-elect proceeded logically enough and in the end satisfied most of the interests desiring a representative close to the White House. His most difficult decisions concerned the future of his campaign manager. McKinley asked Hanna to become postmaster general, a sensible request, but Hanna preferred a seat in the Senate. A way out of the dilemma came with the appointment of John Sherman as secretary of state, which created a senatorial vacancy. Ohio Governor Asa Bushnell then commissioned Hanna to take Sherman's place on Capitol Hill. The Sherman appointment was not a happy one, for the crusty old senator had long since passed his prime. Fortunately, McKinley secured the skills of William R. Day as assistant secretary. It was Day, along with the second assistant secretary, Alvee A. Adee, who was actually to run the Department of State during the demanding months before the Spanish-American War. Day assumed full responsibility as secretary after Sherman's resignation in April 1898.

If for no other reason, the controversy over silver made the appointment of a secretary of the treasury nearly as important as the appointment of a secretary of state. McKinley's first choice was Nelson Dingley, a congressman from Maine; but Dingley's health was poor, and he was reluctant to sacrifice a sure seat and seniority in the House for the uncertainties of administration. After contemplating several other possibilities, McKinley finally settled on Lyman J. Gage, a Chicago banker and staunch upholder of the gold standard. A man of candor as well

as tact, Gage was to become one of the president's closest advisers.

Other outstanding appointments included John Davis Long as secretary of the navy and James H. Wilson as secretary of agriculture. The highly respected Long, who had gained administrative experience as governor of Massachusetts, proved a popular choice. His assistant secretary, Theodore Roosevelt, was far more controversial. Although disliked by Thomas C. Platt, political boss of New York's Republicans, "T. R." had important friends who urged his appointment. No squabbling surrounded "Tama Jim" Wilson of Iowa. Developing a warm relationship with McKinley, he soon became a key member of the cabinet and continued to head the Department of Agriculture until 1913. Also joining McKinley's official family were James A. Gary as postmaster general, Judge Joseph McKenna as attorney general, Cornelius Bliss as secretary of the interior, and Russell Alger as secretary of war. Except for Alger, who was to demonstrate his ineptitude during the war with Spain, the cabinet was competent; Wilson and Gage were unusually able.

Economic Recovery and Foreign Affairs

Once he had assumed the responsibilities of office, McKinley immediately turned his attention to measures for assuring economic recovery. The tariff received first consideration, and even before his inauguration McKinley had worked with leaders of the House to secure legislation that would be acceptable. Nelson Dingley, who chaired the Ways and Means Committee, submitted a bill that did not drastically raise the duties of the Wilson-Gorman Tariff of 1894. While it passed the House quickly at the end of March, the Senate increased the rates, and in its final form it became the highest tariff in American history. McKinley had reservations, but he nevertheless signed the bill into law on 24 July 1897. One reason he did is that the provision for reciprocity trade agreements, though inadequate, promised an opportunity to bring the United States into an international economic system from which the world might secure extraordinary rewards. The distance McKinley had moved from protectionism to market expansion became apparent during the summer of 1897, when he told the Cincinnati Commercial Club that in addition to serving economic ends, good trade ensured goodwill. "It should be our settled purpose to open trade wherever we can," he argued, "making our ships and our commerce messengers of peace and amity."

A second measure for economic recovery involved carrying out the Republican party pledge to secure an international agreement on bimetallism. McKinley appointed a special commission to secure such an agreement, but little came of its efforts. England and France committed themselves to the gold standard, and Japan, Russia, and Germany followed soon after. Apart from positions taken by other nations, however, bimetallism quickly became a dead issue. New discoveries of gold in South Africa, Australia, and Canada brought a dramatic increase in world supplies and a corresponding decline in gold prices. The demand for silver quieted as the need for it disappeared. Production curves and indexes of business activity began to rise during the summer of 1897, and Americans began to turn their attention to other matters.

Economic trends, ideas, and programs interacted during the late nineteenth century. Business fluctuations prompted economic theorists, both professional and amateur, to develop explanations of recurrent crises. Between 1873 and 1896, monetary theories were often central in the arguments of economic analysts, but in those same years an alternative explanatory model attracted increasing attention. That model posited unlimited industrial and agricultural productivity, on the one hand, and a limited home market, on the other. Given such conditions, demand would stagnate while stocks and inventories built up unless American producers found new outlets beyond the home market. Here was a theory that provided not only an explanation of the business cycle but a program for action as well. It was a theory that bypassed controversies over the currency; bimetallists and monometallists could support trade expansion with equal enthusiasm.

No one found overproduction and market-expansion ideas more convincing than did McKinley. In 1895 he had delivered the keynote address to the new National Association of Manufacturers at its organizational meeting. "We want our own markets for our manufactures and agricultural products," he told a receptive audience. "We want a foreign market for our surplus products.. . . We want a reciprocity which will give us foreign markets for our surplus products, and in turn that will open our markets to foreigners for those products which they produce and which we do not." During McKinley's first presidential year his new insight into the importance of commercial expansion provided a frame of reference into which he could fit developments abroad. Increasingly, foreign affairs demanded his most careful consideration.

The first problem in foreign affairs to attract McKinley's attention was the annexation of Hawaii, a matter that had troubled his predecessor. Hoping for American ownership of the islands, sugar growers there had staged a revolution against Queen Liliuokalani in 1893. President Harrison had forwarded a treaty of annexation to the Senate, but Cleveland withdrew it on the grounds that it did not represent the will of the Hawaiian people. The Republican platform of 1896 had included a plank favoring annexation, and in December 1897, McKinley advised Congress to proceed. Troubles in Cuba were exacerbating tensions with Spain, and the president believed that the need for a base in the Pacific justified taking the islands. Congress finally passed a joint resolution annexing Hawaii, and McKinley signed it on 7 July 1898. By that time the United States was at war with Spain.

The Coming of War

The immediate causes of armed conflict lay closer to home than the islands of the Pacific. Cuba, once the center of Spain's New World empire and the richest of Spain's remaining possessions, had long suffered from an oppressive colonial system. During the Ten Years' War of 1868–1878 and again in 1895, the Cuban people rebelled against the mother country. Spanish troops forcibly quelled the first insurrection, and in the second their harsh treatment of the rebels intensified. American sympathy for the Cubans mounted as the yellow press in the United States published lurid details of Spanish atrocities. Yet the pressure of popular support for Cuban independence, though increasing, was not in itself sufficient to bring about intervention. Also important was the growing economic stake in the "Pearl of the Antilles." During the thirty years of unrest in Cuba, American capital investments there had risen to $50 million, and trade had mounted to as much as $100 million. To Americans with financial or commercial interests in Cuba, the rebellion threatened disaster, and they urged a speedy resolution of the difficulty. Unlike the yellow press and the jingoes, most businessmen opposed war. They were fearful that armed conflict might interfere with the orderly process of recovery from depression.

As the fate of Cuba became a subject of national attention, McKinley evaluated the forces at work and considered possible responses to them. Lacking complete confidence in his secretary of state, he himself assumed responsibility for developing a policy. Though he kept his own counsel, he did solicit advice and information. Especially important were the reports he received from Fitzhugh Lee, American consul general in Havana, and Stewart Woodford, who had been carefully though belatedly chosen to serve as American ambassador in Madrid. By the time Woodford presented his credentials to the Spanish foreign minister in the fall of 1897, McKinley had determined that neither war nor the annexation of Cuba would serve the national interest. He therefore proposed that he mediate the conflict so as to secure Cuban autonomy under the Spanish crown. A new liberal government came to power in Madrid coincident with Woodford's arrival, and hopes for a settlement ran high.

The response to McKinley's suggestions was disappointing. Although pledging more humane treatment of the rebels, the Spanish regime of Práxedes Mateo Sagasta rejected mediation and, instead of real autonomy, proposed a Cuban legislature dominated by a council of Spanish appointees. Few Americans and certainly none of the rebels could detect in the proposal much more than the promise of conciliation, and promises were not enough. Yet McKinley was a man of prodigious patience. In his annual message of December 1897 he repudiated the idea of annexation and urged that Spain "be given a reasonable chance to realize her expectations and to prove the asserted efficacy of things to which she stands irrevocably committed." Not fully appreciating the warnings that the presidential message also contained, those who favored military intervention were predictably disappointed that McKinley did not take a firmer position.

Carefully worded though it was, the message also produced some unexpected consequences. Enrique Dupuy de Lôme, the Spanish minister in Washington, found it insincere and hypocritical. He wrote his opinions to a friend in Havana, and in the process, he described McKinley as a cheap, vacillating politician. It was a foolish thing to do. A New York-based Cuban junta had been working vigorously for American intervention, and its spies stole the letter. Anticipating that publication of its insulting contents would add strength to the sentiment for intervention, the junta promptly turned a facsimile over to the *New York Journal*. It appeared on 9 February 1898, and readers were duly enraged by its insolence. Although Dupuy resigned, and the Spanish government forwarded an apology, the harm had been done.

The yellow press and the jingoes were still seething over the de Lôme letter when an even more disturbing communiqué arrived in Washington. McKinley had been concerned with the threat to American lives and property in Cuba, and he had ordered the battleship *Maine* to Havana. Publicized as a courtesy call to reduce tensions with Spain, the visit was clearly intended as a show of strength. On the night of 15 February the ship exploded and sank with a loss of 266 lives. Shaken by news of the disaster, McKinley insisted on an official investigation. If nothing else, it would take time and help avoid precipitate action. Despite public clamor for military confrontation, he did not believe that American forces were adequately prepared for war. From Congress he asked for, and received, an appropriation of $50 million for national defense, to be spent at his discretion.

McKinley's tendency to procrastinate often left doubts about his intentions, and his tendency to keep his own counsel helped to assure neither Congress nor the American people that he had a clear sense of direction. While the nation awaited the report of the *Maine* investigation, administration supporters less patient than McKinley gravitated toward the interventionist camp. Senator Redfield Proctor of Vermont, a fair-minded opponent of war, addressed his colleagues for several hours on 17 March, describing in clinical detail the concentration camps he had seen on a recent trip to Cuba. His conclusion that the rebels would not accept Spanish rule and that peace and justice required intervention was a warning to the president that Congress now expected bold action.

War with Spain

The report from the commission investigating the *Maine* disaster was in the president's hands by 25 March. It concluded that the cause of the explosion was external, and most Americans immediately assumed that Spanish agents had been responsible for it. With war sentiment building up throughout the country and in Congress, McKinley continued to urge caution, still hoping that negotiations might bring an end to problems in Cuba. On 27 March, Secretary Day cabled Woodford outlining the administration's last plan. The final ultimatum called for an immediate armistice and reiterated McKinley's offer of arbitration. Shortly thereafter, Day warned that unless Spain capitulated immediately, public pressure would compel the president to ask for a declaration of war. McKinley feared that if he did not respond to the pressure, his supporters would desert him. Congress might then take matters into its own hands and declare war without McKinley's requesting it.

The Spanish reply to McKinley's ultimatum arrived at the White House on 1 April. It assented to arbitration of the *Maine* affair, abandonment of reconcentration in the western provinces, acceptance of American financial assistance, and a relief program for Cuba. Yet Spain agreed neither to suspend hostilities nor to approve American mediation. In Madrid, Woodford thought that the Spanish ministry knew it had lost Cuba but preferred war to mediation. Nevertheless, he pleaded for more time to work out a solution.

For McKinley, time had run out, and he began drafting a message to Congress asking for a declaration of war. At the last minute, on 10 April, he received a communiqué from Woodford indicating that the queen regent had consented to suspend hostilities and move toward autonomy for Cuba. Given the state of public and congressional opinion, it was too late. McKinley asked for intervention on 19 April, and Congress granted his request the next day, adding only the Teller Amendment, which renounced any intention to annex Cuba. A formal declaration of war followed within a week.

Americans greeted the coming of war with celebration. Patriotic fervor stilled the criticism of McKinley, and as commander in chief he found himself enormously popular throughout the land. Men from all walks of life were eager to share in the expected American triumphs, and enlistments soared. Yet it was with good reason that McKinley had questioned the fighting readiness of the armed forces. Despite a year's warning, they remained unprepared.

Numbering only 28,000 men and officers, the army had watched as the navy, the nation's first line of defense, received most of the $50 million appropriated in March. Now, suddenly increasing to more than 250,000 troops, land forces faced immense if not insurmountable problems in supply and logistics. Half of the volunteers never left training camps during the war, and many of those who did were is-

sued winter woolen uniforms for warfare in the tropics. If all the troops mobilized had seen combat, some of them would have seen it without ammunition, for there was not enough to go around. Selected as the point of embarkation, the Port of Tampa proved an unfortunate choice. Only one railroad connected the city with its inadequate piers. Boxcars backed up for miles, cargoes disappeared in the confusion, and troops found themselves compelled to take matters into their own hands, relying on their wits for survival.

The navy fared better than the army, in part because it escaped the pressures of rapid expansion, and in part because for fifteen years it had kept abreast of innovations in maritime technology. Beyond that, McKinley and his secretary of the navy could rely on commanders who had given much thought to strategy should hostilities begin. It is not surprising, then, that the navy won the first great American victory. In the fall of 1897, Commodore George Dewey had received command of the Asiatic squadron, and with the declaration of war, he was ordered to proceed from Hong Kong to the Philippines. By 30 April the squadron was at the entrance to Manila Bay, where Admiral Montojo had anchored the sizable but decrepit Spanish fleet. The following day, the American force sailed into the bay and annihilated Montojo's fleet without sustaining a loss.

Attributing the *Maine* explosion of the previous February to Spanish treachery may have led many Americans to overestimate enemy strength. At Manila the Spanish were actually incapable of effectively returning fire from their ancient hulks, and mines planted in the channel had no fuses. Yet participants could celebrate the victory as a convincing demonstration of American naval power. When the American people learned of it a week later, they were ecstatic, and they immediately gave Dewey an honored place in their pantheon of heroes. McKinley, more concerned with pursuing the war to a successful conclusion, authorized an expedition to capture and occupy the Philippines. Though the Americans did not take Manila until after Spain had signed a peace protocol, it was clear that the United States had become a power in the Far East. The ramifications of that development were many, and American foreign policy was to undergo momentous changes in the postwar period.

After Dewey's victory, attention turned to the Caribbean theater and to plans for an invasion of Cuba. Actually carrying out the attack was complicated by the confusion in Tampa, by lack of agreement among high-ranking officers in the army, and by Secretary Alger's failure to provide either leadership or coordination. Alger's vanity led him to promise more than was possible, and his arrogance led him to blame others for his inability to meet commitments. In the army itself, supervision of all operations, at least theoretically, rested with Major General Nelson Appleton Miles. The appointment he held provided very little real power, he disliked McKinley personally, and he nurtured hopes of using his military reputation to gain high political office. More important for the moment, Miles opposed rushing off helter-skelter to invade Cuba. He favored postponing the assault until fall, when cooler weather and better training of troops would assure success. A third principal in the military drama that was taking on some of the characteristics of comic opera was General William R. Shafter, who by reason of seniority took command in the field. Cautious and corpulent, he was a prototypical product of the army's bureaucracy. Yet he showed good sense, and while he did not inspire the troops to heroic achievement, his caution reduced casualties.

Although McKinley might have recognized the merit in arguments for postponing an invasion until fall, he was acutely conscious of political pressures that called for immediate action. Furthermore, the navy was to share in the operation, and Secretary Long strongly urged that it get under way. McKinley's patience with Alger and the army was wearing thin, and he finally decided to move. The fleet of Admiral William T. Sampson and Commodore Winfield Scott Schley blockaded Santiago on 6 June, and the following day McKinley ordered Shafter to transport his troops to Cuba. The operation was scarcely a model of military efficiency, but by 29 June it had come within a mile and a half of Santiago.

The Battle of San Juan Hill, which took place on the city's outskirts during the first two days of July, was bloody but inconclusive. Shafter grew despondent and thought of retreat, but then the navy saved the day. Contained in Santiago Bay, the Spanish squadron of Admiral Pascual Cervera y Topete began sailing out of the harbor on 3 July to challenge the ships of Sampson and Schley. Within hours the destruction of Spanish sea power was complete. "The fleet under my command offers the nation as a Fourth of July present the whole of Cervera's fleet," read the cable from Sampson.

The victory at Santiago Bay signaled an early conclusion of hostilities. Rather than attack the city itself, Shafter negotiated its surrender on 17 July. With that surrender the fighting in Cuba petered out, and only Puerto Rico remained as the last vestige of Spanish empire in the western hemisphere. McKinley had already authorized operations to take the island, and an American expedition quickly accomplished that objective a few days before Spain sued for peace. After meeting with the cabinet, McKinley laid down the American terms: Spanish evacuation of Cuba; cession of Puerto Rico to the United States as an indemnity; and American occupation of Manila, pending final treaty agreement. Spain balked at the last provision, but McKinley would not budge. The Spanish finally capitulated on 10 August, and the war came to an end.

The Treaty of Paris

The close of hostilities brought the United States to a critical juncture in international affairs, and along with that development came some important personnel changes in the Department of State. William R. Day cheerfully resigned as secretary—it was an assignment he had accepted with reluctance—and became chairman of the American peace commission that went to Paris to work out the treaty with Spain. To take Day's place, McKinley named John Hay, the brilliant ambassador to Great Britain and a man of long experience in international affairs. Hay was to exercise a profound influence on the shaping of American foreign policy in the twentieth century, but for the moment McKinley and the nation were preoccupied with the treaty negotiations in Paris.

On 16 September the commissioners met with McKinley in the White House and received their instructions. The president reiterated his opposition to the annexation of Cuba and his insistence upon acquiring Puerto Rico. The final disposition of the Philippines presented a more difficult problem. Filipinos under the leadership of Emilio Aguinaldo had, like the Cubans, revolted against Spanish authority and welcomed American assistance in their effort to win independence. Yet McKinley had doubts about the wisdom of independence for the islands. For one thing, many Americans had caught a vision of commercial possibilities in the Orient, and an American outpost in the Philippines might well serve the interests of trade. For another thing, the United States was not alone in its enthusiasm for expansion in the Far East. Germany, in particular, appeared ready for a colonization effort if the United States withdrew.

Characteristically, McKinley reviewed the alternatives for American policy in the Philippines and rejected all but one. Returning the islands to Spain was out of the question. The Spanish had already demonstrated their administrative incompetence, and the American people would oppose such a move. To grant independence without provision for defense of the islands would be tantamount to turning them over to Germany or some other imperialist nation. Taking only one island or establishing an American protectorate would mean accepting responsibilities without power. By such reasoning, McKinley concluded that the only course was to take the Philippines, improve conditions of life for the Filipinos, and eventually grant them independence when they had achieved viability as a nation.

In the end, the American negotiators in Paris followed McKinley's wishes. Signed on 10 December 1898, the treaty provided that Cuba should become independent and that Puerto Rico, Guam, and the Philippines should be ceded to the United States. To placate the Spanish, whose pride had been wounded, the United States agreed to a payment of $20 million for the newly acquired territory. The terms of the Treaty of Paris did not meet universal approval in the United States, but to enthusiasts and critics alike, they marked the path of empire that McKinley had apparently chosen to follow. The acquisition of the Philippines, along with the annexation of Hawaii and, later, of Wake Island and American Samoa, provided coaling stations and bases that could prove useful for the commercial and missionary penetration of Asia. The proponents of empire also found Puerto Rico an admirable possession from which to defend a proposed isthmian canal, should it be completed.

Submission of the treaty to the Senate rekindled old debates over the nature of the Republic and the advisability of territorial expansion. In the discussion of ratification, Senator Henry Cabot Lodge led the fight for the treaty, while his colleague from Massachusetts, Senator George F. Hoar, rallied the opposition. A lively debate also took place outside the Senate chamber as expansionists confronted anti-imperialists on a wide range of issues. Opponents of the treaty argued that it was both immoral and unconstitutional for the United States to impose American rule on an alien people without their consent. Expansionists countered with moral arguments of their own, contending that the United States had a duty to uplift and educate backward populations in order that they might properly appreciate the blessings of liberty. Expansionists also believed that by ful-

filling the American destiny in the Pacific, they would assure the economic well-being of the American people at home. Yet neither American manufacturers nor American workers unanimously favored expansion. Andrew Carnegie thought, for example, that acquisition of the Philippines would threaten the peace and security that were necessary for foreign trade. And Samuel Gompers feared that imperial expansion would open the way for cheap contract labor to enter the United States and drive down the wages of American workers.

On 6 February 1899 the debate in the Senate came to an end, and senators passed the treaty by a vote of fifty-seven to twenty-seven, one vote more than the necessary two-thirds. Except for Hoar and Senator Eugene Hale of Maine, Republicans voted with the majority; although twenty-two Democrats voted no, ten voted for the treaty. Willam Jennings Bryan, front-runner for the Democratic nomination in 1900 and an anti-imperialist, had urged that the treaty be approved in order to end the war and ease the way for Philippine independence. His influence over Democratic senators was important in securing ratification. Yet it was McKinley who had framed the debate so as to make ratification appear to be the only logical alternative. In December he had asked the crucial question: "If, following the clear precepts of duty, territory falls to us, and the welfare of an alien people requires our guidance and protection, who will shrink from the responsibility, grave though it may be?"

American Influence in Cuba and the Philippines

While McKinley accepted congratulations on ratification of the treaty, the reaction in the Philippines was less enthusiastic. Indeed, two days before the Senate voted, Aguinaldo had again taken up the fight for independence. This time it was the Americans rather than the Spanish who stood in the way, and it was the Americans rather than the Spanish who were charged with committing atrocities in a long, bloody guerrilla war. American forces eventually captured Aguinaldo in March 1901, and by 1902 his insurrection had been crushed. The rebellion in the Philippines had turned out to be much more costly in both lives and dollars than the Spanish-American War itself.

The Philippine Insurrection was but the first of many difficulties that were to confront the United

States in distant parts of the world after the Spanish-American War. Victory brought to the McKinley administration responsibility for establishing orderly government in the newly acquired possessions. To the administration came, as well, responsibility for perfecting a foreign policy to guide the United States in the intricate diplomatic maneuvering that took place at the turn of the century. As he wrestled with the problems of policy formation, McKinley came to rely heavily on two new members of his cabinet: John Hay, who assumed office as secretary of state on 30 September 1898, and Elihu Root, who replaced Alger as secretary of war on 24 July 1899.

With governmental arrangements for the former Spanish colonies entrusted to the Department of War, Root immediately set his orderly mind to the task of working them out. His recommendations included removal of tariff barriers between Puerto Rico and the United States so as to promote economic development and "avoid trouble in the island." Although Congress, in 1900, considered a bill to carry out the recommendation, its free-trade provisions offended supporters of tariff protection. A compromise bill then restored a tariff, albeit with reduced rates. It also provided that all duties should cease when a new civil government's system of taxation had become operative. Congress passed the bill, and McKinley signed it on 12 April 1900. Civil government for the island was established on 1 May, and a legislative assembly convened on 3 December. McKinley issued a proclamation removing the tariff on 25 July 1901.

Turning to Cuba, Root insisted that its new constitution include the Platt Amendment, which gave the United States the right to intervene in Cuban affairs, bound Cuba to avoid commitment to another power, and imposed limitations on the size of the Cuban national debt. Though Cubans always resented the intrusion on their national sovereignty, Americans hailed Root's program as a model of efficiency. The military governor under Root's direction, General Leonard Wood, achieved physical, medical, and educational improvements to benefit the island and create a stable regime. In the Philippines, Root acted to strengthen the army, subdue the rebellion, and establish political institutions through the supervision of an American commission. To set the Philippine government on a solid base, McKinley in 1900 selected William Howard Taft as commissioner. It was Taft, acting on instructions from Root, who guided the transition from military to civilian government.

American Foreign Policy and the Open Door

Developing a viable foreign policy for the United States was a responsibility that rested largely with John Hay, but McKinley worked closely with his secretary of state and kept himself well informed of points at issue in the complex series of negotiations that Hay conducted. "The one indispensable feature of our foreign policy," observed Hay in 1899, "should be a friendly understanding with England." McKinley agreed, though he was more reserved in stating the point. Both understood that in relations with Canada and the Latin American nations, the United States and Britain had common objectives. Common interests extended to the Far East as well. Central in McKinley's thinking was the idea that American prosperity had come to depend on healthy commercial relations with the rest of the world. Trade, in turn, depended on international security and the avoidance of war. Security for American trade, not territorial expansion, should therefore be the major objective of American foreign policy. These, then, were the principles that governed McKinley's position in international relations after the Spanish-American War. They found application first in negotiations to assure the construction of an isthmian canal and then in working out an American policy toward China.

The interoceanic canal had long been an objective of naval enthusiasts, and a dramatic demonstration of the canal's importance captured national attention during the war with Spain. The USS *Oregon* had required ninety-eight days to make the voyage from Juan de Fuca Strait around Cape Horn to Cuba, and it was clear that military security required a shortening of the journey. Furthermore, a canal would facilitate trade with nations on the west coast of South America. McKinley had emphasized the desirability of such a "maritime highway" in his annual message of 1898, and Hay set about clearing the way for its construction. One obstacle was the Clayton-Bulwer Treaty of 1850, by which the United States and Britain had agreed to joint construction. Faced with more immediate concerns elsewhere, Britain was now prepared to have the United States proceed alone. Together with Sir Julian Pauncefote, the British ambassador, Hay therefore drafted a treaty in 1899 to provide for American construction of the canal, but the Senate so amended it that the British rejected the pact. Eventually, in 1901, Hay and Pauncefote drafted a new treaty, which both nations found acceptable. Yet by that time McKinley had died, and credit for completing the canal negotiations went to his successor.

Of greater importance, because of the way Americans perceived it, was development of the Open Door policy for China. At the time the United States gained its Philippine foothold in the Far East, the great powers were busy establishing spheres of influence for themselves in a China weakened by internal divisions and by defeat at the hands of the Japanese in the Sino-Japanese War of 1894–1895. Japan extended control over Formosa and the nearby Pescadores, and other nations found themselves attracted to the fabled markets of China itself. Russia obtained special rights in the Liaotung Peninsula; France staked out a sphere of influence on Kwangchowan Bay; Germany secured a leasehold on the Shantung Peninsula; Britain leased the port of Wei-hai, enlarged its leased territory of Kowloon, and secured recognition of economic interests in the Yangtze Valley.

American expansionists, captivated by the thought of economic penetration of the Far East, were perturbed by the partition of China. In 1898, McKinley had informed the peace commissioners in Paris that they could not be indifferent to commercial opportunities in Asia, adding that "we seek no advantages in the Orient which are not common to all. Asking only the open door for ourselves, we are ready to accord the open door to others." What McKinley meant when he referred to an open door became clearer after Hay had sent two sets of notes to the great powers. The first set, sent in September 1899, requested that each recipient avoid interfering with the commercial rights of other nations within its sphere of influence, permit Chinese officials their right to collect existing tariffs, and avoid railroad-rate and port-dues discriminations against the nationals of any country operating within Chinese leaseholds. Receiving an indifferent response, Hay announced in March 1900 that since none of the powers had raised serious objection to his note, he considered their approval "final and definitive."

Through his first Open Door notes, Hay had intended to promote trading opportunities in the Far East, and to that end he had also hoped to prevent the dismemberment of China. Unfortunately he had reckoned only with the great powers, and a society of Chinese nationalists known as the Boxers had other ideas about Chinese affairs. Launching a drive to rid their land of all foreigners, they occupied the city of Peking, cut telegraph lines, and laid siege to the British compound, where members of foreign legations had taken refuge. An international force of eighteen thousand men, including twenty-five hundred Americans, managed to rescue the beleaguered diplomats on 14 August, but the disturbance increased the possibility that China would be carved up by powers determined to secure broader and more binding commitments than they already had.

To avert that possibility, Hay issued the second set of Open Door notes in July 1900. He instructed American envoys in foreign capitals that the United States would adhere to a program of peace for China, that the nation would hold the Boxers accountable for injuries to American citizens, and that in the future the United States would uphold "the principle of equal and impartial trade with all parts of the Chinese Empire." Hay was not committing the United States to the defense of China against other powers; he was pledging only that in the promotion of American interests the United States would maintain respect for China. Through his secretary of state, McKinley had become identified with a policy that was neither as clear nor as forceful as most Americans believed it to be. To his successors he left the difficult task of coping with realities that did not always conform to popular suppositions.

For all McKinley's preoccupation with foreign affairs, he never lost sight of domestic problems, especially if they were likely to become issues in elections. In 1899, for example, he began to study the growth of large business combinations, a development that agitated the minds of reformers and that appeared to require his attention if all citizens were to share the benefits of a restored economic prosperity. Referring to the dangers of trusts and monopolies in his annual message that year, he indicated that the growth of combinations was a matter to which Congress should turn its attention. McKinley's method of handling the trusts was typical of his method of dealing with all potentially controversial matters. He waited until interested parties and persons had discussed the issues and taken positions. Then he acted to find policies for satisfying as many interests as possible. It was an approach that had served him well in the complex politics of Ohio and in Congress. It was also an approach that led to his enormous popularity in all sections of the country and among all classes of people.

McKinley's Reelection Campaign

During his campaign for reelection in 1900, McKinley followed his natural inclination to let the record speak for itself. Garret Hobart, who suffered from a serious heart ailment, had died the previous November, and selecting the vice presidential candidate provided the only real excitement at the Republican National Convention in Philadelphia. McKinley had quietly asked Root and Senator William B. Allison to consider becoming his running mate, but both had refused. In the meantime, sentiment for Theodore Roosevelt was growing. Though the president could not avoid misgivings about the Rough Rider, who had returned from Cuba a national hero, he did not wish to disrupt party unity by opposing his candidacy. McKinley therefore refused publicly to express a preference, saying only that his running mate should be the choice of the convention. Dismayed by this turn of events, Mark Hanna reportedly fretted that if Roosevelt were nominated, only "one heartbeat" would separate "that damned cowboy" from the White House. Nothing could stop the convention's ardor for Roosevelt, however, and when he received the nomination McKinley cordially sent his congratulations. As it turned out, the two made a good team. Roosevelt was a sparkling success on the hustings, allowing McKinley to remain in Canton as the dignified chief executive whose leadership had brought a return to prosperity as well as universal recognition of the nation's importance in world affairs.

For McKinley's opponent, Bryan, the campaign was a disappointing one after the exhilaration of 1896. Deprived of the silver issue by the return of prosperity, he persisted in calling for bimetallism and the inclusion of a silver plank in the Democratic platform. Yet it was imperialism that he hoped to make the paramount issue of the campaign. "History furnishes no example of turpitude baser than ours," Bryan warned, "if we now substitute our yoke for the Spanish yoke." Despite his eloquence, he was unable to persuade voters that American control over the former Spanish colonies remained a live issue after ratification of the Treaty of Paris. The upshot of a lackluster campaign was that McKinley increased his popular vote of 1896 by more than 100,000, and he captured 21 more electoral votes than he had won in 1896.

Assassination

"Your *duty* to the country is to *live* for *four* years from next March," Hanna had written McKinley following the Republican nomination. After his second inauguration, the president decided to go on an extensive tour of the western states, capping it with a visit to San Francisco. To him the journey seemed an appropriate gesture. It would offer abundant opportunities to demonstrate confidence in the future of American leadership among nations of the world. The journey fulfilled McKinley's hopes. Although his wife fell seriously ill in San Francisco, she recovered miraculously, and all along the way cheering crowds greeted the presidential entourage. Resting at home in Canton after his return, McKinley finished preparation of an address he had agreed to deliver at the Pan-American Exposition in Buffalo on 5 September.

The fair was dedicated to peace and amity in the western hemisphere, and a festive spirit prevailed at the exposition when the McKinleys arrived to celebrate President's Day. Their host was John G. Milburn, a leading member of the Buffalo bar. More than 116,000 people had come to greet them, and nearly half that number gathered in the Esplanade to hear what McKinley had to say. His remarks were appropriate to the occasion. Urging an enlightened policy of commercial reciprocity, he argued that the United States could not forever sell the products of American industry abroad without also buying the products of other countries. "The period of exclusiveness is past," cautioned the man who had once been the foremost spokesman of protective tariffs. Capable of adjusting to changing times, he now conceded that "the expansion of our trade and commerce is the pressing problem." Yet he also argued that such expansion must take place under conditions of world peace. "Commercial wars," he warned, "are unprofitable."

It was McKinley's last public utterance. The following day he toured Niagara Falls before returning to the Temple of Music to greet thousands of sightseers and well-wishers. Inconspicuous in the crowd was Leon Czolgosz, who carried in his pocket a .32-caliber Iver-Johnson revolver. Brooding over social injustice, he had been attracted to anarchism, and he had come to kill the president. The day was hot, and handkerchiefs were much in evidence as people mopped the perspiration from their brows. While Czolgosz waited, he surreptitiously wrapped the revolver in his handkerchief. The long line lurched forward as McKinley shook each hand with practiced efficiency. When the assassin reached the head of the line, he fired two shots. The president fell, grasping at his chest and abdomen.

Within minutes McKinley was taken to the emergency hospital on the grounds of the exposition. The physicians who clustered about the operating table saw instantly that the abdominal wound was very serious indeed. Patching it up as best they could under the circumstances, they removed McKinley to the Milburn house, where he had been staying since his arrival in Buffalo. For a week the president seemed to be doing well, and hopes for his recovery ran high; but gangrene gradually spread along the track of the bullet, and by the afternoon of 13 September the attending physicians had abandoned hope.

"Good-bye, good-bye all," murmured the dying man to a small group of friends who had gathered in the room. With his invalid wife at his bedside, he whispered the words of a familiar hymn, "Nearer, My God to Thee." He died shortly after two o'clock the next morning. William McKinley, whose political popularity betokened the skills of a sensitive and experienced political craftsman, was in his personal life a simple man who reiterated platitudes without embarrassment. He had lived with dignity, and with dignity he died.

BIBLIOGRAPHY

Four outstanding studies make available a wealth of information on William McKinley and his times. H. Wayne Morgan, *William McKinley and His America* (Syracuse, N.Y., 1963), the most complete and balanced biography of McKinley, emphasizes McKinley's nationalism to provide an important insight into his administration. A second volume by the same author, *From Hayes to McKinley: National Party Politics, 1877–1896* (Syracuse, N.Y., 1969), theorizes that by subordinating local interests to national concerns, the Republican party laid the groundwork for the modern political system of the United States. Margaret Leech, *In the Days of McKinley* (New York, 1959), is a gracefully written, comprehensive history of the McKinley administration. A more recent volume by Lewis L. Gould, *The Presidency of William McKinley* (Lawrence, Kans., 1980), is persuasive in presenting McKinley as a leader who skillfully used the powers of his office to become the first truly modern president.

Economic developments affecting McKinley's political activities receive attention in Harold U. Faulkner, *Politics, Reform, and Expansion, 1890–1900* (New York, 1959). The detailed study by Milron Friedman and Anna Jacobson Schwartz, *A Monetary History of the United States, 1867–1960* (Princeton, N.J., 1963), is important for understanding monetary issues of the 1896 campaign. Two sophisticated political analyses are valuable for assessing McKinley's advancement to the presidency: the first is Richard Jensen, *The Winning of the Midwest: Social and Political Conflict, 1888–1896* (Chicago, 1971), and the second is Paul Kleppner, *The Cross of Culture: A Social Analysis of Midwestern Politics, 1850–1900*, 2d ed. (New York, 1970). Paolo E. Coletta, *William Jennings Bryan: Political Evangelist, 1860–1908* (Lincoln, Nebr., 1964), the first volume of the most detailed biography of Bryan, provides important information on McKinley's opponent in the elections of 1896 and 1900. Stanley L. Jones presents a thorough, even-handed treatment in *The Presidential Election of 1896* (Madison, Wis., 1964). Another examination of the 1896 election is Paul W. Glad, *McKinley, Bryan, and the People* (Philadelphia, 1964).

In recent years two thorough studies of the Spanish-American War have provided depth to historical understanding of that important development of McKinley's presidency. Throughout *The War with Spain in 1898* (New York, 1981), David F. Trask treats military action with a sure hand. His conclusions are for the most part consistent with the thesis advanced by John L. Offner in *An Unwanted War: The Diplomacy of the United States and Spain over Cuba, 1895–1898* (Chapel Hill, N.C., 1992). Neither scholar views McKinley as committing the nation to war in order to establish the United States as an imperial power.

Nevertheless, the American position in international affairs became increasingly important as McKinley's foreign policy evolved. In *Imperial Democracy: The Emergence of America as a Great Power* (New York, 1961), Ernest R. May portrays McKinley as a man of peace who succumbed to the hysterical clamor for war only because he feared the political effects of remaining neutral. In his *American Imperialism: A Speculative Essay* (New York, 1968), May argues that American leaders were following European precedents in their enthusiasm for overseas expansion. Far less supportive of the notion that "the United States had greatness thrust upon it," William Appleman Williams's thesis in *The Tragedy of American Diplomacy* (Cleveland, 1959) is that all interest groups in American society favored market expansion. Another work by Williams, *The Roots of the Modern American Empire: A Study of the Growth and Shaping of Social Consciousness in a Marketplace Society* (New York, 1969), elaborates on expansionist policy of the 1890s.

American foreign policy at the turn of the century is the topic of several volumes. In *The New Empire: An Interpretation of American Expansion, 1860–1898* (Ithaca, N.Y., 1963), Walter LaFeber argues that the American business community saw market expansion as a solution to economic problems of the 1890s. Thomas J. McCormick develops a related theme in *China Market: America's Quest for Informal Empire, 1893–1901* (Chicago, 1967). Paul A. Varg's study *The Making of a Myth: The United States and China, 1897–1912* (East Lansing, Mich., 1968), rejects the idea of an American economic interest in China. Marilyn Blatt Young, in *The Rhetoric of Empire: American China Policy, 1895–1901* (Cambridge, Mass., 1969), links American imperialism with social and economic anxieties of the 1890s. David Healy's study *U.S. Expansionism: The Imperialist Urge in the 1890s* (Madison, Wis., 1970), also examines the great debate over acquisition of an American colonial empire. While other historians have differed over American foreign policy as it developed during McKinley's presidency, Swedish scholar Göran Rystad provides a reasonable synthesis in *Ambiguous Imperialism: American Foreign Policy and Domestic Politics at the Turn of the Century* (Stockholm, Sweden, 1975).

Recent works include William H. Armstrong, *Major McKinley: William McKinley and the Civil War* (Kent, Ohio, 2000).

Further references can be found in Lewis L. Gould and Craig H. Roell, comps., *William McKinley: A Bibliography* (Westport, Conn., 1988).

Theodore Roosevelt

Richard M. Abrams

Theodore Roosevelt THE LIBRARY OF CONGRESS

THE administration of Theodore Roosevelt was in some respects the first modern presidency. It is with Roosevelt that the most distinctive twentieth-century characteristics of the executive office emerged as more or less permanent traits. Roosevelt put the presidency and the federal government at the center of peacetime political action. He made the White House a national focus for the social mood and did much to set the moral tone of his times. He exploited the president's powers as commander in chief to initiate a forceful, independent foreign policy, deploying military forces abroad without direct (or any) consultation with Congress. And he extended presidential initiatives in policymaking to the do-

mestic scene on an unprecedented scale, putting forward reform proposals for congressional action and using executive orders to promote major innovative programs.

Not all the traits that Roosevelt brought to the White House were admirable. There was sometimes as much truculence as confidence, as much belligerence as goodwill, and as much bravado as good sense. He set some dubious precedents in his bullying of small nations and in his sometimes casual regard for constitutional and international law. He did much to prod Americans to take up their responsibilities as a powerful nation to use their power for good internationally, even though it must be said that his own conception of "good" could not always meet a test for universal approval. He was, in short, not the perfect model for the ideal Philosopher King. But his contributions to good government certainly outweighed his shortcomings.

That Roosevelt went a long way toward persuading the nation of the legitimacy of federal responsibility for regulating business activities and husbanding the country's natural resources, unquestionably counts among his greatest contributions. By 1900, the corporate consolidation of the nation's business had greatly impaired the effectiveness of the market to allocate economic opportunities, advantages, and rewards equitably. Meanwhile, the predominantly interstate and global character of economic activity had rendered state governments constitutionally and administratively incapable of overseeing the nation's industrial and financial affairs so as to redress market imbalances. Nor had the states proved capable of controlling private exploitation of the public's mineral, timber, water, soil, scenic, and recreational resources, much of which by 1900 were beginning their way toward extinction. A longtime governmental vacuum awaited federal attention, which, given the parochial roots of congressional power, only the president could provide. The rise of "The Regulatory State" that gained much of its legitimacy during Roosevelt's presidency was as much an essential part of the modern political economy as was the emergence of the corporate form of business organization and the multinational business firm. Although in the final quarter of the century that began with the Age of Theodore Roosevelt a variety of economic interests came to use "deregulation" as an effective political slogan, in fact none of even those same interests truly envisioned a major withdrawal by the federal government of its regulatory role. Most of what went on in the politics of the 1880s and 1890s aimed chiefly at *rearranging* the structure of competitive costs and advantages that different business and other interests had constructed in previous decades. No one understood the vital importance of the modern regulatory state better than Theodore Roosevelt, and through all the political smoke of the 1890s it remained clear that his perceptions continued to serve modern government.

Meanwhile, the competition for empire among the leading industrial and military powers of Europe and Asia challenged the rationale of America's traditional isolationism and forced heavy responsibilities on the country's commander in chief. These developments greatly magnified the importance of the presidency and inevitably drew the attention of the press beyond state and local events to national politics. Later in the century, as film, radio, and television became public media instruments, the presence of the chief executive and his family would become more potent and more influential. But Theodore Roosevelt achieved such stature in advance of the new technology. It may be that Americans generally get the president who most closely mirrors their mood, but it is at least arguable that presidents shape the nation's mood, its manners, its tastes, and its morals somewhat more than they have been shaped by them. This seems especially true of Theodore Roosevelt.

The Man and His Times

Roosevelt's personality and political philosophy fitted the imperatives far more than they did the fashions of the times, so that the degree to which his behavior in the White House both hastened and shaped the dramatic growth of presidential power over the next seventy-five years must be seriously considered. Temperamentally, Roosevelt craved attention. It was said of him in jest that when he went to the theater, he envied the star; when he witnessed a wedding, he wished to be the bride; and when he attended a funeral, he resented the corpse. Once in the White House, especially in view of the changed national and international circumstances, he could not fail to focus national attention on the presidency.

Roosevelt believed in a strong "National Government" (his preferred term of reference to the federal administration), and he believed in the forceful use of presidential power. In this, he ran against the strong "Jeffersonian" current in nineteenth-century American politics, which treated power with suspicion, federal power with especial distrust, and presidential power as a threat to democratic impulses, which, it was long assumed, resided chiefly in the states and the legislatures. But Roosevelt moved strongly within other nineteenth-century currents that put power in a different perspective. The late Victorian era was, after all, the age of Darwinism, which featured an aggressive confidence in the triumph of the fit. Fit for the nineteenth-century American meant both physical and moral superiority, and moral superiority justified—indeed, mandated—vigorous uses of power. It was a major part of the very meaning of *manliness*, an idea of exceptional importance to contemporary males and to Roosevelt in particular.

Very much in the fashion of his times, Roosevelt viewed the world in terms of struggle between good and evil, between the righteous and the unjust, between civilization and barbarism. For the righteous to shrink from power would be to yield the arena to the unworthy. "I believe in a strong executive; I believe in power," he wrote during his last year in office to the British historian George Otto Trevelyan (and obviously for the historical record). "I greatly enjoy the exercise of power," he added. "While President, I have been President, emphatically; I have used every ounce of power there was in the office," he told Trevelyan. "I do not believe that any President has ever had as thoroughly good a time as I have had, or has ever enjoyed himself as much."

Roosevelt wrote these words by way of explaining why he had declined to run for another term in office. It was not, he made plain, that he felt burdened or disenchanted. It was rather that his view of the presidency required that there be a specific limit on how long any individual should serve. As president, he sought to use power up to, and beyond, the limits that ordinary law and a cautious interpretation of the Constitution set. He owed, he said, his primary obligation to the nation's welfare. That was true of officers in other branches of government, but no other agency of government could act with the efficiency and dispatch that the executive office could; neither did they have so much responsibility. When emergencies arose or unique opportunities beckoned, the president should follow the "higher law" of duty if the secondary law of men or states interfered. It did not trouble him that a president might sometimes play the autocrat—all the best presidents had occasionally done so. It was only important that the people know that after four years they would have the opportunity to dismiss an incumbent and that after eight years they would be assured a new president.

There was both arrogance and innocence in this, traits that, as in so many things, made T. R., as he was called, an archetype of his generation. Only someone so sure as he was of his hold on truth and of his faithful dedication to the nation's interests could be so casual in his regard for law and so certain of his calling to carry out a stewardship of the nation. That was the arrogance in the matter. The innocence consisted in the prevailing contemporary view that the difference between truth and error was plain for all godly and right-thinking persons to see, that virtue was a simple matter, and that honesty of purpose and heart was enough to rectify evil and to serve The Good Society. There was innocence, too, in the belief that no autocrat in the White House within four or eight years could do any permanent or substantial damage to the principles and practices of a free, orderly society ostensibly governed by the rule of law. The sufficiency of democratic, electoral institutions was taken for granted. This was, after all, a generation as yet untouched by the example of what modern technology combined with a populist absolutism could do in the service of the totalitarian state, a concept as yet unborn. It was, as even some contemporaries called it, an "age of confidence," when faith often served as truth, or was mistaken for it, and when values remained as yet unattenuated by pluralistic doubt.

An unquestioning ignorance left Americans at the turn of the century free to assume with certitude the superiority of the "Caucasian race," and, among that race, of Christians; among Christians, of Western civilization; and within that civilization, of the Protestant Teutonic and Anglo-Saxon "races." It was a white, Anglo-Saxon, Protestant God that a majority of Americans acknowledged presiding over the universe in the year T. R. entered the White House. Such conceit—or so we would call it today—permitted those with power to assume that laws were to be applied rigidly for the vicious but could be stretched for the virtuous by the stewards of civic order. It permitted one set of principles to guide policy toward large and powerful nations and another toward smaller or underdeveloped countries; one set for whites, another for nonwhites; one set for the wellborn and well-off, and another for the less well endowed. Such parochial assumptions were in no way novel. They were rather characteristic of the village loyalty and outlook, the clannishness of ethnic and class groupings that has dominated most of human history.

Neither was it a matter of class outlook in Western culture. If Roosevelt could write of his conviction "that English rule in India and Egypt like the rule of the French in Algiers or of Russia in Turkestan means a great advance for humanity," he was only affirming what Karl Marx and Friedrich Engels also had once contended. But whereas Marx and Engels saw European imperialism as serving benevolent historical forces "through the vilest of motives," Roosevelt affected a posture of benign obligation; and whereas Marx and Engels saw Western bourgeois domination as a necessary uplifting stage preceding the ultimate uplift of working-class revolution, Roosevelt committed his life's work to preventing just that eventuality. For Roosevelt, the nation-state was the finest product of social evolution, replacing the tribe and the clan; and it was to the nation that he insisted all class, ethnic, religious, economic, and provincial interests yield their loyalty.

By so insisting, Roosevelt raised a challenge to the prevailing ethos of the times. The country's rapid industrialization since mid-century had sud denly enriched thousands of Americans who had come from modest and, in some cases, lower-class families. In fact, the wealth of the Rockefellers, Carnegies, Hills, and Harrimans substantially dwarfed the family fortunes enjoyed by the country's older, self-conscious "aristocracy," such patrician families as the Adamses, Schuylers, Peabodys, and Roosevelts. And along with the wealth went power. Theodore Roosevelt grew up in a family and in a social set whose political influence had been displaced by the new men of great wealth, men who were guided by a business, rather than a social, ethic and who lacked a family tradition of public service, a sense of noblesse oblige. These men had "made it" through the squalor of industrial conflict to take command of the levers of government and manipulate them in the hard-bitten style of their own experiences. Above all, these men increasingly exemplified the country's new standard of success, a standard built on the workaday values of industry and finance. The old patrician classes of the country could not compete with the men of new wealth on their own terms. By emphasizing nationalism, patriotism, and the virtues of manly and even martial strenuosity, Roosevelt put forward an alternative standard of success.

The Young T. R.

It had been one of Roosevelt's early accomplishments that he had successfully challenged his social set's condescending aloofness by entering the festering New York political scene, against all counsel, without losing his standing in society. "I intended," he said, "to be one of the governing class"; and if the men who then dominated that class were indeed too vulgar and rough for him, then "I supposed I would have to quit, but I certainly would not quit until I had made the effort and found out whether I really was too weak to hold my own in the rough and tumble." Of course, Roosevelt held his own. But more than

that, he helped make politics an attractive career once more for well-educated, talented men and women of goodwill. He, as much as anyone in the country, was responsible for making reform respectable, removing from it the stigmas of radicalism on the one hand and of effeteness on the other. He rehabilitated the idea of the patrician in politics.

It is easy—perhaps too easy—to link Theodore Roosevelt's political philosophy and his behavior in the White House to his childhood and his upbringing. There is a strong consistency in his attitude toward duty, character, and power that runs the extent of the sixty-one years he lived. He was born in Manhattan on 27 October 1858, the second child and the older of two sons in a family of four children. His southern-born mother, Martha Bulloch, could well have been a model for the stereotype of the ineffectual Victorian female. His father, Theodore, Sr., appeared (at least in his older son's revering eyes) a paragon of civic and family virtue, a tall, strong, athletically built man of stern moral commitments, active in philanthropy and on the periphery of politics. His devoted son bore the burden of physical frailty and illness, a burden made doubly heavy by the inevitable comparisons he made to his father. Small-boned, soprano-voiced, nearsighted to the point of virtual blindness in one eye, and severely asthmatic, he wrote later as well as in his childhood diaries of the anguish he felt over his infirmities and of how he had had to depend on his younger brother, Elliott, to help deal with youthful belligerencies. Thoughts on strength and power must have been constant companions for him. In his book *The Strenuous Life* (1901), he would remark, "One prime reason for abhorring cowards is because every good boy should have it in him to thrash the objectionable boy as the need arises." As president in 1906, he wrote, "The chance for the settlement of disputes peacefully . . . depends mainly upon the possession by the nations that mean to do right of sufficient armed strength to make their purpose effective."

When T. R. was about twelve, his father urged him to work on developing his physical strength. The boy put aside his nature books for the regimen of weights, chinning bar, horseback riding, boxing, wrestling, and hunting. It seems to have worked. Although his eyesight would continue to deteriorate, Roosevelt conquered his asthma and built a muscular body capable of the strenuosity he craved, perhaps as proof of his worthiness to be his father's son. ("O, Father, Father how bitterly I miss you, mourn you and long for you!" he wrote when he was nineteen, weeks after his father's death. "I realize more and more every day," he added six months later, "that I am as much inferior to Father morally and mentally as physically.") That was in 1877. Within the next quarter of a century, the energy he poured into sport, scholarship, politics, and actual physical combat must have left him with at least some measure of vindication.

By the time he became president, Roosevelt had in fact accomplishments enough to make him something of a national legend, a career and exploits that might have rivaled any small boy's grandest daydreams. He had engaged in the "rough and tumble" of city and state politics. He had bought a ranch in the untamed Dakota Territory, ridden with cowpunchers, led a posse to capture three armed thieves, and come out the victor in a brief brawl with a (rather drunk) tough in a tavern. Farther west, he had hunted grizzlies and cougars in the Rockies and matched shooting skills with a group of "wild Indians." In that same period, he had written eight or nine books, including two serviceable biographies (*Thomas Hart Benton*, 1887, and *Gouverneur Morris*, 1888), a major four-volume history of the West (*The Winning of the West*, 1889–1896), and *The Naval War of 1812* (1882), which for a time served as a textbook on the subject at Annapolis. He had served on the United States Civil Service Commission (1889–1895) under two presidents, on the New York City Board of Police Commissioners (1894–1896), and as assistant secretary of the navy (1897–1898). On the two commissions, he had managed to attract national attention because of his bold battles for nonpartisan administration of the law (while keeping his fences carefully mended within his party). In the third position, he had found himself in control of the United States Navy on 25 February 1898, ten days after the destruction of the battleship *Maine* in Cuba (Secretary of the Navy John D. Long had taken the day off), and had used that control with a characteristic disregard for lawful authority when the latter stood in the way of the national interest, as he viewed it. Acting with the brashness of a boy suddenly aware of power and heedless of instructions to the contrary, he ordered Commodore George Dewey's Pacific fleet to Hong Kong to prepare (although the country was still at peace) for combat with the Spanish fleet in the Philippines, thereby setting the stage for the Battle of Manila Bay and American annexation of the large Asian archipelago.

With the declaration of war soon after, Roosevelt resigned his office, helped organize a voluntary cavalry unit made up of a few hundred Dakota and other cowboys, a good number of Ivy League football players, a few New York City policemen, and fifteen or so American Indians. Promptly dubbed "The Rough Riders" by the overexcited press, First Regiment of U.S. Volunteer Cavalry with Lieutenant Colonel Theodore Roosevelt as battle commander saw brutal action in the hills overlooking Santiago, Cuba. In taking its assigned target, the regiment suffered extraordinary losses, possibly owing to brief training and its commander's brash amateur leadership; but by some miracle Roosevelt survived, returned quickly to New York in time for the political season, and was elected governor of the country's most populous state that same November, in no small measure on the strength of his wartime notoriety. Two years later, his nomination for the vice presidency was arranged by New York Republicans who had wearied of T. R.'s tempestuous independence and wished him up and away. Then, in September 1901, at the Pan American Exposition in Buffalo, Leon Czolgosz' gun, hidden in his bandaged fist as he approached President McKinley to shake hands, put the Rough Rider in the White House.

In the White House

Although Roosevelt became president in a freakish way and was moreover, at not quite forty-three, the youngest man ever to hold the office, few United States presidents entered the White House who were as well qualified. John Quincy Adams had been at least as well read and had spent more time abroad in diplomatic activities before he, like his father, became president. But Roosevelt's numerous publications showed him to be a man of respectable scholarly accomplishments (his *The Winning of the West* was reviewed seriously in the *American Historical Review* by Frederick Jackson Turner in 1896) and a serious thinker about major contemporary issues, notably military strategy. His western exploits and his brief military career had given experience that Adams conspicuously lacked, to Adams' great disadvantage in his rivalry with Andrew Jackson. And Roosevelt had also traveled abroad frequently, both as a child and as an adult. He moved easily among the genteel and governing classes of England and Germany, and established there lifelong friendships sustained by a massive correspondence. When in 1886 he married

Edith Carow, his second wife (his first, Alice Lee, had died in childbirth in 1884), it was in London, and Britain's future ambassador to the United States, Cecil Spring Rice ("Springy," to Roosevelt), served as his best man.

As John Morton Blum has astutely observed, Theodore Roosevelt spoke and wrote expansively on order, duty, justice, and power—but rarely on happiness, the word that stands at the center of liberal thought. Except for his commitment to a parliamentary and electoral politics, Roosevelt in fact showed few liberal characteristics. He spoke righteously for freedom but placed individual liberty in the context of a greater obligation to the nation. He acknowledged that most individuals probably preferred business as usual, to be left to cultivate their own gardens and to pursue modest livelihoods and comforts, but he viewed such an outlook with scorn. He found peace good but grandeur better. He vigorously defended the rights and privileges of private property, but he would have them subordinated to political priorities. Business competition in an unmanaged, open market, then the centerpiece of the liberal economic order, he regarded with skepticism, as wasteful, disorderly, and given to irrational outcomes. The rule of law, equally central to the legitimacy of power in a liberal state, Roosevelt regarded as an ideal that should be applied to customary matters and ordinary people; but power, he believed, was a better, more reliable guarantor of justice, progress, excellence, order, and nobility. Roosevelt as president strove to build an American national state that could serve as the focus of an orderly justice, but in that cause he himself evaded constitutional and legal constraints that were designed to guarantee orderly government.

In such characteristics lay the greatness, but also the danger, of Theodore Roosevelt. Greatness often requires a reaching beyond conventional limits, a recognition of the possibilities and opportunities that beckon beyond the horizons of ordinary law and custom. The America that Roosevelt contemplated at the turn of the century was about to enter seriously upon international happenings. The nation's business, its size, its expansive history and spirit had thrust it abroad. Yet Americans typically remained ignorant of the implications of such developments, innocent of the country's military and economic vulnerabilities. When, without consulting Congress, Roosevelt "took Panama," sent the fleet around the world, and signed secret agreements with Japan, he filled a void not merely in the constitutional distribution of powers but in the vision of contemporary Americans and their mostly provincial political leaders.

Similarly, the revolution in industrial production, organization, and marketing since 1875 had swiftly made archaic a constitutional and legal system that continued to treat private economic power as if it were still exercised mostly by small proprietary farmers and businessmen who serviced local or state communities. The sudden rise to dominance of a few very large interstate corporations was rapidly turning the open price and market system into a managed continental economy that rewarded the big and the powerful to the gross disadvantage of the masses of smaller business people of the country. Meanwhile, unrestrained private exploitation of natural resources threatened to squander the means whereby future generations might enjoy the same opportunities as did contemporaries. Roosevelt saw both danger and injustice in what was happening and also that the courts and Congress appeared incapable of taking notice. When the president bypassed Congress, expanding the use of executive orders to put some public lands beyond the reach of private exploitation, and when he fought to establish independent administrative agencies in the executive branch to supplement the courts' supervision of private economic behavior, he took the first small steps toward bringing the problems invoked by industrialization within the purview of a national policy. In all these things, in both domestic and foreign policies, Theodore Roosevelt showed remarkable vision, while he also set some precedents for the abuses of power by twentieth-century American presidents.

His private reaction to McKinley's death reveals the raw side of the man. While McKinley lay dying, Roosevelt wrote to his friend Henry Cabot Lodge:

> We should war with relentless efficiency not only against anarchists, but against all active and passive sympathizers with anarchists. Moreover, every scoundrel . . . who for whatever purposes appeals to evil human passion, has made himself accessory before the fact to every crime of this nature, and every soft fool who extends a maudlin sympathy to criminals has done likewise.. . . Tolstoy and the feeble apostles of Tolstoy . . . who unite in petitions for the pardon of anarchists, have a heavy share in the burden of responsibility for crimes of this kind.

The "war" Roosevelt proposed here he meant in a moral sense; he never urged legislation that would in fact bring "soft fools" within the law's definition of an "accessory." But he did sign the Immigration Act of 1903, which permitted the deportation of "alien anarchists" and banned "anarchists" from entering the country or seeking citizenship. For the first time since the long-repudiated Alien and Sedition Acts of 1798, the United States applied a political test for immigration and citizenship. Most insidious, the act left it to local officials to define what kind of activities or speech made one an anarchist.

Roosevelt was not responsible for the act. A great surge of excess and violence followed in the wake of McKinley's assassination, which fed long-standing fires of antiradicalism and nativism. But the new president did and said nothing to deter the nativists' assaults upon civil liberties or to quell the lynch-law "justice" to which they gave expression. Although Roosevelt usually preferred a more orderly and legal form of justice, his own instincts sometimes drifted in other directions, as his behavior in the Brownsville incident suggests. In November 1906, Roosevelt summarily issued dishonorable discharges to more than 160 black soldiers because it had been alleged that members of their battalions rioted in the town of Brownsville, Texas, in August. In the melee, a bartender was killed and a policeman was wounded. No individual was ever indicted; no trial was ever held. But the punishment the president inflicted on the men was severe. Many of the men were close to retirement but were deprived of all benefits because of the dishonorable discharge. Several held the Congressional Medal of Honor, the nation's highest military award. After a congressional outcry against the president's challenge to the Anglo-American legal principles that an individual is innocent until proved guilty and that individual guilt cannot be inferred from membership in a group, Roosevelt compounded his offense, denying that Congress had any right to interfere. In a much publicized speech, he boasted, "The only reason I didn't have them hung was because I could not find out which ones . . . did the shooting." As William Harbaugh points out, it is unlikely that racial bias entered significantly into Roosevelt's action in the case; there is no evidence that he would have treated white troops any differently. That may say something for Roosevelt's racial views but not much for his regard for law.

In office, Roosevelt rarely vented such impulses to impolitic righteousness. As Blum has remarked:

> In order to win office and to make government function, he taught himself to restrain any politically dan-

gerous impulse, to study complex matters of policy before dealing with them, and to balance his objectives against the likelihood of achieving them—an exercise he often obscured by clothing the art of the possible in the rhetoric of the imperative.

Bringing Industrialism Under Control

As in other matters, in his plan to place American industry under national supervision, Roosevelt proceeded cautiously. He well knew that government intervention in the private sector had profound roots in the American tradition and equally profound justification. But the tumultuous politics of the late nineteenth century had aroused a great fear of "mobocracy." The Greenback, Granger, and Populist movements, with their demands that government redress a dangerous imbalance of power between "the trusts" and "the people," had evoked a fierce counterattack not only against the particular regulatory and public-ownership measures proposed by the rural "radicals" but against the legitimacy of government intervention in the economy as a general principle. For decades, court and legislative actions had promoted and protected the growing industrial and transportation companies against foreign competition and against civil and criminal claims pursued by small business, farm, and labor interests. They had done so in the name of the public's interest in rapid industrial growth. But when, especially after 1875, shifting political majorities in several states led to legislation designed to mitigate some of the more conspicuous costs of industrialization, the groups that had grown powerful in the sunlight of government favor now cried foul. The ferocity of the counterattack had the effect of defining the terms of the contemporary debate—that is, of confining the debate to whether the federal government should do anything about restraining the private uses of economic power or even about ascertaining the measure to which the private uses of power had come to confound a consensus on the national interest.

In his first message to Congress, Roosevelt gently suggested that the corporations were, after all, creatures of the state and could therefore be made to serve a public purpose. In his second address, in December 1902, Roosevelt spoke more strongly: "This country cannot afford to sit supine on the plea that under our peculiar system of government we are helpless in the presence of the new conditions. The power of Congress to regulate interstate commerce is an absolute and unqualified grant, and without limitations other than those prescribed by the Constitution." There was, however, a major controversy over how one defined the legal reach of the phrase "interstate commerce" and over just what limitations the Constitution did place on government action. In 1895, for example, the Supreme Court had ruled that a sugar-processing corporation that controlled more than 80 percent of the processed sugar in the country, that purchased all its raw materials from outside the state in which it did its processing, and that sold its finished product across state and international boundaries was nevertheless primarily engaged in manufacturing within the confines of a state and was therefore beyond Congress' reach under the commerce clause. In the face of such obtuseness, a conventional, strictly legal approach to policymaking could only be pathetic.

In fact, on the eve of the twentieth century, the judiciary dominated American policymaking on economic matters. This is not altogether surprising. The American nation rested on no consistent theory of the state. The main features of the Constitution had been shaped to minimize the state, to restrain and deter the exercise of power, essentially to prevent the state from acting arbitrarily or, for that matter, decisively. Through most of the nineteenth century, the state played a small and diminishing role in determining how individuals related to one another and to their society. That was given over largely to private bargaining, with the courts developing, through case law, elaborate doctrines on contracts, liability, trespass, and property. The general antistatist political environment in America meanwhile tended to neutralize both the legislative and executive branches in fixing social and economic priorities as the basis for resolving day-to-day conflicts of interest and ambition. It was the courts, responding to the multitude of mundane claims of right and privilege, that structured the law that gave definition to the "liberty" to which the nation avowed commitment. That is, the doctrines that the courts shaped defined what kinds of social and economic actions enjoyed freedom from sanctions, what kinds ran greater risks, what kinds of access to and use of property were protected against public, community, or second-party claims, and what terms of contracts the state would be prepared to enforce.

Toward the end of the nineteenth century, after a quarter century of industrialization and corporate growth had impaired the marketplace and had turned the struggles for advantage among a multitude of small economic strivers into a massive conflict of groups and classes, the many legislatures of the country moved to intervene. Americans continued to favor economic growth, but the costs borne by traditional business and agriculture, and by insurgent nonbusiness interests as well, gave rise to a sometimes violent politics of protest. The violence reflected a widespread loss of faith in the market's capacity for fairly and impersonally allocating the resources and rewards that the society had to offer. The intervention took many forms and included the creation of state railroad and public-utility regulatory commissions. The commissions were intermediary government agencies, part administrative and part legislative, designed to replace the flawed marketplace with a mechanism characterized by science and technical expertise. They were designed to become the new impersonal and just allocators of advantages. To these agencies, the state legislatures—and Congress, in creating the Interstate Commerce Commission (ICC) in 1887—delegated considerable discretionary power, in effect creating an alternative to the courts for a flexible, law-adjusting response to day-to-day conflicts in the economic order.

Unhappily, to this alternative the courts reacted as to a challenge. Employing a novel interpretation of the due process clause of the Constitution, contriving an exquisitely narrow construction of the commerce clause, and inventing innovative uses of equity proceedings, state and federal judges—and, most important, those on the United States Supreme Court—repeatedly overrode the declared intentions of the legislative branches of American government in antitrust matters, labor relations, employment policies, and the regulation of selected practices of private industry. The number of cases was not large, but the deterrent effect of judicial vetoes had long-lasting and far-reaching impact.

It was these circumstances that Roosevelt confronted when he took office. In addition to the courts, he faced a congressional coalition of Republicans who represented (sometimes rather directly) the new corporate consolidations of economic power that Roosevelt sought to control together with southern Democrats, whose political instincts rebelled fiercely against any enlargement of federal power. So the president moved cautiously. Although more impatient reformers came to doubt Roosevelt's earnestness, although many likened his vigor to that of a rocking chair ("all motion and no progress"), and others charged him outright with "selling out to the interests," the conservatives were so deeply entrenched that one might be as readily impressed by Roosevelt's achievements as by how little was achieved.

Cooking Up the Square Deal

Roosevelt's primary task was to gain popular support for federal restraint of private power and, in this sense, to establish the legitimacy of federal power. The president's huge talent for publicity served him especially well in this. He chose his issues, and his enemies, carefully. The American business community was far from unified in its view of the tide of giant corporate mergers it had been witnessing since 1897. For many conservatives, the private enterprise system itself seemed at stake. When, in 1901, J. P. Morgan concluded the reorganization of the steel industry by buying out Carnegie and consolidating several other major steel producers into the new billion-dollar United States Steel Corporation, even the staunchly conservative *Boston Herald* was moved to remark, "If a limited financial group shall come to represent the capitalistic end of industry, the perils of socialism, even if brought about by some rude, because forcible, taking of the instruments of industry, may be looked upon by even intelligent people as possibly the lesser of two evils." In 1902, Morgan, J. J. Hill, and some other titans of finance and the railroad industry followed up the awesome steel consolidation by forming the Northern Securities Company, a merger of the Northern Pacific, the Great Northern, and the Chicago, Burlington and Quincy railroads. Roosevelt seized the opportunity, instructing his attorney general to prosecute the company for violation of the Sherman Antitrust Act.

The issue and the timing were perfect. The country was newly sensitized to the trusts issue, and not even a pettifogging judiciary could deny that the railroad industry quintessentially concerned interstate commerce. By a 5-4 vote in 1904, the United States Supreme Court did indeed uphold the government's prosecution. (The minority held out on the issue of whether the merger amounted to an illegal restraint of trade.) From this and from the president's attacks on Standard Oil and the "meat trust," long-standing industrial pariahs, T. R. earned his reputation as a trustbuster. Roosevelt himself viewed the Northern Securities prosecution as the most important achievement of his first administration. But

this was not because he generally opposed the business consolidations of the day. It was rather because the president of the United States had successfully called down several of the country's leading business tycoons—an achievement no president in several generations could boast of.

Roosevelt argued during his 1904 presidential campaign that the Northern Securities case was "one of the great achievements of my administration," because "through it we emphasized . . . that the most powerful men in the country were held to accountability before the law." It was a popularly held view. "If Roosevelt had never done anything else," the publisher Joseph Pulitzer wrote to his editor Frank Cobb (a steady Roosevelt critic), "and if he had committed a hundred times more mistakes . . . he would be entitled to the greatest credit for the greatest service to the nation" for his prosecution of the Northern Securities Company. In his autobiography, Roosevelt told the story of how the great J. P. Morgan had come to him after news of the suit broke and in avuncular fashion suggested that the whole scandal could have been avoided if the president's man (the attorney general) had met with Morgan's man to arrange matters. It had become habit for the country's business elite to view the federal government as merely a rival power, even as a lesser power that should consult with its betters before acting. T. R. implied that he had put Morgan in his proper place.

Roosevelt's presidency did much to restore public confidence in the government's ability to hold "the most powerful men in the country" accountable to the law, but there was still the question of what the law should be—or, perhaps more to the point, who should determine what the law should be. In this, Roosevelt was far more accommodating to the men of new corporate power than the bravado about his encounter with Morgan might suggest. In the first place, Roosevelt believed in free-market competition little more than did Morgan and his financier friends. The president acted against Northern Securities less from his concern about monopoly than from his concern about how the public might react to uncontrolled corporate arrogance. He frequently chided conservative critics that revolutionary upheaval was as likely to be inspired from "an attitude of arrogance on the part of the owners of property and of unwillingness to recognize their duty to the public" as by socialist or anarchist revolutionaries. It was more the manner than the substance of the Northern Securities merger that goaded him. Roosevelt himself had small regard for the successful antitrust suits of the McKinley administration, which aimed to break up major railroad traffic associations for fixing rates and routing among the members. "It is difficult to see," he told Congress, quoting the ICC on the subject, "how our interstate railways could be operated . . . without concerted action of the kind afforded through these associations." In his second administration, Roosevelt would urge Congress to amend the Sherman Act to permit cartel-like agreements within the railroad industry.

In 1903 public unhappiness with corporate arrogance permitted the president to push through Congress, against bitter conservative hostility, legislation establishing the Department of Commerce and Labor and, within it, the Bureau of Corporations. The bureau was authorized to investigate and publicize suspect corporate activities. Roosevelt acted from premises about the public's right to know and about the government's need to know in order to hold private economic power accountable. The emphasis on publicity proceeded also from a faith that a common sense of decency would force corporations to be good—not only to be honest but to avoid unscrupulous, even though strictly legal, practices. In other words, in large measure the policy arose from a conviction, not seriously tested by anyone at the time, that the country understood a common definition of such a concept as decency. In practice, of course, men like Roosevelt tended to assume the universality of their own definition.

In any case, Roosevelt had no intention of waging open warfare on big business. In the first place, the big corporations played too important a role in his vision of America's place in international rivalry. Small businesses could scarcely compete successfully for international resources and markets with the European cartels and Japanese *zaibatsu*. But more than that, Roosevelt did not view government and business as adversaries. In the spirit of the "New Nationalism," which he would develop more explicitly in his campaign to recapture the presidency in 1912, Roosevelt pictured the government as a coordinating agency for harmonizing the nation's varied interests and as a referee for interpreting and declaring the rules of the game. In keeping with this view, Roosevelt was prepared to assure corporations of immunity from antitrust prosecutions if he or the appropriate government agencies could be satisfied that their activities were honestly conceived and would benefit the community. When he was not so

convinced, he proceeded, with his usual flare for the dramatic, to "bust the trusts," as when he attacked Standard Oil, the tobacco trust, the meat trust (with antitrust suits and with the Meat Inspection Act of 1906), and the Northern Securities Company.

But through the bureau, the president did enter into a series of gentlemen's agreements with Morgan interests. Companies such as United States Steel and International Harvester (organized in 1903) agreed to open records to the bureau's investigators, on the condition—which Roosevelt accepted—that the president would use such information only as backgrounding for his recommendations of policy to Congress and that nothing would be made public except with the consent of the corporations themselves. To make these arrangements, Roosevelt permitted Commerce and Justice department officials to confer with representatives of Morgan interests such as George W. Perkins, E. H. Gary, and Henry Clay Frick. The meetings gave the Morgan men a chance to debate the legality of their actions and to avoid prosecution by agreeing to correct any "technical" violations of the law in cases where they could not persuade the government otherwise. In spite of Roosevelt's autobiographical boasting, then, Morgan's men were meeting with the president's men to arrange matters.

In 1907, Morgan's men would meet with the president himself to arrange a steel merger that virtually handed the United States Steel Corporation nearly complete domination of the industry. The bankers' panic that year occasioned the conference. Among the feared casualties of the panic was the Trust Company of America (TCA), a major New York City financial institution whose collapse might have deepened the crisis. As it happened, the principal owners of the Tennessee Coal and Iron Company (TCIC) owed the TCA a lot of money. Morgan men Frick and Gary went to the president with a proposition. If they could be assured that there would be no antitrust prosecutions, the Morgan people would buy out the TCIC, thereby allowing its owners to pay off their debt to the TCA and keep the TCA solvent. Roosevelt may or may not have known the degree to which United States Steel's acquisition of the TCIC's steel plants, as well as its resources of coal and iron in Alabama, would substantially reduce competition in the industry. But he did see the virtue of averting a prolonged economic collapse (especially since the financial community was already whining loudly about how the crisis was all the fault of Roosevelt's "radical" attacks on the trusts). Roosevelt gave the green light to the merger. Whether he did so by explicitly approving Morgan's proposal or merely by leaving the matter as a tacit understanding, Roosevelt vigorously defended his role in the merger when he testified about it in 1911—after the Taft administration sued United States Steel for violation of the antitrust laws.

Roosevelt did not have to be apologetic about the steel merger, because he had not concealed his skepticism about the antitrust laws. Addressing Congress in 1907, he argued that the Sherman Act "should be . . . so amended as to forbid only the kind of combination which does harm to the general public." How should it be determined what kinds do harm? "Reasonable agreements between, or combinations of, corporations should be permitted provided they are submitted to and approved by some appropriate Government body." Instead of corporations testing legal limits in the courts by acting and then awaiting retaliatory action from the government or by private litigants, the new order would require the large interstate corporations to consult first with federal agencies established to pass on the acceptability of proposed moves. In the United States Steel case, Morgan had consulted with the president.

More than most of his contemporaries, Roosevelt understood that the corporation revolution had erased the main features of the rationale underlying the American liberal credo on the private uses of property for profit. A big, publicly financed corporation was not a private enterprise; it did not endow an individual entrepreneur with the qualities of independence and self-reliance on which the democratic polity counted; its size negated the competitive rivalry on which the democratic polity and the market economy depended to sharpen efficiency and to prevent arbitrary uses of power; its bureaucratic structure even denied the protection against a permanent preemption of power that mere human mortality afforded in an economy of individual proprietary enterprise. Finally, its managers were employees no less than were factory and mine operatives; the modern business corporation had indeed transformed Americans from a nation of self-employed enterprisers into a nation of hired hands.

Roosevelt's program called for establishment of a number of regulatory agencies modeled after, but with powers that considerably exceeded, those of the ICC and the Bureau of Corporations. His aim, as he later explained, was "to help legitimate business" by making the big corporations answerable to government regulation "as an incident to thoroughly and completely safeguarding the interests of the people as a whole." Roosevelt held such views from the start of his first administration, but it was not until his second that he could feel free to express them publicly. Meanwhile, with the ample rope that they had appropriated, America's corporate leaders prepared to hang themselves and open the way for increased federal intervention.

Their egregious effort to crush the anthracite coal miners in 1902 was a case in point. This was not merely a fight between miners and some coal operators. Seventy percent of the anthracite mines in the country were owned by six railroad companies—which themselves were controlled by financial interests associated with, or directed by, the houses of Morgan, Rockefeller, and closely associated financiers. Moreover, anthracite was the fuel on which millions of voters depended for heat in winter. McKinley's political mentor, Mark Hanna, had averted a strike in 1900 by quietly warning the corporations that an anthracite shortage and high prices in the fall might give Willam Jennings Bryan the edge to defeat McKinley. But in 1902, the companies were ready for a strike, at least in part to crush the United Mine Workers (UMW).

Wages were not the chief issue. Corporate spokesmen refused to countenance the legitimation of collective bargaining, even though collective capital had characterized the industry for decades. Although the public in 1902 cannot be said to have accepted collective bargaining in any substantial sense, neither was it as yet willing to accept fully the legitimacy of corporate collectivism, especially when it controlled one of the necessities of life. When the strike erupted, the national press generally supported the miners. In May, the *Springfield Republican* expressed an increasingly widespread sentiment: "It would be difficult to conceive of a monopoly more perfectly established or operated than this monopoly which holds complete possession of a great store of nature most necessary to the life of the day. There is but one way to deal with [it] . . . public control or ownership." George F. Baer, president of the Reading Railroad and spokesman for the mine. owners, gave point to their arrogance by declaring, in a private letter that was revealed to the press, that God had given the care of the country to the propertied people to protect against labor agitators and their like.

President Roosevelt meanwhile squirmed frantically. On the one hand, he yearned for the power to take control of the industry in the public interest. The mineowners, he wrote to Murray Crane, conservative governor of Massachusetts, "were backed by a great number of businessmen whose views were limited by the narrow business horizon, and who knew nothing either of the great principles of government or of the feelings of the great mass of our people." The "gross blindness" of the corporations, he complained to a Morgan partner, was "putting a heavy burden on us who stand against socialism; against anarchic disorder." To Lodge, he fretted, "That it would be a good thing to have national control, or at least supervision, over these big coal corporations, I am sure; but that would simply have to come as an incident of the general movement to exercise control of such corporations." Understanding that nothing of the sort would come from Senator Nelson Aldrich's and Speaker Joe Cannon's Congress for some time, perhaps generations, Roosevelt shied from even a verbal intervention. Conservatives such as Hanna and Crane took the lead, the latter even urging the president to meet jointly with the operators and the miners. The two party leaders, like Roosevelt, feared what a coal famine might do to Republican prospects that November.

With such encouragement, Roosevelt did force a joint conference. But it failed. For ten hours on 3 October, the president absorbed a barrage of vituperation from the mineowners, led by Baer. John Mitchell, president of the UMW, denied that recognition of the union was an issue in the strike, probably sensing that this was not a matter on which he could expect the public's or the president's support. The operators responded by showing (in Roosevelt's words) "extraordinary stupidity and bad temper," berating Mitchell and accusing the president of encouraging anarchy by suggesting that union leaders should have standing in a dispute between workers and their employers. They would not, they said, "deal with a set of outlaws."

As winter and the congressional elections approached, Roosevelt, enjoying public support, finally decided to act. Characteristically, he planned to act dramatically and not necessarily within the bounds of his acknowledged constitutional power. He would seize the coal mines. "The position of the operators," he later wrote to Crane, "that the public had no rights in the case, was not tenable for a moment." (Actually, Roosevelt himself had earlier accepted his attorney general's advice that the president did not properly have "any concern with the affair" and

could not intervene.) Rumors were flying that trade unions across the country were considering joining the miners in a sympathy strike; that, Roosevelt told Crane, would mean "a crisis only less serious than the civil war." Roosevelt then explained to his conservative New England adviser the obligation he felt to the higher imperatives of government, which moved him beyond the apparent limits of the letter of the law:

> I did not intend to sit supinely when such a state of things was impending.. . . I had to take charge of the matter, as President, on behalf of the Federal Government.. . . I knew that this action would form an evil precedent, and that it was one which I should take most reluctantly, but . . . it would have been imperative to act, precedent or no precedent—and I was in readiness.

Actually, a sudden stirring among "the most powerful men in the country" headed off the crisis. Roosevelt may have been bluffing; we cannot know. But he was too much of a puzzle for his conservative and well-connected advisers to want to test him. Elihu Root, Roosevelt's secretary of war, went to Morgan "as a private citizen," found him irritated with the way Baer and his crew had "botched things," and got him to twist some arms to force the operators to accept arbitration. A coal commission was agreed upon, but not before the operators won on their refusal to accept a labor man on the board. Later, citing the operators' petty obstructionism, Roosevelt chortled in derision that he overcame their objections to a labor man by filling the position designated for a "sociologist" on the commission with the individual whom the UMW had nominated. But the joke was on Roosevelt: the companies won in their insistence that unions per se had no legitimate place in employer-employee negotiations.

The anthracite coal strike is worth detailing because it illustrates several important points about Roosevelt as president. First, T. R. was most comfortable with crisis management, partly (it is at least reasonable to surmise) because crisis laid a gloss on his affinity for direct action beyond the fine points of legal limitation. He was, moreover, not averse to some hyperbole in depicting the troubles (although one must never underestimate the fear of revolution generated among the comfortable classes by contemporary agitation). At the same time, Roosevelt did not accept the view of labor and capital as adversaries. Although he tended to favor collective bargaining, he envisioned unionism as a way of institutionalizing the wage-earner interest vis-à-vis that of the corporate employers, between which interests the government could mediate on a basis of a public interest that was defined by the president and transcended the particular interests of the unions and the corporations. Finally, although Roosevelt did indeed possess a long-term vision of reform, he was above all a practical party man. He rarely challenged the commitments of the party leaders on fundamentals, and consequently much of what he accomplished had more symbolic than substantive value and did more to accommodate prevailing threats to the social order than it did to challenge that order itself.

The symbolism, of course, was not unimportant. Every change in the symbols by which we live foreshadows substantive change. Roosevelt's mediating role in the anthracite strike altered no symbols for employer-employee relations, but there was symbolic force in the federal government intervening in industrial strife without special regard for the longstanding conventions of employer prerogatives. To paraphrase George E. Mowry, American business valued few things more highly than the right to keep its records in secrecy and the right to deal with employees without interference from government. Before the end of his first administration, Roosevelt had challenged both those assumed rights.

The Ripening of the Square Deal

Roosevelt's election to the presidency in his own right in 1904 freed him from many of the inhibitions he felt during his first administration. His popularity was so apparent that the Democrats had trouble finding a candidate to oppose him. Willam Jennings Bryan, the eloquent progressive who had lost twice to McKinley, had no appetite for a third try, this time against a Republican with strong progressive credentials of his own; he threw his support to the then-radical publisher, William Randolph Hearst, but the party was not prepared to accept the father of yellow journalism as its leader. The Democrats nominated instead a virtually unknown party loyalist, Judge Alton B. Parker of the New York State Supreme Court, who promptly alienated the mass of Bryan Democrats on the night of his nomination with a call for affirmation of the gold standard. Against such political clumsiness, T. R. faced no trouble. Nevertheless, unpersuaded of his own already preponderant

strength, Roosevelt risked compromising his progressive standing by making quiet overtures to conservative party, corporate, and financial leaders. The corporate community, antireform though it was, knew more surely than did Roosevelt that Parker was a loser; it put on a happy face, contributed handsomely to T. R.'s campaign when asked, and left Parker to a quiet campaign on his own back porch. On 8 November 1904, Roosevelt swept the country with 336 electoral votes to Parker's 140, and 7.6 million popular votes to Parker's 5.1 million, the most lopsided popular margin of victory since national records had been kept. Roosevelt said he was delightfully "stunned" by the victory.

The year 1906 would be a landmark for progressive legislation, with the passage of the Meat Inspection, Pure Food and Drug, and Hepburn Railroad acts. These measures underlined the federal government's permanent entry as a regulator of the economic life of the nation. Each vested in a federal agency the power to investigate and to fix some of the conditions under which goods could be transported and sold across state lines. In the case of the Hepburn Act, Roosevelt won for the ICC limited rate-making powers, a form of price control that was unprecedented for the federal government.

The measures moved the American polity significantly toward the modern regulatory state, but it is important to understand that all three had powerful support from business groups. Many meat-packers resented the bad name the industry had earned at home and abroad because of the shipment of tainted meats by unscrupulous or simply negligent packaging companies. Similarly, adulteration and misrepresentation of packaged foods and pharmaceuticals hurt more scrupulous businesses, especially those trying to crack foreign markets. Finally, the seemingly arbitrary rate-making practices of the railroad industry had aroused the ire of shippers as well as farmers across the country. Aside from those particular businesses that feared immediate damage to their profits, opposition came from those who worried about where the move to increased federal power might someday lead and from others who saw a threat to orderly government in the arming of administrative agencies with broad discretionary powers of investigation and enforcement. Against these latter arguments, Roosevelt established the point that effective and therefore more orderly government depended precisely on the "continuous disinterested administration" of independent regulatory commissions.

The most enduring triumph of Roosevelt's administration lay in his program for the regulation of the country's natural resources. At the time he became president, private interests were in the process of laying waste to the country's remaining riches, as they had already done to the timber, soil, and water resources of the older settled regions of the continent. During the McKinley administration, millions of acres of public lands had been allowed to slip into the control of private interests without provision for government supervision or restraints on destructive use. Mineral rights had been sold off at prices far below market value. Virtually nothing had been done to safeguard recreational sites or to require replenishment of renewable resources. The movement for conservation (not yet dubbed with that name) had so far been confined to a number of engineers, agronomists, scientists, and public servants—an educated elite that foresaw clearly the ultimate exhaustion of vital assets on which the country had long counted for its economic growth. By winning Roosevelt as an ally, as they did even before he entered the White House, they gained a leader with an incomparable talent for combining the scientific imperatives of modern resource management with an appeal to the moral imperatives of a democratic civilization. It was the latter, of course, that would turn an elite interest into a broad popular cause.

The main lines of Theodore Roosevelt's conservation program were developed by Gifford Pinchot and Frederick H. Newell, easterners with a mission to prevent the continued destruction that uncontrolled private "development" had inflicted on the eastern third of the country, in concert with westerners of similar concerns such as George H. Maxwell of California and Congressman Francis Newlands of Nevada. They called for multiple-purpose projects for development of water and land resources; public-land leasing contracts that required controlled grazing of grasslands and selective cutting and replanting of timber; a land-use fee system that could make public management self-supporting; and the preservation of scenic lands for recreation and the protection of wildlife.

Legislation achieved some of the movement's objectives, but the core of the program depended on the president's use of executive orders and other administrative prerogatives. The Newlands Reclamation Act of 1902 designated revenues from public-land sales to the construction of irrigation projects for the conversion into arable land of the vast arid regions of the American West. During Roosevelt's administration alone, more than thirty such projects, including the Roosevelt Dam in Arizona, were begun. The Newlands Act has been responsible for subsidizing the creation and maintenance of some of the country's most valuable agricultural land today. It is a worthy monument to the Roosevelt administration, although it is flawed by eighty-five years of uncontrolled violations of the act's provision that purported to limit reclaimed and irrigated land to 640 acres per owner.

Congressional legislation in 1905 also set up the Forest Service with broad powers to manage the country's forest reserves, including the water resources within them, and the power to make arrests for violations of its regulations. Roosevelt named Pinchot chief forester, and Pinchot promptly launched a veritable revolution. He used his authority to withdraw from use thousands of acres of land, not only in order to prevent unruly exploitation of timber stands but to keep the fast-growing electric utility companies from preempting valuable waterpower sites before an orderly program could be established.

In the conservation struggle, Roosevelt and his allies made much use of moral rhetoric, frequently appealing to Americans' antimonopoly sentiments and turning the cause into one of "the interests" versus "the people." There is little doubt that the national conservation program disrupted established lines of power between the special interests and state legislative and congressional blocs. Moreover, the entire constellation of issues that was embodied in the conservation movement clashed directly with principles of the business ethic: here was an area where, more clearly than in most, private profit appeared to contradict the social ethic, the public's long-term interest in protection of the national endowment. Yet it is inaccurate to treat the issue in "monopoly" and "antitrust" terms. Roosevelt himself came to acknowledge that he could count more often on the big corporations than he could on smaller and upwardly scrambling business groups for support of his regional programs. The most intractable problem lay in overcoming the parochial interests of state politicians and the shortsighted interests of local businessmen on the make. The big interstate corporations had long-term stakes in efficient resource management almost as much as the general public did. They could be more easily (though not very easily) converted to multiple-purpose uses of forest and water resources than could smaller, single-purpose business firms. And some of them would even enjoy some market advantages in the withdrawal of lands from the entry of potential competitors.

Roosevelt always played the political game with skill. Antimonopoly rhetoric evoked the clearest public response, so he used it. On the other hand, he knew that the more powerful potential antagonist was a public that might come to view conservation as a threat to its ambitions for economic development. Consider his support for San Francisco's plan to flood the Hetch Hetchy Valley, a natural wonder often compared to the Yosemite Valley, for a reservoir to serve the city's growing water needs. He wrote to the outraged naturalist John Muir:

> I will do everything in my power to protect not only the Yosemite, which we have already protected, but other similar great natural beauties of this country; but you must remember that it is put of the question permanently to protect them unless we have a certain degree of friendliness toward them on the part of the people of the State . . . and if they are used so as to interfere with the permanent material development of the State . . . the result will be bad.

Roosevelt asked Muir not to put him "in the disagreeable position of seeming to interfere with the development of the State for the sake of keeping a valley . . . under national control."

Theodore Roosevelt (left) was noted for his conservationist policies as president. Here he stands with naturalist John Muir at Glacier Point, Yosemite Vally, California, in 1906. They collaborated on setting aside forest preserves in the area. BETTMANN/CORBIS

Stretching Presidential Power

Immediately on his election in 1904, Roosevelt committed what most of his advisers and later historians considered his greatest political blunder: he announced then that he would not under any circumstances be a candidate for reelection to a third term in 1908. Certainly the move made him something of a lame duck at the outset of his only full administration. Yet, instead of limiting him, it is possible that lame-duck status served Roosevelt's purposes well. He may have felt in fact that it freed him morally to move to the far side of constitutional law whenever his view of the national interest required it. That, at least, would be consistent with the man's unwillingness to be controlled by anything less than his own moral commitment to serving the public interest as steward of the nation.

Temporal checks on power are not, of course, the equivalent of faithfully regarded constitutional checks. A lot of damage can be done in only a short time by government administrators—regulatory commissioners as well as presidents—when they ex-

ercise power that is restrained by their own sense of justice alone. Blum has written, "It did not require eight years or even four for a president to lead the nation beyond the edge of war, or to employ his 'bully pulpit' to lie to the people, or to employ his authority to subvert the rights of individuals." Roosevelt in fact did none of these things, Blum notes, but he wonders if Roosevelt would have been so restrained if he had confronted global war and massive economic collapse, as some future presidents had to.

On the other hand, although Roosevelt was quite capable of magnifying a sense of crisis as occasion demanded, his presidency did not in fact confront great national or international troubles that might have tested his restraint. More than that, sensitivity to the abuse of presidential power stems from many decades of strong presidential leadership that by the 1970s eventuated in what came to be called—aptly enough—the Imperial Presidency. Theodore Roosevelt's generation faced the opposite problem—decades of weak leadership in which images of governmental usurpation were served up regularly by special interests trying to preserve their immunity from public control and accountability. Moreover, not even the severest critics of modern government (the lunatic fringe aside) would be comfortable now with the relatively small power that resided in the presidency even at the conclusion of T. R.'s reign. As Richard E. Neustadt noted in his landmark book *Presidential Power*, "A striking feature of our recent past has been the transformation into routine practice of the actions we once treated as exceptional.. . . The exceptional behavior of our earlier 'strong' Presidents has now been set by statute as a regular requirement." That Roosevelt acted to the degree that he did in advance of such statutory requirements says more for his intelligence than for his recklessness.

In the area of foreign policy, however, there is room for serious questioning. To cite Blum once more, Roosevelt's "belief in power and his corollary impatience with any higher law presumed that governors . . . possessed astonishing wisdom, virtue and self-control. As much as anything he did, his direction of foreign policy made that presumption dubious."

The key to Roosevelt's foreign policy lay in his division of the world into "civilized" and "barbarous" countries. "Peace cannot be had," he insisted, "until the civilized nations have expanded in some shape over the barbarous nations." Among the civilized nations, his diplomacy sought a balance of power. For the barbarian countries, he was ready to acknowledge an assignment of stewardships among the civilized nations. Russia belonged in Turkestan, Britain in India and Egypt, France in Algiers, and so on.

That there were racial implications in his portrait of global statuses cannot be denied, but that they were "racist" in the modern sense cannot be sustained. Roosevelt's estimate of nations and peoples was, as with so many things, conditioned by considerations of power. When Roosevelt expressed condescension or scorn for nonwhite peoples, his attitude originated in the evident weaknesses of the nations where they predominated; he reacted to the weakness, not to the race. Moreover, he never appears to have begrudged respect to individuals whose personal traits diverged from the stereotypes attributed to the ethnic or racial groups with which they were identified. "I suppose we have all outgrown the belief that language and race have anything to do with

one another." The same thing is true, he suggested, regarding character. "A good man is a good man and a bad man a bad man wherever they are found."

His view of the Japanese should make this clear. Japans' economic and military power won from Roosevelt ungrudging respect for the Japanese people. "I am not much affected by the statement that the Japanese are of an utterly different race from ourselves," he wrote to a British friend during the Russo-Japanese War. To the Japanese, in fact, Roosevelt assigned responsibility for civilizing and policing East Asia, or at least that part which "surrounds the Yellow Sea, just as the United States has a paramount interest in what surrounds the Caribbean." He wrote to his German friend Speck von Sternberg in 1900, "I should like to see Japan have Korea. She will be a check upon Russia, and she deserves it for what she has done." In 1904 he let it be known to both the British and the Germans that Japan ought to have Korea, as well as a role in bringing China "forward along the road which Japan trod" toward membership among the great civilized powers.

With Japan's victory over Russia in 1905, Roosevelt moved quickly to reestablish a balance of power in the Far East. Partly for his role in the Portsmouth, New Hampshire, peace conference that concluded the war, Roosevelt was awarded the Nobel Peace Prize in 1906. But Roosevelt never courted "the odium of being a professional peacemaker." He was concerned rather with assuring that Japan's new ascendancy would not go unchecked. To this end, and without consulting Congress or informing the American people, Roosevelt informally committed the United States to the Anglo-Japanese alliance and recognized Japan's hegemony in Korea and its "paramount interest" in Manchuria, in exchange for a Japanese pledge to honor United States sovereignty in the Philippines. It was not until 1925, as the result of historian Tyler Dennett's research, that the American people first learned of the "Taft-Katsura Agreement" and Roosevelt's secret arrangements.

Roosevelt was aware that the agreement provided for the direct violation of a multipower treaty guaranteeing Korea's independence. When the Germans invaded Belgium in 1914 in defiance of similar international guarantees of that country's neutrality, Roosevelt's public indignation was challenged on the grounds of his earlier acquiescence (indeed, collaboration) in Korea's violation. Roosevelt was infuriated by the analogy. "Any obligation by outside powers," he protested, "is of course dependent upon the power concerned itself standing for its own rights.. . . . If it shows itself impotent . . . it is of course impossible to expect other powers to aid it." He wrote on another occasion:

> To be sure by treaty it was solemnly covenanted that Korea should remain independent. But . . . the treaty rested on the false assumption that Korea could govern herself well.. . . Japan could not afford to see Korea in the hands of a great foreign power.. . . Therefore, when Japan thought the right time had come, it calmly tore up the treaty and took Korea.

It was, he said, a procedure "like that done under similar circumstances by the chief colonial administrators of the United States, England, France, and Germany." With such chilling candor about tearing up "solemnly covenanted" treaties, Roosevelt made clear his view that power established its own legitimacy and that those without power need expect no law to be honored in their favor.

Roosevelt's policies in the Caribbean of course fitted that view perfectly. The establishment of a protectorate in Cuba, the "taking of Panama," and the declaration of what came to be called the Roosevelt Corollary to the Monroe Doctrine all were founded on the assumption that "great powers" have the moral right to "spank" small countries (as Roosevelt put it) whose squabbling or inadequacies imperiled the security or merely the tranquillity of their more civilized neighbors.

The Cuban case in some respects impels a musing that "considering the opportunities" one must wonder at the restraint. The United States had gone to war with Spain in 1898 at least partly to pacify the troubled nearby island of Cuba. To underline its "missionary" objectives, it had declared in advance its commitment to Cuba's independence. Yet independence scarcely would guarantee no further disorders, nor would it prevent other powers from exploiting new disorders to replace Spain on the island. In belated recognition that the whole enterprise lacked logic if the United States simply withdrew without some way of exercising control over what happened to Cuba, the Roosevelt administration drafted, and the Senate ratified, a treaty that recognized Cuba's independence but that included a proviso. Called the Platt Amendment, it forbade Cuba from making any treaties or financial commitments with foreign governments that might compromise its independence, permitted United States oversight of Cuban finances, and authorized the United States to quell any internal disorders that might make Cuba prey to foreign intervention.

Although the reasoning by which Roosevelt justified Japan's annexation of Korea could have been applied to Cuba (to be sure, the United States faced no power so close as Russia was to Japan), the United States minimized its involvement with the Cubans. Cuba did become a protectorate whose internal disorders provoked one three-year military presence beginning in 1906 and several other actions in succeeding decades. But Roosevelt's preferred method of stabilizing the island was to improve its economy. To this end, he persuaded Congress, over ferocious opposition from domestic sugar growers and Republican protectionist ideologues, to give Cuban sugar, the island's biggest economic asset, preferred import status into the United States market.

The Panama episode had its immediate cause, as is legend, in the ocean-to-ocean dash of the USS *Oregon* around Cape Horn in 1898 to join the U.S. squadron off Cuba before the Spanish-American War ended. The epic argued the necessity for a canal across the Central American isthmus. (Californians and other westerners had also clamored for a canal to reduce their dependence on the monopoly power of transcontinental railroad companies.) Original plans for such a canal through Nicaragua blew up with the eruption of a volcano near the proposed site. There remained an abandoned project through Panama begun by a French company that still held a valid charter. Panama at the time was an unruly province of Colombia that had virtually defied governing for eighty years. The trouble lay, as Walter LaFeber writes, in "the type of person the Isthmus attracted—the rootless, lawless transient who obeyed no authority . . . 'a community [according to one contemporary observer] of gamblers, jockeys, boxers, and cockfighters.' " During the course of the nineteenth century, Colombia had to cope with more than fifty insurgencies aimed at secession. At least four times, Colombia called on the United States, with which it had arranged treaty obligations in 1846, to assist in repressing rebellions.

The only asset of the province was that it lay in the way of seagoing traffic between the east and west coasts of North and South America. For this, as the Americans contemplated a canal, Colombia prepared to exact its price. Colombia initiated the negotiations in 1900. In January 1903, Roosevelt offered Colombia $10 million plus $250,000 per year for a ninety-nine-year lease on a six-mile-wide canal zone. In addition,

$40 million was approved by Congress to pay off the Panama Canal Company (PCC), which held the rights to the route. The Hay-Herran treaty embodying the terms was ratified by the United States Senate, but in August the Colombian Senate unanimously turned it down. They wanted more money, including (they later specified) $15 million of the $40 million earmarked for the PCC. Roosevelt exploded, using a variety of tame expletives to describe the Colombian legislators—"inefficient bandits," "a corrupt pithecoid community," "homicidal corruptionists," and so on.

What lay at the heart of Roosevelt's exasperation was the conflict between a political ethic and a social ethic to which he was equally and profoundly committed. The social ethic dictated that reward should go to work and ingenuity. It was the work and ingenuity of others needing to cross the isthmus that gave value to the Colombian property and, indeed, provided livelihoods for the "community of gamblers, jockeys, boxers, and cockfighters" that prevailed there. On the other hand, the political ethic that informed Roosevelt's leadership dictated a strong regard for property rights and national sovereignty. A more conservative nationalist would have yielded the point to Colombia on the principle of sovereign prerogatives. But Roosevelt could not leave it at that. Progress in civilization demanded that legal "technicalities" give way to the more fundamental moral imperatives—at least when the former were unsupported by adequate power.

Meanwhile, suggestions flew from within and without the administration that perhaps the United States ought to encourage, rather than to help Colombia repress, the next Panama rebellion. But as late as October 1903, Roosevelt wrote privately that though he would delight in Panamanian independence, "I cast aside the proposition made at this time to foment the secession of Panama. Whatever other governments do, the United States cannot go into securing [the canal] by such underhand means." He preferred the more direct approach: he drafted a message for Congress asking authority to seize the isthmus. The draft was never completed. Taking the many cues that had been given, the Panamanians revolted. Without Congress' authority, and in spite of United States treaty obligations to Colombia, the president then dispatched the USS *Nashville* with covert instructions to block Colombian military efforts to suppress the new insurgency. With success of the rebellion assured, Roosevelt then negotiated

the terms of United States recognition of Panamanian independence, not with any bona fide representative of the Panamanian government but with Philippe Bunau-Varilla, a French operator who was acting both as political broker and agent for PCC investors. Presented with a fait accompli, the Panamanians accepted the treaty in anguish, having yielded more of their sovereignty and territory than had been included in the pact offered Colombia.

For public purposes, and in deference to the prevailing political ethic, Roosevelt loudly denied any United States complicity in the rebellion. Privately he wrote, "The United States is certainly justified in morals, and therefore . . . in law . . . in interfering summarily in Panama and saying that the canal is to be built and that they [the Colombians] must not stop it." But his attorney general, Philander Knox, is supposed to have said to him, "Oh, Mr. President, do not let so great an achievement suffer from any taint of legality!" Years later, in his autobiography, Roosevelt boasted, "I took the Isthmus, started the canal and then left Congress not to debate the canal, but to debate me."

Having acquired the canal in order to alleviate one kind of strategic problem, Roosevelt acquired for his country new strategic burdens. Outposts beyond the continental borders require protection. Insofar as the canal would become a vital part of the American strategic periphery, the possibility of encroachment in the area by any of the world's powers had to be viewed with concern. The most likely threat came from European powers moving in on Caribbean countries that got into financial trouble with their European creditors. Shortly before becoming president, Roosevelt had written to his German friend Sternberg, "If any South American State misbehaves towards any European country, let the European country spank it." As president in 1904, when the Dominican Republic failed to make its debt payment because of local disorders and several European countries prepared to dispatch warships, Roosevelt stayed cool. "If I possibly can, I want to do nothing," he wrote. But then an international court of arbitration adjudicating the claims of European creditors against Venezuela ruled disproportionate awards to those bondholders whose government (Germany) had sent warships to bombard the Venezuelan coast. Roosevelt finally understood that unless the United States stepped in the Caribbean would teem with European navies. "We must ourselves undertake . . . [to see to it that] a just obligation shall be paid," he told Congress. It was, he pointed out, ultimately a matter of national security. In 1907, when disorders again threatened payments on the Dominican Republic's foreign debts, Roosevelt, acting on his authority as commander in chief, took over the Santo Domingo customhouse. And so the Roosevelt Corollary to the Monroe Doctrine became the foundation for repeated United States intervention in the governing of countries in, or bordering on, the Caribbean. It remains in place today.

The T. R. Administration in Retrospect

As his presidency neared its end, Roosevelt seemed to grow proudest of the things he had done to make the United States into a major military power. In a letter dated 28 December 1908 to a journalist acquaintance who was planning an article on his administration, T. R. cited first of all his "doubling" of the size of the navy. Possibly that was because at that moment, the Great White Fleet was on its trip around the world advertising America's big stick while signaling (with the white paint and the exposure of the American coasts) the country's pacific intentions. Roosevelt also stressed his actions in the coal strike; his steps "toward exercising proper national supervision and control over the great corporations"; his massive increase in the country's forest reserves; the Reclamation Act, which he believed was matched only by the Homestead Act of 1862 in the development of America's farm economy; and "the great movement for the conservation of our national resources." But second on his list was the Panama Canal, about which he wrote: "I do not think any feat of quite such far-reaching importance has been to the credit of our country in recent years, and this I can say absolutely was my own work, and could not have been accomplished save by me or by some man of my temperament." To this he added his pride in the reorganization of the War Department, in the inauguration of regular army and navy maneuvers, and the military interventions in Cuba and the Dominican Republic, which he believed would leave both countries with better prospects for "a stable and orderly independence" than they had ever enjoyed before. He noted furthermore how many of these deeds were "done by me without the assistance of Congress."

Next to such accomplishments, the outgoing president added without elaboration: "I think the peace of Portsmouth was a substantial achievement. You probably know the part we played in the Algeciras conference." In fact, for his efforts in settling the Russo-Japanese War and in calming the tensions between Germany and France over influence in Morocco, Roosevelt was awarded the Nobel Peace Prize in 1906. So it is curious that he used such tame words to note them in a long letter otherwise uncharacterized by modesty. He had no reason to be modest about either the prize or about his triumphs at Portsmouth and Algeciras; they represented Roosevelt at his best as an international leader. Although Roosevelt turned easily to military measures when he treated with small countries, he was the model diplomatist when he negotiated with sizable powers. The prize testified to that. Yet it was clearly strength rather than finesse of which he was most proud, a fact that remains among his most dubious legacies.

When Roosevelt stepped down in 1909, he had set well in motion a powerful current that propelled the American state into the mainstream of its modern responsibilities. His successors, most notably Woodrow Wilson, Franklin D. Roosevelt, and Harry Truman, moved even more substantially toward committing the federal government to restoring the congruity of the American business system to the country's chief priorities, to protecting the nation from the less constructive effects of the industrial and corporative transformation of the economy, and to bringing the country's resources to bear on international problems. Roosevelt himself would contribute further to the current over the remaining ten years of his life, but as a goad and gadfly rather than as a direct force.

At fifty, he was still a young man when he retired from the presidency. In that respect alone it was probably inevitable that he would return to presidential politics. His 1904 vow not to seek reelection in 1908 did not mean he would never seek the presidency again. After a brief interlude in 1909 and 1910 hunting in Africa and hobnobbing with Europe's aristocracy, T. R. returned to the United States amid reform Republicans' growing disenchantment with William Howard Taft, Roosevelt's chosen successor in the White House. Among other things, Taft's dismissal of Gifford Pinchot from the Forest Service rankled particularly because it suggested the undoing of Roosevelt's much cherished conservation program. When Taft chose in the fall of 1911 to prosecute the United States Steel Corporation for antitrust violations in its 1907 merger with the Tennessee Coal and

Iron Company, Roosevelt took the move as a personal affront because of his own role in that affair. That winter T. R. threw his own hat in the ring against Taft for the 1912 Republican presidential nomination.

Taft defeated Roosevelt for the nomination, and T. R. bolted from the Grand Old Party to run for president as the standard-bearer of the newly organized Progressive party. Woodrow Wilson was elected with only 42 percent of the popular vote over both Roosevelt and Taft. It is worth noting that it was in the 1912 election campaign that T. R. gave full expression to the "New Nationalism," a view of government that he had sought unsuccessfully during his presidency to make Republican party policy. It was a program that called upon Americans to put the national interest above their own special competitive interests; to accept government supervision of business, of labor relations, and of resource use and allocation; to take up responsibility for aiding the poor, the disabled, and the aged with federal unemployment, welfare, and retirement insurance plans; to accept both consolidation of economic power and government regulation of such power; and to make cooperation and control rather than competition and cupidity the new model for an American commonwealth.

Roosevelt's New Nationalist campaign forced Wilson to counter with his own version of an industrial policy. Wilson called it the "New Freedom." It contrasted with Roosevelt's proposals in some significant matters, but the two programs held in common a firm commitment to a strong central government prepared to intervene in the nation's business economy whenever compelling reasons of state— including a considered judgment about intolerable levels of human suffering—might require. Except for the regressive Republican interlude in the 1920s, it would become the established political posture of both major parties for almost seventy years.

On the other hand, by leading progressive Republicans out of the Republican party, Roosevelt in effect conceded the party to the reactionaries, who in a single generation turned the GOP into the minority party it basically remained for more than half a century. Meanwhile, Roosevelt quickly abandoned the Progressive party after the 1912 campaign, leaving it to dissolve without a leader or a cause before even the next election came around. It was not a noble performance. Nor did the years after 1912 add stature to Theodore Roosevelt as a citizen or statesman.

In office and campaigning for office, T. R. usually tempered his moral enthusiasm with a strong sense of realism and responsibility. Out of office, and especially on foreign policy matters, Roosevelt often gave in to his less generous impulses. The Great War, as contemporaries referred to it, would bring out the worst in Roosevelt. Long committed to at least an informal Anglo-American alliance, the expresident railed intemperately in public and in private for an early United States intervention on Britain's side against Germany. He denounced President Wilson and others who strained to keep the country neutral as mollycoddles, cowards, hybrid Americans, and even traitors. When the United States did enter the war in 1917, he led the cry for punishment of all dissenters whether they were pacifists who opposed the war on religious or ethical principles or were critics of the government's particular domestic and foreign policies. As always, suggestions about constitutionally protected individual rights won no favor from Roosevelt. In a war, he believed, loyalty to the nation, right or wrong, must be prompt, vigorous, unquestioning, and complete.

That the Woodrow Wilson administration often enough acted on those principles during the 1917–1920 period was in no small measure because of the pressure for a draconian repression that men like Roosevelt persistently demanded. The blows suffered by civil liberties during that period in fact shattered for years the confidence that progressive reformers had once placed in a strong central government. Roosevelt's final years did much to undo what he had achieved for reform as president.

Conclusion

That Theodore Roosevelt is counted among the great heroes of the progressive democratic tradition, alongside Jefferson, Jackson, Lincoln, and Franklin D. Roosevelt, must be counted an oddity of historical circumstance. In essence, he was profoundly conservative, especially in his exaltation of martial values; in his emphasis on duty; in his simplistic view of patriotism; in his absolutistic understanding of morality, justice, and right; in his candid assertion of the moral superiority of the "right people" (defined by their effective organization and uses of power); in his easy distinction between the righteous and the malevolent, the civilized and the savage. But he happened upon the presidency just as the nation confronted seriously for the first time the emergence of a national, interstate corporate power that transformed traditional modes of business enterprise, threatened the integrity of democratic processes, and tampered with the mechanisms for free-market allocation of economic resources, rewards, and opportunities. As champion of a federal government strong enough and willful enough to restrain the men of new corporate power, Roosevelt became a democratic hero. His foreign policy, equally vigorous, bold, and prescient, continues to draw more mixed reviews.

BIBLIOGRAPHY

The indispensable printed source is Elting E. Morison, John Morton Blum, and Alfred D. Chandler, Jr., eds., *The Letters of Theodore Roosevelt*, 8 vols. (Cambridge, Mass., 1951–1954); volumes 2, 4, 6, and 8 also contain perceptive essays by the editors. Henry Cabot Lodge, ed., *Selections from the Correspondence of Theodore Roosevelt and Henry Cabot Lodge, 1884–1918*, 2 vols. (New York, 1925), is far more limited and purposefully edited, but useful nevertheless. John M. Blum, *The Republican Roosevelt* (Cambridge, Mass., 1954; 2d ed., 1977), is a masterful analysis of Roosevelt the man and the president. Blum's chapter on Roosevelt in his *The Progressive Presidents: Roosevelt, Wilson, Roosevelt, Johnson* (New York, 1980), fine-tunes the portrait. Morton Keller, ed., *Theodore Roosevelt: A Profile* (New York, 1967), contains sharply focused excerpts from a variety of books on Roosevelt himself and on the Progressive era.

The best single biography remains William H. Harbaugh, *Power and Responsibility: The Life and Times of Theodore Roosevelt* (New York, 1961; rev. ed., 1975). But Lewis L. Gould, *The Presidency of Theodore Roosevelt* (Lawrence, Kans., 1991), provides more concentrated attention on the presidency than Harbaugh and more detail than the present article. For an account of the young T. R. see David McCullough, *Mornings on Horseback* (New York, 1981). All Roosevelt's biographers continue to be indebted to the keen insights and comprehensive research in Howard K. Beale, *Theodore Roosevelt and the Rise of America to World Power* (Baltimore, 1956), for an understanding of T. R.'s foreign policy. Richard H. Collin, *Theodore Roosevelt's Caribbean: The Panama Canal, the Monroe Doctrine, and the Latin American Context* (Baton Rouge, La., 1990), brings that part of the Roosevelt story in touch with more recent revisionist historiography. An important account of Roosevelt appears in John Milton Cooper,

Jr., *The Warrior and the Priest: Woodrow Wilson and Theodore Roosevelt* (Cambridge, Mass., 1983), an excellent exercise in comparative biography. David H. Burton, *The Learned Presidency: Theodore Roosevelt, William Howard Taft, Woodrow Wilson* (Rutherford, N.J., 1988), treats the extraordinary succession of learned, even scholarly, presidents in that extraordinary era at the turn of the century when the well-earned credentials of intelligence were still important political assets.

Arthur M. Schlesinger, Jr., *The Imperial Presidency* (Boston, 1973); George E. Reedy, *The Twilight of the Presidency* (New York, 1970); and Richard E. Neustadt's pioneering study *Presidential Power*, 2 vols. (Durham, N.C., 1976), deal with Roosevelt only in passing but will help put his presidency in historical perspective, as will James David Barber, *The Presidential Character* (Englewood Cliffs, N.J., 1972), which offers a theoretical framework for "predicting performance in the White House." George E. Mowry, *The Era of Theodore Roosevelt, 1900–1912* (New York, 1958), remains one of the best accounts of T. R.'s administration within the context of the Progressive era.

Richard M. Abrams, *The Burdens of Progress: 1900–1929* (Glenview, Ill., 1978), provides a broader cultural and political context for understanding Roosevelt's personality and leadership. Robert H. Wiebe, "The House of Morgan and the Executive, 1905–1913," in *American Historical Review* 65 (1959), from which a part of the account of Roosevelt's consultations with Morgan was taken, should be supplemented by Wiebe, *Businessmen and Reform: A Study of the Progressive Movement* (Cambridge, Mass., 1962), while there is no better account of the conservation movement than Samuel P. Hays, *Conservation and the Gospel of Efficiency: The Progressive Conservation Movement, 1890–1920* (Cambridge, Mass., 1959). Among the more recent works, Paul R. Cutright, *Theodore Roosevelt: The Making of a Conservationist* (Urbana, Ill., 1985), adds personal detail to the story that Hays treats with a broader brush.

Recent works include Edmund Morris, *Theodore Rex* (New York, 2001), the second of a trilogy profiling the life of the president; this volume focuses on the presidency. The first volume of his early life is *The Rise of Theodore Roosevelt* (New York, 1979). See also Louis Auchincloss, *Theodore Roosevelt* (New York, 2001), H. W. Brands, *T.R.: The Last Romantic* (New York, 1997), and Nathan Miller, *Theodore Roosevelt: A Life* (1994).

William Howard Taft

Paolo E. Coletta

William Howard Taft THE LIBRARY OF CONGRESS

ILLIAM HOWARD TAFT'S parents were of moderate wealth and some political influence in Cincinnati, Ohio, where he was born on 15 September 1857. He graduated from Yale College in 1878 and was awarded a law degree by Cincinnati Law School in 1880. For the next twenty years he received increasingly important judicial positions from Republican hands before serving Presidents William McKinley and Theodore Roosevelt as the first civil governor of the Philippines (1901–1904) and then as Roosevelt's secretary of war (1904–1908). He thus had excellent credentials for achieving his life's goal, a seat on the Supreme Court. However, Helen Herron, whom he married in 1886 and who bore him

three children, sought high political office for him and obtained her wish.

More than six feet tall, weighing 332 pounds at his inauguration, Taft had an infectious chuckle and was usually even-tempered. Although thoroughly honest, he had certain deficiencies that detracted from success in politics. He was devoid of qualities of showmanship, unskilled in managing the fourth estate, conservative in his political and social views, and distrustful of the military viewpoint. In addition, he was afflicted with a craving for quiet, stability, and order that caused him to procrastinate in making decisions and forced him to devote a tremendous amount of energy to completing a task; a corpulence that made him sensitive to heat and increased his natural laziness; a lack of executive leadership, especially of the skill for achieving political compromises; and a perpetual tendency to depend for support upon others, first upon his parents, then upon Mrs. Taft, and particularly upon Theodore Roosevelt. When Roosevelt became president, Taft parroted his ideas; such was his attachment to him that he several times declined his offer of an appointment to the Supreme Court. Yet he disliked politics, saying in 1904 that "a national campaign for the presidency is to me a nightmare."

Legislative Affairs and Tempestuous Politics

As Elihu Root's successor as secretary of war, Taft served Roosevelt less as secretary, because Roosevelt ran the army, than as a provider of sound legal advice, spokesman on the stump, and general troubleshooter. It was only natural then that Roosevelt supported him above all others as his successor because Taft appeared to be an edited version of himself, the best man to carry out "the Roosevelt policies." The most important of these included supporting the right of labor to organize, forcing capital to obey the law, reforming the currency, improving the Sherman Antitrust Act, strengthening the powers of the Interstate Commerce Commission (ICC) over railroads, avoiding government ownership and socialism, and keeping the tariff rates steady.

Until elected president in his own right in 1904, Roosevelt sought only moderate reforms, in order to win the support for his renomination and election by the old guard. Once in power, he followed a "middle-of-the-road, middle-class program of mild reform" and was able to add a bit of constructive legislation to the rolls by appealing to the people over the head of Congress and promising everyone a "square deal." When in 1908 he suggested more radical reforms, the old guard balked. Then, with Roosevelt's strong support, Taft easily defeated Willam Jennings Bryan.

If Taft and Roosevelt agreed on objectives, they differed greatly on methods and interpretation. Both in domestic and foreign affairs, Roosevelt wanted to make the presidency the paramount branch of government. He would act unless constrained by "specific restrictions and prohibitions appearing in the Constitution or imposed by Congress under its constitutional power." As the steward of the people, he sought to do all he could for them, above all to obtain a more equitable distribution of the national wealth. Taft wanted to keep the branches of government in equilibrium and limit government in order to give personal and property rights free rein. He would not act unless he found the power to do so in the Constitution or in law and held that "there is no undefined residuum of power which [a president] can exercise because it seems to him to be in the public interest." He would not use government as an agency to relieve the misery of the masses, whose capability for voting intelligently he doubted. Never during his term did he intervene to settle a labor strike. He depended upon southern whites to solve the blacks' many problems even though the former were racists who equated white supremacy with progressivism. He also opposed the extension of more democratic political methods, including woman suffrage. Yet he did more than any other president before him through mechanistic means devoid of humanitarianism to make the federal government "efficient."

Taft believed, as he noted in his inaugural address, that his tasks would be to "complete and perfect" the progress Roosevelt had made; quiet the popular clamor he had excited, especially among businessmen; and oppose progressive reforms achievable only by the intervention of the federal government.

The most critical domestic problems facing Taft were the obtaining of an income tax that would raise revenue but also serve as a redistributor of the national wealth, the control of big business so as to provide free competition, reform of the tariff and currency and banking systems, the conservation of natural resources, and the improvement of democratic government by the admission of more democratic methods to it that would improve its organization and operations.

To leave Taft alone to run his administration, Roosevelt went hunting in Africa for a year. With Roosevelt's dynamic spell over him broken, Taft returned to his conservative self, thus appearing to progressives as having deserted them and Roosevelt's cause. In addition, his numerous social entertainments, frequent golf games, and long traveling junkets raised the question whether he was truly serving the public or seeking personal pleasure. Another action that helped cause his later split with Roosevelt was his failure to keep Roosevelt's cabinet, which by implication, rather than pledge, he had said he would retain as his own. Of nine men, seven had studied law, five were corporation lawyers, none was a progressive or reformer, and only three had served Roosevelt. He further alienated insurgents—defined as those who rejected dictation by their congressional leaders—and progressives by depending for legislative advice upon the reactionary Joseph Cannon, the dictatorial Speaker of the House, and upon the conservative Nelson W. Aldrich in the Senate, upon his equally conservative brother Henry and half brother Charles, and upon Mrs. Taft, the last three of whom constantly fed him their suspicions of Roosevelt's desire to return to the presidency.

Taft called Congress into special session, on 15 March 1909—the first Republican president to do so since Rutherford B. Hayes—to revise the tariff rates downward and in addition create a tariff commission that would investigate and report each year on those products whose schedules should be raised or lowered. Saying that he was "god-damned tired of listening to all this babble for reform," Cannon wanted to keep the Dingley Tariff of 1897 inviolate, but of his majority of forty-seven men, approximately thirty were insurgents who threatened his control. Believing that he needed Cannon's strength in the battle for tariff reform, Taft withheld his support from the insurgents seeking to unseat Cannon as Speaker. The insurgents naturally wondered how Taft could win progressive reforms by supporting conservatives.

As usual, congressmen sought to protect the economic interests of their own states or regions. Taft failed to give directions to Aldrich or to Sereno E. Payne, chairman of the House Ways and Means Committee, or to threaten opponents with the use of his patronage power. Payne's committee considered four thousand items. While it lowered four hundred duties on products for the benefit of their consumers, in the end it produced a bill that pinched consumers even further. A novelty was a federal inheritance tax of 1 percent on $10,000 or more. After it was passed by a vote of 217 to 161, Taft said it came "as near complying with our purposes as we can hope." He rejected advice from Senator Robert La Follette of Wisconsin and others that it did not square with his platform pledge, adding that he would not interfere with Congress while it was at work; he would veto it if it did not comply with the platform.

Aldrich increased 600 of the 847 items in the Payne bill and demanded its immediate passage so that delay would not disturb business. Instead, a summer of senatorial debate ensued that, for the oratory it produced and the consequences that followed, ranks with the debates over the League of Nations and Franklin D. Roosevelt's attempt to pack the Supreme Court. If the progressives could not move Aldrich, they widely publicized the inequities of his bill. After Aldrich read them out of their party, they told their constituents their side of the story in order to win continued political life. Taft then complained that he had been deceived by some "very astute and expert politicians," including Aldrich, whom he had trusted; but instead of berating Aldrich, he became angry with the insurgents, who were fighting his fight, because he believed that their criticism of the senator was also directed at him.

On 15 April 1909 the insurgents introduced an amendment calling for a flat 3 percent tax on individual and corporate incomes above $5,000 a year as a substitute for Aldrich's inheritance tax. Taft approved but said the Supreme Court would find the income tax unconstitutional and suggested a constitutional amendment for it. Congress passed such an amendment on 28 June. Moreover, he supported an insurgent amendment calling for a 2 percent tax on all corporate income except that derived from banking.

Although Cannon and Aldrich stacked the conference committee with extreme protectionists, Taft did not pressure it or appeal over its head to the public. Instead, he extended patronage to "standpatters" on the ground that his veto of its work would lose him their support for obtaining additional reforms in the subsequent regular session. The House approved the bill on 31 July by a vote of 195 to 183, with 20 Republicans voting nay and only 2 Democrats aye. On 5 August the Senate approved by 47 to 31, with 10 insurgents voting nay.

In addition to modifying the rates of the Dingley Tariff, the Payne-Aldrich Tariff gave Taft the Tariff Commission, which he wanted. It also set minimum and maximum rates and permitted the president to employ the latter against nations that discriminated, in some undefined way, against the United States. Taft concluded that while a veto of it would make him popular with the people, he would lose the support of standpatters. Moreover, he was pleased with the Tariff Commission, the increase of needed revenues, and the reductions in some rates. On 6 August he therefore signed the tariff act. He thereby ended his hundred-day honeymoon with Congress, further separated the regular and insurgent wings of his party, determined the latter to oppose his renomination in 1912, and infused new life into the Democratic opposition. Although he had done more about the tariff than Roosevelt had done in seven years, he decided to explain the new tariff to the people and thus dampen the flames of insurgency that engulfed the West, which was incensed because the tariff cuts had been made largely on western products and therefore helped the eastern manufacturers and trusts.

Rather than carefully preparing his speeches, he vacationed for a month and confessed that "I am putting off those speeches from day to day." His procrastination in the matter and his failure to employ a speechwriter or to submit his writings for editing caused him to make some disastrous gaffs. In Boston on 14 September he highly praised Aldrich. In La Follette's state, instead of thanking the insurgents for their support, he spoke of a postal savings-bank plan. As for a speech to be delivered in Winona, Minnesota, on the seventeenth, he told Mrs. Taft the night before that "it will be a close shave. Speech hastily prepared, but I hope it may do some good." He was never more wrong. While he admitted that he had agreed to some high rates in order to maintain party solidarity, he made a supreme blunder by asserting, "When I do say without hesitation that this is the best tariff bill that the Republican party has ever passed, and therefore the best tariff bill that has been passed at all, I do not feel that I could have reconciled any other course to my conscience than that of signing the bill."

Newspaper headlines, various congressmen, and even his devoted military aide, Captain Archibald W. Butt, saw that he had revealed his lack of proper preparation and ignorance of certain aspects of tariff making. More important, he was standing pat against further tariff revision and, by reading the insurgents from his party, providing them with excellent ammunition for the campaign of 1910. He then added to the animus against him by consorting openly with Cannon and other conservatives. Most important, by aligning himself with conservatives, he opened the door to demands that Roosevelt be reelected in 1912.

Even though controversy over the tariff had not ended, Taft became involved in another, over conservation policy, that engendered mountains of debate and had fantastic political repercussions. The basic argument was between those who would "preserve" what was left of the nation's natural resources for posterity, thus denying them to exploitation by corporate interests and "trusts," and those who would use them under stated conditions for mining, grazing, lumbering, and waterpower. Roosevelt believed conservation the most important contribution he had made to his domestic administration. His way was to employ scientific land-management techniques that would result in orderly resource development, to excuse federal intervention on the ground that the ends justified the means, and to invest the physical values of conservation with social and moral values. By 1908, Congress had blocked further progress in his program.

Taft agreed with Roosevelt on conservation but promised appropriate legislation to regularize various executive orders Roosevelt had used to accomplish his purposes. Roosevelt was pleased that Taft would retain his secretary of the interior, James Garfield, who had enthusiastically supported conservation, and then was disgruntled when Taft replaced him with Richard Achilles Ballinger of Washington State. For conservation, Roosevelt preferred federal control. Taft preferred state control. Taft wanted to lease national lands to private capital for exploitation and let Congress determine whether water should be under federal or state control but limit the reclamation of swamp and marginal lands to the federal government. Above all, he would regularize Roosevelt's extralegal methods, regardless of the results for conservation.

Like Taft a strict constructionist, Ballinger questioned the legality of some of Roosevelt's conservation measures, such as letting Gifford Pinchot, head of the Forestry Service in the Department of Agriculture, grant forest and mineral rights to land whose title was vested in the Department of the Interior. Moreover, Ballinger wanted to sell rather than lease coal lands and waterpower sites. Without specific congressional authority, Roosevelt and Garfield had withdrawn from settlement lands along rivers and streams in the Northwest and failed to inform Ballinger, who within ten days of his taking office stopped granting waterpower permits in the public domain and began restoring the right of private use. Taft supported him against Pinchot by saying that Congress, not the executive, could withdraw lands for conservation purposes. At Taft's request, Congress set aside, between 1910 and 1912, all valuable waterpower sites, thus legitimizing the work begun under Roosevelt yet giving waterpower magnates a lucrative opportunity to develop waterpower on the national domain. Pinchot was soon in disgrace with

Ballinger, and the public quickly became interested in the personal battle between the exemplars of Roosevelt's and Taft's conservation methods and in how Taft would solve this interdepartmental squabble.

Taft's greatest political crisis in the conservation issue came over the coal-lands problem. To foil speculators who merged dummy entries on 160-acre homestead claims in order to exploit coal beneath, in 1905 Roosevelt had directed that coal lands be leased rather than sold. He then withdrew 66 million acres, 7.68 million of them in Alaska, from entry. When one Clarence Cunningham, aided by Ballinger, then a Seattle lawyer, amassed 5,280 acres, rumors began about the impending rape of Alaska's mineral resources by unscrupulous Wall Street interests. Although as land commissioner Ballinger found Cunningham's claim legal, upon the report of a special investigator named Louis R. Glavis he rescinded the approval order. After becoming secretary of the interior, he had still another investigation made. This also upheld Cunningham. Blocked at Interior, Glavis turned to Pinchot in Agriculture, saying he had damaging evidence against Ballinger. Pinchot hoped to be able to drive him from office, but by attacking strict constructionists who favored "the great interests as against the people," he earned Taft's ire.

In February 1907, when Congress verged upon taking the power to establish national forests from the president, Pinchot had helped prepare for Roosevelt a "midnight forests" proclamation covering 16 million acres and Garfield had withdrawn 4 million acres of waterpower sites in the area just before a law creating national forests in six western states went into effect. Deeming Pinchot "a radical and a crank" who utterly worshiped Roosevelt, Taft in December 1908 had refused to use a speech Pinchot had written for him and hinted that because he was not a lawyer he might use illegal methods to accomplish his purposes. Pinchot thereupon concluded that Taft would kill conservation and that Ballinger was a traitor to the cause, but for the moment he kept the argument within the family. In August 1909, Taft accepted reports on the Cunningham claim from both Glavis and Ballinger. After reading them and submitting them to still further examination by his attorney general and others, he decided that Glavis should be fired "for disloyalty to his superior officers in making a false charge against them." He then wrote Pinchot that Ballinger was a true friend of conservation who operated only "within the law and [was] buttressed by legal authority," adding that he would be sorry to have Pinchot leave government service.

In November, in *Collier's* magazine, Glavis publicized his report, soon copied by a number of muckraking publications, which impugned Ballinger. While he praised Ballinger privately, Taft told Pinchot that he was determined to end "public discussion between departments and bureaus" because it was "most demoralizing and subversive of governmental discipline and efficiency." Pinchot pleased Taft by saying that he would not resign but would furnish a bill of particulars against Ballinger. The men parted amicably, yet Pinchot saw a way to keep up his fight for conservation—get himself fired and so dramatize the differences in attitude toward conservation between Roosevelt and Taft. To get himself fired, Pinchot openly attacked Taft in a speech in January 1910 and also in a letter to the chairman of the Senate Committee on Agriculture. Realizing that firing Pinchot would please those who sought to rupture his relations with Roosevelt and stimulate a "Back from Elba" movement that would be supported by the insurgents, Taft decided that others must take the initiative. On the advice of Elihu Root, who at his request read the record of the Ballinger-Pinchot dispute, he wrote Pinchot a letter of dismissal. When the letter arrived at his home, he waved it toward his doting mother and cried, "I'm fired." Eyes flashing, head flung back, and waving an arm over her head, she exclaimed, "Hurrah!"

The House of Representatives held hearings on the charges against Ballinger from 26 January to 20 May 1910. The report exonerated both Ballinger and Taft of evildoing but revealed that Ballinger's actions usually resulted in favors for private enterprise and for the exploitation of the resources desired by the West, thus contradicting Roosevelt's conservation policies. What had been a "tilt between Taft and Ted" then turned the tables on Taft by showing that he had sought to whitewash Ballinger, in part by the use of a predated document. Pressed for time, he had directed his attorney general to date certain papers "prior to the date of my opinion." Not knowing that Ballinger and the attorney general had openly acknowledged the fact, Taft denied it, thus laying himself open to the charge of being a liar and forger. The public press thereupon "convicted" him and "vindicated" Pinchot. Meanwhile, both Pinchot and Norman Hapgood of *Collier's* had gone to Europe to tell Roosevelt how Taft had turned away from his policies.

Proof that Taft was devoted to conservation lies in his withdrawing almost as much land from entry as Roosevelt had. He had regularized Roosevelt's conservation measures but wrecked the inter-departmental arrangements between Agriculture and Interior that had existed under Roosevelt; strengthened the power of Interior over conservation; widened the split in his party over the tariff issue by the conservation controversy; made Pinchot a martyr to progressives; furnished new ammunition to insurgents, especially westerners, who now hoped to add Roosevelt to their ranks; ensured that the House would lose its Republican majority in the elections of 1910; and provided issues for the presidential campaign of 1912. Most important, by firing Pinchot, Taft drove a deep wedge between himself and Roosevelt, who now saw him a failure as a leader.

Although Taft well knew of the serious insurgent and progressive uprising against him, he "walked to his doom 'a gentleman unafraid,'" as William Allen White put it. Having on 4 March 1910 completed a year in office, he alleged that the no-third-term tradition would block Roosevelt. While he admitted that his party was split, he pleaded for solidarity on the grounds that a good beginning had been made in carrying out his party's platform, as instanced by the Payne-Aldrich Tariff, which he still thought was the best tariff bill ever passed; his regularization of conservation; and his undertaking of railroad regulation, an antitrust crusade, and still other reforms. He should not be judged until he had finished his work.

Nonetheless, on the basis of his record, the progressives openly declared war on him as the primaries of 1910 approached. Furthermore, upon his return home on 18 June, Roosevelt submitted to a great popular reception but declined an invitation to visit the White House. Although he said he had no intention of running again and would not take sides in the battle between the regulars and progressives, he could not support Taft for renomination and re-election, despite letters from Taft saying that he had been "conscientiously trying to carry out your policies, but my method of doing so has not worked smoothly." Mrs. Taft's illness—she had suffered a stroke a year earlier—also placed a terribly great strain on Taft. Roosevelt replied that he intended "to keep my mind open as I keep my mouth shut." He broke a promise to Root to keep quiet for sixty days after only four days and conferred with a number of progressives before accepting Taft's invitation to visit him on 30 July at Taft's summer home but excluded discussion of serious political matters, even though he held Taft responsible for splitting their party and

making Democratic victories possible in November. He conceived his task to be the drawing together of the two wings of the party without supporting one against the other. "Taft has passed his nadir," he told Pinchot, but with new advisers he might redeem himself and become worthy of renomination and re-election.

While Roosevelt learned of the difficulties of drawing his party together—the president and the party's old guard defeated him when he sought a "clean-cut progressive program" in New York—Taft, irritated by his failure to keep silent, told Archie Butt on 6 July that "I do not see how I am going to get out of having a fight with President Roosevelt." Of the options available to him of helping, opposing, or bargaining with him, he chose the last. If Roosevelt would endorse him he would drop Aldrich and Cannon as advisers and let him suggest a replacement for Ballinger. If he did not agree, he would fight him.

Roosevelt replied in late August and early September 1910 by undertaking a three-week, sixteen-state western tour to announce the policies of his New Nationalism and so help elect progressives. But instead of cementing his party, he split it still further by demanding advanced social legislation, branding the Supreme Court—Taft's holy of holies—as a barrier to the achievement of social justice, and calling for federal power sufficient to obtain social justice and a president who would be the "steward of the public welfare" and place human rights before property rights. He thus ranged conservatives against himself and by comparison made Taft appear to be the conservator of all worth saving. However, in his customary way of balancing opposed forces, Roosevelt then sought support from conservatives as well as from progressives and so attempted to unite the party. He praised Taft's work on conservation, for example, and agreed to meet him to show the public that they were in harmony. Perplexed, Taft told a friend that "I don't know whither we are drifting, but I do know where every real thinking patriot will stand in the end, and that is by the Constitution," and withdrew even closer into his conservative shell.

Saying that those who had been disloyal to him must be read out of the party, Taft cited Albert J. Beveridge of Indiana, Albert B. Cummins and Jonathan Dolliver of Iowa, La Follette of Wisconsin, and Hiram Johnson of California. By confusing the anti-Cannon insurgents with progressives, he made one of the worst mistakes of his political career, for he drove away men long loyal to their party and divided it by

Presidents have long taken part in the ceremonial aspects of baseball. Here, President Taft attends a Washington Senators game in 1910. THE LIBRARY OF CONGRESS

supporting only its conservatives. Those driven out had their revenge in the primaries. Although Democrats defeated Beveridge, the victory of La Follette foreshadowed the split in the party in 1912. Of the forty-one incumbent Republican congressmen defeated, only one was an insurgent, and all the progressive senators were reelected and would be joined by three others. The insurgent uprising against Cannonism had become a progressive revolution that defeated standpat Republicanism in almost every instance and made Cannon's reelection as Speaker impossible. Moreover, Democratic victories in various eastern states, particularly the election of Woodrow Wilson as governor of New Jersey, offered new leaders of presidential stature. And with a Democratic majority in the House and a Republican majority of only twelve in the Senate, Taft would face a Congress in which either house could block his demands for legislation. With the defeat of almost all of the men he himself had supported, Roosevelt con-

cluded that all talk about his being a candidate in 1912 would end.

Despite the tempestuous primary politics, by the end of the second session of the Sixty-first Congress, on 10 June 1910, Taft had obtained a number of progressive reforms. The House Speaker had been stripped of his most dictatorial powers, and Taft was well on his way toward achieving more reforms, with some fifty new laws, in four years than Roosevelt had won in seven. Among these were more power for the Tariff Commission; a limit on the issue of labor injunctions; postal savings-bank, parcel post, and federal budget systems; streamlining of the post office so as to put it on a paying basis; and creation of the United States Court of Commerce to hear cases arising from decisions of the ICC.

Taft viewed the functions of the ICC in judicial terms, whereas progressives, recalling what the courts had done to its original powers, saw them as economic and political. In a bill introduced by Representative James Mann, Taft tried to lift the antitrust laws and permit railroads to cooperate in drafting freight rates and passenger fares but agreed that the ICC approve the amount of stocks and bonds they issued. However, House insurgents and Democrats amended the bill to bar mergers and to prohibit a greater charge for a short than for a long haul, included telephone and telegraph companies as common carriers, and failed by only one vote to delete the Commerce Court. When progressive and Democratic senators sought to strengthen the bill and thus support Taft, he took their aid as opposition and made the original bill a test of party loyalty.

In the end, he compromised with the House: Arizona and New Mexico could become states, even though they would be Democratic, in return for a railroad bill lacking control over railroad securities. In the Senate, the insurgents deleted from the companion Elkins bill its authorization of traffic agreements and mergers. The greatly changed result, the Mann-Elkins Act, covered not only telephone, telegraph, and cable companies but railroad terminals, bridges, and ferries, and forbade a greater charge for a short than for a long haul but excluded government control over railroad securities. It passed with solid Republican support, but Taft had helped it pass by directing his attorney general to issue an injunction against the presidents of a number of eastern railroads who had joined together to raise their rates. After they rescinded the higher rates and promised to follow the new law, the injunction was dropped. Nevertheless, Taft interpreted the insurgents' attempts to strengthen the law—a great improvement over the Hepburn Act of Roosevelt's day—as opposition to him and determined to seek their defeat in 1912.

Taft pleased businessmen in general by demanding government efficiency and currency and banking reform, by taking the patronage out of politics, by increasing American investments at home, and by obtaining additional foreign markets. Yet he had no word of cheer for the political, economic, and social reforms demanded by progressives. At any rate, finding the government poorly organized and lacking a good accounting system, he reorganized some departments; improved the system of collecting customs duties; cut military appropriations; and, in order to be able to reach administrative decisions, demanded an executive budget, a central purchasing system, and a budget office. The first president to have the federal administration studied in detail—by

the Commission on Economy and Efficiency (1911–1913)—he was able in 110 reports to show Congress how the government could save money and the time and energy of public officials. He wanted to reduce federal spending and the number of public employees, stop pork-barrel legislation, use the best accounting systems adopted by the business world, reorganize and reduce government agencies, and devote a minimum of expenditures to social welfare projects—the last a sore point with progressives.

Desiring to keep its power of the purse, Congress refused to provide the president authority to prepare a federal budget. Saying that his constitutional authority denied Congress power in the matter, Taft, in his budget for fiscal 1914, asked not only for appropriations but for authority to change laws, management procedures, organization, business methods, and even the personnel of the executive branch. Because Congress refused to act, the United States remained the only important nation in the world as yet without a federal budget. What reorganization Taft accomplished, as in the Department of State in 1909, was only mechanistic, because he conceived of administration in terms merely of structure and failed to give it the leadership and spirit good management requires. During his last days as president, he approved the act creating the Department of Labor, theretofore a division of Commerce, and again asserted the need for a thorough reorganization of the executive structure.

While the Payne-Aldrich Tariff was the most generous American one to apply to Canada since a reciprocity treaty of 1854 had been abrogated by the United States in 1866, Taft told the Senate on 26 January 1911 that Canada would have to decide whether to stay out of American markets or become a commercial friend. He then tried to jam a Canadian reciprocity treaty through Congress. By appealing over the head of Congress for popular support for "the most important measure of my administration," he obtained a House bill that lowered some rates of the Payne-Aldrich Tariff and greatly pleased Democrats because it portended the fall of the extreme protectionist system. When the Senate balked at revising the tariff, Taft called Congress into extraordinary session for 1 April 1911.

On the surface, reciprocity promised many benefits. The United States could look for increased sales of manufactures, greater access to Canadian raw materials, and cheaper foodstuffs—at the cost of American farmers, producers of raw materials, and fishermen. Canada would enjoy greater sales of agricultural products to the United States, lower prices for American manufactures, and a drop in taxes—at the cost of increased prices for food and agricultural implements, the destruction of benefits derived from the British imperial preference system, and the end of subsidies for industry. Once the Senate agreed with the House on lower duties, the "legislative agreement" (rather than treaty) had still to run the gauntlet of two national legislatures.

When the new Speaker, Champ Clark, outlined the legislative program, he avoided reciprocity but called for reductions in the tariff that would render ineffective any reciprocity agreement with Canada. The Ways and Means Committee supported him, but he then bungled by saying that "I am for this [reduction] Bill, because I hope to see the day when the American flag will float over every square foot of the British North American possessions clear to the North Pole." In any event, the House passed the bill on 21 April, but on the twenty-fifth it began debating a farmers' free list and wholly disregarded Taft's stentorian call for reciprocity.

In the Senate, Republican insurgents Cummins and La Follette opposed reciprocity because it would hurt American farmers and help the trusts by giving them cheap raw materials. Assuming that the American Congress could not reach agreement before the end of July, the Canadian Parliament on 19 May adjourned for ten weeks. While Taft pressured opposed senators, the House continued to lower agricultural tariff duties, yet on 22 July the Senate passed the Canadian reciprocity bill by a vote of 53 to 27—with Democratic support. It was now Canada's turn, but Taft was also on the spot because the Senate passed bills reducing the rates on various agricultural products and the House went along. Taft thereupon vetoed the bills.

The Canadian Parliament opened on 18 July, but because the majority could not force closure on the question, it was dissolved and new elections were set for September, thus delaying the meeting of Parliament again until 1 October. Taft, on 15 September, began a long tour in which he spoke mostly about the tariff. A week later he learned that Sir Wilfrid Laurier, the Liberal party premier, who favored reciprocity, had been defeated by one who opposed it. Taft, the "father of reciprocity," had thus been repudiated by his northern neighbor.

During the special session Taft called to deal with Canadian tariff reciprocity, Congress admitted Arizona and New Mexico as states, reapportioned the House, provided for free trade with the Philippines, and enacted a number of progressive measures, approving postal savings banks, publicity for campaign contributions, creation of the Industrial Bureau and the Bureau of Mines, an eight-hour day for workers on federal projects, compensation for workers injured on interstate railroads, increased power of the ICC over railroad rates, and a strengthened Pure Food and Drugs Act. Taft vetoed the admission of Arizona because its constitution provided for the recall of judges; he also vetoed several tariff revision bills and was lukewarm toward the popular election of senators. Although the direct-elections bill passed the Senate by only one vote more than the required two-thirds, its popularity was revealed when the House passed it by a vote of 296 to 16.

In January 1911 Senator Aldrich offered recommendations for reforming the currency and banking system distilled from a two-year study. Briefly, he sought to create a great central bank with Reserve Association branches, all under the direction of private bankers, and issue untaxed asset currency. He was attacked by those who variously decried the concentration of lendable funds in the largest cities, demanded public rather than private control, wanted government rather than bank currency, and urged that credit facilities also be provided farmers. Taft approved Aldrich's conclusions after treasury officials were added to the board of directors of the central bank, but he did not push for the plan very hard, and after Aldrich retired from the Senate later in 1911, four standing committees of the House began work on the subject. The Federal Reserve Act, adopted by the succeeding Wilson administration, was based on a report made by a subcommittee of the House Banking and Currency Committee, headed by Carter H. Glass.

Taft's attitude toward the civil service was ambivalent, yet he wished to extend the merit system to all but the most important administrative offices of government and also called for a civil-service pension plan. When Congress balked, he extended the merit system in the postal and consular services and to skilled workers in navy yards.

Taft continued the antitrust cases Roosevelt had begun, adding that he would enforce the Sherman Antitrust Act, pending improved legislation designed to prevent monopoly. He had no quarrel with big business as long as it behaved itself, and he recommended that "good" trusts with a capitalization of

$100 million or more incorporate under a new federal law, thus exempting them from suits brought by states. When a law embodying his ideas was introduced in both houses on 7 February 1910, it was spurned by Democrats and insurgents because it would have destroyed the Sherman Act. Although Taft's unrelenting antitrust crusade far exceeded Roosevelt's—seventy-five suits in four years, compared with forty suits in seven years—by misunderstanding Roosevelt's antitrust policy, he was to cause himself and Roosevelt great personal embarrassment.

On appeal, the Supreme Court on 15 May 1911 decided against the Standard Oil Company of New Jersey, and on the twenty-ninth, against the American Tobacco Company. Roosevelt had entered suit in both cases. But in the Standard Oil case the Court announced a "rule of reason" by which it could decide whether a restraint of trade was "reasonable" or not and what restraints of trade were allowable. More important in expanding the break between Taft and Roosevelt were suits against the United States Steel and International Harvester companies.

During the Panic of 1907, J. P. Morgan and other bankers wished to prevent additional business failures and to shore up confidence in Wall Street by letting United States Steel acquire many shares of the Tennessee Coal, Iron, and Railroad Company (TCI). Fearing an antitrust suit, United States Steel's Elbert H. Gary suggested that the president or the Department of Justice grant approval for the purchase of TCI shares. On 4 November, Gary spoke with Roosevelt, who said that "while he could not advise them to take the action proposed, he felt it no public duty of his to interpose any objection." Wall Street and the nation had thus been saved.

Congressional hearings held on the matter in June 1911 revealed that Gary and George Perkins of United States Steel and International Harvester not only defended the steel company's taking over TCI but disliked the Sherman Act and advocated federal control over industrial corporations and even control of their sale prices—the latter of which Taft saw as state socialism. Asked to testify on the part he had played in the TCI affair, Roosevelt, on 5 August, assumed full responsibility for what had transpired, adding that the result had "justified my judgment." But Taft's entering of a suit against the corporation on 26 October implied that Roosevelt had fostered monopoly and been deceived about the facts of the transaction. This marked the final break between Roosevelt

and Taft. Thereafter, while Roosevelt called for a law that would tell businessmen exactly where they stood with respect to the Sherman Act or, better still, a law granting the federal government power to regulate and supervise business engaged in interstate trade, Taft insisted that the Sherman Act was "clear," thus alienating conservative interests, damaging himself politically, and giving rise to a clamor for Roosevelt to enter the ring against him in 1912.

Roosevelt was also involved in the suit Taft brought against International Harvester, or the "farm machinery trust," in April 1912. Both Taft and Roosevelt had awaited the decision impatiently because each would make it a leading issue in the contest for the presidential nomination. Lacking an agency to control corporations, Roosevelt had not sued Harvester, a "good" trust, but Taft viewed the situation as meaning that he had granted gross executive favoritism to a Morgan interest and was now defending Perkins. But when Taft was secretary of war, he had approved Roosevelt's action; he had then waited three and a half years, until Roosevelt contested the presidential primaries with him, before entering a suit.

Various plans for controlling corporations had been considered by a Senate committee in November 1911, including a plan favored by Roosevelt and Perkins that would "regulate" big business, and Taft's plan, which would have "exterminated" it under what he insisted was the "clear" meaning of the Sherman Act. In consequence of Taft's stand, the voters turned to presidential aspirants who were more friendly than he to big business. In December 1911, Taft sent Congress a special message in which he made three "sanely progressive" proposals that appealed to Wall Street and found favor in all political quarters: (1) that the Sherman Act not be amended; (2) that a supplemental law should be enacted "which shall describe and denounce methods of competition which are unfair and badges of the unlawful purpose denounced in the Anti-trust law"; and (3) that government control of trusts be strengthened by federal incorporation and by the creation of a "special bureau of commission" in the Department of Commerce and Labor.

By highlighting the minatory rather than the reform aspects of these suggestions, he made it difficult for Congress to comprehend his meaning. Moreover, the first regular session of the Sixty-second Congress, which met in December 1911, would not sit until the eve of the national conventions. Last, it could not be expected that the strong Democratic majority in the House and small Republican majority in the Senate would pass any measures he demanded. Congress amended those patent laws that supported monopoly and hindered the enforcement of the Sherman Act, but it did nothing to pass the antitrust laws he demanded. Taft had thus failed to fulfill his platform plank on the matter and driven Perkins and many other businessmen from his side and toward Roosevelt.

Foreign Affairs

Taft differed greatly from Roosevelt in his conduct of foreign, as well as domestic, affairs. Taft's experiences in the Philippines and in the cabinet should have provided him an excellent background in the conduct of diplomacy, but he shunned both Roosevelt's method of proceeding with as much executive action and as little congressional consent as possible and his realistic policy of peace through strength to protect the nation's interests.

Never bellicose, Taft sought to settle international disputes by peaceful means, particularly through the use of the Hague Court of Arbitration or by international commissions of inquiry if diplomatic efforts failed. Pacific means served to settle the Pribilof Islands pelagic sealing question that had for years disturbed the United States, Great Britain, Canada, Russia, and Japan; the fisheries dispute with Newfoundland; and the United States-Canadian boundary. Roosevelt agreed to the arbitration of questions not involving national honor or vital interests, whereas Taft agreed to unlimited arbitration and in April 1911 told Archie Butt that a treaty of this kind with Great Britain "will be the crowning jewel of my administration . . . but also the greatest failure if I do not get it ratified." He failed to take into account a Senate extremely jealous of its prerogatives in the treaty-making process and Roosevelt, who countered that, Britain excepted, "the United States should never bind itself to arbitrate questions respecting its honor, independence, and integrity."

On 3 August 1911, Taft won popular applause when he submitted to the Senate unlimited arbitration treaties with Britain and France. The Senate Foreign Relations Committee deleted the paragraph permitting the referral of arbitral matters to an international commission apart from the Senate, declared that no such commission or court could tell it what was subject to arbitration, and added a long list of items not subject to arbitration, including immigration policy and the Monroe Doctrine. Passed by the Senate mainly to embarrass Taft, the treaties had to be rewritten before being resubmitted to Britain and France, and Taft's appeal to the people in a speaking tour merely strengthened the Senate in its resolve to hold its ground.

Moreover, Taft overlooked the fact that he had refused to arbitrate with Britain over the Panama Canal tolls and thus damaged the principle of arbitration itself. In contrast he agreed to arbitrate the question of the ownership of the Chamizal tract on the Texas-Mexican border, which had hung fire since 1897 and would not be settled until the late 1960s.

Because dictator Porfirio Díaz welcomed foreign investments in Mexico, conservatives, including Taft and his minister to Mexico, disliked the nationalistic and reformist principles of his opponent in the presidential elections of 1910, Francisco Indalecio Madero. While Taft sent military forces to the Mexican border and ships to protect American lives and property during the civil war that broke out between Díaz and Madero and, after the murder of Madero, General Victoriano Huerta, Taft consistently honored his promise not to intervene. Rather than present the incoming Wilson administration with a fait accompli by recognizing the new Huerta regime, he bequeathed it the Mexican problem.

Taft's secretary of state, Philander C. Knox, was an excellent lawyer but an abominable statesman. Moreover, for his first assistant secretary he chose a man who equaled his capacity for antagonizing people, Francis M. Huntington Wilson. In any event, on Knox's advice Taft reorganized the State Department by creating several new positions and the now familiar geographic desks. As for policy, Taft and Knox agreed upon the need for the strategic defense of the Panama Canal, then under construction, by promoting peace in the Caribbean and Central America; support of the Monroe Doctrine; and "dollar diplomacy," the policy of actively encouraging American investments abroad with the object not only of earning profits but of promoting economic and political stability in the areas of investment and thereby world peace. As Taft put it, he was substituting "dollars for bullets." While his strategic and commercial objectives were the same as Roosevelt's, it was hard to believe his saying that dollar diplomacy also appealed to "humanitarian sentiments." On the other hand, conditions south of the border occasionally menaced American interests. Particularly in Central

America, politics were corrupt, economic development lagged, financial indebtedness was prevalent, and revolutions were endemic in those countries that did not have oppressive dictators.

The best examples of the working of dollar diplomacy were in Colombia, Honduras, and Nicaragua. Bitter toward the United States because of its rape of Panama and seeking compensation for the loss, Colombia wanted to arbitrate differences. Taft offered $10 million and a statement sounding like an apology. When Colombia refused, he raised the ante to $25 million, which was also refused; he left office without solving the problem.

To help Honduras liquidate its large foreign debt, Taft suggested a loan to be secured by American control of its customhouses. While various American bankers were willing to assume the great risks involved, the Senate Foreign Relations Committee refused to approve the loan. When a revolution broke out in July 1911, Taft sent warships that landed troops and a special envoy to arbitrate differences. When he offered a new loan arrangement, Honduras refused, thereby leaving this problem also unsolved.

Nicaragua was ruled by an unscrupulous dictator, Europeans held much of its debt, and Washington did not want its alternate canal route to fall into unfriendly or foreign hands. Following a revolution in October 1909 in which two Americans serving with the insurgents were executed, Washington instituted what was popularly called the "Hard Knox Policy." Naval vessels sped to both Nicaraguan coasts, recognition of its government was withdrawn, and a hundred Marines were stationed in its capital, Managua. Nicaragua's request for a loan in September 1910 opened the door for dollar diplomacy, and Taft recognized a new government. The American loan would stabilize Nicaragua's finances, the canal site would be safe, Nicaragua could pay off its foreign debts, and American control of the customs would remove them from the grasp of revolutionaries. Taft therefore concluded that the new financial arrangement and peace treaties with Nicaragua's neighbors would provide "a complete and lasting economic regeneration . . . of inestimable benefit to the prosperity, commerce, and peace of the Republic." But bad luck brewed.

During disorders in 1912 in which insurgents seized some American properties, Taft sent several warships and about twenty-seven hundred Marines to protect American lives and property. When the Senate rejected his financial plan, the new Nicara-guan president asked for $3 million in return for an option on the canal route and certain concessions that would make Nicaragua virtually a financial protectorate of the United States and even permit intervention in its internal affairs. No action was taken in the matter before Taft left office. Taft's dollar diplomacy had generated much ill will south of the border. Arbitration proved useless, Pan-Americanism made no progress, and the Lodge Corollary to the Monroe Doctrine further angered Latin America. (The 1912 corollary blocked the sale of a part of Baja California to a private Japanese syndicate, an act considered a threat to California and the Panama Canal.) Equally poor success marked dollar diplomacy in China. Knowing that he could not get all the nations with spheres of interest therein to abide by the Open Door, Roosevelt had mediated between Russia and Japan in 1905 in great part to prevent Japan from becoming the primary power in the Far East and thus able to close it. He further salved Japan, in return for understandings arranged by Taft as secretary of war that it had no designs on the Philippines, by permitting it to acquire sovereignty over Korea. However, Taft and Knox tried to use the Open Door to increase the export of American surplus goods and to allow America to acquire financial supremacy in China and Manchuria. They thereby challenged vested European and Japanese interests in China and greatly exacerbated Japanese-American relations.

American trade with China was only about 10 percent of its total overseas trade, yet Taft wanted the United States to become a Pacific power. He and Knox agreed to try to buy the Russian and Japanese railroads in China; if Japan would not sell, a competing road would be built with funds provided by the American Banking Group, which American bankers established for China at the request of the State Department. China was of course anxious to have Taft defend it, particularly from Great Britain and Japan, and to grant it loans for railroad construction, currency reform, education, and other undertakings.

Determined to prevent Japan from monopolizing foreign investments in China, Taft asked Japan to let the United States join a Chinese-Japanese mining venture in Manchuria and a British, French, and German railroad consortium—the Hukuang loan. Blocked by the Europeans and China, he took a very unusual step and appealed directly to the Chinese prince regent for equal American participation in the Hukuang loan and, after almost two years, won his point in May 1911. There was also a scheme to build a railroad from Chinchow to Aigun by an international consortium and a plan for still another consortium to acquire, and thus neutralize, all foreign-dominated railroads in China. Although Knox spoke about these measures as attempts to keep the Open Door open, it was easily seen that he was using the Open Door as a financial weapon, and he was defeated by China, Russia, Japan, and the interested European powers.

How well had Taft and Knox aided China? While the Hukuang and currency-reform loans went through, they helped spark a revolutionary outbreak in China and failed to push American capital where it would not go of its own accord. In fact, American exports to China declined from $58 million in 1905 to $15.5 million in 1910. Perceiving Taft and Knox as using the big stick in seeking an economic penetration of China, the Russians, the Japanese, and their respective allies formed a close defensive alliance against the United States.

Although Taft would not give up American extra-territorial rights in China or permit the naturalization of Chinese in the United States, he kept a close eye on attempts by various native reformers to change the Chinese imperial government into a constitutional democracy. When the call for a constitutional convention came late in 1912, he was faced with deciding whether to recognize a Chinese republic unilaterally or in concert with the other five major powers operating in China. He opted for concerted action, but by this time the shadow of the incoming Wilson administration lay over Washington. Taft followed Roosevelt's policies with respect to Japanese landownership and immigration. A renewed Japanese-American treaty of commerce and navigation that went into effect on 5 April 1911 contained nothing about the right of Japanese to own land in the United States and did not change America's Japanese exclusion policy.

The Election of 1912

If Taft was satisfied with what he had accomplished by 1912, the country was not. Although he now shared the patronage and other party honors with progressives and so appeared to be their leader, the insurgents could not forget how he had hounded them in 1910. In addition, La Follette had established the National Republican League, which sought to restore the government to the people by reforms that would provide more democratic procedures not only in government but in political party organiza-

tion as well. Believing the league to be La Follette's instrument for seeking the presidential nomination, Roosevelt had refused to join it, but on 21 January 1911, La Follette and others had created the National Progressive Republican League, which grew so rapidly that both Taft and Roosevelt had to take it seriously into account.

La Follette made great gains in the Middle and Far West by lambasting Taft's lack of policy and direction, but he could not shake off the feeling that his leadership of the league would be lost to Roosevelt if he claimed it and well knew that Taft would control the delegates to the Republican National Convention. Moreover, in an extensive tour in September and October 1911, Taft criticized Roosevelt while nailing down southern delegates. When Roosevelt changed his mind and threw his hat into the ring, Taft felt betrayed and predicted his own defeat in 1912. He nevertheless decided to fight him because "I believe I represent a safer and saner view of our government and its Constitution than does Theodore Roosevelt, and whether beaten or not I mean to continue to labor in the vineyard for those principles."

The delegates to the first National Progressive Republican Conference, held on 16 October, endorsed La Follette and his ideas for returning the government to the people, highlighting presidential primaries, and criticized Taft's antitrust policies. On the twenty-seventh, Roosevelt also opted for presidential primaries and criticized Taft for siding with business and the old guard and never once saying anything "in consonance with humanity." In December, when Roosevelt discounted the no-third-term tradition, it was clear that he was open to a draft. Headquarters for him were opened in important cities, and in February 1912 he announced his platform and hinted to several reform governors that they should ask him to run. This they did, and he promptly accepted. After saying that human rights should be placed above all others, he went on to demand a "fair distribution of property," direct voting methods, and the recall of judicial decisions involving constitutional questions on the state level—the last soon perverted into the recall of judicial decisions. "Nothing but death can keep me out of the fight now," said Taft. It helped Roosevelt that an ill and anguished La Follette broke down while delivering an address in February, even though he did not withdraw from the race.

Thoroughly angered, Taft fought hard in a meeting of his national committee and won convention officers friendly to him. The first president to stump in a primary campaign, he struck hard at Roosevelt, saying that he fought to preserve the Constitution and saw nothing that disentitled him to stand for a second term. So believing, he rejected all progressive demands for direct political action by the people, defended the independence of the judiciary, and spoke contemptuously of the Democratic party. The old guard naturally supported this "regular" conservator of constitutionalism against the "progressive" Roosevelt.

By the end of March, with southern delegates giving him half of the majority he needed, Taft was virtually impregnable, even if many delegates chosen elsewhere were contested by Roosevelt men. By May, Taft began referring in personal terms to Roosevelt and telling his audiences that he was going to "fight him," though he confessed privately that to do so wrenched his soul. After a particularly vicious attack, he blurted out that "Roosevelt was my closest friend," and wept. Roosevelt replied in kind, saying that "it is a bad trait to bite the hand that feeds you" and that this was "a fight to the finish." In any event, the thirteen states using presidential primaries went heavily to Roosevelt, thus making him appear the truly popular choice, whereas states using the convention system generally went to Taft.

By steamroller tactics the national committee gave Taft 235 of the 254 contested delegates, whereupon Roosevelt took the unprecedented step of going to Chicago and personally assuming direction of his lost cause. With Roosevelt's men not participating in the proceedings, Taft was named on the first ballot. On the next day, shouting "We Want Teddy," Roosevelt supporters organized their own party in the greatest revolt against the Republican party since the Silver Republicans had been defeated in 1896. Roosevelt declared himself a presidential candidate and announced the formation of the National Progressive, or "Bull Moose," party. In Baltimore, Democrats chose the progressive Woodrow Wilson as their candidate for president. Since the Democratic platform closely paralleled the Progressive, Taft remained a lonely conservative.

Taft campaigned openly and honestly as a conservative, but by avoiding histrionics he failed to excite his followers. In contrast, Roosevelt's delegates, who met on 5 August at what was more a religious revival than a political meeting, spoke of the need for "social brotherhood" and "representative government" and said they would "Pass Prosperity Around." After naming Roosevelt and, for vice president, Hiram Johnson of California, the "Moosevelt" party adopted the most progressive political and social platform in American history. Roosevelt stumped the West and South; Wilson, the East and Middle West; and Taft abandoned his party. The elections gave the Democrats their greatest victory since 1892—the presidency, both houses of Congress, and twenty-one of the thirty-five gubernatorial contests. The split between Taft and Roosevelt made Wilson a minority president, with the most spectacular gains made by the Socialist candidate, Eugene V. Debs. That the country had not gone Democratic was proved because Taft and Roosevelt together polled 1,311,444 more votes than Wilson. But adding the votes of Debs, Roosevelt, and Wilson showed that 75.26 percent of the vote was progressive. Wilson received 435 electoral votes, Roosevelt 88, and Taft a mere 8 in the worst drubbing a presidential candidate had yet received.

Little was accomplished in the second and last sessions of the Sixty-second Congress by men already repudiated by the public, yet Taft had the pleasure of announcing the ratification of the Sixteenth Amendment and congressional approval of the Seventeenth. Meanwhile, he had accepted a professorship of law at his alma mater, Yale University.

As president, Taft had revealed himself to be a conservative conservator. In his book *Popular Government* (1913), he questioned the validity of enlarging the suffrage and of more democratic methods of achieving political, economic, and social democracy, and in a book published in 1916 he revealed his very restricted view of presidential power. Meanwhile, in March 1913, he went to Yale as Kent Professor of Constitutional Law and served until 30 June 1921, when President Warren Harding fulfilled Taft's lifelong hope by naming him the chief justice of the United States Supreme Court.

Taft took over a bench that was far behind in its work, so badly divided that dissents were offered in about one-fourth of the opinions handed down, and in need of new quarters. He obtained a new building and, by creating a conference of senior circuit judges to work with him, brought the business of the court almost up to date by the time he retired from the court in February 1930 because of heart trouble. As for his own decisions, on the whole he was conservative in his interpretation of the law. In *Bailey* v. *Drexel Furniture Company*, for example, he held that Congress infringed upon the rights of the states and improperly used the tax power when it taxed the products of child labor that went into interstate trade. In the Coronado Coal Company case, he denied federal jurisdiction over coal mining because such mining was not interstate commerce; as for the United Mine Workers, who had struck the company, they had unlawfully used for strike purposes the funds they had accumulated. On the other hand, his most important dissent was against a majority opinion invalidating a 1918 law that fixed a minimum wage for women in the District of Columbia (*Adkins* v. *Children's Hospital*). All in all, he showed a preference for federal, rather than state, control of business, while advocating broad federal power under the commerce clause of the Constitution. Although no leader in judicial thought in the same sense as Oliver W. Holmes, Louis Brandeis, or Benjamin N. Cardozo, he was a good administrator. When he died on 8 March 1930, the new Supreme Court building seemed likely to remain his most enduring monument.

Conclusions

What did Taft accomplish? No great scandal or corruption marred his term, he did not take any steps backward, and his legislative record included many solid achievements: the first tariff revision since 1897, the placing of conservation on a legal basis, improvement of railroad regulation, and an antitrust crusade. To these should be added the building of most of the Panama Canal and, despite cabinet, congressional, and family advisers who counseled against reform measures, the passage of more than fifty minor progressive acts. Two amendments were added to the Constitution, and he had economized on spending yet made government more efficient. He also had peacefully settled a number of international disputes, launched the most ambitious attempt yet made to obtain world peace, and steadily maintained a policy of neutrality toward Mexico.

Against Taft's accomplishments must be weighed several failures: his gaff with respect to the Payne-Aldrich Tariff; his inability to obtain Canadian reciprocity and general arbitration treaties; his poor handling of the Ballinger-Pinchot affair; his failure to follow the Roosevelt policies; and his treatment of the insurgents, which split his party and allowed Democrats and progressive Republicans to win Congress in 1910 and the presidency and Congress in 1912. Liberals were appalled at his refusal to do any-

thing for blacks or to grant independence to the Filipinos. Last, his dollar diplomacy in Latin America and the Far East greatly added to ill will against the United States and failed to earn profits for American business or obtain economic and political stability or peace in the countries to which it was directed, and his "shopkeeper mentality" irritated Britain, Japan, and Russia. Last, in part because of his parsimoniousness, he did little to strengthen the military power of the nation.

Whether Taft was a good, rather than bad, president calls for an examination of personal characteristics that may explain his lack of additional accomplishment. An unpretentious man with singular charm and simple personal desires, high-minded, just-minded, and clean-minded, he was in no way devious or demagogic. A sensitive man, he craved affection and approval, and often deprecated himself in favor of those he thought better men. He was not a competitive or congenital politician like Roosevelt; he simply had no political ambition and could not become another Roosevelt. He took color from those last around him. He lacked the sense to lead the people along the paths they wished to travel. Very lazy, loving tranquillity, no renovator or innovator, he was more suited to inhabit the cloistered serenity of a high court, particularly when he was better at judicial than legislative interpretation.

With a mechanistic view of government, President Taft acted like an engineer trying to make the agencies of government work together. A conservative by education and choice, he did not understand the dynamics of pressure groups and never learned how to mobilize power in the political system, how to balance (as Roosevelt did) the advocates of reform against those of reaction, or how to forgive those who crossed him in politics. Unlike Roosevelt, he sought advice from very few men, disdained publicity, and lacked the flair for engaging the public's emotions. In consequence, he got a bad press. Roosevelt thought of the impact his words would carry; Taft procrastinated in preparing his speeches and too often said the wrong thing. His view of the presidency and of the Constitution was narrow and defensive, and he had high regard for the rights of the business community. In sum, he concerned himself with materialistic rather than social or moral matters, and he was praised most for his great service "to the cause of conservative constitutionalism, which he defended steadily against the assaults of direct democracy." Even when one grants the tempestuous politics of his tenure, his administration alone can be held responsible for the breakup of the Republican party.

Taft's contemporaries placed him "far from the bottom, though not near the top." Neither a Washington nor a Grant, he was as average as Madison or Monroe, a conclusion upheld in several studies of the presidency. Particularly when viewed between the progressive presidents Roosevelt and Wilson, he remains a constitutional conservator.

BIBLIOGRAPHY

Henry F. Pringle, *The Life and Times of William Howard Taft*, 2 vols. (New York, 1939), remains the best full biography of his subject. Paolo E. Coletta, *The Presidency of William Howard Taft* (Lawrence, Kans., 1973), is a study of Taft dealing only with his presidency. Donald F. Anderson, *William Howard Taft: A Conservative's Conception of the Presidency* (Ithaca, N.Y., 1973), accounts for Taft's conservatism and details how his conservative approach affected his dealings, particularly with the insurgents and progressives. Judith Icke Anderson, *William Howard Taft: An Intimate History* (New York, 1981), deals less with Taft's personal relations than with a psychohistorical account of how his obesity contributed to his laziness, thus decreasing his efficiency.

William Howard Taft, *Popular Government: Its Essence, Its Permanence, and Its Perils* (New Haven, Conn., 1913), questions the validity of enlarging the suffrage and of more direct methods of achieving political, economic, and social democracy. *Our Chief Magistrate and His Powers* (New York, 1916) is of all Taft's writings on the office of the president—and he wrote about it more than any other president did—the most noteworthy because it reveals his very restricted view of the chief executive's power.

Walter V. Scholes and Marie V. Scholes, *The Foreign Policies of the Taft Administration* (Columbia, Mo., 1970), stands in a class by itself because it is the only study devoted entirely to the subject, although it does not completely cover it. Paolo E. Coletta, "The Diplomacy of Theodore Roosevelt and William Howard Taft," in Gerald K. Haines and J. Samuel Walker, eds., *American Foreign Relations: A Historiographical Review* (Westport, Conn., 1981), is an evaluation and analysis of the genesis and implementation of the foreign policies of both Roosevelt and Taft that shows divergencies between the two presidents. L. Ethan Ellis, *Reciprocity, 1911: A Study in*

Canadian-American Relations (New Haven, Conn., 1939), is a study of the differing approaches to the subject of tariff reciprocity in both the United States and Canada. Wilfrid Hardy Callcott, *The Caribbean Policy of the United States, 1890–1920* (Baltimore, 1942), though dated, provides an excellent overview of the determination of policy and its implementation in the area covered. Charles Vevier, *The United States and China, 1906–1913: A Study of Finance and Diplomacy* (New Brunswick, N.J., 1955), concludes that Taft's objectives in China were purely materialistic and criticizes his "shopkeeper mentality."

Samuel P. Hays, *Conservation and the Gospel of Efficiency: The Progressive Conservation Movement, 1890–1920* (Cambridge, Mass., 1959), shows that conservation was heartily adopted by Theodore Roosevelt as part of his drive for efficiency in government and that only at the end of Roosevelt's term did it acquire political and especially moral overtones. Elmo R. Richardson, *The Politics of Conservation: Crusades and Controversies, 1897–1913* (Berkeley, Calif., 1962), provides a well-balanced account that includes thorough research into the attitude of the West on conservation. Gifford Pinchot, *Breaking New Ground* (New York, 1947), gives Pinchot's version of the conservation controversy in terms extremely critical of Taft.

William Allen White, *The Autobiography of William Allen White* (New York, 1946), tells of a Republican newspaper editor who opposed Populism but then became a major supporter of insurgency and especially of progressivism. Kenneth W. Hechler, *Insurgency: Personalities and Politics of the Taft Era* (New York, 1940), though dated, provides what may still be considered the best study of the insurgency movement under Taft. Alpheus T. Mason, *Bureaucracy Convicts Itself: The Ballinger-Pinchot Controversy of 1910* (New York, 1941), tries to steer a middle course between Taft and Roosevelt, and Ballinger and Pinchot, even though the last permitted use of his papers.

William H. Harbaugh, *Power and Responsibility: The Life and Times of Theodore Roosevelt* (New York, 1961; rev. ed., 1975), is still the best extant full biography of the subject. George E. Mowry, *The Era of Theodore Roosevelt, 1900–1912* (New York, 1958), relates Roosevelt's relations to contemporaneous affairs for more than a decade. George E. Mowry, *Theodore Roosevelt and the Progressive Movement* (Madison, Wis., 1946), is a superb scholarly study of Roosevelt's shift from mild reforms to full progressivism. William Manners, *TR and Will: A Friendship That Split the Republican Party* (New York, 1969), is a very readable popular account of the conflicts in the personalities and politics of Roosevelt and Taft from 1910 through 1912.

Frank K. Kelley, *The Fight for the White House: The Story of 1912* (New York, 1961), covers all parties and personalities of the campaign of 1912, with an evaluation of the election results. Robert M. La Follette, *La Follette's Autobiography: A Personal Narrative of Political Experiences* (Madison, Wis., 1913), relates his contributions to the growth of the insurgent and progressive movements and how Roosevelt took the presidential nomination of the National Progressive Republican League away from him. Archibald W. Butt, *Taft and Roosevelt: The Intimate Letters of Archie Butt, Military Aide*, 2 vols. (Garden City, N.Y., 1930), is the correspondence of one who, having served Roosevelt before Taft, was caught between being loyal to Taft or to Roosevelt, whom

he preferred (unfortunately, his observations end with 1912, for he went down with the *Titanic*). Paolo E. Coletta, *William Jennings Bryan: Political Evangelist, 1860–1908* and *William Jennings Bryan: Progressive Politician and Moral Statesman, 1909–1915* (Lincoln, Nebr., 1964, 1969), detail the liberal Democratic approach that caused Bryan to support both Roosevelt and Taft when he thought they were right and to oppose them when wrong. Claude Bowers, *Beveridge and the Progressive Era* (Boston, 1932), tells how Beveridge opposed Taft in most instances but supported his quest for the Tariff Commission.

Recent works include William H. Taft, *Four Aspects of Civic Duty; and, Present Day Problems,* ed. by David H. Burton and A. E. Campbell (Athens, Ohio, 2000).

For further sources consult Paolo E. Coletta, comp., *William Howard Taft: A Bibliography* (Westport, Conn., 1989).

Woodrow Wilson

Arthur S. Link

Woodrow Wilson THE LIBRARY OF CONGRESS

THOMAS WOODROW WILSON, twenty-eighth president of the United States, is the only chief executive who has given scholarly attention to the presidency before undertaking the duties of that office. Wilson was born in Staunton, Virginia, on 28 December 1856, the son of Janet Woodrow Wilson and the Rev. Dr. Joseph Ruggles Wilson, a founder of the southern Presbyterian Church. He was graduated from Princeton University (1879), studied law at the University of Virginia (1879–1880), practiced law in Atlanta (1882–1883), and thereafter did graduate work in political science, history, and economics at The Johns Hopkins University, where he received the Ph.D. in 1886.

From his youth onward, Wilson was intensely interested in the problems of modern democracy from a practical, not a theoretical, point of view. Presidential power was at a low ebb in the mid-1880s, and Wilson, in his first book, *Congressional Government* (1885), virtually ignored the presidency and focused on the obstacles that then existed to searching debate and discussion of great national issues. He singled out for particular criticism the committees of the House of Representatives, which, he said, effectively stifled free discussion. The surest way to guarantee that such debate would take place, Wilson said, would be to adopt the British cabinet system and make cabinet members ministers of state responsible to Congress.

Throughout his years as a professor of history, politics, and constitutional law at Bryn Mawr College (1885–1888), Wesleyan University (1888–1890), and Princeton University (1890–1910; president, 1902–1910), Wilson paid close attention to developments in American politics. He admired what he perceived as Cleveland's assertion of the moral leadership of the presidency and noted the impact on that office of the war with Spain and the entry of the United States on the world stage as a colonial and naval power.

It was Theodore Roosevelt's revivification of the presidential office that helped Wilson to come to his mature and definitive understanding of the potential powers of the chief executive. Those powers are described in Wilson's *Constitutional Government in the United States* (1908) in what is perhaps the classic view of the modern presidency. The president, Wilson wrote, is the one single spokesman of the nation:

> Let him once win the admiration and confidence of the country, and no other single force can withstand him, no combination of forces will easily overpower him. His position takes the imagination of the country. He is the representative of no constituency, but of the whole people. When he speaks in his true character, he speaks for no special interest. If he rightly interpret the national thought and boldly insist upon it, he is irresistible; and the country never feels the zest of action so much as when he is of such insight and calibre.

Wilson as Maker and Leader of Public Opinion

This was the kind of president that Wilson was determined to be after his victory on 5 November 1912 over the Republican incumbent, William Howard Taft; the Republican insurgent, or Progressive, Theodore Roosevelt; and the Socialist, Eugene Victor Debs. During the first days of his administration, Wilson moved quickly and decisively to establish himself as the chief maker, educator, and organizer of public opinion to support his domestic and foreign policies.

His first move—to hold regularly scheduled press conferences with the Washington press corps—was an innovation. Wilson appealed to the reporters assembled in the East Room of the White House for his first press conference, on 22 March 1913, to join him in partnership by interpreting the public opinion of the country to him. Wilson's intentions were, of course, to control the flow of information from the capital to the country and to use it to shape public opinion. And this he did successfully, on the whole. Wilson discontinued the regular press conferences in June 1915 because of increasing diplomatic responsibilities. He held only a few afterward—one in September 1916, a few in late 1916 and early 1917, and the final one on 10 July 1919.

Wilson also sought to educate and shape public opinion through state papers, addresses, and public statements. No president in American history has used these media with such remarkable power and success as Wilson did. He rivaled Jefferson and Lincoln in his mastery of the English language, but he used the spoken and printed word far more than they had done to shape the course of events. On the highest level of discourse—when he sought to end the war in Europe, to enunciate American war aims, or to plead for ratification of the Treaty of Versailles—Wilson claimed to speak not for himself but for the American people. In his annual message of 8 December 1914 he said:

> I have tried to know what America is, what her people think, what they are, what they most cherish and hold dear. I hope that some of their finer passions are in my own heart—some of the great conceptions and desires which gave birth to this Government and which have made the voice of this people a voice of peace and hope and liberty among the peoples of the world, and that, in speaking my own thoughts, I shall, at least in part, speak theirs also.

However one judges Wilson's claim, it is beyond doubt that he used the "bully pulpit" of the White House to educate and shape public opinion with remarkable success. And because he invoked Judeo-Christian traditions and appealed to the minds and spirits of people, his rhetoric literally changed the course of history. For example, it is doubtful that any American, other than Wilson, could have so successfully united the people of the United States behind the great war effort of 1917–1918.

Parliamentary Leader

Long study of Anglo-American politics had convinced Wilson that party responsibility was the key to effective government in a democracy. Parties had to enunciate and stand for principles, and a party platform was a covenant with the people. But parties could not play their essential role without leaders. As governor of New Jersey (1911–1913), Wilson had confounded many cynics by fulfilling every pledge in the New Jersey Democratic platform of 1910. He had also invigorated and substantially transformed the Democratic party in his state.

Wilson was determined to unite the fragmented and hitherto leaderless Democrats in Congress into a disciplined phalanx. As he wrote on the eve of his inauguration in 1913, the president

> is expected by the nation to be the leader of his party as well as the chief executive officer of the government, and the country will take no excuses from him.. . . He must be the prime minister, as much concerned with the guidance of legislation as with the just and orderly execution of law.

The White House announced a few days after Wilson's inauguration that the new "prime minister" would help to frame legislation and would confer frequently with Democratic leaders in Congress in the President's Room in the Capitol. This Wilson did throughout his administration. He planned the first legislative program with his spokesmen in Congress even before he was inaugurated. He then broke a precedent, established by Jefferson, by going in person before a joint session of Congress on 8 April 1913 to deliver his message on tariff reform. Wilson kept in close touch with congressional leaders, and no detail of legislation escaped his eye; virtually no legislation was adopted without his prior approval.

Wilson established his leadership of the Democrats in Congress usually through sheer force of personality and moral leadership, by simply reminding them of their obligations to the country. He was courteous, even deferential, in discourse and disarmed potential dissidents by affirming that they, as much as he, wanted to do their duty. As Samuel G. Blythe wrote at the time, he was agreeable, mild-mannered, even solicitous about it all, "but . . . he is firmly and entirely the leader, and insists upon complete recognition as such.. . . The Democratic party revolves around him. He is the center of it; the biggest Democrat in the country—the leader and the chief."

Wilson succeeded as a parliamentary leader mainly because Democratic members admired him intensely, recognized his elevated motives and purposes, and wanted to make their party an effective instrument of government. It was silly to talk about his bending Congress to his indomitable will, Wilson said, for "Congress is made up of thinking men who want the party to succeed as much as I do, and who wish to serve the country effectively and intelligently.. . . They are using me; I am not driving them."

In summation, Wilson was the parliamentary leader par excellence in the history of the American presidency. During the period when he enjoyed a majority in Congress (1913–1919), he broke down the wall between the executive and legislative branches, focused executive and legislative leadership in his own person, and established himself as the spokesman of the American people in domestic and international affairs.

The Cabinet

Wilson's first cabinet reflected the geographical distribution of Democratic strength across the United States and the various factions of the party. The secretary of state, Willam Jennings Bryan of Nebraska, had three times been the Democratic presidential candidate and represented particularly agrarian interests. The secretary of the treasury, William Gibbs McAdoo of New York, spoke for the independent, anti-Wall Street financial elements. The attorney general, James C. McReynolds of New York, had the reputation of a relentless trust-buster. The secretary of war, Lindley M. Garrison, was a New Jersey judge with no political base. The secretary of the navy, Josephus Daniels of North Carolina, represented southern progressivism. Albert S. Burleson of Texas, the postmaster general, had served many terms in the House of Representatives. The secretary of labor, William B. Wilson of Pennsylvania, had been secretary-treasurer of the United Workers of America and was the frank spokesman of the American Federation of Labor (AF of L). Wilson chose the remaining three cabinet members—Franklin K. Lane of California, secretary of the interior; David E Houston of Texas, secretary of agriculture; and William C. Redfield of New York, secretary of commerce—more for their expertise than for their political influence.

There were several changes in the cabinet during the Wilson administration. Bryan resigned in 1915 and was replaced by Robert Lansing of New York, a professional international lawyer. Wilson dismissed Lansing in early 1920 and appointed Bainbridge Colby of New York to succeed him. Garrison resigned in 1916 and was replaced by an Ohio progressive, Newton D. Baker. Carter Glass of Virginia, and then Houston, succeeded McAdoo at the Treasury Department in 1918 and 1920, respectively. McReynolds resigned in 1914 to accept appointment to the Supreme Court. He was succeeded by Thomas W. Gregory of Texas and, in 1919, by Alexander M. Palmer of Pennsylvania. Lane left the cabinet in 1920 and was succeeded by John B. Payne of Illinois. When Houston went to the treasury in 1920, Edwin T. Meredith of Iowa took his place as secretary of agriculture.

Wilson worked closely with his cabinet officers but gave them considerable freedom and initiative and always supported them so long as they executed policies that had his approval. Cabinet meetings, which usually took place once a week, were informal affairs at which Wilson would discuss current problems and seek, as he put it, "common counsel." Wilson formally requested the advice of the cabinet on a specific issue only once—on 20 March 1917, on the question of whether he should ask Congress for a declaration of war against Germany.

Executive Policies

A strong cabinet, composed for the most part of activists, carried out policies that were nearly as important as the legislative achievements for which the Wilson administration is more famous. (Since Wilson tended to make and control foreign policy in all important areas himself, his secretaries of state will be discussed in the sections on foreign policies.)

McAdoo was the most dynamic and vigorous member of the administration; he also had an undisguised lust for power and a habit of invading the jurisdictions of other cabinet officers. His bold and original mind was wedded to a strong determination to make the United States treasury the dominant force in controlling credit, interest rates, and the money supply. He tried, but failed, to make the new Federal Reserve system an adjunct of the treasury. Once the United States entered World War I, McAdoo made the treasury into an all-powerful engine of credit. With the creation in 1918 of the War Finance Corporation, McAdoo enjoyed control of an agency capable of lending money on a large scale. Along parallel lines, the Justice Department, under both McReynolds and Gregory, relentlessly and successfully pursued one single policy: to restore competition through the dissolution of monopolies. Lane, in the Interior Department, took the lead in building the federally owned Alaskan Railroad and in the adoption of a coal-leasing bill for Alaska. Lane was caught between the cross fire of extreme conservationists and private interests in a long struggle for

legislation to permit development of hydroelectric power on navigable rivers and public lands and the exploitation of oil and mineral deposits in the public domain. The adoption of the Water Power and General Leasing acts of 1920 vindicated Lane's long struggle just at the time that he left the cabinet.

Because they were relatively new, the departments of agriculture, labor, and commerce took the lead in the expansion of governmental activities. Secretary of Labor William Wilson in 1913 established an informal conciliation service that frequently settled labor disputes, whenever possible upon the basis of the recognition of the right of labor to organize and bargain collectively. In this matter, the Labor Department was only nominally evenhanded. The secretary also played an active role in attempts to prevent or control child labor. Throughout his tenure, William Wilson maintained a close alliance with Samuel Gompers, president of the AF of L.

Little has been written about Redfield and his work in the Commerce Department. A vigorous free trader, he was also a zealous champion of American business enterprise who sought ardently to stimulate American enterprise abroad. Indeed, Redfield took many of the initiatives in support of American business for which Herbert Hoover, as secretary of commerce from 1921 to 1928, is usually given credit.

Finally, the quiet academic David F. Houston led the Agriculture Department in the most important expansion of the activities of any single department during the Wilson administration. Houston supervised the establishment of the Federal Farm Loan system, created by the Rural Credits Act of 1916. Houston also helped to draft the measures that vastly enlarged the rural service of the federal government: the Cotton Futures Act, the Grain Standards Act, and the Warehouse Act, all of 1916. Even more important were the Agricultural Educational Act of that same year, which provided funds to place agents of land-grant colleges in every agricultural county in the United States; the Smith-Hughes Act of 1917, which provided for federal assistance to vocational and agricultural education in public schools; and the Federal Aid Highway Act of 1916, which was designed at first to benefit rural areas and later became the legislative authority for the construction of a nationwide system of modern highways.

The New Freedom at Home

Wilson came to the presidency in 1913 with clear and precise ideas about the urgent agenda for the reconstruction of the American political economy. Fortunately for him, the Democratic platform of 1912, largely written by Bryan, was either in conformity with Wilson's views or was sufficiently general in language to validate them as pure Democratic doctrine. Wilson believed deeply in the resourcefulness and capacities of the American people. He also believed that the energies of the aspiring middle classes had been stifled by industrial, commercial, and financial monopolists. Wilson laid out his program for reform, which he called the New Freedom, clearly and eloquently during the presidential campaign of 1912.

The first item on Wilson's legislative agenda was, inevitably, a drastic lowering of the high rates of the Payne-Aldrich Tariff of 1909. Low tariffs, to benefit consumers and stimulate competition, had been the most important Democratic policy since the Civil War, and Wilson had pressed the issue vigorously during the campaign of 1912. Moreover, the Payne-Aldrich Tariff stood as the single most glaring symbol of the power of special-interest groups over legislative policy.

Wilson sounded the call for reform in his address to Congress of 8 April 1913: "We must abolish everything that bears even the semblance of privilege or of any kind of artificial advantage." The House of Representatives was ready and eager to act. The Ways and Means Committee, led by Oscar W. Underwood of Alabama, had already introduced a measure that cut most rates drastically, put most consumer goods and articles used by farmers on the free list, and (at Wilson's demand) put farm products, including wool and later sugar, on the free list. The Underwood bill reduced the average ad valorem rates of the Payne-Aldrich Tariff from about 40 percent to about 29 percent; these figures do not take into account the additional reductions effected by the vast expansion of the free list. Finally, in order to compensate for the anticipated decrease in customs receipts, the Underwood bill imposed a modest income tax, the first under the Sixteenth Amendment. The House Democratic caucus made the bill a party measure, and Underwood pushed it through the House by a vote of 281 to 139 on 8 May 1913.

The main danger now was that the slim Democratic majority in the Senate would vanish if senators from the sugar- and wool-producing states bolted. But Wilson stood firm, and he enjoyed the full support of the Finance Committee, headed by Furnifold M. Simmons of North Carolina. Wilson, in a public statement on 26 May 1913, denounced the lobbyists who were hard at work trying to wreck tariff reform. This charge led to a Senate investigation of the private interests of senators that might be affected by tariff reductions. Under the white heat of this investigation and Wilson's steady pressure, Democratic opposition melted, and the Senate, on 9 September, approved what was now called the Underwood-Simmons bill by a vote of 44 to 37. The Senate bill actually decreased the rates of the Underwood bill by 4 percent and brought the general ad valorem rates to a level of about 26 percent; in addition, the Senate bill increased the maximum income tax in the Underwood bill from 4 percent to 7 percent. The House accepted these changes, and Wilson signed the Underwood-Simmons Tariff Act on 3 October 1913.

The measure marked a significant change in federal economic policy. It reflected certain underlying changes in the American economy that had been taking place since the late 1890s, the most important of which was the transformation of the United States from an importer of goods and capital into the leading manufacturing nation of the world, with a surplus of capital and goods that had to be invested and sold abroad.

Much more complex, difficult, and urgent than tariff reform was the restructuring of the nation's banking and currency systems so as to assure a money supply adequate for the needs of a dynamic and growing economy and to open the channels of credit to all worthy borrowers. Bankers, businessmen, and economists had long pointed to the grave weaknesses of the national banking system, established during the Civil War. It tied the money supply in large degree to the gold supply and the bonded indebtedness of the United States, provided only a primitive means of mobilizing and transferring banking reserves from one section to another, and encouraged the concentration of reserves in Wall Street. The National Monetary Commission, headed by Senator Nelson W. Aldrich, Republican of Rhode Island, had exposed these weaknesses in its report to Congress of 1912, but its solution—a single national reserve bank, with branches, owned and controlled by the banks—only intensified the widespread fear that Wall Street wanted to fasten its control over the credit resources of the country.

Wilson had the main outlines of a currency and banking bill in mind at least by November 1912. He explained them a month later to Carter Glass, who would be the next chairman of the House Banking Committee. Wilson proposed the creation of a number of regional reserve banks owned and controlled by member banks. The "capstone," as Wilson called it, would be the Federal Reserve Board, which would control the money supply, determine interest rates, and perform all the functions of a central bank. Moreover, the legislation would provide for new currency, Federal Reserve notes, to be issued by the Federal Reserve banks upon a basis of gold and commercial assets so that the money supply would expand or contract according to the needs of producers and businessmen. Glass and his committee and technical advisers set to work and, about 1 May 1913, completed a draft of a banking and currency bill that conformed to Wilson's concepts.

Circulation of this draft set off a fierce controversy. Bryan could not accept the Glass bill because it stipulated that Federal Reserve notes would be the obligation of the reserve banks, not of the federal government. Neo-Populists in Congress went even further and demanded a reserve and currency system owned and controlled exclusively by the federal government. They were also adamantly opposed to the Glass bill's stipulation that three of the nine members of the Federal Reserve Board should be bankers chosen by the regional banks. McAdoo muddied the waters by drafting a bill that made the Federal Reserve system an adjunct of the United States treasury. Wilson moved decisively but calmly to regain control. He conceded Bryan's point and won his support. Wilson also accepted the advice of Louis D. Brandeis, progressive lawyer and economist of Boston, to the effect that all members of the Federal Reserve Board should be appointed by the president. Glass revised the bill accordingly.

Wilson went again in person before a joint session of Congress on 23 June 1913: "I have come to you, as head of the Government and the responsible leader of the party in power, to urge action now." Glass and Robert L. Owen of Oklahoma, chairman of the Senate Banking Committee, introduced identical bills in their respective houses on 26 June.

By this time, conservatives and many large-city bankers had mounted a furious assault on the Federal Reserve bill. They charged that it was socialistic because it deprived bankers of control over their own property, and they also said that the measure would politicize the banking and currency systems. Other assaults came from agrarian spokesmen because the Federal Reserve bill made no provision for the rediscounting of agricultural paper. Wilson quickly conceded the demand of the agrarians but held firm in his adherence to the principle of public control. The House passed the Federal Reserve bill by an overwhelming majority on 18 September. Wilson waited patiently as conservative Senate Republicans and obstructionist Democrats wore themselves out. The Federal Reserve bill passed the Senate by a vote of 54 to 34 on 19 December. Wilson signed the measure on 23 December 1913.

The Federal Reserve Act was the most important legislation of the Wilson era and one of the most important pieces of legislation in the history of the United States. The cornerstone of the new progressive political economy, it attempted to combine private initiative with public control. The act has been amended significantly only once, in 1935, in order to strengthen the Federal Reserve Board's power over interest rates and the money supply. The Federal Reserve system is still the most important economic instrumentality of the United States.

Achievement of Wilson's third great New Freedom goal—legislation to clarify and strengthen the generalities of the Sherman Antitrust Act of 1890—proved to be nearly as difficult as the writing and enactment of the Federal Reserve Act, but not because of any significant opposition to a stronger federal antitrust policy. The administration's original program was embodied in the antitrust bill introduced by Representative Henry D. Clayton of Alabama on 14 April 1914; in a measure to create an interstate commerce commission with no power to enforce its decrees, introduced by Representative James H. Covington of Maryland on 16 March 1914; and in a measure to give the Interstate Commerce Commission authority over the issuance of securities by the railroads, introduced by Representative Sam Rayburn of Texas on 7 May 1914.

The keystone of the administration's program, the Clayton bill, attempted to outlaw all known methods and devices used to strangle competition and achieve monopoly. It at once drew the fire of the leaders of the AF of L because it did not specifically exempt labor unions from prosecution for acts that the Supreme Court had said violated the Sherman Act. Wilson assuaged labor by permitting the addition of provisions that stipulated that labor unions and agricultural cooperatives should not be deemed to be conspiracies in restraint of trade and that sought to protect labor unions against indiscriminate court injunctions in strikes. The House passed the Clayton, Covington, and Rayburn bills by a huge majority, all on 5 June 1914.

Opposition to the Clayton bill came quickly and vociferously from small businessmen, who claimed that the measure provided jail terms for their day-to-day practices, and from legal authorities, who argued that it was impossible to legislate against every conceivable restraint of trade. Wilson again sought the advice of Brandeis, who urged him to take up a measure that he and a friend had drafted. Known as the Stevens bill, it outlawed all "unfair" competition and established the Federal Trade Commission (FTC) to investigate alleged unfair trade practices; most important, the Stevens bill authorized the FTC to issue cease and desist orders, which would have the force of court injunctions, to alleged perpetrators of unfair competition.

Wilson took up the Stevens bill at once, and a relieved House adopted it as a substitute for the Covington bill on 12 June 1914. Then the Senate undertook the task of generalizing the Clayton bill. The final text may not have "clarified" the Sherman Act, but it strengthened the Sherman Act in two important ways. It made corporation officials personally and criminally liable for the acts of their companies, and it gave individuals and corporations the benefit of decisions in antitrust cases instituted by the government. This meant they could almost automatically collect threefold damages from companies that had injured them once the government had won a suit against the latter. The Rayburn bill was abandoned when the outbreak of war in Europe in August 1914 totally demoralized the securities markets, but would be revived and incorporated in the Transportation Act of 1920. Wilson signed the Federal Trade Commission bill on 26 September 1914 and the Clayton bill on 15 October 1914. The reconstruction of the American political economy was now complete.

Labor and farm organizations and social reformers now increased their pressure upon Wilson and Congress for legislation to benefit special interests and protect disadvantaged groups. Wilson at first yielded gracefully and then championed their causes in 1916, in part because he would need the support of progressive Republicans in the presidential election of 1916 and in part because he was becoming increasingly convinced that federal authority alone could cope with some of the urgent social and economic problems of the day.

Wilson had nothing to do with the origins and passage of the two important pieces of social legislation in 1915. One was the Burnett immigration bill, which attempted to restrict immigration by imposing a literacy test upon newcomers. Organized labor had long demanded this legislation, but social workers

and reformers were badly divided over it. Wilson lost no standing with progressives when he vetoed the Burnett bill on 28 January 1915. It was reenacted over his veto in 1917.

The second measure was the Seamen's Act, drafted by Andrew Furuseth, president of the International Seamen's Union, and championed in Congress by Senator Robert M. La Follette, progressive Republican from Wisconsin. The United States was obliged by treaties with twenty-two maritime nations to arrest their seamen when they deserted in American ports and to return them to their ships. The Seamen's Act freed all seamen in American ports from bondage to their labor contracts; in other words, once seamen were on American soil, they were free to leave their ships and accept whatever employment they chose. Bryan talked to La Follette and Furuseth on 2 March 1915. Wilson was so moved by Furuseth's plea and by the justice of the seamen's claims that he signed the bill on 4 March 1915, and the State Department duly abrogated the treaties.

The pace of Wilsonian reform quickened as the two great parties prepared for their national conventions in 1916. As has been said, Wilson pushed adoption of a comprehensive program to provide to farmers long-term credit, educational and other assistance, and good roads. He advocated and obtained congressional approval for the establishment of the Federal Tariff Commission, which progressives had long demanded. He appointed Brandeis to the Supreme Court and won the Senate's approval of the nomination after a grueling battle. Soon after the adjournment of the Democratic National Convention, Wilson pushed the Keating-Owen child-labor bill and a measure for federal workmen's compensation through the Senate, where they had been stalled for months. In late August and early September, he obtained quick passage of the Adamson Act, which established the eight-hour workday on interstate railroads, thus averting a disastrous nationwide rail strike. At the same time, Wilson approved a Revenue Act that drastically increased taxes upon incomes and estates.

The Democratic platform of 1912 demanded enlarged self-government and early independence for the Philippine Islands and territorial self-government for Puerto Rico. Wilson, who had long since shed whatever imperialistic sentiments he might once have had, became in fact the first de-colonizer among the statesmen of the twentieth century. The Jones Act of 29 August 1916 affirmed the intention of the United States to withdraw entirely from the Philippines as soon as a stable indigenous government was established, created an elective senate to supplant presidential appointees as the upper house of the Philippine legislature, and provided that the governor-general should appoint heads of executive departments, except the Department of Public Instruction, with the consent of the Philippine Senate.

The all-Filipino legislature, which met on 16 October 1916, was the first autonomous legislature established by a colonial power in an overseas possession, except for the self-governing dominions of the British Empire. Moreover, Wilson's governor-general, Francis Burton Harrison, was an ardent anti-imperialist. He transferred virtually all powers of local government to Filipinos, so that the Philippine Islands enjoyed dominion status in fact, if not in name, by the end of the Wilson administration.

For Puerto Rico, Wilson pushed through Congress, and signed on 2 March 1917, the second Jones Act. It gave Puerto Rico territorial status, conferred American citizenship upon residents of the island, and created a virtually autonomous two-house legislature elected by the people.

The New Freedom Abroad

Among all the statesmen of the modern era, Woodrow Wilson stands out as the preeminent champion of liberal humanitarian international ideals. He believed, to the point of religious commitment, that the United States had been created to serve mankind. He detested imperialism and the exploitation of helpless people by the strong and ruthless. He believed in the right of all peoples to govern themselves and in the peaceful settlement of international disputes. He abhorred the use of violence to protect American material interests abroad. Secretary of State Bryan, who shared all of Wilson's views, was easily the leading opponent of imperialism in the United States and was also in the vanguard of the movement to advance peace through arbitration and conciliation. Both Wilson and Bryan were determined to make a new beginning in foreign policy in 1913.

With Wilson's blessing, Bryan, in 1913 and 1914, negotiated with thirty nations—including Great Britain, France, and Italy—treaties that established elaborate machinery to prevent war. Additional evidence of Wilson and Bryan's intentions in foreign policy came early in the new administration, with a forthright repudiation of the "dollar diplomacy" of the Taft administration. At the insistence of the State Department, an American banking group had been admitted in 1911 to an international consortium to finance the construction of the Hukuang Railway in China. Wilson, on 18 March 1913, announced that he could not approve the loan agreement because it would lead to unacceptable outside interference in Chinese domestic affairs, and so the consortium collapsed. Then, on 2 May 1913, Wilson extended diplomatic recognition to the fledgling Republic of China without prior consultation with the other great powers.

A crisis in Japanese-American relations erupted in the spring of 1913, when the legislature of California began to deliberate a bill that forbade persons "ineligible to citizenship" (that is, Orientals) to own land in the state. Wilson sent Bryan to Sacramento to plead with the governor and leaders of the legislature of California to avoid this open insult to the Japanese. But Wilson and Bryan could not budge the intransigent Californians; moreover, the latter put the president and secretary of state in an awkward position when they added to the bill a provision that declared null and void any part of the measure that violated the treaty obligations of the United States.

The Japanese government protested strongly, and there was talk of war on both sides, particularly among American naval leaders; but Wilson and Bryan's conciliatory diplomacy defused the crisis at once. Wilson and Bryan also seemed prepared, in spite of all the obvious political risks at home, to negotiate a treaty with Japan to guarantee the mutual right of landownership. Then, in the early weeks of 1915, a new crisis broke out when the Japanese attempted to impose upon China a treaty that would have made that country a virtual protectorate of Japan. Wilson resisted this assault upon Chinese independence and the Open Door so vigorously that the Japanese gave up their extreme demands.

Another demonstration of Wilson's determination to do the "right" thing in international relations in spite of heavy political risks came out in a controversy with Great Britain in 1913 and 1914. With the Panama Canal nearing completion, Congress, in August 1912, passed legislation that exempted American ships engaged in the coastwise trade from the payment of tolls for use of the canal. The Democratic platform of 1912 had also endorsed such exemption. The British government, soon after Taft signed the Panama Canal Act, sent to Washington a solemn note that argued that the exemption violated the Anglo-

American Hay-Pauncefote Treaty of 1901, which stipulated that the Panama Canal should be open on equal terms to the ships of all nations.

Wilson was convinced, even before his inauguration, that the British were right, but he did not dare to act until the success of his domestic program was assured. Then, on 5 March 1914, Wilson went before a joint session of Congress and asked for repeal of the exemption provision. "The large thing to do is the only thing we can afford to do," he said, "a voluntary withdrawal from a position everywhere questioned and misunderstood."

It was actually one of Wilson's most courageous moves during his presidency. The entire Democratic leadership of the House of Representatives opposed him, and he risked his leadership of Congress and his party by repudiating a prominent plank of the platform of 1912. The British ambassador in Washington believed that Wilson faced certain defeat. However, the House and the Senate approved repeal of the exemption provision on 31 March and 11 June 1914, by votes of 247–162 and 50–35, respectively. "When I think of the obstacles you have encountered and overcome in this conflict for the national honor," one friend wrote to Wilson on 16 June 1914, "the victory seems colossal." It was also a victory over anglophobes and chauvinists, and it secured Wilson's leadership of the Democratic party in Congress.

Wilson and Bryan wanted ardently to draw the two continents of the western hemisphere into intimate economic and diplomatic relationships. As a first step, they negotiated a treaty with the Colombian government to repair the moral and diplomatic damage done by Theodore Roosevelt in 1903, when he encouraged and supported the Panamanian "revolution" that tore the province of Panama from Colombia. The Treaty of Bogotá, signed on 6 April 1914, not only awarded Colombia an indemnity of $25 million, for the loss of Panama; it also expressed the "sincere regret" of the United States that anything should have happened to impair good relations between the two countries. The sight of a great power apologizing to a small country for a wrong done in the past evoked warm approval throughout Latin America. However, Theodore Roosevelt's friends in the Senate were able to block ratification. The Harding administration, in 1921, negotiated a new treaty, which was ratified, that awarded Colombia the $25 million but omitted the apology.

Wilson's great goal in Latin America was the negotiation of a pact to unite all the American republics in an alliance binding them to respect one another's territorial integrity, guarantee one another's political independence, and settle all disputes among themselves by peaceful methods. Such a treaty would in effect have mutualized the Monroe Doctrine, and Wilson, in an address to a Pan-American conference in Washington on 6 January 1916, announced his intention to take this then-radical step. The Monroe Doctrine, he said, was proclaimed by the United States on its own authority; it was a unilateral policy, and it did not restrain the United States in the western hemisphere. Doubts about this matter had to be removed and would be removed by the Pan-American pact, for it was based upon the "handsome principle of self-restraint and respect for the rights of everybody." Wilson's hopes for the Pan-American pact were spoiled by the opposition of Chile, which had an old border dispute with Peru that it would not submit to arbitration.

Whatever their thoughts were about Latin American policy in general, Wilson and Bryan (and subsequent secretaries of state to 1921) regarded defense of the Caribbean area and of the Panama Canal as one of the main objectives of the foreign policy of the United States. They tried to inculcate respect for democratic government among the leaders of the countries in the Caribbean; they also refused, insofar as it was within their power to do so, to permit American business interests to obtain concessions and American bankers loans that would unfairly exploit the people of the Caribbean basin. Nonetheless, Wilson and his secretaries of state deemed the stability of the area to be absolutely essential to the security of the United States and were prepared to take all measures necessary to guarantee that stability.

Bryan continued the Taft administration's support of a corrupt and conservative regime in Nicaragua, not by armed intervention, which Taft had resorted to, but by a treaty that provided for the payment of $3 million to Nicaragua for an option on its canal route and stipulated (at the insistence of the Nicaraguan government) that the United States might intervene in Nicaragua to preserve order, protect property, and defend Nicaraguan independence. The latter provision was unacceptable to antiimperialists in the Senate. Only when the provision was removed from the treaty in 1916 would they consent to its ratification.

The republic of Haiti had always contrived to preserve its independence, but it came on evil times in 1914 and 1915 as governments fell in quick succession to revolutionists with their eyes on the custom-houses. The only remedy seemed to be American control of the Haitian customs, but the Haitians refused to take this strong medicine when Wilson sent a commission to Haiti to offer it. An enraged mob murdered the Haitian president in Port-au-Prince on 27 July 1915; anarchy and starvation threatened. Wilson was reluctant to intervene, but he thought that he had no choice but to rescue the hapless Haitian people. As he wrote to Lansing on 4 August 1915, "I suppose there is nothing for it but to take the bull by the horns and restore order." American marines and sailors occupied Port-au-Prince on 28 July 1915. The American navy proceeded to pacify the country, to set up a puppet government, and to impose upon the Haitian Senate a treaty that made Haiti a protectorate of the United States.

The United States had collected and disbursed the customs revenues of the Dominican Republic since 1905, but Wilson's warnings and Bryan's exhortations failed to prevent the same fatal cycle of revolutions in the Dominican Republic that had devastated Haiti. To Wilson and his advisers, there seemed to be no alternative but to impose peace upon the country. American military forces occupied Santo Domingo, the Dominican capital, on 15 May 1916, and established a military government in the following November.

American marines occupied the Dominican Republic until 1924 and Haiti until 1934. They put an end to revolutions and built schools, roads, and sanitary facilities, and the Dominican and Haitian peoples enjoyed greater peace and protection of their lives and property than they had known before.

Denmark, in desperate straits on account of World War I, indicated in 1915 that it might be willing to sell its West Indian islands, with their potential for naval bases, to the United States if the price was right. Wilson, worried by the possibility that Germany might, by one means or another, force Denmark to cede it the Danish West Indies, was in no mood to haggle over the price of even run-down real estate. The two governments agreed upon a purchase price of $25 million; the treaty was signed on 4 August 1916 and ratified on 17 January 1917; and an American naval commander accepted transfer of the islands from the Danish governor on 31 March 1917.

Wilson fought his first battle against imperialism while dealing with events in Mexico, the country in which imperialism had reached its apogee. Porfirio Díaz, dictator of Mexico since 1877, had given away much of the birthright of the Mexican people to foreigners by 1910. Reformers, led by Francisco Indalecio Madero, drove the senile Díaz into exile and installed Madero in the presidential palace in November 1911. But Madero proved to be an inept ruler, and when the inevitable counterrevolution began on 9 February 1913, the head of the army, Victoriano Huerta, joined the rebels; had Madero murdered; and assumed power as acting president on 18 February. Huerta perpetrated his treachery with the full knowledge and, to some degree, the complicity of Henry Lane Wilson, the American ambassador in Mexico City. Great Britain, Germany, and France, whose citizens owned extensive properties in Mexico, recognized Huerta as the constitutional de facto president, as did Japan and many other nations.

This, then, was the situation in Mexico when Woodrow Wilson took the oath of office on 4 March 1913. Wilson recoiled in disgust at what he called "a government of butchers" and was distressed beyond description when he learned a few months later about Henry Lane Wilson's complicity in Huerta's coup. Woodrow Wilson's goal from March to October 1913 was clear, consistent, and, initially, naive. It was the reestablishment of constitutional government in Mexico through free elections in which Huerta would not be a candidate for president. Wilson's only weapons during those months were moral pressure and the influence that inhered in his power to extend recognition or to withhold it. Thus, he recalled Henry Lane Wilson and, in August 1913, sent John Lind, a former Democratic governor of Minnesota, to Mexico City to offer what amounted to de facto recognition and Washington's approval of a large loan to the Mexican government if Huerta would agree to hold an "early and free" election. The American president also asked for an immediate armistice in the civil war that had begun soon after Huerta's coup, when a large group of Madero's followers, called Constitutionalists, had taken to the field under Venustiano Carranza, governor of the state of Coahuila.

Huerta bluffed and feinted, but by then he had the outright support of the British government and no intention of abdicating. On the contrary, he arrested most of the members of the Chamber of Deputies and instituted an outright military dictatorship on 10 October 1913.

Huerta's move forced Wilson to adopt a policy that took account of the hard realities of the Mexican situation. Support of the usurper was simply not an option with Wilson. There was the possibility of co-operation with Carranza, but the First Chief, as he was called, said plainly that he and his followers did not want Wilson's help, had no interest in "constitutional" elections at this time, and were determined to purge Mexico by the sword. Wilson did not shrink from accepting the logic of his implacable opposition to Huerta. He announced his policy to the powers on 24 November:

> The present policy of the Government of the United States is to isolate General Huerta entirely; to cut him off from foreign sympathy and aid and from domestic credit, whether moral or material, and so to force him out. It hopes and believes that isolation will accomplish this end, and shall await the results without irritation or impatience. If General Huerta does not retire by force of circumstances, it will become the duty of the United States to use less useful peaceful means to put him out.

Wilson could write so confidently because he had just forced the British government to withdraw support from Huerta. When the Constitutionalist campaign faltered, Wilson, on 3 February 1914, lifted the arms embargo against the Constitutionalists that Taft had imposed a year before. Most important, Wilson accepted the Mexican Revolution upon its own terms. Settlement by a civil war was a terrible thing, he wrote in a circular note to the powers on 31 January 1914, "but it must come now whether we wish it or not." From this moment until the end of his administration, Wilson was committed personally and morally to the cause of the Mexican Revolution, "a revolution as profound as that which occurred in France." Wilson's support of the Constitutionalists caused the Roman Catholic Church, the bankers, and the large landowners in Mexico to rally to Huerta's standard, so that the dictator was actually stronger by the spring of 1914 than he had been when Wilson hurled his threats at him. There was no choice now for Wilson but to resort to a show of force. But how could he do this without making open war, which Congress and the American people would probably not support and which Carranza would probably resist? The opportunity came when a Huertista officer arrested the crew of a boat from the USS *Dolphin* at Tampico on 9 April 1914 and the commander of the American fleet in Mexican waters demanded a formal apology and a salute to the American flag with twenty-one guns. When (fortunately for the American president) Huerta balked at rendering the salute, Wilson, on 21 April 1914, ordered the fleet to seize Veracruz, Mexico's largest port. Wilson expected no

resistance because the Huertista commander at Veracruz had promised to withdraw from the city before the Americans landed. He did so, but cadets from the Mexican naval academy and others resisted bravely, and 126 Mexicans and 19 Americans died before the Americans secured their control of Veracruz.

When Carranza denounced the American invasion as angrily as Huerta, what could Wilson do but launch a strike toward Mexico City? But he was determined to avoid general war with Mexico. Wilson was saved from this dilemma by Huerta's acceptance of an offer by the ABC powers—Argentina, Brazil, and Chile—to mediate the controversy. American and Mexican commissioners met at Niagara Falls, Canada, from 20 May to 2 July 1914. Wilson had no intention of submitting to a genuine mediation; on the contrary, he prolonged the charade at Niagara Falls until the Constitutionalists had beaten the weakened, isolated, and weary Huerta. The dictator fled to Spain on 15 July, and Carranza occupied Mexico City on 20 August 1914.

The revolutionary forces had divided even before Carranza rode into Mexico City on his white horse. Carranza faced two bitter foes—Francisco ("Pancho") Villa, former brigand and now commander of the Division of the North, and Emiliano Zapata, leader of a peasant revolt in the state of Morelos, south of Mexico City. Villa and Zapata dominated a convention of revolutionary generals that met at Aguascalientes in October and November 1914. It deposed Carranza and installed a puppet regime in Mexico City. Carranza and the divisions loyal to him retired to Veracruz, which Wilson had recently evacuated.

Wilson tried to persuade the two factions to unite; when this effort failed, he simply withdrew from active interference in Mexican affairs and awaited the outcome of the new civil war. Bryan tried to persuade Wilson to recognize the Villa-Zapata government in Mexico City, but Wilson refused to take sides. Then, when Carranza's chief general, Álvaro Obregón, nearly destroyed the Division of the North in April 1915, several counter-revolutionary Mexican leaders appeared in Washington to seek American assistance. Wilson would have nothing to do with them. As the summer wore on and Carranza gained strength, Robert Lansing, who had replaced Bryan in June and who regarded Carranza as a dire threat to foreign interests in Mexico, concocted a scheme to eliminate the First Chief through Pan-American mediation of the Mexican civil war. Wilson turned Lansing's scheme aside and accorded de facto recognition to the Carranza regime on 19 October 1915.

Villa, who had retreated northward with a small but loyal force, retaliated against Wilson's recognition of Carranza by murdering sixteen Americans in northern Mexico on 11 January 1916. When this act failed to provoke Wilson into military intervention, Villa struck at an army camp at Columbus, New Mexico, on 9 March 1916, burning the town and killing nineteen inhabitants. Wilson did the least that he could in the circumstances: he sent a force of some seven thousand men under General John Joseph Pershing to capture Villa and bring him to justice.

Before he sent Pershing into Mexico, Wilson thought that he had obtained Carranza's tacit consent to the entry of what was called the Punitive Expedition. The problem was the wily Villa, who eluded Pershing and drew him 350 miles southward into Mexico. Carranza, who probably would have been very glad if Pershing had captured Villa, now had to deal with a Mexican public opinion outraged by Pershing's move into the heart of Mexico. In response, the First Chief demanded that Wilson withdraw the Punitive Expedition from Mexican soil. Wilson did withdraw the expedition to the northernmost part of Mexico, but fighting broke out on 21 June 1916, when an American cavalry force attacked a detachment of Mexican regulars at Carrizal. First reports told of a treacherous ambush by the Mexicans, and Wilson wrote an address in which he asked Congress for authority to occupy all of northern Mexico. But both Carranza and Wilson desperately wanted to avoid war. Wilson cried out in a speech on 30 June 1916: "Do you think the glory of America would be enhanced by a war of conquest? Do you think that any act of violence by a powerful nation like this against a weak distracted neighbor would reflect distinction upon the annals of the United States?"

Carranza, on 4 July, proposed that a joint high commission be appointed to investigate and recommend, and Wilson jumped at the chance to seek a diplomatic solution. The commission met at various places in the United States from 6 September 1916 to 15 January 1917, when it broke up because Carranza would accept no agreement that did not provide for the complete withdrawal of all of Pershing's force on a specific date, a promise the Americans were unwilling to make. Wilson, determined to escape from the Mexican imbroglio, called the Punitive Expedition back to the United States on 18 January 1917.

Then Wilson sent a new ambassador to Mexico and, on 3 March, accorded de facto recognition to Carranza and the constitutional government that he had just established at Querétaro.

Through all the confused period in Mexican-American relations from 1914 to 1917, Wilson prevented any counterrevolutionary movements from being hatched on American soil and kept a close watch over American bankers and businessmen who, he suspected, wanted to take advantage of a helpless nation. Over and over, Wilson insisted that the Mexican people had the right to solve their problems in their own way. Ironically, the man who provoked Mexican ill will by his occupation of Veracruz and the dispatch of the Punitive Expedition was in fact the chief defender and guardian of the Mexican Revolution.

American Neutrality, 1914–1916

With the outbreak of a general war in Europe in early August 1914, the great majority of Americans gave thanks for the Atlantic Ocean. Wilson and his advisers acted quickly to establish formal neutrality and to meet the rude shocks caused by the total disorganization of world markets and trade. In addition, Wilson, on 17 August 1914, appealed to his "fellow countrymen" to be "impartial in thought as well as in action."

Wilson then turned his attention to British encroachments against neutral trade with Germany and Austria-Hungary (the Central Powers). He first tried to persuade the British to adhere to the Declaration of London of 1909, which purported to codify existing international law and was extremely protective of neutral commerce. But the British were determined to use their overwhelming sea power to cut Germany off from life-giving supplies, and Wilson had no recourse but to fall back upon ambiguous international law to protect American trading rights. This he did in a note to the British Foreign Office on 26 December 1914.

The European theater of war was in delicate balance by the end of 1914. The British controlled the seas, and the French and British armies had repelled a German advance toward Paris. German armies in the east were on the move in Poland, but they were still far from their main eastern enemy, Russia. In these circumstances of stalemate, American neutrality seemed secure.

The announcement by the German government on 4 February 1915 that it would thereafter use its small submarine fleet to sink all Allied ships within a broad war zone without warning posed a grave threat to American neutrality, since the Germans also said that, because submarine commanders would sometimes find it impossible to discriminate between enemy and neutral ships, neutral ships would not be safe from torpedoes. Wilson, on 10 February, sent a conventional warning to Berlin to the effect that the United States would hold Germany to a "strict accountability" for the destruction of American ships and lives on the high seas. What that warning meant in practical terms, no one, including the leaders in Washington, knew. For example, when a submarine sank a British passenger ship without warning off the coast of Africa on 28 March 1915 and caused the death of one American, Wilson decided not to act or even to protest. However, it was impossible to do nothing when a submarine sank the great British liner *Lusitania* without warning on 7 May 1915, causing the death of more than 1,200 noncombatants, including 128 Americans.

Wilson was in a dilemma worse than the one occasioned by his occupation of Veracruz. It was obvious that the American people wanted him to defend their right to travel in safety upon the seas; it was also obvious that a majority of Americans and of the members of Congress did not want to go to war to vindicate this right. Moreover, the cabinet and Wilson's advisers in the State Department were about evenly divided over a wise and proper response to the sinking of the *Lusitania*. Secretary of State Bryan pleaded with Wilson to acquiesce in the submarine blockade by warning Americans not to travel on Allied ships. Robert Lansing, then second in command of the State Department, pressed Wilson to send a peremptory demand to Germany for an apology, a disavowal, and a promise that submarines in the future would obey international law—that is, commanders would have to warn ships and permit passengers and crews to escape before the ships were sunk.

Wilson, taking high humanitarian ground, addressed two appeals to the German government to abandon the entire submarine campaign, at least against unarmed and unresisting liners and merchantmen. When the German government refused, Wilson, on 21 July, sent a third note, which admitted that it was possible to conduct a submarine campaign in substantial accordance with international law. But the note ended with the warning that the United States government would hereafter regard ruthless attacks on merchant ships and liners, when they affected American citizens, as "deliberately unfriendly"—that is, as an act of war.

Wilson desperately wanted to avoid war. At the very time that he was writing the *Lusitania* notes, he sent two moving appeals to the German government to join him in a campaign to establish real freedom of the seas—that is, to force the British to observe international law. Wilson also planned to rally the other neutrals to win the same objective. But the civilian leaders in Berlin were engaged in a desperate struggle with military and naval leaders over submarine policy and could not return a positive response to Wilson's overtures. Had they done so, the outcome of the war might well have been very different.

Bryan resigned as secretary of state on 8 June rather than continue a correspondence that he said might eventuate in hostilities with Germany. Wilson, somewhat reluctantly, appointed Lansing to succeed Bryan. Wilson continued to maintain close personal control over important foreign policies, but it was hard to do this with Lansing in command at the State Department because the new secretary, bent on war with Germany, tried at critical points to thwart or undermine Wilson's diplomacy. Lansing was also, by Wilson's standards, legalistic and reactionary.

The crisis with Germany came to a sudden head when the commander who had sent the *Lusitania* to the bottom sank another large British liner, the *Arabic*, without warning on 19 August 1915, with forty-four casualties, including two Americans. Wilson did not resort to public correspondence, but he made it clear to the German government that he would break diplomatic relations if it did not disavow the sinking of the *Arabic* and promise that submarines would thereafter warn unarmed passenger ships and provide for the safety of their passengers and crews before sinking them. Kaiser Wilhelm II finally hardened his courage and, on 30 August 1915, ordered his naval commanders to cease the submarine campaign against all passenger ships. Under instructions from his superiors, the German ambassador in Washington, Count Johann Heinrich von Bernstorff, informed Lansing on 1 September, "Liners will not be sunk by our submarines without warning and without safety of the lives of noncombatants, provided that the liners do not try to escape or offer resistance."

Americans hailed the so-called *Arabic* pledge as a great triumph for their president. Actually, what Wilson had done was to narrow the submarine dispute to the sole issue of the safety of unarmed passenger ships. Submarines were still free to prowl the seas and sink merchantmen without warning. The kaiser called all submarines back to their bases temporarily, in order to avoid any further incidents. But the Germans had not renounced the important aspects of the underseas campaign—the war against merchant shipping—and Wilson had in effect withdrawn his demand that they do so.

Confusion and Crises, 1916

The submarine controversy with Germany and disputes with Great Britain over neutral trade convinced Wilson and many other Americans that the world was a jungle, a place where force was more powerful than reason and law, and that the United States, with its limited armed forces, was unable to protect its own security, to say nothing of its worldwide interests.

The administration's plan to strengthen the army was devised by Secretary Garrison and the General Staff. It provided for a 400,000-man reserve force, called the continental army, and for a modest increase in the regular army. In contrast, the plan for naval expansion proposed a five-year building program, aimed obviously at Great Britain and Japan, to give the United States a two-ocean fleet capable of challenging the former and overwhelming the latter. Wilson opened the campaign for these programs in New York on 4 November 1915. Opposition from antimilitarists, pacifists, labor organizations, and Socialists developed very quickly. To complicate matters further for Wilson, the House Military Affairs Committee adamantly opposed the plan for the continental army, mainly because it would replace the National Guard as the first line of defense.

Wilson set out upon a speaking tour in the Middle West in late January to stir up public support for his program. He returned to Washington to find congressional Democrats as stubbornly opposed as ever to the continental army. Wilson was not committed to any single plan to strengthen the land forces; hence, he scuttled the continental army plan and accepted the House committee's demand that the National Guard be greatly strengthened and brought under comprehensive federal control. Garrison's resignation on 10 February, in protest against Wilson's move, cleared the way for easy passage of the revised Army Reorganization Act, signed by Wilson on 3 June. Wilson's great personal achievement was pas-

sage of the Naval Appropriations Act, signed by him on 29 August 1916. It provided for the completion of the Navy Department's building program in three, rather than five, years. "Let us build a navy bigger than hers [Britain's], and do what we please," Wilson said to his confidant, Colonel Edward M. House.

The failure of Wilson and Lansing to coordinate their foreign policies during the early months of 1916 led to confusions and crises that nearly caused Wilson to lose control of foreign policy to Congress. Wilson sent Colonel House to Europe in early January 1916 to work out a plan for Anglo-American cooperation for peace. House went through the formalities of talking with French and German leaders, but he spent most of his time in London. His peace plan stipulated that Wilson should convoke a peace conference in the near future. If the Germans refused to attend, the United States would probably enter the war on the side of the Allies. If a peace conference met and Germany refused to accept a "reasonable" settlement, the United States would probably enter the war on the Allied side. Sir Edward Grey, the British foreign secretary, on 22 February 1916 initialed a memorandum that embodied the plan, but he stipulated that the British, in agreement with the French, should decide when the House-Grey Memorandum was to be implemented.

Meanwhile, Lansing had launched an initiative that threatened to wreck House's negotiations. On 18 January 1916 the secretary of state proposed to the Allies that they disarm their merchant ships in return for a pledge by Germany that submarines would sink merchantmen only after warning them and providing for the safety of their crews. As Grey said, the Allies were being asked to permit submarines to sink their entire merchant fleets. Protests from Grey and House in London caused Wilson and Lansing to reverse course at once. The secretary of state announced on 15 February 1916 that the administration would follow customary rules and require submarines to warn defensively armed merchant ships before attacking them.

The intimation that the United States might break relations or go to war with Germany over the safety of armed ships set off a panic among Democrats in Congress, who threatened to take control of foreign policy by approving resolutions warning Americans against traveling on any armed ships. Wilson responded with his usual boldness, and the Senate and House tabled the resolutions on 3 March and 7 March, respectively. Actually, the safety of armed ships never became an issue between the American and German governments.

When a submarine torpedoed the packet *Sussex* without warning in the English Channel with heavy loss of life on 24 March 1916, Wilson decided to use the incident to force the submarine issue to a clear resolution. He went before a joint session of Congress on 19 April and read the terms of an ultimatum he had just sent to Berlin: if the Germans did not at once abandon their ruthless submarine campaign, he would break diplomatic relations with the German government. The Germans did not yet have enough submarines to conduct a successful blockade; consequently they replied on 4 May that submarines would thereafter observe the rules of visit and search when they attacked merchant ships. Maintenance of this pledge would be contingent upon the success of the United States in forcing Great Britain to observe international law in matters of trade.

Relations with Germany were almost cordial following the so-called *Sussex* pledge, and Americans could turn undistracted attention to the forthcoming national conventions and presidential campaign. The Republicans nominated Associate Justice Charles Evans Hughes, former governor of New York. The Democrats of course renominated Wilson. Repeated demonstrations for peace rocked the Democratic convention hall, and the Democrats adopted a platform plank that hailed Wilson because he had preserved national honor and "kept us out of war."

In the campaign, Hughes appeared petty, legalistic, and quarrelsome. Wilson, in contrast, was never better as a campaigner. Highlighting the themes of progressivism and peace, he kept Hughes on the defensive. Bryan joined other Democrats in trumpeting the cry "He kept us out of war" through the Middle West, the Plains states, and the Far West. In the election on 7 November 1916, Wilson carried New Hampshire, Ohio, the South, and virtually all trans-Mississippi states for a narrow victory (277–254) in the electoral college. Wilson's increase in popular votes in 1916 of nearly 50 percent over his popular vote in 1912 was one of the great electoral achievements in American history.

From Mediation to War, 1916–1917

All through the spring and summer of 1916, Wilson and House tried to persuade Sir Edward Grey to put the House-Grey Memorandum into effect. Grey ada-

mantly refused, and Wilson abandoned all hope of peace through Anglo-American cooperation. This development and others embittered Anglo-American relations and caused Wilson to believe that the British were prolonging the war for conquest and revenge. Ever since the outbreak of the war, Wilson had hoped to bring it to an end. By late 1916, the conflict seemed about to destroy the very fabric of European society; moreover, Wilson knew that both sides would intensify their efforts to end the bloody struggle, and intensification of the war at sea would probably force the United States into the conflict.

To bring peace to the world and to avert the possibility of American participation, Wilson appealed to the belligerents on 18 December 1916 to disclose the terms upon which they would agree to end the fighting. The Germans refused to divulge their terms. The Allies—emboldened by Lansing's assurances, made secretly to the French and British ambassadors, that Wilson was pro-Ally—announced terms that could be achieved only by complete defeat of the Central Powers. Undaunted, Wilson opened secret negotiations with the German government. He was, he told Berlin, prepared to be an independent and impartial mediator, and he could force the Allies to the peace table because they were now totally dependent upon American credit and supplies. While he waited for a reply from Berlin, Wilson went before the Senate on 22 January 1917 to describe the kind of a peace settlement that the United States was prepared to work for and support. It had to be a "peace without victory," he said, one without indemnities and annexations. Above all, it had to be based upon a league of nations to preserve peace.

The Germans were as much determined upon total victory as the Allies. They abhorred the idea of Wilson's mediation and believed that their now large fleet of long-range submarines could bring the British to their knees long before the United States could send a single soldier to France. Hence, they rejected Wilson's hand of friendship, accepted the prospect of war with the United States, and announced on 31 January 1917 that they would begin, the following day, a ruthless submarine campaign against all merchant shipping in European waters.

Wilson was stunned, and he broke diplomatic relations with the German Empire on 3 February. Even so, he said that he hoped that no German aggressions against American ships would force the United States to take sterner measures of protection. American ships refused to enter the war zone, and the nation waited expectantly. Then, in late February, the British disclosed a telegram from the German foreign secretary, Arthur Zimmermann, to the German minister in Mexico. The "Zimmermann telegram" instructed the minister, in the event that the United States entered the war against Germany, to offer to the Mexican government an alliance by which Mexico would go to war against the United States and would receive in return "the lost territory in Texas, New Mexico, and Arizona."

Events thereafter led inexorably to war between the United States and Germany. On 9 March, Wilson announced that the navy would place guns and gun crews on American merchantmen. It soon became obvious that armed neutrality would not suffice to protect American rights, and Wilson, after much agonizing, on 2 April asked Congress to recognize that a state of war already existed between the United States and Germany on account of German aggressions. In a moving peroration, Wilson declared that the world had to be made "safe for democracy" and freed from the threat of German militarism. Congress complied after a brief debate, and Wilson signed the war resolution on 6 April 1917.

The United States at War, 1917–1918

With only recent British experience to guide him, Wilson led Congress, his administration, and the entire American people in one of the speediest and most successful mobilizations for war in history. Congress approved a selective service bill on 18 May 1917, and the War Department set about systematically raising an army of 3 million men. Congress gave Wilson full power over the production, distribution, and prices of food and fuel supplies in the Lever Act of 10 August 1917. Food and fuel administrations mobilized and stimulated production to such an efficient degree that there was never any real danger of critical shortages of fuel and food for the American people, the American army, and the Allies. Through various instrumentalities, but most notably the War Industries Board, Wilson maintained a steady supply of raw materials to war industries. Substantial labor peace was maintained in 1917 through the Labor Department and in 1918 through the National War Labor Board. Wilson launched a large shipbuilding program at the outset of belligerency and, in December 1917, took over operation of the railroads. To pay for this gigantic mobilization, the Treasury De-

partment raised some $23 billion through the sale of bonds and an additional $10.5 billion through heavy taxes on incomes and business profits.

To persuade the public, still badly divided over the wisdom of participation, Wilson established the Committee on Public Information to undertake a nationwide program to convince Americans that they were fighting for justice, peace, democracy, and their own security in the world. To stamp out active opposition to the war effort, Congress adopted the Espionage Act of 15 June 1917 and the Sedition Act of 16 May 1918.

The direct threat to the American and Allied cause in the spring of 1917 was the German submarine campaign, the results of which at first exceeded German expectations. Against British opposition, Wilson insisted upon the institution of the convoy system. Wilson had his way in July, and the Navy Department suspended construction of capital ships and concentrated upon destroyers and smaller antisubmarine craft. The convoy system brought the submarine menace under control by the autumn of 1917 and eliminated it almost entirely by the spring of 1918. In addition, pooled American and British shipping transported nearly 2 million American soldiers safely to France and maintained the flow of American supplies to the Allies.

The American Expeditionary Force, under General Pershing, first saw active service before Paris during the Second Battle of the Marne (21 March–6 August 1918). In mid-August, Pershing's First Army, some 550,000 strong, joined the British and French in a broad counterattack against the German lines. By late September, Pershing's force numbered 1.2 million men; by 1 November it was near the German frontier. American manpower gave the Allied-American armies a predominance of 600,000 soldiers on the western front and turned the tide of battle decisively against Germany.

In his war message to Congress, Wilson had declared that the war aims of the United States were the same as the ones he had enunciated in his Peace Without Victory Address of 22 January 1917. Thus, from the outset of American belligerency, Wilson dissociated his government from the secret treaties and war aims of the Allies and declared that the United States was an associated, not an Allied, power. This meant, theoretically, that the United States was free to wage its own war and to conclude a separate peace when it had achieved its ends. Of course, it was not possible to be so disengaged. The United

States was also committed to total defeat of Germany if necessary, and the only way to wage a total war in the circumstances was through close cooperation, diplomatic as well as military, with Britain and France.

This fact became clear when Pope Benedict XV, on 1 August 1917, called for peace very much along the lines of Wilson's Peace Without Victory Address. Wilson responded as warmly as he thought prudent; when Britain and France rebuffed the pontiff, Wilson had to console himself with the thought that the Allies would be in his hands "financially" at the end of the war and that he could force them to accept his own peace terms.

Wilson was spurred to an independent peace campaign in response to the Bolshevik takeover in Russia in early November 1917. The Bolsheviks, or Communists, appealed to the war-weary peoples of Europe to stop the fighting, called for a general peace conference, and opened separate peace negotiations with the Central Powers. Unable to persuade the Allies to join him in returning a positive response, Wilson went before Congress on 8 January 1918 to announce in precise terms what the United States was fighting for. This peace program, embodied in fourteen points, called for, among other things, an end to secret diplomacy, freedom of the seas, drastic reduction in armaments, an independent Poland, and a "general association of nations . . . affording mutual guarantees of political independence and territorial integrity to great and small states alike."

The Fourteen Points Address at once became the great ideological manifesto of the war and the rallying cry of liberal and labor groups throughout the world. Moreover, in subsequent addresses Wilson challenged the German and Austrian governments to avow their war aims and, better still, to join him in an irresistible campaign for a reasonable peace. The Austrian emperor, Charles, responded warmly and seemed ready to conclude a separate peace based upon the Fourteen Points. However, the French government finessed Charles's move by announcing to the world that the Austrian emperor was eager for peace. Charles could now only proclaim fervent loyalty to his ally, Germany.

The Germans responded to Wilson's appeal with the imposition of the punitive Treaty of Brest-Litovsk upon Russia on 3 March 1918 and with their own peace offensive—the Second Battle of the Marne, designed to knock France out of the war before sub-

stantial American help could arrive. As Wilson said sadly in an address on 6 April, the war now had to be fought to its bitter conclusion. And so it was. As has been said, the second German Marne offensive failed, and the Allies, in July 1918, began a broad counterattack that ended with the armistice.

During the height of the Second Battle of the Marne, the hard-pressed British and French put heavy pressure upon Wilson to join the Japanese in opening a second front in Siberia, in order to prevent the transfer of German troops from Russia to the western front. Wilson suspected, rightly, that the Allies wanted the United States and Japan to make war against the Bolshevik regime. Wilson thought that Allied hopes to reestablish the eastern front were futile and foolish. He also believed very deeply that the Russian people had the right to work out their own destiny and to establish any kind of government that they pleased, without any outside influence or pressure whatsoever. Hence, he vetoed all suggestions for a Siberian operation.

Wilson relented slightly under the pressure of events in the summer of 1918. A force of seventy thousand Czechs, former Austro-Hungarian prisoners of war in Russia, had banded together in what was called the Czech Legion and were fighting to escape along a route from Russia proper to the Siberian port of Vladivostok. Wilson, in a memorandum of 17 July 1918, announced that he would send a small force to Vladivostok to guarantee the safe exit of the Czechs; he also invited the Japanese to join him in this limited operation. In the same memorandum, Wilson reiterated his intention to oppose all efforts to interfere in Russian internal affairs.

Wilson was motivated in large part by the suspicion, which turned out to be well grounded, that the Japanese had designs on Siberia. Thus, Wilson, while he sent only seven thousand men to Vladivostok, did his best to keep the Japanese contingent to the same size. However, the Japanese government eventually sent in seventy thousand men and seized northern Manchuria and eastern Siberia. Wilson, in August 1918, also sent four battalions from Pershing's force to Murmansk and Archangel in northern Russia to cooperate with British and Czech forces there to safeguard large munitions supplies against capture by the Germans.

As British, French, and American armies neared the German frontier in early October 1918, the German government, now in the control of liberals and antimilitarists, appealed to Wilson for an armistice

President Wilson (far right) strolls with David Lloyd George of Great Britain (far left) and Georges Clemenceau of France during the Paris Peace Conference following World War I. ARCHIVE PHOTOS

signed the armistice agreement on 11 November 1918.

Peacemaking, 1919

Wilson now faced the awesome problems of peace-making and the reconstruction of the world order. Yet, even before the guns were silent on the western front, he had gravely impaired his standing by appealing for the election of a Democratic Congress in the off-year election of 1918, on the ground that the return of a Republican majority to either house of Congress would be interpreted in Europe as a repudiation of his leadership. The voters, on 6 November, elected a Congress with slight Republican majorities in both houses. Whether repudiated or not, Wilson proceeded with his own plans for the peace conference without seeking Republican cooperation and support. On 18 November he announced that he would go to the peace conference, scheduled to meet in Paris in January 1919, as the head of an American delegation that was not to contain a single prominent Republican.

Wilson went to Paris in December 1918 determined to achieve a just and lasting peace based upon principles of justice, humanity, and self-determination and upon an effective world organization. All the Allied leaders at Paris were motivated by particular selfish interests. The French wanted large reparations from Germany and a settlement that would remove forever the threat of German militarism from Europe. The British wanted to exact huge payments from Germany, to annex former German colonies, and to destroy the German navy but not destroy the balance of power on the Continent entirely. The Italians had their eyes on former Austrian territory in the Tyrol and along the Adriatic coast. The Japanese demanded former German colonies in the Pacific and the former German concession in the Chinese province of Shantung.

By all accounts, Wilson was the only disinterested principal leader at the peace conference. He wanted nothing for the United States except a just peace that would endure and a world organization that could maintain peace in the future. Wilson fought as hard as any person could to achieve these objectives. With British support, he was able to prevent the dismemberment of Germany in the west, which the French demanded, and vetoed French plans for a "great crusade" to crush the Bolshevik regime. With British and French support, Wilson suc-

based upon the Fourteen Points Address and subsequent speeches by Wilson. Wilson kept in close touch with Allied leaders during the negotiations that followed. Once Wilson was convinced that the German government was prepared to admit defeat, he sent Colonel House to London to obtain British and French consent to an armistice agreement. House claimed that he had won a diplomatic triumph when the British prime minister, David Lloyd George, and the French premier, Georges Clemenceau, agreed to make peace upon the basis of the Fourteen Points. The British said, though, that they would not be bound by the point concerning freedom of the seas, and the French won House's and Wilson's approval for a stipulation to the effect that the Germans should be liable for all civilian damages caused by their aggression. More important, the military and naval terms of the armistice agreement left the Germans powerless to wage even defensive war in the future. Nonetheless, German representatives

cessfully resisted Italian demands for territory along the Adriatic coast that was essential to the new state of Yugoslavia.

Since Wilson had only one vote in the councils at Paris, his one alternative to yielding or to compromising when the British and French ganged up against him was to withdraw from the conference and make a separate peace with Germany. During the direst controversy with the French, Wilson threatened to leave the conference. But, as Wilson knew, the cure in this case was worse than the disease. His withdrawal would wreck his plans for a postwar world organization and result in a Carthaginian peace imposed by the French.

Thus, Wilson yielded on the key question of reparations (the British and French were permitted to demand potentially astronomical payments from Germany) and compromised on the equally important question of French control of the coal-rich Saar Valley of Germany. Moreover, the conferees at Paris said nothing about disarmament. Even so, Wilson was able to vindicate most of his Fourteen Points. Belgium, brutally overrun and occupied by Germany in 1914, was restored. An independent Poland with access to the sea came back into the family of nations. The claims of the Central European peoples to self-determination were satisfied. Alsace-Lorraine was restored to France.

Wilson's most important achievement at Paris was the creation of the League of Nations and the inclusion of its covenant in the Treaty of Versailles between the United States and the former Allies and Germany. The covenant created elaborate machinery for the settlement of international disputes and for united action against aggressors. Moreover, the League was designated as the instrument to carry out the Versailles and other treaties concluded at Paris.

The Treaty Fight in the United States, 1919–1920

Wilson presented the Versailles treaty to the Senate on 10 July 1919, in the supreme confidence that that body would not dare to refuse to give its consent to ratification. There were many signs of danger ahead. One was the persistence of the tradition of isolationism, which before 1914 had been the cornerstone of American foreign policy. Ratification of the Treaty of Versailles would carry heavy new international responsibilities for the United States: Article 10 of the covenant guaranteed the political independence and territorial integrity of all member nations, and support of the covenant's peacekeeping machinery might well entail the risk of war. Moreover, Republicans controlled the Senate, and Wilson's implacable personal and political foe, Henry Cabot Lodge of Massachusetts, was chairman of the Foreign Relations Committee.

Lodge would have preferred to reject the treaty outright, but in order to preserve unity within his party, he accepted a plan offered by more moderate Republicans—to approve the treaty subject to certain reservations. The most important of these was a reservation to Article 10 that stipulated that the United States assumed no obligation under this article unless Congress, by joint resolution or otherwise, should specifically assume such obligation.

Saying that the enemies of the League were poisoning the wells of public opinion, Wilson set out upon a tour of the West in order to purify them. In one of the great forensic efforts in American history, he traveled eight thousand miles and delivered thirty-two major addresses between 3 and 25 September 1919. During the early hours of 26 September, Wilson suffered a stroke warning, which ended his tour. Then, on 2 October, after his return to Washington, Wilson suffered a devastating stroke that paralyzed his left side and for a time threatened his life.

This stroke was only the worst manifestation of cerebrovascular disease that had victimized Wilson at least since 1896, when he suffered loss of dexterity in his right hand for about eight months. Then came small strokes and a serious vascular accident in his left eye in 1906. Dr. S. Weir Mitchell, the distinguished neurologist of Philadelphia, examined Wilson soon after the election of 1912 and reported to the White House physician, Dr. Cary T. Grayson, that he thought Wilson would not live out his first term. Grayson kept Wilson on a regime of simple diet, exercise, and avoidance of stress, but the tasks of overseeing the American war effort blew Grayson's regimen to pieces. Wilson, now suffering from uncontrolled hypertension, went to Paris unwell. There he suffered a viral infection and another small stroke in April 1919. This was followed by a more severe small stroke on 19 July. By the time Wilson went out West, his hypertension was fulminant. The specialist who examined Wilson after his large stroke of October reported that he had long suffered from hypertension, atherosclerosis, and carotid artery disease and was in the lacunar state as a result of small strokes. Wilson was almost completely disabled, both physically and psychologically, from October through December 1919.

A healthy Wilson would almost certainly have found a high ground of compromise with pro-League Republicans and put the treaty across, probably by October 1919. But the sick Wilson, isolated in the White House, was incapable of comprehending political realities, or even of thinking abstractly or strategically. When the treaty came up for a vote in the Senate on 19 November, Wilson commanded Democrats in the Senate to vote against ratification with reservations. The reservation to Article 10, Wilson said, amounted to nullification, not ratification, of the treaty. The Republicans defeated ratification without the reservations; the Democrats then defeated ratification with the reservations.

Democrats tried to find some compromise, but Lodge would not budge on the all-important reservation to Article 10. For his part, Wilson not only refused to yield an inch of ground, but in a public letter (drafted, actually, by his chief of staff, Joseph P. Tumulty), on 8 January 1920 he also made the League issue a partisan question by saying that the coming presidential election should be a "great and solemn referendum" on the question of ratification of the Versailles treaty. Actually, all hopes for Senate approval were by now dead unless enough Democrats were prepared to defy Wilson and join the Republicans to form a two-thirds majority in favor of ratification with reservations. And if that had happened, Wilson would have killed the treaty himself by refusing to go through the process of ratification. But Wilson did not have to do this. In one of the most important presidential letters in history (drafted for the most part by Tumulty), written to his spokesman in the Senate on 8 March 1920, Wilson commanded Democratic senators to vote against ratification with any reservations whatsoever. A second vote in the Senate, on 19 March 1920, failed to find two-thirds of the senators in favor of the treaty in any form. Wilson was only momentarily downcast, if at all. He planned to secure his renomination and to run again for the presidency on a pro-League platform.

The End of the Wilson Administration, 1919–1921

Wilson had passed through the dangerous aftereffects of his stroke and achieved a slight recovery by the end of 1919, but for the balance of his term, he remained a sick man, his physical constitution, psy-

che, and sense of reality shattered. He continued to function on a low level, but he could sit up or concentrate upon a subject for only short periods. He also suffered from severe changes in mood and from some paranoia. Consequently, Wilson was incapable of giving leadership to his party, to Congress, and to the people during one of the most critical periods in American history.

The myth still persists that Edith Bolting Wilson, Wilson's second wife (his first wife, Ellen Louise Axson Wilson, had died on 6 August 1914), ran the presidential office after his first stroke. Edith Wilson, in consultation with Dr. Grayson, did determine to a large degree the persons whom Wilson saw and for how long. She also took important state papers into Wilson's room, read them to him, and recorded her husband's instructions in the margins of the documents. But she neither knew how to serve as an acting president nor wanted to be one. She was interested only in the health and happiness of her husband, whom she worshiped. Mrs. Wilson did make two decisions of momentous importance: in mid-October 1919 she vetoed a plan by Dr. Grayson and his chief consultant, Dr. Francis X. Dercum of Philadelphia, to make a complete disclosure of Wilson's condition. Later, in January 1920, Dr. Grayson persuaded Wilson to resign, and Mrs. Wilson blocked this initiative.

Power in these circumstances fell to Tumulty, who assumed general oversight of the executive office, and to the various departmental heads. Lansing, as the premier of the group, held unauthorized cabinet meetings on his own from October 1919 until Wilson dismissed him on 12 February 1920.

Lansing's successor was Bainbridge Colby, a New York lawyer, appointed on 25 February 1920. The two men presented a study in contrasts. Whereas Lansing was conservative in political outlook, Colby was an advanced progressive who had followed Roosevelt in 1912 and supported Wilson in 1916. Lansing was a professional "realist"; Colby was an idealist and an amateur, at least at the beginning of his incumbency.

When a group of generals led by Álvaro Obregón overthrew Carranza on 8 May 1920, Colby moved at once to mend Mexican-American relations preparatory to a recognition of the Obregón government, but the new rulers in Mexico City were then too afraid of domestic public opinion to come to any understanding with the United States. They deferred serious negotiations until the inauguration of Warren G. Harding.

Wilson seemed to want to wash his hands of European problems after the Senate's second rejection of the Versailles treaty, and the United States government sat on the sidelines while the Allies tidied up the map of Europe. Wilson and Colby also continued the administration's policy of strict noninterference in Russian affairs. The United States, for example, refused to recognize the independence of the new Baltic states of Lithuania, Latvia, and Estonia. Colby coupled the policy of noninterference with one of adamant refusal to recognize the Bolshevik government, on the ground that it did not represent the Russian people.

Departmental heads and Congress met the problems of demobilization without much guidance from the White House. The new attorney general, Alexander Mitchell Palmer, on 8 November 1919, secured an injunction that prevented a nationwide coal strike by the United Mine Workers of America. A federal arbitration commission soon granted most of the miners' demands. Palmer, with an eye on the White House and in response to a mounting fear of Communism, had federal agents, on 1 January 1920, execute a gigantic raid on Communist headquarters throughout the country. It is doubtful if Wilson knew anything about Palmer's raid.

Wilson announced on 24 December 1919 that he would return the railroads to their owners on 1 March 1920 unless Congress instructed otherwise. Congress responded with the Transportation Act of 1920, which affirmed the principle of private ownership but also established comprehensive federal control over all aspects of the railroad business. At the same time, before he left office, Secretary of the Interior Lane was assured of passage of the Water Power and General Leasing acts by Congress in early 1920. Their adoption brought to an end controversies that had worried the Wilson administration since 1913. One of the crowning achievements of the Wilson administration—the Nineteenth Amendment, which conferred the vote upon women—came to fulfillment with ratification of the amendment on 26 August 1920. Finally, Wilson vetoed, on 27 May 1920, a joint resolution ending the war with Germany. A separate peace, he said, "would place ineffable stain upon the gallantry and honor of the United States." (A joint resolution to end the state of war was approved by President Harding in July 1921.) Wilson vetoed, unsuccessfully, the Volstead Act of 1919 for the enforcement of national prohibition under the Eighteenth Amendment. In his last important act as president, he vetoed emergency bills to increase tariff rates and severely limit the admission of immigrants. Congress passed both measures again in May 1921, and the new president signed them.

The Significance of the Wilson Presidency

Wilson and Warren Gamaliel Harding rode together from the White House to the Capitol for the latter's inauguration on 4 March 1921. Wilson, aged and infirm, was a living mind in a dying body; Harding, majestic in appearance, looked every inch a leader. Appearances were never more deceiving. Harding would soon reveal his moral and intellectual bankruptcy, and Wilson lived to attend his funeral services.

Wilson, who died at his home in Washington on 3 February 1924, set an example of leadership, both of public opinion and of Congress, that challenges every incumbent of the White House. His reconstruction of the American political economy still survives in all its important features. Wilson's conviction that the state and federal governments should work actively to protect the weak and disadvantaged remains the main theme of Democratic politics.

The Wilsonian legacy in foreign policy is clear, but the degree to which it continues to guide American foreign policy is ambiguous. Wilson believed very deeply that the United States was called to serve mankind through leadership for peace, democracy, and the uplift of the peoples of the world. But this leadership had to be essentially of the spirit, not of the sword. It may be that the Wilsonian legacy is now only the conscience of American foreign policy.

BIBLIOGRAPHY

Ray Stannard Baker, *Woodrow Wilson: Life and Letters*, 8 vols. (Garden City, N.Y., 1927–1939), is the authorized biography by a contemporary and friend. William M. Leary, Jr., and Arthur S. Link, comps, *The Progressive Era and the Great War, 1896–1920*, 2d ed. (Arlington Heights, Ill., 1978), is the most extensive bibliography of Wilson and his era. Arthur S. Link, *Wilson*, 5 vols. (Princeton, N.J., 1947–1965), provides fullest coverage of Wilson as governor and president, 1913–1917. Arthur S. Link et al., eds., *The Papers of Woodrow Wilson*, 69 vols. (Princeton, N.J., 1966–1994), is the authoritative and basic documentary collection and the starting point for research on Woodrow Wilson and the Wilson era.

August Heckscher, *Woodrow Wilson* (New York, 1991), is the best personal biography. Edwin A. Weinstein, *Woodrow Wilson: A Medical and Psychological Biography* (Princeton, N.J., 1981); Bert E. Park, *The Impact of Illness on World Leaders* (Philadelphia, 1986), and his *Ailing, Aged, Addicted: Studies of Compromised Leadership* (Lexington, Ky., 1993); and the documents and essays in Link et al., eds., *The Papers of Woodrow Wilson*, vols. 58, 63–68, are definitive on Wilson's health history.

John D. Clark, *The Federal Trust Policy* (Baltimore, 1931), is good on the Clayton and Federal Trade Commission acts. Thomas J. Knock and Christine Lunardini, "Woodrow Wilson and Woman Suffrage: A New Look," in *Political Science Quarterly* 95 (1980–1981), gives the closest look at this important subject. Earl Latham, ed., *The Philosophy and Policies of Woodrow Wilson* (Chicago, 1958), provides a good overview. Sidney Ratner, *Taxation and Democracy in America* (New York, 1967), is the best coverage of the Wilson administration's fiscal policies.

Alan P. Seltzer, "Woodrow Wilson as 'Corporate-Liberal': Toward a Reconsideration of Left Revisionist Historiography," in *Western Political Quarterly* 30 (1977), is the definitive monograph on the antitrust policy of the Wilson administration. Frank W. Taussig, *The Tariff History of the United States*, 8th ed. (New York, 1931), is excellent on the Underwood-Simmons Tariff Act and the Federal Tariff Commission Act. H. Parker Willis, *The Federal Reserve System* (Chicago, 1920), provides a documentary history by one of the drafters of the Federal Reserve bill.

Patrick Devlin, *Too Proud to Fight: Woodrow Wilson's Neutrality* (New York, 1974), is by an eminent British legal scholar. N. Gordon Levin, Jr., *Woodrow Wilson and World Politics: America's Response to War and Revolution* (New York, 1968), interprets Wilson's reaction to the war and the Bolshevik revolution from a revisionist point of view. Thomas J. Knock, *To End All Wars: Woodrow Wilson and the Quest for a New World Order* (New York, 1992), is an eloquent antidote to Levin. Frederick S. Calhoun, *Power and Principle: Armed Intervention in Wilsonian Foreign Policy* (Kent, Ohio, 1986), and his *Uses of Force and Wilsonian Foreign Policy* (Kent, Ohio, 1993), are pathbreaking works.

Arthur S. Link, *Woodrow Wilson: Revolution, War, and Peace* (Arlington Heights, Ill., 1979), pres-

ents Wilson as an anti-imperialist, decolonizer, and leader in the fight for world peace. Arthur S. Link, ed., *Woodrow Wilson and a Revolutionary World, 1913–1921* (Chapel Hill, N.C., 1982), gathers articles that reflect the latest research on important topics, such as Wilson and the Mexican Revolution and Wilson and the Russian Revolution. Ernest R. May, *The World War and American Isolation, 1914–1917* (Cambridge, Mass., 1959), provides the worldwide context. Arno J. Mayer, *Political Origins of the New Diplomacy, 1917–1918* (New Haven, Conn., 1959), presents an interesting contrast between Wilson and Lenin as makers of foreign policy.

Dana G. Munro, *Intervention and Dollar Diplomacy in the Caribbean, 1900–1921* (Princeton, N.J., 1964), is a nearly definitive treatment. Robert E. Quirk, *An Affair of Honor: Woodrow Wilson and the Occupation of Veracruz* (Lexington, Ky., 1962), and *The Mexican Revolution, 1914–1915: The Convention of Aguascalientes* (Bloomington, Ind., 1960), cover Mexican-American relations in 1914–1915. Charles Seymour, ed., *The Intimate Papers of Colonel House*, 4 vols. (Boston, 1926–1928), contains the diary and letters of Wilson's confidant on foreign policy.

Daniel R. Beaver, *Newton D. Baker and the American War Effort, 1917–1919* (Lincoln, Nebr., 1966), and Arthur S. Link and John Whiteclay Chambers II, "Woodrow Wilson as Commander in Chief," in Richard H. Kohn, ed., *The United States Military Under the Constitution of the United States, 1789–1989* (New York, 1991), are the best studies of American mobilization. Robert D. Cuff, *The War Industries Board: Business-Government Relations During World War I* (Baltimore, 1973), places too much emphasis on voluntarism as the motif of American mobilization.

For Wilson's wartime diplomacy, see David R. Woodward, *Trial by Friendship: Anglo-American Relations, 1917–1918* (Lexington, Ky., 1993); George F. Kennan, *Russia Leaves the War* (Princeton, N.J., 1956), and his *The Decision to Intervene* (Princeton, N.J., 1958); Betty Miller Unterberger, *America's Siberian Expedition, 1918–1920: A Study of National Policy* (Durham, N.C., 1956), and her *The United States, Revolutionary Russia, and the Rise of Czechoslovakia* (Chapel Hill, N.C., 1989); and Victor S. Mamatey, *The United States and East Central Europe, 1914–1918* (Princeton, N.J., 1957).

For other aspects of the home front, see Horace C. Peterson and Gilbert C. Fite, *Opponents of War,*

1917–1918 (Madison, Wis., 1957); Stephen Vaughn, *Holding Fast the Inner Lines: Democracy, Nationalism, and the Committee an Public Information* (Chapel Hill, N.C., 1980); and Seward W. Livermore, *Politics Is Adjournal: Woodrow Wilson and the War Congress, 1916–1918* (Middletown, Conn., 1966).

The indispensable source for Wilson and the Paris Peace Conference is vols. 53–61 of Link et al., eds., *The Papers of Woodrow Wilson*, to which should be added Arthur S. Link, trans. and ed., *The Deliberations of the Council of Four (March 24–June 28, 1919): Notes of the Official Interpreter, Paul Mantoux*, 2 vols. (Princeton, N.J., 1992). Paul Birdsall, *Versailles Twenty Years After* (New York, 1941), is still the best one-volume account, but see also Inga Floto, *Colonel House in Paris: A Study of American Policy at the Paris Peace Conference 1919* (Princeton, N.J., 1980).

For the period 1919–1921, see Robert K. Murray, *Red Scare: A Study in National Hysteria, 1919–1920* (Minneapolis, 1955); Daniel M. Smith, *The Aftermath of War: Bainbridge Colby and Wilsonian Diplomacy, 1920–1921* (Philadelphia, 1970); Thomas A. Bailey, *Woodrow Wilson and the Great Betrayal* (New York, 1945); Ralph Stone, *The Irreconcilables: The Fight Against the League of Nations* (Lexington, Ky., 1970); Lloyd E. Ambrosius, *Woodrow Wilson and the American Diplomatic Tradition: The Treaty Fight in Perspective* (Cambridge, 1987); and Wesley M. Bagby, *The Road to Normalcy: The Presidential Campaign and Election of 1920* (Baltimore, 1962).

Recent works include Louis Auchincloss, *Woodrow Wilson* (New York, 2000); John Milton Cooper, *Breaking the Heart of the World: Woodrow Wilson and the Fight for the League of Nations* (Cambridge and New York, 2001); and Phyllis Lee Levin, *Edith and Woodrow: The Wilson White House* (New York, 2001).

Warren G. Harding

Robert K. Murray

Warren G. Harding THE LIBRARY OF CONGRESS

W
ITH these words, "I cannot hope to be one of the great presidents, but perhaps I may be remembered as one of the best loved," Warren G. Harding began one of the most corruption-riddled and discredited administrations in the nation's history. Since his day, the name of Harding, rather than evoking praise and admiration, has conjured up scenes of smoke-filled rooms, evil machinations, and raucous poker parties. Few recall anything concrete about his administration except for the infamous Harding scandals. His performance has been rated consistently by American historians as the worst in the national experience, worse than that of Ulysses Grant, worse even than that of the one

president who was forced to resign, Richard Nixon. There is both justice and injustice in this historical verdict.

Warren Gamaliel Harding was born on 2 November 1865 in a tiny clapboard house on the edge of the small village of Blooming Grove, Ohio. His ancestors had migrated from Pennsylvania's Wyoming Valley years before. Harding's father was a self-educated veterinarian who in 1873 attended the Homeopathic Hospital College in Cleveland and thereafter turned his attention from animals to people. His mother, Phoebe Dickerson, who began as a Methodist but became a convert to the Seventh-Day Adventist faith, provided the family with a fundamentalist background and devoutly read her Bible, as Warren's middle name suggests.

Little is known of Harding's boyhood, which was spent in and around Caledonia, Ohio. He was nicknamed Winnie by his family, attended the village school, swam in the local creek, played scrub baseball, and loved animals, especially dogs. As an adolescent, he served as a printer's helper and learned how to stick type, feed press, make up forms, and wash rollers. In 1882 he graduated from Ohio Central College in nearby Iberia. This college's major function was to prepare students for rural teaching, and its curriculum was as meager as its instruction was poor. The year Harding completed his work, there were just three graduates; no records exist to reveal whether he stood at the head, middle, or foot of his class. There is evidence that he did not take his studies too seriously. His main interest was in editing the school paper, the *Iberian Spectator*.

Finding rural teaching not to his liking, Harding left the battle against juvenile ignorance in 1883, tried selling insurance for a year, and then, with two partners, bought a decrepit five-column, four-page newspaper called the *Marion Star*. This paper rapidly expanded under Harding's direction and ultimately achieved an unchallenged position in the bustling Ohio community. Seven years after taking over the *Star*, Harding married Florence Kling De Wolfe, a divorcee with an eleven-year-old child. Flossie, as she was called, was five years older than Warren, plain-featured, somewhat ungraceful, and sharp-tongued. But what she lacked in beauty she compensated for in determination and ambition.

Moving into a wide-porched, gable-roofed house that Harding had built, Florence complemented her husband by further expanding his newspaper. While he concentrated on editorial policy and securing advertisements, she reorganized the carrier delivery system and introduced a streamlined bookkeeping plan. And as the *Star* prospered, so did the importance and influence of its editor. Harding's journalistic activities and his deep involvement in community matters provided an excellent base for launching a political career. Marion offered Harding a suitable background for the projection of his personality and his ideas. For Harding, this small midwestern town represented the common denominator of the nation. Here the farmer and the businessman met on equal ground; here there was no great gulf between employer and employee; here conflict was minimized and divisions were healed. Cooperation, friendship, and local pride constituted a splendid harmony—a harmony that Harding believed was essential for both economic and political success.

Rise in Ohio Politics

Ohio politics needed some harmony at that time. During those years, Senator Marcus A. Hanna, Senator Joseph B. Foraker, and Boss George B. Cox dominated the Republican party in the Buckeye State. When their interests coalesced, they pooled their collective majorities to achieve stunning victories. At other times they leaped at each other's throats, causing defeat through violent intraparty feuds. In this atmosphere, Warren Harding quickly became one of the best-known party pacifiers. He firmly believed that conciliation was a political weapon superior to obstruction and strife, and this fact alone made him increasingly valuable in the acrimonious environment of Ohio politics.

In 1899, Harding ran for his first elective office, the Ohio Senate, and won. He was returned in 1901 for a second term and was elected floor leader. In 1903 he was elected to the post of lieutenant governor on a ticket headed by Myron T. Herrick and for the ensuing two years served as the amiable moderator of the Ohio Senate. At the conclusion of his term as lieutenant governor, he voluntarily returned to Marion and to the Star. However, through his editorials he continued to exert considerable influence on Ohio Republican party politics.

Harding was induced to leave his "retirement" in 1910 to run as a compromise gubernatorial candidate against Judson Harmon, the Democratic incumbent. He lost, but not before making additional friends within Republican ranks because of his sensitivity to the desires of all factions. In 1912, William Howard Taft selected him to place his name in nomination at the Republican National Convention, primarily because of Harding's known conciliatory qualities. Although such soothing tactics did not prevent the Bull Moose secession, Harding returned to Ohio from the 1912 convention an even bigger political figure than when he left. Two years later, he was the party's favorite to succeed incumbent Republican Senator Theodore E. Burton and won the 1914 senatorial election by a stunning majority of one hundred thousand.

The year 1915 was not a propitious one in which to enter the United States Senate. The major legislative battles over Wilson's New Freedom program had already been fought, and fears of war were beginning to overshadow normal partisan activities. During the war itself, there was little opportunity for a junior senator to make much of a reputation, and it was not until the League of Nations question emerged in 1919 that there was an issue capable of evoking serious partisan debate.

What modest reputation Harding acquired before 1919 was secured within the fold of the party rather than on the floor of the Senate. He delivered the Republican National Convention's keynote address in 1916 and was elected its permanent chairman. His call for unity and moderation struck just the proper chord for a party still suffering from the 1912 defeat.

Meanwhile, in the Senate, he carried his committee load, shunned acrimonious debate, and generally followed the old guard—or popular opinion, if that proved more beneficial. He voted for returning the railroads to their private owners after the war and pushed for high tariffs. He was dubious about government subsidies to agriculture, opposed excess-profit taxes and high surtaxes, and took a dim view of strong executive authority. He was mildly conservative in his attitude toward unions and was not swept off his feet by the "Red Scare" of 1919–1920. On woman suffrage and Prohibition he swam with public opinion, personally being committed to neither.

On the League, Harding was generally towed along by the more influential Republican senators. But his position also rested on expediency, since he believed that his Ohio constituents opposed it. He signed Senator Lodge's "round robin" anti-League statement in March 1919 and, as a member of the powerful Foreign Relations Committee, was privy to all discussions regarding the League question. He was also one of the senatorial group that called on the White House, in mid-August 1919, to air its differences with Woodrow Wilson. In the end, Harding declared himself in favor of the Lodge reservations and voted accordingly. Although never one of the "irreconcilables," he joined with such anti-League diehards as William E. Borah, Medill McCormick, and James A. Reed at the home of Nicholas Longworth after the anti-League vote on 19 November 1919 to eat scrambled eggs and celebrate the victory.

Presidential Election of 1920

Harding's emergence in 1920 as a presidential possibility resulted from a confluence of disparate events.

First, as a senator and favorite son from Ohio, "the Mother of Presidents," he automatically was a factor in any presidential equation. Second, continuing acrimony in the Republican party encouraged constant speculation about a compromise candidate. Third, the inability of the major contenders in 1920 to outstrip one another in garnering a majority of the eligible delegates played into the hands of the dark horse. Finally, Harding's cause was pushed by a dedicated and skillful group of supporters, the foremost being Harry Micajah Daugherty.

Daugherty, a Washington Court House, Ohio, political manipulator and lobbyist, had known Harding since the turn of the century, but it was not until after Harding had become senator that their friendship deepened. Sizing up the confused political situation in 1919–1920, Daugherty strongly urged Harding to enter the race and ignored his first negative responses. Contrary to later popular myth, neither Harding nor his wife sought the presidency, and even after Harding was swept along by the enthusiasm of his friends, Florence Harding remained opposed to his running. Although Daugherty later exaggerated his own role in the final decision—"I found him sunning himself, like a turtle on a log, and I pushed him into the water," he once bragged—Daugherty's insistence, along with the favorable circumstances and Harding's own belated ambition, did finally make him an active contender.

Even so, Harding's nomination required considerable luck. Later, when asked by reporters how he would describe his success in capturing the nomination, Harding replied, "We drew to a pair of deuces, and filled." There was much truth in this statement, since only a continued deadlock between front-runners Frank O. Lowden and General Leonard Wood at the convention itself kept open the way for an alternative. That possibility had already prompted Daugherty, who was running Harding's campaign headquarters, to woo both sides assiduously and to prophesy:

> When both realize they can't win, when they're hot and sweaty and discouraged, [they] will remember me and this little headquarters. They'll be like soldiers after a battle, who recall a shady spring along a country road, where they got a drink as they marched to the front. When they remember me that way, maybe both sides will turn to Harding.

Some four months before, Daugherty had made another prophetic statement that, in view of the Friday night activities at the convention (the height of the Lowden-Wood deadlock), gave birth to the smoke-filled-room myth. Said Daugherty:

> I don't expect Senator Harding to be nominated on the first, second or third ballot, but I think we can well afford to take chances that about eleven minutes after 2 o'clock on Friday morning at the convention, when fifteen or twenty men, somewhat weary, are sitting around a table, some one of them will say, "Who will we nominate?" At that decisive time the friends of Senator Harding can suggest him and can afford to abide by the result.

Such a meeting was in fact held on Friday night, 11 June 1920, in a hotel suite rented by the Republican party chairman, Will Hays, and attended by a circulating group of party leaders at which various alternatives to Wood and Lowden were discussed. Among those suggested was Warren Harding, although, contrary to some later accounts, this loosely formed and ever-changing meeting broke up before a consensus was reached. Representing neither a cabal nor a formal gathering, these Friday night discussions did set the stage for the continuation of a search for a solution on the floor of the convention on Saturday morning, which finally resulted in the nomination of the Ohioan on the tenth ballot. Given the circumstances, Harding's selection was no fluke. From the Friday deadlock on, he had emerged as the most available candidate.

Despite caveats in some quarters as to the wisdom of the convention's choice, it was generally agreed that Harding would make a strong candidate. With him on the ticket was Governor Calvin Coolidge of Massachusetts, who had gained widespread fame for his antiradical stand during the Boston police strike the year before.

Opposing Harding for the Democrats was another newspaper editor, James M. Cox, publisher of the *Dayton Daily News* and then governor of Ohio. Cox's running mate was the thirty-eight-year-old assistant secretary of the navy, Franklin D. Roosevelt, a New Yorker. Hampered by certain aggressive personality characteristics and by President Wilson's insistence that the campaign be a "great and solemn referendum" on the League, Cox failed to strike sparks with the public. War-to-peace conversion traumas, the soaring cost of living, widespread labor unrest, alleged radical subversion, and a threatening postwar recession also combined to promote a public desire for change.

Harding capitalized on all of these factors and ran an able campaign. Under the tutelage of Daugherty and other party advisers, he eschewed the temptation to tour the country "bloviating," as he described his free style of speechmaking. Instead, he stayed at home in Marion, reading carefully prepared speeches from his front porch to delegations that came to visit him from across the country. Contrary to some later assertions, Harding was the dominant figure in this campaign, making his own pronouncements, which often were specifically tailored to particular delegations. And the whole tone of the campaign was also distinctly his. The emphasis on pacification, on conciliation, on restoration, and on harmony was not characteristic of most of the aggressively anti-Wilson leaders of his party. Harding said, "America's present need is not heroics but healing, not nostrums but normalcy"—words that the public apparently wanted to hear in the 1920 campaign.

At least that is what the election returns showed on 2 November. It was an astonishing victory, and newspaper headlines groped for superlatives. Whether a result of Harding's own performance or a reaction against Wilsonism, the 16,181,289 votes for Harding, in contrast to the 9,141,750 votes for Cox, represented a resounding mandate. After savoring this victory for a month while on vacation in Texas and Panama, Harding returned to Marion in December to begin the task of selecting his official family. Great time and care were devoted to this job. Calling Marion "the Great Listening Post," Harding sought advice from all quarters and elicited suggestions from all factions. Even leading Democrats were requested by Harding to offer advice.

Presidential Appointments and Style

The result was a curious blend of the best and the worst in cabinet making. Harding shocked many old-guard supporters by naming Charles Evans Hughes, a proponent of the League of Nations, as his secretary of state. Harding considered him as having one of the "finest minds in the country." Similarly, he gave conservative Republicans "gooseflesh," as one phrased it, by appointing Herbert Hoover as secretary of commerce. Somewhat of a political maverick, Hoover was distrusted by a sizable number of powerful old-line Republican politicians, but Harding selected him over their protests because, as he explained to one of them, "I believe he's the smartest 'gink' I know." In another independent decision,

Harding chose Henry C. Wallace, editor of *Wallace's Farmer* and a member of one of the most famous farming families in the United States, as his secretary of agriculture.

Some of his other appointments were more to conservative liking. Andrew W. Mellon of Pittsburgh was given the nod for secretary of the treasury, a selection that delighted such old-guard stalwarts as senators Boies Penrose and Philander Knox of Pennsylvania. The post of secretary of war went to John Weeks of Massachusetts, who was sponsored by Senator Lodge. James J. Davis, an active union member, was made secretary of labor. Will Hays, chairman of the Republican National Committee, was offered the position of postmaster general. Edwin Denby, a former member of the House Naval Affairs Committee, was named secretary of the navy. Albert Fall, senator from New Mexico and a personal friend of Harding's, was given the job of secretary of the interior, despite the cries of some conservationists who were disturbed by his anticonservationist views.

Harding appointed his campaign manager and confidant, Harry Daugherty, as attorney general. Even some old-guard members balked at this selection, being concerned about Daugherty's questionable lobbying past. But Harding was adamant, once telling a disapproving Senator James W. Wadsworth of New York, "I have told [Daugherty] that he can have any place in my Cabinet he wants, outside of Secretary of State. He tells me that he wants to be Attorney General and by God he will be Attorney General!"

The change between the Wilson and the Harding administrations was immediately noticeable. Following a subdued and unostentatious inauguration, the Hardings threw open the White House gates, which had been closed in the last years of the Wilson administration, and quickly chased the gloom of the Wilson illness from the executive mansion. Portions of the White House were even opened to the public. Brighter colors were added to the furnishings and flowers appeared everywhere. Mrs. Harding reinstituted White House teas and gave three garden parties during the first summer. The president immediately restored regular White House press conferences, which Wilson had abandoned. Unquestionably, Harding had the best working relationship with the press of any chief executive in history.

It has often been said that the Hardings represented Main Street come to Washington. The Hardings did move into the White House with their small-town background and ideas intact. They did not hesitate to admit to being "just folks" or to practice small-town ways. To a critic like H. L. Mencken this seemed gauche, but to a majority of citizens it was welcomed as a breath of fresh air. The personality of the president contrasted markedly with that of his predecessor. Gregarious, affable, and handsome, Harding, in the parlance of his own time, "looked like a president." Standing a little over six feet tall and weighing 210 pounds, he had a high forehead, heavy square jaw, and calm, sympathetic gray eyes. His nose was large but in proportion with the rest of his face. He was vain about his person; his straight silver hair was always well brushed, his heavy dark eyebrows neatly trimmed. His suits were immaculate and well pressed, and he varied his dress considerably, more so than most presidents, to fit the occasion. Sometimes he dressed more "sporty" than Mrs. Harding liked.

Harding had a magnetic quality that made both men and women like him. His was not the charisma of a leader but the simple attractiveness of a friendly and engaging individual. Next to Lincoln, Harding was probably the most human man to occupy the White House. As one close associate put it, "W. G. always wore the human side of him out." Harding also had a temper that could vent itself in outbursts of profanity, but he always quickly repented and labeled such lapses with one of his favorite words—"unseemly." Kindliness, friendliness, and generosity were his most winning traits and undoubtedly sprang from his dislike of contention and disharmony and from his compulsive need for friends. Given these traits, it is not surprising that Harding placed a high value on loyalty. An acquaintance once said, "He liked politicians for the reason that he loved dogs, because they were usually loyal to their friends." Harding's fear of offending anyone, his desire to grant requests, and his indiscriminate loyalty placed him in constant danger. Harding's father once remarked that it was fortunate he was not a girl; he would have been in a family way all the time because he could not say no.

Although known at the time and not occasioning any particular adverse comment, certain of Harding's habits were later blown out of proportion and their impact on his presidency exaggerated. Harding liked to play poker and, as a senator, had had a group in every Saturday night for "food and action." After becoming president, he continued playing poker approximately once a week. Beginning sometime after dinner, these games rarely lasted beyond midnight and were for relaxation, not profit. Limited to eight at one sitting, the White House poker group had a fluid membership. Even Hoover and Hughes were invited to play. Later charges that the poker crowd "ran" the government or exercised a hypnotic influence over the president were untrue.

Harding's love of cards was matched by his love of golf. While president, Harding made every professional golfer who came to Washington give him a command performance. The first hint of spring found Harding out on the south grounds of the White House practicing tee shots. There Laddie Boy, a homely Airedale whose affection for Harding caused much comment in the press, chased and retrieved the president's practice balls. On the golf course, the dog was usually at his side while his master, despite all the practicing, struggled to break a hundred. It was fashionable to claim in later years that Harding spent all his time on the golf course, but, again, this was not true. The demands of the presidency clearly prevented him from playing the game as much as he would have liked. During his first two years in the White House, he did play about twice a week, but toward the end of his tenure, he barely had time to play at all.

Harding's drinking and smoking habits while he was in the White House were far more controversial. Harding used tobacco in all forms. He smoked two cigars a day, interspersed with a pipe and cigarettes. Harding also chewed, although he tapered off somewhat after entering the White House because of his wife's nagging. To many, chewing was a filthy habit, but not to Thomas Edison. Harding once shared a plug of tobacco with the famous inventor, causing Edison to remark, "Harding's all right. Any man who chews tobacco is all right."

More controversial was his use of liquor. Throughout his adult life Harding drank and saw nothing wrong in it. He was never personally committed to Prohibition, even though he had voted for it and, like many Americans, pretended the law did not apply to him. He was careful to serve liquor only in his private rooms in the White House and would sometimes take visitors there for that purpose. It was later claimed that Harding was a heavy drinker, although no one ever reported seeing him drunk. Still, such "sneaking around" by the president to break the law, when added to smoking, chewing, and poker playing, raised in some minds the specter of low-life carousals.

In the end, it was the quality of Harding's mind, as much as any personal habits or character traits, that limited his effectiveness as president. Wilson claimed he had a "bungalow mind," and to some extent this was true. Harding tended to accept the pat answer rather than reason through to a more sophisticated solution. His mental powers were undisciplined by hard thought, and he lived his life in the realm of clichés, maxims, and emotionally held opinions. He had never been required to study hard; neither were his closest associates and Senate colleagues noted for their intellectual prowess. Personality counted more with Harding than ideas.

Philosophical discussions and impersonal technical matters like economic theory did not appeal to him. There is no indication that he ever spent much time reading, although his personal library was rather well stocked. He did not possess a deep knowledge of public questions or of their foundations in history, economics, or law. He had managed quite well without such knowledge as a senator. But as president this limitation was constricting. A major difficulty during the Harding years was that the best people in his cabinet had to funnel their collective intelligence through his untrained and ambivalent mind. Sometimes Harding did not understand, other times he was too cautious, occasionally he was too fearful. Often he simply endorsed a solution worked out by others.

Domestic and Foreign Affairs

President Harding inherited from Wilson problems that even the wisest and best-trained chief executive would have found daunting. Calling Congress into special session in April 1921, he delivered to it perhaps the best speech of his career. Declaring that Congress should first turn to domestic problems and put "our own house in order," he mentioned not only increased tariff protection and lower taxes as prime issues but the necessity for a national budget system and economy in administration. He also called for agricultural legislation to help the farmer, construction of "a great merchant marine," encouragement of aviation for civil and military purposes, further development of radio and its effective regulation, passage of an anti-lynching law, and creation of a department of public welfare. With respect to foreign affairs, he expressed hope for some kind of an association of nations "binding us in conference and cooperation for the prevention of war," but he flatly declared that the United States should not enter the League of Nations. He stated that peace should quickly be established with all former enemies and that an orderly funding and liquidation of war debts should be undertaken.

Harding had fully expected to get along well with Congress, but he did not even enjoy a brief honeymoon. Difficulties with congressional leaders over priorities, continued animus emanating from the League struggle, the desire of some congressional leaders to reduce the presidency to a cipher, and Harding's own reluctance to exercise strong leadership combined to get his administration off to a slow start. Indeed, because of the squabbling and indecision, Congress was forced to remain in almost continuous session from April 1921 to September 1922 in order to complete its consideration of Harding's various proposals.

In June 1921, Congress did pass the Budget and Accounting Act, which met Harding's desire for a budget system and opened the way for economy in government administration. Harding's subsequent appointment of Charles Dawes, a Chicago banker, as budget director was a wise move, and under Dawes's leadership a savings of almost $1.5 billion was realized during the first year. In July, after skillful behind-the-scenes maneuvering by Secretary of State Hughes, Congress approved the Knox-Porter Resolution, ending the state of war with Austria and Germany; peace treaties were subsequently concluded with both countries and accepted by the Senate. Following weeks of wrangling over the size and nature of a tax cut and the successful intervention of Harding to prevent passage of a budget-busting soldiers' bonus, Congress finally endorsed the Revenue Act of 1921, reducing the surtax rate from 65 percent to 50 percent and providing for the ultimate elimination of the wartime excess-profits tax.

Under intense prodding from the farm bloc and with the approval of Harding and Secretary of Agriculture Wallace, by early 1922 Congress passed six farm bills that controlled discriminatory practices by packers and stockyard owners (Packers and Stockyards Act); regulated market contracts involving "puts and calls," "bids," and "offers" (Futures Trading Act); expanded the maximum size of rural loans (two amendments to the Farm Loan Act); provided new loans to farmers for the raising and marketing of livestock (Emergency Agriculture Credits Act); and protected farm cooperatives from the operation of the antitrust laws (Capper-Volstead Act).

Congress, reacting to the Harding administration's desire for an "America First" policy, passed

Warren G. Harding and his wife, Florence, share a light moment in the garden. THE LIBRARY OF CONGRESS

both the Tariff Act of 1921 (designed to be only a temporary measure) and the Fordney-McCumber Tariff Act of 1922, which increased for industry and agriculture the rates contained in the old Underwood-Simmons Tariff Act of 1913. Along this same line of protecting "America first," Congress enacted the Immigration Act of 1921, which restricted European migration annually to 3 percent of any nation's nationals living in the United States in 1910. This law resulted in a decrease in the number of admitted immigrants from 805,228 in 1921 to 309,556 in 1922.

Despite his various difficulties, Harding had reason to believe that his administration had acquitted itself rather well by the time of the fall congressional elections of 1922. He had quickly shown his humaneness and his desire for "normalcy" in 1921 by pardoning Eugene V. Debs, who had been placed in jail by the Wilson administration for antiwar activities, and by issuing a general amnesty for other political prisoners of the Red Scare period. Moreover, many of the requests contained in his opening speech in April 1921 had by 1922 been granted by Congress. Actually, the only one flatly rejected by that body was the one to create a new and expanded merchant marine. In the process of compiling this record, Harding and his administration had aroused considerable animosity. Harding's ineffective handling of a railroad shopmen's strike in the summer of 1922 and Attorney General Daugherty's recourse to the infamous Wilkerson injunction to break it enraged organized labor. Further, Daugherty's handling of certain war-related legal matters involving the Justice Department antagonized numerous other elements and kept alive suspicions regarding his competency. Patronage problems also continually plagued the administration, creating some severe internal disputes. But above all, Harding's consistent refusal to support a soldiers' bonus bill, together with his veto of one just prior to the fall elections, angered veterans' organizations and vote-seeking congressmen alike.

The elections of 1922, although not a total rebuff to the administration, did show serious reverses. Such Republican party stalwarts as senators Harry New, Porter J. McCumber, Frank B. Kellogg, and Miles Poindexter were defeated. In the Senate, the Republicans lost seven seats, cutting their majority from twenty-four to ten. In the House, the party lost seventy seats, reducing the Republican majority to twenty. Now more than ever, strong leadership was needed from the White House to keep the depleted Republican congressional ranks working together. There is evidence that Harding increasingly tried to provide it in his brief remaining time in office. But all such attempts would prove to be too little too late. For example, Harding failed once again in getting Congress to consider a merchant marine expansion bill. Congress also turned a deaf ear to his suggestions for a department of public welfare. Although he strongly supported the farm bloc in pushing for new agricultural credits, he demurred from its desire for some sort of direct government subsidy.

Harding's earlier appointment of William H. Taft as chief justice, along with his later selections of George Sutherland, Pierce Butler, and Edward T. Sanford as associate justices, indicated he was still "no friend" of organized labor and wanted the nation to remain "business safe" on economic matters. Further, while he continually supported the passage of an antilynching law (which Congress steadfastly refused to consider), he was not successful in promoting a greater degree of racial justice, and despite his many promises, his appointment policy was not especially pro-black. Finally, even though he officially backed Prohibition enforcement, his own drinking habits vitiated a consistent and forceful stand on the matter.

Some of the successes of Harding's administration by 1923 were as much a result of the efforts of his best cabinet appointees as of himself. Secretary of State Hughes masterminded the successful Washington Naval Disarmament Conference of 1921–1922, which resulted in a strengthening of the Open Door in the Pacific and a reduction in the navies of the United States, Great Britain, Japan, France, and Italy. Hughes also succeeded in improving strained relations with Mexico, left as a legacy from the Wilson years. With Harding's support, a program of military disengagement was begun in the Latin American and Caribbean areas, especially in the Dominican Republic and Haiti. A "heart balm" of $25 million was given to Colombia to atone for precipitate American action in the Panamanian revolution of twenty years before, and in 1922–1923 a Central American conference, held in Washington, began a redefinition of the Monroe Doctrine. Amid trying circumstances, Hughes also formalized the funding of European World War I debts to the United States and secured the necessary congressional agreement. Neither Hughes nor Harding was able to convince the Senate that the United States should join the World Court.

Secretary Hoover added luster to the administration by his skillful handling of the Commerce Department. The successful Unemployment Conference of 1921, whose efforts enabled the nation to weather the last stages of the postwar recession, was essentially Hoover's idea. Hoover's attempts to rejuvenate American overseas trade, his drive for the standardization of measures and products, and his promotion of industrial and scientific research helped restore prosperity and achieve the president's goal of benefiting business. Hoover's initiation of aviation and radio regulations and his cooperation with Harding in forcing an eight-hour day on the steel industry were also major contributions to the Harding years.

Scandals and Illness

Despite his belated attempts at more effective executive leadership and some rather impressive administration successes, Harding found the presidency to be an increasing burden from the summer of 1922 on. He liked the pomp, the ceremony, the attention, and the glitter of the office. But continuing labor strife, protracted wrangling with Congress, squabbling over patronage, mounting Prohibition enforcement problems, concern over the fall election reverses, and the need for constant executive decisions—in short, the magnitude of his presidential responsibilities—threatened to overwhelm him. His old friends found him more solemn and less buoyant around the poker table. He once remarked to the National Press Club, "I never find myself done.. . . I don't believe there is a human being who can do all the work there is to be done in the President's office. It seems as though I have been President for twenty years." From the fall of 1922 on, he spoke increasingly of the day when he could return to Ohio, and once, in an off-the-cuff statement, he declared, "A great many people think it is a fine thing to be President. . . . But I know better, and I would like nothing better than to be a Marionite again."

By the fall of 1922, Harding's growing mental depression rested not merely on political factors nor on the demands of the presidency; his own personal problems had begun to mount. Mrs. Harding, who had lost a kidney a number of years before, suddenly became ill with hydronephritis in late August, and for a time her life hung in the balance. Not long after, his own health began to disintegrate. A severe flu attack that felled him in mid-January 1923 seemed to trigger a visible decline. By April he was complaining that he barely had enough energy to complete nine holes rather than the usual eighteen on his infrequent trips to the golf course. By late spring of 1923, his normally ruddy color had become a pallor and his stamina was at low ebb. He told Hughes at that time that his blood pressure was consistently above 175, which caused the secretary of state to tell his wife, "We have been worrying about Mrs. Harding, but I think it is the President we should be more concerned about."

Harding had other worries. Scandals of serious import were beginning to be rumored in the spring of 1923. Attorney General Daugherty and his activities lay at the root of some of this concern. Several attempts had already been made by Daugherty's enemies, both inside and outside Congress, to force his retirement from the administration. One congressional investigation into the Justice Department had come to naught in January 1923, but it had not deterred many from thinking that despite the lack of damaging evidence, Daugherty was a serious liability to the administration.

Ironically, the first truly disturbing situation arose over Charles Forbes, director of the Veterans Bureau, and not over Daugherty. Appointed by Harding on a whim, Forbes had illegally been selling government supplies from the medical supply base at Perryville, Maryland, to private contractors and at ridiculously low prices. He also was engaged in undercover deals relating to hospital building contracts and site selections. His accomplice in these matters was Charles F. Cramer, general counsel of the Veterans' Bureau.

Brigadier General Charles E. Sawyer, Harding's personal physician and longtime Ohio friend, first suspected Forbes's motives in handling bureau business and voiced his fears to Daugherty, who passed them along to Harding. Shaken by these disclosures, Harding finally summoned Forbes to the White House, grabbed him by the throat "as a dog would a rat," and shouted at him, "You double-crossing bastard!" No record remains of the rest of the conversation, but evidently Harding demanded his resignation, giving him the opportunity to leave the country first. Forbes hastily booked passage for Europe and, once there, resigned on 15 February.

Forbes's resignation took on a more sinister meaning when, on 14 March, Cramer committed suicide by putting a .45-caliber bullet through his right temple while standing before his bathroom mirror in his Washington, D.C., home. At the time, all the public and the press were told was that Cramer had been depressed because of "recent financial reverses."

The Forbes resignation and the Cramer suicide provided natural grist for Washington's rumor mills, but their impact was eclipsed by the sudden death of Jess W. Smith ten weeks later. A diabetic with flabby jowls, scraggly mustache, and large, pleading brown eyes made larger by black, round shell-rimmed glasses, Smith was Harry Daugherty's private secretary and general factotum. As such, he was also a friend of Harding's. Living with Daugherty in the attorney general's Wardman Park Hotel apartment, Smith had used his close contact with the administration to engineer his own scams, which involved the selling of liquor licenses, the granting of paroles, and the arrangement for other types of "fixes."

Helping Smith was a small group of petty scoundrels, collectively known as the Ohio Gang, who used a "little green house on K Street" as a kind of racket headquarters. Just how much of this activity was known to Harding prior to Smith's death is conjecture. But he knew enough to have a long and emotional argument with Smith at the White House on the day before Smith died. Early the next morning

Smith was found slumped on the floor in his bedroom in Daugherty's apartment, still clad in his pajamas, his head in a wastebasket, a pistol in his hand, and a bullet through his temple. The assistant White House physician, Dr. Joel T. Boone, told the press that Smith had had a very severe case of diabetes, had not fully recovered from an appendicitis operation of a year before, and in a state of depression had killed himself.

These events, along with Harding's declining health, did not provide an auspicious background for a much-publicized presidential trip to Alaska in mid-June 1923. The decision to make this trip rested on both medical and political grounds. No fewer than five cabinet officers and twenty-eight bureaus exercised authority over the territory, and the president hoped that a firsthand inspection would help him resolve some of these conflicts. His doctors thought a vacation from the cares of Washington would do him some good.

Later it was claimed that the whole Alaskan venture was suffused with a sense of foreboding and that there was morbid talk of death. The Forbes, Cramer, and Smith tragedies, coupled with Harding's sudden decision to sell the *Marion Star* just before his departure, added credence to these contentions. But if there was no air of morbidity about the presidential party, it was subdued by the realization that the president was very tired and appeared nervous and worried.

During the outward-bound phase of the journey, Harding seemed to recapture some of his old bounce. According to Hoover, as they neared Alaska, Harding displayed the attitude "of a school boy entering on a holiday." Still, Hoover recalled that on the way north Harding once asked him in the privacy of the presidential cabin what Hoover would do if he were president and knew of a scandal brewing. Hoover replied, "Publish it, and at least get credit for integrity on your side." When Hoover pressed for particulars, Harding mumbled something about irregularities in the Justice Department and then "abruptly dried up." When the party turned south toward home, the president became noticeably more morose and his nervousness again increased. By the time he arrived in Vancouver on 26 July, it was obvious that he was again entirely exhausted, and members of the presidential party were deeply alarmed.

A day later, as his train moved down the west coast toward San Francisco, the president complained of pains in the upper abdominal region. By the time the train reached San Francisco, it was clear that he had a cardiac malfunction. Put to bed in the Palace Hotel, he was apparently on the mend when, on the evening of 2 August, while his wife was reading to him from the *Saturday Evening Post*, he suffered an acute coronary artery occlusion, otherwise known as an infarct. In any case, death was instantaneous.

The ensuing cross-country funeral procession allowed Warren Harding for the moment to achieve his goal of being one of America's best-loved presidents. Hundreds of thousands of grieving citizens lined the tracks, singing softly his favorite hymns, "Onward, Christian Soldiers" and "Lead, Kindly Light," as his flag-draped casket, displayed in a specially designed railroad car, passed slowly by. Back in Washington, his coffin was placed in the center of the Capitol rotunda at the exact spot where Lincoln had lain in state. Ten truckloads of flowers lined the walls as thirty-five thousand mourners filed by and another twenty thousand waited in vain outside in lines that were four abreast. Similar scenes were repeated at his burial ceremony in Marion a day later.

Historical Legacy

Death should have brought Warren Harding's problems to an end, but in some respects they were just beginning. Even while the press was eulogizing him as a "man of peace," "an ideal American," and "the greatest commoner since Lincoln," events were in motion that would destroy the Harding reputation almost completely. The general outline of the Harding scandals was known to only a few at the time of his death, but this knowledge spread quickly after his demise. Within three months of his burial, a Senate investigation into the Veterans Bureau uncovered Charles Forbes's improprieties, resulting in his conviction and a two-year jail sentence.

Before this investigation was completed, another was begun into unconfirmed rumors of alleged "oil deals" involving top Harding officials. Centering on Secretary of the Interior Albert Fall, this Senate probe unearthed evidence of the transfer of certain oil reserve lands (the most famous being Teapot Dome in Wyoming) from the Navy Department to the Department of the Interior. Fall then had leased them for development to two oil men, Harry F. Sinclair and Edward L. Doheny, without competitive bids. Fall was later convicted of bribery and conspiracy to defraud the government, and was sentenced to a year in jail and a $100,000 fine. Secretary of the Navy Charles Denby, while not a party to the granting of the leases or the exchange of bribes, was finally forced out of the cabinet because of his naïveté and stupidity.

Far more sensational was the final investigation growing out of the Harding years, one involving Daugherty and the Justice Department. Begun by the Senate in March 1924, it clearly established the perfidy and machinations of Jess Smith and the Ohio Gang, but it was not able to establish "beyond doubt" Daugherty's rumored involvement in these activities. A fortuitous fire destroyed the records in Daugherty's brother's bank in Washington Court House (where the attorney general and Jess Smith kept a joint account) and eliminated evidence that might have proved crucial. Nonetheless, some witnesses (most of them admittedly unreliable and one even known to be a perjurer) told tales of bacchanalian orgies at the little green house on K Street in which both Daugherty and Harding allegedly took part. In the end, the only government official to be convicted as a result of this investigation was Colonel Thomas W. Miller, alien property custodian, who had accepted bribes arranged by Jess Smith to illegally transfer a German-owned American subsidiary to an American firm. He ultimately served eighteen months in jail and paid a $5,000 fine. Daugherty, in turn, went through two trials in 1926–1927, the first ending in a hung jury and the second declaring him not guilty because of insufficient evidence.

All of this naturally raised questions about Harding's own involvement in the scandals. It was difficult for many to believe that the president was not somehow connected with this skulduggery. Even if he were not personally involved, most citizens believed that he must have known about it. Actually, he did not know about Fall, but as we have seen, he did know about Forbes and Smith and had done nothing to expose their corruption. In any case, continued doubts and uncertainties left Harding's reputation badly tarnished.

But it was also Harding's own questionable past that further damaged whatever reputable image he might otherwise have retained. In 1927 there appeared a book entitled *The President's Daughter*, written by Nan Britton, a former Marionite who was years younger than the dead president. In this book, Britton claimed that Harding had fathered a child by her in 1919 and that their illicit contact had contin-

ued on into the presidential years. Rumors also circulated that Harding had had extramarital relations with still another Marion woman who was the wife of one of the town's leading businessmen.

There is considerable doubt that Harding was the father of Nan's child, because medical evidence exists to indicate that he was probably sterile. There is some possibility that the two of them may have maintained a relationship during his senatorial career, but it most certainly did not extend into the White House period. There is no doubt whatever that Harding and Mrs. Carrie Phillips, the businessman's wife, did maintain an intimate relationship for a number of years prior to his becoming a senator.

Whatever the precise truth surrounding these various relationships, they, together with the corrosive effect of the scandals, produced a devastating reaction that prompted much muckraking and mythmaking. Wholly fictional exposés of Harding's life and his alleged carousals now made the rounds. So did increasingly exaggerated stories of the activities of the Ohio Gang. As a result, rumors about Harding's private life and knowledge about the scandals remained, while many of the achievements of the administration were lost to view.

Unjustifiable in some respects as the final verdict may be, Warren Harding must bow to the adverse judgment of history. Extramarital matters aside, fatal flaws obviously existed not only in some of the friends around him, but in Harding himself. Kindliness, friendliness, generosity, and loyalty are not necessarily bad traits for a president to have, but in the case of Harding they were liabilities. Under the circumstances, he probably should never have sought the presidency, and a more discerning electorate would not have elected him.

As it was, throughout the remainder of the 1920s, Warren Harding represented an acute embarrassment for the nation and the Republican party. The great colonnaded marble monument that was erected to him outside of Marion through contributions from his friends immediately following his death stood undedicated because no major Republican figure had the nerve to appear there. Fittingly, President Herbert Hoover, a man who owed much to Harding, finally screwed up his courage, journeyed to Marion in the summer of 1931, and delivered a brief dedicatory address. Standing before a battery of microphones and with Harry Daugherty seated on the platform directly behind him, Hoover faced the issue squarely:

> Here was a man whose soul was seared by a great disillusionment.. . . Harding had a dim realization that

he had been betrayed by a few of the men whom he had trusted, by men whom he believed were his devoted friends. It was later proved in the courts of the land that these men had betrayed not only the friendship and trust of their staunch and loyal friend but that they had betrayed their country. That was the tragedy of the life of Warren Harding.

Perhaps no better or more judicious epitaph for the Harding years exists.

BIBLIOGRAPHY

The Harding papers belong to the Ohio Historical Society and are housed in the Ohio Historical Museum Building in Columbus, Ohio. Samuel H. Adams, *Incredible Era: The Life and Times of Warren Gamaliel Harding* (Boston, 1939), the best-known biography of Harding, is badly flawed because of its emphasis on the scandals and its frequent elevation of rumor to fact. Randolph C. Downes, *The Rise of Warren Gamaliel Harding, 1865–1920* (Columbus, Ohio, 1970), is an exhaustive scholarly treatment of Harding's prepresidential career, based mainly on local Ohio primary sources. Francis Russell, *The Shadow of Blooming Grove: Warren G. Harding in His Times* (New York, 1968), a highly impressionistic biography, places undue emphasis on Harding's extramarital affairs and private traumas.

Andrew Sinclair, *The Available Man: The Life Behind the Masks of Warren Gamaliel Harding* (New York, 1965), is the first attempt to revise the image of Harding as a politician and president following the opening of the Harding papers in 1964. Robert K. Murray, *The Harding Era: Warren G. Harding and His Administration* (Minneapolis, 1969), the most detailed and scholarly work on Harding's presidency, is based largely on manuscripts, including the Harding papers. Eugene P. Trani and David L. Wilson, *The Presidency of Warren G. Harding* (Lawrence, Kans., 1977), represents a relatively brief distillation of the latest scholarship on the Harding administration, relying especially on Sinclair and Murray. Harry M. Daugherty (in collaboration with Thomas Dixon), *The Inside Story of the Harding Tragedy* (New York, 1932), is a sometimes factual, more often fanciful, defense of Harding and Daugherty and their activities, written in reply to Nan Britton's book and Hoover's dedicatory address of 1931. Also see Robert H. Ferrell, *The Strange Deaths of President Harding* (Columbia, Mo., 1996).

Recent works include Carl Sferrazza Anthony, *Florence Harding: The First Lady, the Jazz Age, and the Death of America's Most Scandalous President* (New York, 1998), and John A. Morello, *Selling the President, 1920: Albert D. Lasker, Advertising, and the Election of Warren G. Harding* (Westport, Conn., 2001).

For further sources consult Richard G. Frederick, comp., *Warren G. Harding: A Bibliography* (Westport, Conn., 1992).

Calvin Coolidge

Donald R. McCoy

Calvin Coolidge THE LIBRARY OF CONGRESS

CALVIN COOLIDGE, a shrewd, taciturn, and publicly dignified New Englander, occupied the presidency during the generally prosperous and peaceful period from August 1923 to March 1929. The variety of his accomplishments in the White House was impressive even if their substance was not.

Born in Plymouth Notch, Vermont, on 4 July 1872, he was named John Calvin Coolidge after his father, variously a teacher, storekeeper, farmer, mechanic, and politician, doing whatever would contribute to his modest prosperity. Calvin's mother, Victoria Moor Coolidge, a handsome woman and a lover of poetry and nature, died when the boy was twelve.

Calvin Coolidge's childhood was simple and idealistic. Although his religious ideas were vague, he was taught to believe in a divine intelligence that imposed upon man a duty to give public service. In rugged, rural Vermont, he acquired the attributes of caution, fairness, frugality, honesty, industry, reliability, tolerance, and unpretentiousness. He clung to these qualities throughout his life, and they stood him well in his rise to the presidency. Calvin was the first of the Vermont Coolidges to attend college, going to Amherst College in Amherst, Massachusetts. His Amherst years strengthened his conviction that harmony and stability were essential in the affairs of society. The college also helped him to develop into something of a gentleman, a scholar, an occasionally droll fellow, and an adequate speaker.

After being graduated cum laude from Amherst in 1895, Coolidge read law with John Hammond and Henry Field in Northampton. He was admitted to the bar two years later, after which he opened a law office in Northampton, which he considered his home for the rest of his life. Although he never achieved eminence or riches at the bar, Coolidge was able to earn enough as a lawyer to become financially independent of his father.

Early Career

The law was only Coolidge's first profession. His second career was politics, which satisfied his craving for civic service and supplemented his income. He found his entry into politics easy because his father had been a frequent officeholder in Vermont and because his legal mentors, Hammond and Field, were political leaders in Northampton. In 1896, Coolidge became active in the local Republican party, and in 1898 he was elected to the Northampton city council. From then on, his progress up the political ladder was almost constant. He became city solicitor in 1900, clerk of the Hampshire county courts in 1903, and chairman of Northampton's Republican committee in 1904. Coolidge suffered his only defeat at the polls when he ran for school committeeman in 1905.

That was the year Coolidge married Grace Anna Goodhue, a teacher in Northampton's Clarke Institute for the Deaf. The quiet Coolidge hoped that this charming young woman "having taught the deaf to hear, . . . might perhaps cause the mute to speak." Grace Coolidge was a vivacious, good-humored woman of varied interests who was willing to follow her husband's lead in all things. As such, she was the perfect helpmeet for her affectionate but domestically autocratic mate. Their first son, John, was born in 1906, and another, Calvin, in 1908.

Coolidge resumed his advancement up the political ladder in 1906 with his election to the Massachusetts House of Representatives, where during his two terms he established a mildly progressive legislative record. His ability to appeal unostentatiously to varied ethnic, religious, and economic interests was confirmed in 1909 when he became mayor of Northampton. In 1911, Coolidge was elected to the Massachusetts Senate, where for the first time he attracted notice on the state scene by helping to arrange a fair settlement of the great textile strike in Lawrence. Re-

elected to the state senate in 1912 and 1913, he was chosen president of that body in 1914, becoming the most prominent Republican holding state office. Coolidge performed effectively as senate president in 1914 and 1915, advising his colleagues to "do the day's work" and "be brief." In 1915 he was elected lieutenant governor.

Coolidge gave insight into his political success in a letter to a friend in 1915: "I think I have a reputation of being conservative, which I am, because I do not make so loud a noise as some others. I think I have been in sympathy with practically all legislation intended to improve living conditions." This could be translated into Coolidge's creed throughout his political career: something for everyone so long as it did not cost too much. Add to this the fact that he was a man who got along with almost everybody, who was compassionate with ordinary people while identifying with the well-to-do, and who was effective as an officeholder and remarkably shrewd in his political timing, and one has a politician who, while few could be enthusiastic about him, was acceptable to the majority.

After three years in the lieutenant governorship, Coolidge, recognized as a loyal, astute, and effective wheelhorse of his party in Massachusetts, had acquired enough support to run successfully for governor in 1918. He proved an able governor, one adept at riding the tides of the stormy post–World War I period, in part by skillfully manipulating the platitudes that he believed in and that people wanted to hear. He labored to hold down the escalating cost of living, to increase supplies of items in short supply, to penalize profiteers, to encourage reasonable pay increases, and to settle labor disputes. He successfully advocated ratification of the Nineteenth Amendment (for woman suffrage) and restriction of the workweek of women and children, among other reform measures. Moreover, Coolidge was instrumental in the efficient reorganization of the state's government.

His national reputation did not derive from such accomplishments but from his identification with settling the highly publicized Boston police strike of 1919. The police of Boston had serious grievances, which the authorities largely ignored. Thus, in September 1919 the police walked off their jobs, and disorder came to the Massachusetts capital. Coolidge did not intervene in the situation until peace had been substantially restored. Then the governor took command of the various forces that had been brought into Boston to maintain order. He upheld the police commissioner in refusing to allow the strikers to return to their jobs. When Samuel Gompers, president of the American Federation of Labor, contested him, Coolidge wrote to him, "There is no right to strike against the public safety by anybody, anywhere, any time." For this, during a time when disorder seemed to threaten the nation, Coolidge received America's acclaim. Moreover, that fall he was overwhelmingly reelected governor.

In 1920, Coolidge became a candidate for the Republican presidential nomination, but the efforts on his behalf amounted to little more than a favorite-son movement. After a sharp contest among many candidates, the Republican convention finally nominated Senator Warren G. Harding of Ohio for president. The delegates, in a surprise move, chose the Massachusetts governor to run for vice president. The Harding-Coolidge ticket won a landslide victory that November over Democrats James M. Cox and Franklin D. Roosevelt. As vice president, Coolidge was unimpressive. He sat in on cabinet meetings, but he played no significant role in the Harding administration. He was an uninspiring presiding officer of the Senate, and his speeches were little noted. By 1923, Coolidge was little more than a cipher on the national political scene.

Succession to Presidency

All that quickly changed. President Harding died the evening of 2 August 1923, and Coolidge was thus catapulted from relative obscurity to instant prominence. Senator Henry Cabot Lodge of Massachusetts exclaimed, "My God! That means Coolidge is President!" In a dramatic ritual in his Vermont home, John Coolidge, who was a notary public, swore in his son as the new president by the light of an oil lamp at 2:47 A.M. on 3 August. Calvin Coolidge left for Washington a few hours later to assume his new duties. The style of the presidency would change, if not the administration's basic principles.

Calvin and Grace Coolidge would present a great contrast to their immediate predecessors. The extrovert Harding had worked and played hard, and mixed with people of questionable integrity, while his wife, Florence, had presided over the White House in an imperious, brittle manner. William Allen White wrote in 1925, Coolidge was "not like the run of the herd." The new president was frugal with words, money, and action; easily fatigued; unostenta-

tious; cautious, even secretive; and very much a private person. He had little time for those who were pretentious or of questionable character. His sense of humor was keen, but it was pointed. One example of it was his response to a woman who told him, "I made a bet today that I could get more than two words out of you." "You lose," Coolidge retorted. All this made him into a capital character, "Silent Cal," the man whose idea of a perfect day was one during which absolutely nothing happened. It also made the atmosphere of the White House after Harding, as Alice Roosevelt Longworth observed, "as different as a New England front parlor is from a backroom in a speakeasy."

There was, in fact, more to Coolidge than this. He could be kind, particularly with ordinary people. He could be talkative and loving with his family. If he was sparing in his activities, he did focus his attention conscientiously on public business. If he believed that the government should not act unless necessary, he also believed that when it did act, it should act well. Little of this made him seem less angular, but it did encourage public awareness that Coolidge was doing his job. Moreover, Grace Coolidge was a charming, enthusiastic, and popular First Lady. Although she was limited by the president's control of her schedule and of White House functions, she was an effective counterpoint to her husband's taciturnity, as was the attractiveness of their two teenage sons, John and Calvin. Young Calvin's death in July 1924 from a foot infection stunned the nation and the family, especially the president. The country's outpouring of sympathy was no substitute for the Coolidge family's loss.

Administrative Style

Coolidge's administrative technique was simple, direct, and effective. After consulting with appropriate parties, he laid down the policies that he thought the federal government should follow. He made it clear that he expected his subordinates in the executive branch to do their jobs within those guidelines. He expected appointed officials to run their operations efficiently and economically. If they could not do these things, and do them well, Coolidge impressed upon them that he would find people who could. For civil servants, the president relied heavily on the concept of the merit system in recruitment, retention, and promotion. He made it clear, therefore, that he expected meritorious performance from those who had the security of a federal civil service position. Thanks to his reiterations of these points, Coolidge usually received excellent service from those employed in the executive branch.

In all this, Coolidge made good use of his power of appointment. Equally important, he effectively employed the Budget and Accounting Act of 1921 and the agency established to administer this law, the Bureau of the Budget. The legislation had for the first time given the president substantial control over the appropriations requests of executive agencies and even over their spending of funds, enabling Coolidge to keep a tight rein on the funds, personnel, and programs of the various agencies and therefore on the system of rewards and punishments. Compared to later presidents, he did not have a great deal to administer, but what he did have he administered very well.

Coolidge also proved to be effective at publicizing his policies and activities. Central to this was his regularization of press conferences—his only innovation as president—which he usually held twice a week. Although Coolidge manipulated the news in his press conferences, he made himself a valuable and steady, though normally off-the-record, source of copy. His ability to establish an admirable rapport with news people was to help Coolidge considerably during the 1924 election campaign as well as throughout his presidency.

Coolidge came to the presidency with three obvious disadvantages. First, except for Secretary of War John Weeks of Massachusetts, he was not well acquainted with any of the members of the cabinet. Second, the cabinet he inherited varied considerably in quality. And, third, as a vice president succeeding to the presidency, Coolidge did not feel free to discharge summarily any of Harding's appointees. The new president set out methodically to become acquainted with his chief subordinates and their programs. Moreover, he made it plain to them that he was delegating considerable authority and responsibility to them as well as expecting them to he successful in doing their jobs. He emphasized that he would rely heavily upon them for information and advice, which he expected to be well considered.

This was a good start, but not good enough, considering the character of Harding's appointees. Some, such as Secretary of State Charles Evans Hughes, were outstanding by any measure. Others, such as Secretary of the Treasury Andrew Mellon, easily found accommodation with the new chief executive. Still others were able but independent, such as Secretary of Agriculture Henry C. Wallace. Coolidge's great problem would be with those who would prove to be embarrassments, such as Harding's close associate, Attorney General Harry M. Daugherty. These embarrassments would prove to be substantial, and soon in coming. They pointed up the flaw in the new president's idea: "If you see ten troubles coming down the road, you can be sure that nine will run into the ditch before they reach you and you will have to battle with only one of them."

Scandal

Scandal had touched the Harding administration before the president's death, in the form of massive corruption in the Veterans Bureau and the Office of the Alien Property Custodian. Harding had fired the head of the Veterans Bureau, who later was sent to prison, as was the alien-property custodian. After Coolidge became president, members of Congress probed for the weaker links around Harding. They found them by early 1924.

Senate investigators discovered a remarkable pattern of ineptitude and corruption revolving around Attorney General Daugherty. Sufficient evidence was never found to convict him of anything, but the revelations quickly siphoned off public and official confidence in the attorney general. Coolidge believed that he could not ask Daugherty, especially as Harding's favorite, to resign just on the grounds that he was an embarrassment. Soon Daugherty went beyond the pale when he refused in his own defense to open the files of the Justice Department to Senate investigators. The president could not allow Daugherty to act both as attorney general and as his own defense counsel. "These two positions," Coolidge wrote, "are incompatible and cannot be reconciled." Therefore, on 27 March he demanded that Daugherty resign. Coolidge replaced him with an Amherst friend, Harlan F. Stone, a former dean of the Columbia University Law School.

An even greater scandal had developed earlier in 1924. Senate investigations indicated that oil magnates Harry F. Sinclair and Edward Doheny had bribed Albert Fall, while he was interior secretary, in order to gain leasing rights to the government's Teapot Dome oil reserve in Wyoming and Elk Hills oil reserve in California. Many Democrats and dissident Republicans had a field day with this, and attacks on the administration quickly became vituperative.

Soon there were those who charged that the entire cabinet and even Coolidge had been involved in the oil transactions that had taken place during the Harding administration. President Coolidge remained calm in the face of mounting accusations. He acted quickly, though not precipitately.

While others were hastily arriving at judgments of guilt, Coolidge decided on 26 January to appoint two special counsel, one a Republican and the other a Democrat, to investigate the situation and to take appropriate action. His timing was impeccable, for the Senate was on the verge of taking more extreme action. His appointees, Owen J. Roberts and Atlee Pomerene, were perfect, for they had the professional expertise necessary to conduct an investigation that was neither a whitewash nor a flurry of vindictiveness. Because of their work, Fall was convicted for receiving bribes and so became the first cabinet member sent to prison for misconduct in office. Sinclair was found guilty of contempt of court. Moreover, the Teapot Dome and Elk Hills oil leases were canceled after exhaustive judicial proceedings. The investigations also revealed that Democrats as well as Republicans had been involved in the scandal.

This was not all that resulted from the Teapot Dome and Elk Hills scandal. Much of the investigation of Daugherty stemmed from it. Then, in February 1924, Secretary of the Navy Edwin Denby was forced from office by Senate pressures, although there was no evidence that he was culpable of wrongdoing. Coolidge had refused to ask for his resignation, making clear that he would not "sacrifice any innocent man [or] retain in office any unfit man for my own welfare." Denby volunteered his resignation so that he would not be a burden to the president. Coolidge made a good choice for the new navy secretary in Curtis D. Wilbur, chief justice of the California Supreme Court.

Denby's resignation led the administration's Democratic and Republican critics to try to connect the leadership of the executive branch, including Coolidge, with the oil scandal. Indeed, they sought to find scandal in other situations, especially the Treasury Department's handling of tax rebates to business and Henry Ford's proposal to develop federal property at Muscle Shoals, Alabama. The first of these succeeded in embarrassing its Senate sponsor more than the Treasury Department; the second led to extended debate over the development of Muscle Shoals and Ford's withdrawal of his proposal, but not to a scandal. In all, Coolidge handled the situation masterfully and with little help from the generally timid Republican regulars in Congress. He kept his head while his critics often lost theirs, and he acted as much to retain his self-respect as to win the next election. Moreover, the president benefited from the fact that the investigations demonstrated that, as Charles Evans Hughes said, "corruption knows no party."

The Election of 1924

Coolidge would reap an abundant political harvest from the way in which he met the charges of scandal. He emerged not only as a man of probity but also of coolness under fire. This explains much of the attractiveness of his chief campaign slogan in 1924, "Keep Cool with Coolidge." He apparently had decided soon after he succeeded to the presidency to run for election to the office in his own right. This seemed confirmed by his appointment of C. Bascom Slemp, a professional politician and former Virginia congressman, as his chief White House secretary. Although Coolidge had no significant power base outside Massachusetts, he quickly acquired a team of supporters who worked effectively in raising campaign funds and enlisting convention delegates for him. Moreover, it was his good fortune that by January 1924, Senator Hiram Johnson of California was the only prominent Republican who was striving to contest with him their party's presidential nomination. The crucial showdown between Coolidge and Johnson came in May 1924. Then the president defeated the senator in his home state in the primary election, thanks largely to the efforts of another Californian, Commerce Secretary Herbert C. Hoover. Coolidge was easily nominated by the Republican National Convention in June.

The only mistake of the president's supporters was that they got their wires crossed as to who should be nominated for vice president. The convention delegates took advantage of this to choose a former Illinois governor, Frank O. Lowden, who refused the nomination. The delegates then selected another Illinois figure, the banker Charles G. Dawes, who had recently returned from a highly publicized mission to resuscitate the economy of Germany.

The Democrats in 1924 had a seemingly perfect campaign issue in Teapot Dome, but they managed to carry it too far in both their logic and language. Moreover, their national convention was bitterly divided over issues such as oil-tainted Democrats (of whom there were not supposed to be any), Prohibition, and the Ku Klux Klan. During the record-setting 103 ballots it took the Democratic delegates to agree on a presidential nominee, they laid bare every weakness in their party and knocked out of contention every well-known candidate for the nomination. Their nominee was a relatively obscure Wall Street lawyer from West Virginia, a "dry," John W. Davis, whose running mate, Governor Charles Bryan of Nebraska, seemed to contradict much that Davis stood for. Republican Senator Robert M. La Follette of Wisconsin also ran for president, on the Progressive ticket, with Democratic Senator Burton K. Wheeler of Montana as his vice presidential nominee.

Coolidge's strategy in the 1924 campaign was to stick to presidential business and to ride the rising economic trend. He let Dawes, a colorful and energetic speaker, point up the flaws in their opponents. The conservative Davis was unable either to present much of a contrast to Coolidge or to pull his party together; the aging La Follette succeeded in attracting votes from the Democrats as well as the Republicans, but not in matching the strength of the major parties. The president won election handily, polling 15,718,211 votes to 8,385,283 for Davis and 4,831,289 for La Follette. The electoral vote was divided 382–136–13.

The Early Coolidge Program

During his first fifteen months in office, Calvin Coolidge had shown himself to be an astute administrator and politician. This quality, as well as his basic conservatism, affected his policies. He had no serious disagreement with the policies of the Harding administration. Equally important, he believed that disaster would be visited on an "acting president" who made any wrenching changes in the course being sailed by the administration or the country. Coolidge was fully committed to seeking efficient and economical government. For him, this did not mean cutting back on existing programs, only in making them more effective. He could further cut federal taxes and the national debt in the belief that this would promote the nation's prosperity. This would be augmented by encouragement of business development, for the president believed that the "chief business of the American people is business." Yet Coolidge, no less than Harding, was interested in making changes, however modest.

In Coolidge's first message to Congress, on 6 December 1923, he had called for a moderate develop-ment of flood control, reforestation, electric power, and transportation facilities; the strengthening of the civil service; encouragement of farm cooperatives; and increased regulation of labor disputes, Alaskan fisheries, coastal water pollution, radio, and aviation. He showed his concern for black Americans by requesting action against lynching, increased support of their education, and establishment of a commission to seek harmony between the races in industrial areas. Immigration should be restricted, for, as he knew the great majority of members of Congress agreed, "America must be kept American." Whereas Harding had talked of establishing a federal department of welfare, Coolidge called for a department to encourage character development and education among the people. He also proposed constitutional amendments to set a minimum wage for women and to restrict child labor in industrial employment. All this, of course, was to be achieved within the guideline of having a surplus of federal revenues to apply to reducing the national debt.

The foreign policy goals that Coolidge outlined in his first message to Congress differed little from Harding's. Coolidge reiterated that the United States would not join the League of Nations, although he requested American membership on the World Court. The United States would not cancel the debts of other countries to it, although the administration was willing to negotiate further the terms of those obligations. There would be no recognition of the Soviet Union until it made amends for its perceived transgressions. The merit system should be extended to the nation's foreign service personnel. Overall, there would be a continuation of the Harding administration's foreign policy of promoting peace, goodwill among nations, commercial friendship, and negotiation of disputes. In large part, Coolidge asked Congress for what his executive agencies had recommended. He was to get little of it because of the preoccupation of senators and representatives with questions of scandal in 1924.

Relations with Congress

Coolidge tried valiantly to get along with members of Congress. He was solicitous of the suggestions on legislation and appointments of the Republicans on Capitol Hill. Moreover, he would listen to Democrats who sought his ear. He was cordial to most members of Congress, even to many who embarrassed and opposed him. And the Coolidges so often played host to senators and representatives that the White House sometimes resembled a congressional club. Yet, however shrewd the president was in administration and electoral politics, he was seldom able to achieve harmony with Congress.

This was in part the result of the unfavorable impression Coolidge had made on senators during his lackluster vice presidency. More important was the independent nature of Congress during the 1920s. This, of course, had contributed significantly to the uproar over Teapot Dome and related matters that poisoned relations between president and Congress in 1924. There was also the Republican leadership upon which Coolidge had to rely. Initially, there were the independent Henry Cabot Lodge in the Senate and the genial Speaker Frederick Gillett in the House, both from Massachusetts and both aging. Lodge was no longer a very effective leader and Gillett never had been. In 1925 the congressional leadership passed to Senator Charles Curtis and Speaker Nicholas Longworth, who proved to be more effective than their predecessors, though seldom outstandingly so. Vice President Dawes was of little help. The president regarded him as too independent, and because of his strong opinions, the senators viewed him with suspicion.

As time passed, Coolidge became adept at making friends on Capitol Hill, but he was often unable to convert them into significant legislative allies. Many Democrats and progressive Republicans were unable to forget the scandals of the Harding presidency. Neither could they support the policies of the Harding and Coolidge administrations. For many of these members of Congress, not only had the government pursued economy too far, but its farm and business policies were bones that stuck in their throats. The administration's tax rebates to business, attempt to allow private development of Muscle Shoals, conservative appointments to office, and staunch opposition to a veterans' bonus and to the proposed McNary-Haugen farm legislation—which would have authorized federal purchase of surplus farm commodities at parity and then resale of them abroad at lower prices—had already been points of conflict with Congress in 1924. These issues would return, in one form or another, to plague Coolidge throughout his presidency.

Coolidge would enter his second term in 1925 with a larger Republican majority in Congress—sixty in the House and sixteen in the Senate—which would prove to be of no immediate advantage to

him. First of all, after the 1924 elections he had to face a lame-duck session of the Sixty-eighth Congress. The president made it clear that he had abandoned none of his legislative goals, which did nothing to mollify his opponents. Moreover, Coolidge did not discourage the Senate Republicans from reading out of the party caucus and stripping of their committee seniority Robert M. La Follette and three other Republican senators who had supported the Wisconsinite for president in 1924. These senators and their several sympathizers in the upper chamber would repeatedly embarrass the administration during the next four years.

Early in 1925 the dissenters helped deal the president two major setbacks. Most notable was the passage of Senator George Norris' legislation providing for public development of Muscle Shoals. Although there would be no action on this authorization during Coolidge's presidency, the administration was unable to gain congressional support for private development of the area. Eventually, in 1933, the property became the centerpiece of the Tennessee Valley Authority.

The second problem arose with the president's nomination of Charles Beecher Warren to become attorney general. Earlier Coolidge had easily secured confirmation of William Jardine, an agricultural scientist, to become secretary of agriculture and had encountered some senatorial opposition to his appointment of Attorney General Harlan F. Stone to the Supreme Court, but in nominating a longtime representative of the sugar trust, he presented Democrats and progressive Republicans with a perfect target. Not only did the Senate reject Warren, the first time since 1868 that a cabinet nominee had failed of confirmation, but Coolidge renominated him. Again the Senate rejected Warren. When the president offered him a recess appointment, Warren wisely turned it down. This was hardly shrewd conduct on the part of a president who had been so astute at politics the year before.

Coolidge quickly learned to be more cautious. If his nominees continued to be generally conservative, they were also above reproach. Coolidge replaced one friend, Stone, in the attorney generalship with another, John Garibaldi Sargent of Vermont. The ambassador to Great Britain, Frank B. Kellogg, was appointed secretary of state, and the businessman Dwight F. Davis became secretary of war. Coolidge's cabinet was by 1925 his own. He either had men in it whom he wanted or had tested Harding's holdovers and found them acceptable. The exception was Secretary of Commerce Herbert Hoover. Although he was far from disciplined in Coolidge's eyes either in thought or in minding his own business, Hoover was brilliant, popular, and usually useful to his master in the White House. These two very different men would learn to live with each other, however often they vexed one another. Coolidge also shifted secretaries in the White House. With the 1924 election over, Slemp was replaced as chief secretary by a man of various talents, Everett Sanders, a former Indiana congressman.

However one may assess the members of Coolidge's official family, many of them reached a high level of distinction. Hughes and Stone would become chief justices of the United States; special counsel Owen J. Roberts would also ascend to the Supreme Court; Dawes and Kellogg would receive the Nobel Peace Prize; Hoover would become president; and Interior Secretary Hubert Work and presidential secretary Sanders would become chairmen of the Republican National Committee. Moreover, Henry L. Stimson added luster to his reputation as Coolidge's special envoy by bringing peace to Nicaragua, and Dwight Morrow won fame for his remarkably effective embassy to Mexico.

Coolidge was able to maintain his popularity with the public, to a considerable extent through his astute manipulation of the press and of platitudes acceptable to the people. The only president to have spoken more often in public was Theodore Roosevelt. Coolidge had acquired such a knack for speaking that even if few Americans felt uplifted, few were offended. He seemed always visible, dignified, and full of integrity, even if what he said was seldom memorable.

Coolidge's chief problem remained his inability to bend Congress to his will. Yet he did have his victories, and for him they were usually the essential ones. In his annual messages to Congress between 1925 and 1929, Coolidge largely hewed to his original policies. He told Congress in December 1925, "The country does not appear to require radical departure from the policies already adopted as much as it needs a further extension of these policies and the improvement of details." His key policy was "economy and efficiency." If Congress could restrain itself from meddling in administration, which it largely did after 1924, the executive could provide efficiency. It was also Coolidge's task to persuade Congress not to get carried away with funding new programs or sub-

stantially increasing funds for established programs. In this he was remarkably successful. Appropriations remained low during the Coolidge years, and the officials of the executive branch used the funds allotted them well. With federal revenues constantly exceeding spending, the administration was able to cut the national debt substantially, confident that it was preserving the government's credit for a rainy day as well as curbing inflation.

Neither federal economy nor paring the national debt was significantly controversial during the Coolidge years, but the corollary to these policies, tax cutting, was. Some members of Congress wanted to use the surplus to fund new programs; others charged that the administration's tax-cutting plan favored the rich. Coolidge and Treasury Secretary Mellon did espouse tax cuts that would benefit wealthy Americans, believing that the rich would invest their extra funds in ways that would increase production and therefore jobs and wealth at home. They also believed that this would expand American trade abroad, which would benefit the domestic economy and help stabilize the world economically and politically.

The Coolidge-Mellon plan, which was an outgrowth of Harding's policies, was a clear illustration of the trickle-down theory of national prosperity. It seemed to work, as Coolidge's years in office encompassed a period of increasing prosperity for most Americans. Moreover, Coolidge and Mellon were careful to make sure that all American taxpayers were favorably affected by the proposed tax cuts. Indeed, not only were federal taxes reduced for all, but many low-income Americans wound up not paying any taxes at all by 1929. It is little wonder that, despite sharp debate on Capitol Hill, Coolidge was able to gain legislative approval of his tax program in 1926. Then Congress repealed the gift tax, halved estate taxes, substantially cut surtaxes on great wealth, and reduced income taxes for all.

The tax program was Coolidge's major legislative victory in 1926. It was his best year in Congress, partly because he focused on this major issue. Yet the president also won on a number of other issues. Coolidge kept Prohibition from becoming a major issue by the expedient of occupying the middle ground between drys and wets. As a consequence, wets were slow to criticize the president for fear that he would become an ardent dry, and most drys were reluctant to criticize him too much for fear that he would do even less to enforce the law. As for the farm

President Calvin Coolidge (wearing hat) welcomes representatives of the Sioux tribe to the White House in 1925. THE LIBRARY OF CONGRESS

issue, Coolidge could not avoid it. He was able to scatter support for the McNary-Haugen bill so that it would not pass, while he gained enough votes to advance federal support for cooperative marketing.

In the same year, Coolidge also secured modest increases in appropriations for inland waterways, public buildings, and highway construction as well as additional funding for national parks and forests and Indian programs. It should not be overlooked that 1926 was the year that Coolidge and Congress approved initial funding for the National Archives. The president also astutely exploited the furor created by the court-martial of Colonel William Mitchell for insubordination to develop sentiment for orderly progress in civil and military aviation. The result was that Congress approved subsidies for the growth of the aircraft industry and most of Coolidge's recommendations for the coordination of military aviation and for the regulation of civil aviation.

The president would not do as well with Congress in 1927 and 1928, partly because of Republican losses in the congressional elections of 1926 and

partly because of growing support on Capitol Hill for programs that the administration found unacceptable. He persuaded Congress in 1927 to establish the Federal Radio Commission to regulate the use of wavelengths by radio stations, which had become chaotic. Besides that, in 1927 and 1928 Coolidge asked for some additional funds for public works and national parks and forests, improvement of existing federal farm programs, federal conciliation of labor disputes, and authorization of branch banking, all of which he received, but Congress refused to act on his proposal to consolidate the nation's railways. Coolidge won his chief victory in 1928 when Congress approved additional cuts in income taxes and reductions in corporation taxes.

Besides taxes, the big domestic issues between president and Congress in 1927 and 1928 were the McNary-Haugen legislation, flood control, and public power development. Sentiment had been growing for federal purchase of surplus crops and the selling of them abroad at whatever price they could command. Although the administration offered an alternative proposal—to use cooperatives to extend cheap credit to farmers who would restrict their production—Congress enacted the McNary-Haugen legislation. Even Vice President Dawes championed the McNary-Haugen bill. Coolidge vetoed it in both 1927 and 1928 as unconstitutional class legislation that would benefit neither the nation nor farmers. It would, he contended, only encourage the growing of surpluses and the rearing of tariffs abroad to prevent the dumping of American agricultural commodities. Although much that Coolidge said was correct, the administration did not present an effective plan to deal with the nation's farm problems. Certainly, the administration's cooperative credit plan, which Congress finally accepted in 1929, failed to meet America's agricultural problems.

A time-consuming and heated debate arose over flood control after the inundation of vast areas by the Mississippi, Missouri, and Ohio Rivers during the spring of 1927. The administration moved rapidly to provide relief and loans for reconstruction, but when this proved insufficient, pressure rose for a federal flood control program. Coolidge responded in December 1927 by asking for such a program along the Mississippi. He made a mistake by giving no specifics, and soon Congress was considering a $1.4 billion program instead of the $180 million one he had in mind. By April 1928 the fight between president and Congress had become intense. Only after great effort was he able to get the price marked down to $500 million and thus block legislation that would have jeopardized his stringent economic program.

There was, moreover, the long-standing question of development of the Colorado River basin, which involved not only large appropriations but also the issue of private versus public control. After six years of work and debate, Coolidge finally approved in December 1928 the construction of Boulder Dam, which was central to the Colorado River basin development. He had artfully spun out the issue and passed on to his successor the spending of the $125 million involved as well as the controversial issue of whether the dam would be operated publicly or privately.

Foreign Policy

Domestic questions were not, of course, all that concerned the Coolidge administration. Foreign policy issues also had to be addressed. Coolidge had inherited certain guidelines from Harding, among them that the United States would not join the League of Nations and that foreign debts to America would not be forgiven. The latter he adhered to faithfully, supposedly saying in justification, "They hired the money didn't they?" Nevertheless, Coolidge continued Harding's policy of negotiating lower interest rates, deferral of payments, and other terms relating to foreign debts. The administration also encouraged private American loans to foreign nations in order to help them with their financial problems. Particularly significant in this respect was the Dawes Plan of 1924 to alleviate Germany's economic emergency, which had created an international crisis.

As for the League of Nations, the government gradually increased its unofficial cooperation with the world organization's activities, especially those concerned with promoting disarmament. In this and other things, Coolidge generally followed the advice of his secretary of state. The president did not do so thoughtlessly, for he had his own staunch convictions, his well-developed political sense as to what the American people might accept, and his keen though narrow analytical powers. He was decidedly opposed to war for his own country or any other. War, he believed, only resulted in killing, destruction, and general instability in human affairs.

Although it was not politically feasible for the United States to join the League of Nations, there was interest in finding some other path to international cooperation. Coolidge therefore espoused American membership on the World Court. In January 1926 the Senate agreed to American adherence to the protocol of the World Court, but with five reservations. One of the reservations provided that the United States would not be bound by advisory opinions of the court rendered without American consent. This one many member nations of the court would not accept, and so the question of American membership on the court was ended.

There was continued American interest, too, in forwarding disarmament. When other nations moved too slowly on this, the United States sought to follow up on the naval disarmament arrangements arrived at in the Washington Naval Conference of 1921–1922. Coolidge therefore sponsored an international conference at Geneva, Switzerland, in 1927. It was ill fated at the start, for France and Italy refused to participate. At Geneva, Great Britain and the United States failed to agree, particularly on cruiser tonnages, and the conference collapsed. As a consequence, Congress authorized increased American naval expenditures in 1928.

A prominent and assertive group of Americans had been pressing on the administration the idea of the world's nations agreeing to outlaw war. Coolidge had kept talking to these people for political reasons, but he refused to commit himself to their cause, which he regarded as naive. Foreign Minister Aristide Briand of France saw in the outlawry of war a way in which he might secure a defense alliance with the United States. Therefore, on 6 April 1927, the tenth anniversary of America's entry into World War I, Briand proposed that France and the United States join together to outlaw war. Since Briand had broached the idea publicly, Coolidge could not ignore it, especially as there was considerable public interest in it. The administration stalled the French, hoping that interest in Briand's proposal would wither. This did not happen, so Coolidge and Secretary of State Kellogg in December adopted Senator William Borah's idea that the outlawry of war be multilateral. This was not what Briand wanted, but by now he was so well identified with the outlawry of war that he could not withdraw. So in 1928 the representatives of fifteen nations met in Paris to pledge their countries to "condemn recourse to war for the solution of international controversies, and renounce it as an instrument of national policy in their relations with one another." In 1929, Coolidge successfully pressed the Senate for ratification of the Kellogg-Briand Pact. The agreement turned out to be a swordless sheath, although it seemed dazzlingly promising at the time.

If the Coolidge administration failed to guarantee world peace and to achieve further disarmament, it did meet most of its special problems well. In part this occurred because of the government's improvement of the quality of American representation abroad. This was seen in the passage of the Rogers Act in 1924, which provided for the professionalization of the foreign service, and in Coolidge's increased appointment of professional diplomats to be ambassadors and ministers. It was also a result of the president's concern for avoiding the possibility of conflict. For example, the level of American intervention abroad dropped during the Coolidge presidency, largely because such incursions were expensive and, worse, could lead to war.

China, Mexico, and Nicaragua were the three major instances of the application of Coolidge's policy. During the 1920s, China was plagued by civil strife and threats of foreign intervention; it was also a time when several foreign countries enjoyed special rights that impaired Chinese sovereignty. The United States avoided supporting any of the rivals for power in China and acted to discourage military intervention by foreign nations. In addition, the Coolidge administration insisted, with some effect, on the reduction of the special treaty rights of foreign countries, especially with respect to tariff determination and extraterritoriality in China.

Mexico posed larger problems. Diplomatic relations between America and Mexico had been ruptured in 1920, but Coolidge was able to restore relations in 1923 after agreements had been made to settle property claims and to protect the rights of Americans in Mexico. Rebellion by anti-American elements still plagued Mexico, and its new government under Plutarco Calles soon called upon the United States to lift its embargo on the sale of arms and to encourage the granting of private loans. These things Coolidge did in 1924. This honeymoon did not last long, for in 1925 Mexico restricted American oil operations, and in 1926 President Calles and the Roman Catholic Church were at odds over the government's curbs on religious activities. Moreover, banditry was at a high pitch in Mexico. These developments resulted in hostile reactions in the United States and even pressure for American intervention. Coolidge went to great lengths to calm the American public and to reassure Mexico that disputes would be negotiated. In 1927 he sent Dwight Morrow to Mexico with instructions to "keep us out of war with Mexico." Morrow not only did that but soon reduced tensions between the two countries to their lowest point in decades.

Events in Nicaragua had complicated Mexican-American relations. By the end of 1926 that country was in a state of civil war, with Mexico and the United States backing opposite sides. In 1927, after reversing a decision to settle matters by force in Nicaragua, Coolidge sent Henry L. Stimson, Taft's secretary of war, to Nicaragua to arrange for peace. By May, Stimson had secured agreement to the suspension of hostilities, the restoration of civil rights, and the recognition of an interim government until elections could be held in 1928.

Relations with Japan were another story. Directly upon learning of the disastrous earthquake and typhoon of 1 September 1923, Coolidge ordered the Asiatic fleet to Yokohama to render assistance. This well-received gesture was followed by further private and public American aid. Japanese-American relations became strained when Congress voted overwhelmingly to exclude Japanese from the quotas established in the new Immigration Act of 1924. Despite the strenuous efforts of Coolidge and Secretary of State Hughes, Congress would not budge on the issue and indeed made very clear in debate its strong anti-Asian sentiment. Relations between the two nations would remain touchy thereafter, although the administration took great care in negotiating other issues with Japan.

Coolidge declined to run for reelection as president in 1928. He was satisfied, if not elated, to be succeeded in the White House by Herbert Hoover. After returning to Northampton in 1929, Coolidge busied himself with literary activities, which resulted in the production of his autobiography, some magazine articles, and, for a year, a syndicated newspaper column. He occasionally engaged in civic and political activities, but he was not a political force, nor did he try to be. He was bothered by minor ailments after he left Washington, and he increasingly complained of ill health in 1932. Nevertheless, his death of coronary thrombosis on 5 January 1933 was unexpected. He was buried in the family plot in Plymouth Notch, Vermont.

Assessment

Coolidge was fortunate that his administration faced no great emergencies. It can be said that he met well most of the crises that occurred during his presidency. He astutely handled the Teapot Dome and other scandals, as he did crises in Mexico, China, and Nicaragua and the uproar over the court-martial of Mitchell. Coolidge was shrewd in his efforts to win nomination and election as president in 1924. Moreover, he showed outstanding talents as an administrator and fiscal manager. Although his personality made him seem a throwback to an earlier time, he was skillful at gaining the respect of the public. He was also adept at exploiting America's growing prosperity for political purposes.

Despite all this, Coolidge was not outstanding at exercising leadership. Most of his successes on Capitol Hill were transitory, such as the tax measures of 1926 and 1928, or were routine. He intended to be a president representative of his time and society, and in this he was successful. Speaking for large numbers of Americans, Justice Oliver Wendell Holmes said, "While I don't expect anything very astonishing from [Coolidge] I don't want anything very astonishing." Coolidge obliged. He did the day's work very well, but he felt little motivation to look ahead, to meet future problems. Admittedly, his was not a promising time to do so. He was, moreover, not one to borrow trouble by taking on unnecessary tasks or launching crusades. In sum, what Coolidge did, he usually did as well as could be expected and without indulging in theatrics. He was largely content to preside over the nation, willing to try to rule only when crisis called for it. Americans during his presidency were generally satisfied with that.

BIBLIOGRAPHY

Calvin Coolidge, *The Autobiography of Calvin Coolidge* (New York, 1929), is dry and only seldom revealing. *Have Faith in Massachusetts: A Collection of Speeches and Messages, by Calvin Coolidge* (Boston, 1919) and *The Price of Freedom: Speeches and Addresses, by Calvin Coolidge* (New York, 1924) vary in quality and subject matter; both were intended as election campaign documents.

Claude M. Fuess, *Calvin Coolidge, The Man from Vermont* (Boston, 1940), is a starchy, almost defensive scholarly biography of Coolidge. William Allen White, *A Puritan in Babylon: The Story of Calvin Coolidge* (New York, 1938), is superbly written but often inaccurate. Donald R. McCoy, *Calvin Coolidge, the Quiet President* (New York, 1967; Lawrence, Kans., 1988), is a recent biography of Coolidge. Hendrik Booraem V, *The Provincial: Calvin Coolidge and His World, 1885–1895* (Lewisburg, Pa., 1994), and John Almon Waterhouse, *Calvin Coolidge Meets Charles Edward Garman* (Rutland, Vt., 1984), are good accounts of Coolidge's formative years.

Philip R. Moran, ed., *Calvin Coolidge, 1872–1933: Chronology, Documents, Bibliographical Aids* (Dobbs Ferry, N.Y., 1970), and Clifford A. Pease, Jr., *Calvin Coolidge and His Family: An Annotated Bibliography* (Plymouth, Vt., 1987), are useful to anyone interested in Coolidge studies. Robert K. Murray, *The Politics of Normalcy: Governmental Theory and Practice in the Harding-Coolidge Era* (New York, 1973), provides a general background to the policies of Coolidge's presidency.

Edward Connery Lathem, ed., *Your Son, Calvin Coolidge: A Selection of Letters from Calvin Coolidge to His Father* (Montpelier, Vt., 1968), is a fine collection of letters, sometimes witty, sometimes sad, but almost always revealing of Coolidge's personality. Howard H. Quint and Robert H. Ferrell, eds., *The*

Talkative President: The Off-the-Record Press Conferences of Calvin Coolidge (Amherst, Mass., 1964), offers splendid documentation of how Coolidge handled the press and is also valuable for the content of the president's comments. C. Bascom Slemp, ed., *The Mind of the President, as Revealed by Himself in His Own Words* (Garden City, N.Y., 1926), is a mundane but thoughtful selection of Coolidge's comments. Ishbel Ross, *Grace Coolidge and Her Era: The Story of a President's Wife* (New York, 1962), a good popular biography, supplies interesting insights into the life of the Coolidge family.

Recent works include Robert H. Ferrell, *The Presidency of Calvin Coolidge* (Lawrence, Kans., 1998); Peter Hannaford, comp. and ed., *The Quotable Calvin Coolidge: Sensible Words for a New Century* (Bennington, Vt., 2001), and Robert Sobel, *Coolidge: An American Enigma* (Washington, D.C., 1998).

Herbert Hoover

David Burner

Herbert Hoover THE LIBRARY OF CONGRESS

O N 2 August 1927, on a summer trip in South Dakota, President Calvin Coolidge distributed to reporters copies of a simple message: "I do not choose to run for President in nineteen twenty-eight." He was quietly departing from a presidency that had quietly watched over a country enjoying what seemed to be permanent prosperity, rejoicing in seemingly limitless technological and scientific progress, and enormously proud of its institutions. In Secretary of Commerce Herbert Hoover—an engineer, businessman, humanitarian, administrator, and in many respects political progressive—the nation saw a figure whose brilliantly successful career embodied its technical and economic talents, its gener-

osity, its mythic story of the poor boy whose hard work brings him fame and wealth. Hoover would be the fitting Republican candidate and successor to Coolidge.

The campaign, with Charles Curtis as vice presidential candidate on Hoover's ticket, was all that the Republicans could have wanted. Governor Alfred E. Smith of New York, the Democratic candidate, had the political liability of his Roman Catholicism, which he compounded by appointing a Catholic to be Democratic national chairman. Smith blundered, or at any rate was stubbornly intractable, in his handling of the religious issue. He failed during the campaign to address specifically the fears of those Americans who thought of his religion as alien to the American tradition, and he acted as though any questions about his faith were an affront to be brushed aside. Further, although Smith opposed Prohibition at a time when it was proving itself a failure, this deepened the public perception of him as an eastern urbanite fixed to his Catholic ethnic constituency. Hoover's campaign looked toward an end to poverty, equivocated on Prohibition by calling it an experiment, and promised farmers an agricultural marketing act. But no matter who the Democratic candidate might have been or how the campaign might have proceeded, Hoover had on his side a national prosperity that was irresistible politically. Hoover received 21 million votes, and Smith, 15 million. The electoral vote was divided 444 to 87.

Early Life and Education

What sort of president did the public think it had chosen? How did Hoover perceive himself and his mandate? The course of Hoover's earlier career predicted to some extent the character of his presidency. Amid the rolling farms surrounding West Branch, Iowa, hacked out of the wildwood by his sturdy and independent forebears, Herbert Clark Hoover, born on 11 August 1874, experienced a childhood filled with both the grief and the pleasures of nineteenth-century small-town life. In later years he would reminisce about the pleasures: swimming in streams large enough to dam, eating wild strawberries in the fields, collecting agate and coral along the railroad tracks. The grief that struck the boy came in a form familiar to the western pioneers who frequently lost children and relatives to diphtheria, tuberculosis, and typhoid fever. When Bert was six years old, he lost his father, Jesse, an agricultural implements dealer who had long suffered from a form of heart disease. His mother, always religious, was a hard worker in temperance and Sunday school activities. After becoming a Quaker minister, she traveled to revival meetings, preaching the message of forgiveness and redeeming love. On her return from a winter trip, she died of pneumonia when Bert was nine. The boy himself had a close brush with death while suffering from croup.

The orphan shuttled between relatives on nearby farms until he left to live with an uncle in Oregon in late 1885. Such continuing abandonment and separation could have caused severe problems, but for the most part Hoover was later able to shut out the dark memories of his childhood, preferring not to speak of them and garbling his memory of dates and incidents. Certain possibilities about the emotional relationship between his early life and his adult career do suggest themselves. For example, one of young Hoover's favorite books was *David Copperfield*, the story of an orphan mistreated by adults. Yet Hoover arrived at a sort of rugged, progressive individualism. If he had to be alone, he would make the most of it. He made of his habitually outward-looking life an ideology—heroic individualism, the self-reliant man expressing himself in technological mastery and personal accomplishment. One particular reflection of his early life came in his relief efforts during the era of World War I: helpless, bereaved, abandoned people could count on his aid, though others had not always aided him. Hoover's later dislike of large inheritances also suggests the experience of being left on his own.

The Quaker idea of the Inner Light suggests a real but unseen decency, reasonableness, and harmony within the world. Among the Friends there is a special blend of piety and practical worldliness that expresses itself in business life, and a compound of moral urgency with a certain optimism that the world can be enticed to put its practical arrangements into good moral order. The Quakers immersed themselves in the full variety of nineteenth-century reforms: antislavery (West Branch was a station on the underground railroad, and John Brown spent one winter a mile outside of the town), suffrage for blacks, prison rehabilitation, Indian reform, poorhouses, and care of the insane. The progressive record of Hoover's first eight months in the White House suggests the influence of his Quaker upbringing.

Hoover's years in Oregon, from 1885 to 1891, trained him in business. John Minthorn, the stern uncle with whom he lived, was a doctor, a Quaker minister, and head of a small preparatory school, but his central interest was real estate. Dreaming of enticing settlers to the fertile Willamette Valley, he moved from Newberg to Salem to sell undeveloped land suitable for prune orchards. Hoover dropped out of high school to oversee the day-to-day operations of the Oregon Land Company and attended night school to learn bookkeeping, typing, and office skills. He helped buy and sell land and houses, run saw and flour mills, and arrange advertising in eastern papers. Before Minthorn's company failed in the depression of the 1890s, Hoover had already decided to attend Stanford University.

Hoover, who would later claim that he had been the first boy to take up residence at the new school (founded 1891), took advantage of the innovative curriculum. He received an excellent education in geology, taking about half of his credits in the department under Dr. John Branner and working summers for the U.S. Geological Survey. He also continued a career in business, organizing and selling laundry and newspaper routes. His social views expressed themselves in his disdain for fraternities on account of their snobbishness, and he would not allow his sons to join any at Stanford.

After Hoover was graduated from Stanford in 1895 with a B.A. in geology, he worked briefly as a day laborer in the Reward Gold Mine in Grass City, California. The experience won him a job with an important San Francisco firm that needed his practical knowledge of the Grass Valley mines for a legal case. This in turn led to a position with one of the world's leading mining consultant firms, Bewick, Moreing and Company of London.

Charles Algernon Moreing, desperate for qualified mining engineers willing to work the sultry wastes of the Western Australian goldfields, sent Hoover there in 1897. It was a good arrangement for the firm and for Hoover, who soon successfully recommended to London the purchase of the fabulous Sons of Gwalia gold mine. His other recommendations proved generally fruitful, and he showed increasing versatility as a mine manager and business consultant. Life in the Australian outback was not easy. The temperature frequently rose above 100°, even at night, and Hoover, suffering from physical debilitation brought on by overwork, would sometimes travel hundreds of miles through the desert lying on a mattress in the back of an open wagon. After three years in Australia, at the age of twenty-four, he was a recognized success and authority in his field. He wired Lou Henry, a Stanford geology major from Monterey, California, asking her to marry him, and she did early in 1899 in Monterey just before embarking with him to China on a new adventure.

Sent to China by Bewick, Moreing to find gold, Hoover arranged to exploit extensive and profitable coal deposits instead. He established relations with the Chinese Engineering and Mining Company just before the Boxer Rebellion of 1900 broke out, threatening the Western imperialist spheres of influence that had hitherto dominated China. In exchange for protection by the British, the Chinese signed the company over to Hoover, who in turn bartered it to Bewick, Moreing, in exchange for a partnership in that company. In China the Hoovers were trapped briefly in the city of Tianjin during the Boxer Rebellion; there he carried out relief efforts for the beleaguered European community similar to the famous work he would accomplish during and after World War I.

In 1901, Hoover and his wife made their home in London and raised two sons, Herbert and Allan, taking them sometimes on mining exploration trips around the world. On these ocean voyages, Hoover turned his attention to reading, giving himself some of the liberal arts education he had missed in the narrow curriculum of Stanford. He also wrote technical articles, which appeared in the world's professional mining magazines. He and his wife supervised and annotated the translation from Latin of *De re metallica*, a medieval treatise on mining that they published in 1912. Hoover also contributed thoughtful talks and editorials on the new profession of engineering. In a textbook, *Principles of Mining* (1909), he recommended progressive dealings with labor, favoring collective bargaining, high wages for hard work, and improvements in mine safety.

Hoover's most successful ventures after 1900 involved finding some great supply of base metal near a dependable transportation system. He would supply the world's growing industries, like steel, with needed base minerals. He achieved his greatest success, first with the help of his brother Theodore, after painfully slow experimentation with the extraction of zinc from slag heaps at Broken Hill in New South Wales, Australia. His second successful venture lay with the Burma Corporation, which produced silver, lead, and zinc in abundant quantities. By 1914, Hoover, operating on his own since 1907, had important investments on every continent and offices in San Francisco, London, St. Petersburg, and Mandalay. Once he remarked that if a man "has not made a million dollars by the time he is forty he is not worth much." Hoover was worth about $4 million at the beginning of World War I.

Relief Administrator, World War I

The outbreak of war in 1914 came at a fortuitous time for Hoover. The mining boom in both precious and base metals was beginning to spend itself, except perhaps in Russia. He was thinking now of employing in some philanthropic way his skill in public relations, tested at Stanford and refined in his years of mining promotion. An admirer of Theodore Roosevelt's progressivism, he had been thinking for some years of government service in appointive office. He was in London when war broke out in August, and the American ambassador, Walter Hines Page, asked him to aid Americans who had been stranded abroad at the onset of war. He did this with such efficiency that Page recommended to President Wilson that Hoover be drafted to help provide food for the Belgians, hitherto dependent on the importing of food, after the invasion of their country.

For the next three years Hoover headed the Commission for Relief in Belgium (CRB). Despite the stubbornness of both Germans and British, Hoover, using highhanded and sometimes illegal methods, employed his knowledge of worldwide shipping to bring a steady flow of food to the tiny country. He brought to his work ample technical and administrative skills, but more particularly the relentless energy and forcefulness of his personality. "This man," stated his German passport, "is not to be stopped anywhere under any circumstances."

The relief of Belgium, Hoover enthusiastically proclaimed, was "the greatest job Americans have undertaken in the cause of humanity." The result would be "the greatest charity the world has ever seen." Hoover himself remained shy and averse to publicity. He had, so it seemed, the simple Quaker distaste for such things: in Quakerism good works become tainted if publicized. All his life Hoover made a secret of his hundreds of benefactions.

Unquestionably an ambitious man, Hoover sought from President Wilson the post of United States food administrator even before the country formally entered the war in April 1917. Wilson, who could not question the effectiveness of the CRB, gave Hoover the job. Hoover realized that his earlier work in Belgium was a useful model for wartime administration and that his own reputation for being the "Great Engineer" put him in a unique position to help win the war. His name had become synonymous with thrift and self-denial, so that "Hooverize" came to mean "economize for a worthy purpose."

Propaganda was the main weapon of the Food Administration. It preached meatless and wheat-less days. A massive campaign enjoined those in control of households to cut down especially on the normal use of bread and sugar, and schools and churches joined the crusade. Yet Hoover, while preferring volunteerism, hastened to get congressional legislation, such as the Lever Food Control Act of 1917, which set a government-guaranteed price for wheat.

In 1919, Hoover managed to dispose of much of the wartime food surplus by selling it to European governments, which often borrowed from the United States for the purpose. Whatever the merits of the transaction, Hoover's American Relief Administration (ARA)—a public agency replaced in mid-1919 by a private one bearing the same name—got the job done as well as could be expected. Hoover went to Europe, slashing through red tape everywhere he went. Without functioning European systems of transportation and communications, he had to create his own. Hoover violated laws, made laws, and transgressed the sanctity of international boundaries to get food to where it was most needed. He implicitly urged his subordinates to do likewise and to ignore local or centralized authority.

The Versailles Peace Conference, particularly its representatives from France, urged Hoover to withhold food to discourage the advance of bolshevism in eastern and central Europe. Whether Hoover consistently did so is still a matter of controversy. Hoover's most blatant use of food for political purposes was against a coup d'état by the reactionary Hapsburg monarchy in Hungary. For Hungary, under the leadership of the Bolshevik Béla Kun, Hoover allowed food that had already been purchased to be taken into the country, although the practice ceased after he received explicit directions from Paris not to allow it. By mid-1919, after Kun had ordered hundreds of political executions, Hoover's concern for feeding Hungary had ceased, and he welcomed the government's overthrow by radical trade unions. To him anything was preferable to an Allied invasion of these troubled lands. Hoover's insistence on feeding starving Germans received sharp criticism from the Allies. While he gave some preference to feeding the war-torn nations that had fought with the Allies, he bent the will of Versailles statesmen who would have allowed Germans to starve.

A subsequent episode in Hoover's relief efforts came in Soviet Russia during the great famine of 1921–1923. When the Soviets guaranteed freedom of movement to the ARA, shipments began in huge quantity. When a shrill anti-Communist complained at a public meeting about what Hoover was doing, he replied, "Twenty million people are starving. Whatever their politics, they shall be fed." George Kennan later observed that the ARA "importantly aided" the revolutionary government, "not just in its economic undertakings, but in its political prestige and capacity for survival."

Secretary of Commerce

Frequently mentioned as a presidential candidate for either of the major political parties in 1920, Hoover showed a qualified interest in the possibility. He had been a loyal Wilsonian, at least publicly, ardently championing the League of Nations. As vice chairman of the Second Industrial Conference (1919–1920), he had advanced the cause of collective bargaining for labor. He also denounced elements of the Red Scare. He announced that he was a Republican the same month. After Harding easily swept the election in a public repudiation of Wilson, the new president appointed Hoover to be secretary of commerce.

Hoover brought representatives of industry to Washington conferences to exchange information in order to improve efficiency and standardization. The representatives would agree on a "sense of the meeting" and return home to propagandize for their recommendations. The impetus the trade association movement received from Hoover's office was only temporarily dampened by Justice Department efforts to prevent price-fixing. When progressives protested that he was not using his office to promote business reform, he replied that the Commerce Department was not the appropriate agency. But Hoover had an important part in ending the twelve-hour day in the steel industry and winning the Jacksonville Agreement, which brought temporary labor peace to many of the soft-coal fields. Regulation of radio and the airwaves and the airplane industry also began under Hoover's Commerce Department.

Hoover increased fourfold the personnel of the Bureau of Foreign and Domestic Commerce, to promote a free-flowing international trade. The bureau increased United States business by hundreds of millions of dollars a year. Hoover particularly wanted commercial expansion to replace military adventurism, especially in Latin America. He took it as a matter of faith that an increased American commercial role abroad would bring a higher standard of living both to the United States and to the rest of the world. Through noncoercive means, he strove to divert American loans away from the support of armaments and risky investments.

That commitment to the spread of commerce as a means to a world free of war says a great deal about the mentality of Hoover: his trust in the rational, orderly mind and processes of modern industry and trade, his search for a workable combination of private economic activity and governmental planning,

and his Quaker-like vision of an industrious, peaceful world. It must have seemed, in the sunny year when the former secretary of commerce assumed the presidency, that the planet was ready to be nudged into that future.

In the 1928 campaign, Hoover took a moderate course on the issue of Prohibition, promising a national commission on law observance to study what he cautiously termed "a great social and economic experiment noble in motive and far-reaching in purpose." Hoover respected the attempt at reform because it showed that "property rights did not dominate American ideals." But he also came to accept the belief that Prohibition had failed after being given an "honest trial." As president, he worked to enforce it, within the limits of law, because it was his duty to do so under the Constitution. Yet the report of his commission, which contained only one Prohibitionist, was evasive if not confused. Seven of its eleven members favored revision, but the report also called for a further trial at enforcement. "The findings are wet and the recommendations are dry," the despairing president complained to his secretary of state. Hoover remained the captive of the Prohibitionists through the 1932 campaign, and Roosevelt was the beneficiary of growing sentiments for repeal. The presidency would provide a test of Hoover's Quaker background and prowess as a social engineer.

Domestic Issues

As president, Hoover had a far from perfect record on civil liberties, yet in response to Jane Addams' complaints in 1929 that the government held political prisoners from the Red Scare of 1919, he could investigate and reply that all such prisoners had been released years before, during Harding's administration. He also pleased Addams—who voted for him in both 1928 and 1932—by ordering that a passport be granted the executive secretary of her organization, the Women's International League for Peace and Freedom, with the word *defend* omitted from the oath of allegiance. Hoover asked Attorney General William D. Mitchell to look into the case of the labor martyr, Thomas J. Mooney of California, to see whether his rights had been violated. The president also secured the resignation of Assistant Attorney General Mabel Walker Willebrandt, the flamboyant Prohibitionist whose methods included espionage. Secretary of Labor William Doak had deported aliens to totalitarian countries; years later Hoover would protest to Attorney General Mitchell, "I cannot imagine our Administration violating the very spirit of the Bill of Rights." Unaccountably, he did not protest at the time.

Hoover as secretary of commerce had taken some steps toward desegregating the department after the southern policies of the Wilson years. As chief executive, Hoover acquitted himself quite well on matters of race in contrast to other early-twentieth-century presidents. Like Theodore Roosevelt, Hoover invited a prominent black, Robert Moton of the Tuskegee Institute, to public ceremonies at the White House. Hoover preferred representatives of the Tuskegee philosophy to the less tractable W. E. B. Du Bois of the National Association for the Advancement of Colored People. The wife of a black congressman, Mrs. Oscar de Priest of Chicago, came to a congressional tea, albeit with a carefully pruned guest list that included three cabinet members' wives. Addams' Women's International League for Peace and Freedom formally congratulated Mrs. Hoover on the occasion. Congressman de Priest later ostentatiously used the incident to bait racists. The first sentence Hoover commuted under his presidential pardoning power was that of a black convicted of murdering a white woman. No eyewitness to the crime had appeared, and the verdict had depended on what seemed to be a forced confession.

Hoover sharply increased appropriations for Howard University. He was also sensitive to the need for appointing blacks to government management and to boards such as those guiding federal paroles. The president proposed to foundations that they give tenants and sharecroppers of both races the opportunity to buy the land they worked.

On the subject of lynching, Hoover suggested to an assistant, "With the modern expedition, through aerial and motor forces of Federal troops located at all important centers throughout the country it is possible to bring them almost instantly to the assistance of local authorities if a system were authorized by Congress that would make such action swift and possible." Advised by Mitchell that constitutional restraints prevented the use of federal troops without a request from state government, the president condemned lynching publicly but offered no legislation against it. Evidently he relied on the force of an enlightened public opinion.

Yet under Hoover the Republicans ousted blacks from the party in the South, and Secretary of War Patrick Hurley segregated black gold-star mothers and widows of the World War I dead en route to Europe on ocean liners. Hoover also failed to accomplish much to end discrimination in hiring for government projects.

Hoover's work in prison reform, a field long of interest to Quakers, led to the passage of eight bills. Under the direction of his appointee Sanford Bates, the Bureau of Prisons alleviated prison overcrowding by establishing work camps and building new penitentiaries and reformatories. A federal school for prison guards was founded, and all prison employees came under the Civil Service Administration. Educational opportunities and health benefits were improved, and the number of prisoners on parole multiplied during the Hoover administration.

Again spurred by his Quaker heritage, Hoover sought the reform of Indian policy. He made good appointments when he chose Charles J. Rhoads and J. Henry Scattergood, Philadelphia Quakers, to run the Indian Bureau (now the Bureau of Indian Affairs). Rhoads was appalled by the corruption and insensitivity he found in Washington, but his administration was a transitional one and at odds with itself in many respects. The debate about reform centered on the degree to which Indians should be encouraged to retain their distinct cultural, social, economic, and religious identity. Although the Hoover administration opposed government welfare that "coddled" Indians, expenditures by the bureau almost doubled under Rhoads. The money went chiefly for better schools and health care. John Collier, the New Deal head of the bureau, later acknowledged that the "real shift" toward recognition of Indian rights began under Hoover.

In fulfillment of a campaign pledge, President Hoover, after a special session of Congress in the spring of 1929, signed the Agricultural Marketing Act, which included a $500 million revolving fund to buy surpluses that might be resold in better economic times. The Federal Farm Board speculated in agricultural commodities to hold up farm prices, but to no avail. Farm prices plunged soon after the stock market crash of October 1929, and the board became merely a relief agency. With farmers unwilling voluntarily to reduce crop acreage and the government unwilling to coerce them to do so, the board's funds simply ran out before the Great Depression reached bottom in 1932–1933.

Hoover had made an impressive record while commerce secretary by persuading states through which the Colorado River flowed to agree on a plan to harness its electrical energy, control its flood potential, and distribute its waters fairly. Hoover (formerly Boulder) Dam is a monument to this work. During his presidency Hoover finally managed to negotiate a treaty with Canada for the development of a St. Lawrence waterway. Other projects—the San Francisco Bay Bridge, the Los Angeles Aqueduct, and various public works—also marked his tenure.

The conservation movement advanced under Hoover. Some 2 million additional acres of forestland became national preserves, and the area of national parks increased by 40 percent. But some of the recommendations of Hoover's Commission on the Conservation and Administration of the Public Domain had an ambiguous character. It suggested, for example, that the surface rights to lands useful only for grazing should be returned to the states. Hoover liked the notion of shrinking federal controls and had a naïve idea of state conservation goals. He made plans for building Grand Coulee Dam on the Columbia River but vetoed a proposal by Senator George Norris of Nebraska to develop the Tennessee River valley, objecting to its socialist character and labeling it "degeneration."

Hoover's appointments to the Supreme Court reflected a liberal rather than conservative bias. Charles Evans Hughes, appointed chief justice in 1930, was a judicial moderate who would side with the liberals on most of the critical decisions on New Deal legislation in the 1930s. Justice Owen Roberts was to become known in the 1930s as the "swing vote" on the Court. Hoover's final appointment was perhaps his best. Benjamin Cardozo, known for his integrity and his intellect, had aligned himself with the liberal constitutional philosophy of Oliver Wendell Holmes, Jr. Louis D. Brandeis—who, like Cardozo, was Jewish—was sitting on the Court, and anti-Semites protested the nomination of a second Jew. The famous progressive journalist and Prohibitionist William Allen White wrote to Senator George Norris, I have not had a good drink since I left Kansas City to come to Emporia [Kansas] nearly 40 years ago.. . . Hunt up . . . a good long brown drink of nose-choking, hair-raising, gullet-giggling, hard corn liquor and then and there . . . take one happy untrammeled drink for me in celebration of Justice Cardozo."

Economic Collapse

Hoover had long criticized speculation on the stock market. He had repeatedly asked President Coolidge to seek additional control over private banking and financial practices, especially insider trading and the use of common stocks as security at near-market value for customers' deposits. He also urged Federal Reserve Board members to restrict credit sufficiently to deter speculation. The board pursued confused objectives and showed faulty logic, dropping the rediscount rate, to Hoover's horror, to 3.5 percent in August 1927. There was little that Hoover could do to restrain stock speculation when he entered office in March 1929. He wrote a statement for a reluctant Secretary of the Treasury Andrew Mellon to issue, saying that conservative bonds, in contrast to speculative stocks, were undervalued. Fearing that an assault on the speculative market could start a panic, he was cautious about recommending a rise in the rediscount rate in that year. But probably nothing Hoover could have done would have averted the stock market crash of October 1929.

There were few historical parallels for Hoover to draw on. By late-twentieth-century standards, Hoover reacted slowly to the crisis; by earlier guides he was a remarkable activist. His initial response was to persuade management to maintain wages and to urge a pooling of resources on the part of financial interests to prevent further deflation. Groups of industry and labor representatives came to Washington at the president's invitation, and both took action to try to avert serious trouble, but to no avail. Hoover and the American Economic Association both anticipated a healthy deflation to be followed soon by a business revival. When the depression reached worldwide dimensions toward the end of 1930, Hoover failed to respond freshly to the crisis. He relied principally on increased public works and a balanced budget—timid answers to what by 1931 was obviously a disaster.

Hoover promised in February 1931 that if hunger and suffering could not otherwise be prevented, "I will ask the aid of every resource of the Federal government." But he came only reluctantly to support federal relief. Establishment economic thinking was wary of relief as being unproductive, and Hoover feared that it would bring hordes of subsidy seekers. But he had other reasons for his hesitancy to provide extensive federal relief, and they were of a different sort from those that much historical scholarship has attributed to a cold and reactionary Hoover. In the years before his presidency, Hoover had spent considerable energies in some of the most extensive humanitarian relief in history. Then, acting out of his

Quaker faith and upbringing, he had looked to voluntary, rational acts of compassion and social reformation on the part of the spiritually enlightened. Hoover, it seems, believed that in times of crisis, citizens would take this kind of initiative. It was, then, not only the will of the recipients of relief that would suffer—and Hoover was not given to the right-wing notion that the poor have themselves to blame—but the will of the property holders, who were supposed to behave as Hoover and his volunteers had behaved in days of famine abroad.

Hoover's trust in the generosity and initiative of his fellow citizens was naive, and had he not finally come around to provide some federal aid and then been replaced by the New Deal, it might have proved disastrously naive. But the sharing that he wanted from the citizenry was not so very far from what the democratic left envisions within a workers' democracy. In the years since, when the values of privacy came to be extolled above the virtues of public citizenship, Hoover's belief in the reality of cooperativeness had evidently become only a poignant memory.

It is not inconceivable that Hoover's hesitancy in the face of the depression represented the drag of the past upon the politics of the moment and the sluggishness of prevalent institutions in their first encounter with economic collapse. Hoover had been sympathetic toward the progressive movement, and a vigorous response to the crisis would have been wholly in character for a statesman who in relief work and government service had been so much the activist and innovator. Yet Hoover's failure to launch something like the New Deal was also in character, consistent with his liking for volunteerism and his foolish trust in the business economy with which he had been so intimately and so successfully connected. He knew the productive power of modern industry, its capacity to subdue poverty with goods and jobs; and he knew that cooperative ventures like the CRB and the Red Cross could put the resources of the economy to great public use. His knowledge was also his handicap. He had seen and organized so much that was good that he could not see, or admit to himself, how much a part of the nature of the market economy it was to withhold from one family or region the wealth that it poured into the lap of another. Hoover's inability to recognize this meant that one of the best and most generous administrative minds of the day went stumbling through the presidency and then kept spinning round in a fevered defense of that presidency and of the existing capitalist system while it might have been working toward some new economic order, perhaps an order more radical in its reforms than the New Deal itself.

Late in 1931, after an unsuccessful attempt to persuade private business interests to form an effective credit association, Hoover endorsed the creation of the Reconstruction Finance Corporation (RFC), which passed Congress in January 1932. Based on the War Finance Corporation of World War I, the RFC would lend to banks, corporations, and agricultural groups. A bias in its initial loans led to the charge that the Republicans favored a trickle-down effect by which the unemployed would benefit only when large business organizations could function normally. To a great extent the charge was accurate, but widely accepted historical accounts have failed to recognize that Hoover ultimately saw the necessity of providing federal funds for relief and used the subterfuge of the RFC to lend funds to the states for relief purposes. Hunger marches, beginning in December 1931 and culminating in the famous Bonus Army the next summer, dramatized the urgency of the need. Much farm surplus was released to the unemployed, and early in 1932, Hoover recommended $300 million in RFC loans to the states for relief. A law Hoover finally signed in mid-1932 reversed the government's course on relief. The concept of loans virtually disappeared. Funds would be advanced out of federal aid for highway construction due in 1935, and the states were to repay them later.

The President's Emergency Committee on Employment (PECE) was set up in the fall of 1930 when unemployment had reached about 11 percent. Under the direction of Colonel Arthur Woods, who had played an important role in Hoover's 1921 Conference on Unemployment, PECE strove to generate private charity and prevailed on Hoover and Congress to increase public works spending. But Woods was battling a tidal wave. In August 1931, PECE gave way to the President's Organization on Unemployment Relief (POUR), headed by Walter S. Gifford, president of American Telephone and Telegraph. Some work on expanding, coordinating, and improving relief efforts was accomplished, but unemployment increased still more. Hoover, earlier that year, had signed the Wagner-Graham Stabilization Act, which set up the Federal Stabilization Board to initiate public works. Public works did increase throughout the decade after 1929, but the massive scale needed to cure unemployment never materialized. And in 1931 the mood in Congress remained strongly opposed to federal relief; even the National Council of Social Workers refused to endorse the principle at their convention in May. By this time, shacks derisively called Hoovervilles were rising in the nation's largest cities; New York's Riverside Park was full of them.

In 1932, Hoover continued to adhere, at least publicly, to the economic orthodoxy of a balanced budget. So did Congress, where a national sales tax almost passed under sponsorship from the leadership of both parties. Hoover expressed more progressive sentiments in a memo to Congressman Charles Crisp, arguing for higher excise taxes on luxuries and higher income taxes on the wealthy. Later Hoover said that high estate taxes were essential. The Revenue Act of 1932 embodied most of these ideas.

Foreign Relations

The bad economy was to dominate Hoover's foreign policy. After a postelection goodwill tour to Latin America, Hoover had pursued the enlightened policy there that had originated under Coolidge. Much of the good effect was dissipated by the Smoot-Hawley Tariff of 1930, which raised barriers against foreign imports.

By 1931 the countries of Europe had been badly infected by the virus of worldwide depression. They blamed the American tariff, but it played a comparatively minor role in economic disruptions that were traceable back to the Treaty of Versailles. Congress and the American public believed that the war debts owed to the United States by Europe should be paid, but Europe could not pay. Hoover instituted in 1931 an eighteen-month moratorium on the debts, but even then European countries defaulted. The largest bank in Austria had failed, and Britain soon abandoned the gold standard. Hoover wasted his energies on trying to maintain, with the aid of France, an international gold standard. The depression grew worse.

Always influenced by Quaker pacifism, Hoover advocated international disarmament. The London Naval Disarmament Conference of 1930 attempted to extend the work of the Washington Naval Conference of 1921–1922, which had effectively stabilized the balance of arms in the Pacific. The London conference accomplished some further postponement of the arms race but, along with the Geneva World Disarmament Conference of 1932, was notably inef-

fective against Japanese imperialism, evidenced by Japan's invasion of Manchuria in September 1931.

Hoover and Secretary of State Henry Stimson differed on the proper American response to Japanese militarism. Hoover counseled patience, arguing from his experience that the dominant Chinese culture would ultimately either assimilate or expel the invaders. Stimson was more bellicose and considered supporting world sanctions through the League of Nations. Together they promulgated the Hoover-Stimson Doctrine of January 1932, announcing the American refusal to recognize any arrangement contrary to the Open Door policy. This, the president hoped, would cast "the searchlight of public opinion" on Japan.

Bonus Army March on Washington

Almost nothing that occurred in Hoover's final year in the White House went well for him. The worst event from a political standpoint was the march of the Bonus Army in 1932. About fifteen thousand World War I veterans descended on Washington, D.C., in May to demand early payment of a soldiers' bonus not scheduled for distribution until 1945. The veterans, peaceable protesters except for a tiny minority, settled in abandoned buildings and in tents on the Anacostia Flats. They marched in front of the Capitol and the White House, and when the Senate voted against the bonus in June by 62 to 18, most of the veterans went home at federal expense, but about ten thousand stayed.

When the Senate voted as it did, following the advice of liberals such as Senator Norris of Nebraska and Congressman Fiorello La Guardia and Governor Franklin Roosevelt of New York, many members of Congress avoided confronting the veterans by escaping through subterranean chambers of the Capitol. Until late July, Hoover did nothing except to provide some sanitary facilities, clothing, cots, tents, and food. On 28 July some veterans were evicted from a small downtown area of government buildings. The buildings had been scheduled for demolition to make way for public works projects providing jobs for the unemployed. When a riot ensued in which a veteran died, the District of Columbia commissioners asked for help from the United States Army. General Douglas MacArthur readily obliged.

Hoover gave MacArthur specific orders to remove the veterans from the heart of the district;

troops did so, wielding drawn sabers and carrying tear-gas canisters. But in direct contravention of Hoover's orders, the imperious MacArthur drove the veterans from their pitiful camp at Anacostia Flats into the Maryland countryside. No event staged for the benefit of public opinion could have seemed more cruel. Hoover reprimanded his chief of staff privately, but fearing public instability should the insubordination become known, the president took the blame. Subsequently, both men became enamored of the idea that Communists and criminals had been gaining considerable strength among the remnant of the veterans. The incident marked a turn to the political right on the part of the president and was his final political failure.

When Franklin Roosevelt, the Democratic presidential candidate, heard about the rout of the veterans, he grinned and said to his adviser, Felix Frankfurter, "Well, Felix, this will elect me." But the New Yorker, not yet widely perceived as the easy winner, left nothing to chance. He campaigned tirelessly. Yet the content of his speeches differed only modestly from the president's own views. The contrast between them, at least in 1932, was more personal than political. Roosevelt could instill a sense of security and self-confidence in the nation, qualities that came with inherited wealth. Hoover, the successful self-made engineer, was testimony to the good working order of capitalism in good times but an embarrassment in the depression. Hard times mocked everything Hoover had worked for. And he lacked the kind of deep-rooted conservatism that would allow Roosevelt as president to unite diverse factions and to sense and strengthen a community's innate equilibrium.

Election of 1932 and Postpresidential Years

By 1932 it seemed that Hoover had gone as far as he would in tampering with the economy. His dreary speeches were an unrelieved defense of his record, and he blamed Congress for holding up certain legislation, such as a national system of home loan banks to avoid foreclosures. On 31 October in Madison Square Garden in New York City he launched into a tirade: with no tariff, he warned, "the grass will grow in streets of a hundred cities, a thousand towns; the weeds will overrun the fields of millions of farms . . . their churches and schoolhouses will decay." Secretary of Agriculture Arthur Hyde unleashed a still

more blatant appeal to fear: "If Roosevelt is elected the homes and lives of one hundred million American people might be in jeopardy."

The economy was in fact showing some improvement in the summer and early fall of 1932. Stock prices advanced sharply, bank failures declined, and Hoover would always claim that Roosevelt's election aborted a recovery that was under way. Roosevelt's victory was by 22,810,000 to 15,759,000. By refusing to cooperate with Hoover during the interregnum, the New Yorker, according to Republicans, was threatening to end recovery.

After the election the banking system slumped toward collapse. Nevada's banks closed for six weeks, beginning on 31 October. Unemployment increased to more than 20 percent of the labor force. Many farmers lost their land. In the long interregnum Hoover tried to persuade Roosevelt to join him in advocating a balanced budget, changing the laws on banking, and staying on the gold standard. The president-elect refrained from committing himself. When the two men met at the White House on 22 November, they were superficially friendly. But Hoover thought Roosevelt intellectually incapable of understanding the complexities of international finance.

Late in January a rash of major bank closings filled the country with alarm. In Michigan, banks closed for eight days in mid-February. Panic came at the end of the month when banks lost $73 million in deposits. Hoover unsuccessfully tried to get Roosevelt to promise to guarantee certain bank deposits, but the incoming president refused to participate in any joint solution. The emergency bank holiday and banking legislation of Roosevelt's Hundred Days had been drafted in general terms by Hoover and his staff. On inauguration day, Saturday, 4 March, the wind blew gusts of rain yet a ray of sunlight broke into the weather. The nation could not help but identify the gray bleakness with Hoover and the sunlight with Franklin Roosevelt.

Hoover lived for three decades after leaving office. From his suite in New York's Waldorf Towers he preached isolationism, Republicanism, conservatism, and philanthropy. He saw a threat of Fascism and Communism in the New Deal but approved of many of its specific laws. In 1945 he spoke in revulsion against the use of the atomic bomb: "The only difference between this and the use of poison gas is the fear of retaliation." He returned to public life in the late 1940s, serving for President Truman on a fact-finding international relief trip and then as chairman of the Commission on Organization of the Executive Branch of the Government (the Hoover Commission). Many of his recommendations on saving money were adopted. He chaired a similar commission under President Eisenhower, but with fewer positive results. Hoover died, at the age of ninety, on 20 October 1964.

BIBLIOGRAPHY

Biographies include David Burner, *Herbert Hoover: A Public Life* (New York, 1979); Joan Hoff Wilson, *Herbert Hoover: Forgotten Progressive* (Boston, 1975); Martin L. Fausold, *The Presidency of Herbert C. Hoover* (Lawrence, Kans., 1985); Wilton Eckley, *Herbert Hoover* (Boston, 1980); and Richard Norton Smith, *An Uncommon Man: The Triumph of Herbert Hoover* (New York, 1984). All of these books are being gradually supplanted, at least in matters of detail, by George H. Nash's multivolume life. So far two volumes by Nash have appeared under the main title *The Life of Herbert Hoover:* vol. 1, *The Engineer* (New York, 1983), and vol. 2, *The Humanitarian, 1914–1917* (New York, 1988).

See the following two books by Ellis W. Hawley, the most influential scholar of Hoover studies: *Herbert Hoover as Secretary of Commerce: Studies in New Era Thought and Practice* (Iowa City, Iowa, 1981) and *Herbert Hoover and the Historians* (West Branch, Iowa, 1989). Hawley has also edited *Herbert Hoover: Containing the Public Messages, Speeches, and Statements of the President*, 4 vols. (Washington, D.C., 1974–1977). There are three bibliographies about Hoover: Patrick G. O'Brien, comp., *Herbert Hoover: A Bibliography* (Westport, Conn., 1993); Richard D. Burns, comp., *Herbert Hoover: A Bibliography of His Times and Presidency* (Wilmington, Del., 1991); and Kathleen Tracey, comp., *Herbert Hoover, a Bibliography: His Writings and Addresses* (Stanford, Calif., 1977).

Other important monographs include Donald J. Lisio, *The President and Protest: Hoover, MacArthur, and the Bonus Riot*, 2d ed. (New York, 1994), and his *Hoover, Blacks, and Lily-whites: A Study of Southern Strategies* (Chapel Hill, N.C., 1985); James S. Olson, *Herbert Hoover and the Reconstruction Finance Corporation, 1931–1933* (Ames, Iowa, 1977), and his *Saving Capitalism: The Reconstruction Finance Corporation and the New Deal, 1933–1940* (Princeton, N.J., 1988); Gary Dean Best, *The Politics of American Individualism: Herbert Hoover in Transition, 1918–1921* (Westport, Conn., 1975), and his *Herbert Hoover: The Postpresidential Years, 1933–1964* (Stanford, Calif., 1983); Albert U. Romasco, *The Poverty of Abundance: Hoover, the Nation, the Depression* (New York, 1965); Craig Lloyd, *Aggressive Introvert: A Study of Herbert Hoover and Public Relations Management, 1912–1932* (Columbus, Ohio, 1972); James D. Calder, *The Origins and Development of Federal Crime Control Policy: Herbert Hoover's Initiatives* (Westport, Conn., 1993); George H. Nash, *Herbert Hoover and Stanford University* (Stanford, Calif., 1988); and Allan J. Lichtman, *Prejudice and the Old Politics: The Presidential Election of 1928* (Chapel Hill, N.C., 1979).

Important collections of essays include Lawrence E. Gelfand, ed., *Herbert Hoover: The Great War and Its Aftermath, 1914–1923* (Iowa City, Iowa, 1979); Lee Nash, ed., *Understanding Herbert Hoover: Ten Perspectives* (Stanford, Calif., 1987); and Martin L. Fausold and George T. Mazuzan, eds., *The Hoover Presidency: A Reappraisal* (Albany, N.Y., 1974).

Recent works include Louis W. Liebovich, *Bylines in Despair: Herbert Hoover, the Great Depression, and the U.S. News Media* (Westport, Conn., 1994).

Franklin D. Roosevelt

David M. Kennedy

Franklin D. Roosevelt FRANKLIN D. ROOSEVELT LIBRARY

IT was the worst of times when Franklin Delano Roosevelt assumed the presidency in March 1933. Following the ruinous stock market crash of late 1929, the bottom seemed to drop out of the American economy. By 1933, securities listed on the New York Stock Exchange had lost more than three-quarters of their 1929 value. Industrial production had fallen to half its 1929 level. Agricultural income had plummeted even more sharply. Piles of unmarketable wheat flanked railroad tracks across the plains states. Desperate Iowa farmers blockaded the approaches to Sioux City in the summer of 1932, assaulting vehicles that tried to breach the makeshift barricades of logs and spiked telephone poles.

Americans had earned some $88 billion in 1929. Those still lucky enough to be working earned less than half that amount four years later. One wage earner in four—some 13 million people—had no job in 1933. Some 5,000 banks collapsed in the first three years of the depression, carrying down with them the life savings of tens of thousands of citizens. Those cold statistics only hinted at the human suffering that the Great Depression inflicted. Anxious men and women postponed or canceled plans to marry. Struggling couples had fewer children. Even the divorce rate declined, as the contracting economy sealed the exits from unhappy marriages. Disillusioned immigrants forsook the fabled American land of promise and returned by the thousands to their old countries. Nearly 100,000 down-and-out Americans responded to an advertisement in 1931 offering employment in the Soviet Union. More than a million homeless hoboes drifted about the country in search of work. "Hoovervilles," tar-paper and cardboard shantytowns derisively named for the incumbent president, sprang up on the outskirts of virtually every major city.

One such encampment of the unemployed arose in the summer of 1932 on the damp flatlands along the Anacostia River, in the District of Columbia. Bivouacked in old pup tents and huts fashioned from packing cases, some fifteen thousand veterans of World War I sought by their presence in Washington to wring from Congress the early award of a war-service bonus scheduled to be paid in 1945. President Hoover responded by putting the White House under guard, chaining its gates, and mobilizing four troops of cavalry under the command of General Douglas MacArthur. Exceeding his orders to contain the "Bonus Expeditionary Force" in their campsite at Anacostia Flats, MacArthur cleared the area with tear gas and put the marchers' shacks to the torch.

Against this background of deepening economic distress and rising social tension, Democrats met in Chicago in June 1932 to nominate their presidential candidate. Their party had not commanded the White House since Woodrow Wilson's departure in 1921. In the intervening years, the party had been riven by apparently irreconcilable conflicts between its stunningly disparate factions: agriculturalists opposed industrialists; the largely rural, Protestant, old-stock Anglo-Saxon South, still the party's principal power base, struggled to accommodate the growing influence of the Catholic American body politic. Their effort to coalesce, to agree on a candidate, and to govern thus tested the ability of the society itself to cope with the crisis of the depression in a coherent, effective way.

The Road to the White House

Well before 1932, Franklin Delano Roosevelt had established himself as the favorite candidate of progressive, or liberal, elements in the Democratic party. Yet he was in many ways an improbable progressive. Born on 30 January 1882 into a life of sumptuous privilege, he had passed as a young man through the rituals customary to the upbringing of sons of the Hudson River valley squirearchy: excur-

sions abroad, instruction from tutors, preparatory school at Endicott Peabody's exclusive academy at Groton, Massachusetts, and attendance at Harvard.

Yet, even as an undergraduate, Roosevelt displayed remarkable qualities of leadership and political belief. He remained an extra year at Harvard to serve as editor of the Crimson, the student newspaper. In an undergraduate essay on the decline of the once-famous Dutch families of New York, he made an exception of the Roosevelts. "They have never felt," he wrote, "that because they were born in a good position they could put their hands in their pockets and succeed. They have felt, rather, that being born in a good position, there was no excuse for them if they did not do their duty by the community."

Impelled by that sense of noblesse oblige, Roosevelt set out almost immediately after his graduation from Harvard on a career of public service. He drew inspiration from the example of his fifth cousin, Theodore Roosevelt. With uncanny and Jewish immigrant political machines and labor unions of the northern cities; states' righters battled centralizers; prohibitionist "drys" warred against opposing "wets"; reformist progressives clashed with old-fashioned conservatives. To a far greater extent than Republicans, who tended to be more homogeneous socially and like-minded politically, Democrats contained among themselves the many contentious forces that pulsed in the precision he retraced the path to the White House that Theodore had blazed, serving first as a New York state legislator (1910–1913), then as Woodrow Wilson's assistant secretary of the navy (1913–1920), and as governor of New York (1928–1932).

Stricken by polio in 1921, Roosevelt spent the next several years trying to recuperate, though he never regained the use of his legs. His disease became, in a sense, a political asset. Rising to eminence from birth in a humble log cabin evidenced the indomitability of character of other presidential aspirants; Roosevelt, denied that proof, found its equivalent in his struggle against paralysis. So thoroughly did he triumph over his handicap that many Americans, even after his many years in office as president, remained unaware that Roosevelt could neither walk nor stand unassisted.

Even during the gravest period of his illness, Roosevelt remained politically active, working to modernize the ramshackle organizational structure of the Democratic party and to move it in a progressive direction. "The Democratic Party is *the* Progressive Party of the country," he said in 1924, and two years later he explained that "a nation or a State which is unwilling by governmental action to tackle the new problems, caused by immense increase of population and by the astounding strides of modern science, is headed for decline and ultimate death." Those sentiments were strikingly at odds with the free-market philosophy of 1920s Republicanism and with the Jeffersonian origins of his own party, but they showed Roosevelt's fidelity to the principles of the early-twentieth-century progressive movement that his cousin Theodore had so colorfully led.

As governor of New York, Roosevelt tried to put those principles into practice. He called for the state government to take an active role in developing the St. Lawrence River waterway. He championed reforestation and other resource-management projects under state direction. He proposed legislation to improve credit facilities for farmers and to protect women and children factory workers. In 1931, in telling contrast to the timid response that the Hoover administration made to the problem of unemployment, Roosevelt established the state's Temporary Emergency Relief Administration to provide jobs to victims of the depression.

Democrats knew that they had an excellent opportunity to recapture the presidency from the battered Hoover in 1932, and Roosevelt was clearly the preferred candidate of the progressive wing of the party. But he was not without opposition, particularly from old-guard elements led by John J. Raskob, the enormously wealthy and powerful national party chairman, and from southern Democrats who rallied to the candidacy of Speaker of the House John Nance Garner, a Texan. At the crucial moment in the balloting at Chicago, Garner threw his support to Roosevelt, who secured the nomination on the fourth round of voting.

Many observers were little impressed with the party's choice. One commentator opined that Roosevelt "would probably make the weakest President of the dozen aspirants." Columnist Walter Lippmann offered a judgment destined to become infamous as a monument of underestimation. Roosevelt, he concluded, was "a pleasant man who, without any important qualifications for the office, would very much like to be President." The venerable Supreme Court Justice Oliver Wendell Holmes, Jr., came closer to the mark when he described Roosevelt as a man of "second-class intellect but a first-class temperament."

Unfathomably mysterious is the alchemy that shapes the temperament of leadership out of ordinary human clay, but in Roosevelt's case his aristocratic upbringing and long struggle against disability were crucial elements. He was almost preternaturally self-confident, restlessly active, unflaggingly optimistic, and endowed with a fine instinct for sensing the mood of the nation.

Roosevelt exhibited those qualities immediately upon receiving notice of his nomination. Shattering precedent, he flew to Chicago and gave the first acceptance speech ever delivered to a presidential nominating convention. "I pledge you, I pledge myself," he declared to the assembled delegates, "to a new deal for the American people." But the campaign that followed also seemed to confirm the truth of Holmes's judgment about the nominee's intellectual limitations. Though Roosevelt conscientiously listened to the advice of a "brain trust" of economic nationalists, including Rexford G. Tugwell, Raymond Moley, and Adolf A. Berle, Jr., historians have sought in vain to discover in his 1932 campaign speeches a consciously wrought blueprint for the New Deal. He never mentioned later landmark developments such as the Social Security Act or the Tennessee Valley Authority (TVA). Much of his attack on Hoover focused on the incumbent's alleged determination to expand the federal government and to be "the greatest spending Administration in peace times in all our history"—accusations given a sharply ironic ring by later events.

Roosevelt's warm, ebullient, yet comforting personality contrasted irresistibly with the hapless Hoover's efforts to portray his opponent as a confused and vacillating "chameleon on plaid." On election day, 8 November 1932, Roosevelt rolled up an impressive victory with 22,809,638 votes to Hoover's 15,758,901. He carried all but six states, for an electoral college count of 472 to 59. He pulled into office with him sizable Democratic majorities in both houses of Congress. Roosevelt thus began the longest presidency—three times reelected, twelve years in office—in American history.

Roosevelt's first election marked the last time that a four-month interval separated a president's election and inauguration. (Since 1937, presidents have been inaugurated in January.) The wait in this case was especially long and cruel. The downward-spiraling depression sucked the entire nation's banking and credit structure into its vortex. Nearly five thousand banks failed between 1929 and 1933, wiping out billions of dollars of savings. As the crisis thickened, panicky depositors accelerated their withdrawals from savings accounts, further jeopardizing the precarious liquidity of many institutions. The governor of Nevada ordered a "bank holiday" in October 1932 to slow the vicious cycle. The governor of Michigan followed suit in February 1933, and by inaugural eve, banks had barred their doors in thirty-eight states. Outgoing President Herbert Hoover tried several times to secure President-elect Roosevelt's agreement to various emergency measures, but Roosevelt warily refused to commit himself. On the very morning of the inauguration, the governors of New York and Illinois announced the closing of banks in their states, the twin pillars of the nation's financial edifice. A few hours later, the New York Stock Exchange stopped all trading in securities. This was the grim setting for Roosevelt's inauguration and the occasion for his famous admonition that "the only thing we have to fear is fear itself."

The Hundred Days

"Rulers of the exchange of mankind's goods have failed through their own stubbornness and their own incompetence," Roosevelt charged in his inaugural address. "The money changers have fled from their high seats in the temple of our civilization. We may now restore that temple to the ancient truths." With that belligerent battle cry against the bankers, Roosevelt summoned Congress to convene in special session to deal with the banking crisis. By the time the representatives and senators settled into their seats in the Capitol on 9 March, every bank in the nation was closed by presidential order. Rumors flew that the new president intended to take the radical step of nationalizing the banks.

When the emergency banking bill was read aloud to a tense House of Representatives at 1:00 P.M. (it had been drafted too hastily for copies to be distributed), conservatives were greatly relieved. The bill extended the helping hand of government to assist private bankers back to their feet. It authorized the Federal Reserve Board to issue additional currency secured by bank assets; it directed the Reconstruction Finance Corporation (RFC)—an agency created in the Hoover administration to provide capital to private businesses—to purchase preferred bank stock; it extended the government's control over gold holdings; and it mandated Treasury Department supervision of the reopening and reorganiza-

tion of the banks. Less than eight hours after it was introduced, the banking bill swept virtually unexamined through both houses of Congress and was back on the president's desk for his signature.

Conservatives again took heart six days later when the administration pushed through a stringent budget-cutting measure and followed it up with legislation designed to increase federal revenues from the sale of beer and wine. In a fortnight of dazzling political initiative, the supposedly progressive Roosevelt had enacted almost the entire program of the reactionary Raskob wing of his party. "Capitalism," one New Dealer later reflected, "was saved in eight days."

But the president was not finished. He had shored up the private banking system and had moved to restore business confidence in the soundness of his administration's fiscal policies. Now he saw further opportunities. "Things moved so fast," he wrote of the period just after the Emergency Banking Act was launched, "that during the next two days it became obvious that other matters had to be taken up to meet the financial and economic crisis." Some of the matters next taken up addressed the immediate goals of unemployment relief and economic recovery. Others had their origins deep in the history of the progressive reform movement; they aimed at governmental restructuring of broad areas of American life in ways destined to endure well beyond the depression.

In the next three months, Roosevelt induced Congress to pass a dozen additional pieces of major legislation. The Federal Emergency Relief Act funded the unemployment compensation programs of the states, whose treasuries had long since been overwhelmed by the scale of the depression. The Civilian Conservation Corps (CCC) put hundreds of thousands of jobless young men and a handful of young women to work on federally directed projects in reforestation, road building, and flood control. Financial institutions, as well as homeowners and farmers, were further aided by the Homeowners' Loan Act, the Emergency Farm Mortgage Act, and the Farm Credit Act, all of which provided in various ways for the refinancing of private debts under government auspices. As many as one-fifth of the nation's homes and farms were saved from foreclosure by these measures, securing the lifelong political gratitude of large sections of the middle class. The Glass-Steagall Banking Act created the Federal Deposit Insurance Corporation, insuring bank deposits up to $5,000—a measure that at a single stroke virtually eliminated the prospect of further "runs" on banks by nervous depositors. The Tennessee Valley Authority Act initiated a comprehensive development plan for the vast Tennessee River basin. The Agricultural Adjustment Act sought to stabilize agricultural prices by crop limitation and government subsidy. It also carried an amendment authorizing the president to undertake various steps to inflate the currency. The National Industrial Recovery Act called for the establishment of codes governing production, pricing, and labor practices in major industries; it additionally provided for a $3.3 billion public works program. Other measures promoted the financial reorganization of railroads, as well as tighter federal controls over securities markets and gold.

On 16 June 1933 the special congressional session ended. The famous "Hundred Days" that commenced Roosevelt's presidency left the country somewhat breathless and a bit baffled, but nonetheless bolstered in spirit. The new president had displayed awesome powers of political leadership, though the precise ideological sum of the Hundred Days legislation remained almost impossible to define. Roosevelt seemed to offer something for everybody—but the gift of hope, precious beyond measure at that volatile moment, he offered equally to all.

Roosevelt took extraordinary steps to project his reassuring presence into every American home. He was the first president to master the new electronic medium of radio, with its powerful ability to touch millions of persons instantaneously and simultaneously. He began the second week of his presidency with a radio broadcast explaining in plain, simple language the purpose of his banking program—the first of many such "fireside chats." He cultivated journalists by abolishing the practice of responding only to written questions in press conferences. In studied contrast to President Hoover's treatment of the Bonus Expeditionary Force, Roosevelt provided food and medical services for all the veterans who had remained along the Anacostia River, and sent his wife, Eleanor, to lead them in group singing. This was an early instance of the extraordinary role that Eleanor Roosevelt played in her husband's administrations. A dedicated reformer and humanitarian, she developed an independent public career as an advocate for disadvantaged Americans and served as Franklin Roosevelt's ambassador to such constituencies as blacks, women, farmers, workers, and young

people. She was unquestionably the most activist First Lady in American history up to that time.

The New Deal in Action

The National Recovery Administration (NRA) formed the spearhead of the administration's attack on the economic crisis. Roosevelt had voiced its informing philosophy in a speech to San Francisco's Commonwealth Club in September 1932. His keynote was a call for stability, not stimulus. "Our task now," he had said, "is not . . . necessarily producing more goods. It is the soberer, less dramatic business of administering resources and plants already in hand." Headed by General Hugh Johnson, the NRA set out to secure the agreement of major industries to government-backed codes designed to stop the downward slide of payrolls, prices, and production. Johnson offered exemption from antitrust prosecution to industries that consented to put a floor under wages and to cease cutthroat price slashing. Section 7a of the National Industrial Recovery Act appealed for labor support of these arrangements, by offering guarantees of the right of unions to organize and bargain collectively.

Fearing a court test of the NRAs constitutionality, Johnson avoided legal coercion and relied instead on a massive publicity campaign to achieve his aims. He plastered the country with the NRA symbol, a stylized blue eagle, and organized monster parades to induce businessmen to do their part. Within months, some 2 million employers in most major industries had signed code agreements.

The codes brought stability to the failing economy, but they did not bring instant recovery. More than 20 percent of the work force remained idle in 1934. The codes also brought controversy. Small businessmen in particular chafed under the labor regulations of the codes; virtually all businessmen resented the weight of government bureaucracy with which they were suddenly saddled; other critics charged that the codes maintained prices at artificially high levels and promoted monopoly.

On 27 May 1935 the United States Supreme Court declared the NRA unconstitutional. The administration soon rebounded with a series of "Little NRA" bills targeted on specific industries, including coal mining and oil refining. These measures, together with the Robinson-Patman Act of 1936 and the Miller-Tydings Act of 1937, both of which prohibited "unfair" price competition in the retail trades, showed the persistence of the stagnationist economic philosophy that had originally generated the NRA.

In agriculture, which in the 1930s still employed more than one-fifth of all American workers, the administration pursued similar policies. It aimed at achieving equilibrium, not growth, by raising prices and lowering production. In 1933 those ends compelled the distasteful means of crop destruction. Farmers were required to plow under millions of acres of cotton and to slaughter millions of baby pigs. Thereafter, debate raged within the administration over the best method of increasing farm income. George Peek, head of the Agricultural Adjustment Administration (AAA) and a fierce economic nationalist, favored dumping American surpluses in foreign markets. Rexford Tugwell, then assistant secretary of agriculture and an economist devoted to government-directed economic planning, advocated stricter production controls. For the moment, at least, Tugwell won. In the years immediately following 1933, the AAA relied on loan subsidies and a variety of compulsory crop-reduction laws to reduce the agricultural glut.

Farm income rose nearly 50 percent by 1936, though some of this gain was achieved by exporting rural unemployment to the cities. A combination of spectacular dust storms in the Great Plains and AAA policies forced many small farmers off the land, especially black sharecroppers and tenant farmers in the cotton South. The Resettlement Administration was established in 1935, and its replacement, the Farm Security Administration, in 1937, to deal with the problems of displaced agricultural workers, but neither agency significantly deflected the shift of labor out of agriculture that the depression, the AAA, and the weather had catalyzed.

The Supreme Court declared certain key provisions of the AAA unconstitutional in early 1936, though Congress, as in the case of industrial policy, moved swiftly to replace it with only minor modifications. The Soil Conservation and Domestic Allotment Act of 1936 and the Agricultural Adjustment Act of 1938 perpetuated the early New Deal policies of subsidizing crop reductions. Yet none of these measures solved the problem of over-production, and the growing mountain of agricultural surpluses severely strained the government's ability to maintain prices. By the late 1930s, the United States was dumping millions of bushels of wheat overseas. It would take a world at war to absorb fully the paradoxically baleful bounty of America's farms.

Despite the drama of the Hundred Days and the efforts of the NRA and the AAA, the economy remained sickly. Desperate for some means to raise prices and lift the crushing burdens of debtors, especially farmers, Roosevelt set out in October 1933 on a deliberate program of monetary inflation. He had already cleared the way for such action by taking the United States off the international gold standard on 19 April 1933. A few weeks later, he had repudiated the efforts of the London Economic Conference to stabilize international exchange rates. Now he launched a bold but somewhat ill-advised scheme to devalue the dollar by ordering the Treasury Department to buy gold at ever-increasing prices. These purchases ended in January 1934, with the price of gold pegged at $35 an ounce, the level at which it remained for decades. The dollar had been reduced to about 59 percent of its pre-1933 value relative to gold, but prices had not risen correspondingly.

Roosevelt's disappointment at that result was aggravated by the sharp criticism his gold-buying program evoked in orthodox financial circles. Several high officials in the administration resigned or were fired because of this episode. But pressure to inflate the currency persisted. Congress in June 1934 directed the Treasury Department to monetize large amounts of silver. These inflationary measures, together with chronic though unintended federal budget deficits and the creation in June 1934 of the Securities and Exchange Commission (SEC) to regulate the securities market, helped to precipitate the first organized business opposition to the New Deal—the American Liberty League, chartered in August 1934. Executives of the Du Pont and General Motors corporations, including conservative Democrats like Raskob, dominated the new organization.

If the Liberty League represented the nucleus of an emerging anti-New Deal coalition, its influence was negligible in the congressional elections of 1934. Voters gave the Democratic party a whopping three-to-one majority in the House and an unprecedented sixty-nine seats in the Senate. Many newly elected Democrats came from urban, industrial areas whose unemployed voters hungered for drastic, even radical, solutions to the seemingly endless depression. If anything, the center of political gravity in the new Congress was well to the left of Roosevelt and the New Deal.

The Second New Deal

Other pressures inclining Roosevelt toward the left were also building as the new Congress convened in

1935. Louisiana's flamboyant Senator Huey Long, who had unmistakable presidential ambitions, had founded the national "Share Our Wealth" movement in 1934, advocating sweeping redistribution of national income from the wealthy to the poor. The Reverend Charles Coughlin, Michigan's "radio priest" who claimed a weekly radio audience of some 40 million listeners, increasingly lashed out at Roosevelt for his failure to tame the bankers and unleash an aggressively inflationary program. California physician Francis Townsend championed the cause of the elderly with a warmhearted but actuarially daffy scheme to pay $200 a month to all citizens over sixty years of age. Industrial unionists, led by the president of the United Mine Workers, John L. Lewis, pressed with growing ardor and occasional violence to grasp the benefits that the National Industrial Recovery Act's Section 7a had put so tantalizingly within their reach.

All those forces worked to push the president in a more radical direction. In April he approved the enormous Emergency Relief Appropriation Act, allocating some $4.8 billion dollars to create jobs on public projects under the auspices of the Public Works Administration (PWA) and the newly created Works Progress Administration (WPA). Roosevelt named a close confidant, social worker Harry Hopkins, to head the WPA, which emphasized "work relief," rather than the dole, for the unemployed. Under authority provided by the Emergency Relief Appropriation Act, Roosevelt later created the Rural Electrification Administration to bring electricity to rural areas; the National Youth Administration (NYA) to provide employment and educational benefits to persons under twenty-six years of age; and the National Resources Planning Board to draw up plans for the long-range development of natural resources. (Only the first of these agencies survived World War II.)

Then, on 27 May 1935, the Supreme Court decision that the NRA's code-making activities were unconstitutional removed the centerpiece from Roosevelt's economic program. The Court's action provided the final shove propelling Roosevelt on a fresh round of legislative activity that eventually eclipsed even the formidable achievements of the Hundred Days. The early New Deal had emphasized stabilization and relief, and had made some hesitant efforts to stimulate economic recovery. Roosevelt's legislative program in 1935 emphasized far-reaching social and institutional reforms. It represented a tri-

umphant victory for progressives, who now saw much of their decades-old political agenda finally enacted. And it permanently transformed vast sectors of American society.

The first measure to pass owed more to the new composition of Congress than it did to Roosevelt's leadership. Senator Robert Wagner, whose New York constituents exemplified the urban, working-class elements now rising to dominance in the Democratic party, introduced a bill establishing a permanent National Labor Relations Board (NLRB) to replace an earlier board that had collapsed under management pressure. It provided for considerably stronger government guarantees than the National Industrial Recovery Act's Section 7a had afforded for the rights of workers to organize into unions and to bargain collectively with employers. Neither the president nor Secretary of Labor Frances Perkins (the nation's first woman cabinet officer) bothered until the eleventh hour to lift a finger in support of the bill, which was signed into law on 5 July.

The Wagner Act revolutionized the condition of American labor. Union membership doubled in the half dozen years following 1935. Organizers, protected by the government, rallied workers with the slogan "The President Wants You to join a Union." The Wagner Act also contributed to a profound change in the character of the union movement. It speeded the developing schism between the old-line craft-based unions and the much more rapidly growing industry-based unions, which concentrated on recruiting low-skilled workers. The split became official in 1938 when John L. Lewis led his Congress of Industrial Organizations (CIO) out of the American Federation of Labor (AFL).

Other legislative landmarks followed in quick succession in the summer of 1935. The Banking Act of 1935 brought the Federal Reserve system under closer government control. In the teeth of fierce opposition from privately owned utility companies, the Public Utility Holding Company Act mandated the elimination of monopolistic practices in the utilities industry. It further enabled the Federal Power Commission to regulate the interstate transmission of electrical power, and the Federal Trade Commission to perform a similar function for natural gas.

Most important of all was the passage of the Social Security Act. It provided for joint federal-state programs of unemployment compensation, financed by a federal tax on payrolls. It also created an exclusively federal system of old-age and survivors' insurance funded by a tax shared equally between employers and employees. Though modest in its initial benefits and regressively financed by a uniform tax on the current earnings of workers, the Social Security Act nevertheless represented a milestone on the road to a comprehensive welfare state. It offered a modicum of protection from the historic scourge of unemployment and guaranteed a minimum level of comfort for workers in their old age. It also created the potential for enormous demands on the public purse, diminished incentives for individuals to save, and reduced the sense of responsibility of families to care for their own elderly members. Probably no other New Deal measure did more in the long run to change the character of American life.

Roosevelt now had a broadly based, thoroughly progressive platform on which to stand for reelection in 1936. A handful of unreconstructed conservatives, including the two previous presidential nominees of his own party, bitterly denounced him as a traitor to his own class, a dangerous experimenter with his country's most sacred traditions, and an architect of permanent bloc divisions in the body politic. ("They are unanimous in their hatred for me," Roosevelt told an election-eve crowd at Madison Square Garden, "and I welcome their hatred!") A ragtag coalition of radical populist groups, badly weakened by the assassination in September 1935 of their ablest leader, Huey Long, fielded a Union party presidential ticket, with pathetic results. The Republican party nominated Governor Alf Landon of Kansas, a sincere but inept campaigner who proved no match for Roosevelt.

The president campaigned as a serenely confident incumbent. Though nearly 9 million Americans were still without work, Roosevelt pointed to the progress that had been made against unemployment since 1933. He reaped the political benefits of his myriad programs to halt foreclosures on homes and farms. Black voters, long loyal to the party of Lincoln, switched their allegiance massively to the party of Roosevelt, who had avoided civil rights initiatives but had provided black Americans with unemployment relief and access to newly created agencies like the NYA. Perhaps most dramatic, Roosevelt harvested the rich crop of political goodwill he had sown in the ethnic, working-class communities of the big industrial cities. Fifty-two of Roosevelt's appointments to the federal bench were Catholics; only eight Catholics had been appointed by his three Republican predecessors. John L. Lewis' CIO contributed more than

$770,000 to the campaign, and laborers voted for Roosevelt in overwhelming numbers. Roosevelt carried all but 2 of the nation's 106 cities with populations of a hundred thousand or more. He carried every state except Maine and Vermont, scoring the largest victory margin (523 to 8) in the electoral college since James Monroe in 1820. His share of the popular vote was 27,752,869 to Landon's 16,674,665. Democrats also tightened their grip on Congress, with unassailable majorities of 76 to 16 in the Senate and 331 to 89 in the House.

Roosevelt had thus forged a political coalition that would sustain the Democrats in power for nearly a generation. He had successfully wedded to the traditional southern and agricultural elements in his party the newly potent urban working class, including a variety of ethnic and racial minorities, and large sections of the middle class, grateful for the preservation of their threatened way of life. His party's enormous preponderance in Congress apparently afforded him almost unlimited power. And when he declared in his second inaugural address on 20 January 1937 that I see one-third of a nation ill-housed, ill-clad, ill-nourished," there seemed little doubt that he intended to use that power for progressive ends.

Roosevelt at Bay

Within weeks of that triumphant moment, Roosevelt was ensnared in paralyzing political difficulties. He and his party unquestionably commanded the executive and legislative branches of government, but not the third branch, the judiciary, designedly insulated from the flow and surge of popular political tides. The Supreme Court, made up entirely of pre-Roosevelt appointees, six of them over seventy years of age in 1937, had declared seven major pieces of New Deal legislation unconstitutional by the end of Roosevelt's first term. As he began his second, he determined to confront that judicial obstacle head-on.

On 5 February 1937, Roosevelt proposed to a surprised Congress and nation that he be allowed to appoint one additional justice, up to a maximum of six, for every justice who remained on the Court after reaching the age of seventy. Disingenuously, he tried to justify his proposal with the argument that an overburdened Court needed an expanded membership to handle its caseload—an allegation peremptorily squelched by the respected Chief Justice Charles Evans Hughes.

Roosevelt's "Court-packing plan," as it was soon called, amounted to one of the worst political blunders of his career. Conservatives gagged at the notion of tampering with one of the Republic's sacred institutions. (Though it had been done before, when President Grant had added two justices to the Court, primarily in order to secure a favorable ruling on the Legal Tender Act. Unlike Roosevelt, Grant had taken care to cultivate political support in the Senate before he acted.) Even friends of the New Deal objected to the president's high-handed tactics.

While the battle raged, the Court itself moved to spike Roosevelt's guns. On 29 March 1937 it upheld a Washington State minimum-wage law (in *West Coast Hotel* v. *Parrish*) and two weeks later it declared the Wagner Act constitutional (in *National Labor Relations Board* v. *Jones and Laughlin Steel Corp.*). This shift in judicial sentiment, effected largely by the conversion of Justice Roberts to a more liberal point of view, has been dubbed "the switch in time that saved nine." The president's Court-reform bill died an ignominious death—though eventually Roosevelt appointed eight Supreme Court justices, more than any president save George Washington.

The Court-packing controversy marked the beginning of the end of the New Deal. More than any other single episode, it helped to crystallize a powerfully obstructionist congressional coalition of Republicans and conservative Democrats. In one brief season the president squandered much of the political capital he had so impressively amassed at the polls just a few months earlier.

Other problems soon beset him. Middle-class Americans grew restive at the mushroom growth of industrial unions, especially when daring organizers introduced the "sit-down strike," which amounted to the peaceful seizure of factories by striking workers. The United Auto Workers (UAW) used the sit-down with great effect against General Motors in early 1937. The UAW won recognition as the sole bargaining agent for General Motors employees, but its tactics alienated many nonunionists from the Roosevelt camp.

The worst was yet to come. The economy had improved slowly but perceptibly since 1933, making especially vigorous gains after 1935 under the stimuli of relief expenditures and the one-time-only payment of the budget-busting veterans' bonus, which passed over Roosevelt's veto in January 1936. Incredibly, this display of economic vitality raised the dread specter of inflation in many influential minds, including that of the president. In June 1937, Roosevelt severely curtailed federal spending. Simultaneously,

the new Social Security taxes began to bite into paychecks. By late summer these deflationary developments had precipitated an economic downturn at least as bad as that of 1929. Within months, more than 2 million workers lost their jobs.

The "Roosevelt recession" rubbed salt into the president's already smarting political wounds, but it did bring to eventual resolution a long-running debate within his administration about fiscal policy. Orthodox financial advisers had until then dominated the government's inner policymaking circles. As the devil views holy water, so did they look upon the radical notion that the government might deliberately incur deficits as a means of economic stimulus. Though Roosevelt had not yet produced a single balanced budget, that had continued to be his aim. He had tolerated deficits, not sought them, but now he hearkened to the counsel of another group of advisers. Armed with the recently formulated theories of the British economist John Maynard Keynes, the advisers argued that the government should consciously embrace deficit spending in order to bolster consumption and stimulate the economy.

In April 1938, Roosevelt sent to Congress an avowedly stimulatory multibillion-dollar deficit-spending bill. After almost ten years of depression, this was the first purposeful effort to effect economic recovery through the means of countercyclical fiscal policy. For the millions of Americans who for a decade had paid the price of economic collapse, it came assuredly too late; as events were to prove, it was also woefully too little.

It was also among the last gasps of the New Deal. Roosevelt did manage to push through Congress in June 1938 the Fair Labor Standards Act, which defined a federally guaranteed minimum wage and maximum workweek and outlawed child labor. By then the conservative congressional coalition had crystallized, and even members of the president's own party were openly flouting his will. Roosevelt tried to purge conservatives from his party in the 1938 primary season but failed utterly. In the congressional elections in November, Republicans scored their first gains since 1928, picking up eight seats in the Senate and seventy-nine in the House.

With that, the New Deal was effectively ended. It had carried the country, however minimally, through a dark hour. It left a large and lasting legacy of major institutional reforms. Added together, those reforms embodied the various, often contradictory pressures of the decade—particularly those pulsing in the still disparate Democratic party—rather than a coherent expression of any particular ideology. The problem of the depression, the problem that had been midwife and companion to those reforms, was never solved by the New Deal. Roosevelt's principal achievement was political, not economic. He had enabled his countrymen to keep their heads while peoples all about them in the world were losing theirs. He had, against not inconsiderable odds, maintained social peace in a depressed and sometimes desperate America. As the decade of the 1930s drew on, the president's attention turned more and more to preserving peace in the increasingly brutal world beyond America's borders.

Foreign Policy

To the conduct of American foreign policy Franklin Roosevelt brought credentials that were rare in the history of the presidency. His cosmopolitan upbringing as a late-nineteenth-century American aristocrat, including his intellectual formation on two continents, gave him a sophisticated appreciation of the world that was approximated among modern presidents only by his cousin Theodore. Yet the precise imprint of that international background on his policies was sometimes difficult to define. He had served in the government of the archinternationalist Woodrow Wilson and, as his party's vice presidential candidate in 1920, had faithfully echoed Wilson's call for American membership in the League of Nations. Yet during his own presidential campaign in 1932 he repudiated the idea of American entry into the League.

Roosevelt sounded an especially isolationist note in his first inaugural address when he declared that "our international trade relations, though vastly important, are, in point of time and necessity, secondary to the establishment of a sound national economy." He acted consistently with these sentiments when he helped to scuttle the London Economic Conference in June 1933 and embarked thereafter on a highly nationalist monetary policy of drastically devaluing the dollar.

Yet Roosevelt also displayed distinctly internationalist colors in the early years of the New Deal. He chose Senator Cordell Hull of Tennessee, an indefatigable paladin of liberalized international trade, as his secretary of state. He restrained AAA administrator George Peek from dictating narrowly nationalist agricultural policies. He blessed Hull's campaign to secure passage of the Trade Agreements Act of 1934,

as well as the secretary's subsequent efforts to negotiate reciprocity treaties incorporating the unconditional most-favored-nation principle. Defying the fierce invective of some conservatives—and the scolding of his own mother—he extended diplomatic recognition to the Soviet Union on 16 November 1933. He made partial amends for his destructive role at the 1933 London Economic Conference when he concluded an exchange stabilization agreement with Britain and France in 1936.

Roosevelt also sought to implement the "Good Neighbor policy" with Latin America. He allowed Secretary Hull to vote in favor of a resolution at the Pan-American Conference in Montevideo, Uruguay, in 1933, proclaiming that "no state has the right to intervene in the internal or external affairs of another." That statement effectively repudiated the belligerent "corollary" Theodore Roosevelt had attached in 1904 to the Monroe Doctrine, asserting the claim of the United States to exercise international police power in the western hemisphere. Hull prevailed upon his chief to follow up on that dramatic announcement by renouncing the Platt Amendment (1901), whereby the United States had asserted its right to intervene in Cuban affairs, and by ending in 1934 the twenty-year-old American military occupation of Haiti. Mexico put Roosevelt's good-neighborliness to a demanding test in 1938 when it nationalized its oil industry, expropriating the interests of many American firms. Roosevelt resisted pressure to intervene, and successfully negotiated adequate compensation for the confiscated American properties.

Roosevelt's Latin American policies suggested that he had at most a limited internationalist agenda in the early years of his presidency, confined to making the United States an influential regional power, but no more. That impression was strengthened in March 1934, when Congress mandated the granting of independence to the Philippines within ten years—an apparent signal that the United States intended to diminish its role in Asia.

Roosevelt's halting steps toward a more active international role for the United States took place against a backdrop of gathering isolationist feeling in the country and in Congress. Isolationism had roots sunk deeply into the soil of American history and culture. "Rejection of Europe," the novelist John Dos Passos once wrote, "is what America is all about." The earliest Pilgrims had sought separation from the corruptions of the Old World. George Washington in his farewell address had formulated those sentiments into high political doctrine. "Why . . . entangle our peace and prosperity," he had asked, "in the toils of European ambition, rivalship, interest, humor, or caprice?"

Americans of Roosevelt's generation had temporarily forsaken that ancient wisdom when they entered the European war in 1917. A decade and a half later, many of them deeply regretted that lapse. Fifty thousand of their countrymen had died, Woodrow Wilson had failed miserably to shape a liberal peace, and Europe, so far from being redeemed by the American intervention, had apparently lost its soul in the postwar era to Communism, Fascism, and Nazism. Regret was powerfully reinforced in 1934 when Senator Gerald P. Nye's Munitions Investigating Committee began to publicize sensational accusations that the United States had been cynically maneuvered into the war in 1917 by American bankers and arms manufacturers.

The full force of this isolationist tide was revealed in January 1935, when Roosevelt proposed that the United States join the World Court. Inspired by a savage anti-court radio sermon from Father Coughlin, opponents of the president's plan poured a Niagara of telegrams onto the Senate, drowning the court agreement. Ever sensitive to the public temper, a chastened Roosevelt quickly grasped the implications of this episode for foreign policy: "We shall go through a period of non-co-operation in everything . . . for the next year or two."

For the next year or two and longer, Roosevelt witnessed the simultaneous deepening of the isolationist mood in America and the sorry deterioration of the fragile structure of international peace. Adolf Hitler announced in March 1935 his intention to train a half-million-man army, and a long-simmering dispute between Italy and Ethiopia exploded into a shooting war in October of that year. Alarmed at these events, Congress, in August 1935, passed the Neutrality Act, which imposed a mandatory embargo on arms shipments to all belligerents. Roosevelt disliked the limits on his discretionary power dictated by the act's mandatory features; but, giving top priority to his domestic reform package in that remarkable summer, he did little to shape the neutrality law. The act was strengthened in February 1936 to include a ban on loans or credits to any nation at war. In early 1937, Congress tightened the law still further by confining the sale even of nonmilitary goods to belligerents who could pay cash and carry their cargoes away from American ports in their own ships.

Brazenly flouting the Treaty of Versailles, Hitler marched troops into the Rhineland in March 1936. Four months later, civil war erupted in Spain, which quickly became a proving ground for the newly developed military machines of Fascist Italy and Nazi Germany. "The whole European panorama is fundamentally blacker than at any time in your life . . . or mine," Roosevelt wrote in early 1936 to his ambassador in Paris; these, he said, "may be the last days of . . . peace before a long chaos." Hitler rolled on, virtually unchecked. He marched into Austria in March 1938. At the infamous Munich conference in September 1938, he secured the acquiescence of Britain and France to his annexation of the Sudetenland. Unappeased, he swallowed up the rest of Czechoslovakia six months later. After signing a nonaggression pact with the Soviet Union in August 1939, Hitler invaded Poland on 1 September. Britain and France declared war on Germany two days later.

The Shadow of War

A second world war had "come at last," Roosevelt said on hearing the news from Poland. "God help us all." When the war ended, more than five years and 50 million deaths later, the United States would be indisputably the most powerful nation on the ravaged planet. But in 1939, America wavered uncertainly on the periphery of these ominous events.

Roosevelt hoped to preserve the United States from the scourge of war, but he also hoped, from at least 1935 on, to bring the power of his country to bear against the prairie fire of armed aggression that was licking its way around the globe. Three forces constrained him: the lack of political will in his potential allies, Premier Édouard Daladier of France and Prime Minister Neville Chamberlain of Great Britain, cowering in the face of Hitler's bullying; the isolationist mood in America, codified into formal statutes purposely designed to tie the president's hands; and his own uncertainty, both about the means to be employed abroad and about the political risks of frontally challenging the isolationists at home.

Roosevelt did manage to align the United States with the League of Nations sanctions against Italy in the Ethiopian crisis, simply by enforcing the 1935 neutrality law. It prohibited arms shipments to all belligerents, but since Ethiopia could not have afforded to purchase American arms in any event, the real force of the ban fell exclusively on Italy. Similarly,

Roosevelt artfully invoked the Neutrality Act during the Spanish civil war, reinforcing the Anglo-French Nonintervention Committee's effort—pusillanimous and myopic though it may have been—to contain the conflict within Spain's borders.

Japan in mid-1937 escalated its six-year-old incursion in Manchuria into a full-scale invasion of China, once again testing Roosevelt's ingenuity in finding ways to check aggression while fettered by the neutrality laws. He responded by refusing to proclaim that a formal state of war existed between the two nations. (Japan officially labeled the conflict an "incident.") He thus forestalled activating the arms embargo and cash-and-carry provisions of the neutrality statutes and preserved China's ability to secure supplies in the United States.

Using isolationist legislation to achieve internationalist ends was a kind of political jujitsu, and the president could employ the tactic only so long. "If Germany invades a country and declares war," Roosevelt explained to a senator in 1939, "we'll be on the side of Hitler by invoking the [neutrality] act. If we could get rid of the arms embargo, it wouldn't be so bad." But the president's efforts to revise the neutrality statutes were repeatedly frustrated by congressional isolationists. Their political power waxed while Roosevelt's waned in the declining days of the New Deal. He called for a "quarantine" against aggression in an eloquent speech in Chicago on 5 October 1937, but still smarting from the lacerations of the Supreme Court reform fight and freshly wounded by the sharp recession then setting in, he failed to capitalize on the generally favorable public response. The foreign press accurately described the quarantine speech as "an attitude without a program." Three months later, isolationists in Congress pointedly reminded Roosevelt of the obstacles confronting an avowedly internationalist program when they mustered 188 votes in the House in favor of a constitutional amendment requiring a national referendum on a declaration of war. Throughout the rest of 1938 and most of 1939, Roosevelt could do little to prepare for the inescapable conflict. Only after the German invasion of Poland did Congress, in November 1939, repeal the mandatory arms embargo. The cash-and-carry provisions of the neutrality laws remained.

Roosevelt moved thereafter to make the United States, as he later described it, "the great arsenal of democracy." Yet he and his countrymen had waited so long to make their weight felt in the scales of di-plomacy that the cause they even now so hesitantly joined came perilously close to being lost. After a deceptive lull following his swift conquest of Poland, Hitler unleashed lightning assaults on Denmark and Norway on 9 April 1940. A month later, Germany and Italy invaded France, which crumpled quickly and ingloriously. Jackbooted Fascists now stood astride Europe from the Baltic to the Mediterranean. Only Britain, lonely and besieged, stood between them and the United States.

As Hitler's air force pounded Britain in the summer of 1940, the new British prime minister, Winston Churchill, beseeched Roosevelt for aid, especially for destroyers to secure Britain's sea-lanes. Roosevelt had already, in the opening months of 1940, induced Congress to appropriate several billion dollars for defense measures, including an aircraft production program with the then incredible goal of building fifty thousand planes a year. Now, fulminating against isolationists who deluded themselves that the United States could survive as "a lone island in a world dominated by force . . . handcuffed, hungry, and fed through the bars from day to day by the contemptuous, unpitying masters of other continents," he desperately sought ways to bolster beleaguered Britain. In August he hit upon a bold idea: to give Britain fifty American destroyers in exchange for long-term leases on naval bases in the western Atlantic.

With that exchange, Roosevelt inaugurated a collaboration with Churchill that in the history of relations among sovereign states was uniquely intimate and comprehensive. He also risked the wrath of isolationists—and in an election year. While the Battle of Britain raged, Americans waged their own quadrennial political battle to elect a president. Roosevelt, reluctant to relinquish the stage at such a dramatic historical moment, stood for an unprecedented third term. His opponent was Wendell Willkie, a liberally inclined businessman who had swept out of obscurity to capture the Republican nomination. Fortunately for the cause of American internationalism, Willkie shared much of Roosevelt's appraisal of the international scene and largely refrained from attacking the president's foreign policies. (Roosevelt had earlier taken steps to secure bipartisan cooperation in foreign affairs when in June 1940 he appointed Republicans to head the War and Navy departments.) Roosevelt won by his smallest margin to date, with 27,307,819 popular votes to Willkie's 22,321,018. The electoral tally was 449 to 82.

Both houses of Congress remained safely in Democratic hands.

During the campaign, Roosevelt declared that "this country is not going to war." But in the months after the election, events pushed the United States into ever-closer cooperation with Britain and eventually into what amounted to an undeclared naval war against Germany in the Atlantic. Secret talks between British and American military planners in early 1941 established the cardinal principle that in the event of war with both Germany and Japan, the United States and Britain would give priority to defeating Germany. Churchill wrote the president in December 1940, laying out Britain's military plight with sobering candor. To prevail, even to survive, he must have American war matériel and, above all, American money. Roosevelt, still constrained by the cash-and-carry clauses of the neutrality laws, devised another inventive means to meet Britain's needs: the so-called lend-lease program, pledging American goods secured only by a deliberately vague promise of repayment "in kind" at some unspecified later date. Artfully numbered House Resolution 1776, the Lend-Lease Act passed Congress in March 1941. Its enactment marked the effective end of American neutrality and the opening of a floodgate of American largesse through which more than $50 billion in aid was to flow by the war's end.

Lend-lease provided goods and credits principally to Britain and, after Hitler's invasion of the USSR in June 1941, to the Soviet Union as well. But the task remained of delivering the promised matériel safely to British and Russian ports. Wolf packs of German submarines stalking the Atlantic sea-lanes inflicted enormous losses on British shipping. Churchill pleaded for American naval convoys, but Roosevelt balked. He extended American sea and air patrols to Greenland in April and to Iceland in July, but stopped short of authorizing convoys. He at last took that fateful step in August, after a dramatic meeting with Churchill aboard the American cruiser Augusta, off the coast of Newfoundland. There, in Argentia Harbor, the two leaders formulated the Atlantic Charter, a joint statement of war aims affirming their lack of interest in territorial gain and support for self-determination, a liberalized world economic order, and the creation of a permanent international peacekeeping organization. Having thus secured a public declaration of British war aims, Roosevelt was apparently ready for war, though surely not eager for it.

"Everything [is] to be done to force an 'incident' on the Atlantic, Churchill informed his cabinet. The incidents were not long coming. A German submarine fired on the USS *Greer* off the coast of Iceland on 4 September, and the American destroyer *Kearny* was torpedoed in the same area a few weeks later. On 30 October the *Reuben James* sank under German fire, taking more than one hundred American sailors down with it. But before these deliberately provoked incidents could precipitate war in the Atlantic, an unexpected blow in the far-off Pacific in December at last catapulted the United States into the conflict.

Roosevelt had long opposed the Japanese invasion of China, even while the United States paradoxically remained a major supplier of critical war matériel, including aviation fuel, to Japan. Following Hitler's successes in Europe in mid-1940, Japan began to look covetously on the orphaned French and Dutch colonies in the Far East. On 26 July 1940, Roosevelt sought to discourage the Japanese by slapping an embargo on the shipment of aviation gasoline and high-grade scrap metal to Japan. He cinched the economic noose more tightly when Japan signed a pact of military alliance with Germany and Italy in September 1940, and more tightly still when Japanese troops marched into Indochina in July 1941. Jolted by these American moves, Japan made several last-ditch efforts at reconciliation with Washington in late 1941. But Roosevelt, encouraged by Secretary Hull, insisted that Japan withdraw not only from Indochina but also from China, as the precondition for restoring economic relations with the United States. On other matters the Japanese might have been disposed to yield, but on China they were adamant. Diplomacy reached a dead end in late November. Japan now took the fateful step of breaking the deadlock by military means.

American cryptanalysts in late 1940 had cracked the Japanese diplomatic codes, including the top-secret "Purple Cipher." Military leaders therefore knew, as did Roosevelt, that Japan had abandoned diplomacy in early December and was about to strike an armed blow. American forces throughout the Pacific stood on alert. Because the blow was expected to fall in Southeast Asia, Japan scored a devastating surprise when its aircraft swarmed out of the dawn sky over the American naval base at Pearl Harbor, Hawaii, on 7 December 1941. Within minutes the Japanese sank or crippled several American warships, killing over twenty-five hundred military personnel and civilians. The next day Roosevelt asked Congress for a declaration of war against Japan. Germany and

Franklin Roosevelt, wearing a black mourning armband, holds in his hands the joint Congressional declarations of war against Germany and Italy in December, 1941. THE LIBRARY OF CONGRESS

Italy declared war on the United States three days later. Roosevelt, so long the hesitant neutral, now faced battle on two fronts.

America in World War II

Roosevelt had now to decide which front should command greater attention. The British and American decision in early 1941 to concentrate first on defeating Germany came under question after Pearl Harbor. Japan, treacherous perpetrator of the sneak attack on the Pacific Fleet, loomed as much the more hated enemy in the mind of the American public. Moreover, the Japanese followed their murderous strike at Pearl Harbor with overpowering assaults on Hong Kong, Singapore, Java, Burma, and the Philippines. They seemed to be positioning themselves for further attacks on India or Australia, while

in Europe Hitler was preoccupied on the Soviet front, reducing the immediate danger to the Western Allies.

Disagreement over strategic choices in Europe complicated the issue. The British, remembering the ghastly war of attrition they had fought in 1914–1918, preferred to weaken the enemy by bombing, blockading, and probing about his periphery. The Americans, reflecting the wisdom conventionally taught at West Point and Annapolis, favored an assault in massive force aimed directly at the enemy's stronghold. These differences came to a head during Churchill's visit to Washington in June 1942. The prime minister advocated delaying a massive invasion of France and undertaking instead a joint landing in North Africa, where British forces defending Egypt and the Suez lifeline to India were under heavy German pressure. The chiefs of staff of the army and navy protested to Roosevelt that the American objective should be "to force the British into acceptance of a concentrated effort against Germany, and if this proves impossible, to turn immediately to the Pacific."

The president flatly overruled his military advisers in a decision with far-reaching consequences. The North African invasion went ahead, with American troops under Dwight D. Eisenhower landing in Morocco and Algeria in November 1942. After subduing the Germans in North Africa, the combined Anglo-American force pushed on to Sicily and the Italian mainland in the summer of 1943, further delaying the invasion of France. The Pacific theater remained distinctly subordinate to the effort in Europe, though Roosevelt from time to time found it useful to discipline his British allies by threatening to renege on his Europe-first commitment.

After spectacular American naval victories over the Japanese in the Coral Sea in early May 1942 and at Midway the following month, the United States launched a counteroffensive in the Solomon Islands with an attack on Guadalcanal in August. That bloody engagement initiated a tortuous campaign of fighting up the Pacific island chains to within striking distance of the Japanese homeland. At the price of some forty-five thousand American lives, this effort was to come to a blinding climax on 6 and 9 August 1945, when American aircraft dropped atomic bombs, developed at Roosevelt's initiative, on two Japanese cities. Japan surrendered on 14 August.

In Europe, the prospective landing in France dominated Roosevelt's agenda in the early period of the war. Russia, at frightful cost, bore almost the entire brunt of Hitler's onslaught. The German invasion ultimately cost some 20 million Soviet lives, and Soviet Premier Joseph Stalin ardently urged his Anglo-American allies to open a second front in the west. Roosevelt promised to do so virtually from the outset, but it took him more than two years to make good on his word. In the interim, he sought to reassure Stalin about the reliability of his Western partners by declaring at Casablanca in January 1943 that he would accept nothing less than the "unconditional surrender" of the enemy. Stalin, he suggested, need not worry that Churchill and Roosevelt would cut any deals with the Fascist powers—an assurance that lost much of its credibility just a few months later when the Americans and the British entered into negotiations with the Italians over terms of surrender.

By the time Roosevelt and Churchill conferred in Quebec in August 1943, Roosevelt had clearly established himself as the dominant partner in the Anglo-American alliance. That conference, too, confirmed the spring of 1944 as the target date for the invasion of France. With that issue settled at last and with allied victory in sight, however distantly, Roosevelt began to turn his energies toward planning for the postwar era. He had already, in the opening days of American belligerency, secured the agreement of twenty-six nations, including the major allies, to the United Nations Declaration, which affirmed the principles of the Atlantic Charter. In July 1944 he convened the United Nations Monetary and Financial Conference at Bretton Woods, New Hampshire. There delegates established the International Monetary Fund, to undertake global exchange-rate stabilization, and the International Bank for Reconstruction and Development, to help rebuild the shattered world. The following month Allied representatives, including those from the Soviet Union, gathered at Dumbarton Oaks, in Washington, D.C., to draw up a charter for a permanent international peacekeeping organization.

At meetings with Churchill and Stalin in Teheran in late November 1943 and at Yalta in February 1945, Roosevelt worked to secure Soviet participation in the new organization and to bring the Soviet Union into the war against Japan when the conflict in Europe was settled. His critics later charged that he conceded too much to Stalin to achieve those goals, but he had, in fact, little choice. In Eastern and Central Europe, the Red Army stood supreme and unchallengeable. In Asia, uncertainties about the still untested atomic bomb made it seem imperative that the Soviet Union's weight be added to that of the Western Allies in order to speed Japan's surrender.

The long-awaited invasion of France finally came on D day, 6 June 1944. Within a month a million Allied troops had crossed the English Channel. After breaking out of their Normandy beach-head in August, they raced toward Germany, halted only briefly by a fierce German counterattack in the Ardennes, known as the "Battle of the Bulge," in December. The Allies crossed the Rhine in March.

Roosevelt was victorious at home as well as abroad. He had won reelection in 1944 to a fourth term (though by his smallest margin yet), defeating the youthful Republican Thomas E. Dewey by a margin of 25,606,585 votes to 22,321,018. His electoral count was 432 to 99. The fantastic scale of government spending in the war had finally wiped out the Great Depression. Ending the economic crisis had also extinguished the last sputtering flames of reform. The New Deal spirit was evident in some wartime measures, such as the creation of the Fair Employment Practices Commission, which Roosevelt established to ensure the rights of black workers, and the "G.I. Bill of Rights" of 1944, conferring enormous educational benefits on returning veterans. But the war's effect on reform was best summarized by Roosevelt himself in December 1943 when he declared that the American body politic was no longer to be ministered to by "Dr. New Deal," but by "Dr. Win-the-War." In that spirit, he dropped his exultantly New Dealish vice president, Henry Wallace, from the Democratic ticket in 1944 and replaced him with the supposedly "safer" Harry S. Truman.

On 11 April 1945, while American Marines battled on the beaches of Okinawa and American soldiers sped toward Berlin, Franklin Roosevelt was in Warm Springs, Georgia, working on the draft of a speech for Jefferson Day. His nation's arms were vindicated, his enemies were routed, his principles had everywhere been embraced by men and women of goodwill. This was his triumphal hour; but he was not to enjoy it. The next day, 12 April, he died of a massive cerebral hemorrhage. He had sustained his people through the bleak years of the depression and led them to victory in a nightmarish war. Even at the end, he looked to the future with characteristic buoyancy. The last words that he dictated on that spring afternoon were a fitting epitaph: "The only limit to our realization of tomorrow will be our doubts of today. Let us move forward with strong and active faith."

BIBLIOGRAPHY

James MacGregor Burns, *Roosevelt: The Lion and the Fox* (New York, 1956) and *Roosevelt: The Soldier of Freedom* (New York, 1970), comprise the most exhaustive biography of Roosevelt and deal with the New Deal and the war years, respectively. Two superb one-volume treatments of FDR are Frank Freidel, *Franklin D. Roosevelt: A Rendezvous with Destiny* (Boston, 1990), and Ted Morgan, *FDR: A Biography* (New York, 1985). Arthur M. Schlesinger, Jr., *The Age of Roosevelt*, 3 vols. (Boston, 1957–1960), a brilliantly partisan history, is rich in detail and anecdote, covering the period up to 1936. Frank B. Freidel, *Franklin D. Roosevelt*, 4 vols. (Boston, 1952–1973), is the most detailed of the Roosevelt studies, though these volumes take the story only as far as 1933.

A massive, gripping examination of how FDR was changed by his illness is Geoffrey C. Ward, *A First-Class Temperament: The Emergence of Franklin Roosevelt* (New York, 1989). Betty H. Winfield, *FDR and the News Media* (Urbana, Ill., 1990), is the best of a number of books that have been written on its subject. Invaluable for details is Otis L. Graham, Jr., and Meghan Robinson Wander, *Franklin D. Roosevelt, His Life and Times: An Encyclopedic View* (Boston, 1985). Two contrasting recent interpretations are Philip Abbott, *The Exemplary Presidency: Franklin D. Roosevelt and the American Political Tradition* (Amherst, Mass., 1990), and Robert Shogan, *Hard Bargain: How FDR Twisted Churchill's Arm, Evaded the Law, and Changed the Role of the American Presidency* (New York, 1995).

Anthony J. Badger, *The New Deal: The Depression Years, 1933–40* (New York, 1989), gives an excellent account of Roosevelt's principal social and economic policies. William E. Leuchtenburg, *Franklin D. Roosevelt and the New Deal, 1932–1940* (New York, 1963), is an eminently readable, engaging account of the Roosevelt years up to 1940. Leuchtenburg's *The FDR Years: On Roosevelt and His Legacy* (New York, 1995), is the mature summing-up of one of the preeminent students of FDR's career. Paul K. Conkin, *The New Deal*, rev. ed. (New York, 1975), is the best of the "revisionist" accounts criticizing the New Deal for being too timid, even conservative. Ellis W. Hawley, *The New Deal and the Problem of Monopoly: A Study in Economic Ambivalence* (Princeton, N.J., 1966), is the leading study of New Deal domestic economic policies. Alan Brinkley, *Voices of Protest: Huey Long, Father Coughlin, and the Great Depression* (New York, 1982), is a fresh, suggestive analysis of the two Depression-era figures who had a plausible chance, if anyone did, of wringing radical results from the crisis of the 1930s. The same author's *The End of Reform: New Deal Liberalism in Recession and War* (New York, 1995) examines the economic policy debates of the later Roosevelt years.

Robert Dallek, *Franklin D. Roosevelt and American Foreign Policy, 1932–1945* (New York, 1979), the only complete account of Roosevelt's foreign policies, is an unusually thorough and intelligent work. John Morton Blum, *From the Morgenthau Diaries*, 3 vols. (Boston, 1959–1967), a meticulous history of the Roosevelt years from the perspective of the Treasury Department, is particularly informative about foreign economic policy.

Waldo Heinrichs, *Threshold of War: Franklin D. Roosevelt and American Entry into World War II* (New York, 1988), analyzes in detail the fateful year of 1941. A scintillating evocation of FDR's military leaders is Eric Larrabee, *Commander in Chief: Franklin Delano Roosevelt, His Lieutenants, and Their War* (New York, 1987). Warren F. Kimball, ed., *Churchill and Roosevelt: The Complete Correspondence*, 3 vols. (Princeton, N.J., 1984), is an indispensable source for the war years. John Morton Blum, *V Was for Victory: Politics and American Culture During World War II* (New York, 1976), is a comprehensive and somewhat disillusioned discussion of the home front during World War II.

A mesmerizing estimate of the Franklin Roosevelts as a couple is Doris Kearns Goodwin, *No Ordinary Time: Franklin and Eleanor Roosevelt; The Home Front in World War II* (New York, 1994). It supplements Joseph P. Lash, *Eleanor and Franklin: The Story of Their Relationship, Based On Eleanor Roosevelt's Private Papers* (New York, 1971).

Recent works include James MacGregor Burns and Susan Dunn, *The Three Roosevelts: Patrician Leaders Who Transformed America* (New York, 2001), which examines the roles of Theodore Roosevelt in inspiring his cousins Eleanor and Franklin to work for social and economic justice. Kenneth S. Davis, *FDR: The War President, 1940–1943: A History* (New York, 2000), the latest of the author's books on Roosevelt, is good on the role of Harry Hopkins. Thomas J. Fleming, *The New Dealers' War: FDR and the War within World War II* (New York, 2001), sharply challenges the traditional veneration of Roosevelt as a leader in World War II. Jonas Klein (introduction by George J. Mitchell), *Beloved Island: Franklin and Eleanor and the Legacy of Campobello* (Forest Dale, Vt., 2000), explores the role of the Roosevelts' summer home in shaping their private lives. See also Joseph E. Persico, *Roosevelt's Secret War: FDR and World War II Espionage* (New York, 2001), and David Reynolds, *From Munich to Pearl Harbor: Roosevelt's America and the Origins of the Second World War* (Chicago, 2001).

Harry S. Truman

Robert H. Ferrell

Harry S. Truman THE LIBRARY OF CONGRESS

HARRY S. TRUMAN of Independence, Missouri, once remarked that three experiences prepared a man for high political office—farming, banking, and the army. By the time he entered politics he possessed all three. In his preparation for the presidency he might have added three more: knowledge of small-town America, avid reading of books about the leaders and government of the United States, and extensive participation in local and national politics.

The Formative Years

The future president spent his early years in rural America. He was born on 8 May 1884 in the farm village of Lamar (120 miles south of Kansas City), where his father, John, pursued a horse and mule business, buying and selling in a lot across the street from the small white frame family residence. A few months later the Trumans moved to the first of a succession of farms. In 1890 the family, increased by the birth of a second son, John Vivian, and a daughter, Mary Jane, settled in Independence. There, on the several acres surrounding their house on Crysler Street, John Truman conducted his animal-trading business. Independence grew rapidly during the 1890s, doubling in population to twelve thousand by the turn of the century. In 1896 the Trumans moved to another house near the town's principal residential street.

Since Independence was a farm town and the county seat of a large rural area to the east of Kansas City, Harry Truman's farm roots did not wither and dry up.

When Truman reached manhood, he worked briefly in Kansas City but soon established himself on a farm near Grandview, twenty miles from Independence, where he remained until he entered the army in 1917. Here his lifetime habits became fixed. He often spoke of the farm experience, even during his presidency. Whatever the duties of the presidential years, however late into the evening he presided over dinners or meetings, he awoke each morning at 5:00 or 5:30 and within minutes was at his desk, long before secretaries and assistants.

The farm meant much loneliness, save for the company of horses and mules, and offered opportunity to consider principles, such as the beliefs of the Baptist Church, which Truman joined in Grandview, and the Masons, to which he applied for membership in 1908. He came away from the farm with a sharpened sense of right and wrong, of how principles counted and irresolute positions did not. He understood—when he got into politics—that it often meant compromise, but he interpreted "compromise" as the discovery of a mutually agreeable position, not as a trimming of principles.

During the farm years, Truman became what Americans of another generation might have described as an administrator: he managed six hundred acres. In the early part of the twentieth century, farming necessitated careful management of time and machinery. Plowing, the initial enterprise, required hours for each acre. Cultivating, mowing, and reaping covered areas of only six or eight feet, meaning almost interminable circling of fields. Truman hired farmhands at fifteen or twenty cents an hour, plus meals, to help run his teams, but unlike later management experts, he did much of the work himself.

The second of Truman's preparations for high political office, banking, appears to have meant far less to him than the experience of farming. Perhaps it was because he spent less time at it—three years, beginning in 1903, when he lived in Kansas City and worked in the cages of the National Bank of Commerce and the Union National Bank as a recorder of tellers' transactions or bookkeeper for checks received from, or sent to, country banks. The young bank clerk functioned on a low level, and appears not to have enjoyed the work, or so he told a friend, although he displayed enough interest and ability to increase his salary from $35 a month to $100. From

this experience he may have derived his oft-remarked fascination in later years with the federal budget. As president, he read budgets with intense care, having an acute sense for the reliability—or deviousness—of line items. He saw the director of the Bureau of the Budget almost daily, believing the budget to be the principal management device of the federal government.

In April 1917 the United States entered World War I, and almost immediately Truman entered the army. He had been a member of the Kansas City field artillery battery of the Missouri National Guard for two enlistments, from 1905 to 1911, and when war began, he volunteered to help enlarge the battery into a regiment. There followed his election as first lieutenant in what became, upon reception into federal service, the 129th Field Artillery, attached to the Thirty-fifth Division from Missouri and Kansas. He went overseas in April 1918, was promoted to captain that month, and in July took command of the most unruly battery in the regiment, Battery D, a group of German Catholics and "wild Irishmen" (so he described them) that had broken four previous commanders.

Ability to manage a bewildering variety of tasks had derived from life on the farm, and in the few months that remained of American participation in the war, Truman demonstrated a remarkable skill in the management of men. After an inauspicious beginning, during which the assembled battery greeted him with what one of its members years later described as a "Bronx cheer," he brought the men under control through a careful combination of firmness and friendliness, and took them through several actions, including the battles of Saint Mihiel and the Meuse-Argonne, without losing a man. The battery idolized him, and he became known as Captain Harry. When the men took passage home in April 1919 aboard the German liner *Zeppelin*, a rough rider, they whiled away the time in a day-and-night dice game, during which they set aside a percentage of each pot for purchase of a large engraved silver loving cup for the captain. For the rest of their lives they kept in touch, immensely proud of the man they described as their leader. Each Armistice Day they met in reunion. At the inaugural parade in January 1949, the members of Battery D marched on each side of Captain Harry's automobile.

Among other formative influences was life in Independence during the 1890s. The future president commenced school in 1892 at the age of eight, and in 1894 a near-fatal attack of diphtheria interrupted his studies for months; even so, he graduated with the Independence High School class of 1901 (schooling in those years consisted of ten grades, not twelve). A photograph of the class shows not only Truman but Elizabeth ("Bess") Wallace, who was to become his wife in June 1919. Truman never forgot Independence, in which he was to spend most of his long life. It was, of course, the small town, not the later residential suburb of Kansas City of more than 100,000 inhabitants.

And then there was the reading of books that so influenced him. Just before the Truman family moved to Independence the youngster had been "fine-printed"; that is, fitted with glasses to relieve his farsightedness. As a child in Independence he had been ill with diphtheria. The illness but especially the glasses, which were expensive, kept him out of childhood games, inspired him to study the piano, and made young Truman an inveterate reader during these years. Afterward he tended to exaggerate his reading, but he did spend an unusual amount of time with books. The town library contained seventeen hundred (the president later exaggerated it to four thousand), and he liked to say he had read them all, including the encyclopedias. Perhaps he read several hundred, which seemed like all of them. His taste ran to the historical, especially American history, with an emphasis on the history of American government. He often remembered a four-volume oversized set given him on his twelfth birthday by his mother, who bought it from a door-to-door salesman—*Great Men and Famous Women*, edited by Charles F. Horne. He read Plutarch, Arthurian romances, and biographies of presidential heroes—Washington, Jefferson, Jackson, Polk, Lincoln. The young Truman also admired Grover Cleveland.

Any analysis of Truman's preparation for the presidency must also look to the twenty years of local and national office holding prior to 1945, to the years when he turned to politics as a "profession" (his proud word). His initial participation in American politics occurred in 1892 when he wore a white hat to school bearing the names of Grover Cleveland for president and Adlai Stevenson (grandfather of a future Democratic nominee) for vice president. As he told the story long afterward, some big Republican boys snatched the hat and tore it up. He entered politics after the failure of the haberdashery he had opened in Kansas City in 1919 with his former army sergeant, Edward Jacobson; the business was caught

in a recession that caused shelf stock to plummet in value from $30,000 to less than $10,000. Truman assumed all of the partnership's debts after Jacobson declared bankruptcy in 1925; not until the early 1930s did he pay them off. Indeed, the haberdashery's failure inaugurated a period of twenty years during which he was strapped for funds, for in 1934 and 1940 he had to pay a large share of the cost of two senatorial campaigns.

Truman's political career began because of a chance army friendship. Having met Lieutenant Jim Pendergast during the war, he made the acquaintance of Jim's father, Mike, older brother of the Democratic boss of Kansas City, Thomas J. ("Tom") Pendergast. The Pendergast brothers in 1922 needed a man as "eastern judge" (that is, eastern county commissioner) in the three-man Jackson County court. The eastern part of the county included Independence and its rural hinterland, and Kansas City formed the western part. The court consisted of judges representing each, together with a "presiding judge" elected at large. Truman won the primary, went on to easy victory in November, and served a two-year term (1923–1924). Defeated in 1924 because of a division in local Democratic ranks caused by an anti-Pendergast leader in Kansas City, Joseph G. Shannon, he ran for presiding judge in 1926, was elected, and served two four-year terms (1927–1934).

Association with Boss Tom Pendergast proved a terrible liability once the politician from Independence became prominent nationally; people outside of Missouri did not understand either Pendergast or the politics of Jackson County. The Pendergast association was a complex one and could hardly be reduced to the simplicities employed by Truman's opponents.

Machines no longer manage the big cities of America, but in the era of enormous urban growth that began in the 1880s, the machines did much to make cities endurable for immigrants and poor people; machines constituted the welfare system of their time, the boss helping with groceries, medical care, burial, and other necessities in return for loyalty on election day. His ward heelers ensured victory by getting out the vote. In Kansas City this meant getting out enough votes, real or otherwise, to defeat any state ticket or senatorial nominees put up in primaries by the rival political machine (also Democratic) of St. Louis. Pendergast voted absentees and dead people through use of "repeaters," frequently high school students who voted repeatedly on election day. "Ghost voters" often lived in empty lots, and dozens of them lived in tiny apartments. And then there were always the cemeteries, which inspired the election-day quip "Now is the time for all good cemeteries to come to the aid of the party." Pendergast lieutenants desired to show the boss their vote-getting abilities and frequently brought in more votes than occasions demanded.

Truman probably could not have entered Jackson County politics without support from Pendergast, even had he run only for eastern judge, since Pendergast's brother Mike controlled that part of the county. When running at large for presiding judge, he undoubtedly would have lost without Pendergast votes. He was an honest man, which recommended him to Pendergast, who needed an attractive figure on the court. He was cooperative about patronage, understanding that it was the glue of party loyalty. He always drew a line, which Pendergast respected, between patronage and graft, willing to provide the one but not the other. The two men maintained an easy relationship, and the boss looked to other office-holders, such as the city manager of Kansas City, if there was need for graft. Pendergast refused to support road contractors who thought Truman uncooperative for not giving them preference in contracts, insisting on the lowest bidder. Upon the death of Mike Pendergast in 1929, Presiding judge Truman became Tom Pendergast's lieutenant for the eastern part of the county.

During his years on the court Truman put through two major bond issues, totaling $14.4 million, and gave the county skillfully engineered cement roads, a beautiful art deco skyscraper courthouse in Kansas City, and a remodeled Georgian-style courthouse in Independence. Outside each courthouse he placed an equestrian statue of General Andrew Jackson.

It was contention with St. Louis that persuaded Boss Tom to back Truman for senator in 1934, after at least three prospective candidates refused what looked like a difficult race, but Truman, with a forty-thousand-vote plurality, won the primary, which ensured election in November. During the primary the state's senior senator, Bennett Champ Clark, son of the legendary Speaker of the House "Champ" Clark, fought him tooth and nail, and described Truman's campaign as afflicted with "unexampled mendacity." But, in the way of good politicians after defeat, he took Truman down the aisle of the Senate Chamber

in January 1935 to be sworn in by Vice President John Nance Garner.

As a decade on the Jackson County court had made Truman conversant with the extraordinary convolutions of politics in a metropolitan county and had taught him how to measure factions and how to advance a forward-looking program, so a decade in the Senate taught him how national and even international issues focused on ninety-six men elected from all parts of the country. He learned how progressive legislation emerged from the work of perhaps a dozen relentlessly hardworking, imaginative senators who usually took the other members along in voting for what they produced. In his two terms, the second cut short by elevation to the vice presidency in January 1945, he joined the group of Senate leaders. In his second term, when he headed the Truman Committee to investigate the national defense effort, he became an outstanding member of the upper house.

His first term opened without fanfare, and President Roosevelt in the remote fastness of the White House required weeks before he found time to see the junior senator from Missouri. The president gave Truman a fifteen-minute appointment, but his secretary ushered the senator out after seven minutes. Roosevelt apparently considered him "the senator from Pendergast," a label Boss Tom may have pinned on Truman by relating expansively how steel corporations and railroads sent senators and he therefore had sent his "office boy." One of Truman's primary opponents in 1934 had claimed that Truman would have calluses on his ears, from the long-distance phone to Kansas City, and Roosevelt may have heard of that remark. To make matters worse, the new senator voted a straight New Deal line, which made him invisible; if he had threatened to get out of line during close votes or otherwise given the appearance of being unpredictable, he would have received attention. Roosevelt gave Missouri's patronage to the mercurial Bennett Clark, who took it as if he deserved it.

Truman's fellow senators ignored him, save for the maverick Democrat Burton K. Wheeler of Montana and one or two others. But Senator Wheeler liked Truman, instructed him in Senate ways, and put him on the railroad subcommittee of the Interstate Commerce Committee, where Truman soon was investigating the successive bankruptcies of major roads in the 1920s and 1930s, including the suspicious involvement of bankruptcy courts in high fees to law firms and financiers in New York. The resultant Truman-Wheeler Transportation Act of 1940 brought order out of corporate financial chaos. Truman was also author of the Civil Aeronautics Act of 1938, which provided an independent board and chairman for regulation of the fledgling aviation industry.

At the beginning of his second Senate term, Truman received dozens of letters from Missouri constituents concerning waste in construction at Fort Leonard Wood; in response, he persuaded the Senate to establish an investigating committee with himself as chairman that turned out remarkably well. At the outset the Roosevelt administration displayed no interest and indeed almost no support, and Senator James F. Byrnes allotted only $15,000 to investigate the expenditure of billions. Truman nonetheless brought together several serious-minded senators who made thirty investigations of major aspects of the defense and (after 7 December 1941) war effort, reportedly saving the nation $15 billion. Each Truman Committee report was carefully researched, and the mere threat of an adverse report usually brought correction of abuses.

By 1944, Truman had shown himself an adroit leader, on the local, state, and national levels, and hence was available, to use the political term, for the vice presidency. His achievements in Jackson County politics were almost legendary. On the state level he had managed not merely election to the Senate in 1934 but managed it again in 1940 when he won an extremely close primary campaign against Governor Lloyd C. Stark and another Democratic candidate by a plurality of 7,976 votes. In this campaign the odds had been appalling, be, cause Boss Tom Pendergast had been sentenced to Leavenworth prison for income tax evasion and because the Roosevelt administration favored Stark and refused to endorse Truman (although it did not endorse Stark either). Thereafter Truman showed remarkable leadership with the success of the Truman Committee.

In 1944, Roosevelt allowed party chieftains to recommend Truman as a running mate because the Missouri senator possessed many friends in the upper house and could assist passage of the United Nations treaty. Senators did not respect the vice president at the time, Henry A. Wallace, an aloof figure who took an interest in issues rather than personalities. On their side the party leaders proposed Truman because they considered him presidential timber and were certain that American voters would

As Bess Truman looks on, Harry Truman (left) takes the oath of office from Chief Justice Harlan Stone following the death of President Franklin Roosevelt. CORBIS

reelect Roosevelt to a fourth term and that the president, whose health was deteriorating visibly, would die in office. Truman, let it be said, did not lift a finger for the nomination in 1944, in part because his wife disliked the goldfish-bowl aspect of Washington life and hated the prospect of the vice presidency and presidency; Truman knew, too, that if he had shown any ambition for the vice presidency, Roosevelt would not have liked it, for the president did not like ambitious people. As Truman saw support gathering for his nomination he did not absolutely refuse to accept it; he could have done a "General Sherman," refusing to consider the office under any circumstances, but he did not go that far. One has the impression that he was not unhappy when the office came his way. He knew it meant the presidency.

Following Roosevelt's election to his fourth term, Truman was sworn in as vice president on 20 January 1945, and in subsequent weeks began to accustom himself to his largely ceremonial duties. Then, on 12 April, while he was presiding over a tedious session of the Senate, a tragic scene was being enacted in Warm Springs, Georgia, where the president had gone, as so often before, for treatment of his paralysis. After sitting for his portrait in his small cottage Roosevelt complained of a terrific headache, lost consciousness, and died. Truman was summoned to the White House shortly after five o'clock to learn from Mrs. Roosevelt that he had become president of the United States.

Foreign Policies

When Harry Truman took the oath of office that evening at 7:09 in the Cabinet Room, he was as astonished as were the American people. He knew that the president's health was deteriorating, but the moment was astonishing.

The next day he told a group of newspapermen that he felt as if "the moon, the stars, and all the planets" had fallen upon him, and he asked them to pray for him. This remark, so expressive of his rural Baptist background, was widely quoted. (Privately, Truman doubted if they knew how to pray for him.)

From such remarks people concluded he was an ordinary individual who happened to become president. But he was hardly an ordinary man. Few, if any, leaders in Washington knew more about domestic American politics; the whole of his personal experience had made him a political master. Truman's only obvious lack of qualification for the presidency was his ignorance of international affairs, which were to occupy most of his time during his presidency.

It is a curious fact, not often noticed, that Truman's quickness in learning about foreign affairs—he made errors in foreign policy in his first year of the presidency, but not many—may have been attributable to his knowledge of domestic politics. Truman in retirement ruminated about the qualities he so desperately needed upon entering the presidency after virtually no preparation by the secretive and otherwise absentminded Roosevelt, who (as Truman's assistant Clark Clifford once said) thought he would live forever. The president of 1945–1953 concluded that if a politician knows American domestic politics he can learn quickly about foreign relations. It does stand to reason that if a president, out of long experience, senses what the American people want, he can advance those desires internationally by relying, as Truman did from the outset, upon the negotiating abilities of the Department of State.

The first issue of foreign policy that Truman confronted was the decision to use nuclear weapons against Japan. No decision of his presidency has drawn so much criticism as the dropping of atomic bombs on Hiroshima (6 August 1945) and Nagasaki (9 August). The question is whether he could have done anything else—that is, whether he could have delayed use of the bombs by opting for a demonstration of their immense power or refused to employ what General Dwight D. Eisenhower described many years after its employment as an inhuman weapon.

Truman knew about the bomb before he became president. When he was chairman of the investigating committee his investigators had reported on the huge expenditures at Oak Ridge, Tennessee, and at Hanford, Washington, the two principal production sites for uranium-235 and plutonium. When he and Roosevelt lunched together under a magnolia on the White House lawn in August 1944, just before the vice presidential candidate went out to campaign, the president told him the secret. At that time the bomb had not been tested.

After he entered the presidency, everything moved rapidly. When, on 16 July 1945, scientists tested a plutonium device (only enough U-235 was available for a single bomb, so they could not test the uranium weapon), they expected a low yield, equal to 500–1,500 tons of TNT, and less effective explosive power because everything would be in a single warhead instead of many small bombs. At the very moment of testing, Truman and other high administration officials had just reached the Berlin suburb of Babelsberg in preparation for a Big Three conference that opened next day at Potsdam and lasted until 2 August; the president had no time to think much about a plutonium bomb that he now realized equaled 20,000 tons of TNT. At Potsdam the president spent two weeks in complicated discussion about Germany's occupation and the payment of reparations; the government and borders of Poland; the opening to all commerce of Europe's principal waterways; and a special declaration by the United States, Britain, and China (the Soviet Union did not take part because it had not yet entered the Far Eastern war) warning Japan in general terms to make peace with the Allies.

With the bomb available, and the president at Potsdam, it was necessary to make a decision, and Truman chose to use the new weapon. One reason for his decision was his feeling, and that of virtually all of his countrymen at the time, that the Japanese military—and behind it the Japanese government—did not know how to wage civilized war. The Japanese army not merely had fought well in its campaigns, whether in offense or defense, but it had fought in bestial fashion. The first evidence had appeared in the sack of Nanking in 1937, in which at least 100,000 Chinese, soldiers and civilians alike, were slaughtered. The attack on Pearl Harbor had infuriated the American people, and there had followed the Bataan death march, a terrible affair. The small-scale attack of American bombing planes on Tokyo and other cities in 1942 was followed by another bloodbath of 100,000 or so deaths in China of anyone and everyone suspected of harboring American fliers. The Japanese defense of Manila against the attacking U.S. Army in 1945 may well have added another 100,000 mainly civilian deaths. The same number of American and Allied prisoners were in the hands of the Japanese army and, as it turned out, would have been slaughtered if the United States had invaded the Japanese home islands. And then there was the likely cost of an invasion of the southernmost island of Kyushu scheduled for 1 November 1945, followed by an invasion of Honshu (including the Tokyo plain) on 1 March 1946. At Iwo Jima in 1945 the United States had lost 6,200 men dead, at Okinawa 13,000. Using Okinawa as a measure, the much larger invasion of Kyushu and Honshu would have cost 65,000 deaths, and casualties—missing, wounded, and dead—could have run much higher because of the nearness of bases for the kamikaze planes that might have made chance hits on packed troopships. There was every evidence that Japanese forces would exact frightful casualties, all the while themselves fighting to the death.

The Potsdam Declaration by the United States, Great Britain, and China called upon Japan to surrender, although of course it did not mention the new weapon that might force such a result, as Congress itself, despite having paid the bill, did not know of the nuclear program. The Japanese government, in control of the military, contemptuously refused. The two bombs cost 110,000 lives and gave the military the excuse they needed to consider surrender. But even then the decision to surrender was forced by the emperor, who twice broke a tie vote among his highest advisers. A rebellion by the Tokyo division guarding the imperial palace that was fomented as a protest to the emperor's decision was put down only after the murder of its commander.

Truman's second major decision in foreign relations was to change the American stance in international affairs from abstention to participation, a decision that reversed the long-standing policy advocated by George Washington. This reversal, this change, established Truman's reputation as one of the nation's greatest presidents. His announcement of the change through the Truman Doctrine (12 March 1947), which promised United States support to countries threatened by Communism; the Marshall Plan (5 June 1947), which placed an economic foundation under the struggling nations of Western Europe; and the North Atlantic Treaty (4 April 1949), which assured military assistance, resolved the eco-

nomic and political near-chaos of Europe after World War II. These measures would, he believed, preserve democracy in Western Europe and thereby help preserve the freedom of the United States. The Truman Doctrine applied to Greece and Turkey. The Marshall Plan included most of the nations of Western Europe: Austria, Belgium, Denmark, France, Greece, Iceland, Ireland, Italy, Luxembourg, the Netherlands, Norway, Portugal, Sweden, Turkey, and the United Kingdom. (Switzerland signed the convention creating an organization for the plan, but refused to accept funds.) Congress included China in Marshall Plan appropriations. The North Atlantic Treaty Organization (NATO) comprised the United States, Belgium, the Netherlands, Luxembourg, France, Britain, Canada, Italy, Portugal, Denmark, Norway, and Iceland; Greece and Turkey joined in 1952, West Germany in 1955, and Spain in 1982.

At the time, the logic of Truman's measures may not have been evident to all Americans; many were confused because of proposed policy changes coming so close to the end of World War II, others saw politics in the president's international stance, and still others, having thought little in the past about international affairs, seemed determined to remain in ignorance. The leading figures of the administration, perhaps even the president, were not always sure where they were going; sometimes they were feeling their way. They all had many duties, and the crises came up quickly; they may even have lurched from crisis to crisis.

Confusion often reigned. In the midst of the administration's several measures, the Soviets began the land blockade of the western sectors of Berlin and an airlift became necessary from June 1948 until September 1949. In the Middle East the British government chose the date of 15 May 1948 to give up its mandate over Palestine, resulting not merely in the announcement on midnight of the preceding day, 14 May, of the birth of the State of Israel but in an almost immediate convergence of Arab armies upon the new state, hoping to stifle it at birth. Hostilities lasted until an armistice was worked out the next year. Truman extended almost immediate recognition to Israel, eleven minutes after the state's founding, but the United States remained neutral during the first of the Arab-Israeli wars.

Critics have maintained that Europe could have righted itself without Truman's measures, which, they have said, ensured a permanent cold war. Signs of Soviet weakness, economic and military, were visible at the time and often remarked upon. John Foster Dulles, then a member of an American delegation to a conference in Moscow in 1947, drove from the airport of the Russian capital through the streets to the Kremlin and beheld mile after mile of slums, run-down houses, and aging apartment buildings, the people in tatters. He easily concluded that the Soviet Union had a long way to go before it could match the economic might of the United States. Students of Soviet affairs later concluded that Premier Joseph Stalin in 1947–1949 needed a foreign enemy because the Soviet economy could not produce both peacetime and military goods and he sought to maintain control by threat of war. World War II revealed large groups of the populace, such as the Ukrainians, susceptible to Western—in this case, German—influence. The Soviet Union defeated the German army, so the argument went, largely by masses of troops thrown against German forces and by primitive weapons similarly expended, but was not able to take its crude military might far beyond its borders.

These alarms and contentions could have no effect on President Truman and his assistants, who could act only on the need to do something to save Western Europe—and also, to be sure, on the basis of what they saw, which was Soviet intransigence: vehement protest over peace talks held early in 1945 with German army representatives in Switzerland shortly before surrender of German troops in Italy; looting of territories traversed by the Red Army; indifference to the plight of captured Allied soldiers whose camps Soviet troops overran; demands for huge reparations from Western-occupied zones of Germany; and ruthless domination of the countries of Eastern Europe, despite promises of individual rights and liberties set out in the Yalta Declaration on Liberated Europe, to which the Soviets had promised support. When British, American, and French forces entered their allotted sectors of Berlin in July, they beheld evidences of Russian outrages against the city's population on every side. In ensuing months the Soviets turned the Council of Foreign Ministers, created by the Potsdam Conference to help restore order to Europe, into a debating group, Soviets versus Western Allies.

Then there was the immediate crisis of the spring of 1947. In 1946 it had become obvious that Western Europe's economies could not by themselves recover from the war. The harsh winter of 1946–1947 froze wheat in the ground, threatening dire food shortages. Coal supplies failed to reach cit-ies, where inhabitants were without heat and frequently without electricity.

Truman did not quite sense the crisis until, in February 1947, the British government gave up support of Greece and Turkey, two weakened states on Europe's periphery, one afflicted by years of German occupation and the other threatened by invasion across the long Turkish-Soviet border. The resultant Truman Doctrine, backed by an appropriation of $400 million, inaugurated years of support that mounted to billions of dollars. The European Recovery Plan, announced by Secretary of State George C. Marshall at the Harvard commencement in June 1947, had an initial installment of $5.6 billion (passed by Congress in March 1948) and eventually totaled $13 billion. (In his inaugural address in 1949 the president proposed economic aid to developing countries, and this fourth point in the address—known as Point Four—received modest congressional appropriations for a few years, mostly in the form of pilot projects of a technical nature, such as water systems or plans for increasing crop yields.) The Truman administration could not sign the North Atlantic Treaty until April 1949—that is, until after the president had fought the "whistle stop" campaign of 1948 and become president in his own right. The North Atlantic Treaty Organization did not become an effective military organization until after the outbreak of the Korean War in June 1950. General Dwight D. Eisenhower went to Europe as supreme commander of NATO in January 1951, a clear signal of United States commitment.

The Truman administration perhaps erred in making the Truman Doctrine of 1947 so all-inclusive: the president's enunciation of the doctrine, produced in the State Department, was hard-line and included any threatened country in the world. Administration opponents in Congress immediately raised the question of China, where Communists were fighting Nationalists. Representative Walter H. Judd of Minnesota inquired why the United States sought to protect Greece against Communism when its policy in China, set out clearly in the unsuccessful mission of General Marshall in 1946, was to bring the warring factions together. Undersecretary of State Dean Acheson explained that China's size and population were immensely larger than those of Greece. Actually Acheson had asked a department speechwriter, Joseph M. Jones, to use expansive phrases in the Truman Doctrine speech so as to ensure congressional approval. When the United States in the

1960s involved itself in Vietnam, the phrases came to seem singularly inappropriate. It appeared that the Truman Doctrine had been intended to oppose Communism everywhere, including the Far East—a notion that never entered the minds of Truman and Acheson.

Fortune, as well as statesmanship, may have ensured success of the Marshall Plan, as the plan became known, for $13 billion merely primed Western Europe's economic pump. It was American orders for European goods during the so-called Korean War boom that ensured the revival of the European economies, allowing them to take off into the patterns of consumer consumption that had characterized the American economy since the 1920s.

NATO forces, galvanized by Eisenhower, never numbered much beyond the equivalent of twenty-five divisions, not enough to have prevented a Soviet invasion of Western Europe, although enough to prove that any attack was a serious matter, not a probing effort or an accident. The cost of American forces placed the United States at a disadvantage in trade with allies who did not pay for protecting themselves. And the second largest national contingent of NATO came from West Germany. Inclusion of Germans in NATO occurred only after years of contention with the French government that soured relations between Paris and Washington.

President Truman nonetheless pushed through the three major parts of his program—the Truman Doctrine, the Marshall Plan, and NATO—to effect the permanent alignment of the United States with Western Europe. For a man who achieved the presidency through the death of his predecessor and whose political experience lay almost entirely in domestic issues, it was an extraordinary personal, as well as public, triumph.

The last leading issue of foreign affairs during Truman's presidency, the Korean War, also displayed his resolution, but its domestic political consequences obscured the essential achievement. Not until nearly half a century later, in the 1990s, when the Korean War had passed into history, was Truman's judgment vindicated.

On 24 June 1950 the president was visiting in Independence when he received the news from Secretary of State Acheson that 135,000 North Korean troops had begun crossing the thirty-eighth parallel into South Korea, equipped with Russian tanks and planes—weapons the South Korean forces did not possess—and that tanks were rumbling toward Seoul. The next afternoon, the president returned to Washington and, in his limousine en route to Blair House, where he was living during reconstruction of the White House, told Acheson and Secretary of Defense Louis Johnson, "By God, I'm going to let them have it!" At Blair House that evening his assistants worked out a strategy whereby American naval, air, and, eventually, ground forces entered the fighting in the next few days. Meanwhile, the United Nations Security Council voted to support South Korea. (The Soviet Union was then boycotting its meetings because the Chinese Nationalist representative occupied China's permanent seat, rather than a representative from Beijing, and thus there was no veto.)

In retrospect, it is clear that at the outset of the Korean War, Truman should have asked Congress for a declaration of war. The chairman of the Senate Foreign Relations Committee advised Truman that, as commander in chief of American armed forces and president of a United Nations member state, he had the right to help defend South Korean independence. He also said that the president might run into a long debate with Congress that could tie the chief executive's hands. Truman therefore described Korea as a "police action." A declaration in June 1950 would have been easily obtained, for Congress almost unanimously supported the war at its outset. Unfortunately, later, when the war became unpopular, the idea of a police action gave Truman's domestic political opponents an easy point of criticism, because the war had far outgrown the designation. Moreover, Truman unwittingly provided a precedent for the Vietnam War years later.

American fortunes in the Korean War wavered erratically, but Truman did his best, much to the confusion of the American people, who often failed to understand either tactics or strategy. The United States Army was so weak in June 1950 that it barely stopped the North Korean advance around the tip of the peninsula near the port of Pusan. The Inchon landing high upon the peninsula's west coast, near Seoul, righted matters, but movement into North Korea brought Chinese intervention in November and December, another retreat, and finally establishment of a line approximately at the thirty-eighth parallel. After seemingly interminable parleys, a truce was worked out in July 1953, after Truman had left the presidency.

In the course of the war, General Douglas MacArthur quarreled publicly with the president over strategy and sought to undercut him, and so Truman dismissed him from his Far Eastern commands in April 1951. The general did not merely contend to the president that he believed the Far East a much more important theater of Russian concern and possible aggression than Western Europe; he also talked to newspaper reporters about his strategic opinions and wrote letters voicing them. He also disagreed with the administration on tactics, for when the Chinese intervened, he wanted to use nuclear weapons against them. This, too, became public knowledge. And he made virtually diplomatic points in public, admonishing the North Koreans and Chinese or in other ways undercutting the State Department. The president issued a directive to subordinates, military and diplomatic, to clear their statements with each other, but MacArthur ignored it. When the two men met for a short conference at Wake Island on 15 October, it seemed that they were in agreement, but MacArthur's subsequent pronouncements made their disagreements obvious. America's allies began to doubt that Truman had the general under control; the British government was especially concerned. When Truman at last dismissed MacArthur, he replaced him with General Matthew B. Ridgway.

Truman's task during the long agony of Korea became one of explanation, and the task proved impossible. Few Americans knew much about Korea. It seemed a strangely unimportant peninsula in which to contain Communism. The timing also appeared wrong—mainland China had fallen to the Communists in October 1949. The strategic contentions of MacArthur, with their easy solutions—bombing mainland China, perhaps with nuclear weapons, and sowing a belt of radioactive cobalt across the thirty-eighth parallel with a half-life of sixty-two years (a notion disclosed only after MacArthur's death)—required a return to the prenuclear age. ("There is no substitute for victory," he wrote the Republican minority leader of the House of Representatives, Joseph W. Martin, Jr.) Republican leaders in Congress espied an opportunity for a "great debate" in which they could refuse the bipartisanship so successful in Western Europe; Republican presidential nominees had failed in every election since 1928, and an irresistible opportunity arose for victory in 1952.

Truman's problems—the public's confusion and ignorance, the cries of military and political opponents, and spiraling inflation caused by war orders—were compounded by American casualties of 33,237 men dead, 103,376 wounded, and 410 missing. The American people, Truman often said, understood issues when they were explained to them. That was true of domestic political issues, as the president knew from his whistle-stop explanations, but the international issues in Korea did not lend themselves to explanation from the rear platform of a train.

The trouble with the Korean conflict was that the American people did not yet understand the requirements of statesmanship by a great power in a nuclear age. What really needed to be said—and the administration sought vainly to say it—was that the invention of nuclear weapons had made all-out war in the style of the two world wars impossible and that the differences of the United States and the Soviet Union were likely to flare into limited war in insecure places like Korea and become tests of their resolution. Truman, the Joint Chiefs of Staff, Secretary Acheson, and Secretary of Defense Marshall, who had replaced Johnson, knew that only force, coupled with negotiation, would hold the line, but they were unable to convince many.

The situation was exacerbated by the fact that the purposes of the Soviets in Korea were altogether unclear. The administration was therefore uncertain about what it itself was attempting to do—to prevent the Soviets from taking Korea through use of North Korean or Chinese troops; to save Japan by preserving the Korean buffer; or to convince the Soviets that the United States would fight anywhere, even in East Asia, and thereby prevent the Soviets from overrunning Western Europe before the United States could organize NATO. The memoirs of Soviet Premier Nikita Khrushchev, published years later, undisguisedly admitted Soviet involvement and offered a presumption that weaknesses of the South Korean regime of President Syngman Rhee, together with such American testimony as Secretary Acheson's speech of January 1950 in which he failed to mention South Korea as within the United States' "defense perimeter" in Asia, encouraged the Soviets to explore American resolution. The Kremlin may also have desired to involve the Communist Chinese against the United States, in the hope that the Beijing regime might busy itself in a peripheral area of Asia, away from Soviet borders. Years later, in 1993, an American researcher in the former Soviet archives was given a document proving that Stalin had started the Korean War—by giving the green light to the head of North Korea, Kim Il Sung, and arranging the date of attack. The purpose was to see how far Kim could go.

Domestic Policies

Truman's domestic policies as president took far less of his time, and proved far less successful, than his foreign policies. Here also he dealt with three major issues: administration of the modern American presidency, a legislative program known as the Fair Deal, and Republican accusations of internal subversion and corruption. He managed well with two of these domestic matters.

Students of the Truman presidency do not often realize that Truman was the first chief executive to organize the administration of his high office. He was not the first modern American president; Franklin Roosevelt deserves that distinction. Under Roosevelt the old ways of the presidency disappeared, for during the New Deal and World War II the government became too large; never again could a president conduct his affairs with a few assistants and enjoy leisure that took him out of White House offices for large parts of each day. But none of these presidents had large office staffs, although Roosevelt had expanded the White House staff from thirty-seven people in March 1933 to several times that number in 1945 and had also arranged for a new group of assistants, the Executive Office of the President, created in 1939 at the recommendation of a federal commission. Truman turned the energies of these assistants to presidential problems rather than, as under Roosevelt, internecine rivalries. He deplored Roosevelt's sloppy and sometimes byzantine administrative ways. He sought ideas from his assistants, welcomed arguments over matters of policy, and asked that contentions be set forth in well-reasoned memoranda. Once he set the lines of policy, he expected support from assistants.

In addition to reorganizing the White House staff, Truman vastly expanded the Executive Office of the President, both because he believed it needed expansion and because Congress forced his hand. Uncertain over the economic advice Roosevelt had received, Congress in 1946 created the Council of Economic Advisers, a three-man panel of trained economists. The National Security Act of 1947 and its 1949 amendments then created an organization for presidential coordination of defense and foreign policy, the National Security Council. At first Truman gave it little attention, but after the outbreak of the Korean War, he attended its sessions and used it carefully as a management device. The act created the Department of Defense, reduced the navy and army to subcabinet status, added an air force subde-partment, and created the Central Intelligence Agency.

Truman also brought the sprawling federal bureaucracy under control. At the outset of his tenure, he found that the bureaucracy had grown from 600,000 civilian employees in 1932 to 2.6 million twenty years later, with 4,000 in the judicial branch, 22,500 in the legislative, and 2.57 million in the executive (1.3 million in defense, 500,000 in the post office, and the rest in other activities). He could not have controlled his part of this mass through the White House staff and the Executive Office staff. Moreover, most civilian employees were under civil service; the president appointed only 3,000. Truman therefore had to rely on his cabinet. He trusted that cabinet members would control their departments and thereby do the bidding of his administration. His management of the cabinet hence turned out to be far different from that of Roosevelt and other of his twentieth-century predecessors. Cabinet departments, to be sure, had been far smaller in pre-Roosevelt days, and perhaps it was easier for a president to ignore the cabinet. Truman, upon becoming president, was appalled to learn of the formlessness of the Roosevelt cabinet: Secretary of Labor Frances Perkins had lost almost all of her department's divisions and agencies, and cabinet members fought each other openly, leaking their arguments to newspaper reporters. He dismissed most of the Roosevelt appointees in the initial months of his administration. He insisted upon dealing directly with members of the cabinet, and it was their task, he said, both to show loyalty to him and to control their departments. Not all Truman cabinet appointees proved able; but in the crucial areas of military and foreign affairs, his appointments were generally excellent. Cabinet meetings became business sessions, each official taking up his problems by bringing them before the group, with the president making the decision himself.

The domestic legislation of the Truman era followed carefully the main lines of expansion of economic and social programs advanced by the New Deal. At the outset, in September 1945, Truman sent to Congress a sixteen-thousand-word message proposing full-employment and fair-employment-practices bills, federal control of the unemployment compensation program, a large housing program, and the development of natural resources. The proposals ran into a hail of criticism (''brickbats,'' Truman privately described them), and not much came from this message offered so early in his presidency. Most of his initial months were consumed by arguments whether price controls would prevent inflation while manufacturers sought to fill the huge postwar demand for civilian goods. In 1947–1949 the president offered his major change in American foreign policy—the Truman Doctrine, the Marshall Plan, NATO. In 1948, politics and the Berlin blockade took much time. Only in early 1949 could he go back to his domestic program of three years before. The program of 1949 contained twenty-four points and began with the words "Every segment of our population and every individual has the right to expect from our government a fair deal." This promised development of tried-and-true New Deal themes proposed federal control of prices, credit, commodities, exports, wages, and rents; a broadening of civil rights laws; low-cost housing; and a 75-cent minimum wage. It asked repeal of the Taft-Hartley Act, which had passed over a presidential veto in 1947 and which outlawed industry-wide strikes, closed shops, and mass picketing; made unions liable to suits; required union leaders, before they could use the National Labor Relations Board, to file affidavits declaring that they were not Communists; set up cooling-off periods before strikes; prohibited the use of union funds for political contributions; and gave the president power to obtain antiunion injunctions. The Fair Deal promised increased coverage for Social Security, federal aid to education, and compulsory health insurance. The last issue brought Truman into frontal conflict with the American Medical Association, whose leaders cried "socialized medicine" and eventually helped to establish private programs of health insurance.

The time was not right for the Fair Deal, in either 1945 or 1949. In the immediate postwar years, the desire to relax, to have done with challenges, governed the popular mood; the exertions of the New Deal era followed by those of wartime had been too much. Truman himself bemoaned the public selfishness of the early postwar period when arguments between his administration and Republican leaders in the House and Senate, who wanted to lift price controls because of shortages, notably a meat shortage in 1946, persuaded the president to give up the effort to control consumer prices. He may well have reached the low point of his presidency that year when he wrote out a speech about price controls, which he did not give but which came close to offering his resignation from the presidency. Victory in the election of 1948 and the exhilaration of becoming president in his own right in January 1949 momentarily convinced him that the old American spirit of self-sacrifice and generosity again was abroad in the land, that Americans by voting Democratic had affirmed the New Deal and the Fair Deal. Then he began to sense that his mandate was more personal than public, a recognition of his attractive, fighting personality rather than of his ideas for economic and social legislation. He managed to get parts of his program through the Eighty-first Congress, and the rest of it became a blueprint for successor administrations.

Truman made a valiant attempt to rationalize the nation's agricultural production—to solve what generations of Americans, ever since the opening of the Trans-Mississippi West, had described as the farm problem. Truman's secretary of agriculture during his second term, the able Charles F. Brannan, a longtime high official of the department, proposed what the president announced as the Brannan Plan, perhaps the most promising advance in agricultural policy by the federal government in the present century. The Roosevelt administration had assisted farmers through a crazy quilt of fixed prices and other measurements that tended to assist larger farmers, leaving the American consumer to pick up the check for the support program in the form of higher prices. This policy undercut exports, and the consumer picked up that loss when farmers sold their excess to the government at support prices. The consumer also paid for storing the excess, which the government then usually gave away. Brannan proposed to support all farm products, not just a few, and to translate support into units, such as ten bushels of corn. The plan entitled each farmer to price support for eighteen hundred units, no more, eliminating the advantage of the large farmer. In addition, it proposed direct subsidies instead of government loans and purchase agreements.

But the Republicans would not support his farm program. They preferred to let prices fall and declaimed against subsidies in favor of disguised payments, such as price supports and conservation awards. The Brannan Plan failed of support, and the farm problem staggered on.

The Fair Deal scored a triumph in one important respect—the first national breakthrough in the protection of civil rights of black Americans. (Most earlier civil rights measures had not been reinforced by adequate enforcement legislation.) Truman had grown up in a family that had celebrated the death of Lincoln. The Missouri of his youth was lily-white. But his reading and his plain observation of the realities of life in Missouri and across the nation convinced him that oppression at home was as bad as, or even worse than (because it was far more easily remedied), oppression abroad. Late in 1946 he established the Committee on Civil Rights, which presented its report, *To Secure These Rights*, in October 1947. The cabinet split over the question of asking Congress for legislation, but Truman followed his own course and, on 2 February 1948, sent Congress a ten-point civil rights message calling for a new law against lynching, a federal fair-employment-practices committee, an end to segregation in interstate transportation, and protection of the right to vote. None of these proposals was enacted, and had to await later times.

The Democratic convention of 1948 in Philadelphia turned into a donnybrook over civil rights, with representatives from the Deep South departing the hall in high dudgeon to found their anti-black-rights party, the States' Rights Democrats, a "spoiler" group that hoped to gain attention for its position by throwing the election into the House of Representatives. The Dixiecrats, as the group became known, led by Governor J. Strom Thurmond of South Carolina, presented proof, if such were needed, of Truman's dedication to civil rights. The president already faced a challenge to party unity from the Progressive party, supporters of former Vice President Wallace. Truman could ill afford espousal of black rights in 1948. But he did not hesitate. Neither did Thurmond. A reporter asked the governor why he was taking the drastic step of forming a new party. "President Truman is only following the platform that Roosevelt advocated," the reporter argued. "I agree," Thurmond said. "But Truman really means it." After the election, when civil rights legislation met resistance in Congress, Truman, by executive order, forced compliance with nondiscriminatory rules in government contracts, and by the end of 1951 the order covered a fifth of the nation's economy. During the Korean War the integration of the armed forces, begun in 1948 by executive order, reached completion.

The third major domestic issue during the Truman administration centered on a twin accusation by the Republicans that the president made little effort to clean the Communists out of government departments and that he condoned and covertly supported corruption among members of the White House staff

and within government departments. When the Republicans challenged the Democrats in the election of 1952, it was through a crafty formula suggested by Senator Karl E. Mundt of South Dakota—K^1C^2. The Korea part was clear enough, and C^2 stood for Communism and corruption. The amalgam of charges produced by Senator Joseph R. McCarthy of Wisconsin in 1950, along with the conviction of the onetime State Department officer Alger Hiss for perjury that year and the discovery that spy rings had infiltrated the wartime and postwar nuclear projects, promised to push the GOP to victory in 1952. Combined with charges of Democratic corruption, which had some small basis in fact, the Republican strategy became almost irresistible.

Truman's Republican opponents pressed the Communism-in-government issue, and the president could not easily deny the charge, for a denial would necessarily have forced him to answer many trumped-up charges—and his enemies would always have the advantage of first exposure with their assertions. Moreover, Communists did get into the government, for how else could they have attempted to obtain nuclear secrets or, for that matter, subvert the government? The numbers were minuscule, judging from what the Federal Bureau of Investigation managed to turn up, but the controversy persisted. Truman established the Federal Employee Loyalty Program in 1947, by executive order. By mid-1952 the government had screened 4 million of its employees or prospective employees and dismissed or denied employment to 378 (0.022 percent of the total). The program threatened civil liberties and provided an atmosphere in which character assassins thrived.

The president also had to deal with the charge that the Republicans linked to Communism—namely, corruption. It was in meeting allegations of corruption within the federal government, in the White House staff, and particularly in the Bureau of Internal Revenue (BIR) that the president's patience with his political tormentors nearly ran out. Truman became irritated over this issue of domestic politics, and of course, the more intransigent he became, the harder the opposition hammered at their points about corruption. There may also have been a failure of the president's political experience in this regard, for in his political training with the Pendergast machine he had learned that his efforts at reform had to yield to things as they were. Still another factor entered into his clumsiness in dealing with the corruption issue—loyalty. When a subordinate or a friend got into trouble, he instinctively went to his defense.

One of the president's principal errors in handling the corruption issue was his loyalty to an old Missouri friend from World War I days, his military aide, Major General Harry H. Vaughan, an honest but imprudent man. Despite his friendship for Vaughan, he should have cut him loose. Vaughan accepted several freezers, and one of these appliances found its way to 219 North Delaware Street, the president's house in Independence. Vaughan also was friendly with a few individuals who procured federal contracts for a fee of 5 percent. The term "fivepercenter" became a political epithet. General Vaughan was not transferred but remained in the White House for Truman's entire administration.

More unfortunate was presidential insensitivity to corruption in the Reconstruction Finance Corporation (RFC) and the BIR. The RFC naturally attracted employees who made themselves useful to borrowers and left government employ for private enterprise; one of them, unfortunately from Missouri, presented his wife, a secretary in the White House, with a mink coat worth $9,540, paid for by a lawyer for a firm seeking an RFC loan. Congress abolished the RFC in 1953. The BIR offered similar temptations and too many political appointments to collectorships in regional offices around the country. The BIR was the most sensitive government bureau because its operations touched all taxpayers. The president should have watched it closely and moved against miscreants instantly. In his last months in office, he reorganized the BIR by reducing the numbers of regional districts and collectors and placing almost all of the bureau's personnel under civil service.

Opinion polls reflected Truman's failure to marshal public support during his second term, and by November 1951 his popularity had dropped to 23 percent, down from a July 1945 high of 87 percent. This rating was one point lower than that of President Richard M. Nixon on the eve of his resignation in 1974. For the rest of Truman's administration his popularity rating was very low, and by January 1953 it had risen to only 31 percent.

Part of the reason for Truman's low popularity was the tactics he used to deal with the steel strike of 1952. After appealing to capital and labor, he discovered the animosity and uncooperativeness of both, which seemed especially egregious in the midst of the Korean War. Seeking not to invoke the Taft-Hartley Act, he chose to seize the mills in the name of the government. The mill owners went to court, and the resultant decision, in *Youngstown Sheet and Tube Company* v. *Sawyer*, forced Secretary of Commerce Charles Sawyer to give the mills back to the owners and constituted a sharp blow to Truman's prestige. It was one of the century's most important Supreme Court decisions limiting the power of the president.

Early in 1952, Truman announced that he would not run for another term, which he could have done, since he had not served two full terms. He chose, instead, to support Governor Adlai Stevenson of Illinois, who was chosen Democratic standard-bearer that summer. Stevenson sought to distance himself from the Truman administration because of its low public esteem. For a while the president was angry with Stevenson, whom he believed ungrateful. In the autumn, nonetheless, Truman campaigned against the Republican candidate, General Eisenhower, who triumphed easily in the November election.

All in all it was an immensely successful presidency. Truman had kept at the task of leading the government and nation, in belief that posterity would uphold his purposes, foreign and domestic, and that belief has proved well founded. His indefatigable energy despite his age (he was sixty-eight when he left office), his innate modesty that allowed for judgment without involving personal feelings, and his invincible pride in his country carried him forward despite the confusions of his time. In foreign policy he made the decision to use nuclear weapons, whatever it promised for his historical reputation. He rightly took pride in changing the nation's course, from isolation and occasional intervention to participation through the measures of 1947–1949. The Korean War held the line against Communism. In domestic affairs he left the executive branch securely organized, an extraordinarily helpful inheritance for his successor Eisenhower. The Fair Deal appeared to Truman as a thoroughly reasonable program, a belief justified by its enactment in the 1960s and retention by subsequent administrations, Republican as well as Democratic. The issues of Communism and corruption, which bedeviled his last years in the White House, he firmly believed to be (to use his oftenquoted description for the former) a red herring, and mostly they were, although his usual political judgment failed him in handling the latter.

Truman lived nearly twenty years after his presidency. He returned to Independence and the white Victorian house built shortly after the Civil War, renewing acquaintance with the town through brisk morning walks. He published his memoirs in two thick volumes in 1955–1956, presided over fundraising for construction of the Harry S. Truman Library, and became an active Democratic spokesman. In the mid-1960s he slowed down, for ill health brought his activities virtually to a halt. In his last years he returned to the reading of history, biographies of America's leaders of the past, and narrative accounts of the development of American government. The artist Thomas Hart Benton sketched him in a book-lined room of the Delaware Street house in 1971, piles of books across the desk, the old president holding a book in gnarled, arthritic hands. In this manner he passed the time until his death on 26 December 1972.

BIBLIOGRAPHY

Brief biographies are Robert H. Ferrell, *Harry S. Truman and the Modern American Presidency* (Boston, 1983), Roy Jenkins, *Truman* (New York, 1986), William E. Pemberton, *Harry S. Truman: Fair Dealer and Cold Warrior* (Boston, 1989), and R. Alton Lee, *Harry S. Truman: Where Did the Buck Stop?* (New York, 1991). David McCullough, *Truman* (New York, 1992), and Alonzo L. Hamby, *Man of the People: A Life of Harry S. Truman* (New York, 1995), are views of Truman and his times; Robert H. Ferrell, *Harry S. Truman: A Life* (Columbia, Mo., 1994), focuses on Truman.

Richard Lawrence Miller, *Truman: The Rise to Power* (New York, 1986), stops with the presidency but contains much analysis of the president's early life. So does an authorized biography by Jonathan Daniels, *The Man of Independence* (Philadelphia, 1950), of much interest because Daniels talked with Truman family members and friends in Missouri a dozen years before the Truman Library's oral history program began. See also Alfred Steinberg, *The Man from Missouri: The Life and Times of Harry S. Truman* (New York, 1962), by an able freelancer. Cabell Phillips, *The Truman Presidency: The History of a Triumphant Succession* (New York, 1966), is by a *New York Times* reporter in Washington during Truman's presidency. Robert J. Donovan, *Conflict and Crisis: The Presidency of Harry S. Truman, 1945–1948* (New York, 1977) and *Tumultuous Years: The Presidency of Harry S. Truman, 1949–1953* (New York, 1982), are definitive accounts

by a reporter for the *New York Herald Tribune* during the Truman years. A smaller book on the same subject is Donald R. McCoy, *The Presidency of Harry S. Truman* (Lawrence, Kans., 1984).

Harry S. Truman, *Memoirs*, vol. 1; *Year of Decisions* (Garden City, N.Y., 1955) and vol. 2, *Years of Trial and Hope* (Garden City, N.Y., 1956), constitute a huge analysis of the presidency, with a short narrative of the president's earlier years in the first volume. Francis H. Heller, "Harry S. Truman: The Writing of His Memoirs," in George Egerton, ed., *Political Memoir: Essays on the Politics of Memory* (London, 1994), is by Truman's principal assistant on the memoirs. *Truman Speaks* (New York, 1960) is a collection of lectures Truman gave at Columbia University in 1959; and *Mr. Citizen* (New York, 1960) covers his postpresidential years. Charles Robbins and Bradley Smith, *Last of His Kind: An Informal Portrait of Harry S. Truman* (New York, 1979), is based on interviews with Truman in Independence in 1953, after retirement.

Margaret Truman, *Harry S. Truman* (New York, 1973), and her *Bess W. Truman* (New York, 1986), are of course personally biographical.

Ken Hechler, *Working with Truman: A Personal Memoir of the White House Years* (New York, 1982), is by a White House staffer. Francis H. Heller, ed., *The Korean War: A Twenty-Five-Year Perspective* (Lawrence, Kans., 1977), *The Truman White House: The Administration of the Presidency, 1945–1953* (Lawrence, Kans., 1980), and *Economics and the Truman Administration* (Lawrence, Kans., 1981), are reports of conferences of former administration officials and scholars held by the Truman Library.

Robert Underhill, *The Truman Persuasion* (Ames, Iowa, 1981), is a study of the president's speechmaking but contains much information generally about the presidency. Franklin D. Mitchell, *Harry S. Truman and the News Media: Contentious Relations, Belated Respect* (Columbia, Mo., 1998), offers insight to some of the most frank press conferences in recent history. Monte M. Poen, *Harry S. Truman versus the Medical Lobby: The Genesis of Medicare* (Columbia, Mo., 1979), was another exercise in frankness. Andrew J. Dunar, *The Truman Scandals and the Politics of Morality* (Columbia, Mo., 1984), is excellent for its subject.

Documents appear in Robert H. Ferrell, ed., *Off the Record: The Private Papers of Harry S. Truman* (New York, 1980), selected from letters, memoranda, and diary entries beginning in April 1945; *The Autobiography of Harry S. Truman* (Boulder, Colo., 1980), which draws together autobiographical fragments; and *Dear Bess: The Letters from Harry to Bess Truman, 1910–1959* (New York, 1983), half of the cache of letters discovered in the Truman house after Mrs. Truman's death in 1982. See also Monte M. Poen, ed., *Strictly Personal and Confidential: The Letters Harry Truman Never Mailed* (Boston, 1982), letters Truman wrote and had second thoughts about mailing; and *Truman's Letters Home* (New York, 1984), another drawing on the remarkable resources of the Truman Library.

Robert H. Ferrell, *Truman: A Centenary Remembrance* (New York, 1984), is biography and photographs; James N. Giglio and Greg G. Thielen, *Truman in Cartoon and Caricature* (Ames, Iowa, 1984), shows how its subject lent himself to caricature; and Richard S. Kirkendall, ed., *The Harry S. Truman Encyclopedia* (Boston, 1989), is indeed encyclopedic.

Recent works include Steve Neal, *Harry and Ike: The Partnership That Remade the Postwar World* (New York, 2001) and Michael J. Hogan, *A Cross of Iron: Harry S. Truman and the Origins of the National Security State, 1945–1954* (Cambridge and New York, 2000). The issue of Truman's relations with the political boss of Kansas City in the latter 1920s and 1930s appears in Lawrence H. Larsen and Nancy J. Hulston, *Pendergast!* (Columbia, Mo., 1997); and Robert H. Ferrell, *Truman and Pendergast* (Columbia, Mo., 1999); and Rudolph H. Hartmann, *The Kansas City Investigation: Pendergast's Downfall, 1938-1939*, edited by Ferrell (Columbia, Mo., 1999). On the 1948 election see Harold I. Gullan, *The Upset That Wasn't: Harry S. Truman and the Crucial Election of 1948* (Chicago, 1998), and Zachary Karabell, *The Last Campaign: How Harry Truman Won the 1948 Election* (New York, 2000).

A reprinting of books by or about President Truman, known by its piquant title, the Give 'Em Hell Harry series, begun in 1996, has again made available books mentioned above by Daniels, Donovan, Dunar, Ferrell, Hechler, and Poen, with more to come.

Dwight D. Eisenhower

Fred I. Greenstein

Dwight E. Eisenhower DWIGHT D. EISENHOWER LIBRARY

DWIGHT DAVID EISENHOWER, the thirty-fourth president of the United States, was uniquely popular among post-World War II American presidents. As of 2002, only two other chief executives of that period, had been elected to and completed two terms in office. Apart from John F. Kennedy, who did not live to face the consequences of his policy of increasing military involvement in Vietnam, Eisenhower was the only postwar president who received more positive than negative ratings for his entire time in office.

In spite of Eisenhower's impressive ability to maintain the support of the American people, for roughly the decade and a half after he left the White House most scholars and other writers on the presidency judged him to have been a lackluster leader. In 1962, for example, Arthur Schlesinger, Sr., asked seventy-five leading authorities on the American presidency to rank the chief executives in order of greatness. Eisenhower placed twenty-first, tied with Chester Arthur. The scholars' views of Eisenhower and his leadership fundamentally echoed the 1950s partisan rhetoric of liberal Democrats, who viewed Eisenhower as bland, good-natured, and well intentioned, but politically inept and passive. He seemed to hold a minimalist view of the leadership responsibilities of the chief executive. His success in achieving the potentially valuable political resource of popular support was inescapable. But this support was judged to be based merely on the legacy of acclaim he inherited from his World War II leadership as supreme commander of the Allied forces in Europe, reinforced by the appeal of his broad grin and benign countenance to the politically inattentive bulk of the electorate.

By the mid-1970s, a reappraisal of Eisenhower and his leadership was well under way. Interest in reexamining Eisenhower's presidency was spurred in part by the difficulties encountered by his successors and in part by retrospective assessments of the events that occurred while he was in office. Lyndon B. Johnson had felt obliged not to run again because his backing was so weak; Richard M. Nixon had resigned in the face of certain impeachment and conviction; Gerald Ford and Jimmy Carter had been defeated at the polls. Eisenhower's ability to serve two full terms while maintaining his popularity seemed to call for study and analysis. Moreover, his period in office now seemed to have been one of accomplishment rather than drift. By the summer of 1953 his administration had negotiated an armistice that ended the bloody, stalemated Korean War. Peace prevailed throughout the remainder of his presidency, in spite of major episodes that could have led to East-West military conflict. The divisive internal debate over whether the nation was endangered by Communist subversion from within had ended. Inflation rates were low, and, in general, the economy was performing well.

Other of Eisenhower's actions appeared in retrospect to be highly questionable, perhaps most notably his covert use of the Central Intelligence Agency (CIA) to help overthrow the nationalistic Mossadegh government in Iran in 1953 and the left-leaning Arbenz government in Guatemala in 1954. But the very fact that Eisenhower had policies worthy of attention (whatever their merit), like the fact of his popularity, seemed by the 1970s to make it necessary to reconsider the notion that his presidency was simply a time of leaderless inaction.

Fortunately such reconsideration was by then possible. In the archives of the Eisenhower Library in Abilene, Kansas, and in other repositories, enormous bodies of primary source records on Eisenhower and his conduct of the presidency began to be released, many of them in successive volumes of the Department of State's invaluable documentary volumes entitled *The Foreign Relations of the United States*. These records constitute a window through which to view the unpublicized aspects of a president and presidency whose public and private sides were near antitheses. It is now possible to read private diary notes in which Eisenhower recorded his experiences and clarified his thinking and feelings, as well as similar records by some of his close associates, and it is possible for nonspecialists to explore such matters through a burgeoning scholarly literature on the Eisenhower years.

Eisenhower was a prolific and fluent writer of off-the-record correspondence, which provides important insights into his views and actions. His leadership also is well documented in records of his official and unofficial meetings, phone conversations, and even transcripts of his remarks in prepress conference briefings on what information he did, and did not, choose to make public and what impressions he sought to create. From this evidence and the testimony of people who were closely associated with him, it has become clear that Eisenhower in fact was a presidential activist, but that his activism, which was grounded in a consciously articulated view of how to exercise leadership, took a distinctive and unconventional form.

The Eisenhower Approach to Leadership

Although Eisenhower resented claims that he was a weak leader, his very approach to leadership furthered this impression, at least on the part of those who had access only to the contemporary public record. The impression that he was a passive chief executive president who reigned rather than ruled was engendered both by his approach to organizing the presidency and by the tactics he used to resolve the built-in conflict between what Americans expect from their president in his dual capacity as head of state and principal national political leader.

As head of state, the American president is a symbol of unity. Like a constitutional monarch, he is expected to be an uncontroversial representative of the entire nation. As the nation's chief political leader, however, he must engage in the intrinsically divisive prime-ministerial task of political problem solving. The seeming impossibility of resolving the tension between these contradictory expectations undoubtedly has contributed to the regularity with which Americans become disillusioned with the performance of their presidents.

Eisenhower resolved this contradiction by maintaining the public stance of an uncontroversial chief of state, while concealing or playing down his political leadership, especially those machinations that are essential to effective leadership but that foster animosities and lead the president to be viewed as "just another politician." He carried out this leadership strategy through a number of tactics:

1. In seeking to downplay the political side of his role, he frequently exercised political influence through intermediaries rather than directly or otherwise concealed his part in the cut and thrust of leadership.

2. Similarly, he was studiously artful in employing language. His private communications to close associates are models of analytic clarity and contain informed, realistic accounts of his political strategies. But in press conferences he often was evasive or professed ignorance of matters that he felt were best not discussed, doing so in a homely, idiomatic way that enhanced public affection for and confidence in him. And in his public addresses, he worked with his speechwriters seeking to find language that was dignified yet, as he once put it, simple enough "to sound good to the fellow digging a ditch in Kansas."

3. Eisenhower also took pains never to criticize an adversary by name, lest he demean his own role and arouse underdog sympathies for the opponent. By refusing to (as he put it) "engage in personalities," he also acted on the premise that impugning the motives of others engenders ill feeling that undermines the basic leadership task of welding political cooperation.

4. Although he did not discuss personality publicly, much of his private reasoning and discourse involved sizing up what he called the "personal equation" of other political actors. He did this in order to use aides where they would be most effective and to anticipate how best to exercise influence. His preoccupation with personality analysis helped him to keep the political side of his leadership inconspicuous.

5. He was a vocal proponent of generous delegation of authority, but he varied the magnitude of delegation according to his sense of his associates' capacities and of the likelihood that their actions would be consistent with his desires. Thus, his much publicized commitment to delegation did not lead to abdicating presidential power to subordinates. Nevertheless, by emphasizing this commitment he was able to reward associates by giving them credit for popular administration politics and, more important in terms of protecting himself from controversy, to

allow them to take the blame for unpopular administration policies.

For scholars, most of whom equated effective political leadership with the visible displays of political pulling and hauling of Franklin D. Roosevelt and Harry S. Truman, the apolitical public persona that Eisenhower cultivated seemed evidence of his shortcomings as a chief executive. For most citizens, however, a president who seemed untarnished by politicking was worthy of approval—unless, of course, his remoteness from politics was associated with indications that the nation was being poorly managed. One reason why the public did not become discontented was that Eisenhower used his indirect leadership techniques to defuse potential sources of discontent, quietly resolving matters that, if left unsettled, would have made him vulnerable to criticism.

Just as Eisenhower worked hard at exercising political leadership inconspicuously, he expended much energy in maintaining public confidence in his performance as chief of state. Rather than resting on his prepresidential popularity with a broad spectrum of Americans (including many Democrats), he built on his acclaim as a wartime leader. A striking example of the importance he placed on winning public approval was his insistence on standing in an open car, beaming broadly, and waving to the cheering crowds when he was arriving at, or leaving, a public appearance. This was a bone-crunching physical ordeal for Eisenhower, who was the oldest man to have served in the White House at the time he left office. But he considered it essential to his leadership. More generally, he acted on the premise that in order to carry out his responsibilities with good effect he needed to win the widest possible support for his office and powers.

Eisenhower's tactics for reconciling the political with the chief-of-state aspects of the presidency were complemented by his systematic attention to organizing his presidential leadership. He increased the size of the White House staff, introducing a staff position that was controversial in the 1950s but had become traditional by the 1970s—that of the White House chief of staff. This was the position he assigned to the acerbic former New Hampshire governor Sherman Adams, labeling Adams The Assistant to the President, in contrast to other assistants whose titles lacked the initial article. He also was the first president to employ professional legislative liaison personnel, and he introduced the position of assis-

Dwight D. Eisenhower was the first American president to permit televised press briefings. Here he responds to a White House reporter at his first such event on 19 January 1955. AP/WIDE WORLD

tant to the president for national security affairs, now popularly known as the president's national security adviser.

Eisenhower's organizational leadership was also marked by his extensive reliance on the cabinet and the National Security Council as forums within which he and his aides debated policy. Both bodies normally met weekly. In the case of the cabinet he instituted a planning staff that was responsible for ensuring that items worthy of serious discussion were on the agenda for discussion. He instituted an even more structured forum for foreign affairs discussion in the form of an expanded National Security Council (NSC), with which he also met regularly. An elaborate committee structure ensured that alternative foreign policy options were clearly explicated for

council debate, and that once policies were set, plans for implementing them were made.

At the time many political observers took Eisenhower's seeming departure from the far more informal operating procedures of Roosevelt and Truman as further evidence that he had turned leadership over to a bureaucracy. We now know that Eisenhower's formal committee meetings were supplemented by his extensive informal consultations with a wide range of figures in and out of the government. Further, his cabinet and NSC meetings were as much a means of consolidating his associates around his policies as they were forums for decisive policy discussions. He himself set policy, often in unofficial meetings in the Oval Office before or after cabinet and NSC sessions. The archival record released in the

1970s makes this clear, but when he was in office many of his policies were commonly thought to have been made by committees, or by Sherman Adams, or by Eisenhower's sternly anti-Communist secretary of state, John Foster Dulles.

Antecedents of Eisenhower's Leadership

Eisenhower's approach to leadership was shaped by his military career, much of which had been closely tied to participation in civil government and public affairs for the three decades before he became president. Born in Denison, Texas, on 14 October 1890 and raised in rural Kansas, Eisenhower attended the United States Military Academy in order to get a free education. He was more interested in athletics than studies, graduating sixty-first in a class of 164. He was awakened intellectually and became a keen student of military strategy somewhat belatedly, between 1922 and 1924, when he served in the Panama Canal Zone under the gifted and inspirational General Fox Connor.

Through Connor's intervention Eisenhower was chosen to attend the elite Command and General Staff School at Fort Leavenworth, Kansas. After graduating first in a class of 275, he promptly was selected by the War Department for special opportunities. These included a stint in France writing a guidebook to World War I battlefields, attendance at the Army War College, and, in 1929, assignment as deputy to the assistant secretary of war.

In 1933 Eisenhower became the principal aide to the intensely politicized army chief of staff, General Douglas MacArthur. From 1935 to 1940 he accompanied MacArthur to the Philippines, where they advised the Philippine president and legislature on defense policy, returning to the United States the year before America entered World War II. Just a few days after Pearl Harbor, his meteoric ascent to national and international prominence began. Army Chief of Staff George C. Marshall assigned him to the planning division of the War Department in December 1941. By June 1942 he had so impressed not only Marshall but also Roosevelt and Churchill that he was dispatched to England to head American troops in Europe. In November of that year he commanded the American invasion of North Africa, and by late 1943 he had been advanced to supreme commander of Allied forces in Europe. After leading the Allied invasion of Western Europe and achieving victory in the spring of 1945, he returned home to a hero's welcome.

As supreme commander Eisenhower demonstrated a remarkable capacity both to rally the troops in his command and to bring together larger numbers of civilian and military leaders with widely diverse personalities. This made him a logical prospect for public office. By the end of the war, Gallup polls showed that voters in both parties thought he would make a good president. Immediately after the war ended, President Truman offered to support him for the presidency. In 1948 there was a move by liberal Democrats (squelched by Eisenhower) to draft him for the Democratic presidential nomination.

During the war and in his postwar service—first as chief of staff, next as president of Columbia University (but on leave much of the time to help lead the newly formed Department of Defense), and then as first military commander of the North Atlantic Treaty Organization (NATO)—Eisenhower exhibited the same dualism that was to mark his approach to presidential leadership. The tasks he had to perform made it necessary for him to be closely involved in national and international political maneuvers, but he succeeded in defining them in neutral terms, stressing that all of his actions were based on his official responsibility to serve the wartime and postwar alliances he led and the American national interest. He displayed his buoyant personality in rallying the public, but his private propensity continued to be to act on the basis of cool logic and carefully calculated strategic planning. In short, he did not directly transfer his methods of military leadership to the presidency, but the former provided the template for much of the latter, and neither was politically innocent.

From NATO to the Presidency

Throughout 1951 and the first months of 1952, Eisenhower's base of operations was France and his principal task was establishing working relations among the NATO powers. During this period the press had regular accounts of the campaign to draft him for the presidential nomination. Meanwhile, he was persistently visited by moderate and liberal internationalist politicians and businessmen who urged him to run for president, some of them Democrats but the bulk Republicans.

There is good reason to believe that he could have been elected as a candidate of either party, although the conservative economic views he publicly expressed in 1949 and 1950, when he was not on active military duty, clearly implied what he did not make explicit until early in 1952—that he had been a lifelong Republican in his sympathies. The politicians who were most persistent and influential in pressing Eisenhower to become a candidate were moderates in domestic policy and internationalists in foreign policy. They, like other Republicans, were acutely aware that Democrats had controlled the White House for five terms and that President Truman's unpopularity made it possible to reverse that state of affairs. The Republicans who sought to draft Eisenhower recognized also that the overwhelming favorite among the small-town and rural Republican political leaders who could be expected to dominate the 1952 presidential nominating convention would be a dour, conservative, and distinctly uncharismatic symbol of Republican orthodoxy, Senator Robert A. Taft of Ohio. They were certain that Taft would not win in their own constituencies and probably would not win nationally.

Privately, Eisenhower's domestic policy views were even more conservative than Taft's. Having seen inflation cut deeply into postwar defense budgets, he was a convinced fiscal conservative. He also was skeptical about many welfare policies, but electoral realism led him to insist that his party make clear its commitment to preserve and even incrementally expand the basic New Deal welfare reforms.

Eisenhower's reflections in his private diary make it clear that he did not want to become a candidate and would not have become one simply out of disagreement with Taft's domestic policy positions. But he was deeply concerned that Taft, if elected, would undermine the internationalist foreign and national security policies he had devoted himself to shaping. Early in 1952, Eisenhower cast the die, allowing Senator Henry Cabot Lodge of Massachusetts to enter him in the New Hampshire Republican presidential primary.

This made him a tacit candidate, but as long as he held his NATO office he refused to campaign or make campaign statements. He won the New Hampshire primary, producing clear evidence of his vote-getting power. Then he beat Minnesota's incumbent governor, Harold Stassen, as a write-in candidate in that state's primary. Thereafter he and Taft both won primaries, but the majority of the delegates were selected by party machinery, and a near majority of them were committed to Taft.

Eisenhower turned the tide when he returned to the United States, resigned his commission, and commenced an increasingly persuasive last-minute campaign just before and during the convention. Taft's majority depended on the votes of delegations from southern states, in which the Ohio senator's supporters were being challenged by Eisenhower supporters, who claimed that they had been improperly barred from delegate-selection caucuses. When procedural votes designed to bar the seating of Taft's contested southern delegates succeeded, the convention shifted in Eisenhower's direction. He was nominated by a slim majority on the first ballot, but his victory left Taft supporters embittered.

Eisenhower's campaign strategy and his handling of the period between his election and nomination reflect his preoccupation with consolidating his own forces and reaching out to broaden his strength. He immediately sought to bring his party together, most dramatically by signing a statement of Republican principles that Taft had drafted. His choice of Richard Nixon as the vice presidential nominee also was agreeable to the Taft forces. Nixon, because of the part he played in identifying the New Deal lawyer and foreign service officer Alger Hiss as an alleged Communist agent, personified the right-wing premise that the Democrats had been "soft on Communism."

Eisenhower threw himself into campaigning, traveling more than 50,000 miles by rail and air. The campaign was not without problems. He angered moderate supporters when he gave the appearance of having been conciliatory in Wisconsin to Senator Joseph McCarthy. At one point it became necessary for his running mate, Richard Nixon, to refute the accusation that as a senator he had unethically accepted financial support from a group of California businessmen. In spite of the campaign snags, Eisenhower's powerful public appeal was evident. Unlike his opponent, Governor Adlai Stevenson of Illinois, he did not speak over the heads of his audience. When, late in the campaign, he promised to "go to Korea" if elected, implying that his military expertise would enable him to end the war, political observers correctly judged his victory to be a foregone conclusion. He garnered 55 percent of the popular vote (34 million to 27.3 million) and defeated Stevenson by a 442-to-89 electoral vote margin. He brought into office with him the first Republican Congress since 1947 and the only Republican-controlled Congress until 1995.

Even before the returns were in, Eisenhower exhibited the knowledge of government he had acquired over the years and his predilection for organizing his leadership systematically. On election eve he persuaded a Detroit banker, Joseph Dodge, to become his first director of the key planning organ of the presidency, the Bureau of the Budget. During the time between election and inauguration, it was Dodge's task to act as an observer from within the bureau while Truman's final budget was being prepared and to identify ways it could be cut to Republican dimensions. Eisenhower simultaneously announced the appointments of cabinet members and White House aides, including the aides who were to fill the new staff positions he had devised, such as a White House chief of staff, a presidential national security assistant, and a head of congressional liaison. A little-noted appointment to an unpaid but important position—a body for proposing the reorganization of government agencies—went to his brother and closest confidant, Milton Eisenhower, whose Washington experience had begun in the Coolidge administration.

Several of the announcements of cabinet appointments were delayed and made from his residence between 29 November and 5 December, when (for security reasons) Eisenhower secretly made his inspection trip to Korea. The procession of appointees leaving his home during this period provided his cover story—that he was at his home selecting appointees. Eisenhower arranged for the people he had selected for his cabinet to be flown to Wake Island in the mid-Pacific. Returning to the United States from Korea by ship, he met with this group, beginning his efforts to encourage solidarity and a common sense of purpose among his principal associates.

A Republican Presidency Takes Hold: 1953–1955

In January 1953, when Eisenhower took office, not a single Republican member of the Eighty-third Congress had ever served with a Republican president. To Eisenhower it was as important to build solid links to Capitol Hill as to create a spirit of cooperation among his cabinet and staff. In particular, he cultivated Taft, who was an effective and loyal, if sometimes contentious, administration supporter, serving as Senate majority leader until shortly before his death in the summer of 1953.

The channels from president to Congress had to be numerous in the Eighty-third Congress and the

three Democratic-controlled Congresses that followed. The close balance between the parties and the divisions within them made it necessary for bipartisan coalitions to be shaped to advance Eisenhower's legislative goals. His conservative economic policies received the backing of Taft Republicans and southern Democrats. In seeking to introduce moderate welfare reforms, he relied on the more liberal, mostly eastern members of his own party and on northern Democrats. His internationalist foreign policy programs—for example, extension of the reciprocal trade program and appropriation of foreign aid funds—drew support from the internationalist Republicans, who had been at the forefront in seeking his nomination, but they received more backing from Democrats than from members of their own party.

After Taft's death, Eisenhower developed a working relationship, but one that was less than reliable, with the next Senate Republican leader, the bellicose and politically inept William Knowland. Eisenhower worked officially with Knowland, but following his regular practice of carefully supplementing formal with informal organization, he found a variety of allies who unofficially made up for Knowland's shortcomings. Because bipartisanship was necessary to pass legislation but was controversial to supporters of each party, Eisenhower often met without public announcement in the residential quarters of the White House with the two pragmatic southerners who led the congressional Democrats, Senator Lyndon Johnson and Congressman Sam Rayburn, both of Texas.

Two of Eisenhower's initial policy efforts were in the area of national security. One was the short-run effort to bring the lingering Korean conflict to a close and the other the long-run aim of reconfiguring the nation's general national security posture. Ending the fighting in Korea was by no means simple. The truce talks had long been stalled, and the Chinese Communists and North Koreans were so well entrenched that even if pushing them back had been militarily and politically feasible, it would have been too costly in lives and money to contemplate. Hiding his hand from the American people and the Western allies, who would have undermined his actions by public protest, he leaked through channels friendly to the Chinese the message that he was prepared to use extreme measures (by implication, nuclear strikes) if a truce were not concluded. Since talks promptly resumed and a settlement was reached by

July, Eisenhower felt his implied threat had worked; others have speculated that the death of Soviet leader Joseph Stalin in March may have set the process of accommodation in motion.

Eisenhower's more long-range efforts were to implement Joseph Dodge's efforts to reduce Truman's requests for the fiscal year beginning in June 1953 by $7.2 billion in expected expenditures. The major source of reduction was military spending. The strategy underlying Eisenhower's cut in defense spending came to be known as his administration's "New Look" defense policy. In contrast to the defense intellectuals who dominated strategic planning in the final years of the Truman administration, Eisenhower insisted that national security costs be systematically weighed against their economic effects on the nation. (For this reason, he made his secretary of the treasury and his budget director members of the National Security Council.) Overspending, Eisenhower maintained, was not an effective way of ensuring the nation's defense capacity. Rather, it was an unproductive waste and a self-defeating stimulus to inflation. But how could the government reduce its expenditures and maintain its commitment to contain Communism? (Much less, in the rhetoric Dulles used but never acted upon, rolling it back.) The answer was provided in the ominous-sounding phrase "massive retaliation." The United States would not commit itself to meet Communist expansion at every point where it occurred but rather would respond on its own terms, if necessary with "massive retaliatory power." An attack in an area where American and allied forces could not effectively be used might be responded to elsewhere. And the military could make up for its decreased military manpower by employing low-yield tactical nuclear weapons if necessary or, in dire circumstances, by striking the Soviet heartland.

As a strategist—in the game of bridge as well as in military and political affairs—Eisenhower was aware of the dangers of bluffing. The nuclear component of the New Look was meant to be a deterrent to the adversary, not a response that would readily have been made. Eisenhower's congenital proclivity to play his cards close to his vest makes it impossible to say whether under any circumstance short of a total war he would in fact have used nuclear weapons if circumstances seemed to make that advantageous. His private communications, however, show that he was profoundly aware of the devastating consequences a nuclear war would bring, and he always left tactical ambiguities in those of his statements which implied the possibility of using nuclear weapons.

Typically the hard-line anti-Communist pronouncements of the Eisenhower presidency were made by Secretary of State Dulles, sometimes using phrases Eisenhower himself had drafted. Eisenhower concentrated on playing the contrasting role of peacemaker and seeker of East-West rapprochement. In December 1953 he received accolades for one such effort—a speech at the United Nations proposing that the nuclear powers make available raw materials for research on peaceful applications of atomic energy ("Atoms for Peace"). At still another level, fully concealed from public visibility, Eisenhower and his foreign policy associates periodically employed the CIA in covert Cold War operations, including another 1953 action, the overthrow of Mohammed Mossadegh's government in Iran, and the overthrow of the left-leaning government of Jacobo Arbenz in Guatemala in 1954.

In December 1953, Eisenhower called a three-day White House conclave of Republican congressmen, at which he set forth and won agreement to a carefully worked out domestic program that the administration was to submit to the second session of the Eighty-third Congress. His first year had been one of consolidation, adjustment to power, and response to immediately pressing problems. But his second year in office, leading up to the midterm election, was slated as a time for policy making and the building of a Republican record.

By the midterm elections, Eisenhower, whose active campaigning appears to have held down the normal seat loss of an incumbent party in an off-year election, was in fact able to point to such legislative accomplishments as extension of the coverage of Social Security to a number of categories of citizens who did not have retirement benefits and authorization of construction of the St. Lawrence Seaway. He could also take credit for the Atoms for Peace proposal and the Korean settlement. But the year was punctuated by major activities that had not been on his agenda in December 1953, including the matters of Senator Joseph McCarthy of Wisconsin and the Indochina crisis of 1954.

McCarthy, a political nonentity until 1950, had become almost instantaneously visible in February of that year, when he made the unfounded charge that he had a list of Communists who were presently on the State Department payroll, busily subverting the nation. In that period of preoccupation with internal subversion and with such international events as the Communist victory in China, the very extravagance of his rhetoric—made more newsworthy because President Truman was goaded into replying to him— earned the Wisconsin Republican substantial media attention. On this McCarthy built a grassroots following and became recognized within the Republican party as a figure who, if deeply irresponsible, was nevertheless a political asset.

McCarthy had felt free to allege that the Truman administration was permeated with Communists, oblivious to the negative effects of his unsubstantiated charges on the morale of the executive branch and the perception of the United States by other nations. But what would he do once his own party was in power? Eisenhower sought, with some initial success, to check McCarthy's freewheeling assaults on the loyalty of public servants—for example, by enlisting Taft to certify that McCarthy's claim that career foreign service officer Charles Bohlen was unsuited to be ambassador to the Soviet Union was groundless. Eisenhower also acted to remedy what he himself thought were failures in the government's procedures for screening employees, instituting a program that by extending the reasons for which civil servants could be discharged as security risks took its own toll on morale in the executive branch.

In short order, it became clear that McCarthy was not going to cease his assaults on the loyalty of federal employees and, by implication, on Eisenhower's stewardship of the government. There were widespread demands that Eisenhower reply to McCarthy, some of them from his close supporters. Eisenhower's view was that public mention of a demagogic politician by the president simply enhanced that politician's support. Instead, Eisenhower periodically criticized the kinds of tactics McCarthy employed, leaving it to the press to infer that he was alluding to the Wisconsin senator. Then, in the spring of 1954, when McCarthy overreached himself and allowed his aides to seek favors for a former staff member who had been inducted into the army, the Eisenhower administration orchestrated an oblique campaign against him.

Acting on the premise that presidential efforts to purge a legislator would backfire, Eisenhower worked behind the scenes to encourage the Senate itself to conduct hearings on McCarthy's actions. Carried live on television, the Army-McCarthy hearings contributed to McCarthy's decline in public support

and his subsequent formal condemnation by the Senate. His colleagues began to ostracize him, and he soon became politically impotent. Because Eisenhower's contribution to McCarthy's demise was largely indirect and behind the scenes, his seeming inaction with respect to McCarthy helped reinforce the contemporary impression of Eisenhower's political passivity.

In 1954, Eisenhower circumvented a probable foreign affairs debacle through actions that did not become known in their full dimensions until the 1980s, when the relevant classified documents became available for analysis. In the first months of that year a debate raged within the Eisenhower administration about whether to use American military force to prevent the defeat of the French forces that were at war with the indigenous Communists in Indochina. By January 1954 the Communists had trapped the cream of the French defenders at an isolated military outpost in the hamlet of Dien Bien Phu. Eisenhower feared that a Communist victory would lead to Communist triumphs in neighboring countries, which would succumb, as he put it, like a row of falling dominoes.

He recognized, nevertheless, that there were profound reasons why it would be perilous to use American military force in such an inhospitable environment, a course of action that was favored by the chairman of the Joint Chiefs of Staff, Admiral Arthur Radford, and by Vice President Nixon. In extensive meetings with his associates and members of Congress, Eisenhower established strict preconditions for intervention, including formation of a multinational coalition and a grant of immediate independence to the French colonies. When the preconditions could not be met, he concluded that direct American involvement in the Indochinese conflict would not be politically feasible. Rather than fight, he supported the partition of Vietnam into a Communist North and a non-Communist South Vietnam and provided foreign aid to the latter. He also fostered formation of the Southeast Asia Treaty Organization (SEATO), designed to limit the expansion of Communist North Vietnam and China.

The year 1954 also saw Eisenhower win a major legislative struggle to prevent ratification of a constitutional amendment proposed by Senator John Bricker of Ohio that was designed to limit the president's powers in making international agreements. Success required great political skill, since Bricker had won over sixty-two senators as cosponsors—

more than the necessary two-thirds of the Senate votes required for approval. Eisenhower's strategy was to refuse to acknowledge that his basic desires differed from Bricker's but to object persistently to any wording of the amendment that did not simply make the empty statement that no treaty could violate the Constitution. By converting the issue to one of semantics, he gave sponsors of the amendment a face-saving way to change their votes and cooperate with the extensive lobbying campaign his liaison staff conducted.

From Midterm to Second Term: 1955–1956

The Democratic-controlled Eighty-fourth Congress had barely convened in January 1955 when Eisenhower requested and, after sharp debate, received overwhelming support for a resolution according him power to employ military force in the strait between the Communist-controlled mainland of China and the Nationalist Chinese refuge on Formosa (now Taiwan), one hundred miles from the mainland. When the Nationalists were defeated on the mainland in 1949 and retreated to Formosa, they also maintained control of a number of small islands virtually within sight of the mainland. Late in 1954 the Communists had begun to shell the offshore islands in a seeming prelude to taking possession of them and eventually of Formosa.

Eisenhower viewed a Nationalist-held Formosa as essential to maintaining non-Communist governments on the Pacific "island barrier" running from Japan through the Philippines to Indonesia. In his view the offshore islands were militarily dispensable but politically important for maintaining the morale of the Nationalists, who hoped someday to use them to return to the mainland. The Nationalists had powerful support in the Republican party, including the zealous backing of Senate Republican leader Knowland. Knowland and the Nationalists urged American protection of the offshore islands. Congressional liberals and the British, on the other hand, urged that these vulnerable flyspecks be abandoned.

Eisenhower made certain that the "Formosa Resolution" that authorized him to use American military force to defend Formosa and areas necessary to its defense was vague with respect to those islands. It approved the defense of Formosa, but then added cryptically that the president also was authorized to use American force to defend "such related

positions . . . now in friendly hands . . . required or appropriate in assuring the defense of Formosa." The offshore islands crisis subsided in April 1955, when the Chinese Communists announced at the Bandung, Indonesia, conference of African and Asian nations that as evidence of their commitment to peace they would not seek to gain control of islands in the Formosa Strait by military means.

Shortly after the Chinese action at Bandung, the Soviet Union took a step toward decreasing Cold War tensions, declaring that it was prepared to withdraw from its postwar occupation of Austria and to join the West in signing a peace treaty with that nation. Eisenhower and Dulles, who had resisted calls for a summit meeting, concluded that circumstances now permitted one, for it could be portrayed as a response to Soviet accommodation and might, without excessive danger of raising false expectations, test the Soviet willingness to advance further toward East-West agreement.

The ensuing meeting in Geneva between 18 an 23 July 1955 provided Eisenhower with an opportunity to make a widely acclaimed proposal that was even more dramatic than the Atoms for Peace speech. He called for the United States and the Soviet Union to exchange blueprints of their military establishments and for inspection flights by each nation over the other to eliminate the fear of surprise attack. His speech received widespread accolades in the press, and the conference ended with journalists writing of the promising "Spirit of Geneva." Nikita Khrushchev, whose demeanor at the conference made it clear that he was now top man in the post-Stalin "collective leadership" of the Soviet Union, broadly hinted in conversation with Eisenhower that he considered the proposal no more than a means of spying on the Soviet Union. Apart from being a propaganda coup for the United States, the "open skies" proposal anticipated the later practice, which both nations later came to take for granted, of mutual aerial surveillance by orbiting satellites. Eisenhower was well aware of the potential usefulness of surveillance; in fact, at the time he was setting in motion a highly classified program of overflying the Soviet Union with high-attitude U-2 reconnaissance planes, a program that was to have unhappy consequences in his second term.

Between the Geneva conference and the October foreign ministers' conference at which it became certain that there would be no Soviet acceptance of his program, Eisenhower suffered a major heart attack. He was stricken on 24 September 1955, in Denver, Colorado. Fortunately no international crises or immediate domestic issues required immediate presidential attention. The first session of the Eighty-fourth Congress had adjourned, having enacted a three-year extension of tariff-cutting powers that Eisenhower requested, but not much else of his legislative program.

Eisenhower was soon able to make himself understood and within weeks was conducting rudimentary public business from his bed, using Sherman Adams as his intermediary. He encouraged the cabinet and National Security Council to hold regular meetings. These sessions were presided over by Vice President Nixon, who took pains to make clear that he was serving as a mere stand-in during Eisenhower's absence, but the meetings did serve as a symbol that the government was continuing to function. Meanwhile, the list of Eisenhower's bedside visitors gradually increased, and he even held brief meetings with visiting foreign leaders.

Nevertheless, national and international affairs were bound to be in a state of uncertainty during a period when the president of the United States was hospitalized and the extent of his illness was uncertain. Republican party leaders were distressed with the prospect that their one surefire winning candidate for 1956 might not be fit to run. Individual party members who were prominent enough to seek the nomination—most conspicuously, Knowland—began to jockey for position. Paradoxically, and in spite of the fears of the bulk of Republicans that Eisenhower would not be able to run again, his heart attack had the effect of making him feel obliged to seek a second term.

Just as Eisenhower had originally hoped not to have to cap his military career by serving as president, he had throughout his first term considered it likely that he would serve only a single term. The fall of 1955 was the period when he could have helped enhance the stature of whoever seemed most appropriate as his successor or could have sent out signals that would encourage a field of Republican competitors to emerge. During this period, as he gradually increased his governmental activities, he had to await a medical judgment on his own health, which could not be made until early February. By the time his heart specialist reported him fit for a second term, no other Republican was available who seemed likely to win in 1956, and it was manifest that much of what he hoped to attain as president remained unaccomplished. He announced that he was willing to run again.

Although anticipation of the fall election led to a partisan impasse on many of the issues before the second session of the Eighty-fourth Congress, three administration measures of consequence passed. Each initiated the kind of change that, unlike welfare-state policies, Eisenhower unambiguously favored—investment in natural resources and improvements in the nation's material base. In agricultural policy, the farm subsidy program was adjusted to include a "soil bank," whereby farmers, rather than being paid for growing foods that later would be stored as surplus, were given incentives to take unprofitable land out of cultivation in order to conserve and improve its topsoil. A multiyear program to improve national parks was also approved. Finally, the largest public works bill in American history was passed, creating the interstate highway program, which was to transform the country by constructing a network of limited-access, high-speed roads.

Eisenhower again ran with Nixon as the vice presidential candidate. He had attempted to persuade Nixon to step down, arguing unconvincingly that Nixon's career would be helped by serving as secretary of defense rather than seeming to be second man to the president. Unprepared to split the party by dropping Nixon, he did not achieve his aim of substituting a candidate who might be a better vote getter and more to his liking as the 1960 Republican candidate. The Democrats renominated Stevenson, pairing him with the popular Senator Estes Kefauver of Tennessee as vice presidential candidate. Eisenhower won handily (35.5 million votes to 26 million), increasing his share of the popular vote from 55 percent to almost 58 percent, in what clearly was a personal, not a party, victory. For the first time since early in the nineteenth century, a president was elected without control of Congress by his party.

During the final weeks of the presidential campaign two of the major foreign policy crises of Eisenhower's presidency erupted. The first was the Hungarian uprising. Since Stalin's death in 1953, there had been a series of protests of varying degrees of intensity against Soviet control in Eastern European nations. On 22 October 1956, inspired by concessions won by Polish insurgents, Hungarian students and workers began engaging in protests, seeking to broaden the base of the government and to have Soviet troops removed from their nation. After Soviet forces fired on protesters, a revolt broke out. Fighting with primitive weapons, Hungarian rebels called on the United States to help. As in other instances of Eastern European unrest, Eisenhower was unwilling to act on his administration's rhetorical stance that the Soviet Union should not just be contained but be pushed back. He lodged diplomatic protests, offered food and medical aid, and fostered immigration by Hungarians who escaped to the West before the Soviet Union crushed the rebellion on 4 November. But he would not risk general war or fight a limited war in an area in which the Soviet Union had the advantage and which was not vital to American security.

The other crisis, one that blunted the capacity of the West to brand the Soviet Union as a distinctly aggressive nation, resulted from the coordinated attacks on Egypt by two nations directly allied with the United States—France and Great Britain. Egyptian President Gamal Abdel Nasser had acted to nationalize the Suez Canal in the summer of 1956. Long controlled by the British, the waterway was viewed by the British and French leaders as necessary for their nations' economic survival. The two Western nations provided Israel with the military aid to make an ostensible retaliatory attack on Egypt, which had been the base for commando raids on Israel. On 31 October, on the pretext of protecting the canal, the British and French bombed Egypt and dropped paratroopers in Egypt, and Israeli troops entered the Sinai.

By 1956, Eisenhower was far from enthusiastic about the Nasser regime. The previous year he had been disposed to support Egypt's request for American aid for a major irrigation project—the Aswan High Dam—but Nasser's policies then took an anti-Western tack. Nasser purchased large supplies of arms from the Eastern bloc, recognized Communist China, and berated the West. As a consequence, the United States withheld support for the Aswan Dam, an action that immediately preceded Nasser's nationalization of the Suez Canal.

In spite of his aversion to Nasser, Eisenhower was convinced that open military action against Egypt on a patently hypocritical pretext would infuriate Arab and other Third World nations and would not even accomplish its immediate geopolitical purposes of securing the canal and keeping oil flowing to the West. Rather than allow the Soviet Union to take credit for condemning the Anglo-French-Israeli action, the United States introduced a cease-fire resolution in the United Nations. As a result, the United States ironically found itself voting with the Soviet Union on the same side of a resolution directed against a military intervention by its own allies at the very time it was attempting to muster world condemnation of Soviet action in Hungary. One unintended consequence of the Suez episode that would undermine Eisenhower's long-term goals was British withdrawal from an international role in the Middle East.

The 1956 election victory, as resounding as it was, left Eisenhower with major international problems. Relations with the Soviet Union were less satisfactory than they had been a year earlier and the Western alliance needed mending. His problems in the initial period of his second term, moreover, were not only in foreign policy.

Eisenhower as a Lame-Duck President: 1957–1958

Eisenhower was the first president who was constitutionally limited to two terms under the Twenty-second Amendment. Thus, he took office as an official lame duck. Conventional wisdom is that other leaders will take such an official less seriously, on the assumption they can wait him out rather than reach accommodations with him in order to bring about policy outcomes. Resolving to turn his status as a president who could not run again to his purposes, Eisenhower made it clear that precisely because he did not have to think about reelection, he would feel free to take politically unpopular or unconventional actions.

He began the first session of the Eighty-fifth Congress with an unconventional action, one that, like much that occurs in politics, had unanticipated effects. The budget he was presenting to Congress had been shaped in the latter part of 1956, when he was unable to concentrate single-mindedly on making certain that proposed expenditures were kept to a minimum. Wanting to make clear that budgets of the magnitude of his 1957 recommendation for the 1958 fiscal year should not be viewed as a precedent and evidently also interested in cutting back from his present requests, he took the unprecedented step of having his treasury secretary, George Humphrey, release a statement stressing the importance of holding down spending on the same day the budget went to Congress.

Humphrey's statement was carefully worded so that it did not contradict Eisenhower by criticizing the present budget request, but in the final minutes of the press conference that followed his statement, Humphrey made headlines by using the colorful phrase "a depression that will curl your hair" to refer to the likely consequence of continued large budgets. The press and, more provocatively, Democrats smarting from the recent election defeat took Humphrey's statement to be a revolt against Eisenhower's message of the same day. In subsequent months Humphrey's statement was frequently mentioned by budget-cutting congressmen, who in particular attacked the foreign-aid and overseas-information programs that were central to Eisenhower's program but politically vulnerable. Most of the proposed cuts were restored, but only after special messages to Congress on Eisenhower's part.

While no debacle, Eisenhower's foray into unconventional lame-duck politics led to the kind of polemics and political gamesmanship he deplored and was not an effective maneuver. Indeed, Eisenhower's recollection in his memoirs was that the first session of the Eighty-fifth Congress was the low point of his presidency in executive-legislative relations. The session did, he granted, yield one major enactment—the first national civil rights law since Reconstruction.

Eisenhower held the traditional conservative view that changes in deeply held beliefs and traditions cannot be legislated, but rather must evolve from education and changing social conditions. In 1954, when the Supreme Court reversed its 1896 decision allowing racially segregated schools, Eisenhower was quick to point out that since school segregation had been legal for the past half century, it was understandable that southern whites would initially resist the Court's new reading of the Constitution. He consistently refused to express an opinion about the desegregation decision, arguing that it was improper for a president to enter the judicial domain and pronounce on Court actions. Undoubtedly he also was influenced by his personal background and political base. A number of his prewar army duty stations had been in the South, and some of his strongest supporters were white southerners.

During his first term he had kept his 1952 campaign commitment to take those actions on behalf of civil rights that were clearly within his administrative power as chief executive. These included enforcing desegregation in the District of Columbia and in federal shipyards in the South. The steps taken in desegregating the shipyards typify the kind of nonconfrontational resolution of heated issues that Eisenhower favored. No announcement was made that desegregation was taking place. Instead, teams of maintenance workers were brought in on weekends, when the yards were closed, and instructed to paint out the signs designating race on rest rooms, drinking fountains, and eating places. The employees were quietly encouraged to use any facilities they chose, and the supervisory personnel were instructed not to interfere. Desegregation occurred without conflict. Only after the fact was it made public that Eisenhower had acted on his campaign promise.

A new bill designed to proceed in one of the less deeply emotional, but nevertheless important, areas of racial discrimination—voting rights—was drafted by the Justice Department early in Eisenhower's second term. Eisenhower's reasoning in proceeding in the area of voting was that if southern blacks had the vote, their power at the polls would enable them win other rights. The law that eventually emerged from Congress—the Civil Rights Act of 1957—did not have effective enforcement provisions. Its major accomplishment was the creation of the federal Civil Rights Commission, which through its regular reports focused attention on rights abuses, as well as the Civil Rights Division of the Department of Justice.

School desegregation was a far more explosive issue in the 1950s than voting rights. Many southern white parents were determined at all costs, including use of violence, to ensure that their children were not "mixed" with black children in the schools. Southern political leaders were prepared to back them up. One such leader, Governor Orval Faubus of Arkansas, initiated the kind of direct federal-state confrontation over a racial issue that Eisenhower had been striving to avoid.

In compliance with the Supreme Court ruling that desegregation of schools should proceed with "deliberate speed," the city of Little Rock had instituted a program in which desegregation would begin at the high school level in September 1957 and in later years work down to lower grades. Faubus employed the National Guard to bar black students from entering Little Rock's Central High School, ostensibly to prevent civil disorder. Eisenhower requested Faubus to meet with him and thought he had won Faubus' agreement not to interfere with desegregation. Faubus then withdrew the National Guard and stood aside while a massive mob of anti-integrationists descended on Little Rock, ready to do violence to any black students who entered the high school.

Faced with a blatant disruption of the constitutional order, Eisenhower acted decisively by calling the Arkansas National Guard into federal service so that Faubus could no longer command it and by sending regular army troops into Little Rock to disperse the mob and maintain the peace while black students proceeded to attend the high school. The episode was forced on Eisenhower, but when it became necessary for him to take action, he did so effectively, using a military contingent so large that there was no danger of resistance. He explained to associates that he had substituted federal troops for the National Guard in order not to pit Arkansan against Arkansan.

Eisenhower turned to Congress for foreign policy support early in the Eighty-fifth Congress, as well as for backing on his budget and civil rights proposals. In the aftermath of Suez, Egypt became increasingly tied to the Soviet Union, and the Soviet influence in the area increased more broadly. In addition the Middle East was marked by continuing rivalries between the Arab states and exacerbated Arab-Israeli tensions. Eisenhower met in January 1957 with leading congressmen of both parties to discuss the Near Eastern power vacuum and the danger that the Soviet Union might succeed in establishing itself in that strategically vital area. He requested that Congress pass a resolution, similar to the Formosa Resolution, authorizing a United States commitment of troops to the area if any of the governments requested assistance. It was an indication of the decline in Eisenhower's influence with Congress that the resolution was more hotly debated and approved by a smaller margin than the Formosa Resolution had been.

The most dramatic and politically consequential challenge to Eisenhower's leadership in 1957 was not the budget, civil rights, Little Rock, or the passage by Congress of the Eisenhower Doctrine, as the resolution on the Middle East came to be called. Rather it was an ostensibly scientific event—the launching by the Soviet Union on 4 October of *Sputnik*, the first space satellite. By making it obvious that the Soviet Union had achieved the capacity to produce rockets of sufficient power to propel an object into outer space, *Sputnik* had obvious implications about the respective military strengths of the two superpowers.

In the months before the *Sputnik* launching, the Soviet Union claimed to have rockets capable of propelling intercontinental ballistic missiles (ICBMs) to the United States. The Soviet success in putting a satellite in orbit (and soon after a much larger one) was not matched by the United States until January 1958.

By then, Lyndon Johnson had initiated hearings examining the entire question of American versus Soviet military strength. For the remainder of Eisenhower's time in office, a "missile gap" was alleged to exist by major forces within the Democratic party, led by Johnson, Senator Stuart Symington of Missouri, and the man who was to win the 1960 Democratic presidential nomination, Senator John F. Kennedy of Massachusetts.

The missile-gap controversy continued through the 1960 presidential campaign and contributed to the strategic point of view that led the Kennedy administration to engage in a massive escalation of missile production between 1961 and 1963. In fact, Eisenhower and a handful of his closest associates were well aware that the Soviet Union had virtually no ICBM production under way. Their information came from the highly declassified aerial photographs of the Soviet Union obtained on high-altitude U-2 plane flights that the Soviet leaders privately protested but did not refer to in public, lest they acknowledge an area in which they were vulnerable to the United States.

Eisenhower sought to reassure Americans and their allies that although the Soviet Union might for the moment have greater capacity to produce long-range rockets, in toto the West was well defended, since it could retaliate against a Soviet attack with bombers and with intermediate-range ballistic missiles based in allied nations. Resisting crash increases in spending for missile development programs, Eisenhower took a number of other steps to enhance and highlight the American commitment to retain sufficient military strength to deter a Soviet attack.

In the immediate aftermath of *Sputnik*, Eisenhower set up a presidential science advisory council and installed a full-time science adviser in the White House. In the 1958 legislative session he proposed, and succeeded in having enacted, the National Defense Education Act, which made available college scholarships for students specializing in the sciences, mathematics, and foreign languages. He also used the new atmosphere of national emergency to achieve legislative changes in the organization of the Defense Department that he had been seeking since he was army chief of staff. These changes increased the influence of the secretary of defense and the chairman of the Joint Chiefs of Staff over the individual military services and ostensibly reduced the capacity of the military services to vie with one another for appropriations and duplicate one another's programs.

The American space program was visibly under way by the 1958 midterm election. In addition, two Cold War episodes that, if they had been differently handled, might have caused voter disaffection had been resolved or had subsided. On 15 July, acting consistently with the Middle East resolution, Eisenhower dispatched a force of United States Marines to Lebanon at the request of its president, Camille Chamoun. The Western-oriented Lebanese government seemed to be threatened by the aftereffects of a pro-Nasser coup in Iraq. By 25 October the situation had fully stabilized and American troops were withdrawn. Meanwhile, in August, on the other side of the world, mainland China resumed shelling the anti-Communist forces on the offshore islands. Armed with superior aircraft weaponry by the United States and provided with a technology for supplying the islands, the besieged Nationalists held. By October, shelling from the mainland was reduced to an alternate-day ritual that permitted supply of the islands. The conflict eventually vanished from the headlines.

Although the Eisenhower administration seemed by election time to have allayed the foreign policy concerns of most members of the general public (though not of its Democratic critics), the 1958 off-year voting saw a major Democratic surge in congressional strength. In the House of Representatives, the Democrats' strength increased to 282–154, their greatest margin since 1938. In the Senate the increase from 49 to 64 brought the Democrats to their highest level since 1940. Thus, Eisenhower was fated to spend his final two years with a Congress in which a strong bloc of liberal Democrats would be pressing for social legislation that he found unacceptably liberal and for a more costly military commitment than he was prepared to countenance.

The Democratic gains appear mainly to have had economic causes. Late in 1957 the economy slipped into a major recession. By the middle of 1958 the recession was over, but the experience of a significant economic downturn reinforced the long-standing tendency of voters to associate the Republican party with economic hard times. An undoubted further contribution to the 1958 Republican losses and the election of the liberal Eighty-sixth Congress was the controversy in the months immediately before the election that led to the resignation of the chief White House staff aide, Sherman Adams. When he was governor of New Hampshire, Adams and his family had formed a friendship with the family of the New England textile manufacturer Bernard Goldfine. Early in

1958, congressional investigations of federal regulatory commissions revealed that Adams had telephoned the Federal Trade Commission (FTC) to inquire about cases then pending that had a bearing on whether Goldfine's company was labeling its products in a manner consistent with federal regulations. Further, it came out that Adams had received gifts from Goldfine—a vicuna coat, free use of a hotel suite in Boston, and a Persian rug.

Adams explained that the gifts were part of a pattern of gift giving between his family and Goldfine's, a result of their long friendship. He had intended his phone calls to the FTC as no more than a normal White House service request for information, he maintained, although he now recognized that he had been indiscreet. Eisenhower promptly announced that having acknowledged his error, Adams was to return to his duties as a valued White House aide. No sooner had Eisenhower taken this step than further hearings showed Goldfine to be an entrepreneur who habitually made gifts to public officials and declared them as business expenses. The gifts to Adams took on a new and more questionable meaning.

The recession-beleaguered Republican candidates for reelection were uniform in urging Adams to resign. Eisenhower also was quickly made aware by many of his closest supporters in the Republican party that Adams had become a liability. Evidently this became Eisenhower's own view. Nevertheless, having put himself behind Adams, he did not fire him; rather, he tried indirection, commissioning Vice President Nixon to have an "objective" conversation with Adams that was heavily stacked with arguments for resignation.

Adams declared that he would follow any orders he received from the president, but that he would not resign on his own in the face of unfair charges. Rather than personally order Adams to resign, Eisenhower commissioned Meade Alcorn, the Republican national chairman, to inform him that he was damaging the party's electoral chances and that Eisenhower knew this to be the case but refused personally to fire Adams. With so blunt a message Adams resigned, but so late that questions about the propriety of his performance were grist for the midterm campaign.

"The New Eisenhower": 1959–1961

In January 1959, Eisenhower seemed to be entering his final two years in office as the lamest of lame ducks. The number of congressmen who were ideologically uncongenial to his policies had substantially increased. He had lost the services of Adams. In addition, Secretary of State Dulles was terminally ill with cancer. As it turned out, the period from 1959 to the end of his presidency came be viewed in the press and by many politicians as the period of "the new Eisenhower." Eisenhower was portrayed as a hitherto politically aloof president who had belatedly begun to employ the resources of his office in the political area with a vigor reminiscent of the combative styles of Roosevelt and Truman.

Eisenhower had, of course, not previously eschewed politics. He had been practicing a delicate approach of bargaining privately with congressional leaders, personally and through his personal emissaries, in order to weld legislative majorities in three closely divided Congresses. But during the period of the Eighty-sixth Congress he increasingly found it to his advantage to speak out boldly against and veto legislation that was plainly in conflict with his conception of good public policy.

Ironically, though he was less able to get policy results from the new Congress, his adversarial relationship with a major bloc in it made him seem more like an activist president. Eisenhower furthered this impression by taking highly visible steps to create a political climate that might foster an accommodation with the Soviet Union, though he took the first such step as a result of an error in communication. In the spring of 1959, he was privately urged by British Prime Minister Harold Macmillan to take part with the allied leaders and Soviet Premier Khrushchev in a summit conference on such points of contention as whether West Berlin was to remain under Western control. Meanwhile, Khrushchev, who also favored a summit, proposed publicly that he and Eisenhower exchange personal visits to each other's countries. Eisenhower's general view was that unless summit conferences and personal diplomacy by national leaders followed Soviet concessions or could otherwise be seen as likely to bring about change, they would create complacency in the West and provide the Soviet Union with propaganda forums.

Eisenhower instructed Under Secretary of State Robert Murphy to pass a message of qualified acceptance to the Soviet leader Frol Kozlov, who was then completing an official visit to the United States. In so doing, he meant to stipulate that if there were previous Soviet concessions, he would be open to a summit and an exchange of visits. His qualifications were lost in the transmission, and he discovered to his chagrin that he had conveyed an invitation that was not contingent on some initial act by Khrushchev, such as the withdrawal of the Soviet threat to West Berlin.

Making a tactical virtue of what had inadvertently become a necessity, Eisenhower told reporters that only his personal prestige was at risk in a meeting with Khrushchev and that the stakes were too great for him not to attempt an unorthodox approach to seeking a better understanding with the Soviet leadership. Before Khrushchev's ten-day tour of the United States in September 1959, Eisenhower visited Chancellor Konrad Adenauer of Germany and President Charles de Gaulle of France to stress that he would not make concessions to the Soviet leader without full consultation with them.

Khrushchev's lively ability to command press attention through his American trip persuaded Eisenhower that his own visit to the Soviet Union would at minimum have Cold War propaganda value, advertising to the world that his nation was deeply intent on settling East-West tensions. Even though foreign ministers' conferences were regularly stalemated, he also concluded that some progress in negotiation might be possible at another great-power summit meeting, since his private discussions with Khrushchev had led to a statement that the Soviet Union would not initiate unilateral action affecting West Berlin.

In the winter of 1959–1960, Eisenhower made two international goodwill trips, greeting foreign leaders and publics with a vigor that belied his age. In December 1959 he employed the new technology of the jet plane to visit eleven European, Asian, and North African countries on a nineteen-day trip, replete with enthusiastically cheering crowds as he traveled in motorcades, and earnestly spoke of his nation's desire for peace. His party flew to Rome and then visited the capitals of Turkey, Pakistan, Afghanistan, India, Iran, Greece, Tunisia, France, Spain, and Morocco.

Events in the Caribbean helped ensure that the other goodwill trip Eisenhower was able to take before the spring summit conference would be in Latin America. The Cuban government of Fidel Castro had seemed to be fundamentally nationalistic when it overthrew that nation's military dictatorship in January 1959, but the Eisenhower administration soon became persuaded that the Castro government was Communist-controlled and would provide the Soviet

Union with a base for exercising influence in the western hemisphere. While seeking to destabilize Castro's government (for example, by barring sugar imports from Cuba and training Cuban émigrés for guerrilla war on the island), Eisenhower also worked to strengthen American ties to other Latin American countries. Choosing the four southernmost countries in the hemisphere for his next trip, in February 1960 he visited Brazil, Argentina, Chile, and Uruguay, coordinating these visits with announcements of increases in aid to Latin America. On these trips he also had overwhelming receptions.

Now Eisenhower, rather than Khrushchev, was making international headlines. He hoped his trips would contribute to an international climate in which the Soviet leaders would be more likely to agree to realistic steps to reduce international tensions, both at the summit conference that now had been scheduled and during his follow-up trip to the Soviet Union. Long-pending negotiations between American and Soviet diplomatic representatives and scientists had led to numerous proposals and counterproposals for arms control and nuclear test bans, and it was possible that in a changed international climate, firm agreements might be reached on these matters.

On 1 May 1960, two weeks before the summit meeting of the Western and Soviet leaders in Paris, the fateful U-2 episode occurred. Anticipating disarmament negotiations, Eisenhower had ordered a final surveillance flight over an area of the Soviet Union that he considered to have been inadequately examined for possible nuclear and missile sites. When the U-2 failed to return, a cover story was released that a plane on a meteorological expedition was lost and might have strayed over Soviet air space. Eisenhower had been authorizing overflights on the premise that if at any time the Soviet Union developed the capacity to shoot down a high-altitude "spy plane," the vehicle, including not only its film but also the pilot, would be destroyed, making proof of surveillance impossible.

As it turned out, the Soviet Union recovered the plane, film, and pilot, Francis Gary Powers, who admitted to his mission. The Soviet announcement was not made until after Eisenhower had personally denied that such flights occurred. Eisenhower immediately reversed himself and acknowledged that flights had taken place for five years under his direction and that they were necessary to provide the West with reliable information about Soviet military capabilities and intentions.

Under these unpropitious circumstances, Eisenhower traveled to Paris on 15 May to meet with the Soviet premier. He appropriately titled the chapter in his memoirs on the Paris meeting "The Summit That Never Was." Bringing with him the wreckage of the U-2 plane, Khrushchev insisted that Eisenhower apologize and punish those responsible for its flight—a responsibility Eisenhower already had personally assumed. The demand was couched in terms that left no room for Eisenhower to proceed and effectively terminated his presidential peace-making efforts, including his projected visit to the Soviet Union, although he did make a goodwill trip to Asia.

By early in 1960, Vice President Nixon had succeeded in building up enough delegate support to ensure him the Republican nomination. Running to succeed a still extraordinarily popular president with whom he had been closely associated, Nixon was a more promising bet for election than Senator John F. Kennedy, the Democratic candidate. Although Nixon was better known and Kennedy's Catholicism cost him votes, the Massachusetts senator won in one of the closest elections in American history.

Eisenhower was deeply disappointed by the Republican defeat and the resulting likelihood that many of the policies to which he was committed would be reversed. He turned to preparing the Kennedy administration for its accession to power, personally briefing Kennedy and his associates on two occasions and ordering that all government agencies cooperate with Kennedy's appointees in easing the transition to the new administration.

Aftermath and Retrospect

A few months after Eisenhower left office, Congress restored to him the lifetime rank of General of the Army. His military service, which had begun at West Point in 1911 and continued until he resigned to run for office in 1952, resumed. As had been the case before 1952, Eisenhower assumed the nonpolitical status of a member of the military, although he now felt free to take a moderately active part in the Republican party and speak out for Republican domestic programs.

Behind the nonpolitical facade, he maintained the same private preoccupation with the detailed working of public affairs that had marked his prepresidential career. Private diary entries show that Eisenhower was displeased with the statecraft of both Kennedy and Johnson. Nevertheless, he held it to be his responsibility to support them in public on matters affecting national security. Thus, he made a point of being photographed with Kennedy after his successor's efforts to launch an invasion of Cuba failed, and he met unofficially with Johnson, advising him at length on the conduct of the Vietnam conflict. By the time of Nixon's nomination in 1968, Eisenhower was bedridden after multiple heart attacks. He nevertheless broadcast a message to the Republican convention from his hospital bed and advised the Nixon administration until a few weeks before his death on 28 March 1969.

In retrospect, many of Eisenhower's accomplishments seem to have been what from a latter-day perspective might be described as constructively negative. They were outcomes that did not occur, but that might have ensued were it not for his efforts to resolve conflicts and prevent potential catastrophes. The conflict in Korea was ended; further fighting in Indochina was avoided; McCarthy was defused; inflation rates were held down; the Western alliance held fast; and in spite of many circumstances that might have provoked war, the seven-and-a-half years after the Korean settlement saw no American troops in combat.

Eisenhower's dual policy of limiting the expansion of the welfare state and of curbing costly, potentially provocative military escalation was reversed by his successors. The Kennedy administration greatly expanded missile production. (In later years, opponents of an American weapons buildup often cited Eisenhower's warning in his farewell address against the influence of the "military-industrial complex.") And the Johnson administration expanded welfare programs massively. By the final decades of the twentieth century, however, there was renewed interest in curbing domestic expenditures and limiting weaponry. And there was a new fascination with the statecraft of a president who had succeeded in keeping the support of Americans for two full terms. Thus, the Eisenhower presidency seems both to have had important consequences during his time in office and to provide lessons for future presidencies.

BIBLIOGRAPHY

The most thorough account of Eisenhower's pre-presidential career is Stephen E. Ambrose, *Eisenhower: Soldier, General of the Army, President-Elect, 1890–1952* (New York, 1983). Eisenhower pro-vides a crisp, somewhat impersonal account of his wartime leadership in *Crusade in Europe* (Garden City, N.Y., 1948). For Eisenhower's memoir of his presidency, see his rather dry two-volume report in *The White House Years: Mandate for Change, 1953–1956* and *Waging Peace: 1956–1961* (Garden City, N.Y., 1963, 1965). More of a sense of the man is given in his anecdotal but shrewdly reasoned and wry *At Ease: Stories I Tell to Friends* (Garden City, N.Y., 1967). The fullest picture of the private Eisenhower emerges in *The Papers of Dwight D. Eisenhower* (Baltimore, Md., 1970–); close to thirty volumes are anticipated. See also Robert H. Ferrell, ed., *The Eisenhower Diaries* (New York, 1981).

The most comprehensive scholarly account of Eisenhower's presidency is Stephen A. Ambrose, *Eisenhower: The President* (New York, 1983). The specialized literature on Eisenhower in general and his presidency in particular is growing rapidly. Early contributions to what by the mid-1980s became a steady flow of contributions include Fred I. Greenstein, *The Hidden-Hand Presidency: Eisenhower as Leader* (New York, 1982; rev. ed., Baltimore, 1994); Gary W. Reichard, *The Reaffirmation of Republicanism: Eisenhower and the Eighty-third Congress* (Knoxville, Tenn., 1975); and Richard H. Immerman, *The CIA in Guatemala: The Foreign Policy of Intervention* (Austin, Tex., 1982). A good starting point for grasping Eisenhower's world outlook is H. W. Brandes, Jr. *Cold Warriors: Eisenhower's Generation and American Foreign Policy* (New York, 1988). On Eisenhower's role in sending the first troops to Vietnam see David L. Anderson, *Trapped by Success: The Eisenhower Administration and Vietnam, 1953–1961* (New York, 1991).

A spate of recent scholarship has produced other specialized studies on details and significant issues of Eisenhower's time in office: Craig Allen, *Eisenhower and the Mass Media: Peace, Prosperity, and Prime-Time TV* (Chapel Hill, N.C., 1993); Isaac Alteras, *Eisenhower and Israel: United States—Israeli Relations, 1953–1960* (Gainesville, Fla., 1993); Michael R. Beschloss, *MAYDAY: Eisenhower, Khrushchev, and the U-2 Affair* (New York, 1986); Robert A. Divine, *The Sputnik Challenge* (New York, 1993); Robert J. Donovan, *Confidential Secretary: Ann Whitman's Twenty Years with Eisenhower and Rockefeller* (New York, 1988); Richard G. Hewlett and Jack M. Holl, *Atoms for Peace and War, 1953–1961: Eisenhower and the Atomic Energy Commission* (Berkeley, Calif., 1989); R. Alton Lee, *Ei-*

senhower and Landrum-Griffin: A Study in Labor-Management Politics (Lexington, Ky., 1990); Stephen G. Rabe, *Eisenhower and Latin America: The Foreign Policy of Anti-Communism* (Chapel Hill, N.C., 1988); Duane Tananbaum, *The Bricker Amendment Controversy: A Test of Eisenhower's Political Leadership* (Ithaca, N.Y., 1988); and Raymond J. Saulnier, *Constructive Years: The U.S. Economy Under Eisenhower* (Lanham, Md., 1991).

For a valuable review of the growing body of Eisenhower scholarship see Chester J. Pach, Jr., and Elmo Richardson, *The Presidency of Dwight D. Eisenhower*, rev. ed. (Lawrence, Kans., 1991), pp. 263–272. For further sources consult R. Alton Lee, comp., *Dwight D. Eisenhower: A Bibliography of His Times and Presidency* (Wilmington, Del., 1991).

Recent works include Steve Neal, *Harry and Ike: The Partnership That Remade the Postwar World* (New York, 2001); Geoffrey Perret, *Eisenhower* (New York, 1999); William B. Pickett, *Eisenhower Decides to Run: Presidential Politics and Cold War Strategy* (Chicago, 2000); and Tom A. Wicker, *Dwight D. Eisenhower* (New York, 2002).

John F. Kennedy

Carl M. Brauer

John F. Kennedy THE LIBRARY OF CONGRESS

WENTY years after John F. Kennedy was assassinated, a public opinion poll indicated that he was rated best overall of the nine presidents since Herbert Hoover. Among five positive attributes surveyed, Kennedy "most inspired confidence in the White House," according to 40 percent of those asked, followed by Franklin D. Roosevelt at 23 percent. Sixty percent considered Kennedy as having had the "most appealing personality," followed again by Roosevelt at 11 percent. Kennedy edged Roosevelt on "best in domestic affairs" and on having "cared most about the elderly, the poor and those most in economic trouble." Political scientists, historians, and national journalists have on the whole tended to view Kennedy less favorably than has the general public. Some "experts" hold Kennedy in high regard, but others are extremely critical of him. A significant number probably agree that his promise outstripped his performance and that he left an ambiguous legacy.

Neither popular nor expert opinion would actually be wrong about Kennedy. Indeed, they are in a sense opposite sides of the same coin, for Kennedy's inflation to mythic proportions by the public and his demythologizing by experts both derive significantly from the manner of his death. No one knows how his reputation might have been affected had he served out his first term and the second term to which he likely would have been elected. Alone among modern presidents, Kennedy's place in history revolves around unanswerable questions of what might have been had he lived. Yet this very fact suggests that in his relatively brief presidency—less than three years—Kennedy exerted a profound influence upon both popular and expert hopes and expectations, which endured long after his death. Had Kennedy not had this influence while he lived, the public would not have mythologized him, nor the experts demythologized him, after he was killed. Had he not had this influence, his successors in the White House would have been far less likely to have compared themselves to him, to have sought to emulate him, or to have tried to escape his myth.

Family Background

John F. Kennedy was born on 29 May 1917 in Brookline, Massachusetts, the second son of Joseph P. Kennedy, a self-made multimillionaire who headed the Securities and Exchange Commission under Franklin D. Roosevelt, and Rose Fitzgerald Kennedy. In 1937, Roosevelt made the elder Kennedy ambassador to Great Britain, which marked a significant social breakthrough for an Irish Catholic. (In their native Boston, the Kennedys had sometimes been snubbed by Brahmin society, and Kennedy had moved the family to New York partly as a result of it.) To Roosevelt's dismay, his ambassador sympathized with Prime Minister Neville Chamberlain's appeasement policies toward Nazi Germany. Neither Roosevelt nor Kennedy had ever really liked one another, but until this point they had successfully used one another for their own purposes. But after Kennedy took Chamberlain's side, the two men fell out permanently, and Roosevelt refused even to make use of Kennedy's very considerable business and managerial skills during the war.

John Kennedy, or Jack, as he was known, grew up in a home where political issues were frequently discussed and sometimes debated. His father's strong views evidently influenced his older brother, Joseph P. Kennedy, Jr., more than they did him. All the Kennedy children, but particularly the four boys—Joseph, John, Robert, and Edward—were brought up with a strong sense of noblesse oblige and with little or no interest in enhancing their own very considerable financial fortunes. (Their father set up trust funds for each of them, which made them financially independent when they reached maturi-

ty.) Public service, not private gain, was the ideal instilled in all the Kennedy children. When their private fortunes or family connections could enhance their ability to perform public service, as in getting their views known or in winning elections, for example, the Kennedy boys gladly used them.

Jack Kennedy was a sickly child and adolescent. "When we were growing up together," his younger brother Robert later recalled, "we used to laugh about the great risk a mosquito took in biting Jack Kennedy—with some of his blood the mosquito was almost sure to die." During his illnesses, he became an avid reader and also a fatalist. He never let his frail condition keep him from throwing himself headlong into his family's fierce athletic competitions. At Choate, a predominantly Protestant boarding school in Connecticut, he was an average student, though one who, his teachers believed, performed at less than his potential. His peers liked him for his wit and cleverness, and he proved adept at winning friends. He was admired not for his accomplishments, a teacher later observed, but for his personality. His roommate once noted that he was the only boy who read *The New York Times* every day from front to back. To avoid competing further with his older brother, Joseph, who had also been at Choate, he enrolled at Princeton, instead of Harvard, where his brother was already a campus star. But he became ill once again and dropped out. He enrolled at Harvard the following year.

In college, Kennedy for the most part showed a greater dedication to enjoying himself socially than he did to developing his mind. Once again he was popular and made lasting friends. Once again he suffered from impaired health, including a back injury sustained in playing football. Although he had suffered from backaches even as a child, this injury probably marked the beginning of a chronically bad back. He did have a lively interest in political issues, though he did not have the strongly fixed views of many of his contemporaries, such as his older brother, an isolationist who became a delegate to the 1940 Democratic National Convention and opposed Roosevelt's nomination for a third term.

Using the access to European leaders afforded by his father's position, and with the assistance of hired secretarial help, Kennedy wrote a senior thesis called "Appeasement at Munich." It was awarded second highest honors. Although it sought to explain how Chamberlain had no alternative to appeasement, and in that respect reflected his father's views, it showed Jack's independence by regarding Winston Churchill as an accurate prophet and by emphasizing the importance of American military preparedness. With his father's assistance and connections, the thesis was quickly transformed into a book, *Why England Slept*, a title inspired by Churchill's own *While England Slept*. It received favorable reviews in the summer of 1940, as war clouds gathered in Europe, and it became a best-seller. By the following spring, more than eighty thousand copies had been sold.

During the war, Kennedy commanded a PT boat in the South Pacific. While on patrol one night, the small boat was cut in half by a Japanese destroyer traveling at high speed. Two of the crewmen were killed. Kennedy demonstrated leadership, courage, and stamina in helping to save the eleven survivors. A strong swimmer, he towed a badly burned crewman several miles to a tiny island. Two days later he towed him again to a larger island. The group was finally rescued when they found a pair of natives who took a message to an Australian coast-watcher. The rescue attracted newspaper attention not only for its own sake but because of the identity of the skipper. John Hersey, a journalist, wrote the first long account in the *New Yorker*, which was followed by an abridged version in *Reader's Digest* and eventually by other books and a movie. Kennedy's wartime heroism became a basis and then a staple of his political career. One of Kennedy's charms was that though he never prevented his political supporters from exploiting his heroism, he never personally aggrandized his role either. In a characteristic remark, he explained, "It was involuntary. They sank my boat."

After his rescue, Kennedy commanded another boat and saw some additional action, but his war career was soon cut short by illness and his bad back. After the war, he became a celebrity correspondent for Hearst newspapers at the United Nations charter conference and during the British elections of 1945. He also observed the Potsdam summit conference. But he decided he would rather shape history than report it. His brother Joe, whose political ambitions had been more certain, had died a hero's death in the war. His father later claimed to have been happily surprised by his second son's interest in running for office, and he used his money and contacts to help him get started.

Early Career

John Kennedy began to make speeches around Massachusetts in 1945 and the following spring ran in a

Navy lieutenant John F. Kennedy returned to the United States in 1944 following his heroic exploits in the Pacific as a commander of a PT boat rammed by a Japanese destroyer. AP/WIDE WORLD

primary for a vacant congressional seat in Boston, where nomination was tantamount to election. Although only twenty-nine, he had an impressive war record, his father's financial assistance and personal connections, and excellent name recognition. His wealth and Harvard education were liabilities to be overcome in the working-class districts, but his Irish political pedigree helped. His surviving maternal grandfather, whose last name, Fitzgerald, was Kennedy's middle name, had once been mayor of Boston and a congressman. Kennedy was in effect the first Irish Brahmin. Youthful-looking and handsome, though gaunt and often on crutches, Kennedy proved a tireless campaigner and showed a deft touch in greeting the Irish politicians and working people whose support he needed. His campaign stressed the bread-and-butter needs of his constituents and of the returning veterans. He won the primary impressively and then the general election.

In 1952, Kennedy captured the Senate seat held by Henry Cabot Lodge, Jr. Kennedy received only 51.5 percent of the vote, but his win was remarkable in that it came in the face of an Eisenhower landslide in the state and against a well-respected incumbent who bore a name even more famous than his own. Kennedy owed his victory to his appealing personality and intense campaigning, to his ability both to capitalize on popular disenchantment over the economy and world affairs and to present himself as a new kind of nonpartisan leader, and to his establishment of a personal organization, independent of the Democratic party. On a similar basis, Kennedy won reelection in 1958 with 73.6 percent of the vote, defeating a relative unknown who fashioned himself the poor man's candidate against the millionaire incumbent.

Kennedy did not make a great mark as a legislator. He had served too briefly in the House to acquire much influence there, and his quick move to the Senate reflected both his ambition and his impatience with the career of a junior member of the House. The Senate, which affords more of a forum for addressing major national and international issues, even for junior members, was more to his liking. But there, too, he was always looking beyond, with the presidency as his ultimate goal. His peers respected Kennedy for his intelligence, wit, and independence, but he never became their leader, in name or in fact. He was a critic of certain aspects of Eisenhower's foreign and military policies, particularly the identification with neocolonialism abroad and the economical but supposedly ineffectual "New Look" defense policy.

On domestic issues, he consistently supported unsuccessful liberal efforts to expand federal responsibilities in areas such as civil rights, economic assistance to depressed regions, education, and health, though he spurned ideological labels including that of "liberal." He became an expert and sponsored legislation in the area of labor-law reform, the impulse for which grew out of organized labor's unhappiness with the Taft-Hartley Act of 1947 and out of a Senate investigation of corruption and racketeering in certain unions that captured headlines and a television audience in the mid-1950s. (His brother Robert served as chief counsel to the McClellan investigating committee, of which he was a member.) The bill Kennedy sponsored was too kind to labor unions to be accepted by the fairly conservative Congress, which enacted a less sympathetic one.

In 1953, Kennedy married Jacqueline Bouvier, a beautiful socialite twelve years his junior. After he died, books and articles eventually made the claim, never confirmed by his widow, that their marriage was not happy, that it suffered under the strains of his infidelities and her lavish spending and unease with politics. During his life, they made an extraordinarily attractive couple, with the aura of royalty about them. Rumors of marital difficulties were not widely circulated. If the public was shown less than a completely honest picture of their marriage, that was not an unusual practice in American politics. Neither was it out of the ordinary for a politician to be less than candid about health problems, which in Kennedy's case were much more serious than was publicly acknowledged. But personal adversities, whatever they might have been, failed to impede his energetic pursuit of high office.

While convalescing from back surgery in 1955, Kennedy conceived of a book about political courage. Published in early 1956, *Profiles in Courage* described historical instances of senators placing the national interest above parochial or self-interest. A front-page review in the *New York Times Book Review* hailed the book for restoring "respect for a venerable and much abused profession," politics. The book became a best-seller and won a Pulitzer Prize. More important, it established Kennedy as that American rarity, an intellectual politician, and identified him with political courage. Kennedy took pains to disprove a columnist's challenge to his authorship and even won a retraction, but in 1980, Herbert Parmet, a dispassionate Kennedy biographer, concluded that Kennedy had in fact "served principally as an overseer or more charitably as a sponsor and editor." Much of the writing and the literary craftsmanship were contributed by Theodore Sorensen, Kennedy's talented young assistant. Although there was nothing unusual about a politician using a ghostwriter, Kennedy evidently regarded it as vital to his image to claim sole authorship.

The book's success boosted Kennedy's bid for the Democratic vice presidential nomination in 1956 after Adlai Stevenson, the presidential nominee, surprised the convention by throwing open the choice of his running mate. Kennedy had made an excellent impression at the convention through his narration of a film and through his nominating speech for Stevenson. Kennedy's Roman Catholicism, some hoped, would help woo back Catholic Democrats who had bolted the party in 1952 because Stevenson was divorced; other Democratic activists, including some prominent Catholics, feared that his nomination would stir up intense anti-Catholic sentiment, just as had Governor Al Smith's nomination for president in 1928.

Kennedy's principal rival for the nomination was Senator Estes Kefauver of Tennessee, a populist who had twice sought the presidential nomination and who had a substantial following in the party. Nevertheless, Kennedy came within a whisker of defeating him on the second ballot, thanks in part to support from southerners who regarded Kefauver as a turncoat on civil rights. In a tumultuous scene that followed the second ballot, Kefauver's fellow Tennessean Albert Gore withdrew in his favor, precipitating a series of switches that gave Kefauver the nomination.

Presidential Campaign

"With only about four hours of work and a handful of supporters, I came within thirty-three and a half votes of winning the Vice Presidential nomination," Kennedy told an aide, David Powers, the following November. "If I work hard for four years, I ought to be able to pick up all the marbles." And work hard Kennedy did. He did not become a declared candidate until early 1960, but in the three and a half years before that he delivered hundreds of speeches, appeared frequently on television shows, published many articles, and was often the subject of others. He established contacts with potential Democratic delegates and nurtured them carefully. His efforts were appreciably helped by his family's wealth.

Kennedy's methodical pursuit of the nomination so far in advance of the convention was unprecedented. Some experts and some of his rivals thought he was starting too early, but he proved the experts wrong and stole a march on his rivals. He was, in fact, setting a precedent that has proved enduring. Kennedy's campaign for the nomination in 1960, as described by Theodore H. White in his popular *The Making of the President*, 1960, became Republican Barry Goldwater's model in 1964. All successful non-incumbent candidates for major-party nominations have followed suit, beginning years ahead of the conventions and methodically building personal followings within their parties. The days of the well-positioned favorite son, of the coy disclaimer of presidential ambition, and of the brokered convention seemed to be over.

To a greater extent than at any time since the Civil War, the leading candidates in 1960 were members of the Senate: Kennedy, Lyndon Johnson, Hubert Humphrey, and Stuart Symington on the Democratic side, and the presiding officer of the Senate, Vice President Richard Nixon, a former senator, on the Republican side. In the past, governors had been more prominent in presidential races. The shift in emphasis to the Senate reflected the growing importance of the national news media, particularly television, for they focused attention on broad national and international issues, about which senators presumably had the greatest awareness and expertise.

The 1960 presidential campaign came against an ambiguous background. The country was at peace and there was general prosperity. Eisenhower remained a popular president who, even Kennedy partisans agree, could have been reelected to a third term had not the recently enacted Twenty-second Amendment prohibited it. Yet a series of events, disclosures, and reports suggested that the United States was slipping in its decade-long struggle to contain Communism. The Soviet Union, it appeared, was moving ahead of the United States in winning friends in the new, decolonized nations of the world; was making rapid strides in science and technology, as evidenced by its launching of *Sputnik*; and was besting America in weapons development, presumably causing a "missile gap." At home, a popular argument went, Americans were sated with consumer goods and insufficiently committed to public needs in such areas as job development and economic growth, education, medical care, and civil rights for the nation's black minority. Eisenhower, however popular he remained, seemed to influential opinion leaders, if not to the general public, a passive observer of America's deterioration.

Kennedy ran on the slogans "Get America Moving Again" and "To Seek a New Frontier." His speechwriters in 1960 were instructed to drive home the theme that we had "to summon every segment of our society . . . to restore America's relative strength as a free nation . . . to regain our security and leadership in a fast changing world menaced by Communism." Implicitly his campaign also repudiated Eisenhower's style of leadership. Without ever mentioning Eisenhower by name, he rejected a "restricted concept of the Presidency," advocating that

> the President place himself in the very thick of the fight, that he care passionately about the fate of the people he leads, that he be willing to serve them at the risk of incurring their momentary displeasure . . . [that he] be prepared to exercise the fullest powers of his office—all that are specified and some that are not.

Kennedy defeated his only Democratic opponent, Hubert Humphrey, in Wisconsin and West Virginia, which had the only contested primary elections in 1960. The latter victory was particularly important because it came in a predominantly Protestant state and eased fears that existed within the party of nominating a Catholic. Following it, Kennedy won a string of primaries, but Humphrey had withdrawn and none of Kennedy's potential opponents, Johnson, Symington, or Stevenson, had declared their candidacies. Because of their followings and because of the presence of favorite sons, Kennedy received the required majority for the nomination only as the first alphabetical roll call reached Wyoming, the last state to be called.

Kennedy chose Johnson as his running mate. Johnson had finished second in the balloting and was the overwhelming choice of the South. No Democrat had ever been elected president without carrying the South, and Eisenhower had made significant inroads in that region, so a lot of political history sustained Kennedy's selection of Johnson. Other factors also influenced Kennedy's thinking, including his respect for Johnson's abilities, on the one hand, and his desire not to have Johnson as Senate majority leader should he be elected president, on the other.

The general election pitted Kennedy against Nixon, who held a narrow lead in early public opinion polls. Both men stumped the country energetically, but television played a more important role than ever before. A series of four televised debates drew an enormous audience, especially the first debate, which an estimated 70 million adults watched. Neither man was the clear victor in the debates, but Nixon in a sense was the loser, for his campaign had stressed his advantage over Kennedy in experience and through the debates Kennedy established himself as Nixon's equal. Kennedy was relaxed, handsome, good-humored, and gracious. In a distinct Boston accent, he spoke in cool, rational tones that were well suited to the television medium. Matters of tone and personality seemed to separate the candidates in 1960 more than the issues did.

But even if Kennedy and Nixon were not far apart on substance, the differences between them were nonetheless real, as in the case of civil rights, the most politically sensitive issue they faced. In part through his selection of Johnson, Kennedy reassured white southerners that he was reasonable and moderate on civil rights and that he was not likely to reinstitute a hated Reconstruction. Simultaneously, he promised blacks a wide range of presidential action on their behalf, demonstrated sensitivity to their concerns, and appealed to them on economic grounds. By contrast, Nixon made little effort to win black votes. Instead, he concentrated on the white South, though he did not go far enough in repudiating civil rights activism by the federal government to assure his success there. On election day, Kennedy kept the South quite solidly Democratic and captured a high percentage of black votes nationwide, which made a critical difference in several states, including two in the South.

The election was so close that any one of a variety of different groups and tactics may be said to have determined the outcome. With a popular vote of 34.2 million, Kennedy won by fewer than 120,000 votes out of nearly 70 million cast. His margin in the Electoral College, 303–219, was more comfortable, yet it rested on thin majorities in a dozen states. Had fewer than 12,000 people in five states switched their votes, Nixon would have had an electoral majority. Anti-Catholic sentiment was less overt than in 1928, but postelection analyses by political scientists revealed its continued vitality in the polling booth. In fact, religion was the single most important factor in determining the closeness of the election. Kennedy's church membership won back many disaffected Catholic Democrats, but it lost him a substantially larger number of Protestant Democrats, who apparently were not reassured either by his record of independence from papal influence or by his unequivocal endorsement of the principle of church-state separation. Kennedy's adherence to that principle as president—indeed, he was decidedly less prone to mix religion and government than were several recent Protestant presidents—appeared to quiet anti-Catholic fears. Because no Catholic has received a major-party nomination for president since Kennedy, it is impossible to know how much voting behavior has changed in this regard.

The congressional results likewise constituted less than a ringing endorsement of Kennedy's plan to get the country moving again. For the first time in the twentieth century, the party winning the presidency failed to gain seats in the Congress. The Democrats lost 2 Senate and 21 House seats. This still gave them substantial paper majorities (65–35 in the Senate and 262–174 in the House), but since a conservative coalition of Republicans and southern Democrats had effectively thwarted much liberal legislation in 1959 and 1960, when the majorities were larger, the new numbers did not bode well for legislative activism.

Decisive Leadership

Kennedy publicly rejected the idea that he had failed to get a mandate. "The margin is narrow, but the responsibility is clear," he said. "There may be difficulties with the Congress, but a margin of only one vote would still be a mandate." Nonetheless, Kennedy conducted himself with an acute awareness of the closeness of his win and of the tenuousness of his congressional majority. In the weeks following his election, he took care to appear above partisanship, thereby to reassure the country. His first two announced appointees were incumbents whom he retained in their jobs, Allen Dulles, director of the Central Intelligence Agency (CIA), and J. Edgar Hoover, director of the Federal Bureau of Investigation (FBI). Several weeks later Kennedy chose C. Douglas Dillon, the incumbent under secretary of state, who had contributed money to the Nixon campaign, as secretary of the treasury. Kennedy made a well-publicized and unusual visit to Nixon several days after the election. In addition, he publicly thanked Eisenhower for his cooperation and assistance in the transition, which was marked by a cordiality sometimes lacking in the past, and he revealed that he had asked Eisenhower if he would be available for assignments in his administration.

Kennedy's decision to postpone promised civil rights legislation reflected his recognition of congressional realities. He did not want to alienate southern Democrats, whose support he needed in other areas. Given the makeup of Congress, it would have been a futile gesture to seek civil rights legislation in 1961 anyway.

Within the space of a few months, Kennedy transformed himself from a president-elect without a clear mandate to a highly popular incumbent who raised public expectations of the office. The most visible moment in this transformation came with his inauguration itself, where the contrast between him and Eisenhower could not have been more striking. Eisenhower was the oldest man to occupy the presidency until that time; Kennedy, at forty-three, was the youngest person ever elected president. Eisenhower was the last president born in the nineteenth century; Kennedy was the first born in the twentieth. Eisenhower had been the great World War II commander, and Kennedy, a mere junior officer. Eisenhower had grandchildren; Kennedy had a three-year-old daughter and a son who was born between election and inauguration. Eisenhower had taken care not to endanger his personal popularity by taking on divisive causes and had practiced a kind of indirect leadership, so indirect as often to be undetectable; Kennedy advocated that the president be at the center of the action.

Kennedy's inaugural address vividly underscored the changing of the guard, while promising to uphold America's commitments:

> Let the word go forth from this time and place, to friend and foe alike, that the torch has been passed to a new generation of Americans, born in this century, tempered by war, disciplined by a hard and bitter peace, proud of our ancient heritage, and unwilling to witness or permit the slow undoing of those human rights to which this nation has always been committed, and to which we are committed today at home and around the world.

It was one of the shortest inaugural addresses of this century and the most effective and memorable since Franklin D. Roosevelt's in 1933. Delivered on a cold, clear day following a heavy snowstorm, it would always be remembered by those in attendance and the many millions more who watched it on television or heard it on radio. Young people were particularly stirred by its idealism and inspired by the young man who delivered it so crisply and self-confidently. In the speech's famous climax, Kennedy declared:

> In the long history of the world, only a few generations have been granted the role of defending freedom in its hour of maximum danger. I do not shrink from this responsibility; I welcome it. I do not believe that any of us would exchange places with any other people or any other generation. The energy, the faith, the devotion which we bring to this endeavor will light our country and all who serve it, and the glow from the fire can truly light the world.
>
> And so, my fellow Americans, ask not what your country can do for you; ask what you can do for your country.
>
> My fellow citizens of the world, ask not what America will do for you, but what together we can do for the freedom of man.

Kennedy embraced a universalistic conception of the country's international responsibilities that his successor and the Vietnam War's critics alike cited as a major reason for America's involvement in the war. "Let every nation know," he asserted, "whether it wishes us well or ill, that we shall pay any price, bear any burden, meet any hardship, support any friend, oppose any foe to assure the survival and the success of liberty." Yet even in this tough-sounding speech,

Kennedy declared an interest in opening a dialogue with the Soviet Union to relax tensions and reduce the chance of war. "Let us never negotiate out of fear, but let us never fear to negotiate," he said in one of his most famous contrapuntal sentences. He also promised to help the world's poor help themselves "not because the Communists may be doing it . . . but because it is right. If a free society cannot help the many who are poor, it cannot save the few who are rich." To Latin Americans, he offered a special pledge, "a new alliance for progress, to assist free men and free governments in casting off the chains of poverty."

Just as the inauguration and the inaugural address were studies in contrast, so too was the mood Kennedy set in his first months in office. Kennedy painted a sober, even grim picture of the world as he found it. Things were worse, he said, than he had expected, America's defenses were weaker, its position in certain international situations in greater jeopardy. Yet that sobriety was countered by his youth, vigor, self-confidence, and wit. He flooded Congress with requests, held frequent and impressive press conferences, and proposed bold new national goals, the most important of which was met—to place a man on the moon before the decade was out. "Above all, Kennedy held out such promise of hope," Arthur Schlesinger, Jr., the historian who served as his assistant, wrote. "Intelligence at last was being applied to public affairs. Euphoria reigned; we thought for a moment that the world was plastic and the future unlimited."

Kennedy made an important innovation upon becoming president when he allowed press conferences to be televised live. He used these conferences to communicate directly with the public, which was immediately impressed with his personality, poise, and knowledge of government. As of May 1961, three out of four adults surveyed had seen at least one of his press conferences, and 91 percent had formed a favorable impression of Kennedy from them. The live press conference became Kennedy's communications forte. None of his successors has felt it possible to abandon the practice, though none has done as well by it. Here was a leading example of Kennedy's permanent effect on the presidency and public expectations of it.

Another demanding legacy Kennedy bequeathed his successors lay in press relations. Kennedy, who had been a reporter briefly himself, followed the press closely, had friends among jour-

nalists, and sometimes sought the advice of certain columnists and reporters. Kennedy's immediate successors, Johnson and Nixon, each believed that the press had been infatuated with Kennedy and had treated him with kid gloves, in contrast to the rough treatment they received. In fact, Kennedy received a normal amount of criticism in print and collided with the press on news management (which Kennedy practiced), press self-censorship (which he advocated), and other matters. Like all presidents, he was pleased when he received praise in the press and unhappy when he received criticism. But the fact that his successors forgot the clashes and criticism suggests that Kennedy was at least highly successful in creating merely the impression of good press relations, which may be almost as good as the reality.

Kennedy paid attention to the nation's culture. He honored leading writers, artists, poets, and musicians, and invited them to the White House. The recognition of artistic excellence fit Kennedy's expansive view of the president as the promoter of excellence in virtually all areas of the nation's life. Sympathetic to contemporary intellectual criticisms of mass culture, he appointed as chairman of the Federal Communications Commission Newton Minow, who promptly told the nation's broadcasters that if they ever watched television from morning to night, "I can assure you that you will observe a vast wasteland." At Kennedy's behest, the federal government began to provide aid for educational television. Kennedy also sought to raise aesthetic standards in the design of federal buildings and promoted historic preservation. Not surprisingly, the nation's cultural elite tended to return Kennedy's flattery and then some. Lewis Mumford, for example, in 1964 called Kennedy "the first American President to give art, literature and music a place of dignity in the national life." This was an exaggeration, but Kennedy did set an influential precedent for his immediate successors.

Kennedy likewise encouraged social criticism, and he generated interest in politics and public service. During his presidency, the numbers and impact of published critiques of social conditions and injustices increased appreciably. The Peace Corps, which he created by executive order on 1 March 1961, tapped the idealism of thousands of Americans, many of them young, who volunteered to go to poor countries as teachers, health-care providers, and technicians, and to fulfill other scarce needs. Under Kennedy's direct inspiration, many young people

President John F. Kennedy and First Lady Jacqueline Kennedy stand by the White House Christmas tree in the main entrance hall of the White House, 12 December 1962. AP/WIDE WORLD

embarked on careers in government and politics, which Kennedy gave a respectability and appeal they had usually lacked. Partly as a result of his influence, television news and public affairs broadcasting expanded dramatically.

The social questioning that Kennedy sanctioned and encouraged led some people to ideological conclusions that Kennedy rejected. His presidency saw a rise in both radical and conservative movements, but Kennedy was comfortable with neither extreme. He was not even comfortable with liberalism, though he counted many liberals as his allies and though he espoused many liberal programs. Kennedy described himself as an "idealist without illusions." He was a pragmatist and problem solver who perceived the limitations, as well as the possibilities, of presidential power. As a politician, he worried about his reelection and about how Congress and the public received his suggestions. He believed that many problems called out for new and essentially technical

solutions. The central issues of our time, Kennedy said in a speech at Yale in 1962, "relate not to basic clashes of philosophy or ideology but to ways and means of reaching common goals." Kennedy declared, "What we need is not labels and clichés but more basic discussion of the sophisticated and technical issues involved in keeping a great economic machinery moving ahead."

Liberals sometimes faulted Kennedy for being too rational and cool. They wanted a more passionate and feeling leadership than he usually projected. They hoped he would mount the "bully pulpit," as Theodore Roosevelt described it, to preach to the public and rally it behind just causes. Kennedy certainly liked to think of himself as a leader, but as a practical politician he was disinclined to lead futile crusades. The most compelling moral cause of Kennedy's years as president was civil rights, and it is therefore worth looking at his handling of it in some detail.

Civil Rights

In his campaign for president, Kennedy promised executive, moral, and legislative leadership to combat racial discrimination. After being elected and looking at the congressional situation, he decided to forgo legislative leadership, at least for the time being. But he did exercise executive and some moral leadership in his first year as president. He appointed an unprecedented number of blacks to office, including Thurgood Marshall, who became a federal judge. Marshall was the nation's preeminent civil rights lawyer and had directed the Legal Defense Fund of the National Association for the Advancement of Colored People (NAACP). He had successfully argued the historic *Brown* case, among others, before the Supreme Court. Kennedy also took significant measures against racial discrimination in federal employment and among federal contractors. He was more accessible to civil rights leaders than his predecessors had been and, in contrast to Eisenhower, actually endorsed the *Brown* decision.

Under Attorney General Robert Kennedy, his brother, the Justice Department stepped up enforcement of existing voting rights laws, and the administration encouraged the establishment of the Voter Education Project, which in time registered hundreds of thousands of blacks to vote in the South. Robert Kennedy himself went into the heart of the South to endorse school desegregation. Behind the scenes, the Justice Department endeavored to bring about voluntary and peaceful compliance with court-ordered desegregation.

The administration's symbolic and substantive expressions of support for progress in race relations encouraged the expansion of a preexisting civil rights movement. For the first time, many blacks felt they had real allies in the White House and the Justice Department. Yet participants in the movement, particularly those on the front lines in the South, were sometimes disappointed at certain restraints in the administration's assistance, such as its inability or lack of interest in providing them with federal protection from violence at the hands of local officials and vigilantes.

The Kennedys, for their part, were several times frustrated in their efforts to get state and local officials to carry out their legal responsibilities to obey court orders mandating desegregation of colleges or bus terminals. In May 1961 the administration sent federal marshals to Montgomery, Alabama, to protect Martin Luther King, Jr., the charismatic civil rights leader, from white mob violence during the "freedom rides," which were aimed at desegregating interstate bus transportation.

In September 1962 a long behind-the-scenes negotiation failed to secure Governor Ross Barnett's cooperation in ensuring the safety of James Meredith when he became the first black person to matriculate at the University of Mississippi. Kennedy hoped to avoid sending federal troops, which would stir hated memories of Reconstruction and cause a political backlash among white southerners. Again, federal marshals were sent instead. They performed bravely and with restraint in the face of an angry white mob but, in the end, had to be reinforced by federal troops. Afterward, President Kennedy privately regretted trusting Barnett and was sorry he had not sent in troops earlier, which might have prevented the two deaths that occurred. According to Sorensen, Kennedy also "wondered whether all that he had been taught and all that he had believed about the evils of Reconstruction were true."

In Birmingham, Alabama, Martin Luther King, Jr., led massive demonstrations in the spring of 1963 against that city's segregated public accommodations and against employment discrimination. For a while, the demonstrators were decorously arrested and jailed, a tactic that had broken the back of a comparable campaign in Albany, Georgia, the previous year. But when children began to march in Birmingham, T. Eugene ("Bull") Connor, the police commissioner, changed his tactic to physical repulsion of the demonstrators. Dramatic news photographs and films of defenseless demonstrators being attacked by southern policemen, using vicious dogs, clubs, and fire hoses, appeared around the world. Kennedy sent representatives to the city to mediate the dispute, and he and members of his administration persuaded business executives whose companies had subsidiaries in Birmingham to bring pressure on their local executives to help achieve settlement. These efforts bore some fruit, but were repeatedly endangered by Ku Klux Klan activities, including the terrorist bombings of black homes and businesses, which in turn led to rioting by enraged blacks.

Meanwhile, another crisis brewed in the state, this one over the court-ordered desegregation of the University of Alabama. Governor George Wallace, who had won election as an adamant segregationist, threatened to cause a repetition of the University of Mississippi crisis. Behind the scenes, the Kennedys tried to reason with Wallace and organized business pressure against his causing a violent confrontation. Wallace had sworn to stand in the schoolhouse door to prevent desegregation, and as the day of decision neared, it was not completely clear what would happen if he did. Consequently, President Kennedy federalized the Alabama National Guard. The confrontation came on 11 June 1963. With cameras recording the moment, Wallace stood in the doorway but then stepped aside and let two black students enter the building to register. Wallace kept his defiance symbolic and fulfilled his responsibility to prevent violence as state and local police maintained security; the federal presence was quickly removed.

The events of 11 June gave President Kennedy an excellent moment to address the nation on civil rights. In a period of uncertainty, it seemed a rare instance of unambiguous federal success. The campaign to moderate Wallace's behavior had clearly worked. Although Kennedy had been speaking about civil rights in the previous weeks, he had not made a speech to the nation as a whole. He had already decided to seek broad new civil rights legislation, and, though its details were not complete, Kennedy decided to seize the moment and go on television that evening to address the nation. Sorensen did not even have time to complete writing the speech before Kennedy went on the air, and Kennedy had to extemporize the conclusion.

This time Kennedy unambiguously mounted the bully pulpit and talked about race relations more bluntly and movingly than any president before him. He said:

> The heart of the question is whether all Americans are to be afforded equal rights and equal opportunities, whether we are going to treat our fellow Americans as we want to be treated. If an American, because his skin is dark, cannot eat lunch in a restaurant open to the public, if he cannot send his children to the best public school available, if he cannot vote for the public officials who represent him, if, in short, he cannot enjoy the full and free life which all of us want, then who among us would be content to have the color of his skin changed and stand in his place? Who among us would then be content with the counsels of patience and delay?

Kennedy gave the threat of violence as a principal reason for taking immediate steps to secure black people their rights. Events in Birmingham and elsewhere had increased cries for equality and could not be prudently ignored. National legislation must be enacted, he said, "if we are to move this problem from the streets to the courts." In a sense, Kennedy's

argument could be construed as conservative, for it sought to preserve the social fabric through the provision of a legal outlet. But many conservatives at the time preferred to leave the racial problem in the hands of local officials, even if that meant, as it often did, repression and resistance. Kennedy, on the other hand, believed that America faced a "moral crisis," which could not be "met by repressive police action." He wanted Congress, state and local governments, as well as private citizens, to resolve the crisis by removing its causes. Kennedy manifested a liberal's faith that government had the duty and the ability to correct social injustices.

As he had in the past, Kennedy marshaled economic justifications for eliminating racial discrimination, and he emphasized that the problem was national, not sectional, in scope (which was not only true but politically wise). Kennedy had long emphasized how racial injustices made this country look bad in the eyes of the world. But he argued that the intrinsic moral issue was more important than what the world thought of America:

> We preach freedom around the world, and we mean it, and we cherish our freedom here at home, but are we to say to the world, and much more importantly, to each other that this is a land of the free except for the Negroes; that we have no second-class citizens except Negroes; that we have no class or caste system, no ghettoes, no master race except with respect to Negroes?

For Kennedy, this speech marked a turning point. Most of his advisers had cautioned against it, largely on political grounds. It would cost him the South and the 1964 election, some warned, or it would deadlock Congress. But Robert Kennedy, his most trusted adviser, had argued strongly in favor of a change. Until Birmingham, the administration had managed to stay abreast of, or slightly ahead of, the evolving pressures for the protection of civil rights. But with Birmingham, street demonstrations became a popular, dramatic, and successful tactic, and there were bound to be many more of them. An atmosphere was developing in which Kennedy could only weakly respond to events rather than shape and direct them. Kennedy did not want to find himself in a weak and defensive position when his personality and view of the presidency called for decisive leadership and a measure of control over events. "The situation was rapidly reaching a boil," Sorensen recalled, "which the President felt the federal government should not permit if it was to lead and not be swamped."

The speech also marked a turning point for the country, the beginning of the drive for passage of what became the Civil Rights Act of 1964, the most far-reaching legal instrumentality in the nation's Second Reconstruction. In the ensuing months, the White House became the focal point of efforts to pass this legislation, which in effect meant that Kennedy did succeed in gaining leadership on civil rights. Kennedy held an important and unprecedented series of meetings with groups of lawyers, religious leaders, businessmen, and labor leaders to enlist them as lobbyists for the legislation and to seek voluntary progress against discrimination. Kennedy never expected Congress to fall in line immediately and it did not.

A vital part of Kennedy's legislative strategy was to incorporate suggestions from Republicans so as to win their support for the legislation as a whole. By the time of Kennedy's death in November, this strategy had paid off in the House, resulting in a stronger bill than Kennedy originally submitted and excellent chances of passage. In the Senate, where a filibuster loomed, final passage was more remote, but Everett Dirksen, the Senate Republican leader, had privately promised that the legislation would be brought to a vote. In other words, the filibuster would not be allowed to kill the legislation.

What might have happened to the bill if Kennedy had not been assassinated is one of those things it is impossible to know. Some key participants in the legislative struggle later reflected that essentially the same goal would have been reached. It is possible that Kennedy's death improved the legislation's chances and strengthened it besides. Lyndon Johnson, his successor, immediately made the bill's enactment a memorial to Kennedy. His commitment to the legislation vividly demonstrated that Johnson, a Texan, had a national, not southern, perspective. The civil rights movement had come so far under Kennedy that it would have been politically dangerous for Johnson to have given up the fight, even if he had wanted to. The legislation as finally enacted covered public accommodations, employment, education, voting rights, and the administration of justice.

Other Domestic Policies

In other, less morally compelling areas of domestic life, such as tax reform, social welfare programs, and economic development, Kennedy was less inclined to mount the bully pulpit and more apt to live with the possible. Specifically, this translated into a legislative record that was never as bad as certain critics asserted or as good as administration spokesmen claimed. Legislative initiatives were achieved in manpower training, welfare reform, area redevelopment, and urban renewal and housing. Kennedy also broke some new ground by establishing certain pilot programs through executive authority. Some initiatives were either dramatically watered down by Congress or, in the case of federal aid to education and medical insurance for the aged, blocked by it. With Congress frustrating him, Kennedy looked forward to the 1964 election, when, he hoped, he would receive a stronger popular and legislative mandate. In the off-year elections of 1962, the Democrats had gained four Senate seats and lost two House seats, which was a better record than usual for an incumbent president but not good enough to make much difference legislatively.

In the area of fiscal policy, Kennedy presided over a significant change. At the start of his administration, there was an internal dispute over the budget. Treasury Secretary Dillon and certain other advisers resisted deficits because they were worried about inflation and the weakness of the dollar. On the other side were leading academic economists, such as Paul Samuelson of the Massachusetts Institute of Technology, and the Council of Economic Advisers, chaired by Walter Heller, all of whom had been influenced by John Maynard Keynes, the great English economist. They focused on achieving economic growth through the use of fiscal stimulants and were unafraid of deficits. In 1961, Kennedy came down on the side of the budget balancers, for he accepted conventional thinking, recognized the power of fiscal conservatives in Congress, and could not reconcile tax cuts, proposed by the economists, with his public theme of sacrifice.

In his first year as president, a cyclical recovery from recession encouraged Kennedy in the hope that he could adhere to fiscal orthodoxy and enjoy economic expansion too. But there were some worrisome limitations to the recovery. Business confidence in the administration was shaken in the spring of 1962 when Kennedy became embroiled in a bitter controversy with the head of the United States Steel Corporation. The company had unexpectedly and incautiously increased prices just after the administration's success in getting the steel-workers to restrain their wage demands. By the summer of 1962, the

Council of Economic Advisers had convinced both Dillon and Kennedy that a tax cut was needed to bolster the economy. After the fall elections, Kennedy gave a speech to a business group in New York in which he called for making the kind of tax cuts that would stimulate private investments and "reduce the burden on private incomes and the deterrents to private initiative which are imposed by our present tax system." John Kenneth Galbraith, a liberal Kennedy adviser who dissented from the advice his fellow economists usually offered Kennedy, called it the "most Republican speech since McKinley."

Kennedy's shift on taxes reflected the growing influence of the professional economists who manned the Council of Economic Advisers. It also reflected Kennedy's pragmatism, political interests, and dedication to economic growth. All of these factors were again at play in the spring and summer of 1963 when Kennedy abandoned most of his proposed tax reforms and settled for a program of $11.1 billion in tax cuts for both individuals and corporations. Although certain influential business interests, not surprisingly, got behind the cuts, the projected federal deficit of nearly $12 billion still encountered resistance in Congress, though not enough to prevent enactment early in 1964, an election year.

The tax cut's evident success in bolstering the economic expansion that had begun under Kennedy redounded to the credit of professional economists and neo-Keynesian economics in the United States. The rest of the 1960s saw the economics profession at a high watermark of its influence. Even so, economists proved less persuasive when they recommended tax hikes during the early Vietnam buildup under Johnson than they had when they had proposed tax cuts, which suggests that it was not just the intellectual merits of their case that was compelling but the politics of it. Retrospectively, the Kennedy-initiated tax cuts have been viewed variously as triumphs of modern economic analysis and rational, technically based public policy or as the beginning of the end of fiscal responsibility and the start of an inflationary spiral.

Foreign Affairs

Kennedy's record in foreign affairs has also been subjected to conflicting interpretations. His aides, several of whom are highly skilled writers, have defended him for piloting the United States safely through international crises not of his own making and for be-

ginning the process of détente with the Soviet Union. They have praised him for having a less rigidly ideological view of the world than his immediate predecessor and for accepting a world of diversity, improving America's standing in the Third World. Kennedy's critics, many of whom are on the political left, have charged him with being as much of a cold warrior as Eisenhower and, if anything, less prudent about the application of American power and more provocative and adventuristic. The universalistic language of his inaugural address was applied, they insist, and the world was a more dangerous place as a result.

In the absence of full access to diplomatic records in this country and abroad, it is not yet possible to resolve this debate on Kennedy fully, but certain studies by dispassionate analysts, such as Graham Allison's study of the Cuban missile crisis, lend support to the more friendly view of Kennedy. The president certainly made mistakes in foreign policy, and he raised more hopes than he fulfilled. But he demonstrated a relatively cosmopolitan and sophisticated view of the world, grew in office, and had a feel for diplomacy, which has sometimes been lacking in American presidents.

In contrast to several presidents, Kennedy came to office with a preference for foreign affairs. Issues of war and peace had interested him since his youth, and the awesome responsibility of being president in the nuclear age only reinforced that interest. "Domestic policy," Kennedy often said, "can only defeat us; foreign policy can kill us." He believed, with considerable historical justification, that miscalculation had been the route to war several times in the twentieth century. In Kennedy's view, it was essential to prevent such miscalculation in the future, for there could be no winners in a nuclear war. His military strategy, called flexible response and managed by his highly reputed secretary of defense, Robert S. McNamara, was designed to reduce the chances of war by miscalculation. By building up conventional forces and tightening up command and control procedures, Kennedy and McNamara hoped to provide time for diplomacy in the event of miscalculated Soviet military aggression.

Like several other modern presidents, Kennedy tried to be his own secretary of state, though it is not clear that he originally intended to be. Rather, he hoped to avoid being overly dependent on one person for foreign policy advice; he perceived Truman to have been dependent on Dean Acheson and Eisenhower on John Foster Dulles. Dean Rusk, who became Kennedy's secretary of state through a process of elimination, was hardworking, articulate, and loyal but apparently not highly influential with Kennedy, who, according to his brother Robert, came to depend more on the national security assistant, McGeorge Bundy, and his small staff than he did on Rusk and the State Department.

Kennedy became president at a time when Communism seemed to be gaining ground. The Soviet Union had taken the lead in space exploration, had developed missiles that made the United States vulnerable to nuclear attack, and was using more belligerent rhetoric. Communism and revolution were also on the rise in the world's former colonies, including Cuba, which lay ninety miles from American shores. Just prior to Kennedy's inauguration, Soviet Premier Nikita Khrushchev made a speech promising to support wars of national liberation, and such wars were under way in Southeast Asia. As a candidate for president, Kennedy had stressed the growing Communist menace abroad, and as president, he aimed at thwarting it and meeting new challenges that arose during his time in office. This meant that much of his foreign policy was reactive, though in his last year he showed some initiative in trying to reduce Cold War tensions and improve American-Soviet relations.

Kennedy was sometimes trapped in anti-Communist logic partly of his own making, as in the disastrous Bay of Pigs invasion that occurred soon after he became president. This was a CIA-sponsored invasion of Cuba by thirteen hundred Cubans who had become disaffected with the revolution led by Fidel Castro. Kennedy had reservations about proceeding with the plan; he was worried about its chances of success and about how it might affect his image and the country's to be involved in a foreign, antirevolutionary invasion. For the latter reasons, he refused to authorize overt American involvement in the fighting. But he failed to cancel the operation because it would have been politically embarrassing to call off an anti-Castro effort that had been hatched in the Eisenhower administration, especially when Allen Dulles heartily endorsed it. Kennedy foolishly allowed himself to believe that the United States would be able plausibly to deny involvement in such a large-scale and well-publicized operation. He also allowed himself to be swept along by sheer bureaucratic momentum, and he failed to demand an adequate military review of the invasion plans.

When the invasion came on 17 April 1961, Murphy's Law prevailed: If anything can go wrong, it will.

Most of the invaders were captured, later to be ransomed to the United States; over a hundred were killed; and some were rescued at sea by the United States Navy. Kennedy was stunned and wondered how he could have been so stupid. The invasion plan had turned out to have been based on false, unrealistic assumptions. Some of the invaders and their supporters later grumbled that Kennedy had fatally undermined the plan by denying United States air cover, but retrospectively it appears far more likely that air cover would only have prolonged the inevitable. Castro's military forces were too strong and his regime too popular for a counterrevolution to prevail. The American denial, far from being plausible, became instantly and totally implausible. Kennedy had worried about appearances, but he now appeared naive, weak, or aggressive, depending on where one stood.

About the best that can be said for Kennedy in this instance is that he did a good job of picking up the pieces. He publicly accepted total responsibility for the failure, and he consulted with both Eisenhower and Nixon. These steps helped minimize political fallout. He took care to avoid recriminations within the government, appointing a panel of inquiry that included Allen Dulles and the chief of naval operations, who were in effect investigating themselves; Kennedy thus signaled the military and the CIA that he was not looking for scapegoats. After an appropriate interval, Kennedy did make high-level personnel changes in both the CIA and the military, and he strengthened oversight and coordinating functions. In time, he came to regard the Bay of Pigs as an object lesson in the need for a president to have firm operational control during international crises and not to place too much faith in the experts. This lesson served him well during the Cuban missile crisis.

On the other hand, the Bay of Pigs did not teach Kennedy to stay out of the internal affairs of foreign countries, only to keep down the "noise level." Prodded by Robert Kennedy and Maxwell Taylor, the president's military adviser, the CIA continued to seek Castro's removal, which the CIA interpreted to mean assassination. Although the assassination efforts failed, their discovery by Castro, it has sometimes been speculated, triggered retaliation in the form of President Kennedy's assassination. Although the Bay of Pigs taught Kennedy the need to control the CIA, later investigations made it clear that he was much less than completely successful in achieving it.

The Bay of Pigs also reinforced Kennedy's belief in the need for a better nonconventional or counterinsurgency capability in order to prevent future Castros from obtaining power in the first place. Thus, American advisers taught Latin American governments, including ones far to the right, techniques for crushing leftist opposition. To South Vietnam, where the United States already had a substantial commitment to the anti-Communist government of Ngo Dinh Diem when Kennedy took office, he increased American aid and eventually sent sixteen thousand military advisers, some of whom saw combat, to train Diem's troops in counterinsurgency warfare against the threatening guerrilla forces that had begun to operate there. When Diem, a Catholic, repressed Buddhist monks, who were part of the country's religious majority, he became an embarrassment to the United States. Kennedy's subordinates, if not Kennedy himself, gave a green light to a coup by South Vietnamese generals in the fall of 1963, which resulted in Diem's assassination. Kennedy was shocked and disturbed by Diem's death, though not by the coup, which in effect only further tied American prestige to the success of anti-Communist forces in South Vietnam. That was Kennedy's legacy to Lyndon Johnson, and there is, of course, no way of knowing whether Kennedy would have handled Vietnam any differently than his successor did.

Although he supported counterinsurgency warfare, Kennedy recognized in Vietnam and elsewhere the supremacy of politics over force, and he was skeptical of solutions that required direct American military involvement. Laos, which probably took more of Kennedy's time than any other issue in his first several months in office, had the potential to become another Bay of Pigs. It was in utter crisis in 1961, an obscure and murky battleground of political factions, personalities, feudalism, tribal culture, and social revolution set against the background of the Cold War. Eisenhower had backed a conservative group, but Kennedy, according to Schlesinger, believed that "the effort to transform it into a pro-Western redoubt had been ridiculous and that neutralization was the correct policy." Kennedy nevertheless came close to sending American troops there, and he gave the impression that he would send them; but in the end he managed to arrange a cease-fire and eased the way toward neutralization.

Kennedy often tried to pressure allies endangered by revolution to institute reforms in order to enhance their domestic popularity and the viability of their governments. Yet because these endangered governments often had a lot to lose from the reforms themselves and because they knew that stopping Communism was the higher American priority, they could ignore Kennedy's pressure with impunity. Thus, the Alliance for Progress, the highly touted aid program for Latin America that Kennedy proposed in March 1961, achieved far less social and economic reform than the president had hoped, but the ideals that surrounded the Alliance gave him an unusual degree of personal popularity in Latin America. Similarly, his expressed ideals, youth, and opposition to colonialism enhanced his personal prestige and America's image in the new nations of Africa.

Toward the Soviet Union itself, Kennedy's policies differed little at the start of his administration from those of Eisenhower. Like Eisenhower, Kennedy held a summit conference with Khrushchev, though in contrast to the hopeful spirit that accompanied Eisenhower's summits but evaporated soon afterward, a grim mood emerged from Kennedy's meeting with the Soviet premier in June 1961. The meeting was intended to allow the two men simply to get to know each other, but when Khrushchev challenged him verbally, Kennedy had little choice but to respond in kind.

Repeatedly, during Kennedy's first two years as president, the Soviets made threatening noises about West Berlin and, in August 1961, even built a wall around it to keep East Germans from emigrating. Kennedy responded through words and deeds, including at one point calling up American military reserves. He upheld America's longstanding commitment to defend that city and its access to the West. Finally, in 1963, Soviet pressure receded. When Kennedy traveled to West Berlin on 26 June 1963, he received the most overwhelming public reception of his life. A sea of faces chanted his name and a vast audience roared its approval when he said, "Today, in the world of freedom, the proudest boast is 'Ich bin ein Berliner.' "

Given Soviet provocations over Berlin in particular, it is not surprising that Kennedy called for a significant buildup in America's conventional forces and that he accelerated an expansion of America's missile program that had begun under Eisenhower. Retrospectively, some of Kennedy's own national security advisers regarded the missile buildup as a mistake, an example of the ratcheting effect in the arms race, whereby America built up its forces on the basis of Soviet capabilities, which America interpreted as intentions, and the Soviets then matched the American buildup. It does seem clear that Kennedy accelerated missile deployments more on the momentum of his election campaign charges of a missile gap than he did on the basis of hard intelligence. Information gathered from satellite reconnaissance and from a Soviet spy showed irrefutably that there had been an intelligence gap rather than a missile gap. Kennedy had McNamara acknowledge the missile gap's demise off the record, but Kennedy neither reversed the American buildup nor educated the public on the true nature of the gap.

It has sometimes been argued that the Soviets decided to install missiles in Cuba in 1962 because they were worried about the American buildup. It has also variously been argued that they were seeking a quick and inexpensive strategic advantage, that it was a tactical move which they thought they could get away with because Kennedy was weak, that they were merely trying to protect their client in Cuba from American invasion or subterfuge, or that they did it for some combination of these and other reasons. There can be little question that it was a provocative act and that any American who might have been president when it occurred was bound to respond to it.

Ever since Castro's Communist sympathies had become clear, Cuba had been a sore point in American politics, for Americans were uncomfortable with a Communist government so close at hand. The failure of the Bay of Pigs invasion had made Kennedy and his party vulnerable to charges from the political right. When Soviet military personnel and equipment began to arrive in Cuba in the summer of 1962, the Republican campaign committee announced that Cuba would be "the dominant issue of the 1962 campaign." Several Republicans specifically charged that missile sites were being constructed, and Congress overwhelmingly passed a resolution initiated by the Republican leadership expressing American determination "by whatever means may be necessary, including the use of arms, . . . to prevent in Cuba the creation or use of an externally supported military capability endangering the security of the United States." Kennedy reassured the public that offensive weapons would not be permitted in Cuba and that Soviet representatives had repeatedly assured him that they were not installing such weapons in Cuba.

When, in mid-October, Kennedy received incontrovertible photographic evidence that the Soviets were building launching sites for intermediate-range missiles, he simply had to stop them. Some people, both at the time and since, have discounted the stra-

tegic significance of the missiles on the grounds that it did not matter whether a missile was launched from the Soviet Union or from Cuba. Others emphasized the increased accuracy that the Soviets would have gained from having missiles in Cuba and the possibility that they were seeking a first-strike capability.

More important to Kennedy than technical military considerations were political ones, both international and domestic. Kennedy had to worry about how the Soviets might interpret a capitulation by him on this issue. If they had miscalculated this badly on missiles in Cuba, would they next miscalculate on Berlin, for example, where he would not back down, with the result a nuclear war? If Kennedy did nothing about the missiles, moreover, his political position in the United States would be compromised or destroyed. He would be impeached, Robert Kennedy said. At the very least, the Republicans would mercilessly exploit his weakness in the upcoming congressional elections.

Kennedy wondered about not whether to seek the missiles' removal, but how to achieve that end. For two weeks, an ad hoc group of high government officials deliberated in secrecy about that question. They were divided between those who favored a quick air strike to achieve a fait accompli and those who favored a naval blockade to pressure the Soviets into removing the missiles themselves. Kennedy rejected the air strike because it placed the United States in the position of launching a sneak attack when the onus of world opinion deserved to be on the Soviets and because it might trigger military retaliation. Neither some of the top military commanders nor Democratic congressional leaders were pleased with Kennedy's choice, but on 21 October he proceeded to announce the imposition of a naval blockade, which he called a quarantine, in a crisp and carefully worded television speech.

The crisis was joined, and the world held its breath to see what the Soviets would do. During the tense days that followed, Kennedy personally kept a close watch on the blockade. He decided to let certain tankers and a passenger ship through, but he ordered a Soviet-chartered ship boarded and inspected as a sign of his determination. At the United Nations, Ambassador Adlai Stevenson publicly grilled his Soviet counterpart. Meanwhile, Kennedy and Khrushchev communicated privately by cable and through emissaries. In these communications, Kennedy demonstrated considerable skill and forbearance, ignoring a tough message from Khrushchev and responding to a more conciliatory one. Kennedy carefully avoided humiliating Khrushchev. He gave written assurances against an invasion of Cuba, and his brother Robert told the Soviet ambassador that within a short time after the crisis was over, the United States would remove from Turkey certain missiles that the Soviets wanted removed and that had no bearing on American security. On 28 October, Khrushchev relented and began removal of the missiles. The crisis passed.

In later years, some people downgraded the severity of the crisis by saying that the outcome was a foregone conclusion because the United States enjoyed a huge military advantage over the Soviet Union in the Caribbean. That is, of course, easy to say in hindsight. The United States and the Soviet Union had never gone "eyeball to eyeball" like this before, so everyone was justified in feeling tense waiting for Khrushchev to blink. Everything was at stake, and the world breathed a sigh of relief when the Soviets backed down.

The crisis impelled Kennedy to take new initiatives in seeking an end to the Cold War. At American University on 10 June 1963, he gave one of the most important speeches of his presidency; it marked the beginning of a spirit of détente. Kennedy called for a reexamination of American attitudes toward the Soviet Union and said that both sides in the Cold War had "a mutually deep interest in a just and genuine peace and in halting the arms race." He declared:

> In the final analysis, our most basic common link is that we all inhabit this small planet. We all breathe the same air. We all cherish our children's future. And we are all mortal.. . . We must deal with the world as it is, and not as it might have been had the history of the last eighteen years been different.

He proposed complete disarmament, to be achieved through stages, the first of which would be a ban on atmospheric nuclear tests. As a demonstration of good faith, he promised that the United States would not conduct any further atmospheric tests as long as other countries refrained from doing so.

Khrushchev told Averell Harriman, Kennedy's representative at the test ban talks, that he thought Kennedy had made the "greatest speech by any American President since Roosevelt." The negotiations proved successful, at least in banning atmospheric, though not underground, tests. In August, Kennedy sent the treaty to the Senate; it was the first

arms control agreement between Washington and Moscow. The Joint Chiefs of Staff gave it only grudging approval, and certain military spokesmen vociferously opposed ratification. The public, though, was solidly behind it, and the treaty was ratified on 24 September by a comfortable margin above the required two-thirds. It was only a small step toward disarmament and an end to the Cold War, but Kennedy liked to say that great journeys began with small steps. No other accomplishment gave him greater satisfaction.

The Assassination

On 22 November 1963 the world was stunned to learn that Kennedy had been shot to death as he rode in a motorcade in Dallas, Texas. Within hours of Kennedy's shooting, the Dallas police arrested his alleged assassin, Lee Harvey Oswald, a mysterious, twenty-four-year-old ex-Marine who had lived in the Soviet Union, brought home a Russian wife, and sympathized with Castro. He was unfortunately never brought to trial because two days after his arrest, in full view of a national television audience, he was shot and killed in the basement of the Dallas police headquarters by Jack Ruby, a Dallas nightclub owner who reportedly was grief-stricken over Kennedy's assassination. Less than a year later, a presidential commission headed by Chief Justice Earl Warren concluded that Oswald had acted alone in killing Kennedy, that Oswald had not been part of a conspiracy. But from the time of the assassination itself, a significant part of the public was incredulous at the thought of a lone assassin, and the Warren Commission's findings and methods were subjected to endless second-guessing. In 1979 a special congressional investigation concluded that it was probable that more than one person was involved in Kennedy's assassination, though it was unable to identify anyone besides Oswald or to determine the nature and extent of the conspiracy. Articles and books about the crime number in the thousands and range from careful and thoughtful investigation and analysis to unsupported speculation and maudlin fantasy. On one level, the fascination with the assassination may indicate a psychological denial of Kennedy's death, a mass wish somehow to make it explicable or, in a sense, to undo it.

The depth of the public reaction to Kennedy's assassination can be explained in several ways. Although there had been attempts on the lives of President-elect Franklin D. Roosevelt and President Harry Truman, no American president had been assassinated since William McKinley in 1901. Television brought the Kennedy tragedy into people's lives with an intimacy that had never been known before. Many thousands had stood by the tracks as Lincoln's funeral train passed by, but now the entire country mourned at a presidential funeral. But it is probably safe to say that even if Kennedy had died suddenly of natural causes or through an accident, the public grief would have been great. Kennedy had become identified with many of mankind's hopes and aspirations—peace, racial justice, economic development, public service, social reform, a striving for excellence, and a seeking after New Frontiers on earth and in space. Toward these goals, he brought vitality, grace, and reason. Then, unexpectedly, irrationally, at the age of forty-six, he was dead, and the world was left wondering what might have been. His death at an early age called up the unfairness and tragedy of life.

BIBLIOGRAPHY

Kennedy's aides and friends evocatively and sympathetically portray him in several works, including Theodore C. Sorensen, *Kennedy* (New York, 1965); Arthur M. Schlesinger, Jr., *A Thousand Days: John F. Kennedy in the White House* (Boston, 1965); Paul B. Fay, Jr., *The Pleasure of His Company* (New York, 1966); Pierre Salinger, *With Kennedy* (Garden City, N.Y., 1966); Roger Hilsman, *To Move a Nation: The Politics of Foreign Policy in the Administration of John F. Kennedy* (Garden City, N.Y., 1967); Kenneth P. O'Donnell and David F. Powers, with Joe McCarthy, *"Johnny, We Hardly Knew Ye": Memories of John Fitzgerald Kennedy* (Boston, 1972); and Benjamin C. Bradlee, *Conversations with Kennedy* (New York, 1975).

Herbert S. Parmet has written the biographies *Jack: The Struggles of John F. Kennedy* (New York, 1980) and *JFK: The Presidency of John F. Kennedy* (New York, 1983). Richard Reeves, *President Kennedy: Profile of Power* (New York, 1993), is a well-researched assessment, critical but judicious. In the 1970s and 1980s, many revisionist evaluations of Kennedy appeared. Garry Wills, for example, debunks Kennedy and his defenders in *The Kennedy Imprisonment: A Meditation on Power* (Boston, 1982), while Allen J. Matusow, *The Unraveling of America: A History of Liberalism in the 1960s* (New York, 1984), critically surveys government initiatives that began under Kennedy. Three other recent studies with varying viewpoints are Irving Bernstein, *Promises Kept: John F. Kennedy's New Frontier* (New York, 1991), James N. Giglio, *The Presidency of John F. Kennedy* (Lawrence, Kans., 1991), and Thomas Reeves, *A Question of Character: A Life of John F. Kennedy* (New York, 1991).

Meanwhile, there has been a growing number of monographs and specialized studies, including Graham T. Allison, *Essence of Decision: Explaining the Cuban Missile Crisis* (Boston, 1971); Carl M. Brauer, *John F. Kennedy and the Second Reconstruction* (New York, 1977); Thomas G. Paterson, ed., *Kennedy's Quest for Victory: American Foreign Policy, 1961–1963* (New York, 1989); Montague Kern, Patricia W. Levering, and Ralph B. Levering, *The Kennedy Crises: The Press, the Presidency, and Foreign Policy* (Chapel Hill, N.C., 1983); William J. Rust et al., *Kennedy in Vietnam: American Vietnam Policy, 1960–1963* (New York, 1985); Thomas Brown, *JFK, History of an Image* (Bloomington, Ind., 1988); Michael R. Beschloss, *The Crisis Years: Kennedy and Khrushchev, 1960–1963* (New York, 1991); John M. Newman, *JFK and Vietnam: Deception, Intrigue, and the Struggle for Power* (New York, 1992); and Edwin M. Martin, *Kennedy and Latin America* (Lanham, Md., 1994).

Recent works include Lawrence Freedman, *Kennedy's Wars: Berlin, Cuba, Laos, and Vietnam* (New York, 2000); Barbara Leaming, *Mrs. Kennedy: The Missing History of the Kennedy Years* (New York, 2001); Richard D. Mahoney, *Sons and Brothers: The Days of Jack and Bobby Kennedy* (New York, 1999); Ernest R. May and Philip D. Zelikow, eds., *The Kennedy Tapes: Inside the White House During the Cuban Missile Crisis* (Cambridge, Mass., 1997); and Gerald Posner, *Case Closed: Lee Harvey Oswald and the Assassination of JFK* (New York, 1993).

For further sources consult James N. Giglio, comp., *John F. Kennedy: A Bibliography* (Westport, Conn., 1995).

Lyndon B. Johnson

Henry F. Graff

Lyndon B. Johnson THE LIBRARY OF CONGRESS

N OT since the first President Johnson took office in 1865 has a presidency begun amid such tragedy and turmoil as Lyndon Baines Johnson's did when he took the oath of office on 22 November 1963 aboard *Air Force One*, parked on Dallas' Love Field. It was the plane that earlier in the day had brought President John F. Kennedy to the city on a trip that was to end with his assassination. In its somber aftermath, when President Johnson received at the White House the dignitaries from around the world who had traveled to Washington for Kennedy's funeral, he stood in a brighter limelight than any incoming president had ever had to endure. He faced the daunting challenge of succeeding a martyr figure and of competing instantly with that memory for the public's approbation.

In attaining the White House, Johnson had fulfilled his life's ambition (as a mere twelve-year-old he had told his classmates, "Someday, I'm going to be president of the United States"), but he soon knew he would not inherit with his office the people's esteem. Many of the Kennedy faithful immediately and forever regarded Johnson as a "usurper" of Camelot, unworthy to sit in JFK's chair. Indeed, to them, the new man, notably less handsome and boyish than Kennedy, and "with a few gray hairs in his head" that Johnson liked to say were necessary in a chief executive, seemed virtually an impostor-president. They

[499]

could not adjust to the Texas drawl hitherto unheard in the Oval Office, where it abruptly replaced the Boston-Harvard accent the nation had become accustomed to. Johnson even indulged a brand of humor that they found offensive: it was not witty and literary like their hero's, but often coarse and sometimes scatological.

The keepers of the Kennedy flame gave the appearance of awaiting impatiently the advent of another of the Kennedy brothers to the presidency—and behaving meanwhile as if they represented a kind of government-in-exile. An extremely sensitive man with deep personal insecurities despite the macho image he projected, Johnson felt demeaned, as suggested by his often-repeated reminder, "I'm the only president you have." He lived with his nightmare that in the line of the presidents he would be remembered as sandwiched between two Kennedys.

To be sure, Johnson had a host of admirers, too. Almost immediately he brought a new style to the White House, symbolized by the ending of haute cuisine dinners and their replacement by homelier American fare. Millions appreciated hearing about it. And many people everywhere seemed ready to see in Johnson's older, craggy face and in his long experience in Washington likely evidence of valuable experience and maturity. Finally—and not least of all—Lady Bird Johnson, the president's articulate and tactful wife, quickly won favorable attention which helped give reassurance to the country that this presidential couple was a satisfactory successor to the Kennedys.

Johnson, who for years had been a dominating voice in the Senate, was immensely proud of his reputation as a legislative giant justly compared to the likes of Webster, Clay, and Calhoun. Yet he believed that as vice president, during the thousand days of the Kennedy administration, his talents had been forced to lie fallow. Now, by a sudden turn of fortune, he had the levers of power in his grip, and he fairly lusted to work them—aiming to make his page in history glow as brilliantly as any other president's.

Early Years

Lyndon Baines Johnson was born near Stonewall, Texas, on 27 August 1908. His father, Sam Ealy Johnson, Jr., had been a member of the Texas House and had recently lost several thousand dollars speculating in cotton. His mother, Rebekah Baines Johnson, raised on the outskirts of the little town of Blanco,

was the daughter of Joseph Wilson Baines, an attorney. He had previously occupied the seat that Sam Johnson held in the House. Rebekah worked her way through Baylor College at Belton, where she found encouragement for her lively literary and cultural interests.

When Lyndon was five years old, the family moved to Johnson City. Sam Johnson struggled to earn a living while Rebekah Johnson worked diligently to make ends meet. But there was never enough money, and Lyndon would often speak with disdain of the steady diet of grits, greens, cornbread, and fatback of his early years. Although the family was never as hard up as Johnson later liked to say it had been, he developed what proved to be a lifelong sympathy for ordinary people whose lives were blighted by economic insecurity and deprivation. As a boy, Johnson resented having to wear homemade clothing that once included, to his unspeakable embarrassment, a Buster Brown suit. His mother did private tutoring in elocution in order to pay for dancing and violin instruction for him. He detested the training in both and eventually refused to have any more lessons. He would not be marked a "sissy." Ironically, in the White House his accomplished and tireless social dancing at public functions charmed and sometimes astonished his guests.

Even as a youth, Johnson yearned to have a share in the rising wealth around him, which was based chiefly on the booms in oil and beef. Still he despaired of gaining even a foothold. He put in time working for farmers in and around Johnson City. For a period he was a printer's devil at a local newspaper. He also shined shoes in a barber shop. As he grew up he appeared to be both ambitious and aimless.

Politics had begun to draw the boy's interest when Sam Johnson won back his old seat in the state legislature in 1919. Lyndon became a familiar sight at his father's side on the floor of the Texas House. Soon the youth was bent on becoming a politician as well as a millionaire. After a trip to California with some friends when he finished high school, he yielded to his mother's nagging advice to seek more education. He enrolled in Southwest Texas State Teachers College at San Marcos, from which he was graduated in 1930. To support himself, he had interrupted his studies to take a teaching job at a "Mexican" school in Cotulla, Texas. One day, voting analysts would credit Johnson's close ties with the Mexican-American community with helping to put Texas in the Kennedy-Johnson column in the election of 1960. Johnson also taught briefly in Pearsall and Houston, where he won acclaim training students in public speaking and debating.

But the world of politics proved irresistible. Johnson avidly seized an opportunity in 1931 to become private secretary to Richard Kleberg, son of the owner of the fabled King Ranch, who had just been elected to Congress. In Washington, Johnson quickly became as familiar with the labyrinths of the bureaucracy as he was with the landscape of his Texas hill country. Then, in 1934, he was married in San Antonio to Claudia Alta Taylor of Karnack, Texas, known invariably by her nickname, Lady Bird. Not yet twenty-two years old, Lady Bird Johnson brought much-needed stability to Johnson's life; her winsomeness combined with her shrewd judgment of people from the start helped significantly in furthering his career.

Politically, Johnson was a child of the new opportunities that the era of Franklin D. Roosevelt opened for office seekers eager to have a hand in enlarging and redistributing the nation's resources. After a creative stint as director of the National Youth Administration in Texas, Johnson was elected to the House of Representatives in 1937 to fill the unexpired term of James P. Buchanan in the Tenth District. Already inured to the ways of Congress, Johnson took worshipful counsel from Speaker Sam Rayburn, also a Texan. In turn, Rayburn, who was unmarried, treated Johnson like a son and turned him rapidly into an "insider" despite his lack of seniority. Johnson served in the House until 1948, having been reelected five times on an ever-growing reputation for his craft in directing to his constituents a goodly share of the bounty that New Deal economic programs provided.

Johnson interrupted his tenure in the House shortly after the attack on Pearl Harbor to serve as a lieutenant commander, having been commissioned in the Naval Reserve in 1940. He was the first member of Congress to go on active duty in World War II. General Douglas MacArthur awarded him the Silver Star for "gallantry in action" when the patrol bomber Johnson was flying in was fired upon by Japanese Zeros near Port Moresby, in New Guinea. (Critics would later say that Johnson's political prominence rather than personal valor had won him the decoration. For the rest of his life, however, Johnson proudly wore the insignia of the medal in his lapel.) Almost immediately after receiving the award, Johnson responded to Roosevelt's directive that members of Congress leave military service and resume their legislative duties. After six months in uniform, Johnson was pleased to be back at his desk in Washington.

Johnson won election to the Senate in 1948 (he had failed in a bid in 1941) by a margin of eighty-seven votes, a squeaker that earned him the sobriquet "Landslide Lyndon." He held the seat until he became vice president in 1961. He was minority leader for two years and majority leader from 1956 to 1960, acquiring formidable fame among supporters as a legislative statesman and among detractors as a wheeler-dealer. His selection by Kennedy to be vice president, despite much opposition in the Kennedy camp, was the outcome of a disappointing effort to obtain the nomination for president.

As vice president, Johnson was ignored by many of the administration's prominent figures and was idle much of the time, his vaunted knowledge of Congress largely unused. Although he chaired some significant public committees and was sent on some missions abroad, he was convinced that most of his assignments were little more than busywork. He hid his smoldering resentment even as he made his initial appeal to the people as president an assurance of continuity of policies. Where Kennedy had urged in his inaugural, "Let us begin," Johnson, on 27 November 1963 in his first address to Congress, exhorted, "Today, in this moment of new resolve, I would say to all my fellow Americans, let us continue."

Unfinished Business

What Johnson lacked in Kennedy's urbanity, he made up for in energy so uncommon that one aide credited him with having "extra glands." Despite a severe heart attack in 1955—"the worst a man could have and still live," he liked to tell people—Johnson gave himself unstintingly to his work. Although he climbed into bed for a nap each afternoon, his long hours at his desk—spent mostly on the telephone—topped by his "night reading" left no doubt that he withheld nothing in fulfilling his duties. His desire to be embraced by the people and his constant sense of being unloved drove him to the limit relentlessly as he tried to earn his way into the company of the country's greatest presidents. He was tied to the reputation of Kennedy for his popularity in the beginning, and he struggled to create a devoted following of his own.

The desire to show he was in charge made his first month in office frenetic. From 23 November to

19 December he saw in his office almost seven hundred people alone or in small groups. Possibly to suggest that the new chief executive was economy-minded, the White House let it be known that he went about turning out unused electric lights every night—causing him to be dubbed for a time "Light Bulb Johnson." Still shaken by the circumstances of his own elevation to the presidency, Johnson consulted with Speaker of the House John McCormack of Massachusetts, next in line of succession, regarding any unexpected turnover of the White House.

About fifty pieces of proposed legislation were languishing in congressional committees, but the civil rights bill was the focus of Johnson's labors in the first several months. Its passage as the Civil Rights Act of 1964 would thenceforth be the keystone of Johnson's claim to fame as inheritor and keeper of the urban liberal base of the Democratic party. In seeking support for the bill's passage, he had beseeched Congress on sentimental grounds: "No memorial oration or eulogy could more eloquently honor President Kennedy's memory than the earliest possible passage of the civil rights bill." In short order, the bill that Kennedy had prepared had been made stronger by a number of amendments proposed by ardent advocates. The House passed the revised bill on 10 February. In the Senate it met a filibuster by southerners that lasted eighty-three days, ending on 10 June only with the enactment of a cloture resolution. The bill finally became law on 2 July.

Johnson, feeling special responsibility as a southerner, had made the bill's passage a personal crusade. His efforts can only be called Herculean, for he cajoled and pulled strings to round up support from early in the morning to late at night, day after day, week after week. On more than one occasion in the White House, he upbraided opponents or fence-sitters by fairly screaming as he faced them down—often nose-to-nose, "Do you know what it is to be black?"

The act set in place some of the most fundamental social changes in American history. Among its provisions, it forbade discrimination on account of race in places of public accommodation. It contained protection of the right of blacks to vote. It forbade discrimination on account of race or sex by employers and labor unions. Moreover, to help monitor the law's operation, the Equal Employment Opportunity Commission was established. To accelerate the desegregation of schools, the new law empowered the attorney general to challenge local discriminatory practices in court.

The Great Society

Johnson, having pushed through what he considered Kennedy's bill, now went to work on his own legislative program. He began with the Economic Opportunity Act, the first salvo of a concerted "war on poverty," as he called it, that would become one of the hallmarks of his presidency. The act, signed into law on 20 August 1964, was funded with an appropriation of $948 million. It eventually authorized ten programs under the Office of Economic Opportunity (OEO) established as part of the White House office. The programs included a "domestic Peace Corps" to operate in depressed areas of the country, known as Volunteers in Service to America (VISTA); the Job Corps, designed as a make-work program for the hard-core unemployed; Head Start, to help deprived children compensate for their cultural disadvantages; and community-action programs to give poor people a hand in running government programs. When the session of Congress ended, Johnson, competing in his mind with the legislative achievements of Franklin D. Roosevelt's "Hundred Days," declared grandly, "This session of Congress has enacted more major legislation, met more national needs, disposed of more national issues than any other session of this century or the last."

Johnson was now hitting his stride in the work he was touted to be expert in—persuading Congress to act. The difficulties between the executive and legislative branches that Kennedy had been unable to surmount were apparently vanishing. As they did, so did the memory of Kennedy's New Frontier. Speaking at the University of Michigan on 22 May, Johnson unveiled his own vision of America: "In your time we have the opportunity to move not only toward the rich society and the powerful society, but upward to the Great Society. The Great Society rests on abundance and liberty for all. It demands an end to poverty and injustice, to which we are totally committed in our time."

The possibility of giving life to such a vision brought popular support to the intense new president, who apparently was indeed able to fill Kennedy's shoes. The opinion polls showed Johnson more popular than his predecessor had been at the comparable time in his presidency. An uncommon feeling of confidence and unity seemed to pervade the

Lyndon Johnson (right) was famous for giving the "Johnson treatment" to those he wished to cajole or persuade, closing in on them to make the most of his imposing stature. Here he discusses issues with Roy Wilkins of the NAACP. NATIONAL ASSOCIATION FOR THE ADVANCEMENT OF COLORED PEOPLE (NAACP)

nation, even though perceptive people could see that the excitement connected with the spate of legislation masked the troubles that were brewing in Vietnam. There the Communists in the northern part of the country were bent on overrunning the southern part, which the United States was committed to support.

The Campaign of 1964

With these events—favorable and portentous—as a backdrop, the presidential campaign of 1964 got under way. It was a foregone conclusion that Johnson would have the Democratic nomination, which he received at Atlantic City late in August amid much hoopla over the selection of a vice presidential candidate. Johnson, who played a cat-and-mouse game with several possible candidates (he had already

ruled out Robert F. Kennedy, brother of the late president), was searching for a man, he said, who was "attractive and prudent and progressive." He believed he had found him in Hubert H. Humphrey of Minnesota, who had been his colleague in the Senate from the time they were both elected to it in 1948. (Johnson would keep Humphrey very busy, but on a short tether. When Winston Churchill died in 1965, Johnson could not attend the funeral because of illness. But he would not dispatch Humphrey in his place for reasons he never made public.)

Meanwhile, the Republicans had nominated the conservative Senator Barry Goldwater of Arizona, as they shunted aside the liberal, internationalist, eastern wing of the party, whose leaders included Governor Nelson A. Rockefeller of New York. One of only six Republicans who had voted against the civil rights bill, Goldwater was hoping to win the election by cobbling together support in the South and in the

[503]

West and by providing the nation with what he spoke of as "a choice, not an echo." When eastern Republicans sought to denounce conservative extremists in the party—especially the John Birch Society—Goldwater assured fellow Republicans in his acceptance address that "extremism in the defense of liberty is no vice!" The alarm of moderates was heightened when Goldwater told a reporter that if he could, he would "drop a low-yield atomic bomb on Chinese supply lines in Vietnam."

Johnson campaigned as an experienced man whose restraint and judgment in military matters could be relied upon. It seemed unremarkable in July when five hundred more troops—so-called advisers—were dispatched to Vietnam because Presidents Eisenhower and Kennedy had already been increasing gradually the American military presence there. And the general public seems not to have become exercised when, on 2 and 4 August, in murky circumstances, North Vietnamese torpedo boats allegedly attacked United States destroyers in the Gulf of Tonkin near North Vietnam's coast. Johnson ordered massive air attacks on targets in North Vietnam in retaliation. Moreover, on 7 August he obtained a congressional resolution—ever since known as the Tonkin Gulf Resolution—supporting the president in whatever action he deemed necessary "to repel any armed attack against the forces of the United States and to prevent further aggression" in Southeast Asia. It was not unlike the resolution that Congress had given Eisenhower in 1958 when he sent marines into Lebanon, and its passage was widely approved in the country at large.

Johnson had the support of the middle sector of American political sentiment, which was eager both to avoid a nuclear confrontation and to leave untouched the major domestic reforms, to which people had grown accustomed. Goldwater's broadside attacks on the Social Security Act, the Tennessee Valley Authority, and the graduated income tax played into Johnson's hands. The president could appear the solid man, continuing in international affairs the tried-and-true policies of the Truman, Eisenhower, and Kennedy years. He had shown he was in the tradition of the New Deal by putting Humphrey on the ticket. He showed he was the peace candidate by saying of the conflict rapidly heating up in Vietnam, "We are not about to send American boys nine or ten thousand miles from home to do what Asian boys ought to be doing for themselves." Furthermore, where Republicans were saying of Goldwater, "In

your heart, you know he's right," Democrats were responding, "In your heart, you know he might." Unlike his opponent, Johnson could be counted on, the country was assured, not to press the button that would start a nuclear war. The unabashed way in which Goldwater referred to the Soviet Union as "the enemy" also alarmed many voters, who concluded that Goldwater regarded open war with the Soviets as unavoidable.

In domestic matters Johnson seemed a wizard. Having staunchly supported and pressed upon Congress early in 1964 Kennedy's $80 billion tax cut proposal despite dire predictions by business people of its likely effect, economic activity flourished. All of the usual indicators—consumer spending, gross national product, and federal tax receipts—showed the success the Democrats had predicted.

Johnson received the election results at the Driskill Hotel in Austin. Amid his closest friends he reveled in the greatest popular victory in American history. With 43 million votes, he had run 16 million ahead of Goldwater, carrying 44 states and losing only Arizona and 5 states of the Deep South. The immense triumph had the effect of changing the politics of America, giving Johnson what he labeled "a mandate for unity." On his coattails rode to victory hundreds of Democratic candidates for lesser offices throughout the country. In the House of Representatives the Republicans lost 37 seats, giving the Democrats 295 places to 140 for the Republicans. The 2 seats the Democrats picked up in the Senate enlarged the margin of the Democrats, making it 68 to 32. The nation could see that one effect of Goldwater's anemic candidacy was to open the way for an expansion of the Great Society programs. Johnson would not have to endure the tug-of-war with Capitol Hill that had been Kennedy's lot.

Consensus Politics

Democratic voters thought that Johnson had earned the support he received because of the deftness he had shown in enlarging Kennedy's constituency of four years earlier. Moreover, following so closely on the heels of the assassination, the victory may have revealed the voters' desire not to have another change of president so soon. Johnson took his triumph to mean that he had a blank check to go ahead with an extensive program of social legislation. The president concluded happily that the national unity he had asked for in the sad days of November 1963 had been achieved.

Johnson's goal as president was to achieve consensus—to occupy that common ground on which the general citizenry and Congress alike could stand with him. One of his favorite sayings, "Come, let us reason together," became a rallying call to his banner. As a leader in the Senate he had already made known his fondness for consensus government even across party lines in the close working relationship he established with President Eisenhower. Now he would rely on the force and influence of his own personality rather than on the Democratic party itself. His persuasiveness with erstwhile colleagues on Capitol Hill, often involving psychological arm-twisting that long ago had been labeled the "Johnson treatment," would now be a feature of the relations between the executive and legislative branches.

Already Johnson's first year in office had revealed him a master, too, at self-advertising. Whether holding press conferences, walking his dogs on the White House lawn, or greeting new appointees with lavish fanfare, he was a constant item on the television screen. A photograph of him baring his new surgical scar (he had had his gall bladder removed) seemed undignified to many people, although it stamped him a down-to-earth man for countless others. He was at first an uncertain performer before the television camera, the now indispensable tool of politics, but he nevertheless conveyed a picture of strength. He projected a sense that with his bare hands he could seize the country's problems and subdue them.

The inauguration on 20 January 1965 was itself a symbol of national consensus. The first president elected from the South since Zachary Taylor in 1848, Johnson was serenaded by the Mormon Tabernacle Choir, singing the "Battle Hymn of the Republic." His inaugural address was a ringing call for national unity and noble deeds couched in almost biblical language. The president declared that "the oath I have taken before you and before God is not mine alone but ours together." And in rhetoric that evoked Franklin Roosevelt, he stated, "For every generation there is a destiny. For some, history decides. For this generation the choice must be our own." The destiny was to fulfill the American "covenant with this land"—to achieve justice, liberty, and union. In speaking of the toil and tears that each generation must expend, he unashamedly echoed Winston Churchill. A sentence that called to mind Kennedy's full-throated call four years earlier to defend freedom wherever it was threatened was soon to prove prophetic: "If American lives must end, and American treasure be spilled, in countries that we barely know, then that is the price that change has demanded of conviction and of our enduring covenant."

The new Congress was soon at Johnson's beck and call. It established two new cabinet posts: the Department of Housing and Urban Development, to which Johnson appointed Robert C. Weaver, the first black to hold a cabinet post, and the Department of Transportation. Johnson soon appointed the first solicitor general who was black, Thurgood Marshall (and elevated him in 1967 to the Supreme Court).

The special messages that Johnson sent to Capitol Hill began to inundate the lawmakers, even before the inauguration. On 7 January 1965 he called for Medicare, federally supported medical health services for the elderly, and improved health services for children, the mentally retarded, and the disabled; and he insisted upon millions of dollars for medical research. He traveled to Independence, Missouri, to sign the Medicare bill in the presence of former president Harry Truman, whom Johnson saluted as the law's true progenitor.

Before Congress could catch its breath, he sent it a billion-dollar proposal that became the Education Act of 1965 to aid elementary and secondary public schools, provide preschool programs for young children, grant subsidies to school libraries, finance scholarships and loans to needy students, and extend a variety of help to small colleges. He put his signature on the bill in the one-room schoolhouse he had attended as a boy near Stonewall, Texas. At his side sat "Miss Katie," his first teacher.

Soon the president was pressing Congress to pass a revision of the immigration laws, liberalizing the national origins quota system. Johnson journeyed to the Statue of Liberty to sign the bill into law on 3 October. Meanwhile, under the Voting Rights Act, which Johnson had approved on 6 August, federal examiners went to work immediately, removing impediments to the registration of black voters in the South. No field of reform seemed beyond the interest and reach of the president, and his zeal in dramatizing his concerns was limitless.

Committed to enlarging the "quality of life," Johnson supported legislation for the beautification of highways that Lady Bird Johnson ardently sought. In the field of the arts, Johnson established the National Foundation on the Arts and the Humanities, with a wide agenda of unprecedented duties. The variegated list of laws the administration pursued included the Highway Safety Act and the National Traffic and Motor Vehicle Safety Act.

Johnson reserved special earnestness for the continuing War on Poverty. The Appalachian Regional Development Act of 1965 authorized $1.1 billion to rehabilitate and develop the mountainous region from Pennsylvania to Alabama and Georgia, which was experiencing severe social and economic hardship. The far-reaching Housing Act of 1965 made possible the construction of 240,000 low-rent public-housing units and provided $3 billion in grants for urban renewal. In May 1966, Johnson approved a supplementary appropriation bill to make possible the subsidization of rents for low- and moderate-income families. Said the president as he signed the act, "While every man's house cannot be a castle, it need not be a hovel." Under the Demonstration Cities and Metropolitan Development Act of 1966, Johnson hoped to see large-scale rebuilding of the total economic and social environment of depressed urban communities. The law recognized, he said, "that our cities are made of people, not just bricks and mortar." The Eighty-ninth Congress completed under Johnson's baton the agenda of liberalism opened originally by Franklin D. Roosevelt. Speaker McCormack, who also had formed his views in the 1930s of the role of the federal government, shared Johnson's enthusiasm: "It is the Congress of accomplished hopes. It is the Congress of realized dreams."

Johnson never received the public adulation for his labors that he believed he had earned. In the private quarters of the White House, he had placed on the wall an old photograph of himself facing Roosevelt. Johnson had captioned it, "I listen." And unquestionably he had gone to school to FDR. Johnson's close aide Bill Moyers once said that to Johnson, Franklin Roosevelt was a book to be read and reread. Now, as a reform president, Johnson had "out-Roosevelted Roosevelt," but the beneficiaries did not make Johnson their hero as once they had deified Roosevelt.

By the 1960s the United States had become a welfare state. The largesse of government was no longer a gift but a due. Perhaps the relaxed atmosphere and general prosperity of Eisenhower's time had made it impossible to rekindle enthusiasm for a reforming president. Perhaps, too, many Americans saw Johnson as building a monument to himself as well as sweeping away the problems of industrial America. Where thoughtful people had once hoped to create a good society, Johnson had decided that his legacy to the nation would be Texas-size: the Great Society. He aroused not so much division as disbelief, a contaminant in the brew for immortality.

The liberalism Johnson espoused had been bred into his bones, so he could not see that its time might be drawing to a close. From his father, who taught the young Lyndon how to put his arm on people and serve the cause of social justice in the bargain, he acquired a model and the confidence to go and do likewise. When Johnson was imploring northern city bosses and southern cronies to take his way on civil rights, his nose almost on top of theirs, Texas old-timers could see Sam Johnson alive again.

From his mother the future chief executive acquired a sense of what he could make of himself. Even in his most rebellious time as a destructive and occasionally violent youth, Johnson must have had a picture in his mind's eye of a better young man who one day would please his mother. He later would say that he never made a major decision in his career without consulting her. It is not too much to guess that when Johnson said he wished to be remembered as "the education president," he could feel the influence of his mother who would accompany him to the front gate of their house each morning, reviewing with him the stuff of his lessons for the day.

Finally, Johnson was stamped by the models he took for himself from among the affluent cattlemen and oilmen he admired and envied. They tended to see the world through red-white-and-blue glasses and to regard physical power as the ultimate arbiter of disputes. Moreover, the Texas cowboy tradition of fiction and fact left its impress on Johnson. It reinforced his determination to plump for what was right and to be quick on the draw.

In a nation addicted to television, Johnson's personality became an object of public scrutiny. His penchant for secret conferral and for needlessly refusing to show his hand, which sometimes could seem conspiratorial, grated on associates and, after he entered the White House, on representatives of the media. Many of them began to see a "credibility gap" between the truth and certain White House utterances. The habit of dissimulating thwarted Johnson's hope to be loved by the people. The eager heartiness with which he embraced others by seeming to take them into his confidence may have been an indication of his awareness that he was not really loved in return, although this mannerism may have been accentuated by his considerable deafness, which he never acknowledged publicly.

The bawdy language that notably peppered his conversation suggests that he harbored a deep feeling of inferiority, which even his size—he stood six feet, three inches, and weighed two hundred pounds—could not overcome. The frustration of his youth that there were people richer and luckier than he appeared never to have left him. It seemed to show in his frequent comment that he came from "the wrong part of the country"—an irascible reference to the eastern establishment, which steadfastly regarded him as an outsider. Possibly he compensated for the felt deprivation in his remarkable love of creature comforts and especially in the fervor with which he outfitted his ranch on the Pedernales River.

Never far from his thoughts was the fear that his presidency, like Wilson's, might be destroyed by his physical incapacity. He later wrote, "Whenever I walked through the Red Room and saw Woodrow Wilson hanging there I thought of him stretched out upstairs in the White House, powerless to move, with the machinery of the American government in disarray around him." Johnson may have felt unconsciously that he had no time to lose, that the clock was running against him. Possibly his concern over his health helps explain the frenzy of his presidential activity. Or possibly with his eyes on history's judgment of him he simply wanted to "do it all." The White House staff was aware of Johnson's expressed concern that he might run out of problems to solve—never out of solutions.

Foreign Affairs

In international politics, Johnson was unschooled, and he seemed to lean on precepts gleaned from personal experience. "I know these Latin Americans," he told some newspaper reporters when he had been in the White House only a short while. "I grew up with Mexicans. They'll come right into your yard and take it over if you let them.. . . But if you say to 'em right at the start, 'Hold on, just a minute,' they'll know they're dealing with somebody who'll stand up. And after that you can get along just fine." Still, Johnson was no hothead or saber rattler. The besetting concern over Fidel Castro's regime gave Johnson an opportunity to show his mettle early in his administration. The Cuban dictator was demanding the return to Cuba of the United States naval base at Guantánamo Bay. To underscore his determination, he shut off the water to the American installation. Johnson countered the move immediately by instructing the navy to establish its own water supply. The Cubans working on the base were simply ordered to spend their wages there or be dismissed.

Johnson also showed moderation and self-control when nationalistic rioting took place in the Panama Canal Zone in early 1964. As demonstrators screamed, "Gringos, go home," President Roberto Chiari insisted that the time had come to revise the treaties governing United States-Panama relations. After the violence ended, Johnson agreed to enter into negotiations, declaring afterward that "it was indeed time for the United States and Panama to take a fresh look at our treaties." A United States-Panama treaty was finally signed by President Jimmy Carter in 1978, providing for Panama to assume full control of the canal at the end of 1999.

Latin America presented persistent problems. The Alliance for Progress had created high expectations throughout the region, but it was not yielding the improved standard of living the masses of people had been led to expect. Trouble broke out in the Dominican Republic on 24 April 1965. The civilian government of Donald Reid Cabral came under attack from liberal and radical followers of Juan Bosch. Bosch, heading a reform party, had received 60 percent of the votes in a national election in 1962, but he had been ousted in a coup d'état. The new regime under Reid Cabral received the support of the Department of State, although its leader apparently had little popular support. Moreover, the country was in increasing economic difficulties. In April 1965 a group of young army officers raised the banner of revolt, aiming to restore the exited Bosch to the presidency. Civil war ensued as the senior army officers, backed by conservative elements, opposed the insurgents. In the fierce fighting that followed, the military seemed to be winning. But the pro-Bosch forces gained strength by arming civilians in the city. As the struggle raged on, more than a thousand Americans became trapped in the Embajador Hotel. Ambassador W. Tapley Bennett, concerned for their safety, expressed anxiety over a possible Castro-like government emerging. He cabled President Johnson, urging that troops be landed immediately in order to protect American citizens. On 28 April marines waiting offshore aboard an aircraft carrier were landed and quickly established a cease-fire in Santo Domingo. The following month the Organization of American States (OAS) agreed to station a peacekeeping force in the Dominican Republic to replace the marines.

Johnson had possibly saved American lives and had prevented the rise of a Communist government.

He was able, moreover, to withdraw the American forces gracefully when the OAS troops moved in. Still, he had lost some credibility as he sought to justify the steps he had taken. Two days after the dispatch of troops, he explained his actions on the ground that "people trained outside the Dominican Republic are seeking to gain control." On 2 May he identified the cause of the trouble as a "band of Communist conspirators." In private conversation Johnson stated that "we took out 5,641 people from forty-six nations—without even a sprained ankle.. . . If I hadn't acted, Castro would have had them all." Some Americans were inclined to agree with Bosch's assessment: "This was a democratic revolution smashed by the leading democracy of the world." Johnson had acted on his conviction that "the last thing the American people wanted . . . was another Cuba on our doorstep."

Under Johnson, relations with the Soviet Union seemed less menacing than did those with the People's Republic of China, although Johnson himself was not afraid of China. In 1967 he said: "Why would the Chinese want to take on the United States of America? . . . It would be like an eleven-year-old colored girl from Tennessee going up against Jack Dempsey." And he added, "One way to avoid [war with China] is to quit talking about it." Johnson's dour view of the Soviets possibly had been modified by the cordial meeting he held at Glassboro, New Jersey, with Premier Aleksey Kosygin in June 1967, which may have accelerated progress in the nuclear nonproliferation treaty the president was seeking.

Vietnam: An Entangling Alliance

Despite a folksy manner and intonation, which some Americans took as proof that he was only a regional man, Johnson knew that there was beyond the Pedernales a vastly different world full of treacherous risks. He sensed, too, that his place in history might ultimately depend on how he managed foreign affairs. He was no reader of history, but he had watched intently the doings of his predecessors and had an elephant's memory for their mistakes, particularly those that were politically expensive. He had seen how Truman's experience in "losing" China had hounded the Missourian to the end of his administration. He had pondered the frustration that Castro's coming to power had caused the Eisenhower and Kennedy administrations. Moreover, Johnson could vividly recall—and the details were constantly

at the tip of his tongue—the efforts of Franklin Roosevelt and his people to buck the isolationist tide in the late 1930s and early 1940s. For Johnson that experience was like a remembered time of terror he did not wish to relive. Forthright steps like those he had taken in the Dominican Republic would help prevent it. They became linked with the war in Vietnam when he called upon Congress on 4 May 1965 for the sum of $700 million in additional military appropriations for both undertakings.

The Vietnam situation was a time bomb in the administration. Inherited from Kennedy and Eisenhower, like most of the problems Johnson faced, it gradually became an overwhelming force. During the campaign of 1964, it was beginning to move to the center of public attention. It had been creeping up slowly for years. At the time of Kennedy's assassination more than sixteen thousand Americans were stationed in Vietnam, and the danger of deeper involvement enlarged as the corruption and incompetence of the South Vietnamese government of Ngo Dinh Diem began to cause widespread unrest.

Johnson himself had visited South Vietnam as vice president and had seen at first hand how heavily American prestige was already committed there. Scarcely become president, though, he was privately telling confidants (which we now know from his telephone taping), "I don't think it's worth fighting for." Johnson, nevertheless, was about to become "the Vietnam president," unable to win the war the way he understood it had to be fought and unable to extricate the United States on terms he believed acceptable. Still, he was determined: "I am not going to be the president who saw Southeast Asia go the way China went."

Hardly settled into his own term of office in 1965, Johnson confronted on 6 February a Vietcong attack on the American barracks at Pleiku. Two days before the election a costly attack on the American installation at Bien Hoa had gone unanswered. Now American B-52 bombers assaulted North Vietnam, the beginning of Operation Rolling Thunder, the program of gradually intensified air attacks. Johnson ordered that American dependents be evacuated from Saigon. At the same time, the American military presence in Vietnam was beefed up.

At a news conference on 27 April, Johnson stated the issue as he saw it. The United States, he declared, is "engaged in a crucial issue in Vietnam.. . . Defeat in South Vietnam would deliver a friendly nation to terror and repression. It would encourage and spur on those who seek to conquer all free nations that are within their reach." The "domino theory" of the Eisenhower era received new reinforcement. If North Vietnam succeeded in taking over South Vietnam, said the president, "our own welfare, our own freedom would be in danger." He added: "This is the clearest lesson of our time. From Munich until today we have learned that to yield to aggression brings only greater threats and brings even more destructive war." He was certain that "this is the same battle which we [have] fought for a generation." He stood ready, he declared, to enter into unconditional discussions with the North Vietnamese. Even as he spoke so resolutely, the process was under way that would erode the Johnson administration and gradually turn the nation against him in scenes of fitful violence unprecedented in the history of the presidency. From the beginning of his presidency he was anguished over his plight, musing privately that "when I land troops they call me an interventionist [referring to his move in the Dominican Republic], and if I do nothing I'll be impeached." So, the troubling buildup in Vietnam continued. There were 33,500 American soldiers and marines in Vietnam in April 1965; there were 75,000 by the end of June. And the mission of the troops was gradually broadened from static defense to permit patrolling of the countryside.

Even as the American troop commitment was growing, Johnson had grave doubts about the course he had set the country on. Anxiously, he asked former President Eisenhower: "[Do] you think that we can really get beat out there?" And he was saying to Lady Bird Johnson, his most trusted confidante: "Vietnam is getting worse every day. I have the choice to go in with great casualty lists or to get out with disgrace. It's like being in an airplane and I have to choose between crashing with the plane or jumping out. I do not have a parachute."

In June, American forces took on an active role against the Vietcong in a zone northwest of Saigon. Nevertheless, the troops were instructed not to initiate offensive action. The air strikes, furthermore, were confined to nonindustrial targets some distance removed from Hanoi, the capital of North Vietnam, and Haiphong, its principal port.

In July the military situation in South Vietnam worsened noticeably. The government was shakier than ever, and the Vietcong were pressing the attack. On 28 July the president announced that 50,000 more Americans would be sent to the war zone im-

mediately. And he was looking further down the road: "Additional forces will be needed later, and they will be sent as requested." Johnson talked once again of the stakes: "If we are driven from the field in Vietnam, then no nation can ever again have the same confidence in American promise or in American protection." By the end of 1965, there were almost 185,000 uniformed Americans in Vietnam, and the end was not in sight.

The war, moreover, was spreading beyond Vietnam. The United States felt free to take action in Cambodia if necessary to protect American troops in South Vietnam. The bombing of infiltration routes in Laos was being intensified. And the bombardment of the Ho Chi Minh Trail leading from North Vietnam was raising the specter of possible Chinese intervention in the war. Johnson and his intimates were unable to define what a victory would be, and they were terrified of "another Korea"—a war with an indecisive outcome. Instead of victory, they preferred the phrase *favorable settlement*—defined by Secretary of Defense Robert S. McNamara as coming about when the North Vietnamese ceased feeding "the fires of subversion and aggression in South Vietnam" so that South Vietnam could gradually "expand its control and shape the outcome." The president continued to use the words *winning* and *losing*. Until early 1968 he believed what he had been saying in mid-1965: "I know the other side is winning; so they do, too. No man wants to trade when he's winning." So he concluded that the United States would have to "apply the maximum deterrent until [the enemy] sobers up and unloads his pistol." Johnson persisted in a mistaken conviction that Ho Chi Minh, the North Vietnamese leader, was, like most other politicians, ready sooner or later to make a deal.

At Christmastime 1965 the president conducted a worldwide effort—the "Johnson peace offensive"—aimed at commencing negotiations. Vice President Hubert Humphrey sped off to meet with Soviet Premier Kosygin in New Delhi; Ambassador to the United Nations Arthur Goldberg visited with Pope Paul VI, President Charles de Gaulle of France, and Prime Minister Harold Wilson of Great Britain; and Secretary of State Dean Rusk conferred in Saigon with South Vietnamese officials. The veteran diplomatic troubleshooter Averell Harriman went behind the Iron Curtain to present the position of the administration to ranking officials in Warsaw and Belgrade. The good offices of U Thant, the secretary general of the United Nations, were also earnestly enlisted. The peace offensive, launched with a dramatic and well-publicized halt in the bombing of the North, ended after thirty-seven days on 31 January 1966—an unmitigated failure.

Protest at Home

The war was beginning to threaten Johnson's prized consensus. The first sign had been the votes of Senators Ernest Gruening of Alaska and Wayne Morse of Oregon against the Tonkin Gulf Resolution. But during 1965 other leading senators went into opposition. Two of the best known were William F. Fulbright of Arkansas and Eugene McCarthy of Minnesota. Fulbright, who was opposed to the resumption of bombing after the temporary halt, voiced his fear of an "ever-increasing escalation in the fighting." Morse, the most caustic of the critics, boldly and angrily predicted that the American people "will repudiate our war in Southeast Asia."

Johnson's response was more and more rancorous and hostile. He saw Americans as divided simply "between cut-and-run people and patriotic people." With deep sarcasm he said of his critics: "They have a real feeling for danger.. . . They see a fire and they turn off the hose because it is essential that we not waste any water." Mindful of Fulbright's opposition to the civil rights movement, Johnson pointedly explained the senator's opposition to the war as racist, asserting that the senator from Arkansas "cannot understand that people with brown skins value freedom too."

Johnson never accepted the widely held view of the Democratic "doves" (opponents of the war) that the conflict was a civil war and that the Vietcong had won the allegiance of most South Vietnamese even before the North Vietnamese had began their large-scale infiltration. While Johnson and his people insisted that China was the puppeteer manipulating the assault on South Vietnam, the doves scoffed, maintaining that if the United States restrained itself and did not force North Vietnam to seek Chinese assistance, an independent Communist Vietnam might evolve. The doves rejected, too, Johnson's insistence that the United States had a solemn obligation to act under the provisions of the Southeast Asia Treaty Organization (SEATO). Johnson was adamant, taking pains to point out that Mike Mansfield of Montana, who had succeeded him as majority leader in the Senate and was increasingly opposed to the war, had been a signatory of the treaty establishing SEATO.

A serious defection from the phalanx of Great Society supporters was the Reverend Martin Luther King, Jr. King had concluded that the prosecution of the war was assuming a higher priority than the pledged expansion of civil rights. But Johnson remained adamant, at increasingly heavy cost to the nation's tranquillity and to the base of power that had carried him to his recent electoral victory.

By the end of 1966, the momentum of Johnson's Great Society program was slowing. Worse, the tide of domestic troubles—inflation, a price-wage squeeze, and mounting strikes—was rising, mostly because of the war in Vietnam. Yet the problems could not be managed unless the war ended. Besides, Johnson, having widened the war without calling for public sacrifice, continued to act as if the country could have "both guns and butter." The situation called for a cutback in domestic spending or an increase in taxes, but Johnson was unwilling to break up his immense majority in Congress by asking for either.

The air war in Vietnam had clearly not produced the results sought. Johnson, increasingly testy, even became disenchanted with the Joint Chiefs of Staff, whose chairman, General Earle G. Wheeler, also a victim of heart trouble, he felt kin to. "Bomb, bomb, bomb, that's all you know," Johnson several times complained in frustration. The search-and-destroy operations of the troops under General William C. Westmoreland, the American commander in Vietnam, did not seem to put a strain on enemy manpower. "Westy" now had almost 500,000 men in Vietnam, more than 3,000 helicopters, 28 tactical fighter-bombers, and large numbers of giant B-52 bombers. The Vietnam landscape was so heavily pockmarked by the aerial assaults that experienced pilots could fly to their targets by following bomb craters whose configuration had become familiar to them.

In early August 1967, Johnson formalized to the generals his response to their latest request for troops—for 100,000 more. He would allow them 45,000 and thus bring to 525,000 the strength of the force in Vietnam by the middle of 1968. But he knew that progress in the war was not taking place. He asked Westmoreland, "When we add divisions, can't the enemy add divisions? If so where does it all end?" Expanding the war by calling up the reserves seemed out of the question. The American death toll was rising: by the end of 1967 it was approaching 500 a week. The cost of the war in 1967 was $25 billion, fueling what would prove to be a long cycle of inflation. Moreover, television news was for the first time in

American history bringing the battlefield into the living room regularly. Millions were appalled at the use of napalm on villagers who seemed innocent victims of forces they could not comprehend. In the eyes of the world, the United States was Goliath mercilessly pummeling David.

The war had significantly changed the public's judgment of Johnson. Once seen as a political magician with a sure mastery of people and circumstances, he now seemed battered by events out of his control and beyond his ken. His vaunted capacity for wearing out his young aides was being enlarged by a fury regarding any form of dissent within the ranks. And the people saw a president who wearily wrestled with the politics of the nation's problems rather than with the problems themselves. His ill-temperedness, sometimes combined with disingenuousness, made his public persona unattractive to many Americans. It stood in the way of bringing Johnson the public sympathy a beleaguered president traditionally receives, as Kennedy had received it after the fiasco at the Bay of Pigs. Not even Lincoln in the darkest days of the Civil War had faced such intense dissent and public doubts about his course of action.

The opposition to the Vietnam War was given its most powerful expression by college students. One of their first responses had been the device of the teach-in—hours-long discussions of the war with many participants—the first of which took place on the campus of the University of Michigan on 24 March 1965—a one-day school moratorium during which professors spoke on the war instead of offering their regular lectures. The teach-in became familiar throughout the country. Moreover, it provided an opportunity for students to vent other grievances: against the Reserve Officers' Training Corps (ROTC), against academic support of scientific work for defense purposes, against the exclusion of students from college decision making, and against a medley of real and imagined irritations. The public demonstrations, which may have been an important stimulus to draft resistance, seemed to merge with the uprising known as the youth movement. Johnson, who had never given up the fond hope of being remembered as a friend of education, was publicly taunted at student rallies, often with the stinging refrain, "Hey, hey, LBJ, how many kids did you kill today?"

Concurrently Johnson's relationship with the black community cooled noticeably. Some part of the disaffection was owing to the unpopular war, in-volving as it did the disruption of a land inhabited by people of color, but it also grew out of the alienation from a generally prosperous society of its black people, who did not share in the bounty, and out of a natural evolution of the civil rights movement from a call for integration to a demand for "black power." The neighborhoods of tenements and slums occupied by poor blacks in the North, now denominated ghettos, were notably marked by high unemployment and run-down schools. Even as the presidential campaign had gotten under way in 1964, a riot in New York erupted and lasted five days.

In the next few years the nation experienced "long, hot summers"—riots and the threats of riots in major cities. The Watts district of Los Angeles burst into flames in 1965, and black communities exploded in Cleveland in 1966, in Newark and Detroit in 1967, and in Washington, D.C., in 1968. Anxiety over possible race war gripped many cities as the words "Burn, baby, burn" were reported to be the battle cry of the rioters. The nation was reaping a whirlwind resulting from its long neglect and indifference to the needs of the black poor. As the destruction, including looting and attacks on white policemen, firemen, and National Guardsmen, rent the air, it was easy to find a scapegoat: Johnson and his war in Vietnam. Both he and the struggle in Asia became more unpopular than ever.

The president's response was to appoint the National Advisory Commission on Civil Disorders, chaired by Governor Otto D. Kerner of Illinois. The report delivered to the president on 2 March 1968 blamed white racism for the troubles. The country, it declared, was dividing into two societies, one white, one black—"separate and unequal." Its recommendations included a call for open housing and other "massive" programs. Johnson praised the report, but it distressed him, too, for he said: "They always print that we don't do enough. They don't print what we do." Johnson felt stymied: the War on Poverty he had designed had spent more than $6 billion from 1964 to 1967, and poverty had not disappeared. Indeed, there was extensive proof of widespread malnutrition and even hunger in the country. Fresh evidence came to public attention just as Secretary of Defense Robert McNamara announced that he was proposing a new antiballistic missile defense system that would cost $5 billion. Johnson was now the object of the new accusation that he was unable any longer to discern the nation's true priorities. Many Americans insisted that poverty could be wiped out if the money being spent on the war were diverted to the home front.

In October 1967 a mass protest by a group calling itself the National Mobilization to End the War in Vietnam descended upon Washington. The administration was torn: Should it call a new bombing halt to satisfy the growing opposition at home, or should it intensify the war in order to satisfy the "hawks," who were eager to smite North Vietnam decisively? Before the end of November, a public opinion poll showed that confidence in Johnson's management of the war had dropped to 23 percent—the lowest point yet. Nevertheless, public support of the war effort itself remained at about 45 percent between November and March 1968.

The president and his principal spokesmen were finding it harder each week to avoid the chanting protesters, who seemed to be everywhere. For the first time in history, a president was unwelcome in public in most parts of the country, making him a veritable prisoner in the White House, "hunkered down" there, to use one of his favorite expressions. At the end of 1967 he traveled to Australia, Thailand, Vietnam, and Pakistan in four and a half days, returning to the White House on Christmas Eve after stopping off for a surprise meeting with the pope in the Vatican. Johnson was once again attempting to placate the doves. One means was to state a willingness to accept Vietcong representatives in discussions of the war at the United Nations. The immediate effect was to disrupt relations with South Vietnam, where President Nguyen Van Thieu expressed cold anger at Washington for seeming to have truck with the enemy.

In his State of the Union message of 17 January 1968, Johnson could report that "Americans are as prosperous as men have ever been in recorded history." Still, he took note of the disarray in the country, as he added, "Yet there is in the land a certain restlessness, a questioning." Privately the president was gloomy and depressed. By now, even McGeorge Bundy, who as Johnson's first special assistant for national security affairs had been an architect of the first phase of the war, had come out against its continuation.

The nation's discontent intruded into the White House itself when, on 18 January 1968, Mrs. Johnson held a luncheon for a group of white and black women who had been invited in order to discuss crime in the streets. One of the guests, Eartha Kitt, a prominent singer, rose shortly after the president

had spoken briefly, to assert that young people were rebelling and smoking marijuana because of the war. "Boys I know across the nation feel it doesn't pay to be a good guy. They figure [that] with a [prison] record they don't have to go off to Vietnam." Johnson was furious over what he regarded as an affront to the presidency delivered in the White House itself and over the extensive coverage of the incident in the press and on television.

The Final Days

Johnson's political world was soon a shambles. In November 1967, Senator Eugene McCarthy had announced his audacious intention to run for the Democratic presidential nomination in 1968. McCarthy was opposed not only to the war but also to what he saw as the excessive power of the presidency under Johnson. For a brief time Johnson assumed that McCarthy was only a stalking-horse for Senator Robert Kennedy of New York, which incensed him all the more. The Kennedys, he had come to think, regarded themselves as superior people to himself.

In March 1968, Clark Clifford, Johnson's longtime informal adviser and widely regarded as a hawk, became the secretary of defense. The president did not want another doubting Thomas—as McNamara had become—serving in his cabinet. Nevertheless, events soon overwhelmed traditional categories. On 23 January the USS *Pueblo*, an intelligence-gathering vessel, was seized by North Korean gunboats while on patrol off the North Korean port of Wonsan, and the crew of eighty men imprisoned. The president, provoked and exasperated, restrained himself despite a public outcry for quick military retaliation. He responded by calling to active duty fifteen thousand air force and navy reservists and ordering the nuclear-powered aircraft carrier *Enterprise* to assume a station off the coast of South Korea. His desire was to give assurance that despite the war in Vietnam, he continued to exercise freedom of military action. Following frustrating negotiations, the crew was freed eleven months later, after the United States admitted culpability for violating Korean waters and apologized. Apparently by prearrangement, the "confession" was repudiated after the men's release, for it obviously had been wrenched out of the United States under duress.

A week after the seizure of the *Pueblo*, critical developments changed the scene in Vietnam. While Saigon was celebrating Tet, the lunar new year, the

Vietcong had launched an attack on the city, including the vital Tan Son Nhut Airport. Within two days every significant city or provincial capital in South Vietnam was under assault. General Westmoreland said that the concerted attack had been expected but not its size and destructiveness. The United States and South Vietnamese forces, caught by surprise, recovered quickly. Yet the recapture of the beautiful old capital of Hue, which contained many architectural treasures, took three weeks and some of the costliest fighting of the war. In the end, the city lay in ruins.

The administration insisted that in blunting the Tet offensive it had gained a victory, but the public generally perceived the outcome of the battle as a defeat. In truth, the struggle was a prelude to a decision in Washington to wind down the war. Johnson insisted at a press conference on 2 February that basic United States strategy would remain unchanged. He was relying heavily upon the assessment of the military situation by his generals. He and they, ever mindful of the decisive defeat that the North Vietnamese general Vo Nguyen Giap had inflicted on the French at Dien Bien Phu in 1954, were determined that a similar disaster would not befall the American forces. When crack North Vietnamese units laid siege to the marine garrison and South Vietnamese regulars at Khe Sanh near the Laotian border in late 1967, fear of such an outcome ran high. Johnson anxiously followed the fierce encounter from the war room in the White House. The beleaguered troops—substantially reinforced in response to Johnson's order to hold at all cost—lifted the siege in early April. They had been given the heaviest air support ever accorded to ground forces. Johnson, temporarily relieved by the reports of these momentous battles, continued to rally support in the nation. He even personally bid farewell to a contingent of troops being hurried to the war zone.

The war was entering a new phase. General Wheeler, who had rushed to Vietnam after the Tet offensive, returned with a request from General Westmoreland for additional troops—206,000 of them. To raise and support that many men would require calling up reservists and adding $10 billion to the federal budget. Johnson, seemingly aware now that his goal of "carrying forward the Nation's struggle against aggression in Southeast Asia" was not going to be achieved, instructed Secretary Clifford to undertake a close study of the Westmoreland request. Clifford became the instrument through which the policy of constantly expanding the American presence in Vietnam was eventually reversed.

Johnson, meanwhile, had come to the conclusion that with the military force the United States had in Vietnam the Americans were not going to be able, as he put it, "to nail the coonskin to the wall." Political developments no doubt were determinative in leading Johnson to reexamine his position on staying the course. On 12 March, McCarthy, whom the president personally scorned, won 42 percent of the vote in the New Hampshire primary. Four days later, Robert Kennedy, no doubt emboldened by McCarthy's victory, entered the presidential race too.

The next two weeks were decisive for the president. He had reached certain conclusions, which he announced on 31 March in an address to the nation. He was halting the bombing of North Vietnam in the hope that the step would lead to peace, and he was going to give higher priority than ever to expanding the size of the South Vietnamese forces—that is, to "Vietnamizing" the war once again—and he was authorizing a small increase in the American forces in Vietnam.

At the end of his address he dropped a political bombshell: he would not be a candidate for reelection. He declared, "I have concluded that I should not permit the presidency to become involved in the partisan divisions that are developing in this political year." In his memoirs he later reported that he had decided even as he took the oath in January 1965 that he would never take it again. His health, he had concluded, would not stand the punishment of another term. Johnson did not mention that already the public opinion polls, which he followed intensely on all matters throughout his presidency, showed he would suffer a crushing defeat at the hands of McCarthy in the upcoming primary election in Wisconsin. Following the announcement, Johnson's political fortunes revived briefly as Congress passed his proposals for fair housing (embraced in the Civil Rights Act of 1968) and also a tax increase. But his presidency was soon in the doldrums again as the peace talks seemed to be going nowhere. In October his nominee for chief justice, Associate Justice Abe Fortas, was turned down by the Senate, the first time a president had been thus humiliated since 1795, when Washington's nomination of John Rutledge as the second chief justice was rejected.

Event had piled upon event. Martin Luther King, Jr., was assassinated on 4 April. The riots that ensued added to the dismay of the American people at the low state to which public order and morale had fallen. Two months later Robert Kennedy was assassinated in Los Angeles. When the Democratic National Convention met in Chicago in August to choose a presidential candidate amid violence in the streets, as police and antiwar protesters battled each other, the party named Vice President Hubert Humphrey to carry its banner. Johnson's hold on the party had slipped so badly that he did not even attend the convention.

Humphrey, who felt deeply obligated personally to Johnson, was unable to shake the albatross of Johnson's dealings with the North Vietnamese, now negotiating in Paris with American negotiators. The Republicans had nominated Richard Nixon, who insisted—without specifying his meaning—that "new leadership can end the war in the Pacific and bring peace." The crowning disappointment of the summer of 1968 was the need to cancel Johnson's long-planned trip to Moscow for talks on the limiting of antiballistic missiles. All had been in readiness when, on 20 August, at the height of the tumultuous Democratic convention, 200,000 Russian and Warsaw Pact troops invaded Czechoslovakia to suppress a movement to liberalize society in that Iron Curtain country. The ratification of a proposed treaty was postponed. The president seemed trapped in a maze without an exit.

In retirement, Johnson worked on plans for his presidential library (dedicated in May 1971) on the campus of the University of Texas, in Austin. He devoted time, too, to the preparation of his memoirs, published under the title *The Vantage Point: Perspectives of the Presidency, 1963–1969*. Meanwhile, his heart condition worsened, and it was increasingly difficult for him to exert himself. In considerable physical distress, he presided over a memorable symposium on civil rights at his library only a few weeks before he died on 22 January 1973. He was buried on his beloved LBJ Ranch.

The war remains the dark side of Johnson's moon; domestic legislation is the shining side, particularly the civil rights laws that remain his monument. As his administration drew to a close, Johnson must have felt betrayed by history and by his close associates, whom he had regarded as his choicest inheritance from Kennedy, and by old friends like Senator Fulbright, the carping chairman of the Senate Foreign Relations Committee. Johnson's wondrous hopes for America were not going to be realized in

his time. The civil rights struggle had not yet completely moved from the streets into the courts, although, despite the burning cities of the late sixties, that process was clearly under way.

Johnson came to recognize that he was at the wrong point in history. Although his dream to remake life for the deprived and underprivileged and to be recalled forever as their benefactor had been shattered by the awful bloodletting ten thousand miles from home, the ideal of a land without poverty or racial division remains his legacy to America. Possibly he sensed this when, in an unusual move, he delivered a State of the Union message on 14 January 1969, just before leaving office. His words were a last call for the passage of Great Society legislation. He plainly had not run out of problems requiring attention, as he once had feared he would.

Americans will continue to ponder the incomplete triumph at home and the unfinished and losing war abroad of its first cowboy president, who came out of the hill country of Texas, certain of how society's wrongs could be put right. As he left office to return to his ranch and to the other substantial interests that his political successes had given him the opportunity to acquire, he rested his case with history. And he could hope that one day Americans with a longer perspective on the Vietnam War would judge more favorably than had his contemporaries what he had attempted in Asia and the central role he had played in the tragic epoch that shook the nation to its roots.

BIBLIOGRAPHY

Lyndon B. Johnson, *The Vantage Point: Perspectives of the Presidency, 1963–1969* (New York, 1971), is the president's memoirs, a team effort with loyalist writers. His *My Hope for America* (New York, 1964) is a campaign document containing his philosophy of government culled from some of his speeches. Lady Bird Johnson, A *White House Diary* (New York, 1970), is an impressive book of reminiscences based on the First Lady's daily talks into her tape recorder. Johnson's exchanges with members of the media are found in *The Johnson Presidential Press Conferences*, 2 vols. (New York, 1978).

Irving Bernstein, *Guns or Butter: The Presidency of Lyndon Johnson* (New York, 1996), is the best one-volume treatment, elaborating masterfully how the Vietnam War undermined the Great Society.

Vaughn Davis Bornet, *The Presidency of Lyndon B. Johnson* (Lawrence, Kans., 1983), covers the ground, although it is turgid in style. A lively and penetrating one-volume biography is Paul K. Conkin, *Big Daddy from the Pedernales: Lyndon Baines Johnson* (Boston, 1986). Robert A. Caro, *The Path to Power* (New York, 1982) and *Means of Ascent* (New York, 1990), are the first two volumes of a planned four-volume study, *The Years of Lyndon Johnson*; it is sharply critical and enormously detailed. Ronnie Dugger, *The Drive for Power, from the Frontier to Master of the Senate* (New York, 1982), also critical, is based substantially on many interviews with LBJ; it is the first volume of a projected study entitled *The Politician: The Life and Times of Lyndon Johnson*. Outstanding on Johnson's early career, and elegantly written, is Robert Dallek, *Lone Star Rising: Lyndon Johnson and His Times, 1908–1960* (New York, 1991). Leonard Baker, *The Johnson Eclipse: A President's Vice Presidency* (New York, 1966), is devoted to the most disappointing years in Johnson's public life.

Philip Reed Rulon, *The Compassionate Samaritan: The Life of Lyndon Baines Johnson* (Chicago, 1981), evaluates the man with fervent praise. Alfred Steinberg, *Sam Johnson's Boy: A Close-up of the President from Texas* (New York, 1968), concludes that LBJ failed to grow in office. Merle Miller, *Lyndon: An Oral Biography* (New York, 1980), brings Johnson to life through taped recollections of friends and associates. Louis Heren, *No Hail, No Farewell* (New York, 1970), is a judicious evaluation of the Johnson presidency by the chief Washington correspondent of the *Times* of London. William S. White, *The Professional: Lyndon B. Johnson* (Boston, 1964), is a compelling portrait that served as a campaign biography. The best account of Johnson's election to the presidency is Theodore H. White, *The Making of the President: 1964* (New York, 1965). For the family background, books by Johnson's mother and brother are available: Rebekah Baines Johnson, *A Family Album* (New York, 1965), and Sam Houston Johnson, *My Brother, Lyndon* (New York, 1970).

George C. Herring, *America's Longest War: The United States and Vietnam, 1950–1975*, 2d ed. (Philadelphia, 1986), is the best brief English-language history of the struggle. Herring's *LBJ and Vietnam: A Different Kind of War* (Austin, Tex., 1994), using newly released materials, exposes freshly some basic flaws in Johnson's management of the war. Stanley Karnow, *Vietnam: A History*, rev. ed. (New York, 1991), is a spirited, on-the-battlefield recounting. An-

other instructive review is Brian VanDeMark, *Into the Quagmire: Lyndon Johnson and the Escalation of the Vietnam War* (New York, 1991). Henry F. Graff, *The Tuesday Cabinet: Deliberation and Decision on Peace and War Under Lyndon B. Johnson* (Englewood Cliffs, N.J., 1970), presents the administration's rationale for fighting in Vietnam, based on extensive conversations over a period of years with the principal architects of the war. Frank E. Vandiver, *Shadows of Vietnam: Lyndon Johnson's Wars* (College Station, Tex., 1997), is an accounting of LBJ's performance as commander in chief. David M. Barrett, *Uncertain Warriors: Lyndon Johnson and His Vietnam Advisers* (Lawrence, Kans., 1993), aims to disentangle the sources of Johnson's policies. For a contemporaneous evocation of the atmosphere in which Johnson and his chief lieutenants made decisions, there is none better than David Halberstam, *The Best and the Brightest* (New York, 1972).

The role of Johnson's secretary of state in the shaping of the Vietnam War is set forth unemotionally in Dean Rusk's memoir, *As I Saw It* (New York, 1990). The secretary of defense's belated recounting of the failure of the Johnson policies and of how early he knew they were wrong is in Robert S. McNamara, with Brian VanDeMark, *In Retrospect: The Tragedy and Lessons of Vietnam* (New York, 1995). Clark Clifford, with Richard Holbrooke, *Counsel to the President: A Memoir* (New York, 1991), recounts the author's labors as LBJ's second secretary of defense to begin winding down the war. Jack Valenti, *A Very Human President* (New York, 1975), is one of the best of the insiders' accounts, showing Johnson always reaching for lofty goals. Harry McPherson, *A Political Education* (Boston, 1972), is a superior set of recollections by a special assistant and counsel to the president. Joseph A. Califano, Jr., *A Presidential Nation* (New York, 1975), illuminates problems of the presidency as he saw them while serving as presidential assistant for domestic affairs. Califano's *The Triumph and Tragedy of Lyndon Johnson: The White House Years* (New York, 1991) gives an unsurpassed recital of Johnson at work on his legislative agenda. Doris Kearns, *Lyndon Johnson and the American Dream* (New York, 1976), is based on the author's experience as a White House fellow; psychoanalytically oriented, it purports to shed light on LBJ's relations with his mother. A penetrating appraisal of Johnson by his first press secretary is George Reedy, *Lyndon B. Johnson: A Memoir* (New York, 1982). George Christian, the last press secretary, covers sensitively Johnson's final hundred days in office in *The*

President Steps Down: A Personal Memoir of the Transfer of Power (New York, 1970). Eric F. Goldman, *The Tragedy of Lyndon Johnson* (New York, 1969), derives from his experience as "intellectual-in-residence" at the White House and tells persuasively of the changes that overtook Johnson as the war progressed.

Specialized studies on significant aspects of the Johnson years include Kathleen J. Turner, *Lyndon Johnson's Dual War: Vietnam and the Press* (Chicago, 1985), and Bruce E. Altschuler, *LBJ and the Polls* (Gainesville, Fla., 1990). The series on the administrative history of the Johnson White House published by the University of Texas Press contains W. Henry Lambright, *Presidential Management of Science and Technology: The Johnson Presidency* (Austin, Tex., 1985); James E. Anderson and Jared E. Hazleton, *Managing Macroeconomic Policy: The Johnson Presidency* (Austin, Tex., 1986); Neil D. McFeeley, *Appointment of Judges: The Johnson Presidency* (Austin, Tex., 1987); David M. Welborn and Jesse Burkhead, *Intergovernmental Relations in the American Administrative State: The Johnson Presidency* (Austin, Tex., 1989); Paul Y. Hammond, *LBJ and the Presidential Management of Foreign Relations* (Austin, Tex., 1992); and David M. Welborn, *Regulation in the White House: The Johnson Presidency* (Austin, Tex., 1993). William E. Leuchtenburg, *In the Shadow of FDR: From Harry Truman to Ronald Reagan* (Ithaca, N.Y, 1983), brilliantly illuminates LBJ's connection to Roosevelt in chapter 4. A good brief discussion of Johnson's economic policies by a former chairman of the Council of Economic Advisers under Presidents Nixon and Ford is in Herbert Stein, *Presidential Economics: The Making of Economic Policy from Roosevelt to Reagan and Beyond* (New York, 1984).

Only slightly out of date is *Lyndon B. Johnson: A Bibliography*, 2 vols. (Austin, Tex., 1984–1988). Invaluable still is Robert A. Divine, ed., *Exploring the Johnson Years* (Austin, Tex., 1981), which discusses in eight essays by Johnson scholars the available literature on LBJ and the resources of the Johnson Library in Austin.

A variety of finding aids, selected oral history transcripts, and descriptions of available recordings of Johnson's telephone conversations may be found by consulting the home page of the Johnson Library at http://www.lbjlib.utexas.edu.

Recent works include Michael Beschloss, ed., *Reaching for Glory: The Secret Johnson White House Tapes, 1964–1965* (New York, 2001); Robert A. Caro, *Master of the Senate* (New York, 2002), the third of Caro's planned four-volume study *The Years of Lyndon Johnson,* detailing LBJ's rise in the legislative body; Lloyd C. Gardner, *Pay Any Price: Lyndon Johnson and the Wars for Vietnam* (Chicago, 1995); Robert Mann, *The Walls of Jericho: Lyndon Johnson, Hubert Humphrey, Richard Russell, and the Struggle for Civil Rights* (New York, 1996); H. R. McMaster, *Dereliction of Duty: Lyndon Johnson, Robert McNamara, the Joint Chiefs of Staff, and the Lies That Led to Vietnam* (New York, 1997); and Jeff Shesol, *Mutual Contempt: Lyndon Johnson, Robert Kennedy, and the Feud That Defined a Decade* (New York, 1997).

Richard M. Nixon

Richard Matthew Pious

Richard M. Nixon THE LIBRARY OF CONGRESS

O N 9 August 1974, Richard Nixon arose in the White House and, after meeting briefly with the household staff and his cabinet, took a helicopter from the lawn to Andrews Air Force Base, where he boarded a presidential plane for a trip with his family to the West Coast. But this trip was different from all others, for at exactly noon, while Nixon was flying over Jefferson City, Missouri, his chief of staff, Alexander Haig, delivered a letter to Secretary of State Henry Kissinger that read, "Dear Mr. Secretary: I hereby resign the Office of the President of the United States. Sincerely, Richard Nixon." The thirty-seventh president of the United States had become the first in American history to resign the office in disgrace. The tragedy of the Nixon presidency lies not in its politics or policies, or even in its confrontation with Congress and the courts over the extension of presidential prerogatives, but rather in its use of unconstitutional, illegal, and illegitimate means to achieve its ends.

Politics as War

Nixon had always played politics not merely as a game against worthy opponents but as a war against enemies. His first campaign for a congressional seat, in 1946, in California was conducted against Jerry

Voorhis, a five-term Democratic liberal. Nixon linked Voorhis with a left-wing representative from New York City, Vito Marcantonio, and falsely claimed that Voorhis had been endorsed by a political action committee of the Congress of Industrial Organizations (CIO). He won the election and two years later, taking advantge of the California primary law, entered and won both the Democratic and Republican primaries, thus avoiding potential defeat in an election year that favored Democrats. In 1950, Nixon defeated Helen Gahagan Douglas for a California seat in the United States Senate with the same techniques: he linked Douglas to Marcantonio by distributing the infamous "pink sheet," which tied their voting records together.

Nixon propelled himself into national politics through his skills as a tactician. A member of the California delegation to the 1952 Republican National Convention, he convinced the delegates to vote in favor of the "fair play" resolution that settled a dispute over credentials of rival Taft and Eisenhower delegates in favor of Eisenhower, thus ensuring the general the nomination. As a result, Nixon's name appeared on the shortlist of acceptable vice presidential candidates that Eisenhower submitted to a group of Republican leaders at the convention. The group recommended Nixon, because his anti-Communist credentials and tough campaign tactics would complement Eisenhower's political assets and because Nixon would help Republicans in the West.

Nixon took the low road in the presidential campaign, referring to Adlai Stevenson as an appeaser whose election would be welcomed by the Kremlin. In the midst of the campaign it became known that a group of seventy-six southern California businessmen had contributed to a secret fund that paid Nixon $900 per month (a total of $18,168.87 up to that point). Nixon defended himself by misrepresenting the uses to which the money had been put, claiming it was for office expenses only. In a nationwide television address on 23 September 1952, he claimed that he and his wife did not live well and that Pat Nixon did not even own a fur coat like corrupt Democrats but only "a respectable Republican cloth coat." Revealing that someone had given his children another gift, a dog that they had named Checkers, he said defiantly, "Regardless of what they say about it, we're going to keep it." When the so-called Checkers Speech met with overwhelming public approval, Eisenhower realized that he would be better off keeping Nixon on the ticket. At a meeting a few days later,

he announced, "You're my boy." The two were swept into office in November.

The Vice Presidency

Nixon was given no substantial responsibilities as vice president. He presided occasionally over the Senate and chaired the President's Commission on Government Contracts, which dealt with racial discrimination by government contractors, and the Cabinet Committee on Price Stability for Economic Growth, a group with a long title but short reach in the councils of the administration. The extent of Nixon's influence on administration policy can be judged by Eisenhower's answer at a press conference when asked for an example of Nixon's contributions: "If you give me a week, I might think of one."

During Eisenhower's convalescence from a heart attack in 1955, an ileitis attack in 1956, and a stroke in 1957, Nixon handled himself with restraint. The vice president chaired nineteen cabinet sessions and twenty-six meetings of the National Security Council (NSC), but the reins of government were held by the principal White House aides. The Eisenhower-Nixon agreement on succession in the event of presidential disability served as a model for later administrations, as did Nixon's conduct in these situations.

Nixon was an integral part of the White House political operation. He campaigned for Republican members of Congress in 1954 and 1958. He criticized the Democratic-controlled Congresses. He was part of the White House operation that successfully contained Senator Joseph McCarthy attacks on the administration for being soft on Communism and helped devise the strategy that gave McCarthy enough rope to hang himself with his Senate colleagues. Nixon also participated in the negotiations with Senator John Bricker over changes in the Bricker Amendment, a proposal to place limits on the powers of the president to frame treaties and to ensure that treaties are consistent with domestic law. Eventually the amendment failed to pass Congress.

Nixon positioned himself as a moderate "Eisenhower Republican" on most issues, as well as a unifier within his party. A 1958 trip to Latin America during which he braved the wrath of street demonstrators and, a year later, his famous "Kitchen Debate" in Moscow with Premier Nikita Khrushchev of the Soviet Union also boosted his public standing. By late 1959 half the electorate believed he would make as good a president as Eisenhower or better, and most thought he would be better than Truman. Nineteen Gallup polls of Republican rank-and-file voters all ranked him first among contenders for the 1960 Republican presidential nomination.

Nixon won the nomination easily but ran a poor election campaign, allowing his opponent, Senator John F. Kennedy of Massachusetts, to take the offensive on issues, catch up in the polls, and win the first of four televised debates, which subsequent surveys indicated helped contribute to Nixon's subsequent defeat. The recession and Eisenhower's failure to take strong measures to stimulate the economy also contributed to the results. Nixon believed that voting irregularities in Cook County caused him to lose Illinois, but he was statesmanlike enough not to contest the results. Kennedy's popular-vote total was only 118,574 more than Nixon's. In the electoral college, the results were 303–219.

Nixon returned to California and ran for governor in 1962 in a fierce and somewhat underhanded campaign that included a fraudulent "poll," supposedly conducted by a group of Democrats but actually prepared as a form of campaign literature by the Nixon camp. A court injunction put a stop to this "dirty trick," and Nixon lost the election. In a postelection news conference, Nixon concluded a series of self-pitying remarks by observing that the press would not "have Richard Nixon to kick around any more." After his defeat, Nixon moved to New York City, where he joined a large law firm and continued his activity on behalf of Republican candidates in the 1966 congressional campaign. He continued to travel extensively, sharpening his knowledge of world affairs with wide-ranging discussions among leaders of other nations. By 1967, his financial backers, organized as Richard M. Nixon Associates, were raising funds to bankroll another drive for the White House.

The 1968 Presidential Contest

Nixon was one of several viable contenders for the nomination. Moderates supported George Romney and later Nelson Rockefeller, while Ronald Reagan bid for conservative support. Nixon, situated as a centrist, had to dispel notions that he was a loser and then build a coalition consisting of professional party politicians, personal loyalists, and groups from both the moderate and conservative wings of the party. Nixon's tactical skills again brought success. He made a deal with Senator Strom Thurmond of South Carolina, promising the South that he would appoint "strict constructionists" to the federal judiciary, name a southerner to the Supreme Court, oppose court-ordered busing, and pick someone acceptable to the South for the vice presidency. With this deal set, Nixon was able to win much southern conservative support and head off Reagan. A series of successes in primaries dispelled the loser image, and his standing in the preconvention polls indicated he could win the election, thus undercutting Rockefeller's premise that to back Nixon was to concede the election.

The election results put Nixon in the White House, but under inauspicious circumstances. The third-party candidacy of George Wallace left Nixon with only 43 percent of the vote, hardly a popular mandate. Nixon received 31.7 million popular votes (301 electoral votes); Hubert Humphrey, the Democratic candidate, won 30.8 million votes (191 electoral votes); and Wallace's American Independent party drew 9.4 million votes (46 electoral votes). Nixon won what political scientists call a deviating election—that is, one in which the advantage in party identification remains with the party that lost the election. In Congress, Democrats enjoyed a 57-43 advantage in the Senate and a 243-192 advantage in the House, with Republicans picking up just five House seats to go along with their gain of six in the Senate. Nixon would face a Congress controlled by the opposition and could not rely on a party-based legislative strategy. Instead, he would have to put together shifting coalitions: sometimes center-right, linking most Republicans with the southern Democrats to pay off his debts to the South or to support his foreign policies, and sometimes center-left, with moderate Republicans joining liberal Democrats to pass his own version of modern and progressive Republican social welfare, economic, and environmental legislation. At least in domestic affairs, the Nixon presidency promised to be eclectic and unorthodox.

Nixon never improved on this weak political position. His 1972 victory over George McGovern, with 59.7 percent of the vote, provided him with the support of the "Silent Majority" or "Middle America," as he called it, but he did not lead his party to victory. There were no appreciable changes in Democratic advantages in party identification and voter registration. In 1970 midterm elections the Republicans picked up two Senate seats but lost twelve in the House, and Nixon's strident campaign speeches contributed to this disaster, although the president claimed that he had won an "ideological majority" in the Senate. In 1972 the party lost the two Senate seats but regained the twelve in the House. By 1974 the Watergate investigations (see below) left the party in shambles: Republicans lost four Senate seats and forty-nine House seats, and held less than one-third of governorships and state legislative seats. Republicans did not make a comeback until 1978 and 1980.

Domestic Policies

Nixon refused to follow the Eisenhower pattern of consolidating Democratic programs and attempting to run them more efficiently. He was prepared to make major departures, in part to conciliate the South on race; in part to build a new coalition with policies on aid to parochial schools, opposition to abortion, and support for school prayer, all of which would appeal to Roman Catholics; and in part to appeal to his traditional Republican constituencies with attacks on President Lyndon Johnson's Great Society welfare policies.

Race was the most important domestic issue. The Department of Health, Education, and Welfare (HEW) stalled on implementing desegregation of southern school districts until prodded by federal court orders. By 1970 the administration had bowed to the inevitable, with Nixon setting the tone by declaring that legal segregation was inadmissible; almost all of the all-black southern schools were merged into unitary school districts by 1970, and less than 10 percent of black school-children attended all-black schools by that time, a major advance from the preceding administration.

The president remained strongly opposed to court-ordered busing and came out for the concept of the neighborhood school. He proposed that Congress ban court-ordered busing, ordered the Justice Department to oppose busing orders in pending lawsuits, and called for a $1.5 billion program of new federal aid for school districts in the process of dismantling their segregated facilities. These proposals bogged down in Congress, which did pass several measures, sponsored by southern Democrats, to end the use of federal funds for busing.

Nixon's proposed amendments to the Voting Rights Act of 1965, up for renewal in 1970, were tilted toward the South. The president proposed that its provisions be extended to all states so as not to "discriminate" against one region and that voting-rights lawsuits be tried first in state courts, a change that would have diminished the prospects of effective enforcement of the law. A group of Republicans on the House Judiciary Committee scuttled the Nixon draft, and a bipartisan coalition substituted its own extension of the bill, which also included provisions for granting the vote to eighteen-year-olds.

An unusual departure for the Nixon administration was the plan developed by Secretary of Labor George Shultz to provide training and employment openings for minorities on federally funded construction projects. The government, especially Labor Department and HEW officials, began using racial classifications and numerical goals in implementing their desegregation programs—the first example of "affirmative action."

Law and order was another administration priority. Antiwar and civil rights demonstrations and civil disturbances on the campuses and streets created a backlash among the constituencies Nixon was courting. With children of the post-World War II baby boom coming of age, the crime rates soared. The administration responded with the vigorous use of four measures: the Omnibus Crime Control and Safe Streets Act (1968), the Organized Crime Control Act, the Comprehensive Drug Abuse Prevention and Control Act (1970), and the District of Columbia Criminal Procedures Act. Provisions emphasized wiretapping, preventive detention, and other measures that aroused the opposition of civil libertarians. No appreciable dent was made in the crime rate, which was the province of local law enforcement, and a war on illegal drugs also had little success.

Other Nixon initiatives involved attacks on several of the most visible Great Society programs, which Republicans had strongly opposed. In January 1975, Nixon eliminated the Office of Economic Opportunity (OEO), the coordinating agency for the so-called War on Poverty, begun in 1964. The controversial Community Action Program was reorganized, other OEO programs were moved to other departments, and funding for some activities was cut.

The Nixon administration had its own proposals to fight poverty. It rejected two approaches that were being considered at the end of the Johnson administration—nationalizing the existing welfare program or instituting a guaranteed minimum income through a negative income tax—and instead proposed a program of family allowances developed by the Urban Affairs Council under the direction of Daniel Moynihan. The program was eventually defeated in the Senate in 1970 by an unlikely coalition of conservatives and liberals. The administration did succeed in passing a welfare reform measure that gave the national government complete control over welfare programs for the aged, blind, and disabled, and that provided more than $2 billion in additional payments in the welfare programs annually.

Because Nixon was pragmatic in domestic matters, he could be persuaded or pressured into new initiatives. Bar associations, acting in concert to salvage the Legal Services Program from the wreckage of the Great Society, managed in 1972 to get Nixon to lift his veto threat against legislation converting the Legal Services Program into the Legal Services Corporation with a larger budget and an autonomous board of directors, in spite of Nixon's initial decision to curtail the program severely to please his conservative supporters. The Food Stamp Act of 1964 was greatly expanded to provide billions of dollars of purchasing power to the nation's needy, through the efforts of Senator Robert Dole, Republican of Kansas, and a coalition of farm-state senators and urban liberals. Nixon proposed the New Federalism program in response to the pleas of governors and mayors, hard hit by demands for new services and revenue shortfalls caused by recession. Various narrow categorical grants were consolidated into "block grants" to give states more flexibility in programming funds, although by the time Congress finished with the Nixon proposals, the new grants looked suspiciously like the older narrow grants. Congress also passed a Nixon initiative to provide the states and cities with $30 billion in federal revenues over a five-year period. Responding to the demands of environmentalists, Nixon proposed legislation that led to the creation of the Council on Environmental Quality (1969), the Occupational Safety and Health Administration (1970), and the Environmental Protection Agency (1970). New laws provided tougher standards for water and air quality.

Nixon's domestic record was neither liberal nor conservative, but politically pragmatic. His civil rights policies, judicial appointments, and unsuccessful attempts to appoint southerners to the Supreme Court all represented political payoffs to the South. Nominees Clement Haynsworth and G. Harrold Carswell were blocked by a coalition of legislators sensitive to charges by civil rights organizations that these men, while on the federal bench, had either demonstrated opposition to Supreme Court case law protecting the rights of blacks or demonstrated incompetence in applying the law. In spite of well-publicized attacks on some Great Society programs, transfer payments to the poor, the sick, and the elderly increased greatly. Federal expenditures for intergovernmental grants soared. Early in the Nixon presidency, Attorney General John Mitchell, meeting with a group of civil rights leaders, suggested that they "watch what we do, not what we say" in judging the performance of the administration. By that standard, the Nixon presidency must be adjudged innovative and responsive in practice, although it seemed conservative and uncaring in its rhetoric.

"Nixonomics"

Like most presidents, Nixon had little grasp of complex economic issues but a clear understanding of his political stakes in them. At all costs a recession and high unemployment were to be avoided going into the reelection year of 1972.

The president inherited a mess. Johnson had not followed the advice of his economists, and the result was soaring inflation (up to 5 percent in the last quarter of 1968, double the average rate since 1956). Unemployment was low, at 3.3 percent. Given a trade-off between unemployment and inflation, Nixon would accept higher unemployment rates in order to cool down the inflation, provided it would lead to prosperity by 1972.

Early economic policies, set by Treasury Secretary David Kennedy, Under Secretary Paul Volcker, and Labor Secretary George Shultz, called for a relatively tight budget and a moderately restrictive monetary policy by the Federal Reserve Board. A tax bill passed in 1969 incorporated several Nixon initiatives, including a repeal of the investment tax credit and removal of 2 million of the nation's poor from the tax rolls. But by 1970 it was clear that the program was not working. In June of that year the Council of Economic Advisers began issuing "inflation alerts." By July a shortfall in revenues led Nixon to embrace the concept of the "full employment balanced budget," which provided for large deficits if the amount of expenditures did not exceed the revenues that would have been obtained under conditions of full employment. When Nixon submitted his budget to Congress in January 1971, he used this concept to justify a proposed $11.6 billion deficit and even publicly embraced Keynesian economic principles to argue that government expenditures would pull the nation out of recession. For a Republican president, all this was quite unorthodox, as Democrats gleefully pointed out.

With inflation and unemployment both on the rise, Nixon's appointee to chair the Federal Reserve, Arthur Burns, shifted from a tight-money policy. Early in 1971 the president began to criticize unions and management for agreeing to excessive wage increases in the steel industry. Nixon established the Tripartite Committee to monitor union settlements in the construction industry. By late spring, recently appointed Treasury Secretary John Connally was convinced that bold new measures were needed. By early summer the balance of trade had deteriorated so much that a full-scale flight from the dollar ensued. Unemployment was over 6 percent and climbing.

Meetings held at Camp David in mid-August produced agreement on a new economic program. As outlined by Nixon to the nation on 15 August in a nationwide television address, it included the closing of the gold window and the ending of the convertibility of the dollar into gold; actions that amounted to an 8 percent devaluation of the dollar against other major currencies, thus stimulating American exports; a 10 percent surcharge on foreign imports to discourage their consumption; and measures to stimulate the domestic economy, including an end to the excise tax on automobiles, a 10 percent tax credit for business investment, and a speedup in the personal income tax exemption, to be reflected in reduced withholding taxes in workers' paychecks. To counter the inflationary psychology, Nixon announced a ninety-day freeze on wages and prices (under authority granted to him the year before by the Democratic Congress) and the establishment of the Cost-of-Living Council. These measures, dubbed the "Nixon shocks," were taken without any prior consultation with America's allies, which caused severe strains in relations with them. Inflation was halted temporarily and then slowed as a second phase was implemented on 14 November 1971, with creation of the Pay Board and the Price Commission, which could monitor compliance with guidelines for increases in wages and prices.

By the beginning of 1972, with 2 million more people out of work than in 1969, the administration began to stimulate the economy. The budget sent to Congress in January provided for a $25.2 billion deficit. Government agencies accelerated their purchases from businesses. The Federal Reserve Board expanded the money supply by 9 percent in the elec-

tion year, leading to charges (which Burns vehemently denied) that Nixon and Burns had made a deal to ensure Nixon's reelection and Burns's reappointment. By the autumn the economy seemed to be turning around. Inflation remained under control, unemployment was dropping, and the recession had ended. Later the American public would pay the price for these election-year arrangements. Inflationary forces could not long be suppressed by wage and price controls, and when they were lifted, the effects of increased deficits, an expanded money supply, and the rise in oil prices made themselves felt: inflation increased to 8.8 percent in 1973 and 12.2 percent in 1974, beginning a decade of exceptional price instability marked by increasing inflation rates through the end of the Carter presidency.

The Vietnam War

The priorities of the Nixon presidency lay not in domestic social or economic policies—which were simply the means to the end—but in reelection through creation of a majority coalition. What really interested Nixon was statecraft, the application of American power and diplomatic influence to regional and global problems.

The key problem for his presidency clearly would be the Vietnam War. It had driven his predecessor from office, and if it were not resolved in a way that could be turned to political advantage, it would drive him from office as well. Two months after Nixon assumed the presidency, American combat deaths exceeded thirty-six hundred, and there seemed no end in sight. Nixon was in a dilemma, for during the campaign he had said that he had a "secret plan" to end the war but could not divulge it because it might upset the Paris peace negotiations. If his plan involved escalation, Democrats could charge that he was abandoning attempts to reach a peaceful solution and could point to mounting American casualties and prisoners of war. If he negotiated a solution that led to the fall of the government in Saigon, Democrats could charge that he had abandoned an ally. Nixon had to find a way to cut American commitments while preserving the non-Communist government in South Vietnam—at least for a "decent interval" so that the overthrow of the regime could not be blamed on the United States.

Nixon, his national security adviser Henry Kissinger, and Secretary of Defense Melvin Laird settled on an approach with several elements. First, the

Laird policy for "Vietnamization" was adopted. Responsibility for fighting would be turned over to the Vietnamese, in order to reduce American casualties. Gradually American forces would be withdrawn. This would buy time on the home front. Second, a variant of the "madman" approach in international relations would be adopted. The administration would warn the North Vietnamese that unless they settled soon they would be subjected to carpet bombing of cities, mining of harbors, and even the spread of radioactive debris to halt infiltration of the South. Irrigation dikes would be destroyed and forests defoliated. Third, Nixon and Kissinger would apply the principle of "linkage" in dealing with the Soviet Union: the arms and trade agreements to be proposed to the Soviets (see below) would require a quid pro quo— Moscow would have to pressure Hanoi to agree to a settlement.

The Vietnam policy failed. Nixon announced the withdrawal of a half million troops, and by May 1972 no American forces were on combat missions. By January 1973, only twenty-five thousand American troops remained in Vietnam. The level of fatalities and injuries dropped. But the combat effectiveness of the South Vietnamese did not improve. The invasion of Laos by South Vietnamese forces not only was ineffective but turned into a rout, leaving little doubt that they would be no match for the North Vietnamese.

The escalation of the air war also failed. In mid-March 1969 a secret bombing campaign against Cambodia began; it was kept secret from Congress and the American people for two years. The Ho Chi Minh Trail in Laos, which supplied the Communists in the south (Vietcong), was also bombed, and the number of targets in South Vietnam was increased. In the spring of 1970 bombing was renewed over North Vietnam (reversing a halt ordered by President Johnson in 1968) in the industrial complex between Hanoi and Haiphong.

Ground actions were also stepped up. Incursions into Laos doubled in 1969. South Vietnamese and American troops made incursions into Cambodia in April and May 1970 to clear out enemy units and headquarters in the "Parrot's Beak" salient, which was dangerously close to Saigon. The main effect of the intervention was to drive Cambodian Communist units to the west, into the heart of Cambodia, where together with their North Vietnamese allies they prepared for the overthrow of the existing pro-American regime. Not only was this policy un-

successful militarily, but it triggered renewed antiwar protests at home. At a demonstration on 4 May at Kent State University, National Guardsmen killed four protesters. A huge antiwar demonstration was then held in Washington, D.C., between 6 and 9 May, at which Richard Nixon, in the middle of the night, visited the Lincoln Memorial to talk with some of the protesters about college football, campus life, and other trivialities, not reaching their concerns about the war and the direction of American foreign policy.

North Vietnam meanwhile had its own plans. It prepared for a general offensive in 1972, timed to put pressure on the Nixon administration to settle the war on Hanoi's terms prior to the presidential elections. In view of the failure of Vietnamization, neither the Soviet Union nor North Vietnam had any intention of giving to American negotiators in Paris what the South Vietnamese could not win on the battlefield. The linkage tactic would not work.

Nixon fared better in the home-front battle for public opinion. Although there were large antiwar demonstrations, including the November 1969 "March on Washington," the May 1970 Cambodia protests, and the April 1971 "Mobilization Against the War," there was rising support for Nixon's policies. Escalation of the bombing and the withdrawal of American combat forces resulted in a significant increase in presidential-approval ratings.

Peace negotiations dragged on throughout Nixon's first term. Even before entering office, Nixon had passed word to the South Vietnamese that he could probably get better peace terms for them than the Johnson administration. But in 1969 and 1970, each side rejected the other's eight-point peace plan. In November 1971 peace talks were suspended by Washington, and in 1972 each side in turn temporarily suspended its participation in the talks.

Talks resumed on 19 July 1972, and by the end of the summer two things had become clear to the negotiators: American escalation of the bombing could not induce the North Vietnamese to settle for terms that would require their withdrawal from the South, and no pressure from either the Soviet Union or the People's Republic of China could induce the North Vietnamese to settle. But although the North Vietnamese had made major gains with their spring offensive, they had not achieved all their objectives, and they had been dislodged from several of the cities they had taken. Both sides, having played their hands, were now ready for a settlement.

Henry Kissinger and his North Vietnamese counterpart, Foreign Minister Le Duc Tho, reached an agreement on terms on 12 October 1972, and two weeks later Kissinger announced, "Peace is at hand." But when the South Vietnamese objected to the terms (chief of which involved a cease-fire in place, recognition of the territory controlled by each side, and preparation for a political settlement involving sharing of power), Nixon held up the agreement. Instead, he ordered massive bombing of North Vietnam after his reelection. The purpose seems to have been twofold: to convince the North Vietnamese that the United States would not allow the regime in Saigon to be overthrown and to convince the South Vietnamese that secret commitments (made in an exchange of letters between Nixon and President Nguyen Van Thieu) would be honored after American forces withdrew under terms of the proposed agreement. After more negotiations, an agreement was concluded on 27 January 1973, paving the way for an end to American participation in the war and an exchange of prisoners.

Nixon's commitments to Thieu could not be kept. Congress had imposed restrictions on presidential war-making powers in Southeast Asia, beginning in 1970 with the Cooper Amendment, which provided that no combat troops could be sent to Laos or Thailand, followed by the Cooper-Church Amendment (1970), which prohibited the reintroduction of ground forces into Cambodia, and culminating with passage of the Eagleton Amendment, which called for a halt in all American land, sea, and air military operations in Laos, Cambodia, and Vietnam after 15 August 1973. Any attempt by Nixon or his successors to use American armed forces to guarantee the survival of the Saigon regime would be illegal. Moreover, the War Powers Resolution, passed by Congress over Nixon's veto in 1973, required any American president to obtain congressional approval within sixty days for any military action; this presented yet another problem in shoring up the South Vietnamese government. The Nixon commitments to Thieu were therefore not honored by the Ford administration in 1975, which resulted in the reunification of North and South Vietnam under Communist rule.

The China Card

Vietnam was the great failure, and China the great success, of Nixon's diplomacy. He recognized the advantages that could accrue to the United States by exploiting the Sino-Soviet rift. Peking might put pressure on Hanoi to settle the Vietnam War, while American-Soviet relations might also be affected if Americans and Chinese achieved a détente. During his bid for the presidency Nixon argued, in an article published in the journal *Foreign Affairs* (October 1967), that "we simply cannot afford to leave China forever outside the family of nations, there to nurture its fantasies, cherish its hates, and threaten its neighbors. There is no place on this small planet for a billion of its potentially most able people to live in angry isolation." These comments were surprising, coming from a politician who had made a career of attacking as "soft on Communism" any American political leader who dared to suggest similar ideas.

Hostilities broke out in March 1969 between Soviet and Chinese troops along the Ussuri River, giving Nixon his chance to pursue a diplomatic opening. The first step, recommended by the National Security Council (NSC) and the State Department, was to lift travel and trade restrictions. Then, on visits to President Yahya Khan of Pakistan and General Secretary Nicolae Ceauşescu of Romania, Nixon hinted that he would like better relations with China. By 1970, Walter Stoessel, the American ambassador to Poland, was meeting with Chinese diplomats in Warsaw. In April 1971, signs of a thaw between the two powers became public knowledge, as an American table-tennis team was invited to play in China and was received by Premier Chou En-lai. Later a Chinese team was sent to the United States as part of this "Ping-Pong diplomacy." By the end of April the Chinese indicated privately they would receive a high-ranking emissary from Washington, and Nixon decided to send Henry Kissinger in secret to make arrangements for a summit meeting. On 2 August, Secretary of State Rogers said that the United States would withdraw its opposition to the seating of Communist China in the United Nations, which occurred in October 1971; but the United States resisted the expulsion of Taiwan unsuccessfully. During the summer Nixon announced that he would visit China early in 1972, and Kissinger was then sent to Beijing for another trip. Kissinger and Chou negotiated the outline of a statement dealing with the outstanding issues dividing the two nations.

Nixon's visit to China, which began 21 February 1972, was a field day for the news media. The Chinese permitted American television crews to set up modern studio and transmitting facilities. For ten days the world press followed Nixon as he spoke with Chinese leaders and toured the country. Meanwhile, Kissinger and Deputy Foreign Minister Chiao Kuan-hua continued work on the statement that was to be issued by the two sides at the conclusion of the visit.

The final document, known as the Shanghai Communiqué, summarized points on which the two nations could agree. One point was that there was only one China and that Taiwan was part of China. Another was that the Taiwan issue must be settled peacefully by the Chinese. A third was that the United States was committed to "the ultimate objective of the withdrawal of all U.S. forces and military installations from Taiwan" in the context of a peaceful resolution of the Taiwan issue.

Each of these points contained some ambiguity. The communiqué did not mention which government, the Communist one on the mainland or the Nationalist one on Taiwan, was the legitimate government of "one China." Neither did it mention American treaty commitments to the government on Taiwan. It did not specify a timetable for withdrawal of American forces from Taiwan but only committed the United States to the objective of withdrawal and linked it to a peaceful settlement. Nevertheless, the agreement was the beginning of a new era in Sino-American relations. Trade, tourism and cultural contacts increased.

The new relationship did little to help American diplomacy in other matters. The Chinese were unwilling or unable to bring pressure to bear on Hanoi. The China opening may have convinced the Soviets to negotiate an arms agreement, but it is more likely that it convinced them that a plot to encircle them could be countered only by a massive military build-up. Soviet shifting of forces to the East did bring about an advantage to the allies of the North Atlantic Treaty Organization (NATO) for a brief time until the effects of the Soviet buildup in conventional arms were felt.

Détente with the Soviet Union

Extrication from Vietnam and the opening to China were two strategies of Nixon's statecraft designed to produce a more favorable balance of power in the East. In the West, a policy of political and military détente with the Soviet Union, coupled with expanded East-West trade, formed the cornerstone of Nixon's diplomacy.

Prior to entering the White House, Nixon had been identified with the hard-line anti-Communist politics of the Republican right because of his confrontations with Soviet leaders while vice president and his role in the Alger Hiss case. (Nixon, as a first-term member of Congress, had pursued an investigation of a former State Department employee, Alger Hiss, which had resulted in Hiss's conviction on a perjury charge.) But Nixon had been part of an administration in the 1950s that had negotiated an end to the war in Korea, participated in the accord that led to the withdrawal of Soviet occupation forces from Austria, held summits with Soviet leaders, and proposed major arms-limitation initiatives. Nixon had seen firsthand the political advantages of summit conferences in the Eisenhower administration, as well as observing the worldwide acclaim given to President Kennedy for negotiating the Nuclear Test Ban Treaty of 1963. From the first days of his administration, the major goat of his diplomacy was to conclude an arms-limitation agreement with the Soviet Union, to be capped by a successful summit conference. The enticement was to be the prospect of increased trade; pressure was to come from the Soviet fear of a successful American opening to China.

The first moves toward détente were made by Chancellor Willy Brandt of West Germany. His *Ostpolitik* led to the Moscow Treaty of 1970, in which Bonn recognized the territorial adjustments of World War II and renounced German territorial claims in the East. By April 1971, Soviet General Secretary Leonid Brezhnev, in a speech to the Communist Party Congress, signaled Soviet interest in an arms control agreement. Further negotiations by the West Germans culminated in a treaty between East and West Germany, signed in December 1972.

American arms negotiations with the Soviets were formally conducted in Helsinki, Finland, where Ambassador Gerard Smith, head of the Arms Control and Disarmament Agency (ACDA), led the American delegation. But the real negotiations were conducted between Henry Kissinger, national security adviser and chairman of the NSC's Verification Panel, and Soviet Ambassador to the United States Anatoly Dobrynin. Kissinger, rather than the Central Intelligence Agency (CIA), was responsible for intelligence estimates and the reports reaching the president about Soviet capabilities and intentions in the arms race. These reports painted a grim picture of rapid Soviet escalation, which was not always shared by other agencies, particularly the State Department, the CIA, and the ACDA.

In May 1971, Kissinger and Dobrynin reached preliminary agreement. In the summer they agreed that a summit conference could take place in the spring of 1972. At the Moscow summit, Nixon and Kissinger conducted the crucial negotiations. No representatives from other agencies were allowed in the negotiating rooms, and even the translators were supplied by the Soviets, thus freezing out Secretary of State William P. Rogers, ACDA director Smith, and Secretary of Defense Melvin Laird.

The first set of strategic arms limitation talks (SALT I) agreements, concluded in Moscow in 1972, limited the deployment of antiballistic missile (ABM) defenses to two sites, one of which would be the capital of each nation. This was advantageous for the United States, since the Soviets were considerably ahead in the development and deployment of ABM systems. An interim agreement, to last five years, placed a limit on the number of missiles (referred to as launchers) that each side could deploy. The United States was limited to 1,710 missile launchers, which at the time consisted of 1,054 land-based and 656 sea-based missiles. The Soviets were limited to 2,328 missile launchers; at the time the agreement went into effect, these included 1,607 land-based and 740 sea-based missiles.

The numerical disparity favoring the Soviets had several factors. American rockets were considered more accurate, and more of them were equipped (or soon would be equipped) with "multiple independently targeted reentry vehicles" (MIRVs), or warheads that could be targeted with great accuracy on several different sites. The Soviets had bigger warheads and more powerful rockets but were behind in accuracy and had not yet deployed the MIRV missiles they had been developing. The agreement left the United States with 3,500 war-heads and the Soviets with 2,350 warheads.

In several respects the agreement was not very advantageous to the United States. For one thing, it dealt with the quantity but not the quality of launchers or warheads. Each side could equip its missiles with MIRVs and improve their accuracy, a situation that would have a destabilizing effect as each side moved closer to a first-strike capability in the late 1970s. The agreement did provide that neither side would substitute heavy for light launchers (which would increase the payloads) but did not define terms. The Soviets deployed the SS-19, a heavy launcher, in silos designed for the SS-11, an action that led some commentators in America to charge that they were violating the agreement. These charges, in turn, would make it impossible for the

Carter administration to secure Senate approval of the SALT II agreement.

The American side made several other concessions to obtain the agreement. Although the Soviets had 42 operational submarines for sea-launched missiles, of which a number were obsolete, the agreement set the number on the Soviet side at 48, which would allow them to finish construction of 6 additional vessels without violating the accord. Moreover, under one of the terms, the Soviets could build additional launchers, up to a maximum of 950 launchers for 62 submarines, provided they dismantled as many as 210 of their land launchers. The United States would be permitted to substitute sea launchers for its 54 obsolete Titan missiles. Kissinger, defending these terms, argued that unless an agreement had been reached, the Soviets would have constructed more than 80 submarines with as many as 600 additional missiles. Critics argued that this overstated Soviet capabilities and that the Soviets could not have built more submarines or sea-launched missiles than the agreement permitted, so in effect there was no real arms limitation for the Soviets in the accord.

Finally, the American side gave up its option to convert the obsolete Titans into 3 new submarines, in return for a Soviet agreement to count 30 missiles on their H-class submarines that had not until then been included in their ceilings. The Soviets also agreed to dismantle some of their obsolete ICBMs at the beginning of the agreement and wait until the end before taking advantage of their option to increase their total number of launchers to the ceilings permitted. During the life of the agreement, the Soviets modernized their forces, gained a much more effective sea-launching capability, and improved the accuracy of their MIRVs, but so did the United States. By the end of the first five years, the United States would have 9,000 warheads, and the Soviets, 4,000.

Along with the SALT I accords, Nixon and Kissinger negotiated a major grain deal (with financial credits) at the summit. The secrecy surrounding the negotiations enabled grain dealers to buy large amounts of grain early in the spring from American farmers at depressed prices and then reap windfall profits from their inventories when the Soviet Union entered the grain markets late in 1972. These purchases were followed by a rise in food prices, which in turn contributed to an increase in the cost of living. In the years following, however, American farmers benefited from rising grain prices and exports.

The Moscow summit also produced a memorandum on "Basic Principles of U.S.-Soviet Relations."

The two governments agreed to work for the peaceful resolution of disputes and the reduction of tensions in various areas. There is little evidence that either side paid much attention to them when formulating its approach to regional conflicts. The Soviet resupply of Egypt and Syria during the Mideast war of 1973, the American nuclear alert and resupply of Israel, and successful attempts to freeze out the Soviets from Mideast peace negotiations indicate the limited utility of détente in dealing with regional crises.

The final product of détente was the agreement to hold a conference on European security the following year at Helsinki. Two years of talks there eventually resulted in various agreements between the Warsaw Pact and NATO groupings, most of which would ratify the status quo in Europe. But it also produced the accords on human rights, which the Soviets may have intended as a sop to the West but which became a standard by which public opinion judged repressive regimes all over the world.

The Nixon statecraft had a profound effect on the American military establishment. Withdrawal from the Vietnam quagmire would provide the opportunity to modernize the forces, upgrade the caliber of the men and women serving, and reorient the military toward new missions. The administration went ahead with a new generation of strategic submarines (the Trident program) and increased funding for strategic forces by 15 percent the year after SALT I was concluded. But it also reduced the size of the armed forces from 3.5 million to 2.3 million, withdrew units from several Asian nations, cut the army from nineteen to thirteen divisions and the marines from four to three divisions, ended the draft, and reduced the number of ships in the navy and wings in the air force. The military was ordered to prepare for one major war and one minor war, rather than for two major wars and one minor war, as in the Kennedy and Johnson years.

Prerogatives and Power

Having won a deviating election without the support of an electoral majority and confronted with a Congress controlled by the opposition party, Nixon could not rely on either party leadership or public consensus and support to control domestic and foreign policymaking. He was fairly popular, by historical standards, during his first term and had a surge of popularity in the last year, based on the improved performance of the economy, the reduced role of

American forces in Vietnam, the China summit, and the Moscow summit. Even so, his reelection produced a dramatic personal victory in the context of a failure to make gains against the Democratic party in Congress and the states. Nixon's personal political successes, therefore, would not, and probably could not, be translated into domination of Congress. He would have to control the reins of government almost solely by using his constitutional prerogatives and his own often peculiar interpretation of his responsibilities under the laws of the land.

At times Nixon simply ignored laws. The Federal Comparability Act, for example, required the president to submit a plan for a pay increase for government employees. Nixon refused to submit a plan to Congress during his wage freeze, an act ruled illegal by a federal court of appeals in *National Treasury Employees Union* v. *Nixon* (1974). A law passed in 1972 required the administration to submit the texts of executive agreements negotiated with foreign governments to Congress within sixty days. The law was sometimes circumvented by negotiating at a lower diplomatic level and calling the results "arrangements." Sometimes agreements would be submitted well after the sixty-day deadline. By law, domestic wiretapping requires a judicial warrant, a procedure explicitly upheld by the Supreme Court in *United States* v. *United States District Court* in 1972. The Nixon administration violated the law, which led to federal court decisions that Nixon and other officials were liable for damages in the illegal wiretapping of a National Security Council staff member, in *Halperin* v. *Kissinger* (1976).

Nixon tried to control the bureaucracy with several unconstitutional or illegal ploys. He appointed Howard Phillips as acting director of the OEO, bypassing Senate confirmation, later ruled illegal in *Williams* v. *Phillips* (1973). Phillips issued orders to dismantle the entire agency, based on Nixon's budget requests for the next fiscal year, which provided no funds for OEO. The orders disregarded legislation providing for the continuation of OEO and assumed that a presidential budget request to Congress should take precedence over laws and appropriations. A federal district court ruled these orders illegal in *Local 2677, American Federation of Government Employees* v. *Phillips* (1973).

The Nixon administration impounded funds appropriated for various agencies by Congress, either by delaying outlays or else by rescinding an agency's authority entirely. This power was used as a form of "item veto" to eliminate programs. By 1973, impoundments totaled $18 billion and were justified by Nixon as part of his program of economic stabilization. The problem for the administration was that it did not have any legal authority to make such drastic impoundments. Eventually most of them were ruled illegal by federal district courts and by the Supreme Court in *Train* v. *New York* (1974).

Nixon also refused to fill some offices provided for by law. He sent no nominations to the Senate for the National Advisory Council on Indian Education or for deputy commissioner of Indian education, in an attempt to destroy a program legislated by Congress. Eventually a federal court ordered him to fill the positions and implement the program.

Like other presidents facing hostile congressional majorities, Nixon made free use of the veto threat to force compromises on pending bills. As a result, he was only a little less successful in dealing with Congress, as measured by legislative support for his own initiatives or passage of measures favored by the White House, than were his immediate predecessors. Nixon submitted fewer measures than Kennedy or Johnson, and his successes are best measured not by passage of what he proposed but rather by his ability to block or modify initiatives he opposed. Nixon vetoed twenty-four measures and was overridden only five times, employing these powers more often, but with less success, than his Democratic predecessors.

Nixon also made greater use of the pocket veto. This allows a president to kill a bill sent to him by Congress within ten days of its adjournment, by refusing to sign it or return it. Unlike a regular veto, a pocket veto is final; the bill is not returned to Congress and cannot be passed into law by a two-thirds vote of each chamber. Nixon used the pocket veto sixteen times. He used it during routine short adjournments of Congress when it went on vacation, rather than at the end of a session, as originally intended by the Constitution. His veto of the family practice of medicine bill during a short Christmas break led to a district court decision that overturned the misuse of the pocket veto in *Kennedy* v. *Sampson* (1973). Subsequent presidents have agreed that the pocket veto will be used only at the end of the second session of Congress, though President George Bush briefly revived Nixon's expansive approach.

The Backlash Against Nixon's Prerogatives

Nixon's actions inevitably provoked a strong response. First the federal courts forced Nixon to comply with the Constitution and the laws. Then Congress had its turn. The Budget and Impoundment Act of 1974 set new terms for presidential impoundments. The president would have to propose deferrals, which would go into effect unless either house, by simple resolution, disapproved of his plan, in which case the funds would be spent. Rescissions would be submitted by the president in the form of a legislative measure, which would have to be approved by both houses and signed into law before going into effect.

Congress expanded its use of the legislative veto, a mechanism that permits Congress, by simple resolution of one house or concurrent resolution of both houses, to block an action taken, or proposed to be taken, by the president or some other administration official. Laws may even provide that a committee majority, committee chair, or designated employee of Congress can exercise such a veto over the actions of an official of the executive branch. Legislative vetoes were rarely inserted into laws prior to the Nixon administration. Most involved minor matters; housekeeping items; or matters that Congress did not wish to control, such as reorganization of the bureaucracy, pay for federal employees, or certain tariff decisions.

During the Nixon years Congress more than doubled the number of legislative vetoes. It applied them to important issues: arms sales, transfers of nuclear technology, deferrals of appropriated funds. The most significant provision involved the War Powers Act of 1973. Passed over Nixon's veto, it provided that the president could use the armed forces only pursuant to a declaration of war or other congressional authorization, to repel an attack on the United States, its possessions, or its armed forces. If the president sent troops into hostilities or into a situation in which hostilities were imminent, he was obliged to report this fact to Congress within forty-eight hours.

The key provision of the act was legislative veto over the presidential direction of the armed forces. Once the president issued his first report, he would have sixty days in which to use the military. At the end of that time, unless Congress had authorized continued use of the armed forces, the president would have thirty days to complete their withdrawal.

(If continuation were authorized, he would subsequently report on the use of the armed forces every six months while they were engaged in hostilities.) At any time after the first report was issued, Congress could, by concurrent resolution (not subject to presidential veto), direct that the forces be withdrawn in thirty days.

The legislative veto provision could force the president to withdraw at any time. Unless Congress affirmatively gave its approval, the sixty-day provision would automatically require the president to effect a withdrawal. A president sending troops into hostilities would not only have to avoid the legislative veto at the outset; he also would have to win congressional support within sixty days to pursue his goals.

Nixon denounced the law as an unconstitutional infringement on his powers as commander in chief, a position reaffirmed by all of his successors. Subsequently Ford and Carter acted in ways that minimized the effect of the act. In 1983 the Supreme Court, in *Chadha* v. *Immigration and Naturalization Service*, declared the legislative veto to be a violation of the principle of the separation of powers. Thus, a decade after Nixon left the White House, a Supreme Court dominated by his appointees managed to eliminate many of the checks that had been placed on presidential prerogatives.

Dirty Tricks

Reasonable people might agree or disagree with Nixon's domestic and foreign policies, and in most respects these policies were pragmatic and reasoned responses to the problems facing the nation. The expansive interpretation of constitutional prerogatives was not without precedent either; great presidents—Washington, Jackson, Lincoln, Wilson, Franklin D. Roosevelt, and Truman—had also expanded their powers and minimized legislative authority. Such constitutional trench warfare was part of the political game and could be refereed by the courts and the voters.

But the Nixon presidency had a darker side, a cancer eating away at its legitimacy and the bonds of trust and faith between rulers and ruled. Nixon did not play politics; he practiced war.

What President Ford later referred to as "our long national nightmare" was not a few isolated incidents relating to the 1972 reelection campaign. Rather it was an integral part of the White House political operation from the very first days of Nixon's presidency. The White House in 1969 compiled an "enemies list" containing the names of two hundred people it viewed as political opponents, including politicians, actors, university presidents, and other well-known figures. There was a "shortlist" targeted for immediate political retribution. Background investigations were conducted by White House operatives to find "dirt" that could be leaked to newspapers. Targets of these investigations included Senator Edward Kennedy of Massachusetts and Democratic Speaker of the House Carl Albert. At a meeting of White House staffers on 7 September 1972, Nixon went so far as to order one or two "spies" to be included in the Secret Service detail assigned to Edward Kennedy, believing that if they got lucky and could catch him with a woman companion, it would "ruin him for '76." (There is no evidence that the order was ever carried out.)

The White House used government agencies to harass its opponents. The special services staff of the Internal Revenue Service (IRS) was ordered to conduct audits of organizations opposed to Nixon's policies, and did so until the practice was discontinued by Treasury Secretary George Shultz. The CIA's Special Operations Group conducted "Operation Chaos," which involved spying on New Left and black militant organizations. The Secret Service files on persons who are threats to the president ordinarily include deranged people who threaten the president's life, but during the Nixon administration the files ballooned to forty-seven thousand names, including political opponents. On 28 May 1971, Nixon ordered chief of staff H. R. Haldeman to use wiretaps against leading Democrats, including Kennedy, Edmund S. Muskie, and Hubert Humphrey. "Keep after 'em," he told Haldeman. "Maybe we can get a scandal on any, any of the leading Democrats."

The Federal Bureau of Investigation (FBI), acting on presidential orders, wiretapped people without obtaining judicial warrants, including people in sensitive government positions. Kissinger himself ordered taps placed on staffers he thought were leaking classified information to the press. Then other officials ordered taps on each other, as factions within the White House attempted to discredit others. Attorney General John Mitchell had the FBI tap John Sears, his competitor as campaign adviser to the president. Alexander Haig ordered a tap on speechwriter William Safire. The Joint Chiefs of Staff used a navy ensign assigned to the NSC's communications section to spy on Henry Kissinger, who had his own tap on a defense department official close to Secretary of Defense Laird. Taps placed on Morton Halperin and Anthony Lake were used to gather information on the Muskie candidacy, since these former NSC officials were advisers to his campaign. Altogether seventeen FBI taps on government officials or newsmen were uncovered: seven on NSC staffers, three on White House aides, one on a Defense Department official, two on State Department officials, and four on newsmen.

The White House Special Investigations Unit, directed by Egil Krogh and David Young, hired a group of "Plumbers" to conduct special assignments. Howard Hunt, one of their operatives, conducted an investigation of Edward Kennedy, hoping to obtain damaging information about the accident at Chappaquiddick in which Kennedy drove his car off a bridge and a young female passenger drowned. Hunt also forged State Department cables to make it appear that President Kennedy had been directly involved in the assassination of President Diem of South Vietnam in 1963, and attempted to peddle them to *Life* magazine.

Hunt also organized an operation, ordered by John Ehrlichman, a presidential aide, to obtain damaging information on Daniel Ellsberg, a critic of the Vietnam War. In June 1971, Ellsberg had given the *New York Times* copies of a history of the Vietnam War that had been commissioned by the Pentagon. The "Pentagon Papers" related to the Eisenhower, Kennedy, and Johnson years, but Kissinger persuaded Nixon that the credibility of American statecraft was at stake; other nations would not trust the United States to keep its secrets or protect its allies. He argued that publication of the papers must be stopped. The government won a temporary injunction in federal district court against the Times, barring further publication—the first time such an order had been issued in American history—but other papers then printed their copies. The ban was lifted and in the Pentagon Papers case the Supreme Court rejected the use of a preliminary injunction as a violation of the First Amendment.

Ellsberg was targeted for retribution. The Plumbers believed, on the basis of a wiretap of his conversations with Morton Halperin, that Ellsberg used drugs and had an unorthodox sex life. They then burglarized the offices of his psychiatrist, Dr. Lewis Fielding, to obtain confidential transcripts or notes of their conversations. Ehrlichman decided that no more of these operations would be conducted, and shortly

thereafter the Plumbers unit was disbanded, although other operations continued.

The Resignation of Vice President Agnew

A scandal was brewing in the summer of 1973, involving Vice President Spiro T. Agnew. The United States Attorney's Office in Baltimore, Maryland, was investigating allegations that Agnew, while Baltimore County executive in 1966, had solicited payoffs from contractors doing county business and that as governor of Maryland and later as vice president he had accepted kickbacks from engineers whose firms had received state contracts, even accepting several $2,000 payments in the Executive Office Building next to the White House.

On 31 July, Agnew's lawyers were handed a letter written by George Beall, United States attorney for Baltimore, informing him that he was under investigation for conspiracy, extortion, and bribery. At a meeting with Attorney General Elliot Richardson, Agnew denied all the charges, and on 6 August, as the story broke in the newspapers, he released a statement saying, "I am innocent of any wrongdoing."

Although Nixon called Agnew into the Oval Office and assured him of his support, the White House chief of staff, Alexander Haig, immediately dropped over to Agnew's office after that conference and suggested to the vice president that if he were indicted he should consider how it would affect his performance as vice president—a not so subtle hint to consider resignation. The White House defended Agnew's conduct as vice president but made no mention of what he might have done in Maryland, a significant omission. Meanwhile, Richardson and Assistant Attorney General Henry Petersen pressed the case, while the Baltimore prosecutors found a key witness—the person who had taken the bribes and stored them for Agnew—willing to talk. Nixon backed Richardson and Petersen and kept his distance from Agnew. He refused to allow Agnew's lawyers to work with his own to plan a joint strategy involving presidential claims of executive privilege. His statements of support for Agnew were unenthusiastic.

In September, Agnew began to plea-bargain with the prosecutors, but negotiations dragged on for more than a month as he sought a deal that would not involve any admission on his part of wrongdoing. He tried desperately to get out of the corner: he made an issue of leaks to the press by the prosecutors; he had a 20 September meeting with Nixon, trying to get the president to put pressure on Richardson to agree to a compromise; he asked the House to impeach him so that Congress could conduct an investigation, believing that the courts would have to stand aside while an impeachment inquiry was taking place. But all these maneuvers failed. White House aides refused to pressure Richardson, and the Democratic majority in the House refused to impeach Agnew until judicial proceedings had run their course.

The delay was not to Agnew's advantage. He antagonized Nixon by attacking the Justice Department. His standing in the polls was dropping, a sure sign that he was a political liability. An exhaustive investigation of his finances was completed by the Internal Revenue Service, and the prosecutors now had details about his personal life that conceivably could prove embarrassing if they were revealed. Between 5 and 9 October, Agnew's lawyers and justice department lawyers cut a deal, which on 8 October was agreed to by a federal judge.

Part of the bargain involved Agnew's resignation from office. On 9 October he composed a letter to President Nixon and a formal letter of resignation and took both to the president personally. The resignation was effective the following day at 2:00 P.M., just as the former vice president entered the federal courtroom to plead nolo contendere to the charges, which the judge immediately explained was the technical equivalent of a guilty plea. Then Attorney General Richardson read a lengthy statement into the record outlining the government's evidence against Agnew, which concluded with a plea for leniency (part of the bargain worked out the day before). The judge thereupon decided not to sentence Agnew to jail, pending good behavior for the next three years. He did fine Agnew $10,000 for income tax evasion.

With Agnew out of the way, the president nominated the House minority leader, Gerald Ford, to be vice president, a decision received by Congress with great enthusiasm and strong bipartisan support. With the resignation and succession crises resolved, attention once again turned to the long-simmering Watergate crisis.

Watergate

On 17 June 1972 five burglars were arrested in the Democratic party headquarters in the Watergate apartment and office complex in Washington.

The burglary was the culmination of a series of political dirty tricks that had commenced in the fall of 1971. The White House arranged for operatives to disrupt the primary campaigns of presidential hopefuls Senator Edmund Muskie of Maine and Senator George McGovern of South Dakota. They stole documents, planted false news stories, sent out forged letters on campaign stationery, and spied on campaign headquarters. These activities were approved by Attorney General John Mitchell, chief of staff H. R. Haldeman, and presidential counsel John Dean.

Mitchell and Dean also approved a plan drafted by one of the Plumbers, G. Gordon Liddy, for an operation to break into, and wiretap, the headquarters of the Democratic National Committee. Liddy was given $83,000 in cash from the Committee for the Re-Election of the President (CREEP) for the operation. On Memorial Day weekend, a group broke into the Watergate to search for information and plant the wiretaps. A second break-in, on 17 June, to replace a faulty tap, ended with the arrest of the five burglars who had been hired for the job.

By 20 June, Nixon had been informed of the ties between the arrested burglars and the White House and discussed the matter with Mitchell and Haldeman. On 23 June, Mitchell and Dean recommended to Haldeman, who then recommended to Nixon, that the CIA be used to obstruct the investigation of the burglary by the FBI. Nixon agreed that the CIA should let the FBI know that the investigation involved a national security matter. The president had become implicated in a cover-up and conspiracy to obstruct justice. The CIA refused to carry out the presidential directive, and the FBI investigation moved forward.

The White House then used campaign donations to buy the silence of the arrested burglars, as well as the organizers of the operation, Liddy and Hunt, both of whom had been arrested by the FBI. White House aides perjured themselves in the initial phases of the investigation by arguing that Hunt and Liddy had been hired by CREEP only to provide physical security for the Nixon campaign. Mitchell and his deputy, Jeb Stuart Magruder, lied to a federal grand jury, which then limited its indictments to the burglars Liddy and Hunt without making any further connection to the White House. The incident was

Richard Nixon (far right) is accompanied by Gerald Ford, Betty Ford, and Pat Nixon on the south lawn of the White House on 9 August 1974, the final day of Nixon's presidency. UPI/CORBIS-BETTMANN

contained through the election, which Nixon won in a landslide, gaining 60.7 percent of the popular vote and 520 of 538 electoral votes.

Early in 1973 the dam broke. In January the seven Watergate defendants went on trial. Federal Judge John Sirica postponed sentencing after they were found guilty. Prosecutors urged them to tell the truth before sentencing. During the next two months, stories of illegal campaign contributions surfaced, as well as indications of dirty tricks by various government agencies. On 23 March, Nixon met with Dean to discuss continued payoffs to the burglars. Soon thereafter Dean decided to disclose White House involvement to Justice Department prosecutors.

Nixon then fired Haldeman, Ehrlichman, Dean, and Mitchell (formally accepting their resignations) and claimed that he had known nothing of the initial crimes or their cover-up, although he would take "full responsibility" for Watergate. His new attorney general, Elliot Richardson, was given authority to appoint a special prosecutor. In March he selected Archibald Cox, a Harvard law professor, to head the investigation, and issued guidelines promising the prosecutor full autonomy in pursuing the case.

In May the Senate Select Committee on Presidential Campaign Activities (known as the Ervin Committee after its chair, Senator Sam Ervin of North Carolina) began its nationally televised hearings. Between 25 and 29 June, John Dean testified, claiming that the president had been involved in the Watergate cover-up. But his testimony could not be corroborated, and it was conceivable that he was merely trying to save himself. Then, in July, Alexander Butterfield, a former White House assistant, revealed that the president had used a taping system to record all conversations in the Oval Office. Dean's charges could thus be proved or disproved.

From that point on, the key issue was access to the tapes. President Nixon refused to release them to the Ervin Committee, the special prosecutor, or the press, claiming "executive privilege," the right to maintain the confidentiality of presidential conversations. The Ervin Committee lost a federal court case seeking access to the tapes. The special prosecutor, acting on behalf of the federal grand jury investigating Watergate crimes, also sought access to the tapes and rejected a compromise whereby Nixon would provide only a summary transcript. When Cox rejected this compromise, Nixon ordered Attorney General Richardson to fire Cox. Richardson refused and resigned. The same order was issued to Deputy Attorney General William Ruckelshaus, who was fired when he refused to obey it. Finally, Solicitor General Robert Bork was named acting attorney general, and on 20 October he carried out Nixon's order and fired Cox. The firing was subsequently ruled an illegal violation of Justice Department procedures by a federal district court in *Nader* v. *Bork* (1973). These resignations and firings, known in the press as the Saturday Night Massacre, led to the first calls, in the media and in Congress, for the impeachment inquiry.

Attempting to salvage his position, Nixon was forced to agree to the appointment of another special prosecutor and to an agreement concluded with congressional leaders that he would not fire the prosecutor without their concurrence. Leon Jaworski, a distinguished Texas attorney and former president of the American Bar Association, was chosen. By March 1974, former Attorney General John Mitchell and seven former White House aides, including Haldeman, Ehrlichman, and Dean, had been indicted on charges of conspiracy and obstruction of justice. The president was also named an unindicted coconspirator, although this was kept secret in the hope that he would agree to give up the tapes.

In April the special prosecutor and the House Judiciary Committee, which was beginning an impeachment inquiry, issued subpoenas for the White House tapes. Nixon, on national television, announced that he would release transcripts of most, but not all, of the tapes requested. The transcripts provided damning evidence of the cover-up activities in the White House, but there was still no direct evidence that Nixon himself either ordered the Watergate crimes or attempted to obstruct the investigation—the "smoking gun" that Republican defenders of the president on the Judiciary Committee demanded to see. In district court Judge Sirica upheld Jaworski's subpoena. The president refused to comply, and the special prosecutor then appealed to the Supreme Court.

The final act in the Watergate drama had two scenes, one played before the Supreme Court and the other played on the nation's television screens as the members of the House Judiciary Committee considered the issue of impeachment. A Democratic-controlled committee would be "trying" a Republican president at the bar of public opinion. Its actions must not be, or seem to be, partisan or vindictive. Yet it had no conclusive evidence that Nixon had committed or conspired in criminal activities. The fact that his aides had done so would provide shaky grounds for impeachment.

The Constitution provides that a president is to be impeached for committing "high crimes and misdemeanors" but does not define these offenses. During the impeachment trial of Andrew Johnson in 1868, Democrats argued that the offense must be an indictable crime; Republicans broadened the definition to include abuse of power and failure to execute the laws and the Constitution. But in 1974, Republicans, including the president, opted for the narrow definition, while Democrats argued that the broader definition would be correct.

The Judiciary Committee, denied access to the tapes by Nixon, could not prove that he had committed an indictable crime, although it did have tapes in which Nixon and Dean had discussed the possibility of bribing the burglars to ensure their silence. Beginning 9 May 1974, the committee heard testimony behind closed doors for eleven weeks, during which Chairman Peter Rodino of New Jersey and staff director John Doar presented the members of the committee with a pattern of misuse of presidential power. Most members were prepared to recommend the impeachment of Nixon for abuse of power, but a group of diehard Republicans still demanded evidence of indictable crimes. In late July the committee held televised hearings so that its members could explain their reasoning to the public.

On 27 July 1974, the Judiciary Committee voted to approve the first article of impeachment, which centered on the burglary and cover-up. On 29 July it approved a second article condemning the abuse of power that involved sensitive government agencies such as the IRS, FBI, and CIA. The next day a final article, condemning Nixon for failure to comply with a subpoena to give evidence to the committee, was also approved. The next step would be for the committee to report its findings to the full House.

Meanwhile, at the Supreme Court, Special Prosecutor Jaworski had pleaded for access to the sixty-four tapes withheld by Nixon on the grounds of executive privilege. On 24 July, in a unanimous decision, the Court held, in *United States* v. *Nixon*, that executive privilege was something to be defined by the courts, not the president. In the absence of a valid claim of national security, executive privilege could not be used to withhold evidence from a grand jury about possible criminal actions. Nixon would be forced to turn over the tapes. On 5 August (after the House Committee had voted to recommend three articles of impeachment), he released the tapes to Jaworski. These contained the conversation of 23 June 1972, in which Nixon had discussed the plan to use the CIA to head off the FBI's investigation of the burglary.

It was now clear to the nation that Nixon had known about the burglary's connection to the White House and had attempted to use federal agencies to obstruct justice in a criminal matter. Nixon had violated the law and committed an indictable offense. The smoking gun had finally been found. Nixon now had only two options: he could fight a losing battle against an impeachment vote in the House and drag the nation through a trial in the Senate, or he could resign. After consulting with his closest aides and Senate Republican leaders, he chose to resign. On 8 September his successor, Gerald Ford, pardoned Nixon for all crimes he may have committed during his term of office, blocking any subsequent inquiry into his conduct in the Watergate affair, but Nixon did have to pay back taxes of $467,000 for taking improper deductions on his income tax returns.

The Nixon Legacy

On the morning of his resignation, as Nixon spoke to White House staffers and cabinet secretaries in the East Room of the White House, he cautioned those assembled about giving in to a hatred for those opponents who had brought him down. "Always remember," he admonished, "others may hate you, but those who hate you don't win unless you hate them, and then you destroy yourself." Nixon learned that lesson only after he had destroyed his own presidency. But his observation about hatred is important to remember when attempting an objective and fair assessment of the Nixon years.

His immediate place in history, of course, reflected the feelings of the Watergate era. He resigned office with the lowest public approval rates of any president since polls had begun to be taken. In all the surveys of historians, presidential scholars, and the public since, his administration has ranked at or near the bottom, down with Harding, Grant, Andrew Johnson, and Buchanan.

Nixon pursued innovative policies. Yet an opening to China and détente with the Soviets would certainly have been proposed by other presidents—possibly earlier than the 1970s—if Nixon and the political forces he represented had not fought these initiatives so strongly in prior decades. His constitutional confrontations with Congress were counterproductive and unnecessary, and his assertions of power were checked by the courts. Congress later placed new restrictions on many presidential prerogatives, and the little gain Nixon made in controlling policy was more than offset by new restrictions on authority delegated to the executive branch by Congress. In the aftermath of Nixon's administration, President Ford referred to the "imperial presidency" of the Nixon years as having been transformed into the "imperiled presidency" of the post-Watergate era. Reports both of the swollen powers of the presidency and of its sudden shrinkage were greatly exaggerated. Viewed from the present perspective, it is difficult to conclude that the disruptions of the Nixon years caused permanent damage to the presidency.

The real legacy of the Nixon administration was the introduction of a paranoid style of politics that viewed the struggle for power as a form of warfare against enemies. It countenanced the use of dirty tactics on a scale and magnitude not previously accepted (if one excludes the excesses of local party organizations), especially since these operations were run directly out of the White House and involved the domestic and national security agencies.

The public revelations about Watergate contributed to the steep decline of public confidence in political institutions. Subsequent presidents entered office with lower rates of public approval, suffered steeper declines, and bottomed out at levels approaching Nixon's lows.

The Nixon administration opened the "gates": Lancegate, involving President Carter's OMB director; Koreagate, involving the bribery of members of Congress; Debategate, dealing with the transfer of Carter White House documents to the Reagan camp prior to the national debates between the two presidential contenders in 1980; and Contragate, dealing with an illegal diversion of funds from an arms sale to Iran, in order to aid the Nicaraguan Contras in 1986. In each case the Washington press corps treated the scandal as another Watergate; in each case a beleaguered administration handled matters ineptly, attempting to minimize the issue and contain it. In each incident new revelations and leaks whetted the appetite of the press for more, until eventually heads rolled and reputations were ruined. With each event, confidence in presidents and their aides diminished, and the impression grew that "they all do it." The presentation of scandal and corruption—whether serious or frivolous—had become a major media industry.

A jaded Washington community might even be prepared for a resurrection of the Nixon presidency. A revisionist interpretation would focus on Nixon's policies and applaud his constitutional struggles with Congress, seeing them as a prescient understanding of how obsolete the American system of separated institutions checking and balancing each other had become. It would minimize the dirty tricks, placing them in the context of abuses committed by other presidents. It would see Nixon as a tragic figure, too preoccupied by matters of state to pay attention to the well-meaning transgressions of his aides and too loyal to them to protect his own presidency. His would be the sin of loyalty to his men. In short, it would follow the general lines of Nixon's own subsequent defense of his conduct. But it would be wrong.

After his resignation Nixon attempted to restore his reputation as a statesman. From his home in Park Ridge, New Jersey, he wrote his memoirs and six more books, most of them best-sellers, including several volumes on foreign affairs. Of these, the most influential were *Real Peace* (1983), which focused on relations with the Soviet Union and defended his own approach to détente, and *In the Arena* (1991), which summed up the meaning of his life in politics and lauded those who entered the arena to struggle for their beliefs rather than those who stayed on the sidelines or shied from conflict. He was treated respectfully and even admiringly as an elder statesman on his visits to the United Kingdom, France, China, Russia, and more than a score of other nations.

Nixon's friends raised $21 million to build the Richard Nixon Library and Birthplace at Yorba Linda, California, with Nixon himself contributing $2 million. The library, built entirely with private funds, contains exhibits about the Nixon presidency, but the Nixon papers themselves are kept by the National Archives in its own warehouse. The former president sued to keep 150,000 pages of papers away from presidential scholars.

Nixon suffered a massive stroke in April 1994 and was taken to New York Hospital-Cornell Medical Center. According to his living will, he asked for no extraordinary life support measures. He died at 9:08 P.M., 22 April 1994. In a televised ceremony attended by dignitaries and notables from all over the world, President Bill Clinton expressed the sentiments of much of the nation, particularly editorialists and columnists from the media that Nixon had always despised, when he chose to dwell on Nixon's great positive accomplishments rather than focusing on his unprecedented constitutional crimes.

BIBLIOGRAPHY

Useful general biographies include Stephen E. Ambrose, *Nixon*, 3 vols. (New York, 1987–1991); Roger Morris, *Richard Milhous Nixon: The Rise of an American Politician* (New York, 1990); and Herbert S. Parmet, *Richard Nixon and His America* (Boston, 1990). Irwin F. Gellman, *The Contender: Richard Nixon, the Congress Years, 1946–1952* (New York, 1999), offers an exhaustive account of Nixon's years in the legislature and his controversial election campaigns. Richard M. Nixon, *R. N.: The Memoirs of Richard Nixon*, 2 vols. (New York, 1978), is a sketchy, ambiguous, and incomplete defense of the Nixon presidency; and *Leaders* (New York, 1982), Nixon's reflections on conversations with world leaders such as Churchill and de Gaulle, gives some indication of his own style of leadership.

William Safire, *Before the Fall: An Inside View of the Pre-Watergate White House* (Garden City, N.Y., 1975), discusses Nixon's foreign and domestic policies from the vantage point of a key speechwriter. John Ehrlichman, *Witness to Power: The Nixon Years* (New York, 1982), a gossipy account of the personalities in the Nixon White House, gives a good sense of the level of intellect of Nixon's key aides, as does H. R. Haldeman, with Joseph DiMona, *The Ends of Power* (New York, 1978). *The Haldeman Diaries: Inside the Nixon White House*, (New York, 1994), also available on CD-ROM, provides a day-by-day account of White House operations. Allen J. Matusow, *Nixon's Economy: Booms, Busts, Dollars, and Votes*

(Lawrence, Kans., 1998), discusses the economic policies of the administration and links them to the 1972 election cycle.

Henry Kissinger, *The White House Years* (Boston, 1979) and *Years of Upheaval* (Boston, 1982), give by far the best analysis of Nixon's statecraft, although they also constitute a defense of Kissinger's performance as a presidential assistant. Seymour M. Hersh, *The Price of Power: Kissinger in the Nixon White House* (New York, 1983), is an almost point-by-point refutation of Nixon's and Kissinger's memoirs based on interviews with hundreds of Nixon administration officials, designed to show the political and personal considerations that went into their foreign policy decisions. Larry Berman, *No Peace, No Honor: Nixon, Kissinger, and Betrayal in Vietnam* (New York, 2001), describes the ultimate consequences of Nixon's policies in Vietnam. William P. Bundy, a former Johnson administration official, offers his assessment of Nixon's foreign policy legacy in *A Tangled Web: The Making of Foreign Policy in the Nixon Administration* (New York, 1998).

J. Anthony Lukas, *Nightmare: The Underside of the Nixon Years* (New York, 1976), exposes the dirty tricks of the Nixon presidency. Elizabeth Drew, *Washington Journal: The Events of 1973–1974* (New York, 1975), is the most perceptive and readable of the Watergate narratives. *The Presidential Transcripts* (New York, 1974), transcripts of edited tapes released by the Nixon White House on 30 April 1974, provide conversations between Nixon and his key White House aides, as well as commentary putting them in perspective by the staff of the *Washington Post*. Arthur M. Schlesinger, Jr., *The Imperial Presidency* (Boston, 1973), attempts to place the Nixon and Johnson presidencies in the context of an emerging imperial presidency. Stanley Kutler, ed., *Abuse of Power: The New Nixon Tapes* (New York, 1997) provides transcripts of Nixon's White House tapes.

James L. Sundquist, *The Decline and Resurgence of Congress* (Washington, D.C., 1981), is a study of presidential-congressional conflict during the Nixon administration and how many of these conflicts were resolved in succeeding administrations. Eleanora W. Schoenebaum, ed., *Profiles of an Era: The Nixon-Ford Years* (New York, 1979), is a reference work containing 450 biographies of key figures in the Nixon administration. See also Gerald S. Strober and Deborah H. Strober, *Nixon: An Oral History of His Presidency* (New York, 1994). Another useful effort to put Nixon in the context of political science theories of presidential power is contained in Michael A. Genovese, *The Nixon Presidency: Power and Politics in Turbulent Times* (New York, 1990).

Recent works include Richard Reeves, *President Nixon: Alone in the White House* (New York, 2001), which draws on extensive archival research and interviews to produce a complex portrait of the complex president. Monica Crowley, *Nixon Off the Record* (New York, 1996) and *Nixon in Winter* (New York, 1998), provide a unique trove of Nixon's thoughts on a wide variety of political and personal subjects, written by a foreign policy research assistant of his during his final years. See also Anthony Summers, with Robbyn Swan, *The Arrogance of Power: The Secret World of Richard Nixon* (New York, 2000).

The Social History
of the Presidency

After the British burned the original collection of the Library of Congress during their 1814 invasion of Washington, D.C., Thomas Jefferson sold his beloved personal library to the government to replace it. AP/WIDE WORLD

The earliest published image of the White House appeared on the cover of an 1807 travel guide, and shows the temporary wooden porch and steps that preceded the stone platform of the north entrance. AP/WIDE WORLD

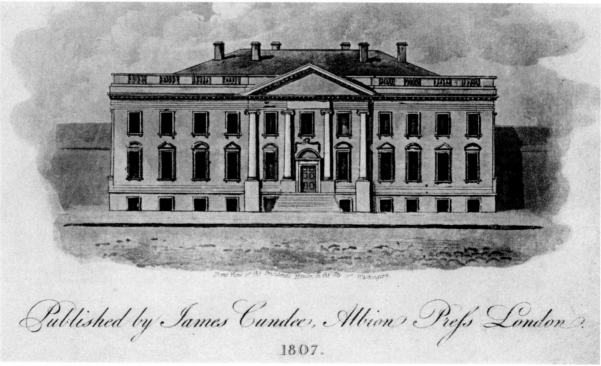

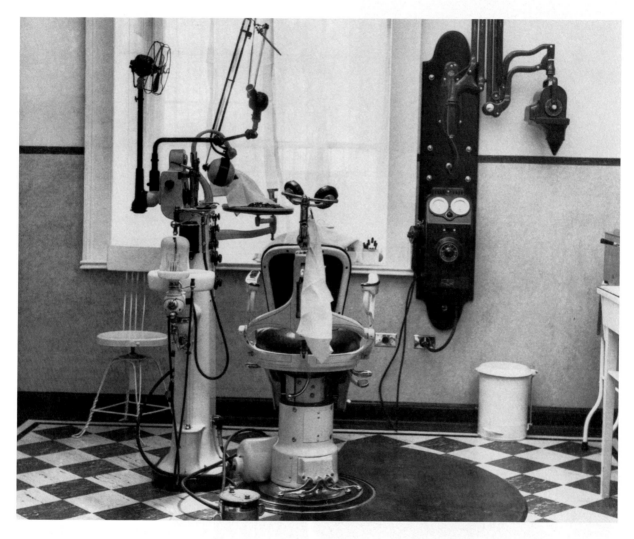

TOP
*Facilities within the White House afford presidents
time-saving convenience. Above is the White House
dental clinic in the 1940s, used by Harry Truman.*
CORBIS

TOP

*An annual White House
event takes place each spring
when youngsters participate
in the Easter egg roll on the
South Lawn.*

AP/WIDE WORLD

BOTTOM

*It is customary for every
presidential couple to add
to the White House china
collection. Here, Mamie
Eisenhower poses in the
China Room in 1959.*

BETTMANN/CORBIS

TOP

On 9 November 2000, former presidents and first ladies joined President and Mrs. Clinton to celebrate the White House bicentennial. Standing from left: Presidents George Bush, Bill Clinton, Gerald R. Ford, and Jimmy Carter. Seated from left: Barbara Bush, Lady Bird Johnson, Hillary Clinton, Betty Ford, and Rosalynn Carter. Nancy Reagan did not attend because of President Ronald Reagan's illness.
REUTERS NEW MEDIA, INC./CORBIS

BOTTOM

The National Christmas tree stands illuminated on the Ellipse near the White House, December 2001. Lighting the tree has become an annual tradition for the First Family, and the 2001 tree reflected the surge of patriotism in the wake of the 11 September attacks on the United States. AP/WIDE WORLD

Gerald R. Ford

Herbert S. Parmet

Gerald R. Ford THE LIBRARY OF CONGRESS

AT noon on 9 August 1974, the day on which President Nixon resigned, everyone in the East Room of the White House rose as Chief Justice Warren Burger entered. Then came Vice President and Mrs. Gerald Ford. She held the Bible, opened to the Book of Proverbs, as Ford placed his right hand on it and was sworn in as the thirty-eighth president of the United States. He told the audience that "our long national nightmare is over. Our Constitution works. Our great Republic is a Government of laws and not of men." Then he urged, "Let us restore the golden rule to our political process, and let brotherly love purge our hearts of suspicion and of hate." Three days later, the new president addressed a joint session of the

Congress and said, I do not want a honeymoon with you. I want a good marriage." He stressed opposition to "unwarranted cuts in national defense" and gave the control of inflation as his first priority. His foreign policy would be a continuation of Nixon's: working toward a cease-fire in Vietnam and a negotiated settlement in Laos, détente with the Soviet Union, and continuation of the "new relationship" with the People's Republic of China. Addressing himself directly to the ethics of government, he promised no "illegal tapings, eavesdropping, buggings, or break-ins by my Administration."

Ford was the first president of the United States to reach the White House by way of the Twenty-fifth

Amendment. He thereby became more a designated, rather than an "accidental," president. Even at the moment of his nomination, mounting revelations about the Watergate scandal had made his ultimate rise to the presidency a distinct possibility. In naming him to replace Spiro Agnew, Nixon had little choice other than to heed the advice of the Democratic leadership that the former House minority leader was the only Republican they would agree to confirm. Ford was simply not viewed as a potent candidate for the presidential nomination in 1976. His elevation made him, in effect, the first congressional president. Contrary to the expectations of its sponsors, the Twenty-fifth Amendment created a presidency that considerably reduced the distance between Capitol Hill and the White House. Ford had not been in office very long before the amendment's implications became obvious. A Ford speechwriter, Robert Hartmann, later wrote that Congress "will never knowingly select the strongest possible Presidential prospect as their opposition. They will pick, at best, someone they see as a competent caretaker until the next election." Ron Nessen, Ford's second press secretary, observed that no other president was routinely described as " 'acting presidential' instead of simply *being* president." Ford never fully recovered from that burden.

Early Career

Jerry Ford's career had always exemplified the Sam Rayburn dictum that "the best way to get along is to go along." As Charles W. Colson told Seymour Hersh, "Nixon knew that Ford was a team player and understood how to work with a wink and a nod." His rise had obviously more to do with availability than with ability. He was the perennial good guy, a product of traditional American midwestern conservatism. That included all the exhortations upholding virtue, patriotism, and individualism, as well as old prejudices against government spending. Jerald ter-Horst, the newspaperman who became Ford's first presidential press secretary, has written that if Ford "saw a school kid in front of the White House who needed clothing, he'd give him the shirt off of his back, literally. Then he'd go right in the White House and veto a school-lunch bill."

Ford's own beginnings were in the best Horatio Alger tradition. Born Leslie King, Jr., in Omaha, Nebraska, on 14 July 1913, he became Gerald Rudolph Ford, Jr., when his divorced mother married a Grand Rapids, Michigan, paint salesman who legally adopted the boy. His athletic abilities at the University of Michigan helped him reach Yale Law School, where he finished in the top third of his class. "He's not dumb," one of his teachers, Eugene Rostow, later recalled. "He got high grades and he coached the freshman football team on the side." His athletic career continued in the navy during World War II, when, after indoctrination at Annapolis, he became director of physical training on a ship that joined the Third Fleet in the South Pacific. He saw combat during many naval engagements and almost lost his life when a typhoon struck the area on 18 December 1944, killing eight hundred men.

Along with many war veterans, the young lawyer became involved in local politics. Even before the war, his own internationalism had led him to work for the nomination of Wendell Willkie in 1940. His continuation of that position inevitably led to support for President Harry S. Truman's programs for European recovery. Nor did he have any doubts about the need to block Soviet expansionism. A conservative who liked to consider himself a centrist, he first won elective office in a 1948 primary contest by defeating a veteran Republican congressman by 23,632 to 14,341. In that overwhelmingly Republican district, he had little trouble against his Democratic opponent that November.

His ambition was to become Speaker of the House, and he seemed to rise toward that quickly, more rapidly, in fact, than Republican progress toward obtaining a congressional majority. Ideologically, he was flexible, more concerned with winning, although he did manage to wind up backing Dwight D. Eisenhower for the Republican nomination in 1952. Making friends as he went along, he also made progress on Capitol Hill, and that included a senior spot on the Appropriations Committee. He joined the "Young Turks" against the continued leadership of Congressman Charles Halleck by becoming chairman of the House Republican Conference during the Eighty-eighth Congress. His prime qualification was that he had made few enemies and was compatible with all elements in the House. That positioned him for the final assault against Halleck, the Hoosier conservative. On 4 January 1965, the Republicans caucused and chose Ford as their new minority leader by a vote of 73–67. As vice president under Nixon, he demonstrated his loyalty and began to hedge only when the Watergate defenses became shaky. His swearing-in as president was accompanied by a national feeling of relief. It was, as Ford put it, "a time to heal."

The First Month

For a while, the new president managed to convince Americans that he could salvage what was best from the past. Ford liked to boast that he had many rivals but no enemies, and this was the most telling mark of his strength. Not only would he keep intact the domestic and foreign policy staffs of the preceding administration—including, of course, Henry Kissinger—but Alexander Haig, who had virtually run the government during Nixon's final days, would remain for the duration as chief of the White House staff. At the same time, the contrast between Ford and his predecessor was emphasized by the creation of a "good old Jerry" image. And Betty Ford, unlike the more reticent Pat Nixon, quickly began to receive a major share of media attention. She became known as an independent, urbane, and sophisticated personality, an image that caught the public's fancy. Indeed, that August was characterized by a collective sense of relief: the American people were eager to admire the human qualities of their first unelected chief executive.

Just about the only discord came from the Republican party's right wing. First, there was Ford's disclosure on 19 August 1974, at a Chicago convention of the Veterans of Foreign Wars, that he would institute a conditional amnesty program for young men who had been draft evaders or military deserters during the Vietnam War. He followed that announcement the next day by nominating Governor Nelson Rockefeller of New York as the second man to fill the vice presidency under the provisions of the Twenty-fifth Amendment. The New Yorker had long been anathema to the party's conservatives. Many disliked him as the prime symbol of the wealthy "eastern establishment." Although his policies as governor had shifted to the right in recent years, he was still associated with liberal attitudes on such issues as social services and civil rights. A nightmarish prospect was the specter of Ford stepping down after 1976 to make way for "Rocky." His presence accelerated the rebellion from what Kevin Phillips called the "new right." Ford quickly attempted to allay such horrors by saying he would probably seek the nomination for himself. As one who could hardly avoid conflict-of-interest involvement, the multimillionaire New Yorker was subjected to lengthy and in-

tense scrutiny instead of a pro forma proceeding. Not until December was Rockefeller confirmed.

Ford was making the most of his presidential honeymoon. By late August, a Gallup poll commissioned by the New York Times showed that 71 percent of the American people approved of his performance. Perhaps even more significant was the fact that only 3 percent had unfavorable impressions. The ratings were significant not only for Ford but for the Republican party as well. The midterm elections were hardly more than two months away. How badly would the voters punish GOP candidates for Watergate? Although not yet perceived, there were already hints of what was to come.

The Nixon Pardon

During Ford's first press conference, correspondent Helen Thomas, asking the opening question, wanted to know whether Ford agreed with Rockefeller that Richard Nixon should have immunity from prosecution. In retrospect, it seems surprising that more significance was not given to the new president's response: he expressed the "hope that our former President, who brought peace to millions, would find it for himself," words received as coming from a healer wanting to avoid controversy. Nevertheless, just before the conference ended, he refused to rule out the possibility that he might grant a pardon even before a trial could take place. That, too, seemed reasonable: he wanted to avoid saying anything that might impede the legal process. *Newsweek* magazine soon reported that 58 percent of the American people polled in its survey opposed any special immunity for Nixon.

Without any advance warning, Ford announced an unconditional pardon for Nixon on Sunday morning, 8 September. That one stroke destroyed the credibility of Ford's presidency. One immediate result was the resignation of Jerald terHorst as press secretary. (TerHorst was replaced by television newsman Nessen.) Overnight, according to a Gallup poll commissioned by the New York Times, Ford's level of popular approval dropped from 71 percent to 50 percent. It was virtually impossible to convince the public that the pardon had not resulted from a secret, if not corrupt, deal. Not only did public opinion surveys reflect powerful anger about pardoning Nixon before he could even be indicted but, by Ford's own admission, there were only seven hundred favorable letters among the four thousand received by the White House within the next few days. The Ford honeymoon was over.

In October, Ford himself testified before the House Judiciary Subcommittee on Criminal Justice in what may have been an unprecedented presidential visit to Capitol Hill. The televised hearing, chaired by Congressman William Hungate of Missouri, was clearly his forum for taking his case to the American people. Ford revealed that the matter had been discussed with General Haig before the resignation but denied that he had made any commitment. "I want to assure you, members of this subcommittee, members of Congress, and the American people, there was no deal, period, under no circumstances," he exclaimed at one point, pounding on the table. "I wanted to do all I could to shift our attentions from the pursuit of a fallen President to the pursuit of the urgent needs of a rising nation," he explained. Nixon, he held, had already paid a sufficient price, and his poor health had been another consideration. And, furthermore, the nation could ill afford a legal circus that might go on for several years. It was time to leave all that behind and go on with the nation's business.

Serious questions have been raised about Ford's denial of a "deal" or "understanding." There is no doubt about the attention given to the pardon option both before and after Nixon's resignation, with Alexander Haig in charge of the arrangements. Ford was a central figure in helping to derail the inquiry by Congressman Wright Patman into the connection between the money found on the Watergate burglars and the Committee for the Re-Election of the President (CREEP).

"Nixon had Ford totally under his thumb," Alexander P. Butterfield, a former Nixon White House appointments secretary, told Seymour Hersh. But Ford held out before he would deliver: he wanted, as Hersh reports, "some concessions from Nixon on the relocation of his papers and tape recordings." Some White House aides also pressed for an act of contrition from Nixon as a prerequisite to a pardon. Hersh also reported that Nixon, impatient and concerned that the understanding would collapse, telephoned Ford on the night of 7 September to warn that he would make public a claim that he had been promised the pardon in exchange for relinquishing the presidency. The new president made his announcement the following morning. The arrangement also involved giving Nixon custody of the papers and tapes, which would be housed in a gov-

ernment storage facility near San Clemente, California.

In what was a masterful example of bad timing, Ford announced the specifics of his amnesty proposal for Vietnam draft evaders only eight days later. Evaders who wanted vindication would have to swear allegiance and perform some low-paid alternate service. Comparisons with the Nixon pardon were inevitable. The discredited ex-president had gotten off scot-free; he had not even been compelled to admit his guilt. A more conservative view was expressed by Barry Goldwater, who charged that Ford's amnesty plan was a "step that is like throwing mud in the faces of the millions of men who had served this country."

Congress, Inflation, and Energy

Rather abruptly, it seemed, Republicans faced the first post-Watergate congressional elections without their newfound buoyancy. Instead of confidence that the past would be safely forgotten, the failure of their credibility loomed as a major problem. With few weeks remaining before November, it hardly seemed possible for the White House to rejuvenate itself by stemming the serious inflation, but nevertheless, that became the major target during the fall of 1974.

All indicators were discouraging: inflation was still in the double digits, unemployment was rising, and the gross national product was in decline. The auto industry was laying off tens of thousands of employees. During Ford's first month in office, the Dow-Jones Industrial Average dropped ninety-nine points, and it fell another fifty in the week after the Nixon pardon. Nations heavily dependent on oil, including the United States, were still reeling from the impact of the Organization of Petroleum Exporting Countries' (OPEC) control of the market. Nixon's proposed "Project Independence," which aimed at making the United States self-sufficient in the production of energy, had never gotten beyond the public relations stage, and prospects of much forward movement were gradually reduced when the supply of fuel returned to more nearly normal levels. A new strategy for coping with the energy situation suddenly seemed less urgent.

Ford's response to the economic difficulties evoked more ridicule than respect. On 8 October he went before the Congress with a program to combat inflation. He proposed a tight lid of $300 billion on the federal budget. To absorb excess purchasing power, he asked for a $5 billion surtax on corporations and on individuals in the higher income brackets. But the centerpiece was a "Whip Inflation Now" plan. Ford introduced it by the acronym *WIN* and said, "There is one point on which all advisers have agreed: We must whip inflation right now."

Ford thought inflation could be whipped by the simultaneous efforts of little people to inhibit pressure on prices. He advised volunteers in the WIN program to "take all you want but eat all you take." Each family should also make a one-hour "trash inventory" to find waste. Within little more than a week after he had introduced the idea, 101,420 citizens announced themselves as recruits by mailing WIN enlistment papers to the White House. By the end of the year, that number had doubled. Some 12 million WIN buttons were in production. All good intentions notwithstanding, the program was soon viewed as more of a public relations gimmick than a serious assault against inflation.

Ford did not have an easy time on Capitol Hill. The heavily Democratic Congress largely disregarded the Ford incumbency. Ford's tax surcharge went nowhere. Congressmen sensitive to Greek-American constituents persistently opposed his desire to continue military aid to Turkey in the face of Turkey's recent use of American arms to invade Cyprus. Ford's veto of a veterans' education bill was easily overridden. Despite another veto threat, Congress passed a bill regulating strip-mining, which Ford managed to pocket veto; the Congress had no opportunity to undo the president's action. Before the second session of the Ninety-third Congress came to an end, Ford had suffered more setbacks on Capitol Hill than any president since Harry Truman (with whom Ford liked to compare himself). In his first three months, he vetoed more bills than had Nixon in eighteen. Furthermore, according to the *Congressional Quarterly*, Ford won only 58.2 percent of the congressional votes on which he took a position, the lowest level of support for any first-year president since that publication had begun keeping records twenty-two years earlier.

The atmosphere created by continued inflation, economic malaise, impotence in the White House, and the uncertainty of what price the GOP would have to pay for Watergate led Democrats to call for the election of a "veto-proof" Congress in the 1974 elections. The real damage to the administration was in the House, where Democrats picked up 43 seats (plus 5 more in special elections) to bring their commanding total up to 291 seats in the Ninety-fourth Congress. A more emphatic result was the ability of the Democrats to take most of their new seats by winning districts with entrenched Republican incumbents. They also won Senate victories in four states and a fifth seat in a special election. Even more disturbing for the Republicans was their performance in the South, where, reversing the trend of recent years, they lost 10 House seats while winning only 2. Also contrary to prevailing perceptions of party growth, Republicans fared poorly in the suburbs. While Democrats fell short of achieving anything resembling the simplistic idea of a veto-proof Congress, the setback to Ford and his party was a dramatic reminder of the great distance to recovery. The locus of power was sufficiently removed from the White House to create a deadlock between Ford and the Ninety-fourth Congress. No issue was more central to this progress, and nothing else had as many implications for both the domestic economy and foreign policy, than energy.

For a year and a half, reaching well back into the Nixon administration, a three-point program had expressed administration policy: developing domestic energy resources, limiting domestic energy consumption, and forging "effective consumer-nation unity." None of the platitudes or vows implicit in something like Project Independence had yet been translated into action. There could not be much optimism when the nation was led by a "congressional president" and a legislature torn between regional and vested interests.

Unlike the crisis that began in 1973 with the oil embargo, the new situation stemmed from a glut on the market. No success had come from efforts to convince OPEC that high oil prices could wreck the international financial system and trigger a global economic recession. Instead, Libya, Kuwait, and Venezuela responded by curtailing output prices, and the Saudi oil minister, Sheik Ahmed Zaki Yamani, revealed that his government, which alone was responsible for 60 percent of OPEC's production, was raising its prices. The implications of the latest manifestation of OPEC's power hardly differed from its use of the embargo, and the situation was fraught with all the dangers of economic nationalism. The latest hard-line response from Washington sounded like brinkmanship and provoked speculation about a desperate resort to military action. In the United States, expressions of frustration inevitably yielded to the realization that the only reasonable alternative was reduced dependence on foreign oil.

But that was more easily said than done. It was easy to find agreement in principle for the notion of belt-tightening, but where would the burden fall most heavily? Further complicating the establishment of any consensus was the widespread suspicion that the major oil companies either had had a hand in creating the situation or were using the crisis to bolster their own profits. Calls for deregulation of petroleum products so that prices could be raised, further exploration of new domestic oil sources could be encouraged, and existing supplies could be conserved only brought more skepticism about motivations. The era that immediately followed the Vietnam War and the Watergate scandals was not the easiest time for a president of the United States to dispel doubts.

Ford's circumstances complicated the effort. First, his February proclamation to increase import fees on petroleum to $3 a barrel over a three-month period required a presidential veto when Congress passed a bill barring the imposition of the new taxes for ninety days. The veto stood, but that was less important than the spectacle of challenges flying back and forth between 1600 Pennsylvania Avenue and Capitol Hill. They became especially shrill when Ford coupled his energy proposals with criticism of congressional failure to act responsibly. The Democratic Senate majority whip, Robert Byrd of West Virginia, struck back by attacking the president's political legitimacy. "After all," said Byrd, "he doesn't have a national constituency, and his is an inherited Presidency, and it's unique in this regard. It doesn't have the national support that it should have."

It readily became clear that the Democrats themselves could not agree on what should be done. Obviously, there was no consensus on issues that pitted one region against the other; furthermore, as the *Congressional Quarterly* pointed out, "divided producer and consumer states had set oil, gas, coal, nuclear and hydroelectric advocates against each other." Others placed the blame squarely upon the White House for failing to provide national leadership. Congress later turned down two Ford proposals for phasing out the federal ceilings on the price of most domestic oil, and the president, in turn, vetoed bills that would have extended the life of those controls past 31 August 1975.

Finally, in December, Ford signaled the end of the debate by signing the Energy Policy and Conservation Act. "The measure was a compromise," Ford has written, "but half a loaf was better than none,

and I decided to sign it." In doing so, Ford swallowed much of what he did not want, including a forty-month period to phase out government price controls on domestic oil and rolling back the price of domestic crude by about 12 percent per barrel. But Frank Zarb, who had replaced John Sawhill as "energy czar," felt it retained sufficient merits to be considered a start toward adoption of a federal energy policy.

That first session of the Ninety-fourth Congress was most notable for a series of confrontations between the administration and the legislature that had mixed results and was largely characterized by stalemate. The Democrats insisted on tax cuts accompanied by programs that they viewed as socially desirable and as potential stimulants for the economy: housing construction subsidies and make-work programs for the unemployed. Ford, repeatedly placing himself in the position of appearing indifferent about mitigating the plight of those who were most helpless, insisted that fighting inflation was the greater priority. This led to his veto of a Democratic bill to create more than a million jobs. Despite an unemployment rate of 9.2 percent, his veto was sustained. Finally, Ford had to make a mild retreat by agreeing on a modified jobs program. He later presented his own package for cutting taxes but linked it to a program for an equivalent reduction in spending.

Irritating some of his own people, especially Defense Secretary James R. Schlesinger, Ford went along with a defense appropriations bill that fell short of the Pentagon's original request by about $7 billion. In March, Ford retreated from his requested anti-inflationary tax increase and accepted a package proposed by the Democrats for a reduction retroactive to the start of 1975. Instead of emerging from the congressional session with a $16 billion one-shot tax rebate to counter the worsening recession, he had to be satisfied with a $22.8 billion tax reduction.

In all, during that session, the president vetoed seventeen bills. The Congress, despite the numerical advantage, was able to override only four. Underlining the philosophical differences between Ford and the Democrats, the overturned vetoes included such social welfare measures as health care funds, appropriations for education, and money for school lunches. The country had neither strong presidential leadership nor viable "Congressional government," which had been the hope of Democrats on Capitol Hill. Speaker Carl Albert finally conceded that Congress would be unable to enact "programs and policies that will return us to full employment, economic prosperity and durable social peace and progress."

What had begun with so much hope after Nixon's resignation yielded to frustration and hard times. Monthly unemployment figures continued to climb, reaching a peak of 9.2 percent by May. The twin forces of inflation and layoffs among such a large portion of the work force added up to the most discouraging figures for the economy since World War II.

The New York City Crisis

Adding to the controversies over both congressional and presidential impotence was the question about the looming financial default of New York City. For eight months, the nation's most populous city, paying the price for attempting to cope with overwhelming economic and social forces, without budgetary discipline, stood at the brink of economic collapse. Only in later months did it become apparent that the New York predicament merely epitomized the problems faced by the nation's older urban centers. Meanwhile, with default virtually a certainty, those with traditionally rural biases against big-city evils found satisfaction that, at last, the "chickens had come home to roost" because of "misguided liberalism." Ford, the conservative, Middle American president, assumed the support of that constituency and kept his distance from the situation even as harried local officials searched for ways to avoid fiscal disaster.

Ford's position was never a mystery. Yet, when he delivered a stern rebuke to the city on 29 October 1975, promising to veto any "bailout" of the nation's premier city, the finality of his statement came as a draconian blow. In one of those journalistic feats that convert a political leader's comments into pungent rhetoric, the *New York Daily News* reported the president's position with the headline FORD TO CITY: DROP DEAD. The Ford rationale, of course, was simple: only by his display of firmness would the city tidy its financial house.

In the days that followed, there was a growing realization that the administration's position had underestimated how much others throughout the country feared the implications of permitting the collapse of New York City. Vice President Rockefeller openly began to suggest that the government might indeed have to play a role. From within the White House itself came similar signals, especially from Treasury Secretary William Simon.

Gerald R. Ford in the Oval Office. Ford's short term was marked by the controversial pardon he gave to President Nixon and the difficult economic circumstances faced by the United States. ARCHIVE PHOTOS

Ford held to his stern justification that he was forcing New York to restore its own fiscal viability, but at the same time, his retreat had become inevitable. Within the city, frantic negotiations took place involving all parties, including banks that had funded the city's short-term securities. Under the pressure, all interested parties came together during additional weeks of negotiations. Drastic reductions were made in the city's work force. Bankers restructured bond issues. The new Municipal Assistance Corporation was established to sell securities. Union pension funds were committed to their purchase. One near disaster after another was averted in a series of cliffhanger scenarios.

Finally, with the city seemingly acting to repair the damage and the broader consequences of a default becoming clearer, Ford changed his stance when he met the press on 26 November. "I have, quite frankly," he announced, "been surprised that they have come as far as they have." Ford then asked Congress to approve federal loans to the city on a seasonal basis through 30 June 1978. He covered his own retreat by emphasizing that New York had "bailed itself out." Finally, by a narrow margin in the House, Congress approved Ford's request for a seasonal financing act to provide up to $2.3 billion for short-term loans during the next three years at 1 percent above the federal cost of money. To further fortify the city against default, in case that assistance failed to work, additional legislation was enacted to facilitate municipal bankruptcy proceedings so that New York and other cities could adjust repayment of their debts. Ford's position, combined with local and federal measures, induced some painful cutbacks but did start the process of rehabilitating New York's finances.

With the coming of the presidential election year, the status of the economy acquired a new urgency. Fortunately, by early 1976, inflation was easing off, and there were tentative signs of recovery, but unemployment would continue to fluctuate throughout the year at undesirably high levels. In his State of the Union message, Ford again urged a slowing down of government spending coupled with incentives for the private sector. "We thought we could transform the country through massive national programs, but often the programs did not work," he said, sounding a theme that became heard more frequently and with varying degrees of stress from Republican critics of the Democratic past. "Too often they only made things worse," he added, and called for a "new realism that is true to the great principles upon which this nation was founded."

In the message and in his budget proposal he was clear about his spending priorities: reductions in a variety of social programs, which would be achieved by a consolidation of fifty-nine programs into four block grants, and a "significant increase" in defense spending. While proposing a comprehensive program of catastrophic health insurance for everybody covered by Medicare, he flatly ruled out any action on a comprehensive national health plan and proposed potentially controversial changes in the federal health programs. His budget also aimed to phase out the emergency public service jobs program for the unemployed as well as extended unemployment benefits. Arguing that the money saved would make feasible tax cuts on a "dollar-for-dollar basis," he renewed his 1975 proposals for permanent tax reductions. In short, Ford had prepared the way not only for his own election but to meet any challenge from the GOP right wing.

Vice President Rockefeller, the former New York governor, was viewed as a "wayout" liberal, which was, of course, one important indication of the direction of the Republican party. In early summer of 1975, the jettisoning of Rockefeller had already been designed when Howard ("Bo") Callaway of Georgia resigned as secretary of the army to head Ford's election campaign. Callaway lost no time in telling reporters that Rocky was the "number-one problem":

"You and I both know that if Rockefeller took himself out it would help with the nomination." When the president met with Rockefeller in the White House on 28 October 1975, only days after the vice president had hinted that something might yet be worked out for New York City, what Rockefeller heard could hardly have been surprising. "I didn't take myself off the ticket, you know," he told Robert Hartmann. "You know—he asked me to do it."

Only a few days later, Rockefeller found ample confirmation of his suspicion that he had been sacrificed as part of a grander design. Rocky, and just about everybody else, was convinced that the real architect of the plan was Donald Rumsfeld. Rumsfeld was a Nixon holdover, a not unusual pedigree in the Ford administration. "Never once, until he left the White House," Hartmann has written, "were there more new Ford faces than there were old Nixon faces." But Rumsfeld, who began to be known by the staff as "a smiling Haldeman" (referring to H. R. Haldeman, Nixon's chief of staff), was more crafty than most. He had served four terms as a congressman from Illinois and had compiled a voting record indistinguishable from Ford's. Fortunate at having been away from the wrong spot at the right time as ambassador to NATO during the Watergate trauma, he joined the Ford staff as Haig's replacement. After six weeks as chief of staff, Haig was eased out with an appointment as commander of NATO. "Six weeks of poisonous leaks to reporters and private complaints to the president from Hartmann and other Ford loyalists," said Ron Nessen, finally helped to get rid of him and to install Rumsfeld. Rumsfeld's opportunity to reach for the brass ring was supplied by the obvious need to create some order within the chaotic Ford staff.

John Osborne, the close "White House watcher" for the *New Republic*, wrote that Ford was being "served by the weakest staff in recent White House history." Ford's own ineptitude had created the opening for Rumsfeld's machinations. A more polite view is that, as Nessen puts it, he "was too much Mr. Nice Guy." Hartmann, often dyspeptic and, more charitably, an "abusive pragmatist," was convinced that Ford had made the fatal error of opting for continuity by taking over Nixon's people; they became Ford's Praetorian Guard, a "fifth column dedicated to Ford's failure" and to an eventual restoration of the old regime. To them, Ford was merely a caretaker. Having moved to the top so suddenly via the Twenty-fifth Amendment, Ford reached the White

House without his own time-tested loyalists. Consequently, the staff was composed of four separate groups that never became unified. The squabbling became endemic; so did news leaks about disorders. At one point, after getting his fill of stories about Kissinger losing his power, Ford pounded his desk and said, "Goddamn it, I don't want any more of this," and threatened "dire consequences" for anyone continuing the practice.

This effort also involved getting his own house in order. The "Halloween Massacre" of a few months earlier exposed the disorder within the White House that had continued to plague the designated presidency. If Ford moved to strengthen the image of his administration, he must have been distressed by the Gallup poll that showed his subsequent level of approval dropping from 58 percent to 36 percent. If his move was designed to placate Republican rightists, as nearly every White House observer assumed, then he was hardly more successful. Governor Ronald Reagan of California, who was still not viewed by Ford's people as ready to risk splitting the party by competing for the presidency, responded in a rather majesterial way, "I am certainly not appeased."

On 3 November 1975, Rockefeller withdrew his name from the 1976 ticket. The announced realignment left the Nixonians in basic control. Rumsfeld was the new majordomo. Defense Secretary James Schlesinger, whose enemies included Ford and Kissinger, was dropped altogether. Kissinger had apparently helped to push Schlesinger overboard by convincing the president that the secretary of defense had sabotaged the possibility of achieving any new strategic-arms limitations agreement with the Russians at Helsinki the preceding summer. Schlesinger, whose strongest support was from the Republican right, was replaced by Rumsfeld. George Bush, who had been the liaison to the People's Republic of China, took over from William Colby as head of the Central Intelligence Agency (CIA). At a time when controversies were swirling about the role of the agency, Bush's new position was not seen as increasing his attraction for higher office.

Among the remaining changes was the downgrading of Henry Kissinger from his dual role as secretary of state and special adviser on national security affairs. The latter post went to Lieutenant General Brent Scowcroft, the intellectual soldier. One objective was to downplay Kissinger's primacy in the area of foreign affairs, but another was to appease conservatives upset by the firing of Schlesinger. Ford's fail-

ure to emerge from all this with enhanced presidential stature seemed to leave Rumsfeld the sole potential beneficiary. Indeed, grumbled Hartmann, "There still was no Ford Administration."

That much had been done to reduce Kissinger's real power is doubtful. His authority had grown rather than decreased. Ford's dependence on his secretary of state dismayed White House insiders. Ron Nessen thought Kissinger was a man who had a "lack of commitment to the truth as a matter of morality. Kissinger bent the truth to serve what he believed were worthwhile foreign policy maneuvers." He dominated the president, noted Hartmann, and "monopolized" him, "sharing the news spotlight and sometimes shouldering him offside" on overseas trips. "This President," John Hersey reported on his privileged view of life within 1600 Pennsylvania Avenue, "who had had a minimal exposure to foreign affairs before he came to office, heard, I was told, only one voice, and a mercurial voice it was, Henry Kissinger's. Yes, this was the most alarming thought I had had all week."

Not surprisingly, Ford's brief presidency was more notable for the continuation of a Kissingerian view of balance-of-power relationships. With the American role in Vietnam having concluded in 1973 and the final victory of Hanoi bringing the war to its real end by April 1975, one remaining concern was the credibility of United States power. Détente, which had come to mean "openings" to both Beijing and Moscow, existed side by side with schemes on the international chessboard to continue Cold War containment and reaffirm the credibility of American power. There was no reason to suppose that such concerns would interfere with the proper noises that had to be made about arms control and peaceful coexistence. Consequently, Ford's brief presidency at no point deviated from its predetermined global course.

An earlier affirmation of continuity was the new president's travels abroad during November 1974. He became the first incumbent American president to visit Japan; he met with the emperor and pledged cooperation on problems of energy and food supplies, and then went on to Korea and Vladivostok. At that Far Eastern Soviet outpost, he met with General Secretary Leonid Brezhnev, and there was a surprising agreement, the groundwork for which had been laid in October during Kissinger's talks with Brezhnev. Both leaders agreed in principle to limit the overall total of nuclear-warhead carriers permitted each country to 2,400 and the total of missiles equipped with multiple nuclear warheads to 1,320. The secretary of state hailed it as a "breakthrough" that had placed a cap "on the arms race for a period of 10 years." When Ford returned to Washington, he explained that what he and Brezhnev had agreed upon was "the general framework for a new agreement that will last through 1985." All this produced some optimism for reviving the stalled second round of SALT talks, but nothing came of it before the end of Ford's administration.

More bitter was the culmination of the final Communist offensive in South Vietnam. On 29 March 1975 came the last refugee flight out of Da Nang. That was followed in Washington by Ford's version of Nixon's clash with Congress over support for administration goals in Southeast Asia. On 10 April, Ford asked for $722 million in emergency military aid and for $250 million in economic and humanitarian assistance to South Vietnam. But, even as he spoke, the Cambodian capital of Phnom Penh was being taken over by the Communist Khmer Rouge forces, and South Vietnam's final capitulation came on 30 April. Ford never did get his requests.

Not only did Congress refuse to act, but the mood on Capitol Hill was turning bitterly against Kissinger, the celebrated diplomat who so recently could do no wrong, and revived talk about Ford's need to disassociate himself from that particular Nixon holdover. Administration policies had to be more clearly identified as Ford's. Not surprisingly, Ford's popular approval, shattered in the wake of the pardon, now hovered in the area of 40 percent.

Disillusionment, even confusion and frustration, was the order of the day. It could hardly have been otherwise after Vietnam, Watergate, and the pardon coming from the man commissioned to do the healing. Because of Seymour Hersh's account in the *New York Times* in December 1974, Americans had heard about intelligence activities having gotten out of hand. They read about the CIA having launched "a massive, illegal domestic intelligence operation during the Nixon administration against the antiwar movement and other dissident groups." The needs of "national security" had been used to justify illegal "break-ins, wiretapping and surreptitious interception of mail." All this followed, by just a few months, revelations about how the CIA had worked to overthrow the Chilean government of President Salvador Allende. As if that were not enough, on 28 February 1975 the television newsman Daniel Schorr, leaking

information from a congressional investigation committee's report, said that the CIA's activities had included assassination attempts against at least three foreign leaders.

Several investigations followed these revelations. The first was a special commission chaired by Vice President Rockefeller to study Hersh's allegations. The Rockefeller findings, issued in June, confirmed illegal CIA activities but minimized the wrongdoing. The report did more to arouse than to quell skepticism.

The *Mayaguez* Affair

Publication of the report came right after a bold presidential stroke to reassert American power, prestige, and presence in Southeast Asia. An American merchant ship, the *Mayaguez*, and its thirty-nine crewmen were seized by Cambodian forces in the Gulf of Siam on 12 May. The Cambodians claimed that the vessel was within their territorial waters. Washington claimed that the *Mayaguez* was exercising its right of innocent passage and that actually it was sixty miles off the coast. Ford, seeking to adhere to the War Powers Act of 1973, had White House aides telephone Capitol Hill to inform legislative leaders that he intended to use force to prevent the ship and its crew from being transferred to the mainland. But not until fifteen hours after the military operation was launched did he personally meet with the congressmen in the White House. Clearly they were informed rather than consulted.

Only two minutes before the first American helicopter approached and was shot out of the sky, Phnom Penh radio announced that the ship had been released. Nothing was said about the crew, and the military operations were, in any case, too advanced to be called off. At that point, Kissinger told Scowcroft, "Let's look ferocious! Otherwise they will attack us as the ship leaves." Two destroyers and an aircraft carrier sped to the scene. Three Cambodian gunboats were sunk and four others damaged. Late on the afternoon of 14 May, Ford ordered a marine attack on a nearby island where the men were believed to be held. American planes also bombed mainland targets to prevent Cambodian interference in the rescue operation. Marines from a United States destroyer then boarded and secured the empty *Mayaguez*, while a small Cambodian boat returned the captured crew to a second American vessel. To rescue the thirty-nine-member crew, about to be released in any case, forty-one Americans had lost their lives and fifty had been wounded.

The legality of the War Powers Act was to be cast into doubt by a Supreme Court decision in 1983, but in 1975, Ford's method of notifying Congress was the immediate center of debate. Another question related to the premature use of force. In hindsight, it is clear that the crew would have been returned without military action and the loss of life. The administration rationalized its actions by citing the unreliability of the Cambodian government, but even that point was debatable. Kissinger, in arguing before the National Security Council, was more direct. He pointed to the important fact that America's NATO and Far Eastern allies were watching. Capturing the boat had enabled Ford to reassert American power, to show that the United States—despite what had just happened in Vietnam—would not allow itself to be further pushed around. Hartmann was more direct: "Did the United States of America, torn internally and with a novice, little-known leader, still have any guts?"

Predictably, public reaction was highly favorable. America had finally stopped "turning tail" and had refused to tolerate harassment from pipsqueak Communist governments. Within the next week, more than fourteen thousand letters, telegrams, and phone calls reached the White House, barely a thousand of which expressed dissent. Ford himself used his memoirs to supply the most candid analysis of the *Mayaguez* affair. "All of a sudden," he wrote, "the gloomy national mood began to fade. Many people's faith in their country was restored and my standing in the polls shot up 11 points. *Mayaguez* wasn't the only reason, of course; the economy was improving at a rapid rate, but the net was that I felt I had regained the initiative, and I determined to do what I could with it."

Foreign Affairs

None of this seemed to have much to do with détente. The Kissinger-directed foreign policy of the Ford administration clearly wanted to go on having it both ways: maintaining the pose of vigorous global anti-Communism while appearing agreeable to accommodations with the many-headed hydra. Ford's European trip, begun in late May, clearly tried to perpetuate that image. He went to NATO headquarters in Brussels, where he assured European leaders that the collapse of American power in Southeast Asia would in no way lessen commitments for their protection. NATO, he asserted, was "the cornerstone of U.S. foreign policy." Then he went on to Salzburg, Rome, and Madrid.

In July, there was another meeting with the Russians. The conference, which brought together thirty-five nations on the question of security and cooperation in Europe, met at the Finnish capital of Helsinki. It was to deal with such issues as security and economic and cultural cooperation. By 1975 the optimum objective had become agreement on a new strategic-arms limitations treaty to augment the SALT I pact of 1972, but in essence, the two sides agreed to disagree, the Americans objecting to the Soviet Backfire bomber with its nuclear weapons delivery capability and the Soviets holding out for limitations on the new American cruise missile. James Schlesinger, then defense secretary, joined the Joint Chiefs of Staff in adamant opposition to accepting any reduction of the cruise missile's capability. "Indeed," as Ford has written, "Schlesinger had become the missile's greatest advocate."

With the cruise missile and the Backfire bomber remaining stumbling blocks, Ford salvaged from Helsinki an accord on human rights. In exchange for American acceptance of the inviolability of the "legitimate" postwar boundaries, the Soviets renounced their right to keep client states in line by unilateral military intervention. They also agreed to observe the basic principles of human rights in their satellite states. Ford wrote in his memoirs:

> They had never recognized such international standards before. If the nations attending the conference failed to live up to their agreements, Europe would be no worse off than it had been previously, but if they made good on their promises, the cause of freedom behind the Iron Curtain would advance. That was a worthwhile goal.

But the accord was inherently more significant than that. It marked the first post-World War II Western acceptance of Soviet domination of Eastern Europe, and that was precisely its weakness for American domestic consumption. A Republican administration had, in effect, ratified the territorial aggrandizement GOP politicians had for so long condemned as the legacy of Yalta. Ford also attempted to explain to representatives of Eastern European nationals in the United States that the effort had been in exchange for a greater commitment to individual freedom and the flow of ideas; in no way did it imply approval of postwar Soviet territorial expansionism. Still, Helsinki sounded to some like another Munich. Too many viewed the outcome as "another Kissinger deal that was forced down the president's throat." In the long run, continued Soviet repression, the anger of Slavic-Americans, and a Ronald Reagan waiting to pounce on the administration as a betrayer of strength against international Communism soured any optimism about détente. Reagan himself expressed the view that all Americans should oppose what had been achieved at Helsinki.

That summer, Ford also went behind the Iron Curtain for visits to Poland and Romania. Another stopover was in Yugoslavia. In December he made a five-day visit to the People's Republic of China, continuing Nixon's opening of the "window on the East."

But, just as the annual American memorials to the post-World War II Sovietization of Eastern Europe, known as "captive nations" resolutions, were not viewed as contradicting the Helsinki accords, neither was the opening to Beijing allowed to permit any disruption of the relationship with Taiwan. The Republican platform that came out of the Kansas City presidential nominations convention in 1976 upheld the efforts to normalize relations with the mainland while pledging to "continue to support the freedom and independence of our friend and ally, the Republic of China, and its 16 million people."

By then, Ford had permitted Kissinger to design a disaster in Angola. Ironically, that involvement was the antithesis of détente and precisely consistent with the international role as prescribed by foreign policy "realists." Furthermore, the entire covert enterprise was mounted even while two congressional committees were investigating the CIA's subversion of other governments. When more became known about what had been happening in that Portuguese part of Africa, critics wondered how such a quagmire could have been risked so soon after Vietnam.

The familiar explanations were ultimately made: the United States could not ignore Soviet and Cuban attempts to gain an African foothold when Angola was to receive independence on 11 November 1975. The actual facts were somewhat different. The "40 Committee," which directed intelligence operations, was dominated by Kissinger. It underwrote and directed covert activities before America's NATO ally Portugal relinquished its colony of Angola. The ostensible idea was to beat the Communists to the punch. Whichever side could win elections scheduled just before independence would control the

new government. Before the enterprise reached its dead end, more than $30 million had been spent and another foreign misadventure had occurred. Moreover, when Congress got wind of all this, both the Senate and the House voted to deny the use of defense funds in Angola for fiscal year 1976.

John Stockwell, the chief of the CIA Angola task force, later revealed how Washington had made the first move. The CIA lied to Congress and to the 40 Committee. Kissinger, pushing the agency into the covert operation, "was determined the Soviets should not be permitted to make a move in any remote part of the world without being confronted militarily by the United States." He was further motivated by the need to repair American relations with neighboring Zaire, where the prospect of a nearby Soviet-backed government raised fears of control of a vital railroad line. The State Department had therefore decided to get behind Zaire by supporting its concerns about Angola. "Clearly, the United States wanted this war," Stockwell found out when arriving to take up the assignment. The American role was hidden from the public, while propaganda stressed the Soviet menace in Africa. Meanwhile, as Stockwell points out, covert military operations were carried out under "suicidal circumstances." The Soviets responded by helping their clients, who turned out to be far more capable.

The revelations that provoked the congressional revolt denying further funds constituted, as John Osborne noted, "a crushing repudiation of Kissinger's and President Ford's view that 'resistance to Soviet expansion by military means must be a fundamental element of U.S. foreign policy' and justifies covert intervention in such places and situations as Angola." The ultimate result was counterproductive. With the cutoff of funds for 1976, the field was left clear for the introduction of far more Cuban troops and Soviet arms. The Russians got their victory by default. Stockwell, summarizing the episode, concluded, "Most serious of all, the United States was exposed, dishonored and discredited in the eyes of the world. We had lost and fifteen thousand Cubans were installed in Angola with all the adulation accruing to a young David who has slain the American Goliath."

Intelligence Reform

All of this further played into the hands of those eager to check runaway intelligence operations. The Senate's Select Committee to Study Governmental

Operations, led by Frank Church of Idaho, published its report in April 1976 with details about assassination attempts against foreign leaders that went back into the Eisenhower and Kennedy administrations. Another study was undertaken by Representative Otis Pike, a New York Republican. The climate for imposing some restraint was established. "Once these two committees began their investigations," Nessen has written, "Ford found himself spending long hours trying to settle disputes among Congress, Kissinger, the National Security Council, the CIA and other agencies over access to classified documents and procedures for handling them. There were no orderly and uniform rules for responding to congressional demands for documents." There was also little reason left for the optimism that had hailed the incoming Ford presidency.

Ford first presented his intelligence reorganization package at a press conference on 17 February 1976. His recommendations failed either to ban covert intelligence operations overseas or to define what would be regarded as improper domestic activities. Inevitably, then, the publication of Church's recommendations led to the establishment of the permanent Senate Committee on Intelligence, with legislative and budgetary authority over the CIA and other federal intelligence activities.

The 1976 Election

None of this had accomplished what Ford needed most: the legitimization of a congressional presidency. In November 1975, he repeated his determination to win a term on his own, even at the price of competing in every primary. He would, he vowed, "go right down to the wire in the convention in Kansas City and win there."

It is quite true, as Tom Braden pointed out, that when "the nation's end men begin to treat a serious politician as a joke, he is through." Precisely that happened to Ford. It started during his trip to Austria in the spring of 1975, when he slipped on a rain-slickened ramp while getting off his plane in Salzburg and fell on the stairs. That the incident happened in full view of reporters and cameramen meant that it was in full view of the world. "The image of klutz would never fade away after that," lamented Ron Nessen. Every time he stumbled, bumped his head, fell to the snow while on his skis, the image was compounded. Ford became famous for his gaffes, whether real or exaggerated.

The national perception was that the president could not be taken seriously. At the start of 1976, as Ronald Reagan announced his own candidacy, several columnists wrote that the first appointed president had become "a joke" and "a caretaker." John Osborne added that Ford was widely viewed as "a loser, a bumbler, a misfit President who for some reason or other . . . was prone to slip on airplane ramps, bump his head on helicopter entrances, entangle himself in the leashes of his family dogs, and fall from skis in front of television cameras that showed him asprawl in snow." The inevitable suspicion linked his difficulties to alcohol. The *New York Times* even speculated editorially that his abdication from competition for the 1976 nomination was not a farfetched possibility. "He fills the mind with the sense of how ordinary he is and how vulnerable," wrote Murray Kempton in *Harper's*. Ford's own pollster, Robert Teeter, found that when asked what the president had done that was particularly impressive, 61 percent replied, "Nothing," which is exactly what 41 percent said when asked what he had done that they did not like. Advised Teeter, "There is no clear perception of his presidency, of his goals, of where he is going." Neither was there "a clear public perception" that anyone was in control of the government.

All this was made to order for a challenge from the Republican right. Not only were the polls confirming Ford's plight, but private surveys were also showing strong support for Reagan. In a single month, the Californian advanced from twenty-three points behind Ford to an eight-point lead in the popularity polls. The very threat of Reagan had sensitized the administration against doing anything that might seem too liberal.

That Reagan would actually oppose the incumbent came as somewhat of a shock to the Ford camp. Even before he appreciated that he would be facing the challenge, Ford disliked the governor intensely. He thought the former movie actor was an opportunist who was milking his position for everything he could get. But he must have disliked the governor's potential power most of all. Fearing that Reagan might actually be nominated, Ford contemplated opposing him by running as an independent. More and more, Reagan was the choice of conservatives. During the California primary, Ford countered Reagan with commercials that warned, "Governor Reagan couldn't start a war. President Reagan could."

The long, hard-fought series of primaries failed to assure either man of the nomination. When Republicans arrived in Kansas City that August, the uncommitted delegates held the balance of power. Ford had begun with a satisfying "first" for his career, winning an election outside his Michigan district by topping Reagan in New Hampshire's kick-off primary. Then, in the northern and border states, he continued to do well, hoping to force his rival to concede the impossibility of removing the incumbent. But Reagan recovered in his own heartland, scoring impressive victories in the South and Southwest, winning especially big in his home state early in June.

Still, Ford had reasons for cautious optimism. His incumbency was a source of strength, balancing the weakness of his record. Another boost had been supplied by Reagan himself. Just as Ford's presidential politics and campaigning were obviously pitched toward the party's conservatives, his competitor's strength reached out toward the liberals with a pre-convention announcement of his intended running mate. The blow stunned conservatives who had regarded their man as a "true believer." Reagan's heretical choice for the vice presidency was Senator Richard S. Schweiker, a Pennsylvania Republican with a liberal voting record. A perceptible drift toward Ford from the GOP right then followed, a development that may have contributed significantly to the outcome.

In the battle between rival conservative factions, the purists behind Reagan managed to dominate the proceedings ideologically. The party platform, traditionally a statement of unifying principles, was clearly painted in Reaganite colors. Ford received only tempered praise and was hardly mentioned by name. The platform expressed reservations about détente and warned that agreements such as those signed at Helsinki "must not take from those who do not have the freedom, the hope of one day gaining it." There was only a vague reference to Watergate, and no direct acknowledgment of the existence of either Nixon or Kissinger. After Ford managed to win the nomination by receiving only 57 more votes than the necessary minimum of 1,130, he asked the convention to designate Senator Robert Dole of Kansas as his running mate. There was not much doubt that Dole's prime qualification was his acceptability to Reagan, but there was also fear that anybody to the left of the Kansan could spark a revolt leading to a draft of Reagan himself to complete the ticket. Osborne was correct in pointing out that substantial hostility to Ford's choice of a vice presidential candidate "would have demolished the flimsy triumph of his own nomination with a nigh unbearable humiliation."

The Democrats had already nominated Jimmy Carter, a former governor of Georgia, and Walter Mondale, a Minnesota, Hubert H. Humphrey-style liberal. Ford hardly ventured beyond the White House for much of the early part of the campaign, accentuating the fact that he was the president. The emphasis was on his role as a post-Watergate healer, reducer of inflation, and opponent of improvident Democrats. Still, without having to spell them out, Carter capitalized on the Nixon pardon and Republican responsibility for Watergate and for the 7.9 percent rate of inflation, the highest since the Great Depression. The campaign itself was dull: the Democrats had chosen their most conservative candidate since the 1920s, a man newly risen from obscurity, and the Republicans, a "nice guy who just couldn't be taken seriously."

Not even three Ford-Carter televised debates did much to relieve the boredom. The highlight was a Ford gaffe about Russian domination of Eastern Europe. In responding to a question from Max Frankel about the Helsinki agreement's seeming recognition of the Soviets' postwar boundaries, Ford said, "There is no Soviet domination of Eastern Europe, and there never will be under a Ford administration." As though matters were not bad enough, his attempted clarification included the statement that "I don't believe that the Poles consider themselves dominated by the Soviet Union. As a matter of fact, I visited Poland, Yugoslavia, and Rumania to make certain that the people of the United States are dedicated to their independence, their autonomy, and their freedom."

Every time Ford tried to clarify himself, he compounded the blunder. In his mind, it was all very clear: the United States did not accept Russian domination of Eastern Europe. Actually, the president thought it was all sound because Kissinger had briefed him about Helsinki. Even the Vatican secretary of state had signed the agreement because Russian control in the area was already a fact of life. But, as Ford later admitted to Jules Witcover, "it certainly came out the wrong way." William F. Buckley, Jr., called it "the ultimate Polish joke."

Ford was crushed by his inability to legitimize his presidency. He held out hope until the end, and he came very close. Of more than 81 million votes cast, Carter's plurality was 1.7 million. By virtually resurrecting the Solid South (except for Virginia and Oklahoma) and reaching into such northern industrial states as Massachusetts, New York, and Pennsylvania,

Carter won 297 electoral votes to Ford's 240. One vote was cast for Reagan. Inflation, unemployment, the Nixon pardon, and Watergate all swayed voters. Blacks voted heavily for Carter, giving the Democrat 94 percent of their vote, and he also won over the bulk of those primarily troubled by unemployment. Meanwhile, two segments of the old Democratic coalition, Jews and Catholics, turned out more heavily for Ford than they had for Nixon. Most telling was the finding that Ford, after his long congressional career and two years in the White House, was considered "experienced" by just 5 percent of the voters questioned. Furthermore, in the first presidential election since Watergate, the Democratic congressional victory was overwhelming.

Having risen to the White House under almost bizarre circumstances, Ford remained a congressional president, one who was designated to fill the void as provided by the Twenty-fifth Amendment. His experience offered little comfort for the prospects of future success under that mode of succession. Neither he nor his vice president, Nelson Rockefeller, the other Twenty-fifth Amendment appointee, was ever able to achieve the legitimacy of elective success. Ford was further burdened by being perceived as merely an extension of the Nixon administration, an impression virtually confirmed by the pardon. Nor did he escape the notion that he was merely the pawn of Henry Kissinger, imprisoned by times that were better left behind.

Postpresidential Career

Perhaps defeat in 1976 was even more galling. Electoral vindication is a normal goal for all accidental presidents, and for Ford that need was much greater. Not surprisingly, defeat brought understandable distress, which included a residue of bitterness toward Reagan for initially having led the intraparty opposition and then undermining him during the 1976 campaign. When Reagan advisers calculated that Ford would strengthen the 1980 ticket by serving as the vice presidential candidate, the ex-president refused to be enticed. The greater his own distance from the White House, the closer Ford moved toward a warm relationship with his successor, especially after Carter completed his own single term.

Ford, as James Reston of the *New York Times* later wrote, soon discovered that being an ex-president was even better than president, with many of the advantages but none of the disadvantages. He

gave the impression of being the happiest politician in the country. "Once a man has been President," he told one interviewer, "he becomes an object of curiosity like those other notorious Missouri characters, Mark Twain and Jesse James." His security protected by the Secret Service, and a lifestyle that included winters in the southern California desert and the Colorado mountains, he seemed devoted to perfecting his golf and enjoying the advantages of more affluence than he had ever known. Eight corporations chose him as a member of their board of directors. He presided over the creation of a Gerald R. Ford Library, which opened its archives in Ann Arbor, Michigan, to researchers in 1982. He joined the college campus speaking circuit, which included becoming the first holder of the Clifford Case Professorship of Public Affairs at Rutgers University. But he was still "good old Jerry," the easygoing Middle Westerner, dressed informally, and always ready for a game of golf.

BIBLIOGRAPHY

Two accounts of the Ford presidency are essential reading, one by a meticulous and judicial historian, John Robert Greene, *The Presidency of Gerald R. Ford* (Lawrence, Kans., 1995), the other by an insider journalist, James Cannon, *Time and Chance: Gerald Ford's Appointment with History* (New York, 1994). These should be read along with Ford's own book, *A Time to Heal: The Autobiography of Gerald R. Ford* (New York, 1979).

Jerald F. terHorst, *Gerald Ford and the Future of the Presidency* (New York, 1974), by the man who served Ford as press secretary until he resigned after the pardon, is a valuable prepresidential biographical study. Jules Witcover, *Marathon: The Pursuit of the Presidency, 1972–1976* (New York, 1977), is the most comprehensive of the several books about the election of 1976.

Robert T. Hartmann, *Palace Politics: An Inside Account of the Ford Years* (New York, 1980), uses Hartmann's long acquaintance with Ford, both before and after the presidency, to produce an often bitter, sometimes dyspeptic indictment of the administration and its surrender to Nixon holdovers. Ron Nessen, *It Sure Looks Different from the Inside* (New York, 1978), another work by an insider that does not place a premium on loyalty to the boss, is a defense of Ford with surprising candor. John Osborne, *The White House Watch: The Ford Years* (Washington, D.C., 1977), is an indispensable collection of perceptive, urbane articles that first appeared in the *New Republic*. Richard Reeves, *A Ford, Not a Lincoln* (New York, 1975), is a well-written view of a man out of his depth. John Hersey, *Aspects of the Presidency: Truman and Ford in Office* (Boston, 1980), originally written as a magazine assignment, provides an indispensable glimpse into the Ford White House.

Seymour Hersh, "The Pardon: Nixon, Ford, Haig, and the Transfer of Power," in *Atlantic* (August 1983), demolishes Ford's public defense of the pardon, concluding that self-interest and political loyalty compromised the democratic process. Clark R. Mollenhoff, *The Man Who Pardoned Nixon* (New York, 1976), too often reads like a diatribe but remains valuable for having asked the right questions and provided information for future skeptics of the pardon explanation. Ken Auletta, *The Streets Were Paved With Gold* (New York, 1979), is the basic book for an understanding of the New York City fiscal crisis.

Coral Bell, *The Diplomacy of Détente: The Kissinger Era* (New York, 1977), a careful and balanced study of the assumptions and contradictions of détente, is particularly insightful about the role of nationalism and Washington-Beijing-Moscow diplomacy. Roger Morris, *Haig: The General's Progress* (New York, 1982), is a most unflattering view of a political general, who emerges as a first-rate schemer; Morris's *Uncertain Greatness: Henry Kissinger and American Foreign Policy* (New York, 1977), is an unflattering portrait. William Colby and Peter Forbath, *Honorable Men: My Life in the CIA* (New York, 1978), is an account by the CIA's director during the first half of the Ford administration that, while inevitably self-serving, is an essential guide to an understanding of intelligence operations during the period. John Stockwell, *In Search of Enemies: A CIA Story* (New York, 1978), contains candid revelations by the man who headed the intelligence venture in Angola.

The First Lady's recollections are in Betty Ford, with Chris Chase, *The Times of My Life* (New York, 1978). For further sources consult John Robert Greene, comp., *Gerald R. Ford: A Bibliography* (Westport, Conn., 1994).

Jimmy Carter

Richard S. Kirkendall

Jimmy Carter THE LIBRARY OF CONGRESS

J IMMY CARTER was an unlucky president. He came to power shortly after the American failure in Vietnam and the Watergate scandals. Since the late 1960s, a "leadership crisis," characterized by widespread, deep, and serious lack of confidence in the leaders the system supplied, had been a major feature of American politics. Also before he became president, an "energy crisis" and other economic troubles had emerged, raising doubts about the future of American power and prosperity. Carter was highly sensitive to these developments and shared the skepticism about "Washington" contained in them. Yet, he had confidence that his own personal qualities could end the leadership crisis. That confi-

dence, coupled with a sense of the limits of power, dominated his approach to the presidency. But, faced with an unusually tough situation, he did not end the crisis. In fact, the American people, many of them convinced that he was weak and lacked direction, gave him only one term to reestablish confidence.

James Earl Carter, Jr., rose to office from a background that, though somewhat varied, was, compared with that of most presidents, quite narrow. The most obvious limitation was lack of previous experience in Washington.

Carter was a southerner, the first one since before the Civil War who had come to the presidency by election. He came from the small-town South—from Plains, Georgia, where he was born on 1 October 1924—the first of four children of Earl and Lillian Carter. A native southerner, Earl was a successful farmer-businessman active in public affairs.

Prior to the presidency, the United States Navy gave Carter his only extended experience outside the South. Following graduation from the segregated public school in Plains and two years at Georgia Southwestern and Georgia Tech, he entered the United States Naval Academy in 1943, an institution that stressed discipline and engineering. A strong student, he graduated in 1946 in the top 10 percent of his class. After marrying Rosalynn Smith of Plains on 7 July, he served as a naval officer until October 1953, mostly in the submarine service, including the nuclear program headed by Hyman Rickover, a man Carter admired greatly.

Following his father's death, Carter returned home to look after the family farm and business, which specialized in peanuts. The business prospered but did not dominate his attention. He became active in public affairs, serving, for example, on the Sumter County Board of Education from 1956 to 1962. In the last year, he was elected to the state senate, where he served successfully for four years, devoting much attention to education. Civil rights was the most prominent issue at the time, but he continued to support segregation and largely avoided the controversy.

In 1966, Carter suffered his first serious failure, and it affected him significantly. He failed in a bid for the Democratic nomination for governor. Depressed, he turned to religion for comfort. Raised a Baptist, he now became much more intense, convinced that he had been "born again."

In 1970, in his second bid for the governorship, Carter succeeded, and for the next four years, he presided over the state's affairs. He embraced a quite eclectic philosophy with a strong conservative bent, especially on fiscal matters, though he liked to present himself as a populist, the representative of the common people against the establishment and the special interests. Proposing a large agenda of welfare reform, educational advance, budget reform, and other matters, he emphasized government reorganization in hopes of making government operate more efficiently and effectively, and he achieved some success. Also eager to promote economic growth, he cooperated with business leaders. And he demonstrated a new, though cautious, interest in reforming race relations.

Campaign for the Presidency

Ambitious and self-confident, Carter decided well before his term as governor ended to run for the presidency in 1976. To strengthen himself for the race, he became better informed on international affairs and better acquainted with certain elites and joined the prestigious Trilateral Commission. He also broke with George Wallace and in other ways improved his image on race relations.

Not a man of national prominence and power, the Georgian surprised the nation by gaining the nomination on the first ballot at the Democratic National Convention in New York. Behind this victory lay strenuous and successful participation in the now numerous primaries throughout the nation. His campaign, which began early in 1975, stressed Washington's defects and his own virtues, not specific issues or a clearly defined ideology. He sensed a widespread yearning for change in leadership and great distrust of and skepticism about established leaders. He tried to persuade the disenchanted that he had the personality and values the situation demanded. He was moral and intelligent, tough yet compassionate. Carter defeated George Wallace in southern primaries, suggesting that the Georgian could solve what had become a major problem for his party, the breakup of the once-solid South. Other candidates had crowded the field, including Senator Henry Jackson of Washington, Congressman Morris Udall of Arizona, and Governor Jerry Brown of California, but one by one they had dropped out as Carter established himself as a winner who could reestablish Democratic control of the White House.

In midsummer, Carter and his vice presidential candidate, Walter Mondale of Minnesota, seemed likely to win the election by a wide margin, but President Gerald Ford gained ground rapidly. He took advantage of his incumbency, spending much of the campaign period in the White House "being president." He attacked his foe as inexperienced, inconsistent, unclear, misguided, and liberal, and charged that the big-spending Democratic Congress was the major source of inflation. He pointed with pride to his record, arguing that no Americans were fighting a war, tension between the United States and the Soviet Union had been reduced, employment was increasing, and inflation was declining. Several blunders, including a statement that the Soviet Union did not dominate Eastern Europe, and Ronald Reagan's less than full support, however, hampered Ford's progress.

Against Ford, Carter did not function as effectively as he had against his Democratic foes. He stressed government reorganization, the reduction of unemployment, the continuation and expansion of government services, tax reform, and fiscal responsibility. He would, he suggested, be both compassionate and frugal. He made much of Ford's shortcomings as a leader. Above all, he emphasized his own virtues and his freedom from the sins of the past, and promised moral regeneration. Although he did not work closely with the Democratic party, he benefited from its strengths and the weakness of the Republicans in the post-Nixon era. Economic troubles also helped him. But doubts about him as a southerner and a born-again Baptist hurt him, especially among liberals, Catholics, and Jews. And his own blunders, especially an unfortunate interview with *Playboy* magazine and the harshness of his attack on Ford, did some damage, raising doubts that he was as good as he suggested. The interview hurt him because of the reputation of the magazine and the nature of the matters discussed, including an appraisal of Lyndon Johnson as a person who had lied, cheated, and distorted the truth and Carter's own opinions about religion and sex. In expressing them, Carter used the terms "shacks up" and "screws" and admitted that he had "committed adultery in my heart many times." Mixed in their views of Ford as a person and as a leader, many voters found Carter puzzling—even contradictory—and untested.

Carter only squeaked through to victory, with a popular vote of 40.8 million to Ford's 39.1 million and an electoral vote of 297 to 240. On election day, the liberals preferred him to Ford, and his fellow southerners gave him more than half of their votes, sharply reversing the southern trend away from Democratic presidential candidates that had been evident for several years. (Many southerners, he has since suggested, yearned for "political redemption.") Catholics and organized labor gave him more support than they had given George McGovern four years before; most Jews stayed with the Democratic party; and more than 90 percent of black voters, including the large number in the South, supported Carter, offsetting the white majority for Ford. Carter carried nearly every southern state and several large northern and midwestern states, pulling back many Democrats who had deserted McGovern but not demonstrating as much strength as pre-McGovern Democrats had shown. Much more successful in the congressional elections, his party maintained control of Congress by wide margins.

Jimmy Carter shovels peanuts on his farm in Plains, Georgia, in 1969. Carter rose to prominence in local and state politics before winning the presidency in his first attempt at national office. ARCHIVE PHOTOS

At the outset of his administration, Carter's position was not substantially stronger than Ford's had been. He had been elected rather than appointed to office and did not have to contend with a Congress controlled by the opposition party, but he had won by only a narrow margin, 50.1 percent to 48 percent, and turnout had been low, with only 54 percent of the eligible voters going to the polls.

The Outsider in Washington

Early on, Carter devoted much of his energy to building popular support. He made great efforts to demonstrate that he was a "people's president," not an "imperial" one. He preached against the sin of pride and spoke of his own limitations. As one commentator observed, he sought in a variety of ways to dramatize "the qualities of morality, frugality, simplicity, candor and compassion for which the voters had been searching." He hoped to restore confidence in government as well as to establish confidence in himself; he cultivated "the people" rather than "the interests," suggesting that the former were good, the latter bad. He relied heavily on both television and direct contacts to accomplish these objectives. And he seemed quite successful.

At the same time and although Carter had campaigned as an "outsider," a critic of America's leadership of the recent past, he drew into his administration people with experience, including experience in Washington. Cyrus Vance became secretary of state; Harold Brown, secretary of defense; James Schlesinger, presidential assistant for energy; and Joseph Califano, secretary of health, education, and welfare. The president also courted business executives, appointing W. Michael Blumenthal as secretary of the treasury. Corporate law, as usual, was also well represented, this time by Vance, Califano, Secretary of Housing and Urban Development Patricia Roberts Harris, and Attorney General Griffin Bell; academia supplied Brown, Harris, Secretary of Commerce Juanita Kreps, Secretary of Labor Ray Marshall, and Zbigniew Brzezinski, the national security adviser. Secretary of Transportation Brock Adams and Secretary of Agriculture Bob Berglund were former congressmen; Secretary of Interior Cecil Andrus had been governor of Idaho. Most had served previously in the national capital. The many roles played by Robert Strauss, a former chairman of the Democratic National Committee, symbolized the importance of established people in the administration. Obviously, Carter's hopes of building support with the establishment outweighed any desire to enlarge his image as an outsider.

Some outsiders did hold important positions in the administration. In particular, the White House staff was dominated by Georgians, including Hamilton Jordan, Jody Powell, and Stuart Eizenstat, who had worked with Carter at home but had never served in Washington. Carter recognized their lack of experience there but had great confidence in them.

The president was quite sensitive to and supportive of the demands of politically active blacks and women. There were now more than forty-three hundred blacks in elected office, more than four times as many as a decade earlier, and they were suf-

ficiently numerous in Congress to have their own caucus. Blacks had moved forward at an especially rapid pace in southern politics, where the number of black voters doubled in the thirteen years following passage of the Voting Rights Act of 1965. And blacks, including Juanita Kreps and Patricia Harris, had some influence in the Carter administration. Wade H. McCree served as solicitor general, Clifford L. Alexander was the first black secretary of the army, Mary Berry was the top official in Washington on educational matters prior to the establishment of the Department of Education, Eleanor Holmes Norton chaired the Equal Employment Opportunity Commission, and Franklin Delano Raines served on the White House staff.

Andrew Young, as United States ambassador to the United Nations, was the most prominent representative of the political advance of southern blacks. He, in fact, was quite conscious of what he represented. "We were protest and now we are *it*," he proclaimed to a largely black audience in 1977. A clergyman and one of Martin Luther King's aides, Young, in 1972, had become the first black elected to Congress from Georgia since Reconstruction. By 1976 he had allied with Carter, helping him move to victory. After the latter moved into the White House, Young became ambassador to the United Nations and emerged quickly as an outspoken and controversial member of the administration, criticizing racism, advocating majority (black) rule in southern Africa, and proclaiming that the American civil rights movement contained lessons of value for black Africans. Eventually, in 1979, Young would become too controversial and would be forced to resign, but Carter would replace him with another black, Donald F. McHenry.

Although Carter refused to endorse all features of the women's movement, he did give it considerable support. He objected to child care centers and abortion, and Congress, supported by the president, Secretary Califano, and the Supreme Court, restricted the use of public funds for abortions, making it difficult for poor women to obtain them. On the other hand, Carter put women in important positions and appointed two, Kreps and Harris, to his original cabinet and a third, Shirley Hufstedler, secretary of education, when that post was created in 1979. Another woman, Patricia Derrian, played a leading role in the human rights campaign, and still others, including Margaret ("Midge") Costanza, Anne Wexler, and Mary Berry, as well as the president's wife, served significantly. Rosalynn Carter, for example, campaigned for ratification of the Equal Rights Amendment. Even more important, she was a close adviser to her husband.

At the same time that he appointed both new-comers and veterans of the Washington scene, Carter hoped to improve the performance of government. He wanted to raise its ethical level and relied heavily on rhetoric for this purpose. He wished also to make it more efficient and effective, and thus, as he had in Georgia, he pushed for government reorganization, eventually enjoying some victories in this area.

At first, Carter's methods seemed to enhance his popularity. By March, over 70 percent of the people, according to the pollsters, approved of his performance. When the battles over policy became hotter, he slipped some, but in July, more than 60 percent of the people still approved. By fall, however, less than 50 percent approved, and by May 1978, the figure was below 40 percent. Carter, it seemed obvious, had not ended the leadership crisis.

The Lance Affair

The turning point had come in late summer 1977 and had been produced by the troubles of another Georgian, Bert Lance, the director of the Office of Management and Budget. During August and September, journalists and government investigators subjected his earlier career as a banker to careful scrutiny and discovered that it contained many questionable practices. Journalists and politicians called for his resignation, as did most people who wrote to the White House or talked to pollsters. Carter continued to express great admiration for, and confidence in, his friend. But the situation became intolerable when a Senate hearing supported the work of government investigators. Before the end of September, Lance resigned, encouraged to do so by Carter because of the damage the controversy was doing, though the president retained confidence in Lance's integrity and believed he was being persecuted. To others, the episode challenged Carter's claim that he demanded a higher code of ethics than his predecessors had. In 1981, however, Lance—and also Carter—would feel vindicated when a jury acquitted the former budget officer of nine charges of bank fraud and the Justice Department dropped the other charges.

Human Rights

As his popularity rose and fell, Carter pushed forward along several lines of policy. Foreign affairs commanded much of his time, and though he had grown up in the 1930s and early 1940s and had served in the navy during World War II and during the years that saw the establishment of the Truman policy of the containment of Communism, he had been affected by the mood of withdrawal from world affairs that had been gaining strength in the United States for a decade. In addition, even though they had served in the Kennedy and Johnson administrations and had supported their policies in Vietnam, many of the men Carter appointed to the top spots in international and military affairs had been influenced by the American failure in Vietnam and by détente. Secretary Brown indicated just before taking office that he had learned from Vietnam that "we must become more cautious about . . . interventions." Carter, according to observers, had by then "made it abundantly clear that the United States ought not to go plunging militarily into under-developed countries." Soon after taking office, he praised the nation for having overcome its "inordinate fear of Communism," and Andrew Young suggested that the administration rejected "military activism."

Carter did embark upon an international campaign for human rights. In part, he did so to distinguish himself from Nixon, Ford, and Kissinger, although the campaign made use of the 1975 Helsinki treaty that the Ford administration had helped to develop. In addition to affirming the boundaries established after World War II in Eastern Europe, the treaty contained promises to respect human rights. Carter hoped the campaign would enable the United States to "regain the moral stature we once had." He explained, "We've been through some sordid and embarrassing years recently, and I felt like it was time for our country to hold a beacon light . . . that would rally our citizens to a cause." But was this policy a response to criticism of past practices as much as it was a basis for renewed activism? "In a nation supposedly instructed in its limitations by its recent failures," a critic charged, "Jimmy Carter . . . has demonstrated how little America has learned"; Carter expressed "that traditional American delusion that, if only America can devise the right . . . formula, then the world will stop being what it is, and become what we wish it to be."

In any event, Carter had difficulty maintaining a firm course on human rights. He regarded this crusade as the centerpiece—the "fundamental tenet"—of his foreign policy. He criticized many countries, not just the Soviet Union, for violating human rights. But many people—inside as well as outside the United States, State Department officials as well as journalists, allies as well as opponents—charged that the campaign was meddling, harmful to international relations, destructive of détente, and a return to the Cold War. The administration often retreated under pressure.

The campaign had mixed results. To the distress of European leaders, it infuriated the Soviet Union, contributing to the emergence of what some called a New Cold War. On the other hand, it pressured authoritarian regimes in Latin America and sub-Saharan Africa and encouraged democratic forces in those parts of the world.

Panama Canal

Carter encountered great difficulties on an issue for which groundwork had been laid by the Johnson, Nixon, and Ford administrations. Foes of two treaties dealing with the Panama Canal forced him to battle for months and nearly defeated him. The key feature of the treaties was to give Panama control of the canal by the year 2000. Opponents in both parties, including Ronald Reagan, actively campaigned against the treaties, charging that the documents would surrender American property that was vital to national security. To these people, the treaties seemed to symbolize American decline.

To the defenders, who denied that the United States owned or had sovereignty over the canal, the treaties represented the proper way for a great nation to behave. Moreover, they insisted, the terms would permit the United States to prevent hostile powers from gaining control of the canal and would enable the United States to use it when necessary. Furthermore, they maintained, the canal was losing its strategic and economic importance. The massive debate, with Carter as an active participant, raged for nearly eight months and ended in victories for the president in March and April 1978. But, in spite of help from Ford and Kissinger, the treaties won by the narrowest of margins. And success in the Senate did not end things, for it was followed by a long battle in the House, lasting until June 1979, over implementation.

SALT II

Picking up where Kissinger left off, Carter also worked for a new strategic arms limitation treaty (SALT II) with the Soviet Union but did not enjoy even a narrow victory. Knowledgeable about nuclear weapons because of his naval service, he feared the destructive power already in existence and hoped to halt the spread of such weapons to other nations and to check the arms race. He pressed the Soviets to agree to cuts in the nuclear arsenals, but Soviet leaders rejected his first proposal. Carter pressed forward, aided by Vance and special arms negotiator Paul Warnke. Negotiations did not break down, and signs of progress emerged from time to time. Yet, foes of a new treaty, such as Senator Henry Jackson, fearful that it would weaken American security, posed the possibility that no treaty acceptable to the Soviets would be ratified by the Senate. The negotiators did not finish work until 1979, and then Republican and Democratic foes in the Senate argued that the Soviets had triumphed in the negotiations, brushing aside the administration's contention that the agreed-upon limits on strategic forces would make the world a less dangerous place and insisting that the United States must increase military spending substantially. The Soviet invasion of Afghanistan weakened prospects still more, persuading Carter in January 1980 to call upon the senators to postpone debate. He continued to favor eventual ratification of SALT II but no longer pressed for it.

The Middle East and Camp David

Worried about the possibilities of Soviet-American confrontation and a new embargo on Middle Eastern oil, Carter sought a "comprehensive" settlement in the Middle East but again ran into tough problems. Apparently seeing Israel's behavior as the key, he pressed Israel to participate in multinational negotiations that would include the Palestine Liberation Organization (PLO), to agree to withdraw to "defensible borders" close to those it had had before the 1967 war, and to accept a homeland for the Palestinian Arabs in exchange for Arab recognition of Israel's right to exist and conduct normal relations. Carter, Vance, and others met frequently with Middle Eastern leaders, and the president also attempted to draw the Soviet Union into the negotiating process.

Although Arab leaders welcomed Carter's efforts, they alarmed Israel and its friends in the United

States. The Arabs hoped that American pressures would succeed, but Menachem Begin, the new Israeli prime minister, was a Polish Jew haunted by memories of the Holocaust, influenced by visions of the boundaries of biblical times, and the leader of a hardline party. Thus, he tried to persuade American leaders that few concessions could be made. Israel's friends in the United States, and they were numerous and influential, were convinced of the strategic importance of Israel, as well as its moral significance. They believed that Carter did not support it as firmly as his predecessors had and reminded him that the PLO was committed to the destruction of the country. They also expressed alarm about the proposals on boundaries and pointed to dangers in efforts to draw the Soviet Union into the negotiating process. Some charged that oil explained the direction that American policies were taking. These pressures forced Carter to insist that he supported Israel, would not harm it, and would not impose a settlement, but he did regard Begin as too inflexible.

A surprise move by Anwar as-Sadat, the president of Egypt, changed the Middle East situation. In November 1977 he visited Israel to initiate face-to-face negotiations between the Egyptians and the Israelis. His country's severe economic problems, the need for peace, and concern about some features of the American peace efforts, including encouragement of Soviet participation, influenced the move. It divided the Arabs, since most refused to talk with a nation whose right to exist they denied, and produced fresh conflict between Egypt and the Soviet Union. But, coupled with Begin's refusal to make major concessions and an Israeli raid into Lebanon, the move gained new admirers for Sadat in the United States and somewhat greater sympathy for the Arab cause.

Carter did what he could to assist the Egyptian president, but after a promising beginning, negotiations ground to a halt as the two sides learned how far apart they were on key issues. Carter then persuaded the two leaders to meet with him at Camp David, Maryland. There, the three men talked for thirteen days in September 1978 and the president achieved a great success: a "framework for peace" in the Middle East and a draft of a peace treaty between Egypt and Israel. To promote the signing of the treaty, Carter traveled to the Middle East. The treaty was soon approved and then signed in Washington on 26 March 1979, and the old enemies established full diplomatic relations. Israel had agreed to withdraw from

the Sinai, but big issues continued to divide the Middle East and generate violence there and problems for the American president.

Earlier in 1978, the Carter administration had announced an arms deal, hoping that it would strengthen Arab moderates and American influence. The deal would send the nation's best fighter plane, the F-15, not only to Israel, as had been expected, but also to Saudi Arabia, an oil-rich country controlled by antiradical and anti-Soviet leaders, and to Egypt. Israel and many of its American friends opposed the deal, doubting that the Saudis could be counted on to restrain Israel's enemies and avoid hostile acts against Israel. To critics, the deal indicated that Carter and his top adviser on foreign affairs, Brzezinski, were insensitive to Israel's security needs and were tilting toward Saudi Arabia. The debate was hot, but the president won when Congress agreed to the arrangement.

China and Taiwan

The administration improved relations with China but paid a price for doing so. Both Vance and Brzezinski visited the People's Republic, eager to break the diplomatic stalemate that had prevailed since 1972 and to normalize relations between the two countries. The Chinese, flanked by the Soviet Union and Soviet-influenced Vietnam, viewed the Soviets as aggressive and worried about what appeared to be an American retreat from containment. Brzezinski, who saw the mounting tension between the Communist giants as opening an opportunity for the United States, assured the Chinese that the United States would remain strong in Asia and would check the Soviets. Taiwan appeared to be a stumbling block. Seeking a formula that would enable the United States to abandon the regime there and recognize Beijing without suffering severe political damage at home and abroad, the Carter administration experienced frequent frustrations. Finally, on 1 January 1979, it recognized the People's Republic as the sole government of China and reestablished normal diplomatic relations with it, breaking its official ties with Taiwan to reach this objective. Taiwan, its friends in the United States, and the Soviets denounced the settlement, but the outcome pleased the president.

The International Economy

The problems Carter confronted abroad were economic as well as political. They included the opening up of a trade deficit as Americans bought more from other countries, especially manufactured goods from Japan and Germany and oil from the Middle East, than those countries purchased in the United States. In addition to working for the reduction of oil imports, the administration pressed its allies, which now had strong economies, to buy more American products, but, to the especially great distress of the American automobile industry, the efforts failed to close the trade gap, and the failure gave a boost to protectionist sentiment in the United States. The administration also struggled unsuccessfully with a weakening of the dollar.

Military Policy

Carter had inherited a wide variety of tough problems in international affairs, and in dealing with them, he was hampered by confusion and uncertainty in Congress and the nation concerning the role the nation should play in the world. A similar state of mind prevailed in the closely related area of military policy, and that state of mind affected the administration. At the beginning of his presidency, Carter pardoned Vietnam War draft evaders and announced that American troops would be withdrawn from South Korea. He also decided against construction of the B-1 bomber as a replacement for the aging B-52, regarding the proposed airplane as costly and obsolete, and also decided to cut back on the navy's shipbuilding program. Champions of military power protested, charging that he was not sufficiently sensitive to the threat of the Soviet Union.

In recent years, the Soviets had strengthened their forces and influence, expanding the army, developing a large navy, and increasing their arms and technicians in the Third World. As Carter's concern about these developments mounted, he alarmed critics of military spending by calling for a significant increase in the military budget for fiscal 1979, a substantial strengthening of North Atlantic Treaty Organization (NATO) forces, and the development and deployment of a new weapon, the neutron bomb. Next, he dismayed advocates of greater military strength by first deciding that the bomb would not be built and then announcing that production would be postponed while the nation waited to see how the Soviets behaved.

In both diplomatic and military matters, the president often found it difficult to stick with his original intentions. He made concessions to de-

mands for more military spending and more activity in Africa and became less critical of American arms sales. He both responded to criticism of the Central Intelligence Agency (CIA) and sought to restore its effectiveness, regarding it as an essential instrument that had been misused.

Critics, including Henry Kissinger, Henry Jackson, and many Republican senators, found him weak and ineffective, confusing and confused. They suggested that his administration had "seen that its neat theories about the world do not fit the difficult realities" and that "it must now come to grips with the world as it is." One close observer, Meg Greenfield of *Newsweek* magazine, wrote in 1978 that while "many of our politicians, more traumatized than instructed by that miserable war [Vietnam], tend to see Vietnams everywhere," more and more congressmen "seem . . . to be getting bored with their own post-Vietnam bemusement," and "under great provocation from abroad, Carter himself is beginning to move."

Domestic Affairs

At the same time that Carter struggled to come to grips with international problems, he also had to grapple with domestic ones, passed on to him by Ford. Unemployment, inflation, and the energy crisis topped the list. At first, slow economic growth and substantial unemployment seemed especially pressing, for 7.3 percent of the workforce did not have jobs when he took office, and the percentage jumped to 7.5 as a result of a severe winter that overtaxed the supplies of natural gas and oil. To stimulate the economy and supply more jobs, Carter proposed a $23 billion to $30 billion program for the next eighteen months. Although the program would increase spending on job-creating programs, it emphasized tax cuts in order to encourage businessmen to increase capital investments. Congress passed much of this economic stimulus package.

Before Congress acted and as economic growth accelerated and unemployment declined, Carter dropped a major feature of his economic program, a tax rebate; shifted his attention to inflation, which hovered around 7 percent; and strengthened his resistance to costly federal job programs and a higher level of spending on welfare. Rejecting price and wage controls, he made several anti-inflation proposals and promised to balance the budget by the end of his term. Yet, when the economy slowed, his concern about unemployment mounted, and he returned to plans for tax cuts. But inflation escalated in 1978, approaching the 1974 level, and Carter soon defined it as the nation's major problem, scaled down his tax-cut proposal, and tried to get prices under control by resisting proposals for increased government spending, promising a balanced budget sometime soon, and using verbal pressure—"jawboning"—to force corporations and unions to exercise restraint in price increases and wage demands. Although he relied heavily on the tested skills of Robert Strauss in the anti-inflation campaign, success eluded him. Spurred by sharp increases in the price of Middle Eastern oil, inflation soared well above 10 percent in 1979 and 1980, and Carter's new chair of the Federal Reserve Board, Paul Volcker, moved quickly to raise interest rates and reduce the money supply.

Carter's somewhat confusing course, influenced by difficulties in deciding whether unemployment or inflation was the greater problem, failed to satisfy the many groups in American life. Businessmen quickly lost confidence in his administration, troubled by divisions within it and by its proposals for tax reform and for higher taxes to protect Social Security. Corporate leaders also insisted that they did not have as much responsibility for inflation as jawboning implied; and conservatives, in and out of corporate ranks, insisted that government spending and deficits were responsible. Reflective of the decline in business confidence, the stock market dropped sharply several times.

Groups that had given Carter his victory in 1976 also grew unhappy with his performance. Union leaders, insistent that big business caused inflation and that workers were its victims, not its cause, lost some of their earlier confidence in the president when he endorsed a bill to facilitate organizing efforts but did not prevent a filibuster in the Senate from blocking passage. Furthermore, labor leaders joined liberals, most notably, Senator Edward Kennedy, in complaining that the administration was not doing enough to reduce unemployment, solve the problems of the poor, or establish national health insurance, and they demanded more government spending. To many of them, Carter seemed little more than a southern Ford. Farmers, dissatisfied with the prices they received for their products, protested against administration farm policies and forced Carter to accept higher price supports than he favored. Still further, many westerners in Congress rose up in anger when, in an effort to cut spending, Carter opposed water projects they favored, and they compelled the president to compromise on the issue.

Although black leaders had reasons to be pleased with Carter, including his support for affirmative action in the *Bakke* case, they objected to some features of his performance. Believing they deserved more influence in the White House, some reminded him that he would not be president if blacks had not voted for him in such large numbers, and charged that he was not paying enough attention to the problems of black Americans, especially the poorer ones. They joined with white liberals in insisting that everyone had a right to a job and that government must do more to increase the number available. To blacks, at least those who had not entered the middle class, unemployment rather than inflation was the most worrisome problem.

Energy Policy

As he grappled with international and economic problems, Carter attempted to build support for an energy program. Energy was, in fact, one of his biggest concerns. In April 1977 he introduced his solutions, employing dramatic terms in doing so. His proposals emphasized conservation and envisioned a smooth transition to an era of scarce and high-priced oil; they relied heavily on the taxing power to encourage people to shift from large automobiles to small ones, to cut back on the miles they drove, to insulate their homes and workplaces, and to shift from natural gas and oil to coal, nuclear power, and solar energy. Warning of a bleak future, praising conservation, appealing to patriotism, and criticizing the "special interests," the president, others in the administration, and the Democratic National Committee waged a massive campaign to build support.

At first, although he had not developed his proposals in cooperation with congressional leaders, Carter seemed likely to succeed. Congress endorsed his proposal for creation of the Department of Energy and his selection of James Schlesinger to head it, and the House—with Speaker Thomas P. ("Tip") O'Neill of Massachusetts cooperating with the administration and providing effective leadership—quickly passed energy legislation that conformed with the administration's proposals.

In the Senate, however, the energy package ran into powerful opposition. A temporary surplus of oil, dislike for the tax features, and demands for deregulation of newly discovered natural gas contributed to the resistance. Republicans and southern Democrats, with Senator Russell Long of Louisiana, head of the Senate Finance Committee, playing an especially large role, combined to revise the package, incorporating the ideas of producers, who assured the people that freeing the industry would lead to solutions. Liberal Democrats and administration representatives battled against them. But lacking support from consumer groups and environmentalists, they lost on key issues, encouraging Carter to denounce the giant oil companies in October. When Senate and House conferees engaged in lengthy negotiations to iron out their differences, the administration embarked on a new, large-scale campaign on behalf of its proposals, with Carter postponing a foreign trip so as to concentrate on building support. But dominated by other concerns, the public was not moved by the campaign, and the administration felt compelled to make concessions.

In spite of Carter's avowed populism, his proposals did not have enough support from the people to overcome opposition from the interests. In fact, most people opposed his energy package. By emphasizing conservation rather than the development of new resources, the program seemed to call upon Americans to change their lifestyle, and most did not want to do that. Furthermore, most people did not believe the energy problem was as serious as the president suggested. With confidence in Carter declining, his ability to shape public opinion on this issue suffered, and he could not rally public support with his attacks on the big oil companies. In addition, the program's heavy reliance on taxes ran head-on into a growing revolt against taxes. Thus, the people did not rise up and help Carter by putting pressure on Congress. Consequently the legislation that finally passed in October 1978, although not unimportant, fell far short of his desires.

As the president struggled with the politics of energy, a coal strike erupted. Lasting 110 days in the winter of 1977–1978, it added to Carter's difficulties. Coal had taken on renewed importance because of the nation's energy problems, and it figured prominently in Carter's solutions. As the strike continued, he resisted pressure to invoke an injunction, hoping that the normal negotiating process would produce a satisfactory outcome. Yet he and others in the administration applied whatever pressure seemed appropriate to them. The miners rebuffed the

president, turning down a contract the administration endorsed, thereby persuading Carter to resort to the injunction, a move that further angered organized labor and did not return many miners to work. Before it ended, the strike had forced many industries and schools to curtail their operations or close down completely. The episode increased awareness of the importance of coal and added to criticism of Carter as a weak president.

The energy situation worsened in 1979. A revolution in Iran reduced oil supplies, and the members of the Organization of Petroleum Exporting Countries (OPEC) raised oil prices sharply. At the same time, an alarming accident at a nuclear power plant at Three Mile Island, Pennsylvania, enlarged doubts about nuclear energy. After holding a "domestic summit conference" at Camp David, Carter gave a major speech on energy, calling for effective action to reduce dependence on foreign supplies. Following another legislative battle, in which some Democratic legislators opposed the president, he achieved some success in 1980. Although Congress had not given him all he requested, what he had achieved in 1978 and 1980 encouraged him to point with pride to lower consumption of oil, lower imports, and more coal production.

The Hostage Crisis

The consequences for the United States of the Iranian revolution were not limited to higher oil prices. Since 1945, the United States had expressed strong interest in this oil-rich country, opposing Soviet efforts to gain a position there in 1945–1946 and opposing also the nationalization of the Iranian oil industry under the leadership of Prime Minister Mohammed Mossadegh in 1951–1953. After contributing to the overthrow of Mossadegh and obtaining access to Iranian oil for American companies, the American government supplied large amounts of aid to the shah, Mohammed Reza Pahlavi, and to his efforts to westernize the country and make it a military power. Those efforts aroused the ire of the Muslim clergy, and the oppressiveness of the shah's regime generated opposition from others. Revolts erupted and gained strength during 1978, forcing the shah to flee early the following year and leading to the establishment of the Islamic Republic of Iran under the leadership of a Shiite Muslim leader, Ayatollah Ruholla Khomeini, who was determined that Islam, not Western influences, should reign in Iran. On 4 November 1979, shortly after the shah entered a New York hospital for treatment of cancer, several thousand Iranian youths seized the American embassy in Teheran and took most members of the staff hostage, demanding that the United States return the shah.

Carter faced another enormously difficult problem. He tried to free the hostages without taking military action, relying chiefly on diplomatic and economic pressures, including the freezing of Iranian assets in the United States. He obtained help from others, such as United Nations Secretary General Kurt Waldheim. Thirteen female and black staff members were released shortly after they had been seized, but the others remained captive. In April 1980 a frustrated president broke with past policy and (over the opposition of Secretary Vance) authorized a military rescue operation. It had to be aborted, however, when three of the eight helicopters involved developed mechanical problems, and, in pulling out, one of the helicopters collided with a transport plane, killing eight men and injuring others. The captors released an ill hostage in July, and the Iranian government, now suffering an invasion from Iraq, soon announced conditions for the release of the remaining fifty-two, but more weeks would pass before they were free.

Afghanistan

In the meantime, in December 1979, the Soviets mounted a large-scale invasion of Afghanistan to protect its Marxist regime. Washington interpreted this as an extension of their ambitions and a threat to American interests in the Persian Gulf area and responded with various forms of pressure, including a grain embargo, a boycott of the Moscow Olympics, reestablishment of registration for the military draft, warnings against any efforts to gain control of the Persian Gulf area, and a sizable military buildup. Carter had embraced Brzezinski's very negative view of the Soviet Union, but the pressures did not persuade the Soviets to withdraw, and the episode doomed SALT II.

Billygate

To further complicate matters for Carter, his younger brother, Billy, came under attack in the summer of 1980. A jovial fellow with a drinking problem, he had already embarrassed his more earnest brother on several occasions. Now, critics filed charges concerning his connections with Libya, a country ruled by the dictator Mu'ammar al-Gadhafi, a financial backer of international terrorism. The complaints included the charge that the president had used American intelligence information to assist Billy. The latter had made a deal with an American oil company to buy Libyan crude oil, had obtained a $220,000 "loan" from the Libyans, and had made various efforts to promote Libyan and Arab interests in the United States. Senate investigators concluded that Libya had cultivated Billy's friendship in hope of gaining influence in Washington and that by responding to these overtures he had acted contrary to the interests of the United States and merited severe criticism. The senators also concluded that Billy had no influence but that the president and some of his aides deserved criticism for ill-advised use of Billy to enlist Libyan aid in the hostage crisis and for possibly giving Libyan officials a false impression that he had influence in Washington. But the investigators found no evidence that anyone had done anything illegal or seriously improper to help the president's brother. The episode damaged the president for only a short time.

Disaffection of the Public

Well before the troubles in Iran and Afghanistan, political commentators had begun to predict that Carter would serve for only one term. To many commentators, he seemed to be a failure and responsible for his own difficulties. Although he was intelligent, worked hard, and was honest, sincere, and emotionally secure, he seemed to suffer from inexperience in dealing in Washington and from heavy reliance on inexperienced advisers. He tried to do too much himself and did not have a chief of staff coordinating work in the White House and its relations with others. He appeared to be indecisive, made too many proposals at a time, did not define his priorities clearly, and did not have a carefully articulated philosophy to help him make such a definition. He seemed to have contempt for the realities of the Washington scene and to be uninterested in working closely with organized groups, congressmen, and his party. He frequently denounced Congress—a Congress controlled by his own party—as dominated by special interests like the oil companies. And he seemed weak in his dealings with people, retreated too readily under pressure, and needed to be much more forceful.

Carter, realizing that many of these criticisms were justified, made changes in 1978. He added some experienced people to the White House staff and conferred more authority on Jordan for the management of it. He made greater efforts to cultivate congressmen and other people in the capital, and at the same time, he went out among the people, beyond Washington. He supplied a definition of his priorities and tried to deal more forcefully with members of his administration, congressmen, and others.

Such efforts did not give Carter a long-lasting boost. Approval of his performance jumped to nearly 60 percent following the Camp David accords, but by the spring of 1979, the rating was below 40 percent again. Many people now saw him as an ineffective president, incapable of moving the nation forward. All of this depressed the president. In July, after meeting at Camp David with a wide range of prominent people, he tried to revive confidence with a major speech that defined a "crisis of spirit" as the country's major problem and called for "confidence and a sense of community." Promising once again to supply the kind of leadership required, he also tried to strengthen his administration by making changes in his cabinet and took another journey of contact with the people. But his approval rating dropped below 25 percent.

The president was trying to provide leadership, but he occupied an office, and presided over a system, that had been discredited for many people by past performances. To one observer from the left, it seemed that "the widespread loss of confidence in our political institutions and leaders, the lack of respect for authority, the alienation from the official values of the society, even the revulsion from politics [were] sensible responses to the debacle accomplished by those in authority."

Many Americans believed that their governments had shown themselves to be immoral, inefficient, and ineffective. They seemed to be very active but to be accomplishing very little; they seemed too big to work. To many people, the tax system seemed unfair, in that it favored the wealthy. To many others, it merely seemed too burdensome for the benefits governments conferred. In California in 1978, the antitax feeling reached a new high with the passage of Proposition 13, which slashed property taxes and threatened funds for schools and other services. Such moves reflected deep unhappiness with what governments were doing and with government officials, as well as with the size of tax bills.

People on the right as well as the left expressed the spirit of discontent. Many intellectuals on the right and left were united in their belief that American realities were sordid. American leaders did not deserve confidence. It would be only a matter of time, according to this scenario, before the nation discovered that Carter was as corrupt as the men who had gone before him. Such skepticism was not restricted to intellectuals and people influenced by them. White-collar workers, blue-collar workers, and middle-class Americans of various occupations also felt like strangers in a nation controlled by a liberal establishment hostile to their values. Country music, popular throughout the nation with working-class, rural, and small-town people, sang of the superiority of the rural South, a surviving symbol of a vanished America, and expressed profound discontent with the now dominant style of life. Although seemingly filled with love of country, the music contained resentment and hostility toward the people in the big cities, who seemed responsible for the rise of the new way of life. Carter, as a small-town southerner, had some appeal for country music fans, but he quickly lost much of it when he became, and behaved like, a man of power.

Evangelical Christianity, a reviving and fast-growing movement of 30 million to 40 million people, also reflected deep discontent with what America, and especially American leaders, had become. "Americans are undergoing a crisis of meaning and self-confidence," one observer noted, "and large numbers of them are turning or returning to religion, usually of the pietistic and evangelical kind." Those in the Southern Baptist contingent especially had had high hopes for Carter's presidency, since they considered him one of them, but he could not satisfy their yearnings for the redemption of government through the election of honest, moral, and simple leaders. Although Carter's Baptist faith continued to influence him and to offend some big-city Americans, he came to seem to many evangelicals as just another politician. Some evangelicals had doubted his religious commitment from the outset, and many of those caught up in what has been labeled "a third Great Awakening" were uninterested in public life and contemporary issues.

Carter also had to contend with a skeptical, often hostile press that had been deeply affected by the traumas of the recent past. Strengthened by the development of television, the press was animated by a new spirit. Often resentful of the efforts of past presidents to manipulate them, media people now frequently expressed mistrust of the presidency and were much more likely to criticize a president than to be used by him. They often aimed their fire at Carter. He, in turn, resented press criticism and frequently expressed a low opinion of newspeople.

In addition, Carter had to deal with an active and critical Congress. Embarrassed by charges of past subservience to the White House, Congress had become more assertive—more determined not to be a rubber stamp. Many new members, shaped by recent experiences, especially Vietnam and Watergate, no longer deferred to senior members, insisted upon a new code of ethics, and demanded that the president avoid the "excesses" of the past at home and abroad. Senior members, possessed of a strong sense of pride and independence, were quick to press views that diverged from those of the president, even when he was a member of their own party. Furthermore, all members of Congress had staffs that were much larger and more professional than they had been only a few years earlier. To many people on Capitol Hill, including many Democrats, it seemed that Carter was not sufficiently respectful of them and their ways, did not consult with them in a timely and consistent fashion, and asked them for too much. Thus, relations between Carter and Congress were seldom smooth and frequently hostile, even after his efforts at improvement in 1978.

Furthermore, the president had, to a significant degree, lost the presidency's strongest allies and defenders, the liberals. Since the days of Theodore Roosevelt and Woodrow Wilson, they had advocated a strong White House, seeing it as the most effective promoter of broad and desirable national interests. But recent events had changed them; they, too, distrusted that office and offered new support for a Congress and press corps that checked, rather than cooperated with, the president. In fact, these new liberals were well represented in the press, Congress, congressional staffs, the bureaucracy, and the public-interest pressure groups.

Carter suffered from still another problem. He could not rally the public by making promises similar to those made by leaders in the past. He could not easily promise victories abroad, continuous growth, and ever higher standards of living. The American defeat in Vietnam, the new complexities of the international situation, and the energy crisis mocked such promises.

Carter understood the difficulties he faced and was, in a sense, a representative of them. Aware of the public's disenchantment with government, he had run against Washington in 1976. Although he frequently turned to government, rather than the private sector, to deal with problems, such as energy, and thought more of making big government more efficient through reorganization than of scaling it down, he often indicated that he did not expect as much from government as some of his predecessors had and many of his liberal contemporaries still did.

Although an active president, he carefully stayed within lines that some of his predecessors had crossed. Although he was active abroad, he worried about the dangers that world affairs contained. He was also sensitive to the implications of the energy crisis, much more so than most Americans. Carter often expressed a sense of the limits on things. He talked of the limits of his own powers and those of the government and the nation. He urged people not to expect too much. Few people derived inspiration from such rhetoric. In addition to his troubles at home, Carter suffered from criticism from his Western allies. Leaders in Western Europe had low opinions of his leadership and his policies.

Not surprisingly, Carter was a one-term president and even had to struggle to obtain renomination by his own party. In the 1980 primaries, Senator Edward Kennedy challenged him, arguing that Carter had betrayed the liberal principles of his party. The president refused to campaign until May, maintaining that the difficulties in Iran and Afghanistan forced him to stay in the White House; and Kennedy, while winning several primaries, did fail to defeat him, in part because Carter used all of the devices at a president's disposal, in part because people for a time rallied behind their president in the Iran and Afghanistan crises, and in part because of concern about Kennedy's moral character. Against Kennedy, a militant liberal, Carter appeared to use quite effectively the argument that people should recognize the great difficulties he faced and not expect too much.

The victories in the primaries did not lead to a smashing success at the Democratic National Convention. The Republicans met first; by the time they did so, Reagan, their leading contender, was ahead of the president in the polls, and during their convention, Reagan moved far ahead of Carter. By August, only about 22 percent of the people, according to the polls, approved of Carter, a new low for presidents, even lower than Nixon in 1974 and Truman in 1951. Fearing that the president would lead the entire ticket to defeat, some Democrats tried to dump him, but they could not come up with a strong contender. "There are no heroes anymore," one explained. So the party nominated Carter without enthusiasm or optimism and remained divided, with Kennedy supplying little support for the ticket.

Election of 1980

In the general election, Carter faced two opponents, Reagan and an independent, Congressman John Anderson of Illinois. Although the economy was plagued by problems, including high levels of inflation and unemployment, each candidate insisted that it had not gone into permanent decline. Carter talked of economic renewal and promised to achieve this by carefully selected spending programs and tax cuts. At the same time, he championed environmental reforms, continued to emphasize conservation as the solution to the energy crisis, and criticized Reagan for proposing surrender to the "merchants of oil." Anderson, too, stressed conservation as the way to guarantee continued growth and proposed a huge increase in the gas tax as one way to encourage conservation.

Critical of some of the conservation measures, Reagan seemed confident that the economy could grow indefinitely. In fact, he proposed a "strategy of growth." To accomplish that, he would cut both income taxes and government regulation of business. He and his platform emphasized energy production, not conservation. He insisted that the nation could get all the oil it needed if the oil industry's opportunities for profit were enlarged and a nuisance, the Department of Energy, were abolished. Along a similar line, he attacked the environmental movement and the government regulations it had successfully promoted.

The candidates said less about race, and none called for major changes in this area. In fact, the chief issue appeared to be the survival of the changes that had taken place in recent years. As a consistent supporter of civil rights legislation, Anderson had no trouble with his record, but as a conservative spokesman since the early 1960s and an opponent of the civil rights legislation of 1964, Reagan had some trouble with his. As a Georgian, so did Carter, although somewhat less; his identification with right-wing southerners in the 1960s was offset by his closeness to Andrew Young and other blacks in the 1970s.

Reagan implied rather vaguely that Carter had some relations with the Ku Klux Klan, and Carter implied more clearly that Reagan was a racist. Although Carter rather quickly denied that he had made such a charge, his words were part of a larger effort to suggest that Reagan would, if elected, set the clock back in this area. The effort took advantage of Reagan's opposition to the 1964 act and his endorsement by the Klan, an endorsement he repudiated. Reagan also said that he no longer opposed the Civil Rights Act of 1964, explaining that it had not worked as he had feared but instead had worked quite well. He called attention to his appointment of many blacks to office while serving as governor of California, and he paid more attention to blacks during the campaign than his party had in its convention. He and his party did continue to oppose the busing of schoolchildren to achieve racial balance.

Wisely perhaps, the candidates tried to ignore the hot issue of relations between men and women. The candidates seemed satisfied to leave it to political participants who were not running for office, including the evangelicals who were campaigning against homosexual rights, sex education in the schools, and other issues of this kind. Anderson associated himself with some of the proposals for change, including liberalization of laws on abortion and protection for the rights of homosexuals. Reagan was quite clearly on the other side of the fence. His platform called for a constitutional amendment banning abortions and for curbs on the use of public funds for them, and he agreed. The platform also ended national Republican support for the Equal Rights Amendment, which he opposed while insisting that he favored equality for women. His positions on these issues were part of his advocacy of traditional values, a major Reagan theme. The platform favored prayer in the schools, and he advocated teaching the biblical theory of creation along with the scientific theory of evolution in the schools, a position championed by critics of evolution.

Carter's positions were somewhere between Reagan's and Anderson's. The Democratic platform contained a strong plank on the Equal Rights Amendment and abortion, reflecting the growing strength of women in the party. The president's own stand on these issues did not fully satisfy feminists.

The candidates spoke much more frequently and also more clearly on the issue of America's role in the world, and none championed a small role. Anderson did oppose some of the military spending proposals, but even he promised to enlarge the main instrument of a large American role, the armed forces.

Reagan was most clearly the advocate of a large role, relying heavily on military power. The party platform spoke of the "Soviet Union's global ambitions" as the "premier challenge" facing the United States, called for "military superiority" through increased spending, a new class of bomber; new ships, planes, missiles, and air defense systems; and higher pay for the armed forces. It opposed arms control that fixed the United States "into a position of military inferiority" and accused the Democrats of weakening the nation.

Reagan, holding to the militant anti-Communism he had embraced in the late 1940s and had expressed in politics since the early 1960s, continued to see the Soviet Union as a real threat and the Cold War as a persistent reality. He expressed the World War II generation's view of the dangers of military weakness and indecision, opposed SALT II, favored a large-scale military buildup, and criticized Carter for weakness and for permitting the United States to fall behind. The challenger also rejected the negative view of the shah of Iran, blaming his fall on Carter's weaknesses rather than the shah's own. Reagan also rejected the negative view of American involvement in Vietnam, a prop of the "little America" point of view, arguing that weak policies were responsible for America's failure there. He also criticized Carter's treatment of Israel and Taiwan.

Although portraying himself as much safer than Reagan, Carter did not advocate a small American role in the world. He represented Reagan as certain to produce a runaway arms race and likely to provoke a war because of his tendency to think of military solutions to crises. The Democratic platform included proposals for strengthening the armed forces through better pay for the military and improvements in the nuclear deterrent and called for resistance to aggression in the Persian Gulf and support for Israel as well as normalization of relations with China and ratification of SALT II. In response to criticism, Carter claimed that he had strengthened the United States and that it was "still the most powerful" nation in the world.

During the campaign, Carter gained ground rapidly. He did so chiefly because of Reagan's ability to generate alarm and to blunder. Seeking to rally Democrats, Carter exploited the widespread doubts about, and fears of, the former movie actor and militant champion of a tougher foreign policy and made use of the advantages that control of the White House supplied, including its ability to distribute federal grants to places in which they could influence votes. Most Kennedy people rallied behind Carter; the economy even improved some. what and soon the gap separating him from Reagan in the polls became insignificant.

If Carter failed, Anderson seemed likely to be a contributing factor. His candidacy rested on the assumption that there was a widespread lack of confidence in both of the leading candidates. "People talk about a spoiler," he remarked in defense of his role. "What's to spoil?" Fearing that Anderson would take votes away from him and detract from his efforts to focus attention on Reagan, the president refused to join in a television debate that included Anderson.

By early October, it appeared that many people believed they had been given an unattractive set of alternatives. It seemed that only about 50 percent of the voters would go to the polls and the winner would obtain fewer than 50 percent of the total and triumph by only a narrow margin. The Republican party seemed likely to make gains, largely because of economic conditions, but it did not seem capable of becoming the nation's majority party once again.

Late in the campaign, two factors gave Reagan a boost. One was a television debate a week before election day that was limited to the two major-party candidates. Reagan was especially effective in his closing statement in which he suggested that there were two basic questions: "Are you better off than you were four years ago?" "Is America as respected throughout the world?" His relaxed and friendly performance helped to dispel fears about him as a warmonger and doubts that he was smart enough for the presidency, while Carter failed to persuade the undecided that he recognized his mistakes, had learned from them, and would govern better in a second term. Another last-minute factor was the frustration of Carter's efforts to obtain an agreement before election day for release of the hostages in Iran. For many people, that failure drove home the theme about Carter's weaknesses. By election day, it competed effectively against his theme that Reagan threatened valuable domestic programs and peace.

Benefiting from a late surge among previously undecided voters and a low turnout among several Democratic groups, Reagan won by a surprisingly large margin, with a popular vote of 43.9 million to Carter's 35.5 million and an electoral vote of 489 to 49. The voter turnout was unusually low, only 52 percent, a phenomenon that seriously damaged the president. Reagan had the support of more than 51

Jimmy Carter has dedicated much of his post-presidential life to good works in the United States and abroad. Here, he and his wife help construct a home in Atlanta, Georgia, in 1988 as part of their deep involvement in Habitat for Humanity. BETTMANN/CORBIS

percent of those who voted to 41 percent for Carter and 7 percent for Anderson. The Democrats maintained control of the House of Representatives but by a narrower margin, and they lost control of the Senate, doing so for the first time since 1952.

After this great failure, Carter achieved three victories before leaving office. Congress accepted two of his proposals for action on the environment, and the United States and Iran agreed on a settlement of the hostage crisis. But they completed their work two days before he left office, and the hostages did not obtain their freedom until 20 January 1981, just as Carter was leaving office, and did not reach American soil until after Reagan had become president. During the presidential campaign, Republicans had feared that the administration would work out a deal just before election day, and later, a former member of the Carter administration, Gary Sick, charged that Republicans themselves worked out a deal to delay the release, a charge that remains unproved.

Although consoled somewhat by his perception of the great difficulties he had faced, Carter left office disappointed and unhappy, the first elected president since Herbert Hoover to fail in a bid for reelection. He recognized that he had not accomplished many of his goals. Above all, he knew he had not ended the leadership crisis.

The task that Carter faced had been enormous. To provide effective leadership in his time, a person needed a compelling vision and political skill of an unusually high order, including great talent in communication. He needed to communicate not only attractive goals but also a sense of realities and of what could be accomplished within them. Perhaps none of the available candidates could have supplied effective leadership in the Carter period.

Out of office and free of the political pressures that had limited his accomplishments as president, Carter became an unusually active and widely admired former president. He found new ways of expressing his humanitarianism: monitoring elections in other countries, mediating international disputes, bringing experts together to develop solutions to pressing problems, and building low-priced housing with the Habitat for Humanity organization.

BIBLIOGRAPHY

In the early 1980s, when the first edition of this book was written, Carter had been out of office only a short time, and the number of books on him remained rather slim. Much of what had been written was by journalists, such as Haynes Johnson, *In the Absence of Power: Governing America* (New York, 1980). A few memoirs had appeared, including Jimmy Carter, *Keeping Faith: Memoirs of a President* (New York, 1982). Only a few scholarly works were available. Good examples of these are Gary M. Fink, *Prelude to the Presidency: The Political Character and Legislative Leadership Style of Governor Jimmy Carter* (Westport, Conn., 1980), and Betty Glad, *Jimmy Carter: In Search of the Great White House* (New York, 1980).

In the decade following the publication of this work's first edition, both memoirs and scholarly writing developed rapidly. For guidance to this literature and the conclusions that are yet emerging, see Burton I. Kaufman, *The Presidency of James Earl Carter, Jr.* (Lawrence, Kans., 1993). The fault line in this literature lies between those who emphasize Carter's shortcomings and those who stress the difficult situation he confronted. Kaufman leans toward the former interpretation, finding it "hard to avoid the conclusion that his was a mediocre presidency and that much of the reason for this was his own doing."

For an excellent summary of "Carter revisionism," see Douglas Brinkley, "The Rising Stock of Jimmy Carter: The 'Hands On' Legacy of Our Thirty-ninth President," in *Diplomatic History* 20 (fall 1996): 505–529.

Carter's account of his political ascendance amid the volatile politics of the 1960s is told in fascinating detail in *Turning Point: A Candidate, a State, and a Nation Come of Age* (New York, 1992). Mrs. Carter's memoir, a warmer and more revealing report than the president's, is Rosalynn Carter, *First Lady from Plains* (Boston, 1984). Carter's rise from obscurity is reported on in Martin Schram, *Running for President, 1976: The Carter Campaign* (New York, 1977). On Carter's defeat for reelection, see Hamilton Jordan, *Crisis: The Last Year of the Carter Presidency* (New York, 1982), the account by Carter's chief of staff. It should be read in conjunction with Richard Harwood, ed., *The Pursuit of the Presidency, 1980* (New York, 1980).

An admiring examination of the Carter years is in *Man of the House: The Life and Political Memoirs of Speaker Tip O'Neill*, with William Novak (New York, 1987). John Dumbrell, *The Carter Presidency: A Reevaluation*, 2d ed. (Manchester, Eng., and New York, 1995), is a laudatory but incisive analysis by a foreigner.

A comprehensive study of the president's conduct of foreign relations is Gaddis Smith, *Morality, Reason, and Power: American Diplomacy in the Carter Years* (New York, 1986). It should be used in conjunction with Zbigniew Brzezinski, *Power and Principle: Memoirs of the National Security Adviser, 1977–1981* (New York, 1983; rev. ed. 1985); Cyrus Vance, *Hard Choices: Critical Years in America's Foreign Policy* (New York, 1983); and Stansfield Turner, *Secrecy and Democracy: The CIA in Transition* (Boston, 1985). To supplement these memoirs see the oral interviews in Kenneth W. Thompson, ed., *The Carter Presidency: Fourteen Intimate Perspectives of Jimmy Carter* (Lanham, Md., 1990). On the hostage crisis, specifically, consult James A. Bill, *The Eagle and the Lion: The Tragedy of American-Iranian Relations* (New Haven, Conn., 1988), and Gary Sick, *All Fall Down: America's Tragic Encounter with Iran* (New York, 1985). On nuclear diplomacy, turn to Strobe Talbott, *Endgame: The Inside Story of SALT II* (New York, 1979).

Recent works include Douglas Brinkley, *The Unfinished Presidency: Jimmy Carter's Journey Beyond the White House* (New York, 1998), which examines Carter's life following his term in office. See also Jimmy Carter, *Living Faith* (New York, 1996) and *An Hour Before Daylight: Memories of a Rural Boyhood* (New York, 2001), and Hamilton Jordan, *No Such Thing As a Bad Day: A Memoir* (Atlanta, Ga., 2000).

Ronald Reagan

Alan Brinkley

Ronald Reagan THE LIBRARY OF CONGRESS

RONALD REAGAN'S election to the presidency in 1980 marked the convergence of two processes, neither of which would have seemed likely to most Americans even a few years earlier. One was Reagan's transformation from a fading film actor into the dominant political figure in the nation. The other was the rise of a powerful conservative movement that profited not only from Reagan's attractive personality but also from a decade of popular disenchantment with politics and government.

Reagan's many successes as president owed much to his actor's instincts and much to the popular pessimism that he inherited and that his sunny temperament helped at least temporarily to dispel.

The same factors contributed as well to the many shortcomings of his administration: its tendency to emphasize style over substance, its emphasis on short-term economic and political benefits at the price of long-term costs, and its insouciant refusal to acknowledge deep domestic and international problems that might undermine the hopeful picture of the world Reagan consistently presented. His presidency coincided with, and contributed to, a long period of dramatic economic growth and the beginning of a momentous change in international relations. But it failed to address, and in many ways intensified, a series of public dilemmas that had been developing for years before Reagan entered the White House and that continued to plague the nation for years after he left.

Youth

Reagan's rise to eminence moved along a path that, in the beginning, resembled that of many other American politicians but that later diverged sharply from the norm. He was born on 6 February 1911 in the small town of Tampico, Illinois. His parents, Jack and Nelle, named him Ronald Wilson for a great-uncle but always called him Dutch (after his father began referring to the strapping baby as his "fat little Dutchman"). Jack Reagan was an unsuccessful sales-man with a serious drinking problem. Nelle Wilson Reagan was a devout farm-woman who raised Ronald and his older brother, Neil, in the Disciples of Christ Church despite their father's Catholicism. The family moved frequently, sometimes in response to new job opportunities, sometimes after Jack had been fired because of his drinking. In 1920 they settled in Dixon, Illinois, where Jack became the proprietor and part owner of a shoe store.

Nelle did occasional work to supplement the family's meager income and became intensely active in church functions. She seemed to live a life of al-most complete self-denial, devoted to her children, defensive of her unsuccessful, alcoholic husband (whom she taught her children to tolerate and for-give). But on occasion, she showed signs of frustrat-ed ambitions, particularly when she traveled around the county giving dramatic readings of poetry and melodrama to church groups and other gather-ings—a popular form of entertainment at the time and one at which Nelle apparently excelled. Her younger son often accompanied her on these out-ings, although he later denied that they were the source of his attraction to acting.

Ronald Reagan was an outgoing, optimistic, pop-ular, and apparently happy youth despite the prob-lems of his family. He was interested in sports from an early age and particularly liked football and swim-ming. His nearsightedness, undiagnosed until he was thirteen, made baseball difficult for him. He was a hardworking and modestly successful student, with a talent for memorization. He was active early in school dramatics. As a teenager, he worked during summers as a lifeguard at the swimming area of the local river and put aside much of what he earned for his education.

His greatest childhood challenge may have been learning to deal with his father's drinking. As an elev-en-year-old, he found his father drunk and passed out on the front porch, dragged him inside, and put him to bed. From then on, he joined his mother and brother in compensating for Jack's "illness," as Nelle explained it to the children. And he began as well to construct a series of defenses, finding ways to wall off the pain of his father's alcoholism from the rest of his essentially happy youth—denying unpleasant reali-ties and viewing his world as he wished it to be. When he graduated from the public high school in Dixon in 1928, he wrote in his yearbook, "Life is just one grand, sweet song, so start the music."

Reagan had been a member of the varsity foot-ball team in high school, and his competent if unre-markable performance on the field was enough to win him a scholarship to Eureka College, a small Dis-ciples of Christ school about a hundred miles from Dixon. He was interested in the school in part be-cause one of Dixon's best football players (and one of Reagan's boyhood idols) had studied there six years earlier, and also because Reagan's high school girlfriend, the daughter of the Disciples of Christ minister in Dixon, would be attending.

Entering college, even one as small and provin-cial as Eureka, was a sign of unusual ambition in Dixon. Fewer than 10 percent of the town's recent high school graduates (and no other member of Rea-gan's own family) had ever done so. But Reagan glided through college without any visible single-mindedness of purpose. His grades were little better than passing (deliberately so, he later implausibly claimed, to keep him from being recruited—as most good students at Eureka were—to be a high school teacher and coach). He played on the football team but rarely started, enjoyed modest success as a varsi-ty swimmer, and was active in the college's drama so-ciety. Even with a scholarship, Reagan had to work hard at several jobs, both during the term and over the summers, to remain in school. But he established himself nevertheless as one of the most visible and popular students on campus.

Reagan's youth was in many ways oddly similar to that of other provincial Americans who rose to po-litical prominence: a boyhood in a small town, a fami-ly struggling precariously on the edges of the middle class, education in small, undistinguished schools. Huey P. Long, Harry S. Truman, Lyndon B. Johnson, Richard M. Nixon, and many others had grown up in comparable circumstances. But unlike most other small-town boys who rose to political greatness, Rea-gan showed little early interest in politics. Jack Reagan, like most American Catholics of his era, was a staunch Democrat; and Ronald inherited his father's unreflective enthusiasm for the party even though, throughout the 1920s, it enjoyed little national success. He became a fervent admirer of Franklin D. Roosevelt in 1932, an attachment that grew stronger when New Deal agencies began providing jobs to unemployed men (among them his father) in depression-ravaged central Illinois. But he never became actively involved in Democratic politics in the state. He found himself drawn occasionally into campus politics at Eureka and in his senior year won election as class president. But when he graduated in 1932, with a B.A. in economics and sociology, politics and public life remained far from his thoughts. He was, he later wrote, drawn to "some form of show business," an interest born in part of his experiences in the Eureka drama society.

Acting Career

Broadway and Hollywood, Reagan recalled, seemed "as inaccessible as outer space." So after graduation he decided to look for a job closer to home, in radio. After an unsuccessful search for work in Chicago, he applied for a position as a sports announcer at station WOC in Davenport, Iowa, about seventy-five miles from Dixon. He got the job by impressing the station manager with a vivid description, entirely from memory, of a Eureka College football game. His skill and enthusiasm won him a growing reputation and, soon, a position as chief sports announcer on WHO, a much larger station in Des Moines. Dutch Reagan quickly became one of the most popular sportscasters in Iowa. His first love was football, but the heart of his job was broadcasting Chicago Cubs baseball games. WHO could not afford to send him to Wrigley Field, so he relied on the running accounts of the games provided by the wire services and extemporized the rest. Reagan modeled his broadcasting on such accomplished and popular myth-makers as Graham McNamee and Grantland Rice—the leading figures in a generation of sports journalists to whom accuracy was far less important than color and uplift. Reagan was a success as a broadcaster because he was skilled at creating appealing fantasies and making effective use of anecdotes. His radio experiences reinforced the storytelling talents his friends and family had already recognized; it also reinforced his tendency to embellish events for dramatic effect.

In the spring of 1937, Reagan accompanied the Chicago Cubs to their spring training camp in southern California, a trip he arranged in order to explore a possible movie career. His good looks and confident manner attracted the attention of an agent, who set up a screen test for him with Warner Brothers. The studio was impressed with Reagan and offered him a seven-year contract starting at $200 a week—many times his salary in Des Moines. Reagan promptly accepted. Six months later, he brought his parents to California to live with him.

Reagan did not soon become a star, but he worked steadily and achieved a series of small successes playing leads in B movies and minor parts in more significant films. His early screen image did not differ greatly from his own personality: good-natured, easygoing, and sincere. The studio considered him a dependable actor who did whatever he was told. In 1939, he was cast in the film version of *Brother Rat*, a Broadway play. It was his most substantial role in a major film yet, but its chief significance for Reagan was that he played opposite the actress Jane Wyman, then in the final stages of a divorce. By the time filming ended, they were engaged. They married in January 1940 and had two children, Maureen, born in 1941, and Michael, whom the couple adopted in 1945, a few days after his birth.

So far, Reagan had moved through his movie career relatively passively, taking the parts he was offered and seldom complaining. But Wyman pressed him to be more assertive, and in 1940 he pursued the part of George Gipp, a famous Notre Dame football player and an important character in the Warner Brothers feature *Knute Rockne—All American*. Reagan was not yet a "name player," and some studio executives resisted his request. But his enthusiasm for the role and his background as a sports announcer finally won him the part. The success of the film, and the critical acclaim Reagan received for it, propelled his career. He began to receive better parts, and his performances in such front-rank films as *King's Row* (1941) and *Desperate Journey* (1942) earned him more critical praise.

His growing success also won him a series of deferments from military service (at the request of Warner Brothers) once the United States entered World War II, and then—after he was called up and commissioned an officer in the cavalry—an assignment with an army film unit. He spent the war in California making army training movies at a military base in Los Angeles, with time off to make feature films at Warner Brothers (among them the successful 1943 tribute to the military, *This Is the Army*). Much of the time, he lived at home with his family. Despite his later claims to the contrary, he never left the country and never saw combat. But he cooperated with studio public relations efforts to portray him as a soldier, who, like other soldiers, left his family to go "off to war." Feature stories described Wyman bravely carrying on, raising the children and maintaining the household while her man was away. Newsreels and magazine photos depicted Reagan "coming home" for leaves and visits. Reagan later sometimes seemed actually to have believed the ruse. Even decades later, he liked to talk about "coming back from the war," like other veterans, eager to take up family life again (a life that in his case had hardly been interrupted).

Reagan's postwar acting career never regained the momentum it had enjoyed in the early 1940s. He had some occasional successes (among them *The Hasty Heart* in 1949), but he found himself working more often now in minor roles or minor films. Jane Wyman's career, in the meantime, was flourishing, and her absorption with it contributed to what were already growing tensions within the marriage. The couple divorced in 1948.

As his career and his marriage languished, Reagan had begun to become active in politics. His first vehicle was the Screen Actors Guild (SAG), the film actors' union. Reagan had been active in SAG since his first months in Hollywood, and his involvement grew with his marriage to Wyman, who was also an important figure in the organization. In 1946, he chaired a union strike committee and demonstrated an energy and a toughness that his SAG colleagues had not previously seen. In 1947, he became president of the union, a position he held for six years. Reagan still considered himself a liberal Democrat, and he used his new political distinction to campaign for Harry Truman in 1948. There was occasional talk of Reagan himself running for Congress as a Democrat, but party leaders apparently opposed the idea because they considered him too liberal.

In reality, Reagan's political views were changing more rapidly than his public activities suggested. During the war, he had harshly criticized the waste and corruption he saw in the awarding of military contracts, and his suspicion of government bureaucracies only grew in the following years. He was also now complaining frequently about taxes. He had signed a million-dollar contract with Warner Brothers in 1944, but the very high wartime tax rates (up to 90 percent in the upper brackets) greatly reduced his income. In 1950, after initially endorsing the actress Helen Gahagan Douglas for the United States Senate, he switched his support to Richard Nixon in mid-campaign. And as president of SAG, he became active in efforts to distance the union from Communist influence (driven to do so, no doubt, by the savagely anti-Communist political climate, but also by his own deep and growing aversion to Communists). By the late 1940s, he was cooperating with the FBI and testifying before the House Committee on Un-American Activities against Communism in the union (although he was not asked to name any individual Communists). Subsequently, he cooperated with the studios as they quietly administered the notorious blacklist of alleged Communists who were to be barred from employment in the movie industry. Reagan later claimed that the effort by Hollywood Communists to "take over the motion picture business," and the unwillingness of many liberals to confront them, was responsible for his political turn to the right.

At least as responsible, however, was his marriage in 1952 to Nancy Davis, a young and largely unknown actress whom he had met at a dinner party in 1949. Davis was the daughter of a once-successful stage actress, Edith Luckett. Her natural parents separated when she was an infant, and she spent most of her childhood in the home of her mother's second husband, Loyal Davis, whose name Nancy took and whose right-wing political views she uncritically absorbed. Her family's conservatism reinforced Reagan's own accelerating drift to the right.

Reagan's second marriage was a happy one. The couple lived in a comfortable home in Pacific Palisades and began to spend time at a ranch Reagan had bought near Santa Barbara. They had two children, Patricia, born in 1952, and Ronald, born in 1958. But Reagan's film career was now in serious decline. Warner Brothers had not renewed his contract, and he was having difficulty finding steady work elsewhere. He was now in his mid-forties, and major stardom was coming to seem beyond his reach.

Corporate Spokesman and Rising Conservative

In 1954, after several years of sporadic acting in minor westerns, Reagan signed a lucrative contract to become the host of the *General Electric Theater*, a new television drama series. Reagan introduced each show and acted in some of them. He also became active in GE corporate relations, touring the company's plants and serving as its "goodwill ambassador" to the public. He spent much time in the company of Earl Dunckel, who handled public relations for the GE Theater and who bombarded Reagan constantly with his deeply conservative political views.

Similar views began to appear more and more often in the increasingly frequent and increasingly political speeches Reagan gave for General Electric in the mid- and late 1950s, when he became not just the host of the company's television series but, in effect, its most prominent corporate spokesman. His subject was almost invariably the wastefulness and intrusiveness of government (which should, he insisted, "be reduced to the barest minimum") and the bankruptcy of the "welfare state." In public, at least, nothing remained of his earlier liberal enthusiasms and his fervent support of the New Deal.

In late 1959, Reagan reluctantly accepted an invitation from the Screen Actors Guild to return as president; he steered the union through a bitter and ultimately unsuccessful strike in which SAG members demanded a share of the profits the studios were receiving for selling film rights to television. But Reagan's main interests now lay elsewhere, and shortly after the unhappy end of the strike he resigned as both president and board member of SAG and never again took an active role in the organization. Instead, he plunged into Republican politics. Although he was still nominally a Democrat, he worked for Richard Nixon in the 1960 presidential campaign (and in 1962 officially changed his party affiliation). But his own politics were, in fact, well to Nixon's right. His fiery speeches for GE in early 1961 and 1962 were fervently anti-Communist and expressed the unhappiness of the party's right wing with the bipartisan commitment to "containment" that had shaped American foreign policy since 1948. Reagan, like the right's great hero of the early 1960s, Barry Goldwater, spoke of the need for "victory" in the battle against Communism.

In 1962, the Kennedy administration launched an antitrust investigation of MCA, one of Hollywood's most powerful talent agencies, which in the 1950s used heavy and some believed illegal pressure to drive competitors out of business and establish a virtual monopoly over large segments of the film industry. Reagan was president of the Screen Actors Guild during the period of MCA's most rapid and ruthless expansion; his own agent was a power in the company; and there were charges that Reagan had used his influence with SAG to help MCA's rise to dominance. The justice Department subpoenaed Reagan's tax returns, and rumors of improper behavior that had begun in 1960 grew to new levels. At about the same time, General Electric canceled the GE Theater, and Reagan was suddenly without employment.

But Reagan's problems did not last long. In September, MCA reached an agreement with the Justice Department to divest itself of some of its divisions; the government then dropped its investigation of Reagan. In the meantime, Reagan found a new role as the host and narrator of *Death Valley Days*, a television western sponsored by Borax. And he accelerated his political activities, speaking now not as a corporate spokesman but as an independent political figure much in demand by the large and growing Republican right wing.

By 1964, Reagan had been socially friendly for more than a decade with Barry Goldwater, who ran for and won the Republican presidential nomination. Reagan eagerly agreed to help Goldwater's campaign. One week before the election, at Goldwater's request, Reagan appeared on national television and gave a memorable speech, "A Time for Choosing," in which he presented the conservative views on major issues he had been promoting in California for years. "You and I have a rendezvous with destiny," he grandiloquently concluded, in a phrase associated with his boyhood idol Franklin Roosevelt. "We can preserve for our children this last best hope of man on earth or we can sentence them to take the first step into a thousand years of darkness. If we fail, at least let our children, and our children's children, say of us we justified our brief moment here. We did all that could be done." The speech created a political sensation. David S. Broder of the *Washington Post* called it "the most successful political debut since Willam Jennings Bryan electrified the 1896 Democratic convention with his 'Cross of Gold' speech." Almost overnight, Reagan became a national political figure—a hero to those on the right who even before the election were losing faith in Goldwater. After the shattering Republican defeat that fall, the party's conservative wing began looking to Reagan for leadership.

Governor of California

Reagan moved immediately to capitalize on the momentum of the Goldwater speech and began appearing before Republican gatherings in California and elsewhere within weeks of the 1964 election. By 1965, encouraged by conservative political leaders and right-wing businessmen in California, he had decided to run for governor; he formally announced his candidacy early in 1966. His opponent was the incumbent governor, Edmund G. Brown, a popular politician running for his third term. (He had defeated Richard Nixon four years earlier.) Brown spoke condescendingly of Reagan's inexperience and ridiculed his film career. But he was no match for Reagan's homespun magnetism. The Reagan campaign capitalized on popular anger at student demonstrations on the Berkeley campus of the University of California, and it portrayed Brown as an old-fashioned politician out of touch with the people: Reagan, in contrast, presented himself as an ordinary citizen fed up with politics and committed to making government more efficient and accountable. He defeated Brown in a landslide.

Reagan entered office surrounded by conservative political outsiders from southern California, fueled with ideological fervor. But the pressures of politics quickly forced the new administration to compromise. In the end, Reagan's governorship was symbolically radical but substantively conventional. Having inherited a substantial budget deficit from the previous administration, Reagan ordered an across-the-board 10-percent reduction in state spending, only to have to restore funds to a host of programs that were already so lean they could not survive the cuts. Within a year he was pressing for a major tax increase—in part to address the budget deficit, in part to give him a fiscal cushion so that he would not have to ask again. Shaped in the end by Democrats in the legislature, the final bill produced a highly progressive tax increase, the highest in the history of California (or of any other state). Reagan signed it, blaming the irresponsibility of his predecessor. When the tax increases produced a budget surplus in subsequent years, he attributed it to his administration's managerial skill.

In the end, Reagan's budget was, in fact, more than twice as high as Brown's; and while much of that growth was a result of inflation, some of it was because of spending increases in the same programs that conservatives had once vowed to cut or abolish—many of them programs important to some of Reagan's critical constituencies. He worked effectively with the Democratic legislature on a series of tax and welfare reforms that were not at all consistent with the more radical agenda of Reagan's most conservative supporters. He oversaw one of the largest (and most expensive) water projects in the nation's history. And despite his harsh rhetorical attacks on the University of California for its alleged coddling of radicals, his administration was generally supportive of the system and helped it to grow. State government under Reagan, according to Gary G. Hamilton and Nicole Woolsey Biggart, did not "shrink and allow private citizens to handle their own affairs," as Reagan had once promised. "Instead government entrenched itself in many ways as a strong, effective force in California society" (*Governor Reagan, Governor Brown* [New York, 1984], p. 214).

Reagan's governing style in California was much like the style he would later adopt in the White House. He was an effective communicator of his administration's broad goals (vague though they often were), and he relished the ceremonial aspects of his job. But he was oddly passive in the day-to-day running of the government. His days were rigidly organized around the typed schedule his assistants always prepared for him and from which he rarely departed. He ceded operating responsibility for his office to a series of energetic aides, many of whom were as inexperienced as he was. (Lyn Nofziger, his first chief of staff in Sacramento, later claimed that the Reagan administration had "materialized out of thin air with no political background, no political cronies and no political machine," and that the new governor was surrounded by "novice amateurs," among them Nofziger himself.)

Reagan disliked bureaucratic conflict, so he permitted his aides and cabinet officers to work out their disagreements among themselves; the governor would then usually ratify a compromise he had played no role in creating. He also relied heavily on existing state agencies. That was one reason his record was so much more moderate than his rhetoric. He left control of education and the environment, for example, to Democrats of progressive inclinations, and his record in both areas pleased many liberals. Reagan won reelection comfortably in 1970 over the Democratic Speaker of the California House, Jesse Unruh, but his victory margin was considerably smaller than it had been four years before. Perhaps that was because he was by then no longer a crusading outsider. He was an incumbent governor with an essentially moderate record.

Presidential Campaigns

But state politics was never Reagan's principal interest. Almost from the beginning of his governorship, he had his eye on national leadership. In 1968 he made a brief foray into presidential politics, entering the race for the Republican nomination shortly before the convention—essentially as a favorite son. From then on, he and his supporters planned for another national campaign in 1976, after Nixon's second term. But Watergate ended the Nixon presidency prematurely, and when Reagan left the governorship at the end of 1974, he unexpectedly found an incumbent Republican president, Gerald R. Ford, standing between him and his hopes. Unwilling to wait, Reagan crafted a harsh conservative critique of Ford's policies and appointments and challenged him with surprising effectiveness in the 1976 Republican primaries. Ford hung on to win renomination by a narrow margin, but Reagan emerged from the campaign the clear leader of the growing Republican right. He hardly paused before beginning preparations for the 1980 campaign.

Only a few years earlier, so many Americans had considered Reagan to be a man of such extreme views that thoughts of him as a potential president had seemed absurd. But much had changed by the late 1970s, both in Reagan's own political credibility (a result of two reasonably successful terms as governor of the nation's most populous state) and in the character of national politics. The booming prosperity and ebullient optimism of the late 1950s and early 1960s had disappeared in the maelstrom of Vietnam; the tumult of racial conflict, urban disorder, and student radicalism; the shambles of Watergate; and perhaps most of all the jarring changes in the American economy after 1973, which did much to increase insecurity and resentment. The American Right,
which had appeared so thoroughly repudiated as recently as 1964, profited enormously from these changes and from its own successful efforts at rebuilding.

By the time Reagan began his campaign for the 1980 Republican presidential nomination, conservatives were the beneficiaries of a remarkable communications and fund-raising organization, developed originally by conservative activist Richard Viguerie from a list of twelve thousand Goldwater contributors and expanded to more than 4 million contributors and 15 million names by the mid-1970s. Gradually, these direct-mail operations came to be accompanied by a much larger conservative infrastructure, designed to match and even exceed what the right saw as the powerful liberal infrastructure. There were now right-wing think tanks, consulting firms, lobbyists, and foundations, staffed by talented, committed men and women eager to promote the conservative cause. There was also a substantial and rapidly growing group of evangelical Christian conservatives who were becoming politically active and developing organizational strength of their own.

The failure of Gerald Ford's presidency did much to damage the fragile equilibrium that had enabled the right wing and the moderate wing of the Republican party to coexist, and convinced many conservatives that they must insist on a candidate true to their beliefs. Unwittingly, perhaps, Ford touched on some of the right's rawest nerves. He appointed as vice president Nelson A. Rockefeller, whom conservative Republicans had reviled for more than a decade. (Goldwater delegates had tried to boo Rockefeller off the podium at the 1964 Republican convention.) Richard Viguerie attributed the birth of the "New Right" to this event alone. Ford proposed an amnesty program for draft resisters, embraced and even extended the Nixon-Kissinger policies of détente, presided ineffectually over the fall of South Vietnam to North Vietnam in 1975, and agreed to cede the Panama Canal to Panama. All of these decisions became potent issues in Reagan's primary campaign against him in 1976. To stave off Reagan's challenge, Ford had to drop Rockefeller from his ticket and accept a solidly conservative platform written largely by one of Reagan's allies, Senator Jesse Helms of North Carolina. Reagan hailed that platform by saying that the party "must raise a banner of no pale pastels, but bold colors which make it unmistakably clear where we stand on all the issues troubling the people."

But the phenomenon that may ultimately have done the most to propel Reagan's rise, and also to shape his presidency, was one that began in 1978. In that year, the conservative activist Howard Jarvis launched the first major, successful citizens' tax revolt in a generation by organizing an elaborate campaign behind Proposition 13, a referendum question on the California ballot rolling back property tax rates. At a time of slow economic growth and stagnating incomes, the revolt against taxes suddenly had a tremendous appeal. Proposition 13 passed easily, and a dozen other states passed similar referenda over the next several years. The tax revolt moved rapidly from local to national politics. Articulate popular economists such as George Gilder and Jude Wanniski created a new, inverted version of Keynesianism, which they called "supply-side" economics (to differentiate it from liberal Keynesianism, which emphasized consumer demand). By cutting tax rates (and offering particularly large cuts to wealthy people), the supply-siders claimed, government would encourage investment and help produce enough growth to generate higher total tax revenues. "There are always two tax rates that yield the same revenues," the economics writer Arthur B. Laffer liked to argue, explaining his briefly famous "Laffer curve." A lower rate could generate as much income for government as a higher one by stimulating growth and increasing taxable income. In 1979 Representative Jack Kemp of New York and Senator William Roth of Delaware proposed a 30-percent reduction in federal income tax rates, without suggesting that such a cut would require any significant reduction in government services. And in 1980 Ronald Reagan—who little more than a decade earlier had pushed the largest state tax increase in American history through the California legislature—accepted the advice of his campaign managers and made a major tax reduction one of the economic centerpieces of his presidential campaign.

Other events helped the Reagan cause as well. The hapless campaign of George Bush, his principal challenger in the Republican primaries, gave Reagan an important boost just before the critical New Hampshire primary. (Bush once referred to Reagan's supply-side program as "voodoo economics," a phrase that haunted both men for years, especially once Bush became Reagan's running mate and vice president.) More important was the deep unpopularity of Jimmy Carter, the incumbent president and Reagan's opponent in the fall campaign. Disenchantment with Carter was so great that Senator Edward M. Kennedy of Massachusetts challenged him in the Democratic primaries—ultimately unsuccessfully, but effectively enough to do serious harm. Particularly damaging to Carter was a crisis that began in November 1979 in Iran, where a fiercely anti-Western Islamic regime, led by the fundamentalist cleric Ayatollah Ruholla Khomeini, had recently seized power. At almost the moment Kennedy announced his candidacy, Islamic militants loyal to Khomeini seized the American embassy in Tehran and took fifty-two Americans hostage. The fate of the hostages soon became a national preoccupation and, over time, a political disaster for the president. A military rescue mission in April 1980 ended in shambles, reinforcing the charges Reagan and other conservatives were making about the dismal state of the nations' defenses. The Soviet Union, in the meantime, had launched an invasion of Afghanistan, raising Cold War tensions to their highest point in years.

In the end, though, popular frustration with the troubled economy was probably Reagan's greatest political ally. Soaring inflation and high interest rates—driven in large part by dramatic price increases in Middle Eastern oil—combined with stagnation and high unemployment to create an unusually sour political climate. The most memorable statement of the campaign was Reagan's question to the American people: "Are you better off today than you were four years ago?"

Election day 1980, then, marked the intersection of many powerful trends: the successful rebuilding of a national conservative movement; growing economic anxiety; rising insecurity about America's place in the world; Jimmy Carter's spiraling unpopularity; and perhaps most of all, the apotheosis of Ronald Reagan. Once a minor film star and a politician whom many Americans considered an extremist, he had emerged as the most magnetic public figure in the nation. His victory in the presidential race was substantial. He won 50.7 percent of the popular vote to Jimmy Carter's 41. (John Anderson, a moderate Republican congressman from Illinois running as an independent, received 6.6 percent; and Ed Clark, the candidate of the Libertarian party, received a surprising 1.1.) Reagan won 489 electoral votes to Carter's 49. Hours before the polls closed, President Carter called Reagan in California to offer his congratulations. Reagan had been taking a shower, and as he later recalled it: "Standing in my bathroom with a wrapped towel around me, my hair dripping with water, I . . . learned I was going to be the fortieth President of the United States."

Perhaps equally important to the future of Reagan's administration as the decisiveness of the presidential vote, Republicans won control of the U.S. Senate for the first time in twenty-eight years; and Democrats retained control of the House by such a narrow margin that, for a time at least, there was an effective pro-Reagan majority composed of Republicans and conservative Democrats (known to many as "boll weevils"). Reagan would be the first Republican president since Eisenhower to enter office with a relatively pliant Congress.

RONALD REAGAN

Presidential Style and Leadership

Reagan's first term began dramatically. He later recalled that, as he stood to take the oath of office on 20 January 1981 on the West Front of the Capitol (the first president ever to do so), "the sun burst through the clouds in an explosion of warmth and light." A much more important symbol of change, however, was Iran's decision to release the fifty remaining American hostages at almost the moment of the swearing in; Reagan was able to announce the news at a luncheon just after the ceremony, as Jimmy Carter, who had negotiated the release in the last hours of his presidency, was flying home to Georgia.

Two other dramatic events punctuated Reagan's first months in office, both of them important in shaping the powerful image he quickly came to assume in the imagination of many Americans. On 30 March, as the president left a Washington hotel after delivering a speech, he was shot in the chest by John Hinckley, Jr., a deranged young man (later found not guilty by reason of insanity) who had been waiting in the crowd outside. Rushed to the hospital, Reagan joked with the surgeons as they wheeled him into the operating room. "I hope you're all Republicans," he reportedly said. He left the hospital eleven days later; and the White House staff arranged a series of carefully crafted public appearances that convinced most Americans that he had recovered from his wounds with remarkable speed. In fact, his injuries were serious, and he followed a sharply curtailed schedule for several months. Disguising that fact was the first of many successes by Reagan's skillful media advisers.

Four months later, on 3 August, thirteen thousand air traffic controllers (members of the Professional Air Traffic Controllers Organization, or PATCO, a union that had supported Reagan in 1980) walked off their jobs. The controllers were federal employees and, by law, forbidden to strike; but their leader, Robert Poli, believed that their ability to shut down the nation's airports would intimidate the administration into accepting their demands. On the advice of Drew Lewis, the new secretary of transportation, Reagan refused to negotiate with the strikers. He gave the controllers forty-eight hours to return to work and then fired those who did not. The government hastily hired replacements, and the disruption of air traffic was brief. The strike was, as Reagan recalled in his memoirs, "an important juncture for our new administration. I think it convinced people who

Ronald Reagan waves to supporters as he leaves a Washington, D.C., hotel, moments before he was shot in an assassination attempt on 30 March 1981. The president was rushed to George Washington University Hospital and spent eleven days there following surgery. CORBIS

might have thought otherwise that I meant what I said."

The assassination attempt and the PATCO strike, critical as they were to shaping the new president's image, were unexpected events. Much more important to his political successes were the everyday efforts of the administration to capitalize on Reagan's engaging personality and make it, and not his sometimes harsh policies, the defining feature of his presidency. Schooled by years in Hollywood, Reagan was a master of self-presentation. He was the most gifted public speaker to occupy the presidency in a generation, and a talented staff of speechwriters ensured that his State of the Union addresses, his televised statements on important events, and ultimately his speeches during his reelection campaign in 1984 were suffused with emotional symbols and powerful, patriotic imagery; statements that would have seemed stilted and in-authentic from a less talented speaker became exhilarating oratory when Reagan spoke them.

Reagan turned seventy years old a few weeks after his inauguration. From his first day in office, he was the oldest man ever to serve as president, and his age was almost certainly an important factor in the way he governed. He worked relatively short hours, sometimes dozed off in meetings, and spent more time on vacations than any president in generations. But through most of his eight years in the White House, Reagan managed to appear energetic, resilient, even youthful—an image his outwardly rapid recovery from the 1981 shooting did much to reinforce. Later, his staff ensured that even his many vacations would seem evidence of his vigor. The most prominent images of Reagan at leisure consisted of pictures of him riding horses and chopping wood at his Santa Barbara ranch.

The principal figures on Reagan's White House staff were James A. Baker III, Edwin Meese III, and Michael K. Deaver. For the first four years of his presidency, they formed a tightly knit triumvirate that ran the daily workings of the White House. They carefully cultivated sympathetic members of Congress of both parties and thus had much to do with the president's early legislative successes. Perhaps more significant, they understood the political importance of the president's image; and they worked energetically, and often brilliantly, to craft that image. They carefully planned the president's every public appearance, chose appropriate backdrops, worked to shape media coverage of him, and tried above all to insulate him from situations where he might speak spontaneously. (Reagan's unscripted remarks were often ill-considered; and when the staff failed to prevent them, it often had to spend considerable energy limiting the political damage they caused.) They received important assistance in their efforts from Nancy Reagan. Her public role in the administration was limited, mostly traditional, and highly social; among other things, she brought a new level of opulence and ceremony to the White House. Privately, however, she was very active and very powerful in shaping public perception of her husband. At times, she played a major role in more substantive decisions as well.

Reagan's enforced absence from the daily business of the White House after his attempted assassination established a pattern that continued in many ways well beyond his convalescence. He was never very interested in, or very well informed about, the details of governance; and his public statements often revealed a startling ignorance of his own policies and the actions of his subordinates. Just as he had while governor of California, he preferred to leave specific decisions to his advisers and to ratify compromises that they forged without him. Just as in California, he reveled in the ceremonial aspects of his job. And just as in California, he rigidly adhered to the daily schedule—a copy of which was neatly typed each day and placed on his desk in a silver frame—and rarely deviated from it. He took great pleasure in checking off meetings and events as he moved through the day.

Many critics of the president, and even some of his own advisers writing later in their memoirs, considered Reagan shockingly aloof from the business of government, a figurehead who played no more than a symbolic role in his own administration. They cited his fondness for anecdotes, his self-deprecating humor, his tendency to tell irrelevant Hollywood stories, and his frequent citation of fictional episodes in his own, or the nation's, past as if they were true; and they argued that together, they revealed a basic lack of interest in, even an unfitness for, his job. But others, including Reagan himself, insisted that he was highly effective in his most important task: establishing broad themes for his administration and keeping his subordinates focused on them despite the immediate pressures of politics. "It was striking how often we on the staff would become highly agitated by the latest news bulletins," one of Reagan's aides later recalled. "Reagan saw the same events as nothing more than a bump in the road; things would get better tomorrow. His horizons were just not the same as ours."

Reagan was, he insisted, more than the Great Communicator (as he was often described)—more than simply a gifted speaker, although he knew that his oratorical skills, and even his avuncular charm as a storyteller, did much to burnish his image and insulate him from criticism. His most important achievement, he insisted, was not how he communicated, but what. He spoke, he said, of "great things," and his words and actions helped the nation move along a fundamentally new course, a course in which he deeply believed and from which he tried not to waver. His most important legacy, he believed, would transcend the particulars of policy. It would be to convince Americans "to believe in themselves again." And for a time, at least, he seemed to succeed in that goal.

Domestic Policy

The most significant element of Reagan's first months in office, however, was not the crafting of his public image or the shaping of his style of governance—as important as both those things were to the future of his presidency. It was his bold effort to transform the nation's economic policies. Relying on the arguments of the supply-side theorists who had been so important to his campaign, he proposed a three-year, 30-percent reduction in both individual and corporate income tax rates—the biggest single tax reduction in American history. The tax cuts affected people in all income groups; but the greatest beneficiaries were people in the highest brackets—those who, according to the supply-siders, would be most likely to use the surplus income to invest in the economy. Congress approved the president's proposal in late July 1981, after lowering the reduction slightly, to 25 percent.

Cutting taxes, Reagan insisted, would stimulate economic growth much more effectively than the traditional liberal approach of increasing government spending. But Reagan, in fact, increased spending too. He proposed an enormous increase in the military budget ($1.5 trillion over five years) to rebuild armed forces that he claimed had been allowed to deteriorate badly in the 1970s. Congress approved that increase, although it was later scaled back significantly. At the same time, the administration set out to make substantial cuts in domestic spending. David A. Stockman, Reagan's talented budget director, supervised an effort to squeeze more than $41 billion out of the government's nonmilitary "discretionary" spending. The task was extremely difficult. The administration could not reduce the 10 percent of the budget committed to paying interest on the national debt (which reached $1 trillion during Reagan's first year in office) and had already agreed to actual increases in the 25 percent of the budget that went to the military. It was not willing to make any significant changes in spending on Social Security, Medicare, and several other broad-based programs. That left a host of much smaller programs, constituting about 10 percent of the budget, many of which were designed to help the poorest Americans. Almost by definition, the bulk of the cuts Stockman proposed came from these programs.

The administration increased the already tight spending restrictions on Medicaid, the major program of medical assistance for the poor, which the federal government financed jointly with the states. It reduced federal subsidies for low-income housing, cut spending on food stamps, reduced federal aid to education and federal contributions to state governments, and placed new restrictions on Aid to Families with Dependent Children (the principal program of direct assistance to the poor). It also substantially reduced spending on government itself—forcing staff and service cuts in almost all departments and agencies. In some cases, the cutbacks eliminated the waste and inefficiency that Reagan argued was characteristic of many government programs. In other cases, they impaired the ability of agencies to function effectively and contributed to the growing popular belief that government could not be trusted to do anything well.

The administration did not win congressional approval of all the budget reductions it requested, but it did much better than most observers had expected. Even many programs that had once seemed unassailable experienced significant reductions. It became clear early in 1981 that the results of the 1980 election had sent shock waves through Congress. Republicans and Democrats alike were scrambling to respond to what they thought the voters had demanded. But they were also responding to evidence of the president's growing popularity. The administration pushed its legislative package through Congress in part through skillful lobbying by the talented White House staff. But equally important were the president's effective television addresses to the nation, which aroused groundswells of popular support for his proposals.

Men and women whom Reagan appointed fanned out through the executive branch of government, committed to reducing the role of government in American economic life. Deregulation, an idea many Democrats had begun to embrace in the Carter years, became the religion of the Reagan administration. Secretary of the Interior James G. Watt had been a major figure in the Sagebrush Rebellion, a movement among western conservatives to fight federal environmental regulations, which they believed had a particularly devastating effect on their region's economy. Watt opened up public lands and water to development and tried to ease other restrictions on the private use of public lands. The Environmental Protection Agency (before its directors were indicted for corruption) relaxed or entirely eliminated enforcement of critical environmental laws and regulations. The Civil Rights Division of the Justice Department eased enforcement of civil rights laws. The Department of Transportation slowed implementation of new rules limiting automobile emissions and imposing new safety standards on cars and trucks. By getting government "out of the way," Reagan officials promised, they were helping to ensure economic revival.

The Reagan administration also transformed the federal judiciary. By the time he left office, Reagan had named more than half of all the federal judges in the nation and three justices of the Supreme Court, among them Sandra Day O'Connor, the first woman ever appointed. Reagan's court appointments, like his appointments to regulatory agencies, had the effect of reversing many of the judicial trends that had been gathering force for over twenty years. The conservative judges and justices who took office in the 1980s set about limiting the effect of some of the decisions of the Warren Court in the 1960s—tempering the strict protections of criminal rights, softening some civil rights measures, and perhaps most notably, weakening (although never eliminating) the right to abortion established by the Supreme Court's 1973 decision in *Roe* v. *Wade*. Symbolic of the conservative shift was Reagan's elevation of William H. Rehnquist, one of the most conservative Supreme Court justices, to chief justice; and his appointment to the Court of Antonin Scalia, a brilliant legal scholar of exceptionally conservative views. Reagan attempted to appoint Robert H. Bork, another fervently conservative judicial activist, to the Supreme Court but was stymied in that effort after a well-organized campaign by liberals and feminists against Bork's controversial views.

Reagan's policies were seldom as radical as his rhetoric (and never as radical as the agenda of the militantly conservative Republican Congress of the mid-1990s). But taken together, the achievements of Reagan's first term represented a significant shift in the direction of public policy. That was visible above all in the administration's economic policies. For the first time since the 1920s, the government was shaping its fiscal policy (its taxing and spending) to promote investment more than consumption and to reduce the tax and regulatory burden on corporations and wealthy people. For the first time since the 1950s (and much more energetically than then), an administration was attempting to stop the growth of many areas of government and to reduce, at times even to eliminate, programs that many Americans had come to consider timeless and unassailable. So distinctive was the new economic program that many began describing it as the Reagan Revolution or, even more frequently and enduringly, Reaganomics.

Both in his campaign and in his early presidential speeches, Reagan had promised not only to reduce taxes and cut spending, but to balance the federal budget. He never did. Instead, his policies contributed to the largest budget deficits in American history and a tripling of the national debt during his eight years in office. Indeed, one of Reagan's most important legacies was his contribution to an enduring fiscal crisis. He helped create a federal budget that was structurally, and radically, unbalanced; and he launched an era in which the national debt grew steadily and dramatically for many years.

The fiscal crisis did little to erode Reagan's popularity. Even though his administration never proposed, let alone achieved, anything approaching a credible balanced budget, the public apparently did not care very much, or accepted the president's explanation that the deficit was the fault of Congress. But the fiscal crisis had a profound and lasting effect on American politics. Over time, it deeply eroded the already weakened faith of the American people in their government and their leaders. And it placed an enormous, even insuperable, obstacle in the way of future leaders who wished to use government to address domestic or international problems. By the mid-1990s, the federal deficit, and efforts to reduce it, had become one of the central facts of American political life.

Reagan had not intended to explode the federal deficit, but his decisions as president led inevitably to that result. He cut taxes substantially and continued to support those cuts even when they did not produce the increase in government revenues that supply-side advocates had promised. He increased the military budget by much more than he was able to cut domestic spending. He refused to consider taking the politically difficult steps of finding savings in popular entitlement programs, most notably Medicare and Social Security, despite strong pressure from members of Congress to do so. His budget officers based their economic projections on dubious, at times even preposterous, assumptions that they themselves knew were false. David Stockman delivered a sharp blow to the administration's image late in 1981 when, in a remarkably candid interview in the *Atlantic Monthly*, he suggested that the Reagan Revolution had failed. The president's tax cut, he claimed, was a "Trojan horse," promising reductions for everyone but really designed to reduce the rates at the top. The administration had never made a serious effort to balance the budget and never had a reasonable idea of how to do so. "None of us really understands what's going on with all these numbers," he conceded.

By the end of Reagan's third year in office, funding for domestic programs had been cut nearly as far as Congress (and, apparently, the public) was willing to tolerate, and still no end to the rising deficits was in sight. Congress responded with the so-called Gramm-Rudman bill, passed late in 1985, which mandated major deficit reductions over five years and provided for automatic budget cuts in all areas of government spending should the president and Congress fail to agree on an alternative solution. Under Gramm-Rudman, the budget deficit did decline for several years from its 1983 high. But much of that decline was a result of a substantial surplus in the Social Security trust fund. (The administration had helped engineer a dramatic increase in Social Security taxes, which for people of low and moderate incomes more than offset the effects of the 1981 income tax reduction.) By the late 1980s, many fiscal conservatives were calling for a constitutional amendment mandating a balanced budget—a provision the president himself claimed to support but did little to promote. (Congress came within one vote of passing such an amendment in 1995.)

Much more damaging to the president's political fortunes was a steep recession that began late in 1981 and soon became the most severe since the Great Depression. Reagan's economic policies were not responsible for the downturn; few of them had yet had a chance to have an impact on the economy. But the administration did little to fight the recession once it began. Reagan took his lead in part from Paul Volcker, the strong-willed chairman of the Federal Reserve Board (appointed by Jimmy Carter), who considered inflation a more serious threat to the economy than recession. Volcker's policies of high interest rates had been one of many causes of the recession, and his slowness to reduce the rates was one reason the recession became so severe. The recession was particularly devastating to American industry. Manufacturers had been suffering from the high interest rates for several years. High rates made it difficult to borrow and invest; they also made the dollar expensive in world markets and sharply reduced American exports. The nation's trade deficit rose from $25 billion in 1980 to $111 billion in 1984. Once the recession began, businesses closed plants and eliminated hundreds of thousands of jobs. Unemployment in 1982 reached 9.7 percent, its highest point in more than forty years. Farmers, even more dependent on exports than manufacturers, fared worse. Hundreds of thousands of them lost their land in the course of the 1980s.

Reagan expressed sympathy for victims of the recession, but he never seriously considered changing course. He supported Volcker's commitment to the anti-inflation strategy even as the economy slid further downward. He refused to alter his economic program, insisting that if the nation would "stay the course" it would emerge healthier and more prosperous at the end. And in fact, the recession lifted more rapidly and impressively than almost anyone had predicted. By the end of 1983, unemployment had fallen to 8.3 percent, and it continued to decline for the next five years. The gross national product had grown 3.6 percent in a year, the largest increase in nearly a decade. Inflation had fallen to below 5 percent. The economy continued to grow, and both inflation and unemployment remained low (at least by the more pessimistic standards the nation seemed to have accepted) for the rest of the decade.

The recovery was a result of many factors. The Federal Reserve finally eased interest rates early in 1983. A worldwide "energy glut" and the virtual collapse of the powerful cartel of Middle Eastern oil producers stopped the upward spiral of energy prices that had done so much to fuel inflation and inhibit economic growth in the 1970s. And the staggering levels of deficit spending pumped billions of dollars into the sagging economy. Reagan's policies had not worked as their initial advocates had expected, and much of his administration's contribution to the economic recovery was inadvertent. The recovery itself, moreover, was less robust than the major economic indicators revealed. The benefits of the economic growth flowed disproportionately to those in the upper income categories, and the boom did not create jobs or increase incomes for working-class and lower-middle-class people in any way comparable to what earlier booms had done. The poverty rate not only failed to decline, but actually rose in the 1980s from its levels of the 1970s. But these problems became visible only slowly. In the meantime, the president reaped enormous political benefits from the prosperity of 1983 and beyond, which his supporters later called, with some justification, "the longest peacetime expansion in American history."

Foreign Relations

Reagan encountered a similar combination of triumphs and difficulties in international affairs. Determined to restore American pride and prestige in the world, he argued that the United States should once again become active and assertive in opposing Communism and in supporting friendly governments whatever their internal policies. The president's rhetoric, and the administration's military spending policies, supported that goal. But in the end, Reagan's foreign policy—although more belligerent than that of his two immediate predecessors—was considerably more cautious than his sometimes bellicose statements suggested.

Unlike recent presidents from Nixon to Carter, whose national security advisers had often overshadowed the cabinet in formulating foreign policy, Reagan appointed prominent men to be secretary of state and secretary of defense and left the White House position to a series of little-known figures whose influence at first rarely matched those of the cabinet ministers. His first secretary of state, Alexander M. Haig, Jr., a man of high self-regard and little patience with politics, resigned after less than a year, complaining that the administration was not following a consistent diplomatic course. His replacement, former secretary of commerce George P. Shultz, served for the remainder of Reagan's term and usually, although not always, dominated the formulation of policy. Shultz's task was complicated by his long-running feud with Secretary of Defense Caspar W. Weinberger, who—despite his unwavering and uncritical support of ever rising defense budgets—was extremely reluctant to endorse any deployment of American troops in situations that carried any element of risk. Over time, the intensity of their disagreements worked to enhance the position of the national security adviser, whose office became increasingly influential as the years passed.

Relations with the Soviet Union, which had been steadily deteriorating in the last years of the Carter administration, grew still more strained in the first years of the Reagan presidency. The president spoke harshly of the Soviet regime, which he once called an "evil empire." He accused it of sponsoring world terrorism, and he declared that any armaments negotiations must be linked to negotiations on Soviet behavior in other areas. Relations with the Russians deteriorated further after the government of Poland (under strong pressure from Moscow) imposed martial law on the country in the winter of 1981 to crush a growing challenge from an independent labor organization, Solidarity.

The president had long denounced the second Strategic Arms Limitation Treaty (SALT II) negotiated by Ford and Carter but as yet unratified by the Senate, although he continued quietly to honor its provisions. The treaty was, Reagan claimed, unfavorable to the United States, and he declined to request ratification. And the early Reagan administration made little progress toward arms control in other areas. In fact, the president proposed the most ambitious (and potentially most expensive) new military program in many years: the Strategic Defense Initiative (SDI), widely known as "Star Wars" after the popular movie of that name. Reagan claimed that SDI, through the use of lasers and satellites, could provide an effective shield against incoming missiles and thus make nuclear war obsolete. The Soviet Union claimed that the new program would elevate the arms race to new and more dangerous levels (a complaint many domestic critics of SDI shared) and insisted that any arms control agreement begin with an American abandonment of SDI. But Reagan remained fervently committed to SDI until the end of his administration, even as the original lofty claims for it proved impossible to sustain and it evolved into a relatively conventional (if unprecedentedly expensive) plan for shielding American missile sites from attack.

The escalation of Cold War tensions and the slowing of arms control initiatives helped produce an important popular movement in Europe and the United States calling for an end to nuclear weapons buildups. In America, the principal goal of the movement was a "nuclear freeze," an agreement between the two superpowers not to expand their atomic arsenals. In what many believed was the largest mass demonstration in American history, nearly a million people rallied in New York City's Central Park in 1982 to support the freeze. Perhaps partly in response to this growing pressure, the administration began tentative efforts to revive arms control negotiations in 1983.

At the same time, however, it began—rhetorically at least—to support forces opposing Communism almost anywhere in the world, whether or not the regimes or movements such forces were challenging had any direct connection to the Soviet Union. This new policy became known as the Reagan Doctrine, and it represented a conscious effort to repudiate the lessons that liberals and others had drawn from the failed war in Vietnam. Reagan called Vietnam a "noble cause," and both he and his supporters seemed to believe that the American defeat had been more the result of insufficient resolve than of the flawed premises of the original commitment. In practice, the Reagan Doctrine meant above all a new American activism in Latin America. In October

1983, the administration sent American soldiers into the tiny Caribbean island of Grenada to oust an anti-American Marxist regime that showed signs of forging a relationship with Moscow. In El Salvador, where first a repressive military regime and later a moderate civilian one were engaged in murderous struggles with left-wing revolutionaries (who were supported, according to the Reagan administration, by Cuba and the Soviet Union), the president provided increased military and economic assistance. In neighboring Nicaragua, a pro-American dictatorship had fallen to the revolutionary Sandinistas in 1979; the new government had grown increasingly anti-American (and increasingly Marxist) throughout the early 1980s. The administration gave both rhetorical and material support to the so-called contras, a guerrilla movement drawn from several anti-government groups and fighting (without great success) to topple the Sandinista regime. Indeed, support of the contras became a mission of special importance to the president, and later the source of some of his greatest difficulties.

In other parts of the world, the administration's bellicose public statements masked an instinctive restraint. In June 1982, the Israeli army launched an invasion of Lebanon in an effort to drive guerrillas of the Palestine Liberation Organization from the country. The United States supported the Israelis but also worked to permit PLO forces to leave Lebanon peacefully. An American peace-keeping force entered Beirut to supervise the evacuation. American marines then remained in the city, apparently to protect the fragile Lebanese government, which was embroiled in a vicious civil war. Now identified with one faction in the struggle, Americans became the targets in 1983 of a terrorist bombing of a U.S. military barracks in Beirut that left 241 marines dead. Rather than become more deeply involved in the Lebanese struggle, Reagan withdrew American forces.

The tragedy in Lebanon was an example of the changing character of many Third World struggles: an increasing reliance on terrorism by otherwise powerless groups to advance their political aims. A series of terrorist acts in the 1980s—attacks on airplanes, cruise ships, commercial and diplomatic posts; the seizing of American and European hostages—alarmed and frightened much of the Western world. The Reagan administration spoke bravely about its resolve to punish terrorism; and at one point in 1986, the president ordered American planes to bomb sites in Tripoli, the capital of Libya, whose controversial leader Mu'ammar al-Gadhafi was widely believed to be a leading sponsor of terrorism. In general, however, terrorists remained difficult to identify or control; and the administration's private resolve in the face of terrorism was never as firm as its public rhetoric suggested.

Reelection and Second Term

Reagan approached the campaign of 1984 at the head of a united Republican party firmly committed to his candidacy. The Democrats, as had become their custom, followed a more fractious course. Former vice president Walter E Mondale established an early and commanding lead in the race by soliciting support from a wide range of traditional Democratic interest groups, and survived challenges from Senator Gary Hart of Colorado (who claimed to represent a "new generation" of leadership) and the magnetic Jesse Jackson, who had established himself as the nation's most prominent spokesman for minorities and the poor. Mondale captured the nomination and brought momentary excitement to the Democratic campaign by selecting a woman, Representative Geraldine Ferraro of New York, to be his running mate and the first female candidate ever to appear on a national ticket.

The Republican party, in the meantime, rallied comfortably behind Reagan, who was now at the peak of his popularity. His triumphant campaign that fall scarcely took note of his opponents and spoke instead of what he claimed was the remarkable revival of American fortunes and spirits under his leadership. His campaign emphasized such phrases as "It's Morning in America" and "America Is Back." Reagan's victory in 1984 was decisive. He won approximately 59 percent of the vote and carried every state but Mondale's native Minnesota and the District of Columbia. But Reagan was much stronger than his party. Democrats gained a seat in the Senate and maintained only slightly reduced control of the House of Representatives. Reagan's triumphant reelection proved to be the high-water mark of his presidency. The administration enjoyed some successes in its second term, and Reagan left office with much of his popularity intact. But beginning in 1985, he suffered a series of painful and damaging blows from which his administration was never able fully to recover.

Two dramatic events shaped the second term of Reagan's presidency. One was the beginning of a momentous change in the structure of international relations—a change that the president played little part in creating but that he prudently accepted and encouraged. The other was a domestic political controversy over a secret initiative about which the president claimed—implausibly to some, all too plausibly to others—to have known nothing.

Shortly after Reagan took his oath of office for the second time (in a small ceremony in the Capitol Rotunda, because bitterly cold weather had forced the cancellation of the traditional outdoor event), a new leader took power in the Soviet Union: Mikhail S. Gorbachev, who was, by Soviet standards at least, a young and energetic head of state. In the beginning, American leaders expected little from Gorbachev. He had, after all, been molded by the same stultifying political system that had shaped his recent predecessors. But to the surprise of almost everyone (including, it sometimes seemed, himself), Gorbachev very quickly became the most revolutionary figure in world politics since the end of World War II. Benefiting from widespread frustration with the rigid and ineffective policies of the preceding twenty years, Gorbachev transformed Soviet politics with two dramatic new initiatives. The first he called *glasnost* (openness). Glasnost led to the dismantling of many of the repressive mechanisms that had been among the most conspicuous features of Soviet life for more than half a century. Gradually it became possible for Soviet citizens to express themselves more freely, to criticize the government, even to organize politically in opposition to official policy. The other initiative Gorbachev called *perestroika* (reform or restructuring). Through it, he attempted to remake the rigid and unproductive Soviet economy by introducing, among other things, such elements of capitalism as private ownership and the profit motive. At the same time, Gorbachev began reshaping Soviet foreign policy. Among the first steps in that effort was his attempt to forge a new relationship with the United States.

He began by reaching out to Washington for major new arms control agreements. Encouraged by British prime minister Margaret Thatcher, a friend and ideological ally of Reagan's and an early champion of Gorbachev's, Reagan too began looking for new avenues to accommodation. At a summit meeting with Reagan in Reykjavfk, Iceland, in 1986 (the second of four between the two leaders), Gorbachev proposed reducing the nuclear arsenals of both sides by 50 percent or more. Continuing disputes over Reagan's commitment to the SDI program, among other things, prevented agreements. But in December 1987, after Reagan and Gorbachev exchanged cordial visits to each other's capitals, the two leaders signed a treaty eliminating American and Soviet intermediate-range nuclear forces (INF) from Europe—the most significant arms control agreement of the nuclear age and the first to make actual reductions in existing nuclear arsenals as opposed to restricting their future expansion. At about the same time, Gorbachev ended the Soviet Union's long and frustrating military involvement in Afghanistan, removing one of the principal irritants in the relationship between Washington and Moscow.

The new arms control agreements, and the rapid moderation of Soviet international behavior, seemed to Reagan and his supporters a clear vindication of the president's earlier policies. By increasing diplomatic and economic pressure on the Soviet Union, and in particular by forcing the Soviets into an expensive new arms race that their staggering economy could not support, the administration had done much to weaken the hard-liners in Moscow and make Gorbachev's reforms possible, even likely. (Reagan had always claimed that the arms buildup he launched was designed, at least in part, to encourage the Soviet Union to agree to arms reductions.) Others were more skeptical and insisted that the decay of the Soviet Union had begun long before Reagan's presidency and had intensified for reasons that had little to do with American policy. In either case, Reagan—a hard-line foe of Soviet Communism for more than forty years—proved flexible enough to respond to the changes and encourage them.

For a time, the dramatic developments around the world and Reagan's continuing personal popularity deflected attention from a series of scandals that might well have destroyed another administration. Top officials in the Environmental Protection Agency resigned when it was disclosed that they were flouting the laws they had been appointed to enforce. Officials of the CIA and the Defense Department resigned after revelations of questionable stock transactions. Reagan's secretary of labor, Raymond J. Donovan, left office after being indicted for racketeering (although he was later acquitted). Edwin Meese, the White House counsel and later attorney general, finally resigned in 1988 after years of controversy over financial arrangements that many believed had compromised his office.

Unnoticed at first were several larger scandals that surfaced only as Reagan was about to leave office. One involved misuse of funds by the Department of Housing and Urban Development, abuses so widespread that by 1990 the survival of the agency itself seemed in question. Another, more serious scandal involved the savings and loan industry. The Reagan administration had sharply reduced regulatory controls over the troubled savings and loan institutions, permitting them to enter into business activities from which they had previously been barred. Many savings banks responded by rapidly, often recklessly, and sometimes corruptly, expanding. By the end of the decade the industry was in chaos, and the government was forced to step in to prevent a complete collapse. The government insured the assets of most savings and loan depositors; and as the banks failed, it found itself saddled with large debts. The eventual cost of the debacle to the public ran to more than half a trillion dollars.

But the most politically damaging scandal of the Reagan years came to light in November 1986. After reports of the episode had begun appearing in foreign newspapers, the White House conceded that it had sold weapons to the revolutionary government of Iran, apparently as part of a largely unsuccessful effort to secure the release of several Americans being held hostage by radical Islamic groups in the Middle East. Even more damaging was the administration's admission that some of the money from the arms deal with Iran had been covertly and illegally funneled into a fund to aid the contras in Nicaragua.

In the months that followed, aggressive reporting and a highly publicized series of congressional hearings exposed a remarkable and previously unsuspected feature of the Reagan White House: the existence within it of something like a "secret government," largely unknown to the State Department, the Defense Department, even parts of the CIA, dedicated to advancing the administration's foreign policy aims through secret and at times illegal means. The principal figure in this covert world appeared at first to be an obscure marine lieutenant colonel assigned to the staff of the National Security Council, Oliver L. North. But gradually it became clear that North was acting in concert with other, more powerful figures in the administration: two national security advisers, Robert McFarlane and John M. Poindexter and, many believed, both the vice president and the president himself. Secretary of State Shultz and Secretary of Defense Weinberger, in a rare display of accord, had vigorously opposed the initiative; but their long-running feud had by then so di-

President and Mrs. Reagan entertain British Prime Minister Margaret Thatcher and her husband, Dennis, prior to a state dinner at the White House in 1988. Reagan and Thatcher were strong allies and like-minded about Cold War strategies. CORBIS/BETTMANN

minished their influence that they proved powerless to stop the effort. The Iran-Contra scandal, as it became known, did serious damage to the Reagan presidency—even though the lengthy investigations it spawned never decisively tied the president himself to the most serious violations of the law.

There were other signs in the late 1980s that the glow of the Reagan Revolution was beginning to fade. In October 1987 the American stock market—the spectacular success of which had been one of the most conspicuous features of the economic boom—experienced the greatest single-day decline in its history; and although stock prices recovered and continued to rise over the next two years, the crash shattered the aura of invincibility that had arisen in the financial markets. The 1987 crash, combined with the continuing budget deficits, gradually eroded popular confidence in Reaganomics.

Ultimately, however, the president retained his hold on public affections despite the many problems of his administration. He was not, as many observers scornfully described him, in any real sense the "Teflon president," a leader to whom no failures or criticisms ever stuck. His popularity rose and fell quite dramatically at times, and the most serious scandals of his administration—Iran-Contra in particular—did him considerable and lasting political damage. But relatively few Americans were ever able truly to dislike him. And as he neared the end of his presidency—his famous energy flagging, his memory failing, his gait far less jauntily confident than it had once been—the allure of his personal style seemed to lodge itself in the public mind more securely than the much more controversial character of his policies. His last year in office was dominated, of course, by a presidential campaign in which he—for only the second time since 1968—was not a candidate. But his presence was palpable nevertheless, for it was in large part on the basis of his popularity that George Bush, his vice president, managed first to win the Republican nomination and then, after a brutal and often ugly campaign, the election. From the beginning to the end of his undistinguished presidency, Bush was dogged by the image of the man he succeeded but somehow never seemed quite to replace.

Reagan retired to a comfortable home in Los Angeles, wrote his memoirs, traveled a bit, and gradually faded from public view. In 1994, after a long silence, he released a handwritten letter informing the nation that he was suffering from the early stages of Alzheimer's disease. With that courageous gesture, his public life came to an end and he entered, as he himself wrote, the "twilight" of his long and eventful life.

Evaluation

Reagan's legacy remains a contested one, and it will be many years before historians will be able to gauge the full effect of his presidency. He set bold goals for his administration, but he paid so little attention to their implementation that his policies often veered in directions he had neither anticipated nor desired. He presided over a long period of prosperity, but one in which poverty increased and the wages of most working people remained stagnant. He was president during the beginning of the end of the Cold War, and he forged a relationship with Mikhail Gorbachev that greatly defused historic tensions between the United States and the Soviet Union; but he also became involved in a series of disastrous misadventures in the Middle East and the Third World that very nearly destroyed his administration. He engineered some of the most profound changes in economic policy in half a century; but he left the government burdened with three times as much debt as it had carried when he entered office.

About one thing, however, there can be little doubt. Reagan's extraordinary personality enabled him to dominate national politics in the 1980s in a way that no president since his boyhood idol, Franklin Roosevelt, had done. Reagan's high-spirited optimism, his unembarrassed patriotism, his soaring, symbol-laden oratory, and his jaunty, almost cocksure public demeanor won him the admiration even of many Americans who disagreed with his policies. He helped restore to public discourse a heady sense of possibilities, a belief in America's moral superiority, and even a faith in leadership. It is clear that many (although far from all) Americans felt better about their society and its future in the 1980s than they had a decade earlier and than they would a decade later. And it is clear that the refurbished nationalism that Reagan so energetically promoted reached out through American culture and became one of the defining characteristics of the era.

The ebullience of the Reagan years faded quickly after his departure, replaced by an increasingly sour and pessimistic political climate and a growing cynicism about leaders and government. But for a moment in the midst of the nation's long, painful transition from its booming industrial past to its uncertain postindustrial future, Reagan allowed many Americans to believe that nothing had really changed—that the problems of the 1960s and 1970s had been mere aberrations, that the country's traditional values and traditional greatness remained intact. In a characteristically exuberant speech in 1986, Reagan himself captured much of what his presidency came to mean to Americans troubled by nearly two decades of turbulence and disillusionment, and eager for reassurance:

> In this land of dreams fulfilled where greater dreams may be imagined, nothing is impossible, no victory is beyond our reach; no glory will ever be too great.. . . The world's hopes rest with America's future.. . . Our work will pale before the greatness of America's champions in the twenty-first century.

BIBLIOGRAPHY

Reagan published two memoirs: *Where's the Rest of Me?* (New York, 1965), an account of his early years and his Hollywood career, written with Richard G. Hubler, and *An American Life* (New York, 1990), a largely unrevealing narrative of his presidency.

Anne Edwards, *Early Reagan: The Rise to Power* (New York, 1987), is the fullest account of Reagan's life up to his election as governor of California in 1966. Dan E. Moldea, *Dark Victory: Ronald Reagan, MCA, and the Mob* (New York, 1986), is a harsh account of some of Reagan's Hollywood activities.

Two works by Lou Cannon, a *Washington Post* reporter who spend many years covering Reagan, provide what is so far the fullest account of his public career: *Reagan* (New York, 1982), which discusses his prepresidential career, and *President Reagan: The Role of a Lifetime* (New York, 1991), which analyzes his presidency. Haynes Johnson, *Sleepwalking Through History: America in the Reagan Years* (New York, 1991), is another, largely critical overview of the Reagan presidency. Garry Wills, *Reagan's America: Innocents at Home* (Garden City, N.Y., 1987), is a provocative interpretation of Reagan and his presidency in midstream. Robert Dallek, *Ronald Reagan: The Politics of Symbolism* (Cambridge, Mass., 1984), and Laurence I. Barrett, *Gambling with History: Ronald Reagan in the White House* (Garden City, N.Y., 1983), are other, highly critical early efforts at analyzing the Reagan presidency. B. B. Kymlicka and Jean V. Matthews, eds., *The Reagan Revolution?* (Chicago, 1988), and Larry Berman, ed., *Looking Back on the Reagan Presidency* (Baltimore, Md., 1990), are collections of essays assessing the impact of Reaganism. Martin Anderson, *Revolution: The Reagan Legacy* (Stanford, Calif., 1990), is a more sympathetic overview.

On Reagan's foreign policy, see Strobe Talbott, *Deadly Gambits: The Reagan Administration and the Stalemate in Nuclear Arms Control* (New York, 1984), a critical discussion of early Reagan administration arms control policies. Kenneth L. Adelman, *The Great Universal Embrace: Arms Summitry—A Skeptic's Account* (New York and London, 1989), is an account of Reagan-era arms control efforts by a participant critical of the idea of arms control. Alexander M. Haig, Jr., *Caveat: Realism, Reagan, and Foreign Policy* (New York, 1984), is a memoir by Reagan's first secretary of state expressing his disillusionment with what he considered the administration's inconsistent course. George P. Shultz, *Turmoil and Triumph: My Years as Secretary of State* (New York, 1993), is a more positive account by the man who served as secretary of state through most of the Reagan years. Robert C. McFarlane, with Zofia Smardz, *Special Trust: Pride, Principle, and Politics Inside the White House* (New York, 1994), is a memoir by one of Reagan's national security advisers, who was implicated in the Iran-contra scandals. Jane Mayer and Doyle McManus, *Landslide: The Unmaking of the President, 1984–1988* (Boston, 1988), is a critical account of the troubled second term, focusing in particular on the Iran-contra scandal.

Several participants in the Reagan administration have published memoirs about the domestic policies of the 1980s. The most celebrated was David A. Stockman, *The Triumph of Politics: How the Reagan Revolution Failed* (New York, 1986), a disillusioned account of the creation of Reaganomics by the president's budget director. Edwin Meese III, *With Reagan: The Inside Story* (Washington, D.C., 1992), offers a more positive assessment by one of Reagan's closest advisers and, ultimately, his attorney general. Peggy Noonan, *What I Saw at the Revolution: A Political Life in the Reagan Era* (New York, 1990), is a generally positive account by the speechwriter responsible for some of Reagan's most memorable public statements. Donald T. Regan, *For the Record: From Wall Street to Washington* (San Diego, Calif., 1988), is a score-settling memoir by the controversial White House chief of staff during Reagan's second term.

Recent works include Edmund Morris, *Dutch: A Memoir of Ronald Reagan* (New York, 1999), a uniquely crafted retrospective on Reagan's life by the Pulitzer Prize–winning author. Peggy Noonan, *When Character Was King: A Story of Ronald Reagan* (New York, 2001), contains many never-before-heard stories from the president's friends, families, and advisers, written by former Reagan speechwriter Noonan. See also *Reagan, In His Own Hand: The Writings of Ronald Reagan That Reveal His Revolutionary Vision of America*, ed. by Kiron K. Skinner, Annelise Anderson, and Martin Anderson (New York, 2001); Nancy Reagan, *I Love You, Ronnie: The Letters of Ronald Reagan to Nancy Reagan* (New York, 2000) and *Ronald Reagan: An American Hero: His Voice, His Values, His Vision* (New York, 2001); Matthew Dallek, *The Right Moment: Ronald Reagan's First Victory and the Decisive Turning Point in American Politics* (New York, 2000); and Michael K. Deaver, *A Different Drummer: My Thirty Years with Ronald Reagan* (New York, 2001).

George Bush

Gaddis Smith

George Bush THE LIBRARY OF CONGRESS

R EPUBLICAN George Herbert Walker Bush took the oath of office as the forty-first president of the United States on 20 January 1989, after serving eight years as Ronald Reagan's vice president and comfortably defeating Democratic candidate Michael Dukakis in the 1988 election. Two years later, after leading a coalition of nations in a swift and decisive war to turn back the aggression of Iraq against Kuwait and negotiating the end of the Cold War with Soviet president Mikhail S. Gorbachev, President Bush's approval rating in public opinion polls was near 90 percent. He appeared to be unbeatable as a candidate for a second term.

But less than two years after that, in the election of 1992, Bush received only 37 percent of the popular vote and lost to Democrat William J. ("Bill") Clinton, governor of Arkansas and a man with no experience in Washington whatsoever. The history of the Bush presidency pivots on that remarkable and rapid reversal. Why had he risen to such heights of popularity and fallen so fast? How could defeat have been snatched so quickly from the jaws of victory? The answers tell us something of the strengths and weaknesses of Bush's leadership, but even more about the post–Cold War shift in American political priorities from foreign policy to domestic issues.

[591]

The Bush years were extraordinarily eventful from a foreign policy standpoint—the Cold War ended, Germany was reunified, the Soviet Union collapsed, relations with China were strained following the lethal suppression of student protest in Beijing, American troops intervened in Panama to overthrow a criminal dictator and in Somalia to save people from starvation, and the United States led a coalition to victory in the Persian Gulf War against Iraq. In domestic affairs, on the other hand, few new programs were launched, there was more gridlock than cooperation between the president and Congress, the economy went into recession, and unemployment increased along with the federal deficit. By 1992 the president was widely perceived as having failed to lead at home while his victories abroad did not translate into votes.

New England, Texas, Washington, D.C.

George Bush was a New England patrician partially transplanted to Texas, where he entered politics after almost two decades in the oil business. He was born on 12 June 1924 in Milton, Massachusetts, and grew up in the affluent New York suburb of Greenwich, Connecticut. His father, Prescott Bush, was a successful investment banker, a friend of President Dwight D. Eisenhower's, and a Republican senator from Connecticut from 1952 to 1963. His mother, Dorothy Walker, was from a prominent family that had migrated in the nineteenth century from New England to St. Louis, Missouri. George Herbert Walker, George's grandfather, established the Walker Cup competition between American and British amateur golfers. George Bush spent summers at Walker's Point, the family's spacious oceanfront compound in Kennebunkport, Maine. Later, Bush would use the residence as his presidential retreat.

In 1942, six months after the Japanese attacked Pearl Harbor, Bush graduated from Phillips Academy, in Andover, Massachusetts, a boarding school with a reputation for preparing boys for future leadership. He rejected the advice of commencement speaker Henry L. Stimson, secretary of war and former secretary of state, to continue his education before rushing off to war. On his eighteenth birthday he joined the navy and soon earned his wings as the country's youngest combat aviation officer. Bush flew fifty-eight combat missions in the Pacific as a torpedo bomber pilot based on the carrier San Jacinto. After

being shot down by the Japanese in 1944 and rescued by an American submarine (his two crew members died), Bush received the Distinguished Flying Cross.

In December 1941 George, age seventeen, met Barbara Pierce, age sixteen, at a country club dance. She was the daughter of a magazine publisher and lived in Rye, New York. In 1943, on the eve of George's combat tour in the Pacific, they became secretly engaged. Barbara briefly attended Smith College but dropped out in her sophomore year. She and George were married in January 1945 and in the next decade and a half had six children: George (elected president of the United States in 2000), Jeb (elected governor of Florida in 1998), Neil, Marvin, Dorothy, and Robin (who died of leukemia before her fourth birthday). Barbara Bush devoted her life to nurturing the close-knit family and to helping her husband's career. As First Lady she chose to avoid the limelight, unlike Eleanor Roosevelt and her successor Hillary Rodham Clinton. She was proud and unapologetic about embracing a traditional lifestyle as helpmate to her husband. In a much publicized address to the women graduating from Wellesley College in 1990 she said: "As important as your obligations as a doctor, a lawyer, a business leader will be, you are a human being first, and those human connections with spouses, with children, and with friends are the most important investment you will ever make."

When World War II ended George Bush followed the tradition of both sides of his family by going to Yale. He graduated in less than three years, in 1948, with a degree in economics, a Phi Beta Kappa key, and membership in the fashionable Delta Kappa Epsilon ("Deke") fraternity and Skull and Bones, the most famous of Yale's secret societies. Tall, gangly, and nicknamed Poppy, he was first baseman (considered a good fielder and a mediocre hitter) and captain of the team that twice went to the finals of the national collegiate baseball championship. He also played soccer. As president he was an avid fisherman, boater, tennis and golf player, and pitcher of horseshoes.

After Yale, Bush turned down a chance for a comfortable career in New York investment banking and moved with his growing family to Texas and an apprenticeship with Dresser Industries, a large oil firm on whose board of directors his father served. Soon he and a partner formed an independent oil exploration company, Bush-Overbey. He and additional partners in 1953 formed Zapata Petroleum and in 1954 Zapata Off-Shore for drilling in the Gulf of Mexico. Bush followed his father's example in switching from financial success in business to politics. He was an unsuccessful Republican candidate for the U.S. Senate from Texas in 1964 and 1970, losing to Democrats Ralph Yarborough and Lloyd M. Bentsen, Jr., respectively. Bush was elected to the House of Representatives in 1966 and again in 1968. Although in 1964 he had followed GOP presidential candidate Barry M. Goldwater in denouncing President Lyndon B. Johnson's civil rights program, in 1968 he voted for open, nondiscriminatory federal housing— thereby alienating conservatives. This was not the first time Bush would be confronted with a contradiction between his own moderate inclinations on social issues and the need for support on the far right.

After losing the race for the Senate in 1970, Bush was appointed by Presidents Richard M. Nixon and Gerald R. Ford to a succession of important positions: U.S. ambassador to the United Nations, 1971–1973; chairman of the Republican National Committee, 1973–1974; liaison (equivalent of ambassador) to the People's Republic of China, 1974–1975; and director of the Central Intelligence Agency (CIA), 1976–1977. At the United Nations he dueled verbally with the tough old Soviet diplomat Jacob Malik on many issues, but was sad to observe the expulsion, in October 1971, of the Republic of China (Taiwan) as a UN member and the seating of the People's Republic (Beijing) in its place.

His stint as chairman of the Republican National Committee coincided with the Watergate scandal and President Nixon's August 1974 resignation in the face of certain impeachment. The scandal originated with a 1972 break-in at Democratic National Committee headquarters by people working for Nixon's personal campaign, the Committee for the Re-Election of the President (CREEP). Neither Bush nor the Republican National Committee had any involvement in Watergate. Bush could only watch, lament, and in the end add his voice to those urging Nixon to resign.

Vice President Gerald Ford became president upon Nixon's resignation on 9 August 1974. Under the Twenty-fifth Amendment to the Constitution it was Ford's responsibility to nominate a new vice president for confirmation by a majority vote of both houses of Congress. Bush hoped he would be selected and was disappointed when Ford picked Nelson A. Rockefeller. As a consolation, Ford offered Bush his choice of diplomatic assignments. Bush chose China.

A quarter century of mutual hostility and isolation between the United States and the Communist People's Republic of China had ended two years before with President Nixon's trip to Beijing, but relations were awkward and not yet "normalized" by the establishment of full-fledged embassies. Bush's assignment was to head the U.S. Liaison Office. During his thirteen months in Beijing he tried to break through the formidable barriers to communication with a regime not yet ready for major reforms, listened to lectures from Chinese officials about the Soviet threat, and created a minor sensation by bicycling around the city with his wife. The position provided more frustration than influence. As he commented afterward, "It was a submarine environment, very restricted. We were engaged in people-watching, watching changing political relationships, analyzing visits, analyzing toasts and the order of protocol, asking other ambassadors what they thought."

Next, President Ford asked Bush to head the Central Intelligence Agency, an institution demoralized by congressional investigations of assassination plots and other dubious practices. The Senate confirmed Bush's nomination by a vote of 64 to 27. The opposition argued that an ambitious politician should not head the nonpartisan intelligence agency. President Ford answered the critics by declaring he would not consider Bush as his vice presidential running mate in 1976. Again Bush was disappointed.

As head of the CIA, Bush was skeptical of optimistic assessments of the Soviet Union. He commissioned the famous Team B report of hard-line anti-Soviet analysts from outside the CIA. Team B warned that Soviet leaders still sought world domination and that under certain circumstances were prepared to wage nuclear war. In January 1977 Bush resigned as head of the CIA so that incoming Democratic president Jimmy Carter, victor over Ford in the 1976 election, could nominate his own choice.

Bush returned to Texas, decided that Carter would be a one-term president, and in 1978 began campaigning for the job himself, with a formal announcement in 1979. He lost the nomination to the more glamorous and conservative Ronald Reagan. Bush's comment that Reagan's proposal to increase federal revenue by lowering taxes was "voodoo economics" earned headlines and years later came back to haunt him.

Reagan, however, picked Bush to be the vice presidential candidate in a traditional gesture of political unity between wings of the Republican party. The Reagan-Bush ticket easily defeated Carter and running mate Walter F. Mondale in the 1980 election and won even more easily in 1984 against Mondale and vice presidential candidate Geraldine A. Ferraro. When President Reagan was shot and seriously wounded by John Hinckley, Jr., in March 1981, Vice President Bush performed the duties of the president with dignity and quiet competence until the president recovered. With a staff of sixty-eight, he kept informed on international issues, maintained his political friendships, and prepared for 1988, when he would again seek the presidency. He headed a task force on the interdiction of the illegal drug trade and another on simplifying and reducing federal regulations. Neither was very successful. Bush also traveled tirelessly at home and abroad, sometimes on substantive missions, more often as a ceremonial representative. He set an attendance record at the funerals of foreign leaders—including three Soviet chiefs of state: Leonid Brezhnev (1982), Yuri Andropov (1984), and Konstantin Chernenko (1985). At Chernenko's funeral Bush met the new, youthful, and energetic leader Mikhail Gorbachev.

Vice President Bush attended many high-level policy meetings in the White House, including those of the National Security Council, of which he was a member. The degree of his knowledge of the illegal sale of arms to Iran and the funding (via profits made from this sale) of rebel soldiers fighting a Marxist government in Nicaragua, in violation of congressional restrictions—the linked scandals known as the Iran-Contra affair of the mid-1980s—remains a matter of dispute. But since he was not a policy maker he suffered no personal political harm from the scandals.

Bush in 1988 was a youthful sixty-four-year-old eastern aristocrat—soft-spoken, courteous, conscientious, considerate (famous for his thank-you letters), cautious, hardworking, better on details than on the big picture, and rather bland. But with Texas as his home base and a need to appeal to anti-eastern elements in the Republican party he affected a fondness for slang and country food. Experience was his strong suit. Ideas were not. His name was associated with no particular program or blueprint for the future. He was first to admit that he was not much for "the vision thing."

The 1988 Campaign

Vice President Bush's most formidable rival for the 1988 Republican nomination was Senator Robert J. ("Bob") Dole of Kansas. The race was close in the beginning, but well before the nominating convention the vice president had accumulated a winning majority of delegates. At the convention in August he sought to conciliate the Republican right wing by selecting James Danforth ("Dan") Quayle, a young, conservative, and relatively unknown senator from Indiana, as his vice presidential running mate. Democrats and critics in the press ridiculed Quayle as an intellectual lightweight, but over the next four years the vice president emerged as an effective, sharp-tongued battler for conservative causes. The Democrats nominated Michael Dukakis, liberal governor of Massachusetts, and conservative senator Lloyd Bentsen of Texas as the vice presidential candidate.

Bush appealed to moderates by promising a "kinder, gentler nation"—an implicit criticism of the abrasive social policies of the Reagan years. He was helped by the apparently healthy state of the economy and the warm afterglow of President Reagan's personal popularity. The broad message of the campaign was, in effect, "If you liked the last eight years, you'll love the next four." The most important theme was Bush's oft-repeated promise: "Read my lips: no new taxes."

A negative theme was the accusation that Governor Dukakis was an extreme liberal ("a card-carrying member of the American Civil Liberties Union") and soft on criminals because he supported furloughs from prison for convicts. In a television blitz organized by political adviser Lee Atwater, the Bush campaign focused on the case of Willie Horton, a convicted murderer who raped a woman while on a weekend pass from prison in Dukakis' Massachusetts. Horton's picture appeared again and again on television with the implication that Dukakis as president would unleash an army of Willie Hortons on a defenseless public. A third theme was the claim that Bush had the experience to handle foreign policy and threats to national security, an area in which Dukakis was a novice. Dukakis made an unsuccessful attempt to overcome this charge by having himself photographed riding around in a tank.

Bush won the election by the wide margin of 426 to 112 in the electoral college, and 53 percent to 46 percent in the popular vote. He was the first sitting vice president to be elected president since Martin Van Buren in 1836. But Democrats made small gains in Congress, resulting in majorities of 55–45 in the Senate and 260–175 in the House. For his entire term President Bush was faced with Democratic control of both houses of Congress. At the same time, he was constrained from seeking common ground with the Democrats because of his dependence on the growing conservative wing of his own Republican party. Unlike Ronald Reagan, Bush refrained from dramatic appeals to the people against Congress, and chose instead to veto many congressional bills and implement others according to his own interpretation. The result in domestic affairs was four years of acrimony between Congress and the White House and a relatively thin record of legislative achievement.

President Bush's inaugural address called for the United States "to make kinder the face of the nation and gentler the face of the world." He subtly rebuked the materialism of the Reagan years by saying "we are not the sum of our possessions.. . . We cannot hope only to leave our children a bigger car, a bigger bank account. We must hope to give them a sense of what it means to be a loyal friend, a loving parent, a citizen who leaves his home, his neighborhood and town better than he found it." He called for a partnership between the government and lauded the "thousand points of light . . . all the community organizations that are spread like stars throughout the nation, doing good." The address, however, lacked any specific agenda for domestic affairs.

In foreign affairs Bush rejoiced that "a world refreshed by freedom seems reborn," but emphasized the importance of maintaining the nation's alliances and military strength. He spoke cautiously about the Soviet Union. "Our new relationship in part reflects the triumph of hope and strength over experience. But hope is good. And so is strength. And vigilance."

The Bush Team

President Bush filled his cabinet and senior White House staff with middle-aged men, many of whom were trusted friends. The only women among his original high-level appointments were Secretary of Labor Elizabeth H. Dole, wife of Senator Dole, and Special Trade Representative Carla A. Hills. Most of the appointees had previous experience in the Reagan or Nixon and Ford administrations. His closest political friend and campaign manager in 1980 and 1988, James A. Baker III, became secretary of state. Although Baker had relatively little experience with foreign affairs, he had been chief of staff for President Reagan (1981–1985) and secretary of the treasury (1985–1988). Baker, a lawyer, had a reputation for negotiating skills and excellent political judgment. As secretary of state he was criticized for ignoring the career foreign service professionals, but he worked closely and effectively with his most important client, the president, especially on relations with the Soviet Union. In August 1992 Baker left the State Department to become Bush's chief of staff in an effort to save the faltering campaign for reelection. Lawrence S. Eagleburger, an experienced foreign policy professional, served as secretary of state for the closing months of the administration.

The only cabinet choice by the president not to be confirmed by the Senate was former Texas senator John G. Tower to be secretary of defense. Tower was rejected because of his reputation for drinking to excess and inappropriate behavior with women. The president's second choice for secretary of defense, former congressman Richard B. ("Dick") Cheney of Wyoming, was easily confirmed. Cheney was a believer in a strong military establishment, doubted that the Cold War was really over, and questioned the supposedly peaceful transformation of the Soviet Union. He was tough, laconic, somewhat humorless, and a strong administrator. Secretary of the Treasury Nicholas F. Brady, a personal friend of Bush's, was a holdover from the Reagan cabinet who did not require reconfirmation. Attorney General Richard ("Dick") Thornburgh, former governor of Pennsylvania, was another holdover from the Reagan cabinet, having been appointed with Bush's approval just before the 1988 election.

Bush inherited Reagan's final director of the CIA, William H. Webster, a former federal judge and director of the Federal Bureau of Investigation (FBI). When Webster retired in 1991 Bush nominated Robert M. Gates, once deputy to the controversial Reagan-era CIA director William J. ("Bill") Casey. In 1987 Gates had been blocked from succeeding Casey because of his connections with the Iran-Contra affair. In 1991 he still faced considerable opposition but not enough to prevent confirmation. Gates was another Cold War hardliner who doubted that the Soviet Union could be trusted.

President Bush's most important military nomination was that of General Colin L. Powell to be chairman of the Joint Chiefs of Staff (JCS). In October 1989 Powell became the youngest officer and the first African American to hold the nation's highest professional military position, as well as the first chairman to have entered the military from the Reserve Officers' Training Corps (ROTC). Powell was the first JCS chairman to operate for his full term under new legislation (the Goldwater-Nichols Act of 1986) giving him the power to advise the president directly and not merely pass on a consensus of the heads of the military services. Powell, a Vietnam combat veteran, was an experienced Washington military insider with previous tours in the White House and Defense Department. He had served in 1988 as Ronald Reagan's last national security adviser, bringing needed order to the National Security Council staff system in the wake of the Iran-Contra debacle.

Powell would be a central player in every foreign policy question involving the actual or potential use of force. In common with most officers of his generation he had been scarred by the experience of the Vietnam War and condemned the leadership of that time for sending Americans to die for unclear objectives and without public support. Powell believed, and so advised Bush, that the nation should use military force only when the objectives were clear, the means fully sufficient, and Congress and the people understood and supported the cause. Sometimes these ideas were called the Powell doctrine. Powell in 1989 stood apart from most high military officers in believing that the Soviet threat was gone. "The Soviet system is bankrupt, and Gorbachev is the trustee.. . . Our bear is now benign," he said.

Two other important Bush appointments were William K. Reilly as administrator of the Environmental Protection Agency and William J. Bennett as director of the National Drug Control Policy. Reilly, a professional environmentalist, worked for effective environmental regulation but often clashed with conservatives in the administration. Bennett, an articulate writer and speaker, garnered considerable press attention for the war on drugs and for himself.

In the modern presidency the senior staff in the White House have more power and influence than most cabinet officers. They do not require approval by the Senate, and they have direct, daily access to the president. In the Bush administration four men were in this category. John H. Sununu, former conservative governor of New Hampshire, became chief of staff and principal domestic adviser. Sununu was sharp-tongued, combative, and often rude—the opposite in manner of Bush. Sununu's job was to manage domestic political affairs, control access to the president, and say no to people asking unacceptable favors of President Bush. Sununu was the president's pit bull. He resigned in December 1991 after being criticized for using government airplanes for personal travel. He was replaced by the less colorful Samuel K. Skinner for eight months and then by James Baker for the final months of the administration.

Brent Scowcroft, a retired Air Force lieutenant general with a Ph.D. in international relations and fluency in Russian, became the national security adviser, the same post he had held under President Ford. Scowcroft, a skeptic about the Soviet Union, was fond of saying that a potential adversary should be treated on the basis of his capabilities rather than on his intentions, since intentions could change. Unlike National Security Adviser Henry Kissinger with Nixon or Zbigniew Brzezinski with Carter, Scowcroft shunned publicity and did not set himself up as a rival to the secretary of state.

Two key domestic policy aides were Richard G. Darman, director of the Office of Management and Budget, and C. Boyden Gray, White House counsel. Darman, who had previously held high positions in the Commerce and Treasury Departments, was the administration's financial watchdog. At first he vigorously defended Bush's promise of no new taxes. But in 1990 he advocated a compromise with Congress— some new taxes in return for budget cuts. He then became the favorite target of criticism from low-tax conservatives. Gray had worked for Vice President Bush in the commission on deregulation. As the president's chief lawyer he crafted strategy for limiting congressional power.

One of a president's most important constitutional and political responsibilities is to appoint judges for the federal courts and justices for the Supreme Court, subject to confirmation by the Senate. During his four years President Bush filled one quarter of the judgeships in the lower courts and two positions on the Supreme Court. He continued Reagan's policy of naming men and women who believe that the powers granted to government under the Constitution are limited and that previous court decisions had granted excessive rights to individuals, especially in criminal proceedings. Bush appointed a record number of women to the federal courts, but gave few appointments to blacks and Hispanics.

During the Bush presidency two liberal justices of the Supreme Court retired: William J. Brennan, Jr., and Thurgood Marshall. To replace Brennan, the president in 1990 nominated a reclusive judicial intellectual, David H. Souter of New Hampshire. Souter refused to indicate in advance how he would decide on specific issues such as a woman's right to an abortion. He was easily confirmed, and once on the bench proved to be less conservative than the president may have expected.

The nomination in 1991 to replace Marshall, hero of the civil rights movement and the first African American to serve on the Court, became a political firestorm. Clarence Thomas, a young federal judge of little experience, was also black. He held the ultraconservative view that the Constitution provided scant authority for federal legislation designed to bring about social change. Political liberals and moderates had legitimate reason to vote against Thomas' confirmation on the basis of his judicial philosophy. But the televised hearings on the nomination before the Senate Judiciary Committee were quickly converted into a seminar on sexual harassment. Anita Hill, a black law professor who had worked for Thomas in two federal agencies, accused him of making improper sexual advances toward her. Thomas denied the charges and described himself as the target of a political lynch mob. The final vote of 52–48 in favor of confirmation reflected divisions in the Senate and the country over which person was telling the truth—Hill or Thomas.

The End of the Cold War

Bush lacked a consuming interest in the domestic policy side of the presidency, but in January 1989 all seemed to be well on the home front. His easy victory as successor to the enormously popular Reagan indicated that most of the American people were happy with the government. The economy, growing spectacularly after a severe recession in the early Reagan years, was still strong. Employment was high, the stock market was up, people with money were making more. It appeared that if Bush simply maintained the domestic status quo he could concentrate on foreign policy, the area of his greatest interest.

Bush occupied the White House during two major events of the twentieth century: the end of the Cold War and the unanticipated collapse of the Soviet Union. Both had deep historical roots. In the 1960s and early 1970s there had been brief thaws in the Cold War and one could argue that the self-destruction of the Soviet Union was inherent in the nature of the Communist system beginning with the Bolshevik revolution of 1917. Accelerated change, however, began only after Gorbachev became the Soviet leader in 1985.

Between 1985 and 1988, Reagan and Gorbachev, along with U.S. secretary of state George P. Shultz and Soviet foreign minister Eduard A. Shevardnadze, began the transformation of Soviet-American relations. They agreed on the first major cuts in long-range nuclear weapons since the beginning of the arms race in the 1940s, eliminated intermediate-range nuclear weapons from Europe, and consented to close inspections of each other's arsenals in order to ensure compliance with agreements. The two superpowers also began tentatively to cooperate in reducing conflicts in the Third World.

Gorbachev was convinced that the survival of the Soviet Union depended on drastic internal economic reform and relief from the crippling burden of military expenditures. Reagan's cooperative posture convinced Gorbachev that he could safely reduce Soviet military strength without tempting the United States to press an advantage. In December 1988 at the United Nations, Gorbachev renounced the Leninist theory of inevitable international conflict between capitalism and socialism, called on all nations to work together to solve universal human problems, and unilaterally announced the withdrawal of half a million troops and thousands of heavy conventional weapons from Eastern Europe.

Did that mean the Cold War was over? When Bush took office as president in January 1989 the answer was not clear. American skeptics in the press and among his advisers warned that it all might be a trick designed to lull the free world. Bush, a staunch Cold Warrior throughout his career, decided to slow the pace of Soviet-American negotiations. He did not believe, as had Reagan, that nuclear weapons could be abolished. He wanted to maintain a strong American nuclear arsenal and was wary of agreements that might give the Soviets an advantage. He was not convinced that the Soviets had abandoned their disruptive behavior in the Third World.

On the other hand, Bush did not rule out the possibility that Gorbachev might really be sincere and trustworthy. As vice president in December 1987 Bush told Gorbachev to ignore his public hard-line remarks, necessary if he was to win the nomination and election. His goal as president, Bush said, would be to improve Soviet-American relations. Gorbachev afterward said this was the most important talk he ever had with Bush.

The president's prudence (a favorite word) led him to underestimate the rapid deterioration of Soviet military and economic power and Gorbachev's desperate determination to jettison military burdens in order to prevent the complete collapse of Soviet society. Bush did not realize at first that nuclear arms control agreements were no longer the major issue or that Gorbachev would agree to almost anything. The real issue was whether Gorbachev would survive as a leader and whether after Gorbachev there would be chaos.

It was not until July 1989 that Bush told Gorbachev that he would consider a meeting—"without thousands of assistants hovering over our shoulders." Meanwhile, Secretary of State Baker and Foreign Minister Shevardnadze met several times and formed a close relationship. Baker was astounded at how frank Shevardnadze was about the Soviet Union's problems. In the autumn of 1989, while Bush watched and waited, Communist regimes throughout Eastern Europe began to topple and Gorbachev publicly renounced the "Brezhnev doctrine," which the Soviet Union had previously invoked to justify armed intervention against freedom movements in Hungary in 1956 and Czechoslovakia in 1968. The message to Communist leaders in 1989 was that they could no longer count on Soviet tanks to keep them in power. With the Soviet Union deliberately standing back, the Berlin Wall came down in November, and soon non-Communist governments were replacing the old regime throughout the former Soviet satellite empire. There were also mounting demands for national independence within the USSR, most notably from the Baltic republics of Estonia, Latvia, and Lithuania.

This was the situation when Bush and Gorbachev met for their first summit—on ships in a storm-tossed harbor of the island nation of Malta in the Mediterranean. The most important outcome of Malta was a secret exchange of assurances. Gorbachev would do what he could to avoid violence in dealing with the problem of Baltic secessionism and the discontent of other nationalities. Bush in turn would avoid public criticism of Gorbachev on this issue.

Bush came away from Malta with a better appreciation of how precarious was Gorbachev's political situation in the Soviet Union. If Gorbachev pressed too hard for economic reforms, made too many concessions to separatist movements, and agreed too easily with the United States, hard-line opponents would charge him with weakness. But if he did not introduce reforms and reduce the economic burden of a Cold War military establishment, the system would collapse.

By 1990 Bush decided that the essential goal of American policy toward the Soviet Union must be to keep Gorbachev in power and to favor the preservation rather than disintegration of the Soviet Union. The alternative was chaos. Sound, mutually advantageous agreements with Gorbachev on arms reduction could be negotiated. Without Gorbachev they might be impossible.

Meanwhile, the Communist government of East Germany collapsed and Germans on both sides of the former Iron Curtain called for reunification. Secretary of State Baker, assuming that Gorbachev would not accept a unified Germany within the North Atlantic Treaty Organization (NATO), in February 1990 initiated some complicated diplomatic negotiations involving the two Germanies plus the United States, Britain, France, and the Soviet Union—the "two plus four" formula. Baker's assumption had been wrong. In July 1990 Gorbachev made his greatest concession. He astonished German chancellor Helmut Kohl by announcing that the Soviet Union would withdraw all its troops from eastern Germany and accept NATO membership for a reunified Germany. Kohl, in return, promised to pay the cost of relocating Soviet troops and provide other economic aid. The line was now dissolving between NATO and the Warsaw Pact, the Moscow-dominated military alliance of Communist governments. The Warsaw Pact was officially disbanded in 1991.

Meanwhile, arms control experts on the Soviet and American sides were making great strides. The most important achievement was the Conventional Forces in Europe (CFE) treaty of November 1990, signed by Bush and Gorbachev in Paris. Among other things, it committed the Soviet Union to reduce by 70 percent its tanks and heavy weapons stationed west of the Ural Mountains. A treaty reducing long-range strategic arms took a little longer. Signed by Bush and Gorbachev in Moscow on 31 July 1991, the START treaty reduced nuclear warheads on both sides to 6,000—a 30-percent reduction. The dangerous category of missiles with multiple independently targeted warheads (MIRVs) was reduced by half. Because of the subsequent collapse of the Soviet Union, the Strategic Arms Reduction Treaty (START I) was not approved by the U.S. Senate until November 1992.

The more the two sides reduced nuclear weapons, the less important arms control became in the relationship. The more pressing issues were cooperation in meeting the challenge of Iraq's August 1990 invasion of Kuwait and the very survival of the Soviet

Union. Bush refrained from criticizing the occasional use of force by the Soviets against independence movements and even warned, in a speech in Ukraine in August 1991, that "Americans will not support those who seek independence in order to replace a far-off tyranny with a local despotism. They will not aid those who promote a suicidal nationalism based on ethnic hatred."

By this time, however, there was nothing Gorbachev or the United States could do to stem the Soviet Union's fall. On 18 August 1991 a group of Communist hard-liners put Gorbachev under house arrest and attempted to take over the country. They were miserably inept. Faced with strong opposition by Boris N. Yeltsin, head of the Russian Federation, and lacking the full support of the Red Army, the coup failed in three days. Marshal Sergei F. Akhromeyev, the most senior of the old military establishment, committed suicide after the coup. He left a note saying that everything he had worked for—the Soviet Union, the Red Army, and the Communist party—was being destroyed. Akhromeyev was right.

Gorbachev returned to the Kremlin as president of the Soviet Union, but he was presiding over an empty husk. On 25 December 1991 Gorbachev resigned. The hammer and sickle flag came down from the Kremlin for the last time. The Soviet Union was no more. All the former dependent republics within the old USSR proclaimed their independence, secured international recognition, and were admitted to the United Nations. The real leader in Moscow now was Yeltsin, president of Russia, a man previously belittled by the Bush administration as a crude self-promoter.

Bush's preference for sustaining a single central government had been overtaken by events. The United States opened embassies in the newly independent states but still concentrated its efforts on Moscow and Yeltsin as the democratically elected leader of the new Russia. The two sides continued to negotiate on nuclear arms and in January 1993, just before Bush left office, agreed to the START II treaty eliminating MIRVs altogether and reducing strategic warheads to 3,500 on the U.S. side and 3,000 on the Russian. This was a 50-percent reduction in the levels set by the START I treaty approved only weeks before by the Senate. Meanwhile, the former Soviet republics in which nuclear weapons were still located—Belarus, Ukraine, and Kazakhstan—agreed in principle that they would be nonnuclear states with the weapons to be dismantled or shipped to Russia.

Yeltsin's political position at home, like Gorbachev's before him, was precarious in large part because of the chaotic state of the Russian economy. Yeltsin begged for massive U.S. economic aid. Bush was generous with words. "If this democratic revolution is defeated," he said, "it could plunge us into a world more dangerous in some respects than the dark years of the Cold War." But the president's inherent caution and the reluctance of Congress meant that aid would be limited to relatively small amounts for humanitarian assistance and help with the dismantling of nuclear weapons. The uncertain future of the Russian economic system made Americans wary of "throwing money down a rathole," and with the United States facing huge deficits itself, public opinion did not support a bailout of Russia.

The only former Communist country undergoing a more chaotic dissolution than the Soviet Union was Yugoslavia. In 1991 the political leaders of the different republics within Yugoslavia could not agree on how to keep the country together. As ethnic violence broke out, the federal Yugoslav army based in Serbia attacked Croatia. The Bush administration applied economic sanctions against Serbia, but was dismayed by the disintegration of a small country into even smaller parts. The United States went along reluctantly in 1992 when Slovenia, Croatia, and Bosnia-Herzegovina were admitted to the United Nations as independent nations. In 1992 the fighting in Croatia subsided, but shifted to Bosnia-Herzegovina, where the Bosnian Serbs launched a war of "ethnic cleansing" against the Bosnian Muslim population. The European Community and the United States tried to broker a political settlement while UN peacekeepers watched helplessly. Bush and the United States were criticized by some commentators for not using military force to punish the Serbs and protect the Bosnian Muslims. But his advisers, including General Powell, believed that the ethnic hatreds in the region were so fierce that outside military intervention would be doomed to failure. Furthermore, no vital security interest of the United States was at stake. Thus, the United States stood back while the Bosnian Serbs continued their attacks, especially on the besieged city of Sarajevo. Not until September 1995, more than halfway through the presidency of Bill Clinton, did the United States and its NATO partners finally use heavy airpower to deter Bosnian Serb attacks on Muslims in an effort to force a peace settlement.

The Persian Gulf War

Bush's close involvement with Gorbachev and the Soviet Union overlapped the biggest headline event of his presidency—the Persian Gulf War waged by an international coalition under American leadership to compel Iraq's dictator Saddam Hussein to end his country's aggression against Kuwait. The February 1991 victory in that war brought Bush the highest public opinion approval ratings of his presidency, overshadowing for a moment the controversial question of whether policy mistakes by the United States were partially responsible for the war in the first place.

Throughout the 1980s it was American policy to overlook the brutal aspects of the Saddam Hussein regime and to support Iraq in its long (1980–1988) and bloody war against Iran. The United States was following the old principle that the enemy of my enemy is my friend—and Iran was an enemy, notwithstanding the Reagan administration's misconceived 1986 effort to curry favor through the secret sale of arms, an aspect of the Iran-Contra scandal. The Bush administration continued to favor Iraq in spite of Saddam Hussein's threats against Israel, overwhelming evidence that he was developing chemical, biological, and perhaps nuclear weapons, and his lethal suppression of the Kurdish minority in Iran (including use of poison gas). The administration believed that Iraq was an essential element in a Persian Gulf balance of power against a resurgent Iran and that the United States could persuade Saddam Hussein to moderate the unattractive features of his regime.

The administration's policy was spelled out in secret National Security Directive 26 in October 1989. It declared: "Normal relations between the United States and Iraq would serve our longer-term interests and promote stability both in the Gulf and the Middle East. The United States should propose economic and political incentives for Iraq to moderate its behavior and to increase our influence." These incentives included massive food exports to Iraq on favorable terms, a boon to American farmers, and the encouragement of trade in high-tech but nonlethal items. The administration resisted demands from human rights activists in Congress to impose sanctions against Iraq and dismissed Saddam Hussein's public threat to destroy half of Israel with chemical warfare as mere bravado. Washington also failed to note that illegal loans to Iraq from an Italian-owned bank in the United States were being used to develop weapons of mass destruction.

In spite of the helpful intentions of the Bush administration, Iraq was in a difficult economic condition. There was widespread unemployment. Oil prices, and hence national revenue, were down. The costs of repairing the damage of the long war with Iran were heavy and the country was deeply in debt to other Arab states. In mid-1990 Saddam Hussein claimed that neighboring Kuwait was draining Iraqi oil from an oil field astride the border. He said the entire field rightfully belonged to Iraq and indicated he might use force to take it. In July 1990 Iraqi armed forces began to move toward Kuwait.

The Bush administration's response was to try conciliation and hope for the best. April Glaspie, the American ambassador in Baghdad, was instructed to tell Saddam that the United States had no position on bilateral differences between Arab states, such as Iraq's dispute with Kuwait, although the use of force would, of course, be contrary to the UN Charter. This statement and the absence of any significant American military preparations probably contributed to Saddam Hussein's decision to invade Kuwait on 2 August.

Kuwait, smaller than the state of New Jersey and with a native population of less than a million (plus a million non-Kuwaiti guest workers from around the Middle East and southern Asia), could not stop the invasion. Within hours Iraqi troops occupied the country. The news reached President Bush while he was on vacation in Maine. He denounced Iraq for "naked aggression," froze Iraqi and Kuwaiti financial assets in the United States, and cut off trade, but said the use of American military force was not under consideration. After talking with British prime minister Margaret Thatcher at a previously scheduled meeting in Aspen, Colorado, however, Bush took a stronger line. Thatcher, whose reputation for courage flowed from her leadership in Britain's 1982 war against Argentina's aggression in the Falkland Islands, compared Saddam Hussein to Hitler. Bush returned to Washington determined that, as he soon declaimed, the aggression against Kuwait would not stand.

The immediate problem, however, was to ensure that Iraqi forces did not press on a few miles and seize the major oil fields of Saudi Arabia—thereby acquiring control of approximately 40 percent of the world's oil reserves. The question of how and when Iraq could be persuaded or forced to retreat from Kuwait came next. The administration moved quickly to secure international support in the United Nations Security Council where, thanks to post-Cold War relations with the Soviet Union and China, American proposals did not face a certain veto. A resolution condemning the Iraqi invasion (2 August) was followed by another imposing mandatory economic sanctions on Iraq (6 August). The protection of Saudi Arabia began with a successful trip by Secretary of Defense Cheney to Riyadh to persuade King Fahd to invite the stationing of American troops on his soil. On 6 August President Bush ordered the first forces of Operation Desert Shield to Saudi Arabia. The commander was General H. Norman Schwarzkopf.

Bush now operated at his best, "working the telephone" with leaders in a dozen different countries, lining up support for the opposition to Saddam Hussein, winning commitments to vote for crucial resolutions in the UN Security Council. His most difficult and sensitive task was to persuade the Soviet Union to be a partner in the enterprise. Bush had to be careful not to undermine Gorbachev's leadership at home; some of the Soviet leader's enemies within the USSR were accusing him of betraying an ally, Iraq, in order to become the lapdog of the United States. In the end Gorbachev provided full support for the coalition in the United Nations, but refused to send any Soviet military forces to participate in the campaign.

U.S. relations with Britain and France on the Iraqi question were good. Both supplied significant military forces and leadership. Relations with two other allies, Germany and Japan, were tricky. Both governments claimed that their constitutions prevented the use of armed forces outside their territory. The United States in these cases sought nonmilitary support. Japan ultimately contributed $14 billion and Germany $11 billion. Along with $16 billion each from Saudi Arabia and Kuwait, a large part of American costs were defrayed. More than forty countries eventually contributed in some way to the effort to expel Iraq from Kuwait.

By October, Desert Shield was providing reliable protection to Saudi Arabia, but economic sanctions had not induced Saddam Hussein to withdraw from Kuwait. Bush decided that Iraq would respond only to military force. He ordered a sharp increase in the number of U.S. troops in the Gulf, thereby creating an offensive capability, but he waited until after the 6 November congressional elections to announce his decision.

At the end of November the United States went to the UN Security Council for authorization for the next stage: the forcible expulsion of Iraq from Kuwait. On 29 November the Security Council passed

Resolution 678, giving Saddam Hussein until 15 January 1991 to withdraw from Kuwait, after which UN members were to employ "all necessary means" to liberate the country. "All necessary means," of course, meant war. The vote was twelve in favor, with Cuba and Yemen opposed and China abstaining.

As the confrontation moved toward probable war, President Bush at first refused to give Congress a role in deciding policy. Critics noted that the U.S. Constitution assigned the responsibility for declaring war to Congress. They conceded that a president, as commander in chief, did have the power to use military force without prior congressional approval when the United States was attacked or in other clear emergencies. But this confrontation was proceeding in slow motion. Bush said that he had the authority to act without Congress—especially in carrying out UN Security Council resolutions.

Critics also called for more time to let the economic sanctions work and warned that a war would be long and very bloody, an impression Saddam Hussein did his best to encourage with his bluster about the approaching "mother of all battles." Bush faced a dilemma. If a war waged without congressional authorization proved long and bloody (some said it could be another Vietnam), the resulting crisis could destroy his presidency. But if he asked for authorization and Congress said no, Saddam Hussein would be the winner. In January 1991 Bush concluded that he had enough votes to secure authorization. He asked for congressional support. Congress debated intensely for two days. A resolution to continue the use of sanctions rather than go to war failed narrowly. On 12 January the Senate by a vote of 52 to 47 and the House by 250 to 183 gave the president authority to use force—although Bush still claimed congressional action was really not necessary. The war—named Operation Desert Storm—began 16 January with a heavy bombing and missile campaign against Baghdad and Iraqi positions in Kuwait.

Iraq responded by firing intermediate-range Scud missiles, with conventional explosive warheads, against Israel. At the time of the invasion of Kuwait, Iraq had suggested that a settlement of the Kuwait question should be linked to Israel's withdrawal from the West Bank and Gaza and the establishment of a Palestinian state. The United States denounced the idea as a device for rewarding aggression and said there could be no "linkage." Now Iraq sought to create linkage by provoking a counterattack from Israel and thereby weakening the resolve of Arab nations to fight over Kuwait. The ploy failed. The government of Israel accepted the U.S. offer to provide Patriot antimissile defenses, manned by Americans, and refrained from retaliatory attacks on Iraq.

Intense air attacks on Iraq continued for more than a month. On the diplomatic front the Soviet government sent a high-level negotiator to Baghdad in an effort to distance itself from the United States. Fortunately, from Washington's point of view, nothing came of the Soviet effort. On 22 February, Bush gave Iraq a twenty-four-hour deadline: withdraw from Kuwait or face an invasion. Iraq responded by setting massive fires in Kuwait's oil fields and hurling verbal defiance. The land war began on 23 February and lasted for one hundred hours. The vaunted battle-hardened Iraqi forces were no match for American and coalition air power. With their communications cut off, without airpower, unable to follow the movement of coalition forces, they were helpless. Thousands were killed, tens of thousands surrendered or fled north toward Baghdad.

Bush, with the full support of General Powell, declared on 27 February that Kuwait had been liberated and Iraq defeated. Offensive operations would end at 8:00 A.M. the following morning, Gulf time. Iraq accepted the cease-fire and agreed to abide by all UN resolutions concerned with its invasion. Did Bush end the war too soon? General Schwarzkopf soon made that charge. Saddam Hussein was still in power and much of his army was intact. But the president had good reasons for the decision. The war had been fought to liberate Kuwait—a clear, single objective. To continue to fight for other reasons would have cost American lives and killed many thousands of Iraqis. The coalition in support of liberating Kuwait would break apart on the question of a larger war. Furthermore, the conquest of Iraq might saddle the United States with long responsibility as an occupying power. And finally, the elimination of Iraq would upset the balance of power in the Gulf to the advantage of Iran.

Victory in the Gulf War was the high point of the Bush presidency. Bush spoke expansively of a "new world order" in which all nations, large and small, would be protected from aggression, and the United Nations, freed from the obstructive use of the veto by antagonistic great powers, would function as originally intended. He also said that the United States had "licked the Vietnam syndrome"—meaning that the country was no longer paralyzed by even the

thought of using military power, for fear of becoming embroiled in a quagmire.

There were other consequences. Although the United States had rejected Iraq's effort to link Kuwait and Israel, linkage in the Middle East was a reality. Secretary of State Baker worked after the war to bring the Israelis, the Palestinians, and the other Arab countries to a peace table for discussions. The first round of talks was held in Madrid, Spain, in October. Bush also brought pressure on Israel to restrict the establishment of new Jewish settlements in the territories occupied after the 1967 war. Specifically, in September 1992 he persuaded Congress not to consider Israel's request for $10 billion in loan guarantees for new housing for emigrants from the Soviet Union. Congress complied, but Bush was strongly criticized by many American supporters of Israel. The pressure worked. In 1992 a new government in Israel agreed to restrict the settlements and the loan guarantee was extended.

The consequences of the Gulf War were less positive in Iraq. Two groups of the Iraqi population—Kurds in the north and Shiite Muslims in the south—used Saddam Hussein's defeat as an opportunity to assert their rights against an oppressive central government. Saddam responded with military force. The United States was in a delicate position. The Kurds and Shiites had legitimate grievances and were victims of Baghdad's brutality. But to support them might lead to the breakup of Iraq, instability in the region, and entangling commitments. The compromise was to provide protection for the Kurds in a safe-haven area and to prohibit Iraq from using airpower against either the Kurds or the Shiites. The United States enforced two no-fly zones for this purpose.

Trade and Foreign Policy in Asia

After the end of the Cold War and victory over Iraq the focus of administration foreign policy changed from maintaining a military-strategic position to expanding trade on favorable terms. Bush worked hard for that objective, concentrating on China and Japan.

Bush's first foreign visit, in February 1989, a month after his inauguration, was to China. He met with Chinese leaders Deng Xiaoping and Premier Li Peng. But the visit was marred when the Chinese blocked dissident Fang Lizhi, a distinguished scientist, from accepting President Bush's invitation to a banquet. The incident was a portent of trouble to come. Throughout the spring of 1989 ever-larger crowds of students in Beijing demonstrated against the government. In May, Premier Li Peng declared martial law. A half a million protesters marched in Shanghai while students in Beijing erected a "Goddess of Democracy" modeled on the American Statue of Liberty in Tiananmen Square. The bloody climax came on 3 and 4 June when the Chinese government responded with the clank of tanks and the rattle of gunfire—while television carried the scene around the world. Hundreds, perhaps thousands, of protesters were killed and wounded.

In public, President Bush joined the American people in condemning the Chinese government's actions. He suspended military sales to China and agreed to provide asylum for Fang Lizhi and his wife in the American embassy. The State Department advised Americans to leave Beijing, evacuated the dependents of diplomatic personnel, and recommended that international financial organizations postpone consideration of loan applications from China. The Bush administration suspended all high-level contacts between American and Chinese officials. Secretly, however, Bush dispatched National Security Adviser Scowcroft and Deputy Secretary of State Eagleburger to Beijing to say that the United States remained interested in good relations. The implicit message was that the Chinese leadership should realize that the administration's measures in response to the Tiananmen events were temporary and connected with American politics.

A crucial question in Chinese-American relations was the continuation or suspension of China's unfettered right to export to the United States. The term for this right, "most favored nation" status (MFN), is somewhat misleading in that it does not confer any special privileges, but only distinguishes states with which the United States has good commercial relations. The withdrawal of MFN was favored by human rights activists and a majority in Congress as a means of punishing China for the human rights violations so vividly symbolized by the Tiananmen massacre. Bush disagreed and fought off congressional pressure to restrict trade, twice vetoing punitive measures. He argued that the best way to encourage reform in China was to have a thriving trade, and that cutting off trade would hurt both the American economy and Chinese men and women who were not responsible for human rights violations.

United States relations with Japan were plagued during the Bush presidency by the perennial problem of unbalanced trade. Japan sold far more to the United States than it purchased and, from the American point of view, used unfair tactics to exclude American products from the Japanese market. The Bush administration continued a twenty-year-old ritual of complaint and negotiation after which the Japanese would appear to make small concessions. The trade imbalance grew worse. Bush made the trade issue the first topic of discussion on a trip to Japan in January 1992, during which he was accompanied by a bevy of American automobile executives. Alas, he caught a stomach virus and vomited on the Japanese prime minister at an official dinner. That embarrassing incident got more headlines than the substance of the discussions.

Not all policy in Asia involved trade. The issue in the Philippines, an American colony from 1899 to 1946 and ally after that, was the future of the huge U.S. naval and air bases at Subic Bay and Clark Field. Washington had long considered the bases essential for the projection of American power in Asia and had used them heavily during the Vietnam War. Successive Philippine governments valued the rent and economic stimulus the bases provided, although many Filipinos considered the American presence demeaning and culturally damaging. While negotiations were in progress in June 1991 the eruption of the Mount Pinatubo volcano severely damaged the bases. In July the negotiators agreed on the terms of a ten-year renewal, but the Philippine senate rejected the agreement. With the Cold War over and the damage from the volcano to confront, the United States no longer considered the bases essential. No effort was made to persuade the Philippine senate to reconsider. On 24 November 1992 the bases were turned over to the Philippine government, ending a near century of American presence.

Bush moved cautiously toward improved relations with Communist Vietnam. Even though American combat in Vietnam ended in 1973, the war left a bitter legacy, especially among those who believed that the Hanoi government was not providing all possible information on American soldiers missing in action (MIA) during the war. The political intensity of the MIA lobby deterred Bush from lifting the prohibition on trade with Hanoi and establishing diplomatic relations. He did authorize the beginning of discussions. Trade and full diplomatic relations were opened by the Clinton administration in 1994–1995.

Backyard Foreign Policy

The Latin American policy of the Bush administration departed sharply from the Cold War concerns of the Reagan years. The Soviet Union gradually withdrew its aid for Cuba, the Sandinista government of Nicaragua, and the leftist insurgents in El Salvador—both because Gorbachev did not want to irritate the United States on an issue of no strategic importance to Moscow and because the USSR had run out of money. The Bush administration, in turn, abandoned the Reaganite military approach to the political problems of Central America and encouraged regional diplomatic solutions and a role for the United Nations. The result was the free election victory in Nicaragua of an anti-Sandinista coalition led by Violeta Barrios de Chamorro in February 1990 and a UN-brokered end to the civil war in El Salvador in late 1991.

Some American liberals urged the administration to open a dialogue with Fidel Castro of Cuba, looking toward a possible lifting of the embargo on trade and the normalization of relations now that the Cold War was over. But on that question Bush held fast to the old policy of tough economic sanctions and verbal denunciation of Castro's totalitarian regime. Castro was no longer a threat to anyone outside of Cuba, but a tough anti-Castro policy was good domestic politics, especially with the well-organized Cuban-American community in Florida.

Elsewhere in the Caribbean and Central America, President Bush dealt with new objectives and problems. The most dramatic episode was the December 1989 U.S. invasion of Panama to oust dictator Manuel Noriega and bring him to trial for his involvement in the illegal drug trade. Noriega's power was based largely on murder and intimidation. He had been on the payroll of the CIA and the Drug Enforcement Agency in the 1980s for assistance in the covert war against the Sandinistas and to help interdict the flow of narcotics into the United States. In fact, he was up to his armpits in the drug trade and money laundering. Finally in 1988 Noriega was indicted on drug charges by a federal grand jury in Florida. The Reagan administration floated the idea, opposed by Vice President Bush, of dropping the indictment if Noriega would give up his power and leave Panama. Noriega was not interested in the deal.

But in May 1989 Noriega, under U.S. pressure, permitted a presidential election in Panama. The democratic opposition, headed by Guillermo Endara, won 68 percent of the vote. Noriega annulled the election. His loyal political roughnecks attacked and severely wounded Endara and other opposition leaders. Noriega was now a bone in Bush's throat. Bush ordered more troops sent to the American base alongside the Panama Canal and tightened economic sanctions. In October 1989 a young Panamanian military officer asked for U.S. help in overthrowing Noriega. The United States hesitated in providing support. Noriega executed the leaders of the attempted coup.

In December, Noriega's puppet National Assembly declared a state of war with the United States. Noriega's army provoked a U.S. response by killing an off-duty marine officer and harassing other Americans. Just after midnight on 20 December, American forces attacked Noriega's headquarters and military installations. Endara, the legally elected president, took office under American protection and declared the Panamanian army disbanded. Armed resistance to the intervention faded quickly, and the great majority of the people of Panama rejoiced in their liberation from a brutal dictator. Noriega took refuge in the residence of the papal envoy to Panama. He soon surrendered and was transported to Florida for trial, conviction, and a long jail sentence. Twenty-five thousand Americans served in the operation, of whom 39 were killed, along with 139 Panamanian troops and about 400 civilians. The Organization of American States condemned the U.S. invasion by a vote of 20 to 1, but Bush, the U.S. Congress, and most Americans, according to public opinion polls, believed the right thing had been done.

Haiti was another nearby problem with no connection to old Cold War issues. The densely populated, impoverished island country had long suffered under corrupt and despotic rule. In December 1990, however, the first reasonably free elections in Haitian history were won by a charismatic hero of the poor, the Reverend Jean-Bertrand Aristide. President Aristide's radical philosophy threatened the army and the wealthy oligarchy. He was overthrown in a military coup on 30 September 1991.

One of the coup leaders, General Raoul Cedras, took over as Haiti's leader. Aristide fled to Venezuela and then to Washington, where he continued to be recognized as the rightful head of government. The United States applied increasing economic pressure against Cedras and supported the futile efforts of the United Nations and the Organization of American States to negotiate Aristide's return. Meanwhile, thousands of poor Haitians tried to escape to the

United States in pitifully unseaworthy wooden boats. Many were lost at sea while thousands of others were picked up by the U.S. Coast Guard. The Bush administration denied the refugees admission to the United States and instead established a temporary camp for them at Guantánamo Bay, the American naval base in Cuba. In 1993 the Clinton administration inherited a standoff with Cedras and in 1994 negotiated Cedras' departure and sent in American troops to prevent violence and permit Aristide's return.

Bush's major economic initiative in Latin America, negotiation of the North American Free Trade Agreement (NAFTA), had large domestic economic and political implications. The agreement brought Mexico into the existing free-trade arrangement between the United States and Canada. It called for the elimination of tariffs (taxes charged on imports) for most trade among the three countries. The Mexican government embraced NAFTA as a boon to manufacturing, and American corporations favored it as a means of lowering the cost of production by using low-wage Mexican workers. Organized American labor, on the other hand, denounced it as a threat to employment in the United States, and environmentalists said it would be a way for American companies to escape U.S. environmental regulations. Ross Perot, an independent candidate in the 1992 election, made opposition a centerpiece of his campaign and warned of the "giant sucking sound" of American jobs flowing down below the border. Bill Clinton was a lukewarm supporter. The agreement was signed by Bush, Mexican president Carlos Salinas de Gortari, and Canadian prime minister Brian Mulroney on 17 December 1992. It was approved by Congress in late 1993 and went into effect 1 January 1994.

Battling with Congress

The political failure of the Bush presidency, defined by Bush's loss in the 1992 election, was entirely in the realm of domestic affairs and may well have been beyond Bush's power to prevent. There had been a sharp recession at the beginning of the Reagan years, with almost 10 percent of the workforce unemployed. But since 1983 the nation's economy had enjoyed extraordinary growth. A cyclical correction was overdue. Growth slowed in 1989 and 1990 and then stopped in 1991. Unemployment rose from 5.3 percent in 1989 to 7.4 percent in 1992. The start of a recovery in late 1992 was not vigorous enough to reduce unemployment and came too late to help Bush at the polls.

Against this economic background, Bush had the political problem of facing a Congress controlled, in both Senate and House, by the opposition party throughout his four years. Other recent presidents—Truman, Eisenhower, Nixon, Reagan—faced a similar problem but encountered less difficulty than Bush. One tactic, used successfully by Truman and Reagan, was to build such popular support for a clear program that members of Congress either cooperated or faced a loss at the next election. Another tactic, mastered by Nixon, was to win support across party lines with a subtle combination of punishments and rewards.

Bush tried neither. He had no compelling program on which to build popular support, and he lacked the taste or talent for bargaining and mutual accommodation. Again, Bush was above all a foreign policy president. His friends and critics agreed on his lack of passion and leadership in domestic affairs. Although he had run for the Senate and served four years in the House, he had few close friends in the legislature. His key advisers on domestic affairs saw Congress as an obstacle, not a difficult partner with whom it was necessary to reach an understanding. Instead, as one analyst of his presidency has written, Bush tried to govern without Congress.

Bush's principal tool was the veto. Under the Constitution the president must sign bills passed by Congress to make them into law. If he disapproves of the legislation, he may refuse to sign it and send Congress a veto. Both houses of Congress need a two-thirds majority to override a presidential veto. Bush wielded the veto successfully forty-three out of forty-four times. The only veto to be overridden, on 5 October 1992, was legislation to regulate the cable television industry. Bush said the law would increase rather than reduce the cost of cable TV to the consumer.

Most of the important successful vetoes reflected Bush's opposition to expanded government regulations and were favorable to business. For example, his first veto, on 13 June 1989, blocked a congressional effort to raise the minimum wage from $3.35 (where it had stood since 1981) to $4.55. Congress offered a compromise at $4.25, which Bush then signed. Bush also vetoed, on 21 June 1990, a bill to require most employers to permit employees to have up to twelve weeks of unpaid leave to care for newborn, recently adopted, or ill children, without risking their job security. Bush said such matters were best left to negotiation between workers and management and that the bill would create "rigid, federally imposed requirements." In October 1991, with unemployment rising, Bush vetoed a bill to extend federal unemployment benefits, saying it would add to the budget deficit.

His most conspicuous veto was exercised against the civil rights legislation of 1990. Recent Supreme Court decisions had narrowed the ability of employees to win redress from employers for discrimination on the grounds of race, sex, religion, and national origin. The Democratic Congress proceeded to strengthen the legislation. Bush's veto message argued that the proposed law would force employers to set quotas in hiring in order to protect themselves from lawsuits. The president said he was all for affirmative action, but vehemently against quotas. He also twice vetoed, as noted above, congressional efforts to deny MFN status to China and a message to restrict textile imports.

Another technique used by Bush to work around Congress was to restrict or eliminate federal regulations on environmental and occupational safety matters deemed burdensome to business, and generally to interpret the will of Congress in the narrowest possible way. A key adviser in this effort was White House counsel Boyden Gray, a lawyer adept at finding ways to reshape the meaning of laws. Another technique was the vigorous use of the Council on Competitiveness headed by Vice President Quayle. The mandate of the Quayle council was to review all federal regulations affecting business and strike down regulations whose cost to business was deemed to exceed the benefits derived. Business interests were invited to appeal directly to Quayle for help.

Bush did work with Congress in passing two major pieces of legislation, both in 1990: the Americans with Disabilities Act and the Clean Air Act. The first required businesses, schools, and public institutions to install facilities providing full access to people in wheelchairs and with other disabilities.

In supporting the Clean Air Act, Bush was acting, to use his own words, as an "environmental president." President Reagan, showing little anxiety over alleged threats to the environment, had for eight years blocked any strengthening of 1977 clean air legislation. The quality of the nation's air had improved little, if at all. Acid rain, caused by smokestack emissions and urban smog from automobiles, was harmful to plants and human beings. Bush agreed something had to be done. He did not accept the sweeping proposals of some members of Congress, but settled for new pollution controls on automobile exhausts and required industry to meet deadlines for the reduction of damaging emissions. The implementation of environmental regulations, however, involved a constant struggle between William Reilly, the administrator of the Environmental Protection Agency, and more conservative, business-oriented members of the administration like Chief of Staff Sununu and Vice President Quayle.

It was not easy for Bush to be simultaneously an environmental president and the protector of business from federal regulations. For example, at first he came out against attending the United Nations Conference on Environment and Development, popularly called the Earth Summit, scheduled for June 1992 in Rio de Janeiro, Brazil. "I am not going to the Rio Conference and . . . sign an agreement that does not protect the environment and economy of this country," he said. In the face of an environmentalist outcry Bush did attend the conference, though the United States refused at Rio to support the Biodiversity Treaty to protect endangered species, because Bush believed it would place undue burdens on American business.

Bush's biggest problem with Congress was the deficit in the federal budget, the gap between revenue and expenditures. The deficit in 1980, Jimmy Carter's last year as president, had been $73.8 billion. By Reagan's last year, 1988, it had doubled to $155 billion. Deficits must be met by borrowing, and borrowing produces a national debt. The debt under Carter was $914 billion. By 1988 it had tripled—requiring more than $200 billion per year just to pay the interest. Bush agreed with his budget director Richard Darman that the deficit and the debt were a serious drag on the American economy, depressing productive investment, costing jobs, weakening the nation's ability to compete for world markets.

But what to do? A deficit can be closed only by reducing expenditures or increasing revenue (taxes), or some combination of the two. Bush had a quadruple problem. First, he had pledged "no new taxes" during the 1988 campaign, and most Republicans were determined to hold him to the pledge. Second, expenditures were rising rapidly because of interest payments, a commitment made in the Reagan administration to bail out failed savings and loan institutions, and the escalating cost of payments under

Social Security, Medicare, and other government "entitlement" programs. Third, the Democratic Congress was loath to cut entitlements but welcomed the opportunity to embarrass Bush with new taxes. And fourth, the economy as a whole went into mild recession in 1990 and 1991. Unemployment rose and wages stagnated. A popular anti-Bush bumper sticker in the spring of 1991 read "Saddam Hussein has a job. Have you?" Bush's dilemma was that he believed the long-term health of the economy required a reduction in federal spending—a measure that in the short term could mean higher unemployment.

Bush kept his pledge on no new taxes in 1989. The budget agreement reached that year kept things as they were: rising expenditures, rising debt, no new taxes. But in 1990 Bush decided to abandon his pledge as part of a comprehensive deal with Congress. He and his staff engaged Congress in prolonged negotiation aimed toward a mix of higher taxes and a substantial cut in expenditures. Representative Dan Rostenkowski of Illinois, the Democratic chairman of the House Ways and Means Committee, was the principal negotiator for Congress. Conservative commentators and some disillusioned members of his own staff believed that Bush was taken to the cleaners by Congress. Under the 1990 budget act taxes went up slightly, but cuts in spending were largely promises for the future. As a result, expenditures continued to grow faster than revenue, the deficit remained high (reaching $290 billion in 1992), and the national debt at the end of Bush's term exceeded $4 trillion.

Bush failed to persuade Congress to enact his favorite economic measure: a reduction in the capital gains tax, the tax incurred when stocks or other assets are sold for more than what they were purchased for. The president argued that a high capital gains tax prevented investors from taking the kind of risk necessary for economic growth and from redirecting funds from old investments to new, more productive ones. He also claimed that a lower capital gains tax would actually mean more government revenue because investors would be more likely to sell stocks when their tax on profits was low, rather than hold onto them and not pay any tax at all. The Democratic-controlled Congress blocked a capital gains tax cut and called it a measure to benefit only the rich— since poor people had no investments and thus no hope of capital gains.

Bush alienated some conservatives by agreeing to new taxes, but he leaned their way on a cluster of noneconomic issues, such as abortion. After the Supreme Court in *Webster* v. *Reproductive Health Services* (1989) extended the power of a state government to restrict abortions, those who believed in a woman's right to choose ("pro-choice") mobilized. The Democratic Congress, with pro-choice majorities, then attempted to strike down existing bans on the use of federal funds for abortions or abortion-related activities. Four times Bush vetoed bills with pro-choice provisions.

Another controversial issue was gun control. Here Bush took a middle-of-the-road position. He declared his strong conviction that Americans had a constitutionally guaranteed right to bear arms and his belief that legislation could do little to keep guns out of the hands of criminals. Better, he said, to deal with crime through longer, tougher prison sentences. On the other hand, he supported restrictions on the importation of certain kinds of automatic weapons unsuitable for sporting purposes.

Defeat in 1992

President Bush always intended to run for a second term and in 1992 faced only one challenger for the nomination—the ultraconservative political commentator and onetime Nixon and Reagan aide, Patrick ("Pat") Buchanan. Although Buchanan gave Bush a scare in the early New Hampshire primary by winning 37.4 percent of the vote, he soon faded. By April 1992 Bush's renomination was locked up. The press did speculate about whether Quayle would be "dumped" from the ticket but Bush stood by his vice president both out of loyalty and as a gesture toward conservative Republicans. Buchanan, however, regained national attention with a ferocious speech at the Republican convention in August, a virtual declaration of war against political and cultural liberals and moderates. Bush's apparent acceptance of Buchanan's extremism may have cost him votes in the November election.

Meanwhile, the Democrats picked Bill Clinton, the youthful governor of Arkansas, and the equally young Albert ("Al") Gore, Jr., senator from Tennessee, as his vice presidential running mate. Businessman Ross Perot, the wealthy and idiosyncratic independent candidate, inspired an enthusiastic band of followers with his call for a simpler, smaller government. Perot never had a chance of winning the election but he received 19 percent of the vote, more at the expense of Bush than Clinton. Had Perot not been running, the contest would have been close, but Clinton would probably still have won.

Clinton's advantage and Bush's liability was the sluggish state of the economy and the perception among disaffected voters, especially traditional Democrats who had voted for Reagan, that Bush did not have a clue about how to stem the deficit and create new jobs. Clinton strategist James Carville defined the key issue of the campaign as "the economy, stupid." Public opinion polling confirmed Carville's analysis. When asked what was the most important issue, most people said the economy and unemployment or the cost of health care; only 6 percent said foreign policy. Bush's championing of NAFTA lost support among workers fearing for their jobs (many of whom probably voted for Perot) and his enthusiasm for a cut in the capital gains tax made him vulnerable among middle- and lower-income voters to the charge that he was the candidate of the rich.

Bush suffered other liabilities. Ironically, the success in foreign policy deprived him of an asset. No longer could he, as in 1988, win votes by pointing to his long experience in foreign and national security affairs. With the collapse of the Soviet Union and Yeltsin's Russia in disarray and the United States avoiding involvement in the civil war in Bosnia, Clinton's foreign policy inexperience did not help Bush the way the inexperience of Dukakis had in 1988. Also, Bush's embrace of a conservative social agenda alienated voters who believed that a woman's right to a legal abortion must be protected.

The election results were devastating. Bush received only 37.4 percent of the vote against 43 percent for Clinton. In the electoral college it was 370 (thirty-two states) for Clinton and 168 (eighteen states) for Bush. Perot received no electoral votes. Democrats retained control of both houses of Congress. Bush was deeply hurt politically, but he pressed on in office, showing a remarkable burst of energy in the "lame-duck" eleven weeks before Clinton's inauguration in January 1993.

On 4 December 1992 Bush ordered the second largest military operation of his presidency, the humanitarian intervention in Somalia to end mass starvation. Drought-plagued Somalia, located on the northeast coast of Africa, was in a state of anarchy as disorganized armed groups terrorized the population, looted relief supplies, and endangered the lives of civilian relief workers. Worldwide television carried excruciating pictures of the suffering. Bush acted. He sent 28,000 American troops to protect the relief efforts and bring food to the starving. President-elect Clinton, Congress, and the American people agreed it was the right thing to do.

Also during his final weeks Bush joined Russian president Yeltsin in proposing additional major reductions in strategic nuclear arms. And on Christmas Eve 1992 he pardoned six Reagan administration officials charged with misleading Congress during the Iran-Contra affair. They were former secretary of defense Caspar W. Weinberger, former assistant secretary of state for inter-American affairs Elliott Abrams, former national security adviser Robert C. McFarlane, and three officials of the Central Intelligence Agency.

George and Barbara Bush returned to Houston, Texas, the day of Clinton's inauguration. Bush chose to be a low-profile ex-president, refusing numerous speaking engagements and making few public pronouncements. The conservative wing of the Republican party blamed him for Clinton's victory and did not invite him to play a prominent role in party affairs. When the Republicans won control of both houses of Congress in the 1994 midterm elections, something they had been unable to do while Bush was president, Bush's name was never mentioned as having contributed to the victory. No one urged him to seek the 1996 Republican nomination and none of the contenders sought his endorsement. Like Gorbachev in Russia, George Bush was no longer a player in high politics.

BIBLIOGRAPHY

There is not yet a detailed biography of George Bush or a comprehensive study of his administration. His autobiography, *Looking Forward* (Garden City, N.Y., 1987), written with Victor Gold, is light and easy reading, written in anticipation of his 1988 campaign for the presidency. *See also* Fitzhugh Green, *George Bush: An Intimate Portrait* (New York, 1989), which ends with the 1988 election. *Barbara Bush: A Memoir* (New York, 1994) presents the social side of life as seen by the president's wife. Vice President Dan Quayle's *Standing Firm: A Vice Presidential Memoir* (New York, 1994) stresses Quayle's conservative credentials.

Michael R. Beschloss and Strobe Talbott, *At the Highest Levels: The Inside Story of the End of the Cold War* (Boston, 1993), is the best account of the interaction of Bush and Secretary of State Baker with Gorbachev and Foreign Minister Shevardnadze. Three excellent books on the background and conduct of the Persian Gulf War are Bruce W. Jentleson, *With Friends Like These: Reagan, Bush, and Saddam, 1982–1990* (New York, 1994); Lawrence Freedman and Efraim Karsh, *The Gulf Conflict, 1990–1991: Diplomacy and War in the New World Order* (Princeton, N.J., 1993); and Michael R. Gordon and Bernard E. Trainor, *The General's War: The Inside Story of the Conflict in the Gulf* (Boston, 1995). Kevin Buckley, *Panama: The Whole Story* (New York, 1991), is good on the 1989 intervention to topple Manuel Noriega.

Most books on the domestic policies of the Bush administration are highly critical. On the conservative side see Charles Kolb, *White House Daze: The Unmaking of Domestic Policy in the Bush Years* (New York, 1994). The title of Michael Duffy and Dan Goodgame's book, *Marching in Place: The Status-Quo Presidency of George Bush* (New York, 1992),

is self-explanatory. The same is true of the highly critical and detailed study by Charles Tiefer, *The Semi-Sovereign Presidency: The Bush Administration's Strategy for Governing Without Congress* (Boulder, Colo., 1994). The best reference work, a rich mine of information, is the 1,300-page compendium by the Congressional Quarterly, *Congress and the Nation*, vol. 8, *1989–1992* (Washington, 1993). See also the 1989, 1990, 1991, and 1992 special "America and the World" issues of the journal *Foreign Affairs*.

Recent works include George Bush, Brent Scowcroft, *A World Transformed* (New York, 1998), by the former president and his national security adviser, which discusses foreign affairs during the first two years of the administration; George Bush, *All The Best, George Bush* (New York, 1999) is a compilation of letters and correspondence from the former president to his family, associates, and others over the course of his life.

William J. Clinton

THE FIRST TERM
David J. Maraniss

THE SECOND TERM
Bernard A. Weisberger

William J. Clinton THE WHITE HOUSE

THE FIRST TERM

David J. Maraniss

ON the afternoon of 16 January 1993, Bill Clinton left the Arkansas Governor's Mansion for his final jog through the familiar streets of Little Rock. This time he carried a shoebox containing the pet frog of his thirteen-year-old daughter, Chelsea. At her request, when he reached the Arkansas River, he released the creature onto the marshy bank where, Chelsea said, it could escape the impending move to Washington and live "a normal life."

Four days later, Clinton stood on the West Front of the U.S. Capitol, placed one hand on his grandmother's King James Bible, and was sworn in by Chief Justice William Rehnquist as the forty-second president of the United States. His normal life was over, but the life he had been yearning for since adolescence had begun. The fable of American democracy is that anyone can grow up to be president and Clinton, unlike most, believed it to be true not as a general proposition, but about himself. He had, from an early age, shaped his life and career around that singular desire. In a letter to a friend after his first year of college, he wrote that he was about to embark on a road that he hoped would "put a little asterisk" by his name "in the billion pages of the book of life." At noon on a brilliant winter's day nearly three decades later, the asterisk was assured. He could not have foreseen that his two-term Presidency as well as his name would pass into history with an asterisk—as the second Chief Executive to be impeached, tried, and acquitted by the Senate.

What assessment of President Clinton would accompany that asterisk? The judgment of history was far off and unknowable when he first took office. In a sense it remained nearly as uncertain even four years later, after he had been reelected to a second term, the first Democrat to achieve that extended status since Franklin D. Roosevelt. It was still more so when he left office in January of 2001. Clinton's White House days repeated the contradictory themes of his career: a counterpoint of hope and disappointment, discipline and chaos, urgency and delay, moral preaching and questionable behavior, lessons learned, forgotten, and relearned. His presidency after one term seemed essentially unresolved. It was neither the personal and policy disaster that his opponents constantly predicted, nor was it as substantively noteworthy as his allies incessantly hoped.

In tone and substance, Clinton's first four years as president can best be described as two distinct subterms of two years apiece. The first subterm (1991–1994), during which Democrats controlled both Congress and the White House, was ambitious if diffuse and ended with a political loss—the Republican majority in Congress—that ranked among the most traumatic of Clinton's career even though his name was not on the ballot. During the second subterm (1995–1996), Clinton resurrected his presidency and ensured himself another four years in the White House by skillfully handling his changed circumstances. He became a diminished yet increasingly popular president dealing with a powerful but increasingly reckless Republican Congress; here defining himself in contrast to the Republicans, there working in ideological concert with them, whichever better suited his political needs.

His comeback was an impressive display of political deftness and willpower, but it was not without cost. Clinton began his second term in 1997 with lowered expectations and a modest agenda. Throughout his mercurial first four years in the White House, two things remained constant about Clinton: his political survival skills and his need to display them after getting into trouble. In his most difficult times, one could see the will to recover and the promise of redemption. In his best times, one

could see the seeds of disaster. The pattern would be intensely and dramatically repeated in the four years that followed reelection. That is how it always was with Bill Clinton. There are repetitive themes in his life and career, cycles of loss and recovery, that go a long way toward resolving the mysteries of an ambiguous man and explaining his performance as president.

Loss and Hope

Bill Clinton's life has been defined more by loss than triumph. The first loss occurred before his birth, when his biological father, a traveling salesman named William Jefferson Blythe, was killed at age twenty-eight in a car accident. William Jefferson Blythe III was born three months later on 19 August 1946 in the small town of Hope in southwest Arkansas, where his mother was staying with her parents. In later years the son would, in his campaigns for president, enjoy the poetry of portraying himself as the man from Hope, but that was largely a myth. No one named Bill Clinton ever lived there. He was known then as Billy Blythe.

His early years were dominated by two strong women who fought for his attention and represented the competing forces that would shape his life. His mother, the young widow Virginia Dell Blythe, was irrepressible and fun-loving. His grandmother, Edith Cassidy, who took care of him for long stretches while his mother studied nursing in New Orleans, was temperamental and frustrated by her position in life. She regimented her grandson's days with metronomic discipline. He would carry both the freewheeling optimism of his mother and the stubborn will of his grandmother into later life.

Most of his childhood was not spent in Hope but in Hot Springs, only fifty miles up the road but an entirely different world, a resort town nestled amid the pine-covered mountains of a national park, with vaporous spas, nightclubs, and the largest illegal gambling operation in the South. He moved there at age five with his mother and stepfather, Roger Clinton, a failed auto dealer and alcoholic. The relationship between Roger Clinton and Bill's mother was tempestuous, marked by divorce and remarriage and sullied by Roger's frequent drunken rages in which he would physically or mentally torment Virginia. Despite that, when Bill was fifteen he took his stepfather's name and became William Jefferson Clinton.

Without diving too deeply into the opaque waters of psychoanalysis, it is apparent that Clinton's status as the oldest son, the guardian of his mother and younger brother (also named Roger) against the unpredictable outbursts of an alcoholic stepfather possibly molded his personality in ways that resurfaced in his career as a politician. In moments of self-reflection, Clinton later attributed this propensity to avoid sharp conflict and please all sides to his constant attempts to bring peace within a dysfunctional family.

The racier side of Hot Springs was counterbalanced by religion and education. Although his mother was more likely to attend the racetrack, Clinton took refuge from his family troubles in the Park Place Baptist Church, to which he walked alone on Sunday mornings. And in a state ranked near the bottom in education, Hot Springs High, which Clinton attended from 1960 to 1964, shined as an exception. It provided excellent courses in mathematics, science, music, and foreign language. Its principal, Johnnie Mae Mackey, who taught her charges to be God-fearing, patriotic, and civic-minded, viewed bright and ambitious Billy Clinton as her prime disciple.

It was under her tutelage that the best-known moment of Clinton's early life occurred. In the summer before his senior year, he was sent to Washington as one of two Arkansas delegates to Boys' Nation, a mock political convention sponsored by the American Legion. There, in the Rose Garden of the White House on a July morning in 1963, Clinton met President Kennedy. Their handshake was captured in photographs and newsreels and later came to symbolize the transfer of power and ambition from one generation to another.

The handshake was no mere accident. On the bus ride to the White House that morning from the Boys' Nation dormitories at the University of Maryland, Clinton stood out among his peers as the boy who kept pestering the chaperon with questions about whether they would have their pictures taken with the president. When the bus stopped at the back gate, it was Clinton who won the barely controlled race-walk to stake out prime handshake position at the front of the crowd at the Rose Garden.

But that calculating element in the youthful Clinton was balanced by a streak of idealism, most evident in his dealings with the thorny issues of race relations. The Boys' Nation representatives convened in Washington during one of the seminal periods of the American civil rights movement. Only one month later, Martin Luther King, Jr. would stand on the steps of the Lincoln Memorial and deliver his his-

toric "I Have a Dream" speech. While most of his schoolmates were still stuck in the prejudicial traditions of Jim Crow and supported resistance to integration, Clinton was an exception, taking a strong civil rights stance and refusing the entreaties of fellow southerners to go along with his regional confederates.

After his week in Washington and his handshake with JFK, "Billy" Clinton returned to Arkansas determined to realize his mother's prediction from his toddler days that he would some day be president of the United States.

The World's Fight

For Bill Clinton the turbulent years that shook the nation from Kennedy's assassination to Watergate—1963 to 1974—were likewise an era of turmoil and transition. He began it as an establishment-oriented student politician at Georgetown University and ended it as a boy wonder law professor and congressional candidate in northwest Arkansas. In between, he ventured to England as a Rhodes scholar to be trained as one of the "best men in the world's fight" and faced the toughest moral dilemma of his life to that point: how to deal with the military draft and the war in Vietnam. It was near the end of that era, while at Yale Law School, that he met his future wife, Hillary Rodham, who would replace his grandmother and mother as the strong woman in his life and play a central role in his political rise.

Clinton's career as a student politician at Georgetown was a curtain-raiser with foretastes of the future. Though an outsider in the predominantly Catholic, upper-middle-class, East Coast school in 1964, he quickly adapted to the system and won over his classmates. He was elected president of his freshman class, then of his sophomore class. But in his junior year, running for president of the student council, he was rejected in favor of a more "populist" candidate.

In his dealings with Vietnam and the draft Clinton behaved like thousands of college students of that era, who adopted different strategies to avoid service in an unpopular war. But as a young man with national political aspirations, he felt pressure to explain in detail every maneuver he made during those anxious days. It turned out that he was better at escaping the military than in leaving an unambiguous account of his actions.

Only 2.2 million of the approximately 8 million young men who served in the armed forces during the 1960s entered the ranks through the Selective Service System. It is hard to pinpoint what percentage of those who volunteered were motivated by patriotism or by more mundane motives like restlessness, or what percentage of those who found ways to avoid conscription were simply seeking to save their skins rather than voicing principled opposition to the Vietnam War. What is certain is that thanks to student deferments, the draft operated unfairly and unequally, with most of the conscripted ranks drawn from lower-income young men from inner cities and farms who did not go to college.

Clinton's own perspective on Vietnam was shaped during his final two years at Georgetown (1966–1968), when he worked as a junior clerk at the Senate Foreign Relations Committee, then chaired by Senator William J. Fulbright of Arkansas. By then, Fulbright, once close to President Lyndon B. Johnson, had broken from LBJ after concluding that the president had deceived him into supporting the 1964 Gulf of Tonkin resolution expanding the U.S. role in what was essentially a civil war pitting anti-Communist South Vietnam against Communist Viet Cong rebels and Ho Chi Minh's North Vietnamese armies. By the time Clinton arrived on Capitol Hill, Fulbright had become one of the war's most pointed critics, claiming that the United States had no moral or practical reason to be in Vietnam save for the "arrogance of power." The senator was an imposing figure and young Clinton became his disciple and his apostle in resisting the steady escalation of the war. He read hundreds of articles and reports on the American role in Southeast Asia, wrote term papers at Georgetown criticizing Johnson's manipulation of Congress and defending conscientious objection to the draft. By February 1968 his convictions were to be put to the test. The Johnson administration changed its draft policy and eliminated virtually all deferments for graduate students when Clinton was only months away from commencement at Georgetown and had just won a prized Rhodes scholarship to attend Oxford University in England for two years of graduate work.

Meantime the war itself was reaching a critical point. The growing casualty lists were fueling a rising antiwar sentiment that was as much practical as moral. Voters were beginning to doubt that the enterprise was worth its human and economic costs, and their skepticism peaked during the Tet Offensive, an uprising of the Viet Cong inside of key cities throughout South Vietnam thought to be secure.

Though the U.S. military "defeated" the offensive, the images of fighting on the grounds of the U.S. embassy in Saigon went far to convince a swelling tide of demands for an end to the failed adventure.

Although Clinton was vulnerable to the draft as soon as he graduated from Georgetown, his draft board in Arkansas delayed calling him and allowed him to sail off to England. This was not unlike the treatment accorded to most of the thirty-two Rhodes scholars in 1968, who were granted temporary deferments despite the new, tighter policy. Others failed induction physicals because of minor ailments that nevertheless left them fit enough to go abroad and begin their studies. Clinton spent most of his two years (1968–1970) enjoying Oxford and holiday trips to Europe, but preoccupation with his draft status and its impact on his future dogged him throughout the experience.

It was a difficult time in his life. He did not receive a degree at Oxford (until the university awarded him an honorary doctorate in civil law in 1994) but did manage to remain a civilian and a two-year student. He first received a draft notice in the spring of 1969 while in England, returned to Arkansas that summer and, with the help of Fulbright aides and others, persuaded the admissions staff of the Reserve Officers Training Corps (ROTC) program at the University of Arkansas Law School to accept him that fall, which entitled him to a reserve deferment that overrode his induction call. Like many contemporaries he was conflicted between opposition to the war and guilt about not serving in Vietnam, where other young Americans were dying. In his case there was the added factor of a strong desire to return to Oxford, and he allowed that to prevail. By the time his name went into the pool again, a three-month freeze on calling up new recruits was in effect, giving him breathing space. He took part in London antiwar demonstrations in the autumn of 1969 and lucked out in December when, in the next draft lottery, his low number (311) guaranteed that he would probably never be called.

Clinton immediately—and unwisely, as it turned out—wrote a letter to Colonel Eugene J. Holmes, director of the ROTC program at Arkansas, thanking the officer for "saving" him from the draft and detailing his inner struggle. He opposed the war on principle, but open resistance to the draft or a plea for conscientious objector status would harm his "political viability" and undercut his life's ambition. His letter, he said, would explain "how so many fine young people have come to find themselves still loving their country but loathing the military." The letter, written when he was only twenty-three, resurfaced in 1992 when Clinton was a presidential candidate. It was pounced upon by opponents, who gave it a politically damaging twist that would haunt his campaigns and administrations, calling it evidence of an ambitious, manipulative young man who had disdain for the military.

Fall and Rise in Arkansas

Clinton was only thirty-two when he entered the Governor's Mansion in Little Rock in January 1979, the youngest governor in the nation since before World War II. Two years later he left office in defeat as the youngest ex-governor in American history.

It all happened so fast. From Oxford he attended Yale University Law School, receiving his degree in 1973, then returned to Arkansas to teach law at the University of Arkansas Law School (1973–1976). In 1974 he launched his elective career with a run for the U.S. House seat in Arkansas' Third District, nearly upsetting a veteran Republican. Elected state attorney general in 1977 and governor two years later, he was the instant golden boy of Arkansas politics. But with a stunning defeat in his reelection, he suddenly became only a bright young man with a great future behind him. That is, until he made the first of his signature comebacks.

Clinton's first presidential term can only be genuinely understood with this prologue: his fall and rise in Arkansas. There are clear parallels between Clinton's first term as governor and his first two years as president, and even more striking similarities in the way he reinvented himself and recovered from the trauma of those two experiences.

He began his governorship with a pent-up idealistic agenda that left him open to the charge of trying to do too much too fast and not focusing on a few major issues. Symbolically he failed to keep one of his earliest promises: that state legislators would have his budget proposals on their desks the first day of the legislative session. His efforts at compromise often ended with both sides angry at him. He had difficulty selling his accomplishments to the voters. He governed during a period of Arkansas politics dominated by angry white men eager to pounce on presumed offenses. Because he pushed through a modest hike in fees for car licenses, for example, he was characterized as a big-tax liberal, arrogant about the plight of the average Arkansan.

He did not have a chief of staff and there always seemed to be some confusion about lines of authority in the governor's office. He constantly fumed at his staff for his own lack of discipline. During his reelection, against an unprepossessing Republican opponent, Frank White, he complained vociferously that his record was being misinterpreted. But after White trounced him, Clinton apologized, said he had been taught a lesson, and went about reshaping his political image to make it more acceptable to the voters.

That 1980 defeat reawakened the trauma of earlier personal losses, but also the sense of loss as being a challenge to overcome. Clinton was now determined never to suffer through such a setback again. From then on, he would become obsessive about raising money and responding to attacks. He developed a brutal metaphor to explain how he would respond in the future: if your opponent is pounding you with a hammer, he said, take out a meat cleaver and cut off his arm.

Whatever guidance to personal behavior he drew from the episode, Clinton also read a larger meaning into the political events of 1980. That year, which saw Jimmy Carter lose to Ronald Reagan, was the culmination of a long, downward spiral for the Democratic party. Clinton had begun as a liberal, first supporting Robert F. Kennedy's bid for the Democratic presidential nomination (tragically cut short by Kennedy's assassination); and two years later, while at law school, serving as the coordinator for the Senate campaign of antiwar Democrat Joseph D. Duffey; and in 1972 serving as the Texas state coordinator for Senator George McGovern's presidential campaign. Both Duffey and McGovern were soundly beaten by the desertion of traditional blue-collar elements of the Democratic coalition, who found the candidates to be too liberal and elitist. And Clinton's Arkansas defeat coincided with the Democratic party's most telling loss, when President Jimmy Carter was beaten by Ronald Reagan. The 1972 and 1980 defeats sent Clinton further down a pathway he had explored with Duffey after that failure, namely a search for a "new politics" by which Democrats could hold some progressive beliefs and not be rejected by an increasingly conservative electorate.

Hillary Rodham, a classmate at Yale Law School whom Clinton married on 11 October 1975, was essential to his personal and political recovery. Both a feminist and an outspoken social advocate, she would remain to the left of Clinton on most political issues. But she was also a practical and effective political operator in her own right. When faced with a choice between ideological purity and political advancement, she would almost always follow the course that benefited her husband's career. Their relationship, one of the more complicated of modern First Couples, went through different phases over the decades. The first lasted from the time they met at Yale in 1970 until 1980. Their attraction from the start was political and intellectual. They shared a passion for literature and politics and agreed that programs and ideals were useless without power to implement them. They quickly realized that together they could get places that they both wanted to go. Still, in their early years together in Arkansas, Hillary played only an occasional behind-the-scenes role in her husband's career. While he was successful, she was free to pursue her own interests as a lawyer and proponent of children's rights issues.

But after Clinton's gubernatorial defeat in 1980, their relationship entered a second phase during which she became politically indispensable to him. She boosted his morale during his two-year exile, brought in pragmatic advisers who would rework his message, and was his top strategic and legal adviser, family breadwinner and investor, and his most dependable governmental aide. She played a major part in his comeback against White and the decade of administration that followed.

The elements of that comeback—a makeover of Clinton's political style—were clearly illustrated not only in the campaign but in the ensuing reelections that spelled ten years of power in Arkansas. His central triumph was an education reform package that Hillary, as chairman of a state task force, put together in 1983 and shepherded through the Arkansas legislature, where her direct manner, in vivid contrast to her husband's easygoing vacillation, impressed veteran state pols. Clinton became known as the education governor, not only in Arkansas but among his gubernatorial colleagues around the country, and the accolade helped him become a national figure during the 1980s as he prepared his inevitable run for the presidency. Throughout that era, the personal relationship of Bill and Hillary was at times tumultuous, but the political partnership was unfaltering as Clinton came to have an implicit faith that whatever his wife did would turn out right. When, later on in the White House, that faith was disappointed by failure in a sterner test, it pushed the marriage into still another, uncertain stage.

During his long second act as governor (1983–1993), Clinton relied on a four-person brain trust—himself, Hillary, chief of staff Betsey Wright, and political consultant Richard Morris—to develop a mode of government that resembled a permanent campaign. Clinton decided never again to push a major initiative without first testing public support and then selling the program. He and Morris were constantly polling the Arkansas electorate to see how voters would respond to different rhetorical arguments. They also kept trying to circumvent the statehouse press corps and using television advertising, leafleting, and telephone banks to build popular acceptance for their proposed measures, and place pressure on state lawmakers.

Along with these tactical changes, Clinton shifted his political emphasis to centrist issues that attracted mainstream support. Morris pushed him to follow his natural instincts and adopt a strategy that Clinton would employ from then on whenever his political future seemed tenuous: co-opt the Republicans on their issues (especially crime, welfare, and taxes). He abandoned years of ambivalence on capital punishment and carried out the death penalty, which was overwhelmingly favored by Arkansas voters. He initiated programs in Arkansas to move welfare recipients into the workforce. At Morris's urging, he became more willing to pick fights, especially with traditional friends and interest groups who were losing public favor. He angered Arkansas public school teachers by forcing them to take competence tests, which they considered belittling. But Clinton, though holding no animus toward teachers, had correctly concluded that the use of such tests was the only way he could receive the necessary corporate and voter support for his educational reforms.

Although the competence tests were seen by some blacks, including Clinton aides, as an indirect attack on black teachers, Clinton consistently attracted stronger black support than any candidate in Arkansas history. He appointed more African Americans to state boards, commissions, and agency posts than all his predecessors combined. His empathetic personality worked well in the black community, as did his facility with scripture and his love of gospel music. At Yale Law School Clinton had been comfortable sitting at what became known as the black table in the cafeteria during the black power era, and as a law professor at Arkansas, he was popular with black students by virtue of his approachable nature and his willingness to help many of them who had struggled on probation. But he understood the complicated role that race played in modern Democratic party history. Black voters were an essential faction in the Democratic coalition, yet there was a line beyond which an increasing number of white voters left the party if it seemed too much money and attention was being devoted to social programs associated with blacks and poor people.

Clinton attempted to reverse that trend as he entered the national political realm. Rhetorically, he argued that race was an artificial issue that had been used historically by segregationist southern Democrats and was now being employed by Republicans for political advantage. The real problems were economic. And to attack those, he helped lead a coalition of centrist Democrats, many from the South, in the Democratic Leadership Council (DLC), of which he had been a founder in 1985. The goal of the DLC was to develop new policies, or at least revise old ones so that the party could lure back a white male majority by making itself more pragmatic and moderate. Clinton became chairman of the DLC in 1990 and used it as his unofficial precampaign vehicle as he traveled and politicked nationwide after announcing that he was a candidate for president on 3 October 1991.

The theme he developed was one of opportunity and responsibility—the government should provide citizens opportunities to succeed, but individuals had corresponding responsibilities to work and contribute to the civil good. This was an effort to link progressive programs to the traditional American ethos of work and fairness, and to shift the Democrats' focus from questions of justice and equality to opening the pathways of economic advancement. That theme became the philosophical foundation of his presidential campaign and the framework for proposed programs ranging from welfare reform to voluntary national service. He called his idea of publicly provided opportunity wedded to private responsibility a "New Covenant." The phrase alarmed some aides by its righteous tone but pleased Clinton, who seemed equally comfortable cursing (in private) and citing scripture. And in fact the theme proved to be a winner, helping Clinton to win both the nomination and election of 1992.

Clinton prevailed in the primaries that year not only by his ideas, but because he proved to be an indefatigable campaigner with a gift for connecting empathetically with his audiences. It allowed him to triumph even as revelations came out in the press about his sexual infidelities, a curious land deal in Arkansas known as Whitewater, and his long-ago effort to avert the draft. And Clinton was willing to counterattack by using negative advertising against his opponents and making promises that he could not keep.

During the general election campaign against President Bush and independent candidate H. Ross Perot, a billionaire entrepreneur from Texas, Clinton's advisers posted a sign at their headquarters in Little Rock that became a daily mantra—"The economy, stupid." While offering centrist "new Democrat" proposals on welfare and trade, Clinton sounded a classic populist message of economic disparity. During the 1980s, he argued, only the wealthiest Americans continued to enjoy real growth in their annual income; for the middle class and poor, the Reagan era had been one of losing ground. Clinton hammered at the burden of the $4 trillion national debt and promised to cut the yearly deficit that swelled it—while also promising a middle-class tax cut and more investments in education, infrastructure, and jobs programs to promote income growth for average American workers. Clinton's diffuse economic brain trust was actually split between "deficit hawks," who warned him that he had to cut the deficit above all else, and those who urged measures to jump-start the economy with a spending program focusing on jobs. Clinton was convinced he could do both.

Actually, less than half the electorate voted for him. He won with 42.95 percent of the vote, compared with 37.40 percent for Bush and 18.86 percent for Perot. Yet as he prepared to take office, the country's mood was turning somewhat optimistic: 1992 recorded growth in gross domestic product and decline in unemployment, signaling the end of a recession during Bush's term. But there was still unease over such trends as the lure of cheap labor overseas, the unequal exchange of manufacturing jobs for low-paying service jobs, the economic drain of interest payments on the huge debt, and the rising cost of health care. Clinton vowed to focus on these economic issues "like a laser beam." Much of the nation thought he would succeed. With Democrats controlling both the White House and Congress after twelve years of divided government, it seemed likely that he could.

Inside the White House

When he moved into the Oval Office, Clinton brought with him busts of his favorite presidents to gaze on daily—Jefferson, Lincoln, Franklin Roosevelt, Truman, and Kennedy. If JFK was Clinton's model for youthful optimism and style, FDR was the one whose whirlwind opening "Hundred Days" had set a standard for swift administrative and legislative action that Clinton hoped to equal. He intended to enact an economic package within the first three months. Then, at the end of his own Hundred-Day Dash, he would unveil a universal health insurance plan that could define his presidency and assure his place in history.

To emphasize with alacrity the speed with which he would move, Clinton issued a set of executive orders immediately after his inauguration. One imposed lobbying restrictions on members of his administration after they left government—a modest opening gesture to the larger, popular, and nonpartisan cause of lobbying and campaign finance reform. The others were in the more controversial realm of abortion. Following through on his pledges as a pro-choice candidate, he lifted the Reagan and Bush moratorium on federal funding for fetal tissue research, suspended the "gag rule" prohibiting patients in federally funded family planning clinics from receiving abortion information, and directed the Department of Defense to allow privately financed abortions at U.S. military facilities.

These executive orders were among the few matters that went according to schedule early in the Clinton regime. His economic and health care proposals would languish incomplete or unattended until late in 1993. And part of the reason for that was because these central policy issues were quickly overshadowed by minor tempests that swept away the traditional "honeymoon" of harmony between a new president and the press and the public. Why did this happen? To some extent because of an initial failure of the baby boomer president and his staff (much as they seemed at home in the information age) to understand and to manage public opinion effectively.

The first defeat came early in the morning of Clinton's second day in office when he announced that his nominee for attorney general, Zoë E. Baird, had withdrawn her name from consideration. Several days earlier, news articles had revealed that Baird, who was being asked to serve as the nation's top law enforcement official, had knowingly broken the law herself. She and her husband had failed to pay taxes for a Peruvian couple they had hired as household help. A minor flap in itself, the episode signaled larger problems.

To meet his campaign promise of high ethical standards in a new, multiethnic, and representative Cabinet that "looked like America," Clinton had privately committed himself to selecting the first female attorney general. When interviewed before her selection, Baird told Clinton aides of her predicament with the housekeepers. They considered the matter insignificant then and later. But the revelation evoked a loud public outcry and the White House and Congress were besieged with calls from angry citizens. Baird's withdrawal became a political necessity.

The lasting significance of this personnel disaster created by sloppy staff work was that Clinton began to lose control of his public image in the face of attacks. The outrage against Baird was fueled by conservative radio talk show hosts who had emerged as influential forces in the American political debate, chiefly Rush Limbaugh, an articulate former disc jockey whose daily syndicated program was hugely popular. Limbaugh was a strong supporter of President Bush, but also, somewhat inconsistently, the voice of middle-class disenchantment with the federal government. To his dismay, many of his followers had joined the Perot movement and helped cost the Republicans the election. The election of a Democrat, however, gave Limbaugh an opportunity to fuse the antigovernment sentiments of his listeners with his own political agenda. Clinton became his target. He portrayed the president and his allies as liberal elitists who claimed to be saviors of the working class while misusing their household help. Baird's infraction was cited as the inevitable product of feminism and affirmative action that Limbaugh's constituency despised.

Ironically, Baird was a corporate lawyer with moderate political instincts, largely unknown to feminist activists. But her nomination was used by conservative denouncers of Clinton as "proof" that his campaign was a centrist was a pose and that once in power he would revert to his true liberal nature.

Clinton's history makes clear that he was not a liberal posturing as a moderate. His moderation as a student politician and his liberalism on race and Vietnam were equal and competing aspects of his ambiguous political personality. But this inner conflict, plus his need to conciliate and please people, his tendency to see both sides of any issue, and his equivocating style all fed the argument that he lacked authenticity and conviction.

Clinton was also weakened at first by his handling of another issue that dominated the news coverage soon after he took office: gays in the military.

Here history conspired against him. Since the year of Clinton's birth, the presidency has been virtually reserved for veterans. Truman—an artillery captain in 1917-1918—was the subduer of Japan, Eisenhower was the military titan of D-Day. Johnson, Nixon, Ford, Carter, and Reagan had all worn the uniform, while Kennedy and Bush had barely escaped heroic death in combat.

Clinton, in contrast, had protested the Vietnam War and avoided service. Military leaders looked on skeptically when he entered the White House. How would this new commander in chief, who once spoke of "loathing the military," treat the armed forces? It might have been easier for a celebrated veteran, not a perceived draft dodger, to lift the ban on gays in the military. But Clinton had latched on to the growing debate. College students had been protesting their schools' sponsorship of ROTC units that enforced the ban on gays. Several returning Gulf War veterans, including a Medal of Honor winner, announced that they were gay, and the discriminatory policy (already questioned by some on grounds of high administrative costs for small results) had been challenged in court and seemed on the verge of being overturned. And some questioned whether it was worth the administrative expenditure of millions to drum a few thousand gays out of the ranks.

Clinton's campaign response to questions on the subject had been that the military's emphasis should "always be on people's conduct, not their status." He was a firm supporter of gay rights and the first major presidential candidate to hold a gay fund-raising event (in Los Angeles in 1992). He pledged that as president he would end the ban. Immediately after taking office he tried to keep that promise, not fully anticipating the strenuous negative reaction that would elicit from the Pentagon and Congress. Soon, this secondary issue was overshadowing his economic agenda.

How did a deft politician let this happen? Clinton underestimated the intense media spotlight the matter would receive as a dramatic story that aroused passionate moral feelings. Then, when the storm broke, his instincts to conciliate and to avert confrontation had the opposite effect and got him into deeper trouble. Seeking to prevent an early showdown with Congress and to avoid more strain on his weak ties with the military, he did not immediately issue an executive order and command the recalcitrant Pentagon brass to change their ways, but instead he gave his staff and the commanders six months to draft a new policy. That allowed time for anti-gay spokesmen to extend the controversy and win over public opinion. Then, when an eventual compromise plan known as "Don't ask, Don't tell"—in which gays would not be discriminated against provided they did not announce their homosexuality—was introduced on 19 July 1993, it did little to diminish the unease about the new president within the military, and it also strained his relations with segments of the gay community who felt sold out by the retreat. And worse, internal White House polls showed that Clinton's defense of homosexuals had provoked a sharp decline in his favorable ratings, especially in the South, which turned against him quickly and perhaps permanently.

In his early reluctance to challenge the congressional leadership, Clinton seemed to be guided by criticisms of Jimmy Carter, another southerner who had arrived in Washington as an outsider. It was said in Washington that Carter's disinclination to engage in political bantering with congressional power brokers had severely hindered his ability to enact his legislative agenda. Yet while seeking to avoid Carter's mistake, Clinton created a new one of his own. He quickly deferred to Democratic leaders of the House and Senate on several issues, most notably on not pressing hard for swift legislation to reform campaign finance and lobbying. He expected that the public would be less concerned with that popular issue if he and Congress broke a decade of gridlock and enacted major legislation on larger economic issues.

But by that compromise, Clinton surrendered the politically useful banner of the newcomer pledged to change Washington's perceived patterns of corruption. His unchanging ends-justify-the-means philosophy would get him into trouble again. To the contrary, he would begin his second term amid calls for another special prosecutor to investigate the questionable manner in which the White House and the Democratic National Committee raised money for the 1996 campaign.

The Economy

From the start of his presidency, Clinton found himself boxed in by apparent contradictions. On the issue that mattered most to him, the economy, he feared that his actions were making him neither a fiscally prudent New Democrat nor a traditional, socially conscious liberal as he was increasingly perceived, but something nebulously in between. "I hope you're all aware we're all Eisenhower Republicans," the president lamented to his economic advisers in April 1993 as his administration moved toward the old-line Republican establishment program of lower deficits, free trade, and supporting the bond market. Secretary of Labor Robert B. Reich warned that Clinton's economic program as described was even more backward-looking and made him "sound like Calvin Coolidge."

The government-activist side of Clinton's plan for the economy had diminished since he took office, while the deficit-reduction side became more prominent. First he abandoned the middle-class tax cut promised during the campaign at the first notice of larger-than-anticipated deficit projections. Next, a separate stimulus bill targeting money for job training, transportation, and technology was rejected by the Senate. It was the first warning signal that one-party dominance of the White House and Congress would not assure swift and cohesive legislative action.

When the larger economic package of which the stimulus had been a party finally reached a vote in August 1993, most of the spending increases for social programs were stripped from the bill and the administration's progressive plan to cut the deficit through a broad-based energy tax was abandoned in the face of strong opposition in the Senate. Instead, an increase in the federal income tax—campaigned against by Clinton—was inserted. A proposed increase in the corporate income tax was cut by half, and attempts to tighten tax breaks for U.S. corporations with plants and operations overseas was stopped.

Some progressive taxation elements remained. An estimated nine-tenths of new revenues came from the top 1 percent of the population, while the working poor benefited from the largest earned-income tax credit in history, a redistribution of wealth shifting sharply away from Reagan-era supply-side economics. But the measure as a whole was seen as more of a deficit-reduction plan than a liberal overhaul of the economy, and its amorphous nature made it difficult for the administration to define and sell to the public.

Congressional Republicans unanimously opposed the president's package, arguing that it raised taxes too much, cut programs too little, and would send the economy into decline. With small defections by liberal and conservative Democrats, the measure barely survived by two votes in the House on 5 August and passed the Senate, 51-50 the next day as Vice President Gore broke the tie.

This first test of the Clinton presidency produced ambiguous results. The predicted slump did not happen. Instead, the deficit shrank, interest rates fell, inflation slowed, home buying and job creation rose—a clear improvement in the nation's economic health for all Americans. Clinton got the credit, though the positive trend had begun before his term. But he emerged with political wounds. The almost straight party-line vote for the program undercut his claim to be a centrist. And although most of the tax bite was taken out of the wealthy, as campaigner Clinton had promised, any tax increase irritated voters, many of whom had abandoned Bush precisely because he broke a pledge not to raise them. Moreover, Clinton now looked like an uncertain waverer between competing ideologies rather than a bold activist who would reinvigorate the economy. Polls showed that 55 percent of the voters disapproved of his economic stewardship and his overall ratings dipped accordingly to the lowest levels of any postwar president that early in a term.

Throughout this period, Clinton often lamented to his advisers that he was having difficult reaching the public with his message. But part of the problem lay in the lack of coherent policymaking at 1600 Pennsylvania Avenue, encouraged by Clinton's own disorganized style. The White House atmosphere he created was the same one in which he had always thrived: a cross between a college dormitory and a think tank, with a constant barrage of interesting people to talk to and policies to debate in a free-wheeling, egalitarian style. The emphasis was on raw energy and brainpower more than strategic order.

What discipline there was at the White House came largely from Vice President Al Gore and First Lady Hillary Rodham Clinton. Their personalities were more structured than Clinton's, and they found that they could usually force him to stop deliberating and make a decision. Sometimes they found themselves competing for Clinton's time and attention. The president's wife, during the early days of the presidency, usually prevailed.

Losing Health Care

On the fifth day of his presidency Clinton announced that his wife would chair his task force on national health care reform. "Of all the people I've ever worked with in my life, she's better at organizing and leading people from a complex beginning to a certain end than anybody," Clinton said. And in turning to Hillary to guide this particular initiative, which he hoped would be the defining issue of his presidency, Clinton followed a long-established pattern. Ever since his defeat as Arkansas governor in 1980, he had asked his wife to handle the most important political and policy matters of his career.

But there was no anticipation of the risks in having the nation's First Lady assume an unprecedented policy role. Would advisers who disagreed with her be reluctant to express their opinions? Would the president himself show less flexibility in accepting compromises in legislation bearing his wife's imprint? Was Hillary herself endangering her larger effort to redefine the role of First Lady with an upfront role in a risky political operation? Clinton himself ignored such potential problems in the implicit faith that, as in Arkansas, she would succeed.

This time, however, she did not succeed. The health care initiative did not move toward a certain end, but grew increasingly more complex. The debate over it dragged on for twenty months before it collapsed. Clinton was ultimately portrayed not as he wished to be—the victor over rising health care costs who provided insurance coverage for all Americans—but as a big-government liberal who tried to dictate and restrict medical choices.

The White House set up the Arkansas model of a legislative campaign operation to push health care, with a "war room," a paid advertising effort, a grassroots organization, and bids for corporate support. But the opposition this time, including insurance coalitions, the small-business lobby, and congressional Republicans, bested him at every turn. They conducted a more expensive and effective advertising campaign and developed a grassroots movement of their own, again relying on the conservative-radio-talk-show network.

Month by month the national fervor for health care form faded. At the beginning, polls showed two-thirds of the public supported Clinton's effort, and congressional action seemed inevitable. By the end, public support had dropped below 50 percent and Republicans were opposing health care reform legislation "sight unseen." What happened? The opposition campaign was only one factor in the defeat of health care, a saga in which everything seemed to go against the Clintons.

Hillary Clinton was distracted for several crucial weeks early in the process by the illness and death of her father on 7 April 1993. She decided not to re-

President Clinton and his family, along with dog Buddy, walk across the south lawn of the White House in 1998. AP/WIDE WORLD

veal the names of the five hundred experts—including doctors, economists, sociologists, and regulators—who, in working groups, molded the plan as members of a task force. Thus, even though she held public hearings around the country and kept in constant touch with Congress, there was an overriding sense that the plan was being concocted in utter secrecy. The staff director of the undertaking, Ira Magaziner, an old friend of Clinton's from his Rhodes scholar days, correctly understood that delays could be fatal and warned him that health care must be handled quickly to get passed at all. But it was not handled quickly. First it was put off for the economic battle over the summer. Then, in the fall, it was delayed again so that Clinton could concentrate on the North American Free Trade Agreement (NAFTA), a tariff-lifting pact with Mexico and Canada signed on 8 December 1993. It was not until 1994 that Congress began considering Clinton's proposal. By then, much of the public pressure for reform had disappeared. The economic recovery that Clinton helped foster worked against him: people were less fearful about losing their jobs and health coverage, while the inflation rate in health care costs fell to a record 5 percent low during the debate.

The Clinton team had started with two central health care goals. One was to contain and eventually lower health care costs for average Americans, who were spending about twice as much money for medical care and health insurance as people in other developed nations. This would be done through government-regulated "managed competition" among insurance groups and health care providers. The second objective was to guarantee health insurance for the 20 million Americans who did not have it. Clinton made the tactical mistake of emphasizing universal coverage—he would accept nothing less—over cost containment. That opened the door for his opponents to attack the plan as a liberal social welfare program.

By the time congressional committees considered the Clinton proposals in 1994 they had become embodied in a 1,342-page bill, whose very length became a symbol of bureaucratic bulkiness. Conservative spokesmen were persuading the public that it forced Americans into an inefficient government-run system. Clinton could not find enough votes in his own majority party to move the measure through either chamber, and uncompromising Republicans increasingly came to embrace the strategy of denying that there was a health care crisis.

In September 1994, one year after Clinton had delivered a well-received speech to Congress on the need for his Health Security Plan, Senate Majority Leader George J. Mitchell of Maine quietly pronounced it dead. Republicans and Democrats both said they would use the defeat of health care to their advantage in the November midterm elections.

Arkansas Revisited

If the Arkansas model failed Clinton in the health care defeat, it was part of a larger pattern of troubles stemming from his past in Little Rock that soon began imposing itself on his administration. Death, scandal, and charges of lawbreaking struck heavily at the Arkansas friends that he brought east with him.

One afternoon in July 1993, Vincent Foster, Jr., the deputy White House counsel, was found dead in a park across the Potomac River in Virginia, a bullet wound in his head. He had committed suicide, an apparent victim, according to a note found in his briefcase, of depression induced by job pressures and the poisonous political atmosphere of Washington. Fos-

ter had been a neighbor of Clinton's in Hope, and a close friend of Hillary's at the Rose Law Firm in Little Rock, where they both worked. Though his death was several times investigated and ruled a suicide, right-wing Clinton critics found enough mystery in the circumstances surrounding the case to shroud it with a lingering afterlife of conspiracy theories.

Other Clinton associates who followed him to Washington fell under the shadow. Webster Hubbell, Jr., general partner in the Rose Law Firm, took a post in the Clinton Justice Department, but left in disgrace after a year to face trial and conviction for double-billing Rose clients. A White House aide and a member of the legal counseling staff were forced to resign for relatively minor ethical lapses. And those old Arkansas associates who stayed at home did not all escape, most notably Clinton's successor as governor, Jim Guy Tucker. Tucker and two former aides from Clinton's gubernatorial years were indicted (and Tucker convicted and forced to quit office) in an investigation that might not have begun had not Clinton become president—an investigation that bore the simple label of "Whitewater."

The name was that of a real estate development scheme along Arkansas' White River, and the original investing partners in 1974 had included Bill and Hillary Clinton. By the time the undertaking went broke it had involved questionable dealings that surfaced during Clinton's first term, provoked reactions from the White House that were denounced as presidential wrongdoing, led to congressional hearings, and finally obliged Clinton to ask for a special prosecutor. Whitewater flowed from Bill Clinton's past into Washington and its churn and roar became the incessant background noise of his time in office. After seven years, many individual state and federal trials, millions of words of court testimony and media polemic, and the expense of millions of dollars by the special prosecutor's office, no basis for indicting either the president or the First Lady was found. Yet the questions persisted: Had the Clintons done anything venal? Or were they persecuted by the exaggerated charges of political enemies who simply hated them?

The two major lines of inquiry were concerned with what happened in Arkansas, and what went on inside the Clinton administration when the story broke and federal regulators zeroed in on the various people and institutions involved. The Clintons were brought into the deal by an old friend, James McDougal, who later ran a savings-and-loan company, regulated by a Clinton appointee at the state level, and represented by the Rose Law Firm. McDougal and his wife, Susan, made most of the payments, though the Clintons were equal partners. The Clintons did lose money when the project went sour in the 1980s, but the unresolved question was whether or not they profited indirectly from the cozy relationship with McDougal, who used his Madison Guaranty Savings and Loan firm as a personal piggy bank until it folded in 1989. Did he divert some of its funds into the Whitewater partnership—and into Clinton's 1984 reelection campaign?

Once Madison Savings and Loan was bankrupt, federal regulators began to examine its connections to the Rose Law Firm. The names of both Clintons appeared in referrals sent up to the Treasury and Justice Departments in Washington. Treasury officials disclosed the contents of the referrals to White House aides. Though the Clintons were not targets of the regulatory probe, the disclosures were improper in that they could lead to an illegal cover-up by presidential command. That was what triggered the call for a special prosecutor.

Each time the issue seemed to be receding, it reappeared and confronted the Clintons with new questions. What role, for example, had Hillary Clinton played as a lawyer for the Rose Firm in dealing with Madison Guaranty? Critical billing records were missing—until, one day in August 1995, they were discovered by a file clerk in the residential portion of the White House. How did they get there? When the story became public, Hillary declared that she had no idea. She was subpoenaed before a federal grand jury—a first for a First Lady.

Whatever the ultimate result of the entire Whitewater probe, it left a stain on the Clinton presidency when combined with other ethical questions that hung over his past. There were his sexual indiscretions, both alleged and acknowledged. There were reports that Hillary, with inside advice from a friend, parlayed $1,000 into $100,000 in the commodities market. There was the discovery in the basement of the White House of FBI files on hundreds of Republicans. There were charges of impropriety in the firing of White House travel coordinators. All these, assiduously boomed into the public ear, left a segment of the public doubting the moral rectitude of these two prominent figures who came of age in the 1960s. And they cast shadows on Bill Clinton's better side, his calls for compassion and common ground in American society.

Foreign Policy

In his nearly hourlong acceptance speech at the Democratic National Convention in 1992, Clinton devoted all of one minute to foreign affairs. During his first year in office, he held no regularly scheduled meetings with his foreign policy team, headed by the terse and phlegmatic secretary of state Warren M. Christopher. Global issues were often regarded by the White House as undesirable interruptions of the domestic business at hand rather than the essential burden of the leader of the free world.

All the same, foreign policy imposed itself on the Clinton administration and, despite typical periods of disarray and contradiction, he scored more diplomatic successes than failures as he matured in office.

Clinton was not, as his critics charged, unknowledgeable in foreign affairs. He had graduated near the top of his class at Georgetown's School of Foreign Service, studied European political systems while at Oxford, and spent two years reading documents and monographs as a clerk to the Senate Foreign Affairs committee. Even as governor of presumably provincial Arkansas, he visited Europe and the Far East twelve times on trade missions.

But even such preparation was hardly adequate to handle the problems of a new, post-cold war era dawning in the world when Clinton entered office. With the collapse of the Soviet Union, unimaginable ten years earlier, there was no longer a clear enemy in opposition to which the United States could define itself and its position in international affairs. The United States and its allies struggled to establish the "New World Order" foreseen but not realized by the Bush administration, without the benefit of clear rules of engagement. It was, as some described it, a period of international deregulation.

In an effort to place the Clinton foreign policy in a cohesive framework, his advisers struck on the theme of a doctrine of "enlargement" to replace the cold war-era doctrine of containment. The goal of enlargement would be to spread democracy and free markets around the world. The doctrine embraced free trade as a tool of foreign policy, and stressed multilateral peacekeeping efforts and international alliances in which the United States would play an important but not singular role. At a time, however, when nationalist and isolationist factions were growing in both political parties, implementing the new doctrine was easier said than done.

There were crises on every continent during Clinton's first term. In Europe, Russia's president

Boris Yeltsin, the United States' choice as the best hope for stability and democracy in that country, moved aggressively against nationalist movements in neighboring states of the Commonwealth of Independent States that had succeeded the old Soviet Union. Moreover, he challenged American support of the expansion of NATO into Eastern Europe by the enlistment of Poland, Hungary, and Czechoslovakia into its ranks. This move converted the old anti-Soviet alliance into one with a broader mission of guaranteeing peace and representative government throughout Europe. Carrying out the change over Yeltsin's opposition while keeping him "onboard" as America's friend was a tricky, but successfully executed, mission.

In Somalia, U.S. troops on a humanitarian mission to combat famine were ambushed in 1993 and 1994 by warlord Mohammed Farah Aidid's gangs, who dragged the bodies of dead American soldiers through the streets of Mogadishu. In Haiti, leaders of a military dictatorship refused to step aside and re-instate democratically elected president Jean-Bertrand Aristide, whom they had ousted in 1991. They relented only on the eve of an American invasion, succumbing to the diplomatic persuasion of former president Jimmy Carter, who seemed for a time to be a semiofficial, one-man State Department. Carter also helped Clinton to move toward an agreement with North Korea to freeze activities that indicated possible progress by the little nation, still a totalitarian state defined as "rogue" by the major powers, toward building nuclear weapons.

But it was the bloody war in the former Yugoslavia, the Serbian aggression in Bosnia, that dominated the foreign policy arena during the 1993–1996 period, and Clinton's handling of it showed both his initial ambiguity in the international arena and his evolution into a world leader.

He started as a hard-liner, at least rhetorically. During the spring and summer of 1992, as Bosnian Serbs began a campaign of ethnic cleansing, driving Muslims from their homes and towns, Clinton accused President Bush of "turning his back" on basic human rights by not taking strong action in defense of the overmatched Muslims. When he was president, Clinton said, he would push the United Nations, with military support from the United States, to do "whatever it takes" to end the slaughter.

Four months into his presidency, Clinton attempted to persuade America's allies in Europe to agree to provide arms to the Bosnian Moslems, lifting an arms embargo that had been placed on all sides in the dispute, and to carry on air strikes against the Serb positions in the Bosnian hills around Sarajevo. The Europeans balked, fearful that such action would escalate the war and further endanger UN troops there. Clinton receded, unwilling to take unilateral action, but grew increasingly frustrated as the war dragged on for two years, with the Bosnian Serbs overrunning three of the UN-protected "safe areas," Gorazde, Srebrenica, and Zepa.

The sight of tens of thousands of Bosnian Muslim refugees fleeing the Serbs sent what one official called "a jolt of electricity" through the White House. Clinton, persuaded that all previous policies were failures, took a new tack. He began attending Bosnia policy review meetings for the first time and fought off congressional pressure to lift the arms embargo, having changed his mind and considering it "the wrong step at the wrong time." Instead, he pressed a twofold plan of military and diplomatic pressure. He pushed NATO to begin major bombing attacks on the Serb positions until they pulled back their artillery. On 8 September 1995, Serb and Bosnian foreign ministers met in Geneva, joined by officials from neighboring Croatia, a third force in the war which actually helped the peace initiative by weakening the Serbs.

In their first meeting in two years, the parties discussed an American plan to apportion territory based on what was called "objective reality." Two months later, the adversaries were brought to the United States for peace talks held at Wright-Patterson Air Force Base outside Dayton, Ohio. After three weeks of intense discussions brokered by deputy secretary of state Richard Holbrooke, all sides agreed on a compromise that called for a unified capital of Sarajevo, a national Bosnian government, and ethnic sub-states within it. As part of the agreement, the Clinton administration promised to send a substantial force of American troops to Bosnia to help keep the peace. This part of the deal was challenged by Clinton's political opponents in Congress, who argued that Bosnia was both too dangerous and too peripheral a place for American forces to be stationed. But Clinton prevailed, with some bipartisan support from the Republican Senate majority leader, Robert Dole.

The naysayers proved wrong. The peace held, however tenuously, and the American presence there was so quiet that it went almost unreported after the first few weeks. Bosnia was barely part of the debate during the 1996 election, and it returned as an issue only very briefly afterward, when Clinton announced that he would not be pulling out the American troops after one year, as he had at first promised.

Peacemaker Clinton

There were two areas, however, in which Clinton stood tall and unwavering, and showed maturing leadership. From 1993 onward he showed a determination to do what was possible to bring peace to two tormented regions—northern Ireland and the Middle East. With regard to the first, risking the displeasure of the British government, he accepted visits from Gerry Adams, the leader of the political wing of the Irish Republican Army, and by such a conferral of legitimacy, helped bring the IRA and the Ulster Protestants to a cease-fire. He followed this up by dispatching a special envoy to moderate ensuing talks looking toward a permanent peaceful settlement. Likewise, he encouraged and endorsed, though did not broker, a significant peace accord achieved in Oslo, Norway, between Israeli prime minister Yitzhak Rabin and Yasser Arafat, chairman of the Palestine Liberation Organization.

Since the Irish peace talks did not reach fruition until 1998—and since the Oslo accords were undercut by tragic developments in 1995 and afterward—the full account of these admirable moves belongs with the story of Clinton's second term.

Revolution and Reinvention

Though he was not on the ballot in 1994, Clinton considered the off-year congressional elections a referendum on the first two years of his presidency. If so, it was a disaster, for he was soundly rejected, as was his party, which lost control of the House and Senate for the first time in forty years.

It was a transformational election that in its sweep took political experts by surprise and yet was a long time coming—the culmination of a slow decline by the Democrats that began when the issues of race and war started to tear apart the New Deal coalition. Clinton had for a long time been working to refashion the party in a more centrist and forward-looking mode to prevent the anticipated fall. But as it occurred on his watch, he was held to blame. Republicans had nationalized the congressional elections, running against Bill and Hillary Clinton as the symbols of big government, and offering their own

"Contract with America" that promised tax cuts, welfare reform, a balanced budget, and laissez-faire deregulation of the business world and the environment.

As the 104th Congress that began in 1995 concentrated on the conservative agenda shaped by House Speaker Newt Gingrich of Georgia, the tactical and intellectual general of the Republican revolution, there was a temptation to dismiss Clinton as inconsequential while media attention focused on Congress. A presidential news conference in April was deemed worthy of coverage by only one major television network, and Clinton was reduced to proclaiming in answer to a question: "The president is relevant here."

But he had already started to put together a comeback plan, reading books on presidential leadership, getting opinions from hundreds of people, and watching videotapes of popular predecessors, including Ronald Reagan, in top form, all to gauge where and how he had failed. Still, during that troublesome spring for Clinton, Speaker Gingrich and his self-styled revolutionary agenda of shrinking government remained at least temporarily preeminent. His every move was observed and analyzed by the press. On the constitutional see-saw of balanced powers, Congress was up and the president was down.

But within a year, the Republican revolution had dissipated. By the time Clinton rode by train from Washington to Chicago in August 1996 to accept his party's uncontested renomination, he seemed miraculously transformed and energized, busting with confidence and in full roar. He seemed, at last, to feel at home in the White House. He had practiced the salute of commander in chief to the point where he could snap it off briskly at any time, even when no military people were in sight.

During the final months of his 1996 reelection campaign against the Republican challenger, Bob Dole of Kansas, the former Senate majority leader, Clinton was confident of winning a second term and already pondering his place in history. He said in an interview that he had finally grown into the job and learned how to play the instruments of power: legislation, executive action, the bully pulpit. To succeed, he said, "a president has to use all those things... and know when it is appropriate to do which... that is a lesson I've learned from my defeats as well as from my successes here in the last four years."

But there were elements other than the education of William Jefferson Clinton to account for this extraordinary return from the political dead. The first was luck. Clinton always seemed to benefit immeasurably from the frailties of his enemies. When he was down, the people who put him there always seemed to sink quickly themselves. The man who defeated him in Arkansas in 1980, Frank White, had quickly fallen from political grace, reminders of which helped to snap Clinton out of his postelection depression.

Newt Gingrich came to serve the same purpose. His tenure as Speaker was marked by strategic blunders and verbal gaffes, and each misstep helped Clinton to recover standing. The Republican takeover of Congress, in fact, might have been a blessing in disguise for Clinton. It took him off center stage as the focus of all anger and disappointment and made Gingrich and his agenda the targets of discontent instead. It was a gift to Clinton, said Democratic senator Russ Feingold of Wisconsin, "and he took it and used it very well."

The second post-1994 change was the return of Richard Morris, the consultant who revived his career after the 1980 gubernatorial defeat. The call went out again to Morris, at first using a code name, in late-night telephone conversations, then more openly. Morris insinuated himself back to the center of Clinton's career and began reshaping his presidency.

The basic strategy that Clinton and Morris developed this time echoed their work in Arkansas: move to the ideological center and frustrate Clinton's conservative opposition by taking away traditional Republican issues. As part of this plan, Clinton restored his promise of a middle-class tax cut and began offering his own balanced budget proposals. Though some congressional Democrats lamented that Clinton's budget-balancing surrender would force unacceptably harsh cuts in programs, the political effectiveness of the move soon became evident. Thereafter, Clinton, seemingly immunized against such complaints, and could wage the debate not on whether to balance the budget but how to do it.

Morris was a fractious presence in the White House at first, with many of the more progressive aides dismayed at the power of this Republican-leading Rasputin. But his stock rose as it became clear that his advice was helping Clinton regain his equilibrium. Morris's "triangulation" plan—whereby Clinton established himself as a moderate third point on the political triangle between liberal Democrats and revolutionary Republicans—paid off

in a way that reconciled even some of those very Democrats.

The president also managed to define himself as a contrast to Congress. He would work with Gingrich and the Republicans, but within boundaries. He would seek compromises on welfare reform and budget cuts, moving rightward, but would use his veto power when the Republicans pushed too far in cutting funds for Medicare, Medicaid, education, and preserving the environment. After never using his veto power during his first two years in office, he suddenly discovered it. As budget-cutting appropriations measures reached his desk, he vetoed several of them until they were revised to his liking. He also vetoed the Republicans' omnibus reconciliation bill to balance the budget in seven years, arguing that it cut too much from federal programs protecting the poor and elderly while providing a tax cut to the wealthy.

The Republicans had been operating on the assumption that Clinton would inevitably relent to their conservative agenda. But they underestimated his political will and overestimated their own public appeal. Clinton's resistance to the harsher aspects of the Gingrich revolution steadily boosted his popularity, as Gingrich would learn when the crunch came at the end of 1995. On two separate occasions, first in November and again in December, House Republicans voted to shut down the federal government in an effort to force Clinton to accept their budget. They assumed that the antigovernment mood was so prevalent across the land that their tactic would be popular. It was instead disastrous. Reports of workers losing their jobs and popular national parks closing dominated the nightly news. Gingrich then partly self-destructed, most prominently by whining about alleged personal slights while attending the funeral of slain Prime Minister Yitzhak Rabin and during the flights there and back. He admitted the role of personal pique in forcing the government shutdown. He became a target of ridicule and his best friends in the House, who once saw him as their irreplaceable leader, began hearing pleas from their constituents to temper their rhetoric and push the outspoken Speaker into the background.

It could be argued that by paralyzing the government the Republicans lost the 1996 presidential race then and there, a year before the election. Forced to back off, their miscalculation renewed Clinton's confidence and strengthened his relationship with congressional Democrats. It gave him flexibility to hold the ideological center ground, occasionally moving to the left without losing public support, or to the right without losing the progressive wing of his party. The loyalty of this faction was sorely tested late in 1996 when Clinton agreed to a Republican-crafted welfare reform proposal that effectively ended the federal guarantee of public assistance for millions of poor women and children. Two prominent members of Clinton's health and social services department resigned in protest, but even the most disappointed liberals preferred a conservative Clinton to the Republican alternative.

The 1996 campaign lacked real competition and luster. Bob Dole's single idea was a promise to cut taxes by 15 percent. The public was skeptical, particularly when Dole himself had built a solid reputation in the Senate as a moderate pragmatist who believed that cutting the deficit made more economic sense than cutting taxes. His election year "conversion" rang hollow; his low-key personality, so useful in engineering Senate cloakroom compromises, failed to capture the public imagination, and he was reduced, in growing frustration, to alternately denouncing Clinton as a liberal and then complaining that the president had co-opted the conservative agenda. Clinton's superior political and rhetorical skills overwhelmed him, and as always, a dull campaign served to the advantage of the incumbent.

On 5 November 1996, William Jefferson Clinton was reelected to a second term. His margin of victory was wider than it had been four years earlier. He captured 379 electoral votes and 49 percent of the popular vote to 41 percent for Dole (and 8 percent for Perot, who was regarded more as a fringe candidate in his second independent bid for the presidency).

No American politician in modern times had run so far so fast as Bill Clinton. It took him merely two decades to move from his first triumph to his last, from attorney general of a small southern state to the youngest Democrat ever reelected to a second term as president. But on election night, as he stood on the portico of the Old State House in Little Rock in the warm autumn darkness and delivered a long and emotional valedictory speech, the moment evoked not just the romance of a life's pursuit coming to an end, but the anxiety of an uncertain future.

THE SECOND TERM

Bernard A. Weisberger

It has traditionally been the case that twice-elected presidents, no matter how successful their first term, have rocky rides in the second. Even George Washington suffered editorial denunciations after 1796. Jefferson left office amid the wreckage of his despised Embargo Act (1807). Jackson was officially censured by the Senate after being reelected in 1832. Franklin D. Roosevelt suffered major political setbacks in 1937 and 1938 and conceivably would not have won—or even been a candidate for—a third term had war not broken out in 1939. Nixon had Watergate and Ronald Reagan Iran-Contra. Bill Clinton managed to extend and exceed the pattern with the Monica Lewinsky scandal. It resulted in his becoming the first duly elected president in U.S. history to be impeached, tried, and acquitted by the Senate (Andrew Johnson, impeached in 1868, had been elected vice president and succeeded Lincoln after his death). It was a distinction that the man from Hope, however eager to leave his mark on history, could hardly have enjoyed.

The Lewinsky scandal, which took more than a year to play out its course, dominated and overshadowed other aspects of Clinton's lame-duck turn on the national stage. In itself a sordid tale of lust, weakness, and arrogance on his part, and of political malice and vindictiveness on that of his accusers, it nonetheless raised serious questions about the meaning of the impeachment clause of the Constitution, the possible political abuse of the process, and the future course of congressional-presidential relations. These were left unanswered by the president's ambiguous victory. The problem for a historian of the episode is in separating the weighty political and cultural issues at its core from the mass of surrounding sleaze. One other serious aspect of the event is its reawakening of the always fascinating question of how the private character of a chief executive affects his role as a national leader. Can anything be learned about the Clinton administration as a whole from the astonishing contrast between the intelligent, politically sensitive, and skillful Bill Clinton of two winning presidential campaigns, and the Bill Clinton who risked his family and the career he had spent a life-

New York City newspapers blare the headlines the day after President Clinton's admission to a national television audience of an inappropriate relationship with a former White House intern. AP/WIDE WORLD

time building for short-lived sexual gratification? That, too, remains an open question.

The one certainty is that the impeachment fitted into the defeat-and-comeback pattern that had marked Clinton's rise to the top. The House vote that placed him on trial for his political life before the Senate took place only two years and one month after his 1996 reelection, which itself followed by just two years the humiliation of having the Democrats lose control of the Congress on his watch. And in the fall of 2000, only eighteen months after his acquittal, his standing in popularity polls was so high that had there been no constitutional amendment prohibiting it, he might well have run successfully for a third term.

There are no simple explanations with Clinton. But clearly, his interludes of success owed much to his flexibility, persuasiveness, and good luck in holding office in relatively prosperous and peaceful times. The first year of the second term gave evidence of all three.

Holding the Center

Consistent with the pragmatic remaking of his liberal image that had followed defeat in the 1980 Arkansas gubernatorial race, Clinton had begun a rightward shift immediately following the 1994 congressional debacle. In his 1995 State of the Union address, he uttered the words "The era of big government is over," and the following year signed welfare-reform legislation that severely limited the decades-old Democratic liberal commitment to making Washington a major source of assistance. He kept on course toward a balanced federal budget, and renewed his endorsement of the tight-money, anti-inflationary fiscal policies of Alan Greenspan, whom he reappointed as chairman of the Board of Governors of the Federal Reserve System. While this dismayed his liberal advisers, the 1996 election results showed that it had not cost him the support of the Democratic party's traditional working-class and minority base. He had won 60 percent of the vote of "labor-affiliated" Americans and 80 percent of the nonwhite vote.

In his second inaugural address in January 1997, therefore, Clinton felt free to advocate "a new government for a new century—humble enough not to try to solve all our problems for us, but strong enough to give us the tools to solve our problems for ourselves; a government that is smaller, lives within its means, and does more with less." Yet on the other hand, he promised, this limited and more frugal government would lead the nation into a triumphant twenty-first century, in which "schools will have the highest standards in the world... and the doors of higher education will be opened to all," where "the knowledge and power of the Information Age will be within reach... of every classroom, every library, and every child," where crime-free streets would "echo again with the laughter of our children," and "new miracles of medicine at last will reach not only those who can claim care now but the children and hardworking families too long denied." Of course, the United States would also maintain a strong defense, promote peace and freedom, and as "the world's greatest democracy [would] lead a whole world of democracies." Likewise, it would be "a nation that fortifies the world's most productive economy even as it protects the great natural bounty of our water, air, and majestic land." Finally, this "land of new promise" would reform its politics "so that the voice of the people will always speak louder than the din of narrow interests."

So there it was—ambitious promises to strengthen education and health care, clean up the environment and politics and the crime-ridden streets—somehow without enlarging the presence and spending of the government. The move to the center was confirmed by Clinton's own choice of a second-term team. This time there would be no nominees with hidden liabilities such as Zoë Baird, Clinton's first-term choice for attorney general, ultimately withdrawn; no controversial choices such as that of law professor Lani Guinier to head the Civil Rights division of the Justice Department, who became such a target for conservative ire that Clinton withdrew her name even before hearings began. The most senior department, State, got a new chief and its first female head in the person of Madeleine Albright, a longtime insider who proposed no particularly radical changes in the nation's foreign policy. Janet Reno continued as attorney general. Andrew M. Cuomo, son of the liberal Democratic former governor of New York, Mario M. Cuomo, gave a liberal tint to the Department of Housing and Urban Development as its new secretary. The new secretaries of Labor and Transportation were African Americans; the new ambassador to the United Nations, Hispanic, and Clinton even included a Republican, the former U.S. senator William Cohen, as his new secretary of defense. Positions at the Treasury and Commerce Departments were filled by appointees respected in investment and banking circles. All were presumably competent; none would rock the boat.

Clinton caught a break early in his second term when House Speaker Newt Gingrich, who had orchestrated the Republican takeover of Congress in Clinton's first term, was found guilty in 1997 by his congressional colleagues of misapplying tax-exempt donations to his educational foundations, and was fined and reprimanded. Though Gingrich continued to serve as Speaker, his rebuke suggested a weakening in the power of the cadre of right-wing revolutionaries that he had helped bring into office in 1994. Given Clinton's step toward center-right, and this possible movement of the Republicans toward the same position, it seemed as if Clinton could realize one of the final promises of his second inaugural speech, a truce to partisanship. Noting that the voters had chosen a president and Congress of different parties, he declared that they surely "did not do this to advance the politics of petty bickering and extreme partisanship.... They call on us instead to be repairers of the breach, and to move on with America's mission." The statement was vintage Clinton—a touch of evangelical zeal and a carefully calibrated set of nods and bows to both right and left, calculated to appease.

Continued prosperity also seemed to promise concord. The economy continued to show growth, low inflation, and low unemployment. Though millions of families still lacked health insurance and job security, and struggled to make ends meet by juggling family commitments with multiple jobs, the managerial and professional workers who were the backbone of the new middle class found the United States a goodly dwelling place, and wanted no political wrangling to disturb the idyll.

But the new Era of Good Feelings was not to be. In 1997 the 105th Congress made no headway in dealing with major issues such as rising medical costs and the codification of standards pertaining to patients' rights; environmental degradation and toxic waste cleanup; campaign finance reform; and the increasing concentration of ownership and wealth by a relatively small segment of the American populace. Proposals on these issues, and on measures such as giving the president fast-track authority to conclude trade agreements, were stymied, not only by partisanship but by the conflicting pressures of lobbying groups that neutralized each others' influence. Under a 1996 law, Clinton had new budgetary authority to exercise the "line-item veto" over individual parts of appropriations bills. (This was declared unconstitutional by the Supreme Court in 1998.) But he could only deny expenditures, not restore cuts, and 1997 ended with another budget standoff. The president refused to sign pared-down appropriations bills unless a few of his favored programs, such as more money for teacher training and modest boosts in the number of subsidized housing units, were reinserted. Yet given his own embrace of budget balancing (which, along with a surplus, was achieved in the spring of 1998), the debate was not so much about which initiatives should be robustly nourished as it was over parceling out what was left in balanced budgets after defense and other priorities had been met.

Nor did the president's apparent move to attach himself to such "Republican" issues as fiscal responsibility silence the steady drumbeat of attacks from the more ardent wing of the opposition. Accusations of improper fund-raising during the 1996 campaign dogged the White House. Clinton was denounced for "selling" audiences with himself and overnight invitations to the White House for campaign cash.

The vice president was charged with making illegal calls from the Executive Office in search of contributions. Money from foreign sources—strictly forbidden—had also supposedly flowed into Democratic coffers through intermediaries. One donor country was China, which wanted to encourage Clinton's efforts to bring it into the international trading community despite public outcry over its human rights abuses. Meantime, the Whitewater probe ground on, producing more file cabinets full of depositions and securing convictions of some of the Clintons' Arkansas associates.

And then in January 1998 the name of Monica Lewinsky first appeared in newscasts; the unfolding story would, throughout the entire year, transfix the nation and imperil the Clinton presidency.

The Year of Unintended Consequences

The story had actually begun in 1994, when Paula Corbin Jones, a former clerical worker for the state of Arkansas, filed a sexual harassment suit in federal district court in Arkansas. She alleged that in 1991, then-governor Clinton, catching sight of her at a public function, had sent a state trooper to invite her to a room at the Excelsior Hotel in Little Rock. Jones claimed Clinton exposed himself to her and suggested that she perform oral sex on him. Though Jones was not threatened with any reprisals when she refused, she nonetheless sued for recompense for her humiliation, pain, and fear of future reprisals. Clinton's lawyers appealed for the dismissal or postponement of the suit as an infringement on the attention and time of the president, from which the national interest might suffer, especially in a time of crisis. The counterargument was that a president could be in office for up to eight years. A reasonable plaintiff's case could be seriously damaged by such a delay— witnesses might die, recollections might fade, materials could be lost. The president was not blessed with "sovereign immunity" and was a citizen like any other.

The president, however, had a pragmatic argument on his side. Lawsuits against future presidents could become a potent political weapon. If well-heeled opponents could finance one frivolous suit after another, they could destroy a president's public reputation and his effectiveness. And in fact, in her legal battle against Clinton, Jones was receiving financial support from several wealthy backers including Richard Scaife, who was outspoken in his dislike of the president on both personal and political terms.

Nevertheless, the U.S. Supreme Court in 1997 decided that the Jones lawsuit could go forward, and so opened the gate into a steadily widening labyrinth. Jones's lawyers were now entitled to attempt to establish a "pattern of conduct" in Clinton's past that would lend credibility to her accusation. They began to collect and probe every rumor of Clinton's past sexual dalliances, and in the process encountered the name of a young woman named Monica Lewinsky, who had been a White House intern in 1995 and 1996. Lewinsky had confided in telephone conversations to a coworker and presumed friend, Linda Tripp, that she had what she thought of as a love affair with the president, including clandestine sexual encounters in the White House and exchanges of gifts. Unknown to Lewinsky, Tripp taped the calls, and the tapes eventually found their way into the hands of Kenneth Starr, the Whitewater special prosecutor, and also, possibly improperly, into those of Jones's attorneys.

The Jones legal team now compelled Clinton to answer questions about Lewinsky. In his deposition in 1998, he denied having had sexual relations with her, which she confirmed by affidavit. Starr's office, with proof in hand that the denials were false, now had a powerful weapon to deploy. Illicit presidential sex was shameful but not a crime deserving special prosecution. But if a chief executive sworn to uphold the law lied under oath, it was an assault on the judicial system itself. Starr now sought permission from the attorney general to add the alleged perjury to the list of charges under his scrutiny. Reno, already under fire for refusing to launch a new special investigation into White House fund-raising, had little choice but to acquiesce.

The trap began to close. Starr summoned witnesses from the White House personnel rosters, including Lewinsky, who at first refused to testify on grounds of self-incrimination. Clinton himself had been busy at the time of the Jones deposition, discussing with Lewinsky what she might say to explain their meetings, trying to arrange a corporate job for her through his political friend Vernon Jordan, and involving his secretary Betty Currie, both in cover stories and in helping to conceal gifts he had given Lewinsky. These actions could be seen as attempts to obstruct justice.

While the legal machinery whirred and clanked, Clinton had to deal with the public relations and political firestorm ignited when the story hit the media. The president informed his advisers and cabinet, and then went on television to tell the nation—wagging his finger for emphasis—that he "did not have sexual relations with that woman, Miss Lewinsky." Through the spring, the rumors swarmed and suppurated, overshadowing all else. A break seemed to fall the president's way in April 1998 when the Jones suit was dismissed in a lower court as unwarranted, since no harm to the plaintiff was proven. But it was too late to save him from two shattering revelations in July and August. On 28 July, under a grant of immunity by Starr's office, Lewinsky agreed to testify. In an appearance before a federal grand jury convened by Starr, she reversed her original denial and confirmed a relationship with Clinton in abundant detail. To clinch matters, she produced a dress she had worn at one of the trysts, never cleaned and still carrying a smear of dried semen. Under court order, the president of the United States on 30 August provided a sample of his DNA from scrapings inside his cheek. The laboratory report brought the devastating and cold truth. DNA matches showed the semen to be Bill Clinton's.

Now Clinton was called on to testify. After long negotiations it was agreed that he could be deposed in the White House on videotape that was carried on a closed circuit to the grand jury. In four hours of grilling by Starr's staff, Clinton split hairs and haggled over words to prove that he had not actually lied in the Jones case, since he had never really "had sex" with Lewinsky as he understood the term. (His understanding seemed to be limited to conventional intercourse.)

But the legalistic bobbing and weaving, designed to avert a criminal prosecution, did not get to the heart of Clinton's personal behavior. He had lied to his closest associates, who innocently repeated his lies to others. He had lied to his wife. And he had lied to the country.

Questions buzzed in Washington's muggy mid-August air. What would Clinton do? What would the people think? What was the duty of Congress? What direction would both political parties take? Were these impeachable offenses? If not, could they merely be overlooked, without appalling consequences to faith in law and leadership? No one had firm answers; strategies were evolved on the fly, and events seemed to unfold without any sense of direction.

The situation was unprecedented. For the third time in twenty-four years the country was facing the possible ouster of an elected president. But Watergate (1974) and Iran-Contra (1987) had been resolved short of an actual Senate trial. Nixon resigned on the advice of senior Republican senators, and in 1987 Democrats had tacitly agreed to make Reagan's subordinates, not the president himself, the target.

But at least three elements made 1998 different. The first was Clinton's determination to fight it out. He remains something of a riddle—the protean personality who could be a Rhodes scholar and "policy wonk," yet have irresistible popular appeal on the campaign trail. The practical politician with an unusual ability to focus on the issues he thought of as central, but who had a violent temper, a streak of gluttony, and a reckless compulsion to sexual adventure. In a strange way, he resembled Richard Nixon. Inner demons (of different kinds) seemed to drive both these men of calculating intelligence into self-destructive behavior better explained by psychiatry than political science. Yet both their stories carried a clear political message: Because of the power of the modern presidency, the office and the nation can be significantly at risk when the conduct of the chief magistrate is unbecoming, let alone unethical or illegal.

A second new element was the information revolution. Clinton was no more goatish, according to fairly well-established evidence, than John F. Kennedy. And surely there were presidents in the past guilty of sexual indiscretions during their tenure. But earlier journalistic codes kept a bright line between the personal and public doings of officeholders. Alcoholics, homosexuals, and philanderers remained "in the closet" even when insiders knew the truth. It was not entirely a matter of ethics. Major newspapers and media outlets were themselves institutions with a built-in interest in good relations with government and the stability of the system of contacts and access. But by the 1990s there was a general frankness about sexual matters that loosened previous inhibitions on reporting subjects once considered "not fit to print." Television talk shows and "celebrity" magazines had democratized gossip and even made disdain for it appear somewhat "elitist."

And then there was the Internet. Any rumor could be posted either in an officially recognized Web magazine or by an independent operator unafraid of libel suits. What should the editors of establishment newspapers, newsmagazines, and news networks do when made aware of such stories? They could, of course, ignore them. But if competitors broke the story, the righteous self-deniers could lose audiences to their rivals, and that was a fearsome prospect. The media themselves had become gigantic business enterprises, often absorbed into mega-corporations with interests in many diverse operations. With large amounts of capital invested in "information packaging," risks could not be taken with the bottom line. So, the "respectable" press, when confronted with the latest "dirt," could not, or at least did not, turn up a fastidious nose. It followed the story, and by that very act elevated it to newsworthiness. By the spring of 1998, the daily output of "Monica" speculation was legitimate news, devouring time and space that might have gone to covering other aspects of the presidency.

Finally, politics in the 1990s had become darker. It was, after all, only four years since the so-called Republican revolution, and Gingrich had risen to the top by utilizing aggressive personal attacks on the Democrats and their electoral base. He had engineered the removal of longtime Democratic House Speaker Jim Wright in 1989 over ethics violations, a feat that he and other Republicans regarded as a payback for Watergate. The new Republican majority in Congress also contained a number of ardent social and religious conservatives, convinced that Clinton and the Democrats were destroying the America of patriotism, piety, and "family values" that they cherished. Democrats responded with their own resentments. There was poison in the air.

And so the lines were drawn and passions prevailed. And each irreversible step contrived to shift a simple, distasteful sex scandal into a major constitutional confrontation.

Rush to Nowhere

Following his grand jury testimony on 17 August 1998, Clinton took to the airwaves to admit to the nation that he had engaged in a relationship with Monica Lewinsky that was "not appropriate," that his testimony in January in a "politically inspired lawsuit" had been "legally accurate," but that at no time had he asked anyone to "lie, to hide or destroy evidence, or to take any other unlawful action." He deeply regretted his "personal failure." But the matter, he argued, should be left between himself and "the two people I love most—my wife and our daughter—and our God." He called for a halt to "the pursuit of personal destruction and the prying into private lives" and expressed a desire to continue the work of the nation.

The speech itself was a classic piece of Clinton triangulation that balanced apology, lawyer-like caution about damaging admissions, and outrage at Starr. Reactions among his intimates varied. Some betrayed members of the presidential staff (though none from the cabinet) resigned, though not immediately. The most important decision was Hillary Clinton's—and she chose once more to be the supportive, wronged, wife. Democrats on Capitol Hill were angry and divided. Some favored asking Clinton to resign. Others were like Connecticut senator Joseph Lieberman of Connecticut, who took to the Senate floor to express his "disappointment and personal anger" at the president's immoral conduct, but said that he would settle for a bipartisan resolution of censure as the correct chastisement.

September was another difficult month for the president. Starr sent two vanloads of documents to the thirty-seven-member House Judiciary Committee, along with a report summarizing the evidence that could be used as a basis for impeachment. Parts of the report were posted on the congressional Web site and immediately became public property. In order to support his contention that Clinton lied even in narrowly defined legal terms about never having "had sex" with Lewinsky, Starr had included her highly explicit testimony about who had touched what body parts, for how long, and with what results. In addition to the public embarrassment brought on by the intimate disclosures, Clinton saw the release and airing of his shifty grand jury testimony. All that was held back was a large accumulation of "raw" data, unverified claims of Clinton misdeeds, including alleged sexual harassment of no fewer than twenty-one women.

Dirt began to fly as the Judiciary Committee, a particularly partisan body, debated on the scope and length of its hearings. In September 1998 the Web site Salon.com unearthed the fact that Chairman Henry Hyde had once conducted an adulterous affair with the wife of a friend. Hyde brushed the matter aside as a "youthful indiscretion" (though he was over forty at the time of the affair) and insisted that smear tactics would not deter him from his nonpartisan and painful duty to investigate wrongdoing.

There was an October truce while Congress was in recess for midterm elections. On Election Day the voice of the people was heard. For a moment, after a rain of steady setbacks, things seemed to brighten for Clinton. The Democrats kept their forty-five senators and picked up enough House seats to whittle the Republican majority down to a mere handful. One immediate reaction was a Republican flight from Gingrich, whom the party held responsible for the electoral losses. House Republicans staged a revolt and named the more moderate Robert Livingston of Louisiana as Speaker-designate for the incoming 106th Congress, from which Gingrich would resign. Next, during a November hearing, Starr defended his report and stated that in all other areas of investigation—Whitewater, "Filegate," and "Travelgate"—he had found nothing worthy of indictment. Meanwhile, attorneys for Paula Jones reached an agreement to give up their appeal to have the sexual harassment case reinstated—a serious possibility in light of the Starr report revelations—for a financial settlement of $700,000. That threat, at least, was now lifted.

But the momentum of the Judiciary Committee was now unstoppable. In the raucous and mesmerizing hearings, Democratic members charged that the committee was railroading the president on flimsy ground, far short of the "high crimes and misdemeanors" required by the Constitution for impeachment. Republicans countercharged that the case was not about sex, but about lies that denied a wronged citizen the justice that was her rightful due. Duty made it impossible for them to look away, even at the risk of political rejection by an electorate impatient to have the matter settled.

It was all good theater—and none of it swayed minds. On 11 December the committee voted to recommend four articles of impeachment to the full House. One accused the president of lying to Starr's grand jury; another of lying in the Jones suit; a third of obstructing justice by concealing evidence related to the Jones case. A fourth catchall article extended the obstruction charge by citing the president's failure to cooperate with Judiciary Committee's investigation. All of the articles passed on straight party-line votes, 21-16, except for the second article, relating to civil perjury, which passed 20-17.

Now it was up to the entire House, and Republicans who might have settled for censure were being heavily pressured by party whip Tom DeLay to vote to impeach. As the representatives gathered for the crucial session in mid-December 1998 there came the announcement that President Clinton had authorized U.S. air strikes against Iraq for noncompliance with the UN arms inspections, which had been going on since the end of the Gulf War. Democratic Majority Leader Richard Gephardt urged a suspension of the impeachment proceedings until the operation

was complete, on the grounds that it would be unseemly not to have Congress united behind the commander in chief when American troops were risking death. The best he could achieve was one day's grace, as Republicans suspected—with some possible justification—that the timing of the attacks was not accidental.

Then another bombshell exploded. Speaker-designate Livingston learned that the publisher of a pornographic magazine had run an investigation and exposed him as an adulterer. On 19 December, Livingston—the second critic of the president to be exposed as a fellow sexual sinner—addressed the president in absentia. "Sir," he said, "you have done great damage to this nation.... I say that you have the power to terminate the damage and heal the wounds that you have created. You, sir, may resign your post." Shouts of outrage broke out from the Democratic side; some members shouted at Livingston: "You resign!" To their astonishment, he did so. "I must set the example that I hope President Clinton will follow. I will not stand for Speaker of the House on January 6." Livingston resigned his seat and left a shaken House whose members now seemed to be looking into a pit that might engulf them all—a series of exposures that would create what Representative Jerrold Nadler, Democrat from New York, called "a developing sexual McCarthyism." Minority Leader Richard Gephardt put it clearly. "Fratricide dominates our public debate." But the debate resumed, precisely on the old savage terms of Democratic accusations that the proceedings were a "constitutional assassination" and a "Republican coup d'etat," and countercharges that nothing less was at stake than the future of freedom from arbitrary power.

One of the Judiciary Committee's articles of impeachment was dropped, another defeated during the House vote. The first and third articles—on perjury before the grand jury and obstruction of justice in the Jones case—passed on almost straight party-line votes. Each article carried the fateful penultimate paragraph: "William Jefferson Clinton has undermined the integrity of his office, has brought disrepute on the Presidency, has betrayed his trust as President, and has acted in a manner subversive of the rule of law and justice, to the manifest injury of the people of the United States." Following the vote the Republicans caucused to name Illinois representative Dennis Hastert as their Speaker-designate for the next Congress. The 105th Congress then concluded its work. Clinton would go to trial.

Yet the Democrats, in the event, had "won by losing." The initial Republican hope had been for the

THE PRESIDENTS

impeachment to carry a bipartisan imprimatur. But the Democrats had held firm and united in insisting that at most only censure was warranted. The strict party-line votes to impeach hung the label around the process of a partisan maneuver to oust Clinton. That meant that Senate Democrats would almost certainly hold together in voting to acquit, which meant that a two-thirds majority necessary to remove the president could not possibly be reached. It looked as if the Senate trial would be a show the final outcome of which was known from the first day. And so it proved. A small group of senators who neither wished to convict nor to let the president go scot-free hoped for a legitimate "finding of fact" on the charges, and censure, but their efforts failed. With respect to impeachment, the Constitution allowed only for an up or down vote.

The six-week trial was a balancing act among objectives. That of Tom Daschle, the minority leader in the Senate, was simply to hold his forty-five senators together against doubts and possible smoking guns hidden in Starr's files. For Majority Leader Trent Lott, it was to satisfy the desire of Hyde's House managers to present a powerful, if doomed, case. Both Daschle and Lott agreed in their desire to keep the Senate from being tied up for months in what easily could become a media circus. The procedures that they persuaded their colleagues to adopt allowed Hyde and the managers only three witnesses—Lewinsky, Jordan, and Clinton assistant Sidney Blumenthal—who would be seen on videotape, not on the Senate floor. The managers would be allowed several days to make their presentations and arguments, with equal time for rebuttal granted to the president's legal team. And finally the senators would have time to pose questions and make their pro-voting statements. Chief Justice Rehnquist would preside, wearing a black robe he chose to adorn with three Gilbert-and-Sullivan-inspired gold stripes on each sleeve.

While the case moved toward resolution, Clinton demonstrated a political astuteness that maddened his enemies. He made only two public statements, reiterating his "profound remorse" for his "shameful conduct," but vowing that he would reclaim the trust of the American people by carrying out the tasks they had chosen him to accomplish. He then withdrew from the fray and focused on appearing "presidential," busy in the Oval Office and supposedly oblivious to the "partisans" howling and raging against him. In his State of the Union address

on 19 January 1999, he was smiling and confident. He recapitulated all the good things that had happened in the United States in 1998 under his guidance, smiled at the Republican side of the chamber, welcomed the usual celebrity guests, and mouthed "I love you" to the First Lady, seated in the gallery. The speech was, in the words of a decidedly unfriendly watcher, the conservative commentator Pat Robertson, "a home run."

On 12 February—Lincoln's birthday—the Senate concluded the trial. On the first count, that of perjury, it found Clinton not guilty 55-45, with ten Republicans in the acquittal column. On the second count, obstruction of justice, it was a dead split, 50-50, five Democrats and five Republicans having joined "the opposition." It was over. As Justice Rehnquist and a disappointed Henry Hyde and managers left the chamber, Tom Daschle and Trent Lott shook hands in the middle of the aisle, proud of having accomplished the objective of a relatively short and dignified proceeding they had established prior to the beginning of the trial. President Clinton spoke briefly after the verdict; when asked if he would "forgive and forget," he answered: "I believe any person who asks for forgiveness has to be prepared to give it." In the end, the public seemed to feel that impeachment itself was sufficient punishment.

In 2002 the historical and political legacy of Clinton's impeachment was still uncertain. For defenders of executive power, the worst-case scenario was that future Congresses of an opposition party could hold an administration hostage to impeachment trials on trivial charges. Those favoring conviction feared that the acquittal had unacceptably lowered the bar for a president's conduct—for what the chief executive might get away with without facing removal. The only historical precedents were Andrew Johnson's trial, after which there was a period of rarely broken congressional supremacy that lasted thirty years, and Watergate, after which there was a period of congressional suzerainty lasting only six years, until the emergence of Ronald Reagan. The events of 11 September 2001 scrambled all predictions of the balance between Congress and the president following an impeachment crisis.

Foreign Policy

Even while the Lewinsky scandal consumed his domestic agenda, Clinton continued to perform in the field that traditionally was reserved for even an unpopular executive—foreign policy. His first-term record had been mixed. There was the failed intervention in Somalia, the indecisiveness characterizing U.S. policy with respect to Haiti, and the unproductive bombings of Iraq. But he had presided over the conversion of NATO from an anti-Soviet alliance into a general instrument for promoting Western and democratic interests, and even compelled Russia to accept its extension into Eastern Europe. (It may have been as a partial offset that he postponed the development of a U.S. missile defense system that Moscow found objectionable). And NATO became, in 1999, a key player in an important victory.

The scene was the Balkans, where a peace agreement signed in Dayton, Ohio, in 1995 still held, but where a new crisis erupted when Yugoslavia's dictatorial leader, Slobodan Milosevic, launched a genocidal campaign of ethnic cleansing among Albanian separatists in the southern province of Kosovo. Faced with indisputable evidence of mass murders, the United States led the UN in protests, and then in March launched an aerial bombing campaign against Yugoslavia, including Belgrade, under NATO auspices. Within a few weeks, Milosevic was forced to pull back his troops and admit neutral monitors, and it all happened with virtually no loss of American lives. Though there was criticism of this kind of "humanitarian" military intervention, which killed a number of innocent Yugoslavs in target areas, Clinton defended it as something that should already have been international policy earlier. And as an aftermath, Milosevic was forced out of power by the Serbs in 2000, and then indicted as a war criminal by a special UN tribunal. If steps were being taken toward the establishment of international legal standards for intervention in states where human rights abuses were being perpetrated, Clinton deserves some of the credit.

In two other peacemaking efforts that had begun in the first term, the consequences of Clinton's actions extended into the second term.

Ireland and Israel

Fighting between Catholics and Protestants in Northern Ireland had gone on for years and cost hundreds of lives, mostly of innocents caught up in terror bombings and retaliations. Following through on a 1992 campaign promise to break the logjam in Ireland, Clinton first sent a delegation of conciliation-minded Irish-Americans to the scene, and then took the bold step of accepting a visit from Gerry Adams, the head of Sinn Fein (Gaelic for "we ourselves"), the political wing of the Irish Republican Army (IRA). Since the British government regarded the IRA as a terrorist organization, it objected strongly to the legitimacy Clinton seemed to be conferring on Adams, especially as the IRA had yet to renounce "armed struggle" to "free" the British-ruled six northern counties known as Ulster. Clinton's hope was that recognition and dialogue would allow Adams to persuade his followers that there was a peaceful road to the IRA's goal. In 1994 the IRA declared a "complete cessation of military operations" for the first time in a quarter of a century. On St. Patrick's Day 1995, Clinton again entertained Adams at the White House, this time in the company of John Hume, leader of the British Labour party. This was followed by other peace-building steps—the promotion of trade and investment measures to boost the stricken economy of Northern Ireland—and a presidential visit. In 1995, ignoring the displeasure of the British government, Clinton sent former senator George J. Mitchell to chair disarmament talks between the warring factions. By 1999 there was almost a complete lull in the violence, and the negotiators were hammering out final details of an agreement for joint control and eventual independence.

On taking office in 1993, Clinton faced a decision on U.S. policy in the Middle East. Except for Egypt, the Arab states continued to refuse to recognize Israel, and the Palestinians continued their resistance to Israel's occupation and ongoing settlement of territories taken in the 1967 war. There was abundant bloodshed—again, mostly of innocent civilians—on both sides. With the cold war over, one rationale for continued support of Israel and for any U.S. intervention to stabilize the region had disappeared, and the administration of George H. W. Bush had given signs of losing interest in the matter. Clinton abandoned that posture, and gave behind-the-scenes encouragement to negotiations taking place in Oslo, Norway, between representatives of Israel and the Palestine Liberation Organization (PLO). These culminated in a historic agreement under which the PLO agreed to recognize Israel's right to exist and Israel in turn recognized the PLO as the legitimate representative of the Palestinian people. Clinton, though he had played no broker's role, arranged to have the September 1993 signing ceremony take place on the White House lawn, where he stood with PLO chairman Yasser Arafat and Israeli Prime Minister Yitzhak Rabin as they exchanged historic handshakes for the cameras. In 1994, those two, joined by Israeli Foreign Minister Shimon Peres, would be jointly awarded the Nobel Peace Prize. But the devil was in the details, and the Oslo agreements were simply a set of promises by both sides to move in a peaceful direction, but without clear road maps. Still, there was an immediate positive spin-off from the eased tensions—the signing of a peace agreement between Jordan and Israel in 1994, embodied in a "Washington Declaration" signed by Jordan's King Hussein and Rabin at the White House. A formal treaty-signing in Jordan later in the year was attended by Clinton.

Clinton continued to be warmly regarded in Israel, even though his efforts could not produce permanent peace. In the autumn of 1995 when Rabin was assassinated by a Jewish fanatic, Clinton attended the funeral. Wearing the traditional kippah, or skullcap, he stood graveside and pronounced aloud the Hebrew words "Shalom, chaver" ("goodbye, friend") in what appeared to be a genuine moment of emotion. Rabin's murder threw the situation into a newly critical phase, as the hard-line right-wing government of Benjamin Netanyahu succeeded to power after new elections. There were more arguments, more accusations of bad faith and fighting. As late as 1998, in the midst of impeachment, Clinton remained involved. He sponsored a new round of talks in western Maryland, spent almost a week in conference with Netanyahu and Arafat, and managed to cobble together an interim agreement, as laid out in the Wye River Memorandum, that put the peace process back on track.

In overall evaluation, Clinton deserves reasonably good marks for leadership in the post-cold war world that he inherited, where the role of the United States was uncertain. Neither a unilateralist like his successor, nor yet a peace-minded internationalist like Jimmy Carter prior to 1979, he was the guardian of an interim arrangement—an era when established international rules were changing, and defining America's interests was a genuine challenge.

However, following the events of 11 September 2001, Clinton found himself attempting to defend his administration against those who charged that his administrations did little to combat the threat of terrorism, citing inadequate responses to the first World Trade Center bombing in 1993 and the bombing of the U.S.S. *Cole* in 2000.

An Ambiguous Legacy

In the domestic arena, Clinton's presidency ended, for all practical purposes, in the spring of 1999. He was not merely a lame duck, but a scarred one, with little congressional confidence behind him. His popularity remained high, as evidenced by the 1998 congressional elections. Perhaps voters were charmed by personality above all, or perhaps they no longer had any sense of structural interaction and interdependence —voting for their congressional representatives and the president as individuals, without regard to their possible cooperation or lack of it in creating legislation.

In any case, the two sessions of the 106th Congress were fairly devoid of legislative accomplishment. The good times rolled on to produce a $184 billion surplus, of which the president boasted in his final State of the Union address, in January 2000. He asked for a limited middle-class tax cut, more money for schoolrooms and teacher salaries, for prescription drug assistance to seniors on Medicare, stricter handgun control, and "fast track" trade-negotiating authority. He got none of them. But Congress did pass limited campaign finance reform, authorize normalization of trade with China, and reformed Depression-era banking laws to allow for new developments in the financial services industry.

During most of 2000 Clinton stayed behind the scenes, doing what he could for Al Gore's candidacy. For the most part, this consisted of letting Gore stand on his own feet, clear of the taint of Clinton's "immorality."

Clinton hoped the 2000 election would be something of a vindication. As it turned out, Al Gore won the popular vote, but not the electoral vote, and George W. Bush became the next president. The 107th Congress was not significantly different from the one preceding it; the Republicans barely kept control of the House and the Senate remained split evenly. A personal victory for the Clintons, however, was Hillary Clinton's election to the Senate from New York, where they would make their post-White House home.

President Clinton's final months in office were a mixture of wins and losses. In October 1999 Kenneth Starr stepped down as Whitewater special prosecutor and was succeeded by Robert Ray. Clinton had outlasted his nemesis in office. Ray did not pursue a perjury indictment to follow Clinton's departure from the White House, but Clinton in exchange admitted to having made a false statement in the now-settled Jones suit. He paid a fine of $25,000, and had his license to practice law in Arkansas suspended for five years. The U. S. Supreme Court also disbarred him, meaning that Clinton would not be allowed to practice before it. In all, the Jones suit set him back millions in legal fees.

The taint of improper fund-raising lingered, and in his last two weeks in office, a final eruption further sullied Clinton's reputation. On 11 January 2001, James Riady, an Indonesian businessman, pleaded guilty to funneling money through various devices to U.S. political parties, mainly Democratic. And on the morning of 20 January, Clinton listed the customary pardons issued by an outgoing president. They included commutation of the sentences of four Hasidic Jews convicted of embezzlement in New York State, who happened to have been active in lobbying the members of their community to support Hillary Clinton's Senate bid. And above all, a man little known to the public, named Marc Rich. Rich was a commodities trader who had fled to Switzerland in 1983 to escape prosecution for conspiracy, racketeering, and illegal trading with Iran, plus some $48 million in unpaid taxes. His ex-wife Denise, however, was a significant contributor to the Democratic party, operatives of which had marshaled an impressive array of friends including Israeli Prime Minister Ehud Barak, to call the White House and press for a pardon for Marc Rich. In the subsequent fallout and flurry of investigations, it also turned out that the First Lady's brother, Hugh Rodham, had received some $400,000 for lobbying on behalf of two convicted felons who received last-minute pardons.

Clinton responded to the outcry with various disclaimers and legalisms. His associates were quick to point out that George H. W. Bush's last-minute pardons in 1992 and 1993 included convicted or about-to-be-tried figures of the Iran-contra affair. Yet the Clintons still made their exit on a distinctly sour note. Accusations hounded them: one, that they had removed gifts that properly belonged to the White House; another, that Clinton's choice of an expensive mid-Manhattan penthouse as his taxpayer-paid ex-presidential office was exceptionally greedy. The departing First Couple again claimed that as always they were the victims of petty harassments. But they returned some thousands of dollars worth of gifts, and the solution to the penthouse office was vintage Clinton. He abandoned the suite in Carnegie Towers for a cheaper one in Harlem, New York's historic black heartland.

What evaluation of Clinton will history render? Will his name invoke the memory of scandal amid prosperity, like that of Harding? Or of riding a business boom that he did not create, like Coolidge? Will political history textbooks record him as the president who led the Democratic party to a new foundation on the essentially midroad sentiments of most Americans? Or as the president who cut the party loose from its moorings in the working class and its emphasis on community responsibility for the general welfare and restraint of private greed? Will he, as he of course wishes, be seen as the chief figure in the era of transition, leading the American people to a new world and a new century? The last seems unlikely given the impeachment. But even if the impeachment were forgotten, and a century hence American textbooks talked about a second Era of Good Feelings, who really remembers James Monroe, the president who presided over the first? Was Clinton a leader, a scoundrel, a figurehead, or a victim? The jury is still out.

BIBLIOGRAPHY

The following books were essential to the writing of the essay detailing Clinton's first term: Elizabeth Drew, *On the Edge: The Clinton Presidency* (New York, 1994), and *Showdown: The Struggle Between the Gingrich Congress and the Clinton White House* (New York, 1996); Bob Woodward, *The Agenda: Inside the Clinton White House* (New York, 1994), and *The Choice* (New York, 1996). David Maraniss, *First in His Class: A Biography of Bill Clinton* (New York, 1995), and David Maraniss and Michael Weisskopf, *"Tell Newt to Shut Up!": Prizewinning* Washington Post *Journalists Reveal How Reality Gagged the Gingrich Revolution* (New York, 1996). Other books that helped frame this essay include E. J. Dionne, Jr., *Why Americans Hate Politics* (New York, 1991), and *They Only Look Dead* (New York, 1996). With his presidency incomplete, Clinton's story is still a breaking story, told largely by newspapers. This essay relied on articles from the *Washington Post*, the *New York Times* and the *Los Angeles Times*.

Other valuable sources include James B. Stewart, *Blood Sport: The President and His Adversaries* (New York, 1996); John Brummet, *Highwire* (New York, 1994). Phyllis Johnston, *Bill Clinton's Public Policy for Arkansas, 1979–1980*, (Little Rock, Ark., 1982); and Ernest Dumas, *The Clintons of Arkansas* (Fayetteville, Ark., 1993). On the First Lady, *see* Rex Nelson, *The Hillary Factor* (New York, 1993); Donnie Radcliffe, *Hillary Rodham Clinton* (New York,

1993); and Judith Warner, *Hillary Clinton: The Inside Story* (New York, 1993).

The following books provide an early accounting of the first term: David Halberstam, *War in the Time of Peace: Bush, Clinton, and the Generals* (New York, 2001); James McGregor Burns, et al., *Dead Center: Clinton-Gore Leadership and the Perils of Moderation* (New York, 1999); Peter Baker, *The Breach: Inside the Impeachment and Trial of William Jefferson Clinton* (New York, 2000); Richard A. Posner, *An Affair of State* (Cambridge, Mass. 2000).

George W. Bush

Nicholas D. Kristof

George W. Bush ARCHIVE PHOTOS

G EORGE W. BUSH was charming the second graders in a classroom in Sarasota, Florida, when the White House chief of staff, Andrew H. Card Jr., walked over to the president and whispered into his right ear. It was 9:05 A.M. on 11 September 2001, and Bush abruptly tensed and his smile vanished. While arriving at the school thirty minutes earlier, he had been given a muddled account of an airplane striking the World Trade Center, but that initial report made it sound like an accident involving a small private plane. Now Card told the president that a second plane had struck both World Trade Center towers, that both were large commercial jets, and that the United States was under attack.

Demonstrating remarkable acting skills, Bush stayed in the classroom, calm and focused on the children. He listened to them read and arched his eyebrows in mock surprise. "Really good readers," he told them warmly. "This must be sixth grade!" After seven more minutes, he finally excused himself and retreated, grim faced, to take over a changed presidency.

The terrorist attacks had a transformative effect on the United States as a whole—indeed, on most of the world—and certainly on the Bush administration. A presidency that had been generally popular but that had seemed, in the words of some aides, "small," suddenly had an enormous embrace. Within

[639]

weeks, Bush was leading a war in Afghanistan, forming an international coalition against terrorism, pushing for a military tribunal to judge terrorist cases, redirecting national resources to combat germ warfare and build up the armed forces, and enjoying extraordinary popularity across America. He had found a new mission for the presidency: to protect the West from terrorist threats. Ever since the British invasion during the War of 1812, the continental United States had remained impenetrable to hostile incursions from outside its borders, and it seemed that the nation was truly vulnerable only to one such threat—Soviet missiles—but now there were new fears: anthrax, smallpox, nuclear weapons, poisoned reservoirs, hijacked planes, and other threats stemming from foreign terrorists on American soil. In leading the West to fight such dangers, Bush reassured America and revitalized his own administration.

In early 2002, it was still far too soon to cast judgment on his presidency. But what is clear—and what historians will have to tangle with—is that in assessing George W. Bush, one encounters countless paradoxes.

He assumed the presidency in an extraordinary way, with a minority of the popular vote and the outcome in the electoral college determined in effect by a close and controversial decision of the Supreme Court. Many pundits thought that he was acquiring a poisoned chalice, that the doubts about his legitimacy would tie Washington in knots and undermine his hopes of creating a meaningful legacy. Yet a year after that disputed election, Bush enjoyed 85 percent approval ratings, the highest of any modern president.

President Bush came into office remarkably uninformed about international affairs, provoking amusement, for example, with his references to Greeks as "Grecians." There were jokes about his vice president, Dick Cheney, being the real decision-maker behind the scenes. But after a year, those jokes had largely vanished: no one doubted that Bush was in control, and his most impressive achievements were in international affairs.

He is a man who sometimes tortures the English language, puzzling audiences with references to the "vile" (instead of "vital") hemisphere and tailpipe "admissions" (instead of "emissions"), and mystifying a group of New Hampshire schoolchildren celebrating "Perseverance Month" in January 2000 when he earnestly counseled them, "You've got to pre-

serve," as if they should all rush out to can tomatoes. Yet he has a dazzling charm, tremendous social skills, a bold self-confidence, and growing political savvy. Most who have worked with Bush, Democrats as well as Republicans, say that contrary to the jokes that prevailed during the campaign about his intellectual shortcomings, he is smart, shrewd, and a quick study.

Early in his presidency, he scored significant accomplishments, including passage of a far-reaching tax bill that cut rates more than at any time since the Reagan tax cut twenty years earlier. He also set the national agenda on education, bolstered military spending, and successfully resolved his first international crisis, the seizure of a military surveillance plane and its crew by China. Yet Bush was also bedeviled by missteps, including—mystifyingly, for a leader who had emphasized how he was going to work well with Congress—perceived disrespectful treatment of a Vermont senator, James Jeffords, a veteran Republican who responded by quitting the party in May 2001, and in the process turning control of the Senate to the Democrats. Bush also worried many American allies, who feared that he planned to establish a unilateralist course and abandon international cooperation on everything from the Balkans, a region plagued by civil war since the breakup of Yugoslavia in the early 1990s, to global warming. And at home, Bush's close association with the energy industry left many middle-of-the-road voters worried that he would pillage the environment in pursuit of oil. His greatest domestic success, the tax cuts, also led to a plunge in the federal budget surplus within months—and to accusations from Democrats that he was endangering the Social Security system with tax breaks for the wealthy.

The paradoxes go on. He is the law-and-order man, the preacher of traditional moral values, and yet he avoided military service in Vietnam, abused alcohol until middle age, and dances around questions about whether he ever used illegal drugs. His administration, at least initially, steered a decidedly conservative path, and yet his speeches often show concern for traditionally liberal audiences: the poor, immigrants, single mothers, and so on. At times he comes across as profoundly ideological, a deeply-rooted conservative whose political values were shaped by the self-reliance and can-do spirit of the Texas oil business. At other times, Bush seems to lack not only an ideology but even a deep interest in public affairs; he can be surprisingly uninformed about the details of public policy and quite flexible about fundamental issues.

When George W. Bush ran for governor of Texas in 1994, his own parents expected him to lose. It was his younger brother Jeb who held the family's confidence and aspirations, who had diligently prepared for his bid to become governor of Florida that same year. George W., in contrast, had come to his ambitions haphazardly, and his mother, Barbara, flatly tried to discourage his seemingly quixotic resolve. Friends and family members remember that the elder Bushes worried that young George would be forced to bow again, as he had repeatedly in his life, to failure.

But that story had a surprise ending: while Jeb lost, George won. And in the process, George Walker Bush launched himself, without any grand plan or intricate forethought, on a most unusual path to the White House. Looking at the trajectory of his life, he comes across—far more than his predecessors—as an almost accidental president, a cocky and cheerful fellow who drifted through much of his life and who was largely unknown in the United States until he assumed his first political office just six years before becoming president.

He is casual and unpretentious, sometimes goofy. Once, before mealtime on a flight during the 2000 presidential campaign, the flight attendant handed him a piping-hot towel, and he did what passengers typically do, rubbing his fingers and mouth. But then he draped the towel over his face and leaned toward the person next to him as if playing peekaboo. Hiding under a square of terry cloth, he pursued an office that embodies gravitas and dignity. Bush has always been quick to lampoon bigwigs, and he used to entertain friends with splendidly cruel impressions of some of his father's more haughty cabinet members. And then this man who delights in deflating important people found himself the most important person in the world.

Youth

The fourth-grade classroom in Midland, Texas, erupted in titters as George W. Bush, one of the class clowns, turned around and faced his friends. He had quietly used a blue ink pen to draw long Elvis Presley–style sideburns down his cheeks.

Frances Childress, the fourth-grade teacher, was a strong disciplinarian who believed that children should be seen but not bearded. She grabbed George by the arm, yanked him out of class, and marched him down the long outside corridor to the principal's office near the main entrance to Sam Houston Elementary School. "Just look at him," Childress told the principal, John Bizilo. "He's been making a disturbance in class." The next step was pretty obvious for anyone in the 1950s version of the West Texas oil town of Midland: Bizilo told George to bend over and then reached for his paddle, a long wooden device the thickness of a Ping-Pong paddle but narrower and twice as long. George got a standard three whacks, and his shrieks filled the office. "When I hit him, he cried," Bizilo later recalled. "Oh, did he cry! He yelled as if he'd been shot. But he learned his lesson."

So he did.

Many of the roots of Bush's policy and political philosophy as president—including his belief in "tough love" for juvenile offenders—seem to go back to his childhood. George W. Bush was born on 6 July 1946, in New Haven, Connecticut, while his father was an overachieving student at Yale, but the family moved to Texas just two years later, in 1948, settling in Midland in 1950. And while George W. packed an impressive family tree (he is a distant cousin of Queen Elizabeth and a relation of President Franklin Pierce on his mother's side, as well as, of course, the son of the forty-first president of the United States, George H. W. Bush), none of this seems to have mattered much in Midland. His grandfather, Prescott Bush, was a senator from Connecticut, but neighbors were only hazily aware of that.

Midland, a conservative, up-from-the-bootstraps town that has grown from 25,000 when he was a boy to almost 100,000 today, mirrors Bush's optimism and his skepticism about government. While playing Little League baseball, or even sobbing in the principal's office, Bush absorbed values that many old friends say are central to understanding who he is today. "I think his political philosophy comes completely from the philosophy of the independent oilman," said Joe O'Neill, a fellow rapscallion in childhood. "His homage to his parents, his respect for his elders, his respect for tradition, his belief in religion, his opposition to abortion—that's the philosophy he grew up with here."

Even in the 1960s, people raised in Midland generally stood with the establishment rather than rejecting it. Very few seem to have been active in the civil rights or anti-war movements, and the generation gap was much smaller in Midland than in American cities. Midland also seems to have bred an optimism about and a faith in capitalism, in part because it rewarded so many people—like the Bushes—with wealth for hard work. For many young people, the moral of childhood was that anybody who struggled in the baking desert of West Texas had a good chance of striking oil, and that capitalism worked. Government was disdained, and churches and civic groups like the Community Chest looked after local needs. Business was what helped people, while government was usually reviled as something in the way.

"What's important for George W. and where he is today is that he was in an isolated environment where there was almost an anti-government streak running through the region," said Bill Minutaglio, a Texan who authored a 1999 biography of Bush. "He felt that people succeeded because they worked hard, they punched holes in the ground and won the lottery. The lesson lasted with George W. for years, and I think he truly believes that people can win the lottery if they work hard, that if they put their nose to the grindstone it'll all work out without government help or intrusion." The values of Midland sometimes seem to emerge in Bush's talk of "compassionate conservatism" and "faith-based initiatives"—that is what his childhood was all about.

Bush has often said that "the biggest difference between me and my father is that he went to Greenwich Country Day and I went to San Jacinto Junior High (in Midland)." That is an exaggeration of the younger Bush's populist credentials, because he is also a product of Andover, Yale, and Harvard. But there is still something to it. The father, chauffeured to and from the private school in Connecticut, suffered politically because of the perception that he was a blue blood who could not relate to ordinary people and their ordinary lives; a famous 1992 news story related Bush's perceived surprise at encountering a supermarket scanner. The younger Bush had a much more ordinary childhood, biking around in jeans and a white T-shirt, and it left him with a common touch that is one of his greatest assets as a politician.

Midland is not the kind of place, though, that generates a lot of postcards. Even its residents, searching for a kind analogy, think of "moonscape." Oil made it a boomtown, attracting ambitious businessmen like the elder Bush and many other out-of-staters as well. Midland had a large proportion of geologists, engineers, lawyers, and accountants, and Ivy

League college graduates were everywhere at the country club. George W. recalls it in Norman Rockwell pastels, and so do many other citizens. Kids bicycled everywhere on their own, crime was almost nonexistent, and if anyone suspicious—say, someone with a beard—showed up in town, then Sheriff Ed Darnell (known as Big Ed) would stop him, escort him to the edge of town, and tell him to get out.

Midland was also rigidly segregated in those days. The town was mostly white, but black children went to their own school rather than to Sam Houston Elementary. The bus station and train station had separate waiting rooms for blacks and whites, and there were different drinking fountains marked "colored" at the stations and at the courthouse. Racial slurs were routine, and Bush picked up the habit of using them as a boy. Once when he was about seven years old he let one slip in his living room in front of his mother, Barbara. She grabbed George by the ear, pulled him into the bathroom, and washed his mouth out with soap as he spluttered indignantly. "His family was probably the only one around that didn't use racial slurs," said Michael Proctor, who lived across the street. "I probably didn't realize it was wrong until I saw that."

By all accounts, life was idyllic, although there was one terrible interruption: in 1953, when George was seven, his younger sister Robin died of leukemia. The loss staggered the elder Bushes, and some writers have described the episode as a crucial turning point that profoundly shaped young George's personality, forcing him to be funny and goofy to help his family get over the grief. It is an interesting and plausible theory, but childhood friends do not remember it that way. They say that Bush recovered relatively quickly, seemed little changed, and in the long run was emotionally unscathed. He has spoken only rarely to friends about his sister's death.

In the summer after Bush finished the seventh grade, the Bush family moved from Midland to Houston, a wrenching transfer for young George. From the nurturing cocoon of rustic Midland, George found himself in the much more competitive world of urban Houston. Things started off poorly when George was rejected by St. John's, the best private school in the city. (During the 2000 presidential campaign, an older acquaintance recalled the rejection, but in an interview, then-Governor Bush said he knew nothing of this. Later, after checking with his parents, he went out of his way to confirm—without any apparent embarrassment—that he had indeed been rejected.) Instead, George W. attended the Kinkaid School, another top-flight private school, for the eighth and ninth grades.

Andover and Yale

Houston seemed to touch his soul much less than Midland had, and in any case, it was understood in the family that George would be attending Phillips Academy in Andover, the Massachusetts prep school where his father had compiled a splendid record a generation earlier. Andover was far more competitive than St. John's, however, and a magazine article from that time says that 80 percent of Andover applicants were then being turned down. It seems unlikely that George would have been admitted to Andover entirely on his own merits.

But he did not need to be. It was at this juncture that he first got a helping hand from the kind of affirmative action that, particularly in those days, helped many wealthy blue-blood offspring. The Andover admissions process calculated a numeric score for each applicant, ranging from 4 to 20, and then gave a three-point bonus to any son of an Andover graduate. This may diminish young George's achievement in getting into Andover, but it does not take it away entirely. Even among sons of Andover graduates, fewer than half were admitted at that time. Bush says he has no recollection of his grades at Kinkaid, but a friend from that time says he was an A student, and it was those grades and his activities as a class officer and athlete that, along with the fact that he was George Bush's son, put him over the top at Andover.

The adjustment to Andover in the tenth grade was a rough one for young George. At Andover, George's first grade on an essay (about his sister's death from leukemia) was a zero, boldly written in red ink along with the teacher's scrawled comment: "disgraceful." Clay Johnson, a fellow Texan in the class of '64, recalled of Andover: "It was a shocking experience. It was far away from home and rigorous, and scary and demanding. The buildings looked different, and the days were shorter. We went from being at the top of our classes academically to struggling to catch up. We were so much less prepared than kids coming from Massachusetts or New York."

Yet despite the pressure, young George seems to have remained remarkably sunny. Classmates remember him as cheerful and exuberant. When snow began falling in October of his first year, he bounded outside in excitement to catch the snowflakes and try to gather enough for a snowball. "My memory of living with George was that it was probably the funniest year of my life," recalled Donald E. Vermeil, a roommate. Andover was rife with cliques, and George fell into the jock crowd, which was disproportionately made up of boys from beyond the Northeast. Those who played basketball, baseball, or football remember George as moderately talented but scrappy—sometimes excessively so. Once the coach had to pull him out of a basketball game when he became angered at a referee's call and hurled the ball at an opposing player. Yet there was one important area where young George did excel: people skills. It was in high school that he first seemed to cultivate them and exhibit them, using wisecracking showmanship to carve out an identity for himself, an identity that is more subdued today but otherwise intact.

Bush in his stump speeches today comes across not as a policy maven or intellectual but as motivated rather by somewhat hazy ideals, optimism and a yearning to "lift the spirit of America," as he puts it. In all this, there is perhaps an echo of the boy at Andover who long ago finally found his niche by building coalitions across cliques and lifting the spirits of his school. In an institution that respected brains and brawn—excellence in the classroom and on the athletic field—George overflowed with neither. He was a mediocre student and no more than a decent athlete, and he paled in comparison to his father and namesake, who had been excellent at everything he did. Yet in the end, George found alternative ways to claim the stage and become popular. Against the odds, he emerged by force of personality as a significant figure on campus. No one thought of George W. Bush as a future politician, and he seemed oblivious to the civil rights struggle and other issues of the day. But he worked hard to remember everybody's name and managed to worm his way into the limelight. Very early on, he demonstrated one of the most fundamental political skills: the ability to make people feel good. "You can definitely see the germination of leadership there, even though the activity was not anything you would call political," Randall Roden, a childhood friend of George who also attended Andover, told The New York Times. "He was learning those skills, or perfecting them, at Andover."

George was chosen head cheerleader, which gave him a chance to ham it up in front of crowds. More than cheerleading, though, George's claim to fame at Andover was organizing an intramural stickball program. At the weekly assembly in April of his senior year, George stood up and announced the formation of a new stickball league. He was wearing a top hat like a circus showman, and instead of a brief announcement, he offered a twenty-minute speech that had much of the audience in stitches. As his time at Andover wound to a close, George fretted among friends about the pressure to get into Yale, which his father and grandfather had attended, and he hit the books largely with that goal in mind. The dean looked over George's transcript and college boards and then suggested in a kindly way that he apply to some less competitive colleges in addition to Yale. So George applied to the University of Texas as his "safe school," but in the end Yale accepted him.

Yale, like Andover, gave a helping hand to alumni sons in the admission process—far more than now—and it seems unlikely that Bush would have been admitted into Yale otherwise. There were no class rankings at Andover, but George never made honor roll even one term, unlike 110 boys in his class. His SAT scores were 566 for the verbal part and 640 for math. Those were far below the median scores for students admitted to his class at Yale: 668 verbal and 718 math. As he graduated from Andover, George was not a finalist in voting for "most likely to succeed," "most respected," "politico," or any of the other main categories. But, in a reflection of his people skills, he did come in second for "big man on campus."

At Yale, George W. Bush distinguished himself primarily as a hard partier, and he managed to be detained by police twice during his university years: once for stealing a Christmas wreath as a fraternity prank and once for trying to tear down the goalposts during a football game at Princeton. Those episodes underscored Bush's approach to rebellion in the 1960s: At a time when university students denounced police as "pigs," Bush stood with the establishment (yet still got himself arrested for pranks). Pressed at Yale to take sides in the great battles then unfolding over politics, civil rights, drugs, and music, Bush mostly was a noncombatant in those great upheavals, but when forced to choose he ultimately retreated to the values and ideals established by his parents' generation. In short, while some students took to the barricades, Bush took to the bar.

Unlike others of his generation including Bill Clinton, Bush never wore his hair long, agonized over Vietnam, wrestled with existentialism, or cranked up Rolling Stones songs to annoy his parents (instead of hard rock music, he listened to soul).

Many young people of privilege who came of age during the 1960s began to question the system and their own values; Bush seems to have grasped his more tightly than ever. He may have broken the law, but he never questioned it. And today, much of his underlying political philosophy rests on the belief that the nation still needs to reverse the psychology of permissiveness and liberalism that began to take root in the country in the late 1960s.

Bush's transcript at Yale shows that he was a solid C student. Although a history major, he sampled widely in the social sciences and did poorly in political science and economics while achieving some of his best grades (the equivalent of a B+) in philosophy and anthropology. The transcript indicates that in Bush's freshman year, the only year for which rankings were available, he was in the twenty-first percentile of his class—meaning that four-fifths of the students were above him. Yet at the same time that he was earning Cs at Yale, Bush displayed a formidable intelligence in another way. At his induction into the Delta Kappa Epsilon (DKE) fraternity, he and others were asked to name all fifty-four pledges in the room. Most were were able to name only five or six. When it was Bush's turn, he named every single one. Later he rose to become president of DKE, and he was also tapped into Skull and Bones, an elite secret society to which his father had also belonged.

Back to Texas

After graduating from Yale in 1968, Bush moved back to Texas and joined the Air National Guard. Bush has said that he wanted to learn how to fly, and the position had another merit: it kept him away from the war in Vietnam. There are many murky aspects to Bush's service in the Air National Guard, and critics believe that his family pulled strings to get him the position and that once in he did not complete his requirements. He denies the charges and insists that he applied for a program that could have sent him to Vietnam as a pilot; in fact, his plane was being phased out, and there was almost no chance that his application would be accepted.

What followed were what Bush has called his "nomadic years," when he partied hard, held a series of jobs, showed little ambition, drank too much, and worried his parents. In one incident, he drank before driving and—when reproached by his father—challenged the elder Bush to a fight. He applied to law school at the University of Texas and was rejected, but Harvard Business School accepted him. And so in the fall of 1973 he moved to Cambridge, Massachusetts, and buckled down to study. This seems to have been a turning point, for afterward he seemed to settle down to some degree and worked reasonably hard in his studies.

After graduating from Harvard Business School in 1975—he is the first president with an MBA—Bush moved back to his childhood stomping ground in Midland, Texas, and entered the oil business. He worked hard, impressed people, and lived so frugally that, according to his friends,his bed was held together with an old necktie. Friends set him up with a young woman whom he had been dimly acquainted with in the seventh grade, Laura Welch, and after a whirlwind courtship, they were married on 5 November 1977. Instead of a honeymoon, they set off together on Bush's next project, to run for an open congressional seat.

Bush campaigned hard and did well in winning the Republican nomination against a prominent local man who had run two years earlier. But in the general election, Bush found himself matched against a popular state senator, Kent Hance, who was from the more northern populous part of the district and who portrayed Bush as an alien from Yankee country. At candidates' forums, Hance would tell the following yarn: As he was working in a field along a rural road, Hance saw Bush driving along in a Mercedes. Bush rolled down the window and asked for directions to a certain ranch. Hance gave Bush directions, telling him to turn right after the cattle guard (a metal grate, ubiquitous on rural Texas roads, that keeps livestock from straying). The yarn ends with Bush asking: "What color uniform is that cattle guard wearing?"

In retrospect, Bush ran an energetic but deeply flawed campaign. He chose a race that may have been unwinnable from the start, and then he muffed up and allowed himself to be portrayed to many voters as an overeducated phony out of touch with ordinary voters—ironically, a bit the way Bush supporters perceived Al Gore during the 2000 presidential campaign. For example, there was the television commercial Bush dreamed up to show how energetic he was: it showed him jogging on a track. In those days, joggers were about as common in West Texas as Martians, and the commercial reinforced the perception of Bush as an affable alien. "The only time folks around here go running," Hance told audiences, "is when somebody's chasing 'em."

The audio text of one of Hance's most effective radio spots is as follows: "In 1961, when Kent Hance graduated from Dimmitt High School in the Nineteenth Congressional District, his opponent George W. Bush was attending Andover Academy in Massachusetts. In 1965, when Kent Hance graduated from Texas Tech, his opponent was at Yale University. And while Kent Hance graduated from University of Texas Law School, his opponent"—the announcer's voice plunged—"get this, folks, was attending Harvard. We don't need someone from the Northeast telling us what our problems are."

When the election came, Hance defeated Bush by a solid 53 percent to 47 percent. The defeat seemed to cause Bush to lose interest in public service, but many years later when he returned to politics he remembered a lesson from that election. As Hance put it in an interview with *The New York Times:* "He wasn't going to be out-Christianed or out-good-old-boyed again. He's going to be the good old boy next door."

After the electoral defeat, Bush threw himself into the oil business. At first he called his company Arbusto (*arbusto* is Spanish for "bush"), but when times grew difficult there were too many jokes about the company going ar-BUST-o. So he renamed the enterprise Bush Exploration. Any assessment of his time in the oil business would be mixed: he proved effective at recruiting investors, but had difficulty running a company profitably. Then as now, he was a brilliant fund-raiser, and through his family and father's friends he raised millions of dollars to drill for oil. But he never found much petroleum, and oil prices virtually collapsed, so that his investors—like many others—did poorly. Bush raised $4.67 million from his limited partners, but his company returned only $1.55 million in distributions (plus hefty tax write-offs). Meanwhile, Bush structured the deals in part to give himself certain financial advantages: His longtime friend and accountant, Robert A. McCleskey, says that his net worth rose from $50,000 in 1975 to more than $1 million by 1988.

But those were tough years for the oil business, and the strains showed in Bush's private behavior. He drank too much, and he often came across as more offensive than amusing. The "bombastic Bushkin," as friends called him, sometimes seemed out of control. While visiting the family retreat in Kennebunkport, Maine, he was cited for drunken driving, and he also managed to insult an old friend of his parents, a prim, well-dressed matron who had recently turned fifty. He wobbled up to her at a cocktail party and, according to a relative, asked her by way of conversation: "So, what's sex like after fifty, anyway?"

It was a vintage Bush moment, the kind that made Bush's friends laugh and cringe at the same time. He could be hilarious company, but also often outrageous and childish. Some acquaintances were offended by what they saw as Bush's arrogance and immaturity, by his penchant for drinking too much and thinking too little. Even Laura wanted him to grow up, old friends say, and by some accounts she signaled that she was so sick of his boorish behavior that she might leave him and take his twin daughters with her. Bush himself has said that he does not know whether he was an alcoholic, and old acquaintances generally concur that he was a borderline case. But he did get drunk regularly, and while he was not a mean drunk, he could be loud and obnoxious.

These pressures, instead of breaking Bush, changed him. There is no neat one-sentence explanation for how he came to terms with himself. It was a gradual process, stretching from his arrival at Harvard Business School in 1973 until after his fortieth birthday in 1986. One turning point, by Bush's own recollection, came in the summer of 1985 when he met with the evangelical religious leader Billy Graham in Kennebunkport. Bush was inspired to begin reading the Bible daily, and back in Midland he began attending a Bible study class. Ever since then, Bush's Methodist faith has been a pillar of his life. Then in July 1986, the Bushes went with a half-dozen friends to celebrate their collective fortieth birthdays at the luxurious Broadmoor Hotel resort in Colorado Springs, Colorado. On one evening, they all stayed up late, drinking a bit too merrily. The next morning, Bush woke up feeling befuddled—and quietly resolved that he would never touch alcohol again. As far as anybody knows, he never did. After that, Bush worked harder and mellowed a bit, so that while he remained mischievous he was less likely to offend people. He did better at controlling his temper. He became a better father. He grew up.

Learning About National Politics

When George H. W. Bush announced his candidacy for president in the 1988 campaign, George W. set aside his oil business and moved to Washington, D.C., to work for his father. It was his first real taste of national politics, and he both enjoyed and demonstrated a talent for it. He also learned from a master

strategist, Bush campaign manager Lee Atwater, how to woo baby boomers and how to undercut opponents. Yet one paradox stands out: Bush managed to be immersed back then in national politics while remaining largely oblivious to its substance, the policy issues. Some people get into politics because they feel passionately about certain issues; Bush joined the 1988 campaign because he felt passionately about his father. He did not push any particular agenda, and no one seems to recall instances when he of his own volition pressed for one policy or another. Likewise, as revealed by the correspondence between father and son during the elder Bush's presidency, George W. often asked his father to send autographs to Texas friends, and occasionally to consider particular people for federal jobs—but in virtually none of the letters does he suggest that his father take a particular position on an issue.

"He'd come in to a meeting with a cup"—his spittoon—"and stick out his hand with a big smile and say, 'Hi, I'm George Bush, and thanks for what you're doing for my dad,'" Richard Bond told *The New York Times*. Bond was then the national political director for the campaign. Bush won over doubters on the campaign in part by poking fun at his own role, sometimes calling himself "Maureen," because Maureen Reagan was then notorious in her father's White House for forever telling staff members what to do. He also sometimes mocked those he regarded as the more pretentious associates of his father, like Nicholas Brady, the future Treasury secretary. Bush was also deployed in the field to make speeches and press the flesh, and he impressed campaign officials with his willingness to slog through Iowa and Michigan snow to meet with groups of voters.

Bush gave the impression that he did not much like Washington, D.C. The 1988 election ended in victory for the Bushes, of course, but George almost immediately moved back to Texas. Still, he visited the White House periodically and became a troubleshooter. "He had a good sense of what wasn't going right," Alan Simpson, a longtime family friend who was then a senator from Wyoming, told *The New York Times*, "and when things weren't going right, George would suddenly be on the front porch." In particular, Bush became disenchanted with the White House chief of staff, John Sununu, and played a role in firing him.

With his father ensconced in the White House, a new opportunity came to George: running a baseball club. An old family friend, Eddie Chiles, was preparing to sell the Texas Rangers and wanted to sell to Bush—if the latter could raise the money. Bush helped put together an investor group, including an old friend from Yale, Roland Betts, and became the general partner responsible for managing the investment. As a baseball owner, Bush proved himself an outstanding manager, still remembered fondly by the players who batted for him, the fans he courted, and even by the executives he fired. Bush helped turn the Rangers into a greatly improved team, and he presided over the complex arrangements for a new ballpark, one of the finest in major-league baseball. He became a multimillionaire in the process, setting himself up financially for his run for the presidency. In one blow, he acquired not only wealth but also the resume he would need to triumph in politics.

Yet the investment was immensely profitable in part because he and his co-owners were shrewd bargainers who charmed and bullied the city of Arlington into giving them a great deal, with the local taxpayers picking up most of the cost—including more than $135 million to help build the Rangers a stadium. Bush and his fellow owners even got the local government to seize the property of landowners for a new stadium and, in effect, hand it over to the Texas Rangers so that they could make a profit on it. In such business dealings Bush displayed both savvy and vision, but critics complain that his actions at the time are hard to reconcile with his later speeches about limited government and private property rights.

Bush's path to becoming a baseball owner was remarkable, because initially he did not put up a cent of his own money. Instead, he borrowed $500,000 from United Bank of Midland, a Texas bank of which he had previously been a director, and used those funds to buy a stake in the Rangers. Bush eventually raised his investment in two stages to an eventual total of $606,000, or 1.8 percent of the team. In 1988 he and his fellow owners sold the Rangers for $250 million. It was a good deal for all the principals, but Bush did particularly well: his cut was $14.9 million.

A Popular Governor

Bush's role with the Rangers was as its public spokesman and cheerleader, and he used the position to give speeches around Texas and win friends. It was in some sense a political role, shorn of policy, and he was very good at it. Increasingly, he also began to

think of using it as a springboard to statewide office. His mother had discouraged him from running while his father was still in the White House, but as the 1994 governor's race approached, that was no longer an issue. Rather, the main concern was whether Bush had any chance to win. Ann Richards, the incumbent Democratic governor, was a national figure and media star with high popularity ratings. Yet Bush, against the advice of friends and family, took her on and ran an artful race.

Richards, who knew that Bush had had problems with his temper, tried to aggravate her opponent into self-destruction by needling him and belittling him as a dull-witted Daddy's boy who never accomplished anything on his own. But Bush simply grinned when Richards goaded him as a "shrub" and a "jerk." One of Bush's insights was that while Texans liked Richards as a person, they often did not agree with her. And so he ran an exceptionally focused, tightly disciplined campaign that hammered home his themes day after day: a tougher juvenile justice system to reduce crime, better schools, tighter restrictions on welfare, and new limits on tort suits.

In the heat of the campaign, Bush went dove hunting, with some thirty reporters in tow. A bird flew up, he blasted away with his shotgun, and proudly held up the prize for the news photographers. The reporters pointed out that he had shot not a dove, but a protected songbird known as the killdee. Bush promptly confessed, paid a $130 fine, and began his news conference that afternoon by saying: "Thank goodness it wasn't deer season. I might have shot a cow." The humor and discipline of the campaign worked: Bush defeated Richards with a healthy 54 percent of the vote. Almost immediately, as the Republican governor of a major state, as a man with a formidable war chest and superb political connections, he was regarded as a national figure.

Bush went out of his way in Texas to work with Democrats and to build bridges with groups that he had offended in his gubernatorial run. During the campaign, Bush had told a reporter of his own belief that the path to Heaven comes from acceptance of Jesus as one's personal savior. Some non-Christians, particularly Jews, were upset that Bush was effectively consigning them to hell. One of the first things he did after becoming governor was to meet a group of Jewish leaders in Houston and soothe the ruffled feelings. Likewise, from the beginning Bush worked exceptionally closely with the Democratic kingmaker of Texas, Bob Bullock, who was nearing the end of his career and came to look on Bush as a protégé and close friend. This spirit of bipartisan cooperation was one of the most striking features of Bush's years as governor, and it maximized his effectiveness.

Bush did not appear to put in long hours as governor—he typically went home at 5:00 P.M. and allocated only fifteen minutes to review death penalty cases and decide whether or not to grant a stay of execution, according to detailed schedules of the governor's time obtained by *The New York Times* under the Texas freedom of information law. But he dominated the legislative agenda, won an education reform package, and attempted unsuccessfully to pass an even more far-reaching tax-restructuring proposal. He also became steadily more popular, and by 1996 he was being mentioned as a potential presidential contender for 2000. In the summer of 1997, one of his aides, Karen Hughes, informed him that there had been an opinion poll of potential Republican candidates for the 2000 race. "You're leading," she told him.

The prospect of a presidential race depended on Bush winning reelection as governor in 1998, and this he did by a landslide. He won 68 percent of the vote and became the first Texas governor reelected to a second consecutive four-year term. Once he was reelected, Bush turned to the question of the presidency and began grappling with what friends say were his two main concerns: his family and his past. Associates say that his wife Laura and his twin girls, who were in high school when he was governor, were not exactly opposed to him running, but that they worried about what the race would mean for their privacy. The girls, the more studious Barbara and the more outgoing Jenna, already were sensitive to the impact on their lives of having a prominent politician as a father.

Bush was also reluctant to face the scrutiny of his past that is the fate of any presidential candidate. Already, he was facing persistent questioning about drug use—he declined to say whether he had used illegal drugs, but his circumlocutions seemed to suggest that he had—and he had never disclosed his arrest for drunken driving in Maine.

Yet in the end Bush did run, and from the beginning he was the overwhelming favorite, both in polls and in fund-raising. His strength extinguished some candidacies in their infancy—like those of Elizabeth Dole, Dan Quayle, and Lamar Alexander—and so his

main rivals in the Republican primaries were Gary Bauer, Steve Forbes, Orrin Hatch, Alan Keyes, and John McCain. Of these, McCain was the only one who had a chance, appealing to a mix of liberals and conservatives alike with his background as a war hero and his calls for campaign finance reform. In contrast to McCain's dynamism, Bush initially ran a hesitant campaign in which he was perceived by voters as aloof and somewhat arrogant. The result was a crushing defeat in the New Hampshire primary on 1 February 2000, with Bush getting just 31 percent to McCain's 49 percent.

After New Hampshire, Bush refurbished his campaign, seizing the reformer label from McCain and becoming far more energetic. He went out of his way to cultivate reporters, whom he had previously seemed to disdain, and he charged into the fray and recovered his footing. Steadily Bush gained states in his column for the Republican nomination, including a decisive win in South Carolina on 19 February and again in nine more states on Super Tuesday, 7 March. By then Bush was effectively the Republican nominee, but the animosity between his staff and McCain's took months to ease.

Bush had asked Dick Cheney, his father's secretary of defense, to lead the effort to find a running mate, but in the end Bush chose Cheney himself to be the vice presidential candidate. It was politically an odd choice, for Cheney was, like Bush, a Texas oilman and did not bring new geographic support to the ticket, but Cheney did bring solidity and experience to the ticket.

The Republican convention in Philadelphia, 31 July to 3 August, was a milestone for the Bush campaign. It sought to reassure the nation that Bush was a centrist, rather than the hard-line conservative depicted by the Democrats, and inclusiveness was a constant theme. Some speeches were given in Spanish, and the large number of African Americans who appeared on the podium led some comedians to joke that the event looked like a Black Entertainment Network broadcast. At the end, Bush gave perhaps the finest speech of his career until that point, a warm and visionary talk that praised President Clinton's talents but suggested that they had been used for no great purpose. Bush managed to raise issues of moral leadership without sounding shrill, and he called for cooperation with Democrats to address traditional Democratic issues like poverty and education. Republicans, he said, are "not the party of repose, but the party of reform." He declared: "We will extend the promise of prosperity to every forgotten corner of this country: to every man and woman, a chance to succeed; to every child, a chance to learn; and to every family, a chance to live with dignity and hope."

The campaign against then-Vice President Al Gore unfolded largely as expected and was tight all the way. Gore's political strength was that he was an incumbent of sorts at a time when the United States was enjoying the longest economic boom in its history, but he also came across as wooden and, to some, as shifty and untrustworthy. Bush was far less knowledgeable about policy issues (he famously mixed up Slovakia and Slovenia, among other lapses), but he impressed many voters as honest and amiable. In a series of campaign debates that perhaps made the difference, he came across to many voters as more knowledgeable than they had expected, while Gore did poorly.

The Bush Presidency

The result was an election that in effect was a tie. Gore won the popular vote but was one vote short in the electoral college of the majority he needed. And with all the other states decided, it was clear that the outcome of the presidential election would depend on Florida, where Bush had the slenderest of leads. After furious rounds of recounting, haggling in the courts and in the media, Florida's secretary of state certified that Bush had won the state. There were indications, though, that more people had tried to vote for Gore in Florida than had tried to vote for Bush, but that enough of their votes were set aside for mistakes (such as punching the wrong hole, or double punching) that Bush had a slight edge. As the battle over whether to recount entered the courts, the dispute was ultimately resolved by the U.S. Supreme Court, which on 12 December 2000 decided—by a 5 to 4 vote on the key issue—that further counting would be impractical and unfair. In effect, the White House was Bush's.

Gore conceded the next day, and Bush accepted the presidency in a speech on 13 December in the Texas House of Representatives—chosen, he said, as a symbol of bipartisan cooperation. "After a difficult election, we must put politics behind us and work together to make the promise of America available for every one of our citizens," he declared. "I am optimistic that we can change the tone in Washington, D.C. I believe things happen for a reason, and I hope

the long wait of the last five weeks will heighten a desire to move beyond the bitterness and partisanship of the recent past."

That did not happen, at least not immediately. Many Democrats were outraged, feeling that the election had been stolen from them. But Bush continued to reach out, and in his inaugural address he sounded again the theme of inclusiveness: "While many of our citizens prosper, others doubt the promise, even the justice, of our own country. The ambitions of some Americans are limited by failing schools and hidden prejudice and the circumstances of their birth. And sometimes our differences run so deep, it seems we share a continent, but not a country. We do not accept this, and we will not allow it." And Bush, always much more welcoming to immigrants than other elements in the Republican Party, added that every immigrant "makes our country more, not less, American."

Upon taking office, Bush selected aides who were generally respected for their experience and competence and who in some cases came from the corporate world: Paul O'Neill, who had been chairman and CEO of the world's largest aluminum manufacturer, Alcoa, was chosen treasury secretary. Politically, the cabinet ranged from John Ashcroft, the conservative attorney general who survived a bitter fight over his nomination, to Norman Mineta, a Democrat, as transportation secretary. Many key figures in the government were recycled from the earlier Bush administration, although there was no evidence that the first President Bush himself played a crucial role in policy formation. Colin Powell, as secretary of state, and Donald Rumsfeld, as secretary of defense, both came across as surprisingly weak until the terror attacks of 11 September—after which they assumed enormous importance. George Tenet, the CIA director, became a close adviser, briefing the president in person for twenty to thirty minutes each morning (he had given Clinton, by contrast, a written daily briefing). But the crucial adviser, in many cases, was Karl Rove, Bush's longtime political strategist. When opposition grew to U.S. military bombing exercises on the Puerto Rican island of Vieques, for example, the Pentagon opposed conciliation, for fear of losing an important site for target practice. But with Hispanics an increasingly important constituency, Bush sided with Rove and announced that the bombing would eventually be halted.

Bush's early focus of attention was the tax cut, and he was successful in getting a landmark cut through Congress. This lowered the top personal rate from 39.6 percent to 33 percent, and started the country on a path toward eventual elimination of the estate tax, a tax on assets held by an individual at the time of death (though this of course could be changed by future Congresses). He also pushed for "faith-based" programs to administer social services, and helped put the issue on the national agenda. Bush was unable to get Congress to institute a system of educational vouchers, in which as an alternative to keeping their children in failing public schools, parents could redeem vouchers to help pay for private or parochial school tuition. As part of his plan for educational reform, however, Bush was able to push through legislation requiring mandatory yearly testing of students in grades three through eight, as a way of making schools accountable for their children's proficiency in reading, math, and science.

One of the toughest issues he faced in his first summer was whether to approve federal funding for research on embryonic stem cells. Proponents urged that stem cells offered immense promise in treating a broad range of diseases, while critics—many of them on the Right—noted that extraction of stem cells destroyed the embryo and a potential human life. Bush discussed the issue widely with aides and outsiders and ultimately came down in the middle. He declared that federal funding of stem cell research would continue, but only for existing stem cells—extracted for the purpose of in vitro fertilization and stored in labs—that otherwise would be destroyed. It was a nuanced position that, while attacked by some on both sides of the issue, seemed to win respect among many in the middle of the road.

Rather less successfully, Bush pushed for a sweeping new energy policy that would put emphasis on increasing production. His assumption of office coincided with a series of power shortages in California, and he argued that the only way to address the power crunch was to increase drilling. In particular, he called for drilling in the Arctic National Wildlife Refuge in Alaska. But these proposals made little headway, and polls found voters deeply suspicious that Bush was too close to big oil and too prepared to destroy the environment. After Enron, a multi-billion dollar energy company headquartered in Houston, collapsed into bankruptcy at the end of 2001, the Bush administration was also embarrassed by the close ties between the company and senior

Bush aides, and between the president and Kenneth Lay, the former chairman of Enron.

Foreign relations were initially a mixed bag, reflecting Bush's lack of confidence in foreign affairs. After initial missteps, he generally was credited with sound handling of his first crisis, the collision in April 2001 of an American spy plane and a Chinese fighter jet off the southern coast of China. The American plane made an emergency landing on the Chinese island of Hainan, but eventually the Bush administration won the return of both the crew and the plane. Bush was given high marks by political analysts for his first overseas trip, to Europe in June, but he benefited from the fact that expectations had been low. He charmed some audiences, but also left many allies infuriated by his insistence on two points: abandoning the Kyoto Protocol to curb global warming, and continuation with America's national missile defense system even if it meant U.S. withdrawal from the Anti-Ballistic Missile Treaty, which had been signed with the Soviet Union in 1972. The Bush administration gave further evidence of its doubts about multilateralism by opposing a treaty establishing an International Criminal Court, by threatening to withdraw from a July 2001 United Nations conference that sought to devise a treaty on small arms trafficking, by rejecting enforcement measures for the 1972 Biological Weapons Convention, and by declining to send a senior delegation to the United Nations World Conference Against Racism in Durban, South Africa. *The Economist* of London, which generally took a pro-Bush stance, asked in its pages on 28 July 2001: "Has George Bush ever met a treaty that he liked?"

In his approach to the presidency, Bush closely followed the Clinton model of constantly campaigning. While he left details of his first budget to others, Bush traveled frequently around the country, making campaign-style appearances to promote his policies. He devoted less attention to states like California and New York that would probably be unwinnable in 2004 and focused on crucial states that might go either way in a reelection fight. Yet for all the energy he showed as a campaigner for his policies, he was not nearly as intricately involved in policy development as Clinton had been, and Bush often took off on Friday afternoons to head for Camp David or his beloved ranch near Waco, Texas. Bush made some inroads with Congress, but his policy there failed catastrophically in one sense, when control of the Senate passed to the Democratic Party due to Senator Jeffords' abandonment of the Republicans.

One of Bush's first challenges was an economic slowdown, and ultimately his reelection prospects may depend on his handling of it. He presented the sagging economy as a problem that he inherited, and in large part he was right: the extraordinary high-tech bubble, which left markets and the real economy buoyant, peaked in the spring of 2000 and steadily deflated after that. Bush sold his tax cut partly as an antidote to the economic weakness, and many economists approved of the tax rebates (up to $600 for a couple) that were sent out in the summer and fall of 2001 and that offered a fiscal stimulus. At the same time, the markets were unnerved by the prospect that America's tremendous progress on reducing the federal debt might be coming apart.

Bush insisted that the tax cut would not threaten the Social Security part of the budget surplus. But he had to tweak accounting rules and come up with very optimistic projections to avoid delving into those retirement funds. In contrast, the Congressional Budget Office, which is nonpartisan, projected that substantial amounts would have to come out of the Social Security surplus between 2001 and 2004. Bush presented the tumbling budget surpluses as desirable—a straitjacket that would prevent Congress from squandering taxpayer money—but they also meant less money available for his priorities, such as education and military spending. And if the United States slips off its sound fiscal track of the mid- to late-1990s, that would be a far-reaching legacy that would force fundamental rethinking within the Bush administration about its priorities.

Six months after taking office, Bush had an approval rating in a Gallup Poll of 57 percent. That was better than the comparable Clinton figure of 41 percent and impressive considering the tumultuous, controversial way in which he had assumed office. But it was well behind the figures for predecessors including his father, Ronald Reagan, Jimmy Carter, Richard Nixon, and John F. Kennedy (who had the highest six-month approval rating, 75 percent).

Responding to Terrorism

Bush's initial response to the attacks on the World Trade Center was inauspicious. He seemed shaken and halting in his first statement, at 9:30 A.M., shortly after stepping out of the classroom in Sarasota. He described the incidents as "an apparent terrorist attack" and vowed "to hunt down and to find those folks who committed this act." The Secret Service then rushed Bush onto Air Force One, and the presidential jet roared off into the sky without delay, headed for Washington.

Once on the plane, according to the *Washington Post,* Bush told aides: "That's what we're paid for, boys. When we find out who did this, they are not going to like me as president. Somebody is going to pay."

Meanwhile, Washington was in chaos. When the Secret Service learned that an airplane was barreling toward the White House, agents burst into the vice president's office, grabbing him by the arms and belt and rushing him downstairs into an underground bunker built to withstand a nuclear blast. Staff were evacuated from key government buildings, with women in the White House and Eisenhower Executive Office Building told to take off their high heels and run for their lives to Lafayette Park. Aides were told to remove the security badges from around their necks, in case snipers were posted to shoot them. Top aides were in the bunker, but it was poorly prepared and at first the audio did not work on the televisions.

The plane that had been thought headed for the White House ultimately crashed into the Pentagon, but now another airplane was detected heading for Washington. Bush, traveling on Air Force One, and Cheney briefly discussed what to do, and Bush gave the order for the Air Force to shoot down passenger planes if necessary. Soon afterward, the second plane heading for Washington, United Flight 93, went down in Pennsylvania. Bush asked, "Did we shoot it down or did it crash?" According to a lengthy reconstruction of 11 September and its aftermath by Bob Woodward and Dan Balz in the *Washington Post,* no one could answer him. (Eventually, it turned out that passengers had fought with the hijackers, causing the plane to crash).

False and exaggerated reports added to the alarm. There were accounts of explosions at the Capitol and State Department, of many more planes hijacked and headed for Washington. Transportation Secretary Mineta ordered all airplanes across the United States down at once, but that took hours to implement. Meanwhile, a phone threat came in to the White House against Air Force One, and because of a mistake in relaying the message it was believed erroneously that the caller had used the plane's code word, "Angel." The term gave the threat credibility, suggesting some knowledge of security procedures, and the Pentagon scrambled fighters to escort Air Force One.

President Bush relied heavily on trusted advisers such as national security adviser Condoleezza Rice in the wake of 11 September 2001. AP/WIDE WORLD PHOTOS

Cheney and Bush's national security adviser, Condoleezza Rice, both urged the president not to return to Washington, citing continuing security concerns. Air Force One eventually landed at Barksdale Air Force Base in Louisiana, where it was immediately surrounded by U.S. troops carrying machine guns. Reporters on the plane were prohibited from describing the location. Bush made a brief television appearance shortly before 1:00 P.M., reading a two-minute statement and taking no questions. His eyes were red-rimmed, he mispronounced words, and the tape of the appearance was jumpy and grainy. "The resolve of our great nation is being tested," he declared.

Soon afterward, Bush was in flight on Air Force One again, this time headed for Offutt Air Force Base in Nebraska, which had an underground bunker and first-rate communications capabilities. While en route, he called his father; on finding out that the former president was in Milwaukee, George W. asked: "What are you doing in Milwaukee?"

"You grounded my plane," his father replied.

Once at Offutt, President Bush convened a teleconference meeting of the National Security Council and then insisted on returning to Washington. There had been a growing chorus of grumbling by politicians, even some Republicans, at the fact that the president was fleeing west when the East Coast was under attack, at his failure to offer a constant reassuring presence to the American public. The Secret Service resisted Bush's desire to return to Washington, but his political aides strongly agreed that he needed to address the nation from the Oval Office. On the evening of 11 September Bush flew back to Washington, arriving at the White House at 7:00 P.M. and addressing the nation live at 8:30.

"None of us will ever forget this day," he declared, "yet we go forward to defend freedom and all that is good and just in the world." He then outlined what came to be regarded as the Bush doctrine: "We will make no distinction between the terrorists who committed these acts and those who harbor them." Even Bush's advisers acknowledged that the speech fell flat, out of tune with the historic nature of the day. But Bush at least conveyed that he was back at the White House, back in command. And from then on, he seemed to regain his footing and sound the right notes in reassuring the nation and responding to the terrorist challenge.

Evidence immediately accumulated that Osama bin Laden and Al Qaida ("The Base"), a radical Islamist terrorist organization, were responsible for the attacks. For years the United States had pursued bin Laden for suspected involvement in terrorist activities; the wealthy Saudi exile had found refuge in Taliban-run Afghanistan. That evening, President Bush and his National Security Council decided to apply all possible pressure on Afghanistan—and its backer, Pakistan—to hand over bin Laden. Otherwise, the United States would use its armed forces to go into Afghanistan itself.

On the morning of 12 September, when Bush and his aides met in the White House Situation Room, Tenet presented the outlines of what would become the strategy in Afghanistan: bomb Taliban positions heavily, send in CIA officers and special forces to bolster the Northern Alliance that had feebly been battling the Taliban, and arm and organize the Alliance so that it could function as a proxy ground force. Also that morning, Bush read a statement that escalated the stakes. "The deliberate and deadly attacks which were carried out yesterday against our country were more than acts of terror," he declared. "They were acts of war.... This will be a monumental struggle between good and evil. But good will prevail."

The speech was much more effective than his previous public appearances, and Bush followed it up with meetings with the congressional leadership and with phone calls with foreign leaders. He asked for and received support from heads of state the world over. Even Russia and China, which normally were anxious about American military deployments near their borders, gave Bush surprisingly strong backings. Indeed, Russian President Vladimir Putin used 9/11 to cement a warmer, more cooperative relationship with the United States, one that was remarkably little disturbed even when Bush announced that he would withdraw from the Anti-Ballistic Missile Treaty. Likewise, the Bush administration—which had its share of hard-liners who saw China as the major long-term threat to the United States—ended up working closely with Chinese leaders and ushering in a period of civility between Washington and Beijing.

The days and weeks following 11 September were wrenching for American citizens, and Bush—who has a deep emotional streak—was no exception. A reporter asked him in front of television cameras on 13 September about his prayers and thoughts, and he struggled to collect himself as he answered: "Well, I don't think about myself right now. I think about the families, the children." His eyes flooded with tears, and he paused. "I am a loving guy, and I am also someone, however, who has got a job to do, and I intend to do it." Bush later said: "Presidents don't particularly like to cry in front of the American public, particularly in the Oval Office, but nevertheless I did." He added, quite rightly, that his "mood reflected the country in many ways."

On the following day, Bush presided over a prayer service at the National Cathedral in Washington, D.C., with three former presidents, much of the Congress, and many other leaders in attendance. At Bush's insistence, a Muslim cleric had also been invited to speak, to underscore that this was not to be a war against Islam. Bush delivered a speech prepared by his most poetic speechwriter, Michael Gerson, and for the first time he hit all the notes perfectly. "We are here in the middle hour of our grief," he began, and he tried to comfort and console the nation. But, although the setting was a house of worship, he also delivered what was close to a declaration of war: "This conflict was begun on the

President Bush stands atop a burnt fire truck at the site of the World Trade Center three days after terrorists hijacked two commercial airliners and slammed them into the towers. Bush toured the wreckage and exhorted rescue workers. AP/WIDE WORLD

timing and terms of others. It will end in a way, and at a time, of our choosing."

On 20 September, Bush spoke to a joint session of Congress to outline his plans. Fighter aircraft circled overhead to defend the Capitol, and some 80 million Americans watched on television. An exhibition professional hockey game in Philadelphia was suspended so that fans could watch the speech on the stadium's screens. Bush delivered a powerful speech that won overwhelming support. He urged Americans to "hug your children" and touched all the emotional bases, but he also outlined a new kind of struggle against global terrorism as a whole, not just against Al Qaida. "Americans should not expect one battle but a lengthy campaign, unlike any other we have ever seen. It may include dramatic strikes visible on TV, and covert operations, secret even in success." He also gave a pledge: "I will not yield. I will not rest. I will not relent in waging this struggle for freedom and security for the American people."

When the Taliban did not respond to Bush's ultimatum—give up bin Laden and end support for Al Qaida—the United States moved quickly to bolster the Northern Alliance and begin bombing targets. At first the fighting was anemic, and for a time there were ominous articles in the American press about an emerging "quagmire." But then supplies worked their way to the forces on the ground and, most helpfully, American Special Forces arrived in Afghanistan to guide the bombing. The result was that the Taliban began to crumble and retreat from northern cities. And once they began to retreat they kept going. There was never a battle in the contested capital city of Kabul; the Taliban fled in the middle of the night.

European and Arab grumbling about the bombing subsided to some degree with the victory in Afghanistan, partly because of scenes of elated Afghans celebrating their newfound freedoms. And the victory itself was a remarkable achievement for the Pentagon. While small numbers of American troops died in friendly fire and in accidents during the liberation of Afghanistan from Taliban control, only a few soldiers were killed by enemy fire (along with one CIA officer). The United States quickly oversaw the installation of a new interim government, led by Hamid Karzai, handpicked by Washington.

The first few months in the war on terrorism had gone remarkably well. But then the picture grew more complex. Osama bin Laden remained at large, along with the Taliban leader, Mullah Muhammad Omar, and Bush administration officials grew increasingly frustrated at the inability to track them down. There was also no immediate success in finding and prosecuting the perpetrator of a series of mailed anthrax attacks in Washington, New York, and Florida, although the FBI came to conclude that the person was probably an American rather than a foreigner. Another attempted attack on a U.S. airliner, in December 2001 by a man with a bomb of plastic explosives built into his shoe, was foiled but reminded Americans of their vulnerability.

There was also a vigorous debate about how to deal with Taliban and Al Qaida prisoners from Afghanistan. President Bush proposed the creation of military tribunals, and he also oversaw the transfer of prisoners from Afghanistan to the U.S. naval base at Guantanamo, Cuba, where they could be interrogated without the protections that would apply if they were on American soil. The administration initially asserted that the Third Geneva Convention, on prisoners of war, would not apply to them, but after an uproar in Europe—and a lesser one in the Pentagon, which did not want precedents that could harm Americans taken prisoner—the White House said that the conventions would apply, but that in any case none of the captured were prisoners of war.

Coverage of the war on terror also became more skeptical. Reporters in Afghanistan began writing about cases in which Americans apparently bombed the wrong targets, killing civilians. After Pentagon officials boasted that they had killed a man whose height made it possible that he was the six-foot-four-inch bin Laden, reporters confirmed that the man was not bin Laden but an impoverished Afghan trying to make ends meet collecting scrap metal. Another raid, initially described by the Pentagon as successful, turned out to have killed anti-Taliban fighters and to have seized guns that had already been confiscated and stockpiled. Afghanistan began to show the strains of rivalries, and there was growing pressure on Washington to provide troops for an international security force in the major cities.

The United States expanded the war on terror by sending troops to the southern Philippines, ostensibly to train Filipino soldiers in counterterrorism techniques. In practice, there were some signs that the Americans intended mainly to pursue the Islamist group Abu Sayyaf, a criminal gang that had kidnapped two Americans but that had few ties to Al Qaida. Doubts began to be raised about the Philippine venture.

By far the most controversial step was the discussion of taking on Iraq. Within a few days of 11 September, there was a push within the administration—led by Paul Wolfowitz, the deputy secretary of defense, to begin planning the overthrow of Iraqi president Saddam Hussein, a longtime adversary of the United States—especially during the 1991 Gulf War—who was known to be trying to accumulate weapons of mass destruction. The Pentagon and National Security staffs generally approved, while the State Department was alarmed at the idea. And those in the world opposed to American unilateralism watched with dismay as the Bush administration began to talk more openly about invading Iraq.

When President Bush addressed these themes in his State of the Union address in January 2002, two paradoxes were striking. First, for a man who took office often denigrated as bumbling and inarticulate, he has often been remarkably eloquent in his prepared speeches. That was evident in the first words of the address: "As we gather tonight, our nation is at war, our economy is in recession, and the civilized world faces unprecedented dangers. Yet the state of our Union has never been stronger."

Second, for a president who initially seemed relatively uninformed and uninterested in international affairs, his presidency has come to focus on matters abroad. Indeed, the most striking aspect of Bush's speech was its hawkish tone—it owed much more to the Pentagon than to the State Department—as it described an "axis of evil" consisting of Iraq, Iran, and North Korea. And, although officials said they had no plans to go after Iran or North Korea militarily, it caused jitters in Europe for what foreigners saw as its jingoism. Bush in effect expanded the list of adversaries from states that support terrorism to those that pursue covert nuclear, chemical, or biological weapons programs: "Our second goal is to prevent regimes that sponsor terror from threatening America or our friends and allies with weapons of mass destruction. Some of these regimes have been pretty quiet since 11 September. But we know their true nature. North Korea is a regime arming with missiles and weapons of mass destruction, while starving its citizens. Iran aggressively pursues these weapons and exports terror, while an unelected few repress the Iranian people's hope for freedom. Iraq continues to flaunt its hostility toward America and to support terror. The Iraqi regime has plotted to develop anthrax, and nerve gas, and nuclear weapons for over a decade.... States like these, and their terrorist allies... [are] arming to threaten the peace of the world. By seeking weapons of mass destruction, these regimes pose a grave and growing danger. They could provide these arms to terrorists, giving them the means to match their hatred. They could attack our allies or attempt to blackmail the United States. In any of these cases, the price of indifference would be catastrophic."

Bush's budget proposal included the largest increase in defense spending in two decades, allowing a push toward new kinds of weaponry and platforms in the coming decades. Other elements of government spending were tightly restrained, creating a measure of dissatisfaction. Early proposals to revise Social Security spending, by allowing workers to put their money into investment accounts, also lost momentum, because of the difficulty in winning consensus on any specific proposal. The administration's economic stimulus package also encountered difficulties, partly because of signs that the economy was recovering in the spring of 2002 on its own and partly because the dramatic decline in the fiscal picture made further tax cuts seem questionable. From an outlook of huge surpluses as far as the eye could see, allowing the complete retirement of America's debt within a dozen years, the picture changed to one of continued deficits. That was partly because of the Bush tax cuts, and partly because of the recession, but it amounted to one of the challenges for the administration in the remainder of its time in office.

This essay takes the reader only up to the State of the Union address in early 2002, and at this writing it is far too early to offer a firm assessment of President Bush. Only the most tentative summation is appropriate: He grew in the job, particularly in his handling of the events of 11 September and overseas terrorism; his public speaking improved dramatically, as a onetime bumbler gave ringing speeches that touched the nation and elevated his own standing; he was immensely popular in the aftermath of 11 September but by early 2002 there was a growing willingness at least among Democrats to criticize administration policies at home and abroad; one of his greatest achievements was an enormous tax cut, but critics charged that it would erode American economic strength and undermine his legacy. Ultimately, the Bush presidency continues to revolve around a series of paradoxes that it is too soon to resolve.

BIBLIOGRAPHY

Bill Minutaglio's biography, *First Son: George W. Bush and the Bush Family Dynasty* (New York, 1999), is excellent and objective, and covers Bush through his years as governor. Elizabeth Mitchell's biography, *W: Revenge of the Bush Dynasty* (New York, Hyperion, 2000), is also very good, particularly on the early years. Frank Bruni has written a fine, engaging and evenhanded account of Bush, focusing on the campaign: *Ambling Into History: The Unlikely Odyssey of George W. Bush* (New York, 2002). Molly Ivins and Lou Dubose authored an entertaining book focusing on Bush's years as governor. It is fiercely critical and makes no attempt to be balanced, but it is generally intelligent and factual: *Shrub: The Short but Happy Political Life of George W. Bush* (New York, 2000).

Bush's campaign biography purports to be an autobiography but was actually written by Karen

Hughes, his key aide. It is very bland but still an important source. *George W. Bush, A Charge to Keep* (New York, 1999). Occasional family letters involving George W. appear in his father's collection of letters: George Bush, *All the Best, George Bush: My Life in Letters and Other Writings* (New York, 1999). Sections on early family life also appear in a campaign book about the father that the son helped to write. It is George Bush with Doug Wead, *Man of Integrity* (Eugene, Ore., 1988).

Information about the Bush administration's reaction to the events of 11 September 2001 comes in a monumental series by Bob Woodward and Dan Balz, "Ten Days in September," *Washington Post*, running each day on the front page from 27 January to 3 February 2002. The immediate aftermath is also well covered in an article by David E. Sanger and Don Van Natta Jr., "In Four Days, a National Crisis Changes Bush's Presidency," *New York Times*, 16 September 2001. Quotations and information in this essay about Bush's handling of the terror attacks came from these articles.

In 2000, the author wrote a series of eleven biographical articles about Bush, covering the period from his childhood through his decision to run for the White House, and they appeared at intervals in *The New York Times* from 21 May through 29 October 2000. Many of the quotations and information in this essay first appeared in those articles.

The Role of First Lady: Martha Washington to Laura Bush

Betty Boyd Caroli

Martha Washington THE LIBRARY OF CONGRESS

Laura Bush AP/WIDE WORLD

EVEN before the federal capital was permanently situated on the Potomac, the president's wife had become a public personage. Martha Washington arrived in New York City one month after her husband's April 1789 inauguration to the acclaim typical of that reserved for a royal consort. On her journey north from Mount Vernon, newspapers reported on the progress of her trip, including the fact that she had been feted at a party in eastern Pennsylvania. George Washington arranged for her to make the crossing from New Jersey to Manhattan on the presidential barge, and New Yorkers lined the streets to cheer "Lady Washington" all the way to the house Congress had rented for the chief executive on Cherry Street.

Until about 1860, the role of president's wife remained largely local. Few people outside the capital city had an opportunity to observe her actions or learn about her activities. But as the city of Washington grew and the number of elected officials and government workers multiplied, the manager of the presidential household became more prominent. Magazines with national circulations began to feature articles about the president's family. As travel conditions in the United States improved, presidents ventured farther away from the capital, and when their wives accompanied them (as Lucy Hayes did on

Rutherford B. Hayes's western journey in 1880) many Americans caught their first glimpse of a president's wife, and they began to take greater interest in her activities.

While the social responsibilities of being First Lady had been apparent from the earliest days of the Republic, much about the role remained for each incumbent to define for herself. Some presidents' wives chose to maintain a distance from their husbands' jobs, while others made no secret of their wish to be involved. As more American women began to define lives for themselves outside the home, working and participating in important public decisions, the role of First Lady expanded, too. Some wives became major players in their husbands' administrations. In 1986, a major newspaper described Nancy Reagan as having achieved something like an "associate presidency"; in 1993, one magazine outlined a First Lady's accomplishments in an article titled "One Hundred Days of Hillary."

Reclusive Roles, Little Political Impact

For much of the nineteenth century, presidential wives were either unavailable to the public or unwilling to assume a prominent role. Widowed presidents and those whose wives preferred to keep a low public profile often turned to young substitutes—daughters, daughters-in-law, and nieces—to handle the social side of the office and the management of the household. The substitutes' youth (all were under thirty years old) evidently excused them from criticism for what might have been judged serious lapses in a mature matron, and the young women drew enormous admiring attention to themselves and to the presidential family.

The death of Rachel Donelson Robards Jackson, the wife of Andrew Jackson, on 22 December 1828 left a saddened president-elect who eventually called in two young women relatives to handle social duties for him. Thomas Jefferson, also a widower, had relied on a daughter to help with entertaining, but Andrew Jackson, who had no female children of his own, turned to Emily Donelson, wife of a nephew who served as the president's secretary. After Emily's death in December 1836, another niece, Sarah Yorke Jackson, wife of Andrew Jackson, Jr., the president's adopted son, helped manage the social calendar.

Martin Van Buren had been a widower for eighteen years when he took up the presidency, and he enlisted the help of his daughter-in-law Angelica Singleton Van Buren after her marriage to Abraham Van Buren in 1838. On a wedding trip to Europe, the son and daughter-in-law of the American chief executive had been treated as royalty, and when they returned to the United States and took up residence in the executive mansion, Angelica Van Buren occasionally incorporated into the president's entertaining some of the royal customs she had observed abroad. Arranging herself and a few women friends in a tableau, she invited guests to walk by and view the courtlike formation.

In March 1841, Anna Symmes Harrison delayed joining her husband, William Henry Harrison, in Washington for his inauguration, on the grounds of ill health and grief. One of the Harrisons' sons had died the previous June, and, at sixty-five years of age, Anna Harrison did not look forward to a journey from Ohio to the capital, especially a winter journey. A widowed daughter-in-law, Jane Harrison, helped manage the White House during the brief Harrison presidency.

Letitia Christian Tyler moved to Washington, D.C., from nearby Virginia when John Tyler ascended to the presidency in April 1841, but she played no public role. A stroke suffered in 1839 had partially paralyzed her, and she died in the White House on 10 September 1842 (the first president's wife to die during her husband's term). Priscilla Cooper Tyler, from a family of Shakespearean actors, became a popular hostess for the president after she married the eldest Tyler son.

On 26 June 1844, John Tyler married Julia Gardiner, a twenty-four-year-old New Yorker whose father had been a friend of the president's. In the remaining eight months of John Tyler's administration, Julia Tyler drew considerable attention to the president's household. A shrewd promoter of herself and of the president, she hired her own press agent—a first for a president's spouse. To emphasize the ceremonial aspects of the chief executive's role, Julia Tyler arranged for the playing of "Hail to the Chief" when the president made public, ceremonial appearances, and she adopted royal trappings for herself. Driving around the capital in a carriage drawn by white horses, she projected a royal image, marked by her preference for receiving guests while seated on a raised platform and wearing a long trained dress and plumed headdress. Although she did no lobbying—in the twentieth-century sense of that term—she used social gatherings to relay her political views, such as her support of the annexation of Texas.

Margaret Mackall Smith Taylor was educated in one of New York City's best schools for young women, but she lived most of her adult life in military and frontier settings and showed little interest in running the White House. She had not wanted her husband, Zachary Taylor, to venture into politics at the relatively advanced age of sixty-three, and she made little secret of her disdain for a public role for herself when her husband won the presidency in 1848. Leaving the hostessing to her youngest daughter, Betty Taylor Bliss, she confined her activities to those involving family and close friends in the private part of the president's residence. Margaret Taylor's reclusiveness prompted many rumors, including the allegations that she smoked a pipe and spoke unintelligibly, all denied by her relatives.

Abigail Powers Fillmore became First Lady in July 1850, but she took little part in the thirty-two-month-long presidency of her husband, Millard Fillmore. Described by acquaintances as a "notable reader" and "remarkably well informed" on the issues of the day, she appeared at few receptions and left most of the hostessing to her teenage daughter, Mary. The library that Abigail Fillmore established on the second floor of the White House served as her strongest legacy—she had been disappointed to find so few books in the executive mansion when she first arrived there.

Jane Appleton Pierce had never shown much interest in politics, and from the time of her marriage to Franklin Pierce in 1834 she expressed clear dislike for the city of Washington. She blamed the capital's full social life for tempting her husband to drink to excess, and she concluded that his political success had exacted its own price—the deaths of two of the Pierces' young sons. She was distressed to hear of her husband's nomination for president in 1852, and she prayed for his defeat. In January 1853, President-elect Pierce, his wife, and their only surviving son, Benjamin, were traveling in Massachusetts when Benjamin was killed in a railroad accident. Grieving Jane Pierce refused to attend her husband's inauguration in March, and she did not take up residence in the executive mansion for several weeks. After she did move in, she relied on female relatives to assist her with hostessing while she kept a low public profile throughout her husband's term.

James Buchanan, a bachelor, turned to a young niece, Harriet Lane, to serve as White House hostess. Twenty-six years old at the time of her uncle's inauguration in March 1857, she achieved great populari-

ty in the next four years, and although her impact was entirely social and ceremonial, she has sometimes been called the first "modern First Lady" because of the favorable attention she called to the role. Her youth and beauty attracted many admirers, and she gave more brilliant parties than had been seen in the capital since the 1820s. Babies were named for her, a song was dedicated to her, and many women imitated her hairstyle and wardrobe. Americans who had little hope of gaining the president's ear went to Harriet Lane instead. She received requests from Native Americans for help, and she drew attention to the arts by inviting painters and writers to the White House.

Eliza McCardle Johnson was ill with tuberculosis when her husband, Andrew Johnson, became president upon the assassination of Abraham Lincoln in April 1865, and she showed little pleasure in the limelight. A married daughter, Martha Johnson Patterson, managed the president's household and won praise for her down-to-earth style. One of Patterson's first public statements after arriving in the capital may have disarmed some potential critics. "We are plain folks from Tennessee, called here by a national calamity," she had said. "I hope not too much will be expected of us." In line with her views on economy and practicality, she arranged for milk cows to graze on the White House lawn, and she covered the mansion's worn carpets with plain muslin. Her mother reportedly made only two public appearances during her entire tenure as First Lady: the first at a dinner party from which she left coughing a few minutes after being seated, and the second at a children's party for her grandchildren and their friends, at which she announced that she was "an invalid" and left soon after her arrival.

Much about Eliza Johnson remains unclear. Although her formal education was superior to Andrew Johnson's at the time of their marriage on 17 May 1827 (when he was eighteen and she was sixteen), the commonly expressed view that she taught him to read and write is an exaggeration. A prospective biographer of Eliza Johnson concluded after years of research that Andrew Johnson valued his wife's judgment as much as that of any of his advisers, leaving unclear how much he relied on anyone. By some accounts, Eliza Johnson showed a keen interest in politics, and in the White House she clipped newspaper articles for her husband, shrewdly separating the good news from the bad. She followed the 1868 impeachment proceedings against President Johnson carefully, announcing at the conclusion that she had been confident of acquittal from the beginning.

Shy and intellectual in her interests, Lucretia Rudolph Garfield had shown little pleasure in the capital social life before her husband, James A. Garfield, won the presidency in 1880, and as First Lady, her main concern for the White House was scholarly. She had been surprised by the lack of information on the building and its furnishings and had gone to the Library of Congress to begin research shortly before she became ill with malaria in May 1881 and went to Elberon, New Jersey, to convalesce. Still there when her husband was shot on 2 July, she returned to Washington and remained with him until his death on 19 September. As Americans read frequent updates on the president's condition, they developed enormous respect for Lucretia Garfield's devotion and considerable affection for the five Garfield children, ranging in age from nine to eighteen. After the president's death, Americans sent in nearly $360,000 in contributions for the support of the family.

Mary Arthur McElroy, wife of an Albany, New York, minister and mother of four children, played the role of White House hostess for her widowed brother Chester Arthur from 1881 to 1885. But her own family responsibilities kept her in Albany most of the time, and she did not reside in the capital or spend much time there.

Rose Cleveland took leave from a teaching career in 1885 to assist her bachelor brother, Grover Cleveland, at the White House. She did not thrive on the social role, much preferring to concentrate on her literary interests, and she admitted that she found receiving lines so boring that she conjugated difficult Greek verbs to keep alert. When she published *George Eliot's Poetry, and Other Studies* in 1885, newspapers congratulated her on "her first book" but generally preferred to report on her hostessing. After Grover Cleveland's marriage in June 1886, Rose Cleveland resumed her own career.

In March 1897, Ida Saxton McKinley began her tenure as First Lady, but poor health impeded her public appearances. Her enfeebled public image was in direct contrast to the vivacious spirit she had shown in her youth. While growing up in Canton, Ohio, she had developed a reputation for independence, even taking a job in her father's bank when such employment was uncommon for women. But after her marriage to William McKinley in 1871, the births of their two daughters, and the daughters' deaths within a few years, she developed a series of maladies, including circulatory problems, which, along with epilepsy, rendered her virtually an invalid for the remainder of her life.

William McKinley was inordinately attentive to his wife's needs and whims, developing a reputation of near saintliness. He stationed himself at her side during important dinners (which she rarely missed) so that he could assist her in the event that she suffered a seizure, and he interrupted important meetings to check on her well-being. In 1898, when the First Lady's brother was murdered by a Canton, Ohio, dressmaker whom he had abandoned after a long liaison, the crime and subsequent trial made national headlines, although neither the president nor the First Lady appeared to give the matter much attention. They attended the funeral in Canton, then immediately resumed their official duties.

Predominantly Social Role with Political Implications

From the beginning of the Republic, the social role played by the president's wife had political implications. Except for the most reclusive, each could have an impact. By extravagant spending or remarkable economy, by altering a guest list and focusing her pleasantries at parties, a First Lady had the power to help or hinder an administration. While some women used the opportunity to great advantage, thus increasing their husbands' popularity and support, others made enemies.

Martha Dandridge Custis Washington, with no precedents to guide her, originated customs that her successors would continue to observe. Although her role is not clear in the decision to combine the chief executive's residence and office on one site, the arrangement required her cooperation because it drew the entire household into politics. Neither guest nor host could label a visit as entirely personal or nonpartisan. Martha Washington's decision to give many parties and to open her home to all callers on New Year's Day drew additional attention to her role. While she appeared to take no notice of nascent political rivalries (and approving Americans rewarded her with the title "Lady Washington"), her successors encountered more difficulty staying out of politics.

Dolley Payne Todd Madison expanded the social role, adding a more rigorous schedule. Even before becoming First Lady, she had some experience with the position—the widowed Thomas Jefferson had asked for her help at White House parties when his daughter could not be present to do the honors. After James Madison's inauguration in 1809, Dolley's charm and popularity proved an asset for the shy, retiring president. She curried favor with legislators' wives by making social visits to all who came to the capital, thus serving as a kind of national Welcome Wagon. Exceptionally egalitarian in her parties, she opened the President's House on Wednesday evenings to almost anyone inclined to call. All persons who had been introduced to the president (or knew someone who had) were invited to make an appearance.

Dolley Madison remained inscrutable about her preferences, except in her admiration for her husband, which was unquestionable. When James Madison dismissed Secretary of State Robert Smith in 1811, she invited Smith and his family to dinner, and when they failed to appear, she called on the family twice, Smith wrote, "with professions of great affection." In James Madison's 1812 bid for reelection, his wife used White House parties to attract support, and some historians have judged her contribution to the November victory as not inconsequential.

Dolley Madison played such a prominent role in running what was still sometimes called the President's House that she cemented into public consciousness a close association between it and the First Lady. The Adamses had resided there only a few weeks, and Thomas Jefferson showed much less interest in it than in his beloved Monticello, so it was left to Dolley Madison to turn it into a showplace. With the help of Benjamin Latrobe, an architect, she furnished the State Dining Room and the suite of rooms on the south side of the first, or public, floor, later known as the Red, Green, and Blue Rooms. When the British troops attacked Washington in August 1814, she arranged for the most treasured possessions in the house, including the Gilbert Stuart portrait of George Washington that Congress had purchased in 1800, to be removed from the mansion and stored in a safe place. Even after the end of her husband's presidency, Dolley Madison remained socially active and prominent up to her death in 1849.

Elizabeth Kortright Monroe did not share Dolley Madison's egalitarian tastes, and her preference for privacy resulted in considerable criticism. A remarkably beautiful woman who retained a youthful appearance well into middle age, she was singled out both in France (where she accompanied her husband, James Monroe, when he served as minister

Dolley Madison is depicted saving the Declaration of Indpenedence before fleeing the White House during the British raids on Washington, D.C., in the War of 1812. BETTMAN/CORBIS

there) and in Washington, D.C., for her stylish appearance. But she showed little interest in using First Ladyship to increase her husband's popularity. She entertained much less than her popular predecessor and refused to make social calls on every legislator's household. Washingtonians wrote her off as snobbish and unfriendly, and some of them boycotted the few parties she did give. When she insisted on inviting only close friends and family to the wedding of her daughter, Maria, in 1820 (the first marriage of a president's child to take place in the White House), she made more enemies. Her long absences from the capital, explained as due either to her own illness or to visits to her married daughters, meant that the president entertained at bachelor parties for men only, leaving the wives of legislators (who had come to the capital expecting a lively social season) miffed to be left out.

Elizabeth Monroe's one positive contribution to her husband's presidency resulted from the particular timing that put the Monroes in the White House immediately following its rebuilding in 1817. Faced with the task of furnishing it, they decided to purchase the materials from France, although James Monroe played a larger part than his wife in the ordering. In the twentieth century, when attention turned to restoration and historic preservation, the Monroes were singled out for their elegant taste and their acquisition of what became the most prized possessions in the White House. Lou Hoover, who furnished rooms on the second floor with reproductions of the Monroes' own furniture in 1932, named the suite for the Monroes.

Louisa Johnson Adams often complained about the heavy social obligations of any woman whose husband aspires to high political office, but she worked hard for John Quincy Adams' success. While he served as secretary of state, she had been among the first women to attend congressional debates, sitting in the visitors' gallery as important matters were discussed, and she worried that people watched her face for some indication of her husband's opinions on matters of state: "Trifling occurrences are turned into political machinery," she wrote. To enhance her husband's popularity, she entertained large numbers of guests and made many calls on legislators' families. She considered the visits particularly unpleasant and complained in her diary that she thought they would make her "crazy" but, heedful of her husband's future, she persevered. "It is understood," she wrote in her diary, "that a man who is ambitious to become President of the United States must make his wife visit the Ladies of the members of Congress first. Otherwise he is totally inefficient to fill so high an office."

The only president's wife to be born in Europe, Louisa Adams knew that some of her critics found her disagreeably foreign, but she won admirers for her charming and self-deprecating manner—a marked contrast to her husband's temperament. Although well educated and sophisticated, she lacked self-confidence, and when she wrote her autobiography for her children, she titled it "Adventures of a Nobody." Although popular in the capital, she saw her duties as entirely social and ceremonial. As for any influence in legislation, she admitted, "I have never once been consulted."

Sarah Childress Polk was singled out by contemporaries and later by historians for holding strong opinions of her own. Educated at one of the best girls' academies in the South, she had married at nineteen, and during the time that James K. Polk served in the House of Representatives, she usually accompanied him to the capital. By the time he became president, she had many influential friends in Washington, both men and women. Just before the 1845 inauguration, Vice President-elect George Dallas wrote of her: "She is certainly mistress of herself and I suspect of somebody else also."

Sarah Polk's letters to her husband indicate that she understood the political controversies of the day and knew where she stood on them, but in line with traditions for women at the time, she did not comment publicly or campaign openly. While her husband was out looking for votes, she remained at home but wrote to inform him of the latest developments, explaining on one occasion that the Democrats' stock had risen ("they are in exstacies [sic]") while that of the Whigs had fallen. With so many of her husband's potential supporters out of town, she complained, "I have not much to opperate [sic] on."

In the White House, Sarah Polk used invitation lists to reward supporters and punish opponents, but she did not voice her opinions on controversial issues. In line with her strict religious observances, she permitted no music to be played on Sunday and attempted to get guests to accompany her to church services. James K. Polk's biographer Charles Sellers concluded that she "became increasingly indispensable, as secretary, political counselor, nurse, and emotional resource" to her frail husband, but that her success in the capital was mainly social.

The tragic circumstances associated with Mary Todd Lincoln's tenure limited her success as First Lady, although she began with rave reviews. National magazines described her costumes and parties in glowing terms, and one of them referred approvingly to the "perfectly molded shoulders" of the "Republican queen."

The Civil War quickly complicated matters for Mary Lincoln. Many of her relatives had sided with the Confederacy, and several of them fought against Union troops. When Mary's half brother was killed in battle, the Lincolns invited his widow to stay with them at the White House, thus feeding suspicions that Mary was a "traitor." The often-repeated story that Abraham Lincoln was called on to defend his wife from such charges in front of a Senate committee is, however, now considered to be untrue.

Although she came from a Kentucky family of substantial means and had been acquainted with national political leaders (including Henry Clay) in her youth, Mary Lincoln showed great insecurity about presiding over the White House, and many people preyed on this weakness. On her way to her husband's inauguration in 1861, she traveled by way of New York to order several new outfits, and her spending continued to grow in the following four years. She lavished large sums on herself as well as on the executive mansion, often without the knowledge or consent of her husband. Merchants extended credit, some of them perhaps hoping for favorable treatment from the president. When Abraham Lincoln was nominated for a second term in 1864, his wife's relief was based partly on the fact that she would not immediately be called on to pay off her debts, then estimated to exceed the president's annual salary.

People seeking access to the president flattered his wife, and his announcement that "women have no influence in this administration" did little to stop them. Observers noted that she frequently appealed to her husband for favors for others, and if he failed to comply, she would invite the supplicant to dine with the president so as to present the case in person.

Even after her husband's death, Mary Lincoln continued to play a public role, and she became one of the most written about of all presidents' wives. The assassination cast her in a martyr role, and she became preoccupied with the subject of money. Living in Europe apparently brought little satisfaction, and after her youngest son, Tad, died in 1871, she became increasingly despondent. In 1875, her one surviving child, Robert, arranged for a sanity hearing that resulted in her being confined briefly to a mental institution near Chicago. With the help of influential friends and a journalist, she plotted her way out a few months later.

Julia Dent Grant, First Lady during the presidency of Ulysses S. Grant, from 1869 to 1877, thrived on the social leadership role accorded the president's wife in the capital. Her tenure coincided with the development of new interest in presidents' families—partly because of the spread of new magazines aimed at a national audience, including women readers. In 1873, *Godey's Lady's Book* began a regular column on Washington under the authorship of the fictional "Aunt Mehitable," who had purportedly accompanied her legislator son to the capital. Actually the writing of Harriet Hazelton, the column enlightened readers about social events, fashion trends, and even the condition of the teeth of some of Washington's most prominent women. Aunt Mehitable made no secret of the fact that she found Julia Grant unattractive, and she pointed out that the First Lady was seen to best advantage in dim light, which concealed the fact that her eyes were crossed.

Julia Grant's good nature and extravagant spending drew favorable attention to herself and the president. The Grants' youngest son, Jesse, nine years old at the beginning of his father's term, and daughter Ellen ("Nellie"), who was fourteen, both became very popular, and their mother did little to restrain public curiosity about them. When Nellie married in 1874, the White House wedding was the social event of the season. Julia Grant's state dinners, consisting of as many as twenty-nine courses and several wines, also attracted praise.

After leaving the White House, Julia Grant decided to write her memoirs, possibly motivated by her husband's success in writing his. Only about thirty pages of the book, which was not published until 1975, deal with the White House years, and these focus on the social and housekeeping aspects of being First Lady. The author did take credit for helping influence the president to veto "the all-important Finance Bill," although her description of how this occurred makes clear that she had very little understanding of what the legislation involved. Her entertaining in the White House, where she invited friends without regard for the political implications, underlined her naïveté.

Lucy Webb Hayes's tenure as First Lady marks a change in the role. The title "first lady" (as in "first lady of the land") came into occasional use by the press in describing her activities. When she accompanied the president on his transcontinental trip in autumn 1880, she was greeted as a heroine. Part of her national prominence resulted from the approval of temperance advocates who were delighted with her ban on alcohol at White House parties. Rutherford B. Hayes apparently shares much of the responsibility for the temperance stand, but it was his wife, ridiculed as "Lemonade Lucy," who took the blame. Her own opinion on the subject was apparently less fixed than was generally assumed. Her biographer Emily Apt Geer concluded that although Lucy Hayes did not drink, she held no strong views about the drinking habits of others. But her decision to endorse temperance evidently attracted favorable attention, and even in a time when virtually no women had the franchise, it won votes. Rutherford B. Hayes's diary entry on 16 January 1881, just before leaving office, endorses that view of her political effectiveness.

Frances Folsom Cleveland, although a young bride when she first moved into the White House, showed other ways that a popular president's wife could enhance his appeal. Only twenty-one when she married, she was the daughter of Oscar Folsom, who had been Grover Cleveland's law partner in Buffalo before his accidental death in 1875. After graduating from Wells College in June 1885, Frances Folsom had spent a year touring Europe with her mother. Her marriage to the forty-eight-year-old president early in his first term was evidently arranged before the trip but kept a secret until the Folsoms returned to New York in late May 1886.

The wedding ceremony on 2 June 1886 in the Blue Room of the White House (the first such ceremony for a sitting president) introduced Americans to a young First Lady whom they would make very popular. Frances Cleveland is usually rated just behind Dolley Madison as the most liked of all nineteenth-century presidents' wives. Her youth and seriousness, her practical down-to-earth approach to White House living, endeared her to many Americans who imitated her in various ways. Women wore their hair à la Frances, twisted in a bun at the nape of the neck, and advertisers incorporated her image in their commercials.

The president's marriage to a young woman of such wholesome, winning ways helped his reputation in some quarters, causing one historian to call it "a master political stroke." Grover Cleveland's relationship with a Buffalo widow, whose child he supported, had become common knowledge in the 1884 campaign and had somewhat tainted his reputation. Aside from that story, his rounded figure and rather lethargic appearance did not make for good copy at a time when news about the presidential household was more and more sought out. Before the end of Grover Cleveland's second term, Frances had given birth to three daughters, who helped establish his image as a devoted family man.

In the summer of 1893, Frances Cleveland assisted her husband in keeping the press from reporting that the president had undergone cancer surgery. Grover Cleveland had been diagnosed with a malignancy in his mouth in May, but he did not want to reveal his condition because of fears that an ailing president might negatively affect the nation's economy. Arrangements were made to operate in secret. On 30 June, the Clevelands left Washington by train,

ostensibly en route to their summer home in Buzzards' Bay, Massachusetts. Somewhere along the way, the president left the train and boarded a yacht that had been fitted out like an operating room. While he underwent surgery, his wife, who was seven months pregnant at the time, proceeded northward with their two-year-old daughter, Ruth.

On 4 July, when the president had not yet arrived in Massachusetts, reporters questioned the First Lady, who asked them not to write about his absence—she assured them that President Cleveland would appear shortly. Except for one account (published at the time and immediately denounced as false) the story of what really happened did not appear until 1917, when one of the attending surgeons wrote about it for the *Saturday Evening Post*.

Caroline Scott Harrison, whose single term as First Lady fell between the two terms of Frances Cleveland, also became a national figure, and although she attempted to keep her job entirely social, it spilled over into matters affecting the president, Benjamin Harrison. Her most publicized effort involved a plan to enlarge the executive mansion, which she deemed too small to accommodate the extended family that accompanied the Harrisons to Washington.

Presidents' families had repeatedly complained of their cramped living quarters, and Caroline Harrison resolved to make a large addition to the White House. Working with architect Frederick Owen, who drew up the plans, she suggested constructing new wings to form a quadrangle, with separate areas for the residence and a museum. Although there appeared to be considerable enthusiasm for the project (and the Senate passed the necessary legislation), it fared less well in the House of Representatives, where the Speaker, angry with the president over an appointment, failed to bring it to the floor.

Had she succeeded in overseeing major alterations at the White House, Caroline Harrison might have become better known for her other efforts. An accomplished artist, she publicized American themes in a White House china pattern featuring a cornstalk-and-flowers border and in her own clothing. Widely respected for her efficient management of the presidential household, she was singled out as a model wife. Her death in the White House on 25 October 1892, just days before her husband failed in his bid for reelection, added a somber final note to her husband's one-term administration.

Edith Carow Roosevelt's nearly eight years as First Lady marked an institutionalization of the role.

Women who preceded her in the job had relied on relatives and friends to assist them in their entertaining and correspondence, and often in their decorating, but Edith Roosevelt preferred hired help. She arranged for Isabella Hagner, formerly secretary to one of Theodore Roosevelt's sisters, to be transferred from the War Department, where she worked as a clerk, to the White House. Operating from a desk on the second floor of the residence, Hagner acted as the First Lady's staff, preparing news releases including information about dinner guests, the president's family, and the First Lady's wardrobe.

More interested in literature than in politics, Edith Roosevelt apparently played little part in discussions of substantive matters affecting the nation. Her impact on the day-to-day running of the White House was, however, enormous. She had a well-earned reputation for economy and the self-confidence to put her ideas into practice. In the extensive 1902 renovation of the White House, she worked with the architectural firm McKim, Mead, and White to reallocate space so that the family had more comfortable quarters. Musicales, featuring performances for small groups of invited guests, had occasionally been scheduled by other First Ladies, but Edith Roosevelt was the first to make them a regular part of the president's entertaining. To help her make choices from among the many artists who sought to perform at the White House, she enlisted the help of Steinway and Sons, the New York piano manufacturers, who provided a consultant.

Although mother of five children (and stepmother to Alice, Theodore Roosevelt's daughter with his first wife, Alice Lee of Boston), Edith Roosevelt maintained a detached demeanor that won her many admirers. She gave no speeches in support of her husband's candidacies, but broke her long silence when she consented to address a large Madison Square Garden rally in 1932. Her subject was Herbert Hoover—and why he would make a better president than his Democratic opponent, Franklin D. Roosevelt, husband of Theodore Roosevelt's niece Eleanor.

Helen Herron Taft is often credited with having had a large role in her husband's political career. William Howard Taft's acceptance of an appointment to head a commission to the Philippines in 1900 was based partly on her enthusiasm for travel. "It was an invitation from the big world," she later wrote, "and I was willing to accept it at once and investigate its possible complications afterwards." When the cou-

ple returned to Washington so that William Howard Taft could enter the cabinet as secretary of war in 1904, Helen appeared set on his becoming president. She had been a guest of the Rutherford B. Hayes family when she was a young girl, she later explained, and she had determined then that she would one day preside over the White House. When President Theodore Roosevelt appeared ready to name her husband to the Supreme Court in 1906, Helen Taft scheduled an appointment with him to express her own views. Although she left no account of that meeting, President Roosevelt's letter to William Howard Taft leaves little doubt about her impact: After "a half hour's talk with your dear wife," he wrote, he had decided against appointing Taft to the Court.

During the 1908 presidential election, Helen Taft was often described as intelligent and forceful, predictably an influence on her husband. She lent credence to such claims with her own announcement that she did not like to be shunted off to lunch with a group of uninteresting women while her husband talked over important matters with other men. After the inauguration, she managed to ride to the White House beside the president, a spot previously reserved for the outgoing chief executive or some other prominent man.

Helen Taft's physical collapse due to a stroke two months after the inauguration curtailed reports of her power and influence. She retired to the Tafts' vacation home in Massachusetts for the summer to recuperate. By October 1909 she was back in the White House, but she kept a low public profile and was often absent on important occasions. The Tafts' one daughter, Helen, and the First Lady's sister helped in White House management and in the social schedule. Helen Taft's main impact on Washington was cosmetic. She arranged for the shipment and planting of several thousand cherry trees along the Potomac.

Immediately after leaving the White House, Helen Taft began writing her autobiography, which was published in 1914. *Recollections of Full Years* thus became the first autobiography of a First Lady to be published (Julia Grant had written hers earlier but it was not yet in print). Only a fraction of Helen Taft's book dealt with the White House years, and that focuses entirely on the social aspects of the role.

Ellen Axson Wilson, although First Lady for only seventeen months, explored new ways that a president's wife could leave her mark on her husband's administration. As a young woman she had studied art in New York City, and during the time her husband was president of Princeton University and then governor of New Jersey she exhibited her paintings, sometimes signing them "E. Wilson" in order to play down her relationship with Woodrow. But rather than concentrating on art projects while in the White House in 1913 and 1914, she turned to housing reform, an interest that had survived since her student days when she had taught in a missionary school in New York. She arranged for housing reformers to meet with legislators at receptions, and she made cars available for touring slums located only a few blocks from the White House. Her efforts helped generate interest in housing reform, resulting in legislation, sometimes called the Ellen Wilson Alley Housing Bill, passed by the Senate just hours before she died on 6 August 1914. The House of Representatives quickly followed suit. Although a lack of funding crippled the law's effects, this marked the first time that a president's wife had been so prominently connected to legislation.

The potential for a woman to participate in her husband's administration was not lost on Florence Kling Harding. She had assisted Warren G. Harding in running his Marion, Ohio, newspaper, and she evidently saw no reason to play a lesser part in his political career. She involved herself in the 1920 campaign, overturning, for example, a decision to reply to rumors that her husband had black ancestry. But her impact on policy matters while First Lady is difficult to assess, partly because she destroyed so many of the papers that would have helped define it. Staff credited her with helping to shape wording of the president's speeches and with vetoing a plan that would have provided an official residence for the vice president, but she herself claimed her role was little more than social and ceremonial. She had a good relationship with the press, and she occasionally scheduled meetings of her own with women journalists.

Ill with a kidney disease for much of her adult life, Florence Harding made a special point of looking strong and healthy. The "Duchess," as her husband called her, enthusiastically greeted tourists who passed through the executive mansion, and whenever she was too sick to appear in public, as happened frequently, she attributed the indisposition to food poisoning. In the end, her attempt to manage the press worked against her. Americans were as unprepared for her death on 21 November 1924 as they had been for her husband's nearly sixteen months earlier.

Grace Goodhue Coolidge, the first president's wife to have earned a university degree, made a point of staying out of politics. She insisted that she did not know the details of her husband's daily schedule or of his decision not to run for a second term in 1928 until she was informed along with the rest of the nation. Her influence was almost entirely one of image—not inconsequential for a less-than-personable, laconic president. Charming and witty, she made self-deprecating comments about herself that won many admirers, and her fondness for animals and small children was legendary. She was frequently photographed with one of her many pets—including a raccoon named Rebecca and a collie, Rob Roy. Her courageous response to the grief that engulfed both her and the president after their younger son, Calvin Coolidge, Jr., died in the summer of 1924 further endeared her to Americans.

Grace Coolidge's attempt to change substantially the furnishings of the White House failed. Following her husband's election to a full term in 1924, she formed an advisory committee composed of experts and connoisseurs, some of whom had just completed an exhibit of American furniture at New York's Metropolitan Museum of Art. She appealed to Congress for an increased allotment and for permission to accept donations of period furniture and art. When controversy developed about the appropriate style for the refurbishing, the plan was dropped, but Grace Coolidge's example prepared the way for other First Ladies, including Jacqueline Kennedy.

Lou Henry Hoover came to the White House with a full understanding of the major issues of the day, but she played the role of First Lady much as it had been played earlier. She neither campaigned for her husband nor gave interviews that revealed any differences between herself and the president. When she gave talks on radio—the first president's wife to do so—she limited herself to topics that reinforced her husband's voluntary approach to solving the problems of the Great Depression. Her efforts to catalog White House furnishings, with the help of friends and volunteers, did not result in a publication, although attention was called to a long-felt need.

Considerable controversy surrounded Lou Hoover's decision to invite Jessie DePriest, wife of African-American congressman Oscar DePriest of Chicago, to a tea for legislators' wives. One southern newspaper editorialized that the First Lady had "defiled the White House"; another suggested that she had offered the nation "an arrogant insult." In other quarters, the incident underlined the First Lady's reputation for egalitarianism.

Opinion is divided on Lou Hoover's impact on her husband's appointments. But in a single term, Herbert Hoover named seven women to jobs requiring Senate approval, bringing the total to more than double what it had been in 1920. She was an enthusiastic supporter of noncompetitive sports for women and of the Girl Scouts. First Ladies had traditionally served as figurehead leader of the Girl Scouts, but she worked hard at the job, helping to raise funds and encouraging membership. Her large personal fortune made possible her support of many ordinary people with hardship cases who asked for her help during the Great Depression, although she refused to publicize her generosity. The largesse continued after she left the White House, and when she died in 1944, her husband was surprised to receive many letters from people he was unacquainted with, wanting to know why their checks had stopped.

Elizabeth ("Bess") Wallace Truman followed a precedent-breaking First Lady, Eleanor Roosevelt, into the White House in 1945, but she played the part her own way. While her husband served as U.S. senator and vice president, she remained virtually unknown in Washington. Her unusually adamant insistence on privacy, later explained by her daughter Margaret as originating in the suicide of David Wallace, Bess's father, when she was eighteen, made her wary of reporters, and she declined to give interviews as First Lady; after finally consenting to answer reporters' questions in writing in 1947, she relied on "no comment" for nearly a third of the thirty questions submitted.

Bess Truman refused to comment on matters of public policy, and her impact remains unclear. Harry Truman credited her many times, saying that she had been his "full partner in all my transactions, political and otherwise." He told reporters that he consulted her on important decisions, including use of the atomic bomb, the Marshall Plan, and Korea, because "her judgment was always good." Staff members concurred that he frequently brought a briefcase to the residence part of the White House and went over the contents with his wife. His letters to her, at least those that have been published in *Dear Bess: The Letters from Harry to Bess Truman, 1910–1959*, frequently seek her advice. Much of the correspondence between the Trumans is unavailable, however, because Bess burned it. Their daughter Margaret wrote after her parents' deaths that her mother often felt shut out of important decisions in the White House.

The one time that Bess Truman made a public statement about a controversial subject involved repairing the White House in 1949 after severe structural problems were discovered. Bess Truman urged retaining the historical value of the original structure rather than demolishing it and building a new residence in its place, an option that would have been less costly. During the extensive renovation the Trumans lived at the Blair House, and when they returned to the White House in early 1952 she left it to the president to conduct a televised tour of the premises. She confined her own appearances to the ceremonial: dedicating hospital planes, posing with poster children, and greeting wounded servicemen.

Mamie Doud Eisenhower, the last First Lady born in the nineteenth century, left the job a ceremonial, social one as she had found it. Many years as wife of a military leader and university president had trained her to be an efficient household manager, and she thrived on the hostessing role. Her press conference in early March 1953 featured a list of her social engagements or, as one reporter summarized it, "tea by inexorable tea." When she published an article in a women's magazine during the 1952 campaign, she took an entirely neutral stand: "Vote for My Husband or for Governor Stevenson," she titled the article, "But Please Vote."

Much about Mamie Eisenhower's style appealed to Americans. She invited popular performers such as Fred Waring to the White House, and she insisted that she and the president often ate their dinners from TV trays, just as millions of her countrymen were doing. Her popular hairstyle, breezy attitude, and recipe for fudge made her first name a household word. Dwight Eisenhower credited her "unaffected manner" with making the White House "livable and comfortable, and meaningful for the people who came in."

First Ladies with Strong Impact on Their Husbands' Presidencies

The presidential campaign of 1960 is generally seen as a turning point in the history of First Ladies. Those who served after that date played a larger, more sig-

Dwight Eisenhower sports a button that shows his support and affection for his better half.
BETTMAN/CORBIS

nificant role in getting their husbands elected and in making their administrations successful. In spite of considerable variation in their clout, all were rated for their value to their husbands' programs, and each was written about in her own right.

Part of the change resulted from timing and from developments entirely outside the First Ladies' control. All were born in the twentieth century, and most had attended college and at one time held jobs of their own. Expanding television coverage, pulling a candidate's entire family into the public eye, focused on their wives. American women, increasingly aware of political solutions for problems they faced in their homes and on their jobs, looked to the president's wife for an example and for help.

The opportunity for a forceful First Lady to involve herself in policy had been present from the beginning of the Republic. The Constitution left a president free to choose advisers at will, without the constraints of a parliamentary system that tied a leader tightly to a party. Chief executives rarely admitted to relying on the counsel of their wives, however, and since much of the communication between presidents and First Ladies was personal and private, it is impossible to assess precisely what role each woman played. By the late twentieth century, accounts were more plentiful. Presidents' wives often

wrote books to tell their own life stories; staff members revealed what they observed about the First Family; and reporters covered the entire White House entourage in detail.

Abigail Smith Adams' tenure as First Lady showed very early how a determined woman could, with her husband's concurrence, exert influence in his administration. John Adams had first been attracted to her by her wit, and during their marriage she often managed family and business matters on her own in her husband's frequent absences. During his eight years as vice president, she observed the careful impartiality and general affability of Martha Washington, and the two women often appeared together on social occasions, but Abigail Adams had her own views about women's roles.

John Adams' presidency, marked increasingly by factionalism, gave his wife the chance to vent her own opinions, if only in letters to relatives and friends and in private conversations. Other people guessed at what she thought—they called her "Mrs. President." Visitors to the President's House reported that she took sides, naming some legislators as "our people" and others as foes. The nearly two thousand of her letters that survive record her views: Albert Gallatin was "sly, artful"; in Alexander Hamilton's eyes she saw "the very devil . . . itself." John Adams' letters underline her role in his administration. After he had made an unpopular appointment while she was in Massachusetts, he wrote to tell her that many people lamented her absence, and called her "a good counsellor." Even though her own illnesses and that of relatives required her to be separated from her husband during much of his presidency, she is generally credited as an important adviser.

As the first occupants of the President's House in the Federal City (yet to be named Washington), the Adamses had a chance to set some precedents that would guide chief executives and their spouses for two centuries. Because her residence lasted only a few weeks, Abigail Adams did not have time to furnish the mansion, even if the plaster had dried, but she transferred some of the customs that had already developed in temporary housing. She opened the residence on New Year's Day to all who wanted to call, a tradition that continued (except during illness or national disaster) until 1932. The party on 1 January 1801 featured the eight-member United States Marine Band, thus associating that ensemble with the president in a special way.

Edith Bolling Galt Wilson is often credited with changing the role of First Lady, although her interest in politics was limited. Before her marriage to Woodrow Wilson on 18 December 1915, she had paid little attention to government, and she confessed that in the 1912 presidential election she could not have even named the candidates. Yet the unusual circumstances that surrounded her tenure pushed her into prominence and gained her an undeserved reputation as one of the most influential of all presidents' wives. During her first years in the White House, she and the president spent a great deal of time together, and she often sat near him as he wrote his speeches or deciphered coded messages. When he traveled to Europe for the talks that ended World War I, she accompanied him, and during a tour of Italy and England she gained considerable admiring attention and was often compared to European queens.

After Woodrow Wilson suffered a devastating stroke in the fall of 1919, Edith Wilson's role changed from romantic companion to diligent nurse. She screened his mail and monitored his visitors and workload, and except for his doctor and trusted secretary, few callers got past her. Rumors circulated that she was taking charge; she was described by a White House employee as an "assistant president," and by a prominent senator as presiding over a "petticoat government."

Evidence that Edith Wilson made important decisions is lacking. She insisted that she only looked out for her husband's well-being, and the facts support her claim. During several major crises throughout the winter of 1919–1920, including the deportation of aliens, a miners' strike, and a steel strike, the White House took little part. Historians have generally concluded that Edith Wilson had neither the ability nor the interest to play a strong political role, but her tenure illustrated the potential for a spouse to control access to the president during a period when he was ill or incapacitated.

Even before she moved into the White House, Eleanor Roosevelt had developed an agenda of her own. Politics was not an unexplored topic in her family (Theodore Roosevelt was her father's only brother), and she had served an apprenticeship of her own, beginning about 1918 when she started doing volunteer work with the Red Cross and meeting women social reformers. After her husband was paralyzed by polio in 1921, she attempted to keep his political future alive by learning to speak in public so that she could represent him. In 1924 she headed a women's delegation that tried unsuccessfully to reach the Resolutions Committee at the Democratic

National Convention and present proposals for a long list of reforms, including equal pay for women workers, regulation of child labor, and improvement of education and working conditions. She campaigned for Al Smith, the Democratic nominee, in 1928 and began publishing magazine articles under her own name.

By 1933, Eleanor Roosevelt's political resources were considerable. She had a large network of competent people who could advise her and accept appointments to high-level jobs. Her husband's physical limitations provided her almost unlimited license to travel in his place, and she frequently said she served as "his eyes and ears." The emotional separation between her and the president, often attributed to his romantic attachment to another woman during World War I, apparently freed her to concentrate on her own projects and goals.

Within days of becoming First Lady, Eleanor Roosevelt indicated that she would take a fresh approach to the job. She invited women reporters to go on a tour of the White House and agreed to meet with them regularly every week. After announcing that she would not touch controversial issues, she soon broke her own rules, causing news agencies to pay more attention to the meetings. She eventually held 348 press conferences, the last just hours before the president's death, and until World War II the conferences were limited to women. News agencies that did not want to miss an important announcement from the presidential household had to hire a woman reporter, and one of them, Ruby Black, thanked the First Lady for getting her a job with United Press.

Although abundant evidence points to Eleanor Roosevelt's large role in New Deal legislation, she played down the amount of power she exercised. At one news conference she announced that she had "never tried to influence" the president "on anything he ever did" and, she continued, "I certainly have never known him to try to influence me." When one man publicly credited her with getting him a job, she objected, saying he had put her in an "embarrassing position."

Her own writings and those of her friends point to her impact. In 1941, Raymond Clapper, a well-known syndicated columnist, named her as one of the ten most powerful people in Washington, playing the part of "cabinet minister without portfolio." Her influence was particularly evident in the formation of the National Youth Administration, in housing reform, and in increasing opportunities for women and minorities. Her letters contain many references to meetings with legislators and agency heads, and in 1942 she testified before a congressional committee, the first president's wife to do so.

Eleanor Roosevelt provided access to government for people who had previously felt deprived. Molley Dewson, chair of the Women's Division of the Democratic National Committee, credited the First Lady with making it possible for her to discuss important matters with the president. Her papers at the Franklin D. Roosevelt Library at Hyde Park, New York, contain many letters from people appealing to her for help—evidence that they thought she could deliver.

The First Lady traveled, both in the United States and abroad, far more than any president's wife before her. None of her predecessors had journeyed abroad on their own when Eleanor Roosevelt decided to go to Great Britain in 1942 to visit army camps, factories, nurseries, and other sites associated with the war. The following year she went to the South Pacific. Her countless trips to Appalachia and to other problem areas of the United States were billed as "fact finding," and they took her to improbable places: into mines, schools, and the dilapidated dwellings of impoverished families.

Eleanor Roosevelt is widely believed to have been more liberal than her husband on many subjects and to have attracted support from quarters where he had less appeal. Her stand on civil rights, especially following her resignation from membership in the Daughters of the American Revolution after that organization barred Marian Anderson, the African-American singer, from performing in its auditorium in 1939, secured her reputation in many quarters. Eleanor Roosevelt made friends with young people, including members of the American Student Union and the American Youth Congress, and she spoke up in their defense. Women's groups also looked to her for leadership, and although she neither joined the Woman's Party nor defended the Equal Rights Amendment as First Lady, she championed the right of married women to work, a right threatened by the Economy Act of 1933.

Although she had a very small staff, Eleanor Roosevelt kept a hectic schedule. Her syndicated newspaper column, "My Day," began appearing in 1936, and she gave hundreds of speeches. The money earned was dedicated to various charities and friends because, although she liked earning money, she

spent little on herself and preferred seeing it "in circulation."

After her husband's death, Eleanor Roosevelt remained a strong political force. President Truman nominated her as a United States delegate to the United Nations, where she helped draft the Universal Declaration of Human Rights in 1948. She campaigned for Adlai Stevenson in 1952 and 1956. In 1961, President Kennedy appointed her to chair the Commission on the Status of Women, but her health had already begun to fail and she died on 7 November 1962, having lived the final years of her life as "First Lady of the World."

Jacqueline Bouvier Kennedy understood the value a popular First Lady could have for her husband's administration, but she did not involve herself in public policy questions. Thirty-one years old at the time of her husband's inauguration, she was the youngest First Lady since Frances Cleveland (1886), and she augmented the attention focused on her by projecting a glamorous image involving designer clothes, expensive jewelry, and a preference "for the best" in food and entertainment. Her savvy in arts and design, her ability in languages, and her extensive travel abroad made her an immensely appealing First Lady, and she was widely imitated.

Ambivalent about a public role (she relished her own privacy and insisted that her two young children be protected from excessive media exposure), Jacqueline Kennedy appointed her own press secretary (the first president's wife to do so) but then encouraged the president's press secretary, Pierre Salinger, to keep reporters away from her and her children.

Besides her glamorous image, Jacqueline Kennedy's strongest legacy was the White House restoration. In 1961 she arranged for a curator to come on loan from the Smithsonian Institution to begin the lengthy process of cataloging the contents of the White House, and she appealed to Congress to pass legislation making the contents of the executive mansion public property so that occupants could not sell or dispose of furnishings "of historic or artistic interest." To restore the mansion to its early-nineteenth-century elegance, she helped form the White House Historical Association, a "not-for-profit historical and educational organization" to "enhance understanding, appreciation and enjoyment of the White House." The sale of guidebooks to finance restoration began on 4 July 1962, and although some critics charged that sales on the premises cheapened the White House, the initial printing of 250,000 copies sold out in a few weeks. When the First Lady showed off the results of the White House refurbishing in a televised tour on 14 February 1962, more than 46 million Americans watched, and interest in the president's residence grew.

After President Kennedy's assassination, his widow helped plan a dramatic funeral, with many of the elements drawn from Abraham Lincoln's. A few days after the interment she summoned Theodore H. White to her Massachusetts home to discuss her own views on the Kennedy administration and how it should be remembered. It was this interview, described in a two-page *Life* magazine article by White on 6 December 1963, that pinned the tag "Camelot" on the Kennedy administration.

Claudia ("Lady Bird") Taylor Johnson called Jacqueline Kennedy a "daunting" act to follow, but she went ahead to make her own mark on the job of First Lady. Her long residence in Washington, beginning with her marriage in 1934, acquainted her with political workings on the national level and she built her own network of powerful friends. Although she had not wanted her husband to accept the nomination for vice president in 1960, she went out to speak in support of the national ticket that year, causing Robert Kennedy, campaign manager for his brother, to pronounce her a major asset. During the Kennedy presidency, Lady Bird Johnson often filled in for the First Lady when she could not, or chose not to, appear at ceremonies.

As First Lady, Lady Bird Johnson named a large, competent staff, headed by Liz Carpenter, a veteran reporter. Although the number of employees was generally about two dozen, the largest any president's wife had named up to that time, additional people came on loan from other agencies and departments to assist in the First Lady's projects and scheduling. Her understanding of reporters' needs (journalism had been one of her majors at the University of Texas) helped her develop a good relationship with members of the press.

In 1964, Lady Bird Johnson campaigned for her husband on her own—the first candidate's wife to do so in such a visible way. Vowing not to write off support in the southern states, where enthusiasm for Lyndon Johnson was weak, she traveled from Washington to Louisiana on a train, dubbed the "Lady Bird Special." Accompanied by staff, advisers, and, for part of the trip, her daughters, she gave speeches along the way urging people to vote for her husband.

After 1965, Lady Bird Johnson staked out a leading role for herself in the Great Society initiatives,

taking an important part in Head Start, a program designed to assist preschool children. Her closest identification, however, was with "beautification." Although the latter suffered from its unfortunate name (which even Mrs. Johnson deemed unsuitable but acknowledged that "we couldn't come up with anything better") and was often denigrated as simply "prettification," it touched on much broader environmental concerns: the upkeep of Washington's monuments and streets, the involvement of Washington residents in neighborhood improvement, a campaign to attract national attention to the value of natural resources, and the struggle to regulate billboards along highways.

While the success of these efforts relied principally on Lady Bird Johnson's ability to attract favorable attention and raise funds from private sources, the last involved national legislation and provoked considerable controversy, particularly after the powerful billboard lobby made its views known. The Highway Beautification Act (sometimes called "Lady Bird's Bill"), passed in October 1965, marked an unprecedented use of the First Lady's implicit power. But the law was seriously weakened during the compromising necessary to passage, and neither she nor the president was very satisfied with the results.

Although Lady Bird Johnson did not take an active part in the burgeoning feminist movement, she developed her own program to recognize the accomplishments of outstanding women and, at the same time, call attention to significant topics at "women-doer" luncheons. Of the nineteen that she eventually hosted, each of them focusing on a single subject, the most publicized was held on 18 January 1968, on street crime. Among the guests was singer Eartha Kitt, who, after listening to the remarks of the First Lady and several others present, expressed her own view that it was not surprising that young people were turning to marijuana and crime when so many of them faced the prospect of being drafted to fight, and perhaps die, in Vietnam. The First Lady later recorded in her diary how important she knew her response would be. She tried to remain calm and dignified as she spoke about her feelings: she hoped that the war would end soon, but while it continued, "that still doesn't give us a free ticket not to try to work for better things—against crime in the streets, and for better education and better health for our people." The incident, widely reported by journalists who were present, illustrated how easily the First Lady could be drawn into important, controversial matters.

The exact role of Lady Bird Johnson in her husband's presidency cannot be fully detailed until all her papers are open and examined. Perhaps not even then. Her own record of her White House years, published in 1970 and titled *A White House Diary*, includes only a fraction of the notes that she made while First Lady. Her biographer Lewis L. Gould concluded that all available evidence indicates that she played a significant part in key decisions and that she altered the institution of First Lady by going beyond what any of her predecessors had done in working for legislation. Other historians have generally rated her a substantial asset to the Johnson presidency.

Patricia ("Pat") Ryan Nixon also brought a long Washington apprenticeship to the White House, but she used it in her own particular way. Although she maintained a busy schedule and took on several projects, she showed little interest in claiming credit for her accomplishments, and the president's staff placed low value on her contribution. Journalists saw her as programmed and distant, but she gained enormous popularity with Americans, who named her to *Good Housekeeping*'s list of "Most Admired Women" every year she was in the White House and for nearly two decades after leaving it.

In her effort to open up the White House "to the little guys," Pat Nixon made special arrangements: persons in wheelchairs and on crutches received extra assistance; blind people were permitted to touch objects; busloads of senior citizens ate Thanksgiving dinner in the State Dining Room. But Pat also traveled to meet people, even those who lived in remote places and were not yet old enough to vote. Her daughter Julie later estimated that Pat had traveled more than any First Lady up to that time, visiting eighty-three nations and criss-crossing North America many times. She persevered whatever the weather, explaining, "I do or I die. I never cancel out."

Although she was overshadowed by the glamour and publicity that had been associated with Jacqueline Kennedy, Pat Nixon worked effectively to gather antiques and artwork for the White House collection. With the assistance of White House curator Clement Conger, who had presided over the refurbishing of the reception rooms at the State Department, she acquired more antique furnishings for the mansion than had been given during the Kennedy and Johnson administrations combined.

Pat Nixon's insistence on privacy gave little opportunity for the public to know what she had done or how she felt on important issues. Frequent staff changes (she named three different press secretaries in just over five years) limited her impact, and when asked to write a syndicated column, she refused, saying, I know a lot but you have to keep it to yourself when you're in this position." Her daughter Julie Nixon Eisenhower, who published a book, *Pat Nixon: The Untold Story* (1986), insisted that her parents were closer than people thought, but she could offer only one instance in which the First Lady tried to influence an important appointment—she hoped that a woman would be named to the Supreme Court.

Betty Bloomer Ford assumed the job of First Lady without the benefit of a national campaign and at a time when the Watergate hearings had diminished public respect for government officials. She frequently said that she had a special responsibility to be candid and honest. At her first press conference, held on 4 September 1974, she admitted that she sometimes disagreed with her husband on important issues and described her position on abortion as much closer to that of Nelson Rockefeller, who supported the Supreme Court's decision leaving the matter for a woman and her physician to decide, than that of Senator James Buckley of New York, who had publicly disagreed with the Court's stand. Her independence (she later admitted she was often tempted to split her ticket when she voted) is generally credited with increasing her husband's popularity in some quarters, and it accounted for campaign buttons in 1976 plugging "Betty's Husband for President."

From the beginning of her tenure as First Lady, Betty Ford announced that she would work for substantive changes, including ratification of the Equal Rights Amendment to the Constitution. She had a separate telephone installed in the White House so that she could lobby state legislators scheduled to vote on the measure. Opponents of the amendment criticized the involvement of a president's wife in such a controversial issue, especially one then before the states, but Betty Ford insisted she would stick with the fight. And she did, although she had to admit defeat when the necessary number of states did not ratify during her term.

Both Gerald and Betty Ford spoke of her influence in his administration. She admitted using "pillow talk" to relay her views on important topics, including the nomination of women to important jobs, and he acknowledged that she had urged him to grant a pardon to Richard Nixon.

Much of Betty Ford's popularity resulted from her candor in dealing with personal problems that other presidential families had hidden. She talked publicly about her sons' possible experimentation with marijuana, her teenage daughter's sex life, and her own use of tranquilizers. (Her frank statement about her alcoholism and her establishment of the Betty Ford Center came after the White House years ended.) In September 1974, when she was diagnosed with breast cancer, she permitted the White House to release all the details to the press. Television programs and magazines featured discussions on radical mastectomies and more limited surgery, on chemotherapy and radiation treatments. Previously almost unmentionable, breast cancer became a household word, and many women were persuaded to seek examinations. Although some criticism charged that the discussions were inappropriate, the First Lady concentrated on the good she had done. "Lying in the hospital, thinking of all those women going for cancer checkups because of me, I'd come to recognize more clearly the power of the woman in the White House."

Rosalynn Smith Carter claimed title to "full partner" throughout her marriage, even in the White House. She had assisted in the Carter family business by keeping the books, and when her husband James Earl ("Jimmy") Carter ran for governor of Georgia in 1966 she went out on the campaign trail (although her fear of making public speeches kept her from anything more than photo opportunity appearances beside the family car). Later, she perfected her speaking skills and grew adept at campaigning so that when her husband began his quest for his party's nomination for president in early 1975, she felt confident about traveling and speaking on her own. She often explained that they could cover more territory if each worked alone.

As First Lady, Rosalynn Carter frequently stood in for the president on ceremonial occasions, and she developed her own abbreviation (BOE for "bottom of the elevator") for the many trips she made to the first floor of the White House to have her picture taken with one delegation or another. But she emphasized the substantive rather than the social and ceremonial parts of the job. She kept an office in the East Wing (where she was sometimes photographed busy at her desk), and she scheduled a working lunch with the president once a week. When subjects that interested her were the focus of cabinet discussion, she joined cabinet members, sitting in "whatev-

Rosalynn Carter broke new ground for a wife of a president by attending Cabinet meetings and actively supporting legislation. THE LIBRARY OF CONGRESS

er seat was available," she later said, even if it happened to be the one normally occupied by the vice president. She was the first president's wife to attend cabinet meetings.

In a precedent-breaking trip, Rosalynn Carter journeyed to seven countries in the Caribbean and South America in spring 1977 to confer with leaders on what the White House billed "substantive matters." After preparing by meeting with members of the State Department and the National Security Council, she talked with leaders about trade and defense. When she returned to Washington she reported to the Senate Foreign Relations Committee on what she had seen and heard. Critics questioned the authority under which she traveled since she was neither appointed nor elected, and some Latino leaders expressed uncertainty about how to treat her remarks. Whether she was responding to the criticism or not, Rosalynn Carter made no more trips of this kind, explaining that her husband had time to "go himself." But she continued with goodwill missions that were more in line with what other First Ladies had done.

Rosalynn Carter had become interested in mental health care reform during the years that her husband served as governor of Georgia, and she continued her efforts as First Lady. As honorary chair of the President's Council on Mental Health, she spoke on the subject in the United States, Canada, and Europe. In February 1979 she went before the Senate Resource Subcommittee to promote mental health programs, thus becoming the first president's wife to testify before a congressional committee since Eleanor Roosevelt.

When President Carter invited Anwar as-Sadat and Menachem Begin to Camp David in September 1978, he asked that Rosalynn and the wives of the other two leaders also be present, saying the negotiations would be more congenial "if all of you are there." Rosalynn Carter's notes on those twelve days later became the basis of one chapter in her autobiography, *First Lady from Plains* (1984), and critics judged it a particularly valuable insight into the Camp David meeting.

Historians have generally rated Rosalynn Carter as an especially effective First Lady, a major asset to her husband's administration. She weathered some criticism for doing what no president's wife had done before, but she emerged as one of a handful of twentieth-century First Ladies judged more successful in their roles than their husbands in the presidency.

Nancy Davis Reagan was not always candid about her impact as First Lady, although it was, by many accounts, substantial. Some associates noted that she had very savvy political instincts and held strong views on the people who worked with her husband. Apparently uninterested in a political base of her own, she took strong exception to those people she deemed harmful to her husband's success and was generally thought to play a major role in the removal of several cabinet and staff members, including Chief of Staff Donald Regan. After he left the job, Regan endorsed that view and added that she had made scheduling of the president difficult by relying on a California astrologer for advice about when Ronald Reagan should travel and attend important meetings. Rather than refuting this charge, Nancy Reagan explained that her fears for her husband's safety, especially after the assassination attempt on him in March 1981, had made her look for help wherever she could find it.

As wife of the governor of California, Nancy Reagan had worked with the Foster Grandparents Program, and as First Lady she published a book on the subject. But her chic image did not seem grandmotherly to many Americans, and the program was not popular. Her ratings dipped in 1981, partly because of what appeared to some people as extravagant spending on the White House and on herself. The timing of a White House announcement on the purchase of nearly $210,000 worth of new china (although paid for by private donations) was particularly unfortunate since it coincided with revelations about cuts in social programs.

At a meeting in late 1981, involving her staff and the president's, a plan was devised to improve Nancy Reagan's image, and she embarked on an antidrug crusade, later billed as "Just Say No." The First Lady insisted that she had a long-standing interest in the topic and would have become involved in an antidrug campaign sooner had her advisers not vetoed the subject as too downbeat. She raised money for school programs and for conferences, including one at the White House that drew spouses of leaders from nations around the world.

Because Ronald Reagan underwent several periods of major illness and lengthy convalescence, Nancy Reagan was watched closely to see what power she held. In July 1985, while he recuperated in hospital following cancer surgery, she returned to the White House to greet visiting dignitaries. Reporters speculated that a triumvirate was in charge: the president, his chief of staff, and the First Lady. Ronald Reagan endorsed this view when he thanked her for "taking part in the business of the nation." She was widely believed to favor an arms limitation agreement with the Soviet Union, and her enthusiasm was sometimes cited as significant in the president's quest for an accord. Before she left the White House, *The New York Times* credited her with expanding the role of First Lady.

Barbara Pierce Bush became First Lady after eight years of relatively inconspicuous preparation while her husband served as vice president. At age sixty-three, she was one of the oldest ever to take on the role and she chose to play it in the style of women a generation earlier. Staying away from decisions involving the president's scheduling and his appointment and retention of staff, she stressed the ceremonial, traditional side of being a White House wife. Her tendency for self-deprecation won her many admirers, and she insisted on retaining the image that had served her well: practical and down-to-earth, without much attention to hair coloring and dress designers. Her mail told her, she said, that there were "an awful lot of white haired, wrinkled ladies out there just tickled pink" with her approach.

In the decade before moving into the White House, Barbara Bush had undertaken a leadership role in the campaign to improve literacy in the United States, and she continued this work as First Lady. Struggling with the dyslexia of one of her sons many years earlier had convinced her, she said, of the importance of the ability to read. Although George Bush billed himself as the "Education President," it was his wife, frequently photographed visiting schools and reading to children, who became most closely identified with the cause. In 1991 she published a humorous book of photographs of the family dog, *Millie's Book*, as Dictated to Barbara Bush, and when it quickly became a best-seller, she donated nearly $800,000 in royalties to the Barbara Bush Foundation for Family Literacy. Had she not given the money away, she would have banked far more than the president's annual salary.

Barbara Bush kept her views on controversial issues to herself although she was widely believed to disagree with her husband on abortion and gun control. Since she had dropped out of college—she had attended Smith—and married at nineteen and had never had a full-time job of her own, she was not widely perceived as a leader among career-oriented feminists. An invitation extended to her by the administration of Wellesley College to speak at graduation ceremonies in June 1990 drew many protests from students enrolled there who objected that she had become a prominent person solely because of her marriage to a famous man. Some students signed a petition asking that the invitation be withdrawn. The First Lady spoke out in defense of students' right to live their lives differently from her, but she did not decline the invitation. Instead, she invited Raisa Gorbachev, who happened to be slated to visit the United States about the time of the graduation, to accompany her to Wellesley and give a speech also. The event, widely covered by the media, underlined Barbara Bush's practical, confident approach to the job, and it helps explain why she remained popular with Americans holding differing opinions about how a president's wife should act.

Hillary Rodham Clinton, the first woman born after World War II to become First Lady, was heralded as ushering in a new era. Her own credentials suggested a departure. She was the first president's wife to have a professional degree from the same institution as her husband and to have had a successful career of her own. After graduating in 1973 from Yale Law School, where she met Bill Clinton, she worked briefly in Washington, D.C., on the legal team employed by the House Judiciary Committee to investigate President Nixon's connection to the Watergate break-in and the events that followed it. When that assignment ended in the summer of 1974, Hillary Rodham moved to Arkansas and taught at the state university law school in Fayetteville. She married Bill Clinton in 1975; he was elected Arkansas attorney general the following year. In 1977 Hillary Clinton took a position in Little Rock at the prestigious Rose Law Firm—one of the first women the firm had hired. Eventually she was made a partner at Rose and won praise from her colleagues, who named her to the *National Law Journal* list of "100 Most Influential Lawyers in America."

During her student days, Hillary Rodham Clinton had become interested in the legal rights of children and of the poor, and as an adult she focused on these concerns. She took leadership roles (often as board member or chair) in the Children's Defense Fund, an organization to protect the rights of minors; the Legal Services Corporation, a federally funded nonpartisan effort to make legal aid available to the indigent; and the New World Foundation, a philanthropy that gave small grants to community groups and minorities.

By 1993, two decades of professional contacts had resulted in a network of savvy, competent men and women who could assist Hillary Rodham Clinton in whatever projects she undertook as First Lady. Many of them went with her and the president to the White House. Two colleagues from the Rose Law Firm achieved particular prominence: Vincent W. Foster, Jr., served as assistant White House Counsel until his suicide in July 1993, and Webster L. Hubbell was associate attorney general until his resignation in March 1994 amid charges that he had approved excessive billing of clients while at the Rose Law Firm.

After her marriage, Hillary Rodham Clinton had taken primary responsibility for the family's financial affairs, and during her husband's run for president in 1992, *Money* magazine titled an article, "How Hillary Manages the Clintons' Money." Her handling of investments came under especially close scrutiny in regard to two matters: one dealt with the Clintons' participation in the Whitewater Development Company, a real estate project in Arkansas that had foundered in the 1970s; the other, a remarkably successful venture into trading in commodity futures in the late 1970s. In the latter, the Clintons had earned a large return (generally reported as nearly $100,000) on a tiny investment of $1,000 in a matter of a few months. When a special prosecutor, Robert B. Fiske, Jr., was appointed to look into the Whitewater affair, he questioned both the president and First Lady separately about their roles—an unprecedented event.

During the 1992 campaign for president, Bill Clinton had insisted that voters would be getting a bonus if they elected him—two excellent people for just one vote. But not all Americans seemed pleased with the idea of a First Lady participating in the presidency, and Hillary Clinton's role was de-emphasized later in the campaign. She often accompanied her husband on the campaign trail, and after the nominating convention she and Tipper Gore, wife of vice presidential candidate Albert Gore, Jr., frequently appeared together, either with their husbands or on their own.

None of this activity broke any new ground for a prospective president's wife, but several months before Bill Clinton was nominated his wife played an important part in keeping his candidacy alive. A tabloid had run a story about Gennifer Flowers, an Arkansas woman who boasted that she had enjoyed a long sexual liaison with Bill Clinton, and other newspapers picked up the story and ran it. To counteract the charges, the Clintons agreed to appear together on the CBS television news program *60 Minutes* and answer questions. While the candidate admitted to causing "pain" in his marriage, he gave no specifics. His wife was more candid, saying that whatever happened, it was the Clintons' business and not a matter for voters to decide. She concluded that if they did not like the candidate, then "don't vote for him."

After the November 1992 election, Bill Clinton welcomed congressional leaders to Little Rock, and when he later described the meeting to the press, he said that his wife had been present, "talked a lot and knew more than we did about some things." Among the very first announcements from the Clinton White House was the First Lady's appointment to chair the Task Force on Health Care Reform and her assignment to an office on the second floor of the West Wing, a few feet from the Oval Office.

Through the first months of 1993, the task force held meetings that resulted in an unusual legal ruling on the role of First Lady. Physicians and others who wanted to participate in the meetings and express their views were barred on the grounds that only "government officials" could attend. Attorneys for the physicians argued that the president's wife did not qualify as a "government official" and that the meetings should be opened. A district federal court agreed, but on 22 June 1993 a federal appeals court reversed that decision, ruling instead that there existed "a long standing tradition of public service by First Ladies . . . who have acted (albeit in the background) as advisers and personal representatives of their husbands." Even a dissenting opinion by Judge James L. Buckley took note of the official status of a president's wife, who is "greeted like a head of state, guarded by the Secret Service, and allowed to spend Federal money." Since the task force had already finished its work, the verdict had no immediate effect, except to codify what had become a general acceptance of the First Lady's status.

Beginning in September 1993, Hillary Rodham Clinton appeared in front of congressional committees to answer questions about the task force report and recommendations. Although she made five such appearances in the course of one week, segments of which were carried on national television, and was generally heralded for her expertise and poised delivery, the task force proposal found little support, either in Congress or with the public. The First Lady was generally thought to have harmed her image and that of the president by being so prominently tied to an effort that failed. Even she conceded that she had tried to do too much.

Hillary Rodham Clinton then turned to more traditional, ceremonial tasks associated with presidents' wives for more than a century. In July 1995 she began writing a weekly syndicated column, "Talking It Over," that ran in newspapers across the nation, but, in the style of Eleanor Roosevelt's "My Day," she usually stuck to safe topics such as visits to art galleries and travel. Her own trips abroad, although not entirely uncontroversial, focused on issues typically defined as women's province such as family planning and human rights. In May 1995 she accompanied the president to Russia, but rather than investigating areas associated with her professional interests she visited museums and laid wreaths on soldiers' graves. After considerable controversy because of the record of the People's Republic of China on human rights, Hillary Rodham Clinton agreed to speak at the United Nations Conference on Women, held in Beijing in September 1995.

Critics complained that Hillary Rodham Clinton could not decide on the image she wanted to project as First Lady. Her competence and sympathies for the underdog propelled her to an activist role, such as that pioneered by Eleanor Roosevelt, but she also recognized that more traditional models, such as Barbara Bush, continued to be very popular.

The Senate run dominated Mrs. Clinton's schedule for the final two years of her husband's second administration. In early 1999, she embarked on "listening tours" through New York State and by January 2000, she had moved into a home the Clintons purchased in Chappaqua so that she could qualify as a New York resident. On 7 November 2000, when she delivered her victory speech, she summed up the campaign as "Sixty-two counties, 16 months, three debates, two opponents and six black pantsuits" but that understated the enormous effort she had expended.

After her election, Hillary Rodham Clinton sought to balance the demands of her two roles-Senator-elect and First Lady. She attended briefing sessions with other newly elected legislators and hosted dozens of receptions and dinners at the White House. A book auction for her memoirs reaped her an $8 million dollar advance, and the Clintons bought a house in Washington, D.C.

Hillary Clinton's early months as New York's junior senator were plagued by continuing attention to pardons her husband had granted just before leaving office. But in each case, even the one which involved her brother Hugh, who admitted taking a payment from a person who received a pardon, she insisted she had known nothing about it. Her first major speech in the Senate dealt entirely with economic development in New York State, but the press persisted in questioning her about her role in Bill Clinton's decisions as president—a unique situation for a senator to be in. Speculation increased that she would run for the nation's highest office herself but she disavowed any intention to do so, saying she meant to concentrate her energy on being a good legislator.

Laura Welch Bush, who had succeeded her in the White House, distanced herself from Hillary's activist record but, at the same time, disavowed the "traditional" label so often attached to her mother-in-law. In fact, Laura Bush combined many of the characteristics of both. Like Hillary, she held a graduate degree, having earned a master's degree in library science in 1972. After enjoying a satisfying career as elementary teacher and school librarian, she had, like many women born after World War II, married

Hillary Clinton publicly supported her husband's denials regarding Monica Lewinsky, beginning with her appearance with the president when he first refuted the charges that he had had an affair with the former White House intern. ARCHIVE PHOTOS

at a much later age than either her mother or mother-in-law. (Laura was 33 when she married George W. Bush in 1977.) But like Barbara Bush, Laura took her husband's name, stopped working soon after marrying, and devoted full time to her family, volunteer work, and her husband's political career.

Although she once quipped that she had agreed to marry George W. Bush only after he had promised she would never have to give a political speech, campaigning was part of Laura's marriage from the beginning. Since he had already decided to run for Congress in 1978 and his father was well on his road to the White House, she could hardly expect to avoid politics.

As popular First Lady of Texas (1995–2001), Laura Bush worked hard to improve literacy. Her most notable achievement was starting the Texas Book Festival which featured local authors and, beginning in 1996, raised hundreds of thousands of dollars to buy books for libraries. Laura later added breast cancer awareness to her agenda, along with attention to the problems of Alzheimer's sufferers and their families after her father died from that disease in April 1995. During her husband's campaign for the presidency (in which she made hundreds of appearances and demonstrated how comfortable she had become in front of the microphone and speaking to large audiences) she indicated that she would concentrate on similar causes as First Lady.

Already familiar with the White House, having visited often during her father-in-law's presidency, Laura Bush put together a staff that included trusted employees she had come to know in Texas and experienced Washingtonians who had worked for Barbara Bush. Frequently cited as a stable emotional anchor for her husband and a major support in his decision to quit drinking alcoholic beverages several years earlier, Laura demurred about a larger role. When asked if she would serve as an adviser to her husband, she once replied, "I'm just his wife. Don't you think that's better?" implying that as American women entered the 21st century, the definition of political wife had expanded greatly. Once free to decline a public role, a First Lady was now expected to be a polished speaker, tireless volunteer, efficient White House administrator, and politically astute assistant. What had once been remarkable had now become routine.

BIBLIOGRAPHY

Carl Sferrazza Anthony, *First Ladies: The Saga of the Presidents' Wives and Their Power*, 2 vols. (New York, 1990–1991), covers the topic from Martha Washington to Nancy Reagan, with the entire second volume devoted to the post-1960 years. Rather than writing about each woman separately, Anthony focuses on the relationships among them and the many instances in which their lives intersected.

Betty Boyd Caroli, *First Ladies* (New York, 1987; expanded ed. 1995), is a history of the job and the women who held it from 1789 to 1995. Written from a feminist perspective, it connects changes in the role of First Lady to changes in the lives of all American women. Margaret Truman, *First Ladies* (New York, 1995), is a personal history of the subject, including anecdotes and observations of a president's daughter.

Lewis L. Gould, ed., *American First Ladies: Their Lives and Their Legacy* (second edition, New York, 2001), has articles on every president's wife, from Martha Washington to Laura Bush. The entries, each written by an outstanding scholar in the field, conclude with bibliographies listing writings by and about the subject. Paul Boller, Jr., *Presidential Wives: An Anecdotal History* (New York, 1988), has entries on each First Lady from Martha Washington to Nancy Reagan.

Myra G. Gutin, *The President's Partner: The First Lady in the Twentieth Century* (Westport, Conn., 1989), grew out of a doctoral dissertation examining the communication roles of presidents' wives after 1920. The book divides twentieth-century First Ladies into several categories: "social hostesses and ceremonial presences," "emerging spokeswomen," "political surrogates and independent advocates," and "a First Lady in transition."

Nearly half of *Presidential Studies Quarterly* 20 (fall 1990) is devoted to articles on the role of First Ladies and recent scholarship on the topic. Ten essays focus on twentieth-century incumbents and their effect on the presidency.

Nancy Kegan Smith and Mary C. Ryan, eds., *Modern First Ladies: Their Documentary Legacy* (Washington, D.C., 1989), includes an introductory article by Lewis L. Gould on the role of First Ladies and articles by individual archivists on the records available for the presidents' wives from the beginning of the twentieth century to the Reagan years.

William Seale, *The President's House*, 2 vols. (Washington, D.C., 1986), is a reliable history of the White House and includes material on First Ladies before 1960.

Recent works include Kati Marton, *Hidden Power: Presidential Marriages That Shaped Our Recent History* (New York, 2001).

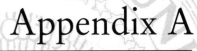

Appendix A

General Bibliography of the Presidency

Basic Sources

Angelo, Bonnie. *First Mothers: The Women Who Shaped the Presidents.* New York, 2000.

Barber, James David. *The Presidential Character: Predicting Performance in the White House.* 4th ed. Englewood Cliffs, N.J., 1992.

Boller, Paul F., Jr. *Presidential Anecdotes.* Rev. ed. New York, 1996.

Brinkley, Alan, and Davis Dyer, *The Reader's Companion to the American Presidency.* Boston, 2000.

Brogan, Hugh, and Charles Mosley. *American Presidential Families.* New York, 1993.

Burke, John P. *The Institutional Presidency: Organizing and Managing the White House from FDR to Clinton.* 2d ed. Baltimore, 2000.

Cooke, Jacob E., ed. *The Federalist.* Middletown, Conn. 1961.

Cronin, Thomas E., and Michael A. Genovese. *The Paradoxes of the American Presidency.* New York, 1998.

Dalin, David G., and Alfred J. Koltach. *The Presidents of the United States and the Jews.* Middle Village, N.Y., 2000.

DeGregorio, William A. *The Complete Book of U.S. Presidents.* Rev. ed. Ft. Lee, N.J. 2001.

Farrand, Max, ed. *The Records of the Federal Convention of 1787.* 4 vols. Rev. ed. New Haven, Conn., 1966.

Hart, John. *The Presidential Branch: From Washington to Clinton.* 2d ed. Chatham, N.J. 1995.

Israel, Fred L., ed. *The State of the Union Messages of the Presidents, 1790–1966.* 3 vols. New York, 1966.

Kane, Joseph Nathan. *Facts About the Presidents: A Compilation of Biographical and Historical Information.* 6th ed., *From George Washington to Bill Clinton.* New York, 1993.

Levy, Leonard W., and Louis Fisher, eds. *Encyclopedia of the American Presidency.* 4 vols. New York, 1994.

Lott, Davis Newton. *The Presidents Speak: The Inaugural Addresses of the American Presidents, from Washington to Clinton.* New York, 1994.

Martin, Fenton S., and Robert U. Goehlert. *American Presidents: A Bibliography.* Washington, D.C., 1987.

McPherson, James, and David Rubel, eds., *To the Best of My Ability: The American Presidents.* New York, 2000.

Mugridge, Donald H., comp. *The Presidents of the United States, 1789–1962: A Selected List of References.* Washington, D.C., 1963.

Ragsdale, Lyn. *Vital Statistics on the Presidency: Washington to Clinton.* Rev. ed. Washington, D.C., 1998.

Smith, Richard Norton, and Timothy Walch, eds. *Farewell to the Chief: Former Presidents in American Public Life*. Worland, Wyo., 1990.

The Institution of the Presidency

Corwin, Edward S. *The President: Office and Powers, 1787–1984: History and Analysis of Practice and Opinion*. 5th rev. ed. New York, 1984.

Cronin, Thomas E. *The State of the Presidency*. 2d ed. Boston, 1980.

Gilbert, Robert E. *The Mortal Presidency: Illness and Anguish in the White House*. 2d ed. New York, 1998.

Greenstein, Fred I. *Leadership in the Modern Presidency*. Cambridge, Mass.,1988.

——. *The Presidential Difference: Leadership Style from FDR to Clinton with a New Afterword on George W. Bush*. Princeton, N.J., 2001.

Guidas, John T., and Marilyn K. Parr, comps. *The Presidents of the United States: The First Twenty Years*. Washington, D.C., 1993.

Hess, Stephen. *Organizing the Presidency*. Rev. ed. Washington, D.C., 1988.

Ketcham, Ralph. *Presidents Above Party: The First American Presidency, 1789–1829*. Chapel Hill, N.C., 1984.

Koenig, Louis W. *The Chief Executive*. 6th ed. Fort Worth, Tex., 1996.

McCormick, Richard P. *The Presidential Game: The Origins of American Presidential Politics*. New York, 1982.

Neustadt, Richard E. *Presidential Power and the Modern Presidents: The Politics of Leadership from Roosevelt to Reagan*. 4th ed. New York, 1990.

Pious, Richard M. *The Presidency*. Boston, 1996.

Rose, Richard. *The Postmodern President: George Bush Meets the World*. 2d ed. Chatham, N.J., 1991.

Rossiter, Clinton. *The American Presidency*. 2d ed. New York, 1960.

Schlesinger, Arthur M., Jr. *The Imperial Presidency*. Boston, 1973.

Thach, Charles C., Jr. *The Creation of the Presidency, 1775–1789*. Baltimore, 1923; repr. 1969.

Presidential Campaigns and Elections

Boller, Paul F., Jr., *Presidential Campaigns*. Rev. ed. New York, 1996.

Brown, W. Burlie. *The People's Choice: The Presidential Image in the Campaign Biography*. Baton Rouge, La., 1960.

Congressional Quarterly. *National Party Conventions, 1831–2000*. Washington, D.C., 2001.

——. *Presidential Elections, 1789–1996*. Washington, D.C., 1997.

Miles, William. *Songs, Odes, Glees, and Ballads: A Bibliography of American Presidential Campaign Songsters*. New York, 1990.

Schlesinger, Arthur M., Jr., et al., eds. *Running for President: The Candidates and Their Images*. Vol. 1, *1789–1896*. Vol. 2, *1990–1992*. New York, 1994.

The White House

Anthony, Carl Sferrazza. *America's First Families: An Inside View of 200 Years of Private Life in the White House*. New York, 2000.

Caroli, Betty Boyd. *Inside the White House, America's Most Famous Home: The First 200 Years*. Garden City, N.Y., 1992.

Clinton, Hillary Rodham. *An Invitation to the White House: At Home With History*. New York, 2000.

Freidel, Frank, and William Pencak, eds. *The White House: The First Two Hundred Years*. Boston, 1994.

Furman, Bess. *White House Profile: A Social History of the White House, Its Occupants, and Its Festivities*. Indianapolis, Ind., 1951.

Monkman, Betty C. *The White House: Its Historic Furnishings and First Families*. Washington, D.C., 2000.

Ryan, William, and Desmond Guinness. *The White House: An Architectural History*. New York, 1980.

Seale, William. *The President's House: A History*. 2 vols. Washington, D.C., 1986.

——. *The White House: The History of an American Idea*. Washington, D.C., 1992.

Presidential History in Pictures

Anthony, Carl Sferrazza. *The Kennedy White House: Family Life and Pictures, 1961–1963*. New York, 2001.

Bassett, Margaret. *Profiles and Portraits of American Presidents*. Intro. by Henry F. Graff. Rev. ed. New York, 1976.

Benbow, Nancy D. Meyers, and Christopher H. Benbow. *Cabins, Cottages, and Mansions: Homes of the Presidents of the United States*. Gettysburg, Pa., 1993.

Beschloss, Michael, ed. *The American Heritage Illustrated History of The Presidents*. Rev. ed. New York, 2000.

Collins, Herbert R. *Presidents on Wheels*. Washington, D.C., 1971.

Collins, Herbert R., and David B. Weaver. *Wills of the U.S. Presidents*. New York, 1976.

Cunliffe, Marcus, and the editors of *American Heritage*. *The American Heritage History of the Presidency*. New York, 1968.

Durant, John, and Alice Durant. *Pictorial History of American Presidents*. New York, 1975.

Hyland, Pat. *Presidential Libraries and Museums: An Illustrated Guide*. Washington, D.C., 1995.

Jones, Cranston, with W. H. Schleisner. *Homes of the American Presidents*. New York, 1962.

Kruh, David, and Louis Kruh. *Presidential Landmarks*. New York, 1992.

Kunhardt, Philip B., Jr., Philip B. Kunhardt III, and Peter W. Kunhardt. *The American President*. New York, 1999.

Laird, Archibald. *Monuments Marking the Graves of the Presidents: A Collection of Photographs and Inscriptions*. North Quincy, Mass., 1971.

Mead, William B., and Paul Dickson. *Baseball: The Presidents' Game*. New York, 1997.

Lorant, Stefan. *The Glorious Burden: The American Presidency*. New York, 1968.

Siuru, William D., Jr., and Andrea Stewart. *Presidential Cars and Transportation: From Horse and Carriage to Air Force One*. Iola, Wis., 1995.

Presidential Libraries and Related Sites

The Presidential Libraries Act of 1955 provides for the preservation and public accessibility of papers and other materials donated to the federal government by U.S. presidents. The National Archives and Records Administration oversees collections of materials for all the presidents since Herbert Hoover, held in nine presidential libraries and two presidential projects included in the list below. Other collections, covering administrations before Hoover, are housed in the Library of Congress. Also listed here are notable presidential sites operated by other organizations.

Office of Presidential Libraries
National Archives at College Park
8601 Adelphi Road
College Park, MD 20740
tel. 301–713–6050
http://www.nara.gov/nara/president

Mount Vernon (home of George Washington)
Mount Vernon, VA 22121
tel. 703–780–2000
http://www.mountvernon.org
Owned and operated since 1858 by the Mount Vernon Ladies' Association

Monticello (home of Thomas Jefferson)
P.O. Box 316

Charlottesville, VA 22902
tel. 804–984–9822
http://www.monticello.org
Owned and operated by the Thomas Jefferson Memorial Foundation, Inc.

The Hermitage (home of Andrew Jackson)
4580 Rachel's Ln.
Hermitage, TN 37076
tel. 615–889–2941
A National Historic Landmark preserved since 1889 by the Ladies' Hermitage Association

Abraham Lincoln Presidential Library
212 North 6th Street
Springfield, IL 62702
http://www.state.il.us.HPH/preslib

Rutherford B. Hayes Presidential Center
Spiegel Grove
Fremont, OH 43420
tel. 800–998–7737
http://www.rbhayes.org
The first presidential library, privately operated with partial support from the Ohio Historical Society

Theodore Roosevelt Birthplace
28 E. 20th St.
New York, NY 10003
tel. 212–260–1616
http://www.nps.gov/thrb
A National Historic Site operated by the National Park Service

Herbert Hoover Library
211 Parkside Dr., P.O. Box 488
West Branch, IA 52358–0488
tel. 319–643–5301
http://www.nara.gov/nara/president/hoover

Franklin D. Roosevelt Library
511 Albany Post Rd.
Hyde Park, NY 12538–1999
tel. 914–229–8114
http://www.academic.marist.edu/fdr

Harry S. Truman Library
500 W. U.S. Highway 24
Independence, MO 64050–1798
tel. 816–833–1400
http://sunsite.unc.edu/lia/president/truman.html

Dwight D. Eisenhower Library
200 S.E. 4th St.
Abilene, KS 67410–2900
tel. 913–263–4751
http://sunsite.unc.edu/lia/president/eisenhower.html

John Fitzgerald Kennedy Library
Columbia Point
Boston, MA 02125–3398
tel. 617–929–4500
http://jfklibrary.org

Lyndon Baines Johnson Library
2313 Red River St.
Austin, TX 78705–5702
tel. 512–916–5137
http://www.lbjlib.utexas.edu

The Richard Nixon Library and Birthplace
18001 Yorba Linda Blvd.
Yorba Linda, CA 92886
tel. 714–993–5075
http://www.nixonfoundation.org

Nixon Presidential Materials Staff
National Archives at College Park
8601 Adelphi Rd.
College Park, MD 20740–6001
tel. 301–713–6950
http://sunsite.unc.edu/lia/president/nixon.html

Gerald R. Ford Library
1000 Beal Ave.
Ann Arbor, MI 48109–2114
tel. 313–741–2218
http://www.ford.utexas.edu

Jimmy Carter Library
441 Freedom Parkway
Atlanta, GA 30307
tel. 404–331–9554
http://www.jimmcarterlibrary.org

Ronald Reagan Library
40 Presidential Dr.
Simi Valley, CA 93065–0666
tel. 805–522–8444
http://www.reagan.utexas.edu

George Bush Library
1000 George Bush Drive West
College Station, TX 77845
tel. 409–260–9557
http://bushlibrary.tamu.edu

William J. Clinton Presidential Materials Project
1000 LaHarpe Blvd.
Little Rock, AR 72201
tel. 501–244–9756
http://www.clinton.nara.gov

Materials will be made available to researchers upon completion of a permanent facility, at which time the project will be renamed the Clinton Library.

Presidential Documents

Every Monday since 2 August 1965 the Office of the Federal Register, National Archives and Records Administration (NARA), has published the Weekly Compilation of Presidential Documents. The "Comp," as it is generally referred to, contains statements, messages, executive orders, proclamations, and sundry other presidential materials released by the press secretary at the White House during the previous week. It is distributed by the Superintendent of Documents, Government Printing Office, Washington, D.C.

Beginning with the Eisenhower administration in 1953, the Federal Register has published annually the Public Papers of the President, which today contain the cumulated contents of the "Comp," except for executive orders and proclamations. Retrospective editions for the Hoover and Truman administrations have also been issued. Below is a list of these and other collections of presidential documents. Editions marked with an asterisk are projects conducted under the auspices of the National Historical Publications and Records Commission (NHPR), a statutory body affiliated with NARA. The NHPR, prodded originally by President Harry S. Truman, is charged to collect, preserve, and publish the public and private writings of prominent Americans, including notably those of the presidents.

Early Compendia
American State Papers: Documents, Legislative and Executive, of the Congress of the United States. 38 vols. Washington, D.C., 1832–1861.
Richardson, James D., ed. *A Compilation of the Messages and Papers of the Presidents.* 20 vols. New York, 1917.

George Washington
Library of Congress microfilm. 124 reels.
Fitzpatrick, John C., ed. *The Writings of George Washington from the Original Manuscript Sources, 1745–1799.* 39 vols. Washington, D.C., 1931–1944.
*Abbot, W. W., et al., eds. *The Papers of George Washington.* 44 vols. of 75 expected. Charlottesville, Va., 1983–.

John Adams
Adams Family Papers. Massachusetts Historical Society microfilm. 608 reels.
Adams, Charles Francis, ed. *The Works of John Adams.* 10 vols. Boston, 1850–1856.
*Butterfield, L. H. et al., eds. *The Adams Family Papers.* 34 vols. of 100 expected. Cambridge, Mass.

Thomas Jefferson
Library of Congress microfilm. 65 reels.

Ford, Paul Leicester, ed. *The Works of Thomas Jefferson.* 12 vols. New York, 1904–1905.

Lipscomb, A. A., and A. E. Bergh, eds. *The Writings of Thomas Jefferson.* 20 vols. Washington, D.C., 1903–1904.

*Boyd, Julian et al., eds. *The Papers of Thomas Jefferson.* 28 vols. of 83 expected. Princeton, N.J., 1950–.

James Madison

Library of Congress microfilm. 28 reels.

Hunt, Gaillard, ed. *The Writings of James Madison.* 9 vols. Washington, D.C., 1900–1910.

*Hutchinson, William T. et al., eds. *The Papers of James Madison.* 23 vols. of 60 expected. Chicago and Charlottesville, Va., 1962–.

James Monroe

Library of Congress microfilm. 11 reels.

Garrison, Curtis W., ed. *James Monroe Papers in Virginia Repositories.* 13 reels. Charlottesville, Va., 1969.

Hamilton, Stanislaus M., ed. *The Writings of James Monroe.* 7 vols. New York, 1898–1903.

John Quincy Adams

Adams Family Papers. Massachusetts Historical Society microfilm. 608 reels.

*Butterfield, L. H. et al., eds. *The Adams Family Papers.* 34 vols. of 100 expected. Cambridge, Mass.

Andrew Jackson

Library of Congress microfilm. 78 reels.

Moser, Harold D. et al., eds. *The Papers of Andrew Jackson.* Microfilm edition. 39 reels. Wilmington, Del., 1986.

*Smith, Sam B. et al., eds. *The Papers of Andrew Jackson.* 5 vols. of 17 expected. Knoxville, Tenn., 1980–.

Martin Van Buren

*West, Lucy Fisher, Walter L. Ferree, and George W. Franz, eds. *The Papers of Martin Van Buren.* Microfilm edition. 55 reels, 134-page guide. Alexandria, Va., 1987.

William Henry Harrison

Library of Congress microfilm. 3 reels.

John Tyler

Library of Congress microfilm. 3 reels.

James K. Polk

Library of Congress microfilm. 67 reels.

Quaife, Milo M., ed. *The Diary of James K. Polk During His Presidency, 1845–1849.* 4 vols. Chicago, 1910.

*Weaver, Herbert et al., eds. *The Correspondence of James K. Polk.* 9 vols. of 11 expected. Nashville, Tenn., 1969–.

Zachary Taylor

Library of Congress microfilm. 2 reels.

Millard Fillmore

*Smith, Lester W., ed. *Millard Fillmore Papers.* Microfilm edition. 68 reels, 47-page guide. Buffalo, N.Y., 1975.

Franklin Pierce

Library of Congress microfilm. 7 reels.

James Buchanan

Moore, John Bassett, ed. *The Works of James Buchanan.* 12 vols. Philadelphia, 1908–1911.

*West, Lucy Fisher, ed. *James Buchanan Papers.* Microfilm edition. 60 reels, 35-page guide. Philadelphia, 1974.

Abraham Lincoln

Library of Congress microfilm. 97 reels.

Basler, Roy P., ed. *Works of Abraham Lincoln.* 9 vols. New Brunswick, N.J., 1953–1955.

Andrew Johnson

Library of Congress microfilm. 55 reels.

*Graf, LeRoy P. et al., eds. *The Papers of Andrew Johnson.* 16 volumes. Knoxville, Tenn., 1967–2000.

Ulysses S. Grant

Library of Congress microfilm. 32 reels.

*Simon, John Y., et al., eds. *The Papers of Ulysses S. Grant.* 22 vols. of 25 expected. Carbondale, Ill., 1967–.

Rutherford B. Hayes

Williams, Charles F., ed. *Diary and Letters of Rutherford B. Hayes.* 5 vols. Columbus, Ohio, 1922–1926.

*Smith, Thomas, ed. *The Rutherford B. Hays Papers.* Microfilm edition. 301 reels, 56-page guide. Fremont, Ohio, 1982.

James A. Garfield

Library of Congress microfilm. 177 reels.

Brown, Harry J., and Frederick D. Williams, eds. *The Diary of James A. Garfield.* 4 vols. East Lansing, Mich., 1967–1981.

Chester A. Arthur

Library of Congress microfilm. 3 reels.

Grover Cleveland
Library of Congress microfilm. 164 reels.

Benjamin Harrison
Library of Congress microfilm. 151 reels.
Speeches of Benjamin Harrison, The. New York, 1892.

William McKinley
Library of Congress microfilm. 98 reels.

Theodore Roosevelt
Library of Congress microfilm. 485 reels.
Morison, Elting, and John Blum, eds. *The Papers of Theodore Roosevelt.* 8 vols. Cambridge, Mass., 1951–1954.

William Howard Taft
Library of Congress microfilm. 658 reels.

Woodrow Wilson
Library of Congress microfilm. 540 reels.
*Link, Arthurs. et al., eds. *The Papers of Woodrow Wilson.* 69 vols. Princeton, N.J., 1966–1994.

Warren G. Harding
*Lentz, Andrea, ed. *Warren G. Harding Papers.* Microfilm edition. 263 reels. Columbus, Ohio, 1970.

Calvin Coolidge
Library of Congress microfilm. 190 reels.

Herbert Hoover
Public Papers of the Presidents of the United States: Herbert Hoover. 6 vols. Washington, D.C., 1929–1933.
Hoover-Wilson Correspondence, The. Ames, Iowa, 1974.

Franklin D. Roosevelt
Rosenman, Samuel I., ed. *Public Papers and Addresses of Franklin D. Roosevelt.* 13 vols. New York, 1938–1950.

Harry S. Truman
Public Papers of the Presidents of the United States: Harry S. Truman. 8 vols. Washington, D.C., 1948–1953.

Dwight D. Eisenhower
Public Papers of the Presidents of the United States: Dwight D. Eisenhower. 8 vols. Washington, D.C., 1953–1961.

*Chandler, Alfred D., Jr., et al., eds. *The Papers of Dwight David Eisenhower.* 21 volumes. Baltimore, 1970–.

John F. Kennedy
Public Papers of the Presidents of the United States: John F. Kennedy. 3 vols. Washington, D.C., 1961–1963.

Lyndon B. Johnson
Public Papers of the Presidents of the United States: Lyndon B. Johnson. 10 vols. Washington, D.C., 1963–1969.

Richard Nixon
Public Papers of the Presidents of the United States: Richard Nixon, 1969–1974. 6 vols. Washington, D.C., 1969–1974.

Gerald R. Ford
Public Papers of the Presidents of the United States: Gerald R. Ford, 1974–1977. 6 vols. Washington, D.C., 1974–1977.

Jimmy Carter
Public Papers of the Presidents of the United States: Jimmy Carter, 1977–1981. 9 vols. Washington, D.C., 1977–1981.

Ronald Reagan
Public Papers of the Presidents of the United States: Ronald Reagan, 1981–1989. 15 vols. Washington, D.C., 1981–1989.

George Bush
Public Papers of the Presidents of the United States: George Bush, 1989–1993. 8 vols. Washington, D.C., 1989–1993.

William J. Clinton
Public Papers of the Presidents of the United States: William J. Clinton, 1993– . 4 vols. to date. Washington, D.C., 1993–1996.

The Presidential Recordings Project

Edited by Philip Zelikow, Ernest May, and Timothy Naftali, and published by W. W. Norton and Company, the Presidential Recordings Project is a comprehensive, accessible written record of all discussions and meetings tape-recorded by recent U. S. presidents. These include recordings from the Eisenhower, Kennedy, Johnson, and

Nixon administrations. The materials are available in book form and CD ROM.

The Presidential Recordings
The Presidential Recordings: John F. Kennedy: The Great Crises, Volumes 1–3. 2000.

Presidents and First Ladies on the Presidency

Adams, John. *Diary and Autobiography of John Adams, 1755–1804.* Ed. by L. H. Butterfield et al. Cambridge, Mass., 1961.

Adams, Abigail. *Letters of Mrs. Adams, the Wife of John Adams.* Boston, 1840.

——. *New Letters of Abigail Adams, 1788–1801* Ed. by Stewart Mitchell. Worcester, Mass., 1947.

Madison, James. *Records of the Federal Convention of 1787.* Ed. by Max Farrand. 4 vols. Rev. ed. New Haven, Conn., 1966.

Madison, Dolley. *The Memoirs and Letters of Dolly [sic] Madison.* Ed. by Lucia B. Cutts. Boston, 1886.

Monroe, James. *A View of the Conduct of the Executive in the Foreign Affairs of the United States. . . .* Philadelphia, 1797.

Adams, John Quincy. *Memoirs of John Quincy Adams, Comprising Portions of His Diary from 1795 to 1848.* Ed. by Charles Francis Adams 12 vols. Philadelphia, 1874–1877. Abridged version, *The Diary of John Quincy Adams, 1794–1845: American Diplomacy, and Political, Social, and Intellectual Life, from Washington to Polk.* Ed. by Allan Nevins. New York, 1951.

Van Buren, Martin. *The Autobiography of Martin Van Buren.* Ed. by John C. Fitzpatrick. Washington, D.C., 1920.

Polk, James K. *The Diary of James K. Polk During His Presidency, 1845–1849.* Ed. by Milo M. Quaife. 4 vols. Chicago, 1910. Abridged version, *Polk: The Diary of a President, 1845–1849.* Ed. by Allan Nevins. New York, 1929.

Fillmore, Millard. *Millard Fillmore Papers.* Ed. by Frank H. Severance. 2 vols. Buffalo, N.Y., 1907.

Buchanan, James. *The Administration on the Eve of the Rebellion: A History of Four Years Before the War.* London, 1865.

——. *The Diary of a Public Man: An Intimate View of the National Administration, December 28, 1860 to March 15, 1861.* 1945.

Grant, Julia Dent. *The Personal Memoirs of Julia Dent Grant (Mrs. Ulysses S. Grant).* Ed. by John Y. Simon. New York, 1975.

Hayes, Rutherford B. *Hayes: The Diary of a President, 1875–1881.* Ed. by T. Harry Williams. New York, 1964.

Cleveland, Grover. *Presidential Problems.* New York, 1904.

——. *Letters of Grover Cleveland, 1850–1908.* Ed. by Allan Nevins. Boston and New York, 1933.

Harrison, Benjamin. *This Country of Ours.* 2d. ed. New York, 1897.

——. *Views of an Ex–President.* Indianapolis, Ind., 1901.

Roosevelt, Theodore. *Theodore Roosevelt: An Autobiography.* New York, 1913.

Taft, William H. *Our Chief Magistrate and His Powers.* New York, 1916.

——. *The Presidency: Its Duties, Its Powers, Its Opportunities, and Its Limitations.* New York, 1916.

Taft, Helen Herron. *Recollections of Full Years.* New York, 1914.

Wilson, Woodrow. *Congressional Government: A Study in American Politics.* Boston, 1885.

——. *Constitutional Government in the United States.* New York, 1908.

Wilson, Edith Bolling. *My Memoir.* New York, 1939.

Coolidge, Calvin. *Autobiography of Calvin Coolidge.* New York, 1929.

Coolidge, Grace. Articles in *Good Housekeeping,* beginning February 1935.

Hoover, Herbert. *The Memoirs of Herbert Hoover.* 3 vols. New York, 1951–1952.

——. *The Ordeal of Woodrow Wilson.* New York, 1958.

Roosevelt, Franklin D. *FDR: His Personal Letters.* Ed. by Elliott Roosevelt. 4 vols. New York, 1947–1950.

Roosevelt, Eleanor. *This I Remember.* New York, 1949.

——. *The Autobiography of Eleanor Roosevelt.* Boston, 1984.

Truman, Harry S. *Dear Bess: The Letters from Harry to Bess Truman, 1910–1959.* Ed. by Robert H. Ferrell. New York, 1983.

——. *Memoirs.* 2 vols. Vol. 1, *Year of Decisions.* Vol. 2, *Years of Trial and Hope, 1946–1952.* Garden City, N.Y., 1955.

—— *Off the Record: The Private Papers of Harry S. Truman.* Ed. by Robert H. Ferrell. New York, 1980.

—— *The Autobiography of Harry S. Truman.* Ed. by Robert H. Ferrell. Boulder, Colo., 1980.

—— *Truman Speaks.* New York, 1960.

—— *Where the Buck Stops: The Personal and Private Writings of Harry S. Truman.* Ed. by Margaret Truman. New York, 1989.

Eisenhower, Dwight D. *The White House Years.* 2 vols. Vol. 1, *Mandate for Change, 1953–1956.* Vol. 2, *Waging Peace, 1956–1961.* Garden City, N.Y., 1963–1965.

Johnson, Lyndon B. *The Vantage Point: Perspectives of the Presidency, 1963–1969.* New York, 1971.

Johnson, Lady Bird. *A White House Diary.* New York, 1970.

Nixon, Richard. *RN: The Memoirs of Richard Nixon.* New York, 1978.

—— *In the Arena: A Memoir of Victory, Defeat, and Renewal.* New York, 1990.

Ford, Gerald R. *A Time to Heal: The Autobiography of Gerald R. Ford.* New York, 1979.

Ford, Betty. *The Times of My Life.* With Chris Chase. New York, 1978.

—— *Betty: A Glad Awakening.* With Chris Chase. Garden City, N.Y., 1987.

Carter, Jimmy. *Keeping Faith: Memoirs of a President.* New York, 1983.

Carter, Rosalynn. *First Lady from Plains.* Boston, 1984.

Reagan, Ronald. *An American Life.* New York, 1990.

Reagan, Nancy. *My Turn: The Memoirs of Nancy Reagan.* With William Novak. New York, 1989.

Bush, George. *All The Best, George Bush: My Life in Letters and Other Writings.* New York, 1999.

Bush, George, and Brent Scowcroft. *A World Transformed.* New York, 1998.

Bush, Barbara. *Barbara Bush: A Memoir.* New York, 1994.

Clinton, Hillary Rodham. *It Takes a Village: And Other Lessons Children Teach Us.* New York, 1996.

Note: *The Autobiography of Thomas Jefferson,* ed. by Dumas Malone (New York, 1959), and *The Autobiography of James Monroe,* ed. by Stuart G. Brown (Syracuse, N.Y., 1959), do not deal with the presidential years of their authors and only tangentially with the presidency itself. The most famous of all autobiographies by a president, *Personal Memoirs of U. S. Grant,* 2 vols. (New York, 1885–1886), covers only the general's Civil War experiences.

Appendix B

*Table of Biographical,
Political, and
Historical Data*

TABLE OF PRESIDENTIAL DATA

George Washington, 1st President (1789–1797)

Life

Birthdate:	22 February 1732
Birthplace:	Westmoreland County, Va.
Parents:	Augustine Washington, Mary Ball
Religion:	Episcopalian
College Education:	None
Wife:	Martha Dandridge Custis
Date of Marriage:	6 January 1759
Children:	None
Political Party:	Nonpartisan but generally sympathetic to Federalist positions
Other Positions Held:	Member, Virginia House of Burgesses (1759–1774)
	Member, Continental Congress (1774–1775)
	Commander, Continental Army (1775–1783)
Date of Inauguration:	30 April 1789
End of Term:	4 March 1797
Date of Death:	14 December 1799
Place of Death:	Mount Vernon, Va.
Place of Burial:	Mount Vernon, Va.

Elections

ELECTION OF 1789

Candidate	Electoral Vote
George Washington	69
John Adams	34
Others	35

ELECTION OF 1792

Candidate	Electoral Vote
George Washington	132
John Adams	77
George Clinton	50
Others	5

DID NOT RUN IN ELECTION OF 1796

POLITICAL COMPOSITION OF CONGRESS

1st Congress (1789–1791)
Senate:	Fed. 17; Opposition 9
House:	Fed. 38; Opposition 26

2d Congress (1791–1793)
Senate:	Fed. 16; Dem.–Rep. 13
House:	Dem.–Rep. 33; Fed. 37

3d Congress (1793–1795)
Senate:	Fed. 17; Dem.–Rep. 13
House:	Dem.–Rep. 57; Fed. 48

4th Congress (1795–1797)
Senate:	Fed. 19; Dem.–Rep. 13
House:	Fed. 54; Dem.–Rep. 52

Vice President

John Adams (1789–1797)

Appointments

Cabinet Members
Thomas Jefferson, secretary of state (1790–1793)
Edmund Randolph, secretary of state (1794–1795)
Timothy Pickering, secretary of state (1795–1797)
Alexander Hamilton, secretary of the treasury (1789–1795)
Oliver Wolcott, Jr., secretary of the treasury (1795–1797)
Henry Knox, secretary of war (1789–1794)
Timothy Pickering, secretary of war (1795)
James McHenry, secretary of war (1796–1797)
Edmund Randolph, attorney general (1789–1794)
William Bradford, attorney general (1794–1795)
Charles Lee, attorney general (1795–1797)

Supreme Court Appointments
John Jay, chief justice (1789–1795)
John Rutledge (1789–1791)
William Cushing (1789–1810)
James Wilson (1789–1798)
John Blair (1789–1796)
James Iredell (1790–1798)
Thomas Johnson (1791–1793)
William Paterson (1793–1806)
Samuel Chase (1796–1811)
Oliver Ellsworth, chief justice (1796–1799)

Key Events

1789   Establishment of Departments of State, War, and the Treasury and Office of the Attorney General; Federal Judiciary Act creates Supreme Court (24 Sept.).

1790   First U.S. census authorized (Mar.): population 3,929,214; Congress locates projected federal capital on Potomac (10 July) and authorizes building of a presidential residence (16 July); federal government assumes state Revolutionary War debts (4 Aug.).

1791   First Bank of the U.S. created (25 Feb.); Whiskey Tax passed (3 Mar.); Bill of Rights added to the Constitution (15 Dec.); plan of Federal City (Washington) laid out.

1792   U.S. Mint opens in Philadelphia; first U.S. political parties (Republican and Federalist) formed; cornerstone of White House laid (13 Oct.); Washington and John Adams reelected (5 Dec.).

1793   Washington issues Neutrality Proclamation (22 Apr.), warning Americans to avoid aiding either France or Great Britain in their war.

1794   Barbary states begin preying on American shipping; Neutrality Act (5 June) forbids enlisting in service of a foreign nation or fitting out foreign armed vessels); Whiskey Rebellion: protest by farmers objecting to whiskey tax, halted by state militias of New Jersey, Pennsylvania, Virginia, and Massachusetts.

1795   Yazoo Land Fraud between Georgia legislators and 4 land companies for present–day Alabama and Mississippi; Pinckney's Treaty (27 Oct.) with Spain gives U.S. free navigation of Mississippi.

1796   Washington's Farewell Address (17 Sept.) warns against U.S. involvement in foreign disputes; Adams and Jefferson elected president and vice president (7 Dec.).

John Adams, 2nd President (1797–1801)

Life

Birthdate:	30 October 1735
Birthplace:	Braintree (now Quincy), Mass.
Parents:	John Adams, Susanna Boylston
Religion:	Unitarian
College Education:	Harvard College
Wife:	Abigail Smith
Date of Marriage:	25 October 1764
Children:	Abigail Amelia, John Quincy, Susanna, Charles, Thomas Boylston

Political Party: Federalist

Other Positions Held:	Member, Continental Congress (1774–1778)
	Minister to France (1778–1779)
	Minister to Great Britain (1785–1788)
	Vice President (1789–1797)
Date of Inauguration:	4 March 1797
End of Term:	4 March 1801
Date of Death:	4 July 1826
Place of Death:	Quincy, Mass.
Place of Burial:	Quincy, Mass.

Elections

ELECTION OF 1796

Candidate	Party	Electoral Vote
John Adams	Fed.	71
Thomas Jefferson	Dem.–Rep.	68
Thomas Pinckney	Fed.	59
Aaron Burr	Dem.–Rep.	30

DEFEATED IN ELECTION OF 1800 BY THOMAS JEFFERSON

POLITICAL COMPOSITION OF CONGRESS

5th Congress (1797–1799)

Senate:	Fed. 20; Dem.–Rep. 12
House:	Fed. 58; Dem.–Rep. 48

6th Congress (1799–1801)

Senate:	Fed. 19; Dem.–Rep. 13
House:	Fed. 64; Dem.–Rep. 42

Vice President

Thomas Jefferson (1797–1801)

Appointments

Cabinet Members:
Timothy Pickering, secretary of state (1797–1800)
John Marshall, secretary of state (1800–1801)
Oliver Wolcott, Jr., secretary of the treasury (1797–1800)
Samuel Dexter, secretary of the treasury (1801)
James McHenry, secretary of war (1797–1800)
Samuel Dexter, secretary of war (1800–1801)
Roger Griswold, secretary of war (1801)
Charles Lee, attorney general (1797–1801)
Theophilus Parsons, attorney general (1801)
Benjamin Stoddert, secretary of the navy (1798–1801)

Supreme Court Appointments:
Bushrod Washington (1798–1829)
Alfred Moore (1799–1804)
John Marshall, chief justice (1801–1835)

Key Events

1797   XYZ Affair: 3 commissioners sent to France to negotiate commerce and amity treaty; Adams discloses to Congress (3 Apr. 1798) refusal of French foreign affairs secretary Talleyrand to receive commissioners unless a loan was granted France and a bribe paid.

1798   Eleventh Amendment prevents individual states from being sued without their consent (8 Jan.); Alien and Sedition Acts: Naturalization Act (18 June), Alien Act (6 July), Alien Enemies Act (6 July), and Sedition Act (14 July) impose severe restrictions on aliens; Kentucky (16 Nov. 1798, 22 Nov. 1799) and Virginia (24 Dec. 1798) resolutions protest Alien and Sedition Acts as unconstitutional and advocate state sovereignty; undeclared naval war ("Quasi–War") with France begins with French seizure of American merchantmen.

1799   Logan Act (30 Jan.) prohibits correspondence with enemy foreign nations; Fries's Rebellion: armed resistance by Pennsylvania farmers led by John Fries to protest federal tax on land and houses, put down by federal troops.

1800   U.S. population: 5,308,483 Harrison Land Act (10 May) facilitates individual land purchases; secret Treaty of San Ildefonso cedes Louisiana to France (1 Oct.); peace with France concluded by Convention of 1800 (30 Sept.); Adams moves into the still–unfinished White House (1 Nov.); Congress convenes in Washington, D.C., for first time (17 Nov.).

1801   John Marshall becomes Chief Justice of the Supreme Court (31 Jan.); House of Representatives chooses Thomas Jefferson over Aaron Burr for president (17 Feb.), the election of 1800 having resulted in a tie vote in the electoral college.

TABLE OF PRESIDENTIAL DATA

Thomas Jefferson, 3rd President (1801–1809)

Life

Birthdate:	13 April 1743
Birthplace:	Goochland (now Albemarle) County, Va.
Parents:	Peter Jefferson, Jane Randolph
Religion:	Deism
College Education:	College of William and Mary
Wife:	Martha Wayles Skelton
Date of Marriage:	1 January 1772
Children:	Martha, Maria, Lucy Elizabeth
Political Party:	Democratic–Republican
Other Positions Held:	Member, Virginia House of Burgesses (1769–1775)
	Member, Continental Congress (1775–1776; 1783–1785)
	Governor of Virginia (1779–1781)
	Secretary of State (1790–1793)
	Vice President (1797–1801)
	Rector, University of Virginia (1825–1826)
Date of Inauguration:	4 March 1801
End of Term:	4 March 1809
Date of Death:	4 July 1826
Place of Death:	Charlottesville, Va.
Place of Burial:	Charlottesville, Va.

Elections

ELECTION OF 1800

Candidate	Party	Electoral Vote
Thomas Jefferson	Dem.–Rep.	73
Aaron Burr	Dem.–Rep.	73
John Adams	Fed.	65
Charles C. Pinckney	Fed.	64
John Jay	Fed.	1

ELECTION OF 1804

Candidate	Party	Electoral Vote
Thomas Jefferson	Dem.–Rep.	162
Charles C. Pinckney	Fed.	14

DID NOT RUN IN ELECTION OF 1808

POLITICAL COMPOSITION OF CONGRESS

7th Congress (1801–1803)
Senate: Dem.–Rep. 18; Fed. 13
House: Dem.–Rep. 69; Fed. 36

8th Congress (1803–1805)
Senate: Dem.–Rep. 25; Fed. 9
House: Dem.–Rep. 102; Fed. 39

9th Congress (1805–1807)
Senate: Dem.–Rep. 27; Fed. 7
House: Dem.–Rep. 116; Fed. 25

10th Congress (1807–1809)
Senate: Dem.–Rep. 28; Fed. 6
House: Dem.–Rep. 118; Fed. 24

Vice Presidents

Aaron Burr (1801–1805)
George Clinton (1805–1809)

Appointments

Cabinet Members:
James Madison, secretary of state (1801–1809)
Samuel Dexter, secretary of the treasury (1801)
Albert Gallatin, secretary of the treasury (1801–1809)
Henry Dearborn, secretary of war (1801–1809)
Levi Lincoln, attorney general (1801–1804)
Robert Smith, attorney general (1805)
John Breckenridge, attorney general (1805–1806)
Caesar A. Rodney, attorney general (1807–1809)
Benjamin Stoddert, secretary of the navy (1801)
Robert Smith, secretary of the navy (1801–1809)

Supreme Court Appointments:
William Johnson (1804–1834)
Henry Brockholst Livingston (1806–1823)
Thomas Todd (1807–1826)

Key Events

1801   Jefferson becomes first president inaugurated in Washington, D.C. (4 Mar.).

1803   Supreme Court, in *Marbury* v. *Madison,* for the first time declares a congressional act unconstitutional (24 Feb.); U.S. purchases Louisiana (828,000 sq. miles) from France (2 May) for $15 million; Meriwether Lewis and William Clark explore the Far West (through 1806).

1804   Alexander Hamilton dies (12 July) from wounds suffered in duel with Aaron Burr the day before; Twelfth Amendment specifies separate ballots for president and vice president in electoral college (25 Sept.).

1805   *Essex* decision by British admiralty destroys principle of broken voyage; British begin seizing U.S. ships carrying French and Spanish goods; impressment by British ships is increased.

1806   Burr Conspiracy: Gen. James Wilkinson warns Jefferson of Burr's expedition allegedly to build a western empire from Spanish territories; Burr arrested (19 Feb. 1807) and acquitted of treason (1 Sept. 1807).

1807   Non–Importation Act (14 Dec.) put into effect against Britain; Robert Fulton's *Clermont* inaugurates commercial steam navigation, Embargo Act (22 Dec.) forbids U.S. ships to leave for foreign countries.

1808   Importation of slaves forbidden (1 Jan.); Madison elected president (7 Dec.).

1809   Non–Intercourse Act (1 Mar.) bans trade with Great Britain and France; Embargo Act repealed.

James Madison, 4th President (1809–1817)

Life

Birthdate:	16 March 1751
Birthplace:	Port Conway, Va.
Parents:	James Madison, Nelly Conway
Religion:	Episcopalian; deist
College Education:	College of New Jersey, now Princeton University
Wife:	Dolley Payne Todd
Date of Marriage:	15 September 1794
Children:	None
Political Party:	Democratic–Republican
Other Positions Held:	Member, Virginia House of Delegates (1776–1780; 1784–1786; 1798–1800)
	Member, Continental Congress (1780–1783; 1787–1788)
	Delegate to Constitutional Convention (1787)
	Member, U.S. House of Representatives (1789–1797)
	Secretary of State (1801–1809)
	Rector, University of Virginia (1826–1836)
Date of Inauguration:	4 March 1809
End of Term:	4 March 1817
Date of Death:	28 June 1836
Place of Death:	Montpelier, Va.
Place of Burial:	Montpelier, Va.

Elections

ELECTION OF 1808

Candidate	Party	Electoral Vote
James Madison	Dem.–Rep.	122
Charles C. Pinckney	Fed.	47
George Clinton	Dem.–Rep.	6

ELECTION OF 1812

Candidate	Party	Electoral Vote
James Madison	Dem.–Rep.	128
DeWitt Clinton	Fed.	89

DID NOT RUN IN ELECTION OF 1816

POLITICAL COMPOSITION OF CONGRESS

11th Congress (1809–1811)
Senate:	Dem.–Rep. 28; Fed. 6
House:	Dem.–Rep. 94; Fed. 48

12th Congress (1811–1813)
Senate:	Dem.–Rep. 30; Fed. 6
House:	Dem.–Rep. 108; Fed. 36

13th Congress (1813–1815)
Senate:	Dem.–Rep. 27; Fed. 9
House:	Dem.–Rep. 112; Fed. 68

14th Congress (1815–1817)
Senate:	Dem.–Rep. 25; Fed. 11
House:	Dem.–Rep. 117; Fed. 65

Vice Presidents

George Clinton (1809–1812)
Elbridge Gerry (1813–1814)

Appointments

Cabinet Members:
Robert Smith, secretary of state (1809–1811)
James Monroe, secretary of state (1811–1817)
Albert Gallatin, secretary of the treasury (1809–1814)
George W. Campbell, secretary of the treasury (1814)
Alexander J. Dallas, secretary of the treasury (1814–1816)
William H. Crawford, secretary of the treasury (1816–1817)
William Eustis, secretary of war (1809–1812)
John Armstrong, secretary of war (1813–1814)
James Monroe, secretary of war (1814–1815)
William H. Crawford, secretary of war (1815–1816)
Caesar A. Rodney, attorney general (1809–1811)
William Pinkney, attorney general (1812–1814)
Richard Rush, attorney general (1814–1817)
Paul Hamilton, secretary of the navy (1809–1812)
William Jones, secretary of the navy (1813–1814)
Benjamin W. Crowninshield, secretary of the navy (1815–1817)

Supreme Court Appointments:
Joseph Story (1811–1845)
Gabriel Duvall (1812–1835)

Key Events

1810   U.S. population: 7,239,881; Rambouillet Decree signed by Napoleon, ordering seizure of U.S. shipping in French ports; Macon's Bill No. 2 passes (1 May) to supplant Non–Intercourse Act; Florida annexed (27 Oct.).

1811   Secret act passed (15 Jan.) authorizing president to take possession of East Florida.

1812   Congress enacts embargo on Great Britain (4 Apr.); Vice President Clinton dies in office (20 Apr.); president authorized to raise 100,000 militia for 3 months; U.S. declares war on Great Britain (18 June) over freedom of the seas, impressment of seamen, and blockade of U.S. ports, beginning War of 1812; Madison elected president (2 Dec.) for second term.

1813   Lord Castlereagh's proposal for peace negotiations reaches Washington (4 Nov.).

1814   White House burned down to its stone walls by the British (24 Aug.); Treaty of Ghent (24 Dec.) ends War of 1812; U.S. rights to Newfoundland fisheries acknowledged, boundary commissions established; Hartford Convention convenes (15 Dec.), at which 26 New England delegates hold secret sessions to consider a convention to revise U.S. Constitution concerning states' rights in national emergencies.

1816   Second Bank of United States established (10 Apr.); Monroe elected president (4 Dec.).

TABLE OF PRESIDENTIAL DATA

James Monroe, 5th President (1817–1825)

Life

Birthdate:	28 April 1758
Birthplace:	Westmoreland County, Va.
Parents:	Spence Monroe, Elizabeth Jones
Religion:	Episcopalian
College Education:	College of William and Mary
Wife:	Elizabeth Kortright
Date of Marriage:	16 February 1786
Children:	Eliza Kortright, Maria Hester
Political Party:	Democratic–Republican
Other Positions Held:	Member, Continental Congress (1783–1786)
	U.S. Senator (1790–1794)
	Minister to France (1794–1796)
	Governor of Virginia (1799–1802; 1811)
	Secretary of State (1811–1817)
	Secretary of War (1814–1815)
Date of Inauguration:	4 March 1817
End of Term:	3 March 1825
Date of Death:	4 July 1831
Place of Death:	New York, N.Y.
Place of Burial:	Richmond, Va.

Elections

ELECTION OF 1816

Candidate	Party	Electoral Vote
James Monroe	Dem.–Rep.	183
Rufus King	Fed.	34

ELECTION OF 1820

Candidate	Party	Electoral Vote
James Monroe	Dem.–Rep.	231
John Quincy Adams	Ind.	1

DID NOT RUN IN ELECTION OF 1824

POLITICAL COMPOSITION OF CONGRESS

15th Congress (1817–1819)
Senate: Dem.–Rep. 34; Fed. 10
House: Dem.–Rep. 141; Fed. 42

16th Congress (1819–1821)
Senate: Dem.–Rep. 35; Fed. 7
House: Dem.–Rep.156; Fed. 27

17th Congress (1821–1823)
Senate: Dem.–Rep. 44; Fed. 4
House: Dem.–Rep. 158; Fed. 25

18th Congress (1823–1825)
Senate: Dem.–Rep. 44; Fed. 4
House: Dem.–Rep. 187; Fed. 26

Vice President

Daniel D. Tompkins (1817–1825)

Appointments

Cabinet Members:
John Quincy Adams, secretary of state (1817–1825)

William H. Crawford, secretary of the treasury (1817–1825)
George Graham, secretary of war (1817)
John C. Calhoun, secretary of war (1817–1825)
Richard Rush, attorney general (1817)
William Wirt, attorney general (1817–1825)
Benjamin W. Crowninshield, secretary of the navy (1817–1818)
Smith Thompson, secretary of the navy (1819–1823)
Samuel L. Southard, secretary of the navy (1823–1825)

Supreme Court Appointment:
Smith Thompson (1823–1843)

Key Events

1817 Rush–Bagot Agreement: an exchange of notes between the U.S. and Great Britain (28–29 Apr.) agreeing to limit naval power on the Great Lakes.

1818 Convention of 1818 (20 Oct.) gives U.S. citizens fishing rights off Newfoundland and establishes Northwest boundary.

1819 Panic of 1819: severe depression in which banks suspend specie payments and much western property turned over to Bank of the U.S.; Adams–On's Treaty (22 Feb.): Spain cedes Florida to U.S. along with claims to Pacific Northwest; *McCullough* v. *Maryland:* Supreme Court interprets implied powers of Congress (6 Mar.); Monroe becomes first president to ride on a steamboat (11 May).

1820 U.S. population: 9,638,453 Missouri Compromise (3 Mar.): Maine admitted to Union as free state, Missouri admitted with no restrictions on slavery.

1821 William Becknell outlines Santa Fe Trail; Monroe inaugurated for second term (5 Mar.)

1822 Bill signed by Monroe reorganizing Latin American republics (4 May).

1823 Monroe Doctrine (2 Dec.) lays down principles that European governments could not establish new colonies in Western Hemisphere and that interference in hemisphere internal affairs would be considered an act of aggression.

1824 Henry Clay coins term "American system" (30–31 Mar.), hoping to check decline of U.S. industry through internal improvements and creation of a home market.

1825 House of Representatives chooses John Quincy Adams as president (9 Feb.).

John Quincy Adams, 6th President (1825–1829)

Life

Birthdate:	11 July 1767
Birthplace:	Braintree (now Quincy), Mass.
Parents:	John Adams, Abigail Smith
Religion:	Unitarian
College Education:	Harvard College
Wife:	Louisa Catherine Johnson
Date of Marriage:	26 July 1797
Children:	George Washington, John, Charles Francis, Louisa Catherine
Political Party:	Democratic–Republican
Other Positions Held:	Minister to the Netherlands (1794–1796)
	Minister to Germany (1796–1801)
	U.S. Senator (1803–1808)
	Minister to Russia (1809–1814)
	Minister to Great Britain (1815–1817)
	Secretary of State (1817–1825)
	Member, U.S. House of Representatives (1831–1848)
Date of Inauguration:	4 March 1825
End of Term:	4 March 1829
Date of Death:	23 February 1848
Place of Death:	Washington, D.C.
Place of Burial:	Quincy, Mass.

Elections

ELECTION OF 1824

Candidate	Party	Electoral Vote	Pop. Vote
John Quincy Adams	Dem.–Rep.	84	30.5%
Andrew Jackson	Dem.–Rep.	99	43.9%
William H. Crawford	Dem.–Rep.	41	13.1%
Henry Clay	Dem.–Rep.	37	13.2%

(ADAMS CHOSEN PRESIDENT BY HOUSE OF REPRESENTATIVES IN THE ABSENCE OF A CANDIDATE WITH MORE THAN 50% OF THE POPULAR VOTE)

DEFEATED IN ELECTION OF 1828 BY ANDREW JACKSON

POLITICAL COMPOSITION OF CONGRESS

19th Congress (1825–1827)
Senate: Admin. 26; Jacksonians 20
House: Admin. 105; Jacksonians 97

20th Congress (1827–1829)
Senate: Jacksonians 28; Admin. 20
House: Jacksonians 119; Admin. 94

Vice President

John C. Calhoun (1825–1829)

Appointments

Cabinet Members:
Henry Clay, secretary of state (1825–1829)
Richard Rush, secretary of the treasury (1825–1829)
James Barbour, secretary of war (1825–1828)
Peter B. Porter, secretary of war (1828–1829)
William Wirt, attorney general (1825–1829)
Samuel L. Southard, secretary of the navy (1825–1829)

Supreme Court Appointment:
Robert Trimble (1826–1828)

Key Events

1826   John Adams and Thomas Jefferson, only presidents who signed Declaration of Independence, both die on fiftieth anniversary of its adoption (4 July); Treaty of Washington: Creek Indians cede lands in Georgia and are removed beyond Mississippi (1827–1829).

1827   Supreme Court rules that president has the final authority to call out the militia (*Martin* v. *Mott*).

1828   Jackson elected president (3 Dec.); Tariff of Abominations passed (19 May); South Carolina Resolves adopted (19 Dec.) declaring Tariff of Abominations unjust and unconstitutional.

Andrew Jackson, 7th President (1829–1837)

Life

Birthdate:	15 March 1767
Birthplace:	Waxhaw, S.C.
Parents:	Andrew Jackson, Elizabeth Hutchinson
Religion:	Presbyterian
College Education:	None
Wife:	Rachel Donelson Robards
Date of Marriage:	August 1791
Child:	Andrew (adopted)
Political Party:	Democratic
Other Positions Held:	Member, U.S. House of Representatives (1796–1797)
	U.S. Senator (1797–1798; 1823–1825)
	Judge, Tennessee Supreme Court (1798–1804)
	Major General, U.S. Army (1814–1821)
	Governor of Florida Territory (1821)
Date of Inauguration:	4 March 1829
End of Term:	4 March 1837
Date of Death:	8 June 1845
Place of Death:	Nashville, Tenn.
Place of Burial:	Nashville, Tenn.

Elections

ELECTION OF 1828

Candidate	Party	Electoral Vote	Pop. Vote
Andrew Jackson	Dem.	178	56%
John Quincy Adams	Nat. Rep.	83	44%

ELECTION OF 1832

Candidate	Party	Electoral Vote	Pop. Vote
Andrew Jackson	Dem.	219	55%
Henry Clay	Nat. Rep.	49	37%
William Wirt	Anti–Masonic	7	8%
John Floyd	Nat. Rep.	11	2%

DID NOT RUN IN ELECTION OF 1836

POLITICAL COMPOSITION OF CONGRESS

21st Congress (1829–1831)
Senate: Dem. 26; Nat. Rep. 22
House: Dem. 139; Nat. Rep. 74

22d Congress (1831–1833)
Senate: Dem. 25; Nat. Rep. 21; others 2
House: Dem. 141; Nat. Rep. 58; others 14

23d Congress (1833–1835)
Senate: Dem. 20; Nat. Rep. 20; others 8
House: Dem. 147; Anti–Masonic 53; others 60

24th Congress (1835–1837)
Senate: Dem. 27; Whig 25
House: Dem. 145; Whig 98

Vice Presidents

John C. Calhoun (1829–1832)
Martin Van Buren (1833–1837)

Appointments

Cabinet Members
Martin Van Buren, secretary of state (1829–1831)
Edward Livingston, secretary of state (1831–1833)
Louis McLane, secretary of state (1833–1834)
John Forsyth, secretary of state (1834–1837)
Samuel D. Ingham, secretary of the treasury (1829–1831)
Louis McLane, secretary of the treasury (1831–1833)
William J. Duane, secretary of the treasury (1833)
Roger B. Taney, secretary of the treasury (1833–1834)
Levi Woodbury, secretary of the treasury (1834–1837)
John H. Eaton, secretary of war (1829–1831)
Lewis Cass, secretary of war (1831–1836)
Benjamin F. Butler, secretary of war (1837)
John M. Berrien, attorney general (1829–1831)
Roger B. Taney, attorney general (1831–1833)
Benjamin F. Butler, attorney general (1833–1837)
William T. Barry, postmaster general (1829–1835)
Amos Kendall, postmaster general (1835–1837)
John Branch, secretary of the navy (1829–1831)
Levi Woodbury, secretary of the navy (1831–1834)
Mahlon Dickerson, secretary of the navy (1834–1837)

Supreme Court Appointments:
John McLean (1829–1861)
Henry Baldwin (1830–1844)
James M. Wayne (1835–1867)
Roger B. Taney, chief justice (1836–1864)
Philip P. Barbour (1836–1841)
John Catron (1837–1865)

Key Events

1829   Kitchen Cabinet, a small group of unofficial advisers, established by Jackson; postmaster general becomes Cabinet–level appointment.

1830   U.S. population: 12,866,020 Webster–Hayne Debate (19–27 Jan.) on interpretation of Constitution; Jackson escapes first assassination attempt on U.S. president (30 Jan.); Indian Removal Act passed (28 May), calling for resettlement of Indians west of Mississippi; north portico of White House completed.

1831   *Cherokee Nation* v. *Georgia*:appeal to Supreme Court by Cherokee to prevent Georgia from enforcing its laws in Cherokee nation, in which court rules Cherokee were not U.S. citizens or a foreign nation and the court lacked jurisdiction; Nat Turner's Rebellion (13–23 Aug.): insurrection by 100 blacks in Virginia, with 55 whites killed, and 20 blacks executed; French spoliation claims (4 July) made by U.S. citizens for losses sustained by French blockade of England.

1832   Bill to renew Bank of United States vetoed (10 July); South Carolina Nullification Ordinance (24 Nov.) nullifies tariffs acts of 1828 and 1832; Jackson issues proclamation (10 Dec.) asserting supremacy of federal government; Jackson elected for second term (5 Dec.).

1833   Force Act (2 Mar.) and a compromise tariff passed; South Carolina suspends ordinance of nullification (15 Mar.); piped running water replaces well water at White House (May).

1834   Bureau of Indian Affairs established (June) in Department of War.

Andrew Jackson (Continued)

1836   Texas settlers revolting against Mexican rule defeated at the siege of the Alamo (23 Feb.–6 Mar.), massacred at Goliad (27 Mar.), vanquish the Mexican army in Battle of San Jacinto (21 Apr.) under Sam Houston; Van Buren elected president (7 Dec.).

1837   Jackson reorganizes Republic of Texas (3 Mar.), following congressional resolutions (July 1836).

Martin Van Buren, 8th President (1837–1841)

Life

Birthdate:	5 December 1782
Birthplace:	Kinderhook, N.Y.
Parents:	Abraham Van Buren, Maria Hoes Van Alen
Religion:	Dutch Reformed
College Education:	None
Wife:	Hannah Hoes
Date of Marriage:	21 February 1807
Children:	Abraham, John, Martin, Smith Thompson
Political Party:	Democratic
Other Positions Held:	Attorney General of New York (1816–1819)
	U.S. Senator (1821–1828)
	Governor of New York (1829)
	Secretary of State (1829–1831)
	Vice President (1833–1837)
Date of Inauguration:	4 March 1837
End of Term:	4 March 1841
Date of Death:	24 July 1862
Place of Death:	Kinderhook, N.Y.
Place of Burial:	Kinderhook, N.Y.

Elections

ELECTION OF 1836

Candidate	Party	Electoral Vote	Pop. Vote
Martin Van Buren	Dem.	170	50.9%
William H. Harrison	Whig	73	36.6%
Others		51	12.4%

DEFEATED IN ELECTION OF 1840 BY WILLIAM HENRY HARRISON

POLITICAL COMPOSITION OF CONGRESS

25th Congress (1837–1839)

Senate:	Dem. 30; Whig 18; others 4
House:	Dem. 108; Whig 107; others 24

26th Congress (1839–1841)

Senate:	Dem. 28; Whig 22
House:	Dem. 124; Whig 118

Vice President

Richard M. Johnson (1837–1841)

Appointments

Cabinet Members:
John Forsyth, secretary of state (1837–1841)
Levi Woodbury, secretary of the treasury (1837–1841)
Joel R. Poinsett, secretary of war (1837–1841)
Benjamin F. Butler, attorney general (1837–1838)
Felix Grundy, attorney general (1838–1839)
Henry D. Gilpin, attorney general (1840–1841)
Amos Kendall, postmaster general (1837–1840)
John M. Niles, postmaster general (1840–1841)
Mahlon Dickerson, secretary of the navy (1837–1838)
James K. Paulding, secretary of the navy (1838–1841)

Supreme Court Appointments:
John McKinley (1837–1852)
Peter V. Daniel (1841–1860)

Key Events

1837   Van Buren's inauguration is first at which "Hail to the Chief" is played (4 Mar.); Panic of 1837 begins with suspension of specie payments by New York banks (May).

1838   Trail of Tears: forced journey of Cherokee from Georgia to Oklahoma, in which 4,000 Indians die.

1839   Helderberg War: New York State militia put down farmers rioting against leasehold system.

1840   U.S. population: 17,069,453

William Henry Harrison, 9th President (1841)

Life

Birthdate:	9 February 1773
Birthplace:	Berkeley, Va.
Parents:	Benjamin Harrison, Elizabeth Bassett
Religion:	Episcopalian
College Education:	Hampden–Sidney College
Wife:	Anna Tuthill Symmes
Date of Marriage:	25 November 1795
Children:	Elizabeth Bassett, John Cleves Symmes, Lucy Singleton, William Henry, John Scott, Benjamin, Mary Symmes, Carter Bassett, Anna Tuthill, James Findlay
Political Party:	Whig
Other Positions Held:	Governor of Indiana Territory (1800–1812)
	Brigadier General, U.S. Army (1812–1813)
	Major General, U.S. Army (1813–1814)
	Member, U.S. House of Representatives (1816–1819)
	U.S. Senator (1825–1828)
	Minister to Colombia (1828–1829)
Date of Inauguration:	4 March 1841
End of Term:	4 April 1841 (died in office)
Date of Death:	4 April 1841
Place of Death:	Washington, D.C.
Place of Burial:	North Bend, Ohio

Elections

ELECTION OF 1840

Candidate	Party	Electoral Vote	Pop. Vote
William H. Harrison	Whig	234	52.8%
Martin Van Buren	Dem.	60	46.8%
James G. Birney	Liberty	0	0.3%

POLITICAL COMPOSITION OF CONGRESS

27th Congress (1841–1843)

Senate:	Whig 28; Dem. 22; others 2
House:	Whig 133; Dem. 102; others 6

Vice President

John Tyler (1841)

Appointments

Cabinet Members:
Daniel Webster, secretary of state (1841)
Thomas Ewing, secretary of the treasury (1841)
John Bell, secretary of war (1841)
John J. Crittenden, attorney general (1841)
Francis Granger, postmaster general (1841)
George E. Badger, secretary of the navy (1841)

Supreme Court Appointments:
None

Key Event

1841 Harrison becomes first president to die in office (4 Apr.).

John Tyler, 10th President (1841–1845)

Life

Birthdate:	29 March 1790
Birthplace:	Charles City County, Va.
Parents:	John Tyler, Mary Marot Armistead Tyler
Religion:	Episcopalian
College Education:	College of William and Mary
First Wife:	Letitia Christian (died 1842)
Date of First Marriage:	29 March 1813
Children from First Marriage:	Mary, Robert, John, Letitia, Elizabeth, Anne Contesse, Alice, Tazewell
Second Wife:	Julia Gardiner
Date of Second Marriage:	26 June 1844
Children from Second Marriage:	David Gardiner, John Alexander, Julia, Lachlan, Lyon Gardiner, Robert Fitzwalter, Pearl
Political Party:	Whig
Other Positions Held:	Member, U.S. House of Representatives (1817–1821)
	Governor of Virginia (1825–1827)
	U.S. Senator (1827–1836)
	Vice President (1841)
	Chairman, Washington Peace Conference (1861)
Date of Inauguration:	6 April 1841 (succeeded to presidency on death of William Henry Harrison)
End of Term:	4 March 1845
Date of Death:	18 January 1862
Place of Death:	Richmond, Va.
Place of Burial:	Richmond, Va.

Elections

DID NOT RUN IN ELECTION OF 1844

POLITICAL COMPOSITION OF CONGRESS

27th Congress (1841–1843)
Senate:	Whig 28; Dem. 22; others 2
House:	Whig 133; Dem. 102; others 6

28th Congress (1843–1845)
Senate:	Whig 28; Dem. 25; other 1
House:	Dem. 142; Whig 79; other 1

Vice President

None

Appointments

Cabinet Members:
Daniel Webster, secretary of state (1841–1843)
Abel P. Upshur, secretary of state (1843–1844)
John C. Calhoun, secretary of state (1844–1845)
Thomas Ewing, secretary of the treasury (1841)
Walter Forward, secretary of the treasury (1841–1843)
John C. Spencer, secretary of the treasury (1843–1844)
George M. Bibb, secretary of the treasury (1844–1845)
John Bell, secretary of war (1841)

John McLean, secretary of war (1841)
John C. Spencer, secretary of war (1841–1843)
James M. Porter, secretary of war (1843–1844)
William Wilkins, secretary of war (1844–1845)
John J. Crittenden, attorney general (1841)
Hugh S. Legaré, attorney general (1841–1843)
John Nelson, attorney general (1843–1845)
Francis Granger, postmaster general (1841)
Charles A. Wickliffe, postmaster general (1841–1845)
George E. Badger, secretary of the navy (1841)
Abel P. Upshur, secretary of the navy (1841–1843)
David Henshaw, secretary of the navy (1843–1844)
Thomas W. Gilmer, secretary of the navy (1844)
John Y. Mason, secretary of the navy (1844–1845)

Supreme Court Appointment:
Samuel Nelson (1845–1872)

Key Events

1841	Tyler becomes first president to come into office upon the death of a president (4 Apr.) and is first president to arrive in Washington by railroad for inauguration; Dorr's Rebellion: President Tyler offers military assistance to Rhode Island governor against malcontents led by Thomas W. Dorr protesting suffrage limitations; state militia quells rebellion (1842).
1842	Webster–Ashburton Treaty (9 Aug.): settles northeastern boundary dispute with England.
1844	Texas annexation treaty signed (12 Apr.); Treaty of Wanghia (3 July) opens 5 Chinese ports to U.S. ships; election of Polk (5 Nov.), whose nomination is first to be reported by telegraph.

James K. Polk, 11th President (1845–1849)

Life

Birthdate:	2 November 1795
Birthplace:	Mecklenburg County, N.C.
Parents:	Samuel Polk, Jane Knox
Religion:	Presbyterian
College Education:	University of North Carolina
Wife:	Sarah Childress
Date of Marriage:	1 January 1824
Children:	None
Political Party:	Democratic
Other Positions Held:	Member, U.S. House of Representatives (1825–1839; Speaker, 1835–1839) Governor of Tennessee (1839–1841)
Date of Inauguration:	4 March 1845
End of Term:	4 March 1849
Date of Death:	15 June 1849
Place of Death:	Nashville, Tenn.
Place of Burial:	Nashville, Tenn.

Elections

ELECTION OF 1844

Candidate	Party	Electoral Vote	Pop. Vote
James K. Polk	Dem.	170	49.6%
Henry Clay	Whig	105	48.1%
James G. Birney	Liberty	0	2.3%

DID NOT RUN IN ELECTION OF 1848

POLITICAL COMPOSITION OF CONGRESS

29th Congress (1845–1847)
Senate:	Dem. 31; Whig 25
House:	Dem. 143; Whig 77; others 6

30th Congress (1847–1849)
Senate:	Dem. 36; Whig 21; other 1
House:	Whig 115; Dem. 108; others 4

Vice President

George Mifflin Dallas (1845–1849)

Appointments

Cabinet Members:
James Buchanan, secretary of state (1845–1849)
Robert J. Walker, secretary of the treasury (1845–1849)
William L. Marcy, secretary of war (1845–1849)
John Y. Mason, attorney general (1845–1846)
Nathan Clifford, attorney general (1846–1848)
Isaac Toucey, attorney general (1848–1849)
Cave Johnson, postmaster general (1845–1849)
George Bancroft, secretary of the navy (1845–1846)
John Y. Mason, secretary of the navy (1846–1849)

Supreme Court Appointments:
Levi Woodbury (1845–1851)
Robert C. Grier (1846–1870)

Key Events

1846   Mexican War: United States declares war (11 May); orders Gen. Zachary Taylor to Rio Grande (28 May) to defend Texas; treaty with Great Britain passes Senate (18 June) and establishes Oregon boundary; central hot–air heating installed in White House.

1848   Gold discovered in California (24 Jan.), Mexican War ends with Treaty of Guadalupe Hidalgo (2 Feb.); California gold rush begins; White House illuminated by gaslight for the first time; Seneca Falls convention for women's rights (19–20 July); Taylor elected president (4 Dec.).

1849   Department of Interior established (3 Mar.).

Zachary Taylor, 12th President (1849–1850)

Life

Birthdate:	24 November 1784
Birthplace:	Orange County, Va.
Parents:	Richard Taylor, Sarah Dabney Strother
Religion:	Episcopalian
College Education:	None
Wife:	Margaret Mackall Smith
Date of Marriage:	21 June 1810
Children:	Anne Margaret Mackall, Sarah Knox, Octavia Pannill, Margaret Smith, Mary Elizabeth, Richard
Political Party:	Whig
Other Positions Held:	Brigadier General, U.S. Army (1838–1846) Major General, U.S. Army (1846–1849)
Date of Inauguration:	4 March 1849
End of Term:	9 July 1850 (died in office)
Date of Death:	9 July 1850
Place of Death:	Washington, D.C.
Place of Burial:	Jefferson County, Ky.

Elections

ELECTION OF 1848

Candidate	Party	Electoral Vote	Pop. Vote
Zachary Taylor	Whig	163	47.4%
Lewis Call	Dem.	127	42.5%
Martin Van Buren	Free–Soil	0	10.1%

POLITICAL COMPOSITION OF CONGRESS

31st Congress (1849–1851)

Senate:	Dem. 35; Whig 25; others 2
House:	Dem. 112; Whig 109; others 9

Vice President

Millard Fillmore (1849–1850)

Appointments

Cabinet Members:
James Buchanan, secretary of state (1849)
John M. Clayton, secretary of state (1849–1850)
William M. Meredith, secretary of the treasury (1849–1850)
George W. Crawford, secretary of war (1849–1850)
Reverdy Johnson, attorney general (1849–1850)
Jacob Collamer, postmaster general (1849–1850)
William B. Preston, secretary of the navy (1849–1850)
Thomas Ewing, secretary of the interior (1849–1850)

Supreme Court Appointments:
None

Key Events

1850   U.S. population: 23,191,876 Clayton–Bulwer Treaty (19 Apr.) calls for joint U.S.–British control of a canal across Central American isthmus; Nashville Convention (10 June) affirms legality of slavery by southern states; Taylor becomes second president to die in office (9 July).

Millard Fillmore, 13th President (1850–1853)

Life

Birthdate:	7 January 1800
Birthplace:	Cayuga County, N.Y.
Parents:	Nathaniel Fillmore, Phoebe Millard
Religion:	Unitarian
College Education:	None
First Wife:	Abigail Powers (died 1853)
Date of First Marriage:	5 February 1826
Children from First Marriage:	Millard Powers, Mary Abigail
Second Wife:	Caroline Carmichael McIntosh
Date of Second Marriage:	10 February 1858
Children from Second Marriage:	None
Political Party:	Whig
Other Positions Held:	Member, U.S. House of Representatives (1833–1835; 1837–1843)
	Vice President (1849–1850)
Date of Inauguration:	10 July 1850 (succeeded to presidency on death of Zachary Taylor)
End of Term:	3 March 1853
Date of Death:	8 March 1874
Place of Death:	Buffalo, N.Y.
Place of Burial:	Buffalo, N.Y.

Elections

DID NOT RUN IN ELECTION OF 1852

POLITICAL COMPOSITION OF CONGRESS

32d Congress (1851–1853)

Senate:	Dem. 35; Whig 24; others 3
House:	Dem. 140; Whig 88; others 5

Vice President

None

Appointments

Cabinet Members:
John M. Clayton, secretary of state (1850)
Daniel Webster, secretary of state (1850–1852)
Edward Everett, secretary of state (1852–1853)
William M. Meredith, secretary of the treasury (1850)
Thomas Corwin, secretary of the treasury (1850–1853)
George W. Crawford, secretary of war (1850)
Charles M. Conrad, secretary of war (1850–1853)
John J. Crittenden, attorney general (1850–1853)
Nathan K. Hall, postmaster general (1850–1852)
Samuel D. Hubbard, postmaster general (1850–1852)
William A. Graham, secretary of the navy (1850–1852)
John P. Kennedy, secretary of the navy (1852–1853)
Thomas M. T. McKennan, secretary of the interior (1850)
Alex H. H. Stuart, secretary of the interior (1850–1853)

Supreme Court Appointment:
Benjamin R. Curtis (1851–1857)

Key Events

1850 Compromise of 1850 (Sept.): 5 statutes admitting California as a free state, Texas and New Mexico with no restrictions, and including Fugitive Slave Act (18 Sept.), placing fugitive slave cases under federal jurisdiction.

1851 *Uncle Tom's Cabin* by Harriet Beecher Stowe published (20 Mar.); Pierce elected president (2 Nov.).

1852 Commodore Matthew C. Perry leaves on expedition to "open" Japan (Nov.)

Franklin Pierce, 14th President (1853–1857)

Life

Birthdate:	23 November 1804
Birthplace:	Hillsborough (now Hillsboro), N.H.
Parents:	Benjamin Pierce, Anna Kendrick
Religion:	Episcopalian
College Education:	Bowdoin College
Wife:	Jane Means Appleton
Date of Marriage:	19 November 1834
Children:	Franklin, Frank Robert, Benjamin
Political Party:	Democratic
Other Positions Held:	Member, New Hampshire legislature (1829–1833; Speaker, 1831–1832)
	Member, U.S. House of Representatives (1833–1837)
	U.S. Senator (1837–1842)
	Brigadier General, U.S. Army (1847)
Date of Inauguration:	4 March 1853
End of Term:	4 March 1857
Date of Death:	8 October 1869
Place of Death:	Concord, N.H.
Place of Burial:	Concord, N.H.

Elections

ELECTION OF 1852

Candidate	Party	Electoral Vote	Pop. Vote
Franklin Pierce	Dem.	254	50.9%
Winfield Scott	Whig	42	44.1%
John P. Hale	Free–Soil	0	5%

DID NOT RUN IN ELECTION OF 1856

POLITICAL COMPOSITION OF CONGRESS

33d Congress (1853–1855)
Senate: Dem. 38; Whig 22; others 2
House: Dem. 159; Whig 71; others 4

34th Congress (1855–1857)
Senate: Dem. 40; Rep. 15; others 5
House: Rep. 108; Dem. 83; others 43

Vice President

William Rufus D. King (1853)

Appointments

Cabinet Members:
William L. Marcy, secretary of state (1853–1857)
James Guthrie, secretary of the treasury (1853–1857)
Jefferson Davis, secretary of war (1853–1857)
Caleb Cushing, attorney general (1853–1857)
James Campbell, postmaster general (1853–1857)
James C. Dobbin, secretary of the navy (1853–1857)
Robert McClelland, secretary of the interior (1853–1857)

Supreme Court Appointment:
John A. Campbell (1853–1861)

Key Events

1853 Gadsden Purchase (30 Dec.): settles boundary question with Mexico for $10 million; first convenient bathing facilities installed in White House living quarters.

1854 Kansas–Nebraska Act passed (30 May) permitting local option on slavery and repealing Missouri Compromise; Canadian Reciprocity Treaty (5 June) opens U.S. markets to Canada and grants U.S. fishing rights.

1856 Kansas Civil War (21 May–15 Sept.): between proslavery and antislavery forces; Buchanan elected president (4 Nov.)

James Buchanan, 15th President (1857–1861)

Life

Birthdate:	23 April 1791
Birthplace:	Stony Batter, Pa.
Parents:	James Buchanan, Elizabeth Speer
Religion:	Presbyterian
College Education:	Dickinson College
Marital Status:	Never married
Political Party:	Democratic
Other Positions Held:	Member, U.S. House of Representatives (1821–1831)
	Minister to Russia (1832–1834)
	U.S. Senator (1834–1845)
	Secretary of State (1845–1849)
	Minister to Great Britain (1853–1856)
Date of Inauguration:	4 March 1857
End of Term:	4 March 1861
Date of Death:	1 June 1868
Place of Death:	Lancaster, Pa.
Place of Burial:	Lancaster, Pa.

Elections

ELECTION OF 1856

Candidate	Party	Electoral Vote	Pop. Vote
James Buchanan	Dem.	174	45.3%
John C. Frémont	Rep.	114	33.1%
Millard Fillmore	Know–Nothing	8	21.6%

DID NOT RUN IN ELECTION OF 1860

POLITICAL COMPOSITION OF CONGRESS

35th Congress (1857–1859)

Senate:	Dem. 36; Rep. 20; others 8
House:	Dem. 118; Rep. 92; others 26

36th Congress (1859–1861)

Senate:	Dem. 36; Rep. 26; others 4
House:	Rep. 114; Dem. 92; others 31

Vice President

John C. Breckinridge (1857–1861)

Appointments

Cabinet Members:
Lewis Cass, secretary of state (1857–1860)
Jeremiah S. Black, secretary of state (1860–1861)
Howell Cobb, secretary of the treasury (1857–1860)
Philip F. Thomas, secretary of the treasury (1860–1861)
John A. Dix, secretary of the treasury (1861)
John B. Floyd, secretary of war (1857–1860)
Joseph Holt, secretary of war (1861)
Jeremiah S. Black, attorney general (1857–1860)
Edwin M. Stanton, attorney general (1860–1861)
Aaron V. Brown, postmaster general (1857–1859)
Joseph Holt, postmaster general (1859–1861)
Horatio King, postmaster general (1861)
Isaac Toucey, secretary of the navy (1857–1861)

Jacob Thompson, secretary of the interior (1857–1861)

Supreme Court Appointment:
Nathan Clifford (1858–1881)

Key Events

1857   Dred Scott Case (6 Mar.): Supreme Court rules slaves are not U.S. citizens and cannot sue in federal courts; Panic of 1857 follows boom after Mexican War.

1858   Lincoln delivers "House Divided" speech (16 June); Lincoln–Douglas Debates (21 Aug.–15 Oct.).

1859   John Brown's Raid (16–18 Oct.): Brown seizes Harper's Ferry, Va., armory; captured by marine force under Col. Robert E. Lee; hanged for treason (2 Dec.); Comstock Lode of silver deposits discovered in Virginia City, Nev.

1860   U.S. population: 31,443,321 Davis Resolutions (2 Feb.): Jefferson Davis introduces in Senate slavery resolutions; Lincoln delivers Cooper Union speech (27 Feb.) on extension of slavery and popular sovereignty doctrine; Lincoln elected president (6 Nov.); South Carolina secedes from the Union (20 Dec.).

1861   Confederate States of America formed at Montgomery, Ala. (8 Feb.), and adopts constitution.

Abraham Lincoln, 16th President (1861–1865)

Life

Birthdate:	12 February 1809
Birthplace:	Hodgenville, Ky.
Parents:	Thomas Lincoln, Nancy Hanks
Religion:	No denomination
College Education:	None
Wife:	Mary Todd
Date of Marriage:	4 November 1842
Children:	Robert Todd, Edward Baker, William Wallace, Thomas ("Tad")
Political Party:	Republican
Other Positions Held:	Member, Illinois legislature (1834–1841)
	Member, U.S. House of Representatives (1847–1849)
Date of Inauguration:	4 March 1861
End of Term:	15 April 1865 (assassinated by John Wilkes Booth)
Date of Death:	15 April 1865
Place of Death:	Washington, D.C.
Place of Burial:	Springfield, Ill.

Elections

ELECTION OF 1860

Candidate	Party	Electoral Vote	Pop. Vote
Abraham Lincoln	Rep.	180	39.8%
Stephen A. Douglas	Dem.	12	29.5%
John C. Breckinridge	Dem.	72	18.1%
John Bell	Constitutional Union	39	12.6%

ELECTION OF 1864

Candidate	Party	Electoral Vote	Pop. Vote
Abraham Lincoln	Rep.	212	55%
George B. McClellan	Dem.	21	45%

POLITICAL COMPOSITION OF CONGRESS

37th Congress (1861–1863)
Senate: Rep. 31; Dem. 10; others 8
House: Rep. 105; Dem. 43; others 30

38th Congress (1863–1865)
Senate: Rep. 36; Dem. 9; others 5
House: Rep. 102; Dem. 75; others 9

Vice Presidents

Hannibal Hamlin (1861–1865)
Andrew Johnson (1865)

Appointments

Cabinet Members:
William H. Seward, secretary of state (1861–1865)
Salmon P. Chase, secretary of the treasury (1861–1864)
William P. Fessenden, secretary of the treasury (1864–1865)
Hugh McCullough, secretary of the treasury (1865)
Simon Cameron, secretary of war (1861–1862)
Edwin M. Stanton, secretary of war (1862–1865)

Edward Bates, attorney general (1861–1863)
James Speed, attorney general (1864–1865)
Montgomery Blair, postmaster general (1861–1864)
William Dennison, postmaster general (1864–1865)
Gideon Welles, secretary of the navy (1861–1865)
Caleb B. Smith, secretary of the interior (1861–1862)
John P. Usher, secretary of the interior (1863–1865)

Supreme Court Appointments:
Noah H. Swayne (1862–1881)
Samuel F. Miller (1862–1890)
David Davis (1862–1877)
Stephen J. Field (1863–1897)
Salmon P. Chase, chief justice (1864–1873)

Key Events

1861   Civil War begins with Confederate firing on Fort Sumter, S.C. (12 Apr.), and surrender of fort; Congress institutes income tax; Committee on Conduct of the War established (20 Dec.).

1862   Department of Agriculture established as federal agency (15 May); Homestead Act enacted (20 May), providing for citizens to acquire 160 acres of public land.

1863   Emancipation Proclamation (1 Jan.) grants freedom to slaves in rebelling states; antidraft riots in New York City (13–16 July).

1865   Confederate surrender to Union forces at Appomattox Courthouse (9 Apr.) ends Civil War; Lincoln assassinated (14 Apr.) by John Wilkes Booth.

Andrew Johnson, 17th President (1865–1869)

Life

Birthdate:	29 December 1808
Birthplace:	Raleigh, N.C.
Parents:	Jacob Johnson, Mary McDonough
Religion:	No denomination
College Education:	None
Wife:	Eliza McCardle
Date of Marriage:	17 May 1827
Children:	Martha, Charles, Mary, Robert, Andrew
Political Party:	Democratic (elected vice president on Republican ticket)
Other Positions Held:	Member, U.S. House of Representatives (1843–1853)
	Governor of Tennessee (1853–1857)
	U.S. Senator (1857–1862; 1875)
	Brigadier General, U.S. Army (1862–1864)
	Vice President (1865)
Date of Inauguration:	15 April 1865 (succeeded to presidency on death of Abraham Lincoln)
Acquittal of Impeachment Charges:	26 May 1868
End of Term:	4 March 1869
Date of Death:	31 July 1875
Place of Death:	Carter's Station, Tenn.
Place of Burial:	Greenville, Tenn.

Elections

DID NOT RUN IN ELECTION OF 1868

POLITICAL COMPOSITION OF CONGRESS

39th Congress (1865–1867)

Senate:	Unionists 42; Dem. 10
House:	Unionists 149; Dem. 42

40th Congress (1867–1869)

Senate:	Rep. 42; Dem. 11
House:	Rep. 143; Dem. 49

Vice President

None

Appointments

Cabinet Members:
William H. Seward, secretary of state (1865–1869)
Hugh McCullough, secretary of the treasury (1865–1869)
Edwin M. Stanton, secretary of war (1865–1868)
John M. Schofield, secretary of war (1868–1869)
James Speed, attorney general (1865–1866)
Henry Stanbery, attorney general (1866–1868)
William M. Evarts, attorney general (1868–1869)
William Dennison, postmaster general (1865–1866)
Alexander W. Randall, postmaster general (1866–1869)
Gideon Welles, secretary of the navy (1865–1869)
John P. Usher, secretary of the interior (1865)
James Harlan, secretary of the interior (1865–1866)
Orville H. Browning, secretary of the interior (1866–1869)

Supreme Court Appointments:
None

Key Events

1865   Johnson is first president to come into office upon assassination of a president (15 Apr.); Reconstruction Proclamation (29 May–13 July) grants amnesty to Confederates who took oath of allegiance; Freedmen's bureau established (24 Nov.); Thirteenth Amendment ratified (18 Dec.) abolishing slavery; Ku Klux Klan established in Pulaski, Tenn.

1866   Supplementary Reconstruction Acts passed (23 Mar., 19 July), providing for registration of all qualified voters; U.S. agrees to purchase Alaska from Russia for $7.2 million (29 Mar.); Civil Rights Act (9 Apr.) bestows citizenship on blacks; Fourteenth Amendment submitted to states (16 June) for ratification, defines national citizenship, ratification necessary for states to be readmitted to Union; Patrons of Husbandry (Grangers) formed (4 Dec.) to promote agricultural interests; White House acquires a telegraph room.

1867   First Reconstruction Act (2 Mar.) divides South into 5 military districts subject to martial law and under military commanders.

1868   Impeachment trial of Johnson (24 Feb.–26 May): president impeached for removal of Stanton as secretary of war as violation of Tenure of Office Act (2 Mar. 1867), president acquitted; Fourteenth Amendment ratified (28 July); first federal 8–hour workday enacted; Grant elected president (3 Nov.).

TABLE OF PRESIDENTIAL DATA

Ulysses Simpson Grant, 18th President (1869–1877)

Life

Birthdate:	27 April 1822
Birthplace:	Point Pleasant, Ohio
Parents:	Jesse Root Grant, Hannah Simpson
Religion:	Methodist
College Education:	United States Military Academy
Wife:	Julia Boggs Dent
Date of Marriage:	22 August 1848
Children:	Frederick Dent, Ulysses Simpson, Ellen Wrenshall, Jesse Root
Political Party:	Republican
Other Positions Held:	Major General, U.S. Army (1862–1864)
	Lieutenant General, U.S. Army (1864–1866)
	General of the Army (1866)
Date of Inauguration:	4 March 1869
End of Term:	4 March 1877
Date of Death:	23 July 1885
Place of Death:	Mount McGregor, N.Y.
Place of Burial:	New York, N.Y.

Elections

ELECTION OF 1868

Candidate	Party	Electoral Vote	Pop. Vote
Ulysses S. Grant	Rep.	214	52.7%
Horatio Seymour	Dem.	80	47.3%

ELECTION OF 1872

Candidate	Party	Electoral Vote	Pop. Vote
Ulysses S. Grant	Rep.	286	55.6%
Horace Greeley	Dem.	N/A	43.9%

(GREELEY DIED BETWEEN GENERAL ELECTION AND MEETING OF ELECTORAL COLLEGE)

DID NOT RUN IN ELECTION OF 1876

POLITICAL COMPOSITION OF CONGRESS

41st Congress (1869–1871)
Senate: Rep. 56; Dem. 11
House: Rep. 149; Dem. 63

42d Congress (1871–1873)
Senate: Rep. 52; Dem. 17; others 5
House: Rep. 134; Dem. 104; others 5

43d Congress (1873–1875)
Senate: Rep. 49; Dem. 19; others 5
House: Rep. 194; Dem. 92; others 14

44th Congress (1875–1877)
Senate: Rep. 45; Dem. 29; others 2
House: Dem. 169; Rep. 109; others 14

Vice Presidents

Schuyler Colfax (1869–1873)
Henry Wilson (1873–1875)

Appointments

Cabinet Members:
Elihu B. Washburne, secretary of state (1869)
Hamilton Fish, secretary of state (1869–1877)
George S. Boutwell, secretary of the treasury (1869–1873)
William A. Richardson, secretary of the treasury (1873–1874)
Benjamin H. Bristow, secretary of the treasury (1874–1876)
Lot M. Morrill, secretary of the treasury (1876–1877)
John A. Rawlins, secretary of war (1869)
William Tecumseh Sherman, secretary of war (1869)
William W. Belknap, secretary of war (1869–1876)
Alphonso Taft, secretary of war (1876)
James D. Cameron, secretary of war (1876–1877)
E. Rockwood Hoar, attorney general (1869–1870)
Amos T. Akerman, attorney general (1870–1871)
George H. Williams, attorney general (1871–1875)
Edwards Pierrepont, attorney general (1875–1876)
Alphonso Taft, attorney general (1876–1877)
John A. Creswell, postmaster general (1869–1874)
James W. Marshall, postmaster general (1874)
Marshall Jewell, postmaster general (1874–1876)
James N. Tyner, postmaster general (1876–1877)
Adolph E. Borie, secretary of the navy (1869)
George M. Robeson, secretary of the navy (1869–1877)
Jacob D. Cox, secretary of the interior (1869–1870)
Columbus Delano, secretary of the interior (1870–1875)
Zachariah Chandler, secretary of the interior (1875–1877)

Supreme Court Appointments:
William Strong (1870–1880)
Joseph P. Bradley (1870–1892)
Ward Hunt (1873–1882)
Morrison R. Waite, chief justice (1874–1888)

Key Events

1869 First transcontinental rail route completed (10 May); Black Friday (24 Sept.), an attempt by James Fisk, Jay Gould, and others to corner the U.S. gold supply.

1870 U.S. population: 39,818,449 Fifteenth Amendment ratified (30 Mar.), stating no citizen can be denied right to vote because of race, color, or previous condition of servitude; Justice Department created (22 June), headed by attorney general.

1871 Enforcement Acts provide federal election law (28 Feb.) and enforcement of Fourteenth Amendment (20 Apr.); Indian Appropriation Act decrees the federal government would not enter into any further Indian treaties; Civil Service Commission established (3 Mar.); Ku Klux Klan Act passes (20 Apr.) to enforce Fourteenth and Fifteenth Amendments and permit president to declare martial law; Treaty of Washington (8 May) between U.S. and Britain lays down rules of maritime neutrality and submits Alabama Claims to arbitration (settled 14 Sept. 1872); Chicago Fire (8 Oct.) destroys 17,500 buildings, causes $200 million in property loss, and leaves 200-300 dead.

1872 Equal Rights party nominates first woman, Victoria Claflin Woodhull, for president and first black, Frederick Douglass, for vice president (10 May); Crédit Mobilier scandal erupts; Grant reelected (5 Nov.).

1873 Panic of 1873 in which 5,000 businesses fail; Coinage Act (12 Feb.) establishes gold standard.

Ulysses Simpson Grant (Continued)

1875   Whiskey Ring conspiracy of revenue officials to defraud government of internal revenue tax.

1876   Alexander Graham Bell patents the telephone; Secretary of War Belknap impeached for receiving bribes for sale of Indian posts.

Rutherford Birchard Hayes, 19th President (1877–1881)

Life

Birthdate:	4 October 1822
Birthplace:	Delaware, Ohio
Parents:	Rutherford Hayes, Sophia Birchard
Religion:	Attended Methodist Church
College Education:	Kenyon College; Harvard Law School
Wife:	Lucy Ware Webb
Date of Marriage:	30 December 1852
Children:	Birchard Austin, James Webb Cook, Rutherford Platt, Joseph Thompson, George Crook, Fanny, Scott Russell, Manning Force
Political Party:	Republican
Other Positions Held:	Brigadier General, U.S. Army (1864–1865)
	Major General, U.S. Army (1865)
	Member, U.S. House of Representatives (1865–1867)
	Governor of Ohio (1868–1872; 1876–1877)
Date of Inauguration:	4 March 1877
End of Term:	4 March 1881
Date of Death:	17 January 1893
Place of Death:	Fremont, Ohio
Place of Burial:	Fremont, Ohio

Elections

ELECTION OF 1876

Candidate	Party	Electoral Vote	Pop. Vote
Rutherford B. Hayes	Rep.	185	48%
Samuel J. Tilden	Dem.	184	51%

DID NOT RUN IN ELECTION OF 1880

POLITICAL COMPOSITION OF CONGRESS

45th Congress (1877–1879)

Senate:	Rep. 39; Dem. 36; other 1
House:	Dem. 153; Rep. 140

46th Congress (1879–1881)

Senate:	Dem. 42; Rep. 33; other 1
House:	Dem. 149; Rep. 130; others 14

Vice President

William A. Wheeler (1877–1881)

Appointments

Cabinet Members:
William M. Evarts, secretary of state (1877–1881)
John Sherman, secretary of the treasury (1877–1881)
George W. McCrary, secretary of war (1877–1879)
Alexander Ramsey, secretary of war (1879–1881)
Charles Devens, attorney general (1877–1881)
David M. Key, postmaster general (1877–1880)
Horace Maynard, postmaster general (1880–1881)
Richard W. Thompson, secretary of the navy (1877–1881)
Nathan Goff, Jr., secretary of the navy (1881)
Carl Schurz, secretary of the interior (1877–1881)

Supreme Court Appointments:
John Marshall Harlan (1877–1911)
William B. Woods (1881–1887)

Key Events

1877	Hayes becomes president after disputed election (4 Mar.); Lucy Webb Hayes becomes first First Lady with a college degree; Thomas Edison patents the phonograph; Reconstruction ends in the South; surrender of Chief Joseph in Nez Perce War (15 Oct.).
1879	White House acquires first telephone (10 May).
1880	U.S. population: 50,155,783 First typewriter arrives at White House (12 Feb.); Garfield elected president (2 Nov.); treaty with China (17 Nov.) limits immigration of Chinese laborers.

James Abram Garfield, 20th President (1881)

Life

Birthdate:	19 November 1831
Birthplace:	Orange, Ohio
Parents:	Abram Garfield, Eliza Ballou
Religion:	Disciples of Christ
College Education:	Williams College
Wife:	Lucretia Rudolph
Date of Marriage:	11 November 1858
Children:	Eliza Arabella, Harry Augustus, James Rudolph, Mary, Irvin McDowell, Abram, Edward
Political Party:	Republican
Other Positions Held:	President, Hiram College (1857–1861)
	Ohio State Senator (1859–1861)
	Brigadier General, U.S. Army (1862–1863)
	Major General, U.S. Army (1863)
	Member, U.S. House of Representatives (1863–1880)
Date of Inauguration:	4 March 1881
End of Term:	19 September 1881 (assassinated by Charles Guiteau)
Date of Death:	19 September 1881
Place of Death:	Elberon, N.J.
Place of Burial:	Cleveland, Ohio

Elections

ELECTION OF 1880

Candidate	Party	Electoral Vote	Pop. Vote
James A. Garfield	Rep.	214	48.5%
Winfield S. Hancock	Dem.	155	48.1%
James B. Weaver	Greenback–Labor	0	3.4%

POLITICAL COMPOSITION OF CONGRESS

47th Congress (1881–1883)

Senate:	Rep. 37; Dem. 37; other 1
House:	Rep. 147; Dem. 135; others 11

Vice President

Chester A. Arthur (1881)

Appointments

Cabinet Members:
James G. Blaine, secretary of state (1881)
William Windom, secretary of the treasury (1881)
Robert T. Lincoln, secretary of war (1881)
Wayne MacVeagh, attorney general (1881)
Thomas L. James, postmaster general (1881)
William H. Hunt, secretary of the navy (1881)
Samuel J. Kirkwood, secretary of the interior (1881)

Supreme Court Appointment:
Stanley Matthews (1881–1889)

Key Event

1881   Garfield assassinated (2 July) by Charles J. Guiteau.

Chester Alan Arthur, 21st President (1881–1885)

Life

Birthdate:	5 October 1829
Birthplace:	Fairfield, Vt.
Parents:	William Arthur, Malvina Stone
Religion:	Episcopalian
College Education:	Union College
Wife:	Ellen Lewis Herndon
Date of Marriage:	25 October 1859
Children:	William Lewis Herndon, Chester Alan, Ellen Herndon
Political Party:	Republican
Other Positions Held:	Collector of the Port of New York (1871–1878) Vice President (1881)
Date of Inauguration:	20 September 1881 (succeeded to presidency on death of James A. Garfield)
End of Term:	4 March 1885
Date of Death:	18 November 1886
Place of Death:	New York, N.Y.
Place of Burial:	Albany, N.Y.

Elections

DID NOT RUN IN ELECTION OF 1884

POLITICAL COMPOSITION OF CONGRESS
47th Congress (1881–1883)
Senate: Rep. 37; Dem. 37; other 1
House: Rep. 147; Dem. 135; others 11

48th Congress (1883–1885)
Senate: Rep. 38; Dem. 36; others 2
House: Dem. 197; Rep. 118; others 10

Vice President

None

Appointments

Cabinet Members:
James G. Blaine, secretary of state (1881)
Frederick T. Frelinghuysen, secretary of state (1881–1885)
William Windom, secretary of the treasury (1881)
Charles J. Folger, secretary of the treasury (1881–1884)
Walter Q. Gresham, secretary of the treasury (1884)
Hugh McCullough, secretary of the treasury (1884–1885)
Robert T. Lincoln, secretary of war (1881–1885)
Wayne MacVeagh, attorney general (1881)
Benjamin H. Brewster, attorney general (1882–1885)
Timothy O. Howe, postmaster general (1882–1883)
Frank Hatton, postmaster general (1883)
Walter Q. Gresham, postmaster general (1883–1884)
Frank Hatton, postmaster general (1884–1885)
William H. Hunt, secretary of the navy (1881–1882)
William E. Chandler, secretary of the navy (1882–1885)
Samuel J. Kirkwood, secretary of the interior (1881–1882)
Henry M. Teller, secretary of the interior (1882-1885)

Supreme Court Appointments:
Horace Gray (1882–1902)

Samuel Blatchford (1882–1893)

Key Events

1881   Arthur becomes second president to come into office upon assassination of a president (20 Sept.).

1882   Peace treaty signed with Korea (22 May).

1883   Pendleton Act (16 Jan.) establishes Civil Service Commission and competitive examinations.

1884   Cleveland elected president (4 Nov.).

Grover Cleveland, 22nd President (1885-1889)

Life

Birthdate:	18 March 1837
Birthplace:	Caldwell, N.J.
Parents:	Richard Falley Cleveland, Anne Neal
Religion:	Presbyterian
College Education:	None
Wife:	Frances Folsom
Date of Marriage:	2 June 1886
Children:	Ruth, Esther, Marion, Richard Folsom, Francis Grover
Political Party:	Democratic
Other Positions Held:	Mayor of Buffalo, New York (1881–1882) Governor of New York (1883–1885)
Date of Inauguration:	4 March 1885
End of Term:	4 March 1889
Date of Death:	24 June 1908
Place of Death:	Princeton, N.J.
Place of Burial:	Princeton, N.J.

Elections

ELECTION OF 1884

Candidate	Party	Electoral Vote	Pop. Vote
Grover Cleveland	Dem.	219	48.5%
James G. Blaine	Rep.	182	48.2%
Benjamin F. Butler	Greenback–Labor	0	1.8%
John P. St. John	Proh.	0	1.5%

DEFEATED IN ELECTION OF 1888 BY BENJAMIN HARRISON

POLITICAL COMPOSITION OF CONGRESS

49th Congress (1885–1887)
Senate:	Rep. 43; Dem. 34
House:	Dem. 183; Rep. 140; others 2

50th Congress (1887–1889)
Senate:	Rep. 39; Dem. 37
House:	Dem. 169; Rep. 152; others 4

Vice President

Thomas A. Hendricks (1885)

Appointments

Cabinet Members:
Thomas F. Bayard, secretary of state (1885–1889)
Daniel Manning, secretary of the treasury (1885–1887)
Charles S. Fairchild, secretary of the treasury (1887–1889)
William C. Endicott, secretary of war (1885–1889)
Augustus Garland, attorney general (1885–1889)
William F. Vilas, postmaster general (1885–1888)
Don M. Dickinson, postmaster general (1888–1889)
William C. Whitney, secretary of the navy (1885–1889)
Lucius Q. C. Lamar, secretary of the interior (1885–1888)
William F. Vilas, secretary of the interior (1888–1889)
Norman J. Colman, secretary of agriculture (1889)

Supreme Court Appointments:
Lucius Q. C. Lamar (1888–1893)
Melville W. Fuller, chief justice (1888–1910)

Key Events

1886   Presidential Succession Act (19 Jan.) delineates line of succession to presidency; Haymarket Riot erupts (4 May) in Chicago; Cleveland marries Frances Folsom (2 June), becomes first president to wed in the White House.

1887   Interstate Commerce Act (4 Feb.) gives federal government right to regulate transportation and business extending beyond state lines.

1888   Harrison elected president (6 Nov.), first grandson of a president to be elected.

1889   Department of Agriculture accorded Cabinet–level status (Feb.).

Benjamin Harrison, 23rd President (1889–1893)

Life

Birthdate:	20 August 1833
Birthplace:	North Bend, Ohio
Parents:	John Scott Harrison, Elizabeth Ramsey Irwin
Religion:	Presbyterian
College Education:	Miami University
First Wife:	Caroline Lavina Scott (died 1892)
Date of First Marriage:	20 October 1853
Children from First Marriage:	Russell Benjamin, Mary Scott
Second Wife:	Mary Scott Lord Dimmick
Date of Second Marriage:	6 April 1896
Child from Second Marriage:	Elizabeth
Political Party:	Republican
Other Positions Held:	Brigadier General, U.S. Army (1865) U.S. Senator (1881–1887)
Date of Inauguration:	4 March 1889
End of Term:	4 March 1893
Date of Death:	13 March 1901
Place of Death:	Indianapolis, Ind.
Place of Burial:	Indianapolis, Ind.

Elections

ELECTION OF 1888

Candidate	Party	Electoral Vote	Pop. Vote
Benjamin Harrison	Rep.	233	47.9%
Grover Cleveland	Dem.	168	48.6%
Clinton B. Fisk	Proh.	0	2.2%
Anson J. Streeter	Union Labor	0	1.3%

DEFEATED IN ELECTION OF 1892 BY GROVER CLEVELAND

POLITICAL COMPOSITION OF CONGRESS

51st Congress (1889–891)
Senate:	Rep. 39; Dem. 37
House:	Rep. 166; Dem. 159

52d Congress (1891–1893)
Senate:	Rep. 47; Dem. 39; others 2
House:	Dem. 235; Rep. 88; others 9

Vice President

Levi P. Morton (1889–1893)

Appointments

Cabinet Members:
James G. Blaine, secretary of state (1889–1892)
John W. Foster, secretary of state (1892–1893)
William Windom, secretary of the treasury (1889–1891)
Charles Foster, secretary of the treasury (1891–1893)
Redfield Proctor, secretary of war (1889–1891)
Stephen B. Elkins, secretary of war (1891–1893)
William H. H. Miller, attorney general (1889–1893)
John Wanamaker, postmaster general (1889–1893)

Benjamin F. Tracy, secretary of the navy (1889–1893)
John W. Noble, secretary of the interior (1889–1893)
Jeremiah M. Rusk, secretary of agriculture (1889–1893)
Supreme Court Appointments:
David J. Brewer (1889–1910)
Henry B. Brown (1891–1906)
George Shiras, Jr. (1892–1903)
Howell E. Jackson (1893–1895)

Key Events

1889 First Oklahoma land run (22 Apr.) by 50,000.

1890 U.S. population: 62,947,714 Sherman Antitrust Act (2 July) declares restraint of trade illegal; Messiah War: an outgrowth of Ghost Dance excitement among the Sioux in the badlands of South Dakota; Sitting Bull is killed while resisting arrest (15 Dec.); principal band of hostile Indians under Big Foot, camped at Wounded Knee Creek, surrender, but are massacred (28 Dec.); final fight between Indians and U.S. Army.

1891 Electric lighting comes to White House.

1892 State militia break up Homestead Steelworkers Strike (12 July); martial law declared in Coeur d'Alene silver mines in Idaho after violence between striking miners and strike breakers; Cleveland elected president (8 Nov.).

Grover Cleveland, 24th President (1893–1897)

Life

Birthdate:	18 March 1837
Birthplace:	Caldwell, N.J.
Parents:	Richard Falley Cleveland, Anne Neal
Religion:	Presbyterian
College Education:	None
Wife:	Frances Folsom
Date of Marriage:	2 June 1886
Children:	Ruth, Esther, Marion, Richard Folsom, Francis Grover
Political Party:	Democratic
Other Positions Held:	Mayor of Buffalo, New York (1881–1882) Governor of New York (1883–1885)
Date of Inauguration:	4 March 1893
End of Term:	4 March 1897
Date of Death:	24 June 1908
Place of Death:	Princeton, N.J.
Place of Burial:	Princeton, N.J.

Elections

ELECTION OF 1892

Candidate	Party	Electoral Vote	Pop. Vote
Grover Cleveland	Dem.	277	46.1%
Benjamin Harrison	Rep.	145	43%
James Weaver	Populist	22	8.5%
John Bidwell	Proh.	0	2.2%

DID NOT RUN IN ELECTION OF 1896

POLITICAL COMPOSITION OF CONGRESS

53d Congress (1893–1895)
Senate: Dem. 44; Rep. 38; others 3
House: Dem. 218; Rep. 127; others 11

54th Congress (1895–1897)
Senate: Rep. 43; Dem. 39; others 6
House: Rep. 244; Dem. 105; others 7

Vice President

Adlai E. Stevenson (1893–1897)

Appointments

Cabinet Members:
Walter Q. Gresham, secretary of state (1893–1895)
Richard Olney, secretary of state (1895–1897)
John G. Carlisle, secretary of the treasury (1893–1897)
Daniel S. Lamont, secretary of war (1893–1897)
Richard Olney, attorney general (1893–1895)
Judson Harmon, attorney general (1895–1897)
Wilson S. Bissell, postmaster general (1893–1895)
William L. Wilson, postmaster general (1895–1897)
Hilary A. Herbert, secretary of the navy (1893–1897)
Hoke Smith, secretary of the interior (1893–1896)
David R. Francis, secretary of the interior (1896–1897)
Julius Sterling Morton, secretary of agriculture (1893–1897)

Supreme Court Appointments:
Edward D. White (1894–1921)
Rufus W. Peckham (1896–1909)

Key Events

1893 Panic of 1893 with failure of 4,000 banks and 14,000 commercial businesses; Diplomatic Appropriation Act (Mar.) creates rank of ambassador; Thomas Francis Bayard appointed U.S. ambassador to Great Britain (Apr.).

1894 Pullman Strike (11 May–20 July): 4,000 members of American Railway Union strike Pullman Palace Car Company and defy blanket injunction prohibiting interference with trains, quelled by federal troops; Edison's kinetoscope has first public showing in New York City.

1896 Supreme Court ruling in *Plessy* v. *Ferguson* upholds legality of separate but equal facilities for races; McKinley elected president (3 Nov.).

William McKinley, 25th President (1897–1901)

Life

Birthdate:	29 January 1843
Birthplace:	Niles, Ohio
Parents:	William McKinley, Nancy Campbell Allison
Religion:	Methodist
College Education:	Allegheny College
Wife:	Ida Saxton
Date of Marriage:	25 January 1871
Children:	Katherine, Ida
Political Party:	Republican
Other Positions Held:	Member, U.S. House of Representatives (1877–1883)
	Governor of Ohio (1892–1896)
Date of Inauguration:	4 March 1897
End of Term:	14 September 1901 (assassinated by Leon Czolgosz)
Date of Death:	14 September 1901
Place of Death:	Buffalo, N.Y.
Place of Burial:	Canton, Ohio

Elections

ELECTION OF 1896

Candidate	Party	Electoral Vote	Pop. Vote
William McKinley	Rep.	271	51.1%
William J. Bryan	Dem.	176	47.7%

ELECTION OF 1900

Candidate	Party	Electoral Vote	Pop. Vote
William McKinley	Rep.	292	51.7%
William J. Bryan	Dem./Populist	155	45.5%
John C. Woolley	Proh.	0	1.5%

POLITICAL COMPOSITION OF CONGRESS

55th Congress (1897–1899)
Senate: Rep. 47; Dem. 34; others 7
House: Rep. 204; Dem. 113; others 40

56th Congress (1899–1901)
Senate: Rep. 53; Dem. 26; others 8
House: Rep. 185; Dem. 163; others 9

57th Congress (1901–1903)
Senate: Rep. 55; Dem. 31; others 4
House: Rep. 197; Dem. 151; others 9

Vice Presidents

Garret Augustus Hobart (1897–1899)
Theodore Roosevelt (1901)

Appointments

Cabinet Members:
John Sherman, secretary of state (1897–1898)
William R. Day, secretary of state (1898)
John Hay, secretary of state (1898–1901)
Lyman J. Gage, secretary of the treasury (1897–1901)
Russell A. Alger, secretary of war (1897–1899)
Elihu Root, secretary of war (1899–1901)

Joseph McKenna, attorney general (1897–1898)
John W. Griggs, attorney general (1898–1901)
Philander C. Knox, attorney general (1901)
James A. Gary, postmaster general (1897–1898)
Charles E. Smith, postmaster general (1898–1901)
John D. Long, secretary of the navy (1897–1901)
Cornelius N. Bliss, secretary of the interior (1897)
Ethan A. Hitchcock, secretary of the interior (1898–1901)
James Wilson, secretary of agriculture (1897–1901)

Supreme Court Appointment:
Joseph McKenna (1898–1925)

Key Events

1898   Spanish–American War: U.S. battleship *Maine* explodes in Havana harbor, Cuba (15 Feb.); U.S. declares independence of Cuba (25 Apr.) and that state of war existed with Spain since 21 Apr.; Treaty of Paris (10 Dec.) establishes independence of Cuba, cedes Puerto Rico and Guam to U.S., and U.S. purchases Philippines for $20 million.

1899   First Hague Conference (18 May-29 July) establishes Permanent Court of Arbitration; Open Door Policy enunciated affirming U.S. commercial and industrial rights in China; McKinley becomes first president to ride in an automobile (Nov.).

1900   U.S. population: 75,994,575 Boxer Rebellion: antiforeign uprising in China by secret society of Boxers (June); McKinley reelected (6 Nov.); Gen. Arthur MacArthur captures thousands (Nov.) of Filipino revolutionaries battling troops of U.S. military government (revolutionaries surrender in 1902); Samoan Partition Treaty (2 Dec.): islands divided between Germany, Great Britain, and U.S.

1901   Platt amendment adopted (2 Mar.), outlining U.S.–Cuban relations and agreements; McKinley assassinated (6 Sept.) by Leon Czolgosz.

Theodore Roosevelt, 26th President (1901–1909)

Life

Birthdate:	27 October 1858
Birthplace:	New York, N.Y.
Parents:	Theodore Roosevelt, Martha Bulloch
Religion:	Dutch Reformed Church
College Education:	Harvard College
First Wife:	Alice Hathaway Lee (died 1884)
Date of First Marriage:	27 October 1880
Child from First Marriage:	Alice Lee
Second Wife:	Edith Kermit Carow
Date of Second Marriage:	2 December 1886
Children from Second Marriage:	Theodore, Kermit, Ethel Carow, Archibald Bulloch, Quentin
Political Party:	Republican
Other Positions Held:	Member, New York legislature (1882–1884)
	Assistant Secretary of the Navy (1897–1898)
	Governor of New York (1899–1901)
	Vice President (1901)
Date of Inauguration:	14 September 1901 (succeeded to presidency on death of William McKinley)
End of Term:	4 March 1909
Date of Death:	6 January 1919
Place of Death:	Oyster Bay, N.Y.
Place of Burial:	Oyster Bay, N.Y.

Elections

ELECTION OF 1904

Candidate	Party	Electoral Vote	Pop. Vote
Theodore Roosevelt	Rep.	336	56.4%
Alton B. Parker	Dem.	140	37.6%
Eugene V. Debs	Soc.	0	3.0%
Silas C. Swallow	Proh.	0	1.9%

DID NOT RUN IN ELECTION OF 1908

POLITICAL COMPOSITION OF CONGRESS

57th Congress (1901–1903)
Senate: Rep. 55; Dem. 31; others 4
House: Rep. 197; Dem. 151; others 9

58th Congress (1903–1905)
Senate: Rep. 57; Dem. 33
House: Rep. 208; Dem. 178

59th Congress (1905–1907)
Senate: Rep. 57; Dem. 33
House: Rep. 250; Dem. 136

60th Congress (1907–1909)
Senate: Rep. 61; Dem. 31
House: Rep. 222; Dem. 164

Vice President

Charles W. Fairbanks (1905–1909)

Appointments

Cabinet Members:
John Hay, secretary of state (1901–1905)
Elihu Root, secretary of state (1905–1909)
Robert Bacon, secretary of state (1909)
Lyman J. Gage, secretary of the treasury (1901–1902)
Leslie M. Shaw, secretary of the treasury (1902–1907)
George B. Cortelyou, secretary of the treasury (1907–1909)
Elihu Root, secretary of war (1901–1904)
William Howard Taft, secretary of war (1904–1908)
Luke E. Wright, secretary of war (1908–1909)
Philander C. Knox, attorney general (1901–1904)
William H. Moody, attorney general (1904–1906)
Charles J. Bonaparte, attorney general (1906–1909)
Charles E. Smith, postmaster general (1901–1902)
Henry C. Payne, postmaster general (1902–1904)
Robert J. Wynne, postmaster general (1904–1905)
George B. Cortelyou, postmaster general (1905–1907)
George von L. Meyer, postmaster general (1907–1909)
John D. Long, secretary of the navy (1901–1902)
William H. Moody, secretary of the navy (1902–1904)
Paul Morton, secretary of the navy (1904–1905)
Charles J. Bonaparte, secretary of the navy (1905–1906)
Victor H. Metcalf, secretary of the navy (1906–1908)
Truman H. Newberry, secretary of the navy (1908–1909)
Ethan A. Hitchcock, secretary of the interior (1901–1907)
James R. Garfield, secretary of the interior (1907–1909)
James Wilson, secretary of agriculture (1901–1909)
George B. Cortelyou, secretary of commerce and labor (1903–1904)
Victor H. Metcalf, secretary of commerce and labor (1904–1906)
Oscar S. Straus, secretary of commerce and labor (1906–1909)

Supreme Court Appointments:
Oliver Wendell Holmes (1902–1932)
William R. Day (1903–1922)
William H. Moody (1906–1910)

Key Events

1901   Roosevelt becomes third president to come into office upon assassination of a president (14 Sept.).

1902   Reclamation Act (June) authorizes president to retain public lands as part of public domain and to construct irrigation works in western states.

1903   Department of Commerce and Labor established (14 Feb.); U.S. warships stand by to protect U.S. interests as Panama revolts against Colombia; Panama independence recognized (6 Nov.); Hay–Bunau–Varilla Treaty (13 Nov.) provides for construction and operation of canal in Panama; Wright brothers' first airplane flight at Kitty Hawk, N.C. (17 Dec.).

1904   Theodore Roosevelt elected president (8 Nov.); Roosevelt Corollary to Monroe Doctrine pronounced (6 Dec.) to prevent intervention in Latin America by European creditors.

1905   Taft–Katsura Memorandum (29 July): U.S.–Japanese cooperation agreement for "maintenance of peace in Far East."

1906   Algeciras Conference (16 Jan.): U.S. obtains privileged position in Morocco; Theodore Roosevelt awarded Nobel Prize for peace; San Francisco earthquake and fire (18–21 Apr.) kills 700.

1907   Gentlemen's Agreement (24 Feb.): U.S. and Japan agree to exclude further Japanese laborers from emigrating to U.S.;

Theodore Roosevelt (Continued)

	Panic of 1907; second Hague Peace Conference (15 June–18 Oct.).
1908	Henry Ford introduces Model T (1 Oct.); Taft elected president (3 Nov.).

William Howard Taft, 27th President (1909–1913)

Life

Birthdate:	15 September 1857
Birthplace:	Cincinnati, Ohio
Parents:	Alphonso Taft, Louisa Maria Torrey
Religion:	Unitarian
College Education:	Yale College; Cincinnati Law School
Wife:	Helen Herron
Date of Marriage:	19 June 1886
Children:	Robert Alphonso, Helen Herron, Charles Phelps
Political Party:	Republican
Other Positions Held:	Judge, Ohio Superior Court (1887–1890)
	U.S. Solicitor General (1890–1892)
	U.S. Circuit Court Judge (1892–1900)
	Governor–General, Philippines (1901–1904)
	Secretary of War (1904–1908)
	Law Professor, Yale University (1913–1921)
	Chief Justice, U.S. Supreme Court (1921–1930)
Date of Inauguration:	4 March 1909
End of Term:	4 March 1913
Date of Death:	8 March 1930
Place of Death:	Washington, D.C.
Place of Burial:	Arlington, Va.

Elections

ELECTION OF 1908

Candidate	Party	Electoral Vote	Pop. Vote
William Howard Taft	Rep.	321	51.6%
William J. Bryan	Dem.	162	43.1%
Eugene V. Debs	Soc.	0	2.8%
Eugene W. Chafin	Proh.	0	1.7%

DEFEATED IN ELECTION OF 1912 BY WOODROW WILSON

POLITICAL COMPOSITION OF CONGRESS

61st Congress (1909–1911)

Senate:	Rep. 61; Dem. 32
House:	Rep. 219; Dem. 172

62d Congress (1911–1913)

Senate:	Rep. 51; Dem. 41
House:	Dem. 228; Rep. 161; others 1

Vice President

James S. Sherman (1909–1912)

Appointments

Cabinet Members:
Philander C. Knox, secretary of state (1909–1913)
Franklin MacVeagh, secretary of the treasury (1909–1913)
Jacob W. Dickinson, secretary of war (1909–1911)
Henry L. Stimson, secretary of war (1911–1913)
George W. Wickersham, attorney general (1909–1913)
Frank H. Hitchcock, postmaster general (1909–1913)
George von L. Meyer, secretary of the navy (1909–1913)
Richard A. Ballinger, secretary of the interior (1909–1911)
Walter L. Fisher, secretary of the interior (1911–1913)
James Wilson, secretary of agriculture (1909–1913)

Charles Nagel, secretary of commerce and labor (1909–1913)

Supreme Court Appointments:
Horace H. Lurton (1910–1914)
Charles Evans Hughes (1910–1916)
Edward D. White, chief justice (1910–1921) (promoted from associate justice)
Willis Van Devanter (1911–1937)
Joseph R. Lamar (1911–1916)
Mahlon Pitney (1912–1922)

Key Events

1909   Robert E. Peary reaches North Pole (6 Apr.); National Association for the Advancement of Colored People (NAACP) founded; Taft converts the White House stables into a garage and acquires 4 automobiles.

1910   U.S. population: 91,972,266. Mann–Elkins Act (18 June) places telephone, telegraph, cable, and wireless companies under Interstate Commerce Commission jurisdiction.

1912   Lodge Corollary (2 Aug.), first application of Monroe Doctrine to Asian nation, prevents Japanese purchase of land in Baja California; marines arrive in Nicaragua (14 Aug.) to support Adolpho Díaz government; token force withdraws in 1925, last marines leave in 1933; Wilson elected president (5 Nov.).

1913   Sixteenth Amendment ratified (25 Feb.), establishing federal income tax; on last day as president, Taft signs legislation creating Department of Commerce and Department of Labor to replace Department of Commerce and Labor (4 Mar.).

Woodrow Wilson, 28th President (1913–1921)

Life

Birthdate:	28 December 1856
Birthplace:	Staunton, Va.
Parents:	Joseph Ruggles Wilson, Jessie Janet Woodrow
Religion:	Presbyterian
College Education:	Princeton University; University of Virginia Law School; Johns Hopkins University
First Wife:	Ellen Louise Axson (died 1914)
Date of First Marriage:	24 June 1885
Children from First Marriage:	Margaret Woodrow, Jessie Woodrow, Eleanor Randolph
Second Wife:	Edith Bolling Galt
Date of Second Marriage:	18 December 1915
Children from Second Marriage:	None
Political Party:	Democratic
Other Positions Held:	President, Princeton University (1902–1910) Governor of New Jersey (1911–1913)
Date of Inauguration:	4 March 1913
End of Term:	4 March 1921
Date of Death:	3 February 1924
Place of Death:	Washington, D.C.
Place of Burial:	National Cathedral, Washington, D.C.

Elections

ELECTION OF 1912

Candidate	Party	Electoral Vote	Pop. Vote
Woodrow Wilson	Dem.	435	41.9%
Theodore Roosevelt	Prog.	88	27.4%
William Howard Taft	Rep.	8	23.2%
Eugene V. Debs	Soc.	0	6.0%
Eugene W. Chafin	Proh.	0	1.5%

ELECTION OF 1916

Candidate	Party	Electoral Vote	Pop. Vote
Woodrow Wilson	Dem.	277	49.4%
Charles E. Hughes	Rep.	254	46.2%
A. L. Benson	Soc.	0	3.2%
J. Frank Hanly	Proh.	0	1.2%

DID NOT RUN IN ELECTION OF 1920

POLITICAL COMPOSITION OF CONGRESS

63d Congress (1913–1915)
Senate: Dem. 51; Rep. 44; other 1
House: Dem. 291; Rep. 127; others 17

64th Congress (1915–1917)
Senate: Dem. 56; Rep. 40
House: Dem. 230; Rep. 196; others 9

65th Congress (1917–1919)
Senate: Dem. 53; Rep. 42
House: Dem. 216; Rep. 210; others 6

66th Congress (1919–1921)
Senate: Rep. 49; Dem. 47
House: Rep. 240; Dem. 190; others 3

Vice President

Thomas R. Marshall (1913–1921)

Appointments

Cabinet Members:
William Jennings Bryan, secretary of state (1913–1915)
Robert Lansing, secretary of state (1915–1920)
Bainbridge Colby, secretary of state (1920–1921)
William Gibbs McAdoo, secretary of the treasury (1913–1918)
Carter Glass, secretary of the treasury (1918–1920)
David F. Houston, secretary of the treasury (1920–1921)
Lindley M. Garrison, secretary of war (1913–1916)
Newton D. Baker, secretary of war (1916–1921)
James C. McReynolds, attorney general (1913–1914)
Thomas W. Gregory, attorney general (1914–1919)
A. Mitchell Palmer, attorney general (1919–1921)
Albert S. Burleson, postmaster general (1913–1921)
Josephus Daniels, secretary of the navy (1913–1921)
Franklin K. Lane, secretary of the interior (1913–1920)
John B. Payne, secretary of the interior (1920–1921)
David F. Houston, secretary of agriculture (1913–1920)
Edwin T. Meredith, secretary of agriculture (1920–1921)
William C. Redfield, secretary of commerce (1913–1919)
Joshua W. Alexander, secretary of commerce (1919–1921)
William B. Wilson, secretary of labor (1913–1921)

Supreme Court Appointments:
James C. McReynolds (1914–1941)
Louis D. Brandeis (1916–1939)
John H. Clarke (1916–1922)

Key Events

1913 Wilson holds first presidential press conference (15 Mar.); Wilson appears before Congress in person to deliver an address, breaking long–standing precedent (8 Apr.); Seventeenth Amendment ratified (31 May), providing for direct election of U.S. Senators; Underwood Tariff significantly reduces tariff rates; Federal Reserve System established (23 Dec.).

1914 Wilson proclaims U.S. neutrality in European war (4 Aug.); Panama Canal opened (15 Aug.).

1915 First transcontinental telephone conversation (25 Jan.); *Lusitania* sinks (7 May) with loss of 128 Americans after attack by German submarine; U.S. marines occupy Haiti after civil war (28 July); treaty signed by Haitian senate (16 Sept.) makes island nation virtual U.S. protectorate.

1916 British steamer *Sussex* attacked by German submarine (24 Mar.), and 2 Americans injured; by executive order an official presidential flag is adopted (29 May); treaty signed for purchase of Danish West Indies (4 Aug.); Wilson reelected (7 Nov.); resistance in Dominican Republic to U.S. customs receivership leads to martial law (29 Nov.) with government headed by U.S. Navy officer.

1917 Wilson's "Peace without victory" speech (22 Jan.); Germany informs U.S. of resumption of unrestricted submarine warfare (31 Jan.); Wilson severs diplomatic relations with Germany (3 Feb.); Zimmermann note of German guarantees to Mexico

Woodrow Wilson (Continued)

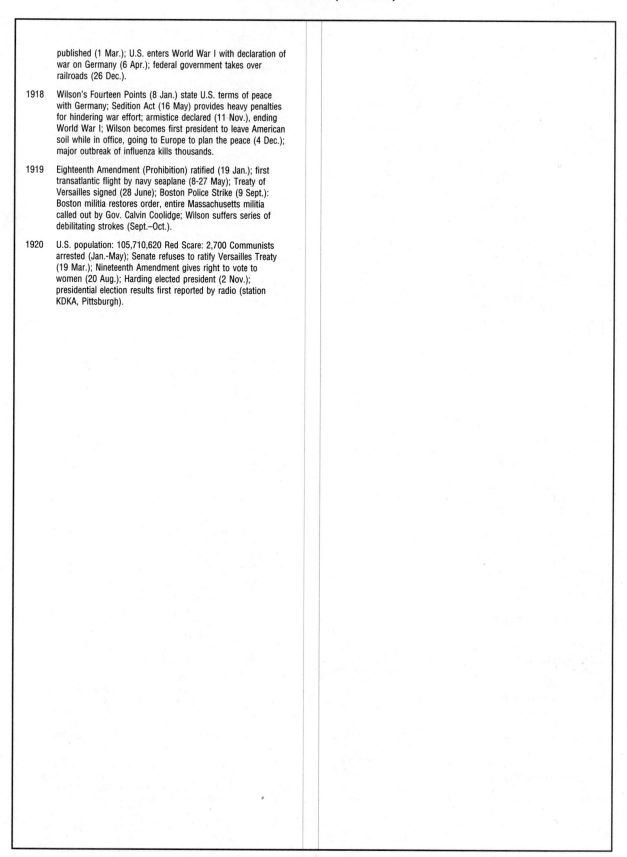

published (1 Mar.); U.S. enters World War I with declaration of war on Germany (6 Apr.); federal government takes over railroads (26 Dec.).

1918   Wilson's Fourteen Points (8 Jan.) state U.S. terms of peace with Germany; Sedition Act (16 May) provides heavy penalties for hindering war effort; armistice declared (11 Nov.), ending World War I; Wilson becomes first president to leave American soil while in office, going to Europe to plan the peace (4 Dec.); major outbreak of influenza kills thousands.

1919   Eighteenth Amendment (Prohibition) ratified (19 Jan.); first transatlantic flight by navy seaplane (8-27 May); Treaty of Versailles signed (28 June); Boston Police Strike (9 Sept.): Boston militia restores order, entire Massachusetts militia called out by Gov. Calvin Coolidge; Wilson suffers series of debilitating strokes (Sept.–Oct.).

1920   U.S. population: 105,710,620 Red Scare: 2,700 Communists arrested (Jan.-May); Senate refuses to ratify Versailles Treaty (19 Mar.); Nineteenth Amendment gives right to vote to women (20 Aug.); Harding elected president (2 Nov.); presidential election results first reported by radio (station KDKA, Pittsburgh).

TABLE OF PRESIDENTIAL DATA

Warren Gamaliel Harding, 29th President (1921–1923)

Life

Birthdate:	2 November 1865
Birthplace:	Corsica (now Blooming Grove), Ohio
Parents:	George Tryon Harding, Phoebe Elizabeth Dickerson
Religion:	Baptist
College Education:	Ohio Central College
Wife:	Florence Kling De Wolfe
Date of Marriage:	8 July 1891
Children:	None
Political Party:	Republican
Other Positions Held:	Editor, *Marion* (Ohio) *Star* (1884–1910)
	Ohio State Senator (1899–1903)
	Lieutenant Governor of Ohio (1903–1905)
	U.S. Senator (1915–1921)
Date of Inauguration:	4 March 1921
End of Term:	2 August 1923 (died in office)
Date of Death:	2 August 1923
Place of Death:	San Francisco, Calif.
Place of Burial:	Marion, Ohio

Elections

ELECTION OF 1920

Candidate	Party	Electoral Vote	Pop. Vote
Warren G. Harding	Rep.	404	60.4%
James M. Cox	Dem.	127	34.2%
Eugene V. Debs	Soc.	0	3.4%
P. P. Christensen	Farmer–Labor	0	1.0%

POLITICAL COMPOSITION OF CONGRESS

67th Congress (1921–1923)
Senate: Rep. 59; Dem. 37
House: Rep. 301; Dem. 131; other 1

68th Congress (1923–1925)
Senate: Rep. 51; Dem. 43; others 2
House: Rep. 225; Dem. 205; others 5

Vice President

Calvin Coolidge (1921–1923)

Appointments

Cabinet Members:
Charles Evans Hughes, secretary of state (1921–1923)
Andrew W. Mellon, secretary of the treasury (1921–1923)
John W. Weeks, secretary of war (1921–1923)
Harry M. Daugherty, attorney general (1921–1923)
Will H. Hays, postmaster general (1921–1922)
Hubert Work, postmaster general (1922–1923)
Harry S. New, postmaster general (1923)
Edwin Denby, secretary of the navy (1921–1923)
Albert B. Fall, secretary of the interior (1921–1923)
Hubert Work, secretary of the interior (1923)
Henry C. Wallace, secretary of agriculture (1921–1923)
Herbert C. Hoover, secretary of commerce (1921–1923)
James J. Davis, secretary of labor (1921–1923)

Supreme Court Appointments:
William Howard Taft, chief justice (1921–1930)
George Sutherland (1922–1938)
Pierce Butler (1922–1939)
Edward T. Sanford (1923–1930)

Key Events

1921   Harding, the first president who could drive an automobile, becomes first to ride to his inauguration in one (4 Mar.); Washington Naval Conference convenes (12 Nov.) to deal with arms race and Pacific security.

1922   Five–Power Naval Treaty (29 Mar.) puts 10–year moratorium on ship construction, fixes ship tonnage ratio, restricts submarine use during war and outlaws poison gas; second Central American Conference convenes (4 Dec.) to settle issues between Nicaragua and Honduras.

1923   Harding dies (2 Aug.).

Calvin Coolidge, 30th President (1923–1929)

Life

Birthdate:	4 July 1872
Birthplace:	Plymouth Notch, Vt.
Parents:	John Calvin Coolidge, Victoria Josephine Moor
Religion:	Congregationalist
College Education:	Amherst College
Wife:	Grace Anna Goodhue
Date of Marriage:	4 October 1905
Children:	John, Calvin
Political Party:	Republican
Other Positions Held:	Member, Massachusetts Senate (1912–1915; President, 1914–1915)
	Lieutenant Governor of Massachusetts (1916–1918)
	Governor of Massachusetts (1919–1920)
	Vice President (1921–1923)
Date of Inauguration:	3 August 1923 (succeeded to presidency on death of Warren G. Harding)
End of Term:	4 March 1929
Date of Death:	5 January 1933
Place of Death:	Northampton, Mass.
Place of Burial:	Plymouth Notch, Vt.

Elections

ELECTION OF 1924

Candidate	Party	Electoral Vote	Pop. Vote
Calvin Coolidge	Rep.	382	54.0%
John W. Davis	Dem.	136	28.8%
Robert M. La Follette	Prog.	13	16.6%

DID NOT RUN IN ELECTION OF 1928

POLITICAL COMPOSITION OF CONGRESS

68th Congress (1923–1925)
Senate: Rep. 51; Dem. 43; others 2
House: Rep. 225; Dem. 205; others 5

69th Congress (1925–1927)
Senate: Rep. 56; Dem. 39; other 1
House: Rep. 247; Dem. 183; others 4

70th Congress (1927–1929)
Senate: Rep. 49; Dem. 46; other 1
House: Rep. 237; Dem. 195; others 3

Vice President

Charles G. Dawes (1925–1929)

Appointments

Cabinet Members:
Charles Evans Hughes, secretary of state (1923–1925)
Frank B. Kellogg, secretary of state (1925–1929)
Andrew W. Mellon, secretary of the treasury (1923–1929)
John W. Weeks, secretary of war (1923–1925)
Dwight F. Davis, secretary of war (1925–1929)
Harry M. Daugherty, attorney general (1923–1924)
Harlan Fiske Stone, attorney general (1924–1925)
John G. Sargent, attorney general (1925–1929)
Harry S. New, postmaster general (1923–1929)
Edwin Denby, secretary of the navy (1923–1924)
Curtis D. Wilbur, secretary of the navy (1924–1929)
Hubert Work, secretary of the interior (1923–1928)
Roy O. West, secretary of the interior (1928–1929)
Henry C. Wallace, secretary of agriculture (1923–1924)
Howard M. Gore, secretary of agriculture (1924–1925)
William M. Jardine, secretary of agriculture (1925–1929)
Herbert C. Hoover, secretary of commerce (1923–1928)
William F. Whiting, secretary of commerce (1928–1929)
James J. Davis, secretary of labor (1923–1929)

Supreme Court Appointment:
Harlan Fiske Stone (1925–1946)

Key Events

1923   Coolidge sworn in as president upon death of Harding (3 Aug.); Teapot Dome Oil Scandal: corruption under Harding administration unearthed by Senate investigation over illegal leases of naval oil reserves at Teapot Dome, Wyo., and Elk Hills, Calif.

1924   Snyder Act (2 June) declares all U.S. Indians citizens; Coolidge elected president (4 Nov.).

1925   First national congress of the Ku Klux Klan in Washington, D.C. (8 Aug.).

1926   Civilian Aviation Act (2 Nov.) establishes bureau in Department of Commerce to map airways and provide flying regulations.

1927   Charles A. Lindbergh makes first solo nonstop transatlantic flight (20-21 May), from New York to Paris.

1928   Merchant Marine (Jones–White) Act (22 May) passes to encourage private shipping; Kellogg–Briand Pact signed (27 Aug.) by 15 nations, renouncing war as an instrument of national policy; Hoover elected president (6 Nov.).

1929   Kellogg–Briand Pact ratified by U.S. Senate (15 Jan.).

Herbert Hoover, 31st President (1929–1933)

Life

Birthdate:	10 August 1874
Birthplace:	West Branch, Iowa
Parents:	Jesse Clark Hoover, Hulda Randall Minthorn
Religion:	Quaker
College Education:	Stanford University
Wife:	Lou Henry
Date of Marriage:	10 February 1899
Children:	Herbert Clark, Allan Henry
Political Party:	Republican
Other Positions Held:	Relief administrator in Europe (1914–1919)
	U.S. Food Administrator (1917–1919)
	Secretary of Commerce (1921–1928)
Date of Inauguration:	4 March 1929
End of Term:	4 March 1933
Date of Death:	20 October 1964
Place of Death:	New York, N.Y.
Place of Burial:	West Branch, Iowa

Elections

ELECTION OF 1928

Candidate	Party	Electoral Vote	Pop. Vote
Herbert C. Hoover	Rep.	444	58.2%
Alfred E. Smith	Dem.	87	40.9%

DEFEATED IN ELECTION OF 1932 BY FRANKLIN D. ROOSEVELT

POLITICAL COMPOSITION OF CONGRESS

71st Congress (1929–1931)

Senate:	Rep. 56; Dem. 39; other 1
House:	Rep. 267; Dem. 167; other 1

72d Congress (1931–1933)

Senate:	Rep. 48; Dem. 47; other 1
House:	Rep. 220; Dem. 214; other 1

Vice President

Charles Curtis (1929–1933)

Appointments

Cabinet Members:
Henry L. Stimson, secretary of state (1929–1933)
Andrew W. Mellon, secretary of the treasury (1929–1932)
Ogden L. Mills, secretary of the treasury (1932–1933)
James W. Good, secretary of war (1929)
Patrick J. Hurley, secretary of war (1929–1933)
William D. Mitchell, attorney general (1929–1933)
Walter F. Brown, postmaster general (1929–1933)
Charles F. Adams, secretary of the navy (1929–1933)
Ray Lyman Wilbur, secretary of the interior (1929–1933)
Arthur M. Hyde, secretary of agriculture (1929–1933)
Robert P. Lamont, secretary of commerce (1929–1932)
Roy D. Chapin, secretary of commerce (1932–1933)
James J. Davis, secretary of labor (1929–1930)
William N. Doak, secretary of labor (1930–1933)

Supreme Court Appointments:
Charles Evans Hughes, chief justice (1930–1941) (promoted from associate justice)
Owen J. Roberts (1930–1945)
Benjamin N. Cardozo (1932–1938)

Key Events

1929   Panic of 1929 results from stock market crash (29 Oct.).

1930   U.S. population: 122,775,046 "Star–Spangled Banner" becomes national anthem (3 Mar.); Smoot–Hawley Tariff (June) raises duties to prohibitive levels on 890 articles.

1931   Scottsboro Case: 8 of 9 black teenagers convicted and sentenced to death for allegedly raping 2 white women (Supreme Court overturns convictions in 1935 and evidence is released in 1966 proving innocence of "Scottsboro Boys").

1932   Reconstruction Finance Corp. established (2 Feb.) with $2 billion to advance loans to failing banks, building and loan societies, and insurance companies; Bonus March on Washington (May–July): 15,000 World War I veterans seek economic relief from Congress and are driven away by U.S. tanks, infantry, and cavalry; Roosevelt elected president (8 Nov.), having been first presidential nominee to address the convention that nominated him (Democratic, 2 July).

1933   Twentieth Amendment ratified (6 Feb.), advancing date of future presidential inaugurations to 20 Jan.

THE PRESIDENTS

Franklin Delano Roosevelt, 32nd President

Life

Birthdate:	30 January 1882
Birthplace:	Hyde Park, N.Y.
Parents:	James Roosevelt, Sara Delano
Religion:	Episcopalian
College Education:	Harvard College
Wife:	(Anna) Eleanor Roosevelt
Date of Marriage:	17 March 1905
Children:	Anna Eleanor, James, Franklin, Elliott, Franklin Delano, John Aspinwall
Political Party:	Democratic
Other Positions Held:	Member, New York Senate (1910–1913)
	Assistant Secretary of the Navy (1913–1920)
	Governor of New York (1929–1933)
Date of Inauguration:	4 March 1933
End of Term:	12 April 1945 (died in office)
Date of Death:	12 April 1945
Place of Death:	Warm Springs, Ga.
Place of Burial:	Hyde Park, N.Y.

Elections

ELECTION OF 1932

Candidate	Party	Electoral Vote	Pop. Vote
Franklin D. Roosevelt	Dem.	472	57.4%
Herbert C. Hoover	Rep.	59	39.7%
Norman Thomas	Soc.	0	2.2%

ELECTION OF 1936

Candidate	Party	Electoral Vote	Pop. Vote
Franklin D. Roosevelt	Dem.	523	60.8%
Alfred M. Landon	Rep.	8	36.5%
William Lemke	Union	0	1.9%

ELECTION OF 1940

Candidate	Party	Electoral Vote	Pop. Vote
Franklin D. Roosevelt	Dem.	449	54.8%
Wendell Willkie	Rep.	82	44.8%

ELECTION OF 1944

Candidate	Party	Electoral Vote	Pop. Vote
Franklin D. Roosevelt	Dem.	432	53.5%
Thomas E. Dewey	Rep.	99	46.0%

POLITICAL COMPOSITION OF CONGRESS

73d Congress (1933–1935)
Senate: Dem. 60; Rep. 35; other 1
House: Dem. 310; Rep. 117; others 5

74th Congress (1935–1937)
Senate: Dem. 69; Rep. 25; others 2
House: Dem. 319; Rep. 103; others 10

75th Congress (1937–1939)
Senate: Dem. 76; Rep. 16; others 4
House: Dem. 331; Rep. 89; others 13

76th Congress (1939–1941)
Senate: Dem. 69; Rep. 23; others 4
House: Dem. 261; Rep. 164; others 4

77th Congress (1941–1943)
Senate: Dem. 66; Rep. 28; others 2
House Dem. 268; Rep. 162; others 5

78th Congress (1943–1945)
Senate: Dem. 58; Rep. 37; other 1
House: Dem. 218; Rep. 208; others 4

79th Congress (1945–1947)
Senate: Dem. 56; Rep. 38; other 1
House: Dem. 242; Rep. 190; others 2

Vice Presidents

John Nance Garner (1933–1941)
Henry A. Wallace (1941–1945)
Harry S. Truman (1945)

Appointments

Cabinet Members:
Cordell Hull, secretary of state (1933–1944)
Edward R. Stettinius, Jr., secretary of state (1944–1945)
W. H. Woodin, secretary of the treasury (1933)
Henry Morgenthau, Jr., secretary of the treasury (1934–1945)
George H. Dren, secretary of war (1933–1936)
Harry H. Woodring, secretary of war (1936–1940)
Henry L. Stimson, secretary of war (1940–1945)
Homer S. Cummings, attorney general (1933–1939)
Frank Murphy, attorney general (1939–1940)
Robert H. Jackson, attorney general (1940–1941)
Francis Biddle, attorney general (1941–1945)
James A. Farley, postmaster general (1933–1940)
Frank C. Walker, postmaster general (1941–1945)
Claude A. Swanson, secretary of the navy (1933–1939)
Charles Edison, secretary of the navy (1939)
Frank Knox, secretary of the navy (1940–1944)
James V. Forrestal, secretary of the navy (1944–1945)
Harold L. Ickes, secretary of the interior (1933–1945)
Henry A. Wallace, secretary of agriculture (1933–1940)
Claude R. Wickard, secretary of agriculture (1940–1945)
Daniel C. Roper, secretary of commerce (1933–1938)
Harry L. Hopkins, secretary of commerce (1938–1940)
Jesse H. Jones, secretary of commerce (1940–1945)
Henry A. Wallace, secretary of commerce (1945)
Frances Perkins, secretary of labor (1933–1945)

Supreme Court Appointments:
Hugo L. Black (1937–1971)
Stanley F. Reed (1938–1957)
Felix Frankfurter (1939–1962)
William O. Douglas (1939–1975)
Frank Murphy (1940–1949)
James F. Byrnes (1941–1942)
Harlan Fiske Stone, chief justice (1941–1946) (promoted from associate justice)
Robert H. Jackson (1941–1954)
Wiley B. Rutledge (1943–1949)

Key Events

1933 Good Neighbor Policy announced (4 Mar.) by Roosevelt to improve relations with Latin America; Roosevelt launches New Deal legislation: Emergency Banking Relief Act (9 Mar.), Civilian Conservation Corps (31 Mar.), Agricultural Adjustment

Franklin Delano Roosevelt (Continued)

Act (12 May), Federal Emergency Relief Act (12 May), Tennessee Valley Authority (18 May), Federal Securities Act (27 May), National Industrial Recovery Act (16 June), Civil Works Administration (8 Nov.); U.S. comes off gold standard (30 Apr.); U.S. recognizes USSR (16 Nov.); with ratification of Twenty–first Amendment, Prohibition ends (5 Dec.).

1934   Export–Import Bank established (2 Feb.); Securities and Exchange Act passes (6 June); Federal Communications Commission established (19 June).

1935   A second New Deal announced by Roosevelt (4 Jan.) for social reform: Soil Conservation Act (27 Apr.), Works Progress Administration (11 May), National Labor Relations Act (5 July), Social Security Act (14 Aug.), Public Utilities Act (28 Aug.); Huey Long (the "Kingfish") assassinated in Baton Rouge (Sept.).

1936   Roosevelt signs second neutrality bill (29 Feb.), banning loans to countries at war; Merchant Marine Act (26 June) creates U.S. Maritime Commission.

1937   Neutrality Act (1 May) prohibits export of arms and ammunition to belligerent nations and the use of U.S. ships for carrying munitions and war materials into belligerent zones; Amelia Earhart lost on round–the–world flight (2 July); U.S. Senate rejects "court–packing" plan by Roosevelt (22 July).

1938   House Committee to investigate Un–American Activities formed (26 May); Civil Aeronautics Act passed (23 June), establishes Civil Aeronautics Authority to supervise nonmilitary air transport; Fair Labor Standards (Wages and Hours) Act passes (25 June).

1939   At opening of New York World's Fair, Roosevelt becomes first president to be televised (30 Apr.); Executive Office of the President established (1 July); U.S. proclaims neutrality in European hostilities (5 Sept.); Roosevelt declares limited national emergency (8 Sept.); Neutrality Act of 1939 passes (4 Nov.) authorizing "cash and carry" sale of arms to belligerents.

1940   U.S. population 131,669,275 National Defense Research Committee established (15 June) with Vannevar Bush as chairman; embargo on exports of scrap iron and steel to non–Western Hemisphere nations except Great Britain (26 Sept.); Roosevelt reelected for record third term (5 Nov.); Office of Production Management established (20 Dec.); Roosevelt calls for production effort to make U.S. "arsenal of democracy" (29 Dec.).

1941   Lend–Lease bill passes (11 Mar.), for lending goods and services to democratic countries in return for services; secret U.S.–British talks in Washington, D.C. (27 Jan.–29 Mar.), produce war plan ABC–1 and set "Germany first" priority in event of war with Germany and Japan; Roosevelt declares unlimited national emergency (27 May); German and Italian consulates ordered closed (6 June); Atlantic Charter formulated (14 Aug.) by Roosevelt and Churchill outlining war aims; Japanese attack (7 Dec.) on Pearl Harbor cripples Pacific fleet; U.S. enters World War II with declarations of war on Japan (8 Dec.) and Germany (11 Dec.).

1942   U.S. signs UN Declaration (1 Jan.); Roosevelt orders (19 Feb.) relocation of Japanese–Americans to interior internment camps; first Moscow Conference (12-15 Aug.): U.S., Soviet Union, and Great Britain decide not to open second front in Europe; Manhattan Project to develop atomic bomb placed under command of Leslie R. Groves (31 Aug.).

1943   Casablanca Conference (14–24 Jan.): Roosevelt and Churchill decide that war would be fought to "unconditional surrender"; first Cairo Conference (22–26 Nov.): Roosevelt and Churchill confer with Chiang Kai–shek regarding war in Far East.

1944   Operation Overlord (D day): massive Allied landings (6 June) on Normandy beaches; Bretton Woods Conference (1–22 July) establishes International Monetary Fund; Dumbarton Oaks Conference (21 Aug.–7 Oct.) establishes basis for UN Charter.

1945   Yalta Conference (4–11 Feb.), Roosevelt, Churchill, and Stalin plan defeat of Germany; United Nations Conference (25 Apr.-26 June) in San Francisco drafts UN Charter; death of Roosevelt (12 Apr.).

Harry S. Truman, 33rd President (1945–1953)

Life

Birthdate:	8 May 1884
Birthplace:	Lamar, Mo.
Parents:	John Anderson Truman, Martha Ellen Young
Religion:	Baptist
College Education:	None
Wife:	Elizabeth Virginia ("Bess") Wallace
Date of Marriage:	28 June 1919
Child:	Margaret
Political Party:	Democratic
Other Positions Held:	Judge, Jackson County (Mo.) Court (1922–1924; 1926–1934); U.S. Senator (1935–1945); Vice President (1945)
Date of Inauguration:	12 April 1945 (succeeded to presidency on death of Franklin D. Roosevelt)
End of Term:	20 January 1953
Date of Death:	26 December 1972
Place of Death:	Kansas City, Mo.
Place of Burial:	Independence, Mo.

Elections

ELECTION OF 1948

Candidate	Party	Electoral Vote	Pop. Vote
Harry S. Truman	Dem.	303	49.5%
Thomas E. Dewey	Rep.	189	45%
J. Strom Thurmond	States' Rights	39	2.4%
Henry A. Wallace	Prog.	0	2.4%

DID NOT RUN IN ELECTION OF 1952

POLITICAL COMPOSITION OF CONGRESS

79th Congress (1945–1947)
Senate: Dem. 56; Rep. 38; other 1
House: Dem. 242; Rep. 190; others 2

80th Congress (1947–1949)
Senate: Rep. 51; Dem. 45
House: Rep. 245; Dem. 188; other 1

81st Congress (1949–1951)
Senate: Dem. 54; Rep. 42
House: Dem. 263; Rep. 171; other 1

82d Congress (1951–1953)
Senate: Dem. 49; Rep. 47
House: Dem. 234; Rep. 199; other 1

Vice President

Alben W. Barkley (1949–1953)

Appointments

Cabinet Members:
Edward R. Stettinius, Jr., secretary of state (1945)
James F. Byrnes, secretary of state (1945–1947)
George C. Marshall, secretary of state (1947–1949)
Dean G. Acheson, secretary of state (1949–1953)
Henry Morgenthau, Jr., secretary of the treasury (1945)

Frederick M. ("Fred") Vinson, secretary of the treasury (1945–1946)
John W. Snyder, secretary of the treasury (1946–1953)
Henry L. Stimson, secretary of war (1945)
Robert P. Patterson, secretary of war (1945–1947)
Kenneth C. Royall, secretary of war (1947)
James V. Forrestal, secretary of defense (1947–1949)
Louis A. Johnson, secretary of defense (1949–1950)
George C. Marshall, secretary of defense (1950–1951)
Robert A. Lovett, secretary of defense (1951–1953)
Francis Biddle, attorney general (1945)
Tom C. Clark, attorney general (1945–1949)
J. Howard McGrath, attorney general (1949–1952)
James P. McGranery, attorney general (1952–1953)
Frank C. Walker, postmaster general (1945)
Robert E. Hannegan, postmaster general (1945–1947)
Jesse M. Donaldson, postmaster general (1947–1953)
James V. Forrestal, secretary of the navy (1945–1947)
Harold L. Ickes, secretary of the interior (1945–1946)
Julius A. Krug, secretary of the interior (1946–1949)
Oscar L. Chapman, secretary of the interior (1949–1953)
Claude R. Wickard, secretary of agriculture (1945)
Clinton P. Anderson, secretary of agriculture (1945–1948)
Charles F. Brannan, secretary of agriculture (1948–1953)
Henry A. Wallace, secretary of commerce (1945–1946)
W. Averell Harriman, secretary of commerce (1946–1948)
Charles Sawyer, secretary of commerce (1948–1953)
Frances Perkins, secretary of labor (1945)
Lewis B. Schwellenbach, secretary of labor (1945–1948)
Maurice J. Tobin, secretary of labor (1948–1953)

Supreme Court Appointments:
Harold H. Burton (1945–1958)
Frederick M. ("Fred") Vinson, chief justice (1946–1953)
Tom C. Clark (1949–1967)
Sherman Minton (1949–1956)

Key Events

1945   Truman becomes president upon death of Roosevelt (12 Apr.); Germany surrenders (7 May); European Advisory Commission (5 June) establishes German occupation zones; Potsdam Conference (17 July–2 Aug.): Truman, Stalin, and Churchill plan future of postwar Europe; U.S. drops atomic bombs on Hiroshima (6 Aug.) and Nagasaki (9 Aug.); Japan surrenders (15 Aug.), ending World War II.

1946   Atomic bomb tests at Bikini Atoll in Pacific (1 July); Philippines given independence (4 July); Atomic Energy Act (1 Aug.) passes control of atomic energy to new Atomic Energy Commission.

1947   Truman Doctrine (12 Mar.): first U.S. attempt to contain Communism; aid to Greece and Turkey approved (22 May); Marshall Plan proposed (5 June) to aid Europe in postwar economic recovery; National Security Act passes (26 July), establishing National Security Council and Central Intelligence Agency; Department of Defense supersedes Department of War and Department of the Navy; Truman delivers first presidential address telecast from the White House (5 Oct.).

1948   USSR blockades Berlin's Allied sectors (1 Apr.); British and U.S. planes' aerial supply operation sustains West; Truman signs Foreign Assistance Act for European Recovery Program (2 Apr.); Truman reelected president (2 Nov.).

1949   Berlin Blockade lifted (12 May); North Atlantic Treaty Organization established (24 Aug.) by U.S., Canada, and 10

Harry S. Truman (Continued)

European nations; a complete reconstruction of the White House begins (12 Dec.); Trumans reside in nearby Blair House.

1950   U.S. population: 150,697,361 U.S. recalls (14 Jan.) consular officials from China after consulate general seized in Peking; H–bomb production authorized (31 Jan.); NSC–68 memorandum calls for massive increase in military spending to face Soviet threat (April); North Koreans cross 38th parallel into South Korea (25 June), provoking Korean War; UN command in Korea formed (7 July) with Gen. MacArthur designated commander (8 July); amphibious Inchon landing (15 Sept.) leads to recapture of Seoul (26 Sept.).

1951   Twenty–second Amendment limits presidential terms (26 Feb.); Julius and Ethel Rosenberg found guilty (29 Mar.) as spies and sentenced to death (executed 1953); MacArthur removed in Korea by Truman over strategy disagreements (11 Apr.); armistice negotiations begin (10 July).

1952   Reconstructed White House ready for occupancy (27 Mar.); Truman seizes steel mills (8 Apr.) to prevent strike; seizure ruled unconstitutional (2 June); Eisenhower elected president (4 Nov.).

Dwight David Eisenhower, 34th President (1953–1961)

Life

Birthdate:	14 October 1890
Birthplace:	Denison, Tex.
Parents:	David Jacob Eisenhower, Ida Elizabeth Stover
Religion:	Presbyterian
College Education:	United States Military Academy
Wife:	Marie ("Mamie") Geneva Doud
Date of Marriage:	1 July 1916
Children:	Doud Dwight, John Sheldon Doud
Political Party:	Republican
Other Positions Held:	Brigadier General, U.S. Army (1941–1942)
	Major General, U.S. Army (1942–1943)
	General, U.S. Army, and Supreme Allied Commander (1943–1945)
	Chief of Staff, U.S. Army (1945–1948)
	President, Columbia University (1948–1953)
	Supreme Commander, NATO forces in Europe (1951–1952)
Date of Inauguration:	20 January 1953
End of Term:	20 January 1961
Date of Death:	28 March 1969
Place of Death:	Washington, D.C.
Place of Burial:	Abilene, Kans.

Elections

ELECTION OF 1952

Candidate	Party	Electoral Vote	Pop. Vote
Dwight D. Eisenhower	Rep.	442	55.1%
Adlai E. Stevenson	Dem.	89	44.4%

ELECTION OF 1956

Candidate	Party	Electoral Vote	Pop. Vote
Dwight D. Eisenhower	Rep.	457	57.6%
Adlai E. Stevenson	Dem.	73	42.1%

INELIGIBLE TO RUN IN ELECTION OF 1960

POLITICAL COMPOSITION OF CONGRESS

83d Congress (1953–1955)
Senate: Rep. 48; Dem. 47; other 1
House: Rep. 221; Dem. 211; others 1

84th Congress (1955–1957)
Senate: Dem. 48; Rep. 47; other 1
House: Dem. 232; Rep. 203

85th Congress (1957–1959)
Senate: Dem. 49; Rep. 47
House: Dem. 233; Rep. 200

86th Congress (1959–1961)
Senate: Dem. 64; Rep. 34
House: Dem. 283; Rep. 153

Vice President

Richard M. Nixon (1953–1961)

Appointments

Cabinet Members:
John Foster Dulles, secretary of state (1953–1959)
Christian A. Herter, secretary of state (1959–1961)
George M. Humphrey, secretary of the treasury (1953–1957)
Robert B. Anderson, secretary of the treasury (1957–1961)
Charles E. Wilson, secretary of defense (1953–1957)
Neil H. McElroy, secretary of defense (1957–1959)
Thomas S. Gates, secretary of defense (1959–1961)
Herbert Brownell, Jr., attorney general (1953–1957)
William P. Rogers, attorney general (1958–1961)
Arthur E. Summerfield, postmaster general (1953–1961)
Douglas McKay, secretary of the interior (1953–1956)
Frederick A. Seaton, secretary of the interior (1956–1961)
Ezra Taft Benson, secretary of agriculture (1953–1961)
Sinclair Weeks, secretary of commerce (1953–1958)
Frederick H. Mueller, secretary of commerce (1953–1961)
Martin P. Durkin, secretary of labor (1953)
James P. Mitchell, secretary of labor (1953–1961)
Oveta Culp Hobby, secretary of health, education, and welfare (1953–1955)
Marion B. Folsom, secretary of health, education, and welfare (1955–1958)
Arthur S. Flemming, secretary of health, education, and welfare (1958–1961)

Supreme Court Appointments:
Earl Warren, chief justice (1953–1969)
John M. Harlan (1955–1971)
William J. Brennan, Jr. (1956–1990)
Charles E. Whittaker (1957–1962)
Potter Stewart (1958–1981)

Key Events

1953   Department of Health, Education, and Welfare established; hostilities halted in Korea (26 July).

1954   McCarthy–Army Hearings (22 Apr.-17 June): investigation by Sen. Joseph McCarthy into charges army was lax in ferreting out Communist spies; *Brown* v. *Board of Education of Topeka, Kansas,* bans racial segregation (17 May); Southeast Asia Treaty Organization formed (8 Sept.) by 8 nations.

1955   Eisenhower holds first televised news conference (19 Jan.); military advisers dispatched to South Vietnam to train army (23 Feb.); Supreme Court orders desegregation "with all deliberate speed" (31 May); black boycott of Montgomery, Ala., bus system inspired by Rosa Parks's refusal to sit at back of bus (1 Dec.).

1956   1st transatlantic cable in operation (25 Sept.); Suez Crisis: Israel invasion of Gaza Strip and the Sinai (29 Oct.) is followed by British and French attacks on Egypt; U.S. leads efforts for a cease–fire (in effect 2 Nov.).

1957   Arkansas National Guard called in (4 Sept.) to bar black students from integrating Little Rock High School; federal court orders Guardsmen removed; federal troops sent in (24 Sept.) and Arkansas National Guard put under federal command; Civil Rights Act (9 Sept.): first since Reconstruction, establishes Civil Rights Commission; Soviets launch *Sputnik 1* (4 Oct.) and *Sputnik 2* (3 Nov.), first artificial satellites.

1959   Alaska (3 Jan.) and Hawaii (21 Aug.) admitted as states; Communist Fidel Castro seizes power in Cuba (Jan.); St.

Dwight David Eisenhower (Continued)

Lawrence Seaway opens (25 Apr.); Soviet Premier Nikita Khrushchev engages in "Kitchen Debate" with Vice President Nixon during 10–day tour of U.S. (Sept.).

1960   U.S. population: 179,323,175 Congress approves voting rights act (21 Apr.) and civil rights act (6 May); U.S. U–2 reconnaissance plane shot down over USSR (1 May); Kennedy and Nixon on television engage in first presidential candidate debates (26 Sept., 7, 13, and 21 Oct.); Kennedy elected president (8 Nov.).

John Fitzgerald Kennedy, 35th President (1961–1963)

Life

Birthdate:	29 May 1917
Birthplace:	Brookline, Mass.
Parents:	Joseph Patrick Kennedy, Rose Fitzgerald
Religion:	Roman Catholic
College Education:	Harvard College
Wife:	Jacqueline Lee Bouvier
Date of Marriage:	12 September 1953
Children:	Caroline Bouvier, John Fitzgerald, Patrick Bouvier
Political Party:	Democratic
Other Positions Held:	Member, U.S. House of Representatives (1947–1953)
	U.S. Senator (1953–1960)
Date of Inauguration:	20 January 1961
End of Term:	22 November 1963 (assassinated by Lee Harvey Oswald)
Date of Death:	22 November 1963
Place of Death:	Dallas, Tex.
Place of Burial:	Arlington, Va.

Elections

ELECTION OF 1960

Candidate	Party	Electoral Vote	Pop. Vote
John F. Kennedy	Dem.	303	49.9%
Richard M. Nixon	Rep.	219	49.6%

POLITICAL COMPOSITION OF CONGRESS

87th Congress (1961–1963)

Senate:	Dem. 65; Rep. 35
House:	Dem. 263; Rep. 174

88th Congress (1963–1965)

Senate:	Dem. 67; Rep. 33
House:	Dem. 258; Rep. 177

Vice President

Lyndon B. Johnson (1961–1963)

Appointments

Cabinet Members:
Dean Rusk, secretary of state (1961–1963)
C. Douglas Dillon, secretary of the treasury (1961–1963)
Robert S. McNamara, secretary of defense (1961–1963)
Robert F. Kennedy, attorney general (1961–1963)
J. Edward Day, postmaster general (1961–1963)
John A. Gronouski, Jr., postmaster general (1963)
Stewart L. Udall, secretary of the interior (1961–1963)
Orville L. Freeman, secretary of agriculture (1961–1963)
Luther H. Hodges, secretary of commerce (1961–1963)
Arthur J. Goldberg, secretary of labor (1961–1962)
W. Willard Wirtz, secretary of labor (1962–1963)
Abraham A. Ribicoff, secretary of health, education, and welfare (1961–1962)
Anthony J. Celebrezze, secretary of health, education, and welfare (1962–1963)

Supreme Court Appointments:
Byron R. White (1962–1993)
Arthur J. Goldberg (1962–1965)

Key Events

1961   Twenty–third Amendment ratified (3 Apr.), granting District of Columbia the vote in presidential elections; Bay of Pigs Invasion (17 Apr.): failed CIA–backed invasion of Cuba by Cuban exiles; Cmdr. Alan B. Shepard in first U.S. manned suborbital space flight (5 May).

1962   Lt. Col. John Glenn is first American in orbit (20 Feb.); first U.S. communications satellite launched (July); federal troops and Mississippi National Guard assist in admitting black student James Meredith into University of Mississippi (30 Sept.–10 Oct.); Cuban missile crisis: buildup of Soviet missiles in Cuba revealed (22 Oct.), Cuba quarantined, USSR removes missiles.

1963   U.S., USSR, and Great Britain agree (25 July) on nuclear test ban treaty, barring all but underground tests; 200,000 people demonstrate for equal rights for blacks in Washington (28 Aug.); hot–line communications installed between Moscow and White House (30 Aug.); South Vietnamese president Diem assassinated (2 Nov.); Kennedy assassinated in Dallas by Lee Harvey Oswald (22 Nov.).

Lyndon Baines Johnson, 36th President (1963–1969)

Life

Birthdate:	27 August 1908
Birthplace:	Stonewall, Tex.
Parents:	Sam Ealy Johnson, Jr., Rebekah Baines
Religion:	Disciples of Christ
College Education:	Southwest Texas State Teachers College
First Lady:	Claudia Alta ("Lady Bird") Taylor
Date of Marriage:	17 November 1934
Children:	Lynda Bird, Luci Baines
Political Party:	Democratic
Other Positions Held:	Member, U.S. House of Representatives (1937–1949)
	U.S. Senator (1949-1961; Democratic Leader, 1953–1961)
	Vice President (1961–1963)
Date of Inauguration:	22 November 1963 (succeeded to presidency on death of John F. Kennedy)
End of Term:	20 January 1969
Date of Death:	22 January 1973
Place of Death:	San Antonio, Tex.
Place of Burial:	Johnson City, Tex.

Elections

ELECTION OF 1964

Candidate	Party	Electoral Vote	Pop. Vote
Lyndon B. Johnson	Dem.	486	61.1%
Barry M. Goldwater	Rep.	52	38.5%

DID NOT RUN IN ELECTION OF 1968

POLITICAL COMPOSITION OF CONGRESS

88th Congress (1963–1965)
Senate:	Dem. 67; Rep. 33
House:	Dem. 258; Rep. 177

89th Congress (1965–1967)
Senate:	Dem. 68; Rep. 32
House:	Dem. 295; Rep. 140

90th Congress (1967–1969)
Senate:	Dem. 64; Rep. 36
House:	Dem. 246; Rep. 187

Vice President

Hubert H. Humphrey (1965–1969)

Appointments

Cabinet Members:
Dean Rusk, secretary of state (1963–1969)
C. Douglas Dillon, secretary of the treasury (1963–1965)
Henry H. Fowler, secretary of the treasury (1965–1968)
Joseph W. Barr, secretary of the treasury (1968–1969)
Robert S. McNamara, secretary of defense (1963–1968)
Clark M. Clifford, secretary of defense (1968–1969)
Robert F. Kennedy, attorney general (1963–1964)
Nicholas deB. Katzenbach, attorney general (1965–1966)
Ramsey Clark, attorney general (1967–1969)

John A. Gronouski, Jr., postmaster general (1963–1965)
Lawrence F. O'Brien, postmaster general (1965–1968)
W. Marvin Watson, postmaster general (1968–1969)
Stewart L. Udall, secretary of the interior (1963–1969)
Orville L. Freeman, secretary of agriculture (1963–1969)
Luther H. Hodges, secretary of commerce (1963–1965)
John T. Connor, secretary of commerce (1965–1967)
Alexander B. Trowbridge, secretary of commerce (1967–1968)
C. R. Smith, secretary of commerce (1968–1969)
W. Willard Wirtz, secretary of labor (1963–1969)
Anthony J. Celebrezze, secretary of health, education, and welfare (1963–1965)
John W. Gardner, secretary of health, education, and welfare (1965–1968)
Wilbur J. Cohen, secretary of health, education, and welfare (1968–1969)
Robert C. Weaver, secretary of housing and urban development (1966–1968)
Robert C. Wood, secretary of housing and urban development (1969)
Alan S. Boyd, secretary of transportation (1966–1969)

Supreme Court Appointments:
Abe Fortas (1965–1969)
Thurgood Marshall (1967–1991)

Key Events

1963   Johnson becomes fourth president to come into office upon death of a president (22 Nov.).

1964   Twenty–fourth Amendment ratified (23 Jan.), banning the poll tax in federal elections; Panamanian riots lead to severing of diplomatic relations with U.S. (9 Jan.) and U.S. offers to negotiate new canal treaty (18 Dec.); Civil Rights Act (29 June) bans discrimination; Sen. Margaret Chase Smith of Maine becomes first woman whose name is placed in nomination at convention of major political party (Republican, 15 July); Gulf of Tonkin resolution (7 Aug.) authorizes Johnson to "repel any army attack" in Vietnam and number U.S. forces increases through 1968; War on Poverty Bill passes (11 Aug.); Warren Commission report (27 Sept.) concludes Oswald was lone assassin of Kennedy; Johnson elected president (3 Nov.).

1965   Lady Bird Johnson becomes first First Lady to participate in husband's inaugural ceremony (20 Jan.); continuous bombing of North Vietnam begins (7 Feb.) by order of Johnson; Voting Rights Act (6 Aug.); establishment of Medicare and Department of Housing and Urban Development.

1966   Department of Transportation established (15 Oct.).

1967   Riots by blacks (July) put down by federal troops and National Guardsmen; Twenty–fifth Amendment ratified, dealing with presidential disability and succession (10 Feb.); Thurgood Marshall becomes first African American named a justice of the Supreme Court (13 June).

1968   Tet Offensive by North Vietnamese (30 Jan.); Martin Luther King, Jr., assassinated (4 Apr.) by James Earl Ray; peace talks on Vietnam open in Paris (10 May); Sen. Robert F. Kennedy assassinated (5 June) by Sirhan Sirhan; U.S. bombing halted in Vietnam (31 Oct.); Richard Nixon elected president (5 Nov.).

Richard Milhous Nixon, 37th President (1969–1974)

Life

Birthdate:	9 January 1913
Birthplace:	Yorba Linda, Calif.
Parents:	Francis Anthony Nixon, Hannah Milhous
Religion:	Quaker
College Education:	Whittier College; Duke University Law School
Wife:	Thelma Catherine ("Pat") Ryan
Date of Marriage:	21 June 1940
Children:	Patricia ("Tricia"), Julie
Political Party:	Republican
Other Positions Held:	Member, U.S. House of Representatives (1947–1951)
	U.S. Senator (1951–1953)
	Vice President (1953–1961)
Date of Inauguration:	20 January 1969
End of Term:	9 August 1974 (resigned office)
Date of Death:	22 April 1994
Place of Death:	New York, N.Y.
Place of Burial:	Yorba Linda, Calif.

Elections

ELECTION OF 1968

Candidate	Party	Electoral Vote	Pop. Vote
Richard Nixon	Rep.	301	43.4%
Hubert H. Humphrey	Dem.	191	42.7%
George C. Wallace	Amer. Ind.	46	13.5%

ELECTION OF 1972

Candidate	Party	Electoral Vote	Pop. Vote
Richard Nixon	Rep.	520	60.6%
George S. McGovern	Dem.	17	37.5%

POLITICAL COMPOSITION OF CONGRESS

91st Congress (1969–1971)
Senate: Dem. 57; Rep. 43
House: Dem. 245; Rep. 189

92d Congress (1971–1973)
Senate: Dem. 54; Rep. 44; others 2
House: Dem. 254; Rep. 180

93d Congress (1973–1975)
Senate: Dem. 56; Rep. 42; others 2
House: Dem. 239; Rep. 192; other 1

Vice Presidents

Spiro T. Agnew (1969–1973)
Gerald R. Ford (1973–1974)

Appointments

Cabinet Members:
William P. Rogers, secretary of state (1969–1973)
Henry A. Kissinger, secretary of state (1973–1974)
David M. Kennedy, secretary of the treasury (1969–1971)
John B. Connally, Jr., secretary of the treasury (1971–1972)
George P. Shultz, secretary of the treasury (1972–1974)
William E. Simon, secretary of the treasury (1974)
Melvin R. Laird, secretary of defense (1969–1973)
Elliot L. Richardson, secretary of defense (1973)
James R. Schlesinger, secretary of defense (1973–1974)
John N. Mitchell, attorney general (1969–1972)
Richard G. Kleindienst, attorney general (1972–1973)
Elliot L. Richardson, attorney general (1973)
William B. Saxbe, attorney general (1974)
Wilton M. Blount, postmaster general (1969–1971)
Walter J. Hickel, secretary of the interior (1969–1970)
Rogers C. B. Morton, secretary of the interior (1971–1974)
Clifford M. Hardin, secretary of agriculture (1969–1971)
Earl L. Butz, secretary of agriculture (1971–1974)
Maurice H. Stans, secretary of commerce (1969–1972)
Peter G. Peterson, secretary of commerce (1972–1973)
Frederick B. Dent, secretary of commerce (1973–1974)
George P. Shultz, secretary of labor (1969–1970)
James D. Hodgson, secretary of labor (1970–1973)
Peter J. Brennan, secretary of labor (1973–1974)
Robert H. Finch, secretary of health, education, and welfare (1969–1970)
Elliot L. Richardson, secretary of health, education, and welfare (1970–1973)
Caspar W. Weinberger, secretary of health, education, and welfare (1973–1974)
George W. Romney, secretary of housing and urban development (1969–1973)
James T. Lynn, secretary of housing and urban development (1973–1974)
John A. Volpe, secretary of transportation (1969–1973)
Claude S. Brinegar, secretary of transportation (1973–1974)

Supreme Court Appointments:
Warren Earl Burger, chief justice (1969–1986)
Harry A. Blackmun (1970–1994)
Lewis F. Powell, Jr. (1972–1987)
William H. Rehnquist (1972–)

Key Events

1969 Stonewall riot in Greenwich Village in New York City marks beginning of gay rights movement (27 June); *Apollo 11* astronauts Neil A. Armstrong and Edwin E. Aldrin, Jr., take man's first walk on the moon (20 July).

1970 U.S. population: 203,235,298 Ohio National Guard kills 4 students at Kent State University, Ohio (4 May), following burning of ROTC building.

1971 Establishment of U.S. Postal Service removes postmaster general from Cabinet; Twenty–sixth Amendment lowers voting age to 18 (30 June); Communist China admitted to UN (25 Oct.), Nationalist China ousted; massive bombing of North Vietnam (Dec.).

1972 Nixon visits Peking (21 Feb.), Moscow (22 May.), first for a U.S. president; North Vietnamese attack in force across demilitarized zone (30 Mar.) and U.S. bombs Hanoi and Haiphong (15 Apr.); break–in of Democratic National Party Headquarters at Watergate (17 June); ABM Treaty between U.S. and USSR enters into force (3 Oct.); Nixon reelected (7 Nov.).

1973 Supreme Court rules in *Roe* v. *Wade* (Jan.) that states cannot categorically ban abortion; cease–fire effective in Vietnam (28 Jan.); China and U.S. agree (22 Feb.) to establish liaison

Richard Milhous Nixon (Continued)

	offices in each country; Vice President Agnew resigns (10 Oct.), pleading no contest to tax–evasion charges; Gerald Ford becomes first appointed vice president (12 Oct.); ban by Middle East Oil nations on exports to U.S. (19-21 Oct., lifted 18 Mar. 1974); War Powers Act (7 Nov.) sets 60–day limit on presidential commitment of troops unless Congress authorizes continued action.
1974	House Judiciary Committee recommends 3 articles of impeachment against Nixon (24–30 July), approved by Congress; Nixon resigns (9 Aug.).

THE PRESIDENTS

Gerald Rudolph Ford, 38th President (1974–1977)

Life

Birthdate:	14 July 1913
Birthplace:	Omaha, Nebr.
Parents:	Leslie Lynch King, Dorothy Ayer Gardner
Religion:	Episcopalian
College Education:	University of Michigan; Yale University Law School
Wife:	Elizabeth ("Betty") Bloomer Warren
Date of Marriage:	15 October 1948
Children:	Michael Gerald, John ("Jack") Gardner, Steven Meigs, Susan Elizabeth
Political Party:	Republican
Other Positions Held:	Member, U.S. House of Representatives (1949–1973; Republican Leader, 1965–1973) Vice President (1973–1974)
Date of Inauguration:	9 August 1974 (succeeded to presidency on resignation of Richard Nixon)
End of Term:	20 January 1977 Resides in Rancho Mirage, Calif.

Elections

DEFEATED IN ELECTION OF 1976 BY JIMMY CARTER

POLITICAL COMPOSITION OF CONGRESS
93d Congress (1973–1975)
Senate: Dem. 56; Rep. 42; others 2
House: Dem. 239; Rep. 192; other 1
94th Congress (1975–1977)
Senate: Dem. 61; Rep. 37; others 2
House: Dem. 291; Rep. 144

Vice President

Nelson A. Rockefeller (1974–1977)

Appointments

Cabinet Members:
Henry A. Kissinger, secretary of state (1974–1977)
William E. Simon, secretary of the treasury (1974–1977)
James R. Schlesinger, secretary of defense (1974–1975)
Donald H. Rumsfeld, secretary of defense (1975–1977)
William B. Saxbe, attorney general (1974–1975)
Edward H. Levi, attorney general (1975–1977)
Rogers C. B. Morton, secretary of the interior (1974–1975)
Stanley K. Hathaway, secretary of the interior (1975)
Thomas S. Kleppe, secretary of the interior (1975–1977)
Earl L. Butz, secretary of agriculture (1974–1976)
John A. Knebel, secretary of agriculture (1976–1977)
Frederick B. Dent, secretary of commerce (1974–1975)
Rogers C. B. Morton, secretary of commerce (1975)
Elliot L. Richardson, secretary of commerce (1976–1977)
Peter J. Brennan, secretary of labor (1974–1975)
John T. Dunlop, secretary of labor (1975–1976)
William J. Usery, Jr., secretary of labor (1976–1977)
Caspar W. Weinberger, secretary of health, education, and welfare (1974–1975)
F. David Mathews, secretary of health, education, and welfare (1975–1977)
James T. Lynn, secretary of housing and urban development (1974–1975)
Carla Anderson Hills, secretary of housing and urban development (1975–1977)
Claude S. Brinegar, secretary of transportation (1974–1975)
William T. Coleman, Jr., secretary of transportation (1975–1977)
Supreme Court Appointment:
John Paul Stevens (1975–)

Key Events

1974 Ford becomes president upon resignation of Nixon (9 Aug.); Nixon pardoned (8 Sept.).

1975 U.S. civilians evacuated from Saigon (29 Apr.), Communists overrun country; *Mayaguez* incident (15 May): merchant ship is rescued from Cambodians by U.S. Navy and marines; Rockefeller Commission reveals (10 June) illegal CIA operations.

1976 United States celebrates bicentennial (4 July); *Viking 2* lands on Mars (3 Sept.); President Ford escapes two assassination attempts (5, 22 Sept.); Carter elected president.

TABLE OF PRESIDENTIAL DATA

James Earl ("Jimmy") Carter, 39th President (1977–1981)

Life

Birthdate:	1 October 1924
Birthplace:	Plains, Ga.
Parents:	James Earl Carter, (Bessie) Lillian Gordy
Religion:	Baptist
College Education:	United States Naval Academy
Wife:	Rosalynn Smith
Date of Marriage:	7 July 1946
Children:	John William ("Jack"), James Earl ("Chip"), Donnel Jeffrey ("Jeff"), Amy Lynn
Political Party:	Democratic
Other Positions Held:	Member, Georgia Senate (1963–1967)
	Governor of Georgia (1971–1975)
Date of Inauguration:	20 January 1977
End of Term:	20 January 1981
	Resides in Atlanta, Ga.

Elections

ELECTION OF 1976

Candidate	Party	Electoral Vote	Pop. Vote
Jimmy Carter	Dem.	297	50.1%
Gerald R. Ford	Rep.	240	47.9%

DEFEATED IN ELECTION OF 1980 BY RONALD REAGAN

POLITICAL COMPOSITION OF CONGRESS

95th Congress (1977–1979)
Senate: Dem. 61; Rep. 38; other 1
House: Dem. 292; Rep. 143

96th Congress (1979–1981)
Senate: Dem. 58; Rep. 41; other 1
House: Dem. 276; Rep. 157

Vice President

Walter F. Mondale (1977–1981)

Appointments

Cabinet Members:
Cyrus R. Vance, secretary of state (1977–1980)
Edmund S. Muskie, secretary of state (1980–1981)
W. Michael Blumenthal, secretary of the treasury (1977–1979)
G. William Miller, secretary of the treasury (1979–1981)
Harold Brown, secretary of defense (1977–1981)
Griffin B. Bell, attorney general (1977–1979)
Benjamin R. Civiletti, attorney general (1979–1981)
Cecil D. Andrus, secretary of the interior (1977–1981)
Bob S. Bergland, secretary of agriculture (1977–1981)
Juanita M. Kreps, secretary of commerce (1977–1979)
Philip M. Klutznick, secretary of commerce (1980–1981)
Ray Marshall, secretary of labor (1977–1981)
Joseph A. Califano, Jr., secretary of health, education, and welfare (1977–1979)
Patricia Roberts Harris, secretary of health, education, and welfare (1979–1981)
Patricia Roberts Harris, secretary of housing and urban development (1977–1979)

Moon Landrieu, secretary of housing and urban development (1979–1981)
Brock Adams, secretary of transportation (1977–1979)
Neil Goldschmidt, secretary of transportation (1979–1981)
James R. Schlesinger, secretary of energy (1977–1979)
Charles W. Duncan, secretary of energy (1979–1981)
Shirley M. Hufstedler, secretary of education (1979–1981)

Supreme Court Appointments:
None

Key Events

1977   Carter holds first presidential call–in broadcast (5 Mar.); Department of Energy created (4 Aug.); Carter pardons approximately 10,000 Vietnam draft evaders.

1978   Congress votes (18 Apr.) to turn over Panama Canal to Panama in 1999; Humphrey–Hawkins Full Employment Act (15 Oct.) sets goals for reducing unemployment.

1979   Nuclear reactor accident at Three Mile Island, Pa. (28 Mar.); Department of Education and Department of Health and Human Services established (17 Oct.), superseding Department of Health, Education, and Welfare; 63 Americans taken hostage at U.S. embassy in Tehran, Iran (4 Nov.).

1980   U.S. population: 226,504,825 U.S. retaliates against Soviet invasion of Afghanistan with grain embargos (4 Jan.); military mission fails (24 Apr.) in attempt to rescue American hostages in Iran, with 8 killed and 5 wounded; Reagan elected president (4 Nov.).

Ronald Wilson Reagan, 40th President (1981–1989)

Life

Birthdate:	6 February 1911
Birthplace:	Tampico, Ill.
Parents:	John Edward ("Jack") Reagan, Nelle Clyde Wilson
Religion:	Episcopalian
College Education:	Eureka College
First Wife:	Jane Wyman (divorced 1949)
Date of First Marriage:	24 January 1940
Children from First Marriage:	Maureen Elizabeth, Michael Edward (adopted)
Second Wife:	Nancy Davis
Date of Second Marriage:	4 March 1952
Children from Second Marriage:	Patricia ("Patti") Ann, Ronald ("Skip") Prescott
Political Party:	Republican
Other Positions Held:	President, Screen Actors Guild (1947–1952; 1959–1960) Governor of California (1967–1975)
Date of Inauguration:	20 January 1981
End of Term:	20 January 1989 Resides in Bel Air, Los Angeles, Calif.

Elections

ELECTION OF 1980

Candidate	Party	Electoral Vote	Pop. Vote
Ronald Reagan	Rep.	489	50.9%
Jimmy Carter	Dem.	49	41.2%
John B. Anderson	Ind.	0	7.9%

ELECTION OF 1984

Candidate	Party	Electoral Vote	Pop. Vote
Ronald Reagan	Rep.	525	59%
Walter Mondale	Dem.	13	41%

INELIGIBLE TO RUN IN ELECTION OF 1988

POLITICAL COMPOSITION OF CONGRESS

97th Congress (1981–1983)
Senate: Rep. 53; Dem. 46; other 1
House: Dem. 242; Rep. 189

98th Congress (1983–1985)
Senate: Rep. 54; Dem. 46
House: Dem. 268; Rep. 167

99th Congress (1985–1987)
Senate: Rep. 53; Dem. 47
House: Dem. 253; Rep. 182

100th Congress (1987–1989)
Senate: Dem. 55; Rep. 45
House: Dem. 258; Rep. 177

Vice President

George Bush (1981–1989)

Appointments

Cabinet Members:
Alexander M. Haig, secretary of state (1981–1982)
George P. Shultz, secretary of state (1982–1989)
Donald T. Regan, secretary of the treasury (1981–1985)
James A. Baker III, secretary of the treasury (1985–1988)
Nicholas F. Brady, secretary of the treasury (1988–1989)
Caspar W. Weinberger, secretary of defense (1981–1987)
Frank C. Carlucci, secretary of defense (1987–1989)
William French Smith, attorney general (1981–1985)
Edwin Meese III, attorney general (1985–1988)
Richard L. Thornburgh, attorney general (1988–1989)
James G. Watt, secretary of the interior (1981–1983)
William P. Clark, secretary of the interior (1983–1985)
Donald P. Hodel, secretary of the interior (1985–1989)
John R. Block, secretary of agriculture (1981–1986)
Richard E. Lyng, secretary of agriculture (1986–1989)
Malcolm Baldrige, secretary of commerce (1981–1987)
C. William Verity, Jr., secretary of commerce (1987–1989)
Raymond J. Donovan, secretary of labor (1981–1985)
William E. Brock III, secretary of labor (1985–1987)
Ann D. McLaughlin, secretary of labor (1987–1989)
Samuel R. Pierce, Jr., secretary of housing and urban development (1981–1989)
Andrew L. Lewis, secretary of transportation (1981–1983)
Elizabeth H. Dole, secretary of transportation (1983–1987)
James H. Burnley IV, secretary of transportation (1987–1989)
James B. Edwards, secretary of energy (1981–1982)
Donald P. Hodel, secretary of energy (1982–1985)
John S. Herrington, secretary of energy (1985–1989)
Terrel H. Bell, secretary of education (1981–1985)
William J. Bennett, secretary of education (1985–1988)
Lauro F. Cavazos, secretary of education (1988–1989)
Richard S. Schweiker, secretary of health and human services (1981–1983)
Margaret M. Heckler, secretary of health and human services (1983–1985)
Otis R. Bowen, secretary of health and human services (1985–1989)

Supreme Court Appointments:
Sandra Day O'Connor (1981–)
William H. Rehnquist, chief justice (1986–) (promoted from associate justice)
Antonin Scalia (1986–)
Anthony M. Kennedy (1988–)

Key Events

1981   American hostages released in Iran on day of Reagan's inauguration (20 Jan.); Reagan survives assassination attempt (30 Mar.); space shuttle *Columbia* launched, the first reusable spacecraft (12 Apr.); Reagan appoints Sandra Day O'Connor first woman justice of the Supreme Court (7 July); largest tax cut in nation's history passes (29 July); federal air traffic controllers strike and are dismissed by Reagan (5 Aug.).

1982   Equal Rights Amendment defeated after 10 years without sufficient ratifications.

1983   U.S. peacekeeping force in Lebanon attacked at marine headquarters with truck bomb (23 Oct.); U.S. invades Grenada (25 Oct.).

Ronald Wilson Reagan (Continued)

1984   Democrat Geraldine Ferraro 1st woman chosen as vice presidential candidate for major political party; Reagan reelected president (6 Nov.).

1985 $1.5 million appropriated (Mar.) for development of MX missile; hijackers seize Italian cruise ship *Achille Lauro* (7 Oct.).

1986   Space shuttle *Challenger* explodes (28 Jan.) shortly after takeoff, killing 7 aboard; U.S. war planes strike Libya in retaliation for Libyan bombing of West Berlin disco (5 Apr.); Congress passes comprehensive Tax Reform Act (Sept.); U.S. and USSR reach agreement on worldwide ban of medium–range missiles (18 Sept.); Iran–Contra scandal emerges (3 Nov.).

1987   First trillion–dollar U.S. budget; 37 sailors killed aboard USS *Stark* by Iraqi missile in Persian Gulf (27 May); Congressional hearings into Iran–Contra scandal (July): Col. Oliver North and Adm. John Poindexter involved in sale of arms to Iran and use of profits to support rebels in Nicaragua; Wall Street crashes (19 Oct.); U.S. and USSR sign INF Treaty dismantling some missiles.

1988   Gen. Manuel Noriega indicted in Florida (4 Feb.) for drug trafficking; more than 1 million illegal aliens apply for amnesty (4 May); Bush elected president (8 Nov.).

George Herbert Walker Bush, 41st President (1989–1993)

Life

Birthdate:	12 June 1924
Birthplace:	Milton, Mass.
Parents:	Prescott Sheldon Bush, Dorothy Walker
Religion:	Episcopalian
College Education:	Yale College
Wife:	Barbara Pierce
Date of Marriage:	6 January 1945
Children:	George Walker, Robin, John Ellis ("Jeb"), Neil Mallon, Marvin Pierce, Dorothy Pierce
Political Party:	Republican
Other Positions Held:	Member, U.S. House of Representatives (1967–1971)
	Ambassador to United Nations (1971–1973)
	Chairman, Republican National Committee (1973–1974)
	Chief U.S. Liaison, People's Republic of China (1974–1975)
	Director, Central Intelligence Agency (1976–1977)
	Vice President (1981–1989)
Date of Inauguration:	20 January 1989
End of Term:	20 January 1993
	Resides in Houston, Tex.

Elections

ELECTION OF 1988

Candidate	Party	Electoral Vote	Pop. Vote
George Bush	Rep.	426	53.4%
Michael S. Dukakis	Dem.	111	45.6%

DEFEATED IN ELECTION OF 1992 BY BILL CLINTON

POLITICAL COMPOSITION OF CONGRESS

101st Congress (1989–1991)
Senate: Dem. 55; Rep. 45
House: Dem. 260; Rep. 175

102d Congress (1991–1993)
Senate: Dem. 56; Rep. 44
House: Dem. 267; Rep. 167; other

Vice President

J. Danforth ("Dan") Quayle (1989–1993)

Appointments

Cabinet Members:
James A. Baker III, secretary of state (1989–1992)
Lawrence S. Eagleburger, secretary of state (1992–1993)
Nicholas F. Brady, secretary of the treasury (1989–1993)
Richard B. Cheney, secretary of defense (1989–1993)
Richard L. Thornburgh, attorney general (1989–1991)
William Barr, attorney general (1991–1993)
Manuel Lujan, Jr., secretary of the interior (1989–1993)
Clayton K. Yeutter, secretary of agriculture (1989–1991)
Edward R. Madigan, secretary of agriculture (1991–1993)
Robert A. Mosbacher, secretary of commerce (1989–1992)
Barbara A. Franklin, secretary of commerce (1992–1993)

Elizabeth H. Dole, secretary of labor (1989–1991)
Lynn Martin, secretary of labor (1991–1993)
Jack F. Kemp, secretary of housing and urban development (1989–1993)
Samuel K. Skinner, secretary of transportation (1989–1992)
Andrew H. Card, secretary of transportation (1992–1993)
James Watkins, secretary of energy (1989–1993)
Lauro F. Cavazos, secretary of education (1989–1990)
Lamar Alexander, secretary of education (1991–1993)
Louis W. Sullivan, secretary of health and human services (1989–1993)
Edward J. Derwinski, secretary of veterans affairs (1989–1992)

Supreme Court Appointments:
David H. Souter (1990–)
Clarence Thomas (1991–)

Key Events

1989　Largest oil spill in U.S. history (24 Mar.) from the *Exxon Valdez* in Prince Edward Sound; Col. Oliver North convicted of obstruction of Congress in Iran–Contra scandal (4 May); legislation passes (9 Aug.) intended to rescue savings and loan industry; 20,000 U.S. troops occupy Panama to apprehend Noriega (20 Dec.–3 Jan. 1990); Department of Veterans Affairs established; while flying in *Air Force One,* Bush uses a fax machine to transmit a veto message to Congress.

1990　U.S. population: 248,709,873 Iraq invades Kuwait (2 Aug.); UN coalition forces including 450,000 U.S. troops stationed in Saudi Arabia to prevent subsequent Iraqi invasion; Clean Air Act passes (15 Nov.): comprehensive plan to reduce 50% of annual level of emissions.

1991　Aerial bombing of Iraq begins (17 Jan.); coalition defeats Iraq in ground war (24–27 Feb.); Iraq accepts UN cease–fire terms (3 Mar.); U.S. and USSR sign START I Treaty; dissolution of Soviet Union (25 Dec.).

1992　An all–white Los Angeles jury acquits 4 L.A. police officers of wrongdoing (29 Apr.) in 1991 beating of Rodney King, a black man, provoking widespread riots; Americans with Disabilities Act takes effect; Clinton elected president (3 Nov.); U.S. troops provide humanitarian aid to famine–stricken Somalia (Dec.–Jan. 1993); Bush pardons former Secretary of Defense Caspar Weinberger and other high–level Reagan administration Iran–Contra scandal figures (24 Dec.); Twenty–seventh Amendment fixes congressional salaries during each term.

TABLE OF PRESIDENTIAL DATA

William Jefferson Clinton, 42nd President (1993–2001)

Life

Birthdate:	19 August 1946
Birthplace:	Hope, Ark.
Parents:	William Jefferson Blythe 3d, Virginia Cassidy
Religion:	Baptist
College Education:	Georgetown University; Rhodes Scholar, Oxford University, England; Yale University Law School
Wife:	Hillary Diane Rodham
Date of Marriage:	11 October 1975
Child:	Chelsea
Political Party:	Democratic
Other Positions Held:	Law Professor, University of Arkansas (1973–1976)
	Attorney General of Arkansas (1977–1979)
	Governor of Arkansas (1979–1981; 1983–1992)
Date of Inauguration:	20 January 1993
Acquittal of Impeachment Charges:	12 February 1999
End of term:	20 January 2001
	Resides in Chappaqua, New York

Elections

ELECTION OF 1992

Candidate	Party	Electoral Vote	Pop. Vote
Bill Clinton	Dem.	370	43%
George Bush	Rep.	168	37%
H. Ross Perot	Ind.	0	19%

ELECTION OF 1996

Candidate	Party	Electoral Vote	Pop. Vote
Bill Clinton	Dem.	379	49%
Robert J. Dole	Rep.	159	41%
H. Ross Perot	Reform	0	8%

POLITICAL COMPOSITION OF CONGRESS

103d Congress (1993–1995)
Senate: Dem. 56; Rep. 44
House: Dem. 258; Rep. 176; other 1

104th Congress (1995–1997)
Senate: Rep. 52; Dem. 48
House: Rep. 230; Dem. 204; other 1

105th Congress (1997–)
Senate: Rep. 55; Dem. 45
House: Rep. 226; Dem. 208; other 1

106th Congress (1999–2001)
Senate: Rep. 54; Dem. 46
House: Rep. 222; Dem. 208; other 1

Vice President

Albert A. Gore, Jr. (1993–2001)

Appointments

Cabinet Members:
Warren M. Christopher, secretary of state (1993–1997)
Madeleine K. Albright, secretary of state (1997–2001)
Lloyd M. Bentsen, Jr., secretary of the treasury (1993–1994)
Robert E. Rubin, secretary of the treasury (1995–2001)
Les Aspin, secretary of defense (1993–1994)
William Perry, secretary of defense (1994–1997)
William S. Cohen, secretary of defense (1997–2001)
Janet Reno, attorney general (1993–2001)
Bruce Babbitt, secretary of the interior (1993–2001)
Mike Espy, secretary of agriculture (1993–1994)
Daniel R. Glickman, secretary of agriculture (1995-)
Ronald H. Brown, secretary of commerce (1993–1996)
Mickey Kantor, secretary of commerce (1996–1997)
William M. Daley, secretary of commerce (1997–2000)
Norman Y. Mineta, secretary of commerce (2000–2001)
Robert B. Reich, secretary of labor (1993–1997)
Alexis Herman, secretary of labor (1997–2001)
Donna E. Shalala, secretary of health and human services (1993–2001)
Henry G. Cisneros, secretary of housing and urban development (1993–1997)
Andrew Cuomo, secretary of housing and urban development (1997–2001)
Federico F. Peña, secretary of transportation (1993–1997)
Rodney E. Slater, secretary of transportation (1997–2001)
Hazel R. O'Leary, secretary of energy (1993–1997)
Federico F. Peña, secretary of energy (1997–1998)
William Richardson, secretary of energy (1998–2001)
Richard W. Riley, secretary of education (1993–2001)
Jesse Brown, secretary of veterans affairs (1993–1998)
Togo D. West, Jr., secretary of veterans affairs (1998–2001)

Supreme Court Appointments
Ruth Bader Ginsberg (1993–)
Stephen G. Breyer (1994–)

Key Events

1993   Clinton invites E–mail messages from the public (Feb.); Congress approves North American Free Trade Agreement (NAFTA) with Canada and Mexico, removing some protectionist trade measures (17–21 Nov.).

1994   Clinton health care reform plans rejected by Congress; in midterm elections Republicans win control of both houses of Congress for first time in forty years (9 Nov.).

1995   U.S. restores full diplomatic relations with Vietnam; NATO peacekeeping forces help maintain cease–fire in war–stricken Bosnia; two blocks of Pennsylvania Avenue adjoining the White House closed to vehicular traffic (20 May); congressional Whitewater hearings investigate possible wrongdoing by Bill and Hillary Clinton in business deal involving a failed Arkansas savings–and–loan.

1996   Secretary of Commerce Ronald H. Brown and 32 others killed in an airplane crash near Dubrovnik, Croatia (3 Apr.); Clinton signs welfare reform legislation (23 Aug.); Clinton reelected president (5 Nov.).

1997   Clinton inaugurated (20 Jan.)

1998   Clinton is first elected president impeached by the House of Representatives (19 Dec.).

William Jefferson Clinton (Continued)

1999   Clinton acquitted by the United States Senate in impeachment trial (12 Feb.).

2000   George W. Bush elected president over Vice President Al Gore (7 Nov.).

2001   United States Supreme Court disbars Clinton, prohibiting him from arguing in front of the Court (1 Oct.).

George Walker Bush, 43rd President (2001–)

Life

Birthdate:	6 July 1946
Birthplace:	New Haven, Conn.
Parents:	George Herbert Walker Bush, Barbara Pierce
Religion:	Methodist
College Education:	Yale University; Harvard Business School
Wife:	Laura Welsh Bush
Date of Marriage:	5 Nov. 1977
Children:	Barbara and Jenna (twins)
Political Party:	Republican
Other Positions Held:	Oil company executive (1976–1988)
	Part–owner, Texas Rangers baseball club (1989–1993)
	Governor of Texas (1995–2001)
Date of inauguration:	20 January 2001
	Resides in Washington, D.C.

Elections

ELECTION OF 2000

Candidate	Party	Electoral Vote	Pop. Vote
George W. Bush	Republican	271	50,455,156
Albert A. Gore, Jr.	Democrat	269	50,992,335

POLITICAL COMPOSITION OF CONGRESS

107th Congress (2001–)

Senate:	Dem. 50; Rep. 49 other 1
House:	Rep. 222 ; Dem. 211; other 1

Vice President

Richard Cheney (2001–)

Appointments

Cabinet Members:
Colin Powell, secretary of state (2001–)
Paul H. O'Neill, secretary of the treasury (2001–)
Donald H. Rumsfeld, secretary of defense (2001–)
John Ashcroft, attorney general (2001–)
Gale A. Norton, secretary of the interior (2001–)
Ann M. Veneman, secretary of agriculture (2001–)
Donald Evans, secretary of commerce (2001–)
Elaine Chao, secretary of labor (2001–)
Tommy G. Thompson, secretary of health and human services (2001–)
Melquiades Rafael Martinez, secretary of housing and urban development
(2001–)
Norman Y. Mineta, secretary of transportation (2001–)
Spencer Abraham, secretary of energy (2001–)
Roderick Paige, secretary of education (2001–)
Anthony J. Principi, secretary of veterans affairs (2001–)

Supreme Court Appointments
None through June 2002

Key Events

2001   New York City and Washington, D.C., attacked by hijacked aircraft, destroying the World Trade Center and damaging the Pentagon, killing thousands (11 Sept.); Bush targets the Al Qaida ("The Base") terrorist network led by Saudi expatriate Osama Bin Laden as the mastermind behind the attacks; United States and Britain attack Afghanistan in an effort to destroy the Al Qaida network and the ruling Taliban regime in Afghanistan.

2002   During the State of the Union address (29 Jan.) Bush states that the fight against terrorism will extend globally. After terrorism and backlash in Israel, Bush tells Israeli prime minister Ariel Sharon to withdraw armed forces from Palestinian cities.

Upon the recommendation of the Brownlow Committee, chaired by prominent political scientist Louis Brownlow, President Franklin D. Roosevelt established the Executive Office of the President (EOP) by the authority of the Reorganization Act of 1939, and in accordance with Reorganization Plan No. 1 and Executive Order 8248. The EOP, designed to improve executive-branch operations by bringing them under better control, came into existence on 1 July of that year. It comprised five divisions: the White House Office (WHO), the Bureau of the Budget, the Office of Government Reports, the National Resources Planning Board, and the Liaison Office for Personnel Management. In addition, the president was empowered to open a sixth division: such office for emergency management as he might deem necessary "in the event of a national emergency, or threat of a national emergency."

The Executive Office of the President (EOP), today enormously expanded from what its founders anticipated, is operated by a total of 1,800 aides, and is concerned with lending support to the president in coordinating the far–flung undertakings and responsibilities of the departments of the executive branch. The EOP is composed of:

1. The White House Office (WHO) which was established to serve the president "in the performance of the many detailed activities incident to his immediate office." Until it was created, the president had no senior aides on his own payroll. He had to rely on the willingness of Congress to provide him with a few clerks and with the housekeeping staff of the White House. At its inception, the WHO consisted of eight officials, three with the title "secretary to the president," four with the title "administrative assistant," and an "executive clerk." At present the number of aides is generally about 500.

The WHO has become the political as well as policy arm of the chief executive, aiming to protect and enhance his public standing and image, and to energize the whole EOP. The WHO is almost invariably staffed by the intimates and insiders who helped the president to reach the White House. Beginning with President Eisenhower in 1953, presidents have usually appointed a chief of staff to organize and direct the work of the WHO. The holder of this position is often a leading spokesperson for the initiatives and policies of the executive branch.

Of all the divisions of the WHO, the Press Office is probably most familiar to the public because its head, the Press Secretary, is frequently seen on television. A highly publicized new division is the Homeland Defense Council. Its director is Assistant to the President for Homeland Security. Other divisions of the WHO are concerned with presidential appointments and scheduling—including those of the First Lady, the management of national security and foreign matters, the development of economic, scientific, and technological policies, the recruitment of high officials, and the arranging of social functions. President George W. Bush created a new Deputy Assistant to the President who would be Deputy Director for Faith–Based and Community Initiatives. The Office of the Cabinet Secretary administers the affairs of the cabinet, known traditionally as the president's "official family." The White House Counsel gives the president legal advice. Subunits are engaged in writing speeches, conducting the president's correspondence, and communicating with governors, mayors, and the media. The Military Office, which handles the "football," the valise containing codes for under taking the use of nuclear weapons, and which superintends the uniformed personnel attached to the White House as military and naval aides, is considered to be part of the WHO. Also so regarded is the White House physician and the medical facilities in his or her charge. The vice–president's office and residence, staffed by about thirty people, is not formally a part of the WHO.

2. The Office of the Vice President, which serves the Vice President in performing the many detailed activities incident to his immediate office.

3. The Council of Economic Advisers, which was established in the Executive Office of the President by the Employment Act of 1946. It now functions under that act and Reorganization Plan No. 9 of 1953. It consists of three members appointed by the President with the advice and consent of the Senate. The president designates the chairman from among the three members. The Council analyzes the economy and advises the President on economic developments, appraises on–going programs, and prepares the economic reports of the President to Congress. It issues the Annual report of the Council of Economic Advisers.

4. The Council on Environmental Quality (CEQ), which was established in the Executive Office of the President by the National Environmental Policy Act of 1969. The Environmental Quality Improvement Act of 1970 established the Office of Environmental Quality (OEQ) to provide professional and administrative support for the Council. Together the CEQ and the OEQ constitute the Council on Environmental Quality. The chair of the CEQ serves also as Director of the OEQ and is appointed by the President. The Council's mission is to develop policies which bring together the nation's social, economic, and environment priorities with the goal of improving the quality of Federal decisions in the field of environmental protection.

5. The National Security Council (NSC), which was established by the National Security Act of 1947 and placed in the Executive Office of the President by

Reorganization Plan No. 4 of 1949), is chaired by the President. The Council advises and assists the President in integrating all aspects of national security policy as it affects the United States. The statutory members, in addition to the President, are the Vice President and the Secretaries of State and Defense. The statutory military advisor to the Council is the Chairman of the Joint Chiefs of Staff and the intelligence advisor is the Director of Central Intelligence. The Secretary of the Treasury, the U.S. Representative to the United Nations, the Assistant to the President for National Security Affairs, the Assistant to the President for Economic Policy, and the Chief of Staff to the President are invited to all meetings. Other officials are invited as deemed appropriate.

6. The Office of Administration, which was established by executive order of 12 December 1977 to supply support services to all units within the Executive Office of the President.

7. The Office of Management and Budget (OMB), formerly the Bureau of the Budget (BOB), which was established in the Executive Office of the President by the Reorganization Plan No 1 of 1939. The OMB monitors and coordinates the budget requests of the various executive departments and agencies and assists the President in preparing the national budget and formulating fiscal policy. It also assists the President in developing and maintaining effective government by reviewing the organizational structure and management procedures of the executive branch to ensure the intended results are achieved.

When President Nixon in 1970 reorganized the BOB making it the Office of Management and Budget, and staffed it with his own people, it began to serve the president in a partisan way. Quickly its credibility became suspect with Congress, which established the Congressional Budget Office to provide what it regarded as more balanced or non–partisan fiscal and financial data. Today the OMB continues to be regarded as being in the president's control.

8. The Office of National Drug Control Policy, established by the National Narcotics Leadership Act of 1988 and the Office of National Drug Control Policy Reauthorization Act of 1988), coordinates Federal, State and local efforts to control illegal drug abuse, and devises national policy and strategies to effectively carry out anti–drug activities.

9. The Office of Policy Development, which is composed of the Domestic Policy Council which was established 16 August 1993 to oversee the development and implementation of the President's domestic policy agenda, and the National Economic Council which was established 25 January 1993 to coordinate the economic policy–making process and provide economic policy advice to the President.

10. The Office of Science and Technology, which was established in the Executive Office of the President by the National Science and Technology Policy, Organization, and Priorities Act of 1976. It serves as a source of scientific, engineering, and technological analysis and judgment for the president with respect to major policies, plans, and programs of the federal government.

11. The Office of the United States Trade Representative, which was created by the Office of the Special Representative for Trade Negotiations by Executive Order on 15 January 1963. The Office was established as an agency of the Executive Office of the

President by the Trade Act of 1974. The Office is responsible for setting and administering overall trade policy.

12. The Office of Homeland Security, which was created by Executive Order dated 8 October 2001, is charged with the mission of developing and coordinating the implementation of a comprehensive national strategy to secure the United States from terrorist threats or attacks.

****

Outside the influence the President exerts through the EOP, he or she exercises power by Executive Orders. These are official documents through which the Chief Executive manages the operation of the Federal Government. The number of EOs issued by a president is one measure of an administration's activity. The tally for the last 13 presidents follows:

Herbert Hoover 1929–33	1,010
Franklin D. Roosevelt 1933–1945	3,728
Harry Truman 1945–1953	896
Dwight D. Eisenhower 1953–1961	486
John F. Kennedy 1961–1963	214
Lyndon B. Johnson 1963–1969	324
Richard Nixon 1969–1974	346
Gerald R. Ford 1974–1977	169
Jimmy Carter 1977–1981	320
Ronald Reagan 1981–1989	381
George Bush 1989–1993	166
William J. Clinton 1993–2001	364
George W. Bush 2001 through April 2002	59

* * * *

The President appoints and receives advice from a vast array of boards, committees, and commissions, some created by Executive Orders, some by acts of Congress. Their membership may carry over from one administration to the next. The range of subjects they study and report upon is as wide as the concerns of government itself. A list running into the high hundreds of such federal executive agencies—including a history of each—which have been terminated, transferred, or changed in name since 4 March 1933, the first day of Franklin D. Roosevelt's presidency, may be found in the United States Government Manual on the World Wide Web. (wais.access.gpo.gov). At present there are fifty–seven active boards, committees, and commissions. Their scope speaks to some of the matters that the President must deal with aside from those that make daily news:

Administrative Committee of the Federal Register
Advisory Council on Historic Preservation
American Battle Monuments Commission
Appalachian Regional Commission
Architectural and Transportation Barriers Compliance Board
Arctic Research Commission
Arthritis and Musculoskeletal Interagency Coordinating Committee
Barry M. Goldwater Scholarship and Excellence in Education Foundation
Chemical Safety and Hazard Investigation Board
Citizens' Stamp Advisory Committee
Commission on Fine Arts

Committee on Foreign Investments in the United States
Committee for the Implementation of Textile Agreements
Committee for Purchase From People Who Are Blind or Severely Disabled
Coordinating Council on Juvenile Justice and Delinquency Prevention
Delaware River Basin Commission
Endangered Species Committee
Export Administration Review Board
Federal Financial Institutions Examination Council
Federal Financing Bank
Federal Interagency Committee on Education
Federal Laboratory Consortium for Technology Transfer
Federal Library and Information Center Committee
Harry S. Truman Scholarship Foundation
Illinois and Michigan Canal National Heritage Corridor Commission
Indian Arts and Crafts Board
Interagency Committee on Employment of People with Disabilities
Interagency Saving Bonds Committee
J. William Fulbright Foreign Scholarship Board
James Madison Memorial Fellowship Foundation
Japan–United States Friendship Commission
Joint Board for the Enrollment of Actuaries
Marine Mammal Commission
Medicare Payments Advisory Commission
Migratory Bird Conservation Commission
Mississippi River Commission
Morris K. Udall Scholarship and Excellence in National Environmental Policy
    Foundation
National Commission on Libraries and Information Science
National Council on Disability
National Park Foundation
Navajo and Hopi Relocation Commission
Northwest Power Planning Council
Panama Canal Commission
Permanent Committee for the Oliver Wendell Holmes Devise
President's Committee on Employment of People with Disabilities
President's Council on Integrity and Efficiency
President's Foreign Intelligence Advisory Board
Presidio Trust
Social Security Advisory Board
Susquehanna River Basin Commission
Textile Trade Policy Group
Trade Policy Staff Committee
United States Holocaust Memorial Museum
United States Nuclear Waste Technical Review Board
Veterans' Day National Committee
White House Commission on Presidential Scholars

Index

A

AAA. *See* Agricultural Adjustment Administration

ABCD ships, 277

Aberdeen, earl of, 160, 161, 162, 163, 165

"A.B. Letter," 84

ABM defense system, 526, 650, 653

Abolitionists. *See* Antislavery sentiment

Abortion
  Bush (George H. W.) position, 607, 608, 618, 675
  Carter position, 556
  Clinton pro-choice pledge, 618
  embryonic stem-cell research and, 650
  Ford (Betty) position, 648-649, 672
  Reagan administration policy, 582

Abrams, Elliott, 608

Abu Sayyaf (Islamic group), 654

Acheson, Dean, 451, 452, 453, 491, 493

Acid rain, 606

Adam, Robert and James, xliv

Adams, Abigail Smith, xxxvi, xliv, 28, 29, 30, 31, 32, 34, 90, 661
  accomplishments of, 24
  letters of, 668
  on Monroe's popularity, 76
  White House residency, 34-35

Adams, Brock, 556

Adams, Charles, xxxv, 36

Adams, Charles Francis, 94, 214, 250

Adams, George Washington, xxxv

Adams, Gerry, 625, 635

Adams, Henry, 55, 69, 293

Adams, John, **23-38**
  and Alien and Sedition Acts, xxvi, 30, 32-35, 41
  assessment of presidency of, 36-37
  benediction for White House, xliv, 34

  on Burr conspiracy, 52
  cabinet, 26-27, 28, 33
  conception of presidency, 26-27, 35, 36
  death of, 36, 56, 86
  early years, 23-24
  fear of Hamilton's ambitions, 30
  as first White House resident, xliv, xlix, 34-35, 668
  foreign policy, 20, 33, 35
  and French crisis, 27-32, 33-34, 35, 36
  Hamilton's personal attack on, 34
  inauguration, 19
  Jefferson relationship, xxi, 25, 26, 35, 37, 55, 56
  judicial reform, 35-36, 44-45
  lame-duck appointments, 36, 43
  Madison correspondence, 72
  "midnight appointments," xliv, 36, 43, 45
  Navy founding by, 29, 31, 33
  political theory, 25-26
  presidency compared with Adams (John Quincy), 87-89
  presidency compared with Jefferson's first term, 49
  and presidential election of 1800, xix, xxxvi, xliv, 34-35
  presidential transitions, xxxvi
  press denunciations of, xix, 17, 30
  slavery criticized by, 203
  sobriquets for, xxiii
  son's presidency. *See* Adams, John Quincy
  as vice president, xxi, 6, 10, 24-25, 26
  wife's (Abigail) influence, 24, 668

Adams, John Quincy, xxxv, **87-99**
  antislavery stance, 87, 91, 97-99, 147, 201
  assessment of presidency of, 99
  cabinet, 89, 90, 91-92, 93
  children of, xxxv
  "corrupt bargain" charges against, xxiii, 90-92, 93, 102, 106
  diplomatic career, 28, 31, 78, 88-89

INDEX

INDEX

INDEX

INDEX

INDEX

INDEX

INDEX

N

INDEX

INDEX

INDEX

INDEX

Syngman Rhee, 454

T

Taft, Charles, 349
Taft, Helen (daughter), xxxiii-xxxiv, xxxv, 665
Taft, Helen Herron, xxxvi, 347, 348, 349, 665
Taft, Henry, 349
Taft, Robert A., xxxvi, 466, 469, 518. *See also* Taft-Hartley Act of 1947
Taft, William Howard, 347-363
  antitrust prosecution by, 335, 355-356
  assessment of presidency of, 361-362
  cabinet, 348-349, 350-351, 357
  children of, xxxiii-xxxiv, xxxv, xxxvi, 665. *See also* Taft, Robert A.
  and conservation controversy, 343, 350-352
  domestic policies, 348-357
  foreign policy, 357-359
  inaugural speech, 348
  personality of, 347-348
  as Philippines commissioner, 347, 665
  post-presidential activities of, xxx, 360-361
  and presidential election in 1908, xxxvi, 348, 665
  and presidential election defeat in 1912, xxxvi, 344, 349-350, 353, 359-360, 366, 390
  and presidential transition, xxxvii
  progressive reforms, 353
  relationship with wife (Helen), 347, 348, 349, 665
  as Roosevelt's (Theodore) political successor, 343, 347, 348-349
  as Roosevelt's (Theodore) secretary of war, 348, 357
  split with Roosevelt (Theodore), xxix-xxx, xxxvi, 343-344, 348-349, 350, 352-353, 357, 359-360
  as strict constructionist, 350, 361-362
  Supreme Court ambitions, 347, 665
  as Supreme Court chief justice, xxx, 360-361, 396
  tariff measures, 349, 350, 352, 353, 354-355, 361
  White House West Wing expansion by, l
Taft-Hartley Act of 1947, 458, 484
Taft-Katsura Agreements (1905), 340
Taiwan (Formosa)
  Communist Chinese shelling of offshore islands, 475
  Eisenhower defense resolution, 470
  Japanese control of (1895), 320
  Nationalist Chinese defeat and retreat to, 453, 470, 475
  and Nixon agreement with Communist China, 524-525
  Republican commitment of support for, 548
Taliban, 652, 654
"Talking It Over" (H. Clinton column), 676
Talk radio, 618, 621
Talk television, xxvii-xxviii, 631
Talleyrand, Charles-Maurice de, 28, 31, 32, 36, 160
Tammany Hall (New York), 264, 282-283, 283, 295
Tampico, Illinois, 572
Tampico, Mexico, 164
Taney, Roger B., 112, 115, 116, 212-213
Tanner, James R., 299
Tariff Commission, 349, 353
Tariff of 1816, 79
Tariff of 1828 (Tariff of Abominations), 95, 113
Tariff of 1832, 113, 143-144
Tariff of 1833. *See* Compromise Tariff of 1833
Tariff of 1842, 144, 145, 179

Tariff of 1890. *See* McKinley Tariff Act of 1890
Tariff of 1921, 395
Tariff of 1930 (Smoot-Hawley), 423
Tariffs
  Arthur reduction measures, 275-276
  Clay protectionism, 127
  Cleveland's proposed lowering of, 284-285, 288, 295
  as election issue, xxi, 286, 295
  elimination under North American Free Trade Agreement, 605, 622
  highest in U.S. history (1897), 313
  as major election issue (1888)
  McKinley (1890), 286, 288, 299, 300, 301, 304, 309-310
  nullification crisis (1832), 113-114, 127, 128, 129
  Polk lowering of, 153, 155, 156
  and Puerto Rican trade, 319
  rate rise bill (1921), 385
  Republican protectionism, 221, 237, 286, 288, 295, 298, 300, 301, 309-310, 313, 394, 423
  Taft reform measures, 349, 350, 352, 353, 354-355, 361
  Tyler vetoes, 144, 145
  Wilson measures to lower, 369
Task Force on Health Care Reform (Clinton administration), 676
Taxation
  Bush (George H. W.) "read my lips...no new taxes" statement, xxviii, 594, 606-607, 620
  Bush (George H. W.) tax raise and efforts to lower capital gains tax, 607, 608
  Bush (George W.) rate cuts, 640, 649-650, 651, 655
  Bush (George W.) rebates, 651
  California citizens' tax revolt (1978), 564, 577
  Clinton promises and policies, 616, 617, 620, 626, 636
  Contract with America and, 625
  Coolidge administration cuts, 406, 408, 409
  first income tax (1913), 369
  Ford anti-inflation cuts, 542, 544
  Fries Rebellion (1799), 32
  Harding administration cuts, 395
  Hoover increase in excise and income tax for the wealthy, 423
  income tax constitutional amendment, 349, 360, 361
  inheritance, 349
  Jefferson's rejection of, 43, 44, 49
  Johnson (Lyndon B.) passage of $80-billion cut, 504
  Kennedy cuts, 493
  Lincoln and graduated income taxes, 221
  Nixon audits-as-harassment policy, 529
  Nixon measures, 521-522
  Reagan federal tax-cut policy, 578, 581, 582, 583, 593
  Reagan's California progressive tax increase, 576, 578
  Social Security, 433-434, 435
  in suppply-side economic theory, 578
  Taft measures, 349
  Whiskey Rebellion (1792), xl 14, 15, 60
Taylor, Claudia. *See* Johnson, Lady Bird
Taylor, John, 64, 74
Taylor, Margaret Mackall Smith, xxxiv, 659
Taylor, Maxwell, 494
Taylor, Robert, xxxiv
Taylor, Sarah Knox, xxxv
Taylor, Zachary, **171-184**, 505
  cabinet, 173, 179
  and California and New Mexico statehood, 173-176
  children of, xxxiv, xxxv

INDEX

INDEX

ISBN 0-684-31226-3

90000

9 780684 312262